Seamounts, Islands, and Atolls

Geophysical Monograph Series
Including
Maurice Ewing Volumes
Mineral Physics Volumes

GEOPHYSICAL MONOGRAPH SERIES

Geophysical Monograph Volumes

1 **Antarctica in the International Geophysical Year** *A. P. Crary, L. M. Gould, E. O. Hulburt, Hugh Odishaw, and Waldo E. Smith (Eds.)*
2 **Geophysics and the IGY** *Hugh Odishaw and Stanley Ruttenberg (Eds.)*
3 **Atmospheric Chemistry of Chlorine and Sulfur Compounds** *James P. Lodge, Jr. (Ed.)*
4 **Contemporary Geodesy** *Charles A. Whitten and Kenneth H. Drummond (Eds.)*
5 **Physics of Precipitation** *Helmut Weickmann (Ed.)*
6 **The Crust of the Pacific Basin** *Gordon A. Macdonald and Hisashi Kuno (Eds.)*
7 **Antarctica Research: The Matthew Fontaine Maury Memorial Symposium** *H. Wexler, M. J. Rubin, and J. E. Caskey, Jr. (Eds.)*
8 **Terrestrial Heat Flow** *William H. K. Lee (Ed.)*
9 **Gravity Anomalies: Unsurveyed Areas** *Hyman Orlin (Ed.)*
10 **The Earth Beneath the Continents: A Volume of Geophysical Studies in Honor of Merle A. Tuve** *John S. Steinhart and T. Jefferson Smith (Eds.)*
11 **Isotope Techniques in the Hydrologic Cycle** *Glenn E. Stout (Ed.)*
12 **The Crust and Upper Mantle of the Pacific Area** *Leon Knopoff, Charles L. Drake, and Pembroke J. Hart (Eds.)*
13 **The Earth's Crust and Upper Mantle** *Pembroke J. Hart (Ed.)*
14 **The Structure and Physical Properties of the Earth's Crust** *John G. Heacock (Ed.)*
15 **The Use of Artificial Satellites for Geodesy** *Soren W. Henriksen, Armando Mancini, and Bernard H. Chovitz (Eds.)*
16 **Flow and Fracture of Rocks** *H. C. Heard, I. Y. Borg, N. L. Carter, and C. B. Raleigh (Eds.)*
17 **Man-Made Lakes: Their Problems and Environmental Effects** *William C. Ackermann, Gilbert F. White, and E. B. Worthington (Eds.)*
18 **The Upper Atmosphere in Motion: A Selection of Papers With Annotation** *C. O. Hines and Colleagues*
19 **The Geophysics of the Pacific Ocean Basin and Its Margin: A Volume in Honor of George P. Woollard** *George H. Sutton, Murli H. Manghnani, and Ralph Moberly (Eds.)*
20 **The Earth's Crust: Its Nature and Physical Properties** *John G. Heacock (Ed.)*
21 **Quantitative Modeling of Magnetospheric Processes** *W. P. Olson (Ed.)*
22 **Derivation, Meaning, and Use of Geomagnetic Indices** *P. N. Mayaud*
23 **The Tectonic and Geologic Evolution of Southeast Asian Seas and Islands** *Dennis E. Hayes (Ed.)*
24 **Mechanical Behavior of Crustal Rocks: The Handin Volume** *N. L. Carter, M. Friedman, J. M. Logan, and D. W. Stearns (Eds.)*
25 **Physics of Auroral Arc Formation** *S.-I. Akasofu and J. R. Kan (Eds.)*
26 **Heterogeneous Atmospheric Chemistry** *David R. Schryer (Ed.)*
27 **The Tectonic and Geologic Evolution of Southeast Asian Seas and Islands: Part 2** *Dennis E. Hayes (Ed.)*
28 **Magnetospheric Currents** *Thomas A. Potemra (Ed.)*
29 **Climate Processes and Climate Sensitivity (Maurice Ewing Volume 5)** *James E. Hansen and Taro Takahashi (Eds.)*
30 **Magnetic Reconnection in Space and Laboratory Plasmas** *Edward W. Hones, Jr. (Ed.)*
31 **Point Defects in Minerals (Mineral Physics Volume 1)** *Robert N. Schock (Ed.)*
32 **The Carbon Cycle and Atmospheric CO_2: Natural Variations Archean to Present** *E. T. Sundquist and W. S. Broecker (Eds.)*
33 **Greenland Ice Core: Geophysics, Geochemistry, and the Environment** *C. C. Langway, Jr., H. Oeschger, and W. Dansgaard (Eds.)*
34 **Collisionless Shocks in the Heliosphere: A Tutorial Review** *Robert G. Stone and Bruce T. Tsurutani (Eds.)*
35 **Collisionless Shocks in the Heliosphere: Reviews of Current Research** *Bruce T. Tsurutani and Robert G. Stone (Eds.)*
36 **Mineral and Rock Deformation: Laboratory Studies—The Paterson Volume** *B. E. Hobbs and H. C. Heard (Eds.)*
37 **Earthquake Source Mechanics (Maurice Ewing Volume 6)** *Shamita Das, John Boatwright, and Christopher H. Scholz (Eds.)*
38 **Ion Acceleration in the Magnetosphere and Ionosphere** *Tom Chang (Ed.)*
39 **High Pressure Research in Mineral Physics (Mineral Physics Volume 2)** *Murli H. Manghnani and Yasuhiko Syono (Eds.)*
40 **Gondwana Six: Structure, Tectonics, and Geophysics** *Garry D. McKenzie (Ed.)*
41 **Gondwana Six: Stratigraphy, Sedimentology, and Paleontology** *Garry D. McKenzie (Ed.)*
42 **Flow and Transport Through Unsaturated Fractured Rock** *Daniel D. Evans and Thomas J. Nicholson (Eds.)*

Maurice Ewing Volumes

1 **Island Arcs, Deep Sea Trenches, and Back-Arc Basins** *Manik Talwani and Walter C. Pitman III (Eds.)*
2 **Deep Drilling Results in the Atlantic Ocean: Ocean Crust** *Manik Talwani, Christopher G. Harrison, and Dennis E. Hayes (Eds.)*
3 **Deep Drilling Results in the Atlantic Ocean: Continental Margins and Paleoenvironment** *Manik Talwani, William Hay, and William B. F. Ryan (Eds.)*
4 **Earthquake Prediction—An International Review** *David W. Simpson and Paul G. Richards (Eds.)*
5 **Climate Processes and Climate Sensitivity** *James E. Hansen and Taro Takahashi (Eds.)*
6 **Earthquake Source Mechanics** *Shamita Das, John Boatwright, and Christopher H. Scholz (Eds.)*

Mineral Physics Volumes

1 **Point Defects in Minerals** *Robert N. Schock (Ed.)*
2 **High Pressure Research in Mineral Physics** *Murli H. Manghnani and Yasuhiko Syono (Eds.)*

Geophysical Monograph 43

Seamounts, Islands, and Atolls

Barbara H. Keating, Patricia Fryer,
Rodey Batiza, and George W. Boehlert,
Editors

American Geophysical Union
Washington, D.C.
1987

Published under the aegis of AGU Geophysical Monograph Board.

Library of Congress Cataloging-in-Publication Data

Seamounts, islands, and atolls.

(Geophysical monograph, ISSN 0065-8448 ; 43)
1. Seamounts. 2. Coral reefs and islands. I. Keating, Barbara H. II. Series.
GC87.6.S4S42 1987   551.46'084   87-19288
ISBN 0-87590-068-2
ISSN 0065-8448

Copyright 1987 by the American Geophysical Union, 2000 Florida Avenue, NW, Washington, DC 20009

Figures, tables, and short excerpts may be reprinted in scientific books and journals if the source is properly cited.

Authorization to photocopy items for internal or personal use, or the internal or personal use of specific clients, is granted by the American Geophysical Union for libraries and other users registered with the Copyright Clearance Center (CCC) Transactional Reporting Service, provided that the base fee of $1.00 per copy plus $0.10 per page is paid directly to CCC, 21 Congress Street, Salem, MA 10970. 0065-8448/87/$01. + .10.

This consent does not extend to other kinds of copying, such as copying for creating new collective works or for resale. The reproduction of multiple copies and the use of full articles or the use of extracts, including figures and tables, for commercial purposes requires permission from AGU.

Printed in the United States of America.

CONTENTS

Dedication to H. William Menard   *Marcia McNutt*   ix

Hotspots: The First 25 Years   *Emile A. Okal and Rodey Batiza*   1

Seamount Abundances and Distribution Near the East Pacific Rise 0°–24° N Based on Seabeam Data   *Daniel J. Fornari, Rodey Batiza, and Mary Ann Luckman*   13

MORPHOLOGIC STUDIES

The South Pacific Superswell   *Marcia McNutt and Karen M. Fischer*   25

Irregularly Shaped Seamounts Near the East Pacific Rise: Implications for Seamount Origin and Rise Axis Processes   *Daniel J. Fornari, Rodey Batiza, and James F. Allan*   35

Structural Failure and Drowning of Johnstone Atoll, Central Pacific Basin   *Barbara H. Keating*   49

Origins of Nonvolcanic Seamounts in a Forearc Environment   *Patricia Fryer and Gerard J. Fryer*   61

GEOPHYSICAL STUDIES

A 3-D Gravity-Tectonic Study of Ita Mai Tai Guyot: An Uncompensated Seamount in the East Mariana Basin   *Bruce Wedgeworth and James Kellogg*   73

Isostatic Compensation and Conduit Structures of Western Pacific Seamounts: Results of Three-Dimensional Gravity Modeling   *J. N. Kellogg, B. S. Wedgeworth, and J. Freymueller*   85

Gravimetric Determination of Densities of Seamounts Along the Bonin Arc   *Takemi Ishihara*   97

Shipboard Confirmation of SEASAT Bathymetric Predictions in the South Central Pacific   *Nicolas Baudry and Michel Diament*   115

Temperature Beneath Midplate Swells: The Inverse Problem   *Marcia McNutt*   123

Paleomagnetic Constraints on the Origin and Evolution of the Musicians and South Hawaiian Seamounts, Central Pacific Ocean   *William W. Sager and Malcolm S. Pringle*   133

SEDIMENTOLOGICAL STUDIES

Post-Eocene Subsidence of the Marshall Islands Recorded by Drowned Atolls on Harrie and Sylvania Guyots   *S. O. Schlanger, J. F. Campbell, and M. W. Jackson*   165

Petrology and Geochemistry of Neogene Sedimentary Rocks From Mariana Forearc Seamounts   *J. A. Haggerty*   175

Textural Characteristics of Sediments on Deep Seamounts in the Eastern Pacific Ocean Between 10°N and 30°N   *Lisa A. Levin and Charles A. Nittrouer*   187

GEOCHEMICAL AND DATING STUDIES

An Isotopic Survey of Pacific Ocean Plateaus: Implications for Their Nature and Origin   *John J. Mahoney*   207

Mineralogical Studies of Samoan Ultramafic Xenoliths: Implications for Upper Mantle Processes   *Elizabeth Wright*   221

Petrologic Evolution of the Louisville Seamount Chain   *James W. Hawkins, Peter F. Lonsdale, and Rodey Batiza*   235

Petrology and Chemistry of Lavas From Seamounts Flanking the East Pacific Rise Axis, 21°N: Implications Concerning the Mantle Source Composition for Both Seamount and Adjacent EPR Lavas   *James F. Allan, Rodey Batiza, and Peter Lonsdale*   255

Isotopic Evidence for a Hotspot Origin of the Louisville Seamount Chain   *Q. Cheng, K.-H. Park, J. D. Macdougall, A. Zindler, G. W. Lugmair, H. Staudigel, J. Hawkins, and P. Lonsdale*   283

$^{40}Ar/^{39}Ar$ Age, Petrology, and Tectonic Significance of Some Seamounts in the Gulf of Alaska   *G. Brent Dalrymple, David A. Clague, Tracy L. Vallier, and H. William Menard*   297

OCEANOGRAPHIC AND BIOLOGICAL STUDIES

A Review of the Effects of Seamounts on Biological Processes   *George W. Boehlert and Amatzia Genin*   319

Effect of Seamounts and Seamount Chains on Ocean Circulation and Thermohaline Structure   *Gunnar I. Roden*   335

Seamount Biota and Biogeography   *Raymond R. Wilson, Jr. and Ronald S. Kaufmann*   355

Seamount Benthic Ecology and Potential Environmental Impact From Manganese Crust Mining in Hawaii   *Richard W. Grigg, A. Malahoff, E. H. Chave, and J. Landahl*   379

Lithospheric Thinning Under the Atlantis-Meteor Seamount Complex (North Atlantic)   *J. Verhoef and B. J. Collette*   391

DEDICATION TO H. WILLIAM MENARD

Bill Menard came to the forefront of marine geology in the 1950's, and never left it. He participated in or lead more than 30 oceanographic expeditions, visited almost every Pacific island group, and scientifically sampled more than 50 islands and every elevated atoll in the Pacific. He was the recognized authority on the geology of the Pacific Ocean. Thus with the passing of the one man who more than any other contributed to our understanding of seamounts, islands, and atolls, it is certainly fitting at this point in time to gather together several decades of progress into this volume dedicated to his memory.

Henry William Menard was born on December 10, 1920 in Fresno, California, although his ancestry remains a mystery. When he was about three years old he was adopted by Henry W. Menard, a commercial decorator, and Blanche Laverne Hodges Menard. His adoptive parents were well-to-do but nonintellectual Los Angeles residents who kept the fact of his adoption a secret from him. He didn't learn the truth until after the deaths of his parents.

Even in his early years, Bill demonstrated characteristics such as an intense intellectual curiosity, the ability to seize opportunities, and persistence (to the point of being downright stubborn) that were the trademarks of his long and creative scientific career. For example, as a child, Bill had an insatiable appetite for reading. He would borrow an arm load of books from the local library, reading one on the way home and saving one for the return trip to the library. By the time he was 10 years old, the librarian had to give him special permission to check out volumes from the adult section since he had already read every book in the children's section. As a senior at Los Angeles High School, Bill learned that several classmates had an extra space in the car they were driving to Pasadena to take the entrance exam for CalTech. At the spur of the moment, Bill decided to join them. He was admitted to CalTech, while his friends were not. After serving as a photo interpreter and air intelligence officer for the Navy during World War II, Bill returned to CalTech for a Masters degree in geology. While lunching at the Atheneum one day, he chanced to observe a young woman dining with her boss, Clark Millikan, the chairman of the Aeronautical Engineering department. She literally took his breath away. Bill could not find anyone who knew her to arrange an introduction, so he boldly presented to her a poem he himself had written. The young woman was intrigued, but not enough to date him. Nine times he asked her out, and nine times she refused. On the tenth try, she agreed. Bill Menard and Gifford Merrill were married four months later in 1946.

This curiosity, ability to recognize opportunities, and persistence paid off very early in his professional career. After completing his Ph.D. from Harvard (studying sediment transport in a flume at Woods Hole Oceanographic Institution), Bill accepted his first job at the Naval Electronics Laboratory in San Diego, in the Sea-Floor Studies section headed by Robert S. Dietz. Almost immediately upon arriving in June, 1949, everyone else in the lab left for an extended oceanographic expedition, leaving Bill on his own in a room filled with depth sounding records of the Pacific gathered by Naval vessels and left virtually untouched since the war. Bill set about studying the records, an exasperating and time-consuming task given the carelessness with which the data had been assembled. He emerged at the end of the summer the World's Authority on the Pacific seafloor, a title he never relinquished. The features he noted from the soundings led to a number of landmark papers coauthored with Bob Dietz and Ed Hamilton on such topics as the origin of the shelf break, the Mendocino Fracture Zone, the geology of the Gulf of Alaska and the Hawaiian swell, moat, and arch. Bill would relate with pleasure the fact that Allan Cox used this story as an example to his students of how even the most seemingly unpromising tasks might lead to something important.

During this period of time, oil exploration was just beginning to move offshore. Bill, recognizing the need for undersea mapping of the California shelf, began a small consulting company with Dietz and Hamilton to offer this service. The venture was immensely successful from a financial viewpoint, but Bill eventually resigned for personal reasons. Gifford recalls that Bill's weekends were so consumed by consulting that they only had Wednesday evenings to themselves. In addition, Bill did not particularly enjoy scuba diving, and as Ed Hamilton relates, that activity was a great feat of personal courage for him. Surprisingly, the great undersea explorer was most comfortable in a body of water no larger than his backyard swimming pool.

Bill's accomplishments at the Naval Electronics Laboratory did not go unnoticed by Roger Revelle, then Director of Scripps Institution of Oceanography. In the mid-1950's, at a party hosted by Sam Scripps at the old family homestead at Miramar Ranch, Roger managed to corner both Bill and Gifford for the purpose of convincing Bill to join the Scripps faculty. Fortunately for all the students he later inspired, Bill agreed. As a teacher and research advisor, he either had a very keen eye for picking students or perhaps simply worked miracles with the raw material at hand. All of Bill's academic offspring - Roger Larson, Tanya Atwater, Jean Francheteau, Clem Chase, Dan Karig, George Sharman, Debbie Smith - have gone on to establish their own distinguished scientific careers. As we all gathered in San Francisco in December, 1985 to celebrate Bill's 65th birthday, we recalled one of his secrets for success: he always treated us as colleagues, not students.

Bill's many contributions to the plate tectonic revolution in the 60's and 70's are readily apparent in his publications and

Copyright 1987 by the American Geophysical Union.

from the citations for the numerous honors he received such as the Penrose Medal from the GSA, the Shepard Medal from SEPM, the Bowie Medal from the AGU, and membership in the National Academy. What is less widely appreciated is Bill's leadership role in the mid-1960's in setting up a computer center staffed by experts and equipped with digitizers, key punches, plotters, and processors, to handle the flood of oceanographic depth and magnetic data supplied by the Scripps fleet. Had it been necessary for Wilson, Morgan, McKenzie, Parker, and the other visionaries of the plate tectonic revolution to wait for the marine data to be reduced by hand, the observational proofs would have been years later in coming. In addition, it was Bill who awakened Scripps to the reality and importance of plate tectonics that by 1967 had gained acceptance in Cambridge, Lamont, Princeton, and Woods Hole. He resurrected the underway marine magnetic program, thus enabling Scripps to participate in the most important revolution in the history of earth science.

Bill's impressive scientific operation was generously funded by the Navy for many years. Both basic science and Navy interests were well served by this productive partnership. During the Viet Nam era, however, Bill became increasingly concerned that the research he performed under Defense Department contract might in some way be sustaining a war effort that his conscience could not support. He quietly went about finding other jobs for all of his research staff, and then turned down continued Navy funding. After the war, when he felt he could once more seek their support without compromising his ideals, he paid dearly for his conscience by never again receiving Navy funding.

In 1978, President Carter appointed Bill to the post of tenth Director of the United States Geological Survey. The decision to move to an administrative post was an extremely difficult one, but it presented a new challenge. To dispel the perception that his move was in any way prompted by languishing research productivity, Bill left Scripps in "a flurry of publications." Bill had always been extremely partial to the USGS, to the point of dedicating one of his books to that organization. With the pivotal roll the Survey would play in estimating offshore oil and mineral resources, Bill considered it his duty to make sure that the USGS would not fall prey to political pressure. He felt that the Geological Survey was one of the few government organizations where one could request information and receive an unbiased answer. Both Gifford and Bill found Washington immensely alive and exciting, although the job was harder physically and emotionally than they had anticipated. It is always a struggle for an outsider placed at the head of a large bureau to gain acceptance from the existing and long-established internal organization. Nevertheless, during his short term as Director, he managed to accomplish a number of his goals, including elevating the Water Resources Department to the same level as the other Divisions within the USGS.

With the change in administration in Washington, a new Director was appointed and Bill and Gifford returned to La Jolla. The transition back to scientific research was not easy. Although his faculty position was waiting for him, Bill faced the immense challenge at age 61 of having to rebuild a research program and funding base from scratch. It is unfortunate that the funding agencies have no provision for easing back into active research those public-spirited individuals who take their turn serving the scientific community, whether it be as an ONR rotator or as the Survey Director. The era of observational marine exploration was past, and the funding was now going to a new breed of seagoing scientists with better tools and the mathematical and computational skills to solve the next generation of problems. At Scripps, the new leaders were John Orcutt, Tom Jordan, and Dick Hey. Bill astutely allied himself with this group, and there ensued several years of stimulating and productive research. The younger members of the team called upon Bill's immense storehouse of observations, experience, and ideas. He, in turn, benefited from their new instruments, quantitative skills, and companionship. All undertakings, whether a Friday business lunch or an oceanographic expedition, were done with style. I had moved to the East Coast by that time, but we continued to work together. Bill installed an automatic dialer on his telephone and was pleased to state that I was "only a button away."

By early 1985, Bill had put aside all commitments except the two books he was writing, the *Islands* monograph and his personal history of the plate tectonic revolution, *The Ocean of Truth*. He was terminally ill with cancer, and wanted to make sure that these works were finished. He was being subjected to frequent and painful chemotherapy treatments but purposely would forego his pain medication in order to have a clear head to continue his work. By shear force of will, his health rallied briefly in December, 1985 for the AGU meeting in San Francisco where he accepted the Bowie Medal. Bill, Jim Natland, and I used the meeting as a convenient *rendez-vous* for planning our upcoming expedition to the Marquesas Islands. Always the optimist, he talked as though he was sure to participate. I remember saying good-by to him on a cold and windy street corner in San Francisco as I left to catch a plane to Boston. He looked so frail and pale that I knew it was the last time I would see him alive.

Less than two months later, Bill died at his home in La Jolla surrounded by his family. He is survived by his wife Gifford, his three children: Andrew Menard, a sculptor in New York City, Elizabeth Menard of Encinitas, California who, with her husband, designs and markets children's clothing, and Dorothy Merrill, an Emergency Medical Technician in Washington, D.C., in addition to four grandchildren: Kate and William Menard, and Alison and Benjamin Kurtz.

In writing this dedication, I drew heavily upon the keen recollections of Gifford Menard. Bill's encouragement and support of women graduate students is by now legendary, and surely his high regard for women's potential stemmed from respect for his own wife. At this writing, Gifford is attempting to establish a women's scholarship fund at SIO in Bill's memory. I cannot imagine a more fitting tribute.

Marcia McNutt
Massachusetts Institute of Technology

FOREWORD

This collection of twenty-six papers arose partly from a special session at the Fall 1985 AGU meeting and reflects the growing research interest in the many diverse aspects of submarine and island volcanoes in the deep sea. Consequently, this book contains research and review articles dealing with a variety of topics including seamount abundances, morphology, geophysical characteristics, sedimentology, geochemistry and dating as well as physical oceanography and biology. We have attempted to select papers for disciplinary balance and also to provide a mixture of research articles and review papers. We dedicate this book to H. W. Menard whose lifelong fascination with seamounts, islands and atolls provided great impetus to their study.

The book starts with a review article on hotspots and a paper on seamount abundances near the East Pacific Rise. The section on "Morphologic Studies" contains four research papers spanning a wide variety of seamount types from tiny volcanic seamounts near the East Pacific Rise, to non-volcanic seamounts occurring in forearcs, to Pacific Ocean islands and large island groups associated with anomalous heating of the lithosphere. The section on "Geophysical Studies" contains six research papers on the gravity and paleomagnetic characteristics of Pacific seamounts and the inferred thermal structure beneath volcanically active regions of the sea floor.

The section on "Sedimentological Studies" contains three research articles on carbonate sedimentation, sedimentary rocks from forearc seamounts and sedimentation processes on volcanic seamounts of the East Pacific. The section on "Geochemical and Dating Studies" has six research papers: two geochemical papers on the Louisville seamount chain, one about the Gulf of Alaska seamounts that includes new age data, and papers about Samoan ultramafic xenoliths, isotopic signatures of oceanic plateaus and the petrology of seamounts near the East Pacific Rise.

The final section on "Oceanographic and Biological Studies" contains a review paper on the physical oceanographic effects of seamounts and four papers on seamount biota, biogeography benthic ecology and biological oceanography.

We have attempted to collect together a modest number of papers giving a representative and capsule view of the state of modern geologic, geophysical, geochemical and oceanographic studies of active and inactive volcanoes arising in the deep sea. While the collection is not meant to be exhaustive, it may be a convenient starting point for those wishing to know more and for active researchers in related topics.

The Editors

Copyright 1987 by the American Geophysical Union.

HOTSPOTS: THE FIRST 25 YEARS

Emile A. Okal and Rodey Batiza

Department of Geological Sciences, Northwestern University, Evanston, Illinois 60201

> "Our extrapolations [...] show that there will be 1,000,000 hotspots by the year 2000. We hope someone proves that hotspots do not exist, before it is too late." [Holden and Vogt, 1977].

Abstract. The Wilson [1963] — Morgan [1971] hotspot hypothesis has been extremely successful for determining past plate motions and has served as a stimulating influence in many fields of Earth Science. In this paper, we provide a brief review of some of the important landmarks in the development of the unified geophysical-geochemical hotspot or plume model for linear island and seamount chains. We briefly review topics under the headings of kinematics, hotspot-plate interactions, and petrology and geochemistry, and then take a closer look at some problems that have developed with the simplest hotspot model in each of these categories. These second-order problems include such items as departure from linearity, prolonged volcanism at certain sites, and isotopic complexity, which are exemplified by such chains as the Cook-Australs, the Marquesas, and the Gulf of Alaska. In such cases, the hotspot model requires additional complexity in order to explain the observations. It is clear that not all oceanic or continental intraplate volcanism can be explained in terms of the classical hotspot hypothesis unless hotspots are part of a continuum which contains upwelling blobs of various size, longevity and isotopic characteristics. Within this context, we discuss some of the possible constraints provided by isotopic and convection modelling, and conclude that not all plumes are created equal.

Introduction

It has now been close to 25 years since J. Tuzo Wilson proposed his famous interpretation of the Hawaiian and other island chains [Wilson, 1963]. The purpose of this paper is to present a brief review of the principal milestones of the hotspot theory in the past quarter-century and of its fundamental remaining problems, and to discuss how the latter may in the future affect our views on the origin and mechanisms of mid-plate volcanism.

Because of the voluminous character of the subject, our review cannot pretend to describe every achievement nor treat every aspect of hotspot theory in the past 25 years (a full book would not suffice; and indeed the literature is rich in reviews on various individual topics). Rather, our purpose is to give a kind of report card of how well the simple model of a universal, long-lasting, radiogenic hotspot, deeply and securely anchored in the mantle, fares against the rapidly growing datasets in many Earth science disciplines. The original notion of fixed hotspots, later correlated with a chemically distinct source in the deep mantle [Schilling, 1973], has been of immense value in unraveling past plate motions and has served as a stimulus for studies of mantle convection and chemical geodynamics [Allègre, 1982]. The hotspot hypothesis has several closely interrelated aspects treated in the literature: (i) kinematic aspects of their fixity and utility for studies of past plate motion [e.g., Minster and Jordan, 1978; Morgan, 1981; Gordon and Henderson, 1987]; (ii) links with the physics of mantle convection [Davies, 1984; Olson and Christensen, 1986], and the dynamics of mantle plumes [Ribe, 1983]; and (iii) the related issue of the chemical diversity of the Earth's mantle [Allègre et al., 1980; Gurnis and Davies, 1986; Zindler and Hart, 1986].

In the first section, we attempt to describe a "simple" universal hotspot model, explaining most first-order observations regarding island and seamount chains, and we list the basic successes of this approach. We then take a closer ("second-order") look at the various characteristics of linear island chains, address a number of problems with their interpretation in the framework of the simple theory, and discuss the constraints they may put on the origin and mechanism of extrusion of ocean island basalts.

A Brief Review of the "Simple" Hotspot Model

As early as the 19th century, Dana [1849] interpreted the degree of erosion of the various Hawaiian islands to infer that volcanic activity along the chain had progressed southeastwards with time; indeed, a correct description of this progression is found in ancient Hawaiian mythology in the form of the successive dwellings of the goddess Pele, although it is not clear that it associated her with the actual building of the islands. The systematic recognition of the linearity of islands chains, notably in the Pacific Ocean, goes back to Wegener [1915] who mentioned in his book on continental drift the existence of oceanic islands aligned perpendicular to the drifting direction of continents.

In 1963, and following systematic dating of igneous rocks from oceanic islands, J. Tuzo Wilson made the fundamental, quantitative observation that the age of an island is usually different from that of the adjoining sea floor, and further established a linear correlation between the age of volcanism and distance along the oceanic chain; he went on to propose his now famous model, in which, as the plate passes over a magma source fixed with respect to the mantle,

Copyright 1987 by the American Geophysical Union.

"the islands are in fact arranged like plumes of smoke [....] carried downwind from their sources"
[Wilson, 1963].

The ensuing success of the model was due to its simplicity, its universality (the same model explains observations in geographically different areas), and to the fact that it could account simply for many observations, which fall grossly into three categories: plate kinematics, hotspot/plate interactions, and origin and chemical nature of the hotspot magmas. We will now review very quickly the principal milestones in the model's development.

Kinematics

The simple hotspot model is based on the assumption that the magma sources are securely anchored in the deep mantle; as such, they can provide a reference frame for the study of the plates' absolute motions both at present and in the past. That this is at all possible as demonstrated for example by Minster and Jordan [1978] (and that the hotspots are therefore, to a precision of about 1 cm/yr, fixed with respect to each other), constitutes in itself a major success of this simple model; further successes in the field of plate kinematics include: (i) the explanation of the linearity and asymmetry of island chains, with the center of present activity located at one end [Wilson, 1963]; (ii) the parallelism of the various island chains inside a given oceanic plate [Wilson, 1963]; (iii) the reconstruction of the change of direction of the Pacific plate's motion about 43 Ma b.p. [Christofferson, 1968] on the basis of the sharp bends observed for example along the Hawaii-Emperor chain; (iv) the linearity of the age-distance relationship along a given chain, and the consistency of the inferred rates of progression amongst chains [Duncan and McDougall, 1976; Jarrard and Clague, 1977].

We must stress that the above are major observations of an absolutely fundamental character, and that they remain the basis for the firm, undeniable success of the hotspot hypothesis.

An implicit assumption of the hotspot model is the long-lived character of the mantle source, in other words that hotspots cannot be born and killed, or turned on and off, at will. It is obvious, for example, that the model would make no sense if the lifetime of the hotspot source were shorter than the age separation between two islands in a chain. At the other extreme, a first-order assumption for the "simple" hotspot model is that of their continuous existence and activity since at least 125 Ma [Anderson, 1982; Chase and Sprowl, 1983], and possibly 200 Ma [Le Pichon and Huchon, 1984]. Such an assumption of long-lived character can then be tested in the oceans by retracing the tracks of hotspots into the geological past, and effecting associations with islands and seamounts; and on continents by looking for evidence of hotspot tracks in the stratigraphic record of uplifts prior to Jurassic time [e.g., Crough, 1981].

Perhaps the most ambitious and successful such study is Gordon and Henderson's [1987], who claim to account for all major islands and plateaux in the Pacific plate by considering 14 hotspots, moving at most 1 cm/yr with respect to each other. In the Southern Atlantic and Indian Oceans, Duncan [1981] and Morgan [1981] similarly accounted for much of the seamount and island volcanism.

Interaction with the Plate

One of the fundamental points in the simple hotspot model is that ideally it considers little mechanical interaction between the plume and the oceanic lithosphere. This idea is indeed inherent in the concept of the oceanic island being the "trace", on the moving plate, of the relative motion of the two systems (plate and deep mantle). Although it was realized early on that this is only an assumption, the following observations seem to confirm it, at least to a first approximation:

While some temporary deviation of the trace of a hotspot chain is observed (e.g., in the Hawaiian chain) when passing over a major fracture zone [Epp, 1978], this signature typically lasts no longer than 300 km, and the linearity of the chain is quickly restored, attesting to the robust character of the plate/mantle velocity vector.

The formation of discrete islands in a chain was explained on the basis of the experimental study of the ascending motion of buoyant pipes under various conditions of density and viscosity contrasts [Skilbeck and Whitehead, 1978]. It was suggested that the characteristic separation between individual islands must increase with plate thickness [Vogt, 1974], which readily explains the formation of discrete islands on older lithosphere, and of continuous plateaux at the ridges. While this model requires the pipe to bend during the formation of an island, the short duration of this process (1—2 Ma) constitutes only a small perturbation to the model.

An alternate model for the upwelling column is that of discontinuous blobs [Schilling and Noe-Nygaard, 1974], explored experimentally by Olson and Singer [1985], who found that such blobs were favored over a continuous plume, under the conditions of large horizontal velocities in the mean mantle flow typically expected in mid-plate regions. Using this model, they calculate a replication time on the order of 5 Ma, generally consistent with a distributed melt model for Hawaii.

Since the oceanic plate has a finite elastic rigidity, it must deform under loading by islands, and a considerable number of studies have addressed this problem [e.g., Walcott, 1970; McNutt and Menard, 1978; Watts et al., 1985]. While a general correlation was established between the flexure of the plate and its age at the time of island formation [Watts, 1978], early studies pointed to a deficiency in the elastic response of the plate, as predicted by adequate models of its rheology and thermal history, leading to the concept of "lithospheric thinning" in the plate [Detrick and Crough, 1978]. As discussed below, some controversy remains as to whether the hotspot is the thinning agent, or results itself from the delamination of the plate. Still, the concept of thinning has been by and large successful in explaining the wealth of geophysical data made available in the past decade from satellite altimetry [McNutt, 1984].

Origin of Hotspots; Petrology and Chemistry

The fixity of hotspots, and the fact that they produce volcanoes, led quickly to the notion that they could be the surface expression of buoyantly rising convective instabilities [Morgan, 1971; 1972a,b]. In this way, the hotspot, or plume, hypothesis became closely linked with questions regarding the possible geometry of mantle convection: mantle plumes could rise from the deep mantle and melt as a result of adiabatic decompression [Turcotte and Oxburgh, 1978], thus producing volcanoes.

In 1965, isotopic analysis of ocean basalts [Tatsumoto et al., 1965] began to provide evidence that the Earth's mantle is chemically and isotopically diverse. In a series of landmark papers, Schilling and others showed that basalts from Hawaii, Iceland, the Azores and other regions were enriched, relative to MORB, in the light rare Earth elements and other so-called incompatible or magmatophile elements [Schilling and Winchester, 1967; Schilling, 1971, 1973; Schilling et al., 1983]. Further, they were able to show that isotope ratios showed a gradual change from normal mid-oceanic ridge basalt [MORB] values to more radiogenic values as hotspot islands were approached. These observations provided an

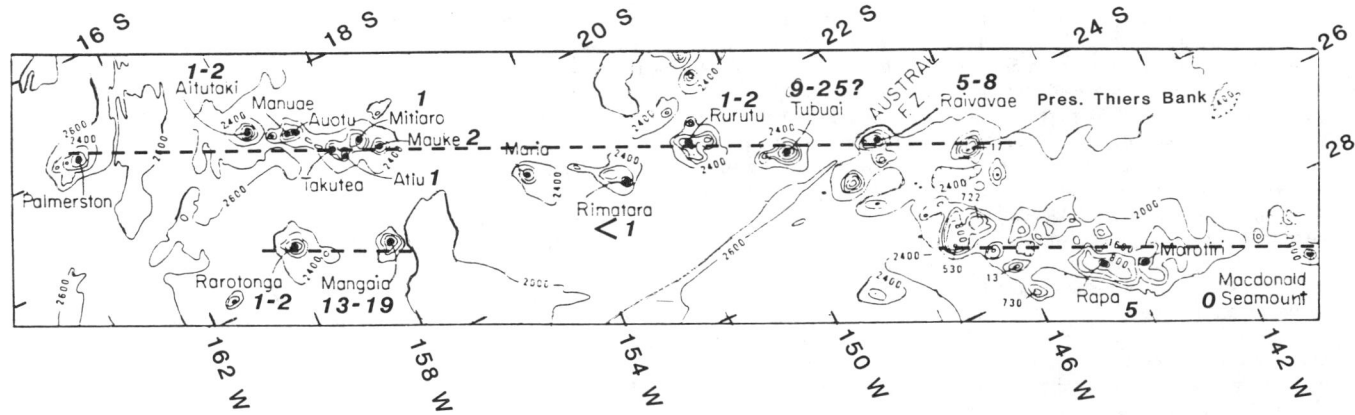

Fig. 1. Map of the Cook-Austral Island chain adapted from Turner and Jarrard [1982]. Numbers in italic indicate ages of islands along the chain (in Ma). The two dashed lines identify the two subchains parallel to each other, offset 250 km at the level of President Thiers Bank, and running concurrently in the Cook Islands. Note the gross violations of age-distance relationships.

important link between diapiric convective instabilities (geophysical plumes) and the evolving idea of mantle heterogeneity, because they provided for simple mixing of two mantle components: a depleted MORB mantle source, and a presumably deeper, enriched, plume source. So, in its simplest form, the combination of rising convective instabilities with chemical and isotopic stratification of the mantle gave rise to a "unified plume theory". This simple model of a convective upper mantle as a source for MORB with a separately convecting deeper layer as the source of the enriched plumes was found to be consistent with both Sr and Nd isotope ratios [DePaolo and Wasserburg, 1976, 1979]. The good correlation between bathymetry and chemical anomalies along mid-ocean ridges has been convincingly demonstrated, though it is best developed along the Mid-Atlantic Ridge [Schilling et al., 1983; Hamelin et al., 1984].

A Second-Order Look; Problems with a Simple Hotspot Theory

In this section, we examine a number of problems and irregularities which surface when attempting to describe all island chains in the framework of the simple theory mentioned above. It must be emphasized that many of these problems are observed in chains other than Hawaii-Emperor, which because of its accessibility, volume of extruded material, present-day subaerial activity, and well-documented history of scientific investigation, has remained the classical model of a hotspot chain. However, as more data (in fields as different as isotope geochemistry and satellite geodesy) become available for islands in the other chains, a long string of problems arise. We address them in the order of the broad categories listed above; however, these problems are often intermixed, through alternate explanations (e.g., the introduction of several hotspots in a single chain).

Plate Kinematics

Failure to remain a linear chain. This problem is particularly acute in the Austral Islands, where lateral offsets on the order of 300 km are frequent (Figure 1). In the southern section, two major portions of the chain, each running for 600 km or more, are offset laterally about 250 km between President Thiers' Reefs and the seamounts to the west of Rapa. This is significantly longer than observed, for example in the Hawaiian chain, upon passage over a major fracture zone; in addition, this offset in the Austral chain is not correlated with a fracture zone, but rather located as much as 300 km east of the Austral Fracture Zone. In the western portion of the Cook-Austral Islands, the two chains run concurrently, parallel to each other (the northern branch from Aituki to Mauke and the southern one from Rarotonga to Mangaia). A possible explanation would involve two hotspots, rather than one; this would require turning them on and off frequently, in order to account for the complex geography of the chain.

A similar problem, though less acute, is the observation that some linear island chains consist not of a single straight line of volcanic edifices, but instead of overlapping, and occasionally alternating, en-échelon systems. Good examples are Hawaii [Jackson et al., 1972], the Society Islands [Talandier and Okal, 1984], and the New England Seamounts. More complex variants, such as "cross-trends" that disturb the linearity of hotspot tracks are also observed, as for example, in the Line Islands [Epp, 1984; Schlanger et al., 1984] (although Gordon and Henderson [1987] interpret the disturbance as a crossover with the pre-existing track of the Marquesas hotspot). Finally, it may be noted that in the case of many large volcanoes within hotspot chains, the forms of individual non circular islands may not be parallel to the trend of the chain: very localized non-linearity of this type is usually caused by the development of long volcanic rift zones and probably reflects local tectonics and edifice effects [Fiske and Jackson, 1972; Vogt and Smoot, 1984].

Duration of volcanism along a chain and/or fluctuation in the rate of extrusion. Some islands chains are clearly much shorter than others: the Marquesas are an obvious example, although Gordon and Henderson [1987] have traced the activity of the Marquesas hotspot backwards in time all the way to the Shatsky Rise (about 130 Ma b.p.), claiming continuous activity evidenced by geoid highs in the absence of major seamounts between the Marquesas and the Line Islands. These authors thus alleviate the need for bringing to life, or "turning on" the Marquesas hotspot as recently as 10 Ma, as would be suggested by the lack of islands or seamounts northwest of Eiao. It must however be accepted that the level of activity of this particular hotspot fluctuated substantially in the past few million years; in particular, there is no evidence, not even seismic, of any activity younger than about 1 Ma. In the continuous upwelling pipe model of Morgan [1971], one must then assume that the burner was adjusted from "sim" to "hot" at 10 Ma, and probably back to "sim" about 1 Ma ago. In the alternate model of the "chain of blobs" [Schilling and Noe-Nygaard, 1974], one would assume that the number or size of the blobs suddenly increased during that same period. Although Olson and Singer [1985] suggest that interaction between rising blobs and the mean flow of the mantle, plus interaction of the rising blobs with the lithosphere, could in general result in such behavior, the specific reasons for the Marquesan sequence eludes us completely. Similarly, Gordon and Henderson [1987] had to introduce the concept of "waning" for several hotspots (Brahms, Rachmaninoff, Gardner, and possibly Louisville) in their Pacific model describing most islands, major seamounts and plateaux as derived from hotspots.

A much more common case is that of more continuously variable extrusion rates along the length of an island/seamount chain [e.g., Vogt, 1981]. An excellent example is the Hawaii-Emperor chain which shows gaps and large variations in the extrusion rate along the chain [Shaw, 1973]. Epp [1978] shows that this is very common in the North Pacific, and recent data from the Louisville Ridge in the South Pacific indicate non-uniform eruption rates as well [Lonsdale, 1987]. Atlantic and Indian Ocean hotspots [Morgan, 1978, 1981, 1983; McDougall and Duncan, 1980; Duncan, 1981; Hartnady and le Roex, 1985] exhibit the same phenomena.

A variation of this problem concerns the massive extrusion of volcanics, together with sill emplacement, during the Cretaceous, in what is now the Western Pacific Basin [Schlanger et al., 1981]. This enigmatic basin-wide event has no modern parallel. We speculate that it could be linked to the dispersal of Pangea [Le Pichon and Huchon, 1984], though this requires a long-time gap between dispersal (Late Triassic - Early Jurassic), and Mid-Pacific volcanism. Alternatively, one can be tempted to explain this volcanism by multiple crossings of hotspot traces; however the presently active hotspots, when traced back in time [Gordon and Henderson, 1987], cannot explain the 3 to 4 episodes of volcanism documented on the plate in the Nauru, Marshall and Mariana basins. Furthermore, in such a model, the interpretation of the apparently simple cooling and subsidence of the region [Schlanger and Moberly, 1986] remains problematic.

A related problem is posed by the vast oceanic plateaux for which hotspot origin has been suggested [Mahoney, 1987]. Alternatively, several plateaux and related sill complexes have been interpreted as large outpourings due chiefly to very rapidly changing spreading patterns [Winterer, 1976; Castillo et al., 1986].

Duration of volcanism on an individual island. It is a basic aspect of the simplest hotspot theory that only one island or seamount be active at a time. At the young end of many hotspot chains, this is not the case. For example, post-erosional basalts are 1-3 Ma younger than shield-building lavas on Oahu and the Samoan Islands [Jackson, 1976; Natland and Turner, 1987]. The petrologic characteristics of these volcanics (i.e., highly alkaline and silica-undersaturated) indicate generation at great depth and their small volumes (considerably less than 1% of the edifice) suggest that they could be remnants from the main thermal event causing shield building. The example of Hawaii and Samoa suggest that post-erosional activity survives for at least 3—4 Ma after shield-building. Most thermal models would indicate that this stretches the upper limit for the continued presence of a single magma body, but such time scales may be characteristic for the waning of deep thermal events. The gravitational anchor model of Shaw and Jackson [1973] provides some rationale for continued eruption of tiny volumes of post-erosional products. On Samoa, the volumes of post-erosional products is much larger, but still only a fraction of the entire edifice.

In some cases, however, prolonged volcanism at a single volcano presents a more serious problem for the simple hotspot model. Excellent examples are the Canary Islands, where active volcanism has occurred for $\simeq$20 Ma [Schminke, 1975], and the Caroline Islands, where volcanism has occurred for $\simeq$ 8 Ma [Mattey, 1982; Dixon et al., 1984]. Clearly, and until more is known about the average active life of oceanic volcanoes, this problem must be held in abeyance. The case of contemporaneous activity at several sites along a chain is similarly problematic: in the Line Islands, Haggerty et al. [1982] and Schlanger et al. [1984] have documented Late Cretaceous volcanism taking place simultaneously over a distance of 2500 km. Similarly, along the so-called Easter hotline, contemporaneous young volcanism has occurred over a linear distance of 2700 km [Bonatti and Harrison, 1976]. Continental examples of this phenomenon are present in Australia [Pilger, 1982].

Violation of age-distance relationships. Some of the linear chains have been found to exhibit strong departures from the predicted age-distance relationships. While some of these inconsistencies may be due to the poor quality of the early datasets, relying heavily on K/Ar ages, there are clear cases of outright violation: In the Southern Cook Islands, only 210 km separate Rarotonga (1.1—2.3 Ma) and Mangaia (13—19 Ma) [Turner and Jarrard, 1982]; in this case, the direction of progression of age itself is wrong. Other examples include Rurutu, located in the middle of the Cook-Austral chain, and dated no older than 1 Ma [Dalrymple et al., 1975].

In the case of Tubuai, the morphology of the island leads to considering two major episodes of volcanism dated 25($\pm$10)—17 Ma and 16—9 Ma, respectively; one Tubuai basanite has been dated as young as 1 Ma. The duration of volcanism on Tubuai is thus at least 16 Ma, and possibly 24 Ma [Mottay, 1976]; indeed, the Austral-Cook chain is clearly the least convincing example of age-distance correlation among Pacific chains [Duncan and McDougall, 1976; Jarrard and Clague, 1977]. Several avenues can be explored to account for this discrepancy: one of them is to use several hotspots (at least three, according to Turner and Jarrard [1982]) to describe the chain; however, each must be turned on and off very fast (in less than a few Ma) to explain the absence of present-day activity, except at the southeastern end of the chain at Macdonald. Another possibility is to interpret the younger, strongly alkalic, formations as comparable to the simple post-erosional activity discussed above for Oahu; the extended period of retention of the magma source involved in this model, is however, difficult to explain by any simple thermal model.

Other examples of age-distance discrepancy include the Pratt-Walker-Bowie chain in the Gulf of Alaska, which has volcanoes that are both too young and too old to be part of a single hotspot chain [Dalrymple et al., 1987]; the Cocos Ridge, which has a 2—3 Ma volcano (Cocos Island) astride a portion of the ridge predicted to be 12—14 Ma [Castillo and Batiza, 1986], and the Caroline Island chain [Dixon et al., 1984; Mattey, 1982], which suffers from age discrepancy and/or prolonged volcanism (up to 8 Ma) on single island volcanoes.

Volcanoes along a chain that are too old to fit the age progression may be explained as having been present on the lithosphere prior to passing over the hotspot. These could be ridge-generated [Batiza, 1981, 1982; Batiza and Vanko, 1984], which can be tested by petrologic means since they would be mostly tholeiitic like MORB. Alternatively, they could be isolated off-ridge volcanoes like Henderson Seamount, in the Eastern Equatorial Pacific [Honda et al., 1987]. In some cases, the flexure response of the lithosphere can be used to determine the age difference between the load (volcano) and the plate [Watts et al., 1980].

Explaining the presence of volcanoes that are much younger than the proper age along a chain can be more problematic, because it is usually difficult to determine whether the young volcanics are a thin cap on a volcano of the correct age or whether the entire edifice is a young volcano. In the former case of volcanic reactivation, renewed volcanism can be caused by passage over a second hotspot; this possibility can be tested kinematically, as done by Gordon and Henderson [1987]. Another alternative is fortuitous volcanic reactivation as discussed by McBirney [1963] and Sykes [1978]. Thus, the presence of volcanoes whose ages violate the predicted age-distance relationship does not necessarily disprove their possible hotspot origin; however, in cases where there are many such volcanoes, as in the Gulf of Alaska [Dalrymple et al., 1987], the hotspot model loses the appeal of its simplicity.

Relative motion between hotspots. Gordon and Henderson [1987] have proposed to account for minor deviations from predicted hotspot tracks by allowing Pacific hotspots to move slowly with respect to each other. When referred to Hawaii, the maximum motion required is 8 mm/yr; the maximum relative motion between two hotspots is about 11 mm/yr between Easter and Tahiti. These numbers are comparable to those mentioned by Morgan [1972a] or Molnar and Francheteau [1975]; in the Pacific, Chase and Sprowl [1984] have proposed to interpret them as representative of the motion of the hotspots away from the geoid high. However, the general difference in order of magnitude between plate/hotspot and hotspot/hotspot velocities constitutes only a minor adjustment to the simple model.

Interaction with the Plate

Action of a hotspot on a ridge system: Trapping. While the general concept of the robustness of the plate/mantle velocity vector with respect to encounter with a hotspot is at first order satisfactory, the conspicuous presence of a large number of hotspots on, or in the immediate vicinity of, mid-ocean ridges arouses suspicion that hotspots may be able to "trap" ridges, or vice versa. Iceland is the perfect example of a hotspot having managed to trap a mid-oceanic ridge through an episode of ridge-jumping, about 9 Ma ago [Morgan, 1981]. The experiments of Olson and Singer [1985] provide some insight into this process, because they show that hotspot fixity is enhanced by the vertical, rather than horizontal, mantle flow expected beneath ridges.

More generally, there is some evidence that the distribution of hotspots is controlled by lithospheric vulnerability [Gass et al., 1978; Pollack et al., 1981], which is a combination of plate speed and thickness. Though this interpretation has been questioned by Vogt [1981] and Stefanick and Jurdy [1984] on several grounds, it is clear that the old, cold and strong lithosphere, though cracked, may act to filter thermal and magmatic events that are transitory, weak, or of small size. The observation that off-ridge non-hotspot volcanoes are added to the lithosphere at rates consistent with plate thickening [Batiza, 1981; Smith and Jordan, 1985] could indicate progressive decrease of availability of magma. Alternatively, it could indicate progressive thermomechanical difficulty for the rising magma to puncture the lithosphere [Spera, 1980; Spence and Turcotte, 1985; Scott et al., 1986].

On the other hand, there exist a number of cases of oceanic islands which were clearly generated on-ridge by a hotspot which is presently an intraplate feature. Examples include the Kerguelen hotspot (which generated the Broken Ridge in an on-ridge geometry), the Tristan da Cunha hotspot [Humphris et al., 1985], and the Northern Tuamotus, which have little if any signal in the geoid, but are abruptly terminated at the Austral Fracture zone [Pilger and Handschumacher, 1981]. One must therefore admit that, just as a ridge can be trapped by a hotspot, it can also escape one. Using the example of the Tuamotu Islands, Okal and Cazenave [1985] speculated that a hotspot had been responsible for rift propagation, in the sense of Hey's [1977] model, an idea already proposed by Vogt [1971] and Vogt and Johnson [1973] to explain "V"-shaped structures at the Mid-Atlantic and Galapagos spreading centers, and by Schilling et al. [1982] on the basis of petrological and geochemical arguments in the Galapagos. This idea has also recently been investigated by Phipps Morgan and Parmentier [1985], who showed that lateral magma-fracture is a plausible mechanism for rifts propagating away from a hotspot; indeed all propagating rifts move away from topographic highs. Okal and Cazenave [1985] proposed that the "circle of influence" of a hotspot for such effects could be on the order of 500 km wide, a figure comparable to estimates of its structural anomaly obtained from seismic probing [e.g., Tryggvason et al., 1983].

Action of a ridge system on a hotspot: Leaking. At the same time, and along the Oeno-Henderson-Ducie-Crough lineament, Okal and Cazenave [1985] noticed that, over a distance of 1000 km, the chain is misaligned by 15° from the azimuth of the plate's absolute velocity. They explained this situation by assuming that conversely, an existing fracture zone can deviate the surficial expression of a hotspot, as long as the lateral distance does not exceed the radius of influence mentioned above. These speculative models fall into the general category of deviated and/or leaking hotspots, which have now been proposed for about a decade. In particular, Schilling [1985] has recently demonstrated a related phenomenon of hotspot-ridge interaction. His evidence shows that hotspots moving off-ridge may maintain a flow channel to the ridge, resulting in predictable geochemical anomaly widths and elevations. This follows the earlier suggestion of Morgan [1978], based entirely on plate kinematics and age-distance relationships, who proposed that in the vicinity of Mid-Ocean Ridges, hotspots could "leak" along horizontal sublithospheric channels into the Mid-Oceanic Ridge, in order to explain the volcanism of such islands as Amsterdam in the Indian Ocean and Darwin in the Galapagos. Okal and Stewart [1982] speculated that interplate earthquakes located at the mouths of such channels may exhibit slow strain release, as a result of thermal decoupling of the transform faults. Epp [1984] lists several examples of these and other perturbations to the simple hotspot model that may obscure or complicate the simplest pattern discussed earlier.

Plate thinning: Plume control vs. delamination. McNutt [1984] reviewed general evidence for an anomalously weak elastic response of the lithosphere under the load from hotspot islands; her observations are readily interpreted in the context of the thinning of the plate. However, as more geoid data become interpreted, it is becoming clear that the response of the plate to hotspot loads, as quantified by its elastic thickness and depth of isostatic compensation, can vary greatly between hotspot chains, and even inside a chain. In a recent review, Calmant [1987] has found elastic thickness values varying from less than 6 km (and thus basically unmeasurable) under the youngest Austral Islands (Rapa, Macdonald) to $\simeq 20$ km in the Marquesas, and $\simeq 30$ km under the Hawaiian swell. Similarly, McNutt [1987] has found that the depth of compensation of the Marquesas is considerably smaller than for the Hawaiian chain (45 vs. 70 km).

In the Austral Islands themselves, Calmant and Cazenave [1986] have pointed out that the extreme southern (and youngest) group, Macdonald and Rapa, are practically not supported elastically, and largely compensated, while the next group to the west, Raivavae, Tubuai, and Rurutu, have elastic thicknesses on the order of 10 km. This situation cannot be explained simply, all the more so since these same authors have estimated that it may take 3—4 Ma before the plate attains its permanent flexural rigidity through initial stress relaxation, as suggested by a strong elastic response under Tahiti already documented by McNutt and Menard [1978].

While the interpretation of the weakened elastic response of the lithosphere must clearly be sought in its thermal regime, a consistent explanation of its observed variation has yet to emerge. McNutt [1987] has put constraints on the depth extent of the temperature anomaly below the Hawaiian and Marquesan swells. Detrick and Crough [1978] showed that lithospheric thinning was taking place too fast to be explained by simple conduction of heat from the plume; a number of models in which convection provides the additional heat flux could better explain the thinning of the plate [Spohn and Schubert, 1982], especially under temperature-dependent rheologies which can reduce the required excess mantle heat flux [Yuen and Fleitout, 1985].

A completely alternate view of lithospheric thinning is the delamination model, in which the location of volcanism may be the result, as opposed to the cause, of the plate's thinning. This model, developed initially for continental volcanoes [Bird, 1979] can reconcile the obviously hot state of the volcanic sites with apparently "colder" geophysical data, such as normal values of whole mantle ScS travel times [Best et al., 1974] and Q [Sipkin and Jordan, 1980], or long-wavelength positive gravity anomalies [Sleep, 1984]. In such a model, one would invoke a form of anchoring of the delaminating plate to ensure the kinematic characteristics of the island chain.

Geochemistry and Origin of Hotspots

Variations in chemistry. When compared to MORB, oceanic basalts generally have higher $^{87}Sr/^{86}Sr$ and lower $^{143}Nd/^{144}Nd$ isotopic ratios. However, a continuum of values is featured between the less radiogenic islands, such as Iceland and Easter, which approach MORB characteristics, and the highly radiogenic ones, such as Tristan, Gough and Samoa. The situation is made more complex when other isotope couples are considered, including the various Pb isotopes and $^3He/^4He$. These recent geochemical observations require at least four and possibly six different endmember mantle components, and we refer to Zindler and Hart [1986] for a complete review of these arguments.

An important aspect of the extreme variability of the isotopic signature of hotspot volcanics is the fact that significant isotopic differences can be documented inside a given chain, or even between various magmatic stages on a single island. For example, in the Austral Islands, Pb and Sr isotope studies indicate that the southernmost group (Macdonald, Marotiri, Rapa) is much less radiogenic than the next one to the north (Tubuai, Rurutu), but that these differences cannot be simply due to a variable degree of mixing [Grall et al., 1985]. Further North, Rarotonga and Mangaia have fundamentally different isotopic signatures, despite being only 200 km apart [Palacz and Saunders, 1986]. This is in agreement with the extreme gradients featured in the Austral Islands region on the so-called "Dupal" anomaly maps [Hart, 1984].

On Ua Pou in the Marquesas Islands, Duncan et al. [1986] have documented an increase in $^{87}Sr/^{86}Sr$ from the shield-building tholeiites to the later-stage alkali basalts. This situation is the opposite of that on Hawaii [Chen and Frey, 1983], and this clearly requires different processes of interaction between the plume and the lithospheric plate in the two chains.

Depth of hotspot sources and/or plumes. That magma is supplied to growing island chains over long periods of time, and that these sources remain reasonably stationary with respect to each other is very well established, although it is clear that kinematic perturbation can occur and that diapirically upwelling mantle and/or mush interacts with the lithosphere in several ways. The major remaining question about the "simple" unified geochemical/geophysical plume hypothesis concerns the depth of origin of the upwelling mantle material (e.g., core-mantle boundary [CMB], lower mantle, transition zone, upper mantle?), and in particular whether this depth is similar for all plumes. This question is important because it is now well-known that while the source of mantle plume magmas is usually different from the MORB source, different plumes may have different mantle sources, and furthermore, enriched plume-like sources exist in the upper mantle [Batiza and Vanko, 1984; Zindler et al., 1984]. These observations provide important constraints for the related questions of chemical and isotopic stratification of the mantle, and of the dominant modes of mantle convection (i.e., whole mantle vs. layered). Also, isotopic systematics and mass balance calculations can provide strong constraints on planetary accretion and differentiation. But accurate calculations of this sort require that the nature of all major reservoirs be well known; in this way, the question of the origin of hotspots magmas becomes pivotal.

Early models, such as Morgan's [1971], argued for a plume source at the core-mantle boundary [CMB]. These were based principally on seismological contentions that significant structural anomalies existed on the CMB below Hawaii [Kanasewich et al., 1973]. These were explained later as artifacts of small scale variations under the receiving seismic arrays [e.g., Capon, 1974; Okal and Kuster, 1975], and indeed the recent tomographic models of the deepest mantle have in general failed to reveal a direct geographical correlation between structure on the CMB and the surface of the planet [Dziewonski, 1984; Morelli and Dziewonski, 1985]; an exception would be Lavely and Forsyth's [1986] observation of a seismic anomaly under the Azores-Gibraltar region. The recent tomography of the CMB carried out at wavelengths of $\simeq$ 1000 km, fails to correlate topographic anomalies on the CMB with hotspot locations at the surface [Gudmundsson et al., 1986].

DePaolo [1980] presented a simple model in which plumes originate within a homogeneous lower mantle that convects separately from the upper mantle region supplying MORB. Chase [1981] and Davies [1984] present both geophysical and geochemical arguments in a favor of a "plum-pudding" model similar to that favored by Allègre et al. [1982], Zindler et al. [1984], and Zindler and Hart [1986]. In these models, the whole mantle or the upper mantle contain heterogeneous domains of variable compositions, size and convective-mixing history. Several recent studies, summarized by Gurnis and Davies [1986] have investigated the question of whether heterogeneities in the mantle can survive intact after diffusion and physical mixing due to convection. They conclude that isotopic heterogeneities, large and small, can survive for long periods, consistent with geochemical evidence.

The difficulty of assigning a depth of origin to island, seamount and MORB sources is due partly to the fact that magmas re-equilibrate during ascent thus masking evidence of a previous higher pressure history. It is for this reason that the plume source has been placed by various workers at a great range of depths: from the CMB [Anderson, 1975] to as shallow as the base of the lithosphere [Anderson, 1985], and even the crust [O'Hara and Yarwood, 1978]. In the absence of direct seismological evidence for the depth of origin of plumes, the debate about the depths and the geometry of plume sources can be expected to continue.

Age and geographical location of hotspots. Studies of the geographical distribution of hotspots indicate that they are preferentially located within a geoid high covering half of the Earth [Chase, 1979; Crough and Jurdy, 1980; Vogt, 1981; Stefanick and Jurdy, 1984]. This geoid high was apparently the former site of Pangea and was located along an equatorial belt [Anderson, 1982; Le Pichon and Huchon, 1984]. In contrast, the geoid low which is also hemispheric and makes a "tennis ball" pattern with equatorial significance with the geoid high marks the site of ancient (200-125 Ma) subduction [Chase, 1979; Chase and Sprowl, 1983;

Jurdy, 1983]. These observations can be interpreted to show that: (i) the location of hotspots and subduction zones control the position of the Earth's spin axis [Crough and Jurdy, 1980; Jurdy, 1983; Le Pichon and Huchon, 1984]; (ii) the present geoid pattern may reflect deep mantle convection [Chase, 1979 and others]; and (iii) the present hotspots were caused by heating from the thermal blanket effect on Pangea over the mantle [Anderson, 1982; Le Pichon and Huchon, 1984].

These suggestions provide a self-consistent scenario in which continents aggregate at the Equator, heat the mantle below by a thermal blanketing effect causing episodic production of many hotspots which then cause fragmentation and dispersal of the supercontinent. This suggestion is consistent with the lack of direct evidence for hotspots older than 200-125 Ma, and has important implications for the evolution of convective patterns within the Earth. It is possible that such a scenario could result in cycles of supercontinent formation and break-up on the order of 400 Ma long [Le Pichon and Huchon, 1984; Bond et al., 1984]. Note however that the continent concentrations necessary to explain the origin of hotspots in this model have not all been proven from a geological standpoint.

If these suggestions prove to be correct, then continental break-up by hotspots may probably indicate a lower mantle source for hotspots initially. If such a source persists over the lifetime of hotspots ($\simeq 200$ Ma), the isotopic differences among hotspots, together with variation along a single chain, and even within a single volcano, permit the conclusion either that the lower mantle is heterogeneous or that the lower mantle material mixes freely with heterogeneous upper mantle material during ascent. Alternatively, after the initial paroxismal event, the convective pattern could change, rooting diapiric convective instabilities at many levels in the mantle.

Clearly, any model linking the geophysical characteristics of mantle plumes has the difficult task of explaining the very common, but inconsistent, interchain, intrachain, and interisland differences in isotopic ratios discussed earlier that document mixing of several distinct mantle sources. Without finer independent constraints on depth of generation, the simplest approach is to invoke a plum-pudding model. In some favorable cases, however, like Ua Pou, it has been possible to obtain some geometric constraints on the mantle sources, but this is unusual and not repeatable.

Conclusions

Not All Hotspots are Created Equal

The first observation resulting from this brief review is that, as more and more geophysical and geochemical data are obtained and analyzed, it appears that substantial differences between chains exist at nearly every stage of the genesis of the islands:

In the first place, the chemical nature of the mantle heterogeneities from which ocean island basalts are derived is clearly variable. Recent advances in isotope analyses now require at least four and possibly six separate reservoirs [Zindler and Hart, 1986], the isotopic signatures of the islands resulting from a mixing between endmembers, whose variability cannot be confined to the shallow region of interaction with the lithosphere.

The obvious differences in rates of lava extrusion between island chains are most probably accompanied by variations in the depth of melting, as witnessed by substantial differences in major element composition (e.g., the absence of tholeiites on the Society Islands). Similarly, the actual mechanism of interaction with the plate during the final stages of magma ascent is highly variable, as evidenced by the differing trends in the evolution of isotopic signatures found in the Marquesas and Hawaiian chains [Duncan et al., 1986]. Despite their relatively low contribution to the total volumes erupted, the level of activity during the posterosional stages also vary significantly.

Finally, the mechanical relationship between plate and island is itself the subject of substantial variation, with no universal correlation with plate age. The degree of thinning and re-heating (or, alternatively, of delamination) undergone by the plate must be adjusted by variations in the thermomechanical properties of the plume/plate system which presently elude us.

A Clear Scofflaw: the Cook-Austral Chain

In Section 2 of this paper, we have often drawn on the Cook-Austral Islands to find examples of substantial deviation from the "simple" hotspot model. This has included: failure to remain a single linear chain (Raivavae-Rapa, Rarotonga-Aituki); violation of age-distance relationships (Rarotonga; Rurutu); prolonged or renewed episodes of volcanism (Tubuai); strong isotopic gradients (Macdonald-Rapa vs. Tubuai-Rurutu; Rarotonga vs. Mangaia); and rapid lateal variations in the mechanical response of the plate to loading (Macdonald-Rapa vs. Tubuai-Rurutu).

These anomalies, and the correlation of some of the properties among smaller geographic entities, suggest that the production of islands involved processes of differing chemical, thermal and mechanical nature, for groups such as Macdonald and Rapa on the one hand, and Rurutu and Tubuai on the other. It is therefore tempting to assume physically different upwelling systems (plumes or blobs), which in turn supports a discontinuous nature for the mantle heterogeneities responsible for island chains [Schilling and Noe-Nygaard, 1974; Schilling et al., 1982].

About the only remaining characteristics of a hotspot chain upheld in this case are its general WNW-ESE orientation, and the location of the only known active volcano (Macdonald) at its eastern end. One may even challenge the latter, since the chain, when prolonged $\simeq 1200$ km over poorly chartered waters, encounters in the vicinity of 35°S, 125°W a geoid high clearly apparent on worldwide maps [e.g., Francheteau, 1983], correlated with an area of anomalously shallow bathymetry, where the very few available shiptracks are densely populated with seamounts. The nature and origin of this volcanism, and its possible relationship with the Cook-Austral hotspot[s] remains an open problem.

When regrouped, all this negative evidence makes a clear maverick, if not an outright scofflaw, of the Cook-Austral chain. Actually, one starts wondering whether the hotspot theory would have emerged as it did, had more cases of Austral-type chains been documented (especially if located in more accessible regions) early in the game.

A Final Perspective

With the above remarks in mind, we must also emphasize that not all intraplate volcanism forms linear island chains. Some may also form isolated volcanoes [Batiza, 1982], large plateaux, which may not all be convincingly explained by hotspots, and even basin-wide volcanic events [Schlanger et al., 1981]. It may then be possible to regard hotspot chains as part of a continuum starting at tiny, ephemeral, blobs, and ranging to vast hemispheric upward surges of hot material. This approach allows for variation in their rate of thermal and magmatic activity, with, for example, the Marquesas representing a single, short-lived burst of thermal activity, Hawaii, a prolonged episode of sustained extrusion, and the other chains having a presumably more complex history [McNutt, 1987]. It also accommodates readily such variations to the hotspot model as described by Epp [1984] or the "hot line" concept of Bonatti and Harrison [1976].

Further, the size and distribution of plumes or blobs may vary with time, and be partly filtered by a cracked, though strong, lithosphere. Treating this speculative notion requires both additional field evidence for the characteristics of volcanism, and laboratory theoretical tests to determine whether such a scheme is permitted by known properties and history.

Acknowledgments. We dedicate this paper to the memory of Bill Menard, who inspired us by his profound knowledge and vision of the Pacific floor and its tenants, large and small. We thank Sy Schlanger, David Epp and Jean-Guy Schilling for careful reviews of an earlier draft of the manuscript. This research was supported by the Office of Naval Research, under Contracts N00014-C-84-0616 (EAO) and N00014-80-C-0856 (RB), and the National Science Foundation under Grants OCE-83-08980 and OCE-85-08042 (RB).

References

Allègre, C.J., Chemical Geodynamics, *Tectonophysics, 81*, 109-132, 1982.

Allègre, C.J., O. Brévart, C. Dupré, and J.-F. Minster, Isotopic and chemical effects produced in a continuously convecting Earth mantle, *Phil. Trans. Roy. Soc. London, 297A*, 447-477, 1980.

Allègre, C.J., B. Dupré, P. Richard, and D. Rousseau, Subcontinental versus suboceanic mantle, 2. Nd-Sr-Pb isotopic comparison of continental tholeiites with mid-ocean ridge tholeiites and the structure of the continental lithosphere, *Earth Planet. Sci. Letts., 57*, 25-34, 1982.

Anderson, D.L., Chemical plumes in the mantle, *Geol. Soc. Amer. Bull., 86*, 1593-1600, 1975.

Anderson, D.L., Hotspots, basalts, and the evolution of the mantle, *Science, 213*, 82-89, 1981.

Anderson, D.L., Hotspots, polar wander, Mesozoic convection, and the geoid, *Nature, 297*, 391-393, 1982.

Anderson, D.L., Hotspot magmas can form by fractionation and contamination of mid-ocean ridge basalts, *Nature, 318*, 145-149, 1985.

Batiza, R., Lithospheric age dependence on the rate of off-ridge volcano production in the North Pacific, *Geophys. Res. Lett., 8*, 853-856, 1981.

Batiza, R., Abundance distribution and sizes of volcanoes in the Pacific Ocean and implications for the origin of non-hotspot volcanoes, *Earth Planet. Sci. Letts., 60*, 196-206, 1982.

Batiza, R., and D. Vanko, Petrology of young Pacific seamounts, *J. Geophys. Res., 89*, 11235-11260, 1984.

Best, W.J., L.R. Johnson, and T.V. McEvilly, ScS and the mantle beneath Hawaii [abstract], *Eos, Trans. Amer. Geophys. Un., 55*, 1147, 1974.

Bird. G.P., Continental delamination and the Colorado plateau, *J. Geophys. Res., 84*, 7561-7571, 1979.

Bonatti, E., and C.G.A. Harrison, Hot lines in the Earth's mantle, *Nature, 263*, 402-404, 1976.

Bond, G.C., P.A. Nickeson, and M.A. Komruz, Breakup of a supercontinent between 625 Ma and 555 Ma: new evidence and implications for continental histories, *Earth Planet. Sci. Letts., 70*, 325-345, 1984.

Calmant, S., The elastic thickness of the lithosphere in the Pacific Ocean, *Earth Planet. Sci. Letts.*, in press, 1987.

Calmant, S., and A. Cazenave, The effective elastic lithosphere under the Cook-Austral and Society Islands, *Earth Planet. Sci. Letts., 77*, 187-202, 1986.

Capon, J., Characterization of crust and upper mantle structure under LASA as a random medium, *Bull. Seismol. Soc. Amer., 64*, 235-266, 1974.

Castillo, P., and R. Batiza, Petrology of the Cocos Ridge: a case study of petrologic evolution of a hotspot [abstract], *Eos, Trans. Amer. Geophys. Un., 67*, 410, 1986.

Castillo, P., R. Batiza, and R.J. Stern, Petrology and geochemistry of Nauru Basin igneous complex: large volume off-ridge eruptions of MORB-like basalt during the Cretaceous, *Initial Repts. Deep Sea Drilling Proj., 89*, 555-576, 1986.

Chase, C.G., Subduction, the geoid, and lower mantle convection, *Nature, 282*, 464-468, 1979.

Chase, C.G., Oceanic island Pb: two-stage histories and mantle evolution, *Earth Planet. Sci. Letts., 52*, 277-284, 1981.

Chase, C.G., and D.R. Sprowl, The modern geoid and ancient plate boundaries, *Earth Planet. Sci. Letts., 62*, 314-320, 1983.

Chase, C.G., and D.R. Sprowl, Proper motion of hotspots: Pacific plate [abstract], *Eos, Trans. Amer. Geophys. Un., 65*, 1099, 1984.

Chen, C.-Y., and F.A. Frey, Origin of Hawaiian tholeiite and alkalic basalt, *Nature, 302*, 785-789, 1983.

Christofferson, E., The relationship of sea-floor spreading in the Pacific to the origin of the Emperor Seamounts and the Hawaiian Islands chain [abstract], *Trans. Amer. Geophys. Un., 49*, 214, 1968.

Crough, S.T., Thermal origin of mid-plate hotspot swells, *Geophys. J. Roy. astr. Soc., 55*, 451-469, 1978.

Crough, S.T., Mesozoic hotspot epeirogeny in eastern North America, *Geology, 9*, 2-6, 1981.

Crough, S.T., and D.M. Jurdy, Subducted lithosphere, hotspots, and the geoid, *Earth Planet. Sci. Letts., 48*, 15-22, 1980.

Dalrymple, G.B., R.D. Jarrard, and D.A. Clague, K/Ar ages of some volcanic rocks from the Cook and Austral Islands, *Geol. Soc. Amer. Bull., 86*, 1463-1467, 1975.

Dalrymple, G.B., D.A. Clague, T.L. Vallier, and H.W. Menard, $^{40}Ar/^{39}Ar$ Age, petrology, and tectonic significance of some seamounts in the Gulf of Alaska, in: *Seamounts, Islands and Atolls, A Memorial to Henry William Menard*, Edited by B. Keating, P. Fryer, R. Batiza and G. Boehlert, American Geophysical Union Monograph, this volume, 1987.

Dana, J.D., *Geology, Volume 10 of the United States exploring expedition during the years 1838-1839, 1840, 1841, 1842*, 756 pp., Sherman and Co., Philadelphia, 1849.

Davies, G., Geophysical and isotopic constraints on mantle convection: an interim synthesis, *J. Geophys. Res., 89*, 6017-6040, 1984.

DePaolo, D.P., Crustal growth and mantle evolution: inferences from models of element transport and Nd and Sr isotopes, *Geochem. Cosmochim. Acta, 44*, 1185-1196, 1980.

DePaolo, D.J., and G.J. Wasserburg, Nd isotopic variations and petrogenetic models, *Geophys. Res. Letts., 3*, 249-252, 1976.

DePaolo, D.J., and G.J. Wasserburg, Neodynium isotopes in flood basalts from the Siberian Platform and inferences about their mantle sources, *Proc. Natl. Acad. Sci. USA, 76*, 3056-3060, 1979.

Detrick, R.S., and S.T. Crough, Islands subsidence, hotspots, and lithospheric thinning, *J. Geophys. Res., 83*, 1236-1244, 1978.

Dixon, T.H., R. Batiza, K. Futa, and D. Martin, Petrochemistry, age and isotopic composition of alkali basalts from Ponape Island, Western Pacific, *Chemical Geology, 43*, 1-28, 1984.

Duncan, R.A., Hotspots in the southern oceans: an absolute frame of reference for motion of the Gondwana continents, *Tectonophysics, 74*, 29-42, 1981.

Duncan, R.A., and I. McDougall, Linear volcanism in French Polynesia, *J. Volcanol. Geotherm. Res., 1*, 197-227, 1976.

Duncan, R.A., M.T. McCulloch, H.G. Barsczus, and D.R. Nelson, Plume versus lithospheric sources for melts at Ua Pou, Marquesas Islands, *Nature, 322*, 534-538, 1986.

Dziewonski, A.M., Mapping the lower mantle: determination of lateral heterogeneity in P velocity up to degree and order 6, *J. Geophys. Res.*, *89*, 5929-5952, 1984.

Epp, D., Age and tectonic relationships among volcanic chains on the Pacific plate, *Ph.D. Dissertation*, 199 pp., University of Hawaii, Honolulu, 1978.

Epp, D., Possible perturbations to hotspot traces and implications for the origin and structure of the Line Islands, *J. Geophys. Res.*, *89*, 11273-11286, 1984.

Fiske, R.S., and E.D. Jackson, Orientation and growth of Hawaiian volcanic rifts: The effect of regional structure and gravitational stresses, *Proc. Roy. Soc. London*, *329A*, 299-326, 1972.

Francheteau, J., The oceanic crust, *Scientific American*, *249*, 114-129, 1983.

Gass, I.G., D.S. Chapman, H.N. Pollack, and R.S. Thorpe, Geological and geophysical parameters of mid-plate volcanism, *Phil. Trans. Roy. Soc. London*, *288A*, 581-597, 1978.

Gordon, R.G., and L.J. Henderson, Pacific plate hotspot tracks, *J. Geophys. Res.*, in press, 1987.

Grall, H.M., B. Hanan, E.A. Okal, and J.-G. Schilling, The Macdonald hotspot: Pb isotopes [abstract], *Eos, Trans. Amer. Geophys. Un.*, *66*, 409, 1985.

Gudmundsson, O., R.W. Clayton, and D.L. Anderson, CMB topography inferred from ISC PcP travel times [abstract], *Eos, Trans. Amer. Geophys. Un.*, *67*, 1100, 1986.

Gurnis, M., and G. Davies, Mixing in numerical models incorporating plate kinematics, *J. Geophys. Res.*, *91*, 6375-6395, 1986.

Haggerty, J.A., S.O. Schlanger, and I. Premoli-Silva, Late Cretaceous and Eocene volcanism in the southern Line Islands, and implications for the hotspot theory, *Geology*, *10*, 433-437, 1982.

Hamelin, B., B. Dupré, and C.J. Allègre, Lead-strontium isotopic variations along the East Pacific Rise and the Mid-Atlantic Ridge: a comparative study, *Earth Planet. Sci. Letts.*, *67*, 340-350, 1984.

Hart, S.R., A large-scale isotope anomaly in the Southern Hemisphere mantle, *Nature*, *309*, 753-757, 1984.

Hartnady, C.J.H., and A.P. le Roex, Southern Ocean hotspot tracks, and the Cenozoic absolute motion of the African, Antarctic, and South American plates, *Earth Planet. Sci. Letts.*, *75*, 245-257, 1985.

Hey, R.N., A new class of pseudofaults and their bearing on plate tectonics, *Earth Planet. Sci. Letts.*, *37*, 321-325, 1977.

Holden, J.C., and P.R. Vogt, Graphic solutions to problems of plumacy, *Eos, Trans. Amer. Geophys. Un.*, *58*, 573-580, 1977.

Honda, M., T. Bernatowicz, F.A. Podosek, R. Batiza, and P.T. Taylor, Age determination of East Pacific Seamounts (Henderson, 6 and 7) — Implications for near-ridge and intraplate volcanism, *Mar. Geol.*, *74*, 79-84, 1987.

Humphris, S.E., G. Thompson, J.-G. Schilling, and R.H. Kingsley, Petrologic and geochemical variation along the Mid-Atlantic Ridge between 46°S and 32°S; influence of the Tristan da Cunha mantle plume, *Geochem. Cosmochim. Acta*, *49*, 1445-1464, 1985.

Jackson, E.D., Linear volcanic chains on the Pacific plate, in: *The Geophysics of the Pacific Basin and its Margins*, Edited by G.H. Sutton, M.H. Manghnani and R. Moberly, *Amer. Geophys. Un. Geophys. Monog.*, *19*, pp. 315-335, Washington, D.C., 1976.

Jackson, E.D., E.A. Silver, and G.B. Dalrymple, Hawaiian-Emperor chain and its relation to Cenozoic circum-Pacific tectonics, *Geol. Soc. Amer. Bull.*, *83*, 601-618, 1972.

Jarrard, R.D., and D.A. Clague, Implications of Pacific island and seamount ages for the origin of volcanic chains, *Revs. Geophys. Space Phys.*, *15*, 57-76, 1977.

Jurdy, D.M., Early Tertiary subduction zones and hotspots, *J. Geophys. Res.*, *88*, 6395-6402, 1983.

Kanasewich, E.R., R.M. Ellis, C.H. Chapman, and P.R. Gutowski, Seismic array evidence of a core boundary source for the Hawaiian linear volcanic chain, *J. Geophys. Res.*, *78*, 1361-1371, 1973.

Lavely, E.M., and D.W. Forsyth, Shear wave velocity anomalies in the lowermost mantle [abstract], *Eos, Trans. Amer. Geophys. Un.*, *67*, 312, 1986.

Le Pichon, X., and P. Huchon, Geoid, Pangea and convection, *Earth Planet. Sci. Letts.*, *67*, 123-135, 1984.

Lonsdale, P., Geography and history of the Louisville hotspot chain in the Southwest Pacific, *J. Geophys. Res.*, in press, 1987.

Mahoney, J., Isotopic survey of Pacific Ocean plateaus: implications for their nature and origin, in: *Seamounts, Islands and Atolls, A Memorial to Henry William Menard*, Edited by B. Keating, P. Fryer, R. Batiza and G. Boehlert, *American Geophysical Union Monograph*, this volume, 1987.

Mattey, D.P., The minor and trace element geochemistry of volcanic rocks from Truk, Ponape, and Kusaie, Eastern Caroline Islands: the evolution of a young hotspot trace across old Pacific Ocean crust, *Contrib. Mineral. Petrol.*, *80*, 1-13, 1982.

McBirney, A.R., Factors governing the nature of submarine volcanism, *Bull. Volcanol.*, *26*, 455-469, 1963..

McDougall, I., and R.A. Duncan, Linear volcanic chains: recording plate motions?, *Tectonophysics*, *63*, 275-295, 1980.

McNutt, M.K., Lithospheric flexure and thermal anomalies, *J. Geophys. Res.*, *89*, 11180-11194, 1984.

McNutt, M.K., Temperature beneath mid-plate swells, in: *Seamounts, Islands and Atolls, A Memorial to Henry William Menard*, Edited by B. Keating, P. Fryer, R. Batiza and G. Boehlert, *American Geophysical Union Monograph*, this volume, 1987.

McNutt, M.K., and H.W. Menard, Lithospheric flexure and uplifted atolls, *J. Geophys. Res.*, *83*, 1206-1212, 1978.

Menard, H.W., and M.K. McNutt, Evidence for and consequences of thermal rejuvenation, *J. Geophys. Res.*, *87*, 8570-8580, 1982.

Minster, J.B., and T.H. Jordan, Present-day plate motions, *J. Geophys. Res.*, *83*, 5331-5354, 1978.

Molnar, P., and T. Atwater, Relative motion of hotspots in the mantle, *Nature*, *246*, 288-291, 1973.

Molnar, P., and J. Francheteau, The relative motion of 'hotspots' in the Atlantic and Indian Oceans during the Cenozoic, *Geophys. J. Roy. astr. Soc.*, *43*, 763-774, 1975.

Morelli, A., and A.M. Dziewonski, Stability of aspherical models of the lower mantle [abstract], *Eos, Trans. Amer. Geophys. Un.*, *66*, 975, 1985.

Morgan, W.J., Convection plumes in the lower mantle, *Nature*, *230*, 42-43, 1971.

Morgan, W.J., Plate motions and deep mantle convections, *Geol. Soc. Amer. Mem.*, *132*, 7-22, 1972a.

Morgan, W.J., Deep mantle convection plumes and plate motions, *Amer. Assoc. Petrol. Geol. Bull.*, *56*, 203-213, 1972b.

Morgan. W.J., Rodriguez, Darwin, Amsterdam..., a second type of hotspot island, *J. Geophys. Res.*, *83*, 5355-5360, 1978.

Morgan, W.J., Hotspot tracks and the opening of the Atlantic and Indian Oceans, in: *The Oceanic Lithosphere*, Edited by C. Emiliani, *The Sea*, vol. 7, 443-487, J. Wiley & Sons, New York, 1981.

Morgan, W.J., Hotspot tracks and the early rifting of the Atlantic, *Tectonophysics*, *94*, 123-139, 1983.

Mottay, G., Contribution à l'étude géologique de la Polynésie Française: — Archipel des Australes — Mehetia (Archipel de la Société), *Thèse de 3ème cycle*, 228 pp., Univ. Paris-Sud, Orsay, 1976.

Natland, J.H., and D.L. Turner, Age progression and petrologic development of Samoan shield volcanoes: evidence from K/Ar ages, lava compositions and mineral studies, in: *Circumpacific*

Earth Series, Edited by T. Brocher, Amer. Assoc. Petrol. Geol., in press, 1987.

O'Hara, M.J., and G. Yarwood, High-pressure-temperature point on an Archean geotherm, implying magma genesis by crustal anatexis, and consequences for garnet-pyroxene thermometry and barometry, Phil. Trans. Roy. Soc. London, 288A, 441-456, 1978.

Okal, E.A., and A. Cazenave, A Model for the Plate Tectonics evolution of the Eastcentral Pacific based on SEASAT investigations, Earth Planet. Sci. Letts., 72, 99-116, 1985.

Okal, E., and G. Kuster, A teleseismic array study in French Polynesia: implications for local and distant structures, Geophys. Res. Lett., 2, 5-8, 1975.

Okal, E.A., and L.M. Stewart, Slow earthquakes along oceanic fracture zones: evidence for asthenospheric flow away from hotspots? Earth Plan. Sci. Lett., 57, 75-87, 1982.

Olson, P., and U. Christensen, Solitary wave propagation in a fluid conduit within a viscous matrix, J. Geophys. Res., 91, 6367-6374, 1986.

Olson, P., and H. Singer, Creeping plumes, J. Fluid Mech., 158, 511-531, 1985.

Palacz, Z., and A.D. Saunders, Coupled trace element and isotope enrichment in the Cook-Austral-Samoa islands, Southwest Pacific, Earth Planet. Sci. Letts., 79, 270-280, 1986.

Phipps Morgan, J., and E.M. Parmentier, Causes and rate-limiting mechanisms of ridge propagation: a fracture mechanics model, J. Geophys. Res., 90, 8603-8612, 1985.

Pilger, R.H. Jr., The origin of hotspot traces: evidence from eastern Australia, J. Geophys. Res., 87, 1825-1834, 1982.

Pilger, R.H. Jr., and D.W. Handschumacher, The fixed hotspot hypothesis and origin of the Easter-Sala y Gomez-Nazca trace, Geol. Soc. Amer. Bull., 92, 437-446, 1981.

Pollack, H.N., I.G. Gass, R.S. Thorpe, and D.S. Chapman, On the vulnerability of lithospheric plates to mid-plate volcanism: Reply to P.R. Vogt, J. Geophys. Res., 86, 961-966, 1981.

Ribe, N.H., Diapirism in the Earth's mantle: experiments on the motion of a hot sphere in a fluid with temperature-dependent viscosity, J. Volcanol. Geotherm. Res., 16, 221-245, 1983.

Schilling, J.-G., Sea floor evolution: rare earth evidence, Phil. Trans. Roy. Soc. London, 268A, 663-706, 1971.

Schilling, J.-G., Iceland mantle plume: geochemical evidence along the Reykjanes Ridge, Nature, 242, 565-569, 1973.

Schilling, J.-G., Upper mantle heterogeneity and dynamics, Nature, 314, 62-67, 1985.

Schilling, J.-G., and A. Noe-Nygaard, Færœ-Iceland plume: rare earth evidence, Earth Planet. Sci. Letts., 24, 1-14, 1974.

Schilling, J.-G., and J.W. Winchester, Rare Earth fractionation and magmatic processes in: Mantles of the Earth and terrestrial planets, Edited by S.K. Runcorn, pp. 267-283, Interscience Publishers, London, 1967.

Schilling, J.-G., R.H. Kingsley, and J.D. Devine, Galapagos hotspot-spreading center system: 1. Spatial petrological and geochemical variations (83°W-101°W), J. Geophys. Res., 87, 5593-5610, 1982.

Schilling, J.-G., M. Zajac, R. Evans, T. Johnston, W. White, J.D. Devine, and R. Kingsley, Petrologic and geochemical variations along the Mid-Atlantic Ridge from 29°N to 73°N, Amer. J. Sci., 283, 510-586, 1983.

Schlanger, S.O., H.C. Jenkyns, and I. Premoli-Silva, Volcanism and vertical tectonics in the Pacific basin related to global Cretaceous transgressions, Earth Planet. Sci. Letts., 52, 435-449, 1981.

Schlanger, S.O., M.O. Garcia, B.H. Keating, J.J. Naughton, W.W. Sager, J.A. Haggerty, J.A. Philpotts, and R.A. Duncan, Geology and Geochronology of the Line Islands, J. Geophys. Res., 89, 11261-11272, 1984.

Schlanger, S.O., and R. Moberly, Sedimentary and volcanic history: East Mariana Basin and Nauru Basin, Initial Repts. Deep Sea Drilling Proj., 89, 653-678, 1986.

Schminke, H.-U., The Canary Islands, Edited by G. Kunkel, pp. 67-184, Junk, The Hague, 1975.

Scott, D.R., D.J. Stevenson, and J.A. Whitehead Jr., Observations of solitary waves in a viscously deformable pipe, Nature, 319, 759-761, 1986.

Shaw, H.R., Mantle convection and volcanic periodicity in the Pacific: evidence from Hawaii, Geol. Soc. Amer. Bull., 84, 1505-1526, 1973.

Shaw, H.R., and E.D. Jackson, Linear island chains in the Pacific: result of thermal plumes or gravitational anchors?, J. Geophys. Res., 78, 8634-8652, 1973.

Sipkin, S.A., and T.H. Jordan, Regional variation of Q_{ScS}, Bull. Seismol. Soc. Amer., 70, 1071-1102, 1980.

Skilbeck, J.N., and J.A. Whitehead, Jr., Formation of discrete islands in linear chains, Nature, 272, 499-501, 1978.

Sleep, N.H., Lithospheric delamination beneath Hawaii: no plume [abstract], Eos, Trans. Amer. Geophys. Un., 65, 1087, 1984.

Smith, D.K., and T.H. Jordan, Abundances and production rates of Pacific seamounts [abstract], Eos, Trans. Amer. Geophys. Un., 66, 1079, 1985.

Spence, D.A., and D.L. Turcotte, Magma-driven propagation of cracks, J. Geophys. Res., 90, 575-580, 1985.

Spera, F., Aspects of magma transport, in: Physics of magmatic processes, Edited by R.B. Hargraves, pp. 268-324, Princeton Univ. Press, Princeton, N.J., 1980.

Spohn, T., and G. Schubert, Convective thinning of the lithosphere: A mechanism for the initiation of continental rifting, J. Geophys. Res., 87, 4669-4681, 1982.

Stefanick, M., and D.M. Jurdy, The distribution of hotspots, J. Geophys. Res., 89, 9919-9925, 1984.

Sykes, L.R., Intraplate seismicity, reactivation of preexisting zones of weakness, alkaline magmatism and other forms of tectonism postdating continental fragmentation, Revs. Geophys. Space Phys., 16, 621-688, 1978.

Talandier, J., and E.A. Okal, The volcanoseismic swarms of 1981-1983 in the Tahiti-Mehetia area, French Polynesia, J. Geophys. Res., 89, 11216-11234, 1984.

Tatsumoto, M., C.E. Hedge, and A.E.J. Engel, Potassium, rubidium, strontium, thorium, uranium, and the ratio $^{87}Sr/^{86}Sr$ in oceanic tholeiitic basalt, Science, 150, 886-888, 1965.

Tryggvason, K., E.S. Husebye, and R. Stefánsson, Seismic image of the hypothetized Iceland hotspot, Tectonophysics, 100, 97-118, 1983.

Turcotte, D.L., and E.R. Oxburgh, Intraplate volcanism, Phil. Trans. Roy. Soc. London, 288A, 561-579, 1978.

Turner, D.L., and R.D. Jarrard, K/Ar dating of the Cook-Austral Island chain: a test of the hot spot hypothesis, J. Volcanol. Geotherm. Res., 12, 187-220, 1982.

Vogt, P.R., Asthenosphere motion recorded by the Ocean floor south of Iceland, Earth Planet. Sci. Letts., 13, 153-160, 1971.

Vogt, P.R., Volcano spacing, fractures and thickness of the lithosphere, Earth Planet. Sci. Letts., 21, 235-252, 1974.

Vogt, P.R., On the applicability of thermal conduction models to mid-plate volcanism: Comments on a paper by Gass et al., J. Geophys. Res., 86, 950-960, 1981.

Vogt, P.R., and G.L. Johnson, Magnetic telechemistry of oceanic crust?, Nature, 245, 373-375, 1973.

Vogt, P.R., and N.C. Smoot, The Geisha Guyots: Multibeam bathymetry and morphometric interpretation, *J. Geophys. Res.*, *89*, 11085-11107, 1984.

Walcott, R.I., Flexure of the lithosphere at Hawaii, *Tectonophysics*, *9*, 435-446, 1970.

Watts, A.B., An analysis of isostasy in the world's oceans, 1. Hawaiian-Emperor Seamount chain, *J. Geophys. Res.*, *83*, 5985-6004, 1978.

Watts, A.B., J.H. Bodina, and N.M. Ribe, Observations of flexure and the geological evolution of the Pacific ocean basin, *Nature*, *283*, 532-537, 1980.

Watts, A.B., D.P. McKenzie, B. Parsons, and M. Roufosse, The relationship between gravity and bathymetry in the Pacific Ocean, *Geophys. J. Roy. astr. Soc.*, *83*, 263-298, 1985.

Wegener, A., *Die Entstehung der Kontinente und Ozeane*, Fried. Wieveg & Sohn, Braunschweig, 1915.

Wilson, J.T., Continental Drift, *Scientific American*, *208*, 86-100, 1963.

Winterer, E.L., Anomalies in the tectonic evolution of the Pacific, in: *The Geophysics of the Pacific Basin and its Margins*, Edited by G.H. Sutton, M.H. Manghnani and R. Moberly, *Amer. Geophys. Un. Geophys. Monog.*, *19*, pp. 269-278, Washington, D.C., 1976.

Yuen, D.A., and L. Fleitout, Thinning of the lithosphere by small-scale convective destabilization, *Nature*, *313*, 125-128, 1985.

Zindler, A., and S. Hart, Chemical Geodynamics, *Annu. Revs. Earth Planet. Sci.*, *14*, 493-571, 1986.

Zindler, A., H. Staudigel, and R. Batiza, Isotope and trace element geochemistry of young Pacific seamounts: implications for the scale of upper mantle heterogeneity, *Earth Planet. Sci. Letts.*, *70*, 175-195, 1984.

SEAMOUNT ABUNDANCES AND DISTRIBUTION NEAR THE EAST PACIFIC RISE 0°-24°N BASED ON SEABEAM DATA

Daniel J. Fornari,[1] Rodey Batiza,[2] and Mary Ann Luckman[1]

Abstract. We have used 10,240 line kilometers of Seabeam data to study the sizes, abundances and distribution of seamounts near the East Pacific rise (EPR) from the equator to 24°N on lithosphere <10 Ma. We find 168 volcanoes with heights over 50 m in this study area of 18,400 km^2 for a mean seamount abundance of about 9000 seamounts/10^{6}km^2 or 1.5 million seamounts for the Pacific assuming constant production rates. Abundances in 49 undivided 1°×1° areas vary widely from values of zero to over 66,000 seamounts/10^{6}km^2 after linear adjustment for percent of area coverage in each 1° square. This indicates highly non-uniform distribution and, in fact, most seamounts are clustered near transform and fracture zones, some large overlapping spreading centers (OSCs) and swollen elevated portions of the EPR. Seamount abundance within 50 km of the EPR is about 10,000±6000/10^{6}km^2 and does not seem to change significantly out to 550 km from the EPR crustal age (4-9 Ma). Size frequency distribution shows similar patterns for 0-0.5 Ma and 0.5-1.0 Ma sea floor, with 70-80% of the volcanoes being smaller than 0.1 km^3 (<100 m high); on older crust, however, only about 45% are in this small size class. If representative, these data indicate that most small seamounts are produced very near the EPR and some may continue to grow as they drift away, in agreement with previous geologic, petrologic, magnetic and radiometric age evidence. This study provides further evidence that seamount production is strongly linked to tectonic and petrologic processes at the EPR near major transform offsets and possibly at some large OSCs. Our data seem to indicate that seamount production on lithosphere <10 Ma occurs almost exclusively very near the EPR axis, which contrasts with earlier findings of a relationship between seamount production and lithosphere age. We attribute this disagreement, in part, to the strong age bias of the data set used in this study, but this disagreement points to the need for more field studies and data to resolve the question of the extent to which seamount production is related to lithosphere age and plate boundary processes.

Introduction

Batiza [1981, 1982] used map counts to infer the sizes, distribution and production rates of seamounts in the Pacific. These studies revealed that the size distribution of seamounts is Poisson-like and that mean and maximum seamount sizes increase with lithosphere age [Vogt, 1974b]. Jordan et al. [1983], Smith and Jordan [1985a,b] and Jordan and Smith [1986], in addition to map counts, used 160,000 line kilometers of conventional echo soundings and limited amounts of Seabeam [Renard and Allenou, 1979] data to investigate the size distribution of seamounts. Their findings about size distribution agreed with those of Batiza [1982], but they were able to study seamounts only 100 m high (using Seabeam) versus minimum sizes of 365 m and 182 m studied by Batiza. One purpose of this study is to extend information on the size frequency distribution of small near-ridge seamounts to seamounts only 50 m high [Luckman et al., 1985]. For this we use 10,240 line kilometers of Seabeam data and find that the size distribution of seamounts remains Poisson-like down to 50 m heights.

Seabeam maps (20 m contours) show 168 seamounts with heights greater than 50 m in our study area of 18,400 km^2 centered on the EPR between the equator and 24°N. Assuming uniform distribution, which we later show to be highly questionable, these data suggest abundances of about 9000 small seamounts per 10^{6}km^2 on lithosphere <10 Ma, or about 1.5 million seamounts in the Pacific Basin with heights less than about 1 km. This estimate assumes constant production rate and agrees with the recent estimate of over 1 million by Smith and Jordan [1985a].

Smith and Jordan [1985a,b] found that most small seamounts in the eastern and south Pacific are produced near the ridge on lithosphere <10 Ma in agreement with the geologic and petrologic findings of Batiza and Vanko [1983, 1984], Batiza and Smith [1986], Fornari et al. [1984], Lonsdale [1985], the magnetic studies of McNutt [1986] and recent radiometric dating results [Graham et al., 1986; Honda et al., 1986]. Batiza [1981] inferred that seamount production was related to t$^{1/2}$ implying highest production near ridges. In this study, we also find that seamount production is very high within 50 km (0.4-1 Ma depending on spreading rate) of the EPR crest: 10,160±6000 volcanoes per 10^{6}km^2. Surprisingly though, production rates remain constant within error as the lithosphere ages out to 550 km (4-9 Ma) from the ridge axis showing that in the vicinity of the EPR volcano production is not a function of lithosphere age. Abers et al. [1987] using 17,000 km of Seabeam data collected on crust 0.5-40 Ma confirm this finding and find that for all sizes, the numbers of volcanoes do not change significantly with age out to 40 Ma. It appears that on lithosphere <10 Ma seamounts are produced only very near the EPR crest. We attribute this result in part to the fact that our data are strongly biased toward very young crust. The observed size distribution of seamounts changes little from 0-0.5 Ma to 0.5-1.0 Ma, but on older crust our data show that small volcanoes decrease in abundance relative to larger ones. We interpret this change as indicating continued growth of seamounts as they drift away from the ridge, though other interpretations are possible [Batiza, 1982].

The data used in this study confirm earlier findings that seamounts near the EPR are preferentially located near transforms

[1]Lamont Doherty Geological Observatory, Columbia University, Palisades, NY 10964
[2]Department of Geological Sciences, Northwestern University, Evanston, IL 60201

Copyright 1987 by the American Geophysical Union.

TABLE 1. Identification number, position, summit depth and calculated volume for the seamounts used in this study

ID #	Seamount Lat.	Long.	Summit Depth (m)	Volume (km^3)
1.	16.185	-105.425	2600	0.055292
2.	16.133	-105.418	2580	0.020944
3.	15.968	-105.407	2860	0.052779
4.	15.912	-105.365	2760	0.006702
5.	15.833	-105.373	2800	0.020944
6.	15.438	-104.583	2840	0.167552
7.	15.413	-104.592	2840	0.020525
8.	15.335	-104.542	3460	0.015080
9.	15.313	-104.537	3220	0.087965
10.	15.258	-104.508	3000	0.215356
11.	15.250	-104.505	3060	0.071942
12.	15.238	-104.495	3060	0.175615
13.	15.183	-104.458	3180	0.025918
14.	15.400	-104.502	2960	0.010472
15.	15.400	-104.518	3040	0.018431
16.	15.450	-104.492	3160	0.006702
17.	15.120	-104.447	2980	0.013404
18.	15.123	-104.438	2960	0.003927
19.	15.087	-104.413	2860	0.004909
20.	15.070	-104.408	2920	0.002618
21.	15.498	-105.332	2860	0.002618
22.	21.982	-110.658	2460	0.753982
23.	15.725	-104.717	2960	0.014726
24.	15.693	-104.715	2980	0.023562
25.	16.152	-104.753	3060	0.030788
26.	16.083	-104.763	3040	0.031416
27.	16.070	-104.762	3060	0.039270
28.	15.727	-104.717	2960	0.006545
29.	15.697	-104.717	3080	0.027489
30.	16.325	-105.387	2760	0.058905
31.	17.427	-105.362	2940	0.027489
32.	17.675	-105.640	2990	0.005236
33.	17.663	-105.402	3200	0.012723
34.	17.658	-105.600	2970	0.011192
35.	17.617	-105.387	2940	0.019007
36.	17.890	-105.462	3150	0.007854
37.	17.825	-105.457	3160	0.016362
38.	17.784	-105.602	2950	0.076969
39.	17.628	-105.342	2860	0.010472
40.	17.580	-105.400	3010	0.009817
41.	17.920	-104.725	2620	0.052360
42.	17.853	-104.748	2660	0.052360
43.	18.467	-104.533	1920	0.047569
44.	19.170	-105.598	4640	0.251327
45.	19.230	-107.840	2280	0.055615
46.	19.228	-107.815	2240	0.104720
47.	19.222	-108.138	3520	0.150796
48.	20.770	-109.397	2520	0.066845
49.	20.680	-109.297	2700	0.002618
50.	20.668	-109.305	2680	0.008836
51.	20.633	-109.328	2840	0.021049
52.	20.540	-109.213	2620	0.020944
53.	20.512	-109.130	2000	0.065450
54.	20.467	-109.147	2800	0.070686
55.	20.483	-109.087	2820	0.010472
56.	20.420	-109.155	2720	0.026180
57.	20.548	-109.412	2840	0.015708
58.	20.552	-109.380	2440	0.070791
59.	20.388	-109.287	2580	0.005131
60.	20.273	-109.400	2720	0.007697
61.	29.243	-109.407	2720	0.005236
62.	20.217	-109.430	2660	0.003927
63.	20.180	-109.463	2640	0.053617
64.	20.127	-109.425	2520	0.020944
65.	20.105	-109.437	2500	0.022644
66.	20.525	-109.325	2720	0.015708
68.	19.958	-109.435	2700	0.068068
75.	19.243	-108.350	3400	6.597344
77.	22.660	-111.353	2560	0.146608
90.	21.043	-109.677	3100	0.037699
91.	21.028	-109.672	3100	0.052779
92.	20.970	-109.603	2900	0.006702
93.	20.958	-109.600	2800	0.021991
94.	20.937	-109.587	2740	0.018850
95.	20.903	-109.557	2820	0.027227
96.	20.813	-109.445	2420	0.005655
97.	21.392	-110.030	3140	0.023562
98.	21.357	-109.975	2940	0.083776
99.	21.317	-109.958	2900	0.092363
100.	21.030	-109.673	3080	0.041050
101.	20.972	-109.605	2860	0.005236
102.	20.958	-109.610	2800	0.010210
103.	20.907	-109.555	2780	0.021991
104.	20.813	-109.447	2440	0.007697
105.	20.770	-109.392	2520	0.101369
106.	20.743	-109.363	2540	0.392524
107.	21.305	-209.940	3000	0.015708
108.	7.800	-102.198	3060	0.014472
109.	7.302	-102.523	2980	0.016339
110.	5.462	-102.328	3180	0.013174
111.	5.585	-102.332	3040	0.008063
112.	5.445	-102.330	3170	0.011211
113.	5.500	-102.447	3060	0.023300
114.	5.550	-102.362	3040	0.154470
115.	2.823	-102.108	2960	0.015287
117.	22.167	-109.017	1900	0.000000
118.	23.033	-108.708	1565	0.000094
119.	21.583	-108.333	1540	0.000000
120.	20.800	-109.283	1860	17.903151
121.	20.800	-109.383	1940	15.084881
122.	21.367	-108.625	2030	22.093250
123.	8.800	-103.900	1625	51.106403
124.	8.783	-104.550	1705	1.356121
125.	11.500	-103.333	2074	66.802971
126.	12.525	-103.300	2030	45.710175
127.	13.725	-101.883	1600	0.000196
128.	11.200	-101.200	2800	1.178097
129.	11.750	-100.667	2880	8.181807
130.	10.867	-101.483	2850	12.498434
131.	11.450	-101.600	2780	18.928045
132.	12.667	-101.550	2270	20.881956
133.	12.533	-100.350	2540	21.609863
134.	12.250	-100.500	2370	32.522762
135.	13.000	-100.833	2200	35.811802
136.	12.000	-101.550	1950	41.238117
137.	12.700	-102.583	1700	53.227417
138.	12.950	-103.200	2200	38.734684
139.	10.367	-100.700	2470	44.981926
140.	13.383	-102.450	860	1684.638794
142.	16.898	-104.740	2940	0.094248
143.	20.742	-109.367	2540	0.376991

TABLE 1. (continued)

ID #	Seamount Lat.	Seamount Long.	Summit Depth (m)	Volume (km³)
144.	19.997	-109.382	2940	0.037699
408.	10.400	-103.773	3020	0.013823
409.	10.200	-103.455	3060	0.015708
410.	10.225	-103.650	3010	0.003351
412.	10.400	-103.772	2980	0.018850
413.	10.125	-103.583	2980	0.015708
414.	10.325	-103.783	3120	0.068211
415.	10.300	-103.750	3040	0.084751
416.	10.267	-103.913	3080	0.029322
418.	10.415	-103.775	2920	0.025133
419.	10.297	-103.753	3060	0.037175
421.	10.053	-104.125	2640	0.016127
422.	10.025	-104.187	2320	0.012566
424.	10.100	-103.580	2800	0.045239
425.	10.100	-103.470	2360	8.042478
426.	10.130	-103.408	2000	10.775662
427.	10.147	-103.337	2580	1.759292
428.	10.140	-103.297	2480	2.178171
429.	12.825	-103.867	2680	1.979203
430.	12.700	-103.850	2500	0.837758
431.	11.492	-103.875	2260	0.080634
437.	10.050	-104.733	1650	13.306808
438.	10.075	-104.680	1830	30.536936
439.	9.958	-104.467	1800	82.267868
440.	9.925	-104.467	1700	28.818615
441.	9.912	-104.400	1890	11.300545
442.	9.558	-103.883	2650	0.160000
443.	12.583	-104.083	2960	0.090000
444.	11.500	-104.000	2590	0.830000
445.	6.150	-105.000	3560	0.270000
446.	6.708	-104.833	3120	4.520000
447.	16.750	-104.400	1950	0.160000
448.	18.533	-104.367	1790	0.260000
449.	7.617	-104.567	2780	5.390000

and fracture zones [Batiza, 1982], some large overlapping spreading centers (OSCs) and elevated portions of the EPR, presumably swollen with abundant magma [Fornari et al., 1984].

Methods

Table 1 gives the position, summit elevation and computed volume of the 168 seamounts we observed. For this study, we used Seabeam contour maps with 10 m and 20 m contours at a scale of 1:72,000 (~60 inches/degree) from Lamont-Doherty, Scripps and the University of Rhode Island. We counted each equant, closed contour high at least 50 m high and for each, we tabulated a set of 37 characteristics including location, summit depth, diameter, shape, presence of caldera, structural lineations and other data. In this study we consider only seamount sizes, abundance and distribution; morphologic and petrologic results of this study will be reported separately.

Figure 1 shows the position of seamounts from Table 1, and an appendix shows their identification numbers. This figure shows that seamounts are clustered at transforms, large OSCs and the elevated portions of the EPR between large offsets. (See Macdonald et al. [1984] and Lonsdale [1985] for EPR elevation profiles.) Plots of seamount abundance (and volume) versus distance from transforms and large OSCs confirm this and show concentration of seamounts within 20 km of these offsets. In contrast, small OSCs, SNOOs [Batiza and Margolis, 1986] and Devals [Langmuir et al., 1986] do not usually have seamounts nearby. This concentration of seamounts near offsets may partly be due to sample bias, as these areas, in general, have more Seabeam coverage. As Table 2 shows, many areas far from offsets are also reasonably well covered, so that we interpret this concentration of seamounts near offsets to reflect actual distribution.

For analysis of the data, we have grouped seamounts into 1°×1° areas. Each of these 49 areas is listed in Table 2 along with percent of the area surveyed with Seabeam, a list of the seamounts found, the normalized seamount abundance (number of seamounts divided by fraction of area surveyed) and the distance of the center of the 1° area from the EPR axis. Figure 2 shows the normalized seamount abundance values as a function of percent of the bin area covered. There is no apparent systematic variation, and the most obvious feature of this plot is the great scatter. A very well surveyed area near the Clipperton Fracture Zone (Figure 3) also shows very large non-uniformity of seamount abundances within subareas and these are not related to percent area covered. One subarea with 22.8% coverage has 5 seamounts whereas another with over twice the coverage (47.7%) has only 2.

As shown in Table 2 and the inset to Figure 2, the data set we use is highly biased; about 50% of the coverage is within 50 km of the EPR and about 75% is within 100 km. The highly non-uniform abundances (Figure 2) make it difficult to quantitatively correct for this strong bias and for this reason we interpret the data with caution, particularly the results for lithosphere over 100 km from the EPR axis.

Results and Discussion

As shown in Figure 1, most seamounts in our study area are located near ridge-transform intersections (RTIs). Since much of the data we use in this study were collected over the axis of the EPR, at transforms and at large OSCs, we regard this result as preliminary. More Seabeam data on the flanks of the EPR both near and far from offset traces will be needed to test our results. Even so, previous studies based on conventional echo sounder surveys and Seabeam have found that seamounts tend to cluster near transforms, their fracture zone extensions and some large OSCs [Batiza, 1982; Batiza and Vanko, 1983; Lonsdale, 1985; Lowrie et al., 1986]. We also find that many seamounts are associated with elevated ridge crest segments between major offsets or near transforms where magma supply seems to be unusually abundant (e.g., western Clipperton-EPR intersection). This agrees with previous suggestions [Searle, 1983; Fornari et al., 1984; Batiza, 1985; Lonsdale [this volume]) and indicates that seamounts form in several distinct tectonic environments near active ridge crests.

Figure 4 shows how normalized seamount abundance (linearly adjusted for percent coverage) varies with distance to the EPR axis. We constructed this plot using data from Table 2, so each point is an average of the 1°×1° areas whose centers are within the same distance range to the EPR axis. The error bars are the means of individual $\sqrt{n}$ counting errors, where n is the number of seamounts found in each bin, propagated through the linear adjustment for percent cover. The error bars are simply counting errors and do not incorporate the effects of observed non-uniform abundance nor strong age bias in track coverage. Also shown on Figure 4 are the data for the Figure 3 control area and the mean seamount abundance (i.e., total number of seamounts found divided by total area surveyed). The abundance values are between 40 and 140 seamounts per 1°×1° area (or 2,500 to 11,600 seamounts/10^6km²). Surprisingly, the lowest normalized abundance is for our control area (Figure 3) which not only has the best track coverage but is centered on the Clipperton transform

TABLE 2. Data for 1°×1° areas

Seamount Abundance Distance to EPR (km)	Coordinate Area	Track Length (km)	Track Width (km)	Surveyed Area (km²)	Map Area (km²)	Percent Cover	Seamounts Counted	ID No.
33±33 54 km	2-3 N 102-103 W	200	1.8	360	11,922	3.0	1	115
294±131 3 km	5-6 N 102-103 W	200	1.8	360	11,862	1.7	5	110,111,112, 113,114
0 330 km	506 N 105-106 W	110	1.8	198	11,862	1.7	0	
117±83 207 km	6-7 N 104-105 W	110	1.8	198	11,862	1.7	2	445,446
111±78 24 km	7-8 N	120	1.8	216	11,802	1.8	2	108,109
55±55 193 km	7-8 N 104-105 W	121	1.8	218	11,802	1.8	1	449
33±33 33km	8-9 N 103-104 W	200	1.8	360	11,742	3.0	1	123
96±96 33 km	8-9 N 104-105 W	68	1.8	122	11,742	1.0	1	124
43±43 80 km	9-10 N 103-104 W	150	1.8	270	11,682	2.3	1	442
29±17 26 km	9-10 N 104-105 W	666	1.8	1,200	11,682	10.3	3	439,440,441
42±42 340 km	10-11 N 100-101 W	155	1.8	279	11,682	2.4	1	139
42±42 230 km	10-11 N 101-102 W	155	1.8	279	11,682	2.4	1	130
33±6 11 km	10-11 N 103-104 W	3,120	1.8	5,616	11,682	48.0	16	404,408,409,410, 412,413,414,415, 416,418,419,424, 425,426,427,428
31±15 96 km	10-11 N 104-105 W	832	1.8	1,498	11,682	12.8	4	421,422 437,438
59±59 358 km	11-12 N 100-101 W	110	1.8	198	11,682	1.7	1	129
177±101 250 km	11-12 N 101-102 W	110	1.8	198	11,682	1.7	3	128,131,136
229±133 142 km	11-12 N 102-103 W	85	1.8	153	11,682	1.3	3	401,402,403
139±68 38 km	11-12 N 103-104 W	187	1.8	337	11,682	2.9	4	125,406, 431,444
0 75 km	11-12 N 104-105 W	15	1.8	27	11,682	.2	0	
176±101 368 km	12-13 N 100-101 W	110	1.8	198	11,682	1.7	3	133,134,135
59±59 261 km	12-13 N 101-102 W	110	1.8	198	11,682	1.7	1	132
57±57 152 km	12-13 N 102-103 W	110	1.8	198	11,621	1.8	1	137
100±50 41 km	12-13 N 103-104 W	250	1.8	450	11,621	4.0	4	126,138, 429,430
43±43 65 km	12-13 N 104-105 W	150	1.8	270	11,621	2.3	1	443
74±54 282 km	13-14 N 101-102 W	170	1.8	306	11,621	2.6	2	127,400
52±52 174 km	13-14 N 102-103 W	125	1.8	279	11,621	2.4	1	140
0 42km	13-14 N 104-105 W	150	1.8	270	11,621	2.3	0	

TABLE 2. (continued)

Seamount Abundance / Distance to EPR (km)	Coordinate Area	Track Length (km)	Track Width (km)	Surveyed Area (km²)	Map Area (km²)	Percent Cover	Seamounts Counted	ID No.
0 / 20 km	14-15 N 104-105 W	174	1.8	313	11,621	2.7	0	
41±41 / 520 km	15-16 N 100-101 W	120	2.3	276	11,441	2.4	1	399
223±59 / 90 km	15-16 N 104-105 W	399	1.8	718	11,441	6.3	14	6,7,8,9,10,11, 12,13,14,15,16, 17,23,23,24
500±166 / 17 km	15-16 N 105-106 W	117	1.8	211	11,441	1.8	9	3,4,5,18,19, 20,21,28,29
142±101 / 524 km	16-17 N 100-101 W	88	1.8	158	11,381	1.4	2	397,398
166±68 / 93 km	16-17 N 104-105 W	227	1.8	409	11,381	3.6	6	25,26,27,141, 142,447
136±78 / 15 km	16-17 N 105-106 W	139	1.8	250	11,381	2.2	3	1,2,31
44±31 / 110 km	17-18 N 104-105 W	285	1.8	513	11,381	4.5	2	41,42
121±38 / 1 km	17-18 N 105-106 W	521	1.8	938	11,381	8.2	10	30,32,33,34,35, 36,37,38,39,40
60±42 / 115 km	18-19 N 104-105 W	209	1.8	376	11,260	3.3	2	43,448
83±83 / 420 km	19-20 N 105-106 W	59	2.3	136	11,260	1.2	1	44
166±117 / 220 km	19-20 N 107-108 W	75	1.8	135	11,260	1.2	2	45,46
77±54 / 125 km	19-20 N 108-109 W	110	2.7	297	11,260	2.6	2	47,75
105±74 / 70 km	19-20 N 109-110 W	124	1.8	223	11,260	1.9	2	68,144
346±57 / 30 km	20-21 N 109-110 W	646	1.8	1,163	11,200	10.4	36	48,49,50,51,52 53,54,55,56,57, 58,59,60,61,62, 63,64,65,66,67, 91,91,92,93,94, 95,96,101,102, 103,104,105,106, 120,121,143,144
104±74 / 41 km	21-22 N 108-109 W	120	1.8	216	11,200	1.9	2	119,122
800±400 / 66 km	21-22 N 109-110 W	29	1.8	52	11,200	0.5	4	98,99,100,107
125±88 / 175 km	21-22 N 110-111 W	102	1.8	184	11,200	1.6	2	22,97
56±56 / 135 km	22-23 N 109-110 W	110	1.8	198	11,079	1.8	1	117
0 / 244 km	22-23 N 110-111 W	22	1.8	40	11,079	.4	0	
154±108 / 353 km	22-23 N 111-112 W	77	1.8	139	11,079	1.3	2	76,77
56±56 / 100 km	23-24 N 108-109 W	110	1.8	198	11,079	1.8	1	118

Area boundaries, Seabeam track length in area, track width (0.75 of the water depth), area surveyed, area of the 1°×1° region, percent of the area surveyed with Seabeam, total number of seamounts found in area plus identification numbers of each seamount (see appendix for map location). At left are listings for normalized seamount abundance (number of seamounts found (n) divided by fraction of area covered ±√n divided by the same fraction) and distance of the center from the 1°×1° area to the EPR.

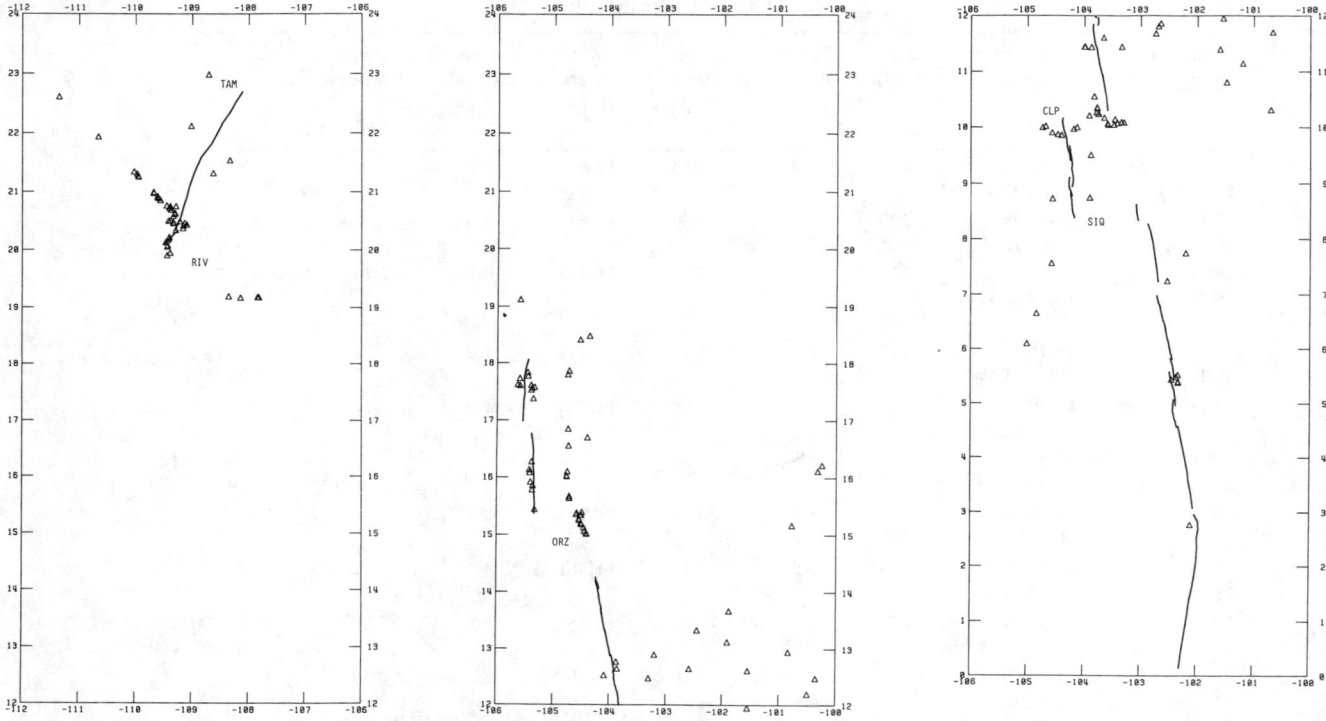

Fig. 1. Map of the East Pacific Rise crest location with seamounts shown as triangles. Note concentration of seamounts at the Rivera (RIV), Orozco (ORZ) and Clipperton (CLIPP) fracture zones and at OSCs at 20.1°N, 13°N and 5.5°N.

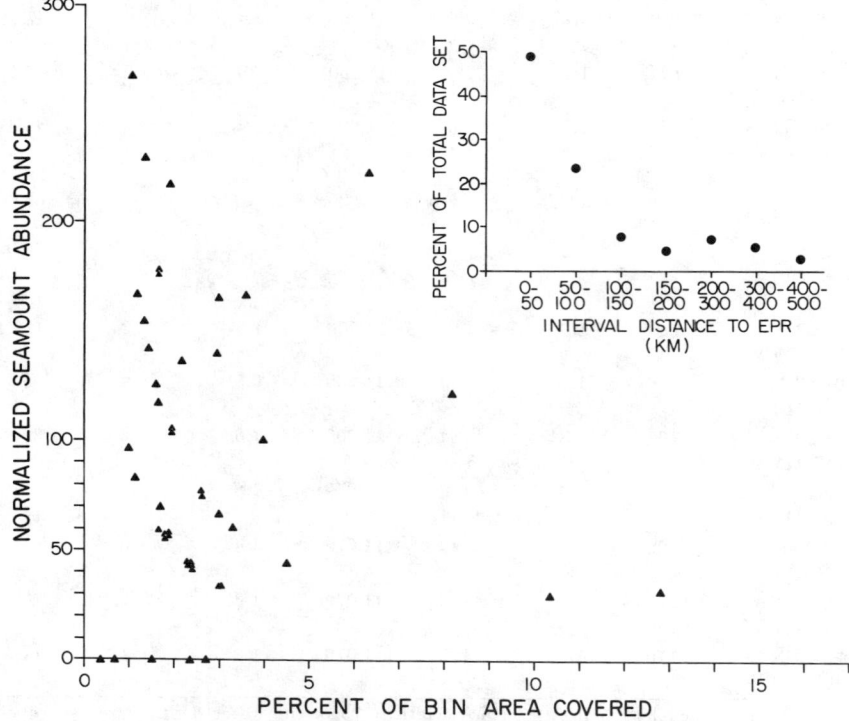

Fig. 2. Normalized seamount abundances (seamounts per 1° area) versus percent of 1°×1° area covered with Seabeam. A point for the area 10°–11°N and 103°–104°W not shown. It has 45% coverage and normalized abundance of 39±0 seamounts per 1° area. *Inset*: Percent of our Seabeam data set as a function of the age of the lithosphere; data from Table 2. Note that most data are near the EPR axis.

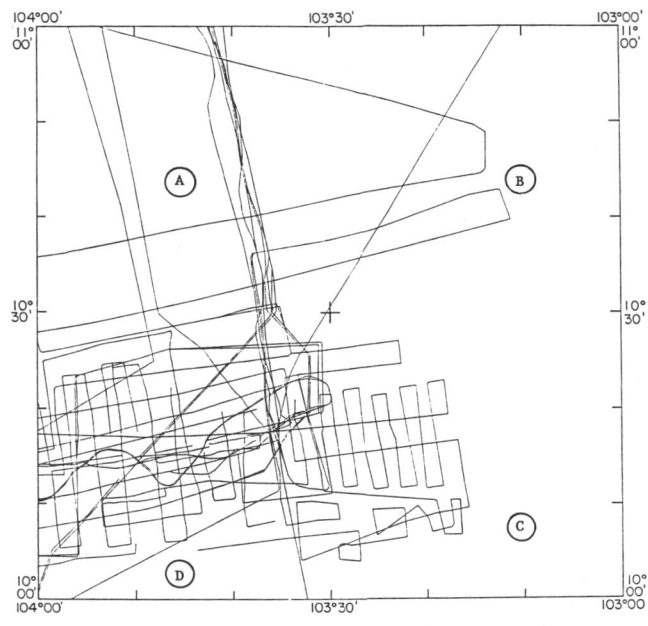

Quarter-bin	Line km	Percent Coverage	Seamounts Counted	Normalized Seamounts
A	775	47.7	2	4±3
B	224	13.9	0	0
C	371	22.8	5	22±10
D	1750	100	9	9
Totals	3120	46.0	16	36±13

Fig. 3. Track line distribution and seamount abundance data for a well-surveyed area near the eastern intersection of the Clipperton transform with the EPR. Note the patchiness of the seamount distribution in each subarea.

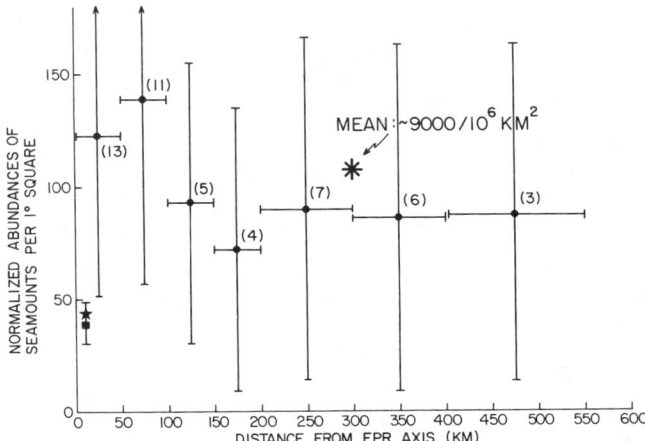

Fig. 4. Normalized seamount abundance (seamounts per 1° area) versus distance to the axis of the EPR from data in Table 2. Each age bin is shown as a filled dot. The square and small star are for the control area shown in Figure 3 and the large asterisk is the average abundance of our study (total number of seamounts divided by total area covered). Since most of the data we used are very near the EPR axis, we believe that extrapolations from data on lithosphere >100 km from the EPR are highly uncertain. See text for discussion.

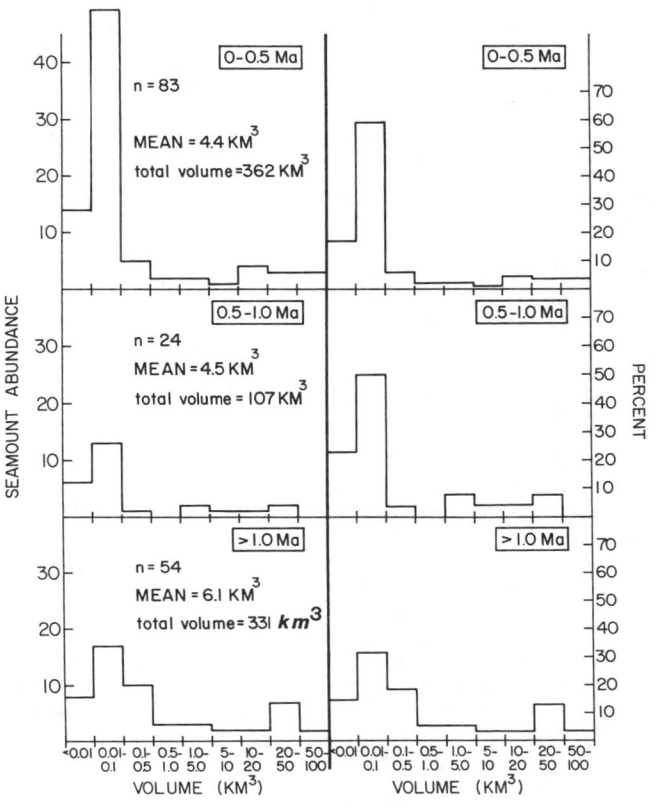

Fig. 5. Histogram of volume (left) and percent of the seamount population (right) for lithosphere 0-0.5 Ma (top), 0.5-1.0 Ma (middle) and >1.0 Ma (bottom). The total number of seamounts in each group (n) and their mean and total volumes are also shown. As found in previous studies, small seamounts are more abundant than larger ones. The smallest-volume group has heights of ~50 m.

and its eastern intersection with the EPR, a setting where seamounts are thought to be preferentially generated. This is difficult to reconcile with the fact that the highest measured abundances are in areas closest to the EPR axis where our data are, overall, most abundant.

There are several possible explanations for this: 1) Our control area does not include the western Clipperton RTI where there are many seamounts [Fornari et al., 1984]; if we consider a 1°×1° area within 35 km of the Clipperton transform and its fracture zone extensions, the normalized abundance increases greatly. 2) Many of the seamounts near Clipperton are much larger than elsewhere along the EPR (Tables 1 and 2), especially near its axis. This means that the total volume of seamount lava near the Clipperton is relatively high but distributed into a smaller number of volcanoes. 3) Any single 1°×1° area is probably not representative. It is clear from Figure 2 that seamount distribution is very patchy and until we know more about the characteristics of this non-uniform distribution and have data to average it out, it will be difficult to strongly defend estimates of mean abundance along the EPR and its flanks. Because of these uncertainties, we favor using the overall seamount abundance of our study area (~9000 seamounts/10^6km^2) as our best estimate for near-EPR seamount density in our study area. We believe that the control area near Clipperton gives a lower than expected abundance value because it does not include the western RTI.

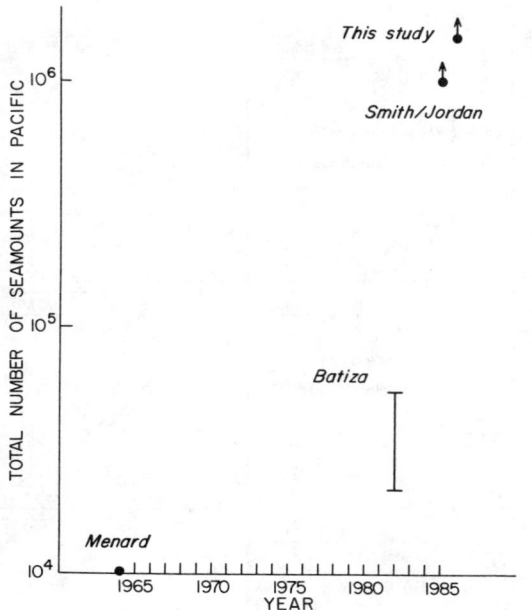

Fig. 6. Seamount abundance in the Pacific (total number assuming that average production rates at the ridge and elsewhere do not vary with time) versus year of estimate. Menard [1964] considered only volcanoes >1 km in height whereas later estimates consider much smaller ones that are very abundant.

Figure 4 also shows that seamount abundances apparently remain constant with distance from the EPR. This is a surprising result, since previous studies have shown that seamount abundances increased with lithospheric age [Batiza, 1981, 1982]. Figure 4 suggests that all the seamounts on crust <10 Ma are produced within 50 km of the EPR in disagreement with previous studies that concluded that new seamounts are added to the lithosphere as it drifts away from the ridge axis. This result must be applied cautiously because of the strong age bias in our data set and the relatively small amount of coverage.

Figure 5 shows the size frequency distribution of seamounts on crust 0-0.5 Ma, 0.5-1.0 Ma and >1.0 Ma. Since the total number of seamounts in each age category is small, it is questionable that these results are fully representative. Nevertheless, they seem to indicate that smaller seamounts are much more abundant than larger ones, in agreement with previous studies. The overall size frequency distribution is Poisson-like except that there is a deficiency of seamounts in the very tiniest size category. It is not clear whether this is real or an artifact of the manner in which we conducted the survey. Such an artifact could be created by our self-imposed 50 m height criterion for seamount selection because by using this we may have selected only the steepest small edifices. There may be a very large number of small volcanic constructs 30-40 m high of similar volume to our smallest size class but with gentler slopes. If so, and submersible studies indicate that this is probably the case, our data for the smallest volume class is biased toward the tallest edifices. Alternatively, artifacts could be created by the Seabeam contouring software. It is possible that near the spatial and depth resolution of the Seabeam system, the contouring program preferentially contours groups of tiny coalesced cones as a single ridge-like or irregular feature. If this deficiency of seamounts in the smallest volume class (Figure 5) is real, it suggests a threshold effect for seamount production. We suspect, however, that it is actually an artifact created by our selection criteria and the charts we used in the study.

Figure 5 also shows that the ratio of small edifices to large ones apparently decreases on crust older than 1 Ma. We cannot assess the significance of this result, but if significant, it suggests that the smallest edifices may continue to grow and are not replaced by new ones of tiny size. Alternatively, tiny edifices could become drowned by sediment accumulating on older crust, as suggested by Batiza [1982]. Clearly, much more data will be needed to confidently use size-frequency distributions to determine the behavior of seamount populations with age.

Conclusions

Our study confirms that seamount abundances on crust <10 Ma are extremely patchy on small scales (1°×1° areas) and that their distribution is primarily controlled by large offsets and magma supply at the EPR. Areas that are well surveyed show up to a factor of three difference in seamount abundance: from about 3000 seamounts/10^6km^2 to ~9000 seamounts/10^6km^2 with large uncertainties.

Because of this great patchiness, we do not attempt to interpret variations of seamount abundance with spreading rate. We find an average abundance on crust <10 Ma of about 9000 seamounts/10^6km^2, which is the largest estimate so far (Figure 6). If correct, and if average production rates are constant with time, the Pacific has many more than 1.5×10^6 seamounts because our estimate is for only relatively small volcanoes.

In this study we also find that seamount abundance does not change with distance from the EPR axis on crust <10 Ma, at variance with earlier studies. Because of the strong age bias in our data set and the patchiness of seamount abundances, we are cautious in interpreting this result. If this result is confirmed by future work, it could be interpreted to mean that true off-ridge seamounts (as opposed to ridge-related ones) are added primarily to lithosphere older than ~10 Ma.

The results of this study and recent high-resolution sonar surveys of the mid-oceanic ridge system clearly suggest that seamount production near ridge axes is an important expression of the accretion process. Along the EPR, where we have the most detailed information, it is clear that the tectonic and magma supply processes occurring along the ridge strongly influence the production and evolution of both large and small seamounts as suggested by their close proximity to the ridge, their preferential location along the ridge and their petrologic characteristics.

<u>Acknowledgments.</u> We thank P. J. Fox, D. Gallo, J. Madsen, W. B. F. Ryan, M. Perfit and D. Epp for constructive comments and discussions. J. Karsten, D. Smith and D. Epp reviewed drafts of this paper and we thank them for their suggestions. D. Smith kindly provided a preprint. J. Madsen supplied computer generated data for Figure 3. P. J. Fox, K. Macdonald, P. Lonsdale, J. Mammerickx, and J. Weissel kindly supplied copies of Seabeam data from the archives of their respective institutions. DJF thanks H. Backer and J. Lange of Preussag for Seabeam data covering the EPR south of the equator not used in this study due to the limitations in data coverage but helpful nonetheless for comparative purposes. This work was supported by the Office of Naval Research under contract N00014-84-C-0132 Scope EPR (DJF) and N00014-80-C-0856 (RB), and the National Science Foundation under grants OCE-83-08980 and OCE-85-08042 (RB) and OCE 84-14614 (DJF). Lamont-Doherty Geological Observatory Contribution Number 4153.

References

Abers, G. A., B. Parsons, and J. K. Weissel, Seamount abundances and distributions in the southeast Pacific, *Earth Planet. Sci. Lett.* (in press).

Batiza, R., Lithospheric age dependence on the rate of off-ridge volcano production in the North Pacific, *Geophys. Res. Lett., 8,* 853-856, 1981.

Batiza, R., Abundance distribution and sizes of volcanoes in the Pacific Ocean and implications for the origin of non-hotspot volcanoes, *Earth Planet. Sci. Lett., 60,* 196-206, 1982.

Batiza, R., A general hypothesis for the origin of seamounts at the near mid-ocean ridges, *Eos Trans. AGU, 66,* 1078, 1985.

Batiza, R., and S.H. Margolis, A model for the origin of small non-overlapping offsets (SNOOs) of the East Pacific Rise, *Nature, 320,* 439-441, 1986.

Batiza, R., and T. Smith, Geologic and volcanic development of a near-ridge seamount: Results from integrated ALVIN/ANGUS and laboratory study, *Eos Trans. AGU, 67,* 1254, 1986.

Batiza, R., and D. Vanko, Volcanic development of small oceanic central volcanoes on the flanks of the East Pacific Rise inferred from narrow beam echo sounder surveys, *Mar. Geol., 54,* 53-90, 1983.

Batiza, R., and D. A. Vanko, Petrology of young Pacific seamounts, *J. Geophys. Res., 89,* 11235-11260, 1984.

Fornari, D. J., W. B. F. Ryan, and P. J. Fox, The evolution of craters and calderas on young seamounts: Insights from SeaMARC I and SeaBeam sonar surveys of a small seamount group near the axis of the East Pacific Rise, *J. Geophys. Res., 89,* 11,069-11,084, 1984.

Fornari, D. J., R. Batiza, M. Perfit, J. Allan, R. Haymon, T. Simkin, A. Barone, W.B.F. Ryan, and T. Smith, The structure and morphological evolution of a small seamount chain near the East Pacific Rise, *Eos Trans. AGU, 67,* 1184, 1986.

Graham, D. W., W. J. Jenkins, M. D. Kurz, and R. Batiza, Helium isotopic disequilibrium geochronology of glassy submarine basalts, *Nature,* in press, 1987.

Honda, M., T. Bernatowicz, F. A. Podosek, R. Batiza, and P. T. Taylor, Age determination of East Pacific seamounts (Henderson, 6 and 7) — implications for near-ridge and intraplate volcanism,, *Mar. Geol.,* (in press), 1987.

Jordan, T. H., and D.K. Smith, Magma body kinetics from seamount population statistics, *Eos Trans. AGU, 67,* 356, 1986.

Jordan, T. H., H. W. Menard, and D. K. Smith, Density and size distribution of seamounts in the Eastern Pacific inferred from wide-beam sounding data, *J. Geophys. Res., 88,* 10,508-10,518, 1983.

Langmuir, C.H., J. F. Bender, and R. Batiza, Petrologic and tectonic segmentation of the East Pacific Rise 5°30′–14°30′ N, *Nature, 322,* 422-429, 1986.

Lonsdale, P., Non-transform offsets of the Pacific-Cocos plate boundary and their traces on the rise flank, *Geol. Soc. Am. Bull., 96,* 313-327., 1985.

Lowrie, A., N.C. Smoot, and R. Batiza, Are oceanic fracture zones locked and strong or weak?: New evidence for volcanic activity and weakness, *Geology, 14,* 242-245, 1986.

Luckman, M. A., D. J. Fornari, and R. Batiza, Seamount distribution along the East Pacific Rise between 20°N and 20°S based on available Sea Beam bathymetric survey data, *Eos Trans. AGU, 66,* 1078, 1985.

Macdonald, K., J.-C. Sempere, and P.J. Fox, East Pacific Rise from Siqueiros to Orozco fracture zones: Along-strike continuity of axial neovolcanic zone and structure and evolution of overlapping spreading centers, *J. Geophys. Res., 89,* 6049-6069, 1984.

McNutt, M., Non-uniform magnetization of seamounts: a least squares approach, *J. Geophys. Res., 91,* 3686-3700, 1986.

Menard, H. W., *Marine geology of the Pacific,* 271 pp., McGraw Hill, 1964.

Renard, V., and J. P. Allenou, Sea Beam multi-beam echo sounding in "Jean Charcot", *Int. Hydrographic Rev., 56,* 35-67, 1979.

Searle, R. C., Submarine central volcanoes on the Nazca plate — high-resolution sonar observations, *Mar. Geol., 53,* 77-102 1983.

Smith, D. K., and T. H. Jordan, Abundances and production rates of Pacific seamounts, *Eos Trans. AGU, 66,* 1079, 1985a.

Smith, D. K., and T. H. Jordan, Seamount population statistics as constraints on the migration of magma bodies through the lithosphere, *Eos Trans. AGU, 66,* 362, 1985b.

Sykes, L. R., Intraplate seismicity, reactivation of preexisting zones of weakness, alkaline magmatism and other tectonism postdating continental fragmentation, *Rev. Geophys. Space Phys., 16,* 621-688, 1978.

Vogt, P. R., Volcano spacing, fracture and thickness of the lithosphere, *Earth Planet. Sci. Lett., 21,* 235-252, 1974a.

Vogt, P. R., Volcano height and plate thickness, *Earth Planet. Sci. Lett., 23,* 337-348, 1974b.

Morphologic Studies

THE SOUTH PACIFIC SUPERSWELL

Marcia K. McNutt and Karen M. Fischer

Department of Earth, Atmospheric, and Planetary Sciences, Massachusetts Institute of Technology, Cambridge

Abstract. Seafloor depths in a broad area of French Polynesia are 250 to 750 m shallower than lithosphere of the same age in the North Pacific and the North Atlantic. The area of shallow seafloor also correlates with a region of high density of volcanoes, low seismic velocity in the upper mantle, and a reduction in the thickness of the elastic plate supporting the volcanoes. The Marquesas fracture zone marks an abrupt transition between normal lithosphere to the north which follows the thermal subsidence curve for a 125-km-thick plate and shallow lithosphere to the south which behaves as though it is only 75-km thick. This age dependence in the French Polynesian depth anomalies, the low elastic plate thickness, and the change in depth at the Marquesas fracture zone, a lithospheric discontinuity, require elevated temperatures in the lithosphere. The pattern and amplitude of the depth anomaly is not consistent with the notion that it results from lithospheric thinning beneath a number of overlapping hot spot swells. Rather, we propose that hot spot traces cluster in this region because the lithosphere is already thinner and more vulnerable to magma penetration. The reduction in the thickness of the thermal plate is presumably due to enhanced small-scale convection resulting from the thermal and/or chemical effect of a broad mantle upwelling beneath the South Pacific as imaged by seismic tomography. The morphologic and petrologic characteristics of this superswell resemble those that existed in the mid-Cretaceous over H. W. Menard's Darwin Rise, a region of the Pacific which includes the Mid-Pacific Mountains, the Marshall Islands, Magellan Seamounts, and Wake Guyots. We propose that the South Pacific superswell is the modern-day equivalent of the Darwin Rise, and that it may be merely an extreme example of global variability in lithospheric thermal structure as a function of temperature, chemistry, and/or state-of-stress in the upper mantle.

Introduction

The observed depth of the seafloor increases from approximately 2500 m on average at the midocean ridges to more than 6000 m in the deep ocean basins, and overall subsidence of the seafloor is quantitatively consistent with the cooling and contraction predicted for an aging lithospheric plate [Sclater and Francheteau, 1970; Parsons and Sclater, 1977]. Parameters describing the average thermal properties of the lithosphere have been determined from fitting large quantities of bathymetric and heat flow data from the North Pacific and North Atlantic to the plate cooling equation [Parsons and Sclater, 1977], and this model provides the standard against which depth anomalies are defined [Menard, 1973].

The GEBCO bathymetric chart [GEBCO, 1978] (Figure 1) displays a large region in the South Pacific to the west of Easter Island where the seafloor subsides less rapidly away from the East Pacific Rise than the standard Parsons and Sclater model predicts [Mammerickx et al., 1975; Cochran, 1986]. The area involved is roughly 15 million km^2, and therefore constitutes a significant fraction of the Earth's surface. The western portion of this anomalous area includes the hot spots of French Polynesia: Macdonald, Pitcairn, Society, and Marquesas [Gordon and Henderson, 1985]. In addition to the unusually shallow depths, the region is also marked by an extremely small value for the effective thickness of the elastic plate supporting the hot spot volcanoes [McNutt and Menard, 1978; Calmant and Cazenave, 1987], a shallow low velocity zone for Love waves [Nishimura and Forsyth, 1985], and a geochemical signature termed the Dupal anomaly [Hart, 1984]. Menard and McNutt [1982] invoke the effects of multiple thermal rejuvenation events due to the passage of the young lithosphere south of the Marquesas Fracture Zone over the numerous French Polynesian hot spots in order to explain the shallow depths, high density of volcanoes, and low values for elastic plate thickness. In this study, we quantitatively examine the predictions from this hypothesis to test whether thermal rejuvenation alone is capable of explaining the observations in French Polynesia.

The Depth Anomaly Map

The first step in testing the thermal rejuvenation hypothesis is to calculate the magnitude and spatial pattern of the depth anomaly in French Polynesia. The depth anomaly map in Figure 2 was calculated from 5' digital SYNBAPS bathymetry [Van Wykhouse, 1973] averaged to one-quarter degree and corrected for the variations of sound speed in water [Matthews, 1939], sediment loading [Ludwig and Houtz, 1979; Le Douran and Parsons, 1982], and seafloor age [Mammerickx et al., 1975; Sclater et al., 1981; Crough and Jarrard, 1981; Menard, personal communication; Handschumacher, 1976] using the thermal model of Parsons and Sclater [1977]. Although the sediment data [Ludwig and Houtz, 1979] do not provide accurate estimates of archipelagic apron thickness due to the difficulty in penetrating the volcaniclastic sediments with conventional seismic profiling

Copyright 1987 by the American Geophysical Union.

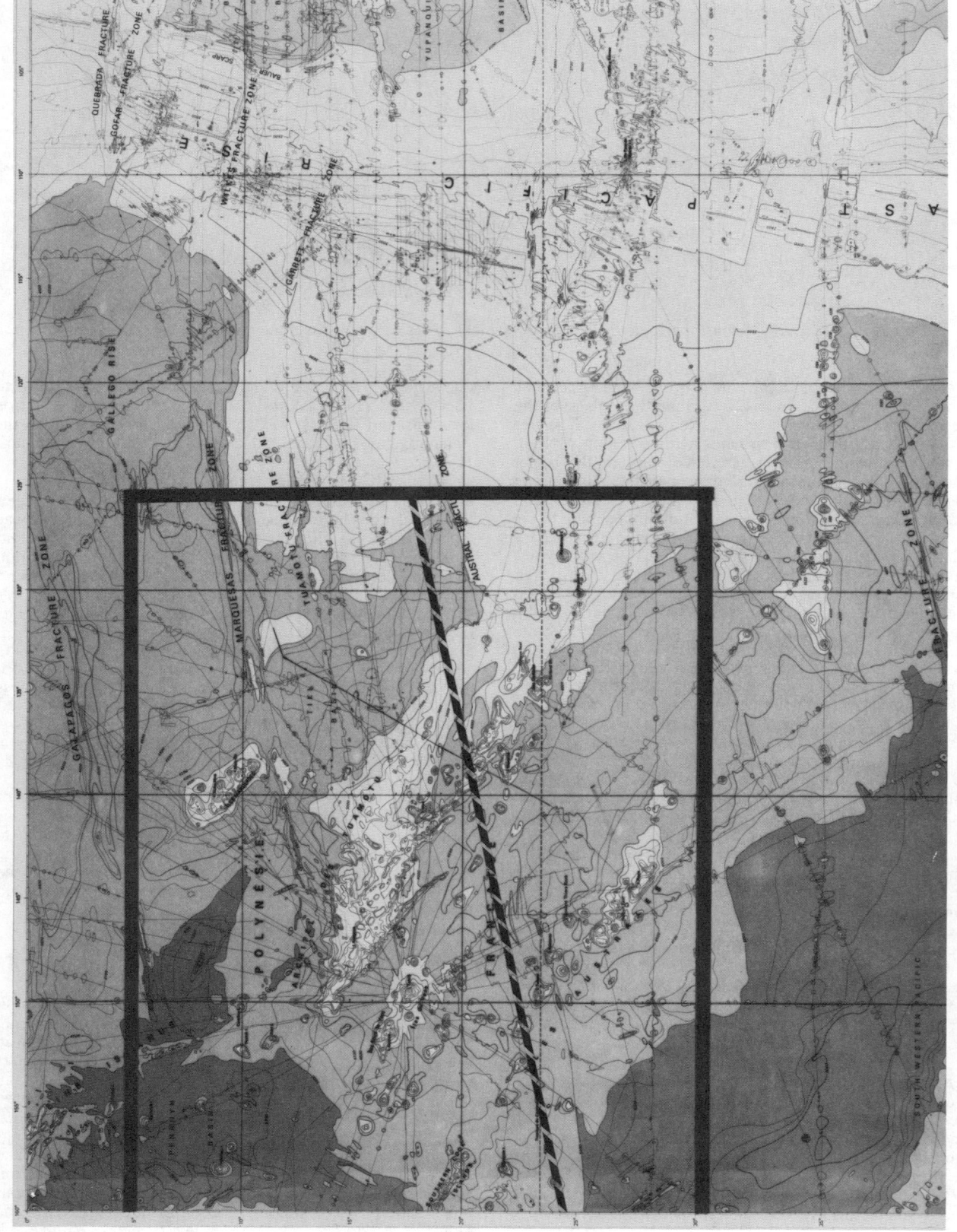

Fig. 1. Bathymetry of the South Pacific [GEBCO, 1978] showing the region of the superswell. Box corresponds to the region for which depth anomalies are calculated in Figure 2. Dashed line shows the location of the profile in Figure 3.

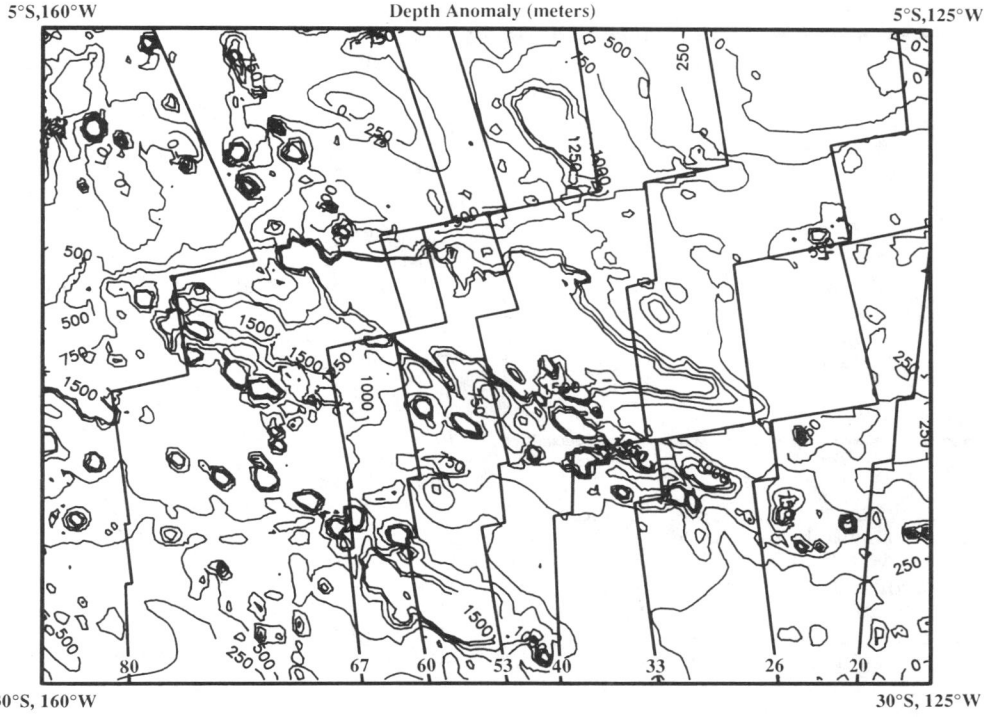

Fig. 2. Depth anomaly map for French Polynesia, showing age- and sediment-corrected bathymetry. Elevation of volcanic islands and platforms clipped at +1500 m. Heavy lines show isochrons in million years before present inferred from magnetic lineations. Area extends from 5°S to 30°S and from 125°W to 160°W. Contours of depth anomaly are in meters.

systems, the resulting errors in the sediment loading correction will be local to the islands. For example, in his classic paper defining archipelagic aprons, Menard [1956] displays echograms from the Marquesas Islands showing that the abyssal hill fabric marking the outer edge of the apron emerges about 250 km from the edge of the islands. Using the flexural rigidity for the lithosphere beneath the Marquesan volcanoes determined from geoid data by Fischer et al. [1986], that distance corresponds to the position of the flexural arch, indicating that the extent of the archipelagic apron is controlled by the width of the flexural moat. The small thickness for the elastic plate observed south of the Marquesas Fracture Zone thus suggests that any errors in our depth anomaly map due to incomplete removal of apron sediments will be confined to within 200 km of the volcanoes, and will not affect any conclusions concerning the magnitude of depth anomalies at wavelengths corresponding to hot spot swells or French Polynesia as a whole.

Our choice of isochrons used in constructing Figure 2 deserves some discussion since there does not appear to be consensus in the published literature on their locations. Isochrons at 33 Ma and younger are based on magnetic lineations which indicate an Early Miocene plate reorganization as proposed by Mammerickx et al. [1975] and Handschumacher [1976]. We include offset on the Tuamotu Fracture Zone (the second fracture zone from the northern edge of Figure 2) which is documented by Menard [unpublished map] and Mammerickx et al. [1975] but discounted by Handschumacher [1976] and Cande [1986].

The rest of the isochrons were interpolated from Crough and Jarrard [1981] and Menard [unpublished map], and, for ages 80 Ma and greater, from Sclater et al. [1981]. These older isochrons place a smaller offset on the Austral Fracture Zone than one might infer from the rather prominent topographic signature of this feature near the Austral Islands, but we hesitate to increase its offset based on the presence of a scarp alone since later tectonism may have influenced its morphologic character. In any case, any errors in age in the western portion of the map will not significantly affect our conclusions due to the small slope in the depth-age relation at older ages. The isochrons shown in Figure 2 vary slightly from the magnetic lineations published by Cande [1986], but, in general, use of his isochrons would only increase the magnitude of the depth anomaly, through not by more than 100 m.

Examination of Figure 2 shows that except for the Marquesas swell [Crough and Jarrard, 1981; Fischer et al., 1986], depth anomalies are near zero north of the Marquesas fracture zone. To the south, however, the seafloor depth, even where unperturbed by islands and seamounts, is consistently shallow with respect to the Parsons and Sclater model. For example, at the eastern edge of the map where the lithosphere is roughly 20 Ma old, the seafloor is already 250 m shallower than predicted. The depth anomalies increase to 750 m in the west where the lithosphere is 80 Ma. While some of the anomaly identifications are tentative in the western area where the fracture zones can no longer be traced, refinement of the details of lithospheric age in this region is

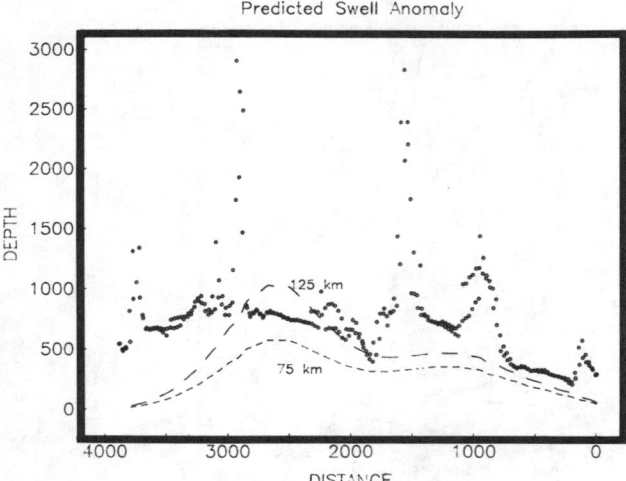

Fig. 3. Profiles of depth anomaly (age- and sediment-corrected) across the superswell along the dashed line shown in Figure 1. The observed depth anomaly (open circles) is compared to the predicted amplitudes from models of overlapping swells. The short-dashed line is the predicted swell amplitude assuming the hot spot reheats a plate only 75-km thick, while the long-dashed line corresponds to a plate 125-km thick.

anomaly is simply due to crustal thickening [Talandier and Okal, 1987] while still traversing the region of significant depth anomalies. If one removes from this profile the very high frequency signal of seamounts, what then remains is a gradual slope in the depth anomaly, increasing from 250 m at 0 km distance to 750 m at 3500 km. Superimposed on this slope are two shorter wavelength undulations, one at 1000-1500 km where the profile crosses the Pitcairn hot spot track, and a second centered near 2500 km where it encounters the Austral chain. We conclude from this profile, and from the map in Figure 2, that the depth anomaly does indeed grow with age, that the lithosphere is anomalously shallow even before it encounters the first hot spot, and that our perception that there is a depth anomaly is not simply the effect of constructional volcanism on islands and seamounts.

Figure 4 presents yet another way of expressing the unusual depth-age relationship south of the Marquesas Fracture Zone. Here we contour the density of depth-age pairs falling in depth-age bins with width 5 m.y. and height 250 m. The dotted, slashed, and hatchured areas denote depth-age bins with at least 100, 300, and 500 depth-age pairs, respectively. Representing the data in this fashion emphasizes the mode, or the most common value, of the depth as a function of age, and therefore avoids the biasing to shallow depths that seamounts introduce into simple depth averages [Renkin and Sclater, 1987]. Superimposed on the contoured data are theoretical depth-age curves for cooling plate models of the lithosphere. The curve for a plate 125-km

not likely to change the basic conclusion that there is a lot of very shallow lithosphere that is not young. By including some offset on the Tuamotu Fracture Zone as we have in Figure 2, the depth anomaly develops in one step going north to south across the Marquesas Fracture Zone, and thereafter the depth anomaly contours remain roughly constant across and perpendicular to the Tuamotu and Austral fracture zones. Had we adopted the model preferred by Handschumacher [1976] with no offset on the Tuamotu Fracture Zone, the total magnitude of the depth anomaly from north of the Marquesas to south of the Tuamotu would remain the same, but the depth anomaly would rise in two steps, a large one just south of the Marquesas and a smaller increment south of the Tuamotu. Therefore, there can be little dispute that the northern boundary of the anomalously shallow region displays fracture zone control, but there is some uncertainty as to whether it is by one or two fracture zones.

While Figure 2 demonstrates the importance of the Marquesas Fracture Zone in determining the locus of shallow lithosphere and the general increase in the magnitude of the depth anomaly from 250 m in the east to 750 m in the west, it is difficult to distinguish the regional pattern of depth anomaly from the local effects of the large number of volcanic edifices. Other methods of representing the depth-age data are better suited for displaying regional as opposed to local anomalies. For example, in Figure 3 we plot a profile of depth anomaly as a function of distance along the dashed line indicated on Figure 2. Individual circles correspond to gridded depth anomaly values within 100 km of the profile, so that the scatter in the values at any one distance give an estimate of the variability perpendicular to the strike of the profile. The location of the profile was chosen to avoid most of the Tuamotu Islands where we know that some of the depth

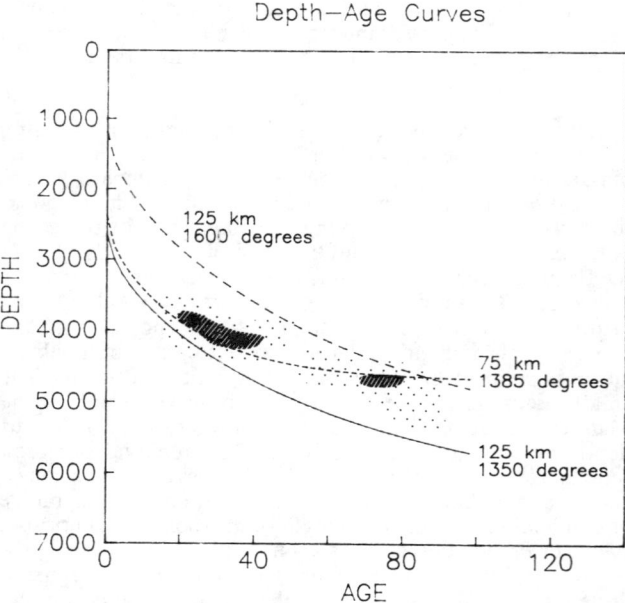

Fig. 4. Depth-age curve for the region south of the Marquesas fracture zone in Figure 2. Shaded contours represent the number of 15' by 15' depth averages which fall within a depth-age bin 5 m.y. wide by 250 m deep, beginning at 100 points and increasing in intervals of 200 points. Continuous curves are predicted depth-age relations for the cooling plate model of Parsons and Sclater [1977] for several values of plate thickness and basal temperature as noted.

thick with a basal temperature of 1350°C is the standard depth-age relationship of Parsons and Sclater [1977] which gives the best fit to the bathymetry and heat flow data in the North Atlantic and North Pacific. The depth anomaly in Figure 2 results from the fact that all of the data fall well above this standard model. The curve for a plate 75 km thick with a basal temperature of 1385°C provides a much better fit to the data. It is not possible to obtain such a fit by varying just the plate thickness or just the basal temperature. The reduction in plate thickness is necessary to cause the depth to begin to flatten at ages as young as 50 Ma, and the increase in temperature at the base of the plate is necessary to explain the depth anomaly on 20 to 40 Ma old lithosphere. However, we recognize that this simple model of a thinner plate over a warmer mantle may not explain the depth-age data in the immediate vicinity of the ridge crest. From a number of bathymetric profiles on lithosphere between the Garret Fracture Zone and the Easter plate, Cochran [1986] calculates an average ridge crest depth of 2700 m and a lower subsidence rate than indicated by our preferred plate model.

Figures 2-4 document the existence and quantify the magnitude of a broad depth anomaly in the region of French Polynesia. Since regional depth anomalies surrounding midplate volcanoes are called "swells" [Dietz and Menard, 1953], here we will use the term "superswell" to refer to a shallow area which encompasses many hot spots.

Possible Causes for the Superswell

We can classify mechanisms that can lead to depth anomalies as
1) Chemical - region stands high because it is made of rock which is less dense than standard crustal or mantle material at the same pressure and temperature;
2) Dynamic - region stands high due to the vertical normal stress exerted on the base of the plate by dynamically-maintained flow in the asthenosphere;
3) Thermal - region stands high because it is warmer and therefore thermally expanded relative to normal lithosphere and/or asthenosphere.
We will consider each of these possibilities in turn.

Certain chemically induced density reductions, such as anomalously thick crust or development of a refractory peridotite layer [Jordan, 1979], are known to cause depth anomalies in the oceans. Once formed, however, such density anomalies maintain a constant offset between the observed depths and the standard model at all later times, and it is difficult to reconcile this prediction with the observation that the depth anomaly grows with age. In addition, neither a thickened crust nor a refractory peridotite layer is consistent with seismic observations in the area. Analysis of P-wave travel times from explosions recorded by the French Polynesian seismic network reveals that probably only the Tuamotu ridge is underlain by a thickened crust [Talandier and Okal, 1987]. The presence of a refractory peridotite layer would lead to higher seismic velocities [Jordan, 1979], whereas Nishimura and Forsyth [1985] find that this depth anomaly in French Polynesia exactly overlies a very prominent low velocity zone in the upper 200 km for Love waves. The age-dependent pattern of the depth anomaly and its other geophysical manifestations, therefore, rule out the possibility that the superswell has a chemical origin.

Alternatively, suppose that the superswell is dynamically maintained by a massive upwelling, i.e. a superplume, beneath otherwise normal lithosphere of the South Pacific. Such an upwelling might naturally be associated with a thermal anomaly which provides the buoyancy, but at this point we will only consider the mechanical effect of the normal stress from a superplume on the overlying lithosphere. The high rate of ocean ridge and off-ridge volcanism in the Central Equatorial Pacific is consistent with this model based on mass balance considerations alone. In addition, an anomalous flux of material from deeper within the mantle would clearly be compatible with the observed geochemical anomalies. Unfortunately, this hypothesis does not explain a number of superswell features. A large-scale mantle superplume would not be expected to show any systematic relationship with the Marquesas (±Tuamotu) fracture zone, a lithospheric feature. Perhaps, however, we could envoke some mechanism, such as a very thin low viscosity zone, to channel the upwelling into a layer at the base of the lithosphere such that the difference in lithospheric thickness across the fracture zone is enough to dam up the flow. In fact, later we will show that such a low viscosity zone is indeed indicated. Once we include a low viscosity channel, however, the upwelling plume becomes less efficient in transmitting its vertical stress to the overlying plate [Robinson et al., 1987]. Furthermore, the dynamic effects of a mantle superplume would not be expected to create an age-dependent depth anomaly. Small-scale convection in a low viscosity layer at the base of the plate would be more apt to produce an age-dependent pattern, but again, the low viscosity would de-couple normal stresses from the base of the plate, leaving the thermal effects of small-scale convection as the more important factor. Essentially the problem with the dynamic hypothesis is that if only stress is transmitted to the overlying plate, it predicts anomalies tied to a mantle reference frame, whereas a number of the superswell features are tied to the lithospheric reference frame.

Unless we appeal to fortuitous circumstances, the data from the superswell appear to be most consistent with the third hypothesis: thermal anomalies within the lithosphere and/or asthenosphere. But to conclude that the depth anomaly is due to thermal anomalies merely leads to the next question: where is the heat and what is its source? For example, the depth-age relation in Figure 4 indicates anomalous heat in both a thinner thermal plate and a hotter upper mantle, but perhaps a number of other models could provide an equally good fit to the observations by appealing to thermal anomalies in either the lithosphere or the asthenosphere alone. Simple arguments, however, demonstrate that both the lithosphere and asthenosphere must be anomalously warm. Since the effective elastic thickness of the elastic plate is controlled by the depth to an isotherm near 550°C [McNutt, 1984], clearly the low value for elastic plate thickness reported for the superswell requires that higher temperatures extend into the upper lithosphere. Furthermore, it is not possible to confine the thermal anomaly to only the lithosphere unless we can find some source for the excess heat other than the asthenosphere below.

A local lithospheric source, such as radiogenic heat production, can be ruled out immediately. In order to produce a depth anomaly of 500 m, the radiogenic heat production in the upper 125 km would have to on average exceed 2×10^{-7} W/m^3, which is larger than that for a tholeiite and more than an order of magnitude larger than the heat production of a

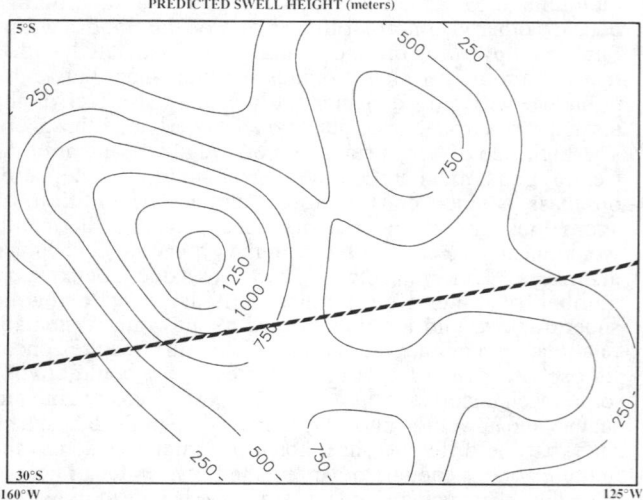

Fig. 5. Map of predicted depth anomalies in French Polynesia based on overlapping swell hypothesis for hot spots of French Polynesia (Pitcairn, Macdonald, Tahiti, and Marquesas). Maximum amplitude of the swell depends on the lithospheric age at the time of heating. Across-strike, the swells are assumed to have a Gaussian shape with half-width (1/e) of 500 km. Contour interval is 250 m.

peridotite. To concentrate the radioactive elements within the crust leads to absurdly large heat production, above that for even a granite. We conclude, therefore, that the superswell exists because both the lithosphere and asthenosphere are warmer than the standard geotherms established for the North Atlantic and North Pacific.

If we literally interpret Figure 4, the plate model best fitting the depth-age observations attributes a few 100 meters of the depth anomaly to thermal anomalies of a few 10's of degrees C in the asthenosphere, and the rest to the reduction in total subsidence for a thinner thermal plate. We can quantitatively test this model by considering the magnitude of the slow seismic velocities observed to lie in the asthenosphere beneath the superswell [Dziewonski and Woodhouse, 1987; Hager and Clayton, 1987]. Hager and Clayton's [1987] tomographic slice through the superswell displays upper mantle slowness anomalies of at least 2×10^{-4} s/km. Using the velocity scaling law of Creager and Jordan [1986], such seismic anomalies, if thermal in origin, would indicate an upper mantle temperature 40°C warmer than the average, similar to the value we derive from fitting the depth-age relation. The remainder of the superswell anomaly we attribute to thermal anomalies within the lithosphere itself. The superswell would be a favorable locus for intraplate volcanism due to easy penetration of hot spot magmas through a thinner and/or less viscous lithosphere. Although this simple explanation fits the available observations, it must be viewed with caution pending complete dynamic calculations since it has been shown that the effect of changing temperature on lithospheric depth can be mimicked by varying viscosity in the asthenosphere alone [Robinson et al., 1987]. Such calculations may alter the proportion of the depth anomaly that we attribute to the lithosphere and our interpretation of the thickness of the plate, but they cannot, without violating the flexure data, change the basic conclusion that the lithosphere is anomalously warm.

Mechanism of Heat Transport Into the Superswell

The source of the excess heat in the lithosphere must therefore be the asthenosphere. But by what mechanism is it transported? Simply elevating the mantle temperature in order to conduct more heat into the base of the plate will not work. For example, in order to produce a 750 m depth anomaly at 80 Ma, the temperature at the base of the plate must be 1600°C. As shown by the theoretical curve in Figure 4 for a normal thickness plate with a 1600°C basal temperature, the resulting depth-age curve does not explain the superswell data at ages other than 80 Ma.

Analysis of subsidence, heat flow, geoid, and elastic plate thickness observations from a number of hot spot swells such as the Hawaiian and Marquesan has shown that in the process of hot spot volcanism, a large amount of heat is rapidly introduced into the base of the lithosphere, temporarily thinning the plate from below [Detrick and Crough, 1978; McNutt, 1987]. The mechanism by which the plate is thinned is not completely understood, but the process occurs so rapidly that it must involve some sort of convective destabilization and downwelling of the lower lithosphere [Fleitout et al., 1986]. At first glance, this process is an appealing explanation for the superswell since we know that it is characterized by a large amount of hot spot activity. Although we do not know exactly the mechanism responsible for lithospheric thinning by hot spots, we do know quite well from a number of observations the amplitude and wavelength of the depth anomalies so produced [Crough, 1978], and the dependence of the process on lithospheric age [McNutt, 1987]. Therefore, by knowing the locations of the hot spots on the superswell, we can quantitatively test the theory that the superswell results from a large number of overlapping hot spot swells. Although this test may not bring us any closer to understanding the physics underlying hot spot volcanism, at least we can determine whether the superswell reflects multiple manifestations of the same process, or a different mechanism.

Figure 5 shows a map of predicted hot spots swells in the same region as Figure 2. The height of the swells as a function of distance from the hot spot was calculated using the age-dependent hot spot model of McNutt [1987] which allows conductive cooling of a 125-km-thick plate which has been thinned to the former depth of the 900°C isotherm and partially rejuvenated to the depth of the 500°C isotherm at the active hot spot. The Gaussian halfwidth of the swells is assigned to 500 km in accordance with observations from numerous examples in the Pacific and Atlantic [Crough, 1978]. Because the depth anomaly only depends on the integral of the anomalous temperature, the details of the lithospheric reheating model are not important. The one adopted predicts the swell height and subsidence data, as well as all the other geophysical observables, from the Hawaiian and Marquesan swells, two hot spots on normal lithosphere.

This overlapping hot spot model is clearly inadequate. First of all, it predicts no depth anomalies on young lithosphere between the Marquesas and Austral fracture zones, where the observed depth anomaly is already 250 m in Figure 2. Nor does it predict any depth anomaly in the southwest corner of the map, but due to the uncertainty in the age contrast across the Austral Fracture Zone at old ages, this deficiency alone may not rule out the model. The most serious failure of the overlapping hot spot model is in predicting the wavelength of the superswell, as best illustrated in Figure 3. The curve with long dashes is a profile across Figure 5 corresponding to the location of the depth anomaly profile. Note that the overlapping swells do not predict the general wavelength of the superswell. In order to better match the observations, the width of the swells would have to be increased by more than a factor of two, and even then the area of low subsidence would not extend to the East Pacific Rise.

The extremely low values for the thickness of the elastic plate supporting superswell volcanoes also appear incompatible with the overlapping hot spot theory. Calmant and Cazenave [1987] have plotted the effective elastic plate thickness T_e of the oceanic lithosphere as a function of its age at the time of loading for a number of dated volcanoes in the Pacific, Atlantic, and Indian oceans. The 42 non-superswell volcanoes show some scatter in T_e versus age due to differences in the amount of thermal rejuvenation of the underlying lithosphere, but essentially yield T_e values between 16 and 30 km for ages greater than 40 Ma at the time of loading. The 17 superswell volcanoes produce a distinctive cluster on their plot that nowhere overlaps the main trend. Elastic plate thickness for the superswell is always less than 14 km even for lithosphere as old as 80 Ma at the time of loading. This result supports our hypothesis that superswell lithosphere is unusually warm, and that the reheating is much greater in magnitude and broader in extent that that which accompanies hot spot activity elsewhere.

Therefore, we conclude that the superswell is not simply a number of overlapping hot spot swells. Even if some sort of convective destabilization is responsible for the superswell, its manifestation is very different from what occurs for simple hot spot swells, and the fact that the lithosphere is too shallow even before it reaches the hot spots suggests that it is not the hot spot which triggers the convective downwelling. Simply put, the lithosphere is not thin only because of the hot spots. The hot spot signatures are there because the lithosphere is already thin even before it encounters the hot spots. Most French Polynesian island chains such as the Cooks, Australs, Tuamotus, and Societies (Marquesas is the notable exception) initiate island formation only after the leading edge of the superswell has passed over their respective hot spots (Figure 1). The possibility exists that due to vagaries of magma supply these hot spots were simply dormant prior to the onset of French Polynesian volcanism. However, the correlation between the passage of the Marquesas fracture zone and the production of volcanoes, at different times in different locations, lends support to the hypothesis that the hot spots simply were not vigorous enough to burn through the normal lithosphere north of the Marquesas.

An internally consistent model for the superswell would include an overprint by individual hot spots and a mechanism for maintaining a thinner thermal plate. The long-wavelength trend in the depth anomaly in Figure 3 could be removed by adopting a thinner thermal plate, as shown in Figure 4. One possibility for the mechanism responsible for the thinner thermal plate is enhanced small-scale convection, which has been proposed in this area from short-wavelength geoid undulations [Haxby and Weissel, 1986], and can produce a similar depth-age relation [E. M. Robinson, personal communication]. The age contrast across the Marquesas Fracture Zone might disrupt the convective pattern by placing higher viscosity rock to the north at depths of 75 to 125 km. The amplitude of individual hot spot swells reheating a 75-km-thick plate along the same profile is given by the short-dashed line in Figure 3 using the same hot spot model of McNutt [1987]. Because the plate is warmer to begin with, the swells are very subdued compared to the case for the 125-km-thick plate. These smaller swells superimposed on the subsidence curve for a 75-km-thick plate would then provide a reasonable approximation to both the long wavelengths and the shorter wavelength undulations of the superswell.

Causes for a Thinner Lithosphere

The flattening of the depth-age curves for the North Pacific and North Atlantic at old ages can be matched if one assumes that a constant temperature boundary condition is imposed on the base of a 125-km-thick plate. Physically, the mechanism by which this apparent boundary condition is maintained is thought to be small scale convection [Parsons and McKenzie, 1978; Fleitout and Yuen, 1984]. As the lithosphere at depth cools, its density as a function of temperature and pressure increases to the point that finally it becomes unstable. The resulting convection supplies heat to the base of the plate thus preventing further thickening of the lithosphere. If the temperature at the base of the plate is increased, the depth for the onset of this instability will be decreased due to the fact that viscosity decreases exponentially with increasing temperature, while density only decreases linearly.

In the case of the superswell, how much must the temperature at the base of the lithosphere be increased in order to produce a thinning of the thermal plate by several tens of kilometers? We have already seen that the depth anomaly on young lithosphere is consistent with a thermal anomaly of several tens of degrees centigrade in the upper mantle, but the decision as to whether this is enough to physically thin the plate depends critically on the choice of viscosity law. For example, the temperature dependence of viscosity is such that a 35°C increase of temperature will reduce viscosity at 125 km depth by a factor of two. Supposing that this reduction is sufficient to allow convective heat transfer to the overlying plate, the hot material will rise and cool adiabatically. The cooling will increase its viscosity, but according to flow laws that include pressure effects, the viscosity increase is partially offset by the decreased pressure at shallower depth. A subject of further research will be to investigate at what depth convective heat transfer is effectively halted. Attempts to model convective thinning of the lithosphere by hot spots [Fleitout et al., 1986], however, suggest that thermal anomalies of the order of two hundred degrees, not several tens of degrees, will be necessary to explain the amount of plate thinning if we invoke only thermal anomalies.

It may not be necessary to invoke higher temperatures to affect the viscosity decrease, however. Small amounts of volatiles can drastically reduce viscosity at a given temperature. In addition, non-Newtonian flow laws predict a further reduction in viscosity with increasing shear stress. The observations that plate velocity with respect to the mantle reaches a maximum on the superswell [Morgan, 1972] and that reduced subsidence is not occurring on the Nazca plate side of the East Pacific Rise [Cochran, 1986] where absolute velocity is greatly reduced both support the notion of some stress effect. We doubt that this is the only factor since depth-age data from both the North Atlantic and North Pacific yield the same thickness for the thermal plate despite the much

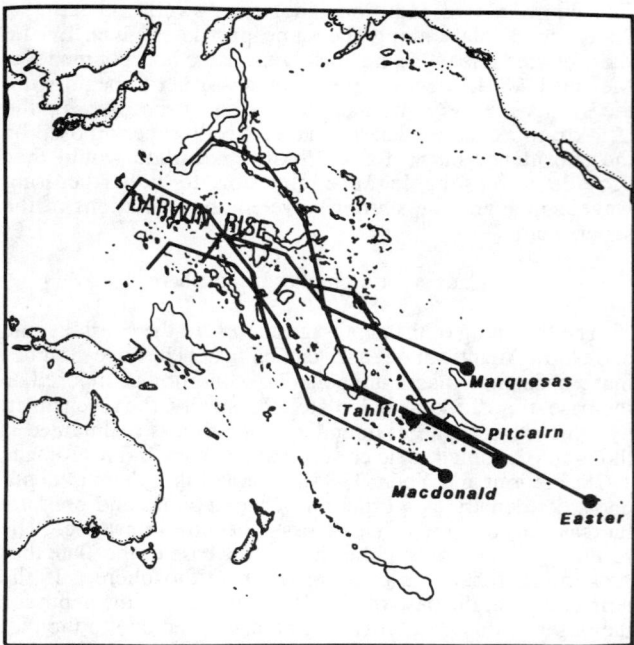

Fig. 6. Location of the proposed Darwin Rise [Menard, 1964, 1984] and tracks of superswell hot spots from Gordon and Henderson [1985].

more rapid absolute velocity of the Pacific plate compared with either the North American or African plates. Nevertheless, the effect of stress on viscosity is nonlinear (power law rheologies have a stress exponent of about 3), perhaps limiting appreciable affects to velocities above some critical value attained only on the superswell.

Other Superswells

Theoretical calculations of convective heat transfer in a fluid with non-Newtonian, temperature-dependent rheology might provide some insight as to the relative contributions of temperature, rock chemistry, and state-of-stress to reducing viscosity beneath the superswell in order to enhance heat transfer to the lithosphere. Unfortunately, the functional form and the constants which calibrate the theoretical flow laws are not well known, especially at the strain rates applicable to geologic processes. Another approach to the problem is to look for other manifestations of the same plate thinning process occurring on the superswell. Is the superswell an isolated occurrence? If not, do other superswells also drift rapidly over the mantle? Do mantle xenoliths recovered from islands indicate a volatile-rich mantle below?

Features on the scale of the superswell may have existed in the past. The morphologic and petrologic characteristics of the superswell are reminiscent of the situation which existed in the mid-Cretaceous on the Darwin Rise [Menard, 1964, 1984], a region of the Pacific that includes the area near the Mid-Pacific Mountains, the Marshall Islands, Magellan Seamounts, and Wake Guyots (Figure 6). One hundred million years ago, the surrounding lithosphere, then 13 to 64 m.y. old, was only 3300 to 4800 m deep, values that match the present-day depth-age relationship in French Polynesia. Several coeval hot spots left short volcanic chains of volcanoes which were frequently overprinted by renewed volcanism, as is the case on the superswell today [Duncan and McDougall, 1976; Bonatti and Harrison, 1976]. In the ensuing 100 million years, the region has only subsided an additional 1000 to 1200 m, on average less than half of that expected from the Parsons and Sclater thermal model for the North Pacific. The initial shallow depths could have been caused by an increase in crustal thickness, but this explanation does not account for the anomalous subsidence as measured by guyot depths. These observations are more easily explained by an age-dependent subsidence as seen on the superswell. Absolute plate motion models [Gordon and Henderson, 1985; Natland and Wright, 1984] trace the source of the midplate Cretaceous volcanism to the hot spots presently beneath the superswell, such as Society, Pitcairn, and Easter (Figure 6). At that time as well as at present, this region contained several spreading ridges and triple junctions [Firstbrook et al., 1979]. Certain petrologic and geochemical similarities between the Cretaceous seamounts of the Darwin Rise and the superswell hot spots suggest that the same variably enriched mantle source with a Dupal signature has existed in this region of the south Pacific in the past [Natland and Wright, 1984]. In summary, both the superswell and the Darwin Rise are extremely broad areas of anomalously shallow seafloor which formed over the same region of the mantle below French Polynesia, include a number of radiogenically enriched hot spots tracks forming short, overlapping chains of volcanoes, and subside more slowly than normal seafloor.

We suspect that even as a general feature, the superswell is merely the most obvious example of a global variability in present-day thermal plate thickness as a function of temperature, chemistry, and/or shear stress in the upper mantle. For example, Cochran and Talwani [1978] note several depth anomalies in the Atlantic Ocean that also appear to be bounded by fracture zones. In future work, we plan to combine models of absolute plate motion with careful studies of heat flow and fluid inclusions from exposed mantle xenoliths on oceanic islands. Applying these models in a number of anomalous areas will help to elucidate the relative contributions of temperature, chemistry, and shear stress to the formation of depth anomalies.

Conclusions

Depth anomalies in French Polynesia south of the Marquesas Fracture Zone are most consistent with a model in which the lithosphere subsides as though it is a thinner thermal plate. Neither chemically-induced density reductions nor uplift from normal stresses at the base of the lithosphere predict the age-dependent pattern. The mechanism by which heat is transfered into the lithosphere is not simply convective destabilization by the French Polynesian hot spots, because the amplitude and wavelength of the superswell is not consistent with the pattern predicted from overlapping hot spot swells. We instead invoke enhanced small-scale convection occurring in this region due to lower viscosities at the base of the plate due to some combination of thermal, chemical, and/or stress effects. The thin lithosphere of the superswell provides a favorable locus for off-ridge volcanism, thus providing significant control on the morphological fabric of the seafloor. We propose that the superswell is not an isolated occurrence, and that it may be the modern-day equivalent of the mid-Cretaceous Darwin Rise.

The principal focus of this study has been to document the existence of the superswell and to demonstrate that some of the commonly-held notions as to what may be causing the depth anomaly are not consistent with the observations. We recognize that numerous questions concerning the superswell are yet unanswered. Why is it found in French Polynesia now, and, if indeed it is related to the Darwin Rise, why is there no continuous band with high density of off-ridge volcanism between the Darwin Rise and the superswell? What is the relationship of the superswell to other anomalies such as the Dupal geochemical signature [Hart, 1984], the slow seismic velocities in the underlying upper mantle [Nishimura and Forsyth, 1985; Hager and Clayton, 1987], and the low order geoid high that centers over French Polynesia when the slab effect in southeast Asia is removed [Richards and Hager, 1985]? What is the long-term fate of the superswell? Careful study of the superswell and other less extreme depth anomalies is needed and may provide useful information on upper mantle heterogeneity and rheology.

Acknowledgements. We are especially grateful to Rodey Batiza for permission to publish this paper in this volume dedicated to Bill Menard. We believe that Bill would have been very pleased with this decision. We thank Tom Jordan for encouragement to write this paper and Peter Molnar, Rodey Batiza, and Jerry Winterer for comments that improved the presentation. Richard Gordon, Anny Cazenave, and Brad Hager kindly provided very useful preprints. This work was supported by NSF OCE-8409157 and ONR N00014-82-C-0019.

References

Bonatti, E. and C.G.A. Harrison, Hot lines in the Earth's mantle, *Nature, 263*, 402-404, 1976.

Calmant, S. and A. Cazenave, Worldwide estimates of the oceanic lithosphere elastic thickness under volcanoes, *Nature*, in press, 1987.

Cande, S., Nazca-South America plate interactions since 50 m.y.b.p., in *Peru-Chile Trench Offshore Peru*, Ocean Margin Drilling Program Regional Atlas Series, Atlas 9, Sheet 14, Marine Science International, Woods Hole, Massachusetts, 1986.

Cochran, J.R., Variations in subsidence rates along intermediate and fast spreading mid-ocean ridges, *Geophys. J. Roy. Astr. Soc., 87*, 421-454, 1986.

Cochran, J.R. and M. Talwani, Gravity anomalies, regional elevation, and the deep structure of the North Atlantic, *J. Geophys. Res., 83*, 4907-4924, 1978.

Creager, K.C. and T.H. Jordan, Slab penetration into the lower mantle beneath the Mariana and other island arcs in the Northwest Pacific, *J. Geophys. Res., 91*, 3573-3589, 1986.

Crough, S.T., Thermal origin for mid-plate hot-spot swells, *Geophys. J. Roy. Astron. Soc., 55*, 451-459, 1978.

Crough, S.T. and R.D. Jarrard, The Marquesas-Line swell, *J. Geophys. Res., 86*, 11,763-11,771, 1981.

Detrick, R.S. and S.T. Crough, Island subsidence, hot spots, and lithospheric thinning, *J. Geophys. Res., 83*, 1236-1244, 1978.

Dietz, R.S. and H.W. Menard, Hawaiian swell, deep, and arch, and subsidence of the Hawaiian Islands, *J. Geol., 61*, 99-113, 1953.

Duncan, R.A. and I. McDougall, Linear volcanism in French Polynesia, *J. Volcan. Geotherm. Res., 1*, 197-227, 1976.

Dziewonski, A.M. and J.H. Woodhouse, Global images of the Earth's interior, *Science, 236*, 37-48, 1987.

Fleitout L., C. Froidevaux and D. Yuen, Active lithospheric thinning, *Tectonophysics, 132*, 271-278, 1986.

Fleitout, L. and D. Yuen, Steady-state, secondary convection beneath lithospheric plates with temperature and pressure-dependent viscosity, *J. Geophys. Res., 89*, 9227-9244, 1984.

Firstbrook P.L., B.M. Funnell, A.M. Hurley, and A.G. Smith, Paleoceanic Reconstructions 0-160 Ma, Deep Sea Drilling Project, La Jolla, 1979.

Fischer K.M., M.K. McNutt, and L. Shure, Thermal and mechanical constraints on the lithosphere beneath the Marquesas swell, *Nature, 332*, 733-736, 1986.

GEBCO, *General Bathymetric Chart of the Ocean*, Canadian Hydrographic Office, 5th Edition, 1978.

Gordon, R.G. and L.J. Henderson, Pacific plate hot spot tracks, unpublished preprint, 1985.

Hager, B.H. and R.W. Clayton, Constraints on the structure of mantle convection using seismic observations, flow models, and the geoid, in *Mantle Convection*, W.R. Peltier, ed., in press, 1987.

Handschumacher, D.W., Post-Eocene plate tectonics of the Eastern Pacific, in *The Geophysics of the Pacific Ocean Basin and Its Margins*, G.H. Sutton, M.H. Manghnani, and R. Moberly, Eds., Geophysical Monograph 19, American Geophysical Union, Washington, D.C., 1976.

Hart, S.R., A large-scale isotope anomaly in the Southern Hemisphere mantle, *Nature, 309*, 753-757, 1984.

Haxby, W.F. and J.K. Weissel, Evidence for small-scale mantle convection from Seasat altimeter data, *J. Geophys. Res., 91*, 3507-3520, 1986.

Jordan, T.H., Mineralogies, densities, and seismic velocities of garnet lherzolites and their geophysical implications, in *The Mantle Sample: Inclusions in Kimberlites and Other Volcanics*, F.R. Boyd and H.O.A. Meyer, eds., American Geophysical Union, Washington, D.C., 1-14, 1979.

Le Douran, S. and B. Parsons, A note on the correction of ocean floor depths for sediment loading, *J. Geophys. Res., 87*, 4715-4722, 1982.

Ludwig, W.J. and R.E. Houtz, Isopach map of sediments in the Pacific Ocean Basin and marginal sea basins, *Amer. Assoc. Petrol. Geol. Map Series*, 1979.

Mammerickx J., R.N. Anderson, H.W. Menard, and S.M. Smith, Morphology and tectonic evolution of the East-Central Pacific, *Geol. Soc. Amer. Bull., 86*, 111-118, 1975.

Matthews, D.J., *Tables of the Velocity of Sound in Pure Water and Sea Water*, Hydrographic Department, Admiralty, London, 1939.

McNutt, M.K., Lithospheric flexure and thermal anomalies, *J. Geophys. Res., 89*, 11180-11194, 1984.

McNutt, M.K. Temperature beneath midplate swells: the inverse problem, in *Seamounts, Islands, and Atolls*, B. Keating and R. Batiza, Eds., American Geophysical Union, this volume, 1987.

McNutt, M.K. and H.W. Menard, Lithospheric flexure and uplifted atolls, *J. Geophys. Res., 83*, 1206-1212, 1978.

Menard H.W., Archipelagic aprons, *Amer. Assoc. Petrol. Geol. Bull., 40*, 2195-2210, 1956.

Menard, H.W., *Marine Geology of the Pacific*, 271 pp., McGraw-Hill, New York, 1964.

Menard, H.W., Depth anomalies and the bobbing motion of drifting islands, *J. Geophys. Res.* 78, 5128-5137, 1973.

Menard, H.W., Darwin Reprise, *J. Geophys. Res., 89*, 9960-9968, 1984.

Menard, H.W. and M.K. McNutt, Evidence for and consequences of thermal rejuvenation, *J. Geophys. Res., 87*, 8570-8580, 1982.

Morgan, J., Plate motions and deep mantle convection, *Mem. Geol. Soc. Amer., 132*, 7-22, 1972.

Natland, J.H. and E. Wright, Magmatic lineages and mantle sources of Cretaceous seamounts in the Central Pacific, *EOS, Trans. Amer.Geophys.Union, 65*, 1075-1076, 1984.

Nishimura, C.E. and D.W. Forsyth, Anomalous Love-wave phase velocities in the Pacific: sequential pure-path and spherical harmonic inversion, *Geophys. J. R. Astr. Soc., 81*, 389-407, 1985.

Parsons, B. and D. McKenzie, Mantle convection and the thermal structure of the plates, *J. Geophys. Res., 83*, 4485-4496, 1978.

Parsons, B. and J.G. Sclater, An analysis of the variation of ocean floor bathymetry and heat flow with age, *J. Geophys. Res., 82*, 803-827, 1977.

Renkin, M. and J.G. Sclater, Age, depth, and residual depth anomalies in the North Pacific: implications for thermal models of the lithosphere and upper mantle, *J. Geophys. Res.*, in press, 1987.

Richards, M.A. and B.H. Hager, The earth's geoid and the large-scale structure of mantle convection, *Proceedings of the NATO Advanced Study Institute: "The Physics of Planets"*, University of Newcastle-Upon-Tyne, April, 1985.

Robinson, E.M., B. Parsons, and S.F. Daly, The effect of a shallow low-viscosity zone on the apparent compensation of midplate swells, *Earth Planet. Sci. Letts., 82*, 335-348, 1987.

Sclater, J.G. and J. Francheteau, The implications of terrestrial heat-flow observations on current tectonic and geochemical models of the crust and upper mantle of the earth, *Geophys. J. R. Astr. Soc., 20*, 509-542, 1970.

Sclater J.G., B. Parsons, and C. Jaupart, Oceans and continents: similarities and differences in mechanisms of heat loss, *J. Geophys. Res. 86, 11,535-11,552*, 1981.

Talandier, J. and E.A. Okal, Crustal structure in the Society and Tuamotu Islands, French Polynesia, *Geophys. J. R. Astr. Soc., 88*, 499-528, 1987.

Van Wykhouse, R., *SYNBAPS*, Tech. Rept. TR-233, National Oceanographic Office, Washington, D. C., 1973.

K. Fischer and M.K. McNutt, Department of Earth, Atmospheric, and Planetary Sciences, Massachusetts Institute of Technology, Cambridge, MA 02139.

IRREGULARLY SHAPED SEAMOUNTS NEAR THE EAST PACIFIC RISE: IMPLICATIONS FOR SEAMOUNT ORIGIN AND RISE AXIS PROCESSES

Daniel J. Fornari

Lamont-Doherty Geological Observatory of Columbia University, Palisades, NY 10964

Rodey Batiza and James F. Allan

Department of Geological Sciences, Northwestern University, Evanston, IL 60201

Abstract. We present new Seabeam and SeaMARC I data for small (<1 km high) volcanoes near the East Pacific Rise (EPR) that exhibit irregular (non-circular) plan-form shapes and whose surfaces are commonly cut by young faults and fissures. The structural control, petrology and close proximity of these irregular seamounts to the EPR strongly suggests a close genetic link between EPR processes and seamount formation and growth. We infer that their irregular shapes are due to early growth from eruptive conduits (fractures) that consist of intersecting sets of EPR-parallel, EPR-perpendicular and oblique faults. Since many small volcanoes near the EPR have irregular shapes, we suggest that larger circular volcanoes may evolve from small irregular ones. This could occur if volcano shape is dominated by the geometry of their conduits in the early stages of growth (in turn controlled by local tectonic stress) but later their shapes are dominated by caldera collapse and gravitational stress within the edifice.

Introduction

Major controls on the shapes of volcanoes are known to include: 1) the shape, size and arrangement of magmatic conduits, 2) eruption rate and magma viscosity, and 3) pre-existing topography and regional and edifice (gravitational) stresses. During and after growth, the primary constructional morphology of volcanoes is frequently modified by the formation of collapse/deformational features, erosion and mass wasting and (for some) tectonic disruption.

The shape, size and geometric relations of magma supply conduits provide important controls on the shapes of volcanic landforms. For example, a point source of magma may build a conical lava pile whereas a long eruptive fissure typically produces a ridge-like feature. The extrusion rate of a linear conduit usually varies along its length producing complex volcanic landforms. Individual fissure eruptions often begin with effusion along the entire length of a fissure, but as the eruption progresses, activity becomes concentrated along a short segment. This sort of eruption produces a long spatter rampart with localized spatter cones or cinder cones and/or lava flows [Williams and McBirney, 1979; Macdonald et al., 1983]. In the deep sea, differences in source geometry probably account for differences between haystacks (point source) and long pillow walls (linear source) [e.g., Fornari et al., 1978].

Eruption rate, distance from vent, magma viscosity and the shape of pre-existing topography are important controls in producing the wide variety of flow forms both subaereally and in the deep sea. In the deep sea, variation in these factors probably accounts for much of the observed variety among individual lava flow forms such as pillow lava, lobate tubes, sheet flows, ponded lava and hyaloclastites [Pieri and Baloga, 1986; Basaltic Volcanism Study Project, 1981; Ballard et al., 1979; Ballard and Moore, 1977; Batiza et al., 1984; Fornari, 1986; A. Barone and W.B.F. Ryan, pers. commun.].

For individual lava flows in the deep sea, it is to be expected that conduit geometry, eruption rate, viscosity and pre-eruption topography exert major controls on morphology. As individual flows pile up to form small cones, the importance of these factors persist but the temporal stability of individual conduits/vents also becomes important. Regional tectonic stress is clearly important in controlling the initial geometry of conduits, but as volcanoes grow and become sizeable, gravitational stresses within the edifice also become important factors in controlling volcano shape.

Oceanic volcanoes range in size over many orders of magnitude, from huge volcanoes like Hawaii at one extreme to tiny cones less than 50 m high along the crest and within the axial rifts at mid-ocean ridges (MORs). Seamount profile shapes also vary widely, from gentle shield shapes like Hawaiian volcanoes, to overturned soup-bowl shapes with flat tops as in the Galapagos [Simkin, 1984], to dome shapes and more complex forms. In plan view, they vary from near circular to elliptical to, as we show in this paper, irregular polygonal shapes. If lateral rift zones develop, elongate and starfish shapes are possible.

Vogt [1974] suggested that volcano size is controlled by lithospheric thickness because, as confirmed also by Batiza [1982], the largest volcanoes seem to be located on the oldest, thickest lithosphere. This issue is more complicated because old lithosphere can be thinned by processes associated with thermal rejuvenation [Detrick and Crough, 1978; Menard and McNutt, 1982; Watts et al., 1980]. Vogt [1974] interpreted the systematic relationship between maximum volcano height and age of the lithosphere as an indication that volcano heights are isostatically limited by the maximum height of a column of magma beneath the volcano [Eaton and Murata, 1960; Basaltic Volcanism Study Project, 1981].

Particular mechanisms of magma ascent and transport have also been invoked to interpret volcano shapes. For example, Lacey et al. [1981] and Angevine et al. [1984] noted the similarity

Copyright 1987 by the American Geophysical Union.

TABLE 1. Structural Data for Small Near-Ridge Volcanoes

Volcano Name	Abyssal Hills or EPR Trend	Ridge Normal*	Sets of Oblique Faults+
N-3	345	- (075)	056(19), 358(77),
N-6	339	073(069)	058(15), 003(70), 017(56)
N-7	340	074(070)	062(12), 005(69),
N-8	355	089(085)	081(8), 007(82),
N-5	338	062(068)	081(19), 014(48), 024(38)
N-1	344	072(074)	065(7), 000(72), 038,023
N-2	350	078(080)	056(22), 355(83),
N-4	340-345	070-075	021-025(45-54)
D	346,351,332	076,090,062	045-024
8	332	053(062)	None
11°30′	348	077±10(077)	354(83), 290(33), 015(62) 002(75), 030(47)
12°50′	355	093(085)	349(14), 317(44), 032(61) 044(49)
12°42′	350	080(080)	006(74), 037(43), 054(26)

* Direction orthogonal to abyssal hills given in parentheses for comparison with actual faults and/or azimuth of line connecting several volcanic centers.
+ Number in parentheses gives angle between fault and the direction of measured ridge-normal features.

Underlined directions correspond to inferred eruptive fissures (see text for criterion).

between the conical and tapered-conical profile shapes of some volcanoes to the expected shapes of surfaces of constant hydraulic potential for porous media flow. This analogy may account for the shapes of large oceanic volcanoes with simple conical forms, but such volcanoes are relatively rare.

Regional tectonic stresses and stresses within the edifice itself have been thought to play important roles in moulding volcano shapes. For example, Nakamura [1977] and Kear [1964] showed how vent alignment and the elongate shapes of volcanoes apparently reflect regional tectonic stresses and fault patterns. In the classic jello-mold study, Fiske and Jackson [1972] demonstrated how gravitational stress within a volcanic edifice can localize eruptions along linear zones of maximum tension, and they used this model to explain the growth of linear volcanic rift zones. Simkin and Batiza [1984] applied this model to flat-topped cratered seamounts that resemble Galapagos volcanoes [Simkin, 1972, 1984]. They suggest that once a doughnut shaped (in plan view) edifice is established by cratering, gravitational stresses will tend to maintain volcanic conduits that are circular in plan.

Gravitational stresses are no doubt important in the growth of large volcanic rift zones such as those commonly found on very large seamounts and guyots [Vogt and Smoot, 1984]. More complex forms, such as some of the volcanoes surveyed by Hollister et al. [1978] may also be explained in this way. Most medium sized oceanic volcanoes (1-2 km high) are roughly circular in plan and have a profile shape (overturned soup bowl) like those of the Galapagos Islands [Simkin, 1984] and Tortuga Island [Batiza, 1978]. Commonly, they have calderas and craters on their flat summits [Fornari et al., 1984; Lonsdale and Spiess, 1979] and in many cases, these may be nested and/or breached. Flank rift zones are usually absent or poorly developed on seamounts, but lava fields and cone fields are common [Fornari et al., 1985]. If the shape of circular, overturned soup bowl volcanoes is controlled by gravitational stresses within the edifice, then clearly this control is by far the most common for medium to large volcanoes. In contrast, very tiny domal volcanoes like those described by Lonsdale [1983] are probably too small for such edifice-related stresses to be important.

One purpose of this paper is to show evidence that many surveyed small (<1 km high) volcanoes near the MORs are irregular, not circular in plan. Thus in ascending order of size, oceanic seamounts appear to vary from tiny conical and dome-shaped lava piles to dominantly irregular or polygonal (up to about 1 km high or less) and finally to dominantly circular upturned soupbowl shapes. Much larger seamounts may be either simple conical edifices or rift-dominated starfish shapes [Vogt and Smoot, 1984]. We argue that irregular or polygonal volcanoes owe their distinctive shapes chiefly to control exerted by the shape and geometry of volcanic conduits in their early stages of growth.

Though available data are not abundant, we also attempt to show that small volcanoes near the EPR are built by volcanic conduits (presumed fractures) with a wide variety of orientations relative to the trend of the EPR. Table 1 and Figure 1 show that presumed eruptive conduits are parallel, oblique and perpendicular to the local trend of the EPR. The trends we have measured and list in Table 1 as being presumably eruptive are linear volcanic ridges, trends defined by linear groups of volcanic cones and linear trends defining the overall plan shape of small seamounts. Non-eruptive trends are either clearly visible faults and fissures, or linear elements in the bathymetry that have not apparently served as conduits. For these measurements we used shaded relief images of digital Seabeam data [Edwards et al., 1984] and attached significance only to linear elements that are reasonably obvious.

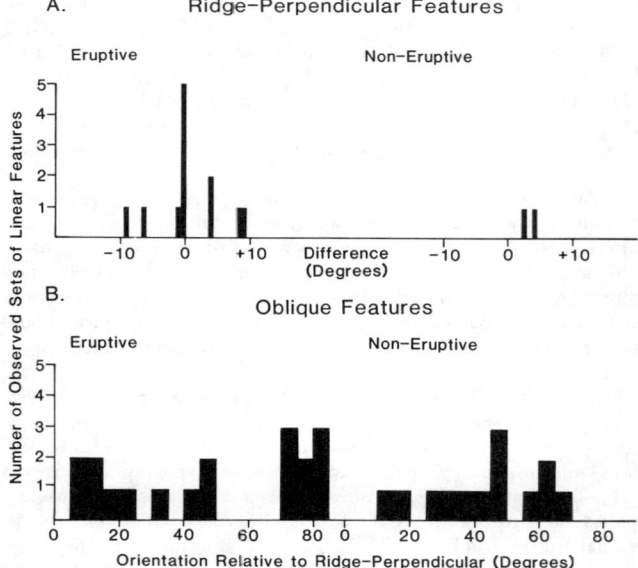

Fig. 1. Histogram of the data in Table 1. Trends that are parallel to the EPR are not plotted. A. Interpreted trends that are within 10° of being perpendicular to the local EPR trend and/or nearly abyssal hills. B. The orientation of oblique trends (angle with measured ridge-perpendicular trends) plotted as a histogram. Eruptive fissures and inferred conduits are mostly parallel to the EPR and oblique. See text for discussion of criteria used to identify the linear elements as well as specific examples.

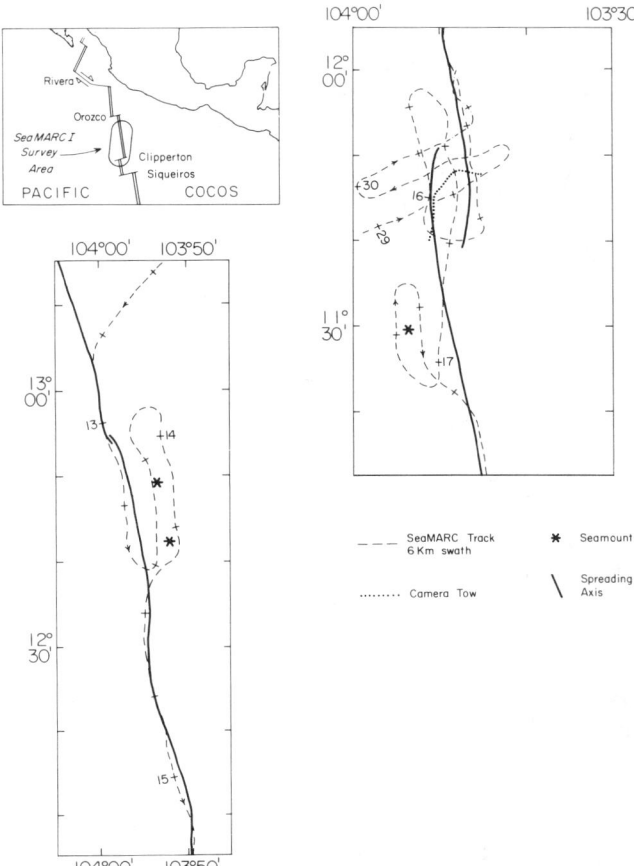

Fig. 2. Location and track coverage for Seabeam and SeaMARC I images shown in Figures 3, 4, 5, and 6.

We recognize that this sort of exercise is necessarily somewhat subjective and furthermore that the nature of some of the measured linear trends is debatable. Despite these problems, we feel that the linear trends we identify are structurally significant. Later, we illustrate the criteria we used for identifying linear structural and volcanic elements by presenting several examples.

Menard [1969] suggested that seamounts may form preferentially at kinks in MORs. Indeed, nearly two decades of more detailed studies have confirmed this and it appears that many individual seamounts and small linear chains originate at MOR offsets. For example, small volcanoes are found within active transform fault zones like Clipperton [Kastens et al., 1986, Figure 8] and form transform parallel and subparallel chains within a few tens of kilometers of the active transform [Gallo et al., 1986]. Inactive fracture zone traces of transforms are also preferred sites for seamount generation [Barr, 1974; Batiza, 1982; Batiza and Vanko, 1983; Lowrie et al., 1986; Searle, 1983; Fornari et al., 1986; Lee and Hammond, 1984]. As suggested by Lonsdale [1985], seamounts also may form preferentially at the dying limbs of some large migrating overlapping spreading centers (OSCs), where, in some cases, they form chains trending at angles that are oblique to both absolute plate motion direction and ridge-perpendicular trends.

Fornari et al. [1984] showed that sites adjacent to elevated ridge segments may be preferential sites of seamount formation; the Larson seamounts near the EPR at 21°N [Allan et al., this volume] may be another example of a small seamount chain built at an elevated ridge segment. In summary, seamounts seem to occur preferentially in several distinct tectonic settings: transforms and fracture zones, some large OSCs and elevated ridge segments. In this paper we present several examples of the latter two types and discuss how the inferred fracture patterns beneath seamounts may help to shed light on the tectonic and volcanic processes in these near-ridge settings.

Pacific Plate Seamount Near the EPR at 11°30′

Figure 2 shows the location of a 600 m high (volume ~50 km³) seamount near the EPR at 11°30′ N. Figure 3 shows a SeaMARC I side-looking sonar mosaic of this volcano, and Figure 4 shows an enlarged SeaMARC I image and Seabeam bathymetric contours overlaid on the geological and structural interpretations of the SeaMARC I mosaic. Viewed along-strike, the EPR axis here forms a gentle dome that rises between bathymetric lows at the 11°15′ offset and the 11°45′N OSC [Macdonald et al., 1984]. The seamount summit is located about 7 km west of the highest part of this dome on crust inferred to be about 110,000 years old. Superimposed on the apex of the axial dome is a local depression, or saddle point [Sempere and Macdonald, 1986]. The EPR 10 km south of the seamount has a central horst 200 m wide with two flanking grabens each about 200 m wide. Northward of this point, the EPR axis narrows toward the saddle point and becomes more triangular in cross section. Abreast of the seamount, the EPR axis is marked by a 300 m wide zone of abundant fissures which widens to about 1 km north of the seamount.

The seamount itself is irregular in shape (see Figure 4). Its form is mostly defined by planar flanks trending 290° (south flank, 2600 to 2800 m depth), 000°-015° (east and west flanks at 2600-2800 m depths) and (less obvious) ~080° (north flank, 2500-2600 m). The 2500 m contour of the summit (Figure 4) trends about 355° on the east and west sides, subparallel to numerous fissures and faults (Figure 3) on the volcano (~345°) and the trend of the EPR (~345°-348°). The 080° trend of the north flank appears to be roughly perpendicular to the trend of the EPR axis, whereas the 290° trend of the south flank and the 000° and 015° trends of the east and west flanks are oblique to the EPR axial trend.

Most of the surface of the volcano is covered by either hummocky, irregular acoustic reflectors (mostly north side, NW flank and east flank) or else patchy, irregular scalloped and dimpled terrain that is less hummocky (see Figures 3 and 4). We interpret both acoustic textures to be principally pillow lava on the basis of submersible observations (R. Hekinian, pers. commun.). In contrast, the summit area consists of smooth, more uniform and less reflective material that we interpret to be smooth sheet flows with a thin coating of sediment. This interpretation seems reasonable for the flat areas of the summit (2460-2480 m) but is problematic for the steep areas of the summit with similar acoustic character (Figures 3 and 4). This sheet flow surface is disrupted by east-facing normal faults with an estimated 20-40 m of displacement, as well as numerous fissures, that roughly parallel the trend of the EPR (330°-350°). Near the highest point of the volcano, a small crater about 300 m diameter is present.

Northward from the summit, the fissures die out and we suggest they are covered by younger, more reflective volcanic units. For example, the flat area just north of the summit is occupied by two darker, oblong patches that we interpret as ponded lava covering fissures and hence younger. Just east of the ponded lava and trending 015° is a broad volcanic ridge consisting apparently of several individual flows and lava cones. Finally, on the NW flank, downslope from and along strike with the lava ponds, is a series of

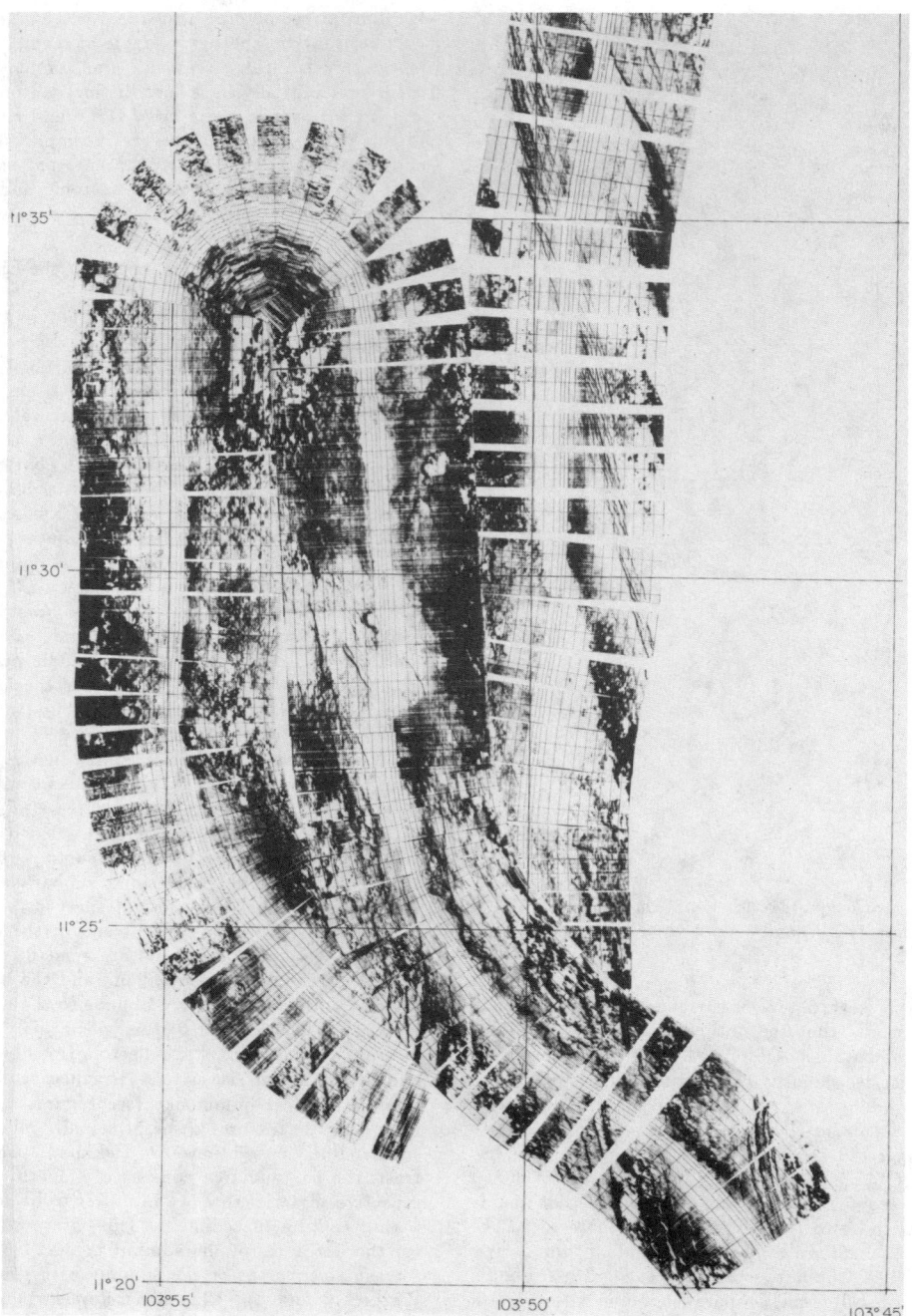

Fig. 3. SeaMARC I image of the EPR and a seamount west of the EPR near 11°30'N. Note the summit crater, abundant EPR-parallel fissures and faults on the seamount and the 015°,030° constructional trends on the north flank of the seamount. Navigation error incurred in fitting Seabeam data to SeaMARC I mosaic is ~300 m.

volcanic ridges or faults that trend 000° to 030° in the hummocky terrain.

The most prominent linear features of this volcano are the EPR-parallel faults and fissures that cut the south flank of the volcano up to the summit, forming notches on the flank topography. These structures and the elongation of the volcanic edifice are all parallel to the orientation of the EPR axis and suggest these patterns are controlled by regional stresses related to the EPR axis.

Similar eruptive activity of EPR-parallel faults at some distance from the axis is evidently quite common. Fornari et al. [1985] and Fornari [1986] show several examples of young volcanic cones and flows erupted from such faults and later we show examples of EPR-parallel faults that are buried by seamount lavas.

The origin of the less well-defined EPR perpendicular trend (080°) plus the oblique trends (290°, 000°, and 015°) are less obvious. In general, they could either reflect the trends of buried

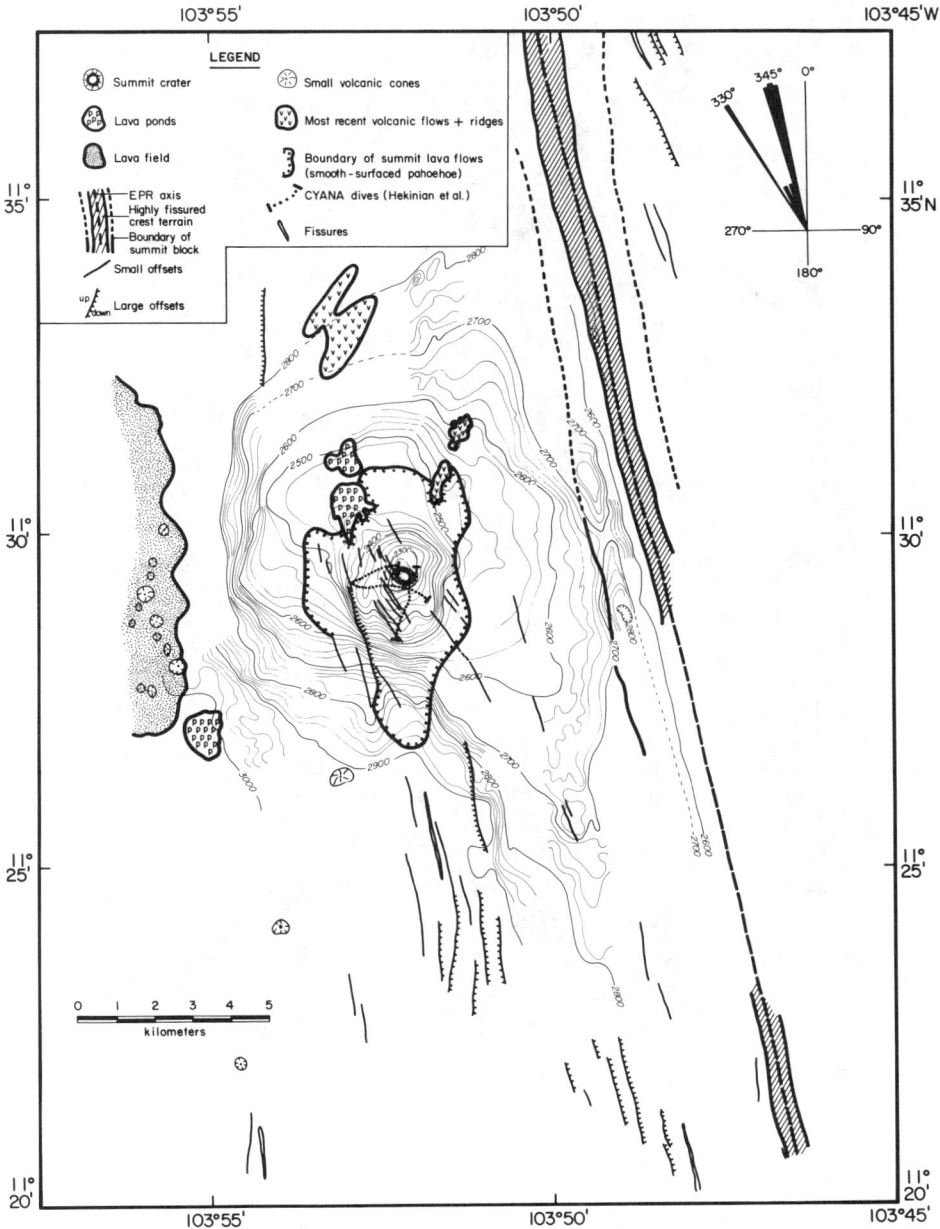

Fig. 4a. Seabeam bathymetry of the 11°30'N seamount in Figure 3 plus interpretation of the SeaMARC I image. See text for additional discussion.

faults that served as eruptive conduits, or else they could be of local origin unrelated to buried faults. In the latter case they could be due either to gravitational stresses in the edifice or represent rotation or perturbations of deeper structures. We favor the interpretation that these trends reflect the trends of linear buried faults/conduits because the EPR-parallel fissures on the volcano are not rotated or perturbed appreciably and the volcano is relatively small.

Cocos Plate Seamounts at 12°42' and 12°50'

Figure 5 shows a SeaMARC I mosaic of the EPR between 12°35' and 13°10'N and Figure 6 shows matching Seabeam bathymetry for part of the area and an enlarged section of the sonar mosaic. This area has been well studied by Hekinian et al. (this volume), Hekinian et al. [1983, 1985], Francheteau and Ballard [1983], Ballard et al. [1984], Gente et al. [1986], Macdonald et al. [1984] and Ryan and Fox (unpublished data). Langmuir et al. [1986] dredged samples from 10 points along the axis in Figure 5 and from the seamount at 12°43.5'N.

In this area, a 32 km long segment of the EPR is bounded on the south by the right-stepping 12°37' OSC and to the north by the left-stepping 12°54' OSC. The linear EPR is domal to rectangular in cross section and the axis is defined by a 200-250 m wide and 30-40 m deep summit graben [Gente et al., 1986]. Along

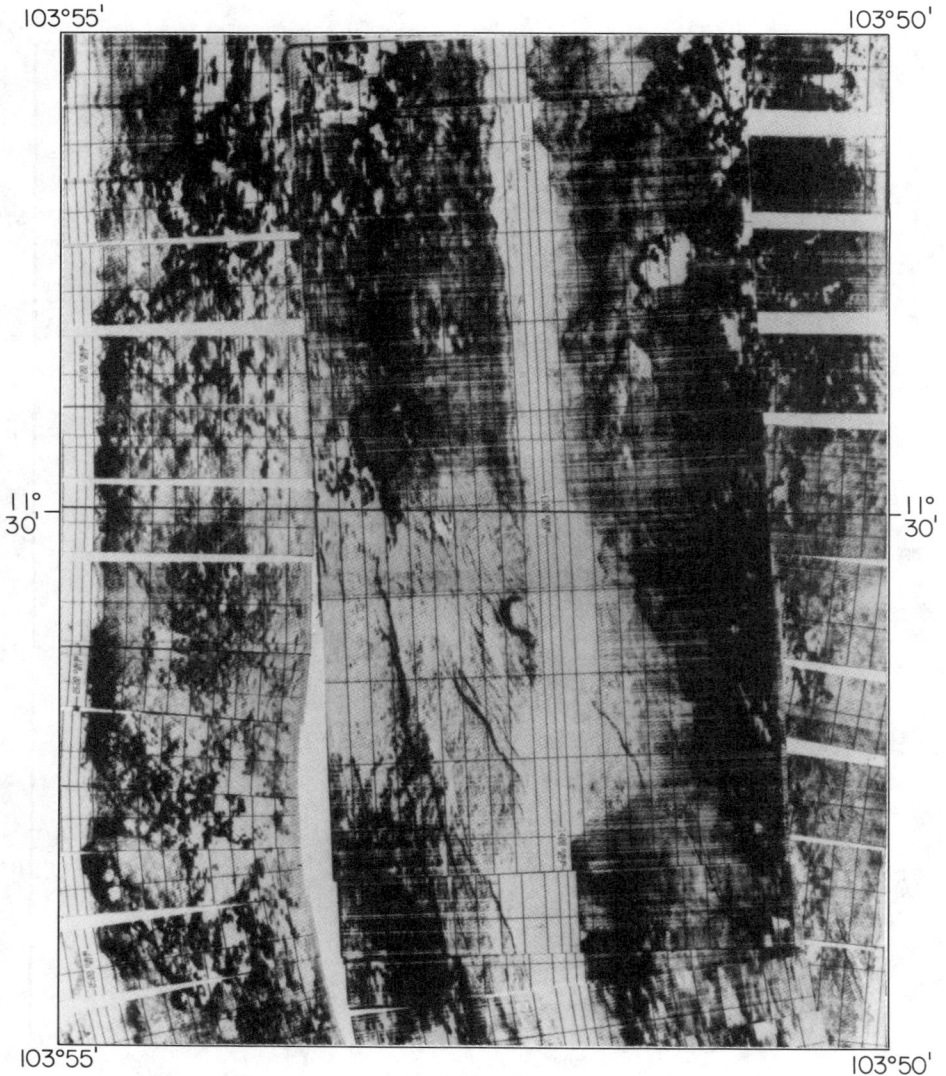

Fig. 4b. SeaMARC I image of the area in Figure 4A. See text for discussion.

strike, the elevation of the ridge axis rises away from both OSCs to define a gentle dome-shaped spreading segment [Macdonald et al., 1984]. On the east side of the EPR, about 5-7 km distant from the axis (inferred crustal age 90,000-130,000 yr) are two irregular-shaped seamounts. The northern seamount is located about 9 km south of the 12°54′ OSC and the southern seamount is about the same distance north of the 12°37′ OSC. Thus, the seamounts lie on seafloor of comparable age and are equidistant from the center of the spreading segment (Figure 6).

The northern seamount at 12°50′N is broader and lower (2680 m) than the southern one (2500 m) but both are somewhat irregular in plan. Fornari [1986] showed that the seafloor between the two volcanoes is covered by young lava flows with channels and tubes that bury EPR-parallel faults. Gente et al. [1986] interpreted that the axial region at 12°50′–12°51′N (at the latitude of the north flank of the northern seamount) as having been volcanically active more recently than the axis at 12°47′N (just south of the southern flank of the northern seamount). They observed that the southern area is dominated by faults and fissures whereas the graben floor to the north at 12°51′N is mostly smooth and covered by young lava flows.

Figure 5 shows the EPR axial graben and prominent EPR-parallel east-facing normal faults on the west flank of the ridge. Several of these may have served as eruptive conduits, as shown by the numerous conical shadows cast by the outline of the upthrown side. On the east flank of the ridge, between the northern and southern seamounts, the eruptive N-S faults described by Fornari [1986] can be seen.

Both seamounts have flat summits and are bounded on some sides by planar flanks. Each is about 200-300 m high and 2-4 km at the base (volume <5 km^3). Figure 5 shows that they bury the underlying EPR-parallel grain of the seafloor and that each consists of rather nondescript hummocky terrane of variable reflectivity. Faintly visible in Figure 6, on both SeaMARC I and Seabeam images, is the NE grain or fabric that transects both seamounts. Figure 6 (and figure 3 of Gente et al. [1986]) show the

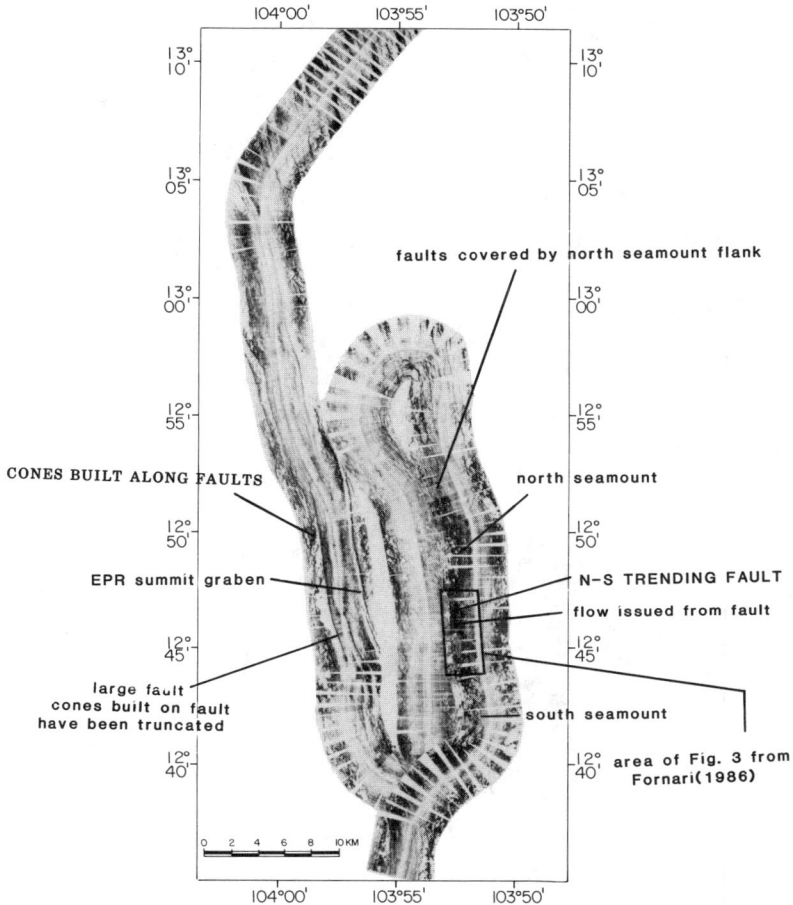

Fig. 5. SeaMARC I image of the EPR between 12°35'N and 13°10'N including the two seamounts at 12°42' and 12°50' on the east side of the EPR. Note the NE structural trends present on both seamounts.

subtly irregular (non-circular) shapes of the two volcanoes. Linear segments of the seamounts' plan form shown in Figures 6 and 7 are: 1) subparallel to the EPR trend of 350°-355° (344° to 349°: somewhat linear west side of the northern seamount, 2800 m contour, and the corresponding side of the southern seamount, 2700 m contour), 2) linear segments perpendicular to 334°-349° trends (080°-095°: e.g., linear portion of the southern 2600 m contour of the southern seamount; southern boundary of the northern seamount, 2700 and 2800 m contour) and 3) oblique trends that vary from 006° to 054° with most being 037° (both seamounts) and 044°. An example of the 044° trend is the NNW boundary of northern seamount defined by the 2800 m contour. Interestingly, this boundary is perpendicular to the trend of the EPR as it veers counterclockwise at the 12°54' OSC. It is also perpendicular to abyssal hills east of the 12°54'N OSC (2900 m contour, Figure 6).

The origin of the oblique-trending controls on the forms of these two seamounts is uncertain. Oblique trends seem to be better developed on the east flank of the EPR at this latitude and are at angles of 37°-47° to the EPR trend. Since they seem to be confined to one side of the ridge only, one could apply the migrating OSC model of Lonsdale [1985] to explain the oblique bathymetric trends as well as the origin of the seamounts. In Lonsdale's model, seamounts form at the dying limbs of OSCs that are migrating along the ridge axis. This migration is inferred from oblique bathymetric trends and, in some cases, seamount chains that point in the direction of migration. If this model applies, it suggests that since about 100,000 yrs ago, both the 12°54'N and 12°37'N OSCs were migrating south along the EPR. The northern seamount could then have formed at a kink in the dying limb of the 12°54' OSC, but the 12°37'N OSC is dextral, so the southern seamount would have to form at the propagating limb, not the dying one. The above scenario is unlikely, however, because it is necessary to invoke a very rapid northward migration of the 12°54'N OSC to explain its present position north of the northern seamount instead of south of it.

Alternatively, both seamounts could have formed at OSCs propagating away from a spreading center high that existed ~100,000 yrs ago. This would explain their symmetric disposition with respect to the present along-axis dome and their equidistant position from each OSC at the present EPR. However, this requires

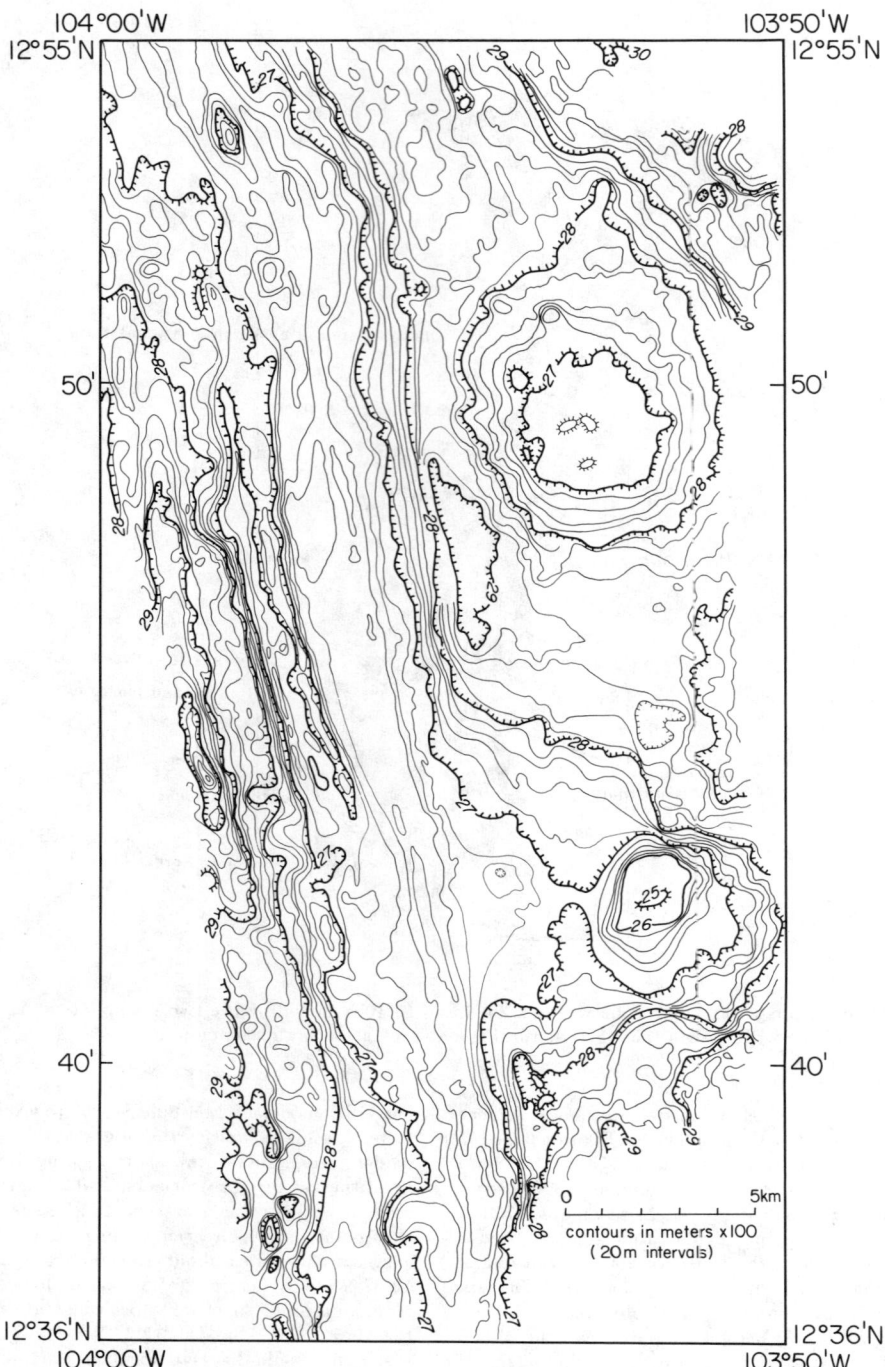

Fig. 6a. Seabeam bathymetry of Figure 5 covering the two seamounts and adjacent EPR. See text for discussion of the shapes of both seamounts.

seamount formation at both dying and propagating limbs or a change of geometry from sinistral to dextral (or vice versa) of one of the OSCs. In summary, there seems to be no completely satisfactory way of deriving both seamounts as well as the near axis oblique trends that presumably controlled their growth from migrating OSCs. Whatever the precise tectonic origin of these two seamounts, it seems clear that ridge parallel faults have played a prominent role in their growth, with subordinate roles for ridge-perpendicular and oblique ones.

Older Seamounts on the Cocos Plate

Figures 8 and 9 show digital shaded relief images of Seabeam data for two small irregularly shaped seamounts on the Cocos

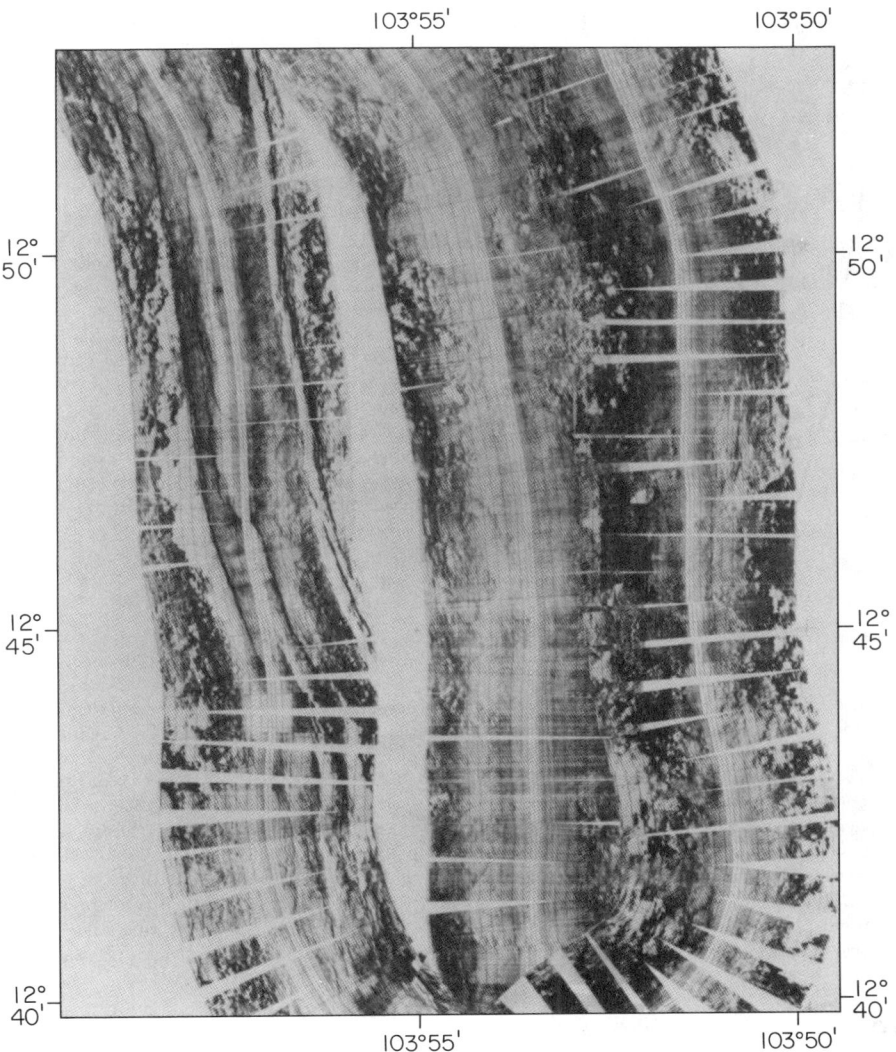

Fig. 6b. SeaMARC I image of the area shown in Figure 6A. See text for discussion.

ridge. Volcano N-6 (Figure 8) is ~7.5 km³ in volume, ~450 m high and located on crust 6.5 Ma in age, whereas N-4 (Figure 9) is about 850 m high, ~20 km³ in volume and is on crust 5 Ma old. Bathymetric charts of these seamounts appear in Batiza and Vanko [1983] and the methods for producing the digital shaded relief images are described by Edwards et al. [1984].

N-6 (Figure 8) has a roughly polygonal outline dominated by straight, steep slopes. The outline of N-4 (Figure 9) appears gently rounded; however, close inspection shows that portions of the rounded outline are actually composed of linear segments. In addition, many linear faults parallel to these segments cut the flat summit region. Also shown on Figures 8 and 9 are abyssal hill (ridge parallel) faults and ridge-perpendicular faults. Each of these volcanoes is located near prominent ridge-perpendicular faults and has well-developed oblique lineations (Table 1) though neither volcano can be traced back to a present offset of the EPR. Table 1 shows that, as with the volcanoes at 11°30', 12°50' and 12°40' described before, N-4, N-6 and other seamounts on the Cocos Plate [Batiza and Vanko, 1983] all show some structural control on their growth from ridge-parallel, ridge-perpendicular and oblique faults.

Discussion

Irregular Morphology of Volcanoes

The shapes of many seamounts in the range 1-50 km³ in volume (up to ~1 km high) are irregular and partly defined by linear trends instead of being perfectly circular or elliptical. Even though many of these volcanoes are also cut by younger faults, we suggest that these irregular forms are mainly primary volcanic growth forms; secondary faulting or mass wasting processes may contribute to their distinctive morphology, but they are probably not the most important processes.

We suggest, as Simkin [1972] did, that the plan-forms of small volcanoes are largely a result of the shape of their main conduits.

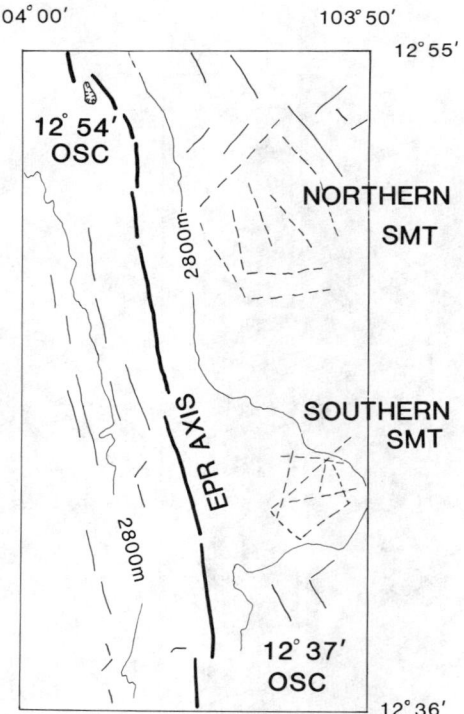

Fig. 7. Structural interpretation of Figure 6A showing inferred faults as light full lines and inferred buried faults as dashed lines.

Large, circular, flat-topped volcanoes have conical (circular in plan) conduits and we suggest that small, irregularly shaped and subtly polygonal volcanoes are fed by a series of conduits controlled by sets of intersecting seafloor faults and fractures that form polygonal outlines in plan view [Batiza and Vanko, 1983]. We further suggest that most seamounts that eventually attain large size and circular form (1-2 km high, >70-100 km^3 volume) may evolve through a growth stage characterized by irregular shape because of the predominance of irregular shapes among small seamounts that have been surveyed. We suggest that eruption from intersecting fractures will initially produce either a series of intersecting linear volcanic ridges or a set of three or more ridges that meet to enclose a polygonal basin. Such a basin would be expected to fill rapidly with further eruption from the linear fissures and their intersections as argued by Simkin [1972]. Growth in elevation by this process is probably limited to a few hundred meters, but at this stage the volcano may be large enough to possess a small magma chamber. Summit collapse caused by the presence of a shallow magma body could subsequently impose a circular symmetry to the growing edifice, which could in turn cause the formation of a new set of conical feeders dominating subsequent growth to form larger circular volcanoes. Alternatively, caldera collapse could be caused by inflation and deflation cycles on a volcano with a well-developed conduit system. Volcano N-3 [Edwards et al., 1984] is diamond-shaped with a tiny crater on its flat top. It may represent a volcano in the early stages of the transition from conduit geometry to gravitational stress as the main control on its shape. While much more data are needed to test this suggestion, we feel that data from available surveys support it.

Origin of Oblique Faults

As we argue earlier, many seamounts near the EPR appear to grow by effusion through EPR-parallel faults plus inferred EPR-perpendicular and oblique faults. The origin of the ridge-perpendicular and oblique faults is problematic because most of the seamounts we have considered in this study are not located near transform faults or their inactive fracture zone extensions.

Oblique faults of many types are commonly found within transforms and at ridge-transform intersections [Fox and Gallo, 1984; Cowen et al., 1986]. Oblique faults are also common at propagating rifts [Hey et al., 1986]. Though less common, oblique faults have been found within the overlap basins of OSCs [Sempere and Macdonald, 1986] and presumably form near migrating OSCs [Lonsdale, 1985]. In this study, we find indirect evidence (at 11°30'N) for oblique and ridge normal faults associated with a sad-

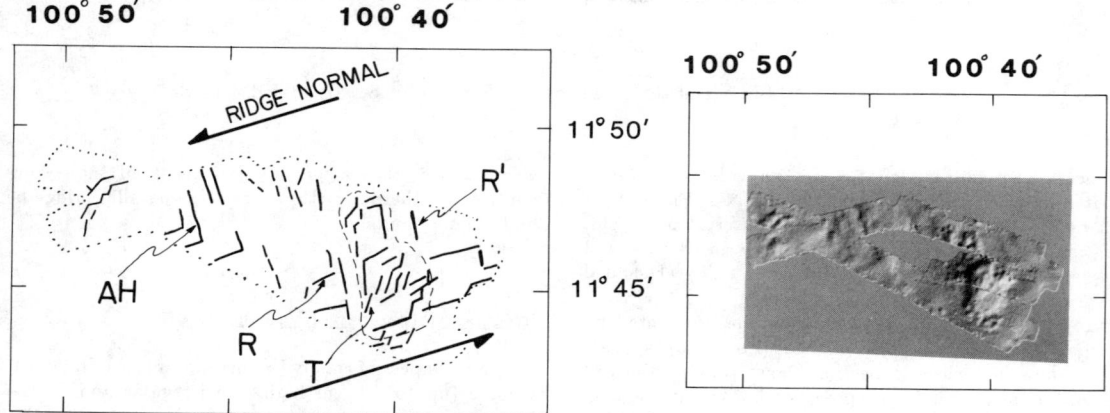

Fig. 8. Shaded relief image of seamount N-6 [Batiza and Vanko, 1983] with line drawing interpretation of structural elements. Note polygonal shape of N-6. AH indicates abyssal hills and "R" and "R'" indicate inferred faults consistent with the directions of Riedel and conjugate Riedel shears if the sense of shear is as shown by arrows. "T" indicates inferred faults with directions consistent with tensional fractures. See Table 1 for summary of the azimuths of the inferred fractures.

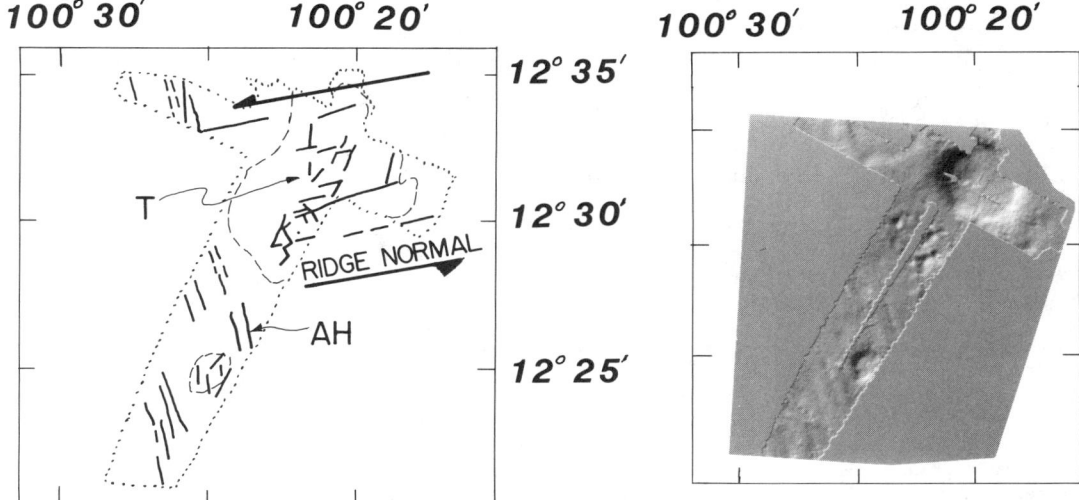

Fig. 9. Shaded relief image of N-4 [Batiza and Vanko, 1983]. Note the presence of young faults on the flat summit that are similar to those on the 11°30'N seamount (Figure 4B) except that these are not ridge parallel as they are on the 11°30'N seamount.

dle point at the ridge axis, though the reason why such faults should form is not clear.

One possibility is that lateral magma transport along the ridge, of the type discussed by Macdonald et al. [1984] and Sempere and Macdonald [1986], can somehow cause deformation if this lateral magma flow is impeded by subsurface structures. Another possibility is that small oblique faults are ubiquitous but also inconspicuous; that they form as a consequence of normal spreading but have not been widely recognized. A third possibility is that they form in association with inferred small offsets by the mechanism proposed by Batiza and Margolis [1986]. According to this model, ridge normal and oblique faults can form away from the axis in association with the formation of small axis offsets by mismatched and uncorrelated spreading behavior of adjacent spreading segments. Mismatched spreading would cause ridge-normal shear away from the axis [Batiza and Margolis, 1985] explaining the presence of oblique lineations: low angle (to ridge normal direction) oblique faults could be Riedel shears [Tchalenko and Ambraseys, 1970], high angle oblique faults could be anti-Riedels and intermediate angle oblique faults could be tensional gashes. There is not yet enough information to tell which of these, if any, is the correct explanation for oblique faults off-axis near saddle points and small offsets; however, it appears that these oblique faults may be more common than previously thought.

Implications of Near Axis Seamounts for Axial Processes

As we attempt to show, near axis volcanoes at 11°30'N, 12°50'N and 12°42'N are closely linked with tectonic and volcanic processes occurring at the ridge axis. Basalts from these seamounts are mostly N-MORB [Batiza and Vanko, 1984] and the structural control for magma supply to the growing seamounts appears to be controlled by axis-related tectonic processes. In fact, axis related normal faults can, as at 11°30', form while the seamount is active. Detailed petrologic comparison between the seamounts at 11°30', 12°50' and 12°42' and the nearby EPR axis, which is in progress, is expected to yield more information about how magma supply to the EPR and seamounts may be related. Elsewhere, it is quite clear that seamount magmas bypass magma chambers present beneath the EPR axis [Allan et al., 1987; Batiza and Vanko, 1984; Fornari et al., 1986].

The preferential origin of seamounts near transforms, fracture zones and OSCs supports the idea that seamount origin is linked to petrologic and tectonic processes near offsets. Even at elevated ridge segments, like 11°30'N near the center of a spreading segment, the seamount seems to have formed at a saddle point in the axis. It is possible that near offsets, where the crust is commonly fractured by more than one set of fractures, there are more magma conduits available. However, the general issue of conduit availability versus magma availability as a control on seamount origin is still unresolved. Doubtless, more and better detailed surveys along with petrologic comparisons between ridge and seamount magmas will greatly help to clarify some of these important questions.

Acknowledgements. DJF thanks W.B.F. Ryan and P. J. Fox, Co-Chiefs, and the scientists and crew on PASCUA Leg 1, who assisted in the acquisition of the SeaMARC I and Seabeam data. W.B.F. Ryan, K. Kastens, and K. Crane all worked on the construction of the SeaMARC I mosaic. The paper was greatly improved by the thoughtful review comments of P. J. Fox, J. Karsten, K. Kastens, and T. Simkin, who we wish to thank. We are grateful to M. A. Luckman for drafting and figure preparation. We gratefully acknowledge support from the NSF (OCE 83-08980 and OCE 85-08042 to RB and OCE 84-14616 to DJF) and the ONR (N00014-80-C-0856 to RB and N00014-84-C-0132 Scope EPR to DJF) for this study. Lamont-Doherty Geological Observatory Contribution Number 4152.

References

Allan, J. F., R. Batiza, and P. Lonsdale, Petrology of lavas from seamounts flanking the East Pacific Rise, 21°N: Implications concerning the mantle source composition for both seamount and adjacent EPR lavas, this volume, 1987.

Angevine, C. L., D. L. Turcotte, and J. R. Ochendon, Geometrical form of aseismic ridges, volcanoes and seamounts, J. Geophys. Res., 89, 11287-11292, 1984.

Ballard, R. D., and J. G. Moore, *Photographic atlas of the Mid-Atlantic Ridge rift valley*, 114 pp., Springer-Verlag, New York, 1977.

Ballard, R. D., R. T. Holcomb, and T. H. Van Andel, The Galapagos Rift at 86°W, 3. Sheet flows, collapse pits and lava lakes of the rift valley, *J. Geophys. Res., 84*, 5407-5422, 1979.

Ballard, R. D., R. Hekinian, and J. Francheteau, Geological setting of hydrothermal activity at 12°50′N on the East Pacific Rise: A submersible study, *Earth Planet. Sci. Lett., 69*, 176-186, 1984.

Barr, S. M., Seamount chains formed near the crest of the Juan de Fuca ridge, northeast Pacific Ocean, *Mar. Geol., 17*, 1-19., 1974.

Basaltic Volcanism Study Project, *Basaltic Volcanism on the Terrestrial Planets*, 1286 pp., Pergamon Press, New York, 1981.

Batiza, R., Geology, petrology and geochemistry of Isla Tortuga, a recent tholeiitic island in the Gulf of California, *Geol. Soc. Am. Bull., 89*, 1309-1324, 1978.

Batiza, R., Abundance distribution and sizes of volcanoes in the Pacific Ocean and implications for the origin of non-hotspot volcanoes, *Earth Planet. Sci. Lett., 60*, 196-206, 1982.

Batiza, R., and S.H. Margolis, A model for the origin of small non-overlapping offsets (SNOO's) of the East Pacific Rise, *Nature, 320*, 439-441, 1986.

Batiza, R., and D. Vanko, Volcanic development of small oceanic central volcanoes on the flanks of the East Pacific Rise inferred from narrow beam echo sounder surveys, *Mar. Geol., 54*, 53-90, 1983.

Batiza, R., and D. A. Vanko, Petrology of young Pacific seamounts, *J. Geophys. Res., 89*, 11235-11260, 1984.

Batiza, R., D. J. Fornari, D. A. Vanko, and P. Lonsdale, Craters, calderas and hyaloclastites on young Pacific seamounts, *J. Geophys. Res., 89*, 8371-8390, 1984.

Cowen, D. S., M. Botros, and H. P. Johnson, Bookshelf tectonics: Rotated crustal blocks within the Sovanco Fracture Zone, *Geophys. Res. Lett., 13*, 995-998, 1986.

Detrick, R. S., and T. S. Crough, Island subsidence, hotspots and lithospheric thinning, *J. Geophys. Res., 83*, 1236-1244, 1978.

Eaton, J. P., and K. J. Murata, How volcanoes grow, *Science, 132*, 925-931, 1960.

Edwards, M. H., R. E. Arvidson, and E. A. Guiness, Digital image processing of Seabeam bathymetric data for structural studies of seamounts near the East Pacific Rise, *J. Geophys. Res., 89*, 11108-11116, 1984.

Fiske, R. S., and E. D. Jackson, Orientation and growth of Hawaiian volcanic rifts: The effect of regional structure and gravitational stresses, *Proc. Roy. Soc. London, 329A*, 289-326, 1972.

Fornari, D. J., Submarine lava tubes and channels, *Bull. Volcanol., 48*, 291-298, 1986. 1987.

Fornari, D. J., A. Malahoff, and B. C. Heezen, Volcanic structure of the crest of the Puna Ridge, Hawaii: Geophysical implications of submarine volcanic terrane, *Geol. Soc. Am. Bull., 89*, 606-616, 1978.

Fornari, D. J., W. B. F. Ryan, and P. J. Fox, The evolution of craters and calderas on young seamounts: Insights from SeaMARC I and SeaBeam sonar surveys of a small seamount group near the axis of the East Pacific Rise, *J. Geophys. Res., 89*, 11,069-11,084, 1984.

Fornari, D. J., W. B. F. Ryan, and P. J. Fox, Seafloor lava fields on the East Pacific Rise, *Geology, 13*, 413-416, 1985.

Fornari, D. J., R. Batiza, M. Perfit, J. Allan, R. Haymon, T. Simkin, A. Barone, W.B.F. Ryan, and T. Smith, The structure and morphological evolution of a small seamount chain near the East Pacific Rise, *Eos Trans. AGU, 67*, 1184, 1986.

Fox, P. J., and D. G. Gallo, A tectonic model of ridge-transform - ridge-plate boundaries: Implications for the structure of oceanic lithosphere, *Tectonophysics, 104*, 205-242, 1984.

Francheteau, J., and R. P. Ballard, The East Pacific Rise near 21°N and 20°S: Inferences for along-strike variability of axial processes of the Mid-Atlantic Ridge, *Earth Planet. Sci. Lett., 54*, 93-116, 1983.

Gallo, D. G., P. J. Fox, and K. C. Macdonald, A Seabeam investigation of the Clipperton transform fault: A morphotectonic expression of a fast-slipping transform boundary, *J. Geophys. Res., 91*, 3455-3467, 1986.

Gente, P., J. M. Auzende, V. Renard, Y. Fouguet, and D. Bideau, Detailed geologic mapping by submersible of the East Pacific Rise axial graben near 13°N, *Earth Planet. Sci. Lett., 78*, 224-236, 1986.

Hekinian, R., J. Francheteau, V. Renard, R.D. Ballard, P. Choukroune, J.L. Cheminee, F. Albarede et al., Intense hydrothermal activity at the axis of the East Pacific Rise near 13 N: Submersible witnesses the growth of sulfide chimney, *Mar. Geophys. Res., 6*, 1-14, 1983.

Hekinian, R., Auzende, J. M., Francheteau, J., Gente, P., Ryan, W.B.F., and Kappel, E. S., Offset spreading centers near 12°53'N on the East Pacific Rise: submersible observations and composition of the volcanics, *Mar. Geophys. Res., 7*, 359-377, 1985.

Hey, R., M. C. Kleinrock, S. P. Miller, T. M. Atwater, and R. C. Searle, Seabeam deeptow investigation of an active oceanic propagating rift system, Galapagos 95.5°W, *J. Geophys. Res., 91*, 3355-3368, 1986.

Hollister, C. D., G. F. Morris, and P. Lonsdale, Morphology of seamounts in the western Pacific and Philippine Basin from multi-beam sonar data, *Earth Planet. Sci. Lett., 41*, 405-418, 1978.

Kastens, K. A., W. B. F. Ryan, and P. J. Fox, Structural and volcanic expression of a fast-slipping ridge-transform-ridge plate boundary: SeaMARC I and photographic surveys at the Clipperton transform fault, *J. Geophys. Res., 91*, 3469-3488, 1986.

Kear, D., Volcanic alignments north and west of New Zealand's central volcanic region, *N.Z. J. Geol. Geophys., 7*, 24-44, 1964.

Lacey, A., J. R. Ochendon, and D. L. Turcotte, On the geometrical form of volcanoes, *Earth Planet. Sci. Lett., 54*, 139-143, 1981.

Langmuir, C. H., J. F. Bender, and R. Batiza, Petrological and tectonic segmentation of the East Pacific Rise, 5°30′N-14°30′N, *Nature, 322*, 422-429, 1986.

Lee, J. S., and S. R. Hammond, Morphology of Heck and Heckle seamount chains, Juan de Fuca Ridge, *Eos Trans. AGU, 65*, 1080, 1984.

Lonsdale, P., Lacoliths (?) and small volcanoes on the flank of the East Pacific Rise, *Geology, 11*, 706-709, 1983.

Lonsdale, P., Non-transform offsets of the Pacific-Cocos plate boundary and their traces on the rise flank, *Geol. Soc. Am. Bull., 96*, 313-327., 1985.

Lonsdale, P., and F. N. Spiess, A pair of young cratered volcanoes on the East Pacific Rise, *J. Geol., 87*, 157-173, 1979.

Lowrie, A., N.C. Smoot, and R. Batiza, Are oceanic fracture zones locked and strong or weak?: New evidence for volcanic activity and weakness, *Geology, 14*, 242-245, 1986.

Macdonald, G. A., A. T. Abbott, and F. L. Peterson, *Volcanoes in the Sea, 2nd ed.*, 517 pp., University of Hawaii Press,, 1983.

Macdonald, K., J.-C. Sempere, and P.J. Fox, East Pacific Rise from Siqueiros to Orozco fracture zones: Along-strike continuity of axial neovolcanic zone and structure and evolution of overlapping spreading centers, *J. Geophys. Res.*, *89*, 6049-6069, 1984.

Menard, H. W., Growth of drifting volcanoes, *J. Geophys. Res.*, *74*, 4827-4837, 1969.

Menard, H. W., and M. McNutt, Evidence for and consequences of thermal rejuvenation, *J. Geophys. Res.*, *87*, 8570-8580, 1982.

Nakamura, K., Volcanoes as possible indicators of tectonic stress orientation—principle and proposal, *J. Volc. Geotherm. Res.*, *2*, 1-16, 1977.

Pieri, D. C., and S. M. Baloga, Effusion rate, area and length relationships for some Hawaiian lava flows, *J. Volc. Geotherm. Res.*, in press, 1986.

Searle, R. C., Submarine central volcanoes on the Nazca plate — high-resolution sonar observations, *Mar. Geol.*, *53*, 77-102., 1983.

Sempere, J.-C., and K. C. Macdonald, Deep tow studies of the overlapping spreading centers at 9°03'N on the East Pacific Rise, *Tectonics*, *5*, 881-900, 1986.

Simkin, T., Origin of some flat-topped volcanoes and guyots, *Geol. Soc. Am. Mem.*, *132*, 183-193, 1972.

Simkin, T., Geology of Galapagos, in *The Galapagos*, edited by R. Perry, pp. 15-41, Pergamon Press, Oxford, 1984.

Simkin, T., and R. Batiza, Flattish summits, calderas and circumferential vents: A morphogenetic comparison of young EPR seamounts and Galapagos volcanoes, *Eos Trans. AGU*, *65*, 1080, 1984.

Tchalenko, J. S., and N. N. Ambraseys, Structural analysis of the Dasht-e Bayaz (Iran) earthquake fractures, *Geol. Soc. Am. Bull.*, *81*, 41-60, 1970.

Thompson, G., W. B. Bryan, R. D. Ballard, K. Hamuro, and W. G. Melson, Axial processes along a segment of the East Pacific Rise, 10°–12°N, *Nature*, *318*, 429-433, 1985.

Vogt, P. R., Volcano height and plate thickness, *Earth Planet. Sci. Lett.*, *23*, 337-348, 1974.

Vogt, P. R., and N. C. Smoot, The Geisha guyots: Multibeam bathymetry and morphometric interpretation, *J. Geophys. Res.*, *89*, 11085-11107, 1984.

Watts, A. B., J. H. Bodine, and N. M. Ribe, Observation of flexure and the geologic evolution of the Pacific Basin, *Nature*, *283*, 532-537, 1980.

Williams, H., and A. R. McBirney, *Volcanology*, 397 pp., Freeman, Cooper and Co., San Francisco, 1979.

STRUCTURAL FAILURE AND DROWNING OF JOHNSTON ATOLL, CENTRAL PACIFIC BASIN

Barbara H. Keating

Hawaii Institute of Geophysics, University of Hawaii, Honolulu, Hawaii 96822

Abstract. Emery (1956) and Ashmore (1973) described the geology of Johnston Atoll (Northern Line Islands chain) and pointed out the anomalous structure of the atoll. These studies led Ashmore (1973) to suggest that the atoll itself is tilted. Johnston Atoll appears to be an example of a seamount that is undergoing a transition from an atoll to a drowned seamount (guyot). Submersible studies of the shallow carbonate bank demonstrate that the carbonate bank displays important karstic features. Recent side-scan sonar studies of the southern flank of this seamount provide evidence that the southern flank of the seamount has undergone substantial mass-wasting. We hypothesize that the mass-wasting of the seamount has loaded the seafloor surrounding Johnston Island unevenly. The southeast Johnston Basin lies 700 m shallower than the southwest Johnston Basin. The loading of the southeast Johnston Basin has resulted in differential subsidence of the sea floor surrounding the seamount which has resulted in the tilting of the seamount (0.016°) and is responsible for the drowning of much of the reef. It is suggested that local structural failure, preferential erosion and drainage, and differential subsidence of seamounts can cause drowning of reefs which may lead to the formation of guyots.

Introduction

Johnston Atoll is situated at 16°45'N 169°30'W; in the central Pacific Basin, near the northern limit of the Line Islands seamount chain (Figure 1). Only Johnston Island (approximately 1 by 3 km) and three small islets (less than 1 km in width or length) rise above sea level to mark the position of a much larger submerged carbonate bank (approximately 17 km in width). This carbonate bank displays unusual morphology in that much of the atoll's ring reef is drowned and the entire carbonate bank slopes to the southeast. Earlier studies of the Johnston carbonate bank by Emery (1956) and Ashmore (1973) suggest that the anomalous morphology resulted from tilting or subaerial erosion. In this paper observations made during several submersible dives along the margins of the Johnston carbonate bank are reviewed. Results from side-scan sonar surveys of the southern flank of Johnston provide evidence of large-scale mass-wasting of Johnston seamount.

Previous Observations

Carbonate Bank Features

Emery (1956) charted the detailed bathymetry of the Johnston Atoll carbonate platform. A simplified version of this bathymetric map is shown in Figure 2. The reef structure of Johnston is described by Emery (1956). Five distinct zones are observed: seaward slope, lithothamnion ridge, coralline algal reef flat, coral slope, and a lagoonward (or leeward) debris slope. The live barrier reef of Johnston Island is restricted to the northwest, i.e., leeward margin (Figure 3). This is a striking observation, because under existing climatologic conditions, reef growth is normally greatest on the windward rather than leeward side of atolls (Emery, 1956).

The Submerged Platform

A distinct rim (interpreted as the fossil ring reef) is revealed by echo sounding along much of the southern and western edges of the platform (Ashmore, 1973). Emery (1956) and Ashmore (1973) both provide evidence that the submerged ridge (not associated with a living reef) has a height approximately the same as the height of the existing barrier reef above the adjoining submarine platform. Based upon geomorphology, this ridge appears to be the drowned eastern margin of the atoll. No central lagoon is obvious in the bathymetry (Figure 2); instead two flat-topped reef terraces cover much of the central platform.

Ashmore's bathymetric studies (1973) describe a submarine ridge upon which Johnston and the small islets (including Sand Island) are situated. The ridge is composed predominantly of dune sands and minor beach rock units (based on

Copyright 1987 by the American Geophysical Union.

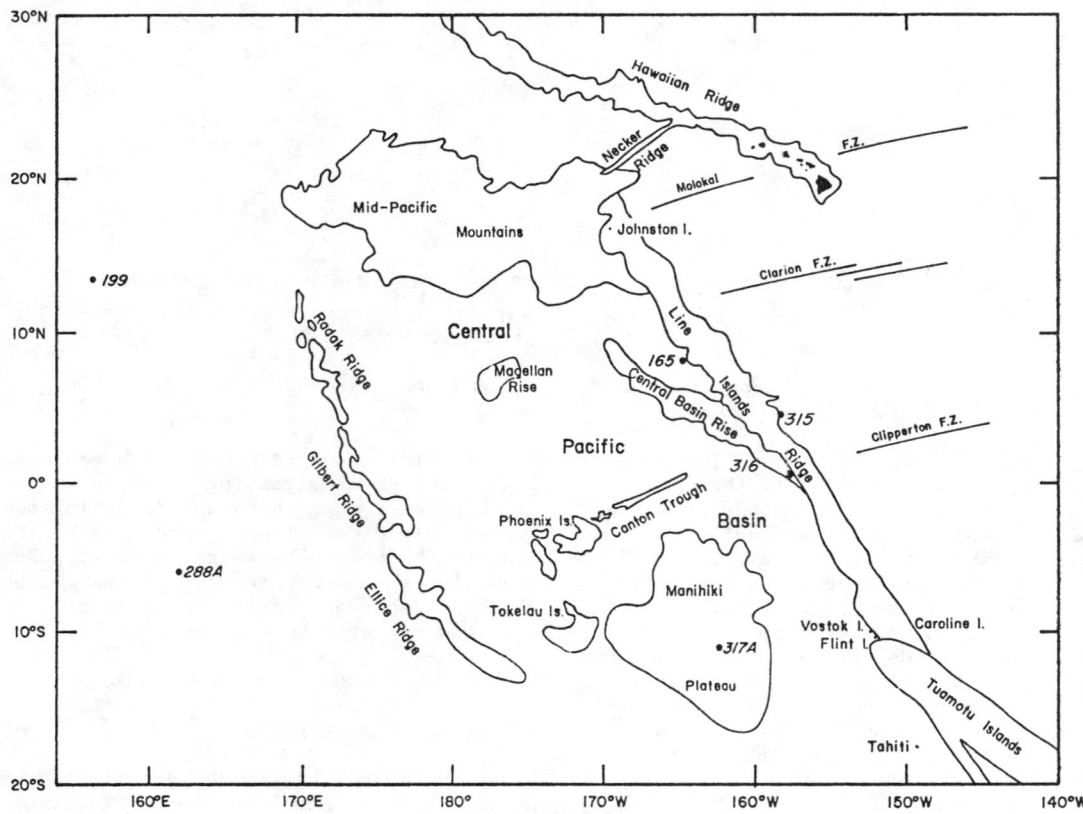

Fig. 1. Map of the southern and equatorial Pacific illustrating the dominant bathymetric features and DSDP site locations. Johnston Island is situated west of Hawaii at the northern end of the Line Island seamount province.

well data and outcrops on Sand Island, Emery, 1956; Maragos, pers. comm., 1983). The sands forming the ridge appear to be largely deposited by wave and wind activity. (Outcrops can be seen on portions of Sand Island. Most outcrops on Johnston Island have now been disturbed by building.) The alignment of the ridge is exactly parallel to the axis of tilt described by Ashmore (1973) and shown in Figure 4. It is also parallel to the dominant wind direction. Dune features, however, suggest a transport perpendicular to the current trade wind direction. The anomalous transport direction could be interpreted as a 90° shift in wind direction but instead probably results from the tilting of the platform and redistribution of sand by wave activity.

Terrace Structures

Ashmore (1973) reported two distinct submarine terrace surfaces at -8 m and -18 m. These reef terraces sit on a sloping carbonate bank surface. The -8 m reef terrace overlies on a deeper reef terrace. Numerous ridges and knolls are found on its surface where live coral and patch reefs are common. Ashmore (1973) reports the most striking feature of this surface to be the abundant sink holes. Many of these sink holes follow contorted, elongate paths, which are open to the -18 m level at one end. Some sink holes are approximately 0.75 km in length. The path of these sink holes is parallel to the dip direction of the larger carbonate terrace. The larger sink holes occur at depths of 20 m in the lower terrace. Since Emery's sediment samples showed that sand and fine debris cover much of the -8 m terrace, it is likely that these sink holes have substantial sediment fill (Ashmore, 1973). The -8 m terrace does not have an observable slope.

The -18 m reef terrace extends over an area of approximately 40 km^2. This terrace is morphologically very distinct from the upper terrace. It is "somewhat dished," suggesting a lagoon topography. There are few knolls, or patch reefs. Ashmore (1973), however, speculated that most minor depressions on this deeper reef terrace are likely to be filled with sands and coral debris.

The on-lapping contact between the upper and lower reef terraces is distinct but very uneven. The horizontal contact extends across the carbonate bank in a north-south direction and is between 500 and 1000 m wide.

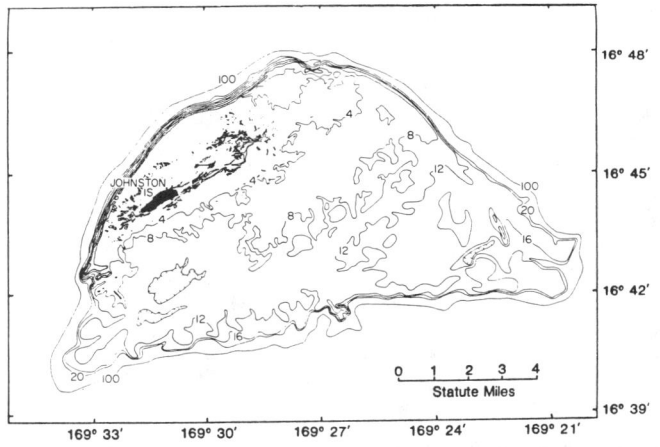

Fig. 2. Bathymetry of the carbonate platform of Johnston. This figure is from Emery (1956).

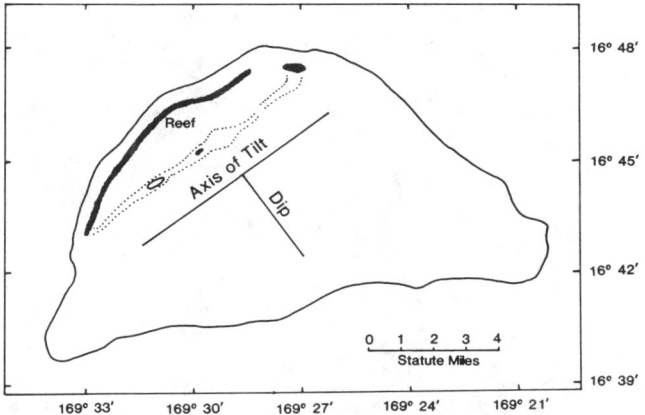

Fig. 4. Map of the Johnston carbonate platform (after Ashmore, 1973) showing the position of the marginal reef and the ridge on which Johnston Island sits. The axis of tilt and dip direction are those proposed by Ashmore. He calculated a slope of 0.016 degrees.

Recent geologic submersible work extends from 30 meters downward, hence the terraces observed by Ashmore (1973) were not examined as part of this study. However, in a separate submersible dive numerous wave-cut cliffs and notches were observed at depths between 30 and 60 m (J. Maragos, pers. communications, 1984). Between 60 and 137 m convex (upward) slopes were observed and below 137 m near-vertical slopes were observed.

Sediment Studies on the Platform

Sediment samples from the shallower portion of Johnston Atoll (Emery, 1956) yielded the following average composition: coralline algae 51%, coral 20%, shell fragments 2%, Halimeda 1%, and fine debris 16%. The coralline algae is composed of high-Mg calcite and is the dominant component of the sands on the surface of the Johnston platform. On the basis of aerial photography, Emery (1956) estimated that about half of the platform floor was dominated by coral growth, and the other half by sandy sediments. While coralline algae is for the most part restricted to the barrier and patch reefs, algal and coral debris contribute significantly to the sediment.

Submersible Observations

Thirty-five submersible dives were completed on the margins of Johnston Atoll as part of an environment assessment of the atoll. The submersible used in these studies was the University of Hawaii research submersible Makali'i, which has a 400-meter depth-capability. Four dives were dedicated to geological studies, and the remainder were biological investigations. The geological dives were distributed about the margins of the carbonate bank in order to examine the geographic variations of rock types and morphology of the slopes and to assess tilt of the carbonate bank (Figure 1). The observations from the four geological dives were augmented by analysis of video tapes of many biological dives which are also reviewed here.

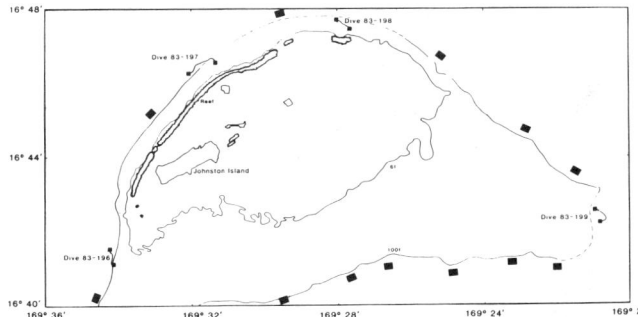

Fig. 3. Map of Johnston Island and the Johnston Island carbonate platform (outlined by the 100 fathom contour). The routes of the four geological dives are shown by the small rectangles marking the ends of the track lines. The locations of additional biological dives are marked by large rectangles. A concentration of biological dives occurred at the southwestern edge of the platform which are not shown in this figure.

Shallow Slopes

The four geological dives concentrated on the geologic structure of the atoll between 122 and 396 meters water depth. The broad, gentle slopes of the atoll surface shallower than approximately 122 m are covered by thick carbonate sands (containing abundant Halimeda fragments). At approximately 122 m, the slope drops away abruptly to become near-vertical (Figure 5).

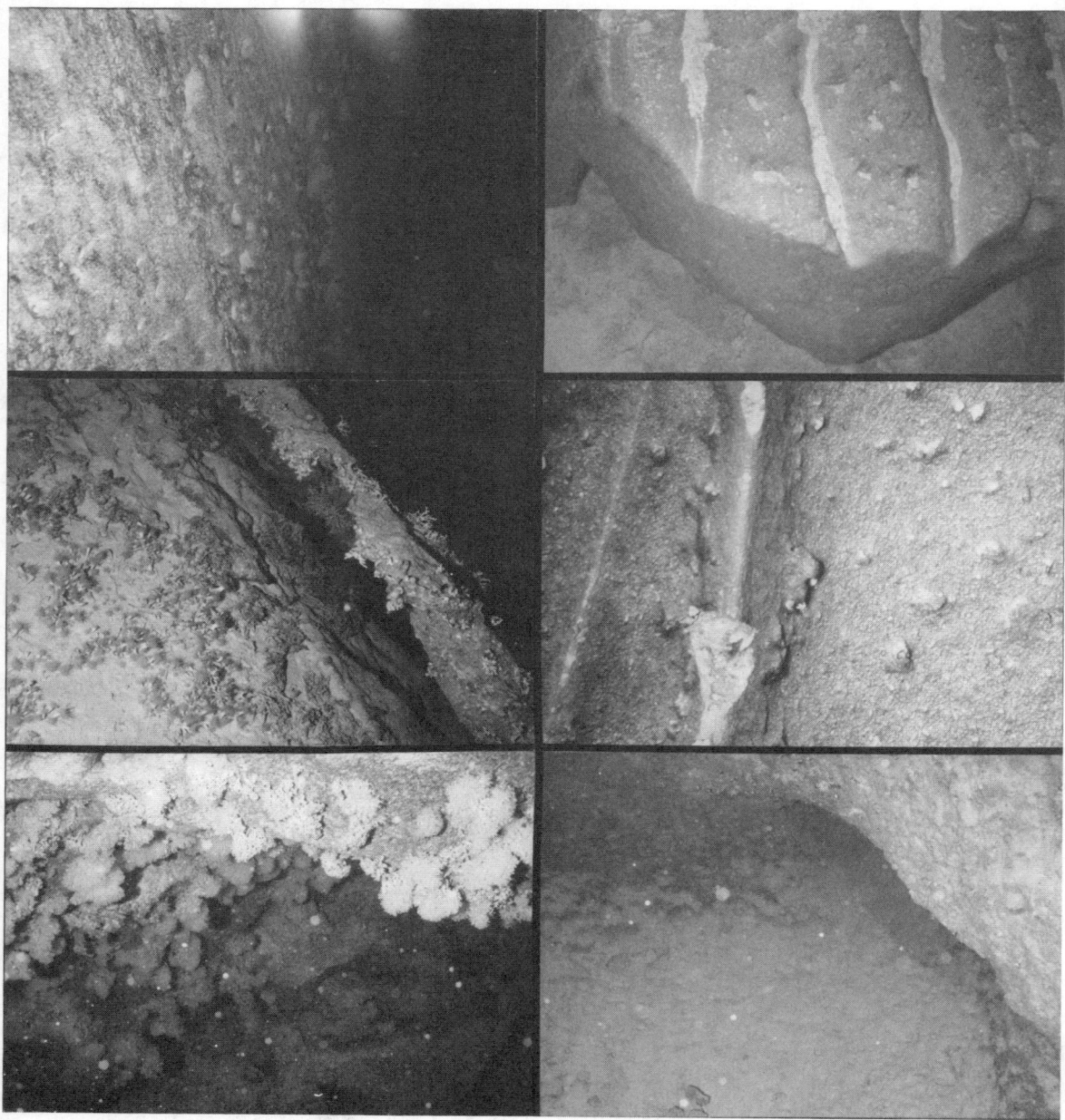

Fig. 5. Photographs of the flanks of Johnston Atoll taken from the University of Hawaii submersible <u>Makali'i</u>. The submersible can dive to 400 m depth. Sediment-free limestone cliffs are shown in the upper left photograph. The dark surface of the outcrop is due to a thin coating of Mn crust. A large "house-size" block is seen perched on the slope in the upper left photograph. The block is several meters in thickness, width and length. Note the sediment chutes on the upper surface of the block. A relatively small block is shown in the center left photograph. The block is less than a meter in thickness but is 4-5 meters wide and 8-10 meters in length. Note the thick sediments under the block and the encrustations on the detrital block and the sediment surface. A close-up of a sediment chute is shown in the center right photograph. Sponges growing on the top of the cave (shown in Figure 6) are shown in the lower left photograph. A small cave with a sediment covered floor is shown in the lower right photograph.

Deep Slopes

In each of the four geological dives, the submersible descended to a maximum depth of slightly more than 400 m and then slowly ascended, in each case within 2 to 3 m of the rock outcrops. At maximum depth the slopes are marked by numerous angular boulders (generally several meters in width and height) that are precariously perched on the slopes, often exceeding the angle of repose (Figure 5). At approximately 244 m, numerous caverns were observed; these appear to be the original setting of the blocks observed at 365 m and greater depths. (Only a few large boulders occur above this level.) Although, wave-cut notched cliffs were expected to occur at depths greater than 50 m they were not observed.

A sediment cover consisting of coarse to fine-grained sand is present locally on the slopes of Johnston Atoll. The sediment cover varies from zero to a maximum thickness of 6 to 10 centimeters (see Figure 5). Halimeda chips are obvious in many of the sediment-covered regions. At Site 199, large mollusca shells are occasionally present on the slope. The living organisms were absent and the shells appear to have been washed from the upper surface of the atoll. Live deep-water corals were observed at two geologic dive sites (199 and 198); however, they do not contribute significantly to the volume of sediments.

The thickness of sediments appears to reflect the current regime at each site. The ocean currents at each of the four sites were found to be extremely variable; multiple changes in direction and velocity are observed with depth. The strongest currents were found on slopes swept clean of sediments.

Where sediments have accumulated to depths of several cm, the sediments give the appearance of having developed a lithified surface. In several instances, land slides have occurred in the otherwise unconsolidated sediments. Where these poorly consolidated sediments have been undermined a thin lithified surface remains visible around the landslide scar.

Sediment Chutes

The most dramatic erosional features observed in this study were the numerous sediment chutes. The chutes resemble karrens found in karst environments and are probably relics of features formed during the Pleistocene lowerings of sea-level. The chutes are generally incised 12 to 15 centimeters into the limestone surface of the carbonate bank (Figure 5). Individual chutes are often blocked by rocks of a few centimeters to 25 cm in diameter.

Caves

At dive site 199, two caves were observed at depths of approximately 200 m. The larger of these caves was approximately 20 m in depth, 20 m in height and 40 m in breadth. The outcrops and walls of the caves were highly pitted, suggesting that significant dissolution has occurred. Both stalagmites and stalactites were observed within the larger cave. Shelfstones (ledges formed at the edges of cave pools) were also observed (Figure 6). No sediments are present on the floor of the larger cave. Sponges can be seen in abundance on the overhanging ledges within the cave (Figure 5). In contrast to the large cave, a small cave shown in Figure 5 does display thick sediment coverage. Shimmering water observed at the cave sites appears to flow from the caves. Currents at this level were strong however, making detailed observations both difficult and hazardous.

Sink Hole

On the southern margin of the Johnston bank a vertical dissolution shaft or sink hole was observed. The feature was approximately 200 m in height and 15 m in width. The outer (southern wall) of the feature is now breached. Very similar features can be seen on land at Puntan dos Amantes on Guam (Mariana Islands) where the sink holes are over 120 m deep. The submerged sink hole observed at Johnston strongly resembles the dissolution features achieved in laboratory acid etching of limestone blocks reported by Purdy (1974).

Outcrops

Only limestones are observed in the submarine outcrops; no basalts or volcaniclastic rocks were observed. The textures of the outcrops vary significantly and it appears likely that several facies are represented. The rock outcrops appear to consist of massive exposures of reef and lagoonal limestones. The surface of these limestones is brown in color and becomes progressively darker with depth, suggesting a thin Fe-Mn crust is present. Where fracture surfaces expose the interior of the rocks they are white. Also, where sediments have been eroded from outcrops, the recently exposed rock is white to very light tan. The brown coating on the exterior of the rock (see Figure 5) was examined by x-ray diffraction and atomic spectrometry and represents an initial precipitation of a Fe-Mn crust (DeCarlo, p. comm., 1985).

Rock Types

Isolated ledges at various depths provided a means of easily collecting rock and sediment samples. These ledges often extend 0.3 to 1 m from the surrounding cliff. No stratification is obvious on the surrounding cliff faces. Occasionally these ledges are partially buried by sediments and rocks that have fallen from above. More often, the ledges had 2 to 3 cm of sediments with a

Fig. 6. Sketch of one of two large caves discovered at depths of 400 meters below sealevel on the margins of Johnston seamount. A series of stalactites and stalagmites were observed with peculiar table-like platforms on the latter. This drawing was made by geophysicist Will Sager after viewing videotapes of the two caves.

few isolated rock fragments (up to 40 cm in diameter) on the surface. Rock samples were collected with the mechanical arm of the submersible from the ledges or from the outflow of a sediment chute. Samples were collected from ledges at Site 196, 197, 198 and 199. The assumption was made that these isolated rocks are from the near vicinity, as a larger rock fall from higher on the cliff would be expected to bury the ledge.

The rocks described here from these dives were analyzed and reported by Aydemir (1985). Aydemir reports that the sample from Site 196 (360 m) consists of angular skeletal fragments (coralline algae, mollusc shells, Halimeda fragments, echinoid spines, foraminifera and ostracod tests) cemented by micrite and crystalline cements. The rock appears to have been transported down-slope as part of a debris flow from a reef-flank facies. The cements are mostly aragonite. Signs of aragonite dissolution occur on the exposed surfaces of the rock sample.

The sample collected from Site 197 (400 m) contained a large hermatypic coral fragment surrounded by coralline algae suggesting the rock originated part of the reef facies. The intra-coralline voids were partially filled by carbonate mud and silt-sized grains. Cements are poorly developed except within the mud infill.

The aragonite and Mg-calcitic cements are still present.

Four rocks were collected during Dive 198. The first (collected at 360 m) contains a large hermatypic coral with a thin rim of small boring and annelid worm tubes. There is little or no crystalline or micritic cement or infill in the interior of the sample. Mud infill is prominent, however, on the exposed surfaces of the rock. The rock appears to be derived from the forereef slope facies. A second rock from this dive, collected at 240 m, is extensively bored. The rock is composed of carbonate sand with Halimeda fragments being the prominent constituent, and appears to have formed in the reef flank facies. The rock is well-lithified and most intergranular pores are filled with cements. The presence of well-developed isopachous Mg-calcite cements suggests formation in a zone where sea water was freely circulating. A third rock from this dive site was collected at 180 m. and is a cemented carbonate sand similar to the last sample but containing a fragment of coral (Porites) and is believed to be derived from the reef front. The exterior of the rock is extensively bored and covered by annelid tubes and solitary corals. There is evidence of recrystallization of micrite and micritic peloids. The final rock collected from Site 198 was collected from 120 m. and is made of crustose coralline algae with an outer rim of extensively bored and encrusted annelid worm tubes and bryozoans. This rock is interpreted as representing reef growth at depths of less than 10 m. An age date of 11,630 ($\pm$ 280) y has been reported for this rock.

The sample collected at Site 199 from 320 m consists of a large hermatypic coral fragment, which is bored and encrusted by corals, bryozoans, and worm tubes. The faunal and floral assemblage is typical Johnston Atoll reef growth. The sample displays little evidence of diagenesis other than minor aragonite cementation. The sample is interpreted as representing reef talus.

The studies of Johnston rocks (Aydemir, 1985) show that most rocks represent shallow-water samples that have been transported down-slope rather than representing rock types at depth, as originally assumed. Aydemir (1985) reports three dates from rocks acquired during the Site 198 dive. The ages are 11,630 ybp ($\pm$ 280), 10,620 ybp ($\pm$ 280) and 10,590 ybp ($\pm$ 290). Aragonite is still present in all these samples and little dissolution has taken place.

The evidence presented by Aydemir challenges the assumption that the rocks collected were at depths near their formation. One could thus conclude that all the rock samples collected by the submersible are young, were formed on the shallow carbonate bank near sea level and were dislodged from the shallow portions of the seamount during the last glacial sea level lowering.

SeaMARC II Side-Scan Sonar Survey Observations

A SeaMARC II side-scan sonar survey was conducted in December 1986 on the southern flank of Johnston Atoll. During the survey, high-resolution seismic profiling was used in conjunction with 3.5-kHz bathymetric profiling. Positioning during the survey used satellite navigation and radar observations of Johnston Island. The side-scan sonar system used in this survey is described in detail by Blackinton et al. (1983). The side-scan sonar image of the bottom (Figure 7) and bathymetry shown here (Figure 8) are shipboard records without subsequent computer enhancement.

Side-Scan Sonar Image

The SeaMARC II survey covers the southeastern corner of Johnston seamount and the southern flank and basins. The track crossing the southeastern flank of the seamount displays an image characteristic of seamount slopes elsewhere in the Pacific. The carbonate cap of the seamount is evident and appears a white-to-light gray shade. Below the carbonate cap, numerous debris flows (black shades) cover the slope and form a debris apron on the abyssal sea floor.

The track parallel to the southern margin of the seamount displays a markedly different character from that crossing the eastern flank. The carbonate bank (light gray shades at the top of the figure) is bound by a cliff whose base grades into extremely steep slope (23°). The dark area in the center of the swath (roughly along the 1300 meter contour) is a second near-vertical scarp. Rocks were dredged from this depth (1400 m) on the southeastern flank of the seamount at 169°40.7'; 16°21.5'N and yielded breccia of carbonate and volcanic clasts in a manganese and phosphate matrix (J. Hein, personal communication, 1984). The rocks which underlie this scarp display steep (15-25°) slopes (black and dark gray shades) and are shown in the southern portion of the image (due south of Johnston Island 16°38-36'; 169°22-28'W). (By comparison the slopes commonly observed in Hawaiian volcanoes are 8-12°.) The surfaces of these slopes are generally covered by debris derived from the carbonate bank or from mass wasting of its margins and underlying volcanic edifice. An example of the latter is a block of carbonate bank debris (white; low reflectivity) over 1 km in diameter seen resting on the debris apron at 169°28'W; 16°38'N.

Three tracks were run to the south of Johnston Island. The track lines, which run roughly north-south, cover a large ridge-feature which appears to be part of the Johnston Island volcanic edifice. The easternmost of these three north-south tracks covers a segment of sea floor displaying extremely rough topography. The center track runs along the summit of the ridge that forms the southern extension of this seamount (hereafter referred to as Johnston Ridge).

The westernmost track records the image of the gradually sloping flanks of Johnston Atoll and Johnston Ridge. The sea floor along the western side of the track line is relatively flat and shows a very gentle slope extending to abyssal sea floor depths. Debris flows of highly reflective material blanket portions of the slopes of the seamount in the upper left portion of the image. High reflectivity debris flows (black shades) are seen on the western flanks of both the seamount and Johnston Ridge.

Side-Scan Sonar Bathymetry

A bathymetric map of the southern flank of Johnston Atoll with 100-m contours was constructed at sea and is shown in Figure 8. The bathymetry of the Johnston Island carbonate bank at depths less than 1000 m has been added using the bathymetry shown on NOAA Hydrographic Map 83637 (1977) as a data source. Slopes on the flanks are greater than 10° throughout the area surveyed except for the regions referred to as the southeast and southwest Johnston Basins and the shallow portion of the platform itself. Steep slopes averaging 22° or more are observed in many areas on the southern margin and many near-vertical faces are present at the margins of the platform itself.

The lower slopes of the southern margin of

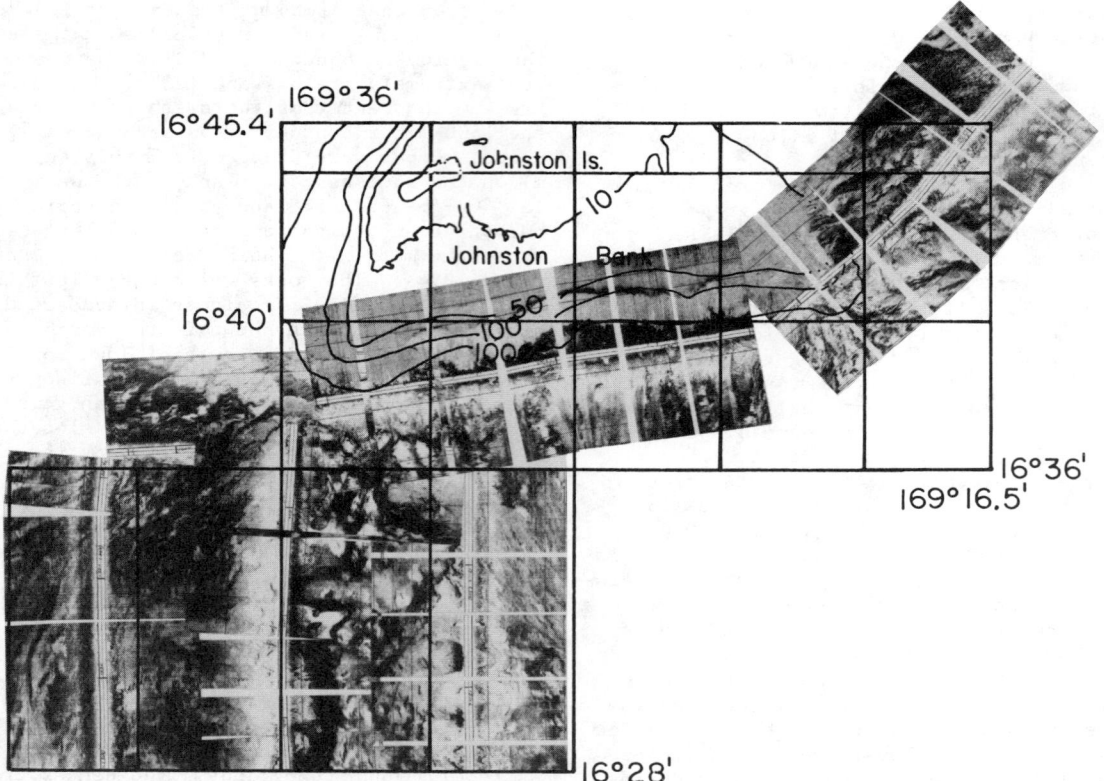

Fig. 7. Side-scan sonar images of the eastern and southern flanks of Johnston seamount. The bathymetric contours shown on the shallow sloping bank are drawn from the NOAA hydrographic map of the atoll (1977). The southeastern and southwestern flanks of the seamount are covered by many debris flows. The southern flank displays a very different outcrop pattern. The margin itself is nearly straight as opposed to curving like most seamount flanks. A thick carbonate bank is obvious (light shades in image: high reflectivity). The slope of the carbonate bank is extremely steep ($23°$) as opposed to that observed for other seamounts. The bank is underlain by high reflectivity basaltic outcrops. These outcrops likewise are anomalously steep ($15°$). The debris apron adjacent is very irregular and extraordinarily thick. A southern unmapped ridge was found which extends south of Johnston. The basin to the east of that ridge is 700 m shallower than that to the west.

Johnston Atoll and the eastern margin of Johnston Ridge are characterized by complex bathymetry, characteristic of both constructional and mass-wasting regimes. The detailed bathymetry (Figure 8) shows the basin southeast of Johnston is strongly channeled. The basin west of Johnston Ridge is nearly flat. The bathymetry of the margins of the southeast basin contrasts with that of the southwest basin. The southeast basin has irregular scalloped margins rather than the smooth margins typical of the southwest basin. This survey shows the depth of the southeast basin is 700 m less than that of the southwest basin. This difference in depth appears to result from in-filling of the basin with debris derived from the southern flank of the Johnston Atoll and eastern flank of Johnston Ridge.

Johnston Ridge itself appears to represent an extension (perhaps a rift zone ? or a remnant) of Johnston seamount, which is free of the thick coral cap which formed at shallow depths on the more northern edifice. An examination of the bathymetric map shows cone-like features on this ridge (Figure 8; $169°24'W$; $16°32'N$ and $169°33'W$; $16°34.5'N$) and in the adjacent basins (one is shown in Figure 7; $169°31'W$; $16°30'N$; another further to the south is outside the area of this map). These cones do not appear to be eroded and are interpreted as products of late stage volcanism.

Evidence for Tilting

Johnston Atoll is characterized by an unusual carbonate platform. Strictly speaking, it is no longer an atoll, since the live reef surrounding the platform is no longer present at sea level. Only a limited barrier reef, approximately 12

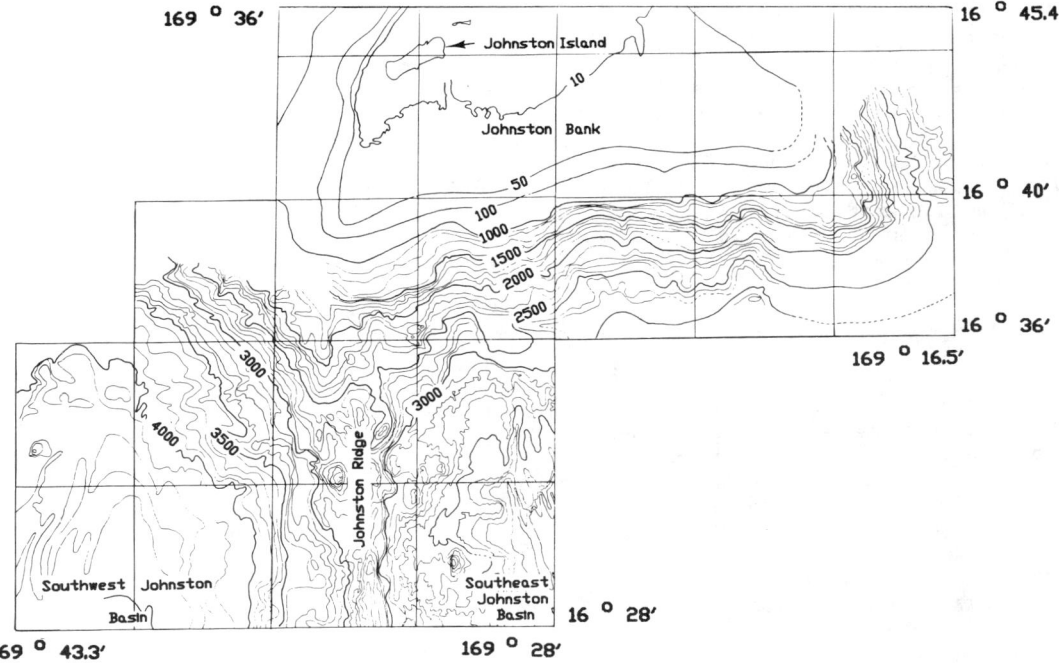

Fig. 8. Bathymetric map of the southern flanks of Johnston seamount. Contour interval is 500 meters unless otherwise noted. The bathymetry on the shallow bank is redrawn from hydrographic maps. The 1200-m and greater depth contours are derived from SeaMARC II side-scan sonar surveys.

kilometers in length, remains near sea level along the western margin of the atoll. While dominant reef growth is normally present on the windward side of islands, the dominant reef growth at Johnston atoll is reported on the leeward side (Emery, 1956). The upper surface of the Johnston Island carbonate platform has two reef platforms at -8 and -18 m which horizontally overlie a sloping bank surface. Ashmore (1973) also reports that sink holes are present in the Johnston carbonate bank which are elongate and dip downward along the dip surface of the carbonate bank.

Another anomalous feature on the Johnston carbonate bank is the ridge upon which Johnston Island and the other islets are situated. The ridge was formed parallel to the present-day leeward barrier reef and is parallel to the mean trade wind direction. This ridge is situated along the tilt axis of the island proposed by Ashmore (1973) shown in Figure 4. Since dune structure within the ridge (Ashmore, 1973) indicates that sand transport was perpendicular to current trade wind direction, it seems highly unlikely that the dominant wind direction has shifted to that extent. It would appear instead that the ridge grew as a result of a tilting process which caused redistribution of the sand.

Two explanations have been suggested (Emery, 1956; Ashmore 1973) to explain the anomalous bathymetry of Johnston. The first is a simple erosional model in which the reefs of the eastern margin have been eroded. The second model proposes that the surface of the atoll has been tilted (Emery, 1956). Ashmore (1973) stated, "...the incompleteness of the reef may be due to partial erosion of an atoll during a glacial epoch of colder water and lowered sea level or to tilting of the atoll so that an original windward reef is now submerged, leaving only the present leeward reef above sea level." Ashmore (1973) suggests the carbonate bank has tilted $0.016°$ to the southeast (Figure 4).

The latter explanation is preferred for several reasons. First, if the reef structure was eroded and killed by a combination of a lower stand of sea level and a lower water temperature during a glacial period, both margins of the atoll would have been affected. Second, the submarine ridge on the eastern margin is comparable in height to the existing barrier reef. If this ridge is the fossil reef that Emery suggested was removed by erosion, it should not be present. All of the major observed bathymetric features reflect tilting of this atoll. The configuration of bathymetric features is inconsistent with existing environmental factors (wind, wave and current directions) which strongly affect reef growth elsewhere.

Discussion of Dive Results

The submersible dives outlined here were intended to evaluate the degree and nature of tilting of the carbonate bank. The absence of stratified sequences at shallow depth (0-400 m), however, precluded this exercise. Instead evidence was found of subaerial karstic dissolution of the carbonate bank. The vertical dissolution shaft and caves with dripstones and shelfstones provide irrefutable evidence of subaerial dissolution. Other important observations include the formation of a "hardened" outer surface on the loose carbonate sediments which is probably a product of initial recrystallization, and initial formation of Mn crusts on these sediments.

Geologic History

The evidence presented by Emery (1956) and Ashmore (1973) strongly supports tilting of the Johnston Island carbonate bank. While no tectonic studies have been directly aimed at the study of Johnston Atoll, the Line Island seamount chain has been studied. The results of three recent cruises are reported by Schlanger et al. (1984) and the results of deep sea drilling in the region is reported by Winterer et al. (1973), Jackson and Schlanger (1979) and Schlanger and Premoli Silva (1981). Assuming that Johnston Island is part of the Line Island chain (and all available evidence suggests it is) then the Johnston seamount was formed by alkalic volcanism during the Late Cretaceous. A radiometric date of 86 Ma is published for the adjacent Karin Ridge. It is likely that the seamount reached sea level before cessation of volcanism since rudistid reef remains have been dredged from the seamounts in this chain. Subsequently, the seamount should have experienced a long period of subsidence that was ended about 45 Ma (Eocene) as a result of renewed volcanism. It is likely that this volcanism again caused the summit of Johnston to reach sea level (Schlanger et al., 1984). Elsewhere in this seamount chain, Eocene reef material has been dredged (Haggerty et al., 1982). Subsidence would resume following this volcanic event. As the volcano subsided, reef growth has kept pace with subsidence and a carbonate island or atoll remained until recent time.

Probably in recent times the seamount has undergone tilting. A Quaternary history is suggested for this tilting, as the youngest levels of reef platforms and reef growth are horizontal and disconformably overlie the sloping edifice. During the Pleistocene, fluctuations of sea level have probably resulted in alternating periods of emergence (suggested by the karstic topography) and submergence. It is very probable that the tilting is associated with the early portion of the Pleistocene history.

The radiometric dating reported by Aydemir suggests reef growth was present on the northern rim of the atoll at 11,000 ybp and modern reef growth continues on the northwest portion of the atoll. If reef growth had been uniformly continuing since the last glaciation it is likely that the evidence of tilting should have been erased (buried) by subsequent reef growth.

Subsidence

The recent studies show that the southern flank of Johnston seamount is exceptionally steep (Figure 8). The margin itself is nearly linear (suggesting faulting) as opposed to the curved seamount margins commonly found in the Pacific (Keating, unpublished results, based upon a search of the hydrographic maps of Pacific Islands). The topography of the debris apron along this south margin of Johnson and the northeastern margin of Johnston Ridge (169°28-33'W; 16°32-38'N) is chaotic. The basin immediately to the south is 700 m shallower than the adjacent basin on the west side of the Johnston Ridge. We suggest structural failure of some of the southern margin of the Johnston Island seamount has occurred and a large load of locally derived detritus fills the basin. We suggest local loading of the sea floor along the southeastern margin of the seamount has resulted in uneven subsidence of the seamount and tilting of the carbonate atoll has resulted.

Implications

There are many reported cases of seamounts having tilted or sloping summits. They have been documented on seamounts in the Hawaiian chain (Kroenke et al., 1987), Line Islands and Gilbert chains (Keating, 1987) and in the Mid-Pacific Mountains (Campbell, per. comm., 1987). Seamounts with tilted or sloping summits have even been observed at mid-ocean rises (Searle, 1983). If some of these occurrences can be associated with mass wasting and non-uniform subsidence of the seamounts on a local basis, then we can resolve a paradox that has long puzzled marine geologists. Purdy (1974) and others have noted that it is common to find guyots and atolls situated adjacent or within a few tens of kilometers from each other. It has been difficult to rationalize how environmental factors which control reef growth could vary over only a few kilometers such that on one seamount the reef community has drowned and a guyot has formed while the adjacent reef complex survives and continues as an atoll (Schlager, 1981). A localized structural discontinuity such as that identified along the south-central margin of Johnston Atoll provides an ideal solution to that problem. In fact, Johnston Atoll appears to be a classic example of an atoll which is in transition from atoll to drowned seamount. Only a fraction of the former reef community continues to grow near sea level, while the majority of the ring reef has been drowned.

Purdy (1974) reports several examples of paired atolls and guyots. Examples include Chagos Bank and shallow atolls of the Solomon Islands, Peros Banthos, Blenheim Reef and Diego Garcia. Surveys of these and other examples in the Pacific using side-scan sonar mapping would prove an ideal method of testing the proposed drowning hypothesis by examining drowned and tilted seamounts that occur paired with atolls to determine if evidence of large scale mass wasting has occurred in such a fashion that debris is localized producing uneven subsidence.

Acknowledgments. Two of the dives in this study were funded by the Department of Army, Pacific Headquarters, Army Corps of Engineers. Support for publication of the results was provided by the Hawaii Institute of Geophysics. I thank Dr. E. DeCarlo of the University of Hawaii for X-ray diffraction and atomic spectrometric analysis of the Mn coating material, and J. Schoonmaker, Eric DeCarlo, C. E. Helsley, and R. Pujalet for reviewing portions of the manuscript. I thank the captain and crew of the University of Hawaii Research Vessel Moana Wave for their assistance in acquiring the side-scan sonar data, the divers of the Hawaii Undersea Research Lab for their assistance on Johnston Island, the members of the SeaMARC II scientific support group, Capt. Mitchell on Johnston Island, and the personnel of the Pacific Headquarters, Army Corps of Engineers for their support of this effort. Hawaii Institute of Geophysics Contribution Number 1859.

References

Ashmore, S. A., The geomorphology at Johnston Atoll. Technical Report TR-237, Naval Oceanographic Office, Washington, D. C., 1-25, 1973.

Aydemir, V., A Geological Study of Reef Margins of Johnston Atoll, Central Pacific Ocean, M.S. Thesis, University of Tulsa, Tulsa, Oklahoma, 1-114, 1985.

Blackinton, J.G., D.M. Hussong, and J.G. Kosalos, First results from a combination side-scan sonar and seafloor mapping system (SeaMARC II), Proceedings, Offshore Tech., Conf., 15th Appendix A (OTC 4478), Houston, TX May 2-5, 307-311, 1983.

Emery, K. O., Marine geology of Johnston Island and its surrounding shallows, Central Pacific Ocean. Geol. Soc. Am. Bull., 67, 1505-1519, 1956.

Froehlich, A. S., Functional aspects of nutrient cycling on coral reefs, ecology of deep and shallow coral reefs (M. I. Reaka, ed.). Symposia Series for Undersea Research, 1, #1, 133-139, 1983.

Haggerty, J. A., S. O. Schlanger, and I. Premoli Silva, Late Cretaceous and Eocene volcanism in the southern Line Islands and implications for hotspot theory, Geology, 10, 433-437, 1982.

Jackson, E.D. and S.O. Schlanger, Regional Synthesis, Line Islands Chain, Tuamotu Island Chain, and Manihiki Plateau, Central Pacific Ocean, in Schlanger, S.O. and Jackson, E.D., et al., Initial Reports of the Deep Sea Drilling Project, 17, U.S. Government Printing Office, Washington, D.C., 915-928, 1976.

Keating, B.H., Morphology of Seamounts in the Gilbert and Phoenix Island Groups: Synthesis of Central Pacific Seamount Morphology Studies, in How Volcanoes Work Symposium, Abtract Volume, 1987.

Kroenke, L., F. Campbell, F., and B.H. Keating, Morphology of seamounts within the Hawaiian Exclusive Economic Zone, How Volcanoes Work, Abstract Volume, 1987.

Purdy, E.G., Reef configurations: cause and effects: in Reefs in Time and Space; Selected Examples from the Recent and Ancient, Soc. Econ. Paleontol. Min., Sp. Public., #18, 9-76, 1974.

Schlager, W., The paradox of drowned reefs and carbonate platforms, Geol. Soc. Am. Bull., 92, 197-211, 1981.

Schlanger, S.O., and I. Premoli Silva, Tectonic, Volcanic, and Paleogeographic implications of redeposited reef faunas of Late Cretaceous and Tertiary age from the Nauru Basin and the Line Islands, Initial Reports of the Deep Sea Drilling Project, 61, p. 817-827 1981.

Schlanger, S. O., M. O. Garcia, J. Haggerty, B. H. Keating, J. J. Naughton, J. A. Philpotts, W. W. Sager, and R. A. Duncan, Geologic evolution of the Line Islands. J. Geophys. Res., 89, 11261-11271, 1984.

Searle, R.C., Submarine central volcanoes on the Nazca plate high resolution sonar observations, Mar. Geol., 53, 77-102, 1983.

Winterer, E.L, Regional Problems, in Winterer, E.L., & J.I. Ewing, et al., Initial Reports of the Deep Sea Drilling Project, 17, Washington D.C., U.S. Government Printing Office, 1973.

ORIGINS OF NONVOLCANIC SEAMOUNTS IN A FOREARC ENVIRONMENT

Patricia Fryer and Gerard J. Fryer

Hawaii Institute of Geophysics, University of Hawaii at Manoa, Honolulu, Hawaii 96822

Abstract. The outer half of the Mariana forearc, the region between the trench axis and the active volcanic arc, contains numerous large seamounts formed entirely by nonvolcanic processes. These seamounts are up to 30 km in diameter and rise as much as 2 km from the seafloor around them. Within about 50 km of the trench axis most of the seamounts are horst blocks of uplifted forearc material. From 50 to about 120 km from the trench axis the seamounts are either sites of updomed forearc material caused by diapiric intrusion, or sites of extrusion of diapirically emplaced serpentinized ultramafics from the lower crust/upper mantle of the underlying forearc. The formation of the diapiric material comprising these seamounts is dependent on the evolution of the thermal structure of the shallow (above 30 km) portion of the overriding plate as a convergence zone develops. Changes in the thermal structure influence the distribution of the stability fields of various regional metamorphic facies within the forearc region. As a convergence zone evolves, the greenschist stability field retreats from the region of the trench axis and is replaced by the stability field of the lawsonite-albite-chlorite facies at shallow levels, and by that of the the blueschist facies at depth. The disappearance of the greenschist facies stability field from the forearc suggests that the serpentinite diapirs are either emplaced early in the history of the forearc or that serpentinite remains metastable within the outer forearc for tens of millions of years. The growth of the chlorite and blueschist stability fields may explain the apparent capacity of forearc regions to accommodate large amounts of fluids driven off the downgoing slab by compaction, desiccation, and dehydration reactions. Although conditions appropriate for the formation of either fault block seamounts or diapirically formed seamounts may exist in any forearc, the occurrence of the seamounts is dependent on the local tectonic environment. In the case of the Mariana forearc the horsts and diapirs are related to fracturing of the forearc and to subduction-related vertical tectonic movement. In those convergent margins with simpler tectonic conditions, horst seamounts may be absent and discrete diapiric seamounts may be replaced by regional upwarp or development of a low forearc ridge.

Introduction

Large seamounts occur on the outer half of the Mariana forearc wedge within 100 km of the trench axis (Figure 1). The seamounts within 50 km of the trench axis are horst blocks of forearc material [Fryer and Smoot, 1985; Fryer and Hussong, 1985], which were probably upthrust in response to the subduction of plate seamounts [Fryer et al. 1985]. In contrast, seamounts occurring between 50 and 120 km from the trench axis were formed by diapiric emplacement of serpentinite and chloritized mafic and ultramafic material [Hussong

Copyright 1987 by the American Geophysical Union.

and Fryer, 1985]. Dredge samples from both horst-block and diapiric seamounts have been described by Bloomer [1983], Hawkins et al. [1984], Fryer et al. [1985], and Haggerty [this volume]; all igneous samples are of arc origin.

The existence of serpentinite and chloritized material at depth in the lower crust or upper mantle of the outer half of a forearc wedge is consistent with dehydration of the upper portion of the downgoing plate and infusion of the overriding forearc wedge with fluids released during that dehydration. The location and extent of such metamorphism is, of course, constrained by the stability fields of regional metamorphic facies within the convergence zone. The distribution of the stability fields changes significantly from the time subduction begins until it reaches a steady state. In order to trace these changes, it is essential to determine the thermal structure of the subduction zone.

Because of the extensive surveying of the Mariana forearc and the clear identification of these non-volcanic seamounts in that forearc, this paper will primarily be concerned with the Mariana system. To map the metamorphic stability fields it is necessary to determine the thermal structure of the forearc and adjacent oceanic plate. No thermal modeling schemes are yet capable of including all tectonic processes which will affect the temperature field, so only qualitative investigation is possible at present. For the purposes of this paper, then, the principles governing the evolution of distribution of stability fields for metamorphic facies in a typical forearc wedge will be demonstrated with a qualitative model. The model used is based on thermal structures of convergent margins presented by Oxburgh and Turcotte [1970], Sydora et al. [1978], Anderson et al. [1978], and Wyllie [1982]. The changes in distribution of the facies stability fields raise some interesting questions regarding the origin of the serpentinite seamounts of the Mariana forearc. A discussion of these questions, of the controls over seamount distribution, and of the possibility of similar seamounts developing in other inter-oceanic forearc regions, is the primary objective of this paper.

Morphology of Mariana Forearc Seamounts

In the Mariana system, the fault-related seamounts close to the trench axis, especially in the central portion of the forearc (17°30'N to 19°N), vary considerably in size and morphology. Most rise above the regional depth by from one to three kilometers. These blocks are interpreted to represent vertical tectonic adjustment of the forearc to the subduction of seamounts on the Pacific plate [Fryer and Smoot, 1985; Fryer and Hussong, 1985]. Horst block seamounts may also result from local plate adjustments unrelated to seamount subduction; in the Mariana system, such horsts are found on the northernmost [Fryer, 1986] and southernmost [Bloomer and Hawkins, 1983; Karig and Ranken, 1983] parts of the outer forearc.

Seamount subduction also has regional effects. A portion of the

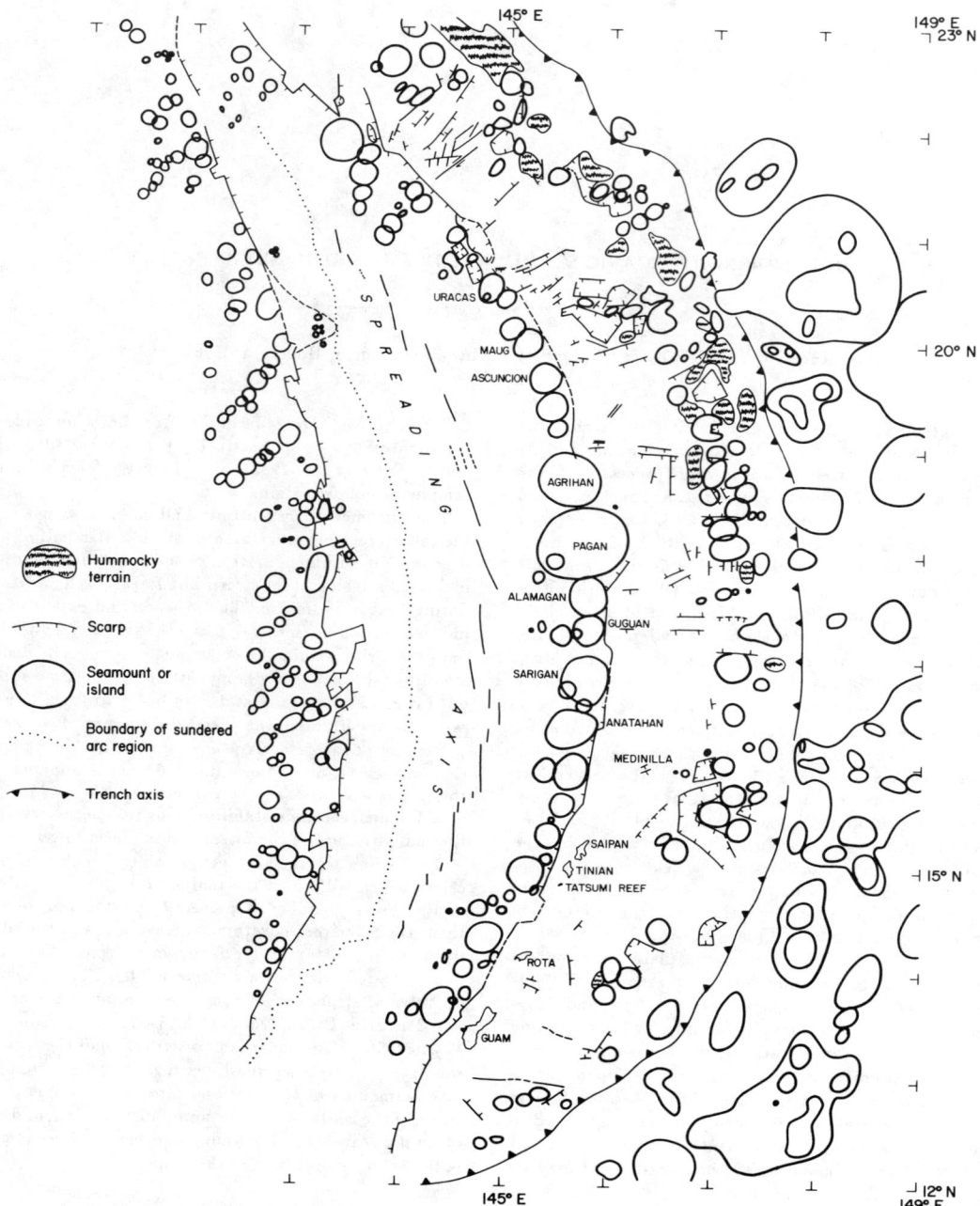

Fig. 1. Geologic sketch of the Mariana island arc region, showing distribution of the major sea-floor features. Positions of seamounts and fractures is based on bathymetric and sidescan data from academic sources, SeaMARC II data and U.S. Navy bathymetry data [Fryer et al., 1985].

inner half of the central forearc, at about 20°N, is uniformly shallower by about 1 km than the rest of the inner forearc (Figure 2). This shallow plateau is situated above what would be the extension of the Dutton Ridge [Smoot, 1983] westward from the axis of the Mariana trench. If large seamounts, similar to the one impinging on the trench at present, were previously subducted beneath this portion of the forearc, they could account for this regional uplift. Further

north along the system, the Ogasawara Plateau, the westernmost seamount of the Michelson Ridge (from 25° to 26°N), is colliding with the Bonin forearc [Vogt et al., 1976; Smoot, 1983]. The effect of this ridge collision may extend far to the south onto the northern half of the Mariana Forearc [Fryer, 1986]. The northern portion of the inner forearc is highly fractured (see Figure 1). The tensional nature of this fracturing is emphasized by the breakup of the volcanic

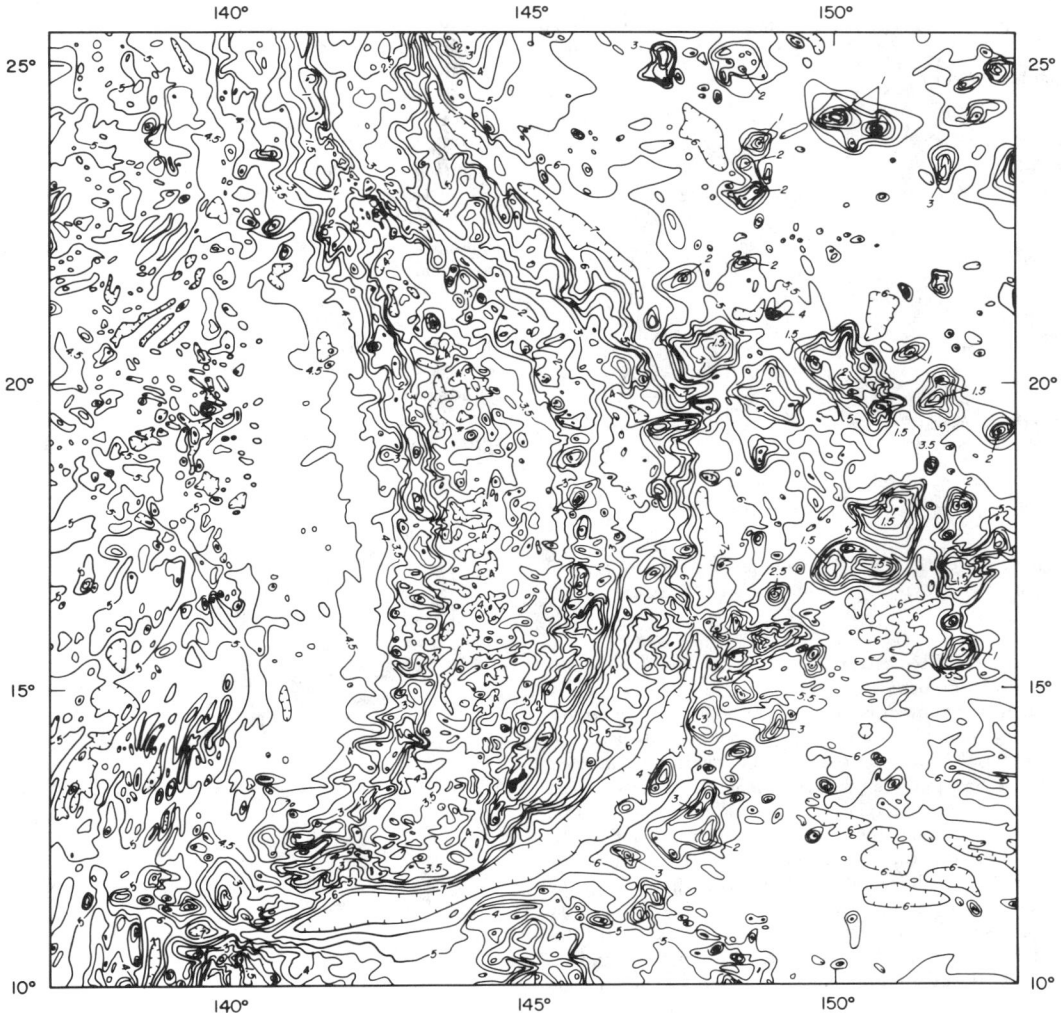

Fig. 2. Bathymetry of the Mariana region (modified after Iwabuchi [1979]).

arc along a large graben at about 22°N (Figure 1) and by the presence of three deep reentrants, north-south trending grabens, in the inner trench wall of the northern Mariana system from 22°N to 24°N (Figure 2). The grabens in the inner trench wall are aligned parallel to some of the fault lineations of the inner forearc and to the large arc-cutting graben. The intervening horsts rise 1 to 2 km above the regional bathymetric grade. Thus, on both local and regional scales, subduction of plate seamounts appears to affect the vertical tectonic processes of the Mariana forearc.

An entirely different type of seamount also occurs on the outer forearc. These are large, conical seamounts up to 30 km in diameter and with up to 2 km of relief which are formed by serpentinite diapirism [Bloomer, 1983; Fryer et al., 1985; Hussong and Fryer, 1985]. They occur from about 50 km to 120 km from the trench axis. Two diapiric seamounts were surveyed by the sidescan and bathymetry system, SeaMARC II, at 19–20°N (Figure 3). These display distinctly different morphologies. One seamount, which is crescent-shaped and referred to informally as "Pacman," is a breached edifice with obviously viscous flow structures on its eastern side (Figure 4). The north and west flanks show muted, apparently older flow structures.

The ovoid flow filling the graben on the eastern flank and the graben walls have been sampled by dredging. The rock samples consist of clasts of serpentinized ultramafic intrusives in a matrix of unconsolidated serpentinite, chlorite, and clay. Preliminary petrologic studies of the clasts show them to contain antigorite, lizardite, and chrysotile secondary after olivine and pyroxene. Also present are chlorite, clay minerals, aragonite, calcite, and quartz as secondary minerals. A few of the rocks show relict fabric that ranges from cumulate to tectonized. Thus, the clasts within the serpentinite matrix probably represent the lower-most crust and upper mantle of the Mariana forearc wedge, but nearly all are highly metamorphosed. Bloomer [1983] and Bloomer and Hawkins [1983] have described similar rocks from other diapiric edifices elsewhere on the Mariana forearc.

The second seamount surveyed by SeaMARC II is a conical feature identified here as "Conical Seamount" (Figure 5). This seamount shows sinuous flows descending its flanks, which are very similar in backscatter characteristics and morphology to the less viscous lava flows occurring on some volcanic edifices surveyed by SeaMARC II. However, when the summit region of the seamount was dredged, no fresh lavas were retrieved, only semi-consolidated vitric siltstones,

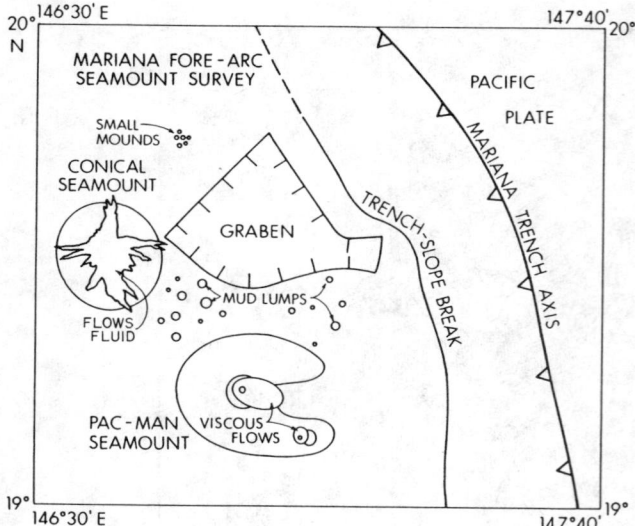

Fig. 3. Geologic sketch of the outer Mariana forearc region surveyed using the sidescan and bathymetry mapping system SeaMARC II.

metabasalts, and serpentinized ultramafics. Hussong and Fryer [1985] suggest that Conical Seamount represents a site of intrusion of serpentinite material into shallow crustal levels. Actually, the uppermost portion of a shallow, possibly rising, diapir may be exposed at this location. The material that comprises the sinuous flows mantling the flanks of Conical Seamount is probably unconsolidated, reworked sediments. The mechanism for initiation of such sediment flows on Conical Seamount is not understood. Uplift of the seamount resulting from rise of the diapir would cause instability of the sediments mantling the slopes of the edifice and facilitate debris flows down the flanks [Hussong and Fryer, 1985]. From diagenetic evidence, Haggerty [this volume] suggests that a similar seamount at 13°N is emitting fluids. The intrusion of a diapir of serpentinite into the crust and its incipient exposure at the summit of Conical Seamount would provide egress for such fluids. If so, then the flows that mantle the lower slopes of the seamount may represent fluidized sediments, essentially mud flows, caused by the venting diapiric fluids. A detailed description of these flows will follow dives by the submersible Alvin in the near future.

Stability Fields of Metamorphic Facies in a Convergent Margin

The effect of inclined isothermal surfaces on the distribution of metamorphic facies in subduction zones has been described by Earle [1980]. This work demonstrated that the distribution of stability fields of metamorphic facies, initially a layered sequence within a lithospheric plate, would "telescope" if an inverted thermal gradient was established on the arc side of a subduction zone. The facies stability fields used by Earle [1980] in this study were those proposed by Ernst [1974], which included the lawsonite-albite-chlorite facies within the blueschist facies. Since the lawsonite-albite-chlorite facies may have an important role in determining the fluid budget of a convergence zone, it is important to map the stability field of this facies explicitly. We have constructed a series of thermal models in a manner similar to Earle [1980], but we have specifically maintained the distinction between blueschist and lawsonite-albite-chlorite fields. In our models the pressure/temperature boundaries of the facies stability fields are those of Turner [1981, Fig. 11.1], shown here in Figure 6. The result-

ing models are shown in Figure 7. No actual numerical modeling was performed to produce these figures. The models were obtained by qualitatively modifying the profiles of Sydora et al. [1978] to match the Mariana geometry, then making further modifications to incorporate the dehydration and corner convection effects of Anderson et al. [1978], Wyllie [1982] and Honda [1985]. The resulting models were adjusted to match the geotherm used by Earle [1980], which is slightly cooler than that used by Sydora et al., and more appropriate for subduction of an old plate. The conclusions of this paper would not change significantly if warmer geotherms were used. Our final models are clearly far from quantitative, but suffice to explain qualitatively the distribution of metamorphic facies in the forearc environment.

Prior to the initiation of subduction, the distribution of the metamorphic stability fields would be that of a layered medium, as is shown in the oceanic plate east of the trench axis (in Figure 7a). As subduction begins, the decrease in temperature and increase in pressure of the upper portion of the descending plate will result in the growth of the lawsonite-albite-chlorite stability field and formation of

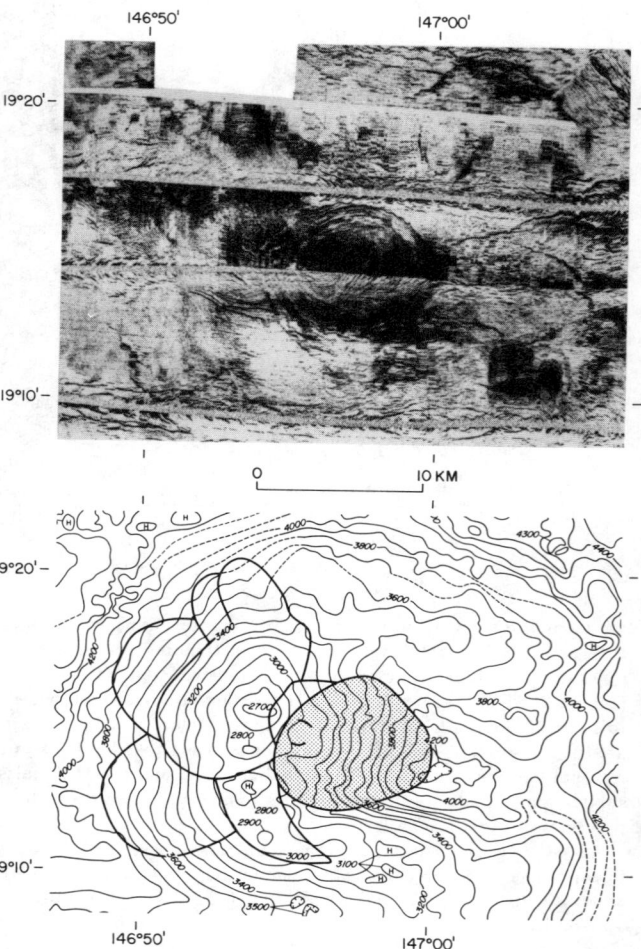

Fig. 4. Bathymetry and sidescan data from the crescent-shaped seamount Pacman, the southern edifice shown in Figure 3. Note the ovoid feature with high backscatter in the center of the image. The position of the feature, a viscous flow of serpentinite, is shown for reference on the bathymetry contour map at the bottom of the figure.

the blueschist field across the décollement surface. This growth takes place at the expense of the greenschist facies field (Figure 7a). As subduction proceeds, a number of changes occur in the greenschist field which pertain to the serpentinite diapirism of the Mariana forearc. As the cooler Pacific plate descends, temperature decreases along the décollement surface and the upper boundary surface of the greenschist stability field is depressed to greater depths. The lower surface of the field is also depressed, but cannot persist beyond about 30 km. Below that depth either blueschist or eclogite facies material is stable, depending on the amount of water present in the environment. Thus, the stability field of the greenschist facies is pinched out within the upper part of the descending slab to be replaced by the blueschist stability field. A lateral separation across the upper part of the subducting plate occurs between limbs of the greenschist stability field. The greenschist stability field on the overriding plate thickens slightly and rolls back, forming a broad hook in the central portion of the forearc (Figure 7b and c). This forearc limb of the greenschist facies field retreats rapidly from the décollement surface because of the roll-back of the isotherms as subduction proceeds.

The rate at which these changes in the distribution of the greenschist field proceed will depend on a number of factors. The angle and rate of convergence, the effects of frictional heating and effects of both exothermic and endothermic chemical reactions in the shallow part of the subduction zone, the degree of fracturing of the overriding plate, and the flux of fluids through the overriding plate all affect the thermal structure of the forearc. The effect of these factors cannot

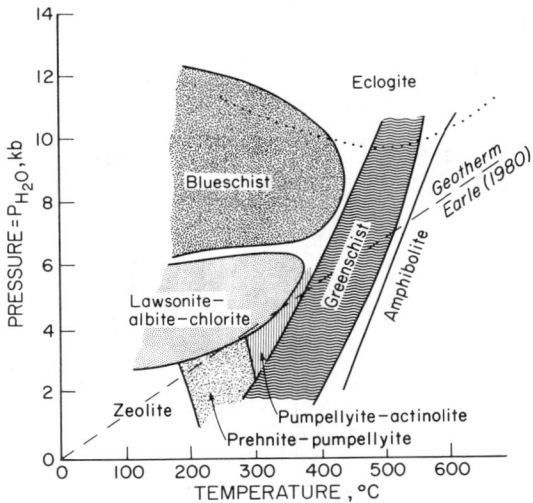

Fig. 6. Pressure/temperature limits for the stability fields of regional metamorphic facies [after Turner, 1981, Figure 11.1, p. 420]. The dotted boundary indicates limits of the eclogite facies under conditions of very low water pressure.

be determined with currently available data, but variations imposed on the stability field of greenschist facies will be minor compared to the effect of the roll-back of the isotherms as the subduction zone develops. The roll-back causes rapid disappearance of the greenschist stability field from the outer half of the overriding plate. This implies either that the serpentinite diapirism which formed the Mariana outer forearc seamounts occurred very early in the history of the development of the subduction system, when greenschist facies material was stable in the outer forearc, or that the material which comprises the serpentinite diapirs of the forearc has existed in a metastable state in the forearc for tens of millions of years.

We do not know the timing of the emplacement of the Mariana forearc diapirs. The interpretation of sidescan data from Pacman Seamount is that the large ovoid flow partially filling the graben in the seamount's east flank represents a recent extrusion of serpentinite [Hussong and Fryer, 1985]. Extrusion of this material may indicate only that recent faulting of the eastern flank of the edifice has exposed a section of an old diapir; any serpentinite exposed by faulting would almost certainly flow downslope. Similar post-emplacement flow of serpentinite in response to gravitational instability is well documented in the Franciscan serpentinite bodies of California [Carlson, 1984]. The apparent source of the flow on Pacman is not the summit of the seamount, but its faulted upper eastern flank [Hussong and Fryer, 1985]. This suggests that faulting is indeed the cause of the flow. If such flows are fault related, then there is no evidence that emplacement of serpentinite diapirs is currently taking place in the Mariana forearc. Documentation of the age of emplacement of these flows must await scheduled *Alvin* work on the seamount.

Subduction-Related Fluids in the Forearc

The change in distribution of the stability fields of the metamorphic facies in a convergence zone may have a profound effect on the budget of fluids within a convergent plate boundary. As can be seen in Figure 7, the growth of the lawsonite-albite-chlorite stability field and the blueschist stability field continues as subduction proceeds, with the arcward boundary of the two stability fields advancing toward the

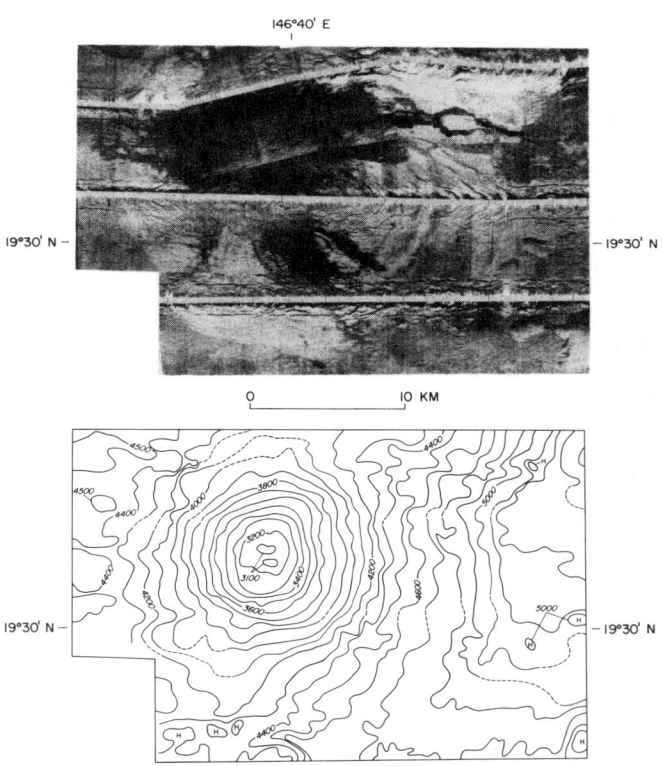

Fig. 5. Bathymetry and sidescan of Conical Seamount, the northern edifice shown in Figure 3. Note the high backscatter from the summit region of the seamount. Also note the sinuous features, fluid flows of remobilized sediment, which appear on the lower flanks of the seamount.

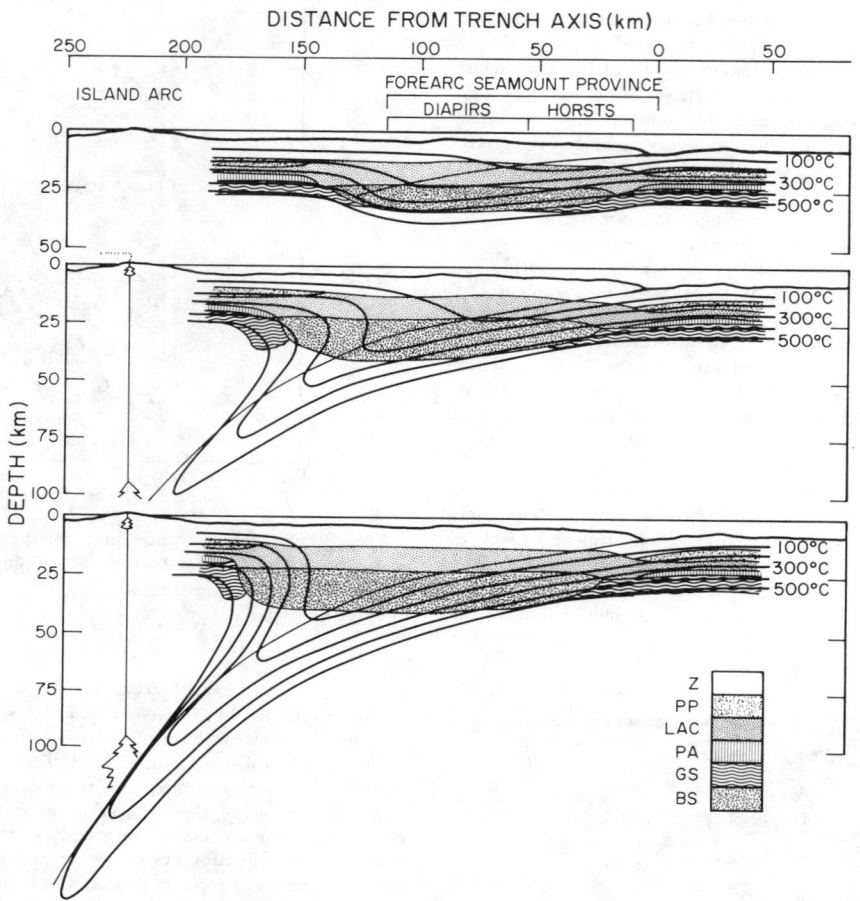

Fig. 7. Stability fields of metamorphic facies in an evolving convergent margin. The bathymetric profile and depth to the top of the downgoing plate are appropriate for the Mariana system at about 18°N. The diagram is drawn at a 1:1 scale. The regions of the outer forearc in which horst block seamounts and diapiric seamounts predominate are shown. Patterns for the various facies are the same as those used in Figure 6. On the legend, Z = zeolite facies, PP = phrenite-pumpellyite, LAC = lawsonite-albite-chlorite, PA = pumpellyite-actinolite, GS = greenschist, BS = blueschist. In the early stages of evolution of a subduction zone (top diagram), the LAC stability field expands and the BS field appears, primarily in the descending slab. As the BS field grows, the GS field pinches out. As subduction continues, the isotherms in the forearc overturn (middle diagram). The LAC and BS fields thicken, and the GS field retreats from the décollement surface back into the forearc. Note the development of a thick overturned trenchward edge within the forearc GS field. The LAC and BS fields continue growing within the forearc until the steady-state is reached (bottom diagram). Arcward retreat of the isotherms is constrained by the requirement that near the arc the environment be hot enough to allow the formation of arc magmas [Honda, 1986].

active arc line. At the same time, the thickness of the fields increases to a maximum of about 30 km. The ultimate barrier to the arcward extent of the thickening of the lawsonite-albite-chlorite stability field and of the occurrence of the blueschist stability field within the forearc wedge will be a thermal barrier imposed upon those stability fields by the thermal structure beneath the active arc. The arcward front of the stability fields will pinch out against the overturned 300°C and 400°C isotherms. The possibility of metamorphism of the forearc wedge to the lawsonite-albite-chlorite grade across nearly the entire width of the forearc to a thickness of 10 km helps to explain the apparent capacity of forearc regions to accommodate large amounts of fluids driven off from a downgoing slab over millions of years of subduction.

An even greater amount of fluid can be accommodated if venting occurs through the overriding plate. If the forearc is fractured, fluids can be vented through the forearc along planes of weakness. Numerous fields of small mounds (hummocky terrain) have been identified in some areas on the Mariana forearc [Hussong and Fryer, 1985]. These may represent venting areas. They are generally located along the periphery of major fault blocks. Some are located within the inner trench wall grabens north of 22°N. These inner trench wall regions are structurally similar to canyon areas of the Japan forearc where venting is occurring [Swinbanks, 1985]. Venting of fluids has also been discovered in other forearcs by Kulm et al. [1986]. If most of the water contained in the sediments of the downgoing plate is released by 15 km, and the geometry of the descending slab is as shown in Figure 7, then the outer 40 to 50 km of the forearc would be the region affected by infusion with these fluids. In a region of tensional faulting the fluids would have easy access to the surface. A much more detailed analysis of the structure of the Mariana forearc is required before these possibilities can be evaluated.

Distribution of Seamounts on the Mariana Forearc

The restriction of the Mariana seamounts to the outer half of the forearc was suggested by Fryer et al. [1985] to reflect the rheological properties of the forearc wedge, the subduction of Pacific plate seamounts, and the local tectonic processes acting on the forearc. Fryer et al. [1985] suggested that the upper 30 km of the forearc wedge behaves as a brittle layer, responding to the subduction of plate seamounts by vertical tectonic activity. This is consistent with the recent work of Honda [1985]. Once an excess mass on the descending plate (a plate seamount) reaches depths greater than 30 km, the more ductile lithosphere of the overriding plate can accommodate the excess mass more readily. Assuming the plate geometry shown in Figure 7, the point at which the top of the descending plate is 30 km below the surface of the forearc is about 100 km west of the trench axis. This is consistent with the restriction of the forearc seamounts to the outer half of the 200 km wide forearc region.

The clustering of seamounts in various parts of the forearc is apparent on Figure 1. This clustering is probably related to variations in tectonic environment along the arc. The largest cluster of seamounts occurs in the mid-latitudes of the forearc from 17°N to 19°N. More seamounts yielding serpentinite have been found in this region than elsewhere on the forearc. The inner forearc in this region is slightly deeper (about 500 m) than elsewhere along the arc system (Figure 2). Multichannel data show deep fracturing of the forearc on an E-W traverses at this latitude [Mrozowski et al., 1981]. SeaMARC II data also show fracturing of the inner forearc along a transit from Pagan to the survey area on the outer forearc [Fryer unpublished data]. The data from DSDP drill sites 458 and 459 [Hussong and Uyeda, 1981] indicate that fracturing in this region occurs on all scales from regional fractures to micro-fractures within the sedimentary sections of the cores. Also, the largest of the arc volcanoes, Pagan and Agrihan, occur within this latitudinal range (see Figure 1). The anomalously large size of Pagan and Agrihan implies a more rapid eruption rate for these volcanoes. This increased rate would be consistent with greater ease of egress of magmas from the arc source to the surface through fractures. These factors indicate that the Mariana arc system is profoundly fractured throughout its central latitudes. The increased depth of the inner forearc may indicate a thinning of the lithosphere resulting from tensional faulting within this region. The cause of this fracturing is not known, but is likely to be related to the increase in curvature of the Mariana arc system with time. If fracturing of the forearc is more common in these latitudes, it is not surprising that a greater number of seamounts formed by serpentinite diapirism occurs here.

Not only do the numbers of seamounts which occur on the forearc vary regionally, but also the nature of the seamounts is different in various parts of the forearc. North of 21°N the forearc seamounts have not been sampled or surveyed with sidescan sonar, however a number of them occur on fault trends evident on the inner forearc (see Figure 1). These may be horst blocks resulting from a regional (rather than local) tension [Fryer, 1986]. Some seamounts in the northernmost part of the forearc are conical in outline and may have formed by serpentinite diapirism. South of 13°N the local highs on the forearc are probably fault blocks resulting from strike-slip motion [Karig and Ranken, 1983; Bloomer and Hawkins, 1983]. No diapiric seamounts have been identified south of 13°N.

Discussion

Few seamounts of these types have been reported from other forearc regions. The primary control over the occurrence of such seamounts appears to be the degree of fracturing of a given forearc. The P/T conditions necessary for the hydration and metamorphism of the outer half of a forearc exist in all convergent margins. However, only in such highly fractured margins as the Mariana may we expect to see a well-developed seamount province. In forearc regions with little or no fracturing, there is little chance for the emplacement of diapiric bodies of serpentinized and chloritized rock, but there may still be a surface expression of this type of metamorphism. Most convergent margins have developed a forearc high, a regional upwarp of the outer half of the forearc. In accretionary plate margins, this forearc high has been suggested to have formed by the underplating of the forearc toe with sediments from the descending plate [Karig 1971]. In non-accretionary margins, like the Mariana system, this forearc high may be caused in part by expansion at depth resulting from hydration and metamorphism of the underlying forearc wedge and descending plate. In order to test this hypothesis, one must calculate the volume increase predicted by the degree of metamorphism of the outer forearc and compare it with the observed increase in volume of the outer forearc. Such calculations would necessitate a detailed structural model for a given forearc, knowledge of the history of subduction at that margin and considerable information about the degree of metamorphism of the forearc. Such calculations are beyond the scope of this paper.

It is possible however, to make this type of calculation on a smaller scale for a more restricted portion of a forearc wedge, one in which the structure and rock types have been studied. The Bonin forearc has been studied in detail by Taylor and Smoot [1984] and Honza and Tamaki [1985]. The Bonin system is the northward continuation of the Mariana arc. It has a similar history of subduction, but quite a different forearc environment. The Bonin system differs in two ways from the Mariana system [Fryer et al., 1985]. The oceanic plate descending beneath the forearc has almost no seamounts of appreciable size on its surface. Thus, breakup of the forearc from disruption caused by subducting plate seamounts is not a factor controlling the structure of the Bonin forearc. Also the Bonin system is remarkably straight, and lacks the faulted regions which, in the Mariana system, appear to be related to increasing curvature with time.

Although no wide zone of seamounts occurs on the Bonin forearc, there is a ridge, roughly 50 km wide, along the length of the outer forearc which is particularly evident from 31°N to 33°N [Honza and Tamaki, 1985]. Rocks dredged from a local high along this ridge are mostly cumulate ultramafics which have been serpentinized and chloritized [Fryer, unpublished data]. The outer 50 km of the Bonin forearc is the region over which water driven off from the sedimentary section of the descending slab would most affect the overriding plate. Assuming that the outer toe of the forearc is fractured to some extent, as is suggested by the reflection profiles given by Honza and Tamaki [1985], then the fluids driven off the descending slab by compaction and desiccation could have percolated upward into the fractured region to cause the metamorphism seen in the dredge samples. If the toe of the forearc is highly metamorphosed, then considerable local expansion must have occurred. The outer forearc ridge is probably a localized arch resulting from such hydration-driven expansion of forearc material.

In order to test this hypothesis, consider the profiles 39 through 42 of Honza and Tamaki [1985] shown schematically in Figure 8. The outer forearc ridge is well-developed in the region of these profiles. If the slope of the upper part of the inner trench wall immediately west of the outer forearc ridge were extended to the trench axis, as shown in Figure 8, the volume of the ridge which extends above this projected inner trench wall surface represents an increase in volume of the outer toe of the forearc by about 25% to 30%. Chloritization and serpentinization of ultramafic rocks to produce the rock types dredged from the ridge is consistent with this degree of expansion.

A number of local highs occur along the summit of the ridge. These

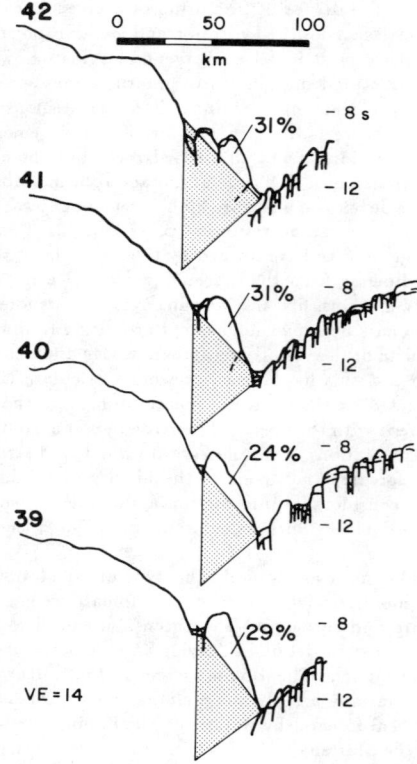

Fig. 8. Line drawings of reflection profiles of the Bonin forearc from about 31°30'N to 32°30'N (after Honza and Tamaki, [1985]). The shaded triangle in each of the profiles was constructed by projecting the slope of the inner trench wall from the trench-slope break to the trench axis (upper boundary), by projecting the surface of the descending slab below the forearc (lower boundary) and by dropping a vertical line from the point at which the inner trench wall changes slope, on the arcward side of the outer forearc ridge, to the top of the descending plate. The smaller, unshaded area above the triangle represents the percent of expansion of the shaded area that could be caused by metamorphism to serpentine and chlorite.

highs are circular in outline and are tens of kilometers in diameter and up to 600 m in relief above the local depth of the ridge [Taylor and Smoot, 1984]. Taylor and Smoot [1984] had suggested that these highs might be analogous to the Mariana forearc seamounts formed by serpentinite diapirism. It now appears more likely that these highs are caused by in situ expansion of the forearc resulting from a locally greater degree of hydration and metamorphism. More detailed investigation of these enigmatic local highs is necessary.

Conclusions

A variety of seamounts, both horst and diapir related, have formed on the outer half of the Mariana forearc. These seamounts represent a variety of tectonic processes active within the forearc wedge. Where vertical tectonic processes predominate, such as in the outer-most 50 km of the forearcs, either horst-block seamounts or local highs within complex deformation fronts may occur. Where regional tectonic processes are indicated by local fracture patterns on the outer forearc from about 50 to 100 km from the trench axis, seamounts related to diapiric rise of serpentinite from the lower crust or upper mantle of the forearc occur.

Material which comprises the Mariana diapiric seamounts is probably mobilized by hydration driven by the dewatering of the downgoing Pacific plate. Conditions necessary for such hydration may not be constant with time and will depend on variations in subduction rate and geometry, and on composition of the descending plate. The hydration-driven metamorphism of the forearc will depend on the changing distribution of stability fields of metamorphic facies as the subduction zone evolves.

Clearly, expansion of the lawsonite-albite-chlorite and blueschist stability fields and change in the distribution of the greenschist field must occur in every active convergence zone. However, not every convergence zone develops forearc seamounts like those of the Mariana system. Without significant forearc fracturing diapiric seamounts and horst blocks will not be formed. Instead, hydration and metamorphism of the outer forearc wedge may result in either regional uplift or the formation of a low forearc ridge.

Acknowledgments. We have benefited from discussions with Kost Pankiwskyj, Beth Ambos, Kris Saboda, Bob Hildebrand, and Brian Taylor. This research was supported by National Science Foundation grants OCE84-11717 and OCE86-14191. Hawaii Institute of Geophysics contribution no. 1868.

References

Anderson, R. N., S. E. DeLong, and W. M. Schwarz, Thermal model for subduction with dehydration in the downgoing slab, *J. Geol., 86*, 731-739, 1978.

Bloomer, S. H., Distribution and origin of igneous rocks from the landward slopes of the Mariana trench: Implications for its structure and evolution, *J. Geophys. Res., 88*, 7411-7418, 1983.

Bloomer, S. H., and J. W. Hawkins, Gabbroic and ultramafic rocks from the Mariana trench: An island arc ophiolite, in *The Tectonic and Geologic Evolution of Southeast Asian Seas and Islands, Part 2, Geophys. Monogr. Ser.*, vol. 27, edited by D. E. Hayes, pp. 294-317, AGU, Washington D.C., 1983.

Carlson, C., Stratigraphic and structural significance of foliate serpentine breccias, Wilbur Springs, in *Society of Economic Paleontologists and Mineralogists, Field Trip Guidebook no. 3*, pp. 108-112, 1984.

Earle, M. M., A note on the relationship between inclined isothermal modeling and reevaluation of isotopic Ar-ages for blueschists in the Franciscan complex of California, *Tectonics, 4*, 421-433, 1980.

Ernst, W. G., Metamorphism and ancient continental margins, in *The Geology of Continental Margins*, edited by C. A. Burk, and C. L. Drake, pp. 907-919, Springer, New York, 1974.

Fryer, P., Tectonics of the Bonin/Mariana arc intersection and effects on alkaline arc magmatism on the Volcano Islands (abstract), *Eos Trans. AGU, 67*, 1277, 1986.

Fryer, P., and D. M. Hussong, SeaMARC II studies of subducting seamounts, in *Formation of Active Ocean Margins*, edited by N. Nasu, pp. 291-306, Terra Scientific Publishing Company, Tokyo, 1985.

Fryer, P., and N. C. Smoot, Morphology of ocean plate seamounts in the Mariana and Izu/Bonin subduction zone, *Mar. Geol., 64*, 77-94, 1985.

Fryer, P., E. L. Ambos, and D. M. Hussong, Origin and emplacement of Mariana forearc seamounts, *Geology, 13*, 774-777, 1985.

Haggerty, J. A., Petrology and geochemistry of Neogene sedimentary rocks from Mariana forearc seamounts: Implications for the origin of the seamounts, *this volume*.

Hawkins, J., A. Volpe, and E. Wright, Ophiolite series rocks of the Mariana forearc seamounts (abstract), *Eos Trans. AGU, 65*, 1136, 1984.

Honda, S., Thermal structure beneath Tohoku, northeast Japan: A case study for understanding the detailed thermal structure of the subduction zone, *Tectonophysics, 112,* 69–102, 1985.

Honza, E., and K. Tamaki, The Bonin arc, in *The Ocean Basins and Margins,* vol. 7A, *The Pacific Ocean,* edited by A. E. M. Nairn, F. G. Stehli, and S. Uyeda, pp. 459–502, Plenum, New York, 1985.

Hussong, D. M., and P. Fryer, Fore-arc Tectonics in the Northern Mariana Arc, in *Formation of Active Ocean Margins,* edited by N. Nasu, pp. 273–290, Terra Scientific Publishing Company, Tokyo, 1985.

Hussong, D. M., and S. Uyeda, Tectonic processes and history of the Mariana arc: A synthesis of the results of the Deep Sea Drilling Project Leg 60, *Initial Rep. Deep Sea Drill. Proj., 60,* 909–929, 1981.

Iwabuchi, Y., General bathymetric chart of the oceans (GEBCO), chart 5.06, Can. Hydrogr. Serv., Ottawa, 1979.

Karig, D. E., Structural history of the Mariana island arc system, *Geol. Soc. Am. Bull., 82,* 323–344, 1971.

Karig, D. E., and B. Ranken, Marine geology of the forearc region, southern Mariana island arc, in *The Tectonic and Geologic Evolution of Southeast Asian Seas and Islands, Part 2, Geophys. Monogr. Ser.,* vol. 27, edited by D. E. Hayes, pp. 266–280, AGU, Washington, D.C., 1983.

Kulm, L. D., E. Suess, J. C. Moore, B. Carson, B. T. Lewis, S. D. Ritger, D. C. Kadko, T. M. Thornberg, R. W. Embley, W. D. Rugh, G. J. Massoth, M. G. Langseth, G. R. Cochrane, and R. L. Scamman, Oregon subduction zone: Venting, fauna, and carbonates, *Science, 231,* 561–566, 1986.

Moore, D. E., Metamorphic history of a high-grade blueschist exotic block from the Franciscan Complex, California, *J. Petrol., 25,* 126–150, 1984.

Mrozowski, C. L., D. E. Hayes, and B. Taylor, Multichannel seismic reflection surveys of Leg 60 sites, *Initial Rep. Deep Sea Drill. Proj., 60,* 57–70, 1981.

Oxburgh, E. E., and D. L. Turcotte, Thermal structure of island arcs, *Geol. Soc. Am. Bull., 81,* 1665–1688, 1970.

Smoot, N. C., Guyots of the Dutton Ridge at the Bonin/Mariana Trench juncture as shown by multibeam surveys, *J. Geol., 91,* 211–220, 1983.

Swinbanks, D., Japan finds clams and trouble, *Science, 315,* 624, 1985.

Sydora, L. J., F. W. Jones, and R. St.J. Lambert, The thermal regime of the descending lithosphere: The effect of varying angle and rate of subduction, *Can. J. Earth Sci., 15,* 626–641, 1978.

Taylor, B., and N. C. Smoot, Morphology of Bonin forearc submarine canyons, *Geology, 12,* 724–727, 1984.

Turner, F. J., *Metamorphic Petrology (2nd. ed.),* 524 pp., McGraw-Hill Book Co., New York, 1981.

Wyllie, P. J., Subduction products according to experimental prediction, *Geol. Soc. Am. Bull., 93,* 468–476, 1982.

Vogt, P. R., A. Lowrie, D. R., Bracey, and R. N. Hey, Subduction of aseismic oceanic ridges: Effects on shape, seismicity and other characteristics of consuming plate boundaries, *Geol. Soc. Am. Spec. Pap. 172,* 1–17, 1976.

Geophysical Studies

A 3-D GRAVITY-TECTONIC STUDY OF ITA MAI TAI GUYOT:
AN UNCOMPENSATED SEAMOUNT IN THE EAST MARIANA BASIN

Bruce Wedgeworth[1] and James Kellogg[2]

Hawaii Institute of Geophysics, Honolulu, Hawaii 96822

Abstract. Ita Mai Tai is a large, locally uncompensated seamount on the eastern edge of the East Mariana Basin. A large positive gravity anomaly of 254 mgal characterizes the summit and a low of -69 mgal, the surrounding moat. Using polygonal prisms to approximate the bathymetry, the observed gravity was inverted to calculate an average density of 2.59 g/cm^3 for the seamount. Observed-calculated gravity residuals are reduced by including the flanking sedimentary basins and a dense volcanic conduit. The drill sites from DSDP Legs 20 and 89 describe a volcanic edifice formed in the Aptian/Albian on Jurassic/Cretaceous crust. The volcanism is recorded in volcanoclastic and epiclastic deposits in the basins nearby. The guyot was covered initially by a succession of reefal and lagoonal sediments followed by a thick mantling of pelagic sediments after it subsided. Gravity models that adequately match the calculated and observed data sets for Ita Mai Tai show little crustal thickening, suggesting that Ita Mai Tai is almost completely locally uncompensated.

Introduction

A major goal in the application of the theory of plate tectonics in the Pacific has been determining the age and location of the oldest part of the Pacific plate. An attempt to reach this objective was made in 1971 when DSDP Leg 20 drilled Site 199 (Fig. 2) in the East Mariana Basin (Fig. 1). It was anticipated that Jurassic lithosphere would be encountered [Larson, 1976; Hilde et al., 1977; Shipley et al., 1983; and others]. Unfortunately, deep water drilling difficulties prevented this primary objective from being reached, and an alternate site was chosen farther east in a cluster of shallow seamounts between the Marshall and Magellan seamount chains (Fig. 1). Three holes were drilled at Sites 200, 201 and 202 on one of these seamounts located at 12° 45'N, 156° 45'E (Fig. 2). This seamount was given the informal name Ita Mai Tai Guyot by Bruce Heezen which means "no damn good" in Tahitian [M. Tharp, pers. comm., 1984], possibly because basement was not reached. A second unsuccessful attempt to reach Jurassic basement was made in 1982 when DSDP Leg 89 drilled Site 585 just north of Ita Mai Tai. Other cruises across Ita Mai Tai include those of Conrad 1205, a Soviet cruise DDM05 in 1971, and Vema 3401 in 1977.

In 1981 the Hawaii Institute of Geophysics research vessel Kana Keoki surveyed Ita Mai Tai (Fig. 2) and other charted and uncharted seamounts in the central and western Pacific collecting bathymetric, gravimetric, magnetic, petrologic and seismic reflection profiling data.

The purpose of this study is to compile and analyze the geophysical data to determine the crustal structure of Ita Mai Tai, its degree of isostatic compensation, and its tectonic history. In order to construct accurate density models it was necessary to have as much information as possible on the bathymetry, sediment distribution, and geology of Ita Mai Tai. Therefore, these topics will be discussed before the section on gravity studies.

Regional Framework

There is a striking dichotomy in morphology and structure between the Eastern Pacific and the Western Pacific (Fig. 1). The picture in the Eastern Pacific seems relatively simple. The seafloor there is characterized by linear island chains with straightforward age progressions, large fracture zones, and simple magnetic lineations. By contrast, the seafloor in the Western Pacific is a complicated collection of large clusters of seamounts and oceanic plateaus.

There have been several hypotheses advanced to explain the distribution of these western Pacific seamounts. The Wilson-Morgan "hotspot" hypothesis for the origin of seamounts predicts linear chains with a progressive age of formation. A second hypothesis is that there was a period of mid-plate volcanism in the Cretaceous during which a widespread area of the western Pacific lithosphere was thinned by a large thermal event [Menard 1964; Schlanger and Premoli-Silva, 1981; Menard, 1984]. Seamounts formed by this mechanism would be expected to show a random distribution, simultaneous regional uplift, and variable paleolatitudes of formation. A third hypothesis is that these seamounts were formed near ridge crests and transform faults. The first and third hypotheses are not necessarily mutually exclusive. (Iceland, the Galapagos and the Mid-Pacific Mountains are possible examples of both mechanisms at work). Seamounts formed near ridge crests should have ages similar to the age of the crust on which they were erupted, a topography reflecting a rectilinear character, and be locally compensated.

Ita Mai Tai, a typical western Pacific seamount, is located on the eastern side of the Mariana Basin. The East Mariana Basin is bordered by the Magellan Seamounts to the north, the Marshall Islands to the east, the Caroline Islands to the south, and the Mariana Trench to the west. The basin is also quite far from well defined magnetic anomaly lineations. The Japanese magnetic lineations are 1500 km to the northwest, the Hawaiian magnetic lineations about 1000 km to the northeast, the Nauru magnetic lineations almost 1000 km to the southeast, and the Phoenix magnetic lineations more than 1500 km

---

[1] Now at Harding Lawson Associates, Honolulu, Hawaii
[2] Now at Department of Geological Sciences, University of South Carolina, Columbia, South Carolina

Copyright 1987 by the American Geophysical Union.

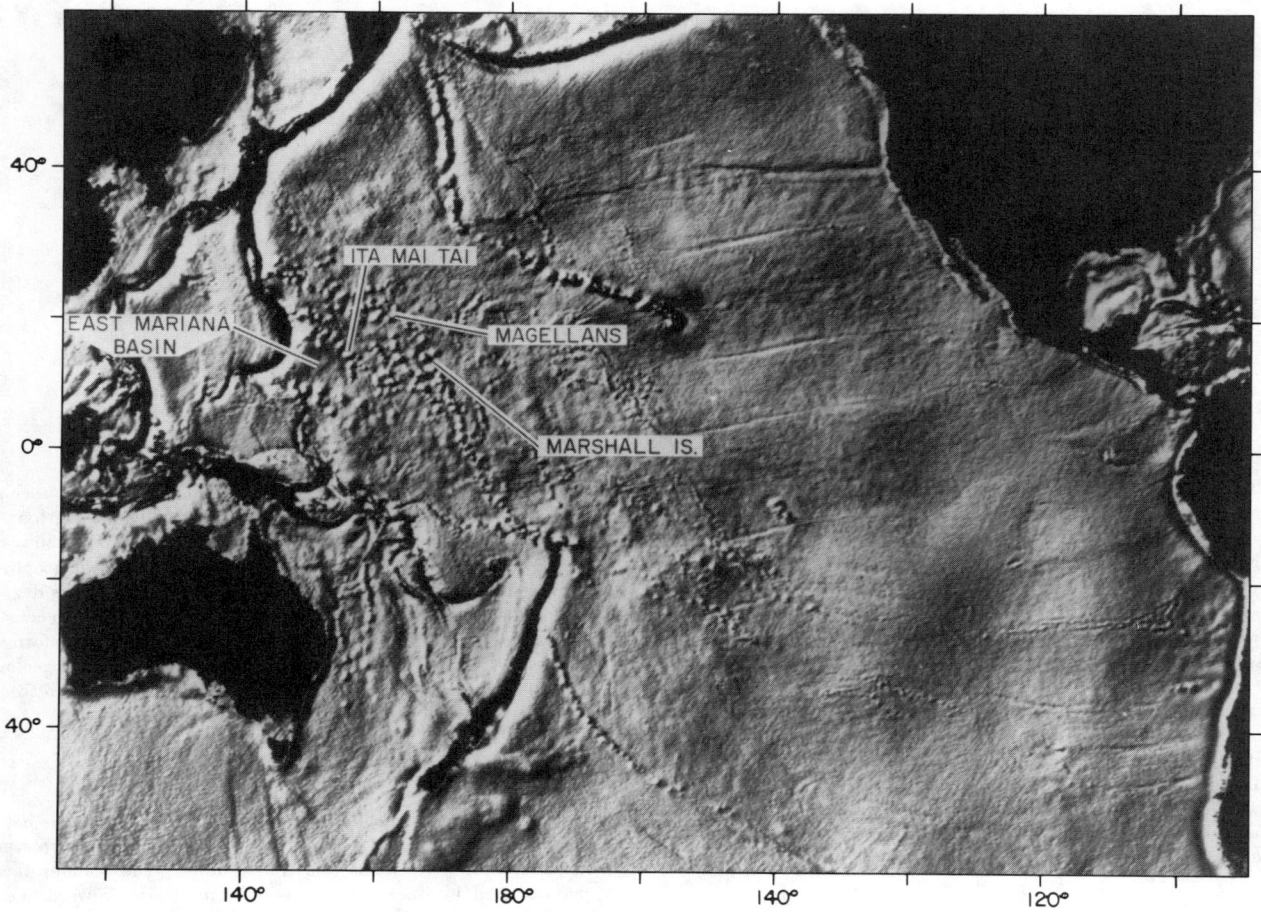

Fig. 1. Gravity image of the Pacific Ocean Basin based upon all Seasat and Geos-3 altimeter data (J. G. Marsh, unpublished data, Code 621, NASA/Goddard Space Flight Center, Greenbelt, Maryland 20771). Data were gridded on a 1/8° grid. A geoid of degree and order 12 has been removed in order to enhance the shorter wave-length features. Ita Mai Tai and nearby seamounts stand out as positive anomalies.

to the east-southeast. The region between these lineations including the East Mariana Basin is characterized by low amplitude or ambiguous magnetic lineations usually referred to as the Jurassic Magnetic Quiet Zone which make determining the age of seafloor near Ita Mai Tai a problem.

Shipley et al. (1983) assumed a half spreading rate of 4.7 cm/yr and extrapolated from M-25 in the Phoenix lineations to estimate the age of the crust in the East Mariana Basin as Jurassic. Paleomagnetic data from DSDP sites 585, 289, and 462 indicate that the western Central Pacific had 4.5 cm/yr of northward drift between the Aptian and Campanian [Scientific Party, Leg 89, 1983]. Other authors have also concluded that the oldest oceanic crust in this part of the western Pacific is Jurassic [Larson and Chase, 1972; Hilde et al., 1976]. However, Kroenke, in Hilde et al. (1977), has suggested that there was an episode of generally north-south intra-plate spreading starting 110 MyBP and that the crust presently beneath the East Mariana Basin is upper Cretaceous. The lowest section of Site 585 encountered late Aptian hyaloclastite- rich turbidite and debris flows from the surrounding subaerial volcanoes. This site stopped just short of sampling the oceanic basement, and thus there is still no direct evidence for the age of the basin.

Seamount Morphology

The bathymetric map of Ita Mai Tai Guyot is shown in Figure 2. Ita Mai Tai rises 4600 m from abyssal depths of around 6000 m to a minimum depth of 1402 m. The height is considerably greater than the average relief of 1 km found for a survey of 6530 Pacific seamounts [Udintsev and others, 1976]. The shape of the seamount is subconical. An 'L' shaped flank ridge extends to the west and turns to the south toward other seamounts in the chain. The basal diameter measures approximately 90 km and covers some 6400 km^2, which is much greater than the mean of north Pacific volcanoes [Batiza, 1982].

The summit area is quite uniform and flat. A break in slope occurs at about 2200 m below which the slope of the upper flanks is as steep as 35°. Gradually the slope decreases to average 9-10° on the lower flanks, a value comparable with that of subaerial volcanoes [Lonsdale and Spiess, 1979]. The northern and southeastern flanks are bordered by a shallow depression or moat as outlined by the 6100 m contour.

Sedimentary Basin Stratigraphy

The shapes and depths of the sediment filled basins to the north and southeast (Profiles A, B and C) (Fig. 2) were determined from

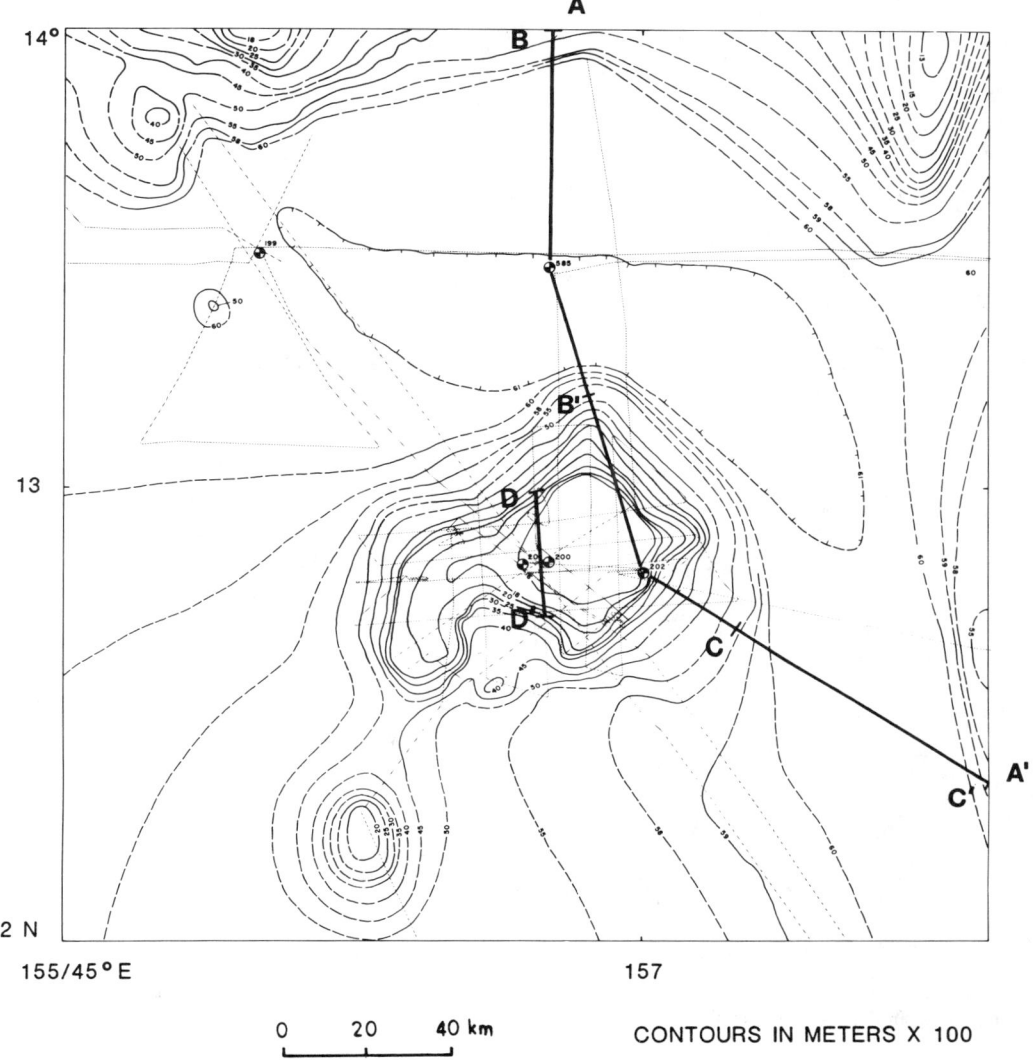

Fig. 2. Bathymetry of Ita Mai Tai Guyot. Track lines are indicated by dotted lines. Seismic cross-sections and five DSDP sites are also indicated.

HIG and DSDP Leg 89 airgun seismic reflection records. The shapes and depths of the pelagic cap units (Profile D) and the northern basin (Profile B) were determined from HIG airgun seismic reflection records. The locations of those profiles selected for this study are shown in Figure 2.

Profile A-A' (Fig. 3) is a complete transect of Ita Mai Tai from north to southeast. It includes a seamount 140 km to the north, a deep sediment filled basin to the north, and another basin to the southeast. The most interesting aspect of this profile is the apparent difference in the depths to acoustic basement in the two basins. The northern basin appears to be much deeper than the southeastern basin.

Profile B-B' (Fig. 4) completely crosses the northern basin shown on Figure 3. The basin is approximately 73 km wide at this point and the sea floor is 6100 m deep. DSDP Site 585 is located about mid-point. The two-way traveltime through the sediments to the floor of the basin is approximately one full second. Five lithologic units in the drilling record are depicted and labeled in the figure. The velocity of each of the lithologic units, their travel-times and maximum thicknesses, are based on closely spaced velocity and density measurements from the drilling record of Site 585 [Scientific Party, Leg 89, 1983] and are shown in Table 1.

The unit thicknesses were independently estimated from HIG airgun seismic reflection records over the northern basin. Acoustic basement begins at about 9 seconds of two-way traveltime or 6900 m. The sediments in the basin are about 900 m thick. The thickest layer, a section containing volcaniclastic turbidites and debris flows (Unit VI), is also the lowest (Fig. 4). There is an especially strong reflector near 8.4 seconds that extends all the way across the section. This has been interpreted as the top of Unit II, where a large density contrast of 0.4 gm/cm^3 is encountered between recent clays and oozes and the Eocene chalks, limestones, cherts and ash beds.

Bright reflectors close to Ita Mai Tai between 8.3 and 8.4 seconds

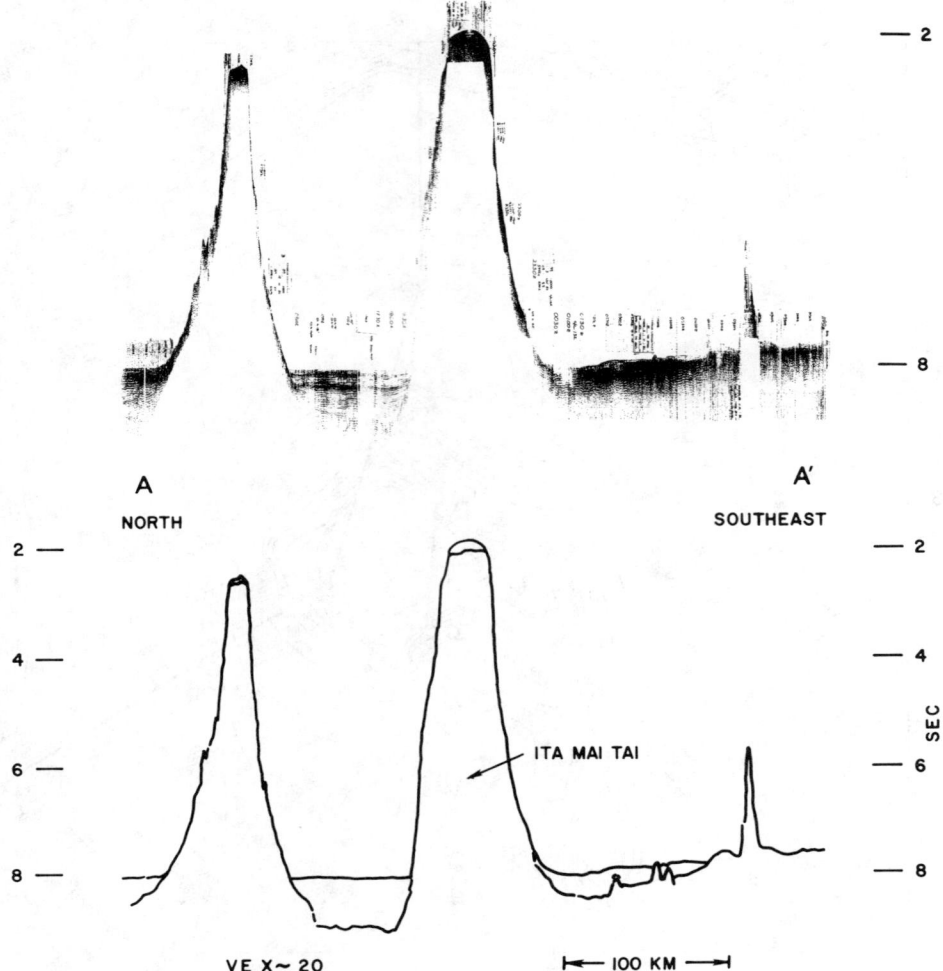

Fig. 3. (a) Photo of airgun seismic reflection record across Ita Mai Tai during DSDP Leg 89 crossing. (b) Line drawing showing the basin depths on either side of Ita Mai Tai. See Figure 2 for location of transect.

TABLE 1. DSDP Leg 89, Site 585 Drilling Record

	Velocity (km/s)	Traveltime (s)	Maximum Thickness (m)
Unit I Clay, nannofossil ooze Pleistocene	1.50	0.17	256
Unit II Nannofossil chalk, zeolitic claystone M. Eocene-Maas.	1.89	0.08	143
Units III + IV Zeolitic claystone, chert Maas.-Campanian	2.01	0.04	86
Unit V Zeolitic claystone, radiolarian siltstone Campanian-M. Albian	2.01	0.05	105
Unit VI Volcaniclastic debris M. Albian-L. Aptian	2.18-3.2	0.09-0.14	303

and which tend to obscure details below them (Fig. 4) are interpreted to be lava flows and sills. Similar flows have been described for the Ontong Java Plateau by Stoeser (1975) and Kroenke (1972). If the sills in Unit II originated from Ita Mai Tai then the edifice must have been active during the deposition of Unit II. Unit VI is interpreted by the authors of this paper to be the main edifice building deposit because it is composed of volcanogenic sediments. The layer that lies on top of Unit II at Site 585 has also been interpreted as volcanogenic in origin, probably from other seamounts such as the one to the north.

Profile C-C' (Fig. 5) crosses the southeastern basin. The width of the basin along track is approximately 100 km. This basin appears to be much shallower than the other, extending to only 8.4 seconds, or about 6300 m. Total sediment thickness contained in the south-

TABLE 2. Pelagic Cap Velocities, Traveltimes, Thicknesses

	Velocity (km/s)	Traveltime (s)	Maximum Thickness (m)
Pelagic cap	1.63	0.07	114
Oolitic limestone	3.83	0.01	35
Lagoonal mud	2.00	0.04	80

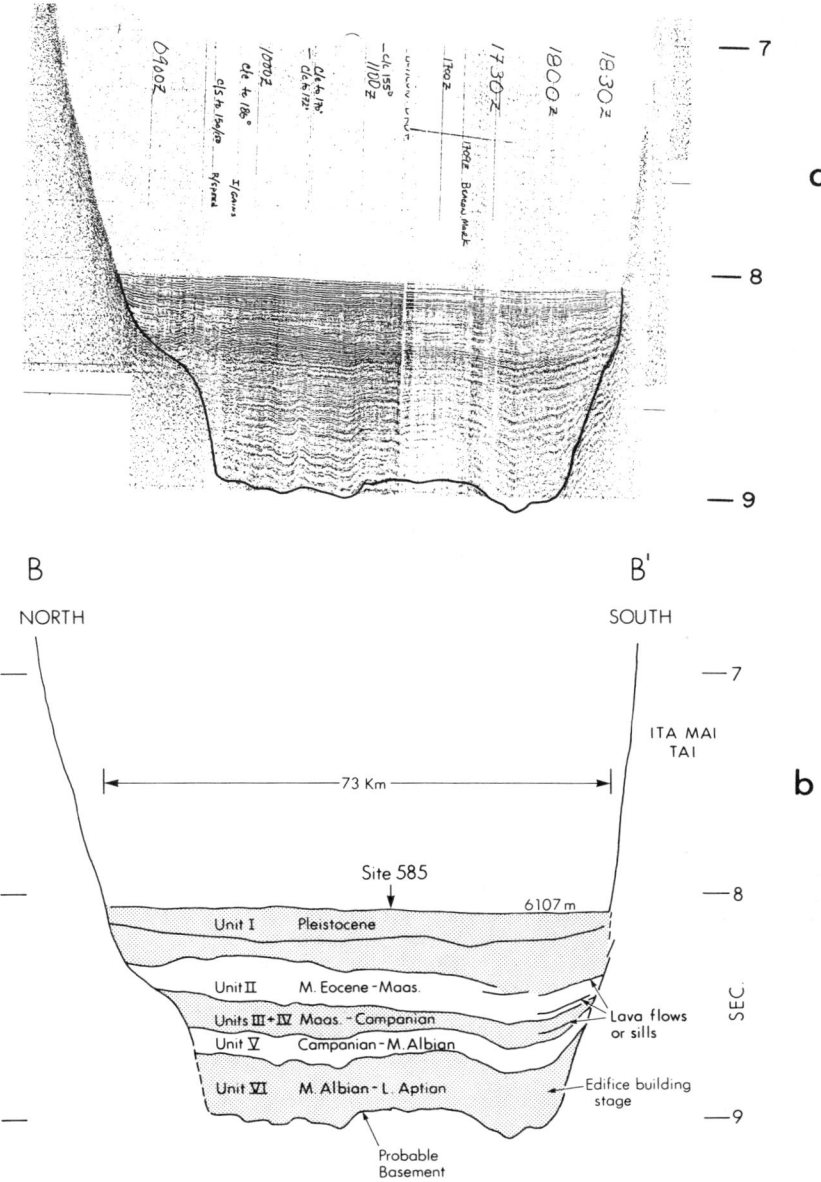

Fig. 4. Photo of airgun seismic reflection record of basin to the north of Ita Mai Tai (Glomar Challenger, Leg 89 profile). (b) Line drawing showing units from Site 585 drilling record, and locations of proposed lava flows and sills.

eastern basin is about 300 m as opposed to 900 m in the northern basin. Again, there is evidence for sills near 8.3 seconds. However, these, and the bright reflector extending across the basin between 8.1 and 8.2 seconds of reflection time, may be obscuring the depth to true basement. Models for these scenarios are described in a following section. Several diapiric or piercement structures extend upward from the basement. One, in fact, stands above the surrounding sediments on the seafloor. These may be intrusive volcaniform features related to the formation of the other seamounts in the vicinity. Their ages are unknown but are probably late Cretaceous because of the late Cretaceous radiometric age determinations of three other nearby seamounts (Scripps, Lamont, and Wilde) [Ozima et al., 1977].

Edifice Structure

There are five different acoustic layers or strata comprising the summit [Nemoto et al., in prep., 1986] (Fig. 6). The smooth and continuous uppermost layer is the pelagic cap which drapes the entire top of the structure except for the northernmost end and is thickest in the middle part of the profile. There is little or no sediment evident on the flanks. The second layer is a thin but bright reflector interpreted as hard oolitic limestone. This layer is sporadically distributed, apparently occuring only where the pelagic sediments are thickest. Beneath this is a series of flat-lying reflectors interpreted as lagoonal muds which are again thickest in the middle portion of

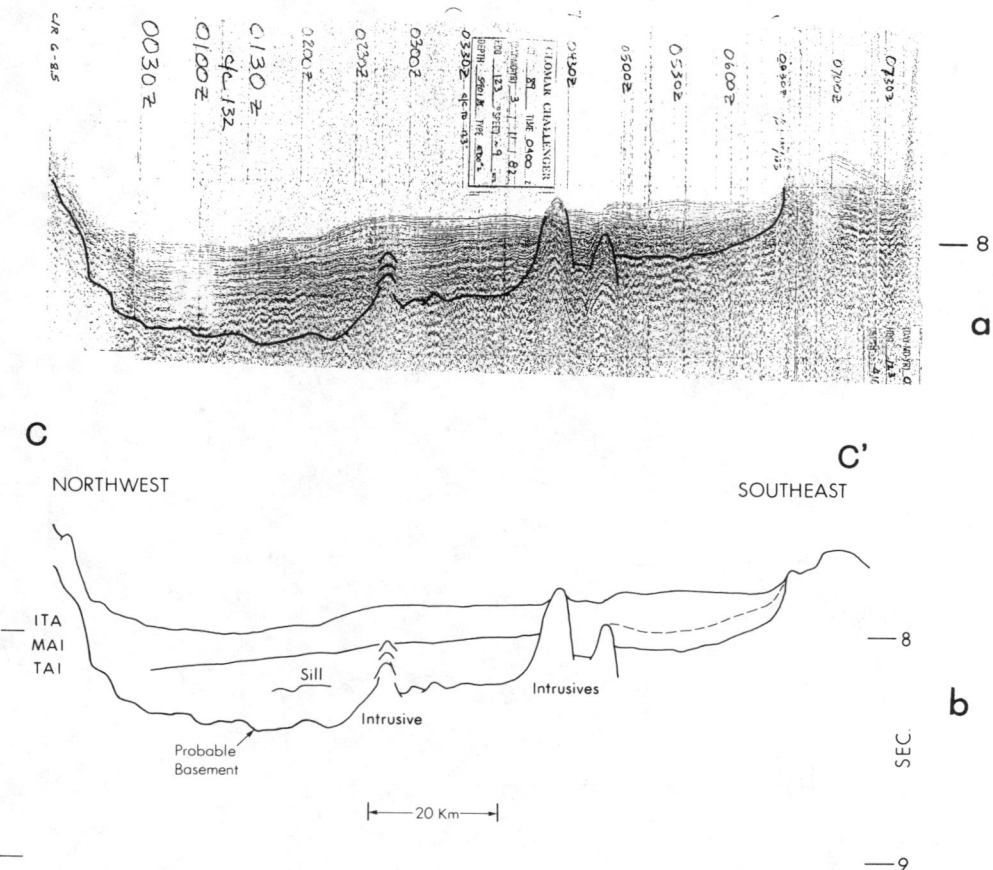

Fig. 5. Photo of airgun seismic reflection record of basin to the southeast of Ita Mai Tai (Glomar Challenger, Leg 89 profile). (b) Line drawing showing the probable depth to basement, and locations of intrusive structures.

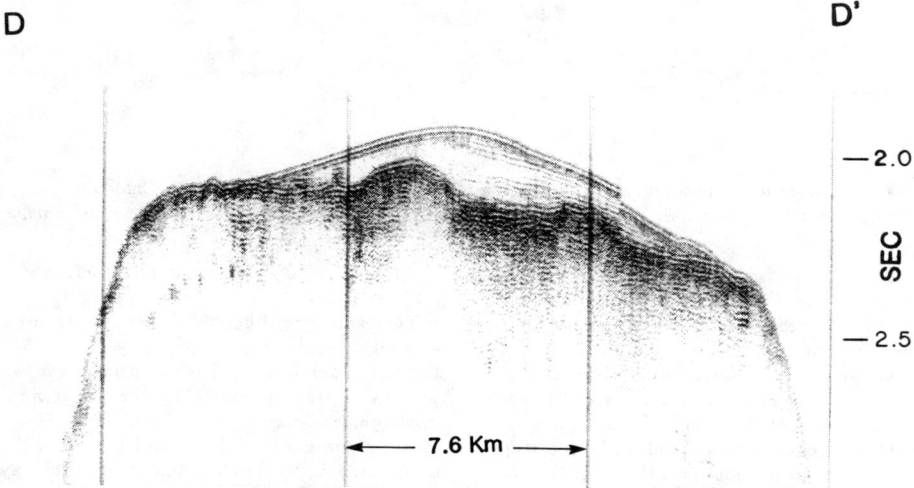

Fig. 6. Photo of airgun EPC seismic reflection record from KK810626 Leg 2 over the summit of Ita Mai Tai. This transect lies between DSDP Sites 200 and 201 (Fig. 2, along line D-D').

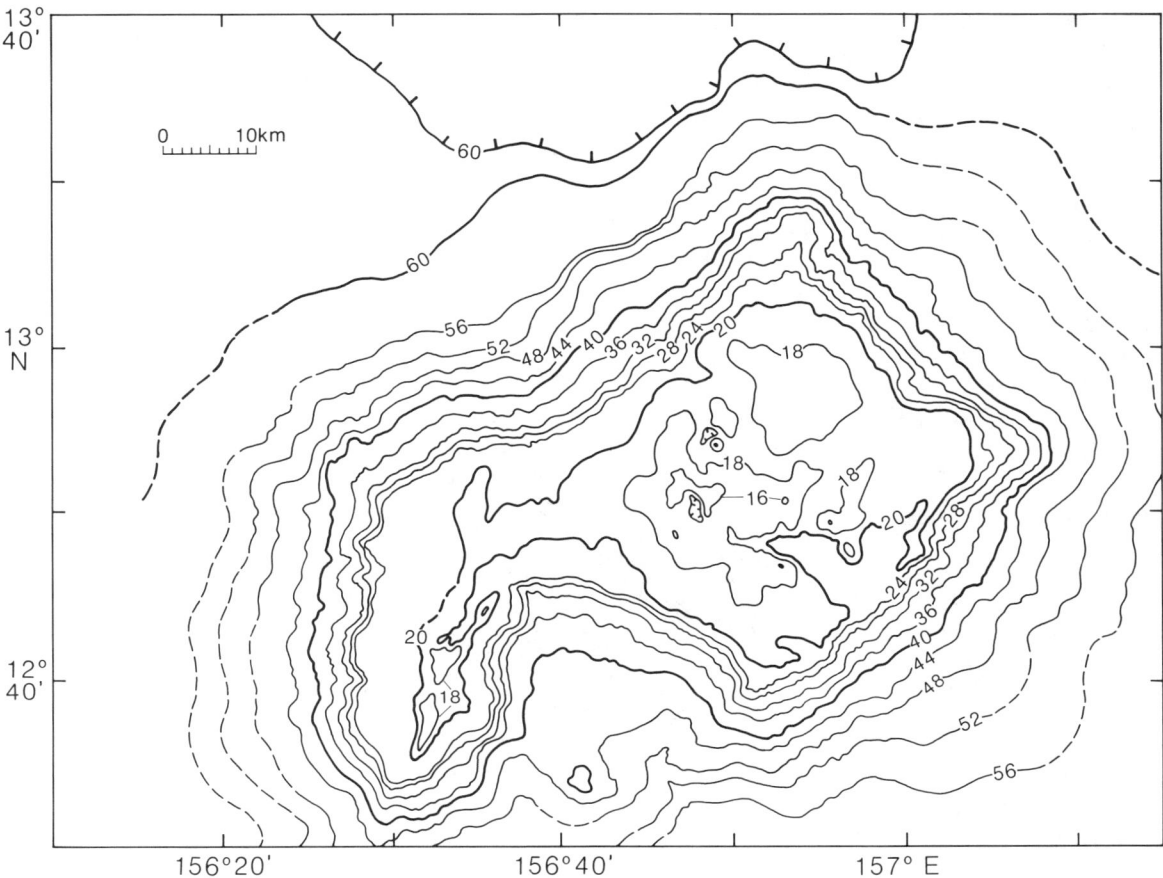

Fig. 7. Map of Ita Mai Tai showing the depth to basement. Sediment thicknesses above the volcanic basement have been removed. Contour interval is 200 m over the summit area, 400 m on the flanks.

the profile. The velocities, traveltimes, and maximum thicknesses for these uppermost three layers are given in Table 2.

The velocities of the pelagic and oolitic layers are taken from Heezen et al., (1973). The oolitic particle velocity was determined to be 3.83 km/sec [Heezen and MacGregor, 1973] which is in good agreement with that determined by others [Press, 1966; Furumoto et al., 1970].

The interpretations of these layers and their thicknesses (Table 2) agree very well with Jones (1973) who used sonobuoy data to compute a velocity of 1.6 km/sec for the pelagic cap and 3.85 km/sec for the oolitic limestone. Below the lagoonal mud is the irregular top of two other components, the reef complex and the volcanic basement. The reef is not continuous across the profile but is indicated only on the flanks where the reef community grew around the edges of the lagoon. The maximum thickness of the reef is 0.1 second of reflection time. The velocity as calculated by the method of Gregory and Kroenke (1982) ranges from 3.0-4.1 km/sec, giving a thickness of 150-205 m.

The irregularity of the volcanic basement is probably due to erosion before the seamount became an atoll. Ita Mai Tai must have subsided a total of 2090 m which is comparable to other seamounts in the area such as Kwajalein (2000 m) and Enewetak (1900 m) [Jones, 1973]. Subsidence apparently was fast enough so that the seamount was not completely leveled, but not fast enough to prevent reefs and a lagoon from forming for a short time. The basement map [Nemoto et al., in prep., 1986] (Fig. 7) shows the aerial extent of the erosional remnants of the original volcano. It is not difficult to imagine looking at an aerial photo of a present day analog, Tahiti for example, and seeing the volcanic remnants standing above the lagoon and the fringing barrier reef.

The foregoing interpretations of the seismic reflection records are based on copies of the DSDP Leg 89 analog shipboard seismic reflection records [R. Moberly, pers. comm., 1985]. Whitman (1985) has independently interpreted the digitally collected seismic data of the Leg. The essential points of our interpretations agree with hers.

The post-eruptive depositional history of Ita Mai Tai is well recorded in the drilling record from Site 202 (Fig. 2). A 75 m thick *Globigerina* sand and sandstone of middle Eocene and early Pliocene age overlies 35 m of lagoonal oolitic limestone of indeterminate age. Below this is a layer of lagoonal coraliferous mud at least 45 m thick containing a few fragments of basalt and feldspar indicating that the volcanic basement is close to outcropping in this area [Heezen et al., 1973; Hesse, 1973].

Neither the reef complex nor the basement were directly sampled in any of the DSDP holes. However, a number of dredges taken by the R/V Kana Keoki in 1981 did sample the reef outcrop, the lagoonal deposits, as well as slump or terrace deposits.

Gravity

The configuration of the free-air gravity anomaly over the seamount is shown in Figure 8. Generally, the shape of the anomaly follows the

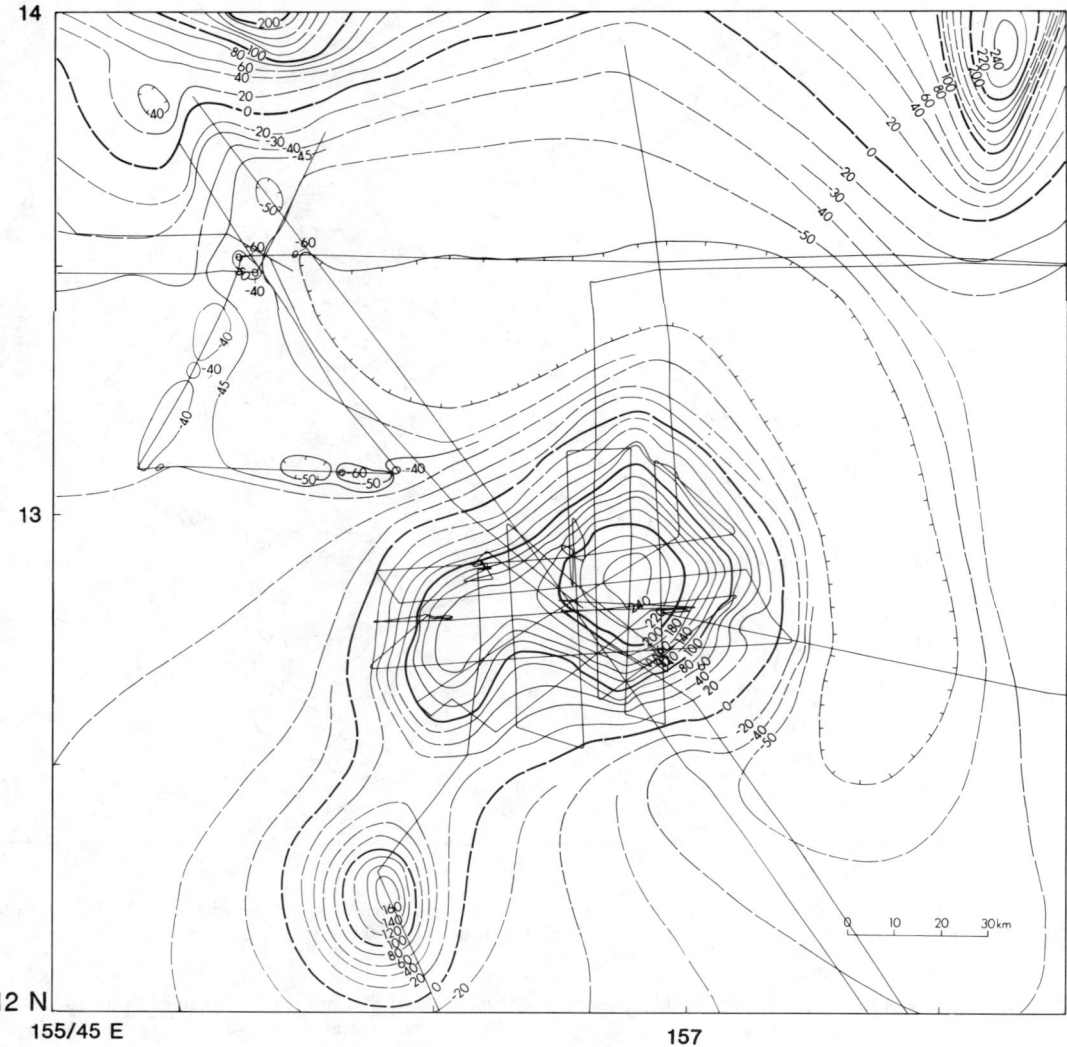

Fig. 8. Free-air anomaly map in mgals of Ita Mai Tai Guyot and surrounding seafloor. Ship tracks are indicated by black lines. Contour interval is 20 mgal except where indicated.

bathymetry. The amplitude ranges from a maximum value of 254 mgal over the summit to a low of -69 mgal observed over the moat on the southeast side of the edifice. The total amplitude range of 323 mgal for Ita Mai Tai is exceeded in the north Pacific only by the much larger and shallower Hawaiian-Emperor chain. The shape of the anomaly also suggests that there was probably only one main volcanic conduit.

The observed gravity data for Ita Mai Tai were estimated for 980 grid points at about 5 km intervals. Ten polygonal layers with vertical sides were used to model the bathymetry (Figures 9 and 10a). The observed gravity was then inverted using a 3-dimensional approach [Talwani and Ewing, 1960; Plouff, 1976]. This technique uses a linear least squares analog to determine the average density of the seamount and assumes internal homogeneity from summit to seafloor.

The model is assumed to be accurate only where there is adequate bathymetry and gravity coverage. No claims are made for those areas with sparse data such as directly south and west of the seamount. However, the model is influenced most by prisms that are shallowest and have the greatest density contrasts. The effect diminishes rapidly with distance from the flanks of the seamount. Nearby seamounts to the northeast and northwest have a negligible effect on the gravity model. The 3-dimensional method was used because the 2-D approach over-corrects the gravity field by 18 percent over the apex of a conical seamount with a 10° slope [Rose and Bowman, 1974].

For the first phase of the gravity model, the calculated density was 2.59 g/cm^3. Both the calculated anomaly for this model and the residual field (observed minus calculated) are shown in Figure 11a. The calculated mean density value agrees well with values for other seamounts such as 2.5 g/cm^3 for Chautauqua Seamount [Schimke and Bufe, 1968], 2.6 g/cm^3 for an unnamed Atlantic seamount [LePichon

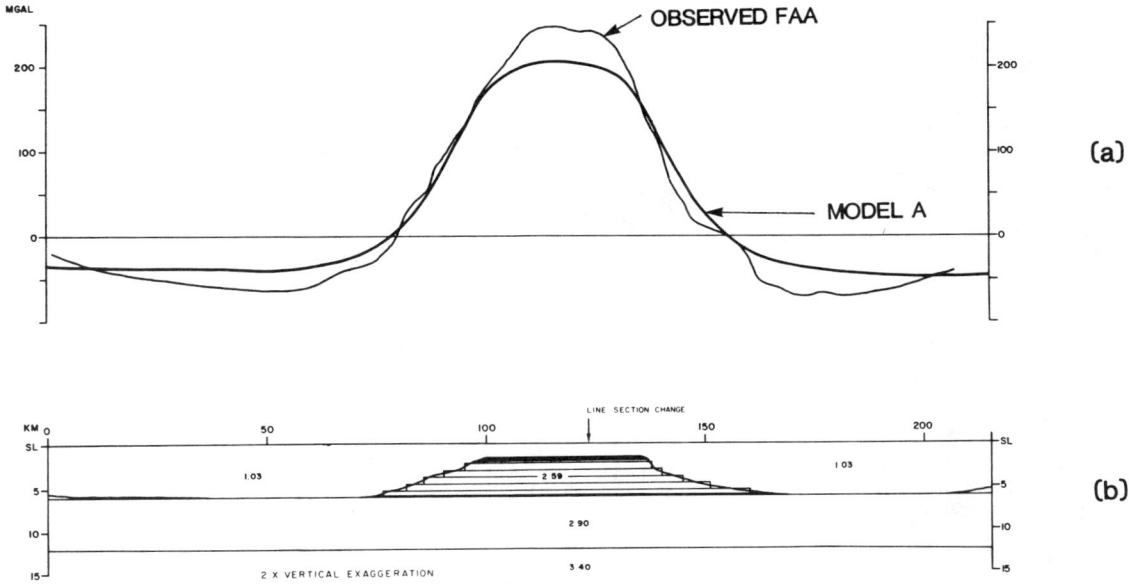

Fig. 9. (a) Cross-section of laterally homogeneous model A, and the observed gravity anomaly over Ita Mai Tai. Location of transect shown in Figure 10. (b) Density model A showing the mean edifice density calculated least squares inversion of the observed gravity.

and Talwani, 1965], and 2.48 g/cm³ for Nagata Seamount [Sager et al., 1982]. Seamount density determinations are summarized in Kellogg and Ogujiofor (1985) and Kellogg et al. (this volume). But the calculated gravity field of model A left residual values of 40 mgal over the summit area and -30 mgal over the basin to the southeast of the seamount.

In the second phase lateral density variations were included in forward models to reduce the gravity residuals and fit geological and seismic reflection data. A dense vertical prism was added (Fig. 10b), extending from the top of the seamount to the oceanic crust. The density used for the prism was 2.95 g/cm³, in accordance with the measured densities of 2.8 g/cm³ for eclogite from Koolau Caldera and 3.0 g/cm³ for nephelinite from Salt Lake Crater on Oahu [M. Manghnani, pers. comm., 1985]. These dense rocks are commonly associated with volcanic conduits or feeder pipes in Pacific seamounts and islands (Kellogg et al., this volume). The average bulk density of the model for Ita Mai Tai then increases to 2.70 g/cm³.

As a third phase, prisms representing the sediment filled basins and incorporating the seismic reflection data were added to model A. The drilling record of Site 585 provided velocities (Table 1) which were converted into densities of 1.9 to 2.1 g/cm³ after G. P. Woollard (1962). A small amount of crustal thickening was added to model A

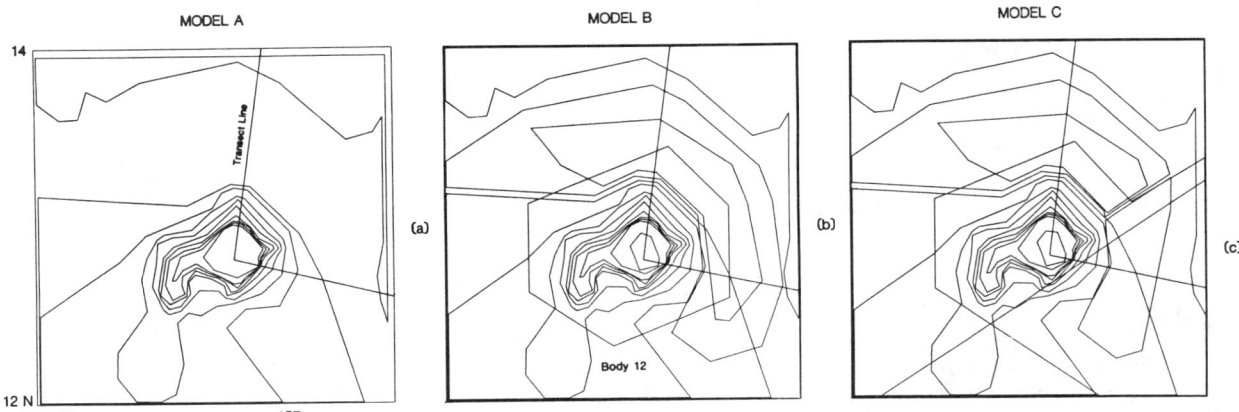

Fig. 10. Plan views of the bathymetric prisms used for models A, B and C. The position of the transect line is shown for figures 9, 12 and 13.

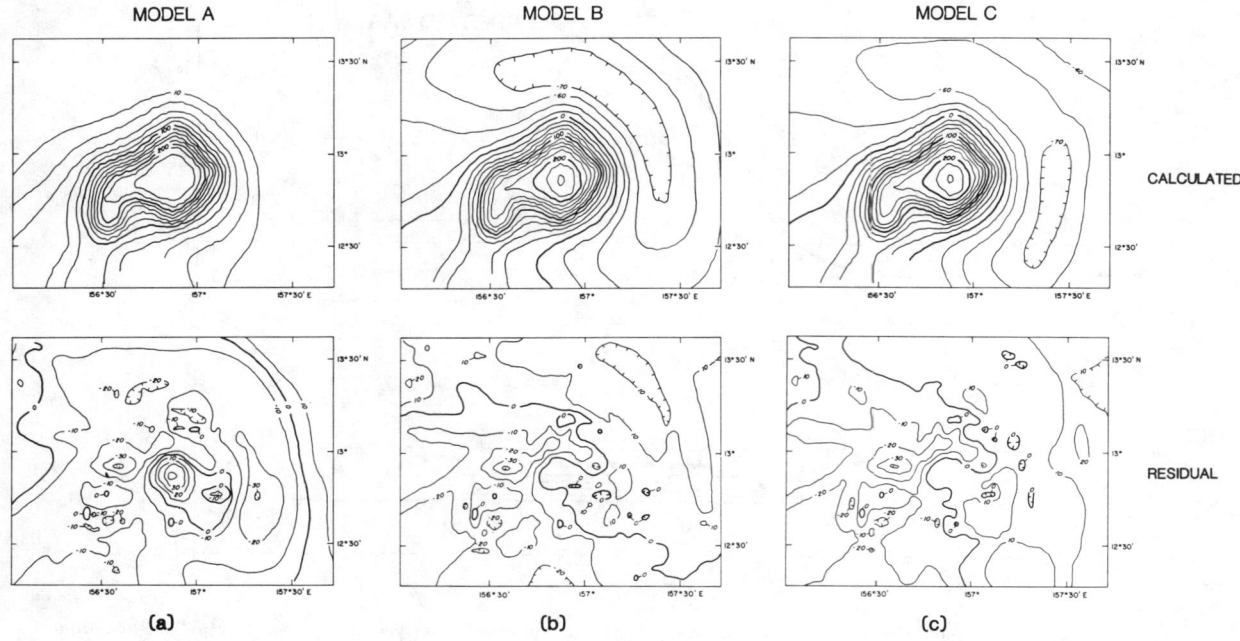

Fig. 11. Calculated and residual (observed minus calculated) gravity fields in mgal for models A, B and C.

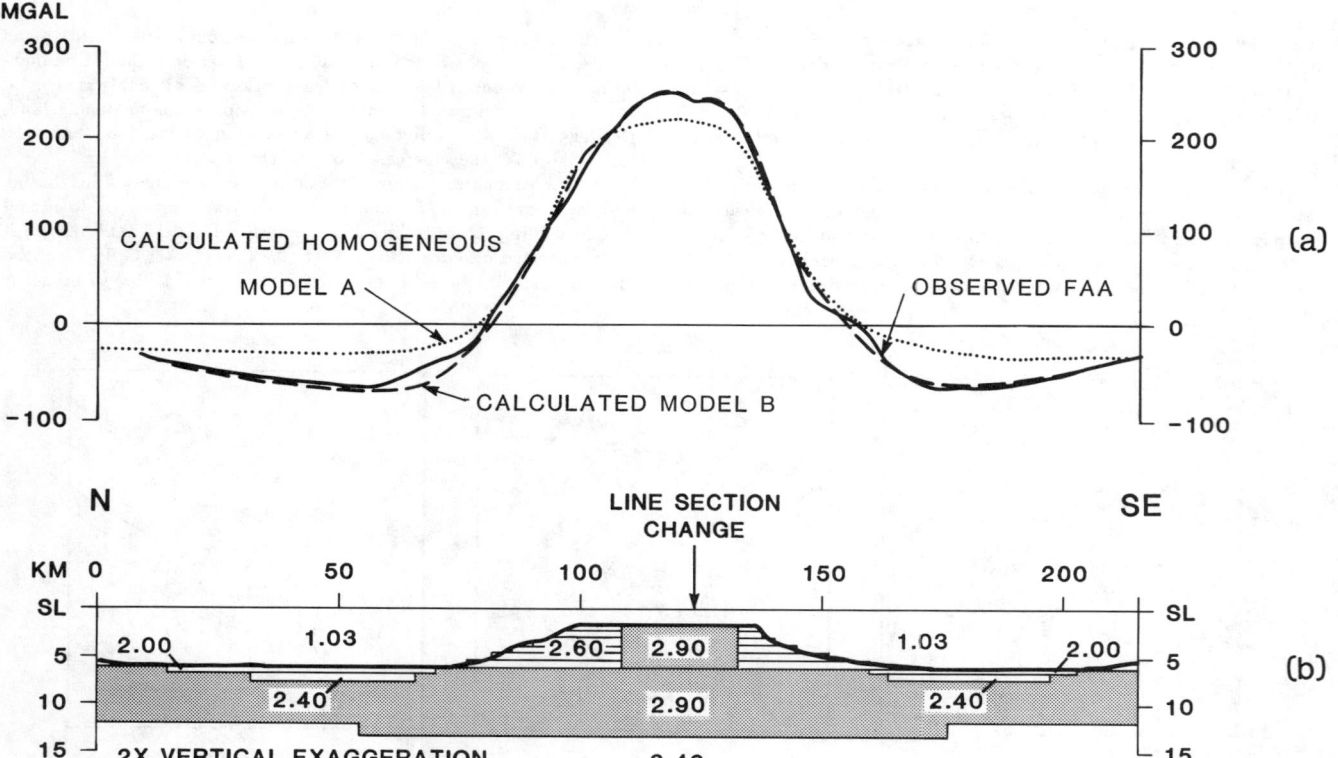

Fig. 12. (a) Cross-section of the observed gravity anomaly (solid line), calculated values for model B (dashed line), and laterally homogeneous model A (dotted line). (b) Cross-section showing the density prisms used in model B. A volcanic conduit, sediment bodies, and crustal thickening were added. Location of transect shown in Figure 10.

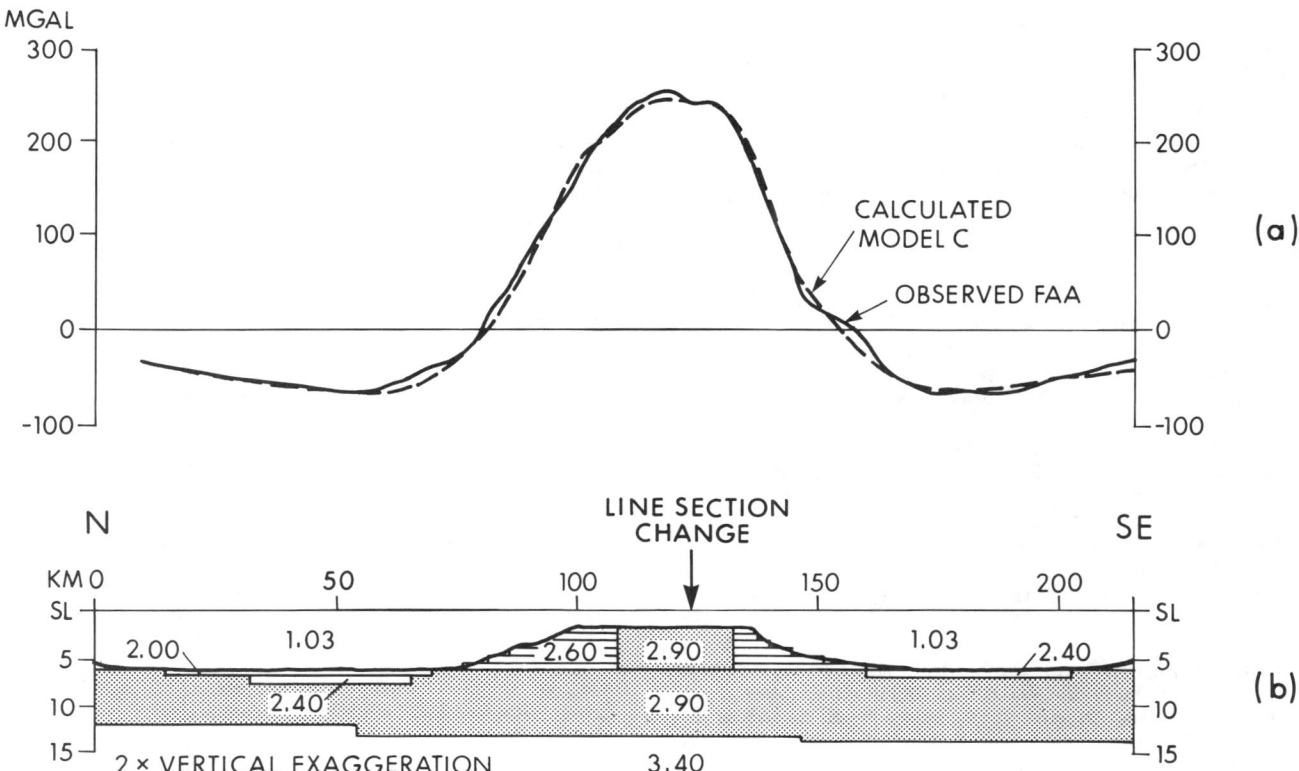

Fig. 13. Same as Figure 12, using model C. Extended crustal thickening toward the southeast.

directly below the seamount (Fig. 12b). The crust-mantle density contrast was assumed to be 0.5 g/cm³.

To achieve the final models, two slightly different approaches were used to achieve the final models. Model B assumes identical sediment bodies to the north and southeast (Fig. 12b), although the southeastern basin was not directly sampled, and 1.0 km of crustal thickening beneath the seamount (body 12, Fig. 10b). The calculated and residual anomalies are shown in Figure 11b. The maximum difference between the observed and calculated along the northern track is about 25 mgal. A cross sectional profile of the observed and the calculated gravity anomalies is shown in Figure 12a. The goodness of fit parameter is 4.87 [Richards et al., 1967], showing that the model adequately describes the observed anomaly.

Model C is very similar to model B except that there is one less sediment body in the southeastern basin, indicating a shallower depth to acoustic basement, and crustal thickening of 1.5 km which extends easterly to the edge of the model (Fig. 13b). The plan view of the prisms is shown in Figure 10c. Figures 11c and 13a show the calculated and residual anomalies. Like model B, the maximum residual is about 25 mgal, along the northern track. The goodness of fit is 4.96, slightly better than model B.

The difference between the two models' calculated anomalies is negligible. Both adequately explain the observed data. The seismic data however would seem to give more credibility to model C with its shallower southeast basin, because it does not require that opaque layers (lava flows, sills, etc.) mask deeper sediments. However, model C does require the assumption of an abrupt change in crustal thickness.

Thus, Ita Mai Tai appears to be almost completely uncompensated locally. This rather dense seamount is, in effect, perched on oceanic crust 6-7.5 km thick causing at most only 1.5 km of crustal downwarping. The lack of isostatic compensation in Ita Mai Tai may be the result of mid-plate eruption on thick inelastic lithosphere with little or no sill injection into the crust.

Conclusions

Ita Mai Tai first erupted during the Aptian/Albian and possibly again during the Eocene. The volcanism is recorded in volcaniclastic deposits in the basins north and southeast of Ita Mai Tai. Gravity models suggest that Ita Mai Tai is a large locally uncompensated seamount that only requires an addition of 1.5 km of crustal thickening. As the oceanic lithosphere moves away from the ridge crest, it cools and thickens so that its effective elastic thickness is increased (Watts and Ribe, 1984). Mid-plate seamounts formed on old seafloor are often associated with long wavelength, high amplitude gravity anomalies, thick effective elastic thicknesses, and the absence of local isostatic compensation. Kellogg et al. (this volume) described an empirical equation relating isostatic compensation and the age of loading t (MyBP) of seamounts:

$$\text{Compensation}(\%) = 68 - 5.6t^{0.5}$$

Thus, the lack of local compensation ($10\% \pm 13\%$, J. Freymueller and J. Kellogg, in prep.) probably resulted from eruption on thick oceanic lithosphere that was at least 30-40 m.y. old and perhaps 100 m.y. old. In other words, the oceanic crust under Ita Mai Tai is probably early Jurassic to early Cretaceous in age.

Acknowledgements. The authors wish to acknowledge the contributions of several individuals who greatly aided the success of this project. They include Frisbee Campbell for the initial data collection and unpublished bathymetry, Loren Kroenke and Kenji Nemoto for unpublished seismic reflection records and stratigraphic interpretations, and J. Marsh for an unpublished Seasat-Geos-3 gravity image (Fig. 1). The paper was improved with comments from John Rose, Al Rudman, and an anonymous reviewer. This study was supported by the Office of Naval Research, Code 425GG. Hawaii Institute of Geophysics contribution no. 1845.

References

Batiza, R., Abundances, distribution and sizes of volcanoes in the Pacific Ocean and implications for the origin of non-hotspot volcanoes, *E.P.S.L., 60*, 195-206, 1982.

Gregory, A. E., III, and L. W. Kroenke, Reef development in a mid-oceanic island; reflection profiling studies of the 500-meter shelf south of Oahu, *AAPG Bull., 66*, 843-859, 1982.

Furumoto, A. S., J. F. Campbell, and D. M. Hussong, Seismic studies of subsurface structure in the Ewa coastal plain, Oahu, Hawaii, *Pacific Sci., 24*, 529-542, 1970.

Heezen, B. C. et al., Tertiary pelagic ooze on Ita Maitai guyot; equatorial Pacific: DSDP sites 200 and 201, in *Initial Reports of the Deep Sea Drilling Project, vol. 20*, edited by B. C. Heezen and I. D. MacGregor, pp. 87-96, U.S. Government Printing Office, Washington, D.C., 1973.

Heezen, B. C., MacGregor, I. D., Oolitic limestone on the Ita Maitai Guyot, Equatorial Pacific: DSDP Site 202, in *Initial Reports of the Deep Sea Drilling Project, vol. 20*, edited by B. C. Heezen and I. D. MacGregor, pp. 97-102, U. S. Government Printing Office, Washington, D.C., 1973.

Hesse, R., Diagenesis of a seamount oolite from the west Pacific, Leg 20, DSDP, in *Initial Reports of the Deep Sea Drilling Project, vol. 20*, edited by B. C. Heezen et al., pp. 363-387, U.S. Government Printing Office, Washington, D.C., 1973.

Hilde, T. W. C., N. Isezaki, and J. M. Wageman, Mesozoic sea-floor spreading in the North Pacific, in *The Geophysics of the Pacific Ocean Basin and its Margin*, Geophys. Monogr. Ser., vol. 19, edited by G. H. Sutton, M. H. Manghnani, and R. Moberly, pp. 205-226, Amer. Geophys. Union, Washington, D. C., 1976.

Hilde, T. W. C., S. Uyeda, and L. Kroenke, Evolution of the western Pacific and its margin, *Tectonophysics, 38*, 145-165, 1977.

Jones, E. J. W., Determination of sedimentary velocities using expendable sonobuoys at DSDP Leg 20 drilling sites, northwest Pacific, in *Initial Reports of the Deep Sea Drilling Project, vol. 20*, edited by B. C. Heezen and I. D. MacGregor, pp. 625-642, U. S. Government Printing Office, Washington, D. C., 1973.

Jordan, T. H., H. W. Menard, and D. K. Smith, Density and size distribution of seamounts in the eastern Pacific inferred from wide-beam sounding data, *J. Geophys. Res., 88*, 10508- 10518, 1983.

Kellogg, J. N., and I. J. Ogujiofor, Gravity field analysis of Sio Guyot: An isostatically compensated seamount in the Mid-Pacific Mountains, *Geo-Marine Letters, 5*, 91-97, 1985.

Kellogg, J. N., B. S. Wedgeworth, and I. J. Ogujiofor, *Invited Paper*, Three-dimensional modeling of the gravity fields of seamounts, Abst., SEG/USN Tech. Symposium on 3-Dimensional Marine Data Collection, Processing, Interpretation, and Presentation, NSTL, Miss., p. 9, 1984.

Kellogg, J. N., B. S. Wedgeworth, and J. Freymueller, Isostatic compensation and conduit structures of Western Pacific Seamounts: Results of three-dimensional gravity modeling, this volume.

Kroenke, L. W., Geology of the Ontong Java Plateau, *Hawaii Institute of Geophysics Report 72-5*, Honolulu, Hawaii, pp. 1-119, 1972.

Larson, R. L., Late Jurassic and Early Cretaceous evolution of the western central Pacific Ocean, *J. Geomag. Geoelectr. 28*, 219-236, 1976.

Larson, R. L., and C. G. Chase, Late Mesozoic evolution of the western Pacific Ocean, *GSA Bull., 83*, 3627-3644, 1972.

Le Pichon, X., and M. Talwani, Crustal structure of the mid-ocean ridges; 1, Seismic refraction measurements, *J. Geophys. Res., 70*, 319-339, 1965.

Lonsdale, P., and F. N. Spiess, A pair of young cratered volcanoes on the East Pacific Rise, *J. of Geology, 87*, 157-173, 1979.

Menard, H. W., *Marine Geology of the Pacific*, 271 pp., McGraw-Hill, New York, 1964.

Menard, H. W., Darwin reprise, *J. Geophys. Res., 89*, 9960-9968, 1984.

Ozima, M., M. Honda, and K. Saito, ^{40}Ar-^{39}Ar ages of guyots in the western Pacific and discussion of their evolution, *Geophys. J. Roy. Astr. Soc., 51*, 475-485, 1977.

Plouff, D., Gravity and magnetic fields of polygonal prisms and application to magnetic terrain corrections, *Geophysics, 41*, 727-741, 1976.

Press, F., Seismic velocities, in *Handbook of Physical Constants*, edited by S. P. Clark, Jr., pp. 202-203, Geol. Soc. America Mem. 97, 1966.

Richards, M. L., V. Vacquier, and G. D. van Voorhis, Calculation of the magnetization of uplifts from combining topographic and magnetic surveys, *Geophysics, 32*, 678-707, 1967.

Rose, J. C., and B. R. Bowman, The effect of seamounts and other bottom topography on marine gravity anomalies, in *Proceedings of the International Symposium on Applications of Marine Geodesy*, pp. 381-396, Mar. Tech. Soa., Washington, D. C., 1974.

Sager, W. W., G. T. Davis, B. H. Keating, and J. A. Philpotts, A geophysical and geologic study of Nagata Seamount, northern Line Islands, *J. Geomag. Geoelectr., 34*, 283-305, 1982.

Schimke, G. R., and C. G. Bufe, Geophysical description of a Pacific Ocean seamount, *J. Geophys. Res., 73*, 559-569, 1968.

Schlanger, S. O., and I. Premoli-Silva, Tectonic, volcanic and paleographic implications of redeposited reef faunas of late Cretaceous and Tertiary age from the Nauru Basin and Line Islands, in *Initial Reports of the Deep Sea Drilling Project, vol. 61*, edited by R. L. Larson et al., pp. 817-827, U. S. Government Printing Office, Washington, D. C., 1981.

Scientific Party, Leg 89, Leg 89 drills Cretaceous volcanics, *Geotimes, 28*, 17-20, 1983.

Shipley, T. H., J. M. Whitman, F. K. Duennebier, and L. D. Petersen, Seismic stratigraphy and sedimentary history of the East Mariana Basin, western Pacific, *Earth Planet. Sci. Lett., 64*, 257-275, 1983.

Stoeser, D. B., Igneous rocks from Leg 30 of the Deep Sea Drilling Project, in *Initial Reports of the Deep Sea Drilling Project, vol. 30*, edited by J. E. Andrews, G. Peckham, et al., pp. 401-414, U. S. Government Printing Office, Washington, D. C., 1975.

Talwani, M. and M. Ewing, Rapid computation of gravitational attraction of three-dimensional bodies of arbitrary shape, *Geophysics, 25*, 203- 225, 1960.

Udintsev, G. B. et al., Seamounts of the Pacific Ocean, in *Volcanoes and Tectonosphere*, edited by H. Aoke and S. Iizuka, pp. 7-33, Tokai University Press, Shimizu, Japan, 1976.

Watts, A. B. and N. M. Ribe, On geoid heights and flexure of the lithosphere at seamounts, *J. Geophys. Res., 89*, 11152-11170, 1984.

Watts, A. B., U. S. ten Brink, P. Buhl, and T. M. Brocher, A multi-channel seismic study of lithospheric flexure across the Hawaiian-Emperor seamount chain, *Nature, 315*, 105-111, 1985.

Whitman, J. M., Tectonic and bathymetric evolution of the Pacific ocean basin since 74 Ma, M.S. thesis, 168 pp., Univ. of Miami, Coral Gables, Dec. 1981.

Woollard, G. P., The relation of gravity anomalies to surface elevation, crustal structure and geology, *Research Report Series No. 62-9*, 330 pp., Aeronautical Chart and Information Center, United States Air Force, St. Louis, Missouri, 1962.

ISOSTATIC COMPENSATION AND CONDUIT STRUCTURES OF WESTERN PACIFIC SEAMOUNTS: RESULTS OF THREE-DIMENSIONAL GRAVITY MODELING

J. N. Kellogg[1], B. S. Wedgeworth[2], and J. Freymueller[1]

Hawaii Institute of Geophysics, Honolulu, Hawaii 96822

Abstract. Detailed three-dimensional polygonal prism models of two large western Pacific seamounts show that the 135 mgal difference in the observed sea surface gravity over the two can be best explained by similar mean densities (2.6 g/cm^3) and crustal thickening under one seamount (Airy isostatic compensation). Observed - calculated residuals are further reduced by including dense (2.9 g/cm^3) vertical feeder pipes or volcanic conduits in the models. Dense conduits or fracture zones 5 to 17 km in diameter are located under many, if not all, craters on volcanic islands and seamounts. Results from the detailed seamount studies can be generalized using exact expressions for the on-axis vertical component of gravity for cones or frustrums of cones. Seamount isostatic compensation levels can then be rapidly estimated by iteratively inverting the on-axis gravity. The estimation algorithm is independent of mechanical assumptions regarding oceanic lithosphere and is particularly useful for the rapid evaluation of large data sets. The results and associated uncertainties are comparable to those of the detailed three-dimensional models and frequency domain studies. As predicted by cooling plate models, the estimated Airy (local) compensation levels μ for seamounts are inversely proportional to the root of the seafloor age at the time of loading t: $\mu(\%) = 68 - 5.6 t^{1/2}$. A map of depth-corrected on-axis gravity values for western Pacific seamounts indicates that seamounts with similar μ values tend to form clusters.

Introduction

The marine gravitational field provides important information regarding bathymetry and the structure of the oceanic crust and upper mantle. The Seasat radar altimeter generated a considerable amount of new information about the short-wavelength (30-400 km) character of the oceanic geoid. A major contribution to the marine geoid is made by seafloor bathymetry, because of the large density contrast at the rock-water interface. Attempts have therefore been made to use satellite altimeter data to predict bathymetry (e.g., Lazarewicz and Schwank, 1982; Dixon et al., 1983). Such a tool would be especially useful in the South and West Pacific where ship crossings are rare. Large areas are known to no better than 100-km resolution, and many first-order features such as seamount chains and fracture zones may be undetected. At the present time, however, successful bathymetric predictions from the Seasat altimeter data have been prevented by (1) uncertainties regarding the distances between the satellite tracks and the axes of bathymetric features and (2) large observed variations in the short-wavelength gravity-depth function.

The first obstacle, estimating off-track distance to a bathymetric feature, can be diminished as the GEOSAT, NROSS, TOPEX, ERS-1, and GRM satellites become operational, thereby substantially increasing the spatial density of sea-surface observations.

Our paper addresses the second obstacle to successful bathymetric predictions from altimeter data: the large variation in the short-wavelength gravity-depth function, that relates maximum sea-surface gravity anomalies and minimum depth to bathymetric features (30-400 km) in wavelength. For example, sea surface free-air gravity anomalies over seamounts of the same size and depth may vary by up to 200 mgal or over 4 meters on the geoid. Vogt et al. (1984) showed that the Seasat radar altimetry and seafloor topography over Bermuda and Gregg Seamount could not be described adequately by a single transfer function. Dixon et al (1983) and Watts and Ribe (1984) related the variations in amplitude of marine geoid anomalies over seamounts to different effective elastic thicknesses of the flexed lithosphere beneath the seamounts. The effective elastic thicknesses are related to the tectonic settings of the seamounts, that is, whether they formed on or near a mid-oceanic ridge crest or off-ridge. Bathymetric prediction from altimeter data directly is therefore difficult unless a priori constraints on the tectonic settings of the seamounts are available. In this paper we will present gravity data from the Mid-Pacific Mountains and the Marshall Island Group indicating that seamounts in lines or spatial clusters have similar gravity-depth relationships and presumably similar tectonic origins.

The gravitational field is the vertical gradient of the potential, and is therefore even more sensitive to nearby shallow mass anomalies than the geoid. The sea surface gravity field over well surveyed seamounts is known better and contains more short wavelength information than the Seasat derived geoid. Previous studies have been limited to gravity anomalies over a relatively few seamounts and oceanic islands (e.g., Watts and Ribe, 1984; Kellogg and Ogujiofor, 1985; Freedman and Parsons, 1986). In this paper, pertinent gravity and bathymetric data are presented together for most of the well-surveyed seamounts and islands in the western Pacific, permitting evaluation of the variations in the short wavelength (30-400 km) gravity-depth function for the western Pacific. We show with three dimensional models that the observed variations in the gravity-depth function can be explained by varying degrees of local Airy isostatic compensation. High resolution surface gravity data permit the quantification of small wavelength (< 30 km) seamount features such as conduit zones. In this paper we estimate the densities and geometries of seamount conduits from gravity and seismic refraction studies and infer their compositions from published petrologic studies. We present a simple iterative in-

---

[1] Now at Department of Geological Sciences, University of South Carolina, Columbia, South Carolina
[2] Now at Harding Lawson Associates, Honolulu, Hawaii

Copyright 1987 by the American Geophysical Union.

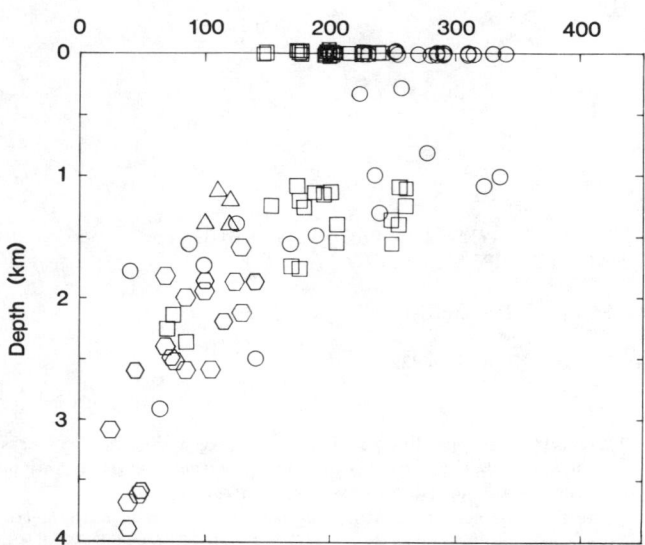

Fig. 1. Maximum free-air gravity anomalies as a function of minimum depths to the tops of 59 seamounts in the western Pacific. For 38 islands and atolls in the western Pacific, maximum Bouguer anomalies (density = 2.3 g/cm³) are plotted at sea level. The Mid-Pacific Mountains are shown as triangles, the Marshall Islands Group and East Mariana Basin Seamounts as squares, the Musicians Seamounts as hexagons, and the Magellan Seamounts, Hawaiian-Emperor Ridge, and Kiribati and Caroline Islands as circles.

verse method to rapidly estimate the degree of isostatic compensation for large numbers of well-surveyed seamounts. Finally, we discuss the implications of the regional clustering of seamounts with similar isostatic compensation levels for bathymetric prediction from satellite altimetry data.

Observed Gravity-Depth Function

The short wavelength (< 400 km) marine gravity field is a function of seafloor topography and lateral density variations in the crust and upper mantle. Sea surface gravity fields observed over seamounts are related to their sizes, shapes, minimum depths, seafloor depths, edifice densities, and density variations in the lithosphere beneath the seamounts. Understanding the relationship between the gravity field and the minimum depths to the tops of seamounts is needed to accurately predict seamount depths from satellite altimetry and is therefore a matter of great importance for submarine navigation and mineral exploration in the many parts of the world's oceans where bathymetric coverage by surface ships is inadequate.

Maximum free-air gravity anomalies are plotted in Figure 1 as a function of minimum depths to the tops of 59 seamounts in the Western Pacific. For 38 islands and atolls in the Western Pacific, maximum Bouguer anomalies ($\rho = 2.3$ g/cm³) are plotted at sea level. Only well surveyed edifices are included to ensure that the gravity anomalies are not underestimated.

Not surprisingly, the data indicate a general inverse correlation between depth and gravity anomalies. A linear estimate for the mean gravity-depth relation is $z = -16g_z + 3800$ m where z is the minimum depth (m) to the top of the seamount and g_z is the maximum gravity anomaly (mgal) observed at the sea surface. There is considerable scatter about the mean however, thus permitting an estimate of the uncertainties in predicting bathymetry directly from gravity or geoid data alone in the Western Pacific. For example, although Sio Guyot, a large seamount in the western Mid-Pacific Mountains (Kellogg and Ogujiofor, 1985), is larger and shallower ($z = 1130$ m) than Ita Mai Tai in the East Mariana Basin ($z = 1402$ m) (Wedgeworth, 1985; Wedgeworth and Kellogg, this volume), it has a maximum free-air gravity anomaly (120 mgal) that is 135 mgal lower than that of Ita Mai Tai (255 mgal) (Figure 2). If we had attempted to predict the minimum depth to Sio Guyot from gravity data alone using our mean gravity depth relation for the western Pacific, $z = -16(120) + 3800 = 1880$ m, or 750 m too deep. Inserting the gravity data for Ita Mai Tai in the same formula gives a value of $z = -16(255) + 3800 = -280$ m, or 280 m above sea level, or 1682 m too high. From Figure 1 we see that gravity values for edifices at the same depth in the Western Pacific vary up to 200 mgal (or over 4 m on the geoid). Thus, with no other constraints, the uncertainties involved in depth predictions for Western Pacific seamounts from gravity data alone are as great as ± 1600 m. This large uncertainty range is unsatisfactory, so we will offer an explanation based on three-dimensional gravity modeling and present possible constraints for depth predictions caused by clustering of seamounts with similar gravity-depth ratios.

Three-Dimensional Models of Sio and Ita Mai Tai Guyots

To better understand the wide variations in gravity fields over seamounts, we modeled the gravity fields of Sio Guyot and Ita Mai Tai Guyot. Sio Guyot consists of two flat-topped summits among a cluster of six large guyots surmounting a broad basement swell or plateau (Nemoto and Kroenke, 1985). The Mid-Pacific Mountains extend over 2000 km eastward almost to the midpoint of the Hawaiian Ridge. The northern summit area of Sio Guyot (2820 km²), lying between 1130 and 1500 m below sea level, is much greater than the exposed summit area of the island of Oahu, Hawaii (1650 km²). At a depth of about 3400 m the 8° slopes of the guyot merge with the broad plateau that slopes gradually to 5500 m abyssal depths. Ita Mai Tai Guyot is smaller, subconical in shape, and has no underlying plateau. The flat-topped summit lies between 1400 and 2200 m and covers an area of about 1500 km².

We found empirically that to limit model density uncertainties to ± 0.1 g/cm³, the gravity field must be calculated with less than 6% error. A three-dimensional method was used because the two-dimensional method (assuming that polygonal prisms extend infinitely perpendicular to the profile) overcorrects the gravity effect by 18% over the apex of a conical seamount with a 10° slope (Rose and Bowman, 1974). The relatively few published three-dimensional models for seamounts include Harrison and Brisbin (1959), Le Pichon and Talwani (1964), Watts et al. (1975), and Sager et al. (1982). The bathymetry for Sio and Ita Mai Tai guyots was approximated with 33 and 11 vertical-sided polygonal prisms respectively (Figures 3 and 4). The observed gravity fields were digitized for 980 grid points each at 9 and 5 km intervals.

Linear least-squares inversion of observed gravity anomalies can sometimes be used to help determine the average density of seamounts. This technique is fundamentally the same as the density-profiling method (Nettleton, 1939). The main assumption is that the wavelength of any subsurface anomalous distribution of mass must be much shorter or much longer than the dimensions of the bathymetric feature being studied. Lewis and Dorman (1970) pointed out that this method is successful only for topography with wavelengths much shorter than those of gravity anomalies produced by regional isostatic compensation. This technique is not valid for a seamount if it has a local gravity "root" or a large magma chamber (Le Pichon and Talwani, 1964). Inversion of the gravity field over Ita Mai Tai produced a calculated mean density of 2.59 g/cm³, but inversion of the field

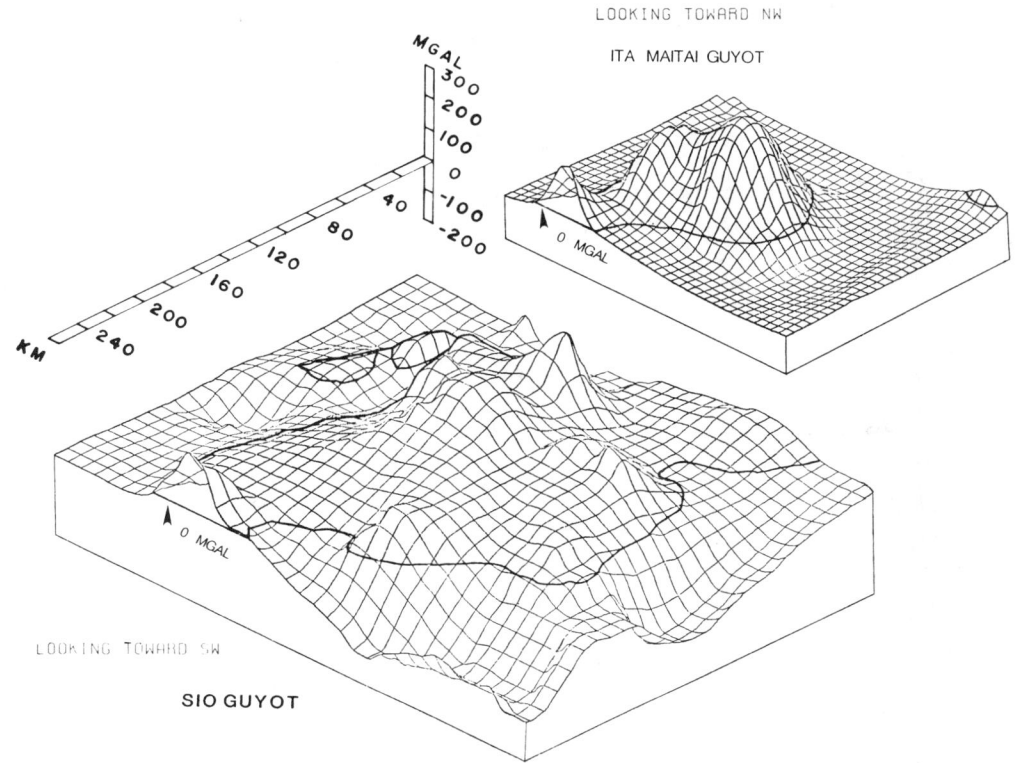

Fig. 2. Free-air gravity anomalies over Sio and Ita Mai Tai Guyots. Although Sio Guyot, a large seamount in the western Mid-Pacific Mountains, is larger and shallower than Ita Mai Tai Guyot in the East Mariana Basin, it has a maximum gravity anomaly 135 mgal lower than that of Ita Mai Tai. Seamount locations are shown in Figure 15.

over Sio Guyot resulted in an impossible low value of 1.95 g/cm^3. Le Pichon and Talwani (1964) obtained a similar density of 1.9 g/cm^3 for a seamount near the Mid-Atlantic Ridge, which they also rejected as erroneous. The fact that the positive gravity anomaly over Sio Guyot has a low amplitude and is flanked by negative anomalies suggests that there may be a broad zone of low density below the plateau with about the same wavelength as the plateau itself. Therefore, for realistic models we must rely on direct measurements of rock densities and seismic refraction velocities from other seamounts.

Measurements of seamount and oceanic island rock densities by Harrison and Brisbin (1959), Nayudu (1962), Kinoshita et al. (1963), Strange et al. (1965), and Manghnani and Woollard (1965) are summarized by Kellogg and Ogujiofor (1985). The measurements suggest that the mean densities of all seamounts lie between 2.3 and 2.9 g/cm^3.

Seismic compressional (P-wave) velocities can also be used to estimate density (Nafe and Drake, 1963). Seismic velocities have been measured for a seamount north of Madeira and two peaks in the Mid-Atlantic Rift Valley (Laughton et al., 1960), Cruiser Seamount (Le Pichon and Talwani, 1964), Bermuda (Officer et al., 1952), Bikini and Kwajalein (Raitt, 1954), the flanks of the Hawaiian Ridge north of Maui (Shor and Pollard, 1964), Oahu (Furumoto and Woollard, 1965; Furumoto et al., 1965; Watts et al., 1985), Tahiti and Rangiroa (Talandier and Okal, in press). The refraction data support the occurrence of a layer of 3.6 to 4.6 km/sec material over basaltic rock of a velocity 5.2 to 6.2 km/sec within the seamount. From the Nafe-Drake curve, these velocities correspond to densities of about 2.30 to 2.50 g/cm^3 and 2.60 to 2.75 g/cm^3, respectively.

The density obtained by inverting the gravity field for Ita Mai Tai (2.59 g/cm^3) is well within the range both of directly measured values and inferred values from seismic compressional velocities for the other seamounts. The density obtained by inverting the data for Sio Guyot (1.95 g/cm^3), however, is too low. We therefore, used realistic densities of 2.5 to 2.7 g/cm^3 for the basal swell or plateau, 2.9 g/cm^3 for the oceanic crust, and 3.4 g/cm^3 for the upper mantle (Figure 5, Kellogg and Ogujiofor, 1985). The first model was "uncompensated" (i.e., the excess mass of the guyot was not balanced by a mass deficit or local "root" directly beneath the guyot) and a uniform crystalline crustal thickness of 6.3 km was assumed (Woollard, 1975). The gravity anomalies of the polygonal prisms were calculated according to the method of Plouff (1976). Correlation between observed and calculated values was poor, along-track residual anomalies were as high as 100 mgal over the abyssal sea floor and as low as -80 mgal over Sio Guyot (Figure 5). From seismic refraction and wide-angle reflection surveys the crust is known to bend and thicken under the Hawaiian Ridge (Shor and Pollard, 1964; Furumoto et al., 1968; Suyenaga, 1979; Zucca et al., 1982; Watts et al., 1985) and under Rangiroa in the Tuamotu Islands (Talandier and Okal, in press), so to account for the apparent mass deficiency beneath Sio Guyot, "compensated" models with a thicker crust were tested. A cross section of the best fitting (minimum along-track residual anomalies) model is shown in Figure 5. In this model, the excess mass of the seamount is 70% "compensated locally" (i.e., balanced by a mass deficit directly beneath the seamount). If we assume that regional compensation is 100%, then 70% is the fraction of the compensation that is purely local. The residual gravity values (observed minus calculated) were

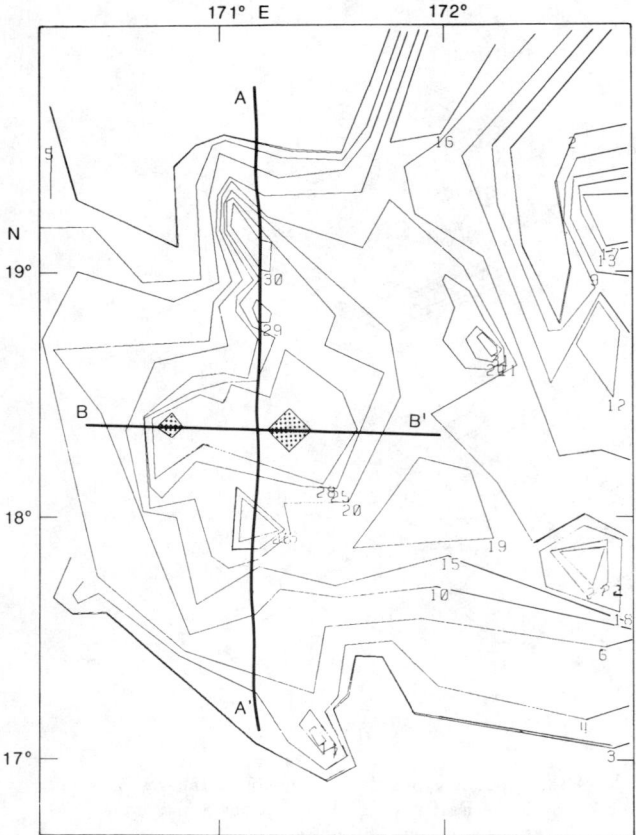

Fig. 3. Plan view of polygonal prisms used to approximate the bathymetry of Sio Guyot (after Kellogg and Ogujiofor, 1985).

low, less than 10 mgal along most of the ship track. The low density root in the compensated model accounts for the low amplitude of the positive gravity anomalies over the guyot as well as the negative anomalies flanking the plateau. In the best-fitting model, the crust underlying the guyot is 16 km thick and extends to a depth of 22 km. An uncertainty in the density contrast at the crust-mantle boundary of ± 0.1 g/cm^3 would result in a Moho depth uncertainty of ± 2 km.

Calculated gravity anomalies assuming a homogeneous edifice density of 2.59 g/cm^3 fit the observed gravity field over Ita Mai Tai fairly well. To explain the gravity lows flanking the seamount, however, the model was corrected for the low density clays and volcaniclastic debris in the basins to the north and east of the seamount (Figure 6; Wedgeworth, 1985; Wedgeworth and Kellogg, this volume). Sediment densities and thicknesses were derived from velocity measurements in the drilling record of DSDP Site 585 (Scientific Party, Leg 89, 1983) as well as HIG and DSDP Leg 89 seismic reflection records. To further reduce residual gravity anomalies, the crust was thickened just 1.5 km in the model. The large difference in the amplitudes of the observed gravity fields over the two seamounts (135 mgal) can be explained by varying levels of local isostatic compensation, with Sio Guyot 70% compensated and Ita Mai Tai only 8% compensated.

Eruptive Centers or Conduits

Although different depths to the crust-mantle boundary can explain the longer wavelength gravity anomalies over Sio and Ita Mai Tai guyots, they do not account for two short wavelength positive anomalies over Sio Guyot and one over Ita Mai Tai. To explain these anomalies, quadrilateral prisms of densities 2.8 to 3.0 g/cm^3 or 0.3 to 0.5 g/cm^3 higher than the surrounding layers were added to the models (Figures 6 and 7). The crustal structure shown along the cross-section B-B' (Figure 7) has a negligible effect on the short-wavelength anomalies.

The density models shown in Figures 6 and 7 could be explained by dense eruptive centers or conduits. Kroenke et al. (1966) modeled the positive gravity anomaly observed over Midway Atoll as the result of a volcanic conduit with a density of 3.2 g/cm^3 at a depth of 2 km. A similar volcanic center has been studied in the Koolau caldera on the island of Oahu (Strange et al., 1965), where nephelinite had a measured density of 3.0 g/cm^3 and seismic velocities were 6.1 km/sec within 1 km of the surface and 7.7 km/sec at a depth of 4 km (Furumoto et al., 1965). The observed positive gravity anomaly over the Koolau Volcano was matched by a calculated anomaly for a wide volcanic pipe with a density of 2.9 g/cm^3 within 2 km of the surface and 3.2 g/cm^3 at greater depths (Strange et al., 1965). The presence of abundant dunite xenoliths in olivine nephelinite vents of the Koolau crater led Sen (1983) to speculate that the dense Koolau plug represents deformed cumulate dunites and Fe-rich spinel pyroxenites frozen in the conduit. Primary CO_2 fluid inclusions in the dunite olivines suggest a maximum pressure of about 5 kbar (15 km depth) for the formation of these dunites (Roedder, 1965).

Conduit diameters estimated from gravity data are approximately 4 to 10 km for seven seamounts along the Bonin Arc (Ishihara, this volume), 5 km for Midway Atoll (Kroenke et al., 1966), 9 and 14 km for Sio Guyot (Figure 7), 17 km for Ita Mai Tai Guyot (Figure 6), and 7 to 17 km for Koolau Volcano on Oahu (Strange et al., 1965). Dense volcanic cores have also been recognized from gravity surveys of Manahiki Atoll, and Mangaia, Mauke, Mitiaro, Rarotonga, Atiu, Manuae, and Nassau Islands in the Cook Group (Robertson, 1967; 1970), Tutuila, Ofu, Olosega, and Tau Islands in American Samoa and Moorea Island in French Polynesia (Machesky, 1965). In Tahiti, positive gravity anomalies are centered over two exposed caldera cores of nepheline monzonites, theralites, and essexites (Williams,

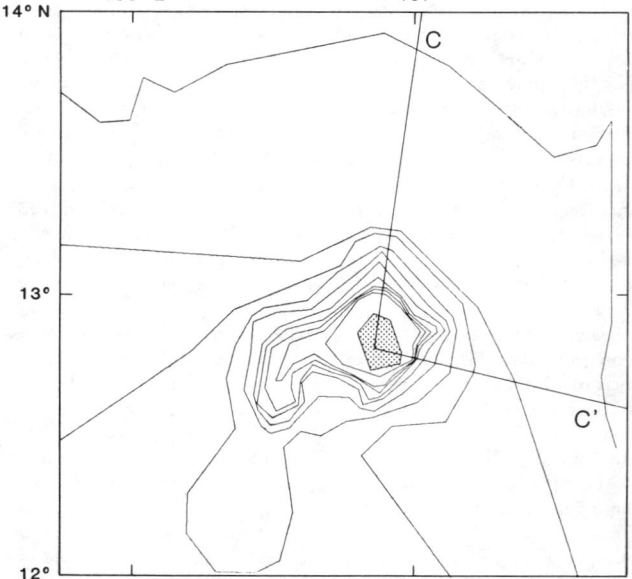

Fig. 4. Polygonal prism model of Ita Mai Tai Guyot (after Wedgeworth and Kellogg, this volume).

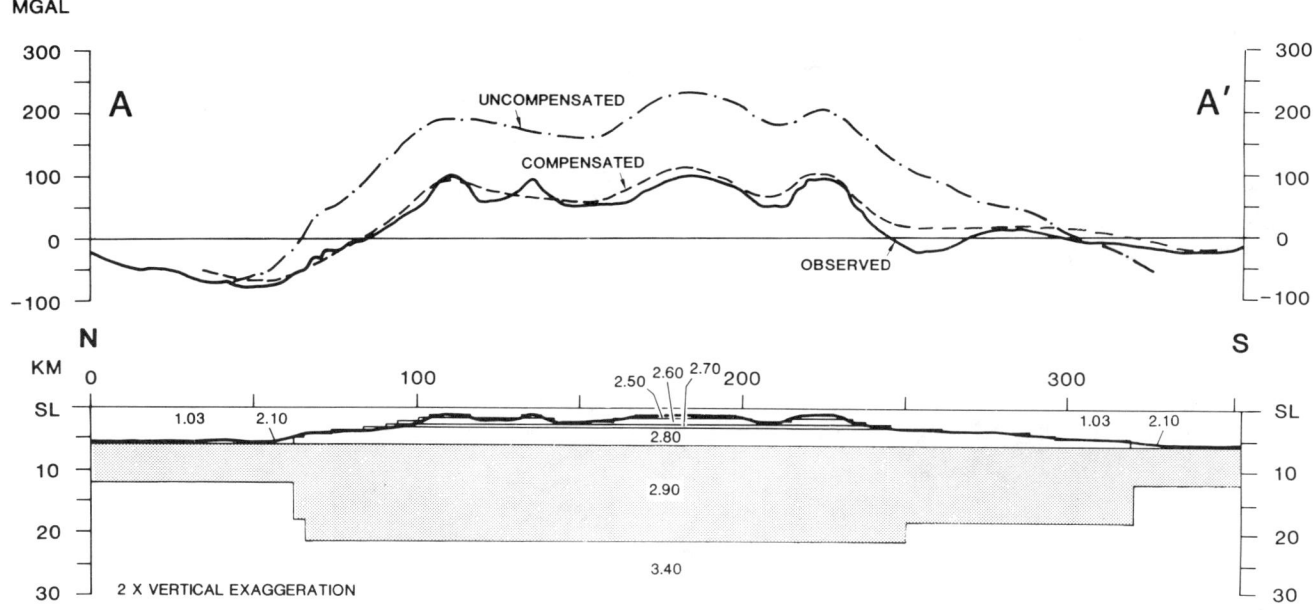

Fig. 5. Cross-section of the compensated density model for Sio Guyot showing observed and calculated free-air gravity anomalies for compensated and uncompensated models (Kellogg and Ogujiofor, 1985). Location shown in Figure 3.

1933; Machesky, 1965). These studies suggest that dense feeder pipes or volcanic conduits may be more common on volcanic islands and seamounts than previously thought, and may in fact be the norm.

Large positive gravity anomalies are located over active Kilauea and Mauna Loa craters on the island of Hawaii. On the basis of seismic activity and tilt data, Eaton (1962) has estimated that magma originates at a depth of 60 km below sea level and rises through a conduit to a magma chamber a few kilometers below the surface, where it remains until sufficient pressure is built up to cause an eruption. Hypocenters of earthquakes induced by the movement of magma define the fracture zone or conduit beneath Kilauea as elliptical in horizontal section with axial dimensions of 1 to 6 km (Ryan et al., 1981). Magma is then intruded from shallow magma chambers through dikes into the summit and east rift zone. P-wave traveltimes, positive gravity anomalies, and triangulation surveys suggest that the rift zone is spreading in response to magma intrusion (Swanson et al., 1976) forming a dense wedge of dikes and submarine pillow basalts covered by hyaloclastic products and subareal basalt flows (Hill and Zucca, 1987).

Generalized Three Dimensional Seamount Gravity Models

To determine whether varying local isostatic compensation levels could also explain the scatter in the gravity-depth function forother seamounts and islands in the western Pacific, we developed three-dimensional models for general cases.

The shapes of seamounts and islands were approximated with vertical-sided polygonal prisms in the form of right circular cones (conical seamounts) and frustrums of cones (guyots and islands) (Figures 8 and 9). The height to basal radius ratios $\xi = h/a_1$, (Figure 10) and the flatness ratios $f = a_2/a_1$ were estimated from wide-beam and side-scan bathymetric surveys of 63 seamounts and islands in the western Pacific. The mean height to basal radius ratio $\xi = 0.187 \pm 0.056$ was obtained by equally weighting the 28 estimates for seamounts with basal radius $a_1 < 25$ km. Jordan et al. (1983) calculated a similar mean ξ of 0.213 ± 0.011 from multibeam and wide-beam surveys of eastern Pacific seamounts. For 35 large western Pacific seamounts with $a_1 > 25$ km, $h = 0.007a_1 + 4254 \pm 488$ m. The decrease in h/a_1 for large seamounts does not reflect a decrease in slope but rather the predominance of flat-topped guyots and atolls. The average slope $\theta = 11 \pm 3°$ is independent of seamount size. There is considerable scatter in the flatnesses $f = a_2/a_1$ for the guyots and atolls. The 42-point sample has a mean of 0.40 ± 0.177.

Seafloor depth was assumed to be 6 km for the modeled seamounts. The edifices were given densities of 2.6 g/cm^3 and gravity anomalies were calculated for all five "uncompensated" models (Figure 8). The excess mass of the five model edifices was then assumed to be completely isostatically compensated by thickening of the crust (2.9 g/cm^3) beneath them, i.e. Airy isostasy, and gravity anomalies were calculated (Figure 8). Note that the model for the completely locally compensated atoll predicts that the crust mantle boundary lies at a depth of 31 km beneath the atoll. The calculated gravity field for the largest compensated model has negative anomalies flanking the edifice and the maximum amplitude (170 mgal) is 200 mgal lower than that calculated for the uncompensated model (370 mgal). This is approximately the range of gravity anomalies observed on western Pacific islands. In Figure 11 the maximum calculated gravity anomalies are plotted as a function of minimum depth to the tops of the models. As the depths to the seamounts increase, the predicted values converge.

We have also modeled seamounts using exact expressions for the on-axis vertical component of the gravity anomaly for a cone or a frustrum of a cone. This problem is one that has been considered before although this derivation was done independently. Previous efforts in this area include the derivation of the anomaly at points off-axis for a circular disk or vertical cylinder (Parasnis, 1961), for a right circular cone (Schwank and Lazarewicz, 1982), and the work of Moon (1981) and Jenkins et al. (1983) which have focused on deriving analytical expressions for more complex cases where the density is laterally varying. Our derivation assumes constant density for the structure, although more complex density distributions may be constructed by superposition.

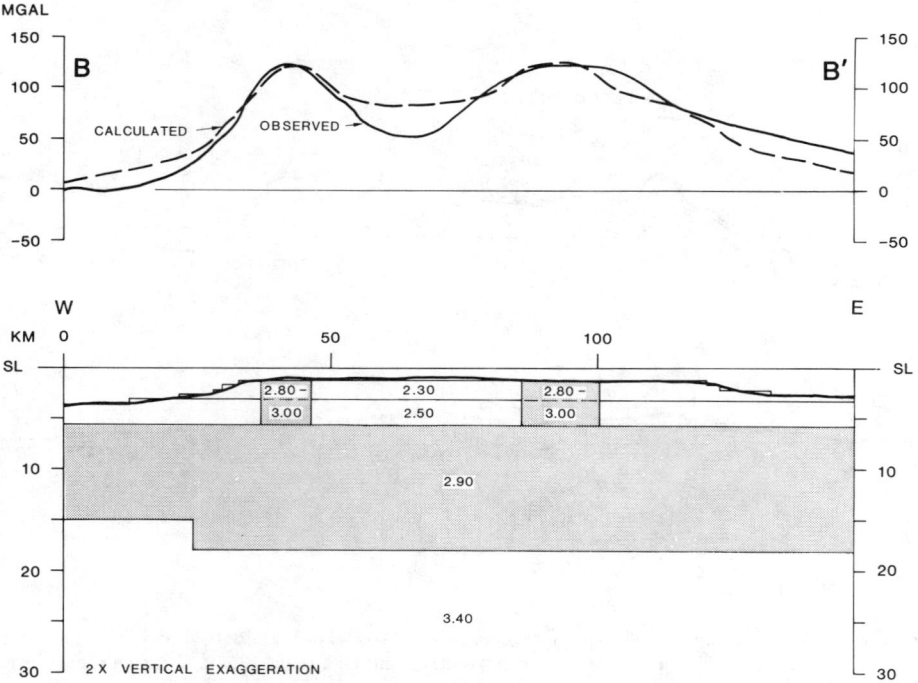

Fig. 6. Cross-section of the density model for Ita Mai Tai Guyot showing observed (solid line) and calculated (dashed line) gravity anomalies (Wedgeworth, 1985; Wedgeworth and Kellogg, this volume). Location shown in Figure 4.

We calculate the anomaly by stacking thin disks of varying radii atop each other and summing the anomaly due to each disk. If the radius of each disk varies linearly with the depth, then the structure obtained is either a cone or a frustrum of a cone. All disks are assumed to have the same density ρ. In the limit that the thickness of each disk becomes infinitesimal, the sum becomes an integral. The on-axis vertical gravitational attraction dg_z of a thin horizontal circular disk of thickness dz and radius a is

$$dg_z = 2\pi G(\rho - \rho_w)dz(1 - z/\sqrt{z^2 + a^2}) \qquad (1)$$

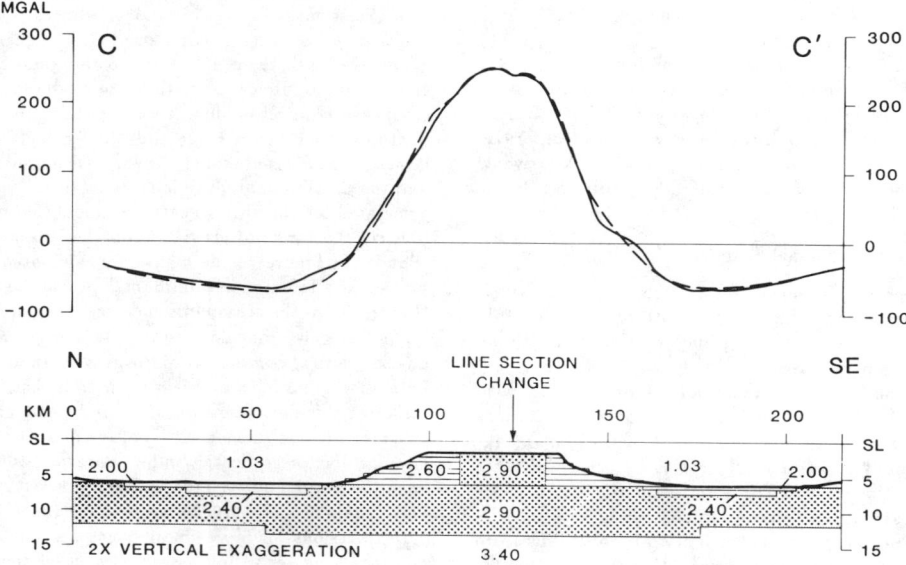

Fig. 7. Cross-section of Sio Guyot with two dense vertical prisms (Kellogg and Ogujiofor, 1985). Location shown in Figure 3.

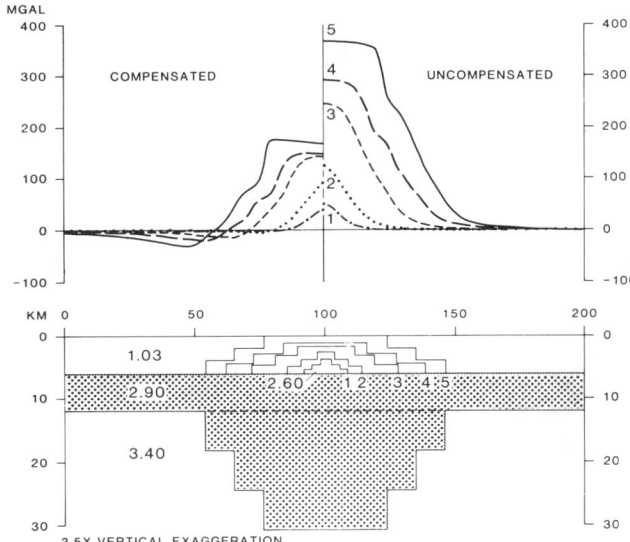

Fig. 8. Cross-sections of polygonal prism models. The calculated gravity is for isostatically compensated seamounts ($\mu = 100\%$) on the left and uncompensated seamounts ($\mu = 0$) on the right. A thickened crustal root is shown for a completely locally compensated atoll.

where G is the gravitational constant, ρ_w is the density of water and z is the depth (e.g. Rose and Bowman, 1974). If $a(z) = bz + c$ in the interval $[z_0, z_1]$, then

$$g_z(z_0, z_1) = \int_{z_0}^{z_1} dg_z \qquad (2)$$
$$= \int_{z_0}^{z_1} 2\pi G(\rho - \rho_w) \left[1 - \frac{z}{\sqrt{z^2 + (bz + c)^2}}\right] dz$$

The evaluation of this integral is straightforward. Writing

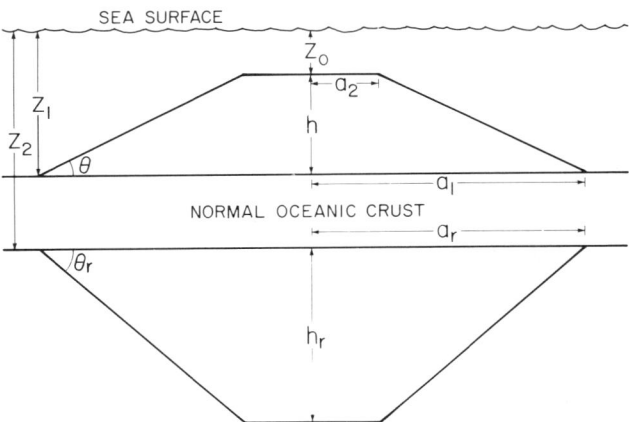

Fig. 9. Cross-section of a flat-topped seamount and thickened crustal root with cylindrical symmetry. Adopting the terminology of Jordan et al. (1983), its shape is described by the flatness $f = a_2/a_1$ and the height-to-radius ratio $\xi = h/a_1$.

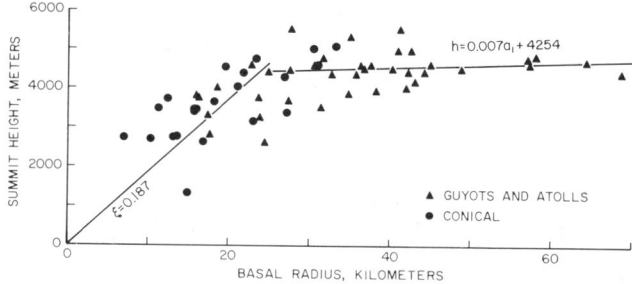

Fig. 10. Summit height h versus basal radius a_1 for 63 seamounts and islands in the western Pacific. For 28 small seamounts ($a_1 < 25$ km), the mean height-to-basal radius ration $\xi = 0.187 \pm 0.056$. For 35 large seamounts ($a_1 > 25$ km), $h = 0.007a_1 + 4254 \pm 488$ m.

$$I(z, b, c) = 2\pi G(\rho - \rho_w) \left[z - \frac{1}{\beta}\sqrt{z^2 + 2bcz/\beta^2 + c^2/\beta^2} \right.$$
$$\left. + \frac{bc}{\beta^3} \ln(z + \frac{bc}{\beta^2} + \sqrt{z^2 + 2bcz/\beta^2 + c^2/\beta^2})\right] \qquad (3)$$

where $\beta^2 = 1 + b^2$, then

$$g_z(z_0, z_1) = I(z_1, b, c) - I(z_0, b, c) \qquad (4)$$

If the slope of the seamount is θ, then $b = \cot\theta$ and $\beta = 1/\sin\theta$. If the radius a at some depth is known, then c can be determined: $c = a(z) - bz$. The calculated gravity-depth functions are plotted in Figure 11 for uncompensated conical seamounts of density 2.6 g/cm^3, slope = 10°, and seafloor depth = 6 km. Values are also shown for Airy compensated seamounts where the excess mass of the seamount edifice is locally compensated by a low density crustal root beneath the seamount (Figure 9). The gravity effect of the root is

$$g_r(z_2, z_2 + h_r) = I(z_2 + h_r, b_r, c_r) - I(z_2, b_r, c_r) \qquad (5)$$

where $z_2 - z_1$ = normal oceanic crustal thickness = 6 km, h_r = thickness of root, $a_r(z) = b_r z + c_r$ gives the radius of the root and $\Delta\rho = \rho_r - \rho_m = -0.5$ g/cm^3. Gravity values are also plotted for shallow (0-2km), flat-topped seamounts (guyots and atolls) with constant flatness ratios $f = a_2/a_1 = 0.37$ (Figure 9).

Figure 12 illustrates the seafloor depth dependence of the on-axis gravity anomalies. Sea surface gravity anomalies are calculated for uncompensated conical seamounts of density 2.3 g/cm^3, slope = 10° for seafloor depths of 1 to 6 km.

Free-air gravity-depth curves calculated from Equations (4) and (5) are superimposed on the observed data for 97 western Pacific seamounts in Figure 13. The curves were calculated for shallow (0-1.75 km) flat-topped seamounts, $f = 0.37$, and deeper (1.5-4.0 km) conical seamounts, $\theta = 10°$, $\rho = 2.6$ g/cm^3. The uncompensated curves shown are for a seafloor depth of 6 km; the compensated curves shown are for a seafloor depth of 4.5 km. The observed data for all 38 islands and atolls and for 55 of the 59 seamounts lies within the range of predicted values. In other words, about 96% of the wide variations in observed gravity signatures for western Pacific seamounts can be explained by different levels of Airy isostatic compensation. The three seamounts to the right of the predicted field (Suiko, Nintoku, and Unnamed) are all part of the Emperor chain and appear to have anomalously high mean densities (2.7 - 2.9 g/cm^3). The seamount to the left of the field (Chatauqua) is located on the Hawaiian arch.

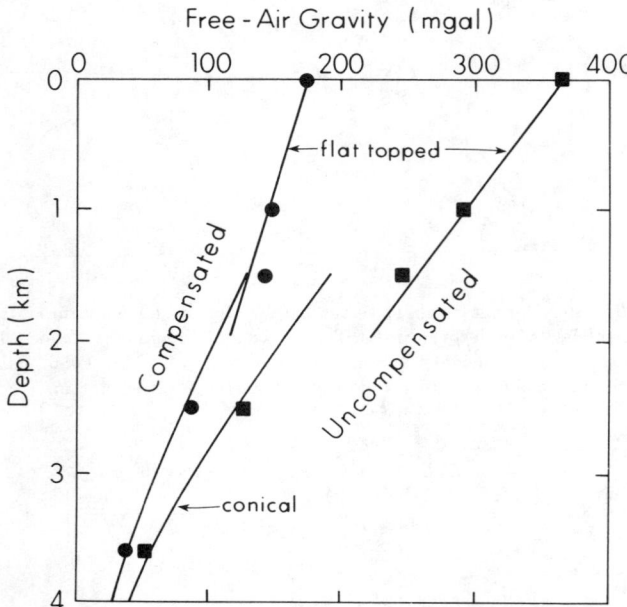

Fig. 11. Maximum calculated gravity anomalies versus minimum depth to seamount models. The squares and circles are for uncompensated ($\mu = 0$) and compensated ($\mu = 100\%$) polygonal prism models respectively (Figure 8). The solid lines are calculated from Equations (4) and (5) for deep conical seamounts ($\theta = 10°$, $z_1 = 6$ km, $z_2 = 12$ km) and shallow flat-topped seamounts ($f = 0.37$).

The abrupt increase in maximum gravity anomalies observed over seamounts shallower than 1.7 km (Figure 13) corresponds approximately to the depth range of guyots in the western Pacific.

Lithospheric Flexure and Crustal Intrusion

Isostatic compensation for seamounts and islands is probably achieved by lithospheric flexure and phase changes or sill intrusions in the lower crust. The gravity signatures that would be produced by lithospheric flexure or crustal intrusion are indistinguishable, so seismic data must be used to determine the compensation mechanism. Many investigations (See for example, Walcott, 1970; Watts et al., 1975) have been undertaken to study the deformation of the oceanic lithosphere by the weight of seamounts. The response of the oceanic lithosphere to long-term surface loads is modeled as that of an elastic plate overlying a weak fluid. Flexure of the lithosphere can explain much of the gravity signature of seamounts. However, a two-ship multichannel seismic experiment around Oahu (Watts et al., 1985) showed that much of the crustal thickening could not be explained by the simple flexural model. The wide-angle seismic profiles obtained by HIG and Lamont-Doherty Geological Observatory in August and September of 1982 show the M-discontinuity dipping 8 km to a depth of 19 km under the Hawaiian Ridge. Reflectors near the top of the crust, however, dip only 2 or 3 km to a depth of 7 or 8 km under the ridge. The remaining 5 or 6 km of crustal thickness may be tholeiitic (Watts et al., 1985) and plagioclase- bearing pyroxene (Sen, 1983) magma intruded into the crust under Oahu.

Isostatic Compensation and Age of Loading

As the oceanic lithosphere moves away from the ridge crest, it cools and thickens so that its effective elastic thickness is increased. Watts and Ribe (1984) noted that seamounts formed on young seafloor near ridge crests are often associated with short wavelength, low amplitude gravity anomalies, and thin effective elastic lithosphere thicknesses. It follows that seamounts formed on young seafloor near ridge crests should also be in local isostatic equilibrium.

We define the degree of local compensation μ as the ratio of the mass deficiency below the normal crust to the excess mass above the normal crust. Since the volume of a right circular cone is proportional to its height, it follows that the thickness of the low-density crustal root h_r (Figure 9) will be proportional to μ, $h_r = \mu h_{Airy}$, where h_{Airy} is the root thickness for a 100% compensated seamount. The free-air gravity anomaly due to the seamount plus the root is

$$g_{observed} = g_z(z_0, z_1) + g_r(z_2, z_2 + \mu h_{Airy}) \qquad (6)$$

Equation (6) can be inverted by an iterative process to determine the degree of compensation μ from the free air anomaly and the shape and depth of the seamount. The expression for g_r includes a term linear in μ and two terms non-linear in μ. We take the first approximation by ignoring the non-linear terms,

$$\mu_{(1)} = \frac{g_{observed} - g_z(z_0, z_1)}{2\pi G(\rho_m - \rho_c) h_{Airy}} \qquad (7)$$

where ρ_c is the density of the crustal root and ρ_m is the mantle density. We can then solve for μ by an iterative process using the equation

$$\mu_{(n+1)} = \mu_{(1)} + \frac{1}{\mu_{(n)} h_{Airy}} \left[\frac{1}{\beta_r} \sqrt{z^2 + 2 b_r c_r z/\beta_r^2 + c_r^2/\beta_r^2} \right.$$
$$\left. + \frac{b_r c_r}{\beta_r^3} \ln(z + \frac{b_r c_r}{\beta_r^2} + \sqrt{z^2 + 2 b_r c_r z/\beta_r^2 + c_r^2/\beta_r^2}) \right]_{z_2}^{z_2 + \mu_n h_{Airy}} \qquad (8)$$

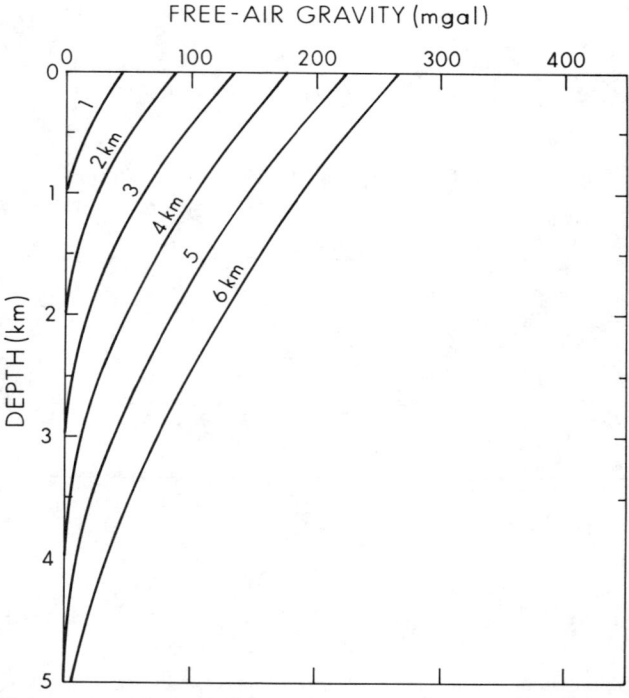

Fig. 12. On-axis gravity versus depth to seamount top for uncompensated conical seamounts of density 2.3 g/cm^3, slope $= 10°$, and seafloor depths of 1 to 6 km.

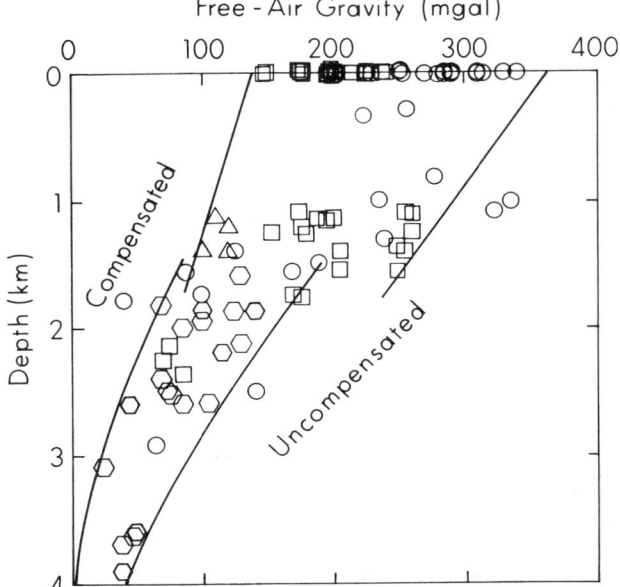

Fig. 13. Free-air gravity/depth curves calculated from Equations (4) and (5) superimposed on the observed data from Figure 1. The curves are calculated for shallow flat-topped seamounts, $f = 0.37$, and deeper conical seamounts, $\theta = 10°$, $\rho = 2.6 g/cm^3$. For uncompensated ($\mu = 0$) curves $z_1 = 6$ km; for compensated ($\mu = 100\%$) curves, $z_1 = 4.5$ km. About 96% of the observed data lies within this range of calculated values.

The algorithm converges more slowly for small structures because there is a smaller difference between the gravity signatures of small uncompensated seamounts and small compensated seamounts than for the corresponding difference for larger seamounts.

Table 1 shows estimates of μ and the age of the oceanic lithosphere at the time of loading t for five well-dated islands and one seamount. The estimated errors in μ are based on the following uncertainties: maximum FAA $\pm$ 10 mgal, $z_0 \pm$ 150 m, $z_1 \pm$ 300 m, $a_1 \pm$ 20%, and $a_2 \pm$ 20%. The uncertainty in the compensation estimate increases with increasing depth z_0, increasing μ, and with decreasing a_1, a_2, and $z_1 - z_0$.

Volcanic edifices erupted on young seafloor, such as Iceland or Galapagos (Isabela Island) are much closer to local isostatic equilibrium than edifices formed on old lithosphere, such as Hawaii and Pohnpei (Figure 14). The curve shown in Figure 14 is a least squares fit to the μ and $t^{1/2}$ values,

$$\mu(\%) = 68 - 5.6 t^{1/2} \qquad (9)$$

The standard deviation is $\pm$ 0.8 for the slope and $\pm$ 6.5 for the intercept. The curve is similar in shape to oceanic isotherms based on the cooling plate model (Parsons and Sclater, 1977) and elastic thickness of the lithosphere at the time of loading (Watts and Ribe, 1984). The similarity in shape suggests that the results of the isostatic compensation algorithm used in this study are quantitatively consistent with the predictions of the lithospheric flexure method and that some of the isostatic compensation is caused by flexure of the lithosphere. Several advantages of the method used here are that it does not rely on a particular mechanical model and it can be rapidly applied to large data sets (Kellogg and Freymueller, 1986).

Potassium-argon ages for 16 rock samples from Kusaie and Pohnpei range from 1.2 $\pm$ 0.1 to 8.6 $\pm$ 0.6 m.y. (Keating et al., 1984). Epp (1984) estimates the ages of loading t as approximately 152 and 160 m.y. respectively for Kusaie and Pohnpei. If correct, these ages double the duration of the window of vulnerability of the lithosphere to seamount formation proposed by Watts and Ribe (1984).

The results in Figure 14 have important implications for studies of the geological evolution of seamounts, oceanic islands, and the ocean basins. By determining the relative isostatic compensation level of a volcanic edifice, it should be possible to estimate the age of the seafloor t at the time the edifice was emplaced. Because of the slope of the curve in Figure 14, these estimates should be most reliable for $t < 30$ m.y. For example, Sio Guyot in the Mid-Pacific Mountains has a maximum FAA of 120 mgal, a minimum depth of 1130 m and average seafloor depth of 5550 m. Using Equation (8), $\mu = 71\% \pm 15\%$, and $h_r = 9.9$ km. The maximum calculated depth to the crust-mantle boundary is 21.5 km. This depth estimate compares well with the 22 $\pm$ 2 km estimate derived from detailed 3-dimensional modeling of Sio Guyot (Kellogg and Ogujiofor, 1985). From Equation (8) the age of loading t is 0-5 m.y., i.e. a ridge-crest origin. Tholeiites of the Mid-Pacific Mountains resemble lavas of Iceland and the Galapagos Islands. Kroenke et al. (1985) interpreted the orthogonal fault system, low gravity anomalies, and lava chemistry of the Mid-Pacific Mountains as the result of plateau eruption along an Early Cretaceous rift system followed by the formation of the upper edifices, including those of Sio Guyot 10 to 20 m.y. later.

Regional Clustering of Compensation Levels

Although variations in isostatic compensation levels can explain the observed range of gravity and geoid anomalies associated with

TABLE 1. Age of Loading and Parameters for Calculating Seamount Compensation

Seamount or Island	Observed Gravity g_{obs} (mgal)	Seafloor Depth z_1 (km)	f	ξ	Compensation μ (%)*	Age of Edifice t_e (myBP)	Age of Lithosphere t_l (myBP)	Age of Lithosphere at Time of Loading $t = t_l - t_e$ (my)**
Iceland	60	2.5	0.56	0.01	65 $\pm$ 10	0.0	5	5 $\pm$ 5
Galapagos***	120	3.0	0.63	0.03	44 $\pm$ 11	0.0	10	10 $\pm$ 2
Tahiti	230	4.4	0.33	0.07	23 $\pm$ 13	1.0	66	65 $\pm$ 5
Great Meteor	250	4.8	0.40	0.08	15 $\pm$ 17	11.0	84	73 $\pm$ 2
Hawaii	307	5.4	0.55	0.05	13 $\pm$ 09	0.0	92	92 $\pm$ 5
Pohnpei	290	4.75	0.27	0.07	3 $\pm$ 14	5.4	165	160 $\pm$ 10

*Computed assuming $z_o = 0$ (except Great Meteor 0.25), $z_2 = z_1 + 6$ km, $\rho_w = 1.03$ g/cm^3, $\rho = 2.6$ g/cm^3, $\rho_c = 2.9$ g/cm^3, and $\rho_m = 3.4$ g/cm^3 from Equation (10).
$f = a_2/a_1$ (Figure 9). $\xi = h/a_1$ (Figure 10).
**Reference for ages: Epp (1984) except Great Meteor from Verhoef (1984).
***Parameters for Isabela Island.

94 SEAMOUNT ISOSTATIC COMPENSATION

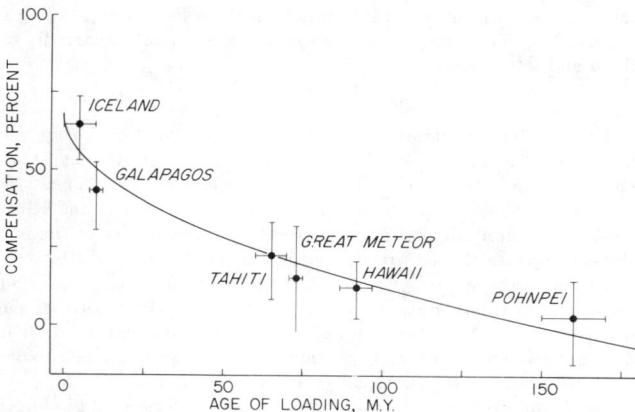

Fig. 14. Plot of degree of isostatic compensation μ against age of the lithosphere at the time of loading t from Table 1. The curve shown is $\mu(\%) = 68 - 5.6t^{1/2}$.

seamounts and islands, it would be impossible to predict bathymetry directly from satellite altimetry unless compensation levels are consistent and known for a region of the ocean.

In Figure 15 depth-corrected free-air gravity anomalies are contoured for seamounts in the western Pacific to see if there are systematic spatial variations in the seamount gravity-depth relationship. The gravity values were corrected for depth by subtracting $(3800 - z_0)/16$ from the observed maximum anomalies.

Seamounts in the East Mariana Basin have positive gravity anomalies, over 100 mgal, in sharp contrast to the negative anomalies, as low as -78 mgal, in the Marshall Island Group and in the Mid-Pacific Mountains. As discussed in this paper, detailed three-dimensional forward modeling of the gravity field for Sio Guyot in the Mid-Pacific Mountains shows that the negative residual may be accounted for by isostatic compensation. Inversion of the gravity field for Ita Mai Tai Guyot indicates that the positive residual may be explained by a lack of compensation. Such systematic spatial variations in compensation levels may be used to infer the tectonic origins (ridge crest versus mid-plate) and ages of seamount clusters.

Discussion

Detailed modeling of two large seamounts in the western Pacific, Sio and Ita Mai Tai Guyots, shows that the large contrast in their sea surface gravity fields is probably not a function of density differences in the two seamounts but rather a function of different depths to the crust-mantle boundary. The depths to the Moho are proportional to the Airy isostatic compensation levels for seamounts and, as predicted by elastic cooling plate models, are inversely proportional to the root of the seafloor age at the time of loading. However, a two-ship multichannel seismic experiment around Oahu (Watts et al., 1985) showed that much of the crustal thickening may not be explained by the simple flexural model. The crust may be thickened by the intrusion of large volumes of tholeiitic (Watts et al., 1985) and plagioclase-bearing

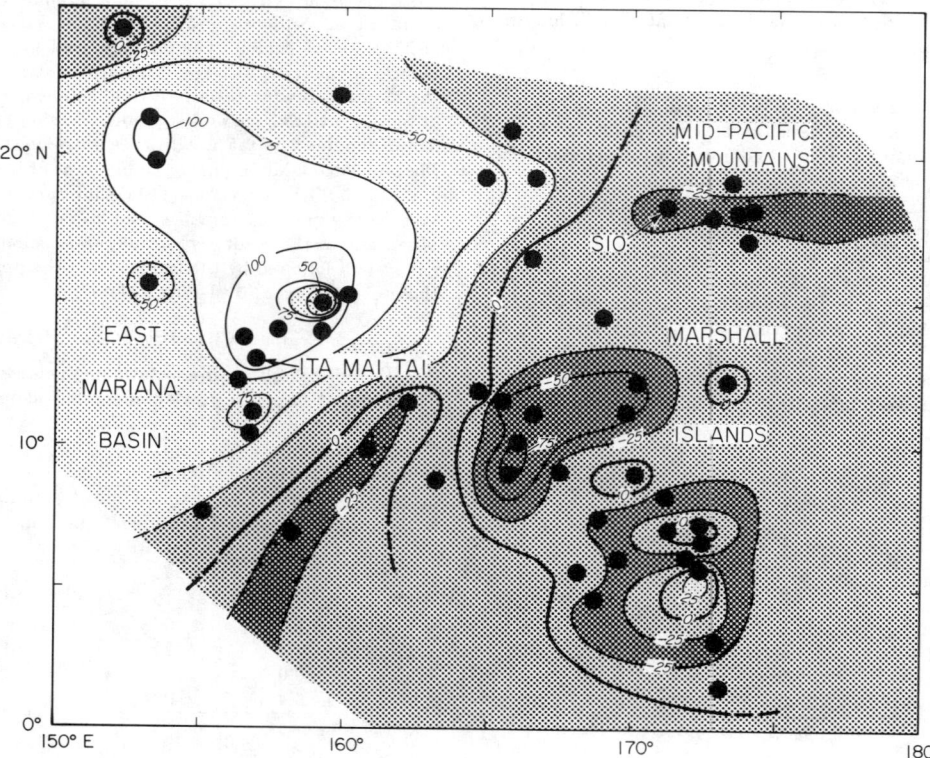

Fig. 15. Depth-corrected on-axis free-air gravity anomalies for seamounts in the western Pacific. The on-axis gravity values were corrected for depth by subtracting $(3800 - z_0)/16$ from the observed maximum anomalies. The discrete point gravity values were contoured to facilitate pattern recognition. Note the clustering of seamounts with positive gravity residuals in the East Mariana Basin.

pyroxene magma (Sen, 1983). Bending and thickening of the crust can explain the anomalously low gravity fields observed over many seamounts and islands that were previously interpreted as caused by magma chambers or thermal anomalies (e.g., Le Pichon and Talwani, 1964; Case et al., 1973).

It is impossible to completely explain the variability in seamount gravity signatures by different edifice densities. In fact, direct measurements of seamount and oceanic island rock densities, seismic compressional velocities, and inversion of the gravity fields over uncompensated seamounts suggest a mean density of 2.6 g/cm^3 with an uncertainty of only about $\pm$ 0.2 g/cm^3. From the gravity fields and bathymetry, Ishihara (this volume) determined the mean density of 19 seamounts in the Bonin Arc to be 2.66 $\pm$ 0.13 g/cm^3. These mean values are lower than the 2.8 g/cm^3 value common in the geophysical literature. Of the 97 seamounts included in this study, only three seamounts in the Emperor chain have anomalously high mean densities (2.7 - 2.9 g/cm^3).

Precise models of Ita Mai Tai (Figures 4 and 6) and Sio Guyots (Figures 3 and 7) and Oahu and Hawaii Islands show that dense conduits contribute substantially to the small wavelength observed sea surface gravity fields. The conduits are fracture zones 5 to 17 km in diameter containing dunites, spinel pyroxenites, nepheline monzonites, theralites, and essexites extending into the lower crust.

A simple method has been presented in this paper for the rapid estimation of seamount isostatic compensation levels. Seamounts are approximated as cones or frustrums of cones, and the observed on-axis vertical gravitational attraction is inverted by an iterative process (Equation 8) to determine the degree of Airy compensation. The algorithm is independent of mechanical assumptions regarding oceanic lithosphere, involves low computational costs, and is particularly useful for the rapid evaluation of large data sets. The results and associated uncertainties are comparable to those of detailed 3-dimensional models and frequency domain studies. The generalized forward problem can also be addressed using exact expressions for the on-axis vertical component of gravity for a cone or a frustrum of a cone. The predicted anomalies for compensated and uncompensated seamounts (Figure 11) converge rapidly at depths of 2 km or greater, making the inversion of the gravity values to estimate compensation levels or flexural parameters much more difficult for small deep edifices such as the Musicians Seamounts (Schwank and Lazarewicz, 1982; Dixon et al., 1983; Freedman and Parsons, 1986).

Because of the wide variation in observed geoid signatures of seamounts, a successful short-wavelength bathymetric transfer function for satellite altimeter data must be based on a statistically representative sample. The data presented in this paper shows the range of gravity/depth values for 97 well-surveyed seamounts in the western Pacific. A depth-corrected maximum free-air gravity anomaly map for seamounts in the western Pacific (Figure 15) suggests regional variations in isostatic compensation levels. Observed gravity and bathymetry can be readily inverted using the algorithm presented in this paper to estimate the compensation levels of well-surveyed seamounts. If the systematic spatial variations observed in the western Pacific are representative, then we can infer the tectonic origin of seamounts elsewhere and develop regional bathymetric-satellite altimetry transfer functions.

Acknowledgments. The first author is thankful to H. William Menard for introducing him to enigmas concerning Pacific seamount morphology in a seminar eleven years ago. We thank L.W. Kroenke and the scientists and crew of the R/V KANA KEOKI for their help in the collection of data from the Mid-Pacific Mountains and for introducing the first author to geophysics at sea. J.F. Campbell kindly provided unpublished gravity data for seamounts in the East Mariana Basin and the Marshall Island Group. J. Rose suggested generalizing seamount gravity models with exact expressions for gravity over right circular cones and frustrums of cones. W. Strange and G. Sen convinced us of the importance of dense conduit zones in the structures of seamounts and volcanic islands. The manuscript was improved with the helpful reviews of A. Lazarewicz and L. Dorman. S. Dang drafted most of the figures, K. Chainey and C. Yasui helped with the typing, and D. Henderson proofread the manuscript. This research was supported by the Office of Naval Research, Code 425GG. Hawaii Institute of Geophysics contribution no. 1866.

References

Case, J.E., S.L. Ryland, T. Simkin, and K.A. Howard, Gravitational evidence for a low-density mass beneath the Galapagos Islands, *Science, 181*, 1040-1042, 1973.

Dixon, T.H., M. Naraghi, M.K. McNutt, and S.M. Smith, Bathymetric prediction from SEASAT altimeter data, *J. Geophys. Res., 88*, 1563-1571, 1983.

Eaton, J.P., Crustal structure and volcanism in Hawaii, in *The Crust of the Pacific Basin, Geophys. Monogr. Ser.*, vol. 6, edited by G.A. Macdonald and H. Kuno, pp. 13-29, AGU, Washington, D.C., 1962.

Epp, D., Implications of volcano and swell heights for thinning of the lithosphere by hotspots, *J. Geophys. Res., 89*, 9991-9996, 1984.

Furumoto, A.S., and G.P. Woollard, Seismic refraction studies of the crustal structure of the Hawaiian Archipelago, *Pacific Science, 19*, 315-319, 1965.

Furumoto, A.S., N.J. Thompson, and G.P. Woollard, The structure of Koolau Volcano from seismic refraction studies, *Pacific Science, 19*, 306-314, 1965.

Furumoto, A.S., G.P. Woollard, J.F. Campbell, and D.M. Hussong, Variation in the thickness of the crust in the Hawaiian Archipelago, in *The Crust and Upper Mantle of the Pacific Area, Geophys. Monogr. Ser.*, vol. 12, edited by L. Knopoff, C.L. Drake, and P.J. Hart, pp. 94-111, AGU, Washington, D.C., 1968.

Freedman, A.P., and B. Parsons, Seasat-derived gravity over the Musicians Seamounts, *J. Geophys. Res., 91*, 8325-8340, 1986.

Harrison, J.C., and W.C. Brisbin, Gravity anomalies off the west coast of North America. 1: Seamount Jasper, *Geol. Soc. Amer. Bull., 70*, 929-934, 1959.

Hill, D.P., and J.J. Zucca, Constraints on the structure of Kilauea and Mauna Loa Volcanoes, Hawaii, and some implications for seismomagmatic processes, in *Transactions of Conference on how volcanoes work*, Hilo, Hawaii, 1987.

Ishihara, T., Gravimetric determination of densities of seamounts along the Bonin Arc, this volume.

Jenkins, A.J.O., D. Messfin, and W. Moon, Gravity modelling of salt domes and pinnacle reefs, *J. Canadian Soc. Expl. Geophys., 19*, 51-56, 1983.

Jordan, T.H., H.W. Menard, and D.K. Smith, Density and size distribution of seamounts in the eastern Pacific inferred from wide-beam sounding data, *J. Geophys. Res., 88*, 10508-10518, 1983.

Keating, B.H., D.P. Mattey, C.E. Helsley, J.J. Naughton, D. Epp, A. Lazarewicz, and D. Schwank, Evidence for a hot spot origin of the Caroline Islands, *J. Geophys. Res., 89*, 9937-9948, 1984.

Kellogg, J.N., and I.J. Ogujiofor, Gravity field analysis of Sio Guyot: An isostatically compensated seamount in the Mid-Pacific Mountains, *Geo- Marine Letters, 5*, 91-97, 1985.

Kellogg, J.N., and J.T. Freymueller, Isostatic compensation of western Pacific seamounts (abstract), *Eos Trans. AGU, 67*, 1229, 1986.

Kinoshita, W.T., H.L. Krivoy, D.R. Mabey, and R.R. MacDonald, Gravity survey of the Island of Hawaii, *U.S. Geol. Surv. Prof. Pap., 475-C*, 114-116, 1963.

Kroenke, L.W., D.A. Walker, and G.L. Maynard, Gravity measurements of Midway Island and reef (abstract), *Proceedings of the Eleventh Pacific Science Congress*, Tokyo, 1966.

Kroenke, L.W., J.N. Kellogg, and K. Nemoto, Mid-Pacific Mountains revisited, *Geo-Marine Letters*, *5*, 77-81, 1985.

Laughton, A.S., M.N. Hill, and T.D. Allan, Geophysical investigations of a seamount 150 miles north of Madeira, *Deep-Sea Research*, *7*, 117-141, 1960.

Lazarewicz, A.R., and D.C. Schwank, Locating uncharted seamounts using satellite altimetry, *Geophys. Res. Lett.*, *9*, 385-388, 1982.

Lewis, B.T.R., and L.R. Dorman, Experimental Isostasy II: An isostatic model for the U.S.A. derived from gravity and topographic data, *J. Geophys. Res.*, *75*, 3367-3386, 1970.

LePichon, X., and M. Talwani, Gravity survey of a seamount near 35°N 46°W in the North Atlantic, *Marine Geology*, *2*, 262-277, 1964.

Machesky, L.F., Gravity relations in American Samoa and the Society Islands, *Pacific Science*, *19*, 367-373, 1965.

Manghnani, M.H., and G.P. Woollard, Ultrasonic velocities and related elastic properties of Hawaiian basaltic rocks, *Pacific Science*, *19*, 291-295, 1965.

Moon, W., A new method of computing geopotential fields, *Geophys. J. Roy. Astron. Soc.*, *67*, 735-746, 1981.

Nafe, J.E., and C.L. Drake, Physical properties of marine sediments, in *The Sea*, vol. 3, edited by M.N. Hill, pp. 85-102, John Wiley and Sons, New York, 1963.

Nayudu, Y.R., A new hypothesis for the origin of guyot and seamount terraces, in *The Crust of the Pacific Basin, Geophys. Monogr. Ser.*, vol. 6, edited by G.A. Macdonald and H. Kuno, pp. 171-180, AGU, Washington, D.C., 1962.

Nemoto, K., and L.W. Kroenke, Sio Guyot: a complex volcanic edifice in the western Mid-Pacific Mountains, *Geo-Marine Letters*, *5*, 83-89, 1985.

Nettleton, L.L., Determination of density for reduction of gravimeter observations, *Geophysics*, *4*, 176-183, 1939.

Officer, C.G., M. Ewing, and P.C. Wuenschel, Seismic refraction measurements in the Atlantic Ocean Basin. 4: Bermuda, Bermuda Rise, and Nares Basin, *Geol. Soc. Amer. Bull.*, *63*, 777-808, 1952.

Parasnis, D.S., Exact expressions for the gravitational attraction of a circular lamina at all points of space and of a right circular vertical cylinder at points external to it, *Geophysical Prospecting*, *9*, 382, 1961.

Parsons, B., and J.G. Sclater, An analysis of the variation of ocean floor bathymetry and heat flow with age, *J. Geophys. Res.*, *82*, 803-828, 1977.

Plouff, D., Gravity and magnetic fields of polygonal prisms and application to magnetic terrain corrections, *Geophysics*, *41*, 727-741, 1976.

Raitt, R.W., Bikini and nearby atolls. 3: Geophysics, Seismic refraction studies of Bikini and Kwajalein Atolls and Sylvania Guyot, *U.S. Geol. Surv. Prof. Pap.*, *260K*, pp. 507-524, 1954.

Robertson, E.I., Gravity survey in the Cook Islands, *N.Z. J. Geol. Geophys.*, *10*, 1484-1498, 1967.

Robertson, E.I., Additional gravity surveys in the Cook Islands, *N.Z. J. Geol. Geophys.*, *13*, 184-198, 1970.

Roedder, E., Liquid CO_2 inclusions in olivine-bearing nodules and phenocrysts from basalts, *Am. Mineral.*, *50*, 1740-1782, 1965.

Rose, J.C., and B.R. Bowman, The effect of seamounts and other bottom topography on marine gravity anomalies, in *Proceedings of the International Symposium on Applications of Marine Geodesy, Marine Technology Society*, 381-396, 1974.

Ryan, M.P., R.Y. Kyonanagi, and R.S. Fiske, Modeling the three-dimensional structure of macroscopic magma transport systems: application to Kilauea volcano, Hawaii, *J. Geophys. Res.*, *86*, 7111-7129, 1981.

Sager, W.W., G.T. Davis, B.H. Keating, and J.A. Philpotts, A geophysical and geologic study of Nagata Seamount, northern Line Islands, *Journal Geomagnetism and Geoelectricity*, *34*, 283-305, 1982.

Schwank, D.C., and A.R. Lazarewicz, Estimation of seamount compensation using satellite altimetry, *Geophys. Res. Lett.*, *9*, 907-910, 1982.

Scientific Party, Leg 89, Leg 89 drills Cretaceous volcanics, *Geotimes*, *28*, 17-20, 1983.

Sen, G., A petrologic model for the constitution of the upper mantle and crust of the Koolau shield, Oahu, Hawaii, and Hawaiian magmatism, *Earth Planet. Sci. Lett.*, *62*, 215-228, 1983.

Shor, G.G., and D.D. Pollard, Mohole site selection studies north of Maui, *J. Geophys. Res.*, *69*, 1627-1637, 1964.

Strange, W.E., G.P. Woollard, and J.C. Rose, An analysis of the gravity field over the Hawaiian Islands in terms of crustal structure, *Pacific Science*, *19*, 381-389, 1965.

Suyenaga, W., Isostasy and flexure of the lithosphere under the Hawaiian Islands, *J. Geophys. Res.*, *84*, 5599-5604, 1979.

Swanson, D.A., W.A. Duffield, and R.S. Fiske, Displacement of the south flank of the Kilauea volcano: the result of forceful intrusion of magma into the rift zones, *U.S. Geol. Surv. Prof. Pap.*, *963*, 39 p., 1976.

Talandier, J., and E.A. Okal, Crustal structure in the Society and Tuamotu Islands, French Polynesia, *Geophys. J. Roy. Astron. Soc.*, in press.

Vogt, P.R., B. Zondek, P.W. Fell, N.Z. Cherkis, and R.K. Perry, Seasat altimetry, the North Atlantic geoid, and evaluation by shipborne subsatellite profiles, *J. Geophys. Res.*, *89*, 9885-9903, 1984.

Walcott, R.I., Flexural rigidity, thickness, and viscosity of the lithosphere, *J. Geophys. Res.*, *75*, 3941-3954, 1970.

Watts, A.B., and N.M. Ribe, On geoid heights and flexure of the lithosphere at seamounts, *J. Geophys. Res.*, *89*, 11152-11170, 1984.

Watts, A.B., J.R. Cochran, and G. Selzer, Gravity anomalies and flexure of the lithosphere: a three-dimensional study of the Great Meteor Seamount, Northeast Atlantic, *J. Geophys. Res.*, *80*, 1391-1398, 1975.

Watts, A.B., U.S. ten Brink, P. Buhl, and T.M. Brocher, A multichannel seismic study of lithospheric flexure across the Hawaiian-Emperor seamount chain, *Nature*, *315*, 105-111, 1985.

Wedgeworth, B.S., Ita Mai Tai Guyot: A comparative geophysical study of western Pacific seamounts, M.S. thesis, 90 pp., Univ. Hawaii, 1985.

Wedgeworth, B.S., and J.N. Kellogg, A 3-D gravity-tectonic study of Ita Mai Tai Guyot, an uncompensated seamount in the East Mariana Basin, this volume.

Williams, H., Geology of Tahiti, Moorea, and Maiao, *Bishop Museum Bull.*, *105*, 3-74, 1933.

Woollard, G.P., The interrelationships of crustal and upper mantle parameter values in the Pacific, *Rev. Geophys. Space Phys.*, *13*, 87-137, 1975.

Zucca, J.J., D.P. Hill, and R.L. Kovach, Crustal structure of Mauna Loa volcano, Hawaii, from seismic refraction and gravity data, *Bull. Seism. Soc. Amer.*, *72*, 1535-1550, 1982.

GRAVIMETRIC DETERMINATION OF DENSITIES OF SEAMOUNTS ALONG THE BONIN ARC

Takemi Ishihara

Geological Survey of Japan, 1-1-3 Higashi, Yatabe, Ibaraki, 305 Japan

Abstract. A new term 'effective depth' is defined as the water depth including the nonlinear effect on a complete Bouguer correction. A least-squares method is used to determine the densities of seamounts from the linear relationship between free-air anomaly and the effective depth, which is calculated by applying a two-dimensional FFT to the bathymetric data. Densities of 19 seamounts along the Bonin Arc are determined using this least-squares method. For seven seamounts including two calderas and two islands, the densities are recalculated removing gravity effects of simple inner structures, which are inferred from the apparent density variations as functions of search radii. Generally speaking, with a track spacing less than 3 nautical miles and with a range of effective depths greater than 1 km, the densities can be determined with an accuracy of 0.05 g/cc. The determined densities have a wide range from 2.4 to nearly 3.0 g/cc. A relationship is recognized between densities of seamounts and their mean depths: the density increases with the depth and a prominent change in the rate of increase is seen at a depth of about 1 km. This is probably due to a decrease in porosity with increase in the depth. A clear pattern of densities is recognized for seamounts with mean depths of about 2 km: a density lower than 2.67 g/cc corresponds to an andesitic volcano and a density higher than 2.67 g/cc corresponds to a basaltic volcano. Two calderas are associated with high Bouguer anomalies.

Introduction

Density of a mountain can be calculated from distribution of gravity values at many points with various heights on and around the mountain. The most simple method of density determination is probably the density profiling method proposed by Nettleton (1939). He drew several Bouguer anomaly curves with various values of density along a traverse. He chose the density for the curve that showed the least correlation with the topography. A least-squares method is mathematically more rigorous. Parasnis (1952) proposed a method, in which, based on an assumption of a linear relation between a free-air anomaly and a complete Bouguer correction with a density of unity, the density is obtained by the slope of the straight line determined by the least-squares of the former data plotted against the latter. He applied this method to determine densities of various geologic formations in English

Copyright 1987 by the American Geophysical Union.

Midlands and obtained fairly good agreements with the laboratory measurements of rock samples from the same formations.

We can apply the same methods to problems in the sea. Although there are many seamounts in ocean basins, very few density values have been determined by the gravity method, and most of them have been obtained by the density profiling method (e.g., Harrison and Brisbin, 1959; Segawa, 1970; Tomoda and Fujimoto, 1981). A least-squares method was used by Sager et al. (1982) to determine the density of 2.48±0.02 g/cc for Nagata Seamount, northern Line Islands. This is a rare case of using least-squares method for determining seamount density. This is probably due to the difficulty of obtaining accurate gravity measurements at sea and also due to the scarcity of detailed sea bottom topographic measurements. Accuracy of the order of 1 mgal has been attained by recent sea gravimeters if combined with good navigation data (Valliant, 1983; Bell and Watts, 1986; Ishihara, 1983), and detailed sea floor topography can be obtained by Sea Beam or similar echo-sounders.

The Bonin Arc is an island arc system in the Western Pacific located between the Northeast Japan Arc and the Mariana Arc. The Bonin Ridge, the Shichito Ridge and the Izu Ridge trend north-south parallel to the Bonin Trench and are mostly submerged. There are many seamounts along the Shichito Ridge (active volcanic chain) and the Izu Ridge (Fig.1). Using detailed bathymetric and gravimetric surveys of this region, I determine the densities of seamounts along the active Shichito Ridge and the young Izu Ridge applying a least-squares method similar to that of Parasnis (1952).

Previous gravity studies have revealed that many volcanoes (including calderas), seamounts, volcanic islands do not have homogeneous density structures. Many volcanoes in Hawaii were interpreted to have high density volcanic pipes (Strange et al., 1965). Gravity surveys of volcanic islands in the Cook Islands are consistent with models of high density cores with radii equal to the radii of the islands (Robertson, 1967, 1970). Low density materials were inferred beneath the centers of many calderas in Japan (Yokoyama, 1963; Ishihara, 1977). Kellogg and Ogujiofor (1985) inferred two dense eruptive centers beneath the northern summit of Sio Guyot, western Mid Pacific Mountains, while Le Pichon and Talwani (1964) found a Bouguer anomaly minimum over a saddle between two seamount peaks in the North Atlantic Ocean, and interpreted it as due to a secondary magma chamber. Some seamounts in the Bonin Arc are also inferred to have high density 'roots' as described later in this paper.

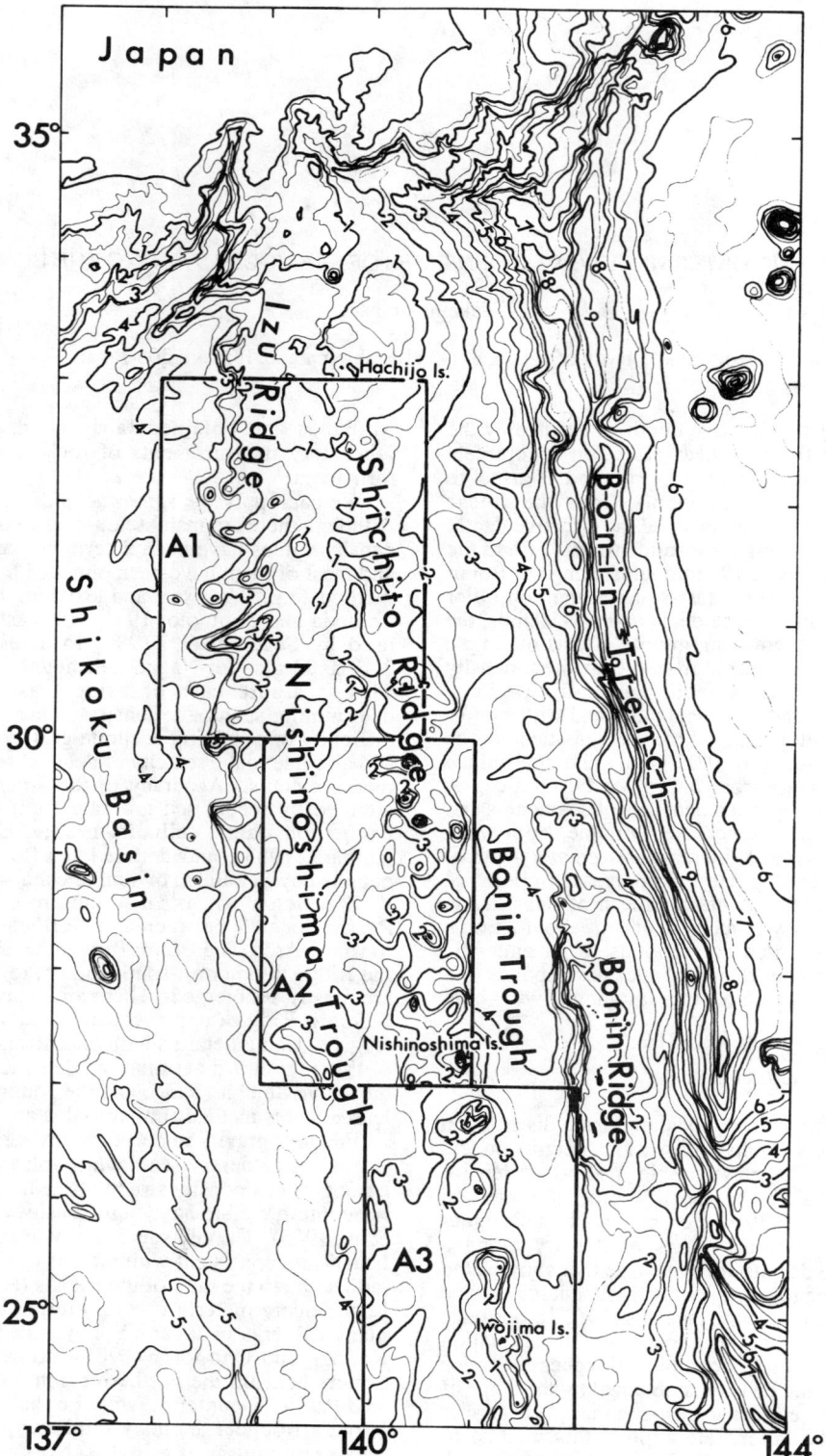

Fig. 1. Bathymetric map of the Bonin Arc. Contours at 500 m interval are drawn by using data compiled by the Japan Hydrographic Department.

Method of Density Determination

The procedure of density determination used in this paper will be shown with an example of Seamount A.

Gravity Effect of Seamount Topography

Parker (1972) showed that a Fourier transform of gravity attraction can be expressed as a sum of Fourier transforms of powers of topography. If we take a cartesian co-ordinate system with the direction of z downwards, and consider the gravity effect of the seawater with the bottom topographic surface $z=d(x,y)=D+h(x,y)$ (i.e., the negative of the complete Bouguer correction at sea), the gravity effect $g(x,y)$ at a point $(x,y,0)$ on the sea surface becomes:

$$g(x,y)=-2\pi G\Delta\rho\, d_{eff}(x,y), \qquad (1)$$
$$d_{eff}(x,y)=D+h'(x,y), \qquad (2)$$

$$F[h'(x,y)]=\exp(-kD)\sum_{n=1}^{\infty}[(-k)^{n-1}/n!]F[h^n(x,y)], \qquad (3)$$

where G is Newton's gravitational constant and F[] denotes a

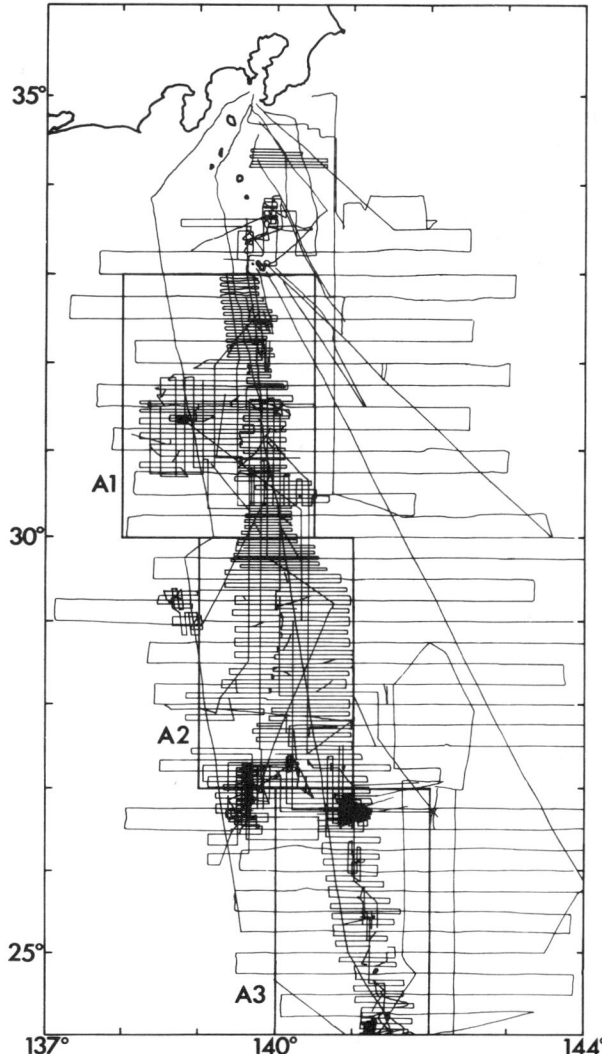

Fig. 2. Geophysical survey tracks of the Bonin Arc conducted by the Geological Survey of Japan by using the R/V Hakurei-maru.

Data

The Geological Survey of Japan conducted regional geological and geophysical surveys of the Bonin Arc in 1979 (Honza et al., 1981; Honza and Tamaki, 1985), and more extensive surveys in 1984-1985. All data have been obtained by the R/V Hakurei-maru. The typical spacing of the survey tracks is 2 to 3 nautical miles (Fig.2). The gravity data were obtained by using a LaCoste and Romberg air-sea gravimeter with a gyro-stabilized platform. The bathymetric data were obtained with a conventional 12 kHz precision depth recorder.

Four seamounts (Seamounts A to D) along the Izu Ridge and 15 seamounts including small islands and calderas (Seamounts E to S) along the Shichito Ridge are analyzed in this paper (Fig.3a-c). They are generally associated with positive free-air anomalies of 50 to 100 mgal higher than the surrounding regional values (Fig.4a-c).

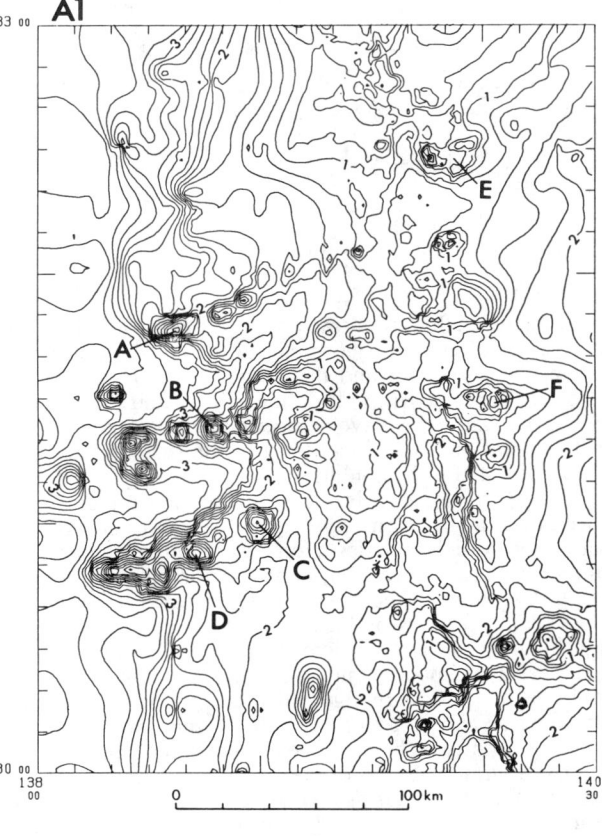

Fig. 3a.

Fig. 3. Sea bottom topography in km of the Bonin Arc contoured using the data obtained by the Geological Survey of Japan. A to S denote the seamounts studied in this paper. (a) Northern area A1; (b) middle area A2; (c) southern area A3 in Fig. 1 and in Fig. 2.

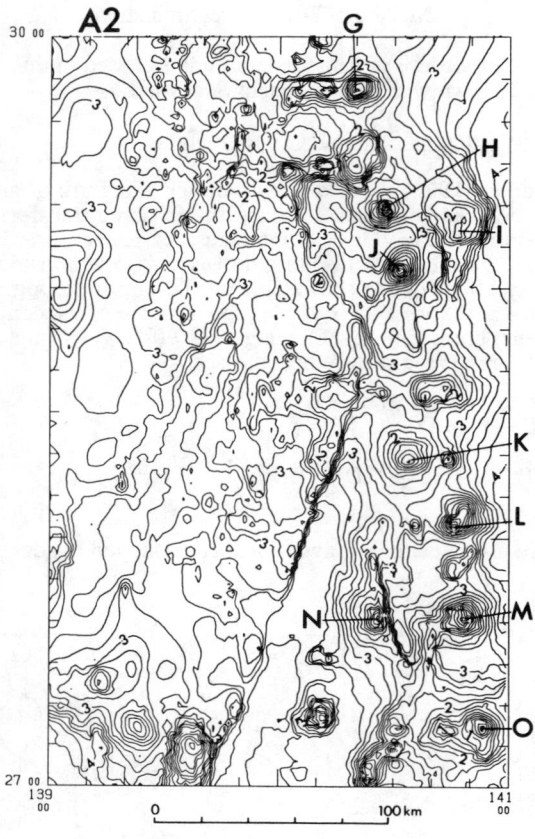

Fig. 3b.

and longitude (about 0.5 km spacing). Where there are no data, grid values are interpolated following the minimum curvature method of Briggs (1974). Each data set, therefore, consists of 180 x 180 gridded points. The contoured bathymetric map around Seamount A obtained from the gridded data is shown in Fig.5. The application of the fast Fourier transform (FFT) method is more feasible with 256 x 256 gridded points. This is done by filling the remaining array points with the values at the edges of the gridded array. Effective depths are calculated from these gridded topographic data by using (2) and (3) with the application of the two-dimensional FFT described above (Fig.6).

It is obvious that short wavelength components of the bathymetric topography (Fig.5) are subdued in the map of the effective depths (Fig.6). Roughly speaking, an effective water depth $d_{eff}(x,y)$ is expressed as an average of water depths of an area around the point (x,y). Owing to this high-cut filtering, the effective depths for tops of seamounts become greater than the corresponding water depths (e.g., the top of Seamount A, which is shallower than 800 m, has an effective water depth greater than 1400 m), while the effective depths for deeps become shallower. If the average water depth becomes deeper, the effect of this high-cut filtering extends to longer wavelengths. Seamount X, which is located in a basin deeper than 3500 m, therefore gives a high in the effective depths much less than Seamount B does, which has an almost the same relative height and an almost the same

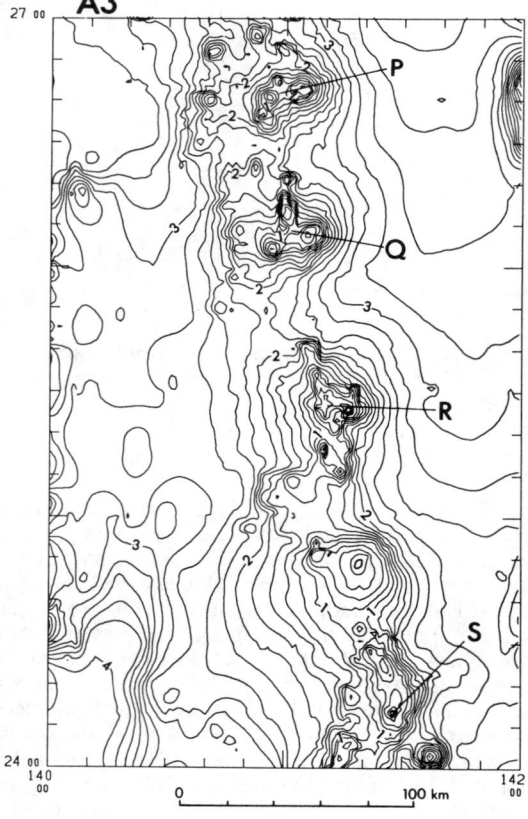

Fig. 3c.

two-dimensional Fourier transform. Equation (1) shows that the gravity effect is proportional to the density contrast Δρ between the seafloor and the seawater. Here a new term, 'effective depth' $d_{eff}(x,y)$ is defined by (2) and (3). Equation (3) means that in the wave number domain, the gravity effect includes not only the linear term of the surface topography $F[h(x,y)]$ but also the nonlinear terms. If we replace $d_{eff}(x,y)$ by $d(x,y)$ in (1), this is a formula of a simple Bouguer correction apart from the sign. A complete Bouguer correction, which includes a terrain correction as well as the simple Bouguer correction, is proportional not to the water depth $d(x,y)$ but to the effective water depth $d_{eff}(x,y)$. So, $d_{eff}(x,y)$ is understood as a water depth including the nonlinearity in a complete Bouguer correction. This nonlinearity is important in the calculation of the gravity effect of large amplitude topographic features like seamounts. However as shown by Parker (1972), this series converges very rapidly if we choose D near the mean of the maximum and the minimum depths of the topography. In the following analysis I take only terms n=1 to 10. Trial calculations with terms n=1 to 20 showed no significant change to the result.

Actual calculation of the Fourier transform in this paper is done as follows. At first, gridded topographic data are calculated from the echo-sounder data obtained simultaneously with the gravity measurements. The bathymetric data are gridded in a 1°x1° area around each seamount with a spacing of 1/3 minute along lines of latitude (about 0.6 km spacing)

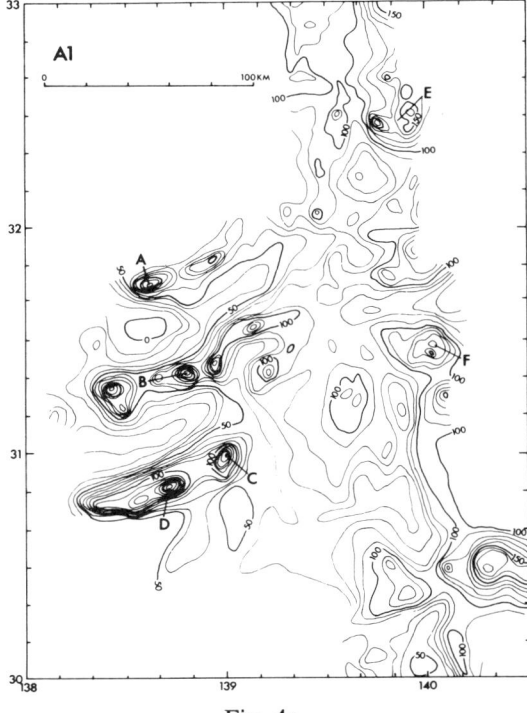

Fig. 4a.

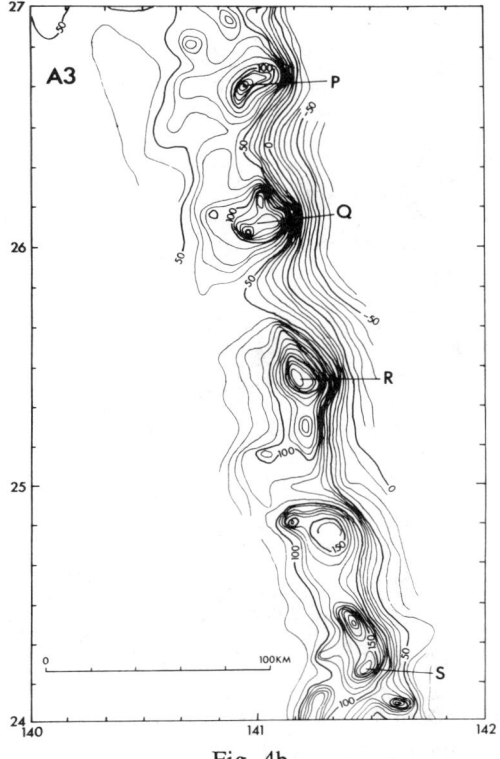

Fig. 4b.

Fig. 4. Free-air gravity anomalies in mgal of the Bonin Arc. (a) Northern area A1; (b) middle area A2; (c) southern area A3 in Fig. 1 and in Fig. 2.

horizontal dimension but located in an area shallower than 2500 m.

Least-Squares Method for Density Determination

If there is no heterogeneous density structure within and around a seamount, a free-air anomaly $g(x,y)$ can be expressed as follows:

$$g(x,y) = -2\pi G \Delta\rho d_{eff}(x,y) + C_x x + C_y y + C, \quad (4)$$

where the first term in the right hand side is the gravity effect due to the seamount topography which is the same as (1) and can be calculated by using the two-dimensional FFT method described in the previous section. The rest of the right hand side of (4) is a regional gravity anomaly approximated as a planar function of x and y.

Using all (=n) gravity data within a definite distance (called henceforth the 'search radius') from the center of the seamount, we can apply a linear least-squares method to (4) with unknowns $\Delta\rho$, C_x, C_y and C:

$$-2\pi G \Delta\rho d_{eff}(x_i, y_i) + C_x x_i + C_y y_i + C = g_i - e_i \quad (i=1, 2,...,n), \quad (5)$$

where e_i is the error of the i-th observation. The four unknowns are determined so as to minimize the sum of the squares of errors e_i^2. We can rewrite (5) as follows:

$$-2\pi G \Delta\rho d_{eff}(x_i, y_i) + C = g_i' - e_i \quad (i=1, 2,...,n), \quad (6)$$

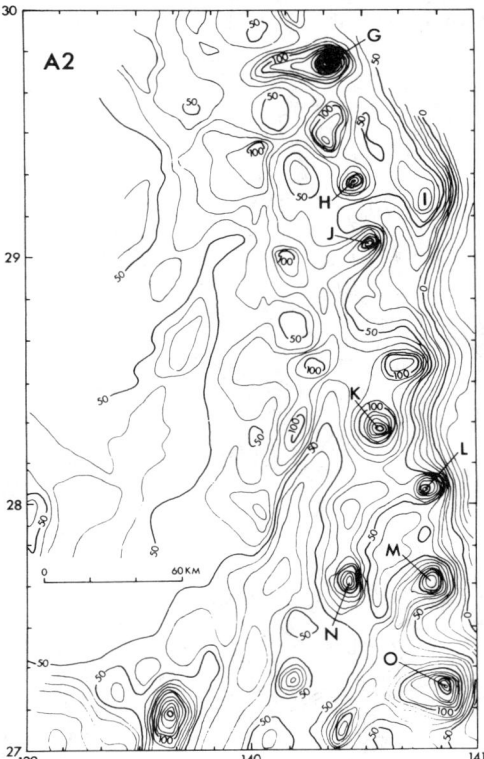

Fig. 4c.

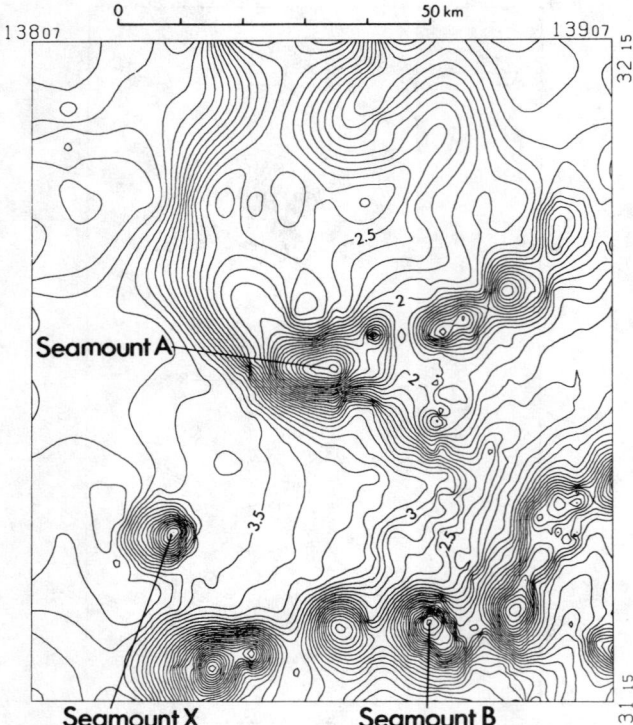

Fig. 5. Bathymetric map of the area of one degree x one degree around Seamount A. Water depth in km. Contours were drawn by using the 180 x 180 gridded bathymetric data.

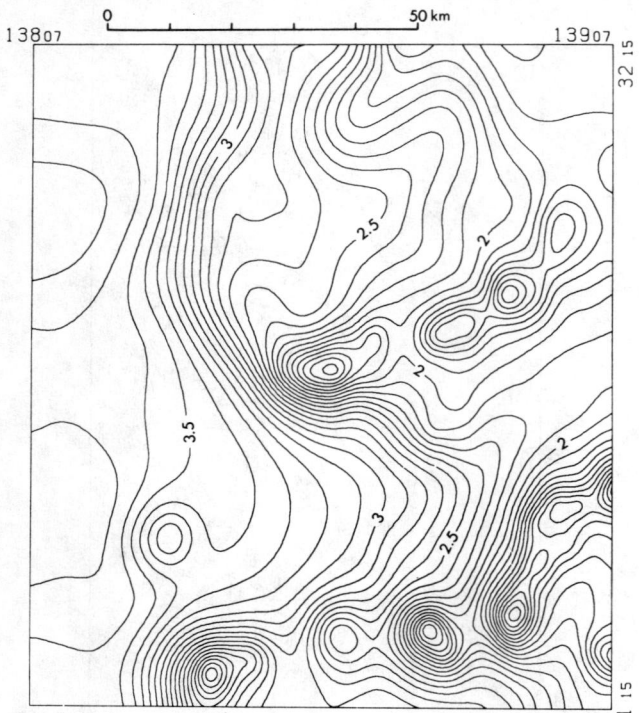

Fig. 6. Effective depths of the same area as in Fig. 5 calculated applying the two-dimensional FFT method to the 180 x 180 gridded bathymetric data shown in Fig. 5.

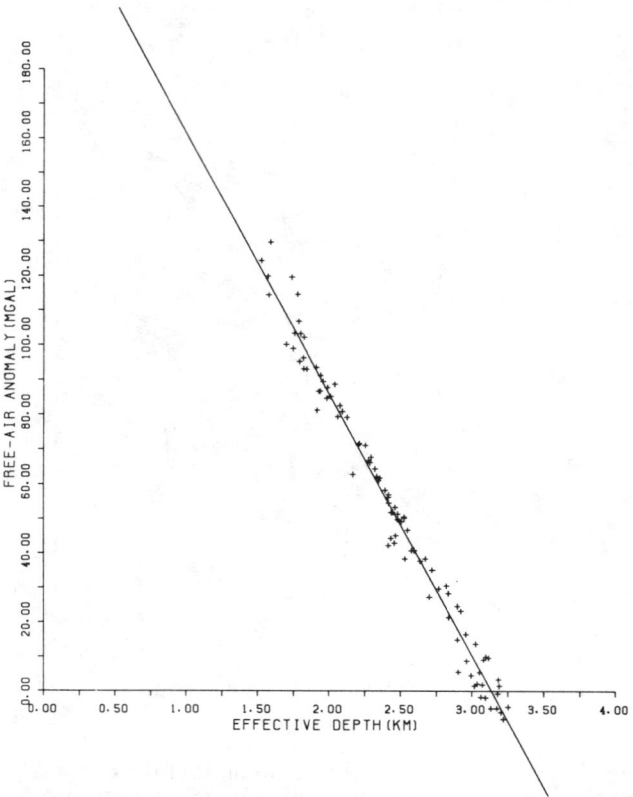

Fig. 7. Free-air anomaly versus effective depth plot for the search radius of 15 km from the center of Seamount A.

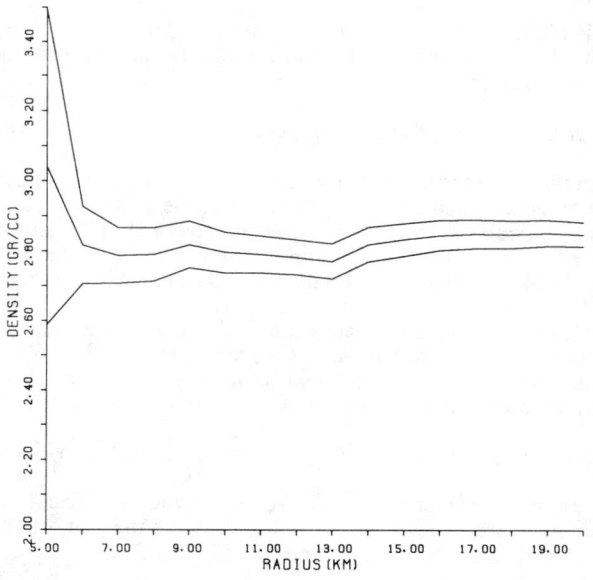

Fig. 8. Density as a function of search radius. The middle curve corresponds to the determined density, while the 1σ error of the density is expessed by the other two.

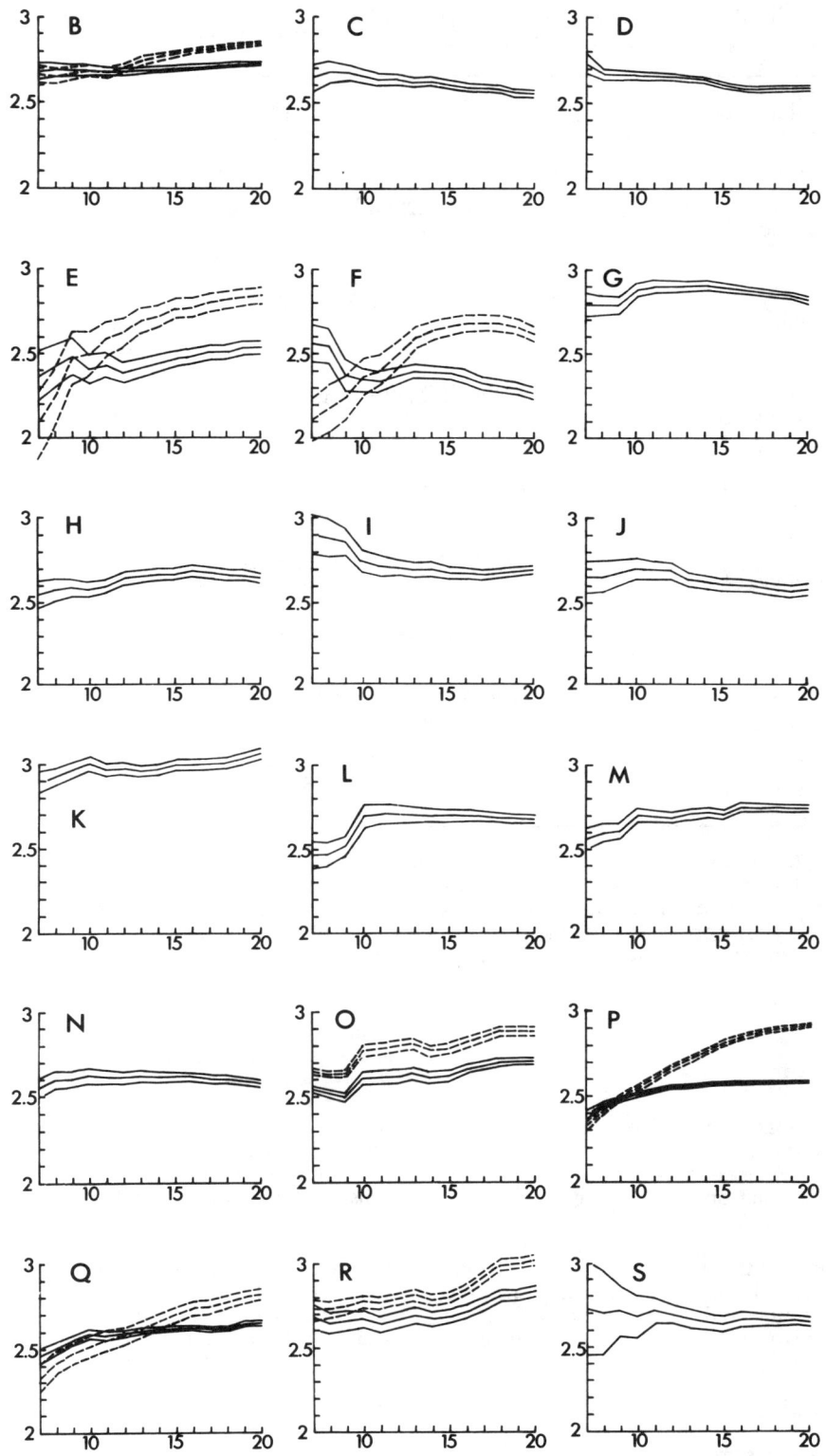

Fig. 9. Results of density versus search radius analysis for Seamounts B to S. For Seamounts B, E, F, O, P, Q and R dashed curves denote the results with homogeneous structures, while solid curves correspond to the results after removing the effect of the assumed structures.

TABLE 1. Parameters of Cylinders or Infinite Horizontal Prisms Assumed Under Seamounts (or Calderas) B, E, F, O, P, Q and R

Cylinder or Prism	Parameter*						
	$\Delta\rho$	r	d_1	d_2	x	y	θ
Seamount B							
cylinder 1	0.1	10	4	10	-12	-4	
2	0.2	5	1.5	5	10	4	
Seamount E (Aogashima Caldera)							
cylinder 1	0.3	3.5	1	5	0	-2	
2	0.3	5	2	5	0	11	
Seamount F (Sumisu Caldera)							
cylinder 1	0.2	4	1.5	5	0	0	
2	0.3	4	2	5	-4	9	
3	-0.3	2	0.3	5	-5	3	
4	0.2	10	5	10	-4	0	
5	0.3	5	5	10	-16	-9	
Seamount O (Nishinoshima Island)							
cylinder 1	0.2	10	5	10	0	5	
Seamount P (Kaikata Seamount)							
prism 1	0.3	8	5	10	0	0	20
Seamount Q (Kaitoku Seamount)							
prism 1	0.3	8	4	10	0	0	160
Seamount R (Kita-Iwojima Island)							
prism 1	0.2	5	5	10	4	0	0

*$\Delta\rho$ is the density contrast of a cylinder or a prism in g/cc. r is the radius for the cylinder or the half width for the prism in km. d_1 and d_2 are its top depth and its bottom depth in km. The center of the cylinder or the prism is located x km eastward and y km northward from the center of the seamount (or caldera), and the horizontal prism extends in a direction θ degrees clockwise from north.

where

$$g_i' = g_i - C_x x_i - C_y y_i . \qquad (7)$$

Equation (6) means that g_i' is a linear function of the effective depth $d_{eff}(x_i,y_i)$ with the linear factor proportional to the density contrast $\Delta\rho$. Observation points of $d_{eff}(x_i,y_i)$, g_i' for the search radius of 15 km from the center of Seamount A are plotted with the line of the least square fit in Fig.7.

In addition to the accuracy of gravity measurements and topographic data, accuracy of the density determination by the least-squares method depends on the range of d_{eff}, i.e., the difference of the maximum and minimum values of the effective depths, and also on the number of observation points.

Density Versus Search Radius Analysis

The preceding analysis presumes no heterogeneous density structure within the seamount. I propose now a method to detect a heterogeneous density structure within a seamount. In this method, the variation of the density determined by the least-squares method is studied as a function of the search radius (called herin 'density versus search radius analysis').

The last procedure of the density determination is as follows. First, the density versus search radius curve of the seamount is drawn with assumption of a homogeneous structure. If the curve is almost flat, the most probable density is determined from the curve. If not, taking Bouguer anomalies around the seamount into consideration, a simple density structure is assumed. The density versus search radius curve is redrawn after removing the effect of the structure, and if the curve is almost flat, the most probable density is determined from the curve. The density versus search radius curve for Seamount A is shown in Fig.8. The curve is almost flat, and the most probable density is calculated from the curve in this case.

Results

Results of density versus search radius analysis for Seamounts B to S are shown in Fig.9. The analysis revealed

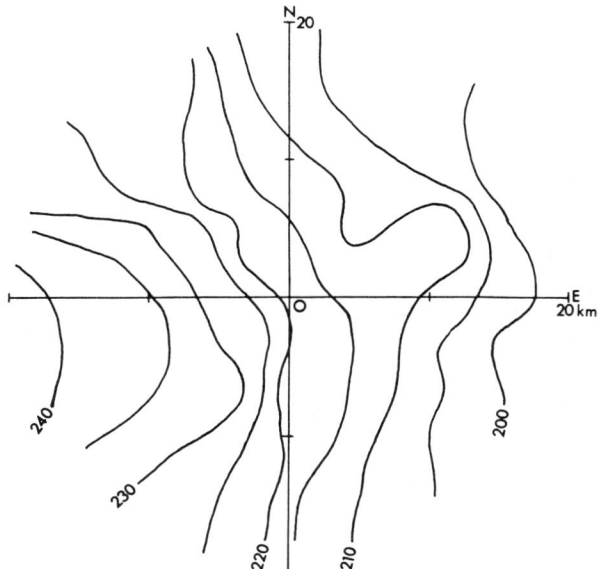

Fig. 10. Bouguer anomalies in mgal around Seamount B. Density for the Bouguer reduction is assumed to be 2.7 g/cc.

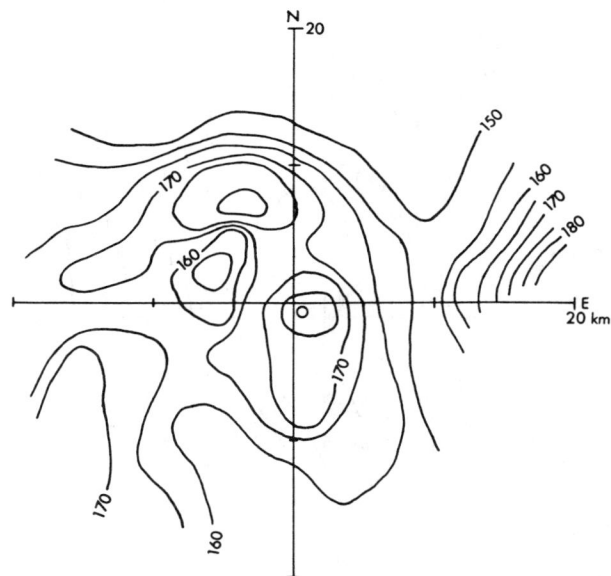

Fig. 12. Bouguer anomalies in mgal around Seamount F (Sumisu Caldera). Density for the Bouguer reduction is assumed to be 2.4 g/cc.

that some seamounts probably have density structures such as roots. Seamounts B, E, F, O, P, Q, and R show significant density variations (dashed lines in Fig.9). Taking Bouguer anomalies around the seamounts into consideration, simplified structures composed of cylinders and horizontal rectangular prisms were determined (Table 1). The following factors were considered in the determination of the parameters of the cylinders and the horizontal rectangular prisms:

1. The density versus search radius curve should be almost flat after the removal of the gravity effect of the heterogeneous structure. The gravity effect of a cylinder was calculated by a numerical integration method for an axisymmetric body (Ishihara, 1977), whereas that of a horizontal rectangular prism was computed using a two-dimensional method (Talwani et al., 1959).

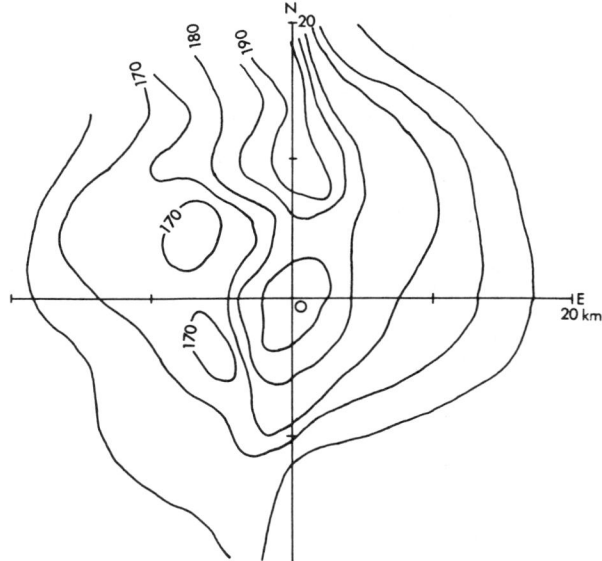

Fig. 11. Bouguer anomalies in mgal around Seamount E (Aogashima Caldera). Density for the Bouguer reduction is assumed to be 2.4 g/cc.

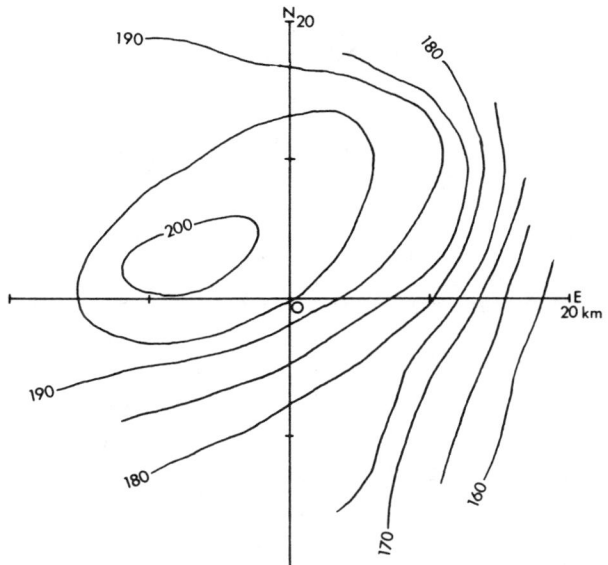

Fig. 13. Bouguer anomalies in mgal around Seamount O (Nishinoshima Island). Density for the Bouguer reduction is assumed to be 2.6 g/cc.

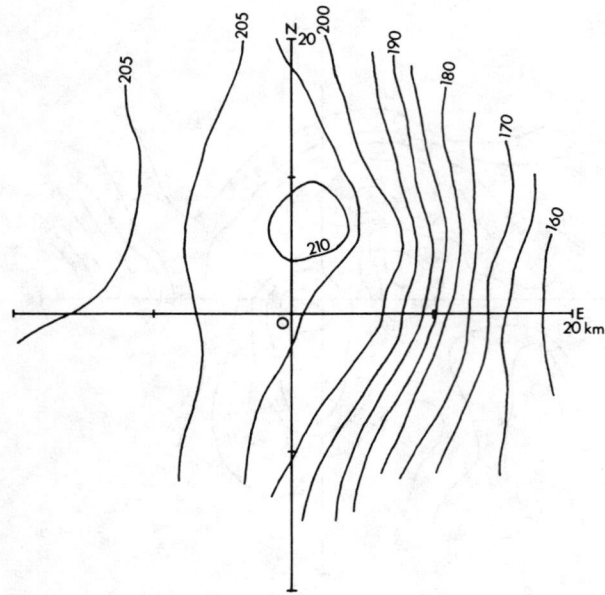

Fig. 14. Bouguer anomalies in mgal around Seamount P (Kaikata Seamount). Density for the Bouguer reduction is assumed to be 2.6 g/cc.

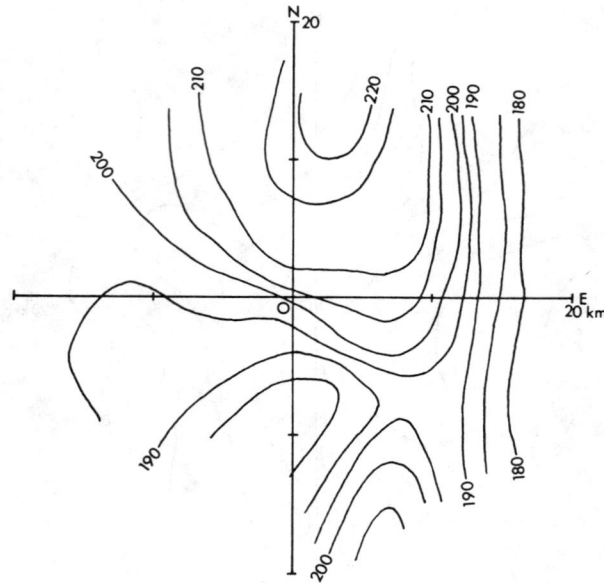

Fig. 16. Bouguer anomalies in mgal around Seamount R (Kita-iwojima Island). Density for the Bouguer reduction is assumed to be 2.7 g/cc.

2. The error of the obtained density should not become greater than before correction.

3. The density used in the calculation of the Bouguer anomalies should be nearly equal to the density determined after the removal of the gravity effect of the structure.

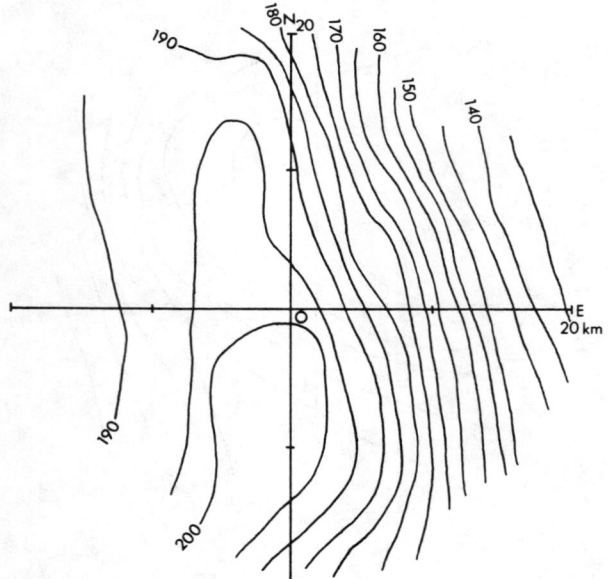

Fig. 15. Bouguer anomalies in mgal around Seamount Q (Kaitoku Seamount). Density for the Bouguer reduction is assumed to be 2.6 g/cc.

Information regarding detailed shapes of the cylinders and the horizontal prisms and their density contrast to the surroundings is less important than that of approximate locations, total excess mass and depths.

Seamounts G, I, L and M also show significant density variations but mainly in the range of search radius less than 10 km. Densities determined for this range of search radius are generally uncertain because of small number of data. No attempt of removing heterogeneous density structures is thus made for these seamounts.

<u>Seamount B.</u> A broad positive Bouguer anomaly high is located in the west of the seamount while another small high occurs in the ENE of the topographic crest (Fig.10). Two high-density cylindrical roots were considered (Table 1), and the resultant density versus search radius curve is almost flat (solid curves in Fig.9).

<u>Seamount E and F.</u> By their topography, these features appear to be calderas (Murakami and Ishihara, 1985). Caldera E is located about 10 km east of Aogashima Island. The caldera rim has a dimension of 5.4 x 9.9 km with the relative height from its floor of about 300 m and the floor is about 600 to 800 m deep. Sumisu Island is located in the southwestern rim of Caldera F. The rim has a dimension of 6.6 x 8.3 km and a relative height up to 700 m. The density versus search radius curves suggest high-density structures under both of the calderas (this problem will be discussed later by using model calculations). A Bouguer anomaly map of Caldera E suggests two high density masses around its center and about 10 km north (Fig.11), but a Bouguer anomaly map of Caldera F is more complicated with a high around its center (Fig.12). The density versus search radius curves after the removal of the structures are flatter than the original ones (solid curves in Fig.9).

<u>Seamount O, P, Q and R.</u> Bouguer anomalies around these seamounts (or islands) suggest broad high-density

TABLE 2. Locations and the Most Probable Densities of Seamounts
Along the Shichito Ridge and the Izu Ridge

Seamount	Location*		Density (g/cc)
A	31°45.2'N	138°37.4'E	2.80±0.05
B	31 21.7	138 48.5	2.69±0.02
C	31 00.0	138 59.6	2.62±0.03
D	30 52.2	138 43.0	2.64±0.03
E (Aogashima Caldera)	32 27.0	139 54.0	2.43±0.06
F (Sumisu Caldera)	31 28.7	140 03.2	2.38±0.05
G (Sofugan Island)	29 47.0	140 21.0	2.90±0.03
H	29 18.0	140 27.5	2.65±0.04
I	29 13.0	140 46.8	2.69±0.05
J	29 03.5	140 31.0	2.64±0.05
K	28 18.5	140 35.0	2.97±0.04
L	28 03.7	140 46.2	2.70±0.04
M	27 41.2	140 48.8	2.70±0.03
N	27 40.8	140 26.0	2.63±0.03
O (Nishinoshima Island)	27 15.0	140 53.0	2.62±0.04
P (Kaikata Seamount)	26 42.0	141 00.0	2.56±0.02
Q (Kaitoku Seamount)	26 06.0	141 03.0	2.61±0.02
R (Kita-Iwojima Island)	25 25.0	141 10.0	2.67±0.05
S (Minami-Iwojima Island)	24 13.0	141 27.0	2.67±0.06

*Locations are approximate latitudes and longitudes of centers of seamounts used in the calculations.

structures under them (Fig.13, 14, 15 and 16). A cylindrical structure is assumed under Nishinoshima Island (Seamount O), whereas horizontal prisms are assumed under Kaikata Seamount (Seamount P), Kaitoku Seamount (Seamount Q) and Kita-Iwojima Island (Seamount R) (Table 1). This approximation is probably good for Seamounts P and Q, while it may be too simple for Seamount R. All deep structures have higher densities. Flatter density versus search radius curves were obtained after removal of the effect of the structures for all seamounts (solid curves in Fig.9). Especially, the curves for Seamounts P and Q are almost flat and the errors of densities are considerably smaller than before the correction.

Bouguer anomalies also show remarkable decrease in the

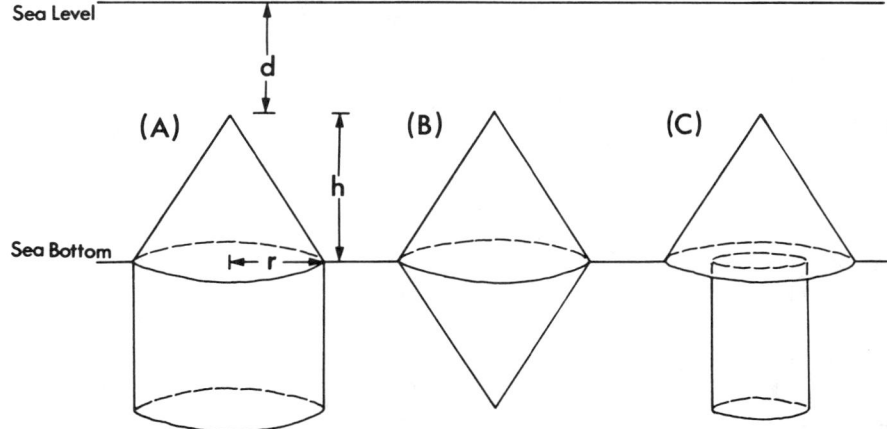

Fig. 17. Three root models. (a) Cylinder with the same radius as that of the seamount bottom. (b) Inverted circular cone with the top of the same radius as the seamount bottom. (c) Cylinder with the radius half of that of the seamount bottom. In the model calculations, the top depth d, the relative height h and the bottom radius r of the seamount are assumed to be 1, 2 and 10 km, respectively, and all the roots are assumed to be 5 km thick.

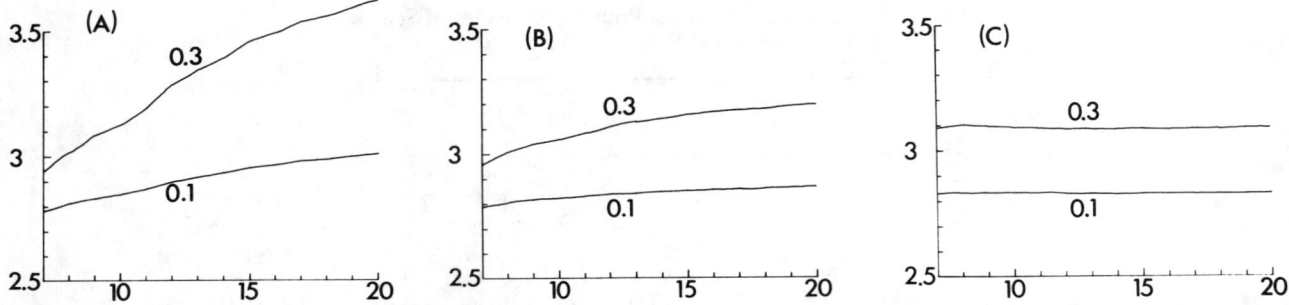

Fig. 18. Apparent densities as a function of search radius for the seamount with three types of roots shown in Fig. 17. The root is assumed to have a density contrast of 0.3 g/cc for the upper curves, and to have a density contrast of 0.1 g/cc for the lower curves.

east of all seamounts. This decrease in Bouguer anomalies is probably due to the thick sediments in the Bonin Trough, which extends north-south in the east of the seamounts. Although no particular heterogeneous structure in the trough is assumed in the above calculation, most of this effect can be probably approximated by the terms of regional trend in (4).

The most probable densities were calculated from the average of the densities for appropriate search radii after removing the gravity effect of the inner structures for seven seamounts described above and without any corrections for the other seamounts. Densities for search radii of less than 10 km are generally uncertain because of small number of data, while densities for greater search radii may include effects outside of the seamount. The most probable density for each seamount was determined by the weighted average of those for five search radii from 11 to 15 km with weights of the reciprocals of the squares of their errors (This weighted average is in effect equivalent to an average with the greatest weight to the data at points within 11 km from the center and with decreasing weight up to the data at a point of 15 km. If all the errors for five search radii are equal, the weight for the data at points within 11 km from the center is about five times greater than that for the data at points apart by 14 to 15 km from the center.):

$$m_0 = \sum_{a=11}^{15}(m_a/\sigma_a^2)/\sum_{a=11}^{15}(1/\sigma_a^2), \qquad (8)$$

where m_a and σ_a are the density and its error for the search radius a, and m_0 is the most probable density.

The most probable densities are shown in Table 2. Generally speaking, with a track spacing of 3 nautical miles or less and with a range of effective depths greater than 1 km, the densities can be determined with an accuracy of 0.05 g/cc. Ranges of effective depths are less than 1 km for Calderas E and F, while the spacing is rather wide for Seamounts R and S.

Discussions

Effect of Heterogeneous Structure of Seamounts

In this paper, density versus search radius analysis was used to detect a density structure under a seamount. Simple model calculations are made to clarify the significance of the results. A circular cone with a density of 2.7 g/cc, a bottom radius of 10 km, a top depth of 1 km and a relative height of 2

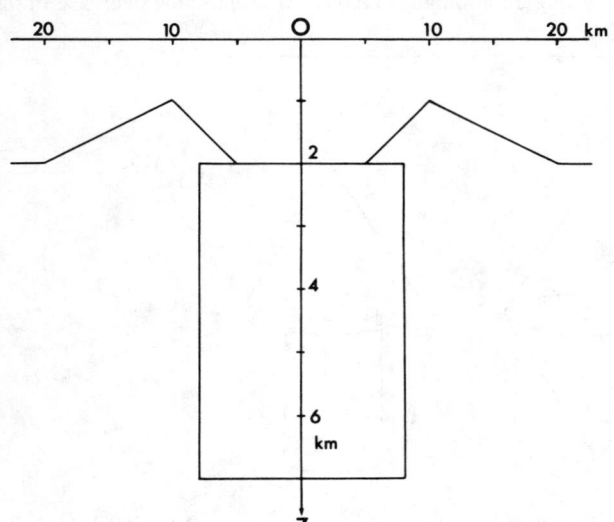

Fig. 19. Model (cross section) of a caldera with a root. Vertical exaggeration 1:5. A cylindrical root 5 km thick, with the radius of 8 km and with the top of 2 km depth is assumed.

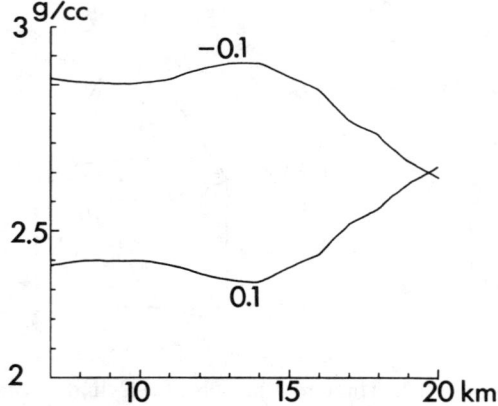

Fig. 20. Apparent densities as a function of search radius for the model in Fig. 19. Density contrast for the root is assumed to be 0.1 g/cc (lower) and -0.1 g/cc (upper).

TABLE 3. Rock Samples Dredged From Seamounts and Collected From Islands
Along the Shichito Ridge and the Izu Ridge (after Yuasa, in preparation)

Seamount	Rock sample
B	augite-olivine basalt
D	hypersthene-augite-olivine basalt, augite-olivine basalt hypersthene-olivine-augite basalt
E (Aogashima Caldera)	augite-hypersthene andesite, augite-hypersthene dacite augite-quartz dacite, hypersthene-augite andesite
F (Sumisu Caldera)	hypersthene-augite andesite, hypersthene-augite dacite augite-olivine basalt
G (Sofugan Island)	hypersthene-augite andesite, hypersthene-augite basalt augite-olivine basalt, hypersthene andesite
H	hypersthene-augite andesite olivine-hypersthene-augite andesite
J	hypersthene-augite andesite
K	olivine basalt, augite basalt
L	olivine-hypersthene-augite basalt
M	olivine-augite basalt
O (Nishinoshima Island)	hypersthene-augite andesite (after Aoki et al., 1984)
P (Kaikata Seamount)	hypersthene-augite andesite, augite-olivine basalt
Q (Kaitoku Seamount)	hypersthene-augite andesite, augite-olivine basalt
R (Kita-Iwojima Island)	augite-olivine basalt, olivine basalt (after Tsuya, 1937)
S (Minami-Iwojima Island)	augite-olivine basalt (after Yuasa and Tamaki,1982)

km is considered as a model seamount. Three 'root' structures are considered as shown in Fig.17. For the first type of the root (cylinder with the same radius as that of the seamount bottom and with a thickness of 5 km), the apparent density determined by the least-squares method increases with the search radius even if the density of the root is 0.1 g/cc higher than the surroundings (Fig.18a). This can be explained qualitatively as follows. The gravity effect of the deeper cylindrical root spreads further than that of the shallower conical seamount with the same radius. Both gravity effects decrease with the distance from the center of the seamount, but the ratio of the gravity effect of the root to that of the seamount increases. The apparent density is calculated from the line of the least-suares fit of the sum of both gravity effects versus the effective depth. If the search radius is small, the gravity effect of the root is relatively small and the density obtained from the least-squares fit is near to the actual density. However, if the search radius increases, the proportion of data, which have high ratios of the gravity effect of the root to that of the seamount, increases, and the apparent density also increases. For the second type of the root (an inverted circular cone with the same radius as the seamount bottom), the apparent density still has a tendency to increase with the search radius for the root with the density contrast of 0.3 g/cc, but little changes in the calculated densities are seen for the density contrast of 0.1 g/cc (Fig.18b). Thus it is possible to identify a root such as the first or the second type, if the estimated density differs by greater than 0.1 g/cc from the true one. For the third type of the root (a cylinder with a radius half of that of the seamount), the density versus search radius curve is almost flat even if the density contrast of the root is 0.3 g/cc so that it is very difficult to identify this type of the root (Fig.18c). This result is quite reasonable when we take into account the ambiguity in gravity interpretation (Nettleton, 1976). It is well known that a deep and concentrated mass can generate nearly the same gravity anomalies as a shallow and broader mass. Nearly the same gravity anomalies can result from a seamount or from a deep cylindrical mass with a radius smaller than that of the seamount.

The results of the caldera models are particularly interesting. A caldera and its root is simplified as shown in Fig.19. The estimated density rapidly increases with the search radius if the root has a positive density contrast and decreases if it has a negative contrast (Fig.20). If we denote a distance from the center of the caldera by r, this can be explained as follows. The gravity effect of the caldera topography varies approximately the same as the topography does: it takes its maximum value at a point $r=r_m$ near the rim of the caldera and decreases in both directions away from the point (i.e., $r \to 0$ and $r \to \infty$). The gravity effect of a positive root, however, decreases monotonically with the distance r. The derivative of the latter effect is thus in the same sense as and therefore intensifies that of the former effect at a point $r>r_m$, but weakens at a point $r<r_m$. The apparent density obtained for a search radius less than r_m is thus less than the real density (Fig.20 shows that the apparent density is 2.4 g/cc or less (less than 2.7 g/cc) for a search radius less than 14 km, when the density contrast of the root is 0.1 g/cc). The apparent density increases with the search radius if the latter is greater than r_m (as in the area of the search radius greater than 14 km in Fig.20), because the proportion of the data in the area $r>r_m$ increases. The relative height of a caldera is generally smaller than that of a seamount (the relative height of the caldera model in Fig.19 is 1 km, i.e., just half of that of the seamount model in Fig.17). The same gravity effect of a root, thus, affects greater to the apparent density of the caldera and results in the greater rate of its increase than to that of the

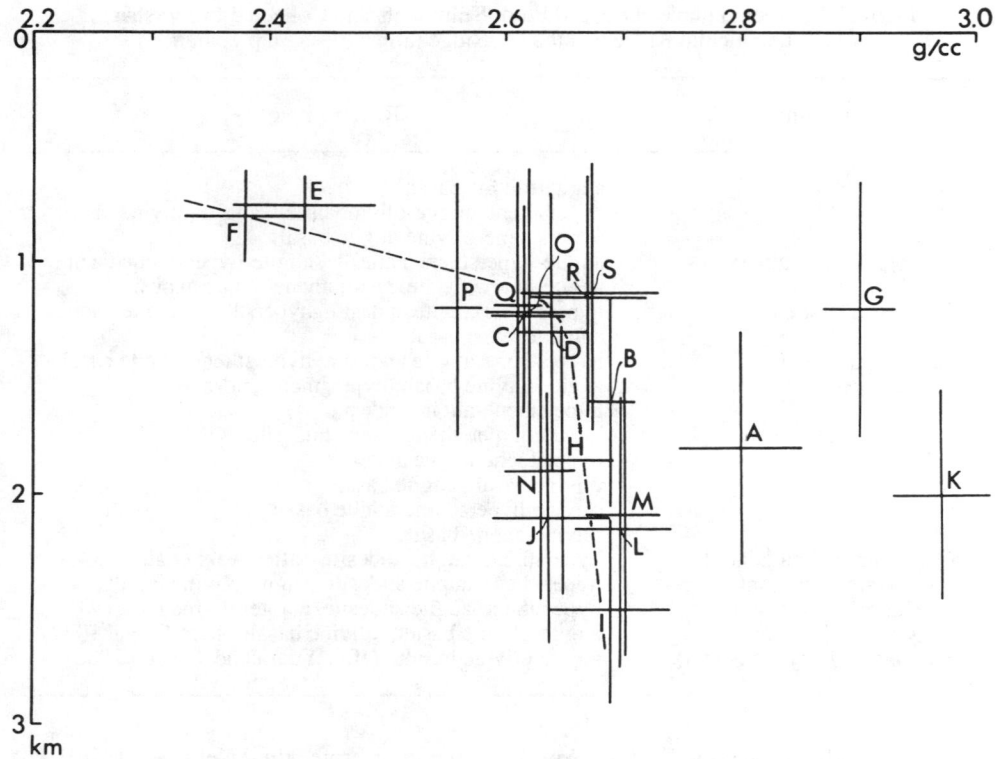

Fig. 21. Plot of most probable densities of Seamount A to S in the Bonin Arc with their mean depths. All seamounts except A, G and K are along the dashed curve. Horizontal bars indicate errors of density estimate and the vertical bars indicate the halves of relative heights.

seamount. The original estimated densities for both of Calderas E and F increase with the search radius (the dashed curves in Fig.9). Bouguer anomalies are high at the centers of these calderas and high-density 'root' structures are very probable under the centers of the calderas. This is consistent with the result of the model calculations shown here. The density versus search radius analysis is especially useful in the detection of a root under a caldera.

The densities of Seamounts B, E, F, P and Q obtained after removal of the dense roots are higher than the original apparent densities in the range of search radii less than about 10 km. This seems strange at first sight. The apparent density is higher than the true density, if a dense root is beneath the center of the seamount in such a case as in Fig.17. This is, however, only true when the derivatives of both gravity effects of the root and the seamount are in the same sense. As described just above, the derivatives of both gravity effects for calderas such as E and F have opposite signs and the apparent densities become smaller than the true ones in the range of small search radii. The centers of the dense roots of Seamount B are apart from the center of the seamount by greater than 10 km. The derivatives of both gravity effects are, thus again, in the opposite sense in the range of small search radius for Seamount B. Seamount Q consists of three or more peaks, and the assumed center of the seamount and the maximum of the gravity effect of the seamount do not correspond each other. The same is true for Seamount P. The derivatives of both effects are in the opposite sense in the range of small search radius for these seamounts. Therefore, it is reasonable that the densities of Seamounts B, E, F, P and Q after the removal of the dense roots is higher than the original apparent densities in the range of small search radii.

Relation of Seamount Densities to Their Depths

Rock densities are highly dependent on their porosities. DSDP basalt samples show a linear relation between bulk density and porosity with the values of 2.8 to 3.0 g/cc for 0 % porosity (Hyndman and Drury, 1976; Hamano, 1980; Kono et al., 1980; Fountain, 1980). On the other hand, Moore (1965) revealed from the studies of dredged submarine samples that their porosities are dependent on the depths where they were collected. From these considerations some correlation is quite probable between seamount density and depth.

The average depth of the top and the foot of each seamount with an error bar of half of the relative height (= difference of foot and top depths) is plotted with its determined density in Fig.21. The analyzed seamounts are mostly quaternary volcanoes, some of which are still active now, and it is reasonable to assume that their depths changed little since their generation. Seamounts A, B, C and D, which are located along the Izu Ridge, are probably a little older. A K-Ar age of 2.2±1.1 Ma was obtained for a basalt sample dredged from a seamount in the Izu Ridge (Yuasa, 1985). One exception is Seamount I. It is an old seamount judging from Late Eocene fossils (Asterocyclina sp. and Biplanispira sp.) dredged from

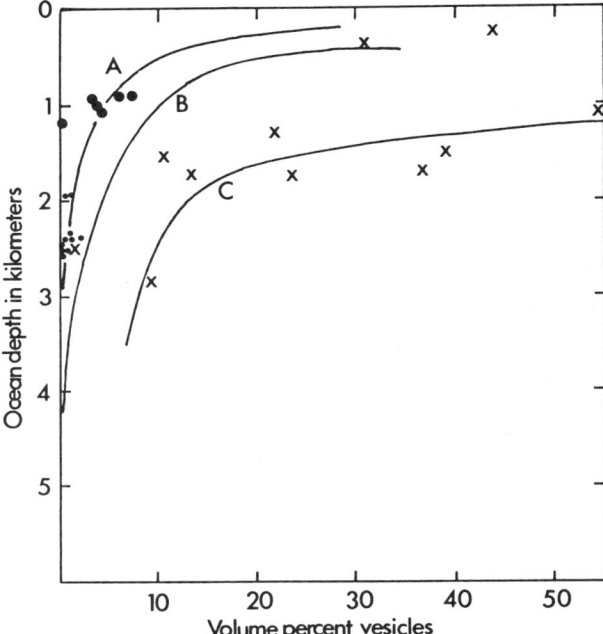

Fig. 22. Vesicularity as a function of depth for three types of submarine basalt (after Moore, 1970). Curve A, K-poor oceanic tholeiites; small dots, Juan de Fuca Ridge samples; large dots, Reykjanes Ridge samples. Curve B, averaged data from submarine part of east rift zone of Kilauea volcano, Hawaii (Moore, 1965). Curve C and crosses, Revillagigedo Island region, Mexico.

the feature (Nishimura, personal communication). If Seamounts A, G and K are excluded, all seamounts are along the dashed curve in Fig.21, which shows a prominent change in slope at a depth of about 1 km, though there are only two seamounts with the average depths less than 1 km. Bulk densities of basalts dredged from the east rift zone of Kilauea also rapidly decreases for the depth less than 1 km, and this density decrease corresponds to the increase of vesicularity (porosity) very well (Moore, 1965). The densities derived for the calderas E and F, 2.38 and 2.43 g/cc are reasonable in comparison with the densities determined for Mt. Fuji (2.3 - 2.4 g/cc, Komazawa, personal communication) and for Mt. Asama (2.46 g/cc, Tajima et al., 1977).

Moore (1970) obtained different curves of vesicularity versus depth for different types of basalts: K-poor tholeiitic basalts are less vesicular and the change of slope is at about 500 m, while alkalic basalts are more vesicular and the change of slope is at a depth of about 1800 m (Fig.22). He suggested that the higher vesicularity of alkalic basalts is due to the higher ratio of water and other volatiles, and also that water-dominated gases become saturated in the melt and exsolve to form abundant vesicles at the confining pressure, which corresponds to the change of slope, while at a deeper depth gases in vesicles may be dominated by sulfer or carbon. Hamilton et al. (1964) have shown that at 1,100°C water is more soluble in andesitic melt than in basaltic melt. No data of water content in rock samples is now available from seamounts along the Bonin Arc. However, if it is true that the change of slope in the density versus depth curve for the seamounts along the Bonin Arc, and, i.e., also in the vesicularity versus depth curve, occurs at a depth of about 1 km, i.e., approximately at the same depth for Kilauean tholeiites, it is inferred that water content of basaltic seamounts in the study area are probably not far from 0.5 percent, which is about the mean water content of Kilauean tholeiites, and that andesitic seamounts may have a higher water content.

Relation of Seamount Densities to Their Petrology

Fig.21 also shows that there are two groups of seamounts for almost the same depth range: one is Seamounts H, J and N and the other is Seamounts B, L and M. The two groups are different in their densities by 0.5 to 1.0 g/cc, although their ranges of density partially overlap. This difference is probably due to petrology. As shown in Table 3, samples of hypersthene-augite andesites were dredged from Seamounts H and J, while basalt samples were dredged from Seamounts B, L and M (Yuasa, in preparation). If porosities are not so different between both groups, this result suggests that a seamount with the average depth of about 2 km is mainly composed of andesites or more acidic rocks if the estimated density is less than 2.67 g/cc and mainly composed of basalts or more basic rocks if greater than 2.67 g/cc. This separation can be recognized also for shallower seamounts. Andesites were mainly collected from lower-density seamounts: Seamounts P (Kaitoku Seamount), Q (Kaikata Seamount) and O (Nishinoshima Island, Aoki et al., 1984). Basalts were collected from higher-density seamounts: Seamounts R (Kita-Iwojima Island, Tsuya, 1937), S (Minami-Iwojima Island, Yuasa and Tamaki, 1982) and D.

Densities of Seamounts G, K and also A are anomalously high. There remained still a possibility of change of density determination due to their inner structures. Although only basalt samples were recovered from Seamount K, gabbros or ultrabasic rocks possibly occur within or under the seamount. Similarly, andesites were mainly dredged from slopes of Sofugan Island (Seamount G). Basalts or more basic rocks probably occur under this island (basalt samples were also recovered from slopes of this island). This is also probable for Seamount A, though no samples were dredged from the seamount.

High Gravity Anomaly Calderas

Yokoyama and Tajima (1957) and Yokoyama (1963) reported that high gravity anomalies are observed at Oshima Caldera in Japan. High Bouguer anomalies are also found at Kilauea Caldera on Hawaii (Krivoy and Eaton, 1961), Koolau and Waianae Calderas on Oahu (Woollard, 1951; Strange et al., 1965) in the Hawaiian Islands. These volcanoes have ejected basaltic lavas and the anomalies were interpreted due to the subsidence of high density basaltic lavas or due to dense volcanic conduits. Low gravity anomalies are observed on other main calderas in Japan: Kuttyaro, Toya, Hakone, Aso, Aira caldera, etc. These are classified as Crater Lake type calderas by Aramaki (1969) and are associated with large amount of dacitic or andesitic ignimbrites around them.

Although high Bouguer anomalies were observed at the center of the calderas E and F (Fig.11 and 12), samples of mainly andesites and dacites were collected from them, not the higher density basalts expected.

One possible explanation is the submarine eruption. Because of water pressure, the eruptions were probably not so explosive as those of a Crater Lake type caldera. Another factor that must be considered is petrology. Volcanic rocks collected from the northern part of the Shichito Ridge including these two calderas and Oshima Volcano are in the region of low alkali tholeiites (Yuasa and Tamaki, 1982). As Moore (1970) suggested for submarine basalts, low alkali tholeiites probably have lower water content and are less explosive than their alkalic counterparts. It is likely that these two factors are combined to form the density structure of these calderas. According to a seismic profiling survey (Murakami and Ishihara, 1985) the sediment thickness inside both calderas is less than 500 m, too thin to give rise to significant low gravity anomalies. On the contrary, the observed gravity anomalies show that high-density material (possibly andesites or basalts) are quite probable at shallow depths (probably shallower than 5 km) beneath both calderas.

Limitation of Homogeneous Seamount Model

I assumed that the seamounts are homogeneous and some of them have deep structures under them. However, if rock density decreases with depth as discussed above, density of shallow parts (i.e., near the top) of a seamount must be lower than that of deeper parts (near the foot). This effect should be especially significant for islands and seamounts with tops shallower than 500 m.

Data of Seamount P (Kaikata Seamount) possibly show this effect. The most detailed survey was carried out around this seamount. The spacings of north-south and east-west tracks are about 1 nautical mile. Accurate density determination can thus be expected. Water depths within a small search radius from the center of the seamount are generally shallow. Therefore, the effects of shallow parts are the major contributions to density determinations using gravity data in a small search radius. The density versus search radius curves for Seamount P (solid curves in Fig.9) show that apparent density after removing the effect of a deep heterogeneous structure still decreases toward smaller search radii from about 12 km. This suggests that densities of a shallow part of Seamount P are lower than 2.56 g/cc, which is determined as the most probable density of the seamount.

This study has not considered either isostatic compensation or lithospheric flexure. These mechanisms work mainly in the long wavelengths. The seamounts along the Bonin Arc are generally of small size. The gravity anomalies dealt with in this study have diameters less than 40 km (i.e., search radii less than 20 km), which correspond to the wavelengths less than 80 km. In the Bonin Arc, the seamount eruptions occurred on lithosphere old and thick enough, and these effects are probably not important in such a short wavelength region.

Conclusion

Gravimetric density determinations of Bonin Arc seamounts revealed the following.

1. With a track spacing less than 3 nautical miles and with a range of effective depths greater than 1 km, the density of a seamount can be determined with an accuracy of 0.05 g/cc using an assumption of a homogeneous structure. More detailed bathymetric data (from Sea Beam or similar devices) are combined with a larger number of gravity data, the accuracy of density determination should be improved.

2. Heterogeneous structure certainly exists in some seamounts. In most cases it can be identified from the density versus search radius analysis. Especially, high-density structures under two calderas along the Shichito Ridge can be clearly identified from this analysis.

3. A relationship was recognized between mean depths of seamounts and their densities. The curve shows a prominent change of slope at a depth of about 1 km. This is due to a close correlation between density and porosity and a correlation between porosity and depth. One density is assumed to one seamount in this paper, but this relation probably holds true also in one seamount: the density is the lowest at the top of the seamount and increases with depth.

4. A clear grouping of density values was recognized for the seamounts with mean depths of about 2 km. Seamounts with densities lower than 2.67 g/cc correspond to andesitic volcanoes and seamounts with higher density correspond to basaltic volcanoes. It is uncertain whether this correlation of seamount densities with petrography exists globally or only along the Bonin Arc. The other important factor, porosity, should be considered. If the porosity of a seamount is known or estimated, the rock type of the seamount may be predicted from the gravity method.

Acknowledgments. The author would like to express his gratitude to Prof. Y. Tomoda for his kind advice and encouragement throughout this study. Fruitful discussions with M. Yuasa were very helpful for the author to complete the geological implication of the results. Careful and critical reviews of the manuscript by Prof. K. Kobayashi and Drs. Y. Shimazaki, W. W. Sager, J. Kellogg and J. Freymueller are gratefully acknowledged.

References

Aoki, H., and Tokai University Research Group for Marine Volcano, Petrochemistry of the Nishinoshima Islands. *La mer 22*, 248-256, 1984.

Aramaki, S., Some problems of the theory of caldera formation, *Bull. Volcanol. Soc. Japan, 2nd Ser., 14*, 55-76, 1969 (in Japanese).

Bell, R. E., and A. B. Watts, Evaluation of the BGM-3 sea gravity meter system onboard R/V Conrad, *Geophysics, 51*, 1480-1493, 1986.

Briggs, I. C., Machine contouring using minimum curvature, *Geophysics, 39*, 39-48, 1974.

Fountain, D. M., Influence of porosity and water saturation on the compressional wave velocities of basalts from the North Phillipine Sea, in G. deVries Klein, K. Kobayashi, et al., *Initial Reports of Deep-Sea Drilling Project*, vol. 58, Washington (U. S. Government Printing Office), 935-940, 1980.

Hamano, Y., Physical properties of basalts from holes 417D and 418A, in T. Donnelly, J. Francheteau, W. Bryan, P. Robinson, M. Flower, M. Salisbury, et al., *Initial Reports of the Deep-Sea Drilling Project*, vol. 51, 52, 53, part 2, Washington (U. S. Government Printing Office), 1457-1466, 1980.

Hamilton, D. L., C. W. Burnam, and E. F. Osborn, The solubility of water and effects of oxygen fugacity and water content on crystallization in mafic magmas, *J. Petrol., 5*, 21-39, 1964.

Harrison, J. C., and W. C. Brisbin, Gravity anomalies off the west coast of North America. 1: Seamount Jasper, *Bull. Geol. Soc. Am., 70*, 929-933, 1959.

Honza, E., E. Inoue, and T. Ishihara (eds), *Geological*

investigation of the Ogasawara (Bonin) and Northern Mariana Arcs, April-August 1979 (GH79-2, 3 and 4 cruises) *Geol. Survey Japan Cruise Report,* no 14, 170 pp., 1981.

Honza, E., and K. Tamaki, The Bonin Arc, in *The Ocean Basins and Margins,* vol. 7A, edited by A. E. M. Nairn, F. G. Stehli, and S. Uyeda, 459-502, Plenum Publishing Corporation, 1985.

Hyndman, R. D., and M. J. Drury, The physical properties of oceanic basement rocks from deep drilling on the Mid-Atlantic Ridge, *J. Geophys. Res., 81,* 4042-4052, 1976.

Ishihara, T., The gravity anomalies on the Kikai caldera and its vicinity, *Bull. Geol. Survey Japan, 28,* 575-588, 1977 (in Japanese).

Ishihara, T., Gravity field around Japan - sea gravimetry by the Geological Survey of Japan, *Marine Geod., 7,* 227-256, 1983.

Kellogg, J. N., and I. J. Ogujiofor, Gravity field analysis of Sio Guyot: an isostatically compensated seamount in the Mid-Pacific Mountains, *Geo-Marine Lett., 5,* 91-97, 1985.

Kono, M., Y. Hamano, and W. J. Morgan, Physical properties of basalts from DSDP leg 55, in E. D. Jackson, I. Koizumi, et. al, *Initial Reports of Deep-Sea Drilling Project,* vol. 55, 715-721, Washington (U. S. Printing Office), 1980.

Krivoy, H. L., and J. P. Eaton, Preliminary gravity survey of Kilauea, *U. S. Geol. Survey Prof. Paper 424-D,* D205-D208, 1961.

Le Pichon, X., and M. Talwani, Gravity survey of a seamount near 35°N 46°W in the north Atlantic, *Marine Geol., 2,* 262-277, 1964.

Moore, J. G., Petrology of deep-sea basalt near Hawaii, *Am. J. Sci., 263,* 40-52, 1965.

Moore, J. G., Water content of basalt errupted on the ocean floor, *Contr. Mineral. and Petrol., 28,* 272-279, 1970.

Murakami, F., and T. Ishihara, Calderas found in the northern part of the Bonin Arc, *Earth Monthly, 7,* 638-646, 1985 (in Japanese).

Nettleton, L. L., Determination of density for reduction of gravimeter observations, *Geophysics, 4,* 176-183, 1939.

Nettleton, L. L., *Gravity and Magnetics in Oil Prospecting,* 464 pp., McGraw-Hill, New York, 1976.

Parasnis, D. S., A study of rock densities in the English Midlands, *Month. Not. Roy. Astr. Soc., Geophys. Suppl., 6,* 252-271, 1952.

Parker, R. L., The rapid calculation of potential anomalies, *Geophys. J. Roy. Astr. Soc., 31,* 447-455, 1972.

Robertson, E. I., Gravity effects of volcanic islands, *New Zealand J. Geol. Geophys., 10,* 1466-1483, 1967.

Robertson, E. I., Additional gravity surveys in the Cook Islands, *New Zealand J. Geol. Geophys., 13,* 184-198, 1970.

Sager, W. W., G. T. Davis, B. H. Keating, and J. A. Philpotts, A geophysical and geologic study of Nagata seamount, northern Line Islands, *J. Geomag. Geoelectr., 34,* 283-305, 1982.

Segawa, J., Gravity measurements at sea by use of the T. S. S. G. part 2, Results of the measurements, *J. Phys. Earth, 18,* 203-247, 1970.

Strange, W. E., G. P. Woollard, and J. C. Rose, An analysis of the gravity field over the Hawaiian Islands in terms of crustal structrure, *Pacific Science, 19,* 381-389, 1965.

Tajima, H., D. Shimozuru, and I. Yokoyama, Gravity surveys over Asama and Kusatsu-shirane volcanos, *Bull. Volcanol. Soc. Japan, 2nd ser., 22,* 161-172, 1977 (in Japanese).

Talwani, M., J. L. Worzel, and M. Landisman, Rapid gravity computations for two-dimensional bodies with application to the Mendocino submarine fracture zone, *J. Geophys. Res., 64,* 49-59, 1959.

Tomoda, Y., and H. Fujimoto, Gravity anomalies in the western Pacific and geophysical interpretation of their origin, *J. Phys. Earth, 29,* 387-419, 1981.

Tsuya, H., On the volcanism of the Huzi volcanic zone, with special reference to the geology and petrology of Izu and the southern islands, *Bull. Earthq. Res. Inst., 15,* 215-357, 1937.

Valliant, H. D., Field trials with the LaCoste and Romberg straight-line gravimeter, *Geophysics, 48,* 611-617, 1983.

Woollard, G. P., A gravity reconnaissance of the Island of Oahu, *Trans. Am. Geophys. Union, EOS, 32,* 358-368, 1951.

Yokoyama, I., Structure of caldera and gravity anomaly, *Bull. Volcanol., 26,* 67-72, 1963.

Yokoyama, I., and H. Tajima, A gravity survey on Volcano Mihara, Ooshima Island by means of a Worden gravimeter, *Bull. Earthq. Res. Inst., 35,* 23-33, 1957.

Yuasa, M., Sofugan Tectonic Line, a new tectonic boundary separating northern and southern parts of the Ogasawara (Bonin) Arc, northwest Pacific, in *Formation of Active Ocean Margins,* edited by N. Nasu, K. Kobayashi, S. Uyeda, I. Kushiro, and H. Kagami, 483-496, Terra Scientific Publishing Company, Tokyo, 1985.

Yuasa, M., and K. Tamaki, Basalt from Minami-Iwojima Island, Volcano Islands, *Bull. Geol. Surv. Japan, 33,* 531-540, 1982 (in Japanese).

SHIPBOARD CONFIRMATION OF SEASAT BATHYMETRIC PREDICTIONS IN THE SOUTH CENTRAL PACIFIC

Nicolas Baudry

ORSTOM, Nouméa, B.P. A5, New-Caledonia
and Laboratoire de Géophysique, (U.A. du C.N.R.S. n°730),
Université Paris-Sud, Bt.509, 91405 Orsay Cedex, France

Michel Diament

Laboratoire de Géophysique, (U.A. du C.N.R.S. n°730),
Université Paris-Sud, Bt.509, 91405 Orsay Cedex, France

Abstract. During the SEAPSO (Leg V) transit cruise of R/V Jean Charcot in the Austral archipelago, we conducted a SEABEAM survey on three unsurveyed seamounts previously precisely located with a new method of SEASAT data analysis. The location site of Fabert Bank was also surveyed and we confirm that, as predicted, no bathymetric feature exists there. The three seamounts were found in the predicted locations and this cruise confirms the 15 km accuracy on the predicted seamounts location. Poorer results have been obtained relating to the predicted heights since it appears that the observed heights of the submarine volcanoes are larger than the predicted ones while the volumes are smaller. This survey confirms also the predictions made concerning the morphological regularity of the seamounts.

Introduction

Detection and location of previously uncharted seamounts using available altimetric data is of major interest from various points of view: in oceanography, since huge seamounts disturb the flow of ocean currents; for geodynamic purposes, since precise location of seamounts is required for a better understanding of the formation of submarine volcanic chains, and for more applied purposes such as fisheries and submarine navigation. Therefore numerous published studies, based on the interpretation of GEOS 3 or SEASAT data offering a more or less dense coverage of vast areas previously unexplored (or poorly explored) by traditional marine geophysics, have dealt with seamount detection and location (Lambeck and Coleman, 1982; Lazarewicz and Schwank, 1982; White et al., 1983; Sandwell, 1984a, Baudry et al., in press). Until now, no result has been published of successful field tests specifically carried out in order to check out such predictions. In this paper, we briefly recall the various prediction techniques based on GEOS 3 and SEASAT data and the results of field tests. We then discuss our results of a SEABEAM survey obtained on some previously unsurveyed seamounts in the Austral archipelago located precisely (Baudry et al., in press, hereafter Paper 1), with the aim of a new location method. Then we describe the location- uncertainties, and the predictions and assumptions of heights and morphology of the seamounts.

Previous Studies

Various techniques have been proposed in order to detect and locate unknown seamounts. Lambeck and Coleman (1982) modelled typical seamount signatures visually detected on altimetric tracks while Lazarewicz and Schwank (1982) and White et al. (1983) used matched filters in order to automatically detect seamount signatures. Transfer functions were also used (Dixon et al., 1983) in order to predict unidimensional bathymetry from SEASAT profiles. Sandwell (1984a) used the deflection of the vertical along the profiles. All these methods yield a location uncertainty of about 15 km along track but much worse cross track. Indeed, since the seamount was generally detected on a single GEOS 3 or SEASAT profile, it could lie on either side of the track at a distance comprised between 0 to about 50 km, the latter value corresponding for example to a very large seamount emplaced on a highly rigid lithosphere (off-ridge seamount). This substantial lateral uncertainty is the main factor which limits the determination of the shape (Groeger, 1981) or height (White et al., 1983) of the sea-

Copyright 1987 by the American Geophysical Union.

mounts. The use of maps does not improve the lateral location uncertainty. Sandwell (1984b) published an image of the sea surface based on the deflection of the vertical on which seamounts are clearly revealed by a characteristic signature. But the precision of the location as given by Sandwell (1984b) is of about 50 km. Geotectonic maps derived from SEASAT data also clearly show subtantial seamounts but the authors do not give any indication as to the exact location of the features (Haxby et al., 1983; Haxby, 1985).

Such inaccurate location determination makes difficult the use of these results for the various topics exposed before. Moreover we believe that it is probably responsible for the failure of previous field tests. Indeed, checks of bathymetric predictions were carried out during four oceanographic cruises (Keating et al., 1984a). As mentioned by Keating et al. (1984a), only about 50% of uncharted seamounts associated with SEASAT anomalies and subsequently tested were actually detected. For example, Keating et al. (1984b) were unfortunately unsuccessful in searching two seamounts in the Caroline Islands detected with matched filters (Lazarewicz and Schwank, 1982) using conventional bathymetry soundings. Such results led Keating et al. (1984a) to conclude that SEASAT detections appear somewhat less reliable than most investigators had thought. As concerns the volume of the seamounts, very few indications were given. Yet, in order to determine the shape and heights of the seamounts it is necessary also to model parameters such as the tectonic setting (see Paper 1). So the amount of parameters which is necessary to model is such that it led Watts and Ribe (1984) to assume that "it may not be possible to use satellite altimeter data to predict bathymetry in the oceans with any degree of reliability". In the previous study we proposed a new method of location in order to locate seamounts precisely, i.e. with an uncertainty of no more than 15 km. This method also predicts the heights of the detected seamounts assuming a simple morphological model. Therefore, we believe that the pessimistic conclusions regarding the ability of detecting bathymetry with SEASAT data are only due to the use of location techniques of insufficient precision.

Location Method

In spite of the irregular coverage of SEASAT data, due to the abrupt disfunctioning of the satellite, it appears that the set of profiles generally consists of groups of two, three or four parallel, ascending or descending, tracks. Each group is about 100 to 200 km distant from the next. Inside a group the profiles are about 10 to 30 km distant. Therefore a seamount is very much likely to give rise to an anomaly detectable on at least two distinct SEASAT tracks. This remark is the base of our proposed location method. To precisely determine the lateral location of the seamount, we achieve a fit between synthetic geoid profiles and each seamount signature visually detected on at least two SEASAT tracks. The synthetic geoid profiles are extracted from two dimensional geoid anomalies above gaussian seamounts. The slope of the gaussian model is chosen after examination of available bathymetric data in the studied area, giving a mean slope for the model. Therefore the only parameter which controls the morphology of the seamount is its height. Results of various tests with both synthetic and real data have shown that it was unnecessary to have an exact idea of the tectonic setting of the seamount to locate it precisely. Indeed, only two classes of tectonic setting have to be taken into account for precise location : on-ridge seamounts and off-ridge seamounts. The first type corresponds to seamounts which were emplaced on a very weak lithosphere (elastic thickness typically less than 5 km) i.e. close to the accretionary center, and the second type to those emplaced on an older and more rigid lithosphere (elastic thickness typically more than 7 km). In that case, the lateral uncertainty is on the order of 15 km, comparable to the along track uncertainty. As for the large intraplate volcanic chains, one can assume with a good confidence that the seamounts have been emplaced off-ridge, even if some complications occur locally along the chain (Calmant and Cazenave, 1986) due for example to the effect of thermal rejuvenation (Menard and McNutt, 1982). If there is no a priori indication concerning the emplacement of the submarine volcanoes in the studied area, it is easy to compute the effective elastic thickness of the lithosphere supporting some known and charted seamounts (e.g., Cazenave and Dominh, 1984; Diament and Goslin, 1986; Calmant and Cazenave, 1986). The hypothesis that other seamounts in the same region have been emplaced through an identical mechanism is then quite reasonable and thus we can assume that the tectonic setting is reasonably well known.

Therefore, once the tectonic setting has been chosen, we compute a broad set of synthetic anomalies varying the distance between the profiles and the axis of the seamount, and the height of the seamount. One can notice that the mean slope of the gaussian shape is constant, whatever the height of the seamount. The minimum r.m.s. of the fit between synthetic profiles and the observed signatures yields a location and a height of the seamount. We interpret the value of the r.m.s. as an indication of the real morphology of the submarine volcano; i.e. the smaller the r.m.s., the closer the real morphology of the seamount to the gaussian model chosen (see Paper 1 for details).

We applied our seamount location method to the Southern Cook and Austral Islands archipelagoes. This area presents some geophysical and petrological complications, and new bathymetric data can be useful for the understanding of the geodynamic evolution of the area. Ten previously

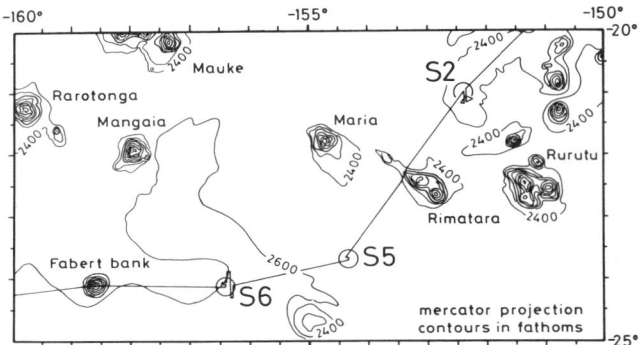

Fig. 1. Bathymetry in fathoms of the surveyed part of the Austral archipelago redrawn after Mammerickx et al. (1973). The locations of three predicted seamounts (S6, S5 and S2) have been added. Also shown is the track of the R/V Jean Charcot during SEAPSO Leg V cruise.

uncharted seamounts were then detected, and named S1 to S10. With the aid of this method, eight seamounts were located with a location uncertainty of 15 km. This study also confirmed the result of Lambeck and Coleman (1982) who postulated that no bathymetric feature was present on the charted location of Fabert Bank (Mammerickx et al., 1973; GEBCO, 1980) since the SEASAT data do not reveal any anomaly above the charted location.

Results of the SEAPSO V Cruise

During the transit Tonga-Tahiti of the SEAPSO (Leg V) cruise (ORSTOM/IFREMER cruise of the R/V Jean Charcot, January 1985), a survey was achieved above the charted location of Fabert Bank and the predicted locations of seamounts S6, S5 and S2 (Figure 1). SEABEAM data, gravity recorded using a KSS30 Bodenseewerk gravimeter and magnetic data were acquired on board. Therefore the existence, exact locations and estimations of height of these features could be checked. Moreover the predictions of location of these three seamounts yield very different r.m.s., thus our assumption concerning the morphology could be checked. A brief preliminary description of the results obtained during the SEAPSO V cruise was presented by Pontoise et al. (1986); we give here a more complete description and interpretation of these data.

Figure 1 displays the ship track in the Austral archipelago. The navigation was achieved using both classical satellite navigation and a G.P.S. system. Figure 2a shows the bathymetry of Fabert Bank as derived from Mammerickx et al.'s (1973) chart. On this chart, the summit of Fabert Bank should be about 400 fathoms below sea level. One can notice that a bank lying at -124 meters beneath sea level is reported on navigation charts. Fabert bank was detected using sounding line by the French warship Fabert, at the beginning of the century. Figure 2b displays sea-floor morphology as obtained on the SEABEAM central beam and the associated gravity anomaly. Since there is no significant gravity anomaly we deduce that no important bathymetric feature is present in the area, even outside the 3 km wide sea-floor stripe covered with SEABEAM data. At the time of the Fabert cruise, a 100 km longitudinal ship mislocation was possible, due to poor navigation. So Fabert Bank could be the seamount S6 located one degree to the east. This first positive result confirms the ability to use altimetric data in order to check the existence of charted bathymetric features or of their possible major mispositioning. Such a study can be easily performed using for example maps of filtered along track geoid or deflection of the vertical (Sandwell, 1984a).

Figures 3, 4 and 5 show the SEABEAM survey performed on each surveyed volcano. The point P and the circle correspond to the predicted seamount location and the 15 km uncertainty respectively. The locations of SEASAT tracks are also

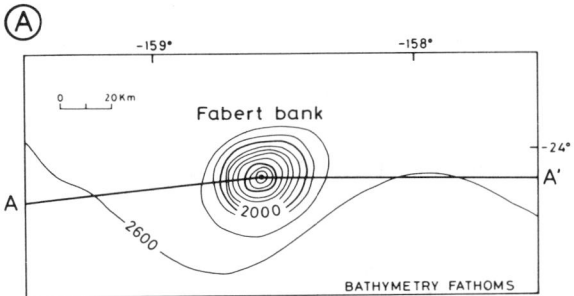

Fig. 2a. Survey of Fabert Bank charted location: Fabert Bank as figured on Mammerickx et al.'s (1973) and GEBCO charts. Contour interval: 200 fathoms. AA' corresponds to R/V Jean Charcot's track.

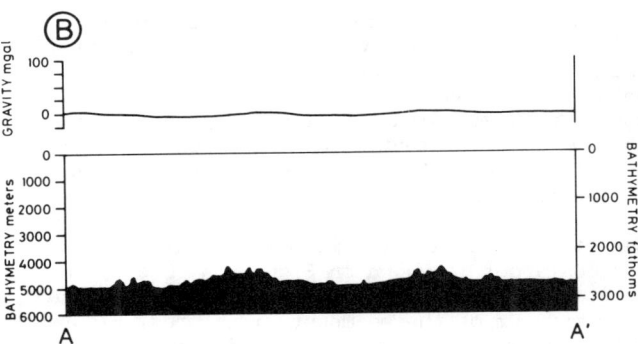

Fig. 2b. Survey of Fabert Bank charted location: Recorded free-air anomaly, and bathymetry obtained from vertical beam of SEABEAM. As predicted from the interpretation of SEASAT data, no such important bathymetric feature exists in the area.

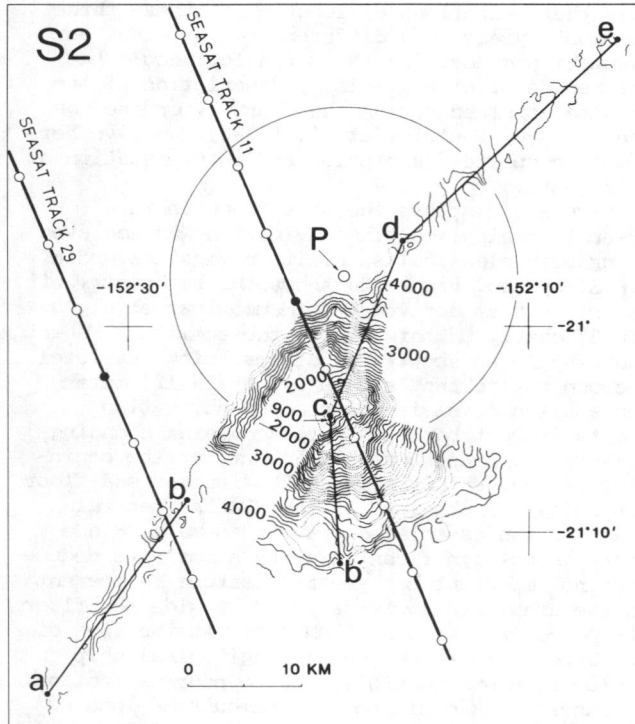

Fig. 3. SEABEAM survey of the location of predicted seamount S2. Contours are in meters with an interval of 100 meters. Point P corresponds to the predicted location and the circle represents the predicted 15 km uncertainty. The SEASAT tracks used for the detection are shown. Open dots are marked at central points of each area represented by one 1/sec data set of the sea surface height survey. Black dots correspond to the relative maxima of the seamount signature on a track. Mercator projection.

displayed. The three seamounts correspond to various location estimates since S2 was located using two parallel SEASAT profiles, S6 using both an ascending and a descending profile and S5 using two descending profiles and an ascending one. We used for that study the average altimetric measurements over 1 second intervals taken at the rate of 10/sec. The instrument field-of-view varies from 2.4 to 12 km, depending on the sea state. Each altimetric measurement of the 1 sec. data set is shown on Figures 3 to 5 by an open dot. The black dots correspond to the relative maximum of the seamount signatures. Figures 3 to 5 show that a seamount was found in each predicted location area. We now discuss each predicted location uncertainty.

Seamount S2 (Figure 3)

The SEABEAM survey reveals the existence of a very regular seamount whose summit (point C) lies 12.5 km south of its predicted location (point P) i.e. inside the "probable circle". This seamount was located using two ascending SEASAT profiles (tracks 11 and 29). The mislocation vector PC can be divided into an along-track error and a cross-track error. The along-track and cross-track errors are respectively parallel and normal to the SEASAT track direction. The along-track uncertainty is of 11 km and corresponds to the misfit between the two relative maxima and the seamount axis. We checked that the various treatments applied to the data, as the removal of the theoretical regional field, did not change the position of the maximum of the geoid anomaly. Therefore this unexpected shift must be attributed to noise in the data set used. This result demonstrates that the along-track location error can be as large as 15 km, which is much larger than the value assumed in some studies (see for example White et al., 1983). The use of a 0.5 sec. data set, although noisier (Vogt et al., 1984), can perhaps reduce this along-track uncertainty. The 6 km cross-track uncertainty is only due to our location method. This value is compatible with the predicted uncertainty.

Seamount S6 (Figure 4)

The survey of this area has shown that the structure responsible for the geoid anomaly consisted in a double cone seamount. Although limited, the SEABEAM data reveal that the western cone is larger than the eastern one. Due to the relative position of these cones and of the two SEASAT tracks used, it was impossible to visually predict the existence of the two summits. Indeed the two signatures overlap and give rise to a single one. Nevertheless, the computed location corresponds roughly to the centroid of the volcanic edifice. Moreover, the two summits are located inside the confidence circle. Thus, here again, the field test confirms the predicted location. This bathymetric feature has been previously detected by Sandwell (1984a) who located it at -24°24'36", -156°18'00"; i.e. 35 km to the south.

Lambeck and Coleman (1982) proposed to locate the seamounts detected on both ascending and descending altimetric profiles at the intersection of the two directions normal to the relative maxima. As shown on Figure 4, such a location yields a location close to the predicted one. Nevertheless, since the along-track uncertainty can reach about 15 km and the angle between the direction of ascending and descending SEASAT tracks is quite small, this method can give rise to a large uncertainty. Therefore, Lambeck and Coleman (1982) proposed to use in addition the less accurate GEOS 3 data since the azimuths of SEASAT and GEOS 3 tracks are quite different. Using both GEOS 3 and SEASAT data, Lambeck and Coleman (1982) located S6 and S5 with an precision identical to ours (Lambeck and Coleman, 1982, Figure 1). Therefore, if a seamount can be detected on intersecting GEOS 3 and SEASAT profiles, it could be located precisely, i.e. with an uncertainty identical with the

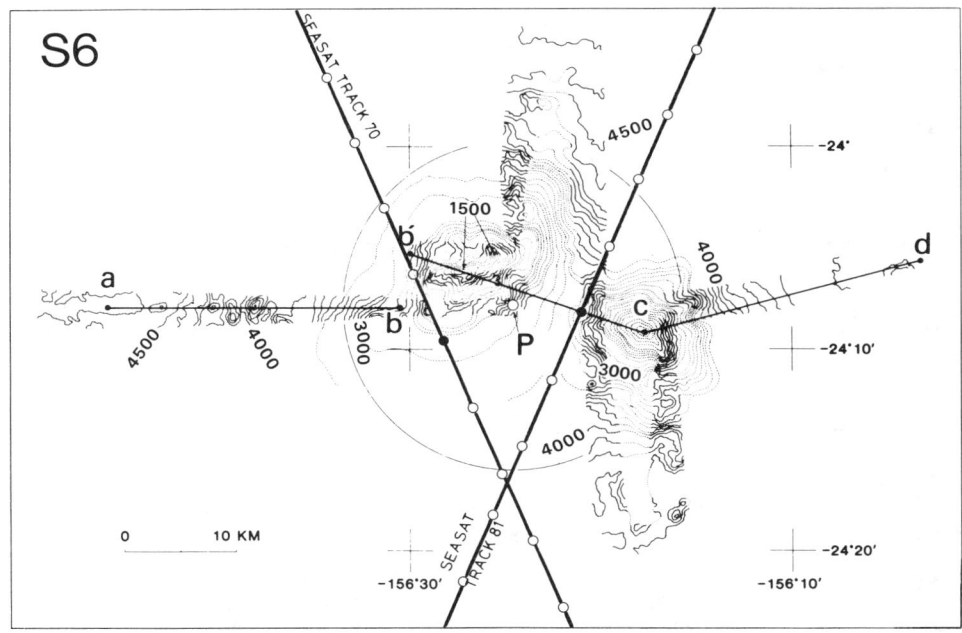

Fig. 4. Same as figure 3 for seamount S6.

detection made using two parallel SEASAT tracks. However, such a figure is quite unusual.

Seamount S5 (Figure 5)

Because of time constraints, we could only perform a simple transect across the confidence circle predicted for the seamount S5. In spite of poor SEABEAM coverage, the surveyed structure seems to be a regular volcano whose summit is located 7.5 km east of the predicted location. Three SEASAT profiles were available in the area. We located the seamount using first the two parallel ones (tracks 30 and 62), and then using the ascending track 51 and the descending track 62. The two computed locations are nearly identical since the distance between the two locations is on the order of 2 km. Point P on Figure 5 corresponds to the mean location. With the two descending profiles the along-track location error is 4 km and the cross-track one is 6 km, while with profiles 51 and 62 the along-track error (roughly north-south) is 1 km and the cross-track error (roughly east-west) is 7 km. These values confirm the previous remarks concerning the use of intersecting altimetric tracks and confirm again the 15 km uncertainty of our proposed location method. Now we turn to the discussion of the predictions of morphology and height of the seamounts.

Heights and Shapes of the Seamounts

Figure 6 represents for each seamount the predicted bathymetry and the observed one. The predicted and observed heights, volumes and upper slopes of the three seamounts are given in Table 1. Obviously, we underestimated the heights and upper-slopes of the seamounts. This is due to the gaussian model chosen after examination of the available maps in the Cook-Austral area. This model was tested successfully (see Paper 1) on some islands and large flat-topped seamounts whose morphology was derived from both GEBCO and Mammerickx et al.'s (1973) charts. But this model probably does not hold for smaller seamounts which present important bathymetric slopes. The

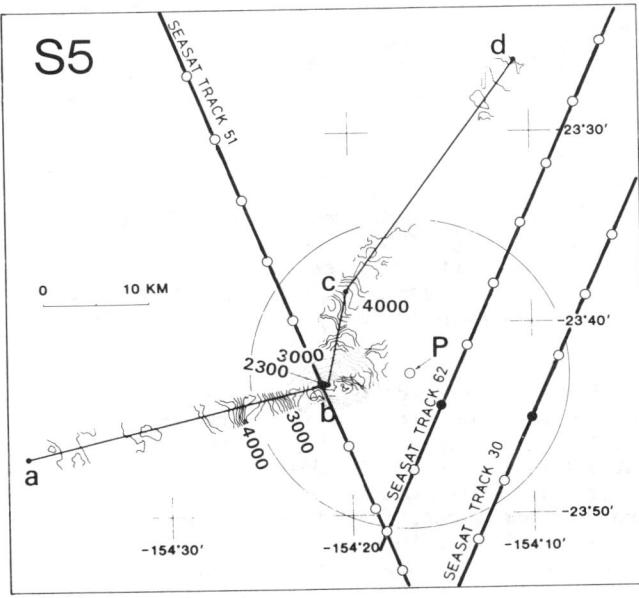

Fig. 5. Same as figure 3 for seamount S5.

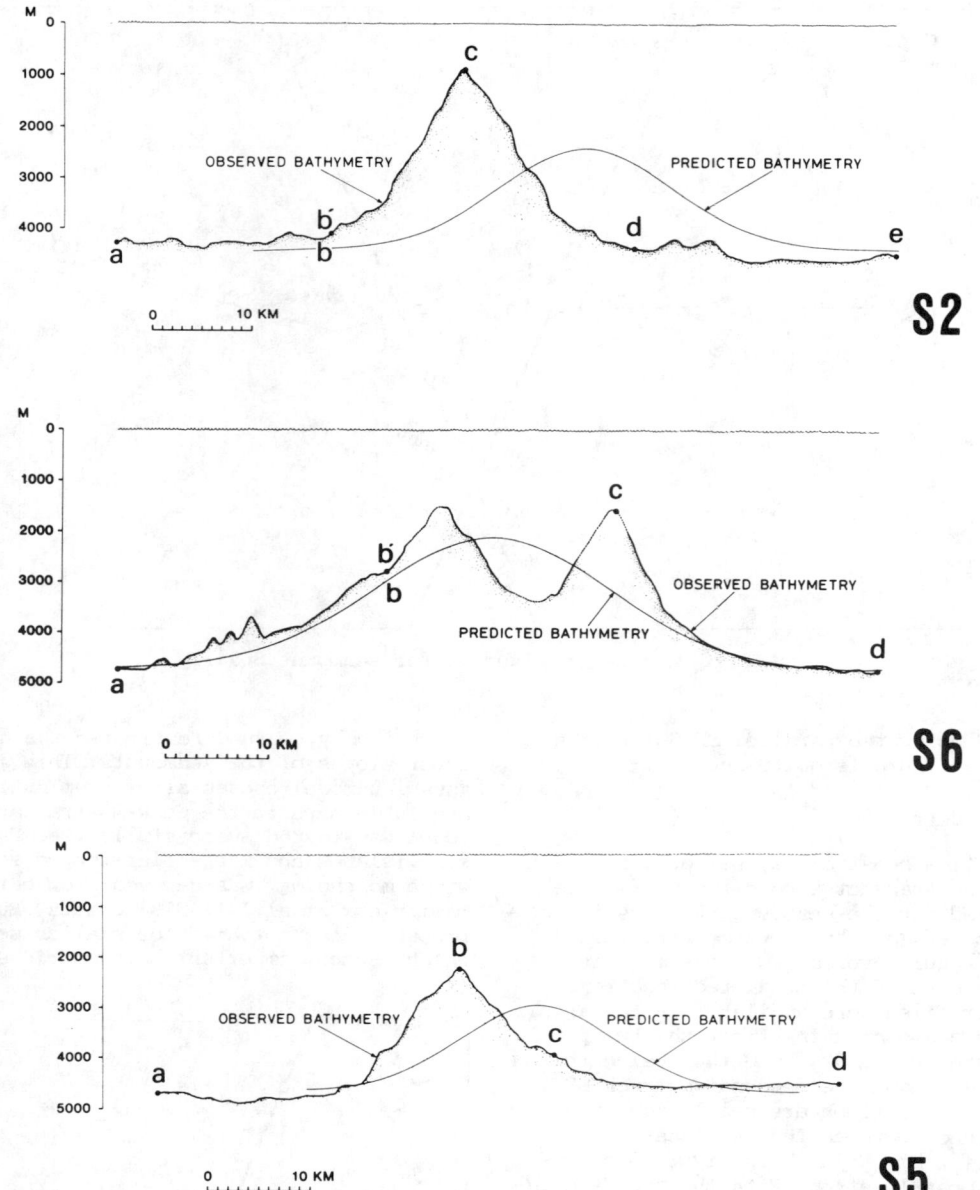

Fig. 6. Comparison between predicted morphologies and locations, shown by the gaussian shape profiles, and the observed bathymetry deduced from SEABEAM surveys. The predicted bathymetry has been projected for each seamount on the observed one in order to show the maximum location error. Letters refer to Figures 3, 4 and 5. Vertical exaggeration: 5X. Adapted from Pontoise et al. (1986).

fit between observed geoid anomalies and synthetic ones computed with a too low upper-slopes model led to underestimating the height and overestimating the volume of the seamounts.

As previously stated, the fit between SEASAT profiles and theoretical ones yielded r.m.s. values which were interpreted as an indication of the conformity between the real morphology and the predicted one. The values obtained for S2 and S5 are small, 3 cm and 8 cm respectively, while the value for S6 is 15 cm (see Paper 1). SEABEAM surveys show that S5 and S2 are indeed regular seamounts with a symmetry axis going through the summit, while S6, which is composed of two distinct cones, does not feature such symmetry. Therefore, we confirm the assumption made in

TABLE 1. Comparison of Predicted and Observed Heights,
Volumes and Upper-Slopes for the Three Seamounts

Seamount	Predicted Values			Observed Values		
	Height m	Volume km³	Upper-Slopes °	Height m	Volume km³	Upper-Slopes °
S6	2600	1650	7.7			
S6 (E)				3100 ?	300	19.0
S6 (W)				3150	770	12.9
S5	1700	500	7.7	2500	390	13.6
S2	2000	750	7.7	3400	430	19.4

Paper 1: a small r.m.s. value, i.e. typically less than 10 cm, indicates that the morphology of the seamount is regular, while a r.m.s. larger than 10 cm indicates some morphological complications. The real morphology was better predicted for S5 than for S2, although the r.m.s. value was lower for S2. This indicates that among the groups with low or high r.m.s., the exact value of the r.m.s. must be interpreted with caution.

During the recent cruise of the R/V Sonne in February 1987, a SEABEAM survey of the seamounts S3 and S7 was achieved (see Paper 1 for the seamounts location). The seamounts were found within the 15 km of the predicted locations, confirming the results obtained during the SEAPSO cruise (U. Von Stackelberg, personal communication).

Summary and Conclusions

Bathymetric data recorded during the SEAPSO V transit across the Austral archipelago confirmed the results of the seamount SEASAT detection technique proposed earlier by Baudry et al. (in press). Therefore, it is possible to locate a seamount precisely, i.e. with a location uncertainty of 15 km, if the seamount signature is detected on at least two altimetric profiles. Exact knowledge of parameters such as crustal model, the accurate effective elastic thickness of the lithosphere and precise morphology is not necessary in order to precisely locate the seamount. As a matter of fact, the 15 km location uncertainty was checked although the real morphology of the surveyed seamounts differs appreciably from the gaussian model used for the prediction. On the other hand, predictions of heights and volumes are very sensitive to the morphological model chosen. The choice of a gaussian model with a small mean slope leads to underestimating the heights by about 35%. Thus, the seamount model must be changed according to the results of statistical studies of the shape of submarine volcanoes in order to improve the location method. According to the precision and spacing of the SEASAT data, we believe that the 15 km uncertainty represents an optimum resolution. Future altimetric data such as those which will be obtained by TOPEX/POSEIDON (Stewart et al., 1986) are necessary in order to improve the location uncertainty.

Apart from the geodynamic and economic interests of such a precise location of previously uncharted seamounts, the 15 km uncertainty also affects the strategy for shipboard seamount survey (see Bracey, 1981). Indeed, such a precision makes possible an easy marine survey even with ships equipped only with traditional echo-sounding, since a seamount 15 km away should give rise to a bathymetric and gravity signature. We believe that such a SEASAT data analysis can be fruitfully performed in order to prepare any oceanographic cruise. For such a purpose, our location method could be linked to such software as the automatic detection of typical anomalies by matched filtering technique (White et al., 1983).

Acknowledgments. We thank B. Pontoise, chief-scientist of SEAPSO (Leg V) cruise, who provided us enough time during the transit to Tahiti. B. Pelletier and two anonymous reviewers largely contributed to the actual form of the paper. We are grateful to M. Le Gouic, from the Service Hydrographique et Océanographique de la Marine, and to J. Mammerickx for useful information about Fabert Bank. We thank the Captain, the officers, the crew, the technical and scientific teams of the cruise for their enthusiasm during the "seamount hunting". Figures were efficiently drawn by J. Butscher.

References

Baudry N., M. Diament and Y. Albouy, Precise location of unsurveyed seamounts in the Austral archipelago area using SEASAT data, Geophys. J.R. Astr. Soc., vol 88, 1987, in press.

Bracey D.R., Morphological characteristics of North Atlantic and North Pacific seamounts as factors for designing effective survey detection strategies, TR-266, 29 pp, Naval Oceanographic Office, Bay St. Louis, MS, 1981.

Calmant S. and A. Cazenave, The effective elastic lithosphere under the Cook-Austral and Society Islands, Earth Planet. Sci. Lett., 77, 187-202, 1986.

Cazenave A., and K. Dominh, Geoid heights over the Louisville ridge (South Pacific), J. Geophys. Res., 89, 11171-11179, 1984.

Diament M., and J. Goslin, Emplacement of the Marion Dufresne, Lena and Ob seamounts (South Indian ocean) from a study of isostasy, Tectonophys., 121, 253-262, 1986.

Dixon T.H., M. Naraghi, M.K. McNutt, and S.M. Smith, Bathymetric prediction from SEASAT altimeter data, J. Geophys. Res., 88, 1563-1571, 1983.

General Bathymetric Chart of the Oceans (GEBCO), Scale 1:10,000,000, Canadian Hydrographic Service, 5th edit., Ottawa, Ont, 1980.

Groeger W.J., Notes on estimating the seamount slope from vertical deflection, NSWC TR 81-2023, 37 pp, Naval Surface Weapons Center, Dahlgren, Virginia, 1981.

Haxby W.F., G.D. Karner, J.L. Labrecque, and J.K. Weissel, Digital images of combined oceanic and continental data sets and their use in tectonic studies, Eos Trans. AGU, 64, 995-1003, 1983.

Haxby W.F., Gravity field of the world's oceans, map, Lamont Doherty Geological Observatory, United States Navy, Office of Naval Research, 1985.

Keating B.H., N.Z. Cherkis, P.W. Fell, D. Handschumacher, R.N. Hey, A. Lazarewicz, D.F. Naar, R.K. Perry, D. Sandwell, D.C. Schwank, P. Vogt, and B. Zondek, Field test of SEASAT bathymetric detections, Marine Geophys. Res., 7, 69-71, 1984a.

Keating B.H., D.P. Mattey, C.E. Helsley, J.J. Naughton, and D. Epp, Evidence for a hot spot origin of the Caroline Islands, J. Geophys. Res., 89, 9937-9948, 1984b.

Lambeck K., and R. Coleman, A search for seamounts in the Southern Cook and Austral region, Geophys. Res. Lett., 9, 389-392, 1982.

Lazarewicz A.P., and D.C. Schwank, Detection of uncharted seamounts using satellite altimetry, Geophys. Res. Lett., 9, 385-388, 1982.

Mammerickx J., S.M. Smith, I.L. Taylor, and T.E. Chase, Bathymetry of the South Pacific, Scale 1:10,000,000, Scripps Institution of Oceanography, 1973.

Menard H.W., and M. McNutt, Evidence for and consequences of thermal rejuvenation, J. Geophys. Res., 87, 8570-8580, 1982.

Pontoise B., N. Baudry, M. Diament, J. Aubouin, R. Blanchet, J. Butscher, P. Chotin, J. Dupont, J.P. Eissen, J. Ferrière, R. Herzer, A. Lapouille, R. Louat, L. d'Ozouville, B. Pelletier, S. Soaki and A. Steveenson, Levés SEABEAM dans l'archipel des Iles Australes: Confirmation d'une nouvelle méthode de localisation de monts sous-marins basée sur l'analyse des données SEASAT. C. R. Acad. Sc., Paris, t. 303, série II, n°7, 563-568, 1986.

Sandwell D., Along-track deflection of the vertical from SEASAT: GEBCO overlays, NOS NGS-40, 8pp, National Oceanic and Atmospheric Administration, Rockville, Md., 1984a.

Sandwell D., A detailed view of the South Pacific geoid from satellite altimetry, J. Geophys. Res., 89, 1089-1104, 1984b.

Stewart R., L.L. Fu, and M. Lefebvre, Science opportunities from the Topex/Poseidon mission, JPL Publication 86-18, 58 pp, Jet Propulsion Laboratory, Pasadena, California, 1986.

Vogt P.R., B. Zondek, P.W. Fell, N.Z. Cherkis, and R.K. Perry, SEASAT altimetry, the North Atlantic geoid, and evaluation by shipborne subsatellite profiles, J. Geophys. Res., 89, 9885-9903, 1984.

Watts A.B., and N.M. Ribe, On geoid heights and flexure of the lithosphere at seamounts, J. Geophys. Res., 89, 11152-11170, 1984.

White J.V., R.V. Sailor, A.R. Lazarewicz, and A.R. LeSchack, Detection of seamount signatures in SEASAT altimeter data using matched filters, J. Geophys. Res., 88, 1141-1551, 1983.

TEMPERATURE BENEATH MIDPLATE SWELLS: THE INVERSE PROBLEM

Marcia McNutt

Department of Earth, Atmospheric, and Planetary Sciences, Massachusetts Institute of Technology, Cambridge

Abstract. Observations pertaining to the thermal structure of midplate swells surrounding hot spots, such as depth anomalies, geoid heights, heat flow, and the thickness of the elastic plate supporting the volcanoes, are inverted using the linear programming algorithm to derive extremal bounds on temperature as a function of depth and time in the lithosphere. The inversion technique makes no assumptions concerning the initial temperature dynamically emplaced in the lithosphere by the hot spot, other than that the temperature be physically plausible, but does assume that the process is steady state and that conductive cooling dominates heat transport once the lithosphere moves past the hot spot. Application of this inversion method to data from the Hawaiian and Marquesan island chains demonstrates that both swells require essentially the same perturbation by the hot spot to the lithosphere's thermal structure. Temperature anomalies of the order of 300-400°C are introduced at depths of 50 to 70 km where the temperature was only 900°C before swell formation.

Introduction

Midplate swells (Figure 1) are broad regions of elevated seafloor surrounding active or recently active oceanic hot spots. The common characteristics of these features include:
1) a depth anomaly Δh which can exceed 2 km relative to normal seafloor of the same age [Morgan, 1972] and gradually subsides as the plate moves away from the hot spot [Detrick and Crough, 1978];
2) a wavelength of 1000 to 2000 km [Crough, 1978];
3) a large geoid anomaly reflecting isostatic compensation for the swell in the mid- to lower lithosphere [Crough, 1978; McNutt and Shure, 1986; Fischer et al., 1986];
4) a heat flow anomaly which may not appear until 10 Ma or more after swell formation [Detrick et al., 1981; Detrick et al., 1986; Courtney and White, 1986];
5) a slight reduction in the thickness of the elastic plate supporting the hot spot volcanoes relative to the elastic plate thickness of normal lithosphere of the same age [Menard and McNutt, 1982; McNutt, 1984].
These observations require a thermal source for swells.

Previous attempts to model the thermal structure of midplate swells and their temporal evolution fall into two general classes. The conductive models specify some initial temperature structure imposed on the lithosphere by the hot spot, such as thermal rejuvenation or lithospheric thinning, without regard to how that structure could physically be established. As the conductively cooling plate moves away from the hot spot, the predictions of the thermal model are then compared to some subset of the above observations to determine one free parameter in the initial temperature structure, such as the younger thermal age to which the lithosphere has been reheated, the depth to which the lithosphere has been thinned, or the magnitude of an arbitrary heat source [Detrick and Crough, 1978; Menard and McNutt, 1982; Sandwell, 1982]. The remarkable fact is that such simple one-parameter models provide an adequate fit to the observations with which they are compared, although I know of no study to date which has simultaneously fit all observations from a given swell.

The other class of models is the dynamics ones which impose an upwelling hot plume on an assumed viscosity structure for the lithosphere [Parsons and Daly, 1983; Courtney and White, 1986; Fleitout et al., 1986]. The subsequent cooling of the dynamically perturbed temperature structure again makes predictions that can be compared with the observations, usually with a less satisfactory fit to the data using the commonly adopted lower limits on lithospheric viscosity and plume temperature. In general, the dynamic models do not produce temperature structures resembling the lithospheric reheating or plate thinning models which do fit most of the data, but there was previously no indication whether those structures were indeed required by the data.

The approach adopted here to determining the thermal structure of midplate swells departs from previous work in that no assumptions concerning temperature variations or viscosity are imposed on the lithosphere at time zero when it encounters the hot spot. Instead, I employ techniques from linear inverse theory to place extremal bounds on temperature within which all models fitting the data must lie. Although this method does not circumvent the problem of how the initial thermal perturbation could be established, at least it provides limits within which dynamically imposed temperatures must fall in order to satisfy the observations. In investigating these limits I will focus on two principal questions. First, how shallow must temperature anomalies be placed at time zero by the hot spot? Can they be confined to the less viscous lower lithosphere or must they extend above 70-km depth? Second, if we look at two very different hot spots, is the answer the same?

Copyright 1987 by the American Geophysical Union.

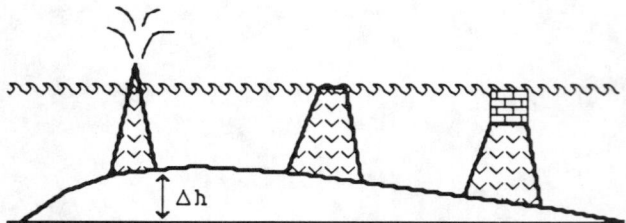

Fig. 1. Schematic view of a longitudinal profile along a midplate swell.

Assumptions

Although I do not specify an initial thermal structure on the swell, several other constraints are adopted and should be justified at the outset. An important assumption is that the hot spot process is steady state. For example, whatever happened to the lithosphere beneath Midway when it passed over the Hawaiian hot spot is also what is happening beneath Hawaii today. Steady-state conditions are also implied in previous studies of swells, although rarely stated explicitly. There is no compelling evidence for a steady state process, and in fact, most hot spots are intermittently active over time periods of several tens of millions of years [Bonatti and Harrison, 1976; Gordon and Henderson, 1986]. There is even evidence from the volume of volcanoes that the relatively steady Hawaiian hot spot waxes and wanes in intensity [Bargar and Jackson, 1974]. Here I assume steady state only as a first approximation for the practical reason that there is no established model for time-dependent hot spot behavior.

Another critical element is the adoption of a conductive cooling model. Regardless of the physical mechanism which introduces a thermal anomaly at time zero, the subsequent observations are explained by conductive cooling downstream from the hot spot. Two situations would obviously violate this assumption. The first is viscous entrainment of a hot plume by the horizontally moving plate, which would effectively sweep some of the dynamic support for the swell downstream from the site of active volcanism. However, recent models of asthenospheric convection predict a low viscosity zone immediately beneath the plate [Yuen and Fleitout, 1985; Buck and Parmentier, 1986; Craig and McKenzie, 1987] which would serve to decouple the motion of the plate from the asthenosphere below. The conductive cooling assumption would also be violated if large volumes of magma are transported to the surface in the process of post-erosion volcanism and associated intrusions [Watts et al., 1985]. This effect is probably of minor importance in explaining the gross features of midplate swells.

One-dimensional heat conduction is another simplification incorporated into this analysis. Given the fact that the wavelength of the swell is large compared to the thickness of the lithosphere, this assumption is valid. A two-dimensional treatment is feasible with the linear programming technique, but is hardly justified by the present density of data over swells.

The Forward Problem

Before describing the inverse problem of determining temperature given observations of swell height, geoid anomaly, heat flow, and elastic plate thickness, I begin by reviewing the forward problem of calculating these time-dependent functions of temperature given an initial geotherm. The simplest solution for temperature T as a function of depth z and time t in a plate when radioactive heat production and latent heat of fusion are neglected is [McKenzie, 1967]:

$$T(z,t) = T_m \left[z/\ell + \sum_{n=1}^{\infty} c_n \sin(n\pi z/\ell) \exp(-n^2 t/\tau) \right] \quad (1)$$

in which

T_m = fixed temperature at the base of the plate
ℓ = thickness of the lithosphere
τ = nondimensional time = $\ell^2/(\pi^2 \kappa)$
κ = thermal diffusivity

The coefficients c_n are similar to Fourier coefficients and depend on the initial temperature structure.

The swell height, geoid anomaly, heat flow, and elastic plate thickness are all functions of the temperature T. Since the first two of these quantities are commonly reported as anomalies relative to the plate model, they are more easily expressed as functions of the anomalous temperature ΔT:

$$\Delta T(z,t,t_o) = T(z,t) - T_{plate}(z, t_o+t)$$

where T_{plate} is also given by (1) with $c_n = 2/(n\pi)$. Time t for the swell is simply $t = x/u$ in which x is distance along the swell from the hot spot and u is the absolute plate velocity. For lithosphere of age t_o when it encounters the hot spot, time t_o+t in the plate model is the absolute age of the lithosphere since it was created at the ridge crest.

In terms of the temperature anomaly ΔT, the depth anomaly Δh is

$$\Delta h = \frac{\rho_s}{\rho_s - \rho_w} \int_0^\ell \alpha \, \Delta T \, dz$$

in which ρ_s and ρ_w are the mean densities of the lithosphere and water, respectively, and α is the coefficient of thermal expansion. This integral can be easily performed analytically using the expressions for T and T_{plate} to yield the depth anomaly in terms of the coefficients c_n:

$$\Delta h = \frac{\alpha \rho_s T_m}{\rho_s - \rho_w} \sum_{n=1}^{\infty} \left\{ e^{-n^2 t/\tau} \frac{\ell}{n\pi} \left[c_n - \frac{2}{n\pi} e^{-n^2 t_o/\tau} \right] \left[1 - \cos n\pi \right] \right\} \quad (2)$$

The heat flow Q measured on the swell depends on the temperature gradient at $z=0$:

$$Q = k \, dT/dz \,|_{z=0}$$

where k is the thermal conductivity. Substituting for T from (1):

$$Q = k T_m \left[1/\ell + \sum_{n=1}^{\infty} c_n \, n\pi/\ell \, \exp(-n^2 t/\tau) \right] \quad (3)$$

The elastic plate thickness roughly corresponds to the depth of the 450°C to 600°C isotherm, which marks the transition from long-term elastic behavior to ductile behavior [Watts et al., 1980; McNutt and Menard, 1982]. Therefore, the predicted thickness for the elastic plate is simply the depth z such that T given by (1) equals T_e, the temperature chosen to mark the base of the elastic plate.

The geoid anomaly N is related to the temperature anomaly via [Ockendon and Turcotte, 1977; Parsons and Richter, 1980]:

$$N = \frac{-2\pi G \alpha \rho_s}{g} \int_0^\ell z \, \Delta T \, dz$$

in which G is Newton's constant and g is gravitational acceleration at the Earth's surface. Substituting for ΔT, this expression becomes

$$N = \frac{-2\pi G \alpha \rho_s T_m}{g} \sum_{n=1}^{\infty} \frac{\ell^2}{n\pi} (-1)^n \, e^{-n^2 t/\tau} \left(c_n - \frac{2}{n\pi} e^{-n^2 t/\tau} \right) \quad (4)$$

Using equations (1)-(4), one could calculate the elastic plate thickness of the lithosphere beneath the swell, its depth anomaly relative to the plate model, the heat flow, and its geoid anomaly relative to the plate model as a function of time given the infinite set of coefficients c_n which describe the geotherm at the time of hot spot volcanism.

The Inverse Problem

The problem addressed here is the inverse of that stated above. Given a few estimates, with associated uncertainties, of the depth anomaly, heat flow, geoid anomaly, and elastic plate thickness of the lithosphere as a function of distance along a midplate swell, what can we determine about its temperature structure? The problem is classically nonunique since the set of unknown coefficients is infinite. Therefore, we seek properties that are common to all solutions consistent with the data. In the formulation presented here, linear programming is used to place bounds on the temperature as a function of depth within which all possible solution must fall. The development follows closely that presented by McNutt and Royden [1987] for inverting metamorphic geothermometers and geobarometers to characterize the thermal history of eroded mountain belts.

The linear programming algorithm can find any finite number of unknown quantities that enter (1) linearly subject to constraints imposed by the geophysical data and other physically reasonable linear inequalities and such that a specified quantity (the penalty function) is extremal [Gass, 1975]. For this particular application, I use the revised simplex algorithm to find the solution vector

$$x = \{T_m, c_1, c_2, c_3, \ldots c_{max}\}$$

subject to constraints

(a) the thermal model fits all depth anomaly observations $\Delta h(t)$ to within their uncertainties $\partial h(t)$;
(b) the thermal model fits all heat flow observations $Q(t)$ to within their uncertainties $\partial Q(t)$;
(c) the thermal model predicts a geoid anomaly over the swell such that its compensation depth z_ℓ given by

$$z_\ell = \frac{-N}{\Delta h} \frac{g}{2\pi G (\rho_s - \rho_w)} \quad (5)$$

agrees with the observed compensation depth z_ℓ to within the uncertainty ∂z_ℓ;
(d) the thermal model predicts that the 600°C isotherm was never shallower than $z_e(t)$, the elastic plate thickness observed now;
(e) the initial geotherm is bounded by $(z \cdot T_{min}/\ell) < T(z) < T_{max}$;
(f) the temperature at the base of the plate is bounded by $T_{min} < T_m < T_{max}$; (g) at a specified depth z_b and time t_b, the temperature is either maximized or minimized.

Constraints (a) and (b) are straightforward, but several of the others require some discussion. The geoid observation is only indirectly satisfied via the compensation depth in constraint (c). The reason for this approach is that it easily allows the incorporation of results from gravity studies in addition to geoid studies and avoids having to deal with baseline problems. Some studies of swell compensation remove only a long-wavelength global reference field, others perform an age correction also, and some additionally remove a best-fitting plane. Since the compensation depth given by (5) is calculated using the component of the geoid at the same wavelength as the depth anomaly, such differences in base level do not affect z_ℓ (see McNutt and Shure [1986]), but obviously can produce vastly different estimates of the geoid height. Using the Ockendon-Turcotte formula in (4) to calculate the geoid height N in (5) provides only a long-wavelength approximation which overestimates the true geoid by 10-20% at the 1000-2000-km wavelengths typical of swells. This error is comparable to the uncertainty in the observed compensation depths used to constrain the inversions, and little affects the bounds on temperature.

The elastic plate constraint in (d) is expressed in a very conservative way. The rationale is that if at any time between the formation of the hot spot volcano and now the 600°C isotherm became shallower than z_e, we would observe a smaller elastic plate thickness unless that isotherm grossly underestimates the temperature at the base of the elastic plate, which it probably does not [Watts et al., 1980; McNutt and Menard, 1982]. The constraint allows the temperature to be very much colder at the depth z_e, such as might be reasonable if the isotherm controlling the base of the elastic plate is only 450°C or if a small elastic plate thickness is due to local reheating of the lithosphere in the immediate vicinity of the volcano that does not reflect the overall thermal structure of the swell.

Constraints (e) and (f) ensure that the solution will correspond to a physically realizable initial model. The lower bound for (e) is the linear geotherm only achieved in very old lithosphere. It is extremely unlikely that the hot spot process produces overlying lithosphere anywhere colder than this limit. The choice for T_{max} can be based on petrological arguments concerning the expected temperature at depth of surface magmas or on other geophysical/geodynamic

TABLE 1. Hawaiian Swell

t Ma	Δh km	∂h km	Q mW/m³	∂Q mW/m³	z_e km	z_ℓ km	∂z_ℓ km
0.	1.25	.25					
2.						70.	10.
4.			53.	4.	33.		
5.			55.	4.	32.		
7.			58.	4.	32.		
13.	1.0	.25					
22.			59.	4.			
28.	.5	.25					

estimates of temperatures within the convecting asthenosphere.

Potentially the greatest limitation in this sort of analysis is the fact that we can only solve for a finite number of unknowns which enter the equations linearly. For example, the lithospheric thickness ℓ, the thermal diffusivity κ, and the coefficient of thermal expansion α might rightfully be considered variables. I have assigned values to these parameters based on the best fit to depth and heat flow observations in the North Pacific and North Atlantic from Parsons and Sclater [1977] in order to be consistent with the fact that several of the observations are referenced to this plate model. The only parameter which might reasonably be expected to vary over the swell is the lithospheric thickness ℓ. However, the solutions derived below for the Hawaiian and Marquesas swells both show hot, nearly isothermal conditions in the lower lithosphere. The subsequent cooling history over the next 30 or so Ma is therefore practically insensitive to the lithospheric thickness in the same way that the plate model agrees with the predictions of simple halfspace cooling at young ages.

The fact that the expansion for the thermal model must be truncated at some c_{max} is not a serious drawback. First of all, the number of terms taken in the expansion does not depend on the number of data and is only limited by computer size. The fact that temperatures are intially bounded above and below means that any individual c_n is likewise bounded. Since the influence of the higher order terms decays as $exp(-n^2 t/\tau)$, there will always be a time $t>0$ such that the true extremal temperature is reached even with a finite number of c_n's. At time $t=0$, no damping occurs. By constructing the initial geotherm with only a finite set $\{c_n\}$, we can only look at the temperature averaged over a finite depth interval roughly given by $\ell/(nmax+1)$.

Results

This algorithm was applied to data from two swells, Hawaii and Marquesas. Much better heat flow data exist over the Bermuda Rise [Detrick et al., 1986] and the Cape Verde Rise [Courtney and White, 1986] in the Atlantic Ocean, but because the African and North American plates move slowly in the hot spot reference frame relative to the Pacific rate, there is no estimate of the change in depth and heat flow with time since hot spot volcanism. In the Pacific cases presented below, tight constraints are obtained on the thermal model for the reason that the geotherm at any position beneath the swell must satisfy not only the geophysical data at that location, but also the earlier and later observables via the physics of conductive heat transport.

Hawaii

Table 1 lists the observations that were inverted to produce the extremal bounds on the temperature beneath the Hawaiian swell. The depth and heat flow values are from Detrick et al. [1981] as measured along the flexural arch to the south of the island chain to avoid the disturbing effects of the islands themselves. The uncertainties in the heat flow values are taken from the error bars in Detrick et al. [1981], while that for the depth anomalies is uniformly set at 250 m. Beneath Hawaii, where some of the elevation may be dynamically supported in the mantle, this error estimate is probably reasonable. For the older portions of the swell, the depth anomaly is better constrained, but retaining the larger uncertainty allows more generous bounds on temperature. The compensation depth and associated uncertainty from McNutt and Shure [1986] is considered to be an average over the young portion of the swell. The values for elastic plate thickness are those of Watts [1978]. The ages are estimated from the date of the adjacent portion of the Hawaiian ridge as given by K-Ar when available, otherwise from assuming constant motion of the Pacific plate over a fixed hot spot at the rate of 110 mm/yr.

Of most interest is the time zero geotherm beneath Hawaii since it provides the most detailed view of the thermal perturbation from the hot spot before the onset of conductive cooling which smooths the temperature anomalies. Unfortunately, the true extremal bounds on the time zero geotherm found by performing the linear programming inversion as $n \rightarrow \infty$ are intrinsically uninteresting. Except at shallow depths where the maximum temperature is limited by the elastic plate constraint, the true $t=0$ extremal bounds are given by constraint (e) alone. With infinite degrees of freedom in the expansion for the temperature, the linear programming solution can construct a model fitting the data with a hot or cold thermal spike at any depth. The thermal spike achieving the extremal bound at the target depth z_b is always coupled with thermal spikes of opposite sign at adjacent depths such that the spikes instantly annihilate each other so as not to violate the data. However, by producing the extremal bounds from a truncated expansion, we can average over these thermal spikes to view the more useful bounds on the depth-averaged thermal structure.

Figure 2a shows the extremal bounds on temperature in the upper 100 km of a 125-km thick plate beneath the island of Hawaii from the linear programming inversion with $n_{max}=10$, $T_{min}=1350°C$, $T_{max}=1400°C$ and all of the constraints in Table 1. With only 10 terms in the expansion, the temperature is effectively averaged over a 10-km depth interval. The upper and lower extremal bounds themselves are not

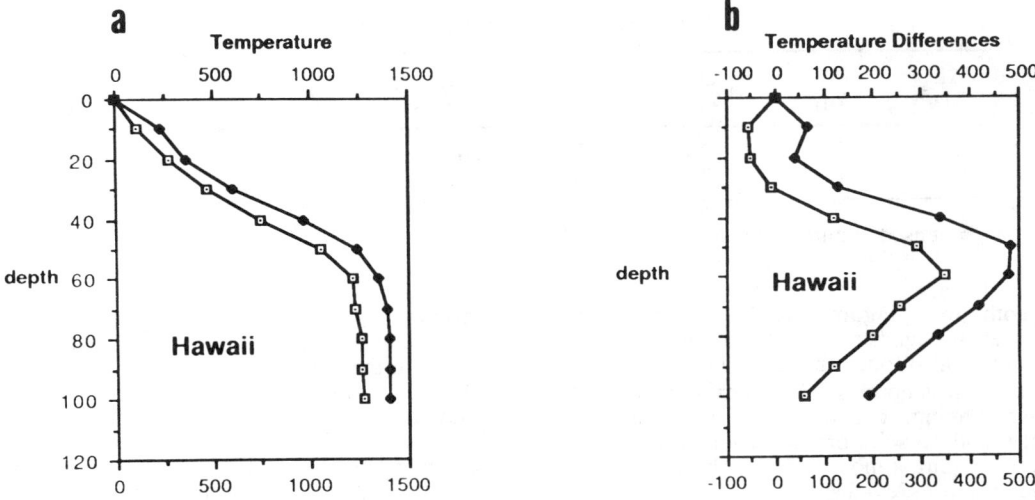

Fig. 2. (a) Extremal bounds on temperature as a function of depth beneath the island of Hawaii as obtained from a linear programming inversion of the data in Table 1 using 10 terms in Equation (1) to describe the thermal structure. (b) Same bounds as (a) but with the expected temperature as a function of depth according to Parsons and Sclater [1977] for 80-Ma old lithosphere subtracted from each bound to yield temperature differences.

geotherms which fit the data, but between the bounds lie an infinite number of models fitting the constraints. The bounds are indeed extremal; i.e. there is no $n=10$ model consistent with the data which anywhere exceeds the bounds. They are also optimal; i.e. each point on the bounds does correspond to a feasible solution. The temperature bounds show a relatively low geothermal gradient in the upper 30 km, followed by a steepening geotherm between 30 and 60 km, and finally very hot, nearly isothermal conditions in the lower lithosphere.

Another way to view the extremal bounds is in terms of temperature anomalies (Figure 2b) relative to the thermal model of Parsons and Sclater [1977] for lithosphere of 80 Ma, the age of the Pacific plate beneath Hawaii. The bounds on anomalous temperature indicate that absolutely no change in the temperature is required in the upper 30 km of the plate.

The anomalous temperature peaks at values of 300 to 500°C at 60-km depth, just above the compensation depth of the swell. The temperature differences taper off at greater depths where the lithosphere was hot even before reheating.

Figure 3 shows the temperature and temperature anomaly beneath Hawaii for a second inversion using the same parameters as those in Figure 2 except that $n_{max}=6$. Therefore, we are viewing the temperature through an averaging window 18 km wide. Compared with Figure 2, these bounds are everywhere tighter, but do not basically change any of the conclusions stated above. Obviously some of the latitude allowed in the geotherms enclosed by the bounds in Figure 2 is due to correlated short-wavelength variability over distances between 10 and 18 km, which probably is not physically real. (i.e. One can imagine a

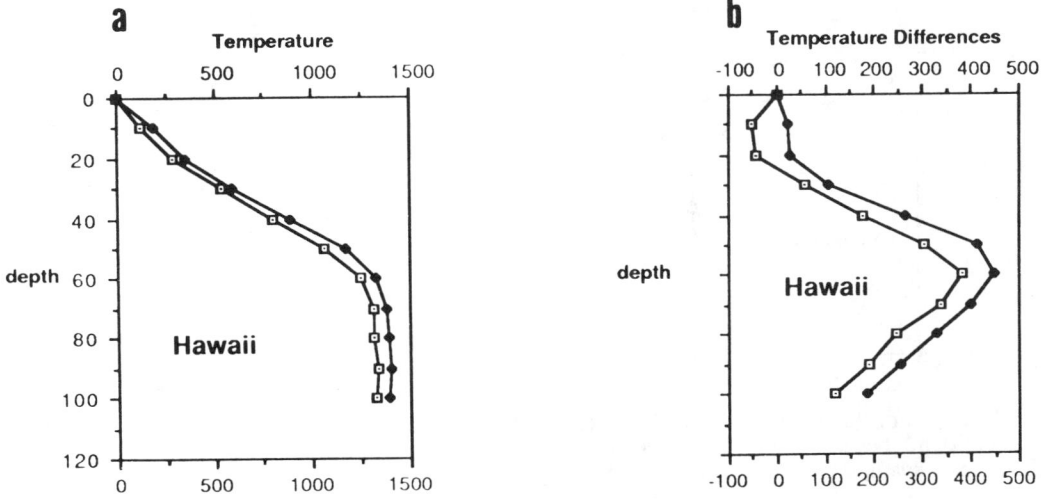

Fig. 3. Same as Figure 2, but with only 6 terms in the expansion for the temperature.

TABLE 2. Marquesas Swell

t Ma	Δh km	∂h km	Q mW/m³	∂Q mW/m³	z_e km	z_ℓ km	∂z_ℓ km	km
2.	1.		.25	(45.	20.)*	20.	45.	10.
9.	1.		.25					

*not used in initial inversion

permissible geotherm in Figure 2 rattling back and forth between the extremal bounds such that every time it hits the upper bound it must also touch the lower bound within the next 10 to 18 km.) It is not possible to perform any further depth averaging. Attempts to invert the observations with an $n_{max}=5$ model found no solutions consistent with the data. The observations require a model that resolves temperature differences over distances less than 20 km.

Marquesas

The Marquesas hot spot chain differs considerably in its attributes from the Hawaiian case. For example, as shown in Table 2, the height of the swell is lower than the Hawaiian swell, its compensation depth is much shallower, and its elastic plate thickness is less [Fischer et al., 1986]. Furthermore, compared to the long continuous chain of volcanoes produced by the Hawaiian hot spot, the Marquesas chain only exhibits a 7 Ma span of continuous activity. By inverting geophysical data from the Marquesas swell, we can determine whether these differences extend to the subsurface temperature structure in the swell.

The first attempt to invert the Marquesas data was disappointing. Figure 4a shows the extremal bounds on temperature beneath Fatu Hiva, the youngest of the Marquesan islands, using the same parameters for the first Hawaiian inversion ($n_{max}=10$, $T_{min}=1350°C$, $T_{max}=1400°C$). The bounds are much less restrictive, and about all that can be said from the temperature differences relative to 50-Ma-old lithosphere (Figure 4b) is that some thermal anomaly is required between 30 and 70 km depth. Without heat flow data, there is little constraint on the near-surface thermal gradient. Uncertainty in the surface temperature propagates down through the entire lithosphere allowing a large range in permissible temperatures.

In the second attempt to invert the Marquesas data, I added a heat flow estimate of $Q=45\pm20$ mW/m², which is the average plus/minus one standard deviation of all the heat flow observations anywhere on the Marquesas swell [Jessop et al., 1976]. Although it might appear that the 50% uncertainty in this number would place little further constraint on the inversion, in actual fact the bounds in Figure 5a are considerably tighter. The heat flow is so low that it rules out any significant thermal anomaly in the upper 20 km (Figure 5b), thus lowering the upper bound in the upper lithosphere and raising the lower bound in the lower lithosphere. It might be argued that this heat flow estimate is not truly representative of the Marquesas swell, but based on observations from other hot spots and on physical principles it appears that any constraint that limits the amount of reheating at the top of the lithosphere at the young end of hot spot swells is reasonable.

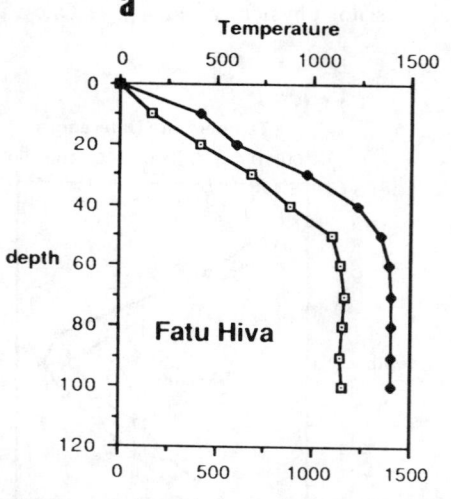
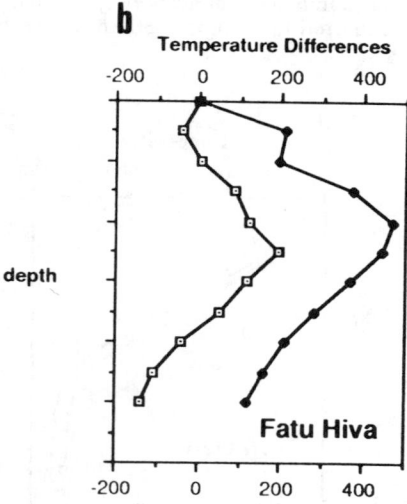

Fig. 4. Bounds on (a) temperature and (b) temperature differences relative to 50-Ma old lithosphere as function of depth beneath Fatu Hiva. Inversion is the same as for Figure 2, but using the data in Table 2 for the Marquesas swell, without the heat flow estimate.

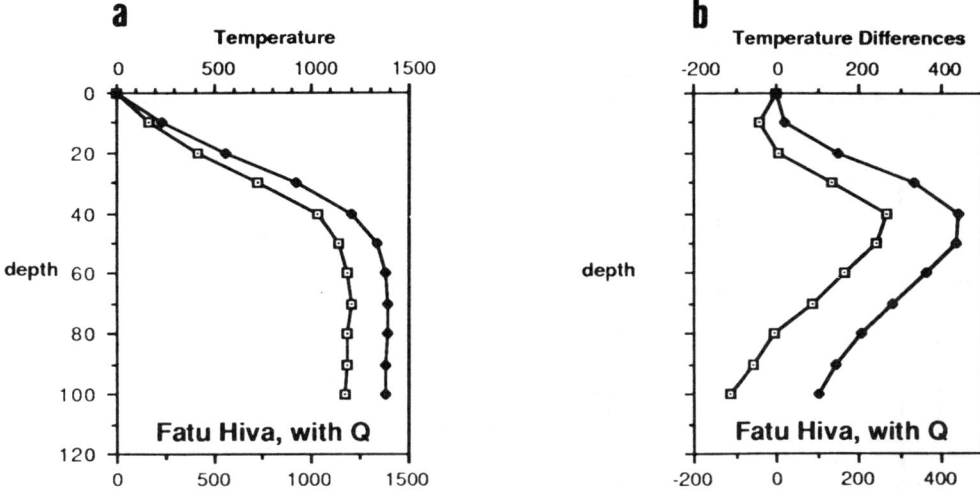

Fig. 5. Same as Figure 4, but including the heat flow estimate from Table 2.

The pattern shown in the temperature differences in Figure 5b is similar to that in Figure 2b for the Hawaiian swell, although shifted to shallower depths. No thermal anomaly imposed by the hot spot is required in the upper 20 km. The maximum temperature difference reaches 250-450°C at 50 km, just about the compensation depth of the swell. In the lower lithosphere, where temperatures were hot even before encountering the hot spot, temperature differences return to zero.

When we factor in the differences in the temperature of the lithosphere before hot spot reheating, the profiles for both the Hawaiian swell (Figure 2b) and the Marquesas swell (Figure 5b) imply the same perturbation by the hot spot. For both swells the base of the "unaffected" region at the surface is marked by the 500°C isotherm before hot spot reheating (Figure 6). The region of the lithosphere with the maximum thermal anomaly corresponds to the position of the 900°C isotherm before reheating in both cases (Figure 6). Therefore, if we imagine that the extent to which the hot spot can penetrate to reheat the lithosphere at time zero is dependent on the lithosphere's initial viscosity, which in turn depends on temperature, we conclude that significant penetration must occur at depths as shallow as the 900°C isotherm, with a smaller degree of reheating extending as shallow as the 500°C isotherm. The differences in the geophysical characteristics of the Marquesas and Hawaiian swells are entirely due to the different ages of the lithosphere at the onset of hot spot volcanism. There is no indication that whatever process led to the geotherm presently beneath Hawaii is any different from that responsible for the geotherm beneath Fatu Hiva.

The elastic plate constraint for both swells prevents temperatures from exceeding 600°C above 20 km for Fatu Hiva and above 30 km for Hawaii. In neither case was that constraint actually needed. For Hawaii (Figure 3), the bounds on the temperature at the depth of the elastic/ductile transition are 538-578°C. At Fatu Hiva, the bounds are 412-553°C. Therefore, the elastic plate thickness is not constraining the inversion. The bounds from the inversion predict that the isotherm controlling the base of the elastic plate is about 550°C, in agreement with that derived by McNutt [1984] from considering the slower strain rates for seamount loading compared to deformation of the outer rise seaward of subduction zones. Temperatures as cold as 460°C are allowed at the base of the elastic plate according to the more generous bounds in Figure 2. Any local heating by magma injection in the vicinity of individual volcanoes would necessarily raise the estimate of the isotherm controlling the base of the elastic plate.

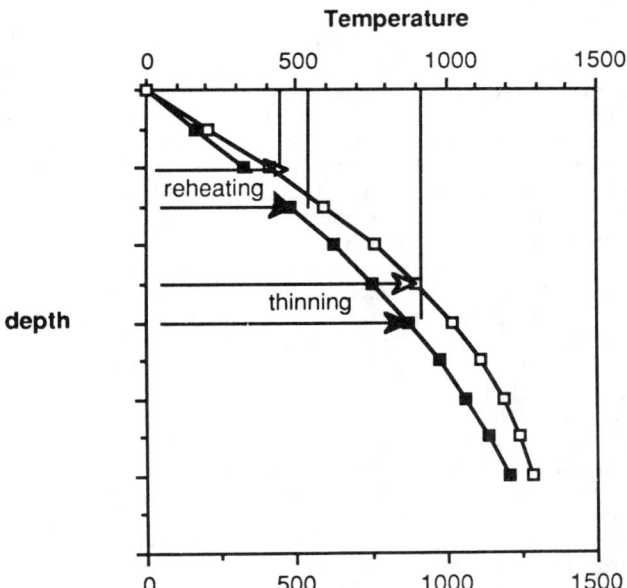

Fig. 6. Geotherms for normal 80-Ma old lithosphere (open symbols) and 50-Ma old lithosphere (closed symbols) from the plate model of Parsons and Sclater [1977]. Arrows show the depth of lithospheric thinning and the shallowest depth of partial reheating for each case as determined from the bounds in Figures 2 and 4.

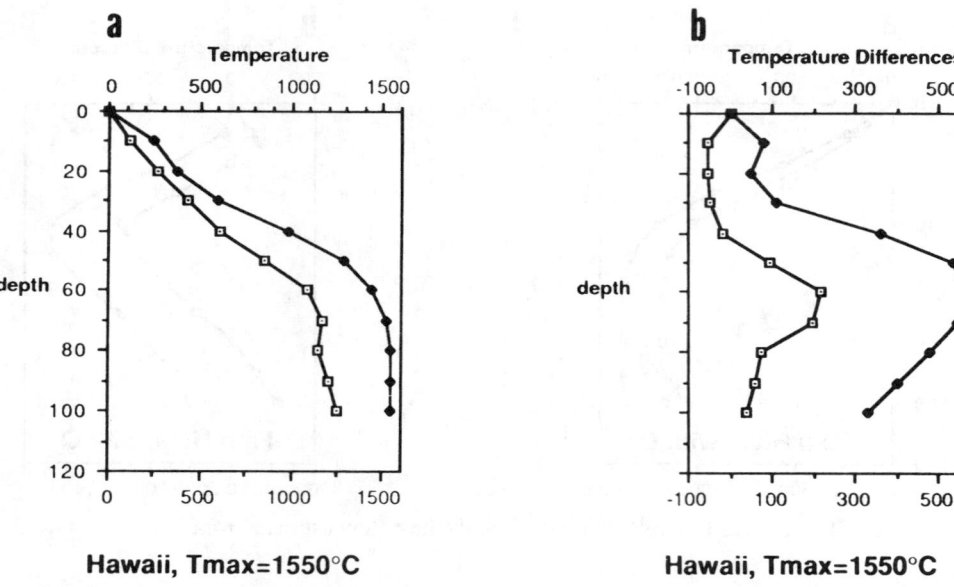

Fig. 7. Same as Figure 2, but increasing the bound on the maximum permissible temperature in the lithosphere from 1400°C to 1550°C.

Discussion

The results from the linear programming inversion of data from the Hawaiian and Marquesas swells are extremely similar. In the terminology of earlier conductive cooling models, it appears that in each case the lithosphere has been "thinned" to the depth of the 900°C isotherm before encountering the hot spot and partially "rejuvenated" to depths as shallow as the 500°C isotherm. Since the Hawaiian swell rises from the depth of normal seafloor to its peak at Hawaii in the space of only 8 Ma [McNutt and Shure, 1986], whatever dynamic model describes the interaction between the upwelling plume and the plate must inject a significant amount of heat into the lithosphere in a time period of less than 10 Ma.

The extent to which the results stated above can be defended depends upon the validity of the assumptions constraining the extremal inversions. Here I will attempt to anticipate some of the possible objections to this analysis.

1) The compensation depth should not be used as a constraint on the solution because models exist with density anomalies everywhere below z_ℓ that mimic the geoid anomaly from compensation at z_ℓ. From numerical experiments of two-dimensional convective flow in a box, Robinson et al. [1987] show that the depth of compensation can appear shallow even when the thermal anomaly remains deep if a thin low viscosity zone underlies the conducting portion of the lithosphere. In their models, they assume a conducting lid 75 km thick overlying a 125-km thick zone with viscosity 1 to 2 orders of magnitude less viscous than the underlying mantle. If the shallow compensation depths for the Marquesas and Hawaiian swells are a non-physical artifact of assuming too simple a model, then the temperature anomalies in Figures 2 through 5 may be forced into the mid lithosphere in order to satisfy an erroneous constraint. To investigate this possibility, I again inverted the Hawaiian data as for Figure 2 but without the compensation depth constraint. The bounds obtained are identical to those in Figure 2. In other words, the compensation depth is in no way constraining the solution. In fact, any conductive cooling model which explains all of the other observations predicts that the compensation depth must lie within 70±10 km. This result does not rule out a low viscosity zone beneath the plate. In fact, such a zone is needed to decouple the motions of the plate from the flow of the relatively stationary upwelling plume. It means that the evidence for reheating of the lithosphere above 70-km depth does not rest on the interpretation of the compensation depth. For the Marquesas, the compensation constraint is more important due to the absence of good heat flow data. Nevertheless, extremal models unconstrained by the compensation depth never predict a compensation depth greater than 65 km for the Marquesas swell.

2) The value of T_{max} is too low. By not allowing larger temperature differences in the lower lithosphere, some of the thermal anomaly is forced above 70 km to fit the depth anomaly data. I chose $T_{max}=1400°C$ based on the maximum predicted temperature at the base of the lithosphere for Hawaiian lavas assuming upwelling at constant entropy [McKenzie, 1984]. However, most dynamic models for plume formation involve maximum temperature differences of 200°C between the normal mantle (1350°C) and the upwelling plume [Fleitout et al., 1986; Robinson et al., 1987]. The extremal bounds on temperature and temperature differences beneath Hawaii for an inversion with $T_{max}=1550°C$ are shown in Figure 7. This model was also run without the constraint on compensation depth in order to allow models with very high temperatures confined to depths greater than 70 km if consistent with the other data. Allowing hotter initial temperatures, the bounds are much broader but have the same overall configuration as those in Figure 2. It is still necessary to have thermal anomalies of at least 200°C at depths of 50 to 80 km in order to fit the data. In addition, all of the geotherms which attained the upper bounds in excess of 1400°C in Figure 7 set the temperature at the base of the plate to values near 1350°C so that heat is discharged back into the mantle at early times in order to fit the subsidence data at later times. Increasing the upper bound on temperature to 1600°C only

widened each bound by about 20°C below 50-km depth, without eliminating the need for elevated temperatures in the mid-lithosphere.

3) The depth interval l over which thermal anomalies are considered is too shallow. Consideration of deeper anomalies would allow cooler temperatures at shallow depth. It would be possible to increase the thickness of the lithosphere such that hot rock deeper than 125 km is carried downstream with the Pacific plate. I have not attempted an inversion with a thicker plate because a change in l would require redefining all of the anomalies relative to something other than the Parsons and Sclater [1977] plate model. In addition, it is not clear that a larger effective thickness for the plate would be compatible with the existence of a low viscosity zone below 75-km depth, as predicted by the temperature and pressure dependence of viscosity.

Conclusions

Observations of depth, geoid, heat flow, and elastic plate flexure can be used to bound the temperature in the lithosphere beneath midplate swells using the technique of linear programming. The advantage of this approach is that it requires no assumptions concerning the initial temperature dynamically imposed by the hot plume and easily incorporates realistic bounds on the size of physical parameters. Of the several types of observations, the depth and heat flow are most critical in defining the extremal bounds on temperature. The compensation depth of the swell is predicted by all models consistent with the other data, as is the elastic plate thickness if the elastic/ductile transition occurs at a temperature near 550°C beneath seamounts.

If the temperature within the lithosphere cannot exceed 1400°C, the bounds on temperature beneath Hawaiian and Fatu Hiva, the youngest Marquesa volcano, display a similar, well-constrained pattern. The lithosphere has been "thinned" to depths of 70 and 50 km, respectively, with some "thermal rejuvenation" extending to within 30 km of the surface. In both cases, the depth to which the lithosphere is thinned correlates with the position of the 900°C isotherm and the depth to which some reheating occurs correlates with the 500°C isotherm before reheating. If temperatures reach as high as 1550°C within the lithosphere, the constraints are not as tight, but a thermal anomaly of at least 200°C is still required above 70-km depth beneath Hawaii.

This paper does not attempt to address how such geotherms might be established during the 8 to 10 Ma rise time of a midplate swell. Dynamic models that confine the thermal anomaly to below 70-km depth, however, will not be able to explain the observations.

Acknowledgments. I thank Emile Okal and David Sandwell for reviewing the manuscript. This work was supported by NSF OCE-8409157 and ONR N00014-82-C-0019.

References

Bargar, K. E. and E. D. Jackson, Calculated volumes of individual shield volcanoes along the Hawaiian-Emperor chain, *J. Res. U. S. Geol. Surv.*, 2, 545-550, 1974.

Bonatti, E. and C. G. A. Harrison, Hot lines in the earth's mantle, *Nature*, 263, 402-404, 1976.

Buck, R. and E. M. Parmentier, Convection beneath young oceanic lithosphere: Implications for thermal structure and gravity, *J. Geophys. Res.*, 91, 1961-1974, 1986.

Courtney, R. C. and R. S. White, Anomalous heat flow across the Cape Verde Rise: Evidence for a thermal plume in the Earth's mantle, *Geophys. J. Roy. Astr. Soc.*, 87, 815-869, 1986.

Craig, C. H. and D. P. McKenzie, The existence of a thin low viscosity layer beneath the lithosphere, *Earth Planet. Sci. Lett.*, in press, 1987.

Crough, S. T., Thermal origin of mid-plate hot-spot swells, *Geophys. J. Roy. Astr. Soc.*, 55, 451-469, 1978.

Detrick, R. S. and S. T. Crough, Island subsidence, hot spots, and lithospheric thinning, *J. Geophys. Res.*, 83, 1236-1244, 1978.

Detrick, R. S., R. P. von Herzen, S. T. Crough, D. Epp, and U. Fehn, Heat flow on the Hawaiian swell and lithospheric reheating, *Nature*, 292, 142-143, 1981.

Detrick, R. S., R. P. von Herzen, B. Parsons, D. Sandwell, and M. Dougherty, Heat flow observations on the Bermuda Rise and thermal models of mid-plate swells, *J. Geophys. Res.*, 91, 3701-3723, 1986.

Fischer, K., M. McNutt, and L. Shure, Thermal and mechanical constraints on the lithosphere beneath the Marquesas swell, *Nature*, 322, 733-736, 1986.

Fleitout, L., C. Froidevaux, and D. Yuen, Active lithospheric thinning, *Tectonophysics*, 132, 271-278, 1986.

Gass, S. I., *Linear Programming: Methods and Applications*, 4th ed., McGraw-Hill, New York, 1975.

Gordon, R. G. and L. J. Henderson, Pacific plate hot spot tracks, *J. Geophys. Res.*, submitted, 1986.

Jessop, A. M., M. A. Hobart, and J. G. Sclater, The world heat flow data collection - 1975, *Geothermal Series Number 5*, Earth Physics Branch, Ottowa, Canada, 1976.

McKenzie, D. P., Some remarks on heat flow and gravity anomalies, *J. Geophys. Res.*, 72, 6261-6273, 1967.

McKenzie, D. P., The generation and compaction of partially molten rock, *J. Petrol.*, 25, 713-765, 1984.

McNutt, M. K., Lithospheric flexure and thermal anomalies, *J. Geophys. Res.*, 89, 11,180-11,194, 1984.

McNutt, M. K. and H. W. Menard, Constraints on yield strength in the oceanic lithosphere derived from observations of flexure, *Geophys. J. Roy. Astr. Soc.*, 71, 363-394, 1982.

McNutt, M. K. and L. Royden, Extremal bounds on geotherms in eroding mountain belts from metamorphic pressure-temperature conditions, *Geophys. J. R. Astr. Soc.*, 88, 81-95, 1987.

McNutt, M. K. and L. Shure, Estimating the compensation depth of the Hawaiian swell with linear filters, *J. Geophys. Res.*, 91, 13,915-13,923, 1986.

Menard, H. W. and M. K. McNutt, Evidence for and consequences of thermal rejuvenation, *J. Geophys. Res.*, 87, 8570-8580, 1982.

Morgan, W. J., Plate motions and deep mantle convection, *Geol. Soc. Am. Mem.*, 132, 7-22, 1972.

Ockendon, J. R. and D. L. Turcotte, On the gravitational potential and field anomalies due to thin mass layers, *Geophys. J. R. Astr. Soc.*, 43, 425-451, 1975.

Parsons, B. and S. Daly, The relationship between surface topography, gravity anomalies, and the temperature structure of convection, *J. Geophys. Res.*, 88, 1129-1144, 1983.

Parsons, B. and F. M. Richter, A relation between driving forces and geoid anomaly associated with mid-ocean ridges, *Earth Planet. Sci. Lett.*, 51, 445-450, 1980.

Parsons, B. and J. G. Sclater, An analysis of the variation of ocean floor bathymetry and heat flow with age, *J. Geophys. Res.*, 82, 803-827, 1977.

Robinson, E. M., B. Parsons, and S. Daly, The effect of a shallow low viscosity zone on the apparent compensation of mid-plate swells, *Earth Planet. Sci. Lett.*, in press, 1987.

Sandwell, D. T., Thermal isostasy: Response of a moving lithosphere to a distributed heat source, *J. Geophys. Res.*, 87, 1001-1014, 1982.

Watts, A. B., An analysis of isostasy in the world's oceans, 1, Hawaiian-Emperor seamount chain, *J. Geophys. Res.*, 83, 5989-6004, 1978.

Watts, A. B., J. H. Bodine, and M. S. Steckler, Observations of flexure and the state of stress in the oceanic lithosphere, *J. Geophys. Res.*, 85, 6369-6376, 1980.

Watts, A. B., U. S. ten Brink, P. Buhl, and T. M. Brocher, A multichannel seismic study of lithospheric flexure across the Hawaiian-Emperor seamount chain, *Nature, 315,* 105-111, 1985.

Yuen, D. A. and L. Fleitout, Thinning of the lithosphere by small-scale convective destabilization, *Nature, 313,* 125-128, 1985.

M. McNutt, Department of Earth, Atmospheric, and Planetary Sciences, Massachusetts Institute of Technology, Cambridge, MA 02139.

PALEOMAGNETIC CONSTRAINTS ON THE ORIGIN AND EVOLUTION OF THE MUSICIANS
AND SOUTH HAWAIIAN SEAMOUNTS, CENTRAL PACIFIC OCEAN

William W. Sager[1]

Department of Oceanography, Texas A&M University, College Station, Texas

Malcolm S. Pringle[1]

U. S. Geological Survey, Menlo Park, California

Abstract. Twenty-two new paleomagnetic poles, 24 paleoinclinations, and 14 new radiometric ages have been determined for seamounts and ridges in the Musicians Seamounts and the South Hawaiian Seamounts. The geologic and tectonic implications of these data are presented in this report. Paleolatitudes show that the seamounts were formed astride the equator and are consistent with coeval volcanism over a range of 10°-20° of latitude. These data show no clear evidence for the origin of any of the seamounts at fixed-latitude hotspots; however, a progression of ages in the NW-SE trending chain in the Musicians implies a hotspot formation. Two mean paleomagnetic poles defining the Pacific plate Cretaceous apparent polar wander path at 80 and 87 Ma of age were calculated. Age estimates were made for un-dated seamounts by comparing their paleomagnetic poles to the updated apparent polar wander path. The results imply volcanism over a period greater than 20 Ma, from before 90 Ma to after 70 Ma, in both the Musicians and South Hawaiian seamounts. The similarity of ages of many edifices in both provinces implies that they may have been generated by the same mechanism. The paleomagnetic results from several seamounts in each of the two provinces are interpreted to indicate a possible 15°-26° counterclockwise rotation of two small crustal blocks. A tectonic model is proposed to explain the location and timing of the formation of seamounts in the region using a hotspot to create some of the Musicians Seamounts and tectonic deformation caused by a salient of Farallon plate, trapped between the Murray and Molokai transform faults during a change in spreading direction, to account for the remainder.

---

[1] Formerly at Hawaii Institute of Geophysics, 2525 Correa Road, Honolulu, Hawaii 96822.

Copyright 1987 by the American Geophysical Union.

Introduction

To the northwest of the Hawaiian Islands lies a Cretaceous submarine mountain range known as the Musicians seamounts. Other generally smaller volcanoes, known as the South Hawaiian seamounts, extend farther south around the Hawaiian Islands (Figure 1). Despite the large amount of geophysical data that has been collected in this region, the origin of these volcanoes remains obscure.

We report 18 new paleomagnetic poles for Musicians seamounts, 24 paleolatitudes for Musicians ridges, and 6 new paleomagnetic poles for South Hawaiian seamounts. Additionally, we report ^{40}Ar-^{39}Ar radiometric ages for rocks dredged from 14 of these volcanoes. Together with 11 paleomagnetic poles [Richards et al., 1967; Schimke and Bufe, 1968; Francheteau et al., 1970; Harrison et al., 1975] and several ages [Dymond and Windom, 1968; Clague and Dalrymple, 1975] previously published for seamounts in the region, these data provide valuable constraints on the origin and evolution of the volcanoes in the Musicians and South Hawaiian provinces. In this article we address the paleomagnetic data in particular and its geologic and tectonic implications. Such age data as is appropriate is included; however, a detailed account of the radiometric age determinations will be presented elsewhere [Pringle, in preparation].

Geologic and Tectonic Background

The Musicians seamounts are bounded to the north by the Pioneer fracture zone (Figure 2), but to the south their termination is unclear. Most of the larger seamounts in the region are located north of 25°N, which is often regarded as the southern geographic limit of the province. However, the South Hawaiian seamounts are scattered nearby to the south around the Hawaiian Islands. Although the juxtaposition of the two

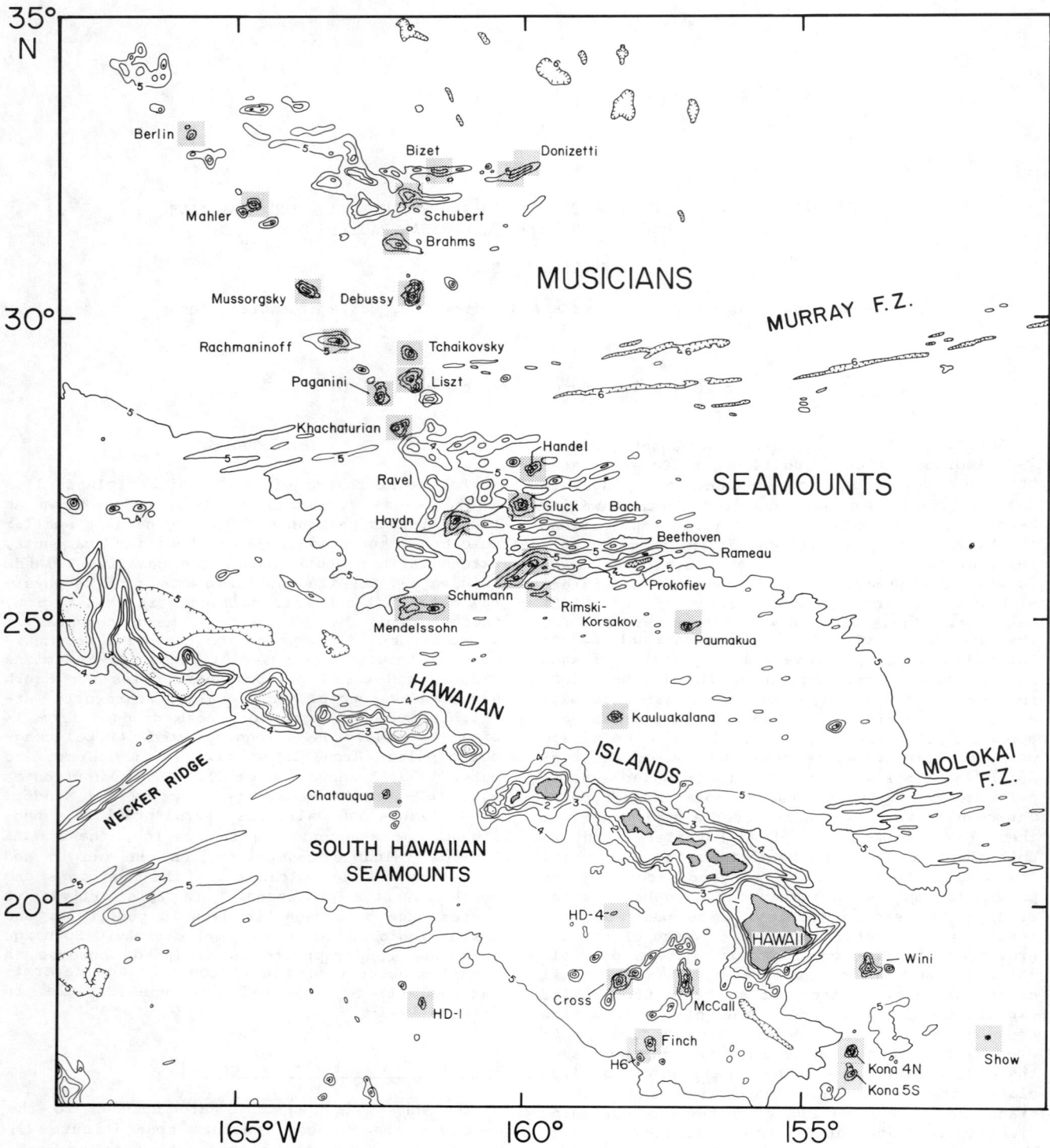

Fig. 1. Generalized bathymetric chart of the central Pacific Ocean showing the locations of the Musicians Seamounts and South Hawaiian Seamounts (after Mammerickx and Smith [1985]). The stippled boxes indicate the seamounts that have been modeled to obtain paleomagnetic poles. The bathymetric contour interval is 1 km.

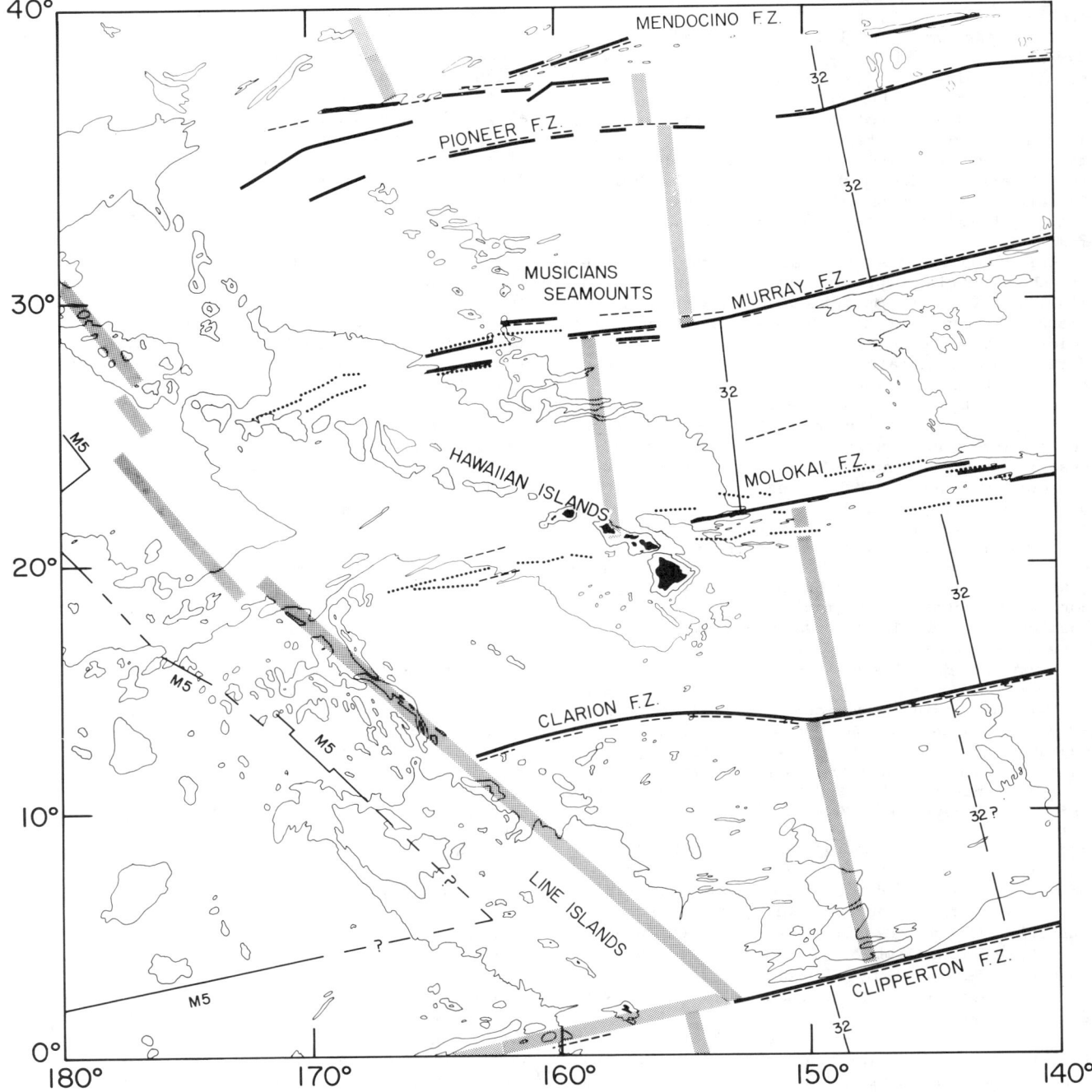

Fig. 2. Chart of tectonic features of the central Pacific. Heavy lines show the bathymetric trends of the major fracture zones (from Mammerickx and Smith [1985; 1981]). Dashed lines indicate fracture zone trends derived from the deflection of the vertical from SeaSat altimeter data (from Sandwell [1985]). Dotted lines indicate lineated magnetic anomalies caused by fracture zones (from Malahoff et al. [1966]; Rea [1970]). Magnetic isochrons M5 and 32 (see text for sources) are shown to indicate the isochron trends for anomalies of the late JK-M and early KTQ-M superchrons. The extrapolated edges of the Cretaceous Quiet Zone (K-N superchron) are shown by the stippled pattern.

seamount groups is suggestive, their relation is unclear.

The seamounts, atolls, and islands of the Hawaiian ridge (Figure 1) in this vicinity were formed within the last 10 Ma (see review by Dalrymple et al. [1980]) as the Pacific plate drifted northwestward over a melting anomaly, herein called a "hotspot," in the mantle. The massive volcanism and the voluminous sediments of the Hawaiian ridge doubtlessly hide morphologic features that would aid in understanding the origin of the Musicians and South Hawaiian seamounts.

Three populations of seamounts were recognized in the Musicians province by Rea and Naugler [1971]: (1) the Musicians Horst, an elevated block of crust, located between the Murray and Molokai fracture zones, elongated in an east-west direction and containing several large volcanoes; (2) a series of five large east-west trending ridges located in the southern part of the province; (3) individual seamounts scattered throughout the province, but concentrated mainly in the western half. Interestingly, two predominant trends, one about N90°E and the other about N70°E, are displayed by many of the elongated edifices in the first two groups. Furthermore, in the latter group two distinct linear chains are notable (Figure 1). One, we call the "Bending Line" chain (for reasons explained below), trends northwest-southeast beginning with a cluster located at 34°N, 167°W. At the Murray fracture zone this chain blends with the southern ridges and consequently its extension farther south is unclear. The other chain trends north-south along 162°W. It includes seamounts on a line between Schubert and Mendelssohn, perhaps including a few seamounts to the south of the Hawaiian ridge. This lineament we call the "North-South" chain.

The boundaries of the South Hawaiian seamounts are also uncertain. Most are scattered, small volcanoes similar to many others of Cretaceous age found in the central and western Pacific. The greatest concentration of South Hawaiian seamounts is found near the island of Hawaii (Figure 1). Of particular note is a grouping of seamounts directly west of Hawaii that forms an inverted "V" shape. One limb of the "V," including Cross Seamount, is formed by a ridge-like feature similar to those in the southern Musicians, but with an azimuth of N50°E.

Two large fracture zones, formed at transform faults on the Pacific-Farallon ridge, cross the study area. The Murray fracture zone, consisting of numerous linear troughs and ridges, trends east-northeast through the middle of the Musicians province. It causes no perceptible offset of the seamounts, suggesting that many, if not all, formed after the active Murray transform had moved off to the east. The topographic expression of this fracture zone fades a few hundred kilometers west of the Musicians seamounts, but it can be traced westward by its magnetic anomalies to the vicinity of Laysan Island in the Hawaiian chain [Rea, 1970]. Farther south, similar bathymetric and magnetic features delineate the Molokai fracture zone. Although its topographic expression disappears slightly east of the Hawaiian Islands, it has also been traced westward, nearly to the Line Islands, by its magnetic [Malahoff et al., 1966] and geoid anomalies (Figure 2).

The Musicians and South Hawaiian seamounts sit atop ocean crust that apparently formed during the Cretaceous normal polarity superchron (K-N). In Figure 2 the probable edges of the K-N seafloor are shown. The western edge of the K-N in Figure 2 has been extrapolated eastward from the Jurassic-Cretaceous mixed polarity superchron (JK-M) isochrons observed in the Pacific west of the Line Islands [Hilde et al., 1976; Larson, 1976; Tamaki et al., 1979; Tamaki and Larson, 1987]. Because the actual edge of the K-N, chron M0, has only been identified with certainty in the Hawaiian lineations north of 25°N, the actual edge of the K-N in this region is somewhat uncertain. However, several isochrons of the late JK-M sequence have been recognized to the south in a limited area slightly west of the Line Islands [Tamaki and Larson, 1987].

The eastern edge of the K-N in Figure 2 has similarly been extrapolated westward from the isochrons of the Cretaceous-Tertiary-Quaternary mixed polarity superchron (KTQ-M) observed east of the Hawaiian Islands [Atwater and Menard, 1970; Malahoff and Handschumacher, 1971; Addicott et al., 1982]. The actual location of the eastern boundary of the K-N is also uncertain because the oldest magnetic isochron reliably identified to the east of the Musicians seamounts is anomaly 32b [Malahoff and Handschumacher, 1971; Addicott et al., 1982] rather than the actual edge of the K-N, chron 34. It is unclear whether this boundary of the K-N is missing in the region or has simply remained unmapped. If the extrapolation used to approximate the eastern boundary of the K-N is correct, the age of the seafloor beneath the northern Musicians seamounts (north of the Murray) and the South Hawaiian seamounts (south of the Molokai) is about 95-100 Ma. In between, the age of the seafloor beneath the seamounts is extrapolated to be approximately 80-85 Ma.

Evidently the Musicians and South Hawaiian seamounts were erupted within a relatively short period after the formation of the seafloor upon which they reside. Several studies of the compensation and lithospheric flexure of these edifices have concluded that they were mostly formed near the spreading ridge [Watts et al., 1980; Schwank and Lazarewicz, 1982; Freedman and Parsons, 1986]. However, variations in the compensation and amplitudes of gravity anomalies of the Musicians seamounts have led to the suggestion that some of these volcanoes may have been constructed some tens of million years after the crust upon which they are found [Schwank and Lazarewicz, 1982; Freedman and Parsons, 1986]. The flexural evidence for the age of these seamounts is in accord with the few reliable published radiometric ages which range from 66-89 Ma [Dymond and Windom, 1968; Clague and Dalrymple, 1975].

Because few geologic data complement the extensive geophysical data sets from the Musicians and South Hawaiian provinces many ideas concerning the evolution of these seamounts are based on geometric constraints and little else. Several bathymetric trends within the Musicians have invited speculation. As a result, at least five scenarios have been developed to explain their origin. Conversely, the South Hawaiian seamounts are a largely amorphous collection of volcanoes with few compelling bathymetric trends to suggest their origin. To our knowledge, no one has tried to explain the genesis of this particular group.

Hypotheses of the origin of the Musicians seamounts can be divided into two categories, hotspot and non-hotspot related. Of the latter type, there are three. According to Rea [1970] and Rea and Naugler [1971], the Musicians seamounts formed along a line coincident with the western chain of volcanic edifices at which many of the north Pacific fracture zones appeared to bend, given the geophysical data available at the time (hence the name "Bending Line" chain). They supposed that the line corresponded to a zone of highly fractured crust caused by a change in the spreading direction. Another possibility is that the Musicians seamounts are the result of a ridge jump, either beginning or ending at the Bending Line chain [Epp, 1978; Rea and Dixon, 1983]. The basis for this hypothesis are observations that the Bending Line chain is roughly perpendicular to the trends of the Late Cretaceous mid-Pacific fracture zones and that the zone of K-N seafloor is particularly wide in this region. Yet another explanation for the formation of these seamounts is that they are a part of the widespread pulse of mid-plate volcanism that erupted throughout most of the present central and western Pacific during the Late Cretaceous [Schlanger et al., 1981; Haggerty et al., 1982].

Seamount lineations within the Musicians province are very suggestive of edifices built by hotspot volcanism. The Bending Line chain is copolar (i.e., parallel to a small circle around the same Euler axis) with the northern Line Islands seamounts, whereas the North-South chain of seamounts is copolar with the Emperor seamounts [Epp, 1978]. Available age data from both the Emperors and Line Islands display age progressive trends that strongly suggest both were formed by hotspots [Dalrymple et al., 1980; Schlanger et al. 1984]. A single hotspot explanation [W. J. Morgan, personal communication, 1978] for the formation of the Musicians is that the Bending Line chain is the trace of a hotspot that moved southeast until it reached the area of the Murray Fracture Zone. Coincident with a change in plate motion near the end of the Cretaceous, the hotspot then moved due south along the North-South chain. A two-hotspot hypothesis has also been offered to explain the origin of the Musicians seamounts [Henderson and Gordon, 1981]. In this scenario, the Bending Line formed from 95-80 Ma as the Pacific drifted northwestward over the first hotspot. The north-south chain was subsequently erupted as the plate changed direction at the end of the Cretaceous to a more northerly drift and the Musicians province passed over a second hotspot during the period 72-55 Ma. In either hotspot hypothesis, the Musicians Horst and the east-west ridges may have formed along leaky transform faults by hotspot magma shunted toward the nearby spreading ridge [Morgan, 1978; Lowrie et al., 1986].

Our research has convinced us that the evolution of the seamounts in the Musicians and South Hawaiian provinces was complex. Although the data do not allow a completely unequivocal choice of a tectonic model, they provide important constraints. Based on this information, we favor a hybrid model combining the hotspot and spreading ridge reorganization models.

Seamount Paleomagnetism

Seamount paleomagnetism is of particular interest and importance in the study of oceanic plates, such as the Pacific, because it is extremely difficult to obtain fully-oriented samples from the oceans for laboratory paleomagnetic studies. However, an inversion of the magnetic anomaly of a seamount can yield essentially the same information.

The observed magnetic anomaly caused by a seamount can be mathematically formulated as a linear combination of the Cartesian components of its mean magnetization vector and volume integrals of its shape. Usually the volume integrals of a body of arbitrary shape cannot be solved analytically, so the shape is approximated by simple geometric bodies whose volume integrals can be readily calculated [Vacquier, 1962; Talwani, 1965; Plouff, 1976]. The components of the magnetization vector can then be determined through an over-determined linear least-squares inversion. Once the mean magnetization vector of a seamount is determined, the results may be used like any other paleomagnetic datum [e.g., Francheteau et al., 1970; Harrison et al., 1975; Sager, 1983].

Seamount magnetic anomaly inversion requires that several assumptions be made about the formation of a seamount and the character of its rocks. The edifice is assumed to have formed over a long enough period of time to have averaged out secular variations. Furthermore, the contributions of induced magnetization, viscous remanent magnetization, or any other secondary magnetic component to the mean magnetization vector are assumed to be negligible. In addition, for reasons of mathematical simplicity and the inherent non-uniqueness of potential field analysis, the magnetization is assumed to be homogeneous throughout the edifice.

As these assumptions are rather stringent, their validity has been a source of some concern.

Two questions about these assumptions arise most frequently: (1) are seamount geomagnetic poles (GPs) accurate if the volcano is not homogeneously magnetized and (2) are not seamount GPs seriously biased by secondary magnetization components including induced and viscous magnetism. The obvious answer to each is that a seamount pole can be misleading in a worst-case scenario. A seamount whose magnetization contains many reversals can give an erroneous GP [Lumb et al., 1973]. Furthermore, a seamount whose magnetization has a large induced component will yield a GP too close to the present-day geomagnetic north pole, if it is normally polarized, or too far away, if it is reversely polarized.

Concerning the problem of magnetization homogeneity, two factors tend to restrict the use of non-uniformly magnetized seamounts for the calculation of paleomagnetic data. Those with highly non-uniform magnetizations rarely yield acceptable values of the reliability parameters that are used to test the fit of the modeled and observed magnetic field. Such data are rejected as unreliable on this basis. Moreover, many of the seamounts that have been studied paleomagnetically in the Pacific were probably formed during the K-N and thus are likely to have a relatively uniform, normally polarized magnetization [Hildebrand and Staudigel, 1986]. Fortunately, most of the Musicians Seamounts have remarkably uniform magnetic anomalies that respond well to the linear least-squares inversion technique, yielding a relatively consistent data set.

The question of the composition of the magnetization residing within seamounts has recently engendered considerable debate. The large ratio of seamounts with normal polarity anomalies versus those with reversed anomalies has led some authors to suggest that seamount magnetizations contain a significant induced or viscous component [Williams et al., 1983; Merrill, 1985; Verhoef et al., 1985]. On the other hand, it has been argued that much of the polarity bias results from the fact that the Pacific seamounts most likely to have magnetic anomalies amenable to least-squares inversion are those that formed during the K-N [Hildebrand and Staudigel, 1986]. Moreover, a comparison of well-dated seamount and non-seamount Pacific paleomagnetic data found that there is no noticeable offset between the two types of data that would imply a significant contribution of induced or viscous magnetization [Sager, 1987].

Unfortunately, there is very little evidence to be had from actual rock samples taken from the interior of seamounts. Magnetic studies have been undertaken on samples from only two deep drill holes on seamounts. Kono [1980] found that rocks from Deep Sea Drilling Project Hole 433C on Suiko Guyot, in the Emperor chain, had undergone little low temperature alteration. These samples had an average Koenigsberger ratio of 9.4 and magnetizations resistant to alternating field demagnetization. Samples from the other deep drill hole, in Bermuda [Rice et al., 1980], revealed that highly differentiated alkalic sheets of Tertiary age had intruded into the original Cretaceous tholeiitic basalt pile causing extensive remagnetization and hydrothermal alteration. Not only are many of these rocks remagnetized, but chemical changes have lowered their Koenigsberger ratios and rendered them more susceptible to acquire secondary components. Thus, although most available data indicates little bias of seamount GPs by secondary components [Sager, 1987], their existence cannot be entirely ignored in the interpretation of this type of data.

Data

For the inversion of seamount magnetic anomalies to calculate paleomagnetic poles, the data needed are bathymetric soundings to delineate the shape of a volcano and measurements of its magnetic anomaly. The primary data used in this study were from two Hawaii Institute of Geophysics (HIG) cruises of the R/V Kana Keoki. Cruises KK80041402 and KK80071500 were undertaken specifically to gather data in the Musicians Seamounts for testing various hypotheses of their origin. On these cruises, eight seamounts were surveyed with the intent of inverting their magnetic anomalies for paleomagnetic data. Additionally, several dozen dredges, scattered throughout the province, successfully obtained rock samples for petrologic and radiometric age study. Depths were determined with a 3.5 kHz echo sounder and corrected for the velocity of sound in seawater [Matthews, 1939]. Seismic reflection profiling was also carried out using an 80-in^3 (1311 cm^3) airgun source and ship tracks were positioned using Doppler satellite navigation.

Geomagnetic field intensity measurements were digitally recorded with a proton precession magnetometer towed 200 m behind the ship. Total field residual anomaly values were obtained by subtracting the 1975 International Geomagnetic Reference Field (IGRF) [Baraclough and Fabiano, 1977] from the observed magnetic field values. As solar quiet day diurnal variations are typically less than 40 nT at Honolulu and decrease rapidly northward to about 35°N [Chapman and Raja Rao, 1965; Matsushita, 1967], diurnal corrections were made only for the magnetic surveys of South Hawaiian and Musicians seamounts with smaller magnetic anomalies. These corrections were made by subtracting either hourly average field values recorded at the Honolulu magnetic observatory or an average diurnal variation curve suitable for the latitude of the survey [Matsushita, 1967].

It would have been impossible to undertake a study of this scope without geophysical data from many other sources. Two Musicians seamounts, Mendelssohn and Schumann, were surveyed in detail in a HIG project to assess mineral resources in the Hawaiian Exclusive Economic Zone (cruises KK84080600 and KK84082402). The bathymetric data for Mendelssohn Seamount were derived with the

SeaMARC II side-scan sonar system. Finch and Finch-W, both located in the South Hawaiian province, were surveyed on HIG cruise KK78080700. The rest of the geophysical cruise data, too numerous to detail here, were taken from the archives of the National Geophysical Data Center. Two notable contributions are detailed bathymetric and magnetic surveys conducted during the 1960's by the Environmental Sciences Service Administration (ESSA) in the region north of the Hawaiian Islands [Naugler, 1968; Rea, 1969; Rea and Naugler, 1971] and by the U.S. Naval Oceanographic Office in the region southwest of the Hawaiian Islands [U.S. Naval Oceanographic Office, 1962].

Magnetic Anomalies

Bathymetric and magnetic anomaly maps of the Musicians and South Hawaiian seamounts examined in this study are shown in the Appendix (microfiche). The average peak-to-peak magnetic anomaly amplitude for the Musicians seamounts studied here is approximately 850 nT; for those in the South Hawaiian Seamounts, the average is about 750 nT. Mendelssohn Seamount has the largest magnetic anomaly of the Musicians seamounts studied at 1415 nT and Rimski-Korsakov has the smallest, 220 nT. Of the South Hawaiian seamounts we examined, Finch has the largest anomaly, 1320 nT, and its neighbor, Finch-W, has the smallest, 215 nT.

Perhaps the most remarkable aspect of the magnetic anomalies of the Musicians seamounts is their uniformity (e.g., Figure 3). All but three features in the province are predominantly normally polarized. The reversely polarized edifices are Rameau and Prokofiev ridges and nearby Paumakua Seamount. As discussed in the sections that follow, the age and paleomagnetic data from the Musicians seamounts indicates that they formed during the period of approximately 95-65 Ma. Few reversals occurred between the end of the Cretaceous Quiet Period and 65 Ma [Harland et al., 1982], so the magnetic field was normally polarized 75-80% of the time during which these seamounts formed. Thus the preponderance of normally magnetized edifices probably reflects the polarity bias of the period of time spanned by volcanism in this province.

Not only are the anomalies of these seamounts uniform in polarity, but homogeneity also seems to be characteristic of their magnetizations as well. Nearly all of the Musicians seamounts that were analyzed in this study have simple, usually dipolar, magnetic anomalies. This characteristic made possible the inversion of the large number of seamount anomalies presented here. Although only eight Musicians seamounts were surveyed for paleomagnetic study, the smooth shapes of the anomalies allowed the contouring of magnetic anomaly maps for many others by using one or more recent Kana Keoki tracks as tie lines for the older data. Furthermore, the smoothness of the magnetic anomalies suggests that many of these seamounts do indeed have relatively homogeneous magnetizations, as implicitly assumed by the magnetic modeling procedure.

Not all of the seamounts in this region have anomalies that indicate uniform magnetization, however. Ravel, Mendelssohn, and Schumann seamounts, in the southwest part of the Musicians province, all have complex magnetic anomalies. Ravel was the only seamount in the province examined in this study that yielded paleomagnetic results considered to be unreliable. Both Mendelssohn and Schumann (four volcanic peaks in all) appear to incorporate reversely magnetized rocks into edifices that are largely normal in polarity. Likewise, Cross Seamount, in the South Hawaiian group, also has a complex magnetic anomaly. Because these seamounts apparently violate the assumption of a uniform magnetization, it was necessary to take special steps to model some of them.

Paleomagnetic Models (3D)

Magnetization parameters were calculated for seamounts in the Musicians and South Hawaiian provinces using both two and three-dimensional magnetic inversion techniques. These data are listed in Tables 1-3 and the locations of the seamounts studied are shown in Figure 1. Most of the paleomagnetic data discussed here were derived using the three-dimensional (3D) method. Paleolatitudes from the east-west ridges in the southern Musicians were derived using a two-dimensional magnetic inversion and are discussed below. The three-dimensional method used was Plouff's [1976] extension of the Talwani [1965] algorithm. This technique utilizes a stack of polygonal prisms with vertical sides to approximate the shape of the magnetic body. Other paleomagnetic poles, taken from previous work, were calculated using either Vacquier's [1962; also in Richards et al., 1967] or Talwani's [1965] modeling techniques. All of these methods produce results that are analogous.

Most magnetic anomaly inversion routines calculate a regional field along with the magnetization components. In many previous studies the regional field was assumed to be a sloping plane. Theoretically, the determination of this plane should pose little difficulty as the inversion is highly over-constrained. However, in practice the calculated plane is sometimes correlated with the seamount's anomaly, particularly if the anomaly is complex or the survey is incomplete [Sager, 1983; McNutt, 1986]. As an incorrectly modeled planar regional can lead to errors in the determination of a seamount's paleomagnetic pole we calculated only the constant offset between the observed and calculated anomalies. We did not deem it necessary, however, to recompute the previously published magnetic models of seamounts in the region that included a planar regional.

In calculating magnetic parameters we proceeded in the following fashion. A bathymetric model was created by fitting polygons to the contours

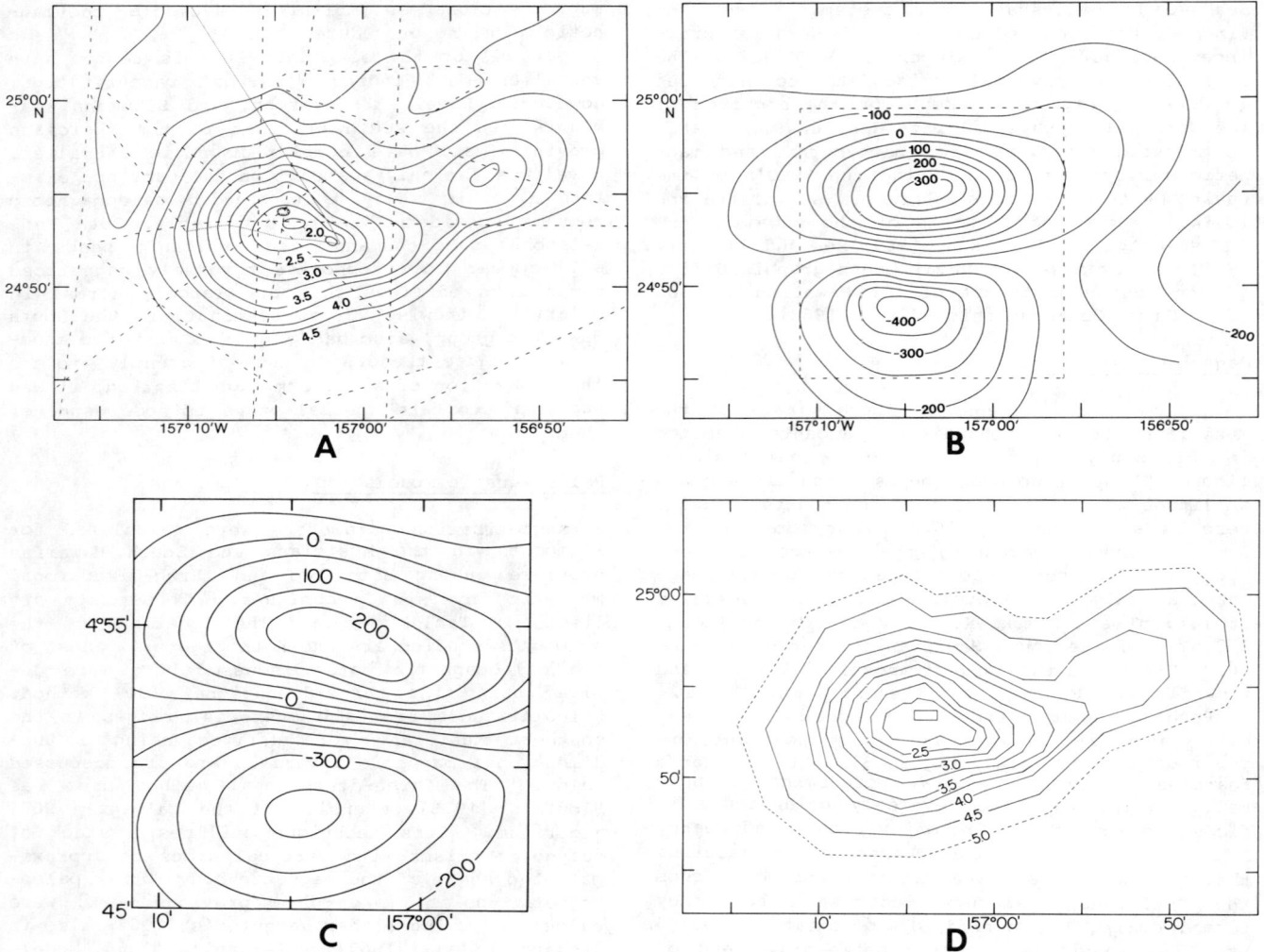

Fig. 3. Magnetic model of Paumakua seamount, an example of a homogeneously magnetized seamount. (A) and (B) are bathymetric and total field magnetic anomaly contour charts. The contour interval in (A) is 250 m and in (B), 50 nT. The dashed lines in (A) show the locations of the shiptracks used to make the contour charts. In (B) the dashed box is the area of the magnetic anomaly gridded for input into the magnetic modeling calculations. The calculated magnetic anomaly (C), from the best-fitting magnetic model, corresponds to the box in (B). (D) shows polygons representing the edges of vertical-sided prisms making up the bathymetric model for the magnetic calculations. The dashed polygon was added below the seafloor to make a closer fit of the observed and calculated anomalies (see text for discussion).

of each seamount (Figures 3, 4). The vertices of these polygons were digitized and entered into the magnetic inversion program to describe the sides of vertical prisms used to approximate the shape and volume of the seamount. Input magnetic anomaly values were either digitized in a grid of 1.85-3.70 km spacing or at intervals of 1.0-3.0 km along tracklines for those surveys in which the data was too sparse for gridding.

Usually the resemblance of the calculated to the observed magnetic anomaly is taken as an indicator of the validity of the magnetization parameters calculated in an inversion. The parameter most widely used for this purpose is the "goodness-of-fit ratio" (GFR) [Richards et al., 1967]. It is simply the mean magnitude of the observed magnetic anomaly divided by the mean magnitude of the residuals (observed minus calculated anomaly values). Although there is no theoretical precedent for selecting a minimum accept-

TABLE 1. Magnetization Parameters of Musicians Seamounts

Name	ID	Location Lat(°N)	Lon(°W)	Inc (+Down)	Dec (+East)	Int (A/M)	GFR	Paleopole Lat(°N)	Lon(°E)
Berlin	M1	32.9	166.0	5.1	7.1	12.1	3.9	59.4	358.8
Mahler	M2	31.8	165.0	4.1	17.5	6.0	6.7	56.0	342.6
Mussorgski*	M3	30.4	163.9	0.9	11.2	5.6	3.3	58.2	354.5
Rachmaninov*	M4	29.6	163.3	11.9	26.6	9.3	2.5	55.6	324.6
Paganini	M5	28.7	162.6	12.2	356.3	8.3	3.2	67.2	26.9
Khatchaturian*	M6	28.1	162.3	5.9	23.0	12.8	5.3	56.5	332.5
Schubert	M7	31.9	162.1	17.9	9.2	6.4	4.3	65.7	355.3
Brahms*	M8	31.2	162.1	19.8	11.6	7.4	2.0	66.3	348.2
Debussy	M9	30.3	162.1	16.2	5.7	5.9	3.2	67.3	3.1
Tchaikovsky	M10	29.4	162.3	6.7	9.6	7.8	3.4	62.4	356.6
Liszt	M11	29.0	162.3	10.6	20.9	7.0	5.1	59.2	333.8
Handel	M12	27.5	159.9	14.0	3.5	4.2	7.4	69.3	10.2
Rimski-Korsakov	M13	25.3	159.7	12.8	6.8	2.9	9.3	70.1	0.0
Gluck	M14	26.9	160.1	4.3	4.4	6.7	5.2	64.9	9.5
Mendelssohn-W	M15	25.1	162.8	-12.4	7.5	9.7	3.3	57.8	3.1
Mendelssohn-E	M16	25.1	161.7	6.8	1.5	7.3	3.5	68.3	14.3
Haydn	M17	26.6	161.3	13.8	7.3	7.7	3.3	69.2	357.9
Schumann-W	M18	25.7	160.2	-3.1	14.8	3.3	2.3	59.2	349.9
Schumann-E	M19	25.9	159.9	-5.3	19.8	4.4	2.3	55.6	343.3
Donizetti-W	M20	32.2	160.3	10.8	23.6	5.6	3.5	55.3	333.2
Donizetti-E	M21	32.2	160.0	2.3	358.1	3.0	5.0	58.9	23.4
Bizet	M22	32.3	161.6	-15.0	2.8	4.3	3.6	50.1	32.1

GFR = Goodness of Fit Ratio
INC = Inclination; DEC = Declination; INT = Intensity
*From Harrison et al. (1975)

able GFR value, seamount anomaly inversions with GFRs below 1.8-2.0 are generally considered unreliable [Harrison et al., 1975; Sager, 1983].

The GFR values of the Musicians and South Hawaiian seamounts are generally large. For the three-dimensional calculations, 18 of 22 Musicians seamounts and 8 of 13 South Hawaiian seamounts have GFRs greater than 3.0. Significantly, the Musicians seamount with the lowest GFR value is Brahms, whereas the South Hawaiian seamount that yielded the lowest GFR value is McCall. Even though this reliability parameter suggests that

TABLE 2. Magnetization Parameters of South Hawaiian Seamounts

Name	ID	Location Lat(°N)	Lon(°W)	Inc (+Down)	Dec (+East)	Int (A/M)	GFR	Paleopole Lat(°N)	Lon(°E)
Kauluakalana	H1	23.3	158.4	40.8	5.2	2.0	5.7	85.2	289.9
Chatauqua*	H2	22.2	162.6	12.7	189.3	4.8	--	60.0	358.7
HD1†	H3	18.3	161.8	-24.2	21.8	1.9	4.7	52.0	342.0
HD4†	H4	20.0	158.2	-6.7	350.7	4.3	3.4	66.0	40.0
Finch	H5	17.7	156.7	-7.7	4.6	8.3	4.4	68.0	10.0
Finch-W	H6	17.4	157.9	-13.8	2.3	4.1	3.0	65.5	16.6
Kona 4N**	H7	17.3	154.2	-8.4	13.5	5.8	2.9	64.6	352.8
Kona 5S**	H8	17.1	154.2	35.3	196.4	0.9	2.9	49.8	1.5
Show**	H9	17.9	152.7	18.0	199.8	3.8	3.2	56.5	350.1
Wini**	H10	19.0	153.8	0.2	2.9	3.9	2.3	70.9	17.1
Paumakua	H11	24.9	157.1	-7.8	187.0	4.0	4.9	67.7	1.8
Cross	H12	18.5	158.0	1.8	0.8	2.7	4.2	72.4	19.4
McCall	H13	18.8	157.2	-3.1	355.7	4.5	2.1	69.2	35.0

GFR = Goodness of Fit Ratio
INC = Inclination; DEC = Declination; INT = Intensity
* From Schimke and Bufe (1968)
† From Richards et al. (1967)
** From Francheteau et al. (1970)

TABLE 3. Magnetization Parameters of Musicians Ridges*

ID	Feature	Location Lat(°N)	Lon(°W)	Effective Inclination (+Down)	Intensity (A/M)	GFR	Ridge Azimuth	Polarity	@Paleo-Latitude
Rameau Ridge									
R1	A	25.84	159.50	1.5	3.3	3.7	71	N	0.7
R11	E	26.04	158.06	-175.6	1.8	6.2	78	R	2.1
R12	F	26.08	157.91	-161.0	2.8	8.7	78	R	9.1
R13	F	26.07	157.95	-164.9	1.8	8.1	78	R	7.2
R14	F	26.08	157.87	-170.6	3.6	9.5	78	R	4.4
Beethoven									
BE1	A	26.22	160.16	22.5	6.5	4.0	90	N	11.6
BE4	B	26.24	159.68	5.3	3.4	22.3	80	N	2.5
BE5	B	26.24	159.67	3.7	3.4	4.3	80	N	1.8
BE6	C	26.23	159.35	-0.9	3.1	4.2	88	N	-0.4
BE7	C	26.23	159.16	-4.2	2.2	2.8	88	N	-2.1
BE11	D	26.24	158.41	8.3	2.1	6.1	88	N	4.1
BE12	D	26.25	158.32	14.4	1.9	4.2	88	N	7.2
Bach Ridge									
BA2	B	26.58	160.72	8.7	4.7	3.5	76	N	4.0
BA6	D	26.55	160.01	-7.5	3.5	8.1	90	N	-3.7
BA7	D	26.55	160.00	-8.2	4.6	5.4	90	N	-4.1
BA10	F	26.62	159.53	12.1	4.5	2.8	85	N	5.9
BA13	H	26.63	159.01	11.4	3.7	6.1	92	N	5.7
BA14	H	26.63	158.91	24.1	4.7	4.5	86	N	12.3
BA15	H	26.63	158.80	20.9	4.8	4.6	92	N	10.7
BA17	I	26.66	158.31	-8.9	2.1	3.4	80	N	-4.2
BA18	I	26.67	158.20	1.3	2.2	9.9	80	N	0.6
BA19	I	26.68	158.12	-6.4	1.7	3.2	80	N	-3.0
Prokofiev Ridge									
P1	A	25.83	157.94	-171.8	3.3	9.1	65	R	3.4
P2	A	25.85	157.89	-174.9	2.8	7.2	65	R	2.1

*Complete listing of data from all 2D inversions is given in Table A-1, Appendix
GFR = Goodness of Fit Ratio
@Paleolatitude: Determined Using Assumption D = 10°

these magnetic inversions may not be reliable, these results are of considerable importance in the interpretation of the paleomagnetic data because rocks from both seamounts have been radiometrically dated.

For many of the magnetic models, modifications of the seamount's shape improved the match between the observed and calculated anomalies. Most of the modifications consisted of extending the bottom of a seamount below the seafloor and the removal of some of its summit. Such modifications have been found in other studies to improve the magnetic models of many seamounts [Harrison, 1971; Harrison et al., 1975; Sager, 1983]. These modifications are needed if the observed magnetic anomaly has a longer wavelength than can be reproduced with the measured shape of the seamount. They effectively increase the distance between the plane of observation and the magnetic source, thereby increasing the wavelength of the calculated anomaly. The geologic implications of such model modifications are discussed elsewhere [Harrison, 1971; Harrison et al., 1975; Sager, 1984; Sager and Keating, 1984].

The bottom extensions were usually accomplished by adding one or two layers beneath the seafloor. Where seismic reflection records were available and of suitable quality, they were used to determine the shape of the added sub-seafloor layers. However, if no suitable reflection records were available (as was most often the case) or the bottom extension required was deeper than the penetration observed with the reflection records, the lower prisms were constructed to follow the shape and slope of the lower portions of the seamount. The summit layers were removed in the magnetic model by excluding one or more of the prisms, representing the top of the edifice, from the calculations. For all of these modifications, the best model was taken to be the one that yielded the highest GFR.

In the models of Musicians and South Hawaiian seamounts the bottom extensions were generally small. All but four had best models with 250 m

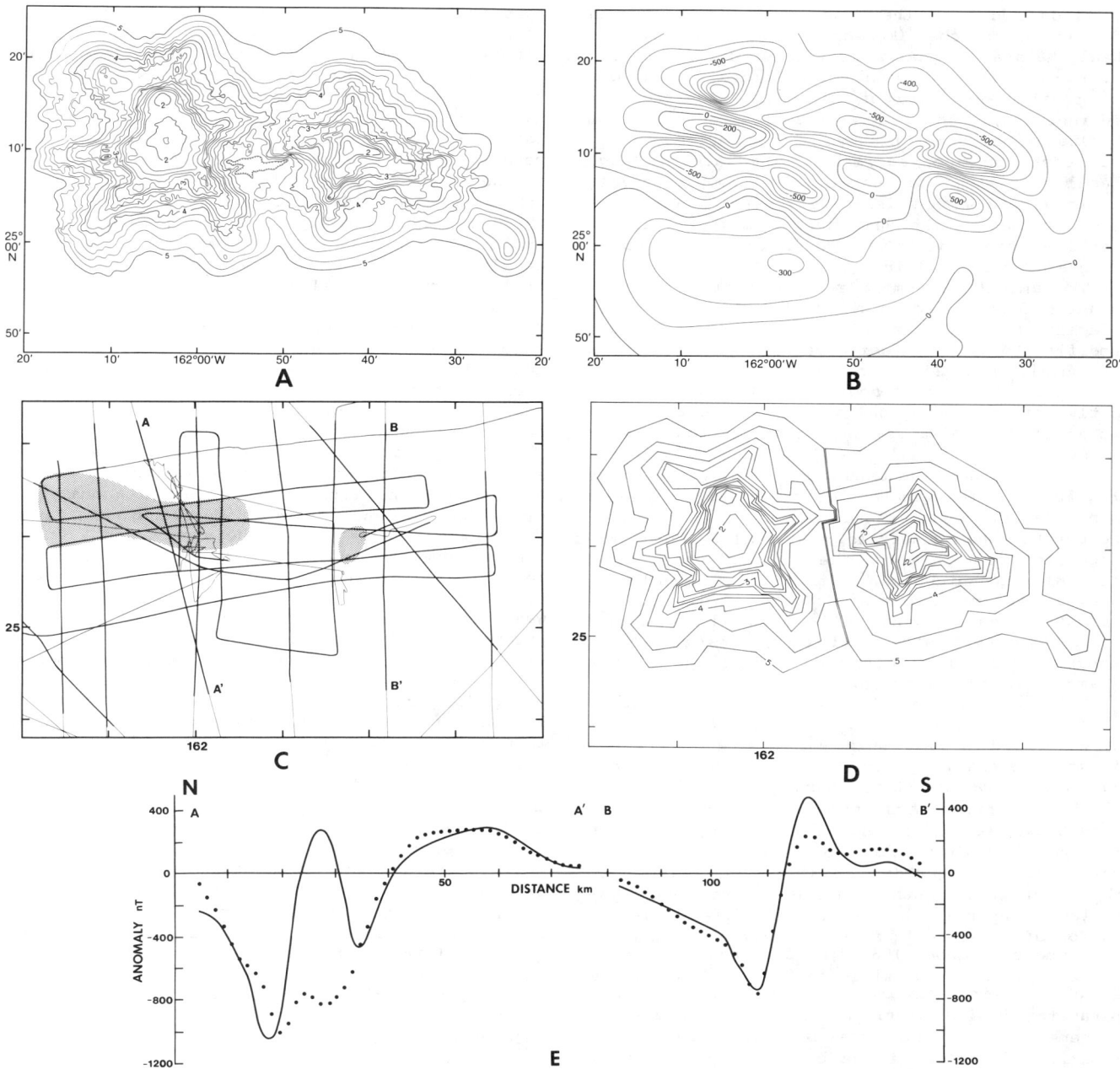

Fig. 4. Magnetic model of Mendelssohn seamount, an example of an inhomogeneously magnetized seamount. A bathymetric chart constructed from SeaMARC II side-scan and conventional echo sounding is shown in (A). The contour interval is 200 m. In (B) the total magnetic field anomaly is displayed with a contour interval of 100 nT. (C) is a chart of shiptracks used to construct the maps in (A) and (B). The heavy lines denote the portions of the tracks with magnetic data used for paleomagnetic modeling. The stippled areas show where data was excluded from the magnetic inversion calculations to minimize the effects of the inhomogeneities (see discussion in text). Chart (D) shows polygons that represent the vertical-sided prisms making up the bathymetric model used in the magnetic calculations. A comparison of observed and calculated magnetic anomalies along two north-south tracklines is shown in (E). The solid line in each case is the observed anomaly and the dots represent the anomaly calculated from the best-fitting homogeneous model. The locations of the lines, A-A' and B-B', are shown in (C).

or less added on the base. Of the four with deeper extensions (Mahler, Liszt, Handel, and Kauluakalana) the areal coverage of the surveys of two are limited, thus the extended foundations of their models are of uncertain significance. Furthermore, seismic reflection data from Kauluakalana Seamount shows that it is buried by at least 800 m of sediment. The lack of large basal extensions on most of the seamount models is in accord with seismic reflection and refraction studies in the Musicians seamounts indicating that the sedimentary cover in the region is generally thin [Wallin, 1982].

The amount of summit removed from these seamount models varied considerably. Four seamounts (Rachmaninoff, Brahms, Liszt, and Handel) had unmodified tops. The rest have from 250 m to 750 m of summit removed. No obvious regional trend exists for the summit modifications. They apparently reflect individual variations in the character of the volcanism and magnetization of each seamount.

Some of the seamounts modeled in this study required special treatment because their magnetic anomalies are complex and indicate that they incorporate inhomogeneities. Several authors have suggested ways in which the linear least-squares inversion technique can be modified to model such seamount anomalies (see McNutt, 1986). These methods appear to work well enough if the amount of inhomogeneity is small or covers a limited area in comparison with the uniform part of a seamount's magnetization.

The magnetic anomaly of the western edifice of Mendelssohn Seamount consists of a broad, normally polarized anomaly surrounding a shorter wavelength, reversely polarized feature (Figure 4). We first inverted this anomaly using McNutt's [1986] algorithm with the assumption that the summit magnetization is different from that of the base and that their boundary is horizontal. This model indicated that the magnetization of the upper part of the seamount is reversely polarized. Whereas the calculated magnetic declination of the base is approximately 7.5°, that of the summit is about 188.7°, a difference of nearly 180°. It was impossible, however, to determine a reliable inclination for the summit as this parameter varied significantly with the assumed placement of the horizontal boundary. The magnetization direction of the base of the seamount, which encompassed most of the volume of the model, appeared to be affected only slightly by changes in the location of the polarity boundary. Nevertheless, to avoid a bias caused by the reversed summit, the inversion was run with the magnetic anomaly observations from over the summit (about 35% of the total number of data) removed from inverse calculations (Figure 4). The results of this model are those listed in Table 1.

A similar technique was used to obtain paleomagnetic data from the eastern edifice of Mendelssohn Seamount. The magnetic anomaly of this feature appears to be a strong dipole that is split into two parts along a north-south line across the summit. From our modeling it appears that the western half of the upper kilometer of this volcano is reversely polarized. The observed magnetic anomaly values over the reversed part (about 3% of the data for this feature) were removed from the inverse calculations (Figure 4).

The morphology of the magnetic anomaly of Schumann Seamount indicates that both edifices of this seamount probably also incorporate a small amount of reversely polarized material. Magnetic models with areas of reversed polarity were tried, but none yielded a significantly better fit of the observed and calculated anomalies. Because of the non-uniformity, the GFR parameters calculated in the magnetic inversion routine were low. However, the consistency of the paleopoles from Schumann Seamount compared with other Musicians GPs of the same age implies that the calculations produced reasonable results.

Different approaches were taken in the analysis of Cross and McCall seamounts, located in the South Hawaiian group. The magnetic anomaly of Cross has a band of short wavelength features trending east-west across the summit and eastern flank. Upward-continuation by 6 km was used to low-pass filter the anomaly, a method discussed by Sager [1984], and the upward-continued field was used to constrain the inversion for magnetic parameters. The main difficulty with the inversion of the magnetic anomaly of McCall Seamount was the paucity of survey data. This seamount is elongated north-south and has two peaks, but the southern peak is poorly surveyed. We used a recent bathymetric chart of the South Hawaiian seamounts [Wilde et al., 1980] to constrain the shape of this part of the seamount. Furthermore, it was necessary to model the southern peak with a stronger magnetization than the northern peak. We formulated a model in which the southern peak was constrained to have a magnetization with the same direction, but twice the intensity, as that of the northern peak. Although these assumptions may appear to be somewhat contrived, greater degrees of freedom of the magnetic model are probably not justified considering the scarcity of magnetic and bathymetric survey data.

Paleomagnetic Models (2D)

Volcanic ridges have only rarely been used for the determination of paleomagnetic data by magnetic anomaly inversion. Because they are elongated features, the components of magnetization that contribute most to the magnetic anomaly are the vertical and the projection of the horizontal into a plane normal to the strike of the ridge. Thus, the magnetic anomaly of an elongated feature is highly dependent on its azimuth and it is difficult to determine the declination of the magnetization vector.

The volcanic ridges in the southern Musicians province are, however, ideally suited for two-

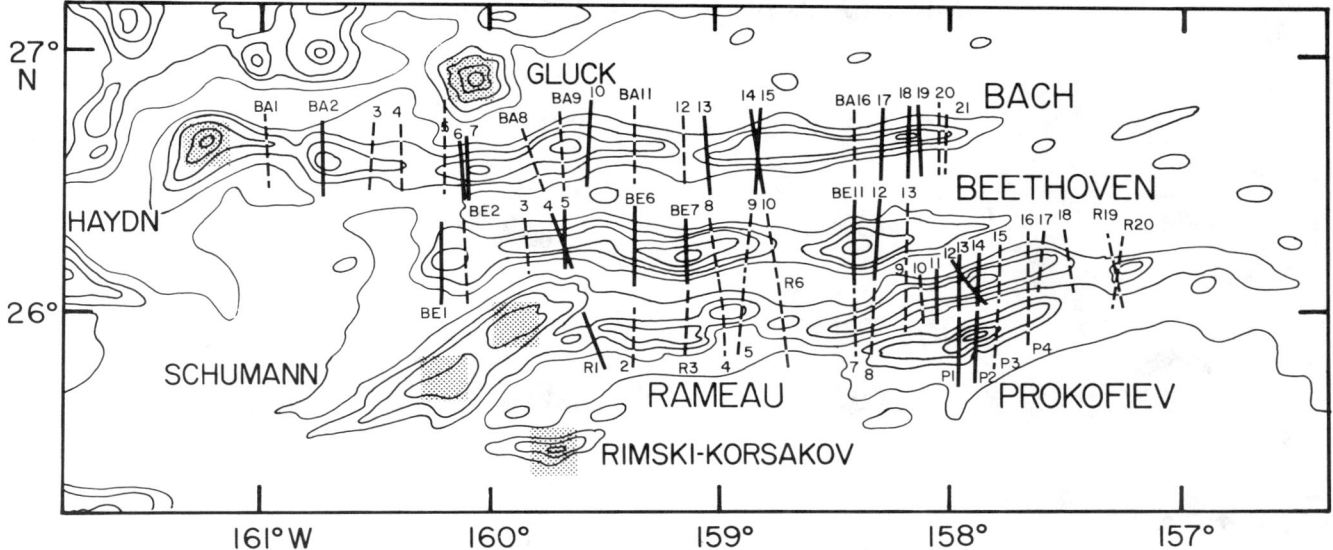

Fig. 5. Generalized bathymetric chart of the southeast Musicians ridges (redrawn from Mammerickx and Smith [1985]) showing the locations of shiptracks used in the 2D magnetic calculations. The heavy lines represent tracks that yielded paleomagnetic data deemed reliable, whereas the dashed lines produced data considered unreliable. The stippled boxes show seamounts that were studied with the 3D magnetic modeling method. Results from the 2D calculations are given in Table 3 and in the Appendix.

dimensional (2D) paleomagnetic modeling. They all trend nearly east-west and are crossed by a large number of ship tracks, primarily from the ESSA Seamap survey, oriented nearly north-south. Thus a 2D form of the inversion routine can be employed to determine paleomagnetic parameters for these features. The 2D magnetic inversion technique is similar to the 3D method. It consists of a 2D algorithm, devised for forward modeling of magnetic anomalies by Talwani and Heirtzler [1964], into which we programmed a least-squares solution for the magnetization parameters. A constant offset was used for the regional in these calculations as it was for the three-dimensional computations.

The horizontal and vertical components of the magnetization derived by this method give the "effective inclination" which is the projection of the inclination angle into a plane perpendicular to the strike of the two-dimensional body. This datum is essentially the same as those determined from the analysis of magnetic lineation skewness [Schouten and Cande, 1976]. The effective inclination, I', is related to the actual inclination by

$$\tan I' = \tan I/\sin(A-D), \qquad (1)$$

where I and D are the inclination and declination of the magnetization and A is the strike of the elongated feature. Because I and D cannot be determined independently, the locus of the paleomagnetic pole is half of a great circle on the earth's surface. In the case of the Musicians ridges, their azimuths are nearly 90° and the average declination of all of the other volcanoes in the province is approximately 10° ± 8°. Thus, the effective inclination and actual inclination should be nearly the same.

Paleomagnetic data calculated from the Rameau, Beethoven, Bach and Prokofiev ridges are given in Table 3 and the Appendix (Table A-1). The locations of the ship tracks used to compute these data are shown in Figure 5. In all, effective inclinations were calculated for 58 crossings of the ridges. These inversions showed that Bach and Beethoven are normally magnetized, whereas Prokofiev and all but the western tip of Rameau are reversely polarized. Interestingly, both Rameau and Prokofiev are near Paumakua Seamount, which has the same polarity. Thus virtually all of the reversely polarized volcanoes in the entire province are located within a short distance of one another (Figures 2, 5).

The effective inclinations determined in these calculations show a considerable scatter, demonstrating the need for some sort of quality control. First we eliminated from consideration all of those data calculated in inversions that produced a GFR less than 2.5. Further, we felt that the data yielded by edifices with low intensities of magnetization may display an unacceptable contribution by induced magnetism. Thus, we considered all of the inversions that yielded intensities of less than 1.5 A/m to be of lesser reliability. By the former criterion 8 data were

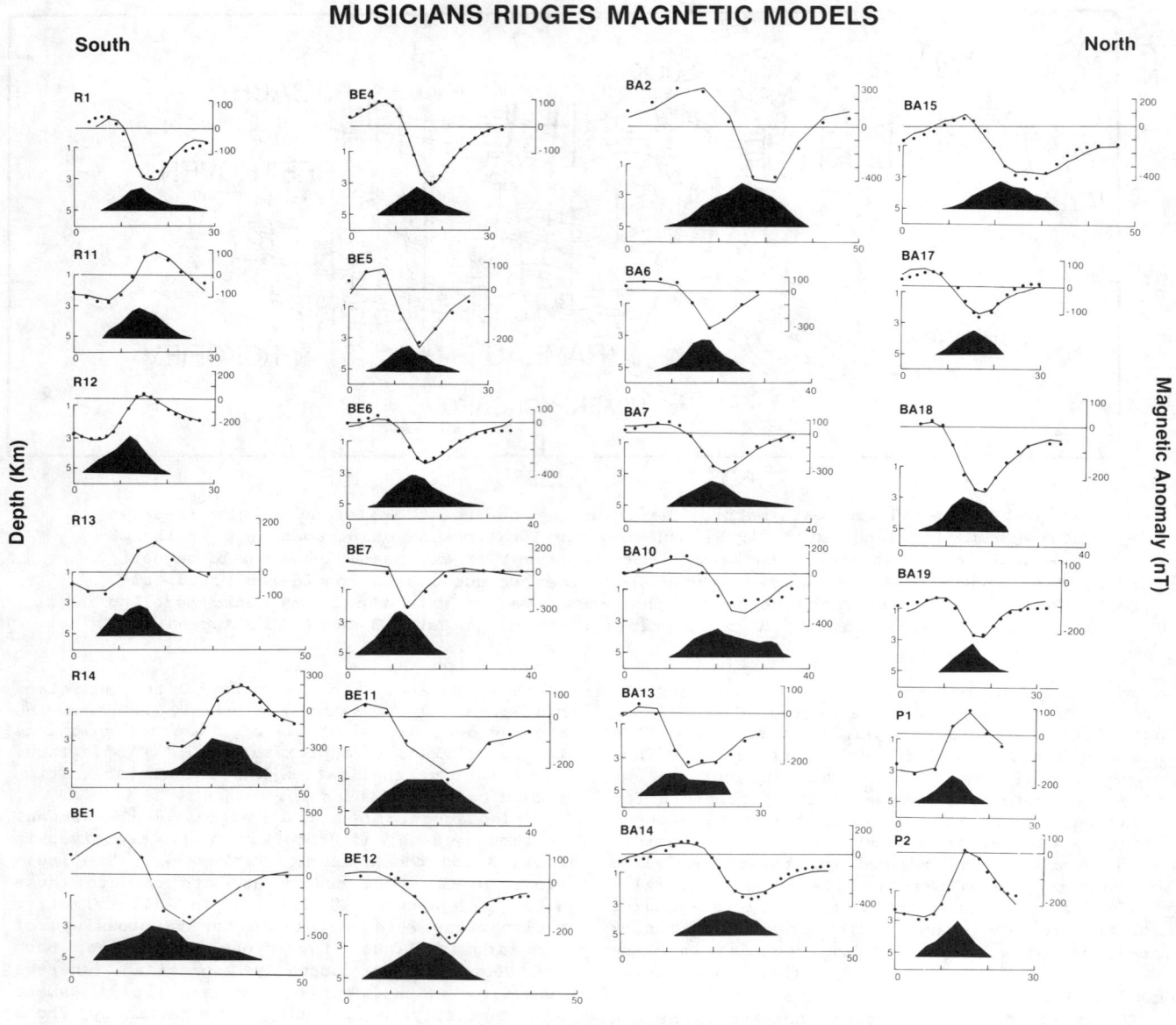

Fig. 6. Comparison of observed and calculated magnetic anomalies for the reliable 2D magnetic models. Solid lines denote the observed anomalies and dots represent the calculated anomalies. The bathymetric model is shown by the solid polygon beneath each set of anomalies. North is to the right and south to the left of all plots. The labels correspond to the line identifiers in Figure 5 and Table 3.

removed from further consideration and by the latter, 3 additional data were eliminated.

As seen in Figure 5, the Musicians Ridges are not truly two-dimensional. In many locations, the ridges more nearly resemble a string of volcanoes connected on their lower flanks than truly two-dimensional ridges. The effective inclinations calculated from ship tracks crossing over the flanks of an edifice were often systematically different from those computed from tracks over its summit. An examination of the seamount magnetic anomaly maps (Figures 3, 4, and Appendix) shows the reason for this problem. If a feature is three-dimensional and has a magnetization declination that is non-zero, then a north-south line over a flank will have the zero line and the high and low of the anomaly shifted with respect to the shallowest point of bathymetry as compared to their configuration over the summit. Thus an incorrect inclination is obtained from an inversion over the flank. Recognizing this difficulty, the individual volcanoes making up each ridge were identified (these are the "features" listed in Tables 3 and A-1) and the position of each line with respect to the summit of the nearest volcano was noted. Only those lines passing near a summit were deemed to have yielded a reliable effective inclination.

Twenty-four of the track lines fit this criterion. The agreement of the observed and calculated magnetic anomalies along these tracks are shown in Figure 6. A paleolatitude was calculated for each line using a declination of 10°. The paleolatitudes from the same edifice are consistent and generally agree to within a few degrees.

Seamount Ages

K-Ar and ^{40}Ar-^{39}Ar total fusion ages have been reported for five seamounts (exclusive of the Hawaiian ridge) in the region of this study. Clague and Dalrymple [1975] determined ages of 88.8 ± 5.2 Ma and 66.9 ± 2.9 Ma, respectively, for Rachmaninoff and Khatchaturian seamounts, located in the Musicians. Dymond and Windom [1968] determined ages of 87.6 ± 2.0 Ma and 87.6 ± 1.8 to 91.3 ± 2.1 Ma for Seamount HD1 and Cross Seamount, in the South Hawaiian province. They also reported an age of 0.7 Ma for a seamount located 120 km northwest of HD1 but it appears the dated sample was mislabeled and actually dredged elsewhere far removed from the study area. All of these ages have been corrected for new K-Ar decay constants determined since their publication [Steiger and Jäeger, 1977].

Although the K-Ar radiometric decay clock has been widely used to date oceanic lavas, care must be used to avoid the effects of seawater alteration. During normal submarine weathering, both K addition and radiogenic ^{40}Ar loss will lower the apparent K-Ar age. Clague et al. [1975] and Dalrymple and Clague [1976] found that ^{40}Ar-^{39}Ar total fusion ages of altered Hawaiian basalts were a better estimate of the crystallization age than conventional K-Ar ages of the same rocks. They attributed this effect to the proportional loss of radiogenic ^{40}Ar and K-derived ^{39}Ar from alteration products such as clays. Dalrymple et al. [1980] used ^{40}Ar-^{39}Ar incremental heating experiments to test the degree to which K-Ar crystallization ages had been disturbed, and recommended a set of conservative criteria to test whether a sample is too disturbed or altered to yield reliable, independent crystallization ages. Further work (for example, Walker and McDougall [1982] and Pringle [1984]) has emphasized that whole rock total fusion ages, at best, must be cautiously interpreted in the absence of age spectra data.

We have determined ^{40}Ar-^{39}Ar ages for 14 sea-

TABLE 4. Summary of Ages from the Musicians and South Hawaiian Seamounts

Name	Age ± 1 sd
Condordant Incremental Heating Ages	
Khatchaturian*	81.7 ± 1.6
Brahms	88.9 ± 0.6
Mendelssohn-E	77.0 ± 1.9
Mendelssohn-W	81.7 ± 1.2
Central Bach Ridge	73.8 ± 1.7
Schumann-W	82.2 ± 1.0
Concordant Total Fusion Ages	
Rachmaninov*	85.6 ± 1.2
Haydn	76.5 ± 1.4
Liszt	83.8 ± 1.6
Paumakua	65.5 ± 4.3
Kauluakalana	80.5 ± 1.6
McCall	82.7 ± 0.5
Somewhat Discordant Total Fusion Ages	
Mahler	86.4 ± 2.6
Cross*	84.6 ± 3.8
Conventional K-Ar Age	
HD1**	87.6 ± 1.8 - 91.3 ± 2.1
Magnetic Polarity Ages	
Chatauqua	79
Kona 5S	81
Show	81
Prokofiev Ridge	65
Rameau Ridge	65

*Weighted average includes most reliable of previously published values.
**From Dymond and Windom [1968]

mounts (Table 4), based mainly on concordant incremental heating experiments and mineral total fusion ages (Tables A-2, A-3 in Appendix). Ages from concordant incremental heating experiments should be accurate to the reported analytical precision, no better than 0.5 percent. Feldspar total fusion ages, usually within analytical precision of the best age estimate, may be as much as 10% too young. Whole rock total fusion ages can deviate at least 30% from the true crystallization age, but may be within ± 10% for carefully selected samples. A complete discussion of the accuracy of conventional K-Ar and ^{40}Ar-^{39}Ar ages of altered oceanic lavas is beyond the scope of this report; however, a detailed analysis of this problem will be presented elsewhere [Pringle, in preparation].

Nine samples from seven seamounts yielded concordant ^{40}Ar-^{39}Ar incremental heating age plateau

148 MUSICIANS AND SOUTH HAWAIIAN SEAMOUNTS

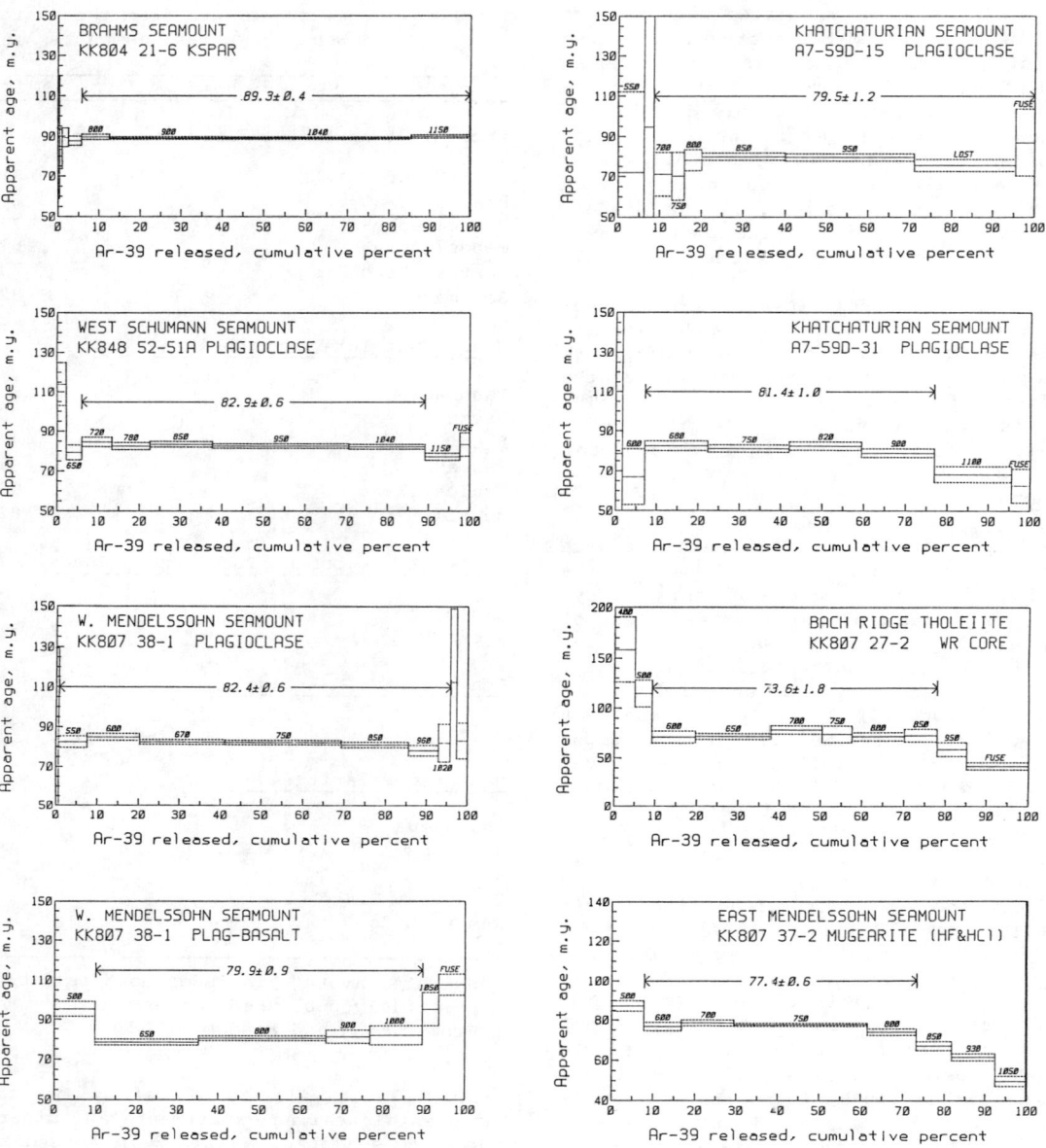

Fig. 7. ^{40}Ar-^{39}Ar age spectra for samples from the Musicians seamounts. The age indicated is the weighted plateau age in Ma and the temperature for each increment are in degrees Celsius. Dashed lines indicate the estimated standard deviation about the calculated age (solid lines) for each increment.

and isochron ages (Table A-2, Appendix) following the criteria of Dalrymple et al. [1980]. Figure 7 shows the age spectra and weighted plateau age for the best of these experiments. We prefer the isochron age instead of the weighted plateau age because (1) no assumption of the composition of non-radiogenic ^{40}Ar is required and (2) the error estimate includes both an estimate for the experimental precision of each increment and an estimate for the scatter about the final isochron age. We adopt the isochron age as the best estimate for the age of six of these seamounts: Khatchaturian, Brahms, East Mendelssohn, West Mendelssohn, Schumann, and central Bach Ridge (Table A-2, Appendix). Clague and Dalrymple [1975] reported a conventional K-Ar age of 66.9 ± 2.6 Ma for one of these samples, a plagioclase separate (A7-59D-15) from Khatchaturian Seamount. This is 18% lower than the incremental heating age reported here and highlights the problem of dating even apparently fresh-looking feldspar separates with the conventional K-Ar technique. The incremental heating experiment for a sample from the sixth seamount, Mahler, did not reveal a very precise age estimate and we prefer to use an average of the total fusion ages for that seamount.

Ages for seven seamounts (Rachmaninoff, Haydn, Schumann, Liszt, Paumakua, Kauluakalana, and McCall) are based on at least two plagioclase $^{40}Ar-^{39}Ar$ total fusion experiments on each seamount (Table A-3, Appendix). A few alkalic whole rock total fusion ages have been included where these are concordant with the plagioclase total fusion ages. We included the two coarser-fraction plagioclase total fusion ages reported by Clague and Dalrymple [1975] in the weighted age for Rachmaninov Seamount. Additionally, plagioclase total fusion ages confirm the $^{40}Ar-^{39}Ar$ incremental heating ages for Brahms seamount and central Bach Ridge.

Total fusion ages from Mahler and Cross seamounts are somewhat discordant at the 95% confidence level (Table A-3, Appendix). We prefer the arithmetic average of the individual total fusion experiments as the best estimate of these seamount ages, and the standard deviation of this mean as the best estimate of the accuracy of these ages. The preferred age for Mahler Seamount is concordant with the plagioclase incremental heating age reported above. We have included the conventional K-Ar biotite age determined by Dymond and Windom [1968] in the preferred age for Cross Seamount.

Three seamounts (Chatauqua, Kona 5S, and Show) and two ridges (Prokofiev and Rameau) can be dated by their reversed magnetic polarity. Following Gordon and Cox [1980a] we note that the three seamounts were evidently formed earlier than 69 Ma as their GPs are located on the Pacific APWP, but farther south than the 69 Ma mean pole (see next section and Figures 9-11). Between the end of the Cretaceous Quiet Period and 69 Ma, only three reversals took place, 31r, 32r, and 33r [Harland et al., 1982]. Chrons 31r and 32r occurred between 68-72 Ma, but chron 33r occurred between 79-83 Ma. The positions of the GPs of these seamounts, near other data of approximately 80 Ma age, implies that these seamounts formed during chron 33r. Kona 5S and Show are assigned the mean age of this reversed period, 81 Ma. Chatauqua, on the other hand, has a normally polarized summit. Thus it is assumed to be the age of the end of chron 33r, 79 Ma. We note that different versions of the geomagnetic reversal time scale assign ages of 79-83 Ma for the beginning of Chron 33r [Ness et al., 1980], thus a reasonable estimate of the error of these magnetic polarity ages is about 5% or 4 Ma.

The two ridges are the same polarity as nearby Paumakua Seamount, dated at 65 ± 5 Ma. Because of their proximity and the fact that these are the only three edifices in the Musicians Seamounts that are entirely reversed in polarity, it seems reasonable to assume that they formed contemporaneously during the same reversed polarity chron. In addition, their paleolatitudes, 2.8° and 5.7°, are close to that of Paumakua, 3.9°. Thus we infer an age of 65 ± 5 Ma for both ridges.

Discussion and Interpretation

Before exploring the implications of the data set it is important to consider its limitations. In this study and elsewhere, it was found that on the average random errors in reliable GP positions amount to about 4°-6° [Gordon, 1983; Sager, 1983; Sager, 1987]. Furthermore, the GP data, with its errors, must be interpreted with age data that also contain errors. The error in an "acceptable" age determination depends, of course, on the type and quality of the datum, but it usually ranges from 1-2% for the best data to 10-30% for the worst. In many other geologic settings pole and age errors of these magnitudes would pose few problems. However, apparent polar wander for the Pacific plate appears to have been rapid during the mid to Late Cretaceous [Gordon, 1983; Sager, 1983]. As a consequence, the paleomagnetic and age data are pushed to the limit of their resolution. Therefore, we must endeavor to carefully extract the consistent overall pattern from the data while filtering out the errors.

A New Pacific Apparent Polar Wander Path

The magnetization parameters (Tables 1-2) have been used to calculate a geomagnetic pole for each of the seamounts in the study area. These data can be used in two different, but important ways. First, the GPs with reliable ages can be used to refine the apparent polar wander path (APWP) of the Pacific plate. Second, the APWP can be used as a benchmark against which the paleomagnetic poles of undated seamounts can be compared to obtain constraints on geologic and tectonic models.

Realizing that our well-dated seamounts could greatly improve the resolution of the Pacific APWP, we recalculated two of the mean poles that define it (Tables 5 and A-4, Appendix). In Figure 8 we plotted the pole positions for the seamounts that have been dated in this study along with poles from other seamounts with ages from the literature that appear to be reliable. The general trend of the poles is southward with increasing age, towards the north central Atlantic Ocean, from the early Tertiary to Late Cretaceous. From about 70-90 Ma APW appears to have accumulated rapidly as the GPs of these ages are smeared out over a large area. At approximately 80 Ma the trend appears to bend to the west.

Details of the calculations for paleomagnetic poles 39 and 69 Ma of age are reported elsewhere [Sager, 1987]. No data from the Musicians or South Hawaiian Seamounts were used in the determination of the former; however, GPs from Haydn and Paumakua were used for the latter. These two

TABLE 5. Pacific Plate Apparent Polar Wander Path

Age (Ma)	Pole Location Lat (°N)	Lon (°E)	95% Confidence Ellipse Semi-Axis Length (°) Major	Minor	Azimuth of Major Axis (°E)	Ref
39 ± 2	77.6	7.6	3.5	2.4	91	1
69 ± 4	70.2	0.8	3.0	1.9	91	1
80 ± 4	58.5	358.3	3.1	2.9	91	2
87 ± 3	57.0	331.6	4.2	3.8	56	2

References: (1) Sager [1987]; (2) This Study

paleopoles comprised 19% of the data utilized for the calculation of the 69 Ma pole.

Seamount paleomagnetic poles from this study, Pacific poles previously published, and other Pacific paleomagnetic data with ages between 78-94 Ma were collected and divided into two groups by age. The older group, consisting of the data with ages in excess of 83 Ma has a mean age of 87 Ma. The younger group has a mean age of 80 Ma. Because we wished to combine the GPs with other Pacific paleomagnetic data of the appropriate age, a least-squares, maximum-entropy method designed for this purpose by Gordon and Cox [1980b] was used to calculate mean paleomagnetic pole positions. This routine determines an ellipse of 95% confidence by linear propagation of the errors from the input data to the best fit average pole.

An empirical method was used to determine the standard errors of the seamount GPs. Using Fisher statistics the θ_{63} [McFadden, 1980] of the GPs in each group was determined and assumed to be the standard error of each datum in that group for input into the mean pole calculating routine. For the 80 Ma and 87 Ma groups, the standard errors are 5° and 6°, respectively. Special statistics

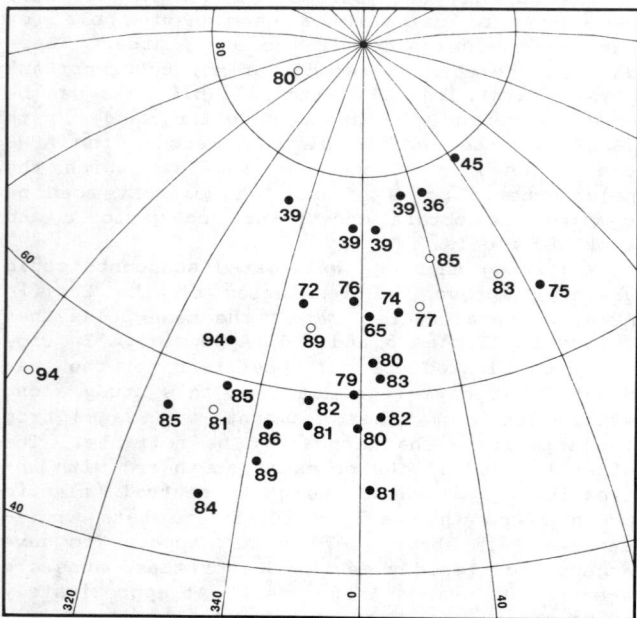

Fig 8. Dated Pacific seamount paleomagnetic poles. Filled circles denote those poles used in the calculation of mean paleomagnetic poles defining the Pacific apparent polar wander path (see text and Sager [1987]). Open circles are poles not used in the mean pole calculations.

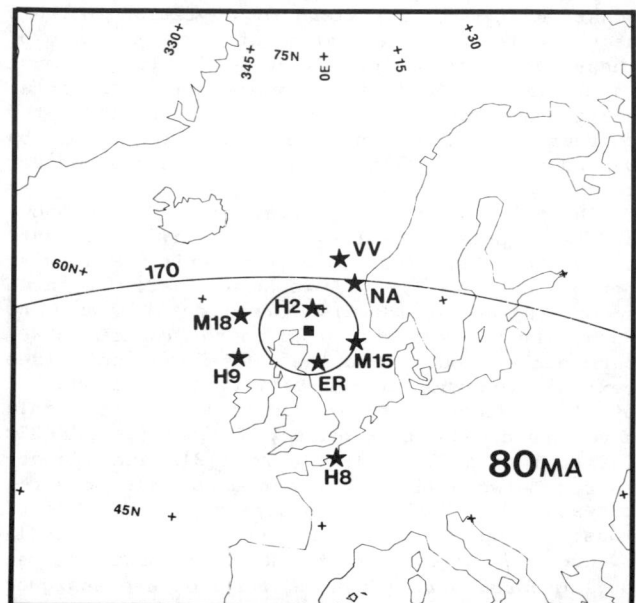

Fig. 9. The 80 Ma mean Pacific paleomagnetic pole and the data used for its calculation. The stars are seamount paleomagnetic poles and the curved arc is a segment of the polar locus determined from azimuthally-unoriented paleomagnetic samples from DSDP Site 170. The letters are seamount identifiers from Tables 1 and 2 or the first two letters of the seamount name if from other than the study area. The filled square is the location of the mean pole and the surrounding ellipse is its 95% confidence region (see Table 5). A complete listing of the data used in the mean pole calculation is given in the Appendix.

derived for inclination-only paleomagnetic data [Cox and Gordon, 1984] were applied to published DSDP core measurements from sites 170, 171, and 317A to determine a mean paleocolatitude and the standard error of the mean for each site (Table A-4, Appendix).

Eight seamount GPs (from Von Valtier, Nagata, Erimo, Kona 5S, Chatauqua, Show, Schumann, and Mendelssohn-W) and a single paleocolatitude from a DSDP sediment core taken at Site 170 were used to determine the position of the 80 Ma mean paleomagnetic pole (Figure 9). Six seamount GPs (from Liszt, Mahler, Rachmaninoff, HD1, Kapsitotwa, and Makarov) plus two DSDP sediment core paleocolatitudes, from Site 171 and 317A, were utilized for the computation of the 87 Ma mean pole (Figure 10). These data are listed in Table A-4 (Appendix) and the mean paleomagnetic poles defining the new Pacific APWP presented in Table 5.

Not all of the available Pacific paleomagnetic data of the appropriate ages were used in these calculations. Because Pacific paleomagnetic data are not abundant, it is undesirable to use deviant pole positions or data that do not properly average secular variation. Paleoinclination data from seven DSDP basalt cores (sites 61, 163, 165A, 313A, 315A, 462A, and 465A) were not used because none contained more than four independent samples [Cox and Gordon, 1984] and thus they constitute only spot measurements of the magnetic field direction. In addition, DSDP sediment core inclinations from three sites (167, 315A, and 462A) were excluded because their reported biostratigraphic age control appeared insufficiently precise for the task of constraining the paleomagnetic poles considering the rapidity of the APW that occurred in the Late Cretaceous.

In order to exclude deviant paleomagnetic data from the calculation of each mean pole, we calculated θ_{95} for the GPs of each age group. This is the angle that should enclose 95% of the samples of a Fisherian distribution [McFadden, 1980]. Poles located outside a circle of this radius centered at the mean pole position can be considered to be unrepresentative of the sample population at the 95% confidence level. For the 80 Ma group, this angle is 9.8° and for the 87 Ma group, 13.7°.

Using this criterion, several well-dated seamount GPs were excluded from the mean pole calculations. These poles may be discrepant for several reasons. If the GP is located near the APWP, then the error seems most likely to be in the age assignment. Those GPs located well away from the APWP may reflect errors in the determination of the paleomagnetic parameters. GPs from Z-43 [Vacquier and Uyeda, 1967], Kauluakalana, Mendelssohn-E, and Khatchaturian, appear to fall into these categories. An alternative explanation for inconsistent GPs is that they reflect actual tectonic motion. We believe that this may be the correct hypothesis for the data from Brahms, Cross, and McCall seamounts.

The GP for Kona 5S is located 8° south of the mean 80 Ma pole nearly on a line connecting this pole and the north geomagnetic pole. Considering the seamount's low intensity of magnetization, 0.9 A/m, it is possible that the position of this pole is affected by induced magnetization. However, it is not so distant from the mean pole so as to be inconsistent with the amount of scatter observed in the GPs of the same age. Consequently, this datum was used in the calculation of the 80 Ma mean paleomagnetic pole despite the possible bias. Its inclusion in the calculations did not change the pole location significantly. Without Kona 5S, the mean pole location is found to be only 1.3° farther to the north.

Despite the fact that seamounts from the Musicians and South Hawaiian provinces provide much of the constraint for the calculations of the mean poles, the new mean pole locations are in good agreement with previously published Pacific APWPs [Sager, 1983; Gordon, 1983; Cox and Gordon, 1984]. Furthermore, the APWP follows the trend of undated seamount GPs and other paleomagnetic data from other parts of the Pacific. Thus, the seamount paleomagnetic data derived in this study greatly improve the precision with which the Pacific APWP is known, but do not provide an obvious systematic bias in its calculation.

Paleopoles, Magnetic Ages, and Possible Rotations

The geomagnetic poles calculated for the undated Musicians and South Hawaiian seamounts (Tables 1 and 2) were plotted and compared with

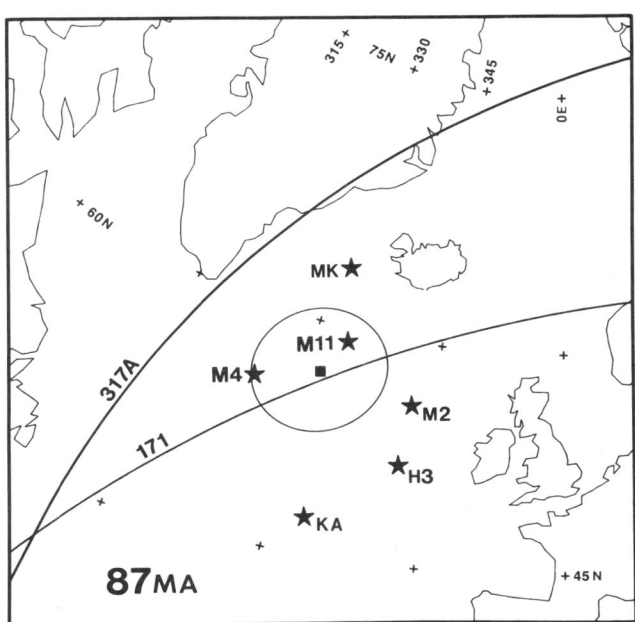

Fig. 10. The 87 Ma mean Pacific paleomagnetic pole and the data used in its calculation. Conventions as in Figure 9.

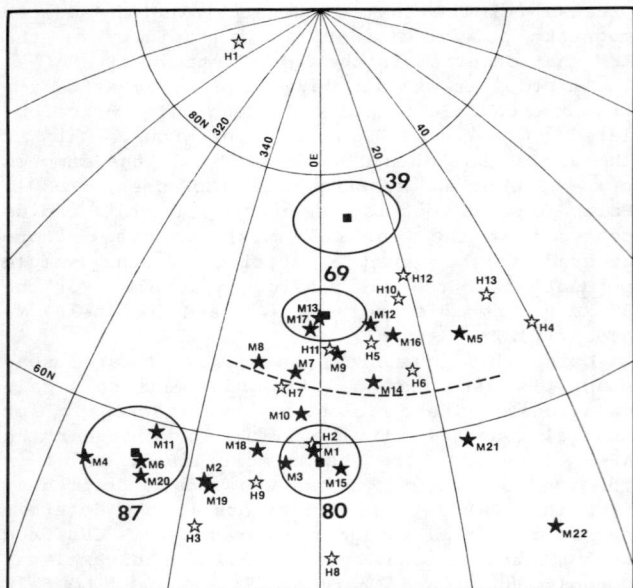

Fig. 11. Comparison of Musicians and South Hawaiian seamount poles with the Pacific apparent polar wander path. Filled stars denote poles of Musicians seamounts; open stars denote South Hawaiian seamount poles. Labels correspond to the identifiers in Tables 1 and 2. The larger numbers indicate the ages of the mean paleomagnetic poles in Ma. The location of each mean paleomagnetic pole is shown by the filled squares and is surrounded by its 95% confidence ellipse. The dashed line divides the paleomagnetic poles into two groups for the estimation of magnetic ages (see text for discussion).

the Pacific APWP discussed above (Figure 11). With few exceptions, most of the GPs from both seamount groups lie close to the APWP on the sections corresponding to the periods of rapid polar wander from 69 to 87 Ma. Only one GP, from Kauluakalana Seamount, is located to the north and west of the main cluster of GPs. The age of this seamount, 80 Ma, is clearly inconsistent with the location of its paleopole. From the location of its GP, between the geomagnetic and geographic north poles, the magnetization of this particular volcano must be almost entirely induced. Interestingly, none of the other seamounts in this study obviously shows such an obvious induced bias.

Several GPs are located to the south and east of the APWP. Six to eight South Hawaiian and Musicians seamount GPs are located slightly east of the 69 Ma pole. As explained below, we believe the placement of these GPs may have a tectonic cause. The GPs of Donizetti-W and Bizet are both found well to the east of the APWP. The locations of both of these poles may be the result of errors in the determination of the magnetization parameters of the seamounts. The magnetic anomaly inversions of both were based on sparse geophysical data sets consisting mainly of tracks from the twenty-plus year old ESSA Seamap survey.

As the majority of the Musicians and South Hawaiian GPs are located near the Pacific APWP we can make a rough estimate of the age of each of the seamounts from the position of its GP along the path. In Figure 11 a dashed line between the 69 and 80 Ma mean poles separates the GPs into two groups: those located along the younger part of the APWP and those located along the older part. An age of 65-75 Ma is implied for the "younger" seamounts and an age of 80-90 Ma is inferred for the "older" seamounts. This exercise makes the assumption that each GP accurately reflects the age of the seamount for which it was determined. From the preceding analysis, we know that the GPs have an average error of 4°-6°, consequently poles located near the dashed line may be assigned an incorrect age. This factor must be considered in the interpretation of such age estimates. In order to avoid confusion with standard age dating techniques, we refer to these estimates as "magnetic ages."

In general, the magnetic ages of nearby seamounts in the study area are consistent (Figure 12). Most of the seamounts along the Bending Line chain belong to the older group as do those on the northeast side of the Musicians Horst. Many of the edifices in the eastern Musicians and central South Hawaiian seamounts belong to the younger group. The South Hawaiian volcanoes with younger magnetic ages appear surrounded by older edifices. In the southeast Musicians province, around the east-west ridges, the magnetic ages are mixed. Most of these seamounts have younger magnetic ages, but Mendelssohn-W and Schumann are both indicated to be older.

Because dated Musicians and South Hawaiian seamounts provided much of the constraint for the calculation of the APWP, the magnetic ages of these seamounts should agree with their radiometric ages. Brahms, Cross, and McCall seamounts are notable exceptions. All three yield paleopoles that are located near the 69 Ma mean pole (Figures 8, 11 and 13), yet all three have radiometric ages in the range of 83-89 Ma. The GPs are located relatively near the APWP at a sizable distance from the mean paleomagnetic poles of the appropriate ages. The fact that the three GPs are located relatively close to one another implies consistency. Thus, the magnetic age discrepancy cannot be easily explained as a more or less random error in either the radiometric ages or the GPs because they would have to be systematically biased by almost exactly the same amount in both age and in location. Furthermore, the age determination for Brahms Seamount comes from an ^{40}Ar-^{39}Ar concordant incremental heating experiment that produced an exceptionally good age plateau (Figure 7). Consequently, this age should be particularly reliable. In addition, the discrepant poles are unlikely to be caused by induced or viscous magnetism as they are not displaced

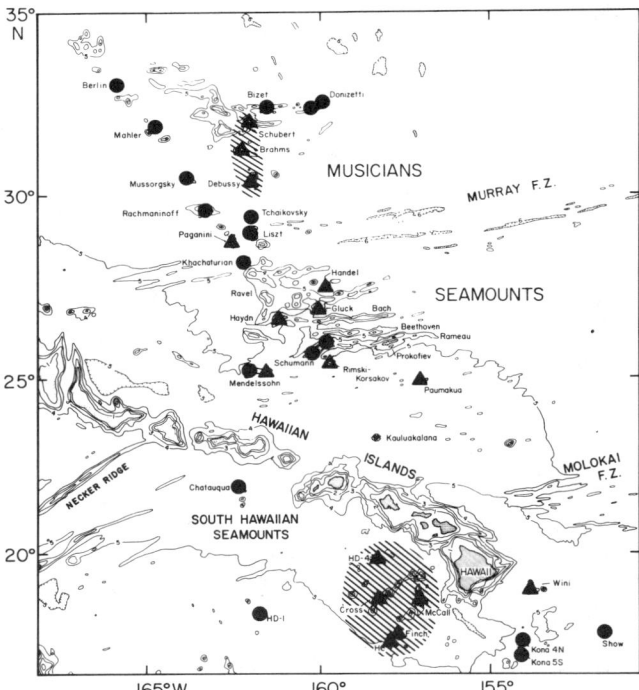

Fig. 12. Magnetic ages. The triangles correspond to seamounts having poles that are located closest to the 69 Ma mean Pacific paleomagnetic pole and the filled circles denote those that have poles located closest to the 80-87 portion of the Pacific apparent polar wander path (see text for discussion). Crosshatching indicates seamounts with pole positions that may indicate rotation and hence incorrect magnetic ages.

Hawaiian Islands, six have ages in the range of 79-85 Ma. The one younger seamount of this group, Jaggar, is located near Cross and McCall and has an age of 68 Ma, but this is only a total fusion reconnaissance date [Pringle, in preparation]. Unfortunately, geophysical data from this seamount were too sparse to allow a magnetic inversion to be performed.

We are left with a dilemma because these data can be interpreted in several different ways, none of which is entirely satisfactory. One can assume that the radiometric ages of Brahms, Cross, and McCall are all low by 17-22% so that their ages agree with the locations of their GPs. This hypothesis forces us to discount one excellent and two very good $^{40}Ar-^{39}Ar$ age data. Another possibility is that Brahms, Cross, and McCall are indeed older than their neighbors, but have GPs that are in error and happen to be located, unluckily, near the GPs of the younger

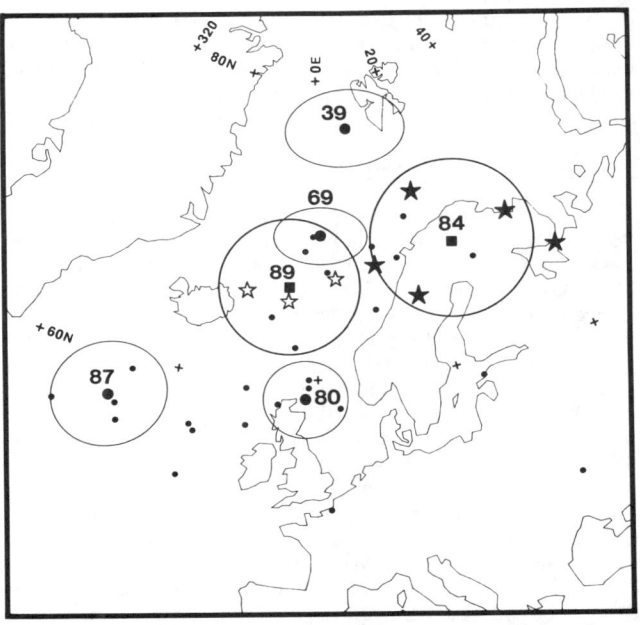

Fig. 13. Possible anomalous paleomagnetic poles. The open stars represent the paleomagnetic poles of Brahms, Debussy, and Schubert, three seamounts in the northern Musicians that may have rotated with respect to the rest of the Pacific plate. The solid stars denote the poles for Cross, McCall, and three other nearby seamounts in the South Hawaiian province that also may have rotated. Solid squares show the mean positions of the anomalous poles and the surrounding circles are their 95% confidence regions. Poles of the Pacific apparent polar wander path are shown as filled circles and are surrounded by their 95% confidence ellipses. The small dots denote the paleomagnetic poles of other Musicians and South Hawaiian seamounts. Large numbers indicate the average age of each mean pole.

toward the present geomagnetic pole from their expected positions. Instead, their deflection is nearly at right angles to this direction.

A detailed examination of the GPs (Figure 13) shows that the two seamounts next to Brahms in the North-South chain (shown by hatchures in Figure 12), Schubert and Debussy, both have GPs that are located very close to that of Brahms. Because of the proximity of these GPs to the 69 Ma mean paleomagnetic pole and the fact that neither has been dated, it is possible that both volcanoes are nearly 20 Ma younger than Brahms. However, no younger volcanoes have been found in this part of the Musicians seamounts as has been the case farther south in the province. A similar situation exists in the South Hawaiian seamounts. Both Cross and McCall seamounts have GPs that are located to the east of the 69 Ma pole and thus inconsistent with their radiometric ages. Moreover, three nearby undated seamounts (shown by hatchures in Figure 12) yield GPs close to those of Cross and McCall (Figure 13). Likewise, these three seamounts may be near 69 Ma in age, but of seven dated South Hawaiian seamounts south of the

seamounts surrounding them. This hypothesis calls for a rather unlikely, albeit possible, set of coincidences. Our preferred interpretation is to take the data at face value. The results for these three seamounts are relatively consistent and indicate a counterclockwise rotation with respect to the rest of the Pacific plate.

If we assume that the other seamounts near Cross, McCall, and Brahms that yielded suspect GPs are approximately the same age, then mean poles can be determined with Fisher statistics to quantify the amount of rotation (Figure 13). The three seamounts in the northern Musicians (including Brahms) suggest a counterclockwise rotation of 15° ± 9°, whereas the seven seamounts in the South Hawaiian province imply a similar rotation of 26° ± 9°. We interpret the data to indicate that the tectonic rotation occurred in two small blocks or microplates, rather than one large block, because seamounts that show no evidence of rotation separate the two deviant groups and the circles of 95% confidence of the two groups do not overlap (Figure 13). The rotation hypothesis must be treated as tentative at this time because it is founded on some of the least reliable data. However, the hypothesis is testable with further age and paleomagnetic data.

Duration of Volcanism

Paleomagnetic poles for both Musicians and South Hawaiian seamounts are scattered more or less uniformly along the segment of the Pacific APWP bounded by the 87 Ma and 69 Ma mean poles, suggesting that the volcanism in both provinces was coeval and lasted for 20 Ma or more. Additionally, none of the reliable GPs are located on the APWP west of the 87 Ma mean pole, nor north of the 69 Ma mean pole. This is in agreement with the available age data for the Musicians and South Hawaiian seamounts that are all in the range of 95-65 Ma [Pringle, in preparation].

The major differences in the distribution of the GPs from the two groups is that most of the GPs found at the western (oldest) end of the APWP are from the Musicians seamounts and most of the GPs located to the east of the 69 Ma pole are from the South Hawaiian province (Figure 11). The first observation seems to indicate that the oldest Musicians seamounts may be slightly older than the oldest South Hawaiian seamounts. This finding is supported by the radiometric age data that suggests the seamounts of the Bending Line chain in the northwest Musicians are as old as 95 Ma, whereas the oldest dated South Hawaiian seamount is 5-6 Ma younger. The location of numerous South Hawaiian GPs to the east of the 69 Ma mean pole may be a result of the hypothesized rotation of a small crustal block located south of the present Hawaiian Islands. Alternatively, it may simply indicate that there are many younger (i.e., around 70 Ma) seamounts in this province and that the estimated position of the 69 Ma pole is slightly in error.

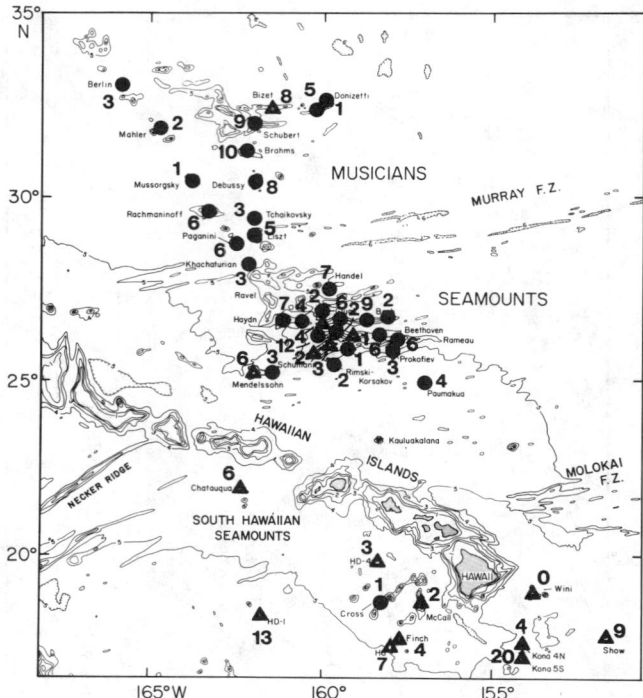

Fig. 14. Paleolatitudes of Musicians and South Hawaiian seamounts and ridges. Filled circles represent seamounts that formed north of the equator, whereas triangles denote seamounts formed south of the equator. The numbers labeling each symbol show the paleolatitude (in degrees north or south) at which each volcano formed.

Paleolatitudes

Paleolatitudes for each seamount are plotted in Figure 14 along with the reliable paleolatitudes from the Musicians ridges. Most of the values fall between 10°S and 10°N, indicating that the seamounts in this region were formed while this part of the Pacific was near the paleoequator. With only one exception, the Musicians seamounts to the north of the east-west ridges formed slightly to the north of the equator. Conversely, with a single exception, the seamounts of the South Hawaiian group located to the south of the Hawaiian Islands formed slightly to the south of the equator. The east-west ridges and the seamounts among them show a mix of north and south paleolatitudes.

The distribution of paleolatitudes in Figure 14 suggests that the seamounts in both provinces formed more-or-less coevally over a latitude range consistent with their geographic spread. Despite the northward drift of the Pacific plate during the Late Cretaceous implied by hotspot seamount chains [e.g., Engebretson et al., 1985] there is no obvious roughly north-south trending subset of volcanoes with a nearly constant paleolatitude that might indicate they were formed by a hotspot. Instead, the highest paleolatitudes are found in the northern Musicians and in the South Hawaiian seamounts, whereas the lowest paleolatitudes are found in the area in between.

Having a considerable number of data from both the Bending Line and North-South chains, we can examine the implications of the paleomagnetic data for their formation. In Figure 15 the paleolatitudes of the volcanoes in each chain have been plotted versus distance along the chain. If the seamounts were formed at a hotspot that remained nearly fixed in latitude, their paleolatitudes would plot on a horizontal line. Alternatively, if the seamounts erupted more or less contemporaneously and formed in their present latitudinal spread, their paleolatitudes should plot along a line tilted at 45°. Unfortunately, the data for the Bending Line chain are equivocal. Considering the error bounds of the paleolatitudes, all of the points plot within reasonable scatter for either model. On the other hand, the seamounts in the North-South chain clearly did not form at a single latitude. Instead, the trend of their paleolatitudes is close to 45°, suggesting that they formed in approximately their present latitudinal distribution. This finding agrees with the radiometric age data from this chain which display no age progressive trend [Pringle, in preparation].

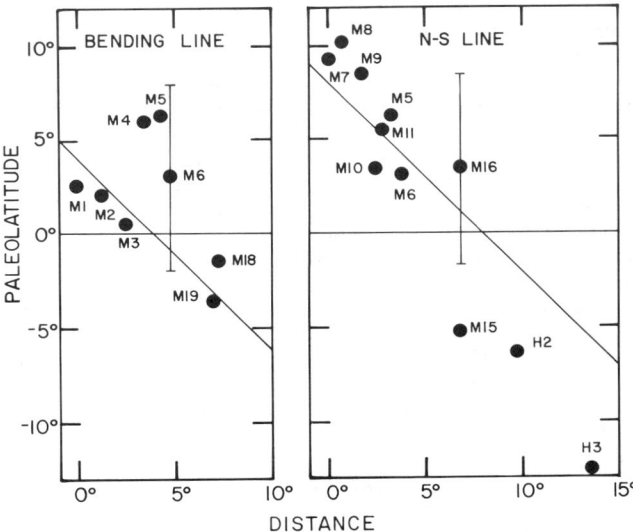

Fig. 15. Paleolatitude versus distance plots for the seamounts in the NW-SE trending (Bending Line) and N-S trending linear chains. Distance is plotted in degrees of arc from Berlin seamount (Bending Line) and Schubert seamount (N-S line). The error bars shown for the point in the middle of each plot are average estimates believed to be representative for the seamounts examined in this study. Note that seamounts M5 and M6 (Paganini and Khatchaturian) are included in both plots as it is unclear to which chain they belong.

Tectonic Model

The paleomagnetic and radiometric age data provide a number of useful constraints for geologic models of the formation of the Musicians and South Hawaiian seamounts. Such a model should explain the following findings. The age data displays an age-progressive trend in the Bending Line chain [Pringle, in preparation] suggesting that it resulted from hotspot volcanism. However, both the age and paleomagnetic data imply that this is not the case for the North-South chain. Furthermore, the data show no obvious trends elsewhere in either province that might indicate hotspot volcanism. Moreover, the model should explain the widespread and prolonged volcanism that apparently occurred in both provinces for over 20 Ma from about 90-70 Ma. In addition, a mechanism for the possible rotation of small crustal blocks, containing several seamounts each, is desirable.

None of the published evolutionary schemes for the formation of the Musicians and South Hawaiian seamounts fits all of the geophysical observations well. A simple ridge jump model explains neither the protracted length of volcanism, nor the age trend in the Bending Line chain, nor the genesis of the majority of the seamounts in these provinces. Additionally, the Cretaceous volcanic pulse model, essentially ad hoc, provides no testable hypothesis to account for the locations and distributions of these seamounts. However, in the "bending line" and hotspot hypotheses are elements that can be used to account for most of the observations.

Although the single "bending line," along which Pacific-Farallon spreading direction changed, probably never existed as originally envisioned by Rea [1970] because of the large offsets across the Murray and Molokai transforms, we believe that he correctly postulated a relation between the formation of these seamounts and a change in spreading direction. A single hotspot model cannot easily account for the ages, paleolatitudes and locations of all of the Musicians and South Hawaiian seamounts. Furthermore, the evidence presented here shows that the North-South chain was not formed by a second hotspot as suggested by Henderson and Gordon [1981]. Nevertheless, the Musicians age data imply that a hotspot played a role in their genesis. Our model for the evolution of these seamount groups incorporates aspects of both the "bending line" and hotspot models.

We preface our story by examining the central Pacific crust surrounding the study area. In Figure 2 the traces of the major mid-Pacific fracture zones, as expressed by bathymetry, magnetic anomalies, and satellite-derived geoid anomalies, are shown. Also shown in the figure are major bathymetric features and selected magnetic isochrons. The area pertinent to this study is that south of the Mendocino fracture zone and north of the Clipperton fracture zone.

The Mendocino fracture zone appears complex and probably represents the boundary between two different regimes of spreading. During the K-N, the Mendocino transform may have been part of the boundary between north and south Farallon plates [Rea and Dixon, 1983]. At the end of the K-N, the Mendocino appears to have separated the Pacific from the Chinook microplate [Rea and Dixon, 1983; Mammerickx and Sharman, 1987].

The Clipperton and other major fracture zones to the south of it appear linear east of the Line Islands. However, the Pioneer, Murray, Molokai, and Clarion fracture zones, located between the Mendocino and Clipperton, clearly curve convex to the north (Figure 2). The bends in these fracture zones occur slightly west of the younger boundary of the K-N, suggesting that a change in the relative plate motion happened near the end of the K-N. It is not clear whether the difference in fracture zone trends north and south of the Clipperton represents another, as yet unidentified, plate boundary or whether the curved portions of the Clipperton fracture zone and others farther south were lost through a boundary reorganization. The proximity of isochron 32 to the extrapolated position of the older boundary of the K-N south of the Clipperton (Figure 2) suggests that the latter hypothesis may be true.

The Murray and Molokai fracture zones are diffuse belts of deformation, 100 km or more in width, but the Pioneer and Clarion fracture zones are much narrower and well-defined (Figure 2). This difference appears to be a result of the size of the offset across each fracture zone. Crossing the Murray, anomaly 32 is offset sinistrally by about 750 km [Rea and Dixon, 1983]. Across the Molokai, it appears to be offset dextrally by a slightly greater distance [Addicott et al., 1982]. These offsets indicate that a long westward salient of the Farallon plate once protruded into the Pacific between the two fracture zones. If the width of the deformed area indeed reflects the offset across a fracture zone, then the wide traces of the Molokai and Murray suggest that the large offsets may have persisted throughout most of the K-N. The offsets of magnetic isochrons across the thinner Clarion and Pioneer fracture zones, on the other hand, appear to be less than 100 km [Atwater and Menard, 1970].

Examination of the trends of magnetic isochrons near the Line Islands suggests that the Pacific-Farallon ridge was nearly parallel to that chain at about the beginning of the K-N. Not long thereafter a change in the direction of spreading must have taken place and the trend of the ridge became more nearly north-south. The arcuate fracture zone trends in the central Pacific imply that the relative pole of rotation describing the northern Pacific and Farallon plate moved to a point near the equator. We drew great circles perpendicular to five points on each of the Clarion and Pioneer fracture zones inside the swath of K-N seafloor. From these circles an Euler pole of rotation at 11.0°S, 154.6°W was found. As the curve of the fracture zones appear continuous through the K-N seafloor, spreading around this pole of rotation must have continued throughout most of the rest of the K-N.

At about 95 Ma volcanism apparently began on the Bending Line chain in the Musicians seamounts as the Pacific plate moved in a northwesterly direction over a hotspot located near the equator. Why the Bending Line begins abruptly south of the Pioneer fracture zone is not clear. The hotspot may have erupted on the Farallon plate to the north of the Mendocino fracture zone and then come beneath the Pacific plate as the Mendocino passed northward over it.

Just prior to the end of the K-N, a change in spreading direction took place once again along the Pacific-Farallon ridge. The evidence for this ridge reorganization is the change in fracture zone trends near the younger edge of the K-N seafloor. Additionally, the bathymetric signatures of the Pioneer and Clarion fracture zones, well-defined elsewhere, are difficult to trace at this point (the hatchured zones in Figure 16). The hotspot was at this time located slightly north of the long salient of Farallon plate that protruded into the Pacific plate between the Murray and Molokai fracture zones. Before the change in spreading direction occurred, the ridges were oriented approximately north-south and spreading was east-west. In Figure 16 we have extrapolated the position of the Pacific-Farallon ridge at about 90 Ma to show its configuration before the change. After the change in spreading direction, the ridges were oriented about 20° west of north and the direction of spreading was about N70°E.

As a consequence of the change in spreading direction the transform boundaries along the long interfingered salients of the Pacific and Farallon plates were no longer parallel to the direction of maximum stress along which the two plates were forced to move. Thus compression must have occurred along some fracture zones and extension along others. The Farallon salient, trapped between pieces of Pacific plate, caused fracturing of the Pacific on either side as it rotated with the pivoting Farallon plate. Many of the Musicians and South Hawaiian seamounts were formed at this time as magma, perhaps some or all of it from the nearby hotspot, found its way to the seafloor along these fractures.

During this period of deformation and adjustment along the Pacific-Farallon ridge system there may have existed crustal blocks that rotated in relation to the surrounding major plates. Two such possible microplates are shown in Figure 16, delineated by the locations of the seamounts whose anomalous paleomagnetic poles suggest a rotation with respect to the Pacific plate. Given the limited data available it is impossible to precisely define the boundaries of these microplates or provide a unique geologic model for their origin and development. However, we note

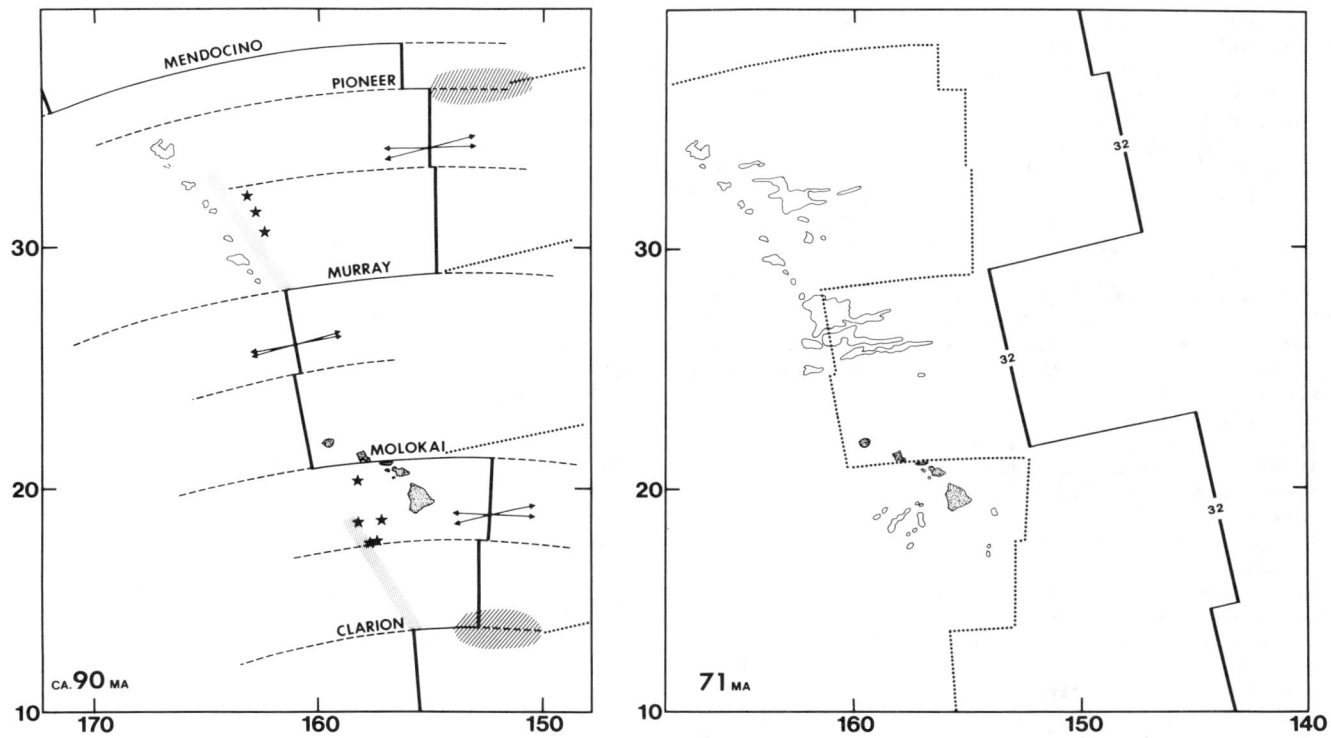

Fig. 16. Tectonic model for the formation of the Musicians and South Hawaiian seamounts. (left) An approximation of the position of the Pacific-Farallon ridge at about 90 Ma, just before a change in the direction of spreading. The Hawaiian Islands are shown for positional reference, but did not exist at the time. The bending line chain (light lines) was forming due to the Pacific plate's northwestward drift over a hotspot. The hatchured areas show unclear portions of the otherwise well-defined Pioneer and Clarion fracture zones. These ill-defined segments of the fracture zones may have formed during the change in ridge orientation accompanying the spreading direction change. The arrows show the directions of spreading along each ridge segment both before and after the change in spreading direction. The dotted lines show the fracture zone trends of the new spreading direction and the dashed lines show fracture zone trends of the old spreading direction. A small transform offset is shown on each ridge segment between the major fracture zones to indicate that there probably existed smaller fracture zones in addition to the major fracture zones. The stippled lines trending northwestward show the direction along which fractures may have propagated in the lithosphere as a result of compression along the longer transforms caused by the change in spreading direction. Stars show locations of seamounts that may have rotated on microplates. (right) Volcanism ends at about 71 Ma (anomaly 32 time) as the Farallon plate salient clears the obstructing region of the Pacific plate corresponding to the 90 Ma location of the Murray and Molokai fracture zones (dotted lines).

that if a thin sheet of brittle material has an interfingering boundary, as the Pacific and Farallon plates apparently had, and there are forces placed oblique to the strike-slip boundaries, there is a tendency for the larger "fingers" to break off at their bases. This type of fracturing may have allowed the reorientation of some segments of the Pacific-Farallon ridge by the rotation of microplates rather than by ridge rotation.

Evidence for ancient and currently active microplates has been found recently in many areas of the Pacific [Rea and Dixon, 1983; Hey et al., 1985; Anderson-Fontana et al., 1986; Mammerickx et al., 1986; Mammerickx and Sharman, 1987], yet tectonic models for microplate evolution are still rather crude [e.g., Engeln and Stein, 1984]. Although our evidence for microplate rotations in the Musicians and South Hawaiian seamounts is based on somewhat tenuous evidence, if the postulated rotations can be confirmed, this data will shed new light on the poorly understood dynamics of such features.

It should have taken 10-15 Ma for the Farallon salient to withdraw from the obstructing pieces of Pacific plate surrounding it. Thus volcanism continued in the Musicians and South Hawaiian seamounts as brittle deformation and fracturing occurred as a consequence of the interactions of the two plates. The ridges and elongated volcanic edifices, and perhaps the Musicians Horst, possibly formed along lines of weakness that may have been fracture zone traces. The Murray and Molokai were the major fracture zones in the area, but there is evidence that other smaller fracture zones offset the Pacific-Farallon ridge. One possible fracture zone has been noted south of the island of Hawaii [Handschumacher and Andrews, 1975]; another can be seen in the magnetic lineations east of the Musicians Seamounts between the Murray and Molokai fracture zones (recognized in Figure 2 of Malahoff and Handschumacher [1971] by R. Moberly [personal communication, 1982]). The elongated features in the Musicians are oriented approximately east-west and also north-northeast corresponding to the two directions of spreading. Finally, at about 71 Ma the Farallon salient cleared the impinging pieces of Pacific plate that had confined it and the volcanism in the Musicians and South Hawaiian seamounts ended. The configuration of the Pacific-Farallon ridge at about this time is shown in Figure 16.

This tectonic model has several features that are worth noting. First it explains why the Musicians and South Hawaiian seamounts formed where they did. The necessary ingredients were a reorganization of a spreading ridge plate boundary with long interlocking sections and a nearby hotspot to provide anomalous magma. It also offers an explanation for the extended duration of the volcanism in these seamount provinces as a consequence of the lengthy interaction of the Pacific and Farallon plates along their interlocked boundary. The formation of the linear volcanic features is accounted for by the eruption of magma along lines of weakness fractured by the plate interactions. These may have been coincident with fracture zone traces. Additionally, this model offers a framework for the explanation of the apparent rotation of small crustal blocks during the plate boundary reorganization.

Conclusions

Many new paleomagnetic and age data from the Musicians and South Hawaiian seamount provinces have been combined in this study with previously existing data to provide constraints on the origin and geologic history of these seamounts. We have presented evidence that suggests volcanism occurred throughout the Musicians seamounts from about 95 to 70 Ma. The volcanism in the South Hawaiian seamounts may have begun 5-10 Ma later, but seamounts in both provinces were apparently active at the same time and so the two groups are probably related. The seamounts all appear to have formed near the equator. During the time they erupted, the paleoequator was located at about the location of the Musicians ridges. Thus the northern Musicians display paleolatitudes that are slightly to the north of the equator and the South Hawaiian seamounts show paleolatitudes that are slightly to the south. The paleolatitudes also suggest that the seamounts of the North-South chain in the Musicians were formed nearly contemporaneously at different latitudes rather than at a nearly fixed latitude by a hotspot.

The new paleomagnetic data and ages have allowed the recalculation of two new mean paleomagnetic poles on the Pacific apparent polar wander path. One, located at 58.5°N, 358.3°E, has a mean age of 80 Ma and the other, located at 57.0°N, 331.6°E, has a mean age of 87 Ma. By comparison with the polar wander path we have calculated magnetic ages for the undated Musicians and South Hawaiian seamounts. They suggest that the oldest Musicians seamounts are located in the Bending Line chain and in the northern part of the Musicians horst. The youngest are located in the southeast Musicians and perhaps in the South Hawaiian provinces. Several seamounts with reliable ages have paleomagnetic pole positions consistent with one another, but displaying large deviation from the other dated paleomagnetic poles of the same age. We have interpreted these data as indicating that at least two small crustal blocks may have rotated with respect to the rest of the Pacific as microplates.

Our preferred tectonic model for the formation of the Musicians and South Hawaiian seamounts calls upon the proximity of a hotspot to a long section of Farallon plate that protruded into the Pacific plate. A change in spreading direction caused this salient of Farallon plate to deform the pieces of Pacific surrounding it causing volcanism in the province for a period of 10-15 Ma. Many of the volcanic features in both seamount groups were formed by the eruption of hotspot magma along fractures caused by the plate interactions.

APPENDIX: Miscellaneous Tables and Seamount Maps
Contents:

Section A: Miscellaneous Tables

A-1: Magnetization Parameters of Musicians Ridges (complete listing)

A-2: Age Spectra and Isochron Analysis Summary of Concordant $^{40}Ar/^{39}Ar$ Incremental Heating Experiments

A-3: $^{40}Ar/^{39}Ar$ Total Fusion Ages

A-4: Paleomagnetic Data Used for the Determination of New Mean Paleopoles for 80 Ma and 87 Ma

A-5: Age Discordance Between $^{40}Ar/^{39}Ar$ Incremental Heating Age and Conventional K-Ar Age and $^{40}Ar/^{39}Ar$ Total Fusion Age

Section B: Seamount Maps

The seamount maps are done in the following manner. Part A shows the bathymetry and magnetic anomaly maps. Bathymetry is contoured at 250 m intervals whereas the magnetic anomaly is contoured at 50 or 100 nT intervals. On the bathymetric map, the dashed lines correspond to the shiptracks used to construct both maps. On the magnetic map, the dashed lines indicate the data used for the magnetic inversion. A dashed box indicates a gridded area used as input and dashed lines denote shiptracks along which data were digitized. Parts B and C are plots of calculated and residual anomalies. A map lot corresponds to the gridded area of the magnetic map of part A. If inverted anomaly was digitized along tracklines, then a comparison of the observed and calculated anomalies are shown in part B. This line is labelled A-A' on the corresponding part A.

B-1: Berlin (M1)
B-2: Mahler (M2)
B-3: Paganini (M5)
B-4: Schubert (M7)
B-5: Debussy (M9)
B-6: Tchaikovsky (M10)
B-7: Liszt (M11)
B-8: Handel (M12)
B-9: Rimski-Korsakov (M13)
B-10: Gluck (M14)
B-11: Haydn (M17)
B-12: Schumann W & E (M18, M19)
B-13: Donizetti W & E (M20, M21)
B-14: Bizet (M22)
B-15: Kaulaukalana (H1)
B-16: Finch, Finch-W (H5, H6)
B-17: Cross (H12)
B-18: McCall (H13)

Acknowledgments. We are indebted to Ralph Moberly, John Sinton, and J. Frisbee Campbell for their efforts to make this study possible. We also thank them for the interest, knowledge, and encouragement that they provided. We thank the captain and crew of the R/V Kana Keoki for their hard work and would also like to express our gratitude to L. Neil Frazer and Brooks Wallin for their work at sea and later. Reviews by Victor Vacquier, John Hildebrand, Tracy Vallier, Jon Hagstrum, and David Clague proved valuable in revising this article. The funding to collect the data presented here and to perform the initial analyses was provided by the Office of Naval Research.

References

Addicott, W. O., P. W. Richards, and Circum-Pacific Map Committee, Plate Tectonic Map of the Circum-Pacific Region, Pacific Basin Sheet, Amer. Assoc. Petrol. Geol., Tulsa, Oklahoma, 1982.

Anderson-Fontana, S., J. F. Engeln, P. Lundgren, R. L. Larson, and S. Stein, Tectonics and evolution of the Juan Fernandez microplate at the Pacific-Nazca-Antarctic triple junction, J. Geophys. Res., 91, 2005-2018, 1986.

Atwater, T. and H. W. Menard, Magnetic lineations in the northeast Pacific, Earth Planet. Sci. Lett., 7, 445-450, 1970.

Baraclough, D. R. and E. B. Fabiano, Grid values and charts for the IGRF 1975.0, IAGA Bull no. 38, 28 pp., IUGG Publications Office, Paris, 1977.

Chapman, S. and S. K. Raja Rao, The H and Z variations along and near the equatorial electrojet in India, Africa and the Pacific, J. Atm. Terr. Phys., 27, 559-581, 1965.

Clague, D. A. and G. B. Dalrymple, Cretaceous K-Ar ages of volcanic rocks from the Musicians Seamounts and the Hawaiian Ridge, Geophys. Res. Lett., 2, 305-309, 1975.

Clague, D. A., G. B. Dalrymple, and R. Moberly, Petrography and K-Ar ages of dredged volcanic rocks from the western Hawaiian ridge and southern Emperor seamount chain, Geol. Soc. Amer. Bull., 84, 991-998, 1975.

Cockerham, R. S. and R. D. Jarrard, Paleomagnetism of some Leg 33 sediments and basalts, Init. Rept. DSDP, 33, 631-647, 1976.

Cox, A. and R. G. Gordon, Paleolatitudes determined from paleomagnetic data from vertical cores, Rev. Geophys. Space Phys., 22, 47-72, 1984.

Dalrymple, G. B. and D. A. Clague, Age of the Hawaiian-Emperor bend, Earth Planet. Sci. Lett., 31, 313-329, 1976.

Dalrymple, G. B., M. A. Lanphere and D. A. Clague, Conventional and $^{40}Ar/^{39}Ar$ ages of volcanic rocks from Ojin (Site 430), Nintoku (Site 432), and Suiko (Site 433) seamounts and the chronology of volcanic propagation along the Hawaiian-Emperor chain, Init. Rept. DSDP, 55, 659-676, 1980.

Dymond, J. and H. L. Windom, Cretaceous K/Ar ages from Pacific Ocean seamounts, Earth Planet Sci. Lett., 4, 47-52, 1968.

Engebretson, D. C., A. Cox and R. G. Gordon, Relative motions between oceanic and continental plates in the Pacific basin, Spec. Paper 206, 59 pp., Geol. Soc. Amer., Boulder, Colorado, 1985.

Engeln, J. F. and S. Stein, Tectonics of the Easter plate, Earth Planet. Sci. Lett., 68, 259-270, 1984.

Epp, D., Age and tectonic relationships among volcanic chains on the Pacific plate, Ph.D. Thesis, 199 pp., University of Hawaii, Honolulu, 1978.

Francheteau, J., C.G.A. Harrison, J. G. Sclater, and M. L. Richards, Magnetization of Pacific seamounts: a preliminary polar curve for the northeastern Pacific, J. Geophys. Res., 75, 2035-2061, 1970.

Freedman, A. P. and B. Parsons, Seasat-derived gravity over the Musicians Seamounts, J. Geophys. Res., 91, 8325-8340, 1986.

Gordon, R. G., Late Cretaceous apparent polar wander of the Pacific plate: evidence for a rapid shift of the Pacific hotspots with respect to spin axis, Geophys. Res. Lett., 10, 709-712, 1983.

Gordon, R. G. and A. Cox, Paleomagnetic test of the early Tertiary plate circuit between the Pacific basin plates and the Indian plate, J. Geophys. Res., 85, 6534-6546, 1980a.

Gordon, R. G. and A. Cox, Calculating palaeomagnetic poles for oceanic plates, Geophys. J. R. Astr. Soc., 63, 619-640, 1980b.

Haggerty, J. A., S. O. Schlanger, and I. Premoli-Silva, Late Cretaceous and Eocene volcanism in the southern Line Islands, and its implications for hotspot theory, Geology, 10, 433-437, 1982.

Handschumacher, D. W. and J. E. Andrews, Kana Keoki Fracture Zone: interaction with the Hawaiian ridge, Geology, 3, 25-28, 1975.

Harland, W. B., A. V. Cox, P. G. Llewellyn, C. A. G. Pickton, A. G. Smith, and R. Walters, A Geologic Time Scale, pp. 63-84, Cambridge Univ. Press, 1982.

Harrison, C. G. A., A seamount with a nonmagnetic top, Geophys., 36, 349-357, 1971.

Harrison, C. G. A., R. D. Jarrard, V. Vacquier, and R. L. Larson, Palaeomagnetism of Cretaceous Pacific seamounts, Geophys. J. R. Astr. Soc., 42, 859-882, 1975.

Henderson, L. J. and R. G. Gordon, Oceanic plateaus and the motion of the Pacific plate with respect to the hotspots (abstract), EOS, Trans. AGU, 62, 1028, 1981.

Hey, R. N., D. F. Naar, M. C. Kleinrock, W. J. Phipps Morgan, E. Morales, and J.-G. Schilling, Microplate tectonics along a superfast seafloor spreading system near Easter Island, Nature, 317, 320-325, 1985.

Hilde, T. W. C., N. Isezaki, and J. M. Wageman, Mesozoic seafloor spreading in the north Pacific, in The Geophysics of the Pacific Ocean Basin and its Margin, Geophys. Mon. Ser. 19, edited by G. H. Sutton, M. H. Manghnani, and R. Moberly, pp. 205-226, Amer. Geophys. Union, Washington, D. C., 1976.

Hildebrand, J. A. and H. Staudigel, Seamount magnetic polarity and Cretaceous volcanism of the Pacific basin, Geology, 14, 456-458, 1986.

Jarrard, R. D., Paleomagnetism of Leg 17 sediment cores, Init. Rept. DSDP, 17, 365-375, 1973.

Kono, M., Paleomagntism of DSDP Leg 55 basalts and implications for the tectonics of the Pacific plate, Init. Rept. DSDP, 55, 737-752, 1980.

Larson, R. L., Late Jurassic and Early Cretaceous evolution of the western central Pacific Ocean, J. Geomag. Geoelectr., 28, 219-236, 1976.

Lowrie, A., C. Smoot, and R. Batiza, Are oceanic fracture zones locked and strong or weak?: new evidence for volcanic activity and weakness, Geology, 14, 242-245, 1986.

Lumb, J. T., M. P. Hochstein, and D. J. Woodward, Interpretation of magnetic measurements in the Cook Islands, southwest Pacific Ocean, in The Western Pacific Island Arcs, Marginal Seas, Geochemistry, edited by P. J. Coleman, pp. 79-101, Crane, Russak and Co., New York, 1973.

Malahoff, A. and D. W. Handschumacher, Magnetic anomalies south of the Murray fracture zone: new evidence for a secondary seafloor spreading center and strike-slip movement, J. Geophys. Res., 76, 6265-6275, 1971.

Malahoff, A., W. E. Strange, and G. P. Woollard, Molokai fracture zone: continuation west of the Hawaiian ridge, Science, 153, 521-522, 1966.

Mammerickx, J., D. F. Naar, L. L. Guthrie, and D. Naar, Paleo-plates in the Pacific Basin (abstract), EOS, Trans. Amer. Geophys. Union, 67, 1199, 1986.

Mammerickx, J. and G. F. Sharman, Evolution of the north Pacific during the Cretaceous Quiet Period, J. Geophys. Res., in press, 1987.

Mammerickx, J. and S. M. Smith, Bathymetry of the northeast Pacific, Map Series MC-42, Geol. Soc. Amer., Boulder, Colorado, 1981.

Mammerickx, J. and S. M. Smith, Bathymetry of the north central Pacific, Map Series MC-52, Geol. Soc. Amer., Boulder, Colorado, 1985.

Matsushita, S., Solar quiet and lunar daily variation fields, in Physics of Geomagnetic Phenomena, v. 1, edited by S. Matsushita and W. H. Campbell, pp. 302-424, Academic Press, New York, 1967.

Matthews, D. J., Tables of the velocity of sound in pure water and sea water for use on echo-sounding and sound ranging, 2nd ed., 52 pp., H. D. 282, Admiralty Hydrogr. Dept., London, 1939.

McFadden, P. L., Determination of the angle in a Fisher distribution which will be exceeded with a given probability, Geophys. J. R. Astr. Soc., 60, 391-396, 1980.

McNutt, M., Nonuniform magnetization of seamounts: a least squares approach, J. Geophys. Res., 91, 3686-3700, 1986.

Merrill, R. T., Correlating magnetic field polarity changes with geologic phenomena, Geology, 13, 487-490, 1985.

Morgan, W. J., Rodriquez, Darwin, Amsterdam, ..., a second type of hotspot island, J. Geophys. Res., 82, 5355-5360, 1978.

Naugler, F. P., Bathymetry of a region (PORL-421-2) north of the Hawaiian Ridge, ESSA Tech. Rept. ERL 82-POL 1, 13 pp., U.S. Government Printing Office, Washington, D. C., 1968.

Ness, G., S. Levi, and R. Couch, Marine magnetic anomaly time scales for the Cenozoic and Late Cretaceous: a precis, critique, and synthesis, Rev. Geophys. Space Phys., 18, 753-770, 1980.

Ozima, M., M. Honda, and K. Saito, ^{40}Ar-^{39}Ar ages of guyots in the western Pacific and discussion of their evolution, Geophys. J. R. Astr. Soc., 51, 475-485, 1977.

Ozima, M., I. Kaneoka, and S. Aramaki, K-Ar ages of submarine basalts dredged from seamounts in the western Pacific area and discussion of oceanic crust, Earth Planet. Sci. Lett., 8, 237-249, 1970.

Plouff, D., Gravity and magnetic fields of polygonal prisms and application to magnetic terrain corrections, Geophys., 41, 727-741, 1976.

Pringle, M. S., A primer on K-Ar whole rock

dating of oceanic lavas: I. conventional and $^{40}Ar/^{39}Ar$ total fusion analysis, examples from the Musicians Seamounts (abstract), EOS, Trans. AGU, 65, 1082, 1984.

Rea, D. K., Bathymetry and magnetics of a region (POL-21-3) 29° to 35°N, 155° to 165°W, ESSA Tech. Rept. ERL 146-POL 4, 23 pp., U.S. Government Printing Office, Washington, D. C., 1969.

Rea, D. K., Changes in structure and trend of fracture zones north of the Hawaiian ridge and relation to seafloor spreading, J. Geophys. Res., 75, 1421-1430, 1970.

Rea, D. K. and J. M. Dixon, Late Cretaceous and Paleogene tectonic evolution of the north Pacific Ocean, Earth. Planet. Sci. Lett., 65, 145-166, 1983.

Rea, D. K. and F. P. Naugler, Musicians seamounts province and related crustal structures north of the Hawaiian ridge, Mar. Geol., 10, 89-111, 1971.

Rice, P. D., J. M. Hall, and N. D. Opdyke, Deep drill 1972: a paleomagnetic study of the Bermuda Seamount, Can. J. Earth Sci., 17, 232-243, 1980.

Richards, M. L., V. Vacquier, and G. D. Van Voorhis, Calculation of the magnetization of uplifts from combining topographic and magnetic surveys, Geophys., 32, 678-707, 1967.

Sager, W. W., Seamount Paleomagnetism and Pacific Plate Tectonics, Ph.D. Thesis, 472 pp., University of Hawaii, Honolulu, 1983.

Sager, W. W., Paleomagnetism of Abbott Seamount and implications for the latitudinal drift of the Hawaiian hot spot, J. Geophys. Res., 89, 6271-6284, 1984.

Sager, W. W., Late Eocene and Maestrichtian paleomagnetic poles for the Pacific plate: implications for the validity of seamount paleomagnetic data, Tectonophys., in press, 1987.

Sager, W. W., G. T. Davis, B. H. Keating, and J. A. Philpotts, A geophysical and geologic study of Nagata Seamount, northern Line Islands, J. Geomag. Geoelectr., 34, 283-305, 1982.

Sager, W. W. and B. H. Keating, Paleomagnetism of Line Islands seamounts: evidence for Late Cretaceous and early Tertiary volcanism, J. Geophys. Res., 89, 11135-11151, 1984.

Saito, K. and M. Ozima, ^{40}Ar-^{39}Ar geochronological studies on submarine rocks from the western Pacific area, Earth Planet. Sci. Lett., 33, 353-369, 1977.

Sandwell, D. T., Along-track deflection of the vertical from Seasat: GEBCO overlays, Map. No. 7, NOAA Tech. Memorandum NOS NGS-40, U.S. Dept. of Commerce, Rockville, Maryland, 1985.

Schimke, G. R. and C. G. Bufe, Geophysical description of a Pacific Ocean seamount, J. Geophys. Res., 73, 559-569, 1968.

Schlanger, S. O., M. O. Garcia, B. H. Keating, J. J. Naughton, W. W. Sager, J. A. Haggerty, J. A. Philpotts, and R. A. Duncan, Geology and geochronology of the Line Islands, J. Geophys. Res., 89, 11201-11272, 1984.

Schlanger, S. O., H. C. Jenkyns, and I. Premoli-Silva, Volcanism and vertical tectonics of the Pacific Basin related to global Cretaceous transgressions, Earth Planet. Sci. Lett., 52, 435-449, 1981.

Schouten, H. and S. C. Cande, Palaeomagnetic poles from marine magnetic anomalies, Geophys. J. R. Astr. Soc., 44, 567-575, 1976.

Schwank, D. C. and A. R. Lazarewicz, Estimation of seamount compensation using satellite altimetry, Geophys. Res. Lett., 9, 907-910, 1982.

Steiger, R. H. and E. Jäeger, Subcommission on geochronology: convention on the use of decay constants in geochronology and cosmochronology, Earth Plaet. Sci. Lett., 36, 359-362, 1977.

Talwani, M., Computation with the help of a digital computer of magnetic anomalies caused by bodies of arbitrary shape, Geophys., 30, 797-817, 1965.

Talwani, M. and J. R. Heirtzler, Computation of magnetic anomalies caused by two dimensional structures of arbitrary shape, in Computers in the Mineral Industries, edited by G. A. Parks, Stanford University, Stanford, California, 1964.

Tamaki, K., M. Joshima and R. L. Larson, Remanent Early Cretaceous spreading center in the central Pacific basin, J. Geophys. Res., 84, 4501-4510, 1979.

Tamaki, K. and R. L. Larson, Mesozoic tectonic history of the Magellan microplate in the western central Pacific, J. Geophys. Res., in press, 1987.

U.S. Naval Oceanographic Office, A marine magnetic survey south of the Hawaiian Islands, Technical Rept. 137, 56 pp., U.S. Naval Oceanographic Office, NSTL Station, Mississippi, 1962.

Uyeda, S. and M. L. Richards, Magnetization of four Pacific seamounts near the Japanese Islands, Earthquake Res. Inst. Bull., Univ. Tokyo, 44, 179-213, 1966.

Vacquier, V., A machine method for computing the magnitude and direction of a uniformly magnetized body from its shape and a magnetic survey, in Proceedings Benedum Earth Magnetism Symposium, 123-137, 1962.

Vacquier, V. and S. Uyeda, Paleomagnetism of nine seamounts in the Western Pacific and of three volcanoes in Japan, Earthquake Res. Inst. Bull., Univ. Tokyo, 45, 815-848, 1967.

Verhoef, J., B. J. Collette, and C. A. Williams, Comment on "Hawaiian hotspot volcanism mainly during geomagnetic normal intervals", Geology, 13, 314-315, 1985.

Walker, D. A. and I. McDougall, $^{40}Ar/^{39}Ar$ and K-Ar dating of altered glassy volcanic rocks: the Dabi volcanics, P.N.G., Geochem. Cosma. Acta., 46, 2181-2190, 1982.

Wallin, B. H., The northern Hawaiian deep and arch: interpretation of geologic history from reflection profiling and echo character mapping, M.S. Thesis, 133 pp., University of Hawaii, Honolulu, 1982.

Watts, A. B., J. H. Bodine, and N. R. Ribe, Observations of flexure and the geologic evolution of the Pacific Ocean basin, Nature, 238, 532-537, 1980.

Wilde, P., T. E. Chase, W. R. Normark, J. A. Thomas, and J. D. Young, Oceanographic data off southern Hawaiian Islands, LBL Pub. 359, Lawrence Berkeley Laboratory, University of California, Berkeley, 1980.

Williams, C. A., J. Verhoef, and B. J. Collette, Magnetic analysis of some large seamounts in the north Atlantic, Earth Planet. Sci. Lett., 63, 399-407, 1983.

W. W. Sager, Department of Oceanography, Texas A&M University, College Station, TX 77843-3146

M. S. Pringle, U.S. Geological Survey, 345 Middlefield Road, Menlo Park, CA 94025

Sedimentological Studies

POST-EOCENE SUBSIDENCE OF THE MARSHALL ISLANDS RECORDED BY DROWNED ATOLLS ON HARRIE AND SYLVANIA GUYOTS

S. O. Schlanger

Department of Geological Sciences, Northwestern University, Evanston, Illinois

J. F. Campbell[1] and M. W. Jackson[2]

Hawaii Institute of Geophysics, University of Hawaii, Honolulu

Abstract. Geophysical and geological surveys of Harrie and Sylvania Guyots in the northern Marshall Islands show that both of these volcanic edifices are capped by drowned atolls of Early Eocene age. The volcanic eruptions that formed both of these guyots were apparently coeval with the eruptions that formed the volcanic edifice below Enewetak Atoll. These Eocene eruptions took place in an off-ridge setting in a region that had experienced a complex history of Cretaceous mid-plate volcanism. Present depths to the tops of these drowned Eocene atolls are 1520 m at Harrie and 1480 m at Sylvania which, taken together with the coeval subsidence of Enewetak atoll of ~1300-1400 m and the post-Late Cretaceous subsidence of the Nauru Basin of ~1600 m, show that this region has subsided rapidly, as a unit, atop a thermally rejuvenated lithosphere of Middle Jurassic age. The Eocene atolls on Harrie and Sylvania Guyots drowned during a rapid sea level rise ~49 Ma that followed a period of relatively high sea levels in Early Eocene time.

Introduction

In two of his last papers, "Origin of Guyots: the Beagle to Seabeam" [1984a] and "Darwin Reprise" [1984b], Bill Menard continued to explore the potential drowned ancient volcanic islands (DAVI in his terminology) have to inform us of the history of volcanism and vertical motion of the sea floor that underlies the vast Pacific Basin. In these two papers Menard reviewed the history of the study of the subsidence of the Pacific basin from Darwin's identification of DAVI in 1842 through Harry Hess's WWII surveys of guyots, the discovery of drowned Cretaceous reefs in the Mid-Pacific Mountains on the mid-Pacific Expedition of 1950 [Hamilton, 1956], the mapping of the Mesozoic magnetic anomalies that dated the Pacific Plate [Larson et al., 1972], the development of plate tectonic theory [Morgan, 1972] which provided a basis for determining the horizontal motions of the lithosphere and the evolution of ideas on regional subsidence due to thermal aging of the plate [Parsons and Sclater, 1977; Detrick and Crough, 1978].

Menard accepted, as most geologists do today, that plate tectonic theory provided "... an adequate basis for tracking horizontal motion of the lithosphere" and that "first order vertical motion is also adequately described by thermal subsidence with aging" [1984a, pg. 11,117]. However, he also emphasized that "... substantial variations from predicted depths occur in midplate swells, and few means exist to track these vertical motions of the lithosphere associated with these swells." He argued that the study of DAVI would continue to be useful in attacking the problem of the history of ancient swells, such as his "Darwin Rise," because "given the age of the DAVI and any cap of coral or sediment, its subsidence history can be established. This would be very useful information regarding midplate swells, provided DAVI can be identified" [1984a, pg. 11,117].

It is the purpose of this paper to present and interpret data on two DAVI in the Marshall Islands, Sylvania Guyot and Harrie Guyot. Marine geological and geophysical data gathered from these in 1981 identify them as DAVI capped by drowned atolls of Eocene age. These data confirm the argument of Detrick and Crough [1978, pg. 1243] that the Marshall Islands region has, since Eocene time, subsided "...much more than would be expected from the normal thermal subsidence of the surrounding sea floor." They ascribed this excess subsidence to the fact that the Marshall Islands formed on anomalously shallow sea floor that had undergone uplift due to thermal rejuvenation of the underlying old lithosphere. Menard and McNutt [1982, pg. 8579], after an extensive study of of the subsidence histories of isolated guyots, seamounts, banks, and islands also came to the conclusion that the mechanism of thermal rejuvenation "... provides a plausible explanation for a wide range of geological and geophysical observations such as the rapid subsidence of atolls and guyots...." As Menard [1984a] pointed out, only 13 of the 431 guyots he counted in the world ocean are identified as being capped by drowned atolls or barrier reefs that were once unequivocally at sea level. Therefore, we consider it useful, in the context of this volume dedicated to the memory of Bill Menard, to document and interpret these two reef-capped drowned atolls which confirm the magnitude and regional extent of subsidence in the heart of "Darwin Rise" country.

Regional Setting and History of Volcanism in the Marshall Islands

The atolls of the northern Marshall Islands lie atop northwest-southeast trending ridges disposed roughly perpendicular to magnetic anomalies M21 through M29 (Figure 1). These anomalies

---

[1] Now at Seafloor Surveys International, Inc., 1221 Kapiolani Blvd., PH-40, Honolulu, HI 96814
[2] Now at EXXON Company, U.S.A., Houston, TX 77210

Copyright 1987 by the American Geophysical Union.

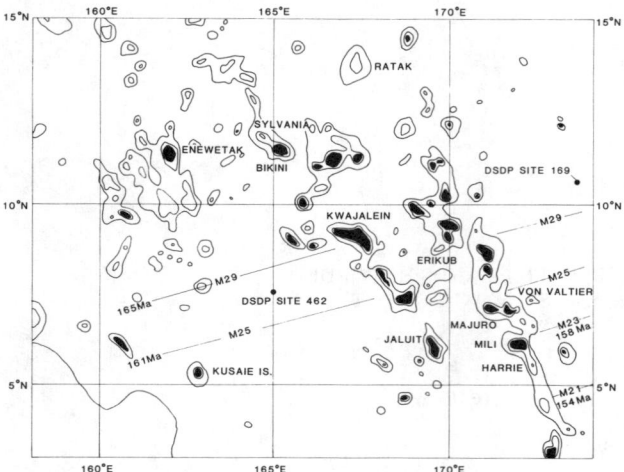

Fig. 1. Map of the northern Marshall Islands and adjacent areas showing the locations of the atolls, guyots, and seamounts discussed in the text. Locations of the magnetic anomalies shown were compiled from Larson [1976] and Cande et al. [1978].

define the age of the lithospheric plate to be, according to the Harland et al. [1982] time scale which is used in this paper, 158 Ma in the vicinity of Harrie Guyot, 165 Ma at Kwajalein Atoll, and >165 Ma at the present position of Enewetak and Bikini Atolls which lie in the Jurassic Quiet Zone [Larson and Hilde, 1975; Hilde et al., 1976; Larson, 1976]. This portion of the Pacific plate has been moving northward at least from Aptian time to the present (see review in Ogg, [1985]). Following the formation of this segment of the plate at a ridge crest the plate was subjected to a number of off-ridge volcanic events over the period from ~130 Ma to ~55 Ma. Beyond the summary of these events given below details of this complex volcanic history can be found in Winterer [1973, 1976], Watts et al. [1980], Schlanger and Premoli Silva [1981], Larson and Schlanger [1981], Schlanger et al. [1981], Rea and Vallier [1983], and Schlanger and Moberly [1985].

Results of drilling in the Nauru Basin at DSDP Site 462 on DSDP-IPOD Legs 61 and 89 [Larson and Schlanger, 1981; Schlanger and Moberly, 1985] showed that following the formation of the Pacific plate in the region from ~150 Ma to ~165 Ma a thick section of submarine flows were extruded in Early Cretaceous time, probably in the Valanginian at ~130 Ma. A period of sill intrusion then took place in the Aptian or Albian, or both, ~100 to ~110 Ma. These episodes were followed by further intrusions of sills in Campanian time. The presence of abundant terrestrial plant fragments in volcanoclastic sediments of Aptian age [Jenkyns and Schlanger, 1981] testify to the presence in the area around the Nauru Basin of forested, high volcanic islands. Therefore Aptian edifice building took place in addition to sill intrusions. That the entire northern Marshall Islands province experienced Cretaceous volcanism can be inferred from K/Ar ages of 82 Ma obtained from the volcanic edifice of Erikub Seamount and 79 Ma from Ratak Seamount [Hein et al., in press]. Dredging on von Valtier Seamount recovered pelagic foraminifera-bearing limestone with abundant included volcanic material. Planktonic foraminifera in the limestone showed them to be Coniacian-Santonian, 83-87.5 Ma, in age. This edifice is taken to be of Late Cretaceous age. Also, a basalt sill drilled within the pelagic sediment section at DSDP Site 169 just east of the Marshall Islands is considered to be of Late Cretaceous, post-Cenomanian, age [Winterer, Ewing et al., 1973].

In a wider regional context these volcanic episodes fit into the picture of widespread Cretaceous volcanism in the Pacific Basin [Winterer, 1976]. Drilling in the East Mariana Basin [Schlanger and Moberly, 1985] showed that during Aptian time major edifices were built. The compilation of volcanic chronologies by Schlanger and Premoli Silva [1981] showed major pulses of volcanic activity in the time envelopes covering the periods from ~115 Ma to ~90 Ma and from ~83 Ma to ~65 Ma. Rea and Vallier [1983] compiled data on the volcanogenic component of sediments from the Pacific Basin and came to the conclusion that the periods from 110 Ma to 95 Ma and from 80 Ma to 65 Ma were times of intense and widespread volcanic activity. Studies in the Line Islands [Haggerty et al., 1982; Schlanger et al., 1984] also revealed widespread Cretaceous volcanism along that chain.

Evidence for Eocene volcanism in the Marshall Islands is less abundant. K/Ar dates of 50 Ma and 59 Ma were determined from basalts cored from the volcanic edifice below Enewetak Atoll [Kulp, 1963]. The oldest limestones drilled just above this volcanic edifice at Enewetak are of Eocene age. This fossil date does not contradict the K/Ar ages. As discussed below the Early Eocene age determined for the drowned reef cap on Harrie Guyot could be taken as indicating that the underlying edifice is the same age as the edifice below Enewetak.

Previous Studies on the Timing and Magnitude of Subsidence in the Region

These off-ridge volcanic episodes affected the aging Pacific plate when it was between ~35 Ma and ~110 Ma considering the ~130 Ma event in the Nauru Basin to have taken place on lithosphere

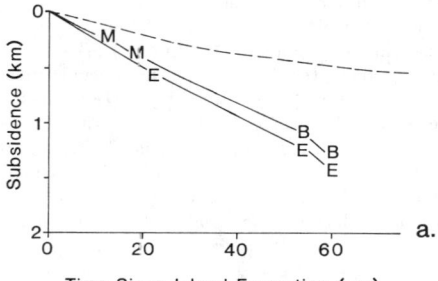

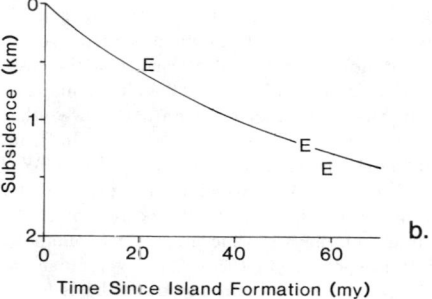

Fig. 2. Upper figure a shows the subsidence history of Enewetak (E), Bikini (B), and Midway (M) Atolls derived from drilling and biostratigraphic dating. The dashed line is the predicted subsidence curve assuming that these islands formed on 90 m y old crust and have subsided according to an empirical age-depth relation for the normal sea floor. Lower figure b shows the predicted subsidence history of Enewetak assuming that the lithosphere was thinned to the equivalent of normal 25 m y old lithosphere. Solid line is the predicted subsidence path of the atoll; E's are dated horizons derived from drilling on Enewetak (figure and caption after Detrick and Crough [1978]).

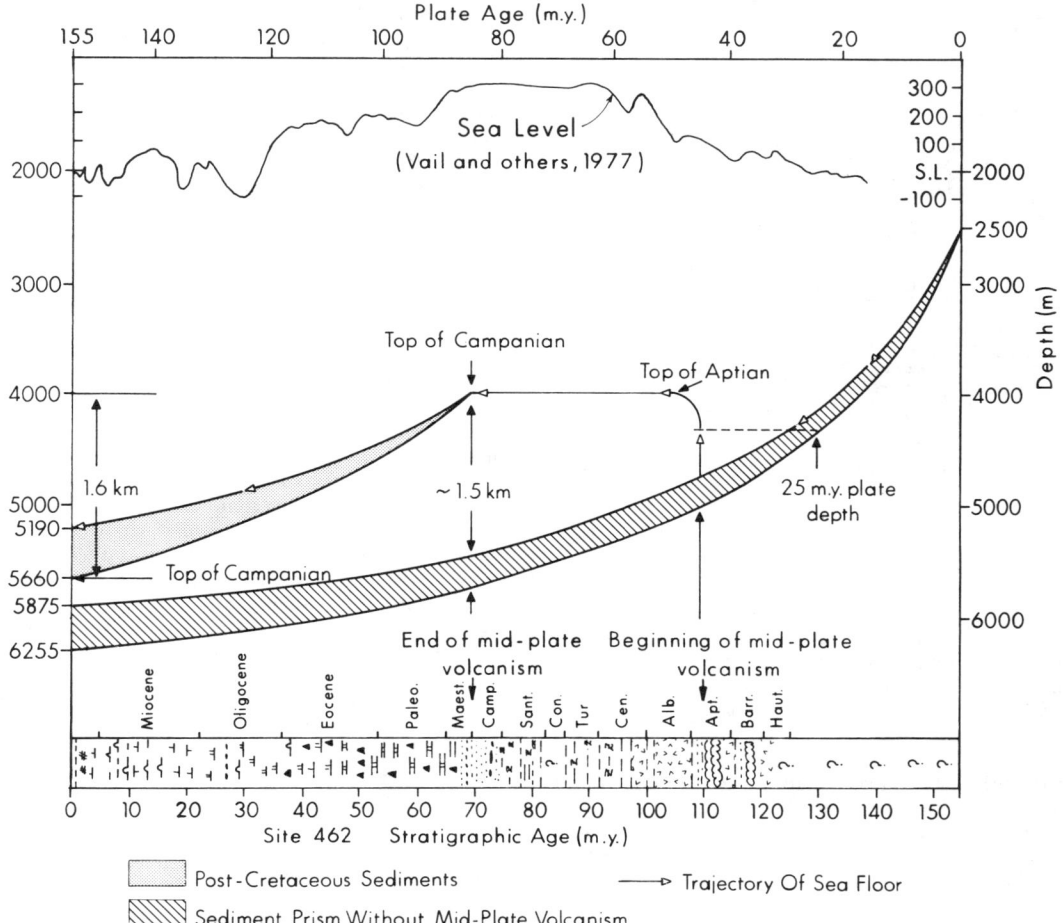

Fig. 3. Uplift and subsidence history of the Nauru Basin based on drilling results from DSDP-IPOD Leg 61 (after Schlanger, [1981]). The subsidence path of the Nauru Basin, had there not been Cretaceous mid-plate volcanism, is shown as the diagonally striped sediment prism according to data from Parsons and Sclater [1977, table 4]. Due to mid-plate volcanism the area was uplifted. The trajectory shown by the open-headed arrows is the interpreted sea floor path. It is proposed in this analysis that the region stayed anomalously shallow until the cessation of mid-plate volcanism in Late Cretaceous time. The uppermost Campanian sediments then being deposited now lie at a depth of 5660 m below sea level; the top of the basin fill of Cenozoic sediments shown as the shaded prism is at the present depth of the Nauru Basin, 5190 m. The post-Late Cretaceous subsidence of the Nauru Basin of ~1.6 km is slightly greater than the post-Eocene subsidence of Sylvania and Harrie Guyots. The discovery, on Leg 89, of a ~130 Ma volcanic event in the Nauru Basin would not affect the interpretation of the magnitude of post-Cretaceous subsidence derived from this analysis.

that is now ~165 Ma and the Eocene volcanism at Enewetak to have taken place ~55 Ma. Some or all of these episodes resulted in thermal rejuvenation of the maturing lithosphere and interrupted its "normal" subsidence. In light of the multiplicity of events and our still imprecise knowledge on the regional extent of each episode it is probably not possible now to sort out individual perturbations in the vertical component of the plate trajectory. If each episode resulted in lithospheric thinning and uplift the trajectory would have a saw-tooth aspect.

Detrick and Crough [1978], in their study of Pacific island subsidence histories in terms of lithospheric thinning and uplift due to the passage of the plate over hotspots, compared the actual subsidence path of Enewetak and Bikini Atolls derived from drilling on these atolls [see Emery et al., 1954; Schlanger, 1963] to a predicted subsidence path assuming that the volcanic edifices formed on crust that was 90 m y old and that the crust subsequently subsided along a Parsons and Sclater [1977] path (Figure 2a). They came to the conclusion (Figure 2b) that these atolls have subsided as if they had formed on 25 my old crust, the inference being that the 90 my old crust had been thermally rejuvenated. We now know that Enewetak and Bikini formed on ~110 Ma crust and that therefore the segment of the Parsons and Sclater curves shown in Figure 2a should be slightly flatter than the segment used. This change would only increase the difference between the predicted and actual paths. Drilling in the Nauru Basin revealed not only an unexpected volcanic history of the region but also the fact that the sedimentary section of post-Campanian age lies at depths that are shallower than would have been predicted from the Parsons and Sclater curve (Figure 3). In order to account for the anomalously shallow position of these sediments Schlanger [1981] proposed that the last resetting of the

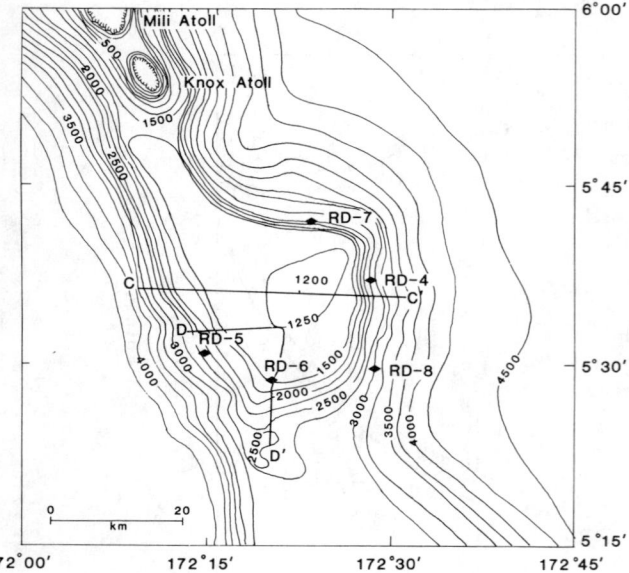

Fig. 4. Bathymetric chart of Harrie Guyot based on seismic reflection profiles run by R/V Kana Keoki, Hawaii Institute of Geophysics Cruise KK 810626, Leg 2. Uncorrected depths shown on contours are in meters. Dredge haul locations are shown as are the track lines of the seismic profiles shown as Fig. 5a and b.

thermal age of the lithosphere in the Nauru Basin took place during the Late Cretaceous volcanic episode that spanned Campanian-Maestrichtian time, 73 Ma to 65 Ma. See also Larson and Schlanger, [1981] and Schlanger and Premoli Silva, [1981] for other treatments of the subsidence history of the Nauru Basin.

Geology and Geophysics of Harrie Guyot

Harrie Guyot lies submerged on the easternmost ridge of the northern Marshall Islands (Figure 1). Immediately to the northwest along this ridge are Knox and Mili Atolls. The volcanic edifice of Harrie Guyot is attached to these adjacent edifices by a narrow ridge only a few miles wide at a depth of ∼1500 m. Harrie Guyot (Figure 4) rises from surrounding depths of ∼4500 m to the summit of the pelagic cap now at a corrected depth of ∼1330 m (corrected depths given in this paper were determined by using water column velocities given in Emery et al., 1954, figure 3). Seismic profiles, of which two representative ones are shown on Figure 5, show the pelagic cap is ∼120 m thick based on a Vp of 1.6 km/sec for globigerinid ooze and a two-way travel time through it of 0.15 sec. The top of the reef cap, where it is exposed on the rim of the guyot, is at a corrected depth of 1520 m. The volcanic edifice, which exhibits considerable relief, reaches a minimum depth of ∼1700 m based on a two-way travel time through the cap near the center of the edifice of .25 sec and an assumed Vp of 2.0 km/sec. The cap at this point has a thickness of ∼250 m. The relief on the top of the volcanic edifice of ∼200 m is the same order as that seen by drilling at Enewetak where the basement has a relief of ∼120 m [Schlanger, 1963] and by drilling at Midway where the Miocene volcanic edifice has a relief of ∼230 m [Ladd et al., 1970].

SeaMARC II mapping of Harrie Guyot (Figure 6) combined with interpretation of the seismic profiles, was used to produce the geologic map of the guyot shown as Figure 7. Of the 5 dredge hauls attempted on Harrie Guyot (Figure 4) 4 — RD-4, RD-6, RD-7, and RD-8 — were successful in recovering large pieces of limestone. The faunal, floral, and textural characteristics of these limestones as described below show that the limestone cap displays the facies common to Eocene reef complexes in the Pacific Basin [Schlanger, 1963, 1964]. These limestones have been dated as middle Early Eocene, P7/P8 planktonic foram biochronozones, by I. Premoli Silva based on the Eocene *Asterocyclina* fauna and associated planktonics such as several species of *Morozovella*. RD-4, taken at a depth of 1500 to 1700 m, in an attempt to sample the reef, recovered rocks typical of two distinct facies. The first is a shallow-bank facies characterised by the presence of abundant, packed, well-preserved, oriented tests of large benthonic foraminifera of the discocyclinid type including the genus *Asterocyclina* of Eocene age and abundant miliolids and rotalids. Also present are echinoid spines and plates and fragments of calcareous red algae and bryozoans. The second is a reef-wall facies characterised by massive encrustations several inches thick of encrusting red calcareous algae on gastropod shells and corals. *Asterocyclina* tests indicate that the reef-wall facies was coeval with the shallow-bank facies. Dredge haul RD-7 recovered limestone made up of fragments of coral, calcareous red algae, echinoid debris, molluscs, and bryozoans and discocyclinid foraminifera. In addition to these fossil elements these limestones contain common ooids and coated grains. Ooids are rare in atoll settings. A survey of oolitic limestone occurrences in the Pacific Basin [Schlanger, in press] shows that they are present in limestones of Cretaceous to Recent age. Their settings suggest that the oolite facies in atoll settings is an ephemeral one that forms during the rapid submergence of a reef platform during times of rapidly rising sea level. RD-8 recovered limestone with several features indicative of a complex history. Prominent within a coarsely crystalline calcite cement are fragments of pre-existing limestone such as miliolid-rich pelletal limestone of probable lagoonal origin and limestone identical to those from the shallow-bank facies described from RD-4. Abundant fragments of coral, *Asterocyclina*, red calcareous algae, encrusting foraminifera, and small benthic foraminifera float in the pervasive calcite mosaic cement. In addition to the shallow-water fossil elements the interstices between the larger fossil fragments contain abundant tests of planktonic foraminifera. The abundance of planktonic foraminifera is taken to indicate that indurated fragments of shallow-water limestone were eroded from a reef complex and redeposited in a deep-water fore-reef bathymetric setting. Further, large (up to 2.5 cm long) angular fragments of basalt are common within these limestones. These are olivine basalts with olivine phenocrysts in an intersertal to intergranular groundmass of plagioclase, pyroxene, olivine and black opaques. The presence of these basalt clasts and shallow-water limestone fragments in the planktonic rich matrix is taken to indicate that erosion of both the volcanic edifice and a reef complex took place. An attempt to date this erosional event is of course problematic. However, if we take the age of the limestone to be middle Early Eocene, we could argue that the marked ∼150 m sea level fall shown on the most recent EXXON sea level curve of Haq et al. [1986] that took place in the P9 planktonic foram zone of latest Early Eocene age resulted in erosion of both the volcanic island and its surrounding embryonic fringing reef.

These observations allow the piecing together of a history of Harrie Guyot as follows:
(1) the volcanic edifice formed and grew upwards into the photic zone allowing reef growth to start by middle Early Eocene time. That the edifice formed in an off-ridge setting is evidenced by the free-air gravity anomaly over Harrie Guyot of 178 milligals; the contours of the anomaly map roughly parallel the bathymetric contours. As shown by Watts et al. [1985] a free-air gravity anomaly of this magnitude indicates eruption of the volcano on old crust. Based

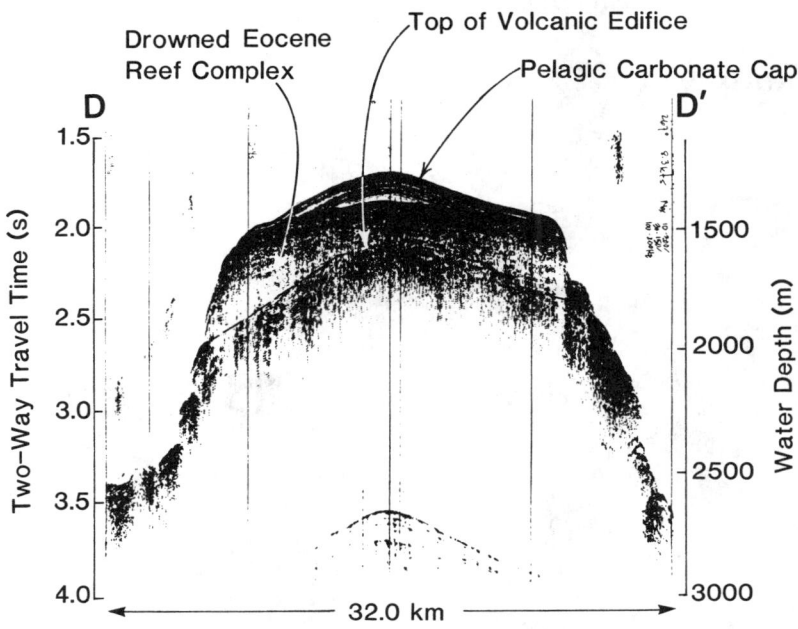

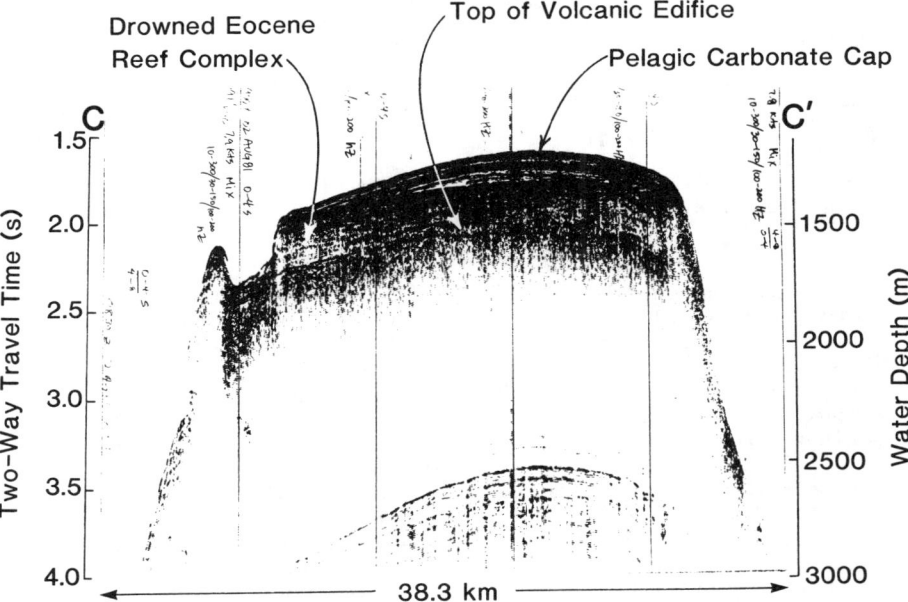

Fig. 5. Seismic profiles across Harrie Guyot. These are shipboard records obtained using an air gun source. Upper figure a is along track segment D-D' and the lower figure b is along track segment C-C'. The geological interpretation is based on the seismic stratigraphy and the dating and facies analysis of the dredged limestones as discussed in the text. The top of the drowned Eocene reef cap is at a corrected depth of 1520 m below sea level.

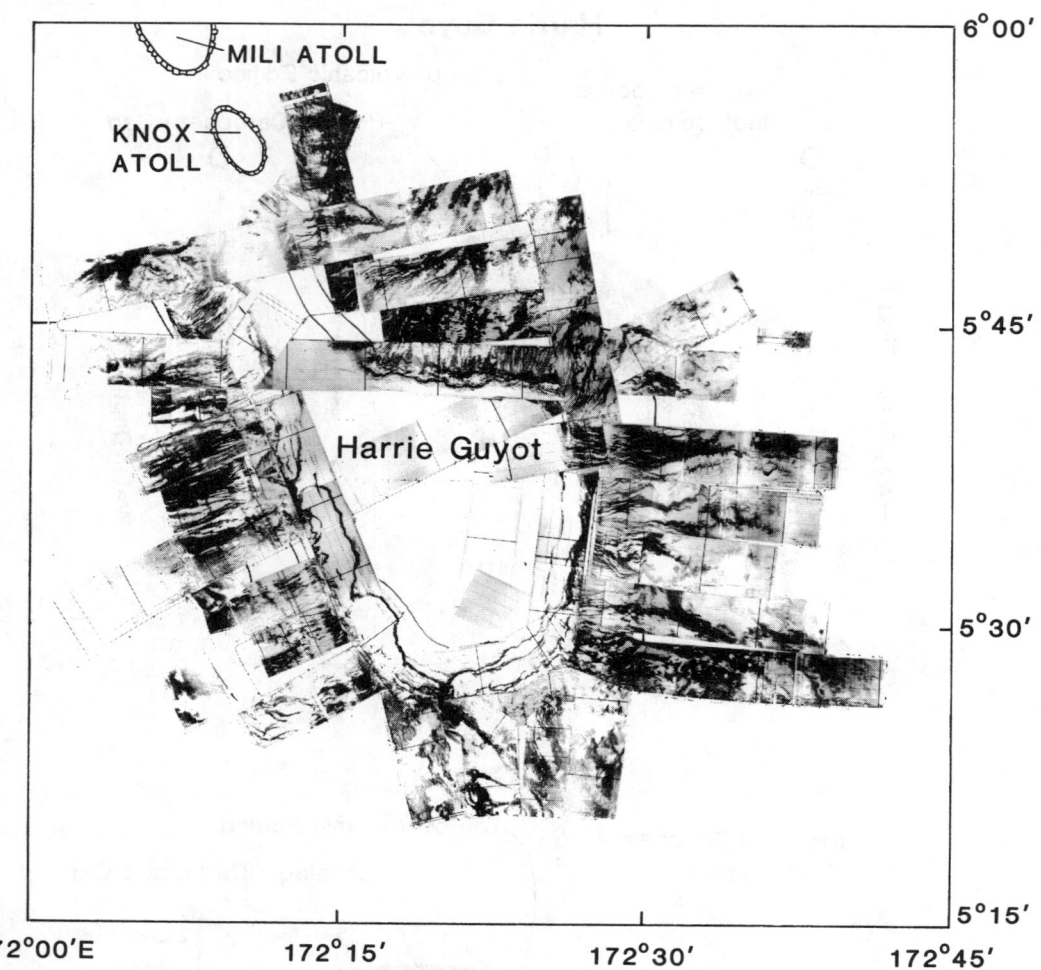

Fig. 6. Sea MARC II mosaic of Harrie Guyot from surveys run from R/V Kana Keoki, Hawaii Institute of Geophysics by J.F. Campbell. The distinct reflectivity patterns allow mapping of the various sediment and rock types at the sea floor.

on the lack of any Cretaceous or Paleocene faunal elements in the dredge hauls we propose that the edifice had formed by Early Eocene time.
(2) The volcanic foundation subsided on its thermally rejuvenated crust and the Early Eocene reef complex developed and thickened.
(3) Reef growth was interrupted during an emergent period as a result of a rapid fall in sea level in latest Early Eocene time and erosion took place.
(4) Continued subsidence coupled with a rapid rise in relative sea level in earliest Middle Eocene time [Haq et al., 1986] drowned the reef on Harrie Guyot.

Geology and Geophysics of Sylvania Guyot and Bikini Atoll

As background for any discussion of Sylvania Guyot it is necessary to also consider the information in hand on Bikini Atoll. Both of these structures were extensively studied during Operation Crossroads in 1946 and 1947 [see Emery et al., 1954]. Two deep holes were drilled on Bikini in an attempt to reach the volcanic basement and therefore obtain direct proof of Darwin's subsidence theory for the formation of atolls. Both of these holes failed to reach the volcanic edifice but the deeper of the two penetrated 780 m of shallow-water reefal sediments and reached strata of Early Miocene and Oligocene (?) age. The stratigraphic sections drilled at Bikini, as deep as they penetrated, are equivalent to the sections drilled at Enewetak [Schlanger, 1963]. The basement at Enewetak was reached in two holes on opposite sides of the atoll at depths of 1271 m and 1388 m. The correlation of the dated horizons between Enewetak and Bikini shows that these two atolls had similar subsidence histories. Seismic refraction studies on Bikini Atoll [Raitt, 1954] revealed the presence of a layer — the third layer of Raitt — with a velocity of ~ 4 km/sec at a depth of 1300. The upper surface of this layer has considerable relief and was considered by Raitt [1954] to be the top of the volcanic edifice. Aeromagnetic surveys of Bikini Atoll [Alldredge et al., 1954] were interpreted as indicating the volcanic basement at a depth of ~ 1500 to 1600 m below sea level.

The bathymetric mapping of Sylvania Guyot (Figure 8) showed the flat top of the Guyot as corresponding to a terrace on the northeast end of Bikini Atoll. The seismic surveys across Sylvania

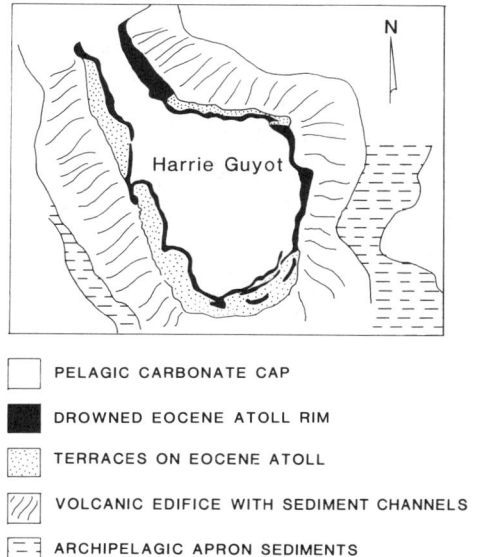

(Figure 9) confirmed the earlier results and show the summit of the pelagic cap to be at a corrected depth of 1400 m.

The geological interpretations of these seismic profiles are somewhat more speculative than those made for Harrie Guyot because, in contrast to the dredging results from Harrie where large blocks of richly fossiliferous limestone were recovered from the reef cap, dredging on Sylvania Guyot failed to recover such material. Dredge hauls made on Sylvania during the Mid-Pacific Expedition of 1950 [Emery et al., 1954; Hamilton and Rex, 1959] recovered basaltic rock and a tuff breccia, the cracks of which contained phosphatised planktonic foraminifera of Early Eocene age. According to Emery et al. [1954] the scoriaceous, highly vesicular nature of the volcanic rocks indicated eruption of the edifice in shallow water. The high proportion of pyroclastic material in the dredge hauls indicated submarine eruptions. A dredge haul on the south side of Sylvania Guyot taken in 1981 [Duennebier and Petersen, 1982] recovered rocks similar to those taken on the Mid-Pacific Expedition. J. Haggerty (pers. commun., 1986) found these rocks to include vesicular basalt and phosphatised pelagic sediment of Early to Middle Eocene age. A piece of hyaloclastite contained a limestone fragment with shallow-water peloids, fragments of a large benthonic foraminifera, calcareous red algae, and bryozoan remains. This piece of limestone is the only direct evidence that the volcanic edifice is capped by a shallow-water limestone facies.

Despite the lack of dredged unequivocal reef limestone from Sylvania, we argue that the seismic character of the several units shown on Figure 10 are typical of a completely developed atoll. The high, massive rim around the guyot encloses bedded lagoonal deposits that are distinctly different than the relatively transparent pelagic cap. Discontinuous, hummocky reflectors show the high relief characteristic of volcanic edifices below atolls. The continuous rim around Sylvania would be difficult to interpret as a relic volcanic land form unless we revert to Lyell's pre-Darwin theory of atoll formation.

Fig. 7. Geologic map of Harrie Guyot. This map was made by considering the bottom characteristic patterns shown on Fig. 6, the seismic profiles across Harrie Guyot and the rocks dredged from it. The broad central expanse of the pelagic cap, determined from piston cores to be a globigerinid ooze, lies within the exposed Eocene reef complex rim. Lower down are exposed the slopes of the volcanic edifice that present a furrowed aspect possibly due to sediment debris flows. These lower slopes merge downward into archipelagic apron deposits at depths of from 4 to 4.5 km below sea level.

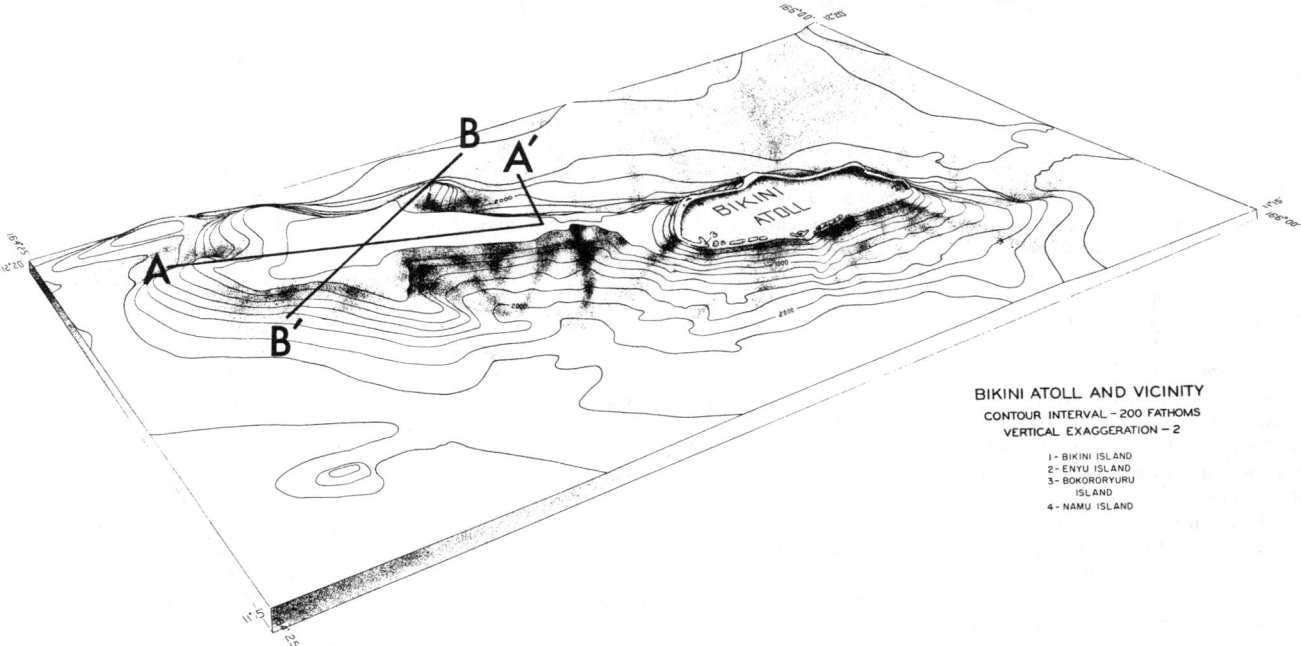

Fig. 8. Perspective diagram of Bikini Atoll and adjoining Sylvania Guyot (from Emery et al., [1954]). Lines A-A' and B-B' indicate the locations of the seismic profiles shown as Fig. 9a and b.

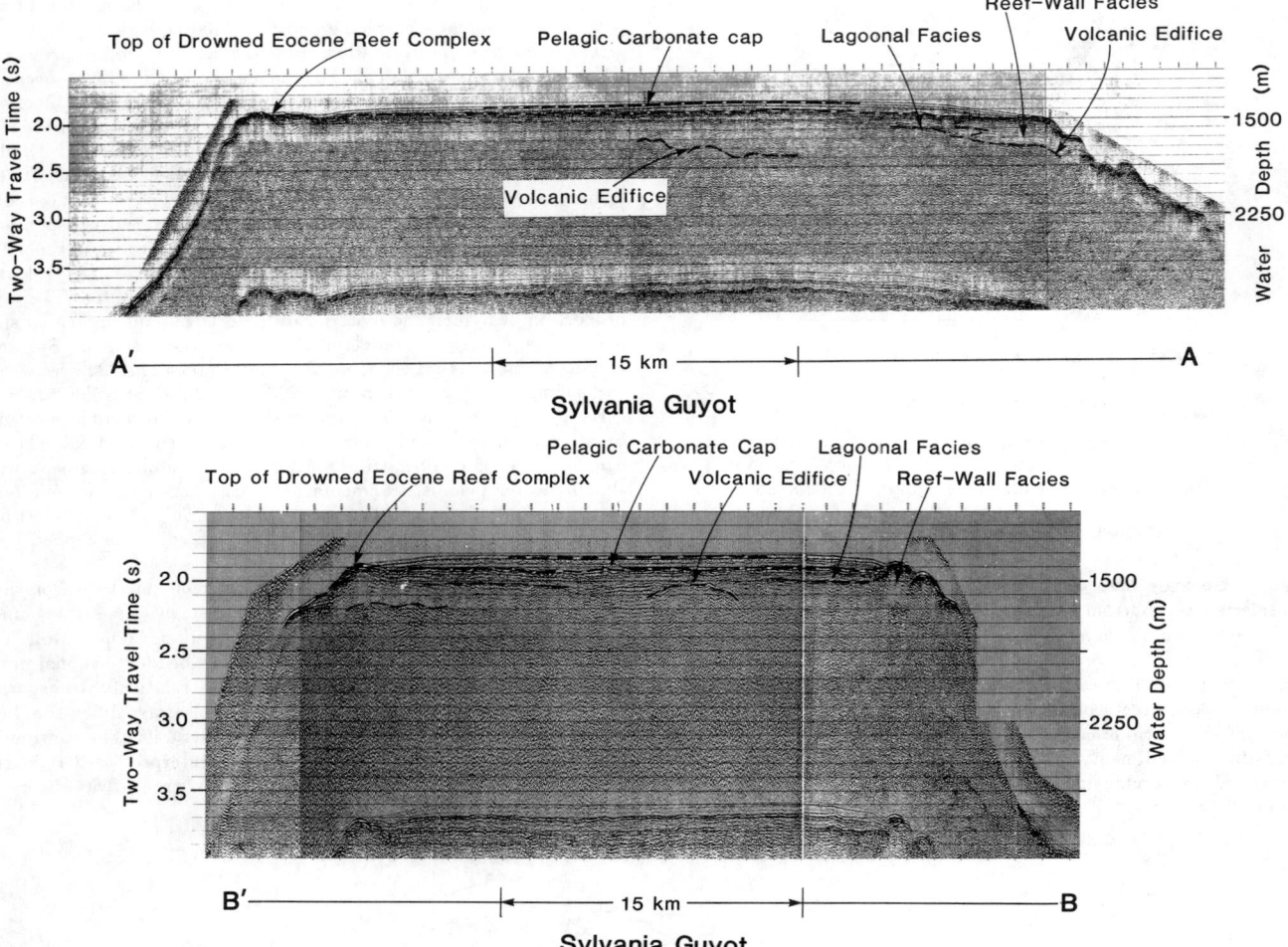

Fig. 9. Seismic profiles across Sylvania Guyot. Upper figure *a* is along track A-A' and lower figure *b* is along track B-B'. These profiles were run from R/V Kana Keoki, Hawaii Institute of Geophysics Cruise KK 810626, Leg 4 by F. Duennebier. The energy source was an 80 cu in water gun. The digitally recorded data was processed by T. Shipley at the Scripps Institution of Oceanography. The geological interpretations are by the authors. The top of the drowned Eocene reef cap is now at a corrected depth of 1480 m below sea level.

The pelagic cap has a two-way travel time of ~0.1 sec which constrains its thickness to be ~80 m assuming a Vp of 1.6 km/sec for these sediments. The lagoonal layer above the highest point on the volcanic edifice, near the center of profile B-B' is ~100 m thick assuming a Vp of 2 km/sec. The highest peak on the volcanic basement then would be at 1580 m below sea level. The top of the reef-wall facies that forms the raised rim of the guyot is at a corrected depth of 1480 m, a depth that is very close to the 1520 m depth of the reef cap on Harrie Guyot.

The geological history of Sylvania Guyot then appears to be quite similar to that proposed for Harrie Guyot.

(1) Submarine volcanic activity built an edifice into the photic zone by Early Eocene time. As in the case of Harrie Guyot, Sylvania has a free-air gravity anomaly of 180 milligals and therefore formed in an off-ridge setting on old crust [Duennebier and Petersen, 1982].
(2) The presumed Eocene reef cap developed and thickened as subsidence took place on thermally rejuvenated lithosphere.
(3) Reef growth was interrupted during an emergent period resulting from a rapid sea level fall in latest Early Eocene time.
(4) Continued subsidence coupled with a rapid rise in sea level in earliest Middle Eocene time drowned the reef on Sylvania Guyot.

Conclusions

Interpretations of seismic profiles and rocks dredged from Harrie and Sylvania Guyots are taken as indicating that both of these volcanic edifices are capped by drowned atolls of Early Eocene age. The lack of any pre-Eocene fossils in dredged rocks and the Early Eocene/ Late Paleocene K/Ar dates determined from basalt recovered in drill holes at Enewetak Atoll suggest that the volcanic eruptions that formed Harrie and Sylvania Guyots were coeval with the eruptions at Enewetak. These eruptions took place in a region that had undergone widespread, repeated episodes of volcanism in Cretaceous time.

Comparison of the eustatic sea level curve of Haq et al. [1986] with the Early Eocene age of these drowned reefs suggests that the reefs flourished atop subsiding edifices during a period of high sea level, approximately 200 m above present sea level, between ~54 and 50 Ma, were exposed during a sharp drop in sea level at ~50 Ma, and then drowned as they failed to keep up with a sharp rise in sea level ~49 m. y. years ago. The depths to the reef caps at Harrie and Sylvania Guyots of 1520 m and 1480 m show that these structures have subsided, relative to present sea level, by those amounts over the past 49 m.y. The volcanic basement at Enewetak has subsided somewhat less over this same period of time, ~1300-1400 m. The Nauru Basin has subsided ~1600 m since Late Cretaceous time. It is apparent that the entire northern Marshall Islands province has subsided as single tectonic unit. This regional subsidence took place at the northwest end of Bill Menard's Darwin Rise and involved Middle Jurassic lithosphere that subsided along a path such as that proposed by Detrick and Crough [1978] for thermally rejuvenated older lithosphere.

The question of why the Eocene reefs at Harrie and Sylvania Guyots failed to survive while the nearby reefs at Mili and Bikini Atolls survived to the present day remains unanswered.

Acknowledgments. Both the sea-going and shore-based aspects of this work were supported by the Office of Naval Research. We wish to thank the captain and crew of the R/V Kana Keoki for their efforts as well as those of the technicians of the Hawaii Institute of Geophysics who participated. F. Duennebier and L. Petersen of the Hawaii Institute of Geophysics and T. Shipley made available results of their work on the seismic surveys of Sylvania Guyot. The fossil identifications made by I. Premoli Silva of the University of Milan allowed the dating of the drowned reef cap on Harrie Guyot. J. Haggerty supplied the data on the dredged rocks from Sylvania Guyot and reviewed the manuscript. Hawaii Institute of Geophysics contribution 1821.

References

Alldredge, L. R., F. Keller, and W. J. Dichtel, Magnetic structure of Bikini atoll, *U. S. Geol. Surv. Prof. Paper, 260-M*, 529-536, 1954.

Cande, S. C., Larson, R. L., and J. L. La Brecque, Magnetic lineations in the Pacific Jurassic quiet zone, *Earth Planet. Sci. Lett., 41*, 434-440, 1978.

Detrick, R. S., and S. T. Crough, Island subsidence, hot spots, and lithospheric thinning, *J. Geophys. Res., 83*, 1236-1244, 1978.

Duennebier, F. K., and L. D. Petersen, *Summary report, IPOD Site Surveys in the western Pacific, R/V Kana Keoki cruise KK810626, Leg 4*, Hawaii Institute of Geophysics, 1982.

Emery, K. O., J. J. Tracey, Jr., and H. S. Ladd, Geology of Bikini and nearby atolls, *U. S. Geol. Surv. Prof. Paper, 260-A*, 1-262, 1954.

Haggerty, J.A., S.O. Schlanger, and I. Premoli-Silva, Late Cretaceous and Eocene volcanism in the southern Line Islands and implications for hot spot theory, *Geology, 10*, 433-437, 1982.

Hamilton, E. L., Sunken islands of the Mid-Pacific Mountains, *Geol. Soc. Amer. Mem., 64*, 97p, 1956.

Hamilton, E. L. and R. W. Rex, Lower Eocene phosphatized *Globigerina* ooze from Sylvania Guyot, *U.S. Geol. Surv. Prof. Paper 260-W*, 785-797, 1959.

Haq, B. V., J. Hardenbohl, and P. R. Vail, Chronology of fluctuating sea levels since the Triassic (250 million years ago to present), *Science*, in press, 1986.

Harland, W. B., A. V. Cox, P. G. Llewellyn, C. A. G. Pickton, A. G. Smith, and R. Walters, *A Geologic Time Scale*, Cambridge Univ. Press, Cambridge, MA, 131 p. 1982.

Hein, J. R., W. C. Schwab, and A. F. Davis, Cobalt and platinum-rich ferromanganese crusts and associated substrate rocks from the Marshall Islands, *Mar. Geol.*, in press.

Hilde, T. W. C., N. Isezaki, and J. M. Wageman, Mesozoic seafloor spreading in the North Pacific, in *The Geophysics of the Pacific Ocean Basin and its Margin,*, edited by G. Sutton, et al., pp. 205-226, AGU, Washington, D.C., 1976.

Jenkyns, H. C. and S. O. Schlanger, Significance of plant remains in redeposited Aptian sediments, Hole 462A, Nauru Basin, to Cretaceous oceanic-oxygenation models, *Initial Reports of the Deep Sea Drilling Project, 61*, 557-562, 1981.

Kulp, J. L., Potassium-argon dating of volcanic rocks, *Bull. Vulcanol., 26*, 247-258, 1963.

Ladd, H.S., J.I. Tracey, Jr., and M.G. Gross, Deep drilling on Midway Atoll, *U.S. Geol. Survey Prof. Paper 680-A*, 1-21, 1970.

Larson, R. L., Late Jurassic and Early Cretaceous evolution of the western central Pacific Ocean, *J. Geomag. Geoelec., 28*, 219-236, 1976.

Larson, R. L., and T. W. C. Hilde, A revised time scale of magnetic reversals for the Early Cretaceous and Late Jurassic, *J. Geophys. Res., 80*, 2586-2594, 1975.

Larson, R. L., and S. O. Schlanger, Cretaceous volcanism and Jurassic magnetic anomalies in the Naura Basin, western Pacific Ocean, *Geology, 9*, 480-484, 1981.

Larson, R. L., S. M. Smith, and C. G. Chase, Magnetic lineations of Early Cretaceous age in the western equatorial Pacific Ocean, *Earth Planet. Sci. Lett., 15*, 315-319, 1972.

Menard, H. W., Origin of guyots: the *Beagle* to Seabeam, *J. Geophys. Res., 89*, 11,117-11,123, 1984a.

Menard, H. W., Darwin reprise, *J. Geophys. Res., 89*, 9960-9968, 1984b.

Menard, H. W., and M. McNutt, Evidence for and consequences of thermal rejuvenation, *J. Geophys. Res., 87*, 8570-8580, 1982.

Ogg, J. G., Paleolatitudes and magnetostratigraphy of Cretaceous and Lower Tertiary sedimentary rocks, DSDP Site 585, East Mariana Basin, western central Pacific, *Initial Reports of the Deep sea Drilling Project, 89*, 629-646, 1985.

Parsons, B., and J. G. Sclater, An analysis of the variation of ocean floor bathymetry and heat flow with age, *J. Geophys. Res., 82*, 803-827, 1977.

Raitt, R. W., Seismic refraction studies of Bikini and Kwajalein atolls, *U. S. Geol. Surv. Prof. Paper 260-K*, 507-527, 1954.

Rea, D. and T. Vallier, Two Cretaceous volcanic episodes in the western Pacific Ocean, *Geol. Soc. Amer. Bull., 94*, 1430-1437, 1983.

Schlanger, S. O., Subsurface geology of Eniwetok atoll, *U. S. Geol. Surv. Prof. Paper 260-BB*, 991-1066, 1963.

Schlanger, S. O., Petrology of the limestones of Guam, M.I., *U.S. Geol. Surv. Prof. Paper 403-D*, 1-50, 1964.

Schlanger, S. O., Shallow-water limestones in ocean basins as tectonic and paleoceanographic indicators, in, The Deep Sea Drilling Project: A Decade of Progress, edited by J. E. Warme, R. G. Douglas, and E. L. Winterer, *Soc. Econ. Mineral. Petrol. Spec. Pub. 32*, 209-226, 1981.

Schlanger, S. O., The oolite facies as a transitional unit in deepening-upward sequences in atoll, seamount and guyot settings in the Pacific Basin, *Amer. Assoc. Petrol. Geol. Abstracts Volume*, 1987 Annual Meeting, in press.

Schlanger, S. O., and R. Moberly, Sedimentary and volcanic history: East Mariana Basin and Naura Basin, *Initial Reports of the Deep Sea Drilling Project, 89*, 653-678, 1985.

Schlanger, S. O., and I. Premoli-Silva, Tectonic, volcanic, and paleogeographic implications of redeposited reef faunas of Late Cretaceous and Tertiary age from the Nauru Basin and the Line

Islands, *Initial Reports of the Deep Sea Drilling Project, 61*, 817-827, 1981.

Schlanger, S. O., H. C. Jenkyns, and I. Premoli-Silva, Volcanism and vertical tectonics in the Pacific Basin related to the global Cretaceous transgression, *Earth Planet. Sci. Lett., 52*, 435-449, 1981.

Schlanger, S. O., M. Garcia, B. Keating, J. Naughton, J. Haggerty, and W. Sager, Geology and geochronology of the Line Islands, *J. Geophys. Res., 89*, 11261-11272, 1984.

Watts, A. B., J. H. Bodine, and M. S. Steckler, Observations of flexure and the state of stress in the oceanic lithosphere, *J. Geophys. Res., 85*, 6369-6376, 1980.

Watts, A. B., D. P. McKenzie, B. E. Parsons, and M. Roufosse, The relationship between gravity and bathymetry in the Pacific Ocean, *Geophys. J. R. Astron. Soc., 83*, 263-298, 1985.

Winterer, E.L., Bathymetry and regional tectonic setting of the Line Islands chain, *Initial Reports of the Deep Sea Drilling Project, 33,*, 731-748, 1976.

Winterer, E. L., J. I. Ewing, and et al., *Initial Reports of the Deep Sea Drilling Project, 17*, 930 p., 1973.

PETROLOGY AND GEOCHEMISTRY OF NEOGENE SEDIMENTARY ROCKS FROM MARIANA
FOREARC SEAMOUNTS: IMPLICATIONS FOR EMPLACEMENT OF THE SEAMOUNTS

J.A. Haggerty

Department of Geosciences, University of Tulsa, Tulsa, OK 74104

Abstract. Sedimentary rocks recovered from the Mariana forearc seamounts differ in age and environment of deposition from rocks recovered from the Magellan Seamounts, and all other Pacific mid-plate seamount provinces. Sedimentary rocks from the Mariana forearc seamounts are Neogene in age, and some contain either chloritized igneous rock fragments, or serpentinized ultramafic rock fragments. Faunal assemblages are typical of the pelagic environment, and are not environmental equivalents of the Cretaceous and Tertiary fauna or flora found in dredge hauls recovered from nearby Magellan Seamounts on the Pacific plate.

Overgrowths of equant calcite spar, and extensive inter-crystalline porosity of the dredged carbonate rocks are not observed in mid-plate seamounts. Authigenic aragonite occurs in Mariana forearc seamount sediments and adjacent serpentinites. This mineral is anomalous in Pliocene sediment at water depths deeper than 3000 m in the Pacific, which is below aragonite compensation depth. Aragonite associated with Mariana forearc seamount serpentinite differs in elemental and isotopic composition from normal marine aragonite, and from aragonite associated with fracture zone serpentinite.

This study yields no evidence that the Mariana forearc seamounts formed as exotic, oceanic plate seamounts prior to trench formation, nor as ones accreted onto the forearc region. The unusual diagenetic texture of extensive porosity, overgrowths of calcite, and the presence of aragonite may result from migration of fluids other than normal seawater through the sediment. The distinct chemistry of the Mariana aragonite suggests the samples were dredged from forearc seamounts that are not horsts, but serpentinite diapirs venting fluids.

Introduction

Very little is understood of the origin and evolution of intra-oceanic forearcs, including

Copyright 1987 by the American Geophysical Union.

vertical movements across forearcs, the character of deformation in forearcs, and the nature of igneous and metamorphic activity. Geochemical research combined with biostratigraphic dating can help determine the history of vertical motion and related tectonic processes associated with the formation of oceanic forearc regions. This information is essential because the style and magnitude of movement or deformation, by whatever combination of uplift and subsidence, places constraints on thermal and mechanical models for the evolution of active margins.

Fryer et al. [1985] mapped seamounts, grabens, and regions of hummocky terrain that are confined to the outer forearc region of the Mariana arc-trench system (see Figure 1 in Fryer, this volume). These features are interpreted as being formed by either diapiric emplacement of serpentinite, or horsts associated with faulting and vertical tectonic movement in the outer forearc region [Evans and Hawkins, 1979; Bloomer, 1983; Fryer et al., 1985]. The timing of formation of these features, the details of the process of emplacement, and their relationship to regional tectonics is not understood.

Samples were dredged during a Hawaii Institute of Geophysics cruise (KK810626-03) in 1982, from forearc seamounts located close to the trench-slope break and upper slope of the inner trench wall of the Mariana forearc, from seamounts in the Mariana trench, and from seamounts adjacent to the Mariana trench in the Magellan Seamount Province. Paleontological, sedimentological, and geochemical studies of samples dredged from locations shown in Figure 1, have helped decipher processes associated with development of these features.

Background

Forearc Tectonics

The Mariana forearc is an intra-oceanic forearc that lacks extensive sediment accumulation, and its evolution was never influenced by a continent. The initial formation of the Mariana arc-trench system may have

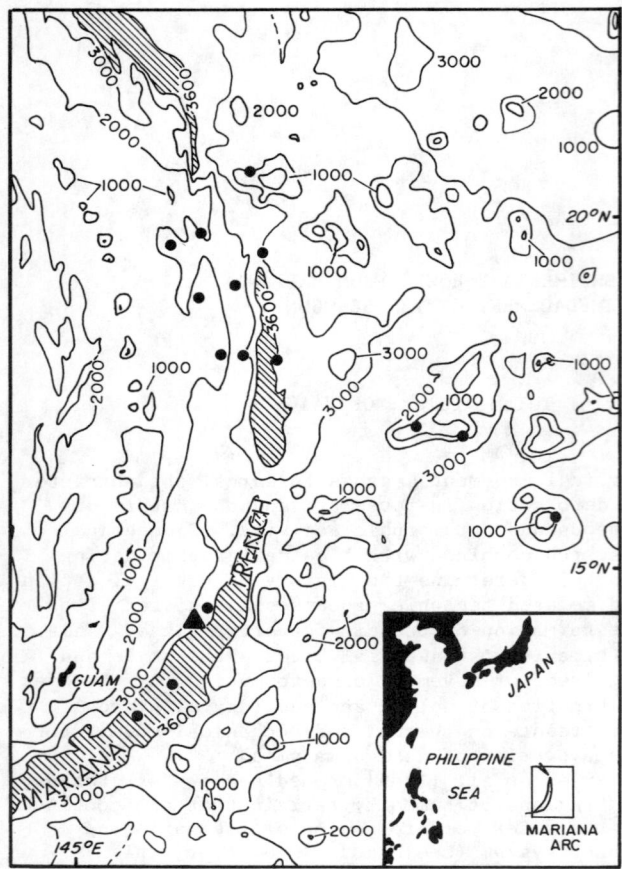

Fig. 1. Location map of the Mariana arc-trench system and the adjacent Magellan Seamount Province. Solid circles represent the location of the Hawaii Institute of Geophysics dredge sites. The triangle represents the location of a forearc seamount from which dredge samples were geochemically analyzed. (Figure modified from HIG cruise report.)

occurred during the Eocene [Karig, 1971; Hussong and Uyeda, 1981]. The subsequent development of this arc-trench system, specifically the tectonics associated with the forearc region, is not agreed upon by the various investigators.

Recent tectonic models of forearcs, specifically the landward inner trench slopes associated with oceanic island arcs or continental regions, require either uplift and accretion of the downgoing oceanic plate [Seely, 1979; Dickinson and Seely, 1979], or subsidence and erosion of the overriding plate [von Huene et al., 1980; Hussong and Uyeda, 1981]. Very few models address deformation of sediments immediately prior to their subduction or addition to the accretionary prism, and the subsequent impact on forearc tectonics [Shreve and Cloos, 1986]. The forearc may be the product of several episodes of tectonic erosion or accretion or both [Uyeda, 1982], and recent studies have revealed this complex variability [Arthur and von Huene, 1980; Scholl et al., 1980; von Huene, 1981; Hussong and Uyeda, 1981; von Huene and Arthur, 1982; Moore et al., 1982; Karig and Ranken, 1983; Lundberg, 1983; Aubouin et al., 1984; Smoot, 1984; Cochrane and Lewis, 1984; Kulm et al., 1986; Zhao et al., 1986]. Most of these recent investigations concentrate on forearcs associated with continental margins, or those with significant sediment accumulations, or both. Only a few studies address formation and development of intra-oceanic forearcs that lack high sediment accumulation, such as the Mariana forearc.

The Mariana arc-trench system is used by Uyeda [1982] as an example of an active margin characterized by tensional stress and seafloor spreading in the backarc region, erosion of the outer forearc, and subsidence of the inner trench wall. The central Mariana forearc, from 17 to 20°N, is one of the most extensively studied regions. Seismic reflection studies, dredging operations, and drilling results do not show evidence of significant accumulations of accreted sediment and rock from the downgoing oceanic plate. These data are interpreted as revealing tectonic erosion and subsidence of the central Mariana forearc [La Traille and Hussong, 1980; Mrozowski and Hayes, 1980; Hussong and Fryer, 1981; Hussong and Uyeda, 1981; von Huene and Uyeda, 1981; Bloomer, 1983; Fryer and Hussong, 1985; Fryer et al., 1985; Hussong and Fryer, 1985; Fryer, this volume].

Uplift in addition to subsidence and erosion, has also been proposed to be a process of primary importance in the Mariana forearc [Karig and Ranken, 1983; Fryer and Smoot, 1985; Fryer and Hussong, 1985; Fryer et al., 1985]. Karig and Ranken [1983] propose that some uplift has occurred on the basis of studies in the southern portion of the Mariana arc-trench system. They suggest that a set of ridges trending parallel to the trench axis are thrust slices of disrupted forearc basement or accreted oceanic crust. Results from bathymetric surveys also indicate that regional uplift occurs in the Mariana forearc where large oceanic plate seamounts are near the trench axis [Fryer and Smoot, 1985; Fryer and Hussong, 1985].

Conflicting interpretations of uplift and accretion vs. subsidence and tectonic erosion may result from a change in response of the arc over time [Karig and Ranken, 1983], or even a change in response along the arc or across the arc [Hussong and Fryer, 1985].

Mariana Forearc Seamounts

Bathymetric data from site surveys for DSDP Leg 60 revealed the existence of large seamounts in the forearc region [Hussong and Fryer, 1981]. These seamounts are roughly conical or ovoid in shape, sometimes elongated subparallel to the

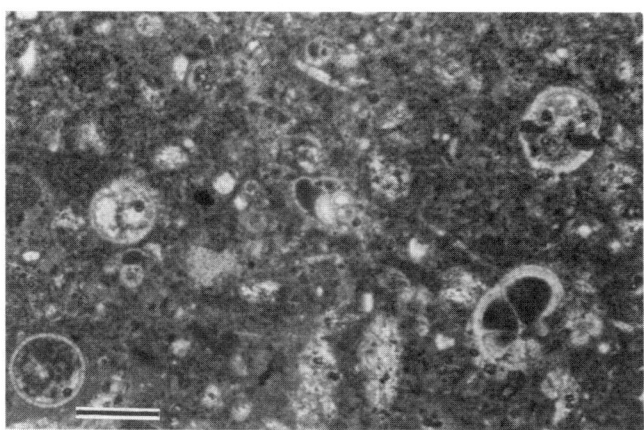

Fig. 2. Pliocene foraminiferal limestone from seamount indicated with a triangle in Figure 1. Transmitted light. Scale bar represents 0.5 mm.

trench, and have 2-3 km of relief from the surrounding forearc seafloor [Hussong and Fryer, 1981; Bloomer and Hawkins, 1983; Fryer et al., 1985]. Proximity of these seamounts to the trench, their distant position relative to any known magma source, and serpentinized ultramafic rocks recovered from topographic highs near the trench-slope break, argue against a volcanic origin [Evans and Hawkins, 1979; Hussong and Fryer, 1981; Hussong and Uyeda, 1981; Bloomer and Hawkins, 1983; Fryer et al., 1985; Fryer, this volume]. The forearc seamounts are interpreted as either horst blocks of forearc crust uplifted by vertical tectonic movement in the forearc, or diapirs of serpentinized ultramafic rocks that rose from the lower crust or upper mantle of the forearc wedge [Evans and Hawkins, 1979; Bloomer, 1983; Fryer et al., 1985].

Fryer et al. [1985] developed a thermal model for the Mariana forearc region that shows the outer half of the forearc wedge, near the trench axis, as being cooled by contact with the downgoing plate. Zeolite and chlorite facies metamorphism is expected to occur within a few tens of kilometers of the trench axis. Uplifted blocks of zeolite bearing, chloritized mafic material, and some serpentinized ultramafic rocks occur within 50 km of the trench [Fryer et al., 1985]. Serpentinization is predicted to occur from 70 to 150 km west of the trench axis depending on the stage of evolution of the subduction zone. Temperatures in this area are proposed to be within the stability field of greenschist metamorphism. Serpentinized ultramafic rocks dredged from Mariana forearc seamounts from 50 to 120 km west of the trench axis are cited as evidence of diapiric emplacement of these seamounts [Fryer et al., 1985]. Fryer [this volume] discusses the stability fields of the metamorphic facies, and the distribution of the different types of forearc seamounts as controlled by local tectonic processes.

Methods

Faunal assemblages were identified and used to determine biostratigraphic age of the sediment and the paleoenvironment. Biostratigraphic zonation schemes used for planktonic foraminifera are from Blow [1969], and Kennett and Srinivasan [1983]. Mineralogy of the sedimentary rocks was determined by standard petrographic techniques, and by x-ray diffraction using a Norelco diffractometer with a high energy Ni-filtered, Cu-K$_\alpha$ source.

Electron microprobe analysis was used to determine chemical composition of carbonates recovered from a seamount indicated with a triangle on Figure 1. Thin sections were coated with silver following the method of Smith [1986] to inhibit thermal decomposition of carbonates during electron bombardment, maintain spatial resolution, increase analytical precision, and lower trace element detection limits. An ARL, five-spectrometer electron microprobe was operated at an accelerating potential of 20 kV with a sample current of 10 nA and a one micron focused beam. All trace elements in the carbonates were analyzed with 80-s counting times on the peak, as well as on the high and low background sides of the peak.

Carbon and oxygen isotopic composition of carbonates, from the same rocks that were analyzed with the electron microprobe, were determined with a Finnigan MAT 251 stable isotope ratio mass spectrometer. Carbon dioxide was evolved from 10-15 mg of carbonate sediment reacted with 100% phosphoric acid, and extracted for isotopic analysis following the procedure outlined by McCrea [1950]. The values reported are with respect to the PDB standard. Analytical error was no greater than ±0.2°/oo.

Results

Paleontology and Depositional Environments

The faunal assemblages are typical of a Pliocene to Recent pelagic environment. Foraminiferal tests have moderate to poor preservation, and the assemblage is composed primarily of the genera: Globigerina, Globorotalia, Orbulina, Pulleniatina, and Sphaeroidinella (Figure 2). Some of the rocks contain Globorotalia plesiotumida Blow and Banner, which ranges from late Miocene Zone N17A into early Pliocene Zone N19 [Kennett and Srinivasan, 1983], associated with Sphaeroidinella dehiscens (Parker and Jones), which ranges from early Pliocene Zone N19 to Recent [Kennett and Srinivasan, 1983]. There is no evidence of redeposition or of mixing of assemblages. The rocks with both G. plesiotumida and S. dehiscens are therefore interpreted as being deposited during the early Pliocene.

Fig. 3. Radial acicular bundles of aragonite needles in foraminiferal limestone immediately adjacent to the serpentinite. Sample recovered from the forearc seamount marked with a triangle in Figure 1. Under crossed nicols. Bar scale represents 2 mm.

Some rocks dredged from these forearc seamounts contain chloritized igneous rock fragments, whereas others have sediment associated with serpentinized ultramafic rocks. No shallow-water benthic foraminifera or shallow-water debris are found in any of the forearc dredge samples.

The forearc seamount assemblages are not environmental equivalents of the upper slope Cretaceous and Tertiary fauna or flora found in dredge hauls recovered from the nearby Magellan Seamounts on the Pacific plate. The Mariana forearc sedimentary rocks also do not exhibit evidence of a platform terminal facies of oolite as found in Cretaceous deposits from some Magellan seamounts [Haggerty and Premoli Silva, 1985]. The breccia and conglomerates from these forearc seamounts do not contain igneous rock fragments that are similar to basalts recovered in debris flow conglomerates from the Magellan seamounts or other oceanic plate seamounts.

If the forearc seamounts were previous oceanic plate seamounts accreted onto the forearc, then the adjacent Magellan Seamount province, of which some of the seamounts are in the process of being subducted [Fryer and Hussong, 1985; Fryer and Smoot, 1985], is the best analogue for comparison. The results from this study yield no evidence for formation of the Mariana forearc seamounts as exotic, oceanic plate seamounts that existed prior to the formation of the trench or as ones accreted onto the forearc region. These data combined with geophysical evidence of gravity and magnetic anomalies [Hussong and Fryer, 1981; Fryer et al., 1985], and the petrology of the magmatic rocks [Evans and Hawkins, 1979; Bloomer, 1983; Bloomer and Hawkins, 1983; Hawkins et al., 1984; Fryer, 1985; Fryer et al., 1985], argues against an origin as an accreted oceanic plate seamount, or as uplifted crust from the oceanic plate by tectonic activity.

Diagenesis

Sedimentary rocks recovered from the Mariana forearc seamounts not only differ in age and environment of deposition from rocks recovered from the Magellan Seamounts, they are also atypical of the lithologies observed in any other Pacific mid-plate seamount province. Detailed geochemical analyses were performed on rocks recovered from 3810 to 3930 m water depth on a forearc seamount at 13° 46'N, 146° 04'E (indicated by a triangle in Figure 1). These rocks contain authigenic aragonite precipitated as acicular crystals in serpentinized harzburgite, as well as in carbonate sediment that is in contact with serpentinite. The carbonate sediment is predominantly low-Mg calcite and contains planktonic foraminifera of Pliocene age.

Authigenic aragonite is anomalous in Pliocene sediment at these water depths in the Pacific for several reasons. Seawater below a few hundred meters in the present day Pacific is undersaturated with respect to aragonite [Li et al., 1969; Berner and Honjo, 1981]. The aragonite compensation depth (ACD) is as shallow as 400 m in some regions of the Pacific [Berger, 1970]. Samples from the forearc seamounts were recovered from below 3000 m water depth, in depths significantly below the ACD, and aragonite is still preserved.

Abiotic aragonite placed in water depths below 3000 m in the Pacific would be expected to exhibit evidence of extensive dissolution, if not complete dissolution, after a year [Berger, 1970]. The Pliocene sediment from these forearc seamounts was deposited between 4.8 to 3.1 Ma. If aragonite associated with the serpentinite and this sediment did not form during the Pliocene, but relatively recently, then it probably precipitated from interstitial waters with a chemistry unlike normal seawater at those depths. If the aragonite did precipitate during Pliocene time, then ever since its crystallization, the water chemistry of the local environment must be sufficiently different than normal seawater to preserve the aragonite in depths below the ACD. The fact that aragonite needles are found in these carbonate sediments as well as in the serpentinites, demonstrates that aragonite preservation is not merely the result of a protective coating from the serpentinite. The aragonite could also acquire an organic coating to inhibit dissolution [Berger, 1970], but this is considered unlikely in this circumstance.

The non-biogenic aragonite has several different growth habits. Rocks containing foraminiferal tests and serpentinite have abiotic, radial acicular bundles of aragonite needles in the adjacent sediment (Figure 3), or

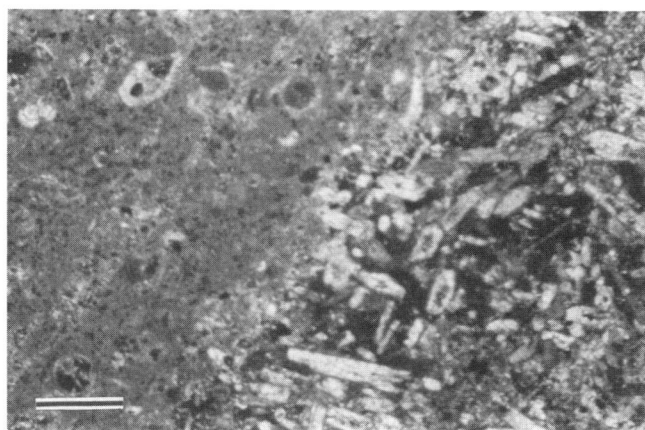

Fig. 4. Needles of aragonite in Pliocene sediment (upper left) and shot through the serpentinite (lower right). Some of the aragonite needles in the serpentinite are hollow. Sample recovered from seamount indicated with a triangle in Figure 1. Under crossed nicols. Bar scale represents 0.5 mm.

needles of abiotic aragonite shot through the sediment and the serpentinite (Figure 4). In some cases these aragonite needles are hollow, which implies rapid growth. In twelve hollow needles of aragonite, the average magnesium and strontium concentrations are significantly higher than the concentrations observed in a solid aragonite needle (see Table 1). The greater abundance of magnesium and strontium in the hollow aragonite supports the idea that they grew more rapidly than the solid aragonite needles.

A transect from rim to core in the solid aragonite needle also revealed interesting variations in the trace element compositions. Average concentrations from fourteen analyses revealed slightly lower strontium and sodium contents than Veizer's [1983] predicted trace element contents of marine aragonite precipitated in equilibrium with seawater (see Table 1). Furthermore, the manganese concentrations observed in the transect are unusually high compared to Veizer's [1983] calculations, and also compared to analyses of natural aragonites [Brand and Veizer, 1980].

Aragonite needles also occur as multiple layers of nearly isopachous crusts that surround what appears to be a tube through the sediment (Figure 5). Needles truncate at the edge of each layer in a zone of micrite (Figure 6). These structures are suggestive of small vents. The orifice or tube appears to have closed by precipitation of aragonite as an isopachous lining.

High-Mg calcite spar, that fills a chamber of a planktonic foraminifera test composed of low-Mg calcite, contains magnesium, manganese, iron, and sodium in excess of Veizer's [1983] predicted values of calcite precipitated in equilibrium with seawater (see Table 1). Calcite precipitated in the deep sea realm is also expected to have a very low-Mg calcite composition [Fuchtbauer and Hardie, 1976]. The very magnesian composition of the chamber-fill calcite also indicates precipitation in an environment that is not in equilibrium with normal marine waters.

TABLE 1. Elemental Compositions of Aragonite and Calcite from Mariana Forearc Seamount Sediments, and Calculated Compositions in Equilibrium with Seawater

	Mg (ppm)	Sr (ppm)	Mn (ppm)	Fe (ppm)	Na (ppm)
Hollow Needle Aragonite	1200	9000	130	330	710
Solid Needle Aragonite	700	5940	90	150	760
Calculated Values for Aragonite[1]	750 to 6300	7000 to 9400	0.1 to 0.6	–	1500
Chamber-fill High-Mg Calcite	91600	B.D.[2]	90	190	1470
Calculated Values for Calcite[1]	16300 to 75400	1000	1	2 to 39	200 to 300

[1] From Veizer [1983].
[2] Below detection limit on electron microprobe.

Fig. 5. Aragonite needles as nearly isopachous layers lining what may have been a vent through the sediment. Sample recovered from the seamount indicated with a triangle in Figure 1. Under crossed nicols. Bar scale represents 1 mm.

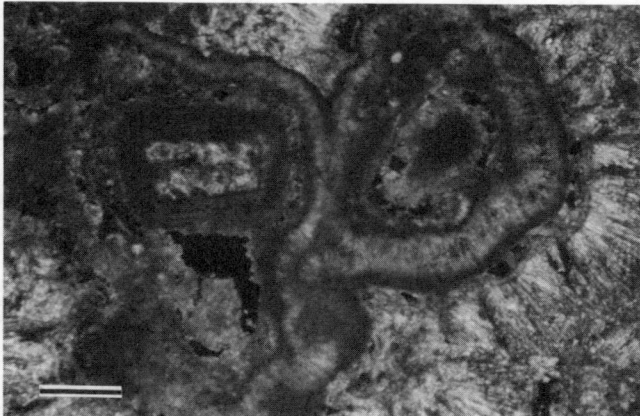

Fig. 6. Close-up of Figure 5. Under crossed nicols. Bar scale represents 0.5 mm.

distinct negative carbon isotopic signature and a positive oxygen isotopic signature (see Figure 7). The carbon isotopic composition of the aragonite and low-Mg calcite crystals are more negative than nearly all other marine carbonates.

The carbon reservoir contributing to the isotopic composition of the crystals shows a decided change from normal seawater, whereas the oxygen reservoir does not. Carbon isotopic compositions of the calcite and aragonite vary widely from -1.2 to -21.2°/oo with constantly positive oxygen isotopic values (+5.1 to +7.6 °/oo). Positive oxygen isotopic compositions may indicate low temperatures of formation, consistent with an oxygen reservoir from cold seawater contributing to the isotopic composition of carbonate precipitated near the sediment/water interface. The carbon isotopic values can not be attributed to precipitation of a carbonate mineral in equilibrium with ambient seawater.

Aragonite crystals from this Mariana forearc

The bulk rock composition of the carbonate sediments is primarily low-Mg calcite. Some of the carbonate rocks display a fine-grained sugary texture, composed of equant, low-Mg calcite spar with multiple generations of overgrowths, retaining extensive inter-crystalline porosity. The degree of porosity and the diagenetic features in the Mariana forearc sediments make these atypical of lithologies observed from any other oceanic seamount province.

The isotopic signature of these aragonite and low-Mg calcite crystals (see Table 2) in sediment dredged from this forearc seamount is unlike other marine limestones that have not undergone burial. Most deep-sea limestones have a slight positive carbon and oxygen isotopic signature reflecting the composition of seawater from which they were precipitated. Results from eight different analyses of calcite and aragonite extracted from forearc seamount samples show a

TABLE 2. Stable Isotopic Composition of Aragonite and Calcite from Mariana Forearc Seamount Sediments

	$\delta^{18}O$	$\delta^{13}C$
Aragonite needles in sediment adjacent to serpentinite	+5.1	-21.2
Aragonite needles in serpentinite	+5.3	-19.6
Isopachous aragonite crusts	+5.3	-15.7
Low-Mg calcite	+6.3	-10.9
	+6.0	-11.1
	+6.1	-11.8
Aragonite needles in pelagic sediment	+4.5	-9.0
Calcite pelagic sediment	+7.6	-1.2

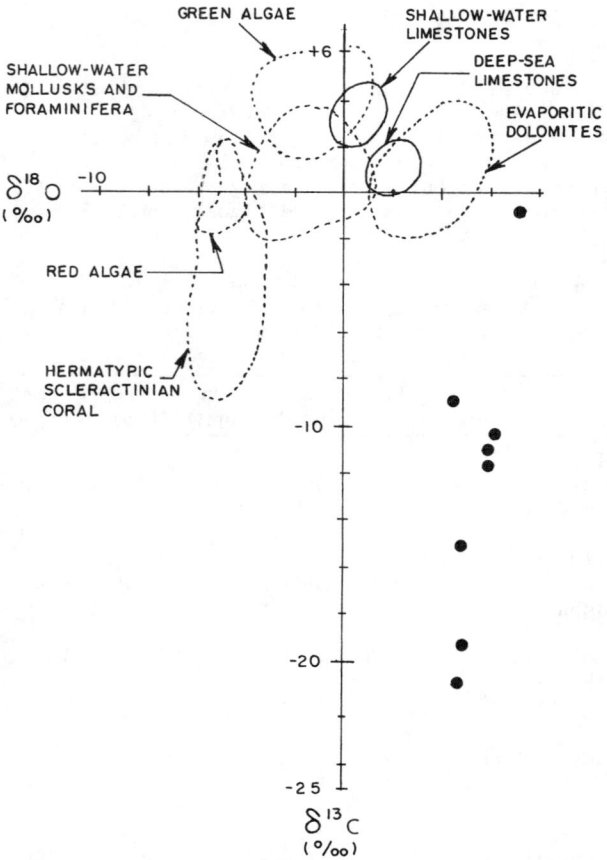

Fig. 7. Solid circles represent stable isotopic compositions of calcite and aragonite (listed in Table 2) extracted from samples recovered from the seamount shown with a triangle in Figure 1. Data from this study added to a figure modified from Milliman (1974).

serpentinite are also chemically unlike those associated with deep-sea serpentinized ultramafic rocks from fracture zones studied by Thompson et al. [1968], Thompson [1972], and Bonatti et al. [1980]. The aragonite associated with fracture zone ultramafic rocks has significantly higher strontium (9500 to 11600 ppm Sr) and lower magnesium contents (<300 ppm Mg) than normal marine precipitated aragonite, and Mariana aragonite. The fracture zone aragonite displays two distinct morphologies: radial aggregates of acicular crystals, and veins which cut through the rock. Bonatti et al. [1980] reported the isotopic compositions of seven aragonite samples taken from their collection of serpentinized ultramafic rocks. The carbon isotopic composition ranges between +0.03 and +1.12 $^o/oo$ PDB, along with an oxygen isotopic composition ranging between +3.16 and +4.87 $^o/oo$ PDB. The Mariana aragonite is depleted in strontium, enriched in magnesium, and displays a significantly lighter carbon isotopic signature and heavier oxygen isotopic signature than aragonite associated with fracture zone serpentinites.

Bonatti et al. [1980] also analyzed $^{87}Sr/^{86}Sr$ ratios of aragonite and combined this data with carbon and oxygen isotopic compositions as well as the elemental chemistry. They concluded that the fracture zone aragonite precipitated at ocean floor temperatures from solutions that circulated through fissures and fractures within the ultramafic rocks. On the basis of relic carbon isotopic and strontium isotopic compositions of the aragonites being similar to seawater, the solutions are interpreted as having originally been seawater that reacted with the host rock at or below the seafloor, and subsequently became enriched in calcium and magnesium. The distinctly different chemistry of the Mariana aragonite, is therefore interpreted as indicating a distinctly different mode of genesis. A source of water that is unique to subduction zones may be derived by dewatering of the downgoing plate as theorized by Anderson et al. [1976]; perhaps such a source of water is responsible for this unique aragonite chemistry.

Discussion

The unique chemistry of the Mariana aragonites indicates that they did not form by the same mechanism as the fracture zone aragonites. Mariana aragonites have a significantly lighter carbon isotopic signature that can not be accounted for by normal sea water alone. Marine carbonates in isotopic equilibrium with sea water have carbon isotopic compositions about 0 $^o/oo$, whereas organic matter has a carbon isotopic composition of about -25 $^o/oo$. Modification of organic matter during diagenesis, and its effect on pore water and precipitation of carbonate cement has been derived for a closed system [Irwin et al., 1977; Curtis, 1978]. Bacterial oxidation, sulfate reduction, and fermentation dominate the upper diagenetic zones, while abiotic or thermogenic reactions dominate the lower zone. These reactions all generate carbon dioxide which enters the pore water and increases the bicarbonate concentration. Diagenetic carbonates precipitated not far below the sediment/water interface, incorporate carbon dioxide generated from organic matter by bacterial sulfate reduction, and typically have moderately negative carbon isotopic compositions. Isotopically light carbonates can also be precipitated by incorporating carbon dioxide generated by the oxidation of methane produced from organic matter [Hathaway and Degens, 1969]. Methane and other hydrocarbons (that are capable of aiding formation of diagenetic carbonates with light carbon isotopic signatures) are usually associated with an initial biogenic origin [Rice and Claypool, 1981; Schoell, 1983].

The Mariana diagenetic carbonates may not have precipitated in an environment dominated by sulfate reducing bacteria, or oxidized biogenic methane. Abiogenic sources of light carbon must also be considered. Mantle carbon ranges between -5 and -8 $^o/oo$, based upon interpretations from a variety of rocks: carbonatites, diamonds, MORB, etc. [Deines and Gold, 1973; Faure, 1977; Javoy et al., 1986], and possible mantle dolomite associated with greenschist facies metamorphics [Bogoch et al, 1986]. Some controversial views expressed by Soviet scientists [Porfir'ev, 1974] favor outgassing of the upper mantle to explain the origin of natural gas and petroleum, and Gold [1979] invokes mantle outgassing as a possible source of methane. Javoy et al. [1986] suggest that the mantle carbon isotopic composition can become contaminated from sedimentary carbonate and organic matter, or fractionated by outgassing effects, yielding a wider range of carbon isotopic values from -2.5 $^o/oo$, in carbon dioxide outgassed from subduction zones, to -32.5 $^o/oo$, in placer diamonds. Javoy et al. [1986] also point out that work by Mattey et al. [1984] shows that the carbon isotopic composition of samples from the Mariana Arc are depleted (-28$^o/oo$) with respect to samples from the Mariana Trough and Scotia Sea (-18 $^o/oo$). If this Mariana forearc seamount formed by diapiric emplacement of serpentinized ultramafics, then water driven off the subducting plate may have aided serpentinization and greenschist metamorphism of deep-seated plutonic rocks, and imparted a characteristic signature in the authigenic minerals.

In recent publications [Neal and Stanger, 1983; Coveney et al., 1987], hydrogen and other gas mixtures emanating from serpentinized ultramafics in the Semail ophiolite, Oman, and hypothesized serpentinized ultramafics in Kansas, are attributed to inorganic formation at relatively low temperatures. Gas formation associated with igneous rocks was previously interpreted as a product of magmatic activity (outgassing) or hydrothermal activity, but in the above cited locations, isotopic and chemical evidence indicates formation can also occur by low-temperature redox reactions in a closed groundwater system. Gas mixtures associated with ultramafic rocks is not unusual, and the carbon contribution to the gases is usually thought to be secondary, possibly from solutions generated post-serpentinization [Morency and Zeller, 1986].

At this stage of the investigation it appears that the light carbon isotopic composition of the carbonates from this Mariana forearc seamount has several possible origins: 1) oxidized methane or carbon dioxide from reactions with serpentinized ultramafic rocks, 2) dewatering of the downgoing plate associated with diapiric emplacement of seamounts during greenschist metamorphism, 3) oxidized biogenic methane, 4) carbon dioxide evolved from organic matter during sulfate reduction by microbial activities, 5) some a combination of the above, or 6) some mechanism not yet considered.

Wada and Okada [1982] analyzed carbonate nodules from sedimentary strata associated with methane in the Japan Trench. The carbonate mineralogy varied from magnesium calcite, dolomite, manganese calcite, and rhodochrosite. The isotopic composition of the calcites showed slightly more negative carbon values (-5.9 to -35.2 $^o/oo$) and not as positive oxygen values (+3.6 to +5.0 $^o/oo$) as the Mariana carbonates. The samples from the Japan Trench are interpreted as being authigenically formed at or near the position they were found, and the carbon isotopic signature is attributed to carbon dioxide evolved during bacterial sulfate reduction.

Other carbonates with negative carbon isotopic signatures (-33.6 to -66.7 $^o/oo$) and positive oxygen isotopic signatures (+1.71 to +6.79 $^o/oo$) were recovered from Joes River Melange on Barbados [Larue and Suess, 1985], and off Oregon [Kulm et al., 1986]. These isotopic compositions are attributed to venting of methane-rich pore waters that oxidized to form carbonate crusts. At both of these cool-water vent sites, biological communities were noted [Suess et al., 1985; Larue and Suess, 1985]. At the Oregon site, the macroorganisms are reported as using methane as an energy and food source in symbiosis with microorganisms. Chemosynthesis of methane by organisms is also reported in an abyssal seep community in the Gulf of Mexico [Paull et al., 1985]. The methane at all of these sites is interpreted as a diagenetic product from organic matter that was previously deposited.

Since the 1984 discovery of a cool-vent biological community associated with a subduction zone off of Oregon, several other discoveries of similar communities have been noted on the landward inner trench wall of the Nankai Trough, and the Japan Trench at 5640 m water depth [Kulm et al., 1986]. Kulm, Suess, and Thornburg also dredged specimens of the giant clam *Calyptogena*, usually associated with vent communities, from the Peru continental margin in April 1985. Swinbanks [1985] reported on another discovery of giant clams in Tenryu Canyon off the Pacific Coast of Japan. All circum-Pacific discoveries, with the exception of Peru, are associated with an inner trench wall and thick sediments in an accretionary prism. The Peru discovery is the only margin representing a subduction erosion tectonic setting [Kulm et al., 1986].

The above cited cool-water vents located on margins with thick accretionary prisms are thought to be associated with oxidized biogenic methane; there is no evidence of serpentinized ultramafic rocks exposed in these areas. In the Mariana samples, multiple isopachous layers of aragonite needles line what appears as tubes through the sediment; these may actually be small vents that began to clog by the precipitation of aragonite within the tube, perhaps during periods of relatively slow fluid flow. Mariana forearc authigenic carbonates differ in texture and mineralogy from those that form in subduction accretion settings. In the Mariana forearc, the possibility of methane or carbon dioxide produced by deserpentinization, and the potential of parent fluids derived from dewatering of the downgoing plate must also be considered. The fluids responsible for aragonite authigenesis may be associated with local diapiric emplacement of serpentinized ultramafic rocks and indirectly related to dewatering reactions of the downgoing plate.

Conclusions

Fryer et al. [1985] mapped seamounts, grabens, and regions of hummocky terrain that are restricted to the outer forearc region of the Mariana system. Studies since DSDP Leg 60 show that seamounts associated with the trench-slope break, and on the nearby trench wall in the Mariana intra-oceanic forearc are horsts and diapirs of metamorphosed forearc material [Bloomer, 1983; Fryer et al., 1985], and are not volcanic [Hawkins et al. 1979; Fryer, 1985] or accreted oceanic plate seamounts [Haggerty, 1985]. Fryer et al. [1985] consider these horsts and diapirs of metamorphosed forearc material a new class of seamounts.

The Pliocene to Recent fossil assemblages recovered from the Mariana forearc seamounts are not environmental equivalents of the upper slope Cretaceous and Tertiary fauna or flora dredged from the nearby Magellan Seamounts. This study yields no evidence that the Mariana forearc seamounts are exotic, oceanic plate seamounts that existed prior to trench formation, nor as ones accreted onto the forearc region.

Lithologies of sedimentary rocks recovered from the Mariana forearc seamounts are unlike those observed in any other Pacific seamount province. Authigenic aragonite occurs in these sediments and the associated serpentinites. Crystallization and preservation of aragonite in these depths requires a pore water chemistry unlike that of normal seawater. Aragonite in the sediment and the serpentinite may be evidence of cool-water venting in the Mariana forearc region.

The isotopic signatures of low-Mg calcite and aragonite crystals in limestones dredged from a Mariana forearc seamount are unusual compared to other marine limestones that have not undergone burial. Elemental and isotopic compositions of the aragonite associated with serpentinite from a Mariana forearc seamount differ not only from normal marine aragonite, but are also distinctly different from aragonite associated with marine fracture zone serpentinites.

Two types of seamounts occur within the Mariana forearc, horsts of uplifted forearc crust and serpentinite diapirs [Fryer et al., 1985; Fryer, this volume]. The possibility that the Mariana aragonite and serpentinite formed as a result of fracturing and uplift of parts of the forearc as horsts must be considered. In this scenario, circulation of seawater through the uplifted ultramafic rock to induce serpentinization and aragonite growth would be expected to be produce aragonite that is chemically and isotopically similar to those from the fracture zone serpentinites. The distinctly different chemistry of the Mariana aragonite, compared with the fracture zone aragonite, argues against this possibility. Aragonite needles are associated with serpentinite on several of the other dredged forearc seamounts.

The unusual diagenetic texture and geochemistry observed in the sedimentary rocks and serpentinites recovered from Mariana forearc seamounts are interpreted as the result of migration of fluids through the sediment other than normal seawater. This form of diagenesis may also be associated with serpentinite diapirism on forearc seamounts.

Acknowledgements. Collection of forearc dredge samples used in this research was sponsored by the National Science Foundation. Biostratigraphic research was supported by NSF grant OCE-8215749. The author thanks M.P. Smith for aid with the electron microprobe analyses, J.B. Fisher for comments on an earlier version of this manuscript, and the reviewers for their comments. Stable isotope compositions were determined at the Stable Isotope Laboratory at Amoco Production Company, Tulsa Research Center.

References

Anderson, R.N., S. Uyeda, and A. Miyashiro, Geophysical and geochemical constraints at converging plate boundaries- Part I: Dehydration in the downgoing slab. Geophysical Jour. Royal Astronomical Soc., 44, 333-357, 1976.

Arthur, M.A., and R. von Huene, Sedimentary evolution of the Japan Fore-arc region off northern Honshu, Legs 56 and 57, Deep Sea Drilling Project, in Initial Reports of the Deep Sea Drilling Project, 56, 57, pp. 521-568, 1980.

Aubouin, J., J. Bourgouis, and J. Azema, A new type of active margin: the convergent-extensional margin, as exemplified by the Middle America Trench off Guatemala, Earth Planet. Sci. Lett., 67, 211-218, 1984.

Berger, W.H., Planktonic foraminifera: selective solution and the lysocline, Mar. Geol., 8, 1-11, 1970.

Berner, R.A., and S. Honjo, Pelagic sedimentation of aragonite: its geochemical significance, Science, 211, 940-942, 1981.

Bloomer, S.H., Distribution and origin of igneous rocks from the landward slopes of the Mariana Trench: implication for its structure and evolution, Jour. Geophys. Res., 88, 7411-7428, 1983.

Bloomer, S.H., and J.W. Hawkins, Gabbroic and ultramafic rocks from the Mariana Trench: an island arc ophiolite, in The Tectonic and Geologic Evolution of Southeast Asian Seas and Islands, Part 2, Geophys. Monogr. 27, edited by D.E. Hayes, AGU (Washington, D.C.), pp. 274-317, 1983.

Blow, H.W., Late middle Eocene to Recent planktonic foraminiferal biostratigraphy, in Proceedings of the First International Conference on Planktonic Microfossils in Geneva, v. 1, edited by Bronnimann, P. and H.H. Renz, Brill Publishers (Leiden, Netherlands), pp. 199-422, 54 plates, 1969.

Bogoch, R., Magaritz, M., and A. Michard, Dolomite of possible mantle origin, southeast Sinai, Chem. Geol., 56, 281-288, 1986.

Bonatti, E., Lawerence, J.R., Hamlyn, P.R., and D. Breger, Aragonite from deep sea ultramafic rocks, Geochim. Cosmochim. Acta, 44, 1207-1214, 1980.

Brand, U., and J. Veizer, Chemical diagenesis of a multicomponent carbonate system - 1: Trace elements, J. Sed. Petrology, 50, 1219-1236, 1980.

Cochrane, G.R., and B.T.R. Lewis, Comparison of structures in underthrusting and overthrusting lower slope sediments of the Washington-Oregon convergent margin [abs.], Eos Trans. AGU, 65, 1089, 1984.

Coveney, R.M., Goebel, E.D., Zeller, E.J., Dreschhoff, G.A.M., and E.E. Angino, Serpentinization and the origin of hydrogen gas in Kansas, Am. Assoc. Petrol. Geol., 71, 39-48, 1987.

Curtis, C.D., Possible links between sandstone diagenesis and depth-related geochemical reactions occurring in enclosing mudstones, Jour. Geol. Soc. Lond., 135, 107-117, 1978.

Deines, P., and D.P. Gold, The isotopic composition of carbonatite and kimberlite carbonates and their bearing on the isotopic composition of deep-seated carbon, Geochim. Cosmochim. Acta, 38, 1147-1164, 1973.

Dickinson, W.R., and D.R. Seely, Structure and

stratigraphy of forearc region, Am. Assoc. Petrol. Geol. Bull., 63, 2-31, 1979.

Evans, C., and J.W. Hawkins, Mariana arc-trench system: Petrology of 'seamounts' on the trench-slope break [abs.], Eos Trans. AGU, 60, 968, 1979.

Faure, G., Principles of Isotope Geology, John Wiley & Sons (N.Y., N.Y.), 464 pp., 1977.

Fryer, P., Morphology of seamounts in the Mariana Island Arc System [abs.], Eos Trans. AGU, 66, 1082-1083, 1985.

Fryer, P., E.L. Ambos, and D.M. Hussong, Origin and emplacement of Mariana forearc seamounts, Geology, 13, 774-777, 1985.

Fryer, P., and D.M. Hussong, Seamarc II studies of subducting seamounts, in Formation of Active Ocean Margins, edited by N. Nasu et al., pp. 291-306, Terra Scientific, Tokyo, 1985.

Fryer, P., and N.C. Smoot, Morphology of ocean plate seamounts in the Mariana and Izu/Bonin subduction zone, Marine Geology, 64, 77-94, 1985.

Fuchtbauer, H., and L.A. Hardie, Experimentally determined homogenous distribution coefficients for precipitated magnesium calcites: Applications to marine carbonate cements, Geol. Soc. Am. Ann. Meeting, 8, 877, 1976.

Gold, T., Terrestrial sources of carbon and earthquake outgassing, J. Pet. Geol., 113, 3-19, 1979.

Haggerty, J.A., Comparison of diagenetic textures and lithologies from fore-arc seamounts and mid-plate seamounts in the western Pacific [abs.], Eos Trans. AGU, 66, 1083, 1985.

Haggerty, J.A., and I. Premoli Silva, Ooids and shallow-water debris in Aptian-Albian sediments from the East Mariana Basin, Deep Sea Drilling Project Site 585: Implication for the environment of formation of the ooids, in Initial Reports of the Deep Sea Drilling Project, 89, pp. 399-412, 1985.

Hathaway, J.C., and E.T. Degens, Methane-derived marine carbonates of Pleistocene age, Science, 165, 690-692, 1969.

Hawkins, J., S. Bloomer, C. Evans, and J. Melchior, Mariana arc-trench system: Petrology of the inner trench wall [abs.], Eos Trans. AGU, 60, 968, 1979.

Hawkins, J., A. Volpe, and E. Wright, Ophiolite series rocks in the Mariana forearc seamounts [abs.], Eos Trans. AGU, 65, 1136, 1984.

Hussong, D.M., and P. Fryer, Forearc tectonics in the northern Mariana Arc, in Formation of Active Ocean Margins, edited by N. Nasu et al., pp. 273-290, Terra Scientific, Tokyo, 1985.

Hussong, D.M., and P. Fryer, Structure and tectonics of the Mariana arc and fore-arc: Drillsite selection surveys, in Initial Reports of the Deep Sea Drilling Project, 60, pp. 33-44, 1981.

Hussong, D.M., and S. Uyeda, Tectonic processes and the history of the Mariana Arc: A synthesis of the results of the Deep Sea Drilling Project Leg 60, in Initial Reports of the Deep Sea Drilling Project, 60, pp. 909-929, 1981.

Irwin, H., Curtis, C., and M. Coleman, Isotopic evidence for source of diagenetic carbonates formed during burial of organic-rich sediments, Science, 269, 209-213, 1977.

Javoy, M., Pineau, F., and H. Delorme, Carbon and nitrogen isotopes in the mantle, Chem. Geol., 57, 41-62, 1986.

Karig, D.E., Structural history of the Mariana island arc system, Geol. Soc. Am. Bull., 82, 323-344, 1971.

Karig, D. E. and B. Ranken, Marine geology of the forearc region, Southern Mariana Island Arc, in The Tectonic and Geologic Evolution of Southeast Asian Seas and Islands, Part 2, Geophys. Monogr. 27, edited by D.E. Hayes, AGU (Washington, D.C.), pp. 266-280, 1983.

Kennett, J.P. and M.S. Srinivasan, Neogene Planktonic Foraminifera, Hutchinson Ross Publishing Co. (Stroudsburg, PA), 265 pp., 1983.

Kulm, L.D., E. Suess, J.C. Moore, B. Carson, B.T. Lewis, S.D. Ritger, D.C. Kadko, T.M. Thornburg, R.W. Embley, W.D. Rugh, G.J. Massoth, M.G. Langseth, G.R. Cochrane, and R.L. Scamman, Oregon subduction zone: Venting, fauna, and carbonates, Science, 231, 561-566, 1986.

Larue, D.K., and E. Suess, Eocene subduction-driven vent community, Joes River Melange, Barbadoes [abs.], Eos Trans. AGU, 66, 1097, 1985.

LaTraille, S.L. and D.M. Hussong, Crustal structure across the Mariana Island Arc, in The Tectonic and Geologic Evolution of the Southeast Asian Seas and Islands, Geophy. Monogr., 23, edited by D.E. Hayes, AGU (Washington, D. C.), pp. 209-222, 1980.

Li, Y.-H., Takahashi, T., and W.S. Broecker, Degree of saturation of calcium carbonate in the oceans, J.Geophys. Res., 75, 5507-5525, 1969.

Lundberg, N., Development of forearcs of intraoceanic subduction zones, Tectonics, 2, 51-61, 1983.

Mattey, D.P., Carr, R.H., Wright, I.P., and C.T. Pillinger, Carbon isotopes in submarine basalts, Earth Planet. Sci. Lett., 70, 196-206, 1984.

McCrea, J.M., On the isotopic chemistry of carbonates and a paleotemperature scale, J. Chem. Phys., 18, 849-857, 1950.

Milliman, J.D., Marine Carbonates, Recent Sedimentary Carbonates, Part 1, Springer Publishers (N.Y., N.Y.), 375 pp., 1974.

Moore, J.C., J.S. Watkins, T.S. Shipley, K.J. McMillen, S.B. Bachman, and N. Lundberg, Geology and tectonic evolution of a juvenile accretionary terrane along a truncated convergent margin: Synthesis of results from Leg 66 of the Deep Sea Drilling Project, southern Mexico, Geol. Soc. Am. Bull., 93, 847-861, 1982.

Morency, M., and E. Zeller, Are all fossil fuels really fossils? Oil and Gas Journal, 84, 92-95, 1986.

Mrozowski, C.L., and D.E. Hayes, A seismic reflection study of faulting in the Mariana forarc, in The Tectonic and Geologic Evolution of the Southeast Asian Seas and Islands, Geophys. Monogr., 23, edited by D.E. Hayes, AGU (Washington, D. C.), pp. 223-234, 1980.

Neal, C. and G. Stanger, Hydrogen generation from mantle source rocks in Oman, Earth Planet. Sci. Lett. 66, 315-320, 1983.

Paull, C.K., A.J.T. Jull, L.J. Toolin, and T. Linick, Stable isotope evidence for chemosynthesis in an abyssal seep community, Nature, 317, 709-711, 1985.

Porfir'ev, V.B., Inorganic origin of petroleum, Am. Assoc. Pet. Geol., 58, 3-33, 1974.

Rice, D.R., and G.E. Claypool, Generation, accumulation, and resource potential of biogenic gas, Am. Assoc. Pet. Geol., 65, 5-25, 1981.

Schoell, M., Genetic characterization of natural gases, Am.Assoc.Petrol.Geol., 67, 2225-2238, 1983.

Scholl, D.W., R. von Huene, T.L. Vallier, and D.G. Howell, Sedimentary masses and concepts about tectonic processes at underthrust ocean margins, Geology, 8, 564-568, 1980.

Seely, D.R., The evolution of structural highs bordering major forearc basins, in Geological and Geophysical Investigations of Continental Margins, AAPG Mem. 29, 245-260, 1979.

Shreve, R.L., and M. Cloos, Dynamics of sediment subduction, melange formation, and prism accretion, J. Geophys. Res., 91, 10,229-10,245, 1986.

Smith, M.P., Silver coating inhibits electron microprobe beam damage of carbonates, J. Sed. Petrology, 56, 560-561, 1986.

Smoot, N.C., Multi-beam surveys of the Michelson Ridge guyots: Subduction or obduction, Tectonophysics, 99, 363-380, 1984.

Suess, E., B. Carson, S.D. Ritger, J.C. Moore, M.L. Jones, L.D. Kulm, and G.R. Cochrane, Biological communities at vent sites along the subduction zone off Oregon, Biol. Soc. Wash. Bull., 6, 475-484, 1985.

Swinbanks, D., Japan finds clams and trouble, Science, 315, 624, 1985.

Thompson, G., A geochemical study of some lithified carbonate sediments from the deep sea, Geochim. Cosmochim. Acta, 36, 1237-1253, 1972.

Thompson, G., Bowen, V.T., Melson, W.G., and C. Cifelli, Lithified carbonates from the deep sea of the equatorial Atlantic, J. Sed. Petrology, 38, 1305-1312, 1968.

Uyeda, S., Subduction zones: An introduction to comparative subductology, Tectonophysics, 81, 133-159, 1982.

Veizer, J., Chemical diagenesis of carbonates: theory and application of trace element technique. Chapter 3, in Stable Isotopes in Sedimentary Geology, SEPM Short Course Notes 10, 3-1 - 3-100, 1983.

von Huene, R., Review of early results from drilling of the IPOD-1 active margin transects across the Japan, Mariana, and Middle-America convergent margins, in The Deep Sea Drilling Project: A Decade of Progress, SEPM Special Publication 32, pp. 57-66, 1981.

von Huene, R., and M.A. Arthur, Sedimentation across the Japan Trench off northern Honshu Island, in Trench-Forearc Geology, Geol. Society Spec. Pub. No. 10, edited by J. K. Leggett, Blackwell Scientific Publications (London, Eng.), pp. 27-48, 1982.

von Huene, R., M. Langseth, N. Nasu and H. Okada, Summary: Japan Trench transect, in Initial Reports of the Deep Sea Drilling Project, 56, 57, pp. 473-488, 1980.

von Huene, R. and S. Uyeda, A summary of resultsd from the IPOD transects across the Japan, Mariana, and Middle-America convergent margins, Oceanol. Acta., 1981, Proceedings 26th International Geological Congress Geology of Continental Margins Symposium, Paris, July 7-17, 1980, pp. 233-239, 1981.

Wada, H. and H. Okada, Nature and origin of deep-sea carbonate nodules collected from the Japan Trench, in Studies in Continental Margin Geology, AAPG Memoir 34, pp. 661-674, 1982.

Zhao, W.-L., D.M. Davis, F.A. Dahlen, and J. Suppe, Origin of convex accretionary wedges: Evidence from Barbados, J. Geophys. Res., 91, 10,246-10,258, 1986.

TEXTURAL CHARACTERISTICS OF SEDIMENTS ON DEEP SEAMOUNTS
IN THE EASTERN PACIFIC OCEAN BETWEEN 10°N AND 30°N

Lisa A. Levin and Charles A. Nittrouer

Department of Marine, Earth and Atmospheric Sciences,
North Carolina State University, Raleigh, NC 27695

Abstract. A review of sedimentation on seamounts provides a perspective for understanding the processes which affect sediment texture on seamounts. To examine these processes in the eastern Pacific Ocean, between 10°N and 30°N, forty cores were collected from 16 seamounts using DSRV ALVIN. Visual observations combined with analyses of grain size and carbonate content indicate that sedimentation on seamounts is complex and highly variable. Sediment texture, composition, and color vary greatly between latitudinal regions, between seamounts within the same region, and between environments within seamounts. Seamount latitude, water depth, and age influence large-scale (over 10^3 km) supply and removal patterns of sediment through changes in productivity, calcium carbonate dissolution, and production of hydrothermal precipitates. Localized volcanic settings within seamounts (e.g., calderas, benches, bases) experience hydrodynamic conditions associated with different degrees of winnowing and deposition, which give rise to highly varied sediment textures over intermediate spatial scales (kms). Physically and biologically generated surface roughness (e.g., ripples, mounds, tests) modifies sediment texture and composition on cm scales by causing differential deposition and removal of particles. Feeding activities and test construction by agglutinating protozoans (xenophyophores) also contribute fine-scale heterogeneity. Thus, the processes influencing the character of the sediment which accumulates on seamounts occur on spatial scales spanning eight orders of magnitude, from 10^{-5} to 10^3 km.

Introduction

Seamounts (and guyots) are common features in the marine environment and represent a significant percentage of the seafloor [e.g., 6% in the Pacific Ocean; Jordan et al., 1983]. Early observations indicate that the sediment covering seamounts is much different than that found on the surrounding seafloor. This results from variable bathymetric and topographic characteristics and multiple sediment sources. Although seamounts are volcanic in origin, the sediment which accumulates on them is extremely diverse and includes biogenic, lithogenic, authigenic, volcanogenic and hydrothermal material. In addition to the diverse sediment types supplied to localities on seamounts, physical and biological processes may redistribute sediments, and topographic relief creates a variety of depositional settings. Seamount sedimentation is therefore complex, and patterns of sediment accumulation on seamounts are highly variable.

Some previous studies have described seamount sediments, however, few have investigated sediment differences within and between seamounts. This is, in part, due to sampling difficulties. Steep slopes, rock outcrops, and coarse sediments cause conventional shipboard sampling devices to be of limited use. Submersibles allow precise placement and location of samples, but they are expensive and large data sets are difficult to acquire.

In this study, forty cores were collected from sixteen seamounts in the eastern Pacific Ocean (Fig. 1) by the DSRV ALVIN. These 16 seamounts were also sites of volcanological and biological investigations. The cores represent an unusually comprehensive collection of seamount sediment. Whereas previous studies (on other seamounts) have examined the composition and origin of seamount sediment, the present study focuses on the texture and evaluates the influence of physical, biological, and topographic factors. Textural variability is examined on a variety of spatial scales. Effects of latitude, depth and age are considered over tens to hundreds of kilometers. Different topographic settings such as caldera floors, walls, summits, flanks, and bases influence texture over kilometers within individual seamounts (see Fig. 2) and biogenic features, such as agglutinated protozoan tests, modify sediments over centimeters. The objectives of this paper are to (1) provide a comprehensive review

Copyright 1987 by the American Geophysical Union.

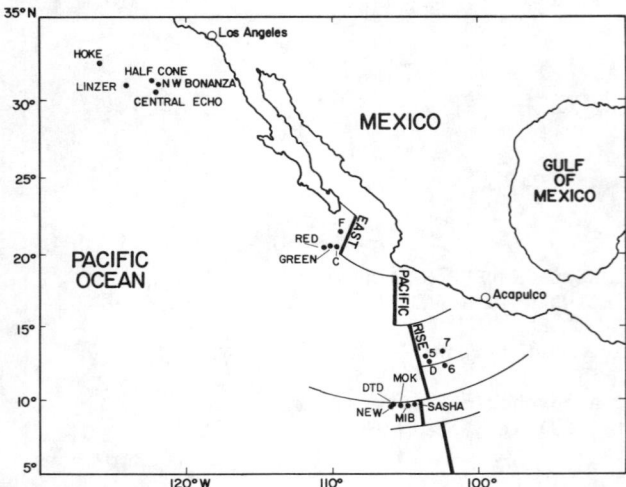

Fig. 1. Locations of seamounts sampled between 1982 and 1985 in the eastern Pacific Ocean. Sample depths ranged from 788 m to 3563 m.

of sedimentation on seamounts (2) describe sedimentary characteristics (especially grain size) for the cores collected and (3) to evaluate environmental factors affecting these characteristics.

Background

Seamount Sedimentation

Seamounts are submarine volcanoes, which, by rigorous definition, stand at least 910 m above the surrounding seafloor [Heezen et al., 1959; Menard, 1964]. However, smaller volcanoes are more common [Batiza, 1982; Jordan et al., 1983; Fornari et al., 1987], and usually are referred to as seamounts also. The production rate of seamounts decreases with the age of oceanic crust [Batiza, 1981], but the number of seamounts increases with age [Batiza, 1982]. After volcanism ceases, erosion and deposition modify the height and morphology of seamounts.

Sediment origin and composition. Seamount sediments can be of varied composition, representing diverse mechanisms of supply and redistribution. The igneous origin of seamounts leads to the presence of much volcanogenic sediment on many seamounts. Although the interior core of a seamount is probably tholeiitic basalt, the exposed extrusive rocks are commonly alkalic [e.g., Palmer, 1964; Herzer, 1971; Fornari et al., 1979; Taylor et al., 1980; Batiza and Vanko, 1984]. Sediment can be composed of a range of volcanic debris, including fragments of basaltic glass, pillows, bombs, tuffs, and tephra [Natland, 1976]. Hyaloclastites form discrete volcanic deposits which extend down the flanks of seamounts [Lonsdale and Batiza, 1980; Batiza et al., 1984]. Alteration of volcanogenic debris into palagonite introduces finer sediment to the seabed [Nayudu, 1962; Taylor and Hekinian, 1971; Herzer, 1971].

Volcanic rocks and sediment are buried by biogenic oozes composed primarily of Globogerina forams. These oozes may also include Globorotalia [Taylor et al., 1975] and Globigerinoides forams [Schwab and Quinterno, 1986], pteropods [Pratt, 1967], nannoplankton, [Lonsdale et al., 1972; Schwab and Quinterno, 1986], and siliceous organisms [Lonsdale et al., 1972]. Carbonate oozes form acoustically transparent layers over seamounts. On the lower flanks of some seamounts, the oozes contain internal seismic reflectors, which are turbidite layers composed of lithogenic sediment transported from a continental margin [Taylor and Hekinian, 1971; Lonsdale et al., 1972]. Other mechanisms for supplying lithogenic sediment to seamounts include aeolian transport [Stanley et al., 1981], ice rafting [Pratt, 1967], and even kelp rafting [Palmer, 1964].

Besides biogenic and lithogenic sediment input to seamounts, authigenic sedimentation can be a significant process. This results primarily from precipitation of ferromanganese oxides in the form of crusts [Pratt, 1967; Lonsdale and Batiza, 1980; Halbach et al., 1982], nodules [Lonsdale et al., 1972; Hein et al., 1985], and pavements [Aumento et al., 1968]. Authigenic sediments which have been observed much less commonly are glauconite and phosphorite [Palmer, 1964; Hein et al., 1985; Schwab et al., 1986]. On some young and active seamounts, hydrothermal sediments are present. These consist of metallic oxides and sulfides which reveal a wide range of compositions [Lonsdale et al., 1982; Malahoff et al., 1982; Exon and Cronan, 1983; Hekinian and Fouquet, 1985; Alt et al., 1987].

Sediment texture. Little data exist concerning grain size of seamount sediment. A medium sand (median size about 1.8 ϕ) composed primarily of foram tests has been reported as the surficial

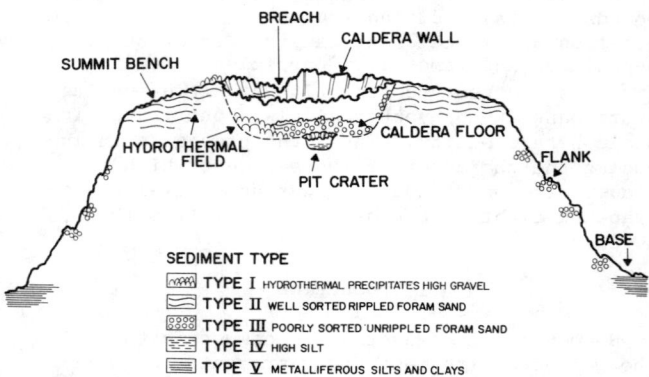

Fig. 2. Schematic diagram of topographic settings and generalized sediment types on a typical young seamount in the eastern Pacific Ocean. See Fig. 5 for histograms of sediment types.

sediment on top of Great Meteor Seamount [Pratt, 1963]. Several seamounts west of the Hawaiian Islands contain a surficial lag of foram sand (median size about 1.8 ϕ), which is deficient in a silty nannoplankton fraction present beneath the lag [Karig et al., 1970; Lonsdale et al., 1972]. On Horizon Guyot these lag deposits can reach thicknesses of several meters [Schwab and Quinterno, 1986]. The surfaces of foram oozes on seamounts commonly contain a thin (mm's to cm's) layer of dark material [Budinger, 1967; Schwartz and Lingbloom, 1973], usually described as finer iron-stained sediment [Lonsdale et al., 1972].

Physical and biological processes. The elevation of seamounts above the surrounding seafloor affects numerous aspects of seamount sedimentation. Upward deflections of isotherms have been observed above several seamounts [e.g., Roden and Taft, 1985; Genin and Boehlert, 1985] and are consistent, in some cases, with the Taylor column theory [Taylor, 1923; Huppert and Bryan, 1976] which addresses interactions between currents and seamounts. Taylor column events may be more likely to occur over shallow seamounts, under conditions of unidirectional flow. The theory may be less applicable in areas close to the equator and in regions dominated by decoupled internal tidal currents. Entrapment of nutrient-rich, upwelled waters in seamount-generated eddies can occur for periods of weeks [Cheney et al., 1980] to months [Owens and Hogg, 1980] and can lead to enhanced phytoplankton production [Genin and Boehlert, 1985], depending on the location and depth of the event. Subsequently, increased biomass at higher trophic levels may result from in situ population growth (numerical response) of zooplankton or through behavioral aggregation (functional response) of consumers above seamounts. The abundant populations of pelagic and epibenthic fishes associated with Pacific seamounts [Uda and Ishino, 1958; Boehlert and Seki, 1984; Uchida and Tagami, 1984] might be attracted by enhanced abundances of prey. Increased production and grazing in overlying waters influences the biogenic sediments which reach the seabed on seamounts.

Accumulation rates on seamounts are typically about 1 cm/1000 yr [Budinger, 1967; Taylor et al., 1975; Lonsdale et al., 1972], and where rates are locally high [e.g., Corner Seamounts; McGregor et al., 1973] slumps can occur down relatively steep flanks [Taylor and Hekinian, 1971; Taylor et al., 1975]. A cause of steepening which can lead to localized slumping is current erosion [Kayen et al., 1986]. The most frequent physical motion of sediment on seamounts is related to transport by currents. Moats around the bases of seamounts result from current erosion [Roberts et al., 1974; Hollister et al., 1978], or from downwarping of the surrounding seafloor by crustal subsidence near a seamount [Watts et al., 1980]. The two modes of moat formation can be distinguished by seismic analysis.

Ripples on the surface of foram sands provide the most common evidence of current activity [Schwartz and Lingbloom, 1973; Pratt, 1967; Fornari et al., 1979]. On Horizon Guyot, ripples are straight and sharp-crested with wavelengths of 10-35 cm, and are superimposed on sand dunes which are about a meter high and 30 m in wavelength [Lonsdale et al., 1972]. The ripples are nearly symmetrical, probably as a result of similar ebb and flood transport by tidal currents. Maximum tidal currents on Horizon Guyot are found around its perimeter and reach velocities of 30 cm/sec [Cacchione et al., 1986]. Total current velocity is greater when the tidal component is superimposed on ambient oceanic currents of about 15 cm/sec [Cacchione et al., 1986]. The sand waves on Horizon Guyot are asymmetrical and indicate some net transport upslope [Lonsdale et al., 1972]. Besides ripples and dunes, evidence on other seamounts suggests strong bottom current activity: coarse lag deposits, crag-and-tail features, and scour pits [Taylor et al., 1975; Stanley and Taylor, 1977]. Hummocks 12 m high and with 750-m wavelengths indicate large-scale erosional processes on Horizon Guyot [Lonsdale et al., 1972]. After formation, bedforms can be reworked and destroyed by bioturbation [Stanley and Taylor, 1977]. Substantial biological reworking of seamount sediments has been reported from bottom photographs and submersible observations [Pratt, 1967; Heezen and Hollister, 1971; Stanley and Taylor, 1977; Hein et al., 1985].

Seamounts of the Eastern Pacific Ocean

The study area of this investigation includes four regions in the eastern Pacific Ocean, between 10°N and 30°N (Fig. 1). Crustal ages for these regions are: 0.2 - 0.9 my at 10°N [Fornari et al., 1984]; 0.9 - 7.5 my at 13°N [Batiza and Vanko, 1983, 1984; Vanko, 1984]; 0.3 - 1.0 my at 20°N [Lonsdale and Batiza, 1980]; and 25 to 30 my at 30°N [Sclater et al., 1981]. Many of the seamounts provide evidence of more recent volcanic activity, and several at 13°N and 20°N still have anomalously high heat flow [Lonsdale et al., 1982; Alt et al., 1987; Vanko, 1984]. Seamounts in the eastern Pacific are better surveyed than those in most of the world ocean [see Batiza, 1982; Fornari et al., this volume]. In recent years several studies have focused on seamounts in the study area and have provided insights to the regional topography, sediments, and environmental processes [Batiza et al., 1984; Batiza et al, this volume].

Morphologically, many seamounts in the study area resemble Galapagos shield volcanoes [Batiza and Vanko, 1983; Lonsdale and Spiess, 1979; Taylor et al., 1980]. Basal slopes are 1°-2°, increase to greater than 30° on the flanks, but decrease on the summit, where flat benches can be found (Fig. 2). The summits of many seamounts in the eastern Pacific contain calderas (i.e., with diameters > 1 km) or some type of central crater

[Lonsdale and Spiess, 1979; Lonsdale and Batiza, 1980; Batiza and Vanko, 1983]. These depressions are typically several kilometers across and several hundred meters deep, with steep walls (vertical in some places) and irregular floors. They contain pillow mounds, talus piles, and pit craters [Batiza et al., 1984]. Pit craters are typically about a hundred meters wide and deep, and are bounded by fault scarps [Lonsdale and Spiess, 1979]. The variations among seamounts in the eastern Pacific result from differences in volcanism, which create a diversity of shapes [Batiza and Vanko, 1983].

Seamount sediments in this region reveal a range of origins and compositions. Young seamounts located near the East Pacific Rise (EPR) can release hyaloclastites and may possess delicate chimneys which discharge hydrothermal solutions [Lonsdale et al., 1982]. The seafloor of these seamounts contains polymetallic oxides and sulfides formed by cooling and precipitation of the hydrothermal solutions [Lonsdale et al., 1982; Hekinian and Fouquet, 1985; Alt et al., 1987]. Where volcanic and hydrothermal activity has terminated, hyaloclastites and other volcanic debris become encrusted and cemented by ferromanganese deposits [Lonsdale and Batiza, 1980] and may be buried by the rain of foraminiferal tests, which are supplied at a rate of about 1 mg/cm^2/y near 10°N [Fischer, 1984].

Infaunal densities in seamount sediments of the eastern Pacific recently have been quantified and have average values of about 1500 individuals/m^2 [Levin et al., 1986, 1987]. The observed abundances are highest for a group of seamounts near 10°N and lowest for seamounts near 30°N. Within individual seamounts, pit craters and summit benches are the environments supporting the greatest faunal abundances, and bases of seamounts and hydrothermal fields have the lowest abundances. Benthic foraminifera on several seamounts at 13°N provide evidence of low oxygen at water depths < 1000 m (J. Nienstedt and A. Arnold, personal communication, 1987).

Biological mixing rates on several seamounts in the eastern Pacific have been measured from Th-234 profiles, and range between 8 to 17 cm^2/y in the vicinity of giant, agglutinated protozoan tests (xenophyophores) [Levin et al., 1986]. These values are comparable to mixing rates observed in both shallow waters [i.e., continental margins; Nittrouer et al., 1984; DeMaster et al., 1985b] and high-energy deep-sea environments [e.g., Nova Scotian continental rise; DeMaster et al., 1985a].

Methods

Field Work

Sample collection. The DSRV ALVIN, which was operated from the RV LULU until 1983 and from the RV ATLANTIS II subsequently, was used to collect sediments from 16 seamounts in the eastern Pacific Ocean (Fig. 1). Sediments were obtained during five cruises concentrated in four latitudinal regions.

10°N - ATLANTIS II Cruise 112-25,
   13 May - 1 June, 1985
13°N - ATLANTIS II Cruise 112-8,
   29 May - 23 June 1984
20°N - LULU, Pluto Cruise 7,
   23 January - 7 February 1982
   ATLANTIS II Cruise 112-30,
   31 August - 17 September 1985
30°N - ATLANTIS II Cruise 112-13,
   12-29 October 1984

From 1 to 5 locations were sampled on each seamount, and a total of 40 sediment samples were obtained from depths of 788 m to 3563 m (Table 1). These samples represent a range of environmental settings: base, flank, summit bench, caldera wall, caldera floor, and pit crater (Fig. 2). In addition, active hydrothermal fields were examined at 13°N (Seamount 5) and at 20°N (Red Seamount).

Sediments obtained on most cruises were collected in acrylic cylindrical cores (diameter 7 cm, length 20 cm). Cores were subsampled on board ship with plastic tubes (diameter 2 cm, length 10 cm). The tubes were removed, sealed with parafilm, and frozen. The upper 5 cm of these tube cores were examined in the laboratory for grain size and carbonate content. In several cases (Dives 1395, 1400, 1402, and 1642) material was retained (and frozen) from depth intervals of 10-15 cm in box cores (cross-section 15 cm x 15 cm, length 15 cm) collected for biological studies. These sediments were analyzed when no other samples were available. Sediments from 20°N, Pluto Cruise 7 (ALVIN dives 1179-1187) were collected in small, Ekman-style box cores. On board ship a square, acrylic subcore (1.5cm x 1.5cm x 15 cm) was inserted, removed, and frozen as described above. Giant (4-13 cm test diameter) sediment-agglutinating protozoans (Phylum Sarcodina: Class Xenophyophorea) were collected from the sediment surface in cylindrical cores or box cores. On board ship, tests were removed gently and preserved in 10% buffered formalin prior to grain-size analysis of incorporated sediment particles.

Visual and photographic observations. Visual observations were made during 14 dives, 4 each at 10°N and 13°N, and 3 each at 20°N and 30°N. Hand-held, 35-mm camera photographs taken during these dives provide close-up documentation of small-scale bedforms and biogenic structures on the sediment surface. The present study examines six photographic transects made by the ANGUS camera sled [Ballard, 1980] at 13°N and five transects made by a LDGO sled at 10°N. Both sleds contained downward facing 35-mm cameras, which were towed approximately 2-10 m above the bottom. Each transect ran 4-11 hours, photographed 3 or 4 frames per minute, and covered 3-15 km of seafloor. Bedform dimensions were measured from camera sled photographs taken at 13°N using a Hipad digitizer and Bioquant software.

Laboratory Work

Grain-size analyses. Approximately 25 gm of wet sediment were placed in a jar with distilled water and were disaggregated by adding sodium hexametaphosphate and then sonifying the sample. This sediment was wet-sieved to separate sand and mud fractions. The sand fraction was analyzed at a 0.5 φ class interval by sieving techniques. The mud fraction (silt and clay) was analyzed with a Micromeritics Sedigraph 5000 ET, which uses a collimated x-ray beam to measure the reduction of suspended sediment within a settling cell. This allows determination of settling velocities and calculation of the distribution of particle sizes, also at a 0.5 φ class interval.

Grain-size analyses were performed on 38 sediment samples. Duplicate samples from two cores (dives 1389 and 1391) were analyzed to examine the precision of the technique. Tests of 14 xenophyophores were analyzed for grain size as described above, and results were compared to those for ambient seabed sediment collected about a meter away (i.e., compared to samples among those mentioned above).

Carbonate analyses. A technique similar to that used in this research is described by Gross (1974). Approximately 2 gm of dried and ground sediment were leached by 0.1 N HCl on a hot plate (about 50°C). The sample was washed on filter paper with distilled water, and then dried and weighed. Weight loss represents carbonate sediment. Carbonate content was measured for 29 samples; duplicate analyses were performed on two of the samples (dives 1402 and 1565) to examine the precision of the technique.

Results

Visual and Photographic Observations

Observations which provide relevant information about the physical and biological characteristics of the seamount sediment in the 4 regions surveyed are described below.

10°N. - Sediments on all 4 seamounts observed (MIB, MOK, DTD, and NEW; Fig. 1) exhibit similar bedforms and biogenic structures, and share a similar fauna. ALVIN dives and camera tows surveyed water depths between 1700 and 2300 m. Sediments are uniformly cream-colored and coarse-grained, though a surficial layer of dark material is present in localized deposits. Distinct ripple marks are present: (1) on summit benches of all seamounts; (2) in the breached calderas of MIB and NEW; (3) in the saddles between DTD and NEW (2100 m); and (4) between the two calderas of MOK (1900 m). Hummocks (25 cm high) and larger swales and basins were observed on the SE breached wall of MIB. Further evidence of strong bottom-current motion is present as scour pits around rocks, xenophyophore tests (Fig. 3a), and other protrusions. Mounds (0.05 to 1.5 m diameter), elongate furrows (up to 3 m long) (Fig. 3b), pits (5-25 cm deep), tubes, and animal tracks are common features on unrippled sediments for all these seamounts. Agglutinated xenophyophore tests (2-15 cm diameter) are reticulate (Fig. 3a) or platy in form and commonly attain densities of 1-5/m^2 on caldera rims and floors. A dark material and a light-colored debris (possible protozoan agglutinations) collect in ripple troughs or other depressions (Fig. 3b). Large patches (often > 1 m diameter) of this surficial dark material are present on unrippled sediments and are commonly the site of aggregations of sea urchins, brittle stars and gastropods.

13°N. - The caldera floors of seamounts 6, 7 and D (Fig.1) are covered with cream-colored foraminiferal sands, often overlain by dark micronodules of Mn and basalt glass similar to those observed at 10°N. On the caldera floors of seamounts 6 and D, these sands are covered with a pavement of manganese nodules (2-6 cm diameter). Mounds and pits (about 10% cover) are superimposed on the nodule carpet. Foram sands are burying volcanic debris on the seamount summits and flanks (Fig. 3c). Where deposits have become extensive on summits, rippled sands are present with wavelengths varying from 5 to 100 cm. Dark detritus and agglutinated debris are common in ripple troughs.

Xenophyophore tests are present on rippled sediment (Fig. 3d), but are much more abundant (as are pits, mounds, furrows and tracks; Fig. 3e) on unrippled surfaces. The sediments of seamounts 6, 7, and D are inhabited by large numbers of xenophyophores and brittle stars. Unusually high concentrations of shrimp, galatheid crabs, and rattail fish are present in the shallow (788 m) caldera of seamount 7.

Seamount 5 exhibits fresher basalt and much less sediment cover than the other 3 seamounts investigated. Rippled sediments are observed on the eastern summit bench only. Hydrothermal deposits are present at 1200-1300 m in fields (> 400 m^2) on the upper northeastern and western flanks of the seamount. Orange-yellow oxide precipitates form crusts, mounds and chimneys (having spouts a few mm in diameter) with 10-50 cm relief (Fig. 3f). Temperatures range from +0.1°C at 5 cm depth to +1.8°C above ambient ($\simeq$ 4°C) at 50 cm depth in these precipitates [Vanko, 1984]. Shrimp were the dominant organisms visible on hydrothermal deposits (Fig. 3f), and white chitons and small white fish were the only other epifauna observed. Signs of subsurface biological activity are not obvious, though a variety of small infaunal taxa were sampled in sediment cores. Manganese-coated siliceous skeletons (sponge or microbial in origin) protrude from the oxides. A

TABLE 1. Sampling Sites and Summary Characteristics of Sediments on

Dive	Seamount	Depth (m)	Setting
10°N			
1558	Sasha	1999	Caldera breach
1560	MIB	1898	Pit crater
1561	MOK	2254	Crater floor
1562	MOK	1925	Caldera floor
1564	MOK	1913	Caldera wall
1565	MOK	1764	Summit bench (rim)
1566	MIB	1741	Summit bench
1568	MIB	1701	Summit bench (rim)
1570	MOK	1990	Summit bench
1572	NEW	1882	Summit bench (rim)
13°N			
1387	6	2324	Caldera floor
1389	6	1775	Summit bench
1390	6	3009	S. base
1391	6	2324	Caldera floor
1392	7	788	Summit bench
1393	7	1790	Summit bench
1394	7	2850	S. base
1395	7	3353	N. base
1397	5	1247	Bench (hydrothermal)
1398	5	1197	Flank (hydrothermal)
1400	5	1225	Bench (hydrothermal)
1401	5	1239	Flank
1402	D	2344	Caldera floor
20°N			
1179	Green	1980	Caldera floor
1180 A	Green	2138	Flank
1180 B	Green	1955	Crater floor
1181	C	2450	Flank
1182	Red	2083	Summit bench
1183	Red	1950	Caldera wall
1184	Green	2034	Pit Crater wall
1185	Green	1989	Caldera floor
1187	Red	2062	Caldera floor (hydrothermal)
1639	Green	1957	Caldera floor
1640	Green	1952	Pit Crater
1642	Red	2060	Crater floor (hydrothermal)
30°N			
1465	Linzer	2942	Caldera floor
1466	Hoke	1101	Flank
1468	Echo	3332	Crater floor
1469	NW Bonanza	2776	Caldera floor
1473	Half Cone	3563	Summit bench

*Sediments were 10-15cm vertical fraction from ALVIN box cores.
+0-2cm fraction from a 7cm diameter tube core.

pale yellow, fine-grained material, probably bacterial in origin, dusts pillow basalts at depths < 1200 m over much of the seamount [Alt, 1986].

20°N. - Sediment cover on Green and Red seamounts (Fig. 1) is minimal (0-10 cm thick), and pit craters within the calderas are the only environments with significant sediment thicknesses (i.e., > 50 cm). Sediments are generally finer than those present at the lower-latitude sites, and ripples are absent. Hydrothermal precipitates are present on both seamounts. Crusts and mounds of orange-red iron oxides are found in great abundances in the caldera floor of Red seamount and to a lesser extent on Green seamount, where sulfide mounds form near the caldera and pit-crater walls. Water temperatures up to

Eastern Pacific Seamounts. (See Figure 1 for seamount locations.)

Mean Grain Size (φ)	Sorting (S.D.)	%Gravel	%CaCO$_3$	Histogram Type (See Fig. 5)
3.61	2.81	0.8	82.3	II
5.66	3.17	0.9	64.1	IV
4.13	2.35	0	88.5	IV
3.74	2.47	0	83.7	III
3.51	2.87	0.2	85.4	II
3.26	2.37	0.1	85.8	II
3.77	2.27	0	86.3	IV
3.50	2.54	1.5	73.5	III
2.92	2.47	2.5	91.0	II
+2.06	2.35	9.1	---	II
4.00	2.83	0	79.7	III
2.32 (2.33)	1.75 (1.84)	0	---	II
7.15	3.19	5.6	27.7	V
4.11 (3.99)	2.42 (2.32)	0	50.5	III
3.03	2.67	0	88.7	II
3.45	2.21	0	90.7	III
7.10	3.46	0	---	V
*7.37	3.22	0	36.2	V
2.62	3.49	17.8	3.4	I
1.69	3.75	24.8	18.9	I
*3.12	4.31	27.2	6.8	VII
3.65	2.78	2.1	84.7	III
*3.66	2.62	0	85.3	III
5.25	3.28	0	---	III
4.76	4.03	6.1	---	VI
4.25	3.88	4.0	---	VI
5.99	4.52	1.1	---	VII
3.37	4.56	30.4	---	I
3.23	3.14	2.7	---	III
2.50	4.04	33.3	---	I
4.44	3.63	0.8	10.3	III
5.78	4.15	0.5	---	VI
5.64	3.71	0.2	55.1	IV
3.83	4.13	13.7	50.6	IV
* --	--	--	30.0	--
7.27	3.04	0	60.7	V
2.95	2.79	2.7	84.8	III
8.19	2.89	0.7	38.7	V
6.26	3.68	3.4	65.1	VI
7.56	3.09	0	55.8	V

13.5°C were measured in active oxide chimneys at 2060 m on the caldera floor of Red seamount (Alt et al., 1987). The only epifauna observed at the active hydrothermal sites consisted of fan-shaped xenophyophores and shrimp, and infaunal counts were extremely low.

The nonhydrothermal sediments on Red and Green seamounts are characteristically light, cream-colored carbonates covered by a thin layer of gray-green fine-grained material (Fig. 3g). Where sediment thickness is greater than about 5 cm, evidence of biological activity is common. Pits (Fig. 3g), burrows, mounds, fecal casts, tubes, and xenophyophore tests are abundant. The light-colored sediment is typically brought to the surface as mounds of feces and pseudofeces.

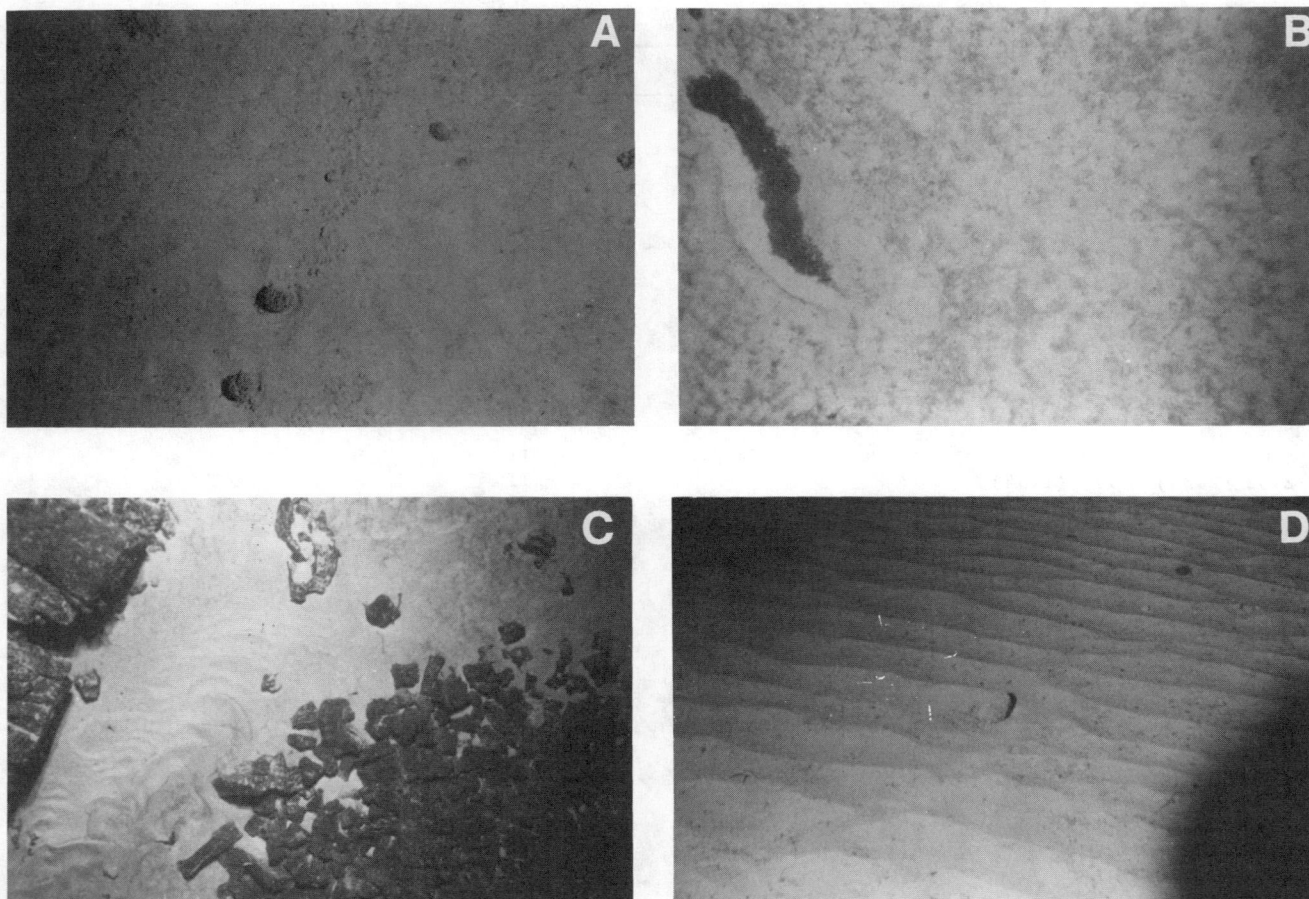

Fig. 3. a) MOK Seamount, LDGO Camera Tow #1 (5/17/85). 1800 m. Xenophyophores atop foram sand. Note scour pits around large tests. Discolored material on the sediment surface may be disaggregated xenophyophore tests. b) MOK Seamount, LDGO Camera Tow #1 (5/17/85). 1800 m. Foram sand with dark surficial sediments. A deep furrow contains dark, low density material. c) Volcano 6, Angus Tow #220 (6/2/84), Time 05:50:14. 1710 m. Basalt talus and sediment chute of foram sand. Note bedforms and mottled appearance of the sediment. d) Volcano 7, Alvin Dive 1393 (6/7/84). 1800 m. SE bench on flank. Rippled foram sands with a xenophyophore test at the center of the photograph. Ripple wavelength approximately 7-10 cm. e) Volcano 7, ANGUS Tow #226 (6/9/84), Time 08:37:24. 3100 m. South volcano base. Xenophyophores and tracks of urchins and crabs visible on dark, fine, metalliferous sediments. f) Volcano 5, Alvin Dive 1397 (6/11/84). 1230 m. Mounds of iron oxides at a hydrothermal field on the upper NE flank of the volcano. Relief is approximately 50 cm. A large caridean shrimp sits atop oxides at the center of the photograph. g) Green Seamount, Alvin Dive 1639 (9/8/85). 1958 m. Pits ($\approx$ 10 cm diameter) in the caldera floor sediments are created by an unidentified infaunal organism. Note dark surficial sediments overlying light calcareous ooze. h) Northwest Bonanza Seamount, Alvin Dive 1469 (10/22/84). 2770 m. Manganese nodules carpet light calcareous ooze on the caldera floor. Sediment mounds approximately 25 cm diameter were deposited atop the nodules.

Pebble-size chips of basalt and glass are common in most sediments. Maldanid polychaetes form aggregations (5 cm diameter) of these particles in the caldera floor of Green seamount. Reticulate and fan-shaped xenophyophores are the dominant epifaunal form on sediments and basalts of caldera floors, walls and rims.

30°N. - Most seamount sediments at this latitude are cream-colored, calcareous oozes. They range from coarse-grained at shallow depths (1101 m) on Hoke seamount, to very fine-grained on the other seamounts investigated (2700-3600 m) (Fig. 1). Manganese nodules (5 cm diameter) carpet the caldera floor and summit benches of NW Bonanza

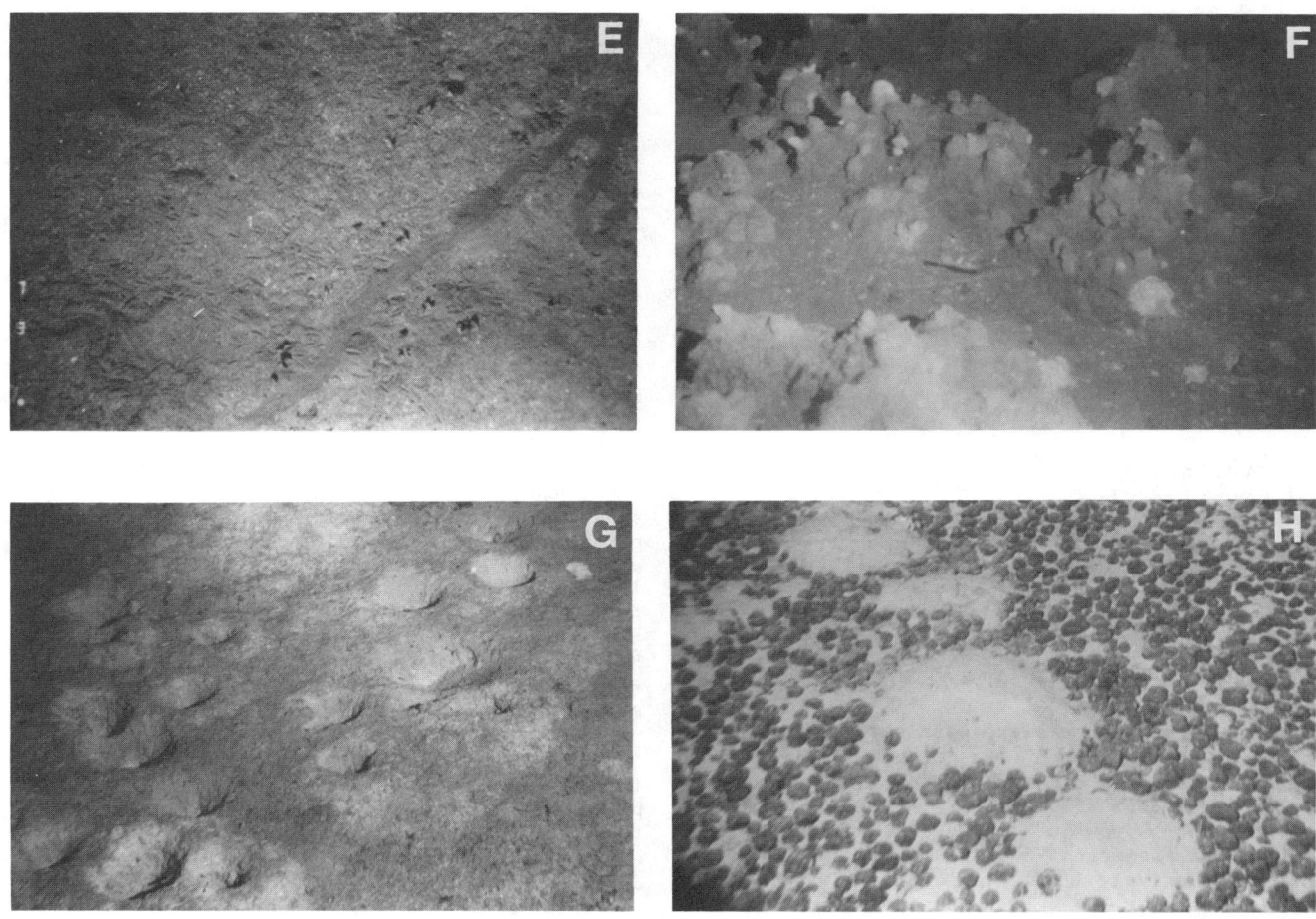

Fig. 3. (continued)

(Fig. 3h), and are also present on West Bonanza, Linzer, West Echo, and Central Echo seamounts. Thick Mn encrustations cover basalts on all seamounts except Hoke. Mounds (up to 50 cm diameter; Fig. 3h) and pits, fecal casts, tubes and xenophyophore tests (up to $1/m^2$) are present atop or poking through manganese nodules on the caldera floor and summit of NW Bonanza. On several seamounts, narrow furrows or gouges (width < 0.5 m, length 1-10 m), cut through the nodule cover into the sediment. Large (1 m diameter, 15 cm high) sediment mounds, apparently of biological origin, are present on solid manganese crusts of three seamounts, isolated from sources of sediment below. The mound sediments contain many smaller tubes, casts, pits, mounds and tracks. Densities of epifauna on sediments (primarily echinoderms and xenophyophores) at this latitude are much lower than those present at the other three study areas.

Sediment cover is sparse on the flanks of all seamounts in this region. Patches of salt-and-pepper-colored foram sands are present between volcanic flows on the slopes of Hoke seamount. Many of these patches contain ripples with wavelengths about 20 cm. A single savonius rotor measurement made from ALVIN indicated instantaneous current speeds of 5 cm/sec. Currents on Echo seamount were strong enough to make submersible operations difficult, but sediment ripples were not observed. The ripples on sandy sediment of Hoke Seamount were the only ripples viewed on any of the seamounts in this region of the study area. A patch of rust-colored oxides, probably an ancient hydrothermal field, was observed on the flank of Hoke Seamount at about 920m.

Grain-Size Analyses

Statistical measures. The summary of grain-size statistics is presented in Table 1. The two sets of duplicate analyses suggest that the reproducibilities of measurements for mean grain size and sorting (standard deviation) are both good to about ±0.10 φ. Several histograms for individual samples appear to be polymodal (see section on histograms). For these samples, the values of mean grain size and sorting have uncertain significance, but they are presented in

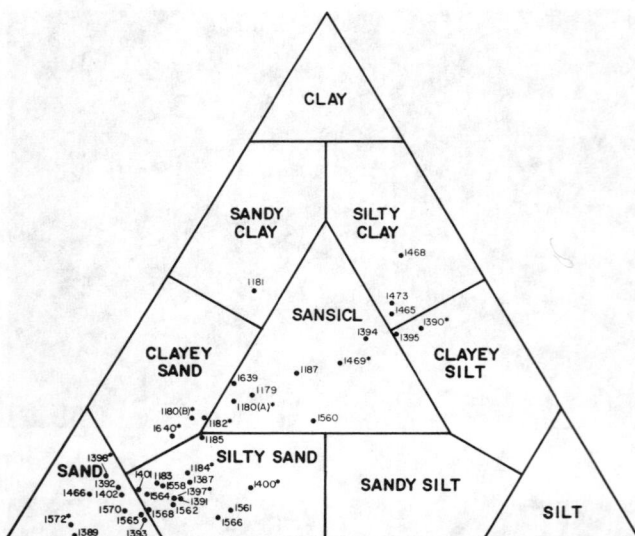

Fig. 4a. Ternary diagram of sediment texture. Each ALVIN dive number corresponds to a sample described in Table 1. Dives marked with an * are samples with > 3% gravel. The gravel and sand fractions were combined for plotting purposes.

order to provide a complete data set. The gravel component (coarser than -1 φ) of the samples is primarily composed of volcanic debris or cemented hydrothermal deposits.

The samples from 10°N represent the upper portions of the seamounts and are mostly sand. They exhibit relatively little variability, with mean grain sizes near 3.4 φ (fine sand) and sorting about 2.2-2.8 φ. As a group, these sandy sediments exhibit the best sorting of the four latitudinal regions. Samples from 13°N cover a greater range of environments on the seamounts, and grain size is more variable. Mean sizes range from 1.7 φ (medium sand) to 7.1 φ (silt), and sorting commonly exceeds 3.0 φ. Samples from 20°N are largely from within calderas and craters, but although mean grain sizes are more restricted [about 3.3 φ (very fine sand) to 5.5 φ (coarse silt)] sorting is very poor, typically > 4.0 φ. The northernmost latitudinal region, 30°N, is characterized by silts typically 6.0-8.0 φ, and by intermediate levels of sorting (2.8-3.7 φ).

Ternary diagrams. The textural data are displayed on a ternary diagram [Shepard, 1952] in Figure 4a. Gravel percentages (coarser than -1 φ) have been combined with sand (-1 to 4 φ), so all samples can be presented on the diagram. More than half of the samples are sand or silty sand. However, the complete set of data points stretches as a band from the sand apex to the silty clay/clayey silt boundary. Some effects of latitudinal distribution can be seen in Figure 4b. Samples from 10°N are primarily found near the sandy end of the band, but one of the samples has < 50% sand. Samples from 30°N are primarily silty clay, but one of the samples has > 80% sand. Samples from 13°N and 20°N stretch over various portions of the band of grain sizes. Additional insights can be obtained from the effects of water depth in Figure 4c. Shallow samples tend to be coarse-grained and deep samples tend to be fine-grained. However, significant overlap occurs between samples of intermediate depths.

Histograms. Seven distinct histogram patterns

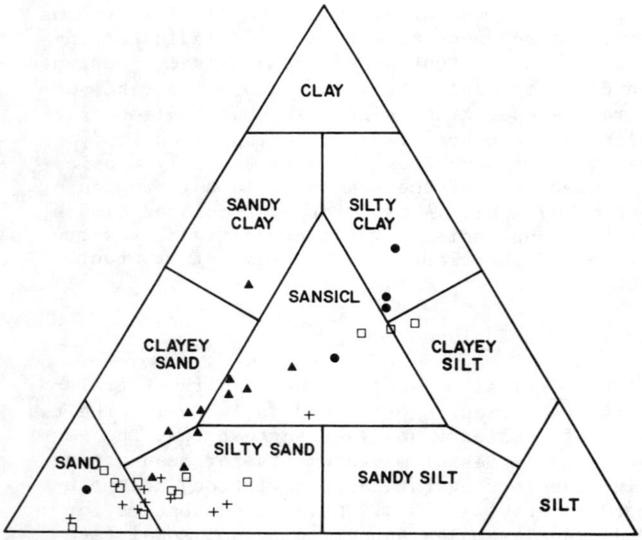

Fig. 4b. Ternary diagram of sediment texture with samples presented by latitudinal regions.
● 30°N, △ 20°N, □ 13°N, + 10°N.

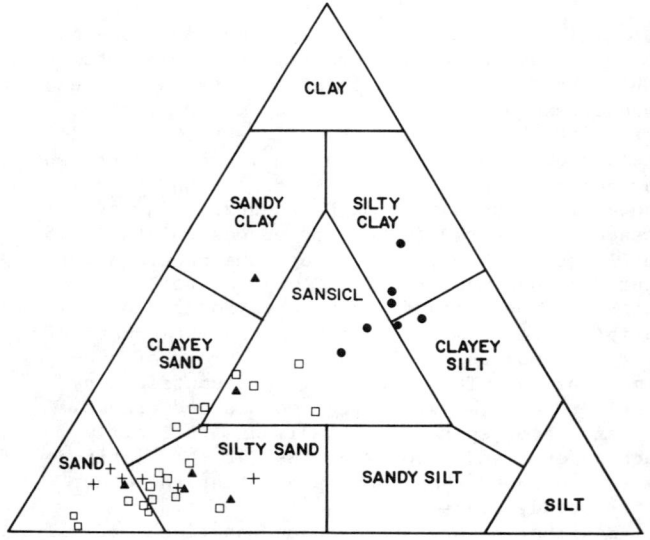

Fig. 4c. Ternary diagram of sediment texture with samples presented by depth category.
+ 700-1550 m, □ 1700-2100 m, △ 2100-2500 m, ● > 2700 m.

of grain size can be recognized in the study area (Fig. 5). Type I samples have high gravel content with uniformly low amounts of sand, silt and clay. These samples primarily are found in hydrothermal areas at 13°N and 20°N. Type II samples have a dominant sand mode at 1-2 ϕ, with no gravel and small amounts of silt and clay. Summit benches, at 10°N and 13°N, characterized by ripples and other evidence of current activity, are the locations for Type II samples. Type III samples are similar to those of Type II except that uniformly large amounts of sand (1-4 ϕ) are present without a dominant mode. Type III sediment is typically found on the floors and walls of calderas. Type IV histograms gradually build to a mode located at the sand/silt boundary, between about 3-6 ϕ. This mode is disected at 4 ϕ because of the discontinuity in analytical techniques. These samples are typical of pit craters and some caldera floors at 10°N and 20°N. Type V samples have large amounts of silt and clay with little sand and gravel, and are found on seamount bases at 13°N and on some deep caldera floors at 30°N. Types VI and VII are miscellaneous categories including, respectively, a uniform size distribution ranging from sand to clay and a distinctly bimodal size distribution with modes of coarse sand and of clay.

The most conspicuous biogenic structures on seamount sediments are the agglutinated tests of xenophyophores. They are reticulate, platy, or fan-shaped, 1-15 cm in diameter, and attain densities of 1-25 individuals/m^2 in all seamount environments except hydrothermal settings. Grain size analyses performed on 14 xenophyophore tests (many belonging to the genus Reticulammina) have been compared to ambient sediment sampled within 100 cm of the tests (Fig. 6). Eleven of the fourteen tests contain a greater proportion of sand and a lesser proportion of gravel, silt, and clay (Fig. 6). The sand particles included in most xenophyophore tests are 1-4 ϕ planktonic foram tests, although the test of at least one xenophyophore species is dominated by volcanic glass fragments. Much of the silt and clay in xenophyophore tests is contained within brown-black stercomes (fecal pellets) stored within the tests. The effective density of this material is less than that of calcareous sediment.

Carbonate Analyses

The carbonate content of samples is shown in Table 1. Duplicate analyses suggest values are reproducible to within 5%. Values range from a few percent to about ninety percent carbonate. Several relationships exist between the carbonate content and characteristics of the sedimentary environments. Low carbonate content is associated with hydrothermal environments (see Table 1, Fig. 7). If these hydrothermal settings are ignored, then a strong positive correlation (R = 0.83, p < 0.01) is observed with respect to sand content (Fig. 7). Carbonate content is negatively correlated with sample water depth (R = -0.70; p < 0.01).

Discussion

Large-Scale Factors Affecting Sedimentation

The samples collected for this study were predominantly from the shallower flanks of seamounts, as has been the case for most previous studies. The general results are also similar to previous work: the dominant sediments observed on deep seamounts of the eastern Pacific Ocean are cream-colored foram sands. However, such a general statement is misleading because it ignores the less common (but significant) sediments, which are present in a vast array of colors, compositions and textures. The variability of sediment on seamounts is as important an observation as the general character of sediment, as it provides knowledge about the range of processes supplying and accumulating sediment on seamounts.

Large-scale textural relationships can be examined by displaying en masse data from the individual samples. Sediment samples stretch as a linear band across the ternary diagram (Fig. 4a), suggesting the presence of two end-member sediments and the mixing of these in various proportions. One end member is the sandy biogenic sediment. Extrapolated to the extreme case of 100% sand-size particles (see Fig. 7), this material would be about 95% carbonate material (foram tests). The additional 5% predominantly includes hydrothermal and volcanic sediment. The second end member is silty clay/clayey silt; and extrapolated to its extreme of 0% sand-size particles (see Fig. 7), this material would be about 35% carbonate material (juvenile and fragmented forams, nannoplankton). The additional 65% probably includes Fe-Mn oxides, fine-grained hydrothermal materials, basalt glass, and volcanic clays.

The importance of carbonate sediment on seamounts suggests that factors affecting the supply and removal of this material should modify the texture of seamount sediment. Oceanic productivity in the eastern Pacific Ocean is generally less at 30°N than at 10°N [Parsons et al., 1984], and the supply of foram sand-sized particles to the seabed would be expected to decrease similarly. The distinct difference between samples from 10°N and 30°N, as shown in Figure 4b, supports this hypothesis. However, the overlap of samples from these and other latitudes indicates that additional factors also must be important. Dissolution of carbonate sediment generally increases with water depth, as reflected in the negative correlation between carbonate content and water depth. This suggests that removal of foram sand-sized particles from the seabed also would increase with depth. The distinct difference between shallow and deep samples, as shown in Figure 4c, supports this hypothesis. However, the overlap of samples from various depths indicates that water depth is not the sole factor controlling texture.

Latitude and water depth increase with age for

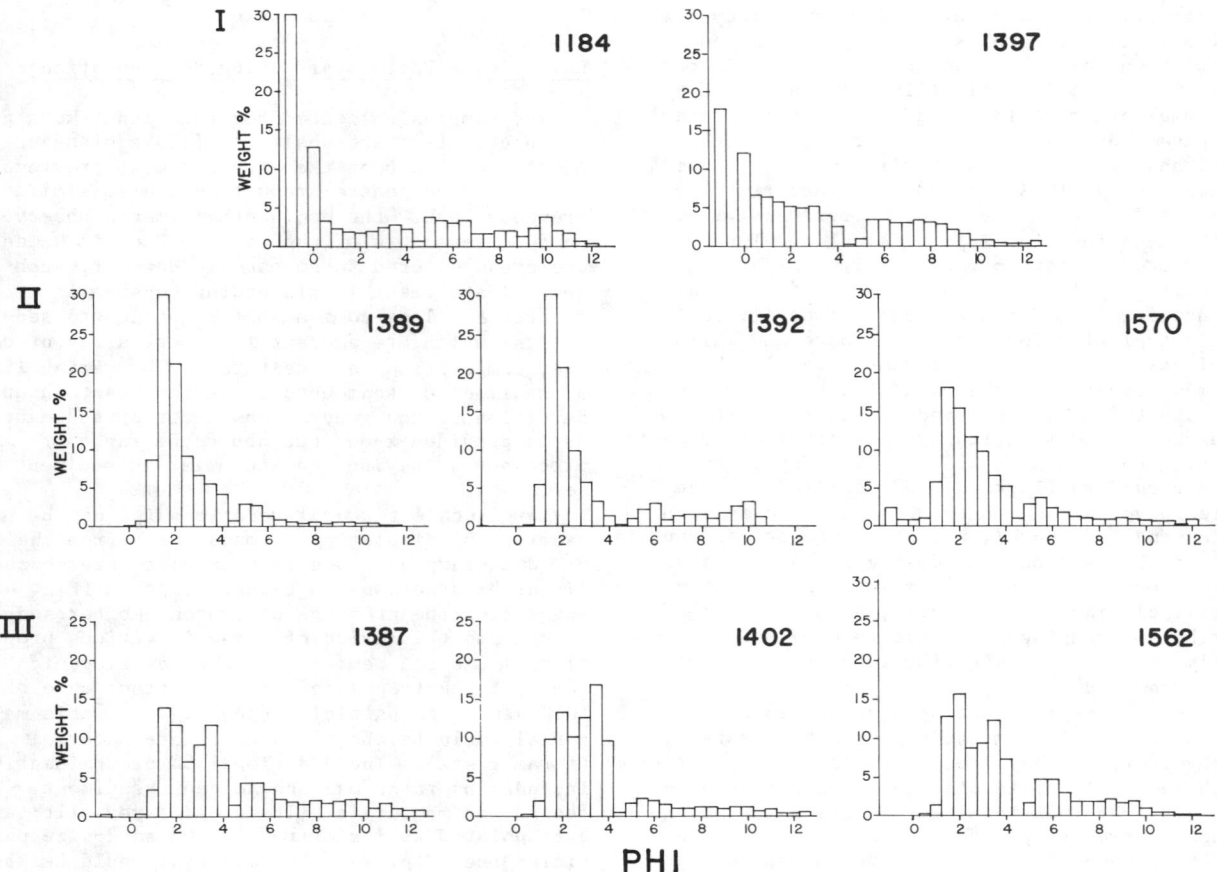

Fig. 5. Grain-size frequency histograms for selected sites which typify 7 commonly observed distributions (see Fig. 2). I-Hydrothermal sediments; II-Summit benches and breached calderas; III-Caldera floors; IV-Pit craters; V-Bases and deep caldera floors; VI and VII-Miscellaneous. ALVIN dive numbers given for each histogram correspond to sampling sites listed in Table 1.

seamounts west of the EPR. The seamounts at 30°N are old, deep, and relatively far north, and for all these reasons tend to be fine-grained. However, seamount age can affect sediment supply to the seabed in a manner independent of latitude and depth. In particular, hydrothermal sediments are commonly exposed on seamounts (e.g., at 13°N and 20°N) which are active or recently have been active. Where hydrothermal sediments are common, they can overwhelm carbonate sediment (see Table 1, Fig. 3f, Fig. 7). The textural signature of hydrothermal sediments is distinct from that of carbonate-rich sediments (Table 1; Fig. 5). Notably different is the presence of gravel-sized particles, formed from the cementation of metallic oxides and sulfides or mass-wasted from steep caldera walls. The properties described above should be generalizable to all deep seamounts. Seamounts which are older are expected to have greater sediment cover and lack surface hydrothermal precipitates. Those which are deeper should exhibit progressively finer particles.

Intermediate-Scale Factors Affecting Sedimentation

Sedimentary environments associated with seamounts have a number of characteristics which differ from those of other marine environments. Seamount sediments can have extremely diverse origins, are affected by intense physical and biological processes, and accumulate within a framework of variable and rugged topographic relief. The resulting strata bear textural evidence of each of these characteristics, as demonstrated by the various sediment types described in the Results. Type I sediment reflects a hydrothermal and/or volcanic origin, and contains the coarsest material associated with seamounts. Type II is found as rippled and scoured sand on

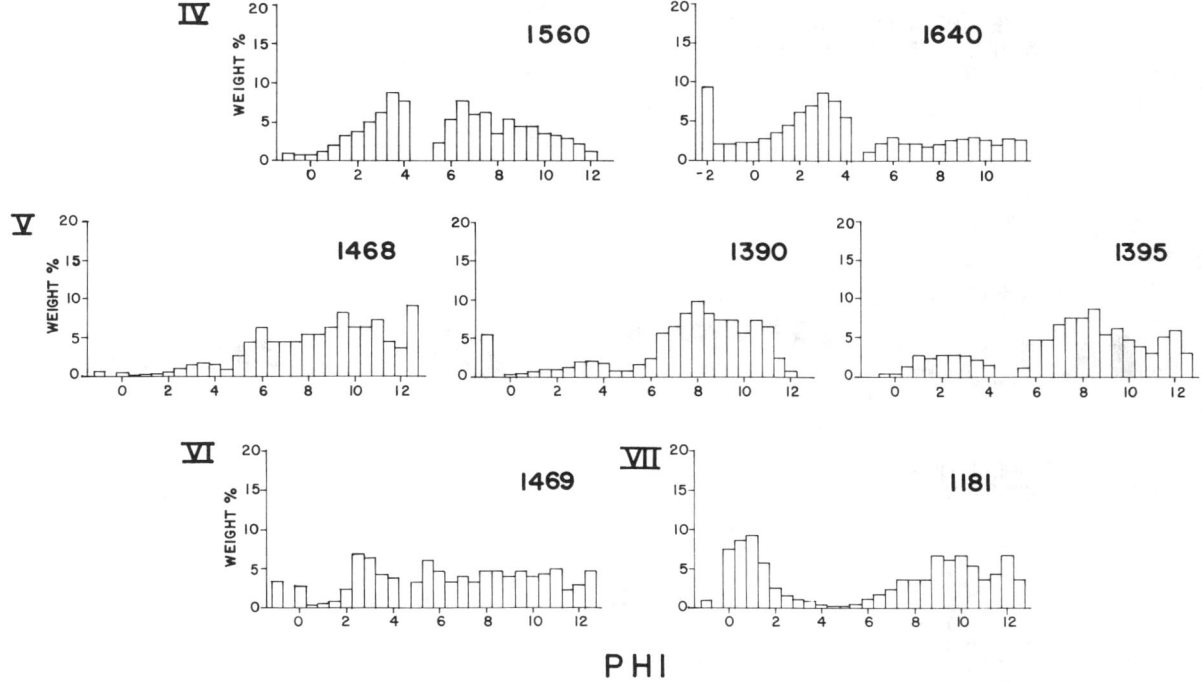

Fig. 5. (continued)

the summits (or topographic highs) of seamounts, and clearly is influenced by strong current activity. The well-sorted sediment and the relatively coarse mode at 1.75 φ suggest winnowing by currents, and removal of the fine fraction. This is the sediment which most closely approaches that described for the summits of Great Meteor Seamount [Pratt, 1963] and Horizon Guyot [Lonsdale et al., 1972].

Sediment Types III and IV are found, respectively, on caldera floors and walls and in pit craters of relatively shallow seamounts. These are areas of weak current activity, and they effectively trap material deposited. Most sediment supply to seamounts, especially supply of carbonate sediment, occurs as pelagic fallout. Therefore, sediment reaching caldera floors and pit craters probably remains, and Types III and IV most closely represent the distributions of particle sizes being supplied to seamounts. Type V lacks a carbonate sand-size fraction, and is found at seamount bases or on deep caldera floors (at 30°N). Dissolution of the carbonate (foram) sand and relative enhancement of the silt and clay fractions (including less corrosive nannoplankton) is reasonable for depths > 3000 m in the eastern Pacific Ocean. Type V sediments resemble those found on deep seamounts of the Sohm abyssal plain in the Atlantic [Stanley et al., 1981]. The enhancement of silt and clay fractions to form Type V sediments also could result from down-slope transport of fine sediments winnowed from seamount summits (i.e., in the formation of Type II sediment).

Exposure of hydrothermal and volcanic sediment is most common on young seamounts. Hydrothermal deposits occur in areas of relatively thin sediment cover (see the observations of seamounts at 20°N and of seamount 5 at 13°N). Therefore, Type I sediment represents an early stage in the evolution of seamount sedimentation. Types II through IV represent an intermediate stage, during which carbonate sedimentation dominates. Type V sediment represents a late stage of evolution, when much of the seamount is near or below the CCD. These transitions lead to a progressive fining of sediment texture. Similar transitions with age can be expected for seamounts generated in other oceans or other parts of the Pacific Ocean (e.g., over hot spots) though rates of change may vary.

Small-Scale Factors Affecting Sedimentation

Textural variability within sediments can occur on scales of centimeters, as a result of physical and biological processes. Ripples and other bedforms almost certainly concentrate distinct sediment sizes within different portions of their waveform (e.g., crest versus trough). Similarly, scour pits and crag-and-tail features associated with biological relief (especially xenophyophore tests) introduce small-scale heterogeneity in sediment texture. Unfortunately, such

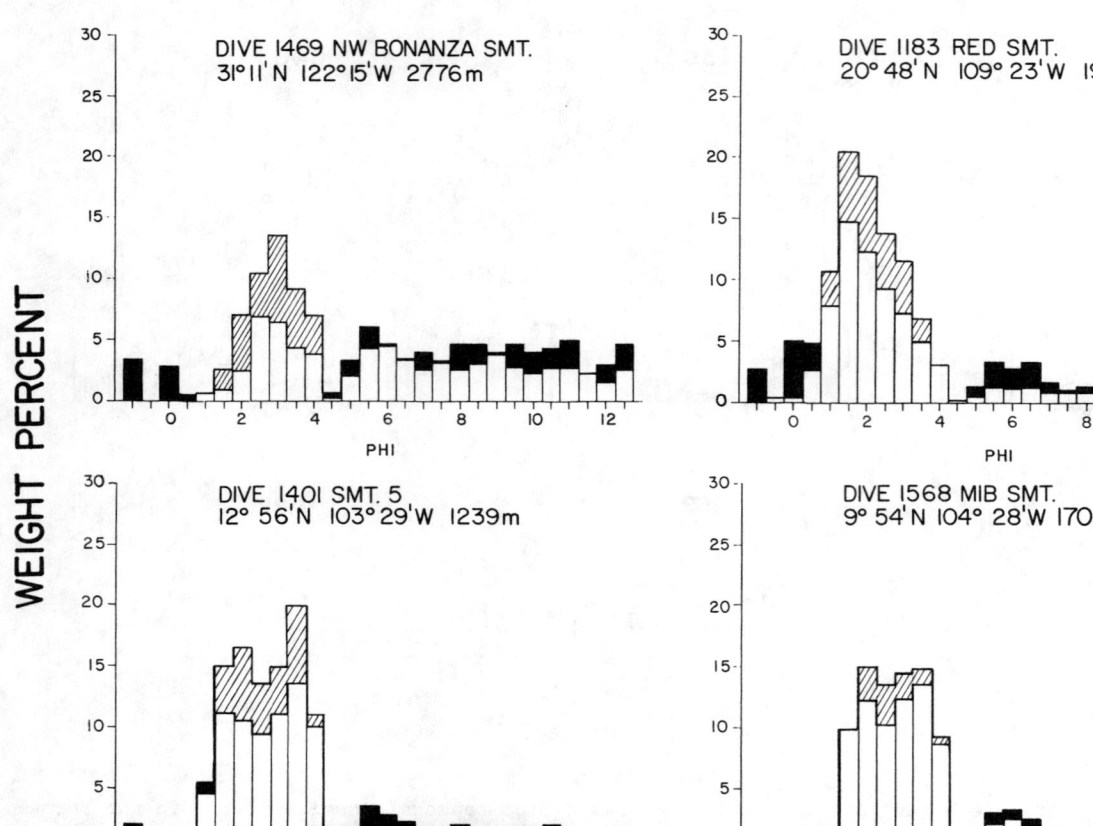

Fig. 6. Grain-size frequency histograms of particles comprising the tests of giant, agglutinating protozoans (xenophyophores) overlain with histograms of ambient bottom sediments collected approximately 1 m away. The white area indicates regions of overlap between histograms. Particle sizes for which the protozoan tests exhibit excess are depicted with hatch marks. Particle sizes in which the tests are deficient relative to ambient sediments are depicted in black.

types of textural variability resulting primarily from physical processes could not be examined with the samples collected for this study. However, the dominant biological effects were examined. Xenophyophores (up to 15 cm in diameter) concentrate sand-sized particles within their tests (Fig. 6). High activities of Th-234 and Pb-210 within xenophyophore tests [Levin et al., 1986; Swinbanks and Shirayama, 1986] indicate that these protozoans also enhance the flux of fine particles to the seabed through active or passive particle trapping (biodeposition). Enhanced macrofaunal abundances in sediments associated with xenophyophores might increase particle mixing rates in sediments surrounding them [Levin et al., 1986].

Upon destruction of xenophyophore tests, light-colored wall material (largely foram sand) and dark-colored stercomes (fecal pellets containing silts and clays) are released to the seabed. These are similar to materials observed in furrows, pits, and ripple troughs of the seamounts. Dark-colored surficial layers are very common on the seamounts of this and other study areas. They are usually described as basalt glass fragments on younger seamounts and as Fe/Mn oxides or iron-stained sediment on older seamounts (see Background). Apparently the dark material has a low preservation potential, because exposures of subsurface sediment (e.g., biological mounds formed from excavation of underlying sediment) are distinctly lighter in color (Fig. 3g). This is also true in areas where the dark material is metallic oxide; for example, mounds and furrows extending through Mn-nodule layers at 30°N reveal predominantly light-colored sediment (Fig. 3h).

Unfortunately, the sampling largely of surface sediment in this study precluded examination of small-scale vertical trends in sediment texture,

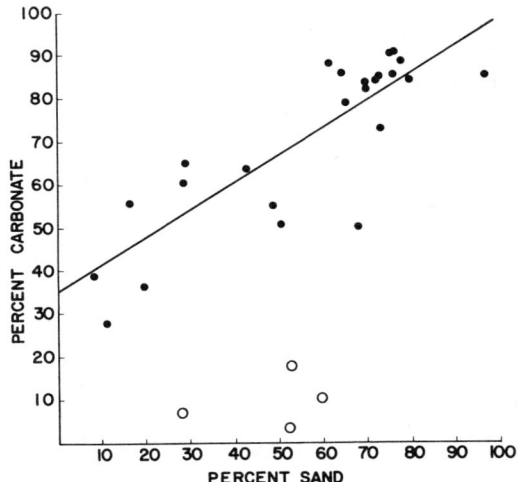

Fig. 7. Percent carbonate as a function of sand content. Open circles denote hydrothermal oxide samples. All other samples are represented as solid circles. Linear regression omits hydrothermal samples. R = 0.83, n = 24, p < 0.01.

such as those described above and in the sand lag deposits present on Horizon Guyot. The possibility of vertical sorting of sediment suggests that data for the few non-surface samples in Table 1 should be cautiously compared with data for the other surface samples.

Conclusions

1) Sediments on seamounts in the eastern Pacific Ocean are comprised primarily of carbonate-rich foram sands with texture influenced by latitude and water depths. Very young seamounts can be dominated by hydrothermal and volcanic sediments, with unique grain-size characteristics. Much variability in sediment texture results from smaller-scale factors than latitude, depth and age of seamounts.

2) Textural characteristics of sediment Types I through V differ as a result of seamount evolution and local topography. Type I deposits form during periods of volcanic and hydrothermal activity. Subsequently, Types III and IV deposits accumulate in the natural sediment traps formed by calderas and pit craters. Coarse, Type II deposits occur on topographic highs (summits) where current activity concentrates sands. Fine, Type V deposits are found at the bases of seamounts where carbonate dissolution is greatest and where sediment winnowed from summits can accumulate. These latter deposits generally become more widespread with the evolution of seamount sedimentation. Vertical sections through old seamounts should reveal a general fining upward in sediment texture.

3) Physical and biological processes cause small-scale textural variability of seamount sediment. Bedforms and scour features resulting from currents cause local segregation of particle sizes, which was not examined in this study. Xenophyophores are dominant epibenthic organisms on seamount sediment in the present study area. These organisms affect textural variability through selective use of sand particles to make their tests and through biodeposition of silt and clay within their tests. Fine-grained, dark-colored surficial material, whether from glass fragments, metallic oxides, or xenophyophores appears to be poorly represented in preserved sediments.

Acknowledgments. The authors thank Rodey Batiza and Dan Fornari, who, as Chief Scientists, possessed a special spirit of collaboration which enabled the collection of sedimentological and biological samples on eastern Pacific seamounts. Rodey and Dan also provided access to the ANGUS and LDGO camera sled filmstrips. The efforts of the ALVIN and Atlantis II pilots, masters and crews were critical to the success of the sampling program. The authors also thank P. Lonsdale, J. Edmond and the many participants of Pluto leg 7, and ALVIN/ AII legs 112-8, -13, -25 and -30 for their assistance with observations, and with sample collection and processing. C. Thomas tirelessly performed grain-size and carbonate analyses, and assisted with filmstrip analysis and presentation of data. K. Thornbjarnarson also assisted with grain-size analyses. Drafting was done by P. Bowers, and typing by Brenda Batts. E. L. Creed and C. Thomas assisted with the manuscript preparation. We thank W. Schwab, P. Taylor, R. Batiza and D. Stanley for their helpful reviews of the manuscript. This research was supported by ONR contract N00014-84-0081 (to L. Levin), and NSF Grants OCE 83-08980 (to R. Batiza) and OCE 84-14616 (to D. Fornari).

References

Alt, J.C., Hydrothermal/bacterial iron deposit from a seamount near 21°N, East Pacific Rise, Geol. Soc. Am. Annual Meeting. Abstracts with Programs 18, 526 (Abstract), 1986.

Alt, J.C., P. Lonsdale, R. Haymon, and K. Muehlenbachs, Hydrothermal sulfide and oxide deposits on seamounts near 21°N, East Pacific Rise, Bull. Geol. Soc. Am., in press, 1987.

Aumento, F., D.E. Lawrence, and A.S. Plant, The ferromanganese pavement on San Pablo Seamount, Geol. Survey Canada Paper 68-32, 30 pp., 1968.

Ballard, R.D., Mapping the mid-ocean ridge: Proc. 12th Annual Meeting Offshore Tech. Conf., OTC-3682, 55-64, 1980.

Batiza, R., Lithospheric age dependence on the rate of off-ridge volcano production in the North Pacific, Geophys. Res. Lett., 8, 853-856, 1981.

Batiza, R., Abundances, distribution and sizes of volcanoes in the Pacific Ocean and implications for the origin of non-hotspot volcanoes, Earth and Planet. Sci. Lett., 60, 195-206, 1982.

Batiza, R. and D. Vanko, Volcanic development of small oceanic central volcanoes on the flanks of the East Pacific Rise inferred from narrow-beam echo-sounder surveys, Mar. Geol., 54, 53-90, 1983.

Batiza, R. and D. Vanko, Petrology of young Pacific seamounts, J. Geophys. Res., 89, 11,235-11,260, 1984.

Batiza, R., D. Fornari, D. Vanko, and P. Lonsdale, Craters, calderas and hyaloclastites on young Pacific seamounts, J. Geophys. Res., 89, 8,371-8,390, 1984.

Batiza, R., D. Fornari and J.F. Allan, Polygonal seamounts near the East Pacific Rise; Implications for seamount origin and rise axis processes, (this volume).

Boehlert, G.W. and M.P. Seki, Enhanced micronekton abundance over mid-Pacific seamounts EOS Trans. Am. Geophy. Union, 65, 928 (Abstract), 1984.

Budinger, T.F., Cobb seamount, Deep-Sea Res., 14, 191-201, 1967.

Cacchione, D.A., W.C. Schwab, G.B. Tate, and M. Noble, Current meter and temperature measurements on Horizon Guyot and implications for sediment transport, U.S. Geol. Survey Open File Report 86-433, 104-132, 1986.

Cheney, R.E., P.L. Richardson, and K. Nagasaka, Tracking a Kuroshio cold ring with a free-drifting surface buoy, Deep-Sea Res., 27, 641-654, 1980.

DeMaster, D.J., B.A. McKee, C.A. Nittrouer, D.C. Brewster, and P.E. Biscaye, Rates of sediment reworking at the HEBBLE site based on profiles of naturally occurring Th-234 and Pb-210, Mar. Geol., 66, 133-148, 1985a.

DeMaster, D.J., B.A. McKee, C.A. Nittrouer, J. Qian, and G. Cheng, Rates of sediment accumulation and particle reworking based on radiochemical measurements from continental shelf deposits in the East China Sea, Cont. Shelf Res., 4, 143-158, 1985b.

Exon, N.F. and D.S. Cronan, Hydrothermal iron deposits and associated sediments from submarine volcanoes off Vanuatu, Southwest Pacific, Mar. Geol., 52, M43-M52, 1983.

Fischer, K.M., Particle fluxes in the eastern tropical Pacific Ocean-sources and processes, Ph.D. Thesis, Oregon State University, Corvallis, OR, 225 pp., 1984.

Fornari, D., R. Batiza, and M.A. Luckman, Seamount abundances and distribution near the East Pacific Rise 0-24°N based on Sea Beam data, (this volume).

Fornari, D.J., A. Malahoff, and B.C. Heezen, Visual observations of the volcanic micromorphology of Tortuga, Lorraine and Tutu seamounts: and petrology and chemistry of ridge and seamount features in and around the Panama Basin, Mar. Geol., 31, 1-30, 1979.

Fornari, D.J., W.B.F. Ryan, and P.J. Fox, The evolution of craters and calderas on young seamounts: insights from sea marc I and sea beam sonar surveys of a small seamount group near the axis of the East Pacific Rise at 10°N, J. Geophys. Res., 89, 11,069-11,083, 1984.

Genin, A., and G.W. Boehert, Dynamics of temperature and chlorophyll structures above a seamount: An oceanic experiment, J. Mar. Res., 43, 907-924, 1985.

Genin, A., P.K. Dayton, P.F. Lonsdale, and F.N. Spiess, Corals on seamount peaks provide evidence of current acceleration over deep-sea topography, Nature, 322, 59-61, 1986.

Gross, M.G., Carbonate determination, in Procedures in Sedimentary Petrology, edited by R.E. Carver, pp. 573-596, Wiley Interscience, New York, 1974.

Halbach, P., F.T. Manheim, and Otten, P., Co-rich ferromanganese deposits in the marginal seamount regions of the central Pacific basin-results of MIDPAC '81, Erzmetall, 35, 497-453, 1982.

Heezen, B.C. and C.D. Hollister, The Face of the Deep, Oxford University Press, New York, 659 pp., 1971.

Heezen, B.C., M. Tharp, and M. Ewing, Physiography of the North Atlantic, Geol. Soc. Am. Spec. Paper 65, 122 pp., 1959.

Hein, J.R., F.T. Manheim, W.C. Schwab, A.S. Davis, C.L. Daniel, R.M. Bouse, L.A. Morgenson, R.E. Sliney, D. Clague, G.B. Tate, and D.A. Cacchione, Geological and geochemical data for seamounts and associated ferromanganese crusts in and near the Hawaiian, Johnston Island, and Palmyra Island exclusive economic zones, U.S. Geol. Survey Open File Report 85-292, 1985.

Hekinian, R. and Y. Fouquet, Volcanism and metallogenesis of axial and off-axial structures on the East Pacific Rise near 13°N, Economic Geology, 80, 221-249, 1985.

Herzer, R.H., Bowie seamount. A recently active, flat-topped seamount in the Northeast Pacific Ocean, Can. J. Earth Sci., 8, 676-687, 1971.

Hollister, C.D., M.F. Glenn, and P.F. Lonsdale, Morphology of seamounts in the western Pacific and Phillipine Basin from multi-beam sonar data, Earth and Planet. Sci. Lett., 41, 405-418, 1978.

Huppert, H.E. and K. Bryan, Topographically generated eddies, Deep-Sea Res., 23, 655-679, 1976.

Jordan, T.H., H.W. Menard, and D.K. Smith, Density and size distribution of seamounts in the Eastern Pacific inferred from wide-beam sounding data, J. Geophys. Res., 88, 10,508-10,518, 1983.

Karig, D.E., M.N.A. Peterson, and G.G. Shor, Sediment-capped guyots in the mid-Pacific Mountains, Deep-Sea Res., 17, 373-378, 1970.

Kayen, R.E., H.J. Lee, and W.C. Schwab, Geotechnical analysis and physical properties of sediment from Horizon Guyot, U.S. Geol. Survey Open File Report 86-433, 29-103, 1986.

Levin, L.A., D.J. DeMaster, L.D. McCann and C.L. Thomas, Effects of giant protozoans (class:-Xenophyophorea) on deep-seamount benthos, Mar. Ecol. Progr. Ser., 49, 99-104, 1986.

Levin, L.A., L.D. McCann, and C.L. Thomas, The ecology of polychaetes on deep seamounts in the Eastern Pacific Ocean, in Proc. 2nd-International Polychaete Conference, edited by J. Kirkegaard and M. Petersen, E.J. Brill/W. Backhuys, Leiden, in press, 1987.

Lonsdale, P. and R. Batiza, Hyaloclastite and lava flows on young seamounts examined with a submersible, Geol. Soc. Am. Bull., 91, 545-554, 1980.

Lonsdale, P., R. Batiza, and T. Simkin, Metallogenesis at seamounts on the East Pacific Rise, MTS Journal, 16, 54-61, 1982.

Lonsdale, P., W.R. Normark, and W.A. Newman, Sedimentation and erosion on Horizon Guyot, Geol. Soc. Am. Bull., 83, 289-316, 1972.

Lonsdale, P. and F.N. Spiess, A pair of young cratered volcanoes on the East Pacific Rise, J. of Geology, 87, 157-173, 1979.

Malahoff, A., G.M. McMurtry, J.C. Wiltshire, and H.W. Yeh, Geology and chemistry of hydrothermal deposits from active submarine volcano Loihi, Hawaii, Nature, 298, 234-239, 1982.

McGregor, B.A., P.R. Betzer, and D.C. Krause, Sediments in the Atlantic Corner Seamount: control by topography, paleo-winds, and geochemically-detected modern bottom currents, Mar. Geol., 14, 170-190, 1973.

Menard, H.W., Marine Geology of the Pacific, McGraw Hill, New York, N.Y., 271 pp., 1964.

Natland, J.H., Petrology of volcanic rocks dredged from seamounts in the Line Islands, Initial Reports of Deep Sea Drilling Project, 33, 749-777, 1976.

Nayudu, Y.R., A new hypothesis for origin of guyots and seamount terraces, in The Crust of the Pacific Basin, Geophys. Monogr. 16, edited by G.A. Macdonald and H. Kuno, pp. 171-180, 1962.

Nittrouer, C.A., D.J. DeMaster, B.A. McKee, N.H. Cutshall, and I.L. Larsen, The effect of sediment mixing on Pb-210 accumulation rates for the Washington continental shelf, Mar. Geol., 54, 201-221, 1984.

Owens, W.B. and N.G. Hogg, Oceanic observations of stratified Taylor columns near a bump, Deep-Sea Res., 27, 1029-1045, 1980.

Palmer, H.D., Marine geology of Rodriguez Seamount, Deep-Sea Res., 11, 737-756, 1964.

Parsons, T.R., M. Takahashi, and B. Hargrave, Biological Oceanographic Processes, Pergamon Press, Oxford, 330 pp., 1984.

Pratt, R.M., Great Meteor Seamount, Deep-Sea Res., 10, 17-25, 1963.

Pratt, R.M., Photography of seamounts, Johns Hopkins Oceanogr. Stud., 3, 145-158, 1967.

Roberts, D.G., N.G. Hogg, D.G. Bishop, and C.G. Flewellen, Sediment distribution around moated seamounts in the Rockall Trough, Deep-Sea Res., 21, 175-184, 1974.

Roden, G.I. and B.A. Taft, Effect of the Emperor Seamounts on the mesoscale thermohaline structure during the summer of 1982, J. Geophys. Res., 90, 839-855, 1985.

Schwab, W.C., J.R. Hein, A.S. Davis, L.A. Morgenson, C.L. Daniel, and J.A. Haggerty, Geological and geochemical data for seamounts and associated ferromanganese crusts in the Ratak Chain, Marshall Islands, U.S.Geol. Survey Open File Report 86-338, 26 pp, 1986.

Schwab, W.C., and P.J. Quinterno, Geologic setting and sedimentologic environment of Horizon Guyot, U.S. Geol. Survey Open File Report, 86-433, 3-28, 1986.

Schwartz, M.L. and K.L. Lingbloom, Research submersible reconnaissance of Cobb seamount, Geology, 1, 31-32, 1973.

Sclater, J.G., B. Parsons and C. Jaupart, Oceans and continents; similarities and differences in the mechanisms of heat loss, J. Geophys. Res., 86, 11,535-11,552, 1981.

Shepard, F.P., Nomenclature based on sand-silt-clay ratios, J. Sed. Petrology, 24, 151-158, 1954.

Stanley, D.J. and P.T. Taylor, Sediment transport down a seamount flank by a combined current and gravity process, Mar. Geol., 23, 77-88, 1977.

Stanley, D.J., P.T. Taylor, H. Sheng, and R. Stuckenrath, Sohm abyssal plain: evaluating proximal sediment provenance, Smithsonian Contrib. Mar. Sci., 11, 1-47, 1981.

Swinbanks, D.D. and Y. Shirayama, High levels of natural radionuclides in a deep-sea infaunal xenophyophore, Nature, 320, 354-357, 1986.

Taylor, G.I., Experiments on the motion of solid bodies in rotating fluids, Roy. Soc. Lond. Proc., 104A, 213-218, 1923.

Taylor, P.T. and R. Hekinian, Geology of a newly discovered seamount in the New England seamount chain, Earth and Planet. Sci. Lett., 11, 73-82, 1971.

Taylor, P.T., D.J. Stanley, T. Simkin, and W. Jahn, Gilliss seamount: detailed bathymetry and modification by bottom currents, Mar. Geol., 19, 139-157, 1975.

Taylor, P.T., C.A. Wood, and T.J. O'Hearn, Morphological investigations of submarine volcanism: Henderson Seamount, Geology, 8, 390-395, 1980.

Uchida, R.N. and D.T. Tagami, Groundfish fisheries and research in the vicinity of seamounts in the North Pacific Ocean, Mar. Fish. Rev., 46, 1-17, 1984.

Uda, M. and M. Ishino, Enrichment pattern resulting from eddy systems in relation to fishing grounds, J. Tokyo Univ. Fish., 44, 105-119, 1958.

Vanko, D.A., Hydrothermal activity on a seamount on 0.9 ma crust, East Pacific Rise flank at 13°N, EOS, Trans. Am. Geophys. Union, 65, 1079 (Abstract), 1984.

Watts, A.B., J.H. Bodine, and N.M. Ribe, Observations of flexure in the geologic evolution of the Pacific Ocean Basin, Nature, 283, 532-537, 1980.

Geochemical and Dating Studies

AN ISOTOPIC SURVEY OF PACIFIC OCEANIC PLATEAUS: IMPLICATIONS FOR THEIR NATURE AND ORIGIN

John J. Mahoney

Hawaii Institute of Geophysics, 2525 Correa Road, Honolulu, HI 96822

Abstract. Available basement samples from Pacific oceanic plateaus show oceanic island or plume-type Nd and Sr isotopic signatures, in contrast to their chemical characteristics which tend to be broadly similar to those of MORB. No clear indication of continental affinities is found in any of the plateau lavas. Other evidence suggests the plateaus could have been formed at ancient spreading ridges, possibly near triple junctions. The isotopic results argue for proximity to hotspots as well, and a near-ridge hotspot origin is proposed here. Seawater alteration has disturbed Sr isotopic values in the plateau basalts, in some cases severely, though Sm-Nd systematics generally remain unaffected. A multiple step acid-leaching procedure removes nearly all the isotopic effects of alteration, however, and allows recovery of Sr isotopic ratios very close to those with which the lavas were erupted.

Introduction

The large oceanic plateaus of the Western Pacific (Figure 1) are among the least understood features in the ocean basins. Possibly related--and just as poorly understood--edifices also exist in the Atlantic and Indian oceans. The Pacific plateaus cover extensive areas ranging to more than 1.5 million km^2 (Ontong Java Plateau) and are characterized by thick, 20-40 km crusts with a distinctive elevated morphology 2-3 km above the surrounding ocean bottoms. Seamounts (not necessarily all volcanic) punctuate the surfaces of most. Although portions of several plateaus show evidence of originally having been at quite shallow depths, all are now submerged and blanketed by thick layers of marine sediments, in some places exceeding 1.5 km. The latter feature has effectively thwarted recovery of basement rocks; very few samples are available and for the most part they represent only the uppermost few meters (or centimeters) of basement. Not surprisingly, sample-based geochemical, petrological, and geochronological data are correspondingly sparse. Remote sensing, geophysical studies provide the bulk of information but have thus far yielded no conclusive answers about plateau composition, large-scale structure, or early history. As a result several largely speculative theories for plateau origins have been advanced, including subsidence of rifted continental fragments [e.g., Heezen, Glass, and Menard, 1966; Nur and Ben-Avraham, 1982] and asteroid impacts on the seafloor [Rogers, 1981]; however, many marine geologists believe that they are likely to be wholly oceanic in nature. A number of authors have argued for plateau formation at ancient spreading ridges, particularly in the vicinity of migrating triple junctions or major transform offsets during periods of anomalously heavy volcanism and/or ridge jumping [Kroenke, 1972; Winterer et al., 1974; Winterer, 1976; Hilde et al., 1977; Kroenke and Nemoto, 1982; Vallier et al., 1983].

The rare samples that have been obtained from the basement carapaces of these plateaus (mostly from five Deep Sea Drilling Project (DSDP) holes) are predominantly tholeiitic basalts, although several alkalic and acidic lavas have been dredged or drilled on plateau seamounts [e.g., Scott, 1981; Vallier et al., 1983] and exotic intrusions of alnoite exist on the southwestern margin of the Ontong Java Plateau [e.g., Hughes and Turner, 1977; Nixon, 1980]. Because of the altered condition of the prevalent tholeiites it generally has not been possible to classify them rigorously. Whereas many chemical characteristics imply affinities with mid-ocean ridge basalts (MORB), several trace elements suggest some similarities to oceanic island basalts [Bass et al., 1973; Stoeser, 1975; Jackson et al., 1976; Scott, 1981]. Tholeiitic basalt also is a very common rock type on continents, of course, particularly near rifted margins; but on the basis of lithological and chemical evidence no rocks that are incontrovertibly continental have yet been discovered on any of these plateaus.

Basal sedimentary rocks and igneous samples from the top of basement yield Lower Cretaceous ages, linking the upper surfaces of the edifices

Copyright 1987 by the American Geophysical Union.

208 PACIFIC OCEANIC PLATEAUS

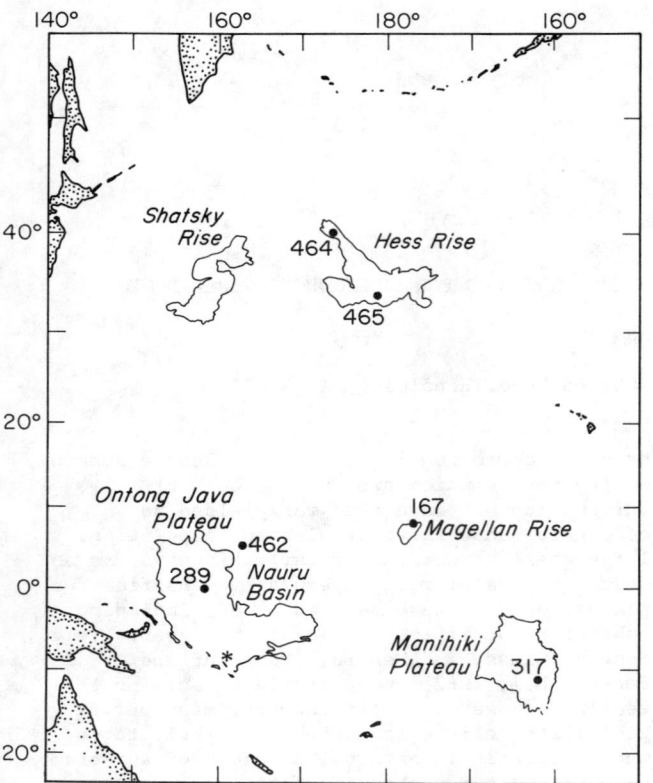

Fig. 1. Map of the western Pacific showing locations of Cretaceous oceanic plateaus, Nauru Basin, and associated DSDP sites reaching basement. Plateau outlines follow 5-km depth contours except for the Ontong Java Plateau, which is represented by its 4-km contour and its approximate boundary with the Solomons (in the southwest). Asterisk marks location of Malaita.

to a period of excessively heavy, widespread seafloor volcanism throughout the Pacific [e.g., Watts et al., 1980]. Calculated paleolatitudes indicate that all were in the Southern Hemisphere at this time [Hammond et al., 1975; Cockerham and Jarrard, 1976; Vallier et al., 1983]. Magnetic anomalies tend to be small and ambiguous over the plateaus themselves [Uyeda and Vacquier, 1968; Larson et al., 1972; Winterer, 1976]; however, with respect to the surrounding seafloor several plateaus are situated near bends in the magnetic anomaly patterns. This feature, plus the fact that they are in isostatic equilibrium [e.g., Moberly and Kroenke, 1974; Watts et al., 1980; J. Kellogg, personal communication, 1986] have in part prompted the suggestions of association with ancient ridges at triple junctions [e.g., Winterer, 1976; Hilde et al., 1977; Scott, 1981; Vallier et al., 1983].

The existing seismic evidence can in several cases be interpreted as favoring either amplified sections of otherwise normal oceanic crust, more or less typical continental crust, or some combination of the two [Hussong et al., 1979; Carlson et al., 1980; Nur and Ben-Avraham, 1982]. Rather than being continental blocks it has been suggested that the plateaus represent "protocontinents" in the early stages of true continent formation, capped by the extensive submarine analogues of continental flood basalts [Kroenke, 1974; Nixon, 1980]. In any event, because their ultimate fate must be to collide with convergent plate margins, they appear to be related to continents as likely sources of displaced terranes such as Wrangellia [e.g., Kroenke, 1974; Nur and Ben-Avraham, 1982].

Given the incomplete and unsettled status of present knowledge, a Nd and Sr isotopic survey of available basement rocks was undertaken with the aim of adding a new type of information to the limited body of sample-based data; this paper presents and discusses the results. Because of their power in discriminating between otherwise subtle oceanic ridge, intraplate, and continental signatures in basalts, even limited multi-element isotopic data offer help in resolving the true nature of these plateaus. To do so, however, requires a means of evaluating possible modifications of isotopic ratios by the sometimes substantial seawater alteration that has affected many of the basement lavas.

Samples and Methods

The samples used in this study, begun in 1983 and carried out at the Scripps Institution of Oceanography and the University of Minnesota, were taken mainly from DSDP cores from sites 317A (Manihiki Plateau), 167 (Magellan Rise), 464 and 465A (Hess Rise), and 289 (Ontong Java Plateau). Three additional basement samples from the island of Malaita on the southwestern edge of the Ontong Java Plateau were provided by the Ministry of Natural Resources of the Solomon Islands. Three from the extensive, tabular sheet-flow and sill complex filling the Nauru Basin (site 462A) adjacent to the Ontong Java Plateau (Figure 1) also were analyzed. Although Nauru Basin magmatism never constructed an elevated plateau, the strong geochemical similarities of the rocks to known plateau basalts suggest they may be related [e.g., Tokuyama and Batiza, 1981]. Other than a trachyte drilled on a Hess Rise seamount (site 465A) all the samples are tholeiitic basalts. All were in contact with seawater at least briefly in their history and have been affected variably by low-temperature seawater alteration; for the most part there is little indication of high-temperature alteration, however [but see Bass et al., 1973], and subaerial leaching is likely to have been a factor mainly for the uplifted basalts from Malaita. The samples range from moderately fresh (Nauru Basin, some Manihiki samples) to extremely altered (Magellan and Hess Rise basalts), with different amounts of secondary palagonite, smectite, chlorite, carbonate, and/or zeolites. In several cases these phases comprise the dominant constituents of the rock [for more detailed descriptions see the pertinent Initial Reports of the DSDP, and Hughes and Turner, 1977].

Fresh glass was carefully handpicked from two of the Nauru Basin specimens (Table 1); the remaining samples were all fine to very fine grained crystalline rock chips. Initial preparation involved cleaning of any extraneous surficial material (drill or saw marks, primarily) by abrading, then washing briefly in acetone and weak HCl in an ultrasonic bath. This step was followed by pulverization to fine powder in a boron carbide or agate mortar. Splits of the powders (~30 mg) were in some instances dissolved directly for processing for isotopic analysis (designated as "U", for unleached, in Table 1). In order to assess--and hopefully diminish or remove--the effects of alteration on isotopic ratios, aliquants of several powders spanning the range of alteration present were first subjected to a rather harsh, multiple step acid-leaching procedure ("L" or leached samples in Table 1). This technique differed significantly from the commonly used one-step method of hot or cold HCl-leaching in its use of an ultrasonic bath and the repeated changing of the leaching solution. First worked out in an earlier study [Mahoney et al., 1983], the procedure is broadly similar to one used by H. Staudigel [personal communication, 1986] and also to a related technique utilized by Cheng et al. [this volume] on a highly altered suite of rocks from the Louisville Ridge.

For a given sample, about 200-300 mg of powder were placed in a teflon vial, to which was added 10 ml or more of either 4N or 6N ultra-pure HCl. The vial was capped and agitated ultrasonically for about 20 minutes, by which time the solution was invariably an intense yellow-green color (indicative of dissolved Fe) and milky with suspended particles. The liquid--particles and all--was then removed by pipetting and the vial replenished with fresh HCl; sample powder remaining on the bottom was stirred into suspension and the vial replaced in the ultrasonic bath. This cycle was repeated several times, the acid growing progressively less colored and turbid as HCl-soluble and easily suspended material was consumed. After about 2 hours, on the average, the liquid would remain colorless despite new additions of HCl. At this point the final leachate was removed, the sample rinsed with ultra-pure water and dried. Typically only about 10% of the original volume of powder remained at this stage. X-ray diffraction traces of residues showed peaks of well-crystallized plagioclase and clinopyroxene; no carbonate, clay, or zeolite peaks could be observed [cf. Mahoney et al., 1983] despite the prevalence of these phases in some of the corresponding unleached specimens. Experiments with less severe leaching generally resulted in some smectite being left in the residue.

Nd and Sr isotopic measurements and Sm, Nd, Rb, and Sr isotope dilution concentration analyses were carried out on selected unleached and leached powders, mostly at Scripps. The results are listed in Table 1. After adjustment to the same standard values, splits of several non-plateau basalt samples (Central Indian Ridge MORB) run in both the Scripps and Minnesota laboratories yielded the same ($^{143}Nd/^{144}Nd$) and ($^{87}Sr/^{86}Sr$) within errors [Mahoney et al., 1987, in prep.]. Isotopic fractionation corrections, standard reference values, and experimental uncertainties are given in Table 1. The uncertainties listed with individual samples are either internal (within-run errors) or external (based on repeated analyses of standards), whichever is greater, as defined in the table caption.

Results

Alteration and the Effects of Leaching

The Nd and Sr isotopic data are listed in Table 1 and presented graphically in Figure 2, "age-corrected" to basal sediment and/or top-of-basement ages given in the relevant DSDP volumes. Measured ($^{147}Sm/^{144}Nd$), ($^{87}Rb/^{86}Sr$), and Nd and Sr isotopic ratios were used for the age adjustments for both the leached and unleached samples. This procedure almost certainly does not give true initial Sr isotopic ratios for the unleached rock powders as low-temperature seawater alteration of the type affecting these rocks tends to modify ($^{87}Sr/^{86}Sr$) towards seawater values; it also may add Rb, which over time can increase ($^{87}Sr/^{86}Sr$) as well [e.g., Staudigel et al., 1981]. The former effect is apparently the greater in several of the unleached tholeiites whose Rb and Rb/Sr are very small despite their altered state. High-temperature alteration can remove Rb [e.g., Mottl and Holland, 1978; Menzies and Seyfried, 1979], but there is little evidence of it in most of the low Rb rocks [Jackson et al., 1976; Floyd, 1986].

In all cases, leaching reduced calculated ($^{87}Sr/^{86}Sr$)$_T$ significantly in comparison to the respective unleached samples. For three of the more altered specimens large reductions occurred: from 0.70389 to 0.70284 in MR167-94-3, the most severely altered of the set; from 0.70428 to 0.70346 in OJ289-132-3; and 0.70446 to 0.70401 in M317A-31-3. Rb abundances dropped dramatically with leaching; this is not too surprising considering the clinopyroxene- and plagioclase-rich makeup of the residues, for neither mineral holds Rb. On the other hand, Sr concentrations generally changed little, either increasing or decreasing slightly, probably depending on the

Table 1. Isotopic Ratios and Isotope Dilution Data for Pacific Plateau and Nauru Basin Lavas

	$\left(\frac{^{143}Nd}{^{144}Nd}\right)_0$	$\left(\frac{^{87}Sr}{^{86}Sr}\right)_0$	$\left(\frac{^{147}Sm}{^{144}Nd}\right)_0$	$\frac{^{87}Rb}{^{86}Sr}$	Sm	Nd	Rb	Sr	$\left(\frac{^{87}Sr}{^{86}Sr}\right)_T$	$\left(\frac{^{143}Nd}{^{144}Nd}\right)_T$	$\varepsilon_{Nd}(T)$
			Manihiki Plateau	($T = 110$ m.y.)							
M317A-34-4(72-74)											
Flow 10* U	0.512742 16	0.70444 3	0.1851	0.016	2.683	8.762	0.641	115.9	0.70442	0.512609	+2.2 .3
L	0.512805 14	0.70431 3	0.2713	0.009	0.8346	1.860	0.392	122.6	0.70430	0.512610	+2.2 .3
M317A-34-1(141-143)											
Flow 8 U	0.512676 22	0.70454 3	0.1883	0.027	2.822	9.060	0.920	99.36	0.70450	0.512541	+0.8 .4
L		0.70432 3		0.005			0.199	120.4	0.70431		
M317A-34-1(56-58)											
Flow 7 U	0.512746 14	0.70452 3	0.1853	0.012	2.317	7.560	0.491	115.6	0.70450	0.512613	+2.2 .3
L	0.512808 14	0.70429 3	0.2630	0.005	0.6334	1.456	0.188	118.0	0.70428	0.512619	+2.3 .3
M317A-33-3(124-126)											
Flow 6 U	0.512812 22	0.70432 3	0.1998	0.019	2.011	6.085	0.641	99.32	0.70429	0.512668	+3.3 .4
L	0.512905 30	0.70402 3	0.2991	0.010	0.7530	1.552	0.258	77.52	0.70401	0.512690	+3.7 .6
M317A-32-1(27-29)											
Flow 5 U	0.512813 14	0.70423 4	0.1978	0.008	2.119	6.477	0.292	109.6	0.70422	0.512671	+3.4 .3
M317A-31-3(40-42)											
Flow 3 U	0.512902 22	0.70451 3	0.2039	0.030	2.207	6.544	1.17	112.8	0.70446	0.512755	+5.0 .4
L	0.512946 30	0.70401 3	0.25	0.005	0.40	0.9662	0.161	103.3	0.70401	0.512766	+5.2 .7
			Ontong Java Plateau	($T = 110$ m.y.)							
OJ-289-132-3(52-55)											
U	0.512969 14	0.70457 3	0.1969	0.182	3.272	10.04	8.30	131.7	0.70428	0.512827	+6.4 .3
L	0.513022 16	0.70359 3	0.2788	0.081	1.739	3.770	2.13	75.72	0.70346	0.512821	+6.3 .3
OJ P43 U	0.512841 16	0.70423 3	0.1872	0.034	3.291	10.63	1.63	137.5	0.70418	0.512706	+4.0 .3
OJ P384 U	0.512884 16	0.70421 3	0.1920	0.008	3.255	10.25	0.324	122.9	0.70421	0.512746	+4.8 .3
OJ 8393 U	0.512832 14	0.70456 3	0.1847	0.125	2.581	8.448	6.00	138.5	0.70436	0.512699	+3.9 .3

Nauru Basin (T = 110 m.y.)

Sample	$^{143}Nd/^{144}Nd$	$\pm$	$^{87}Sr/^{86}Sr$	$\pm$	$^{147}Sm/^{144}Nd$	$^{87}Rb/^{86}Sr$	Sm	Nd	Rb	Sr	$(^{87}Sr/^{86}Sr)_T$	$(^{143}Nd/^{144}Nd)_T$	$\epsilon_{Nd}(T)$	$\pm$
N462A-21-1(91-93) U	0.512955	14	0.70398	3	0.1940	0.013	3.676	11.45	0.566	127.4	0.70396	0.512815	+6.2	.3
N462A-51-4(28-30) Glass	0.512964	24	0.70366	3	0.2046	0.044	2.085	6.158	1.40	91.68	0.70359	0.512817	+6.2	.5
N462A-56-1(9-10) Glass	0.512975	14	0.70367	3	0.2047	0.044	2.091	6.173	1.42	93.11	0.70360	0.512828	+6.4	.3
U			0.70390	3										
L	0.512993	14	0.70363	3	0.2211	0.008	1.625	4.443	0.223	78.02	0.70362	0.512834	+6.5	.3

Magellan Rise (T = 135 m.y.)

Sample	$^{143}Nd/^{144}Nd$	$\pm$	$^{87}Sr/^{86}Sr$	$\pm$	$^{147}Sm/^{144}Nd$	$^{87}Rb/^{86}Sr$	Sm	Nd	Rb	Sr	$(^{87}Sr/^{86}Sr)_T$	$(^{143}Nd/^{144}Nd)_T$	$\epsilon_{Nd}(T)$	$\pm$
MR167-94-3(132-133) U	0.513050	14	0.70401	3	0.1972	0.065	3.284	10.07	3.94	174.1	0.70389	0.512876	+8.0	.3
L	0.513195	14	0.70288	3	0.2736	0.025	0.6680	1.476	1.33	152.7	0.70284	0.512953	+9.5	.3
MR167-95-1(143-145) L	0.513019	16	0.70324	3	0.2216	0.048	1.165	3.176	4.34	261.7	0.70315	0.512823	+7.0	.3

Hess Rise (T = 110 m.y.)

Sample	$^{143}Nd/^{144}Nd$	$\pm$	$^{87}Sr/^{86}Sr$	$\pm$	$^{147}Sm/^{144}Nd$	$^{87}Rb/^{86}Sr$	Sm	Nd	Rb	Sr	$(^{87}Sr/^{86}Sr)_T$	$(^{143}Nd/^{144}Nd)_T$	$\epsilon_{Nd}(T)$	$\pm$
H464-34-CC U	0.513044	14	0.70405	3	0.1821	0.170	2.975	9.875	7.90	134.0	0.70379	0.512913	+8.1	.3
H465A-42-2(76-78) U	0.512851	14	0.70447	3	0.0962	0.445	10.94	68.70	34.8	226.6	0.70378	0.512782	+5.5	.3

Indian Ocean (T = 35 m.y.)

Sample	$^{143}Nd/^{144}Nd$	$\pm$	$^{87}Sr/^{86}Sr$	$\pm$	$^{147}Sm/^{144}Nd$	$^{87}Rb/^{86}Sr$	Sm	Nd	Rb	Sr	$(^{87}Sr/^{86}Sr)_T$	$(^{143}Nd/^{144}Nd)_T$	$\epsilon_{Nd}(T)$	$\pm$
238-58-1(123-136) Glass	0.513022	14	0.70347	3	0.2312	0.070	2.801	7.323	2.43	100.1	0.70343	0.512969	+7.3	.3
L	0.513027	14	0.70341	3	0.2454	0.015	2.946	7.254	0.520	97.74	0.70340	0.512971	+7.3	.3

- Isotopic fractionation corrections: $(^{86}Sr/^{88}Sr) = 0.1194$; $(^{148}NdO/^{144}NdO) = 0.242436$ [$(^{148}Nd/^{144}Nd) = 0.241572$] Scripps $(^{146}Nd/^{144}Nd) = 0.7219$ Minnesota

- Isotopic data are all reported relative to standard values measured at Scripps: $(^{87}Sr/^{86}Sr) = 0.71026$ for NBS 987 Sr and 0.70804 for E&A Sr; $(^{143}Nd/^{144}Nd) = 0.511859$ for La Jolla Nd and 0.512632 for BCR-1. $(^{143}Nd/^{144}Nd) = 0.51264$ corresponds to $\epsilon_{Nd}(0) = 0$.

- In many cases within-run errors on individual samples $(2\sigma_m)$ are smaller than the ranges measured for La Jolla Nd and NBS 987 Sr standards; the latter, external uncertainties are given instead. The Scripps total range for NBS 987 is ±0.000026; for La Jolla Nd it is ±0.000014 (0.3 ε units). At Minnesota $2\sigma_m$ was ±0.00003 for NBS 987 and ±0.000022 (0.4 ε units) for La Jolla Nd.

- Uncertainties on Scripps concentration measurements are as reported in Stosch and Lugmair (1984).

* Manihiki flow numbers are those given in Jackson et al. (1976).

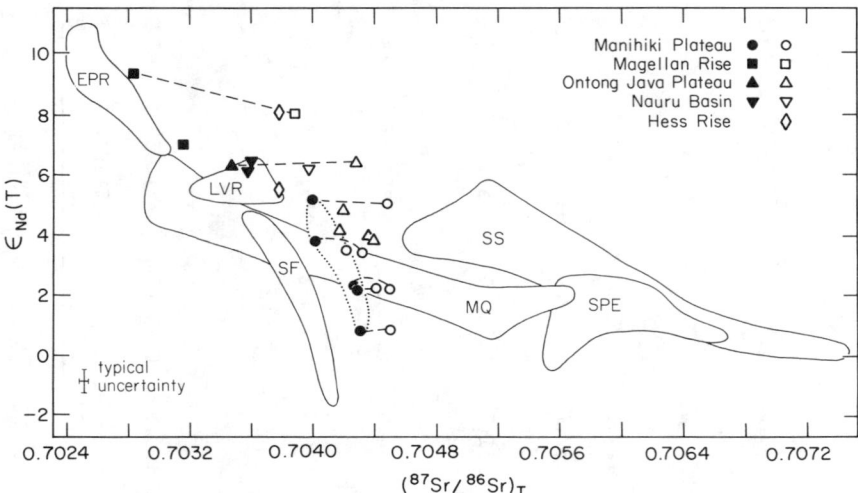

Fig. 2. Age-adjusted Nd and Sr isotopic data for plateau and Nauru Basin igneous rocks. Fields for some Pacific islands, island chains, and ridge basalts are shown for reference. Open symbols represent unleached samples, filled symbols are leached samples or glasses. Dashed lines connect points for leached and unleached splits of the same sample. Dotted field is for leached Manihiki basalts. Data are from Table 1, excepting one Ontong Java point from Bielski-Zyskind et al. [1984]. EPR: field of East Pacific Rise, Easter Microplate, and Easter Island basalts of Macdougall and Lugmair [1986]. LVR: Louisville Ridge [Cheng et al., this volume]. MQ: Marquesas Islands [Vidal et al., 1984; Duncan et al., 1986]. SF: San Felix and Juan Fernandez islands [Gerlach et al., 1986]. SS: Samoan shields; SPE: Samoan post-erosional lavas [Wright and White, 1987].

relative enrichment of plagioclase to clinopyroxene in the residues, on their proportions in the original rocks, and of course, on Sr abundances in both the altered and unaltered (glass, mesostasis, for example) components removed by leaching. In conjunction with indications from XRD traces these results all suggest that the leached residues contained very little altered material; as such their calculated $(^{87}Sr/^{86}Sr)_T$ values should be quite close to the true initial ratios for the corresponding whole-rocks. There is further evidence that this is true (see below).

Leaching also caused pronounced decreases in concentrations of Nd and Sm, and substantial increases in $(^{147}Sm/^{144}Nd)$ and present-day $\varepsilon_{Nd}(0)$. These results are consistent with clinopyroxene enrichment in particular, and also emphasize that the leaching procedure removes some unaltered, as well as altered, portions of the rock; elemental abundances in the residues therefore do not represent original bulk-rock compositions. Significantly, calculated initial $\varepsilon_{Nd}(T)$ values are identical, within errors, between respective leached and unleached powders in 5 out of 6 cases, confirming expectations that Sm-Nd systematics are disturbed negligibly by moderate degrees of seawater alteration. For most of the plateau samples, therefore, $\varepsilon_{Nd}(T)$ calculated from $(^{147}Sm/^{144}Nd)$ and $\varepsilon_{Nd}(0)$ on unleached powders should indeed represent erupted whole-rock initial values. On the other hand,

for extremely altered basalts such as MR167-94-3 this conclusion is not necessarily valid. In this sample secondary smectite, carbonate, sulfides, and even feldspars have almost completely replaced the original phases (however, no Mn coating is present) [Bass et al., 1973]. Here leaching resulted in a 1.5 unit increase in calculated $\varepsilon_{Nd}(T)$ (from +8.0 to +9.5) implying that some extraneous, low ε_{Nd} Nd became incorporated into leachable portions of the rock. Whether or not it was derived directly from circulating seawater (with a mere $\sim 3 \times 10^{-6}$ ppm Nd, a very large seawater/rock ratio would seem to be required), from solutions carrying remobilized Nd from metalliferous sediments in the vicinity, or even represents a pre-alteration, late-stage magmatic contaminant from earlier basalt flows or suspected sediment layers reposing beneath the upper basalts at this site [cf. Bass et al., 1973] cannot be ascertained at present. The sense of change towards greater $\varepsilon_{Nd}(T)$ with leaching is consistent with all these possibilities; given the condition of the sample, however, it seems reasonable to ascribe the change to alteration. Even so, nothing quantitative can be said about this secondary component as the leaching procedure irreproducibly removes suspended, unaltered primary material, soluble primary material (i.e., glass), along with secondary suspended and dissolved species, thus precluding mass balance calculations. A case of even more extreme modification of Nd isotopic ratios during severe alteration of submarine lavas is documented by Cheng et al. [this volume].

As a direct test of how effectively the leaching procedure used in this study recovers alteration-free whole-rock $(^{87}Sr/^{86}Sr)_T$, a sample of altered (smectite + carbonate) crystalline basalt from the same rock chip as glass N462A-56-1 (9-10) was powdered and leached. The leached powder gave a value of 0.70362 ($\pm$0.00003), within uncertainty the same result as the fresh glass (0.70360; Table 1). Additionally, powder of an altered, carbonate-veined, ca. 38 m.y. Central Indian Ridge pillow basalt interior (from DSDP site 238-58-1 (123-136)) was leached, analyzed, and compared isotopically with the corresponding fresh glass from the pillow rim. Again the values were essentially identical (0.70343 for the glass, 0.70340 for the leached powder). In both cases, calculated initial Nd isotopic ratios for glasses and leached powders were the same within errors (Table 1).

One of the two Hess Rise specimens is a basalt (unleached) whose elevated $(^{87}Sr/^{86}Sr)$ relative to its MORB-like $\varepsilon_{Nd}(T)$ (Figure 2) is consistent with its advanced degree of alteration. The other is a trachyte (also unleached) from site 465A; in spite of some alteration its comparatively low $(^{87}Sr/^{86}Sr)_T$ (Figure 2) indicates that its greater Sr (226.6 ppm) and Rb (34.8 ppm) concentrations probably minimized seawater modification of its Sr isotopic ratio.

In contrast to the very rare specimens of basement rocks available from the large plateaus, many were recovered from the deep drillholes at sites 462 and 462A, which penetrated some 650 m into the non-edifice-building Cretaceous volcanic complex filling the Nauru Basin. Interestingly, the three Nauru Basin lavas analyzed in this study, as well as two measured recently by Castillo et al. [1986] all possess identical $\varepsilon_{Nd}(T)$ (~+6.2), within errors. A larger range has been documented in Sr isotopes (0.70354 to 0.70403) based on 34 analyses, 31 of which were performed on crystalline whole-rocks or density separates [Fujii et al., 1981; Notsu et al., 1986; Castillo et al., 1986; this study]. Fujii et al. [1981] and Castillo et al. [1986] considered the Sr isotopic ratios to represent true mantle source variation because one-step HCl leaching of a single sample produced no decrease in $(^{87}Sr/^{86}Sr)$. In the present work the two unleached, crystalline samples gave relatively high values of 0.70398 and 0.70390; the two fresh glasses, the leached powder, plus a plagioclase separate analyzed by Castillo et al. [1986], possess lesser initial values between 0.70354 and 0.70362, suggesting that alteration has elevated Sr isotopic ratios somewhat in some of these rocks.

Note that $(^{147}Sm/^{144}Nd)$ for the unleached basalts clusters narrowly around the chondritic average of ~0.196 [Jacobsen and Wasserburg, 1980]. Thus ε_{Nd} of these rocks has changed only negligibly since their eruption in the Lower Cretaceous (with the probable exception of MR167-94-3), and the ε_{Nd} notation is convenient for comparing the plateau data with results from present day mantle-derived volcanic rocks. Likewise, the basaltic whole-rock Rb/Sr values tend to be quite small, notwithstanding the undoubted elevation of Rb contents by alteration in some instances, implying sources with even lesser Rb/Sr; had the plateau basalt sources not been melted until today, their $(^{87}Sr/^{86}Sr)$ would not be very different than in the Lower Cretaceous.

Summary of Plateau Basalt Isotopic and Chemical Data

The plateau isotopic data span a wide range: $\varepsilon_{Nd}(T)$ varies from +9.5 to +0.8, $(^{87}Sr/^{86}Sr)_T$ for leached powders from 0.70284 to 0.70431. Points for the leached (as well as many of the unleached) specimens all plot well within the field of isotopic values defined by volcanic rocks from mid-ocean ridges, intraplate oceanic islands and island chains in the modern Pacific (Figure 2). The Manihiki lavas, for example, describe a trend closely paralleling that recently reported for the San Felix and Juan Fernandez islands [Gerlach et al., 1986], whereas the leached Magellan Rise basalt data fall very near values for East Pacific Rise (EPR) MORB, the Easter Microplate, and Easter Island [Macdougall and Lugmair, 1986].

Sm, Nd, and Sr contents in the unleached samples (Table 1) are very similar to levels in MORB. Based on published analyses, other incompatible element abundances among the Manihiki, Ontong Java, and Nauru Basin lavas (which are both more numerous and less altered than the existing Hess Rise or Magellan Rise basalts) are generally within a factor of ~2 of concentrations in average N-type MORB [Stoeser, 1975; Jackson et al., 1976; Hughes and Turner, 1977; Fujii et al., 1981; Batiza, 1981; Seifert, 1981; Floyd, 1986; Saunders, 1986; Castillo et al., 1986]; that is, within the variations typically found in MORB itself (see Figure 3). The Manihiki flows from site 317A actually have smaller average concentrations of most incompatible elements (0.7-0.8X) than average MORB (Table 1; Jackson et al., 1976). Scrutiny of interelement ratios, however, reveals that the existing plateau and Nauru Basin basalts possess slight but apparently consistent enrichments over N-type MORB in highly incompatible elements resistant to seawater alteration (Figure 3). The broadly chondritic Nd/Sm ratios mentioned above, for instance, contrast with the Nd/Sm less than chondritic of normal MORB; and where available, plateau Nb/Y, La/Yb, Ta/Zr, Th/Ti, etc. are somewhat greater than in average normal MORB [e.g., Scott, 1981; Batiza, 1981; Castillo et al., 1986; Floyd, 1986; Saunders, 1986].

In terms of bulk compositions most of the plateau and Nauru Basin basalts are quartz- and/or hypersthene-normative tholeiites. Major

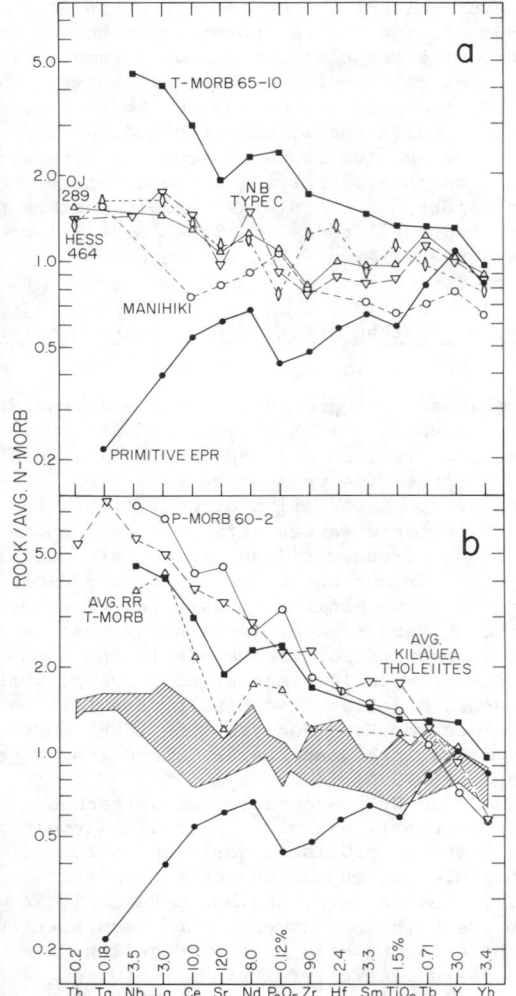

Fig. 3. Alteration-resistant incompatible element patterns, normalized to average N-type MORB [Pearce, 1983; supplemented by values in Saunders, 1986]. (a) Patterns for analyzed oceanic plateau basalts compared with the primitive EPR MORB of Puchelt and Emmermann [1983] and T-type MORB 65-10 of Le Roex et al. [1983]. Manihiki: average of site 317A samples [Jackson et al., 1976; this paper]. OJ 289: site 289 Ontong Java basalt [Stoeser, 1975; Batiza, 1981; this paper]. Hess 464: site 464 Hess Rise basalt [Vallier et al., 1983; this paper]. NB type C: Nauru Basin site 462A average of type C of Floyd [1986], supplemented by pertinent values from Castillo et al. [1986] and Saunders [1986]. (b) Includes information in (a) except hatched band replaces individual plateau basalt patterns. Also shown are patterns for average Reykjanes Ridge (RR) T-type MORB [from Saunders, 1986], an average of Kilauea tholeiites [Leeman et al., 1980; with BHVO-1 values for Nb, Sr, P, and Y from Sun et al., 1979], and P-type MORB 60-2 of Le Roex et al. [1983].

element and mineral compositions, particularly spinel compositions of Manihiki and Nauru lavas--which are characterized by very high Cr-numbers relative to MORB--indicate that they are products of quite high degrees of partial melting at relatively shallow levels [Clague, 1976; Tokuyama and Batiza, 1981; Dick and Bullen, 1984; Castillo et al., 1986]. Considering the sum of mineralogical and chemical characteristics, Tokuyama and Batiza [1981] have proposed that the existing plateau and Nauru Basin lavas represent a new category of oceanic basalt, which they term "oceanic plateau basalt."

Discussion

The Sources of the Pacific Plateaus

Perhaps most relevant for theories of plateau origins is that the Manihiki, Ontong Java, and Nauru Basin lavas possess ocean-island-type isotopic signatures, whereas Nd isotopic ratios of the Magellan and Hess Rise tholeiites approach those of present-day EPR MORB (Figure 2). Tholeiites erupted onto continental interiors can have MORB-like or ocean-island-like isotopic characteristics too, but in a given suite or province some lavas usually display values not found (so far) among products of the oceanic mantle. Particularly diagnostic are large negative $\varepsilon_{Nd}(T)$ and Sr isotopic compositions causing data to fall well away from the oceanic mantle field in plots such as Figure 2 [e.g., Carter et al., 1978; Mahoney et al., 1982; Hawkesworth et al., 1983; Menzies et al., 1983; Carlson, 1984]. In some continental basalt provinces lavas with such properties constitute a large majority [e.g., Hawkesworth et al., 1983; Menzies et al., 1983]. Additionally, continental tholeiites typically exhibit chemical characteristics distinct from those of any of the Pacific plateau basalts, especially in their highly variable but often very substantial enrichments in the more incompatible elements. As noted above, the modest enrichments and comparatively uniform chemical properties of the plateau lavas more naturally have invited close comparisons with MORB. The lack of any samples with clear continental isotopic or chemical signatures thus weakens the case for any significant involvement of old continental lithosphere in their petrogenesis (either as a contaminant or a source of magmas). In a study of ultramafic mantle nodules from the southwestern tip of the Ontong Java Plateau (Malaita) Bielski-Zyskind et al. [1984] likewise found no evidence for continental influences. Of course, no definitive conclusions can be reached for such large edifices on the basis of the very scanty existing sample populations. The data at hand, however, argue against the presence of extensive, old continental basements under the volcanic caps of these plateaus.

If a predominantly oceanic nature is indicated,

the question of plateau origins is nevertheless far from answered. In particular, the broadly MORB-like chemical characteristics of the available basalts do not obviously tally with the distinctly oceanic-island-like or plume-type isotopic signatures of the Manihiki, Ontong Java, and Nauru Basin samples. Intraplate oceanic island tholeiites generally exhibit marked enrichments in highly incompatible elements, in which respect they are grossly similar to many continental basalts [e.g., Thompson et al., 1983]. There appear to be several possible ways to reconcile the plateau isotopic data with the low incompatible element contents, slight enrichments in highly incompatible elements, and evidence that many of these lavas are the products of high degrees of partial melting. It is worth noting that aside from their relevance for understanding oceanic plateaus themselves, observation of such features in an allochthonous terrane on land could be critical in deciphering its early history.

1) The Pacific plateaus could simply be enormously thick accumulations of otherwise ordinary, Lower Cretaceous MORB [Hussong et al., 1979]. A spreading ridge origin during periods of slow or restrained spreading, and/or excessive volcanic output has been championed by several authors, as noted earlier. In light of the present geochemical data this hypothesis would require that the mantle sources feeding the Lower Cretaceous ridge crests be isotopically and compositionally distinct from those now supplying the EPR (or the Atlantic and Indian ridges, for that matter). No Nd or Sr isotopic analyses of "normal" Lower Cretaceous or Jurassic Pacific MORB exist, to my knowledge. Significantly however, major and trace element data on available samples show that they are depleted in highly incompatible elements and chemically indistinguishable from modern EPR N-type MORB--quite unlike the mildly incompatible-element-enriched plateau lavas [Saunders, 1986]. Future results on Mesozoic Pacific seafloor could change the picture, of course, but currently this explanation is not favored.

2) A second possibility, envisioned by Fujii et al. [1981] specifically for the non-edifice-building Nauru Basin complex, involves large-scale remelting of oceanic island mantle source regions that had been depleted previously of oceanic island magmas. Based upon the new results indicating extreme isotopic homogeneity in the Nauru Basin [Castillo et al., 1986; this paper], the mantle source would have had to be isotopically quite homogeneous to begin with, and then be depleted more or less uniformly of its oceanic island magmas relatively shortly before the Nauru Basin melting episode.

A conservative estimate of the volume of the Nauru Basin volcanics is 250,000 km^3 (assuming an average thickness of some 600 m and an areal extent of more than 400,000 km^2 [e.g., Floyd, 1986]). If the basalts are the products of ca. 20% partial melting, as suggested by Castillo et al. [1986], then their mantle source would have occupied at least 1.3×10^6 km^3. In comparison, the large oceanic island of Hawaii is made up of several (isotopically distinct) volcanoes with volumes between 16.6×10^3 km^3 and 42.5×10^3 km^3, comprising a total volume of about 117×10^3 km^3 [Shaw et al., 1980]. Supposing the erupted lavas represent 10% partial melts of their sources, a roughly 1.1×10^6 km^3 residual mantle region is available for later remelting. Such a reservoir would be more or less sufficient in size for the Nauru Basin complex.

This mechanism appears to be incapable, however, of accounting for the vastly greater volumes of magma required to form the large oceanic plateaus. The Ontong Java Plateau, for example, has an area in excess of 1.5×10^6 km^2 and an average crustal thickness of about 36 km [Hussong et al., 1979], corresponding to a volume of $\sim 5.4 \times 10^7$ km^3. A previously depleted mantle source yielding secondary 20% partial melts would encompass at least 2.7×10^8 km^3; that is more than 245 times the volume of depleted mantle beneath the big island of Hawaii. Even if the initial source depletion were by oceanic island magmas corresponding to only 1% partial melts, the available depleted mantle region would still be 25 times too small. Conceivably the proto-Ontong-Java source could have been tapped by numerous, large, closely adjacent oceanic islands draining non-overlapping zones of the mantle; but such a model appears cumbersome and contrived, especially if also applied to the other large Pacific plateaus. It also begs the question of how and where the plateaus were actually formed.

3) An alternative and presently preferred explanation is that the Manihiki, Ontong Java, and presumably the Hess and Magellan lavas represent high degree partial melts of ocean-island-type mantle material mixed with variable amounts of MORB mantle. Mixing of two end members (each of which could consist of more than one isotopic "component" [e.g., White, 1985]) is suggested in particular by the observed correlations between Sm/Nd and $\varepsilon_{Nd}(T)$ for the Manihiki and Ontong Java samples (Figure 4)--the only edifices for which several specimens are available. More generally this idea is consistent with the incompatible element ratios of the plateau lavas, which are to a first order intermediate between those of N-type MORB and oceanic island basalts; whereas their small incompatible element contents can be accounted for by a combination of advanced melting and mixing.

The most likely plate tectonic environment for generating such voluminous volcanic piles with the observed geochemical features would appear to be where a melting anomaly known as a hotspot is situated near or under a slow-spreading ridge. This idea fits well with other evidence suggesting ridge crest origins [e.g., Kroenke, 1972; Winterer et al., 1974; Vallier et al.,

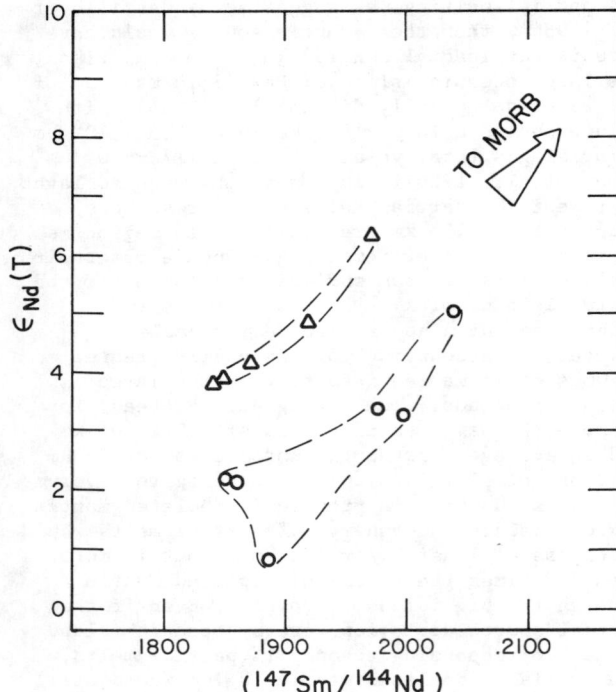

Fig. 4. $\varepsilon_{Nd}(T)$ vs. $(^{147}Sm/^{144}Nd)$ for unleached Ontong Java and Manihiki samples. Note that correlations appear to trend towards values typical of MORB. Uncertainty on $\varepsilon_{Nd}(T)$ is as shown in Figure 2; uncertainty on $(^{147}Sm/^{144}Nd)$ is less than width of symbols. Interestingly, "ages" of ca. 1500 m.y. are obtained from pseudo-isochrons fitted through the data for the two plateaus; these are much older than the ca. 200 m.y. figures derived from some suggested mixtures of oceanic-island-type and MORB mantle [e.g., Le Roex et al., 1983]. In the context of the mixing hypothesis discussed in the text the correlations need not have any age significance.

1983]. Modern hotspot plateaus, such as the Icelandic and Galapagos plateaus, are much less extensive than most of the Pacific Cretaceous ones but possess broadly similar morphology and appear to be formed in just such settings. The Icelandic example is by far the best-studied; significantly, several workers have pointed out that although not perfect (see Figure 3), the closest chemical analogues to the Nauru Basin basalts--and by inference, to the existing plateau lavas--are tholeiites from the Reykjanes Ridge [Floyd, 1986; Notsu et al., 1986; Saunders, 1986; Castillo et al., 1986].

In the framework of a mantle plume model, Schilling et al. [1983] have argued that much of the trace element and isotopic variation among Icelandic rift zone basalts reflects differences in proportions of plume and MORB mantle source material owing to temporal variations in plume flux and spreading rate. The generally modest incompatible element enrichments of the Pacific plateau basalts may indicate MORB-dominated rather than plume-dominated (or more generally, blob- or ocean-island-mantle-dominated) magma sources; so too may evidence that the plateau surfaces, although initially at relatively shallow depths, were never much, if any, above sea level [cf. Schilling et al., 1983]. Of the analyzed samples, the Manihiki lavas have the lowest $\varepsilon_{Nd}(T)$; because they appear to be products of high degrees of melting, their alteration-resistant incompatible element ratios should resemble those of their immediate sources fairly closely. Model calculations using plausible isotopic parameters, and Sm/Nd characteristics within the range of values presumed for the sources of many oceanic islands (i.e., Sm/Nd ~ 0.26-0.28) and EPR MORB (i.e., Sm/Nd ~ 0.34-0.40) can reproduce the observed isotopic and trace element ranges for the Manihiki plateau with a MORB-dominated source if the ε_{Nd} of the oceanic-island-type end member is slightly negative. In this context the incompatible element enrichment of the Magellan and Hess Rise tholeiites [e.g., Bass et al., 1973; Vallier et al., 1983], coupled with their more MORB-like Nd and leached Sr isotopic signatures, could suggest oceanic-island-type end members isotopically more like Pacific MORB than those of the Manihiki and Ontong Java lavas; or they could reflect a greater contribution of MORB source material and slightly lesser degrees of partial melting.

The analogy with Iceland cannot be carried very far, at least at present. Although about 50% of Icelandic rift zone tholeiites can be classified on a major element basis as MORB-like [Imsland, 1983], volcanic rocks from Iceland exhibit much greater lithological and chemical variation than observed so far on the Pacific plateaus. In large part the apparent difference may prove to be an artifact of the acute undersampling of the latter. Recalling that on all the Pacific plateaus only five drill holes reached the top of basement, the thick trachyte sequence encountered on the Hess Rise at site 465A [Vallier et al., 1983] and the alkalic lavas of Malaita [Hughes and Turner, 1977] indeed suggest that a wide range of rock types actually exists on the plateaus. The Icelandic case is further complicated by the migration of the Mid-Atlantic Ridge over Icelandic lithosphere produced earlier; the consequent reworking of this older material [Oskarsson et al., 1985] leads to magmas whose detailed provenance is uncertain. Such a process may have operated on some or all of the Cretaceous Pacific plateaus as well, but cannot be assessed without much more detailed information than currently is available.

Note that whereas the isotopic and chemical data can be explained by high degree partial melts of mixed oceanic-island-type and MORB-type mantle, they do not themselves require the direct presence of hotspots per se. In conjunction with other information—not the least of which is their great volume—near-ridge hotspot origins provide a plausible explanation for the large plateaus. On the other hand, the comparatively diminutive, Lower Cretaceous Nauru Basin complex appears to have been erupted in an intraplate location onto Jurassic crust already 20-40 m.y. old, based on well-defined Jurassic magnetic lineations crossing the Basin [e.g., Castillo et al., 1986]. There are other conceivable ways of introducing oceanic-island-type material into MORB mantle, however; for instance it could be spread out into streaks by convective dispersion along flow lines far from a point of origin [e.g., Fitton and James, 1986]. If ultimately derived from an enriched blob or plume at a hotspot, such material could even have been slightly depleted of incompatible elements before leaving the vicinity of the hotspot, thereby reducing elemental abundances without immediately disturbing isotopic ratios and thus facilitating subsequent generation of basalts with Nauru Basin-type trace element signatures [cf. Fujii et al., 1981]. Of course, other geometries also are possible [e.g., Le Roex et al., 1983]. The Nauru Basin complex lies adjacent to and is roughly contemporaneous with the huge Ontong Java Plateau (Figure 1); no known tectonic discontinuity divides them, and it has been proposed that they may be related to the same volcanic event [Batiza et al., 1981; Kroenke et al., 1986]. The virtually identical Nd and Sr isotopic ratios of the two Nauru Basin glasses and the leached sample from site 289 on the northern Ontong Java Plateau (Figure 2; Table 1) indeed are suggestive of related mantle sources. In the framework of a rise crest hotspot model it is thus possible that the plume-type component in the Nauru Basin could have an association with the presumed hotspot supplying magmas to the Ontong Java Plateau.

Which Hotspots for Which Plateaus?

On plate tectonic grounds Gordon and Henderson ["Pacific plate hotspot tracks," preprint, 1986] have also recently proposed a near-ridge hotspot origin for the Pacific oceanic plateaus, and further, specified as sources known or postulated hotspots thought to have later created major Pacific island and seamount chains. They contend that the Magellan Rise formed above the Easter hotspot, for example, and that the putative Louisville hotspot gave rise to the Ontong Java Plateau; a possible Easter hotspot link to the Manihiki Plateau is also speculated. Earlier, Duncan and Hargraves [1984] suggested a Galapagos hotspot origin (off-ridge, however) for the thickened core of the Caribbean region. Ultimately plate tectonic evidence will probably decide the viability of these hypotheses; it is not yet clear how helpful isotopic data will be in testing them. The extent to which hotspots represent compositional as well as melting anomalies in the convecting upper mantle is not known with certainty. Perhaps more important in the present discussion, geochemical variations in the erupted products of a hotspot are not well documented as a function of time, particularly in the South Pacific. However, isotopic studies of the Ninetyeast Ridge [Mahoney et al., 1983], New England Seamounts [Taras and Hart, 1983], and Louisville Ridge [Cheng et al., this volume] suggest that at least some hotspots may "breed true" for periods of 20-80 m.y.; that is, that the range of isotopic values associated with a hotspot in the recent past may not have changed dramatically during much longer periods.

If the major assumption of a fixed range of isotopic compositions since the Lower Cretaceous is made for a given hotspot, then an associated oceanic plateau would be expected to exhibit isotopic ratios between the extreme low $\varepsilon_{Nd}(T)$ values observed for products of the hotspot and those of MORB. Inasmuch as the leached Magellan Rise basalts bear a close isotopic resemblance to the field described by present day Easter Island, Easter Microplate, and EPR lavas (Figure 2), Gordon and Henderson's [1986] proposed relationship thus is supported, whereas an Easter hotspot origin for the Manihiki Plateau is not. Isotopic compositions of seamounts along ~4000 km of the Louisville Ridge are remarkably constant ($\varepsilon_{Nd}(T)$ = +5.2 to +6.4; $(^{87}Sr/^{86}Sr)_T$ = 0.7035 $\pm$ 0.0003) and nearly independent of rock type or age of underlying oceanic lithosphere; as such they indicate a long-lived (ca. 70 m.y.), isotopically quite homogeneous mantle source whose isotopic signature does not vary significantly with degree or depth of melting [Cheng et al., this volume]. The single leached Ontong Java sample has suitably low $(^{87}Sr/^{86}Sr)_T$ = 0.70346; Sr isotopic values of the other Ontong Java tholeiites are greater but the samples have not yet been leached. However, four of the five Ontong Java basalts analyzed possess lesser $\varepsilon_{Nd}(T)$ (+3.8 to +4.8) than any of the Louisville Ridge seamounts. The available data therefore do not appear to offer much support for a Louisville hotspot connection to the Ontong Java Plateau. Overall, although it is tempting to make these sorts of evaluations, such exercises are at best premature. Much more extensive sampling—and analysis—of plateau crusts is required, along with work on seamount chains emanating from postulated parental hotspots. Planned Pb isotopic measurements on the existing plateau basalts should help in further assessing individual hotspot influences, as well as the roles and relative importance of MORB and oceanic-island-type sources in plateau genesis.

Conclusions and Summary

Nd and Sr isotopic data on Pacific oceanic plateaus provide new insights into their nature and possible origins. Seawater alteration has elevated $(^{87}Sr/^{86}Sr)$ in the plateau basalts, in some cases substantially; however the multi-step acid-leaching procedure described here reduced ($^{87}Sr/^{86}Sr$) to values that are probably very close to whole-rock initial ratios. For all but extremely altered samples Sm-Nd systematics are not disturbed measurably by alteration. Thus initial Nd isotopic ratios determined from both leached and unleached powders appear to give reliable estimates of original rock values in moderately altered specimens. The plateau isotopic data strongly suggest oceanic island or plume-type affinities, particularly for the Manihiki and Ontong Java basalts; this result stands in contrast to their chemical characteristics, which are essentially those of slightly enriched MORB. If discovered in basalts of an accreted terrane, such a combination might be a key indication of an early stage as an oceanic plateau. So far, neither the isotopic nor chemical data give any clear indication of old continental basements beneath the surfaces of these plateaus. Rather, it is suggested that geological and geophysical information favoring ridge crest origins is compatible with the isotopic and chemical evidence if plateau formation took place in the vicinity of near-ridge hotspots. Such settings provide plausible environments for a) voluminous, edifice-building magmatism, b) high degrees of partial melting, and c) mixing of ocean-island-type mantle with MORB mantle, all of which appear consistent with current, very limited knowledge about these plateaus. Known hotspots may have produced some or all of the plateaus, but understanding of both hotspot-related geochemical variations as a function of time and of the full isotopic spectrum existing on individual plateaus is as yet too incomplete for comparisons of plateau and hotspot-produced island chain data to be diagnostic of such relations.

Acknowledgments. This research was supported in part by NSF grants to J. D. Macdougall, G. W. Lugmair, and V. Rama Murthy, and a U. of H. grant to the author. The assistance of Qun Cheng and Chris MacIsaac, who helped with various aspects of the work, including the preparation and measurement of two samples at the last minute, is greatly appreciated. The Ministry of Natural Resources of the Solomon Islands is thanked for the Malaitan samples, and the DSDP for providing the others. Reviewers Bill White, James Rubenstone, and Rick Carlson provided many helpful, thoughtful comments. This is Hawaii Institute of Geophysics contribution no. 1848.

References

Bass, M. N., R. Moberly, J. M. Rhodes, C.-Y. Shih, and S. Church, Volcanic rocks cored in Central Pacific, Leg 17, Deep Sea Drilling Project, Init. Rep. Deep Sea Drill. Proj., 17, 429-503, 1973.

Batiza, R., Trace element characteristics of Leg 61 basalts, Init. Rep. Deep Sea Drill. Proj., 61, 689-696, 1981.

Batiza, R., S. Shcheka, H. Tokuyama, K. Muehlenbachs, T. L. Vallier et al., Summary and index to petrological and geochemical studies of Leg 61 basalts, Init. Rep. Deep Sea Drill. Proj., 61, 829-840, 1981.

Bielski-Zyskind, M., G. J. Wasserburg, and P. H. Nixon, Sm-Nd and Rb-Sr systematics in volcanics and ultramafic xenoliths from Malaita, Solomon Islands, and the nature of the Ontong Java Plateau, J. Geophys. Res., 89, 2415-2424, 1984.

Carlson, R. L., N. I. Christensen, and R. P. Moore, 1980, Anomalous crustal structures in ocean basins: continental fragments and oceanic plateaus, Earth Planet. Sci. Lett., 51, 171-180, 1980.

Carlson, R. W., Isotopic constraints on Columbia River flood basalt genesis and the nature of the subcontinental mantle, Geochim. Cosmochim. Acta, 48, 2357-2372, 1984.

Carter, S. R., N. M. Evensen, P. J., Hamilton, and R. K. O'Nions, Neodymium and strontium isotope evidence for crustal contamination of continental volcanics, Science, 202, 743-747, 1978.

Castillo, P., R. Batiza, and R. J. Stern, Petrology and geochemistry of Nauru Basin igneous complex: large-volume, off-ridge eruptions of MORB-like basalt during the Cretaceous, Init. Rep. Deep Sea Drill. Proj., 89, 555-576, 1986.

Cheng, Q., K.-H. Park, J. D. Macdougall, A. Zindler, G. W. Lugmair, J. Hawkins, P. Lonsdale, and H. Staudigel, Isotopic evidence for a hotspot origin of the Louisville seamount chain, this volume, 1987.

Clague, D. A., Petrology of basaltic and gabbroic rocks dredged from the Danger Island troughs, Manihiki Plateau, Init. Rep. Deep Sea Drill. Proj., 33, 891-911, 1976.

Cockerham, R. S., and R. D. Jarrard, Paleomagnetism of some Leg 33 sediments and basalts, Init. Rep. Deep Sea Drill. Proj., 33, 631-648, 1976.

Dick, H. J. B., and T. Bullen, Chromian spinel as a petrogenetic indicator in abyssal and alpine-type peridotites and spatially associated lavas, Contrib. Mineral. Petrol., 86, 54-76, 1984.

Duncan, R. A., and R. B. Hargraves, Plate tectonic evolution of the Caribbean region in the mantle reference frame, Geol. Soc. Am. Mem., 162, 81-93, 1984.

Duncan, R. A., M. T. MuCulloch, H. G. Barsczus, and D. R. Nelson, Plume versus lithospheric sources for melts at Ua Pou, Marquesas Islands, Nature, 322, 534-538, 1986.

Fitton, J. G., and D. James, Basic volcanism associated with intraplate linear features, Phil. Trans. R. Soc. Lond. A, 317, 253-266, 1986.

Floyd, P. A. Petrology and geochemistry of oceanic intraplate sheet-flow basalts, Nauru Basin, Deep Sea Drilling Project Leg 89, Init. Rep. Deep Sea Drill. Proj., 89, 471- 497, 1986.

Fujii, N., K. Notsu, and N. Onuma, Chemical compositions and Sr isotopes of Deep Sea Drilling Project Leg 61 basalts, Init. Rep. Deep Sea Drill. Proj., 61, 697-700, 1981.

Gerlach, D. C., S. R. Hart, V. W. J. Morales, and C. Palacios, Mantle heterogeneity beneath the Nazca plate: San Felix and Juan Fernandez islands, Nature, 322, 165-169, 1986.

Hammond, S. R., L. W. Kroenke, and F. Theyer, Northward motion of the Ontong-Java Plateau between -110 and -30 m.y.: a paleomagnetic investigation of DSDP site 289, Init. Rep. Deep Sea Drill. Proj., 30, 415-418, 1975.

Hawkesworth, C. J., A. J. Erlank, J. S. Marsh, M. A. Menzies, and P. van Calsteren, Evolution of the continental lithosphere: evidence from volcanics and xenoliths in southern Africa, in Continental Basalts and Mantle Xenoliths, edited by C. J. Hawkesworth and M. J. Norry, pp. 111-138, Shiva Publishing, Ltd., Cheshire, 1983.

Heezen, B. C., B. Glass, and H. W. Menard, The Manihiki Plateau, Deep-Sea Res., 13, 445-458, 1966.

Hilde, T. W. C., S. Uyeda, and L. Kroenke, Evolution of the western Pacific and its margin, Tectonophys., 38, 145-165, 1977.

Hughes, G. W., and C. C. Turner, Upraised Pacific Ocean floor, southern Malaita, Solomon Islands, Geol. Soc. Am. Bull., 88, 412-424, 1977.

Hussong, D. M., L. K. Wipperman, and L. W. Kroenke, The crustal structure of the Ontong Java and Manihiki plateaus, J. Geophys. Res., 84, 6003-6010, 1979.

Imsland, P., Iceland and the ocean floor: comparison of chemical characteristics of the magmatic rocks and some volcanic features, Contrib. Mineral. Petrol., 83, 31-37, 1983.

Jackson, E. D., K. E. Bargar, B. P. Fabbi, and C. Heropoulos, Petrology of the basaltic rocks drilled on Leg 33 of the Deep Sea Drilling Project, Init. Rep. Deep Sea Drill. Proj., 33, 571-630, 1976.

Jacobsen, S. B., and G. J. Wasserburg, Sm-Nd isotopic evolution of chondrites, Earth Planet. Sci. Lett., 50, 139-155, 1980.

Kroenke, L. W., Geology of the Ontong-Java Plateau, Hawaii Inst. Geophys. Rept., HIG-72-5, 119 pp., 1972.

Kroenke, L. W., Origin of continents through development and coalescence of oceanic flood basalt plateaus, Eos Trans. AGU, 55, 443, 1974.

Kroenke, L. W., and K. Nemoto, Marine geology of the Hess Rise. 2. Basement morphology, sediment thickness, and structural geology, J. Geophys. Res., 87, 9259-9278, 1982.

Kroenke, L. W., J. M. Resig, and P. A. Cooper, Tectonics of the southeastern Solomon Islands: formation of the Malaita Anticlinorium, in Geology and Offshore Resources of Pacific Island Arcs - Central and Western Solomon Islands Region, edited by J. J. Vedder and D. L. Tiffin, Circum-Pacific Council for Energy and Mineral Resources, Earth Science Series, 4, 109-116, 1986.

Larson, R. L., S. M. Smith, and C. G. Chase, Magnetic lineations of early Cretaceous age in the western equatorial Pacific Ocean, Earth Planet. Sci. Lett., 15, 315-319, 1972.

Leeman, W. P., J. R. Budahn, D. C. Gerlach, D. R. Smith, and B. N. Powell, Origin of Hawaiian tholeiites: trace element constraints, Am. J. Sci., 280A, 794-819, 1980.

Le Roex, A. P., H. J. B. Dick, A. J. Erlank, A. M. Reid, F. A. Frey, and S. R. Hart, Geochemistry, mineralogy and petrogenesis of lavas erupted along the Southwest Indian Ridge between the Bouvet triple junction and 11 degrees east, J. Petrol., 24, 267-318, 1983.

Macdougall, J. D., and G. W. Lugmair, Sr and Nd isotopes in basalts from the East Pacific Rise: significance for mantle heterogeneity, Earth Planet. Sci. Lett., 77, 273-284, 1986.

Mahoney, J. J., J. D. Macdougall, G. W. Lugmair, A. V. Murali, and K. Gopalan, Origin of the Deccan Trap flows at Mahabaleshwar inferred from Nd and Sr isotopic and chemical evidence, Earth Planet. Sci. Lett., 60, 47-60, 1982.

Mahoney, J. J., J. D. Macdougall, G. W. Lugmair, and K. Gopalan, Kerguelen hotspot source for the Ninetyeast Ridge?, Nature, 303, 385-389, 1983.

Menzies, M. A., and W. E. Seyfried, Basalt-seawater interaction: trace element and strontium isotopic variations in experimentally altered glassy basalt, Earth Planet. Sci. Lett., 44, 463-472, 1979.

Menzies, M. A., W. P. Leeman, and C. J. Hawkesworth, Isotope geochemistry of Cenozoic volcanic rocks reveals mantle heterogeneity below western USA, Nature, 303, 205-209, 1983.

Moberly, R., and L. W. Kroenke, Sedimentary record on oceanic plateaus, Proc. Ann. Meet. AAPG-SEPM, April, 1974.

Mottl, M. J., and H. D. Holland, Chemical exchange during hydrothermal alteration of basalt by seawater. I. Experimental results for major and minor components of seawater, Geochim. Cosmochim. Acta, 42, 1103-1115, 1978.

Nixon, P. H., Kimberlites in the south-west Pacific, Nature, 287, 718-720, 1980.

Notsu, K., N. Onuma, and N. Fujii, (1986) Rb-Sr isotope systematics and Sr/Ca-Ba/Ca ratios of Nauru Basin basalts, Deep Sea Drilling Project Leg 89, Init. Rep. Deep Sea Drill. Proj., 89, 523-527, 1986.

Nur, A., and Z. Ben-Avraham, Oceanic plateaus, the fragmentation of continents, and mountain building, J. Geophys. Res., 87, 3644-3661, 1982.

Oskarsson, N., S. Steinthorsson, and G. E. Sigvaldason, Iceland geochemical anomaly: origin, volcanotectonics, chemical fractionation and isotope evolution of the crust, J. Geophys. Res., 90, 10,011-10,025, 1985.

Pearce, J. A., Role of the sub-continental lithosphere in magma genesis at active continental margins, in Continental Basalts and Mantle Xenoliths, edited by C. J. Hawkesworth and M. J. Norry, pp. 230-249, Shiva Publishing, Ltd., Cheshire, 1983.

Puchelt, H., and R. Emmermann, Petrogenetic implications of tholeiitic basalt glasses from the East Pacific Rise and the Galapagos spreading center, Chem. Geol., 38, 39-56, 1983.

Rogers, G. C., Oceanic plateaus as meteorite impact structures, Nature, 255, 126-128, 1981.

Saunders, A. D., Geochemistry of basalts from the Nauru Basin, Deep Sea Drilling Project Legs 61 and 89: implications for the origin of oceanic flood basalts, Init. Rep. Deep Sea Drill. Proj., 89, 499-517, 1986.

Schilling, J.-G., P. S. Meyer, and R. H. Kingsley, Rare earth geochemistry of Iceland basalts: spatial and temporal variations, in Structure and Development of the Greenland-Scotland Ridge, edited by M. H. P. Bott, S. Saxov et al., pp. 319-342, Plenum Press, New York and London, 1983.

Scott, R. B., Geochemistry of igneous rocks in Deep Sea Drilling Project hole 465A, Hess Rise: significance to oceanic plateau petrology and evolution, Init. Rep. Deep Sea Drill. Proj., 62, 955-960, 1981.

Shaw, H. R., E. D. Jackson, and K. E. Bargar, Volcanic periodicity along the Hawaiian-Emperor chain, Am. J. Sci., 280-A, 667-708, 1980.

Siefert, K. E., Geochemistry of Nauru Basin basalts from the lower portion of hole 462A, Deep Sea Drilling Project Leg 61, Init. Rep. Deep Sea Drill. Proj., 61, 705-708, 1981.

Staudigel, H., S. R. Hart, and S. H. Richardson, Alteration of the oceanic crust: processes and timing, Earth Planet. Sci. Lett., 52, 311-327, 1981.

Stoeser, D. B., Igneous rocks from Leg 30 of the Deep Sea Drilling Project, Init. Rep. Deep Sea Drill. Proj., 30, 401-444, 1975.

Stosch, H.-G., and G. W. Lugmair, Evolution of the lower continental crust: granulite facies xenoliths from the Eifel, West Germany, Nature, 311, 368-370, 1984.

Sun, S. S., R. W. Nesbitt, and A. Y. Sharaskin, Geochemical characteristics of mid-ocean ridge basalts, Earth Planet. Sci. Lett., 44, 119-138, 1979.

Taras, B., and S. R. Hart, Sr, Nd and Pb isotopic compositions of the New England Seamount Chain, Eos Trans. AGU, 64, 907, 1983.

Thompson, R. N., M. A. Morrison, A. P. Dicken, and G. L. Hendry, Continental flood basalts ... arachnids rule OK?, in Continental Basalts and Mantle Xenoliths, edited by C. J. Hawkesworth, and M. J. Norry, pp. 158-185, Shiva Publishing, Ltd., Cheshire, 1983.

Tokuyama, H., and R. Batiza, Chemical composition of igneous rocks and origin of the sill and pillow-basalt complex of Nauru Basin, Southwest Pacific, Init. Rep. Deep Sea Drill. Proj., 61, 673-687, 1981.

Uyeda, S., and V. Vacquier, Geothermal and geomagnetic data in and around the island of Japan, in The Crust and Upper Mantle of the Pacific Area, edited by L. Knopoff, G. L. Drake, and P. J. Hart, p. 349-366, AGU, Washington, D.C., 1968.

Vallier, T. L., W. E. Dean, D. K. Rea, and J. Thiede, Geologic evolution of the Hess Rise, central North Pacific Ocean, Geol. Soc. Am. Bull., 94, 1289-1307, 1983.

Vidal, Ph., C. Chauvel, and R. Brousse, Large mantle heterogeneity beneath French Polynesia, Nature, 307, 536-538, 1984.

Watts, A. B., J. H. Bodine, and N. M. Ribe, Observations of flexure and the geological evolution of the Pacific Ocean basin, Nature, 283, 532-537, 1980.

White, W. M., Sources of oceanic basalts: radiogenic isotope evidence, Geology, 13, 115-118, 1985.

Winterer, E. L., Anomalies in the tectonic evolution of the Pacific, in The Geophysics of the Pacific Ocean Basin and its Margin, edited by G. H. Sutton, M. H. Manghnani, and R. Moberly, p. 269-278, AGU, Washington, D.C., 1976.

Winterer, E. L., P. F. Lonsdale, J. L. Matthews, and B. R. Rosendahl, Structure and acoustic stratigraphy of the Manihiki Plateau, Deep-Sea Res., 21, 793-814, 1974.

Wright, E., and W. M. White, The origin of Samoa: new evidence from Sr, Nd and Pb isotopes, Earth Planet. Sci. Lett., in press, 1987.

MINERALOGICAL STUDIES OF SAMOAN ULTRAMAFIC XENOLITHS: IMPLICATIONS FOR UPPER MANTLE PROCESSES

Elizabeth Wright

Department of Geological Sciences, University of Illinois, Chicago, IL 60680

Abstract. Two types of ultramafic xenoliths are included in Samoan post-erosional lavas: harzburgite-lherzolite (HL) nodules showing porphyroclastic and equigranular-mosaic textures, and dunite-wehrlites (DW) showing tectonized cumulate textures. Signs of reaction and equilibration with the host lavas include zonation within olivine and chromite grains in the xenolith and reaction of xenolith orthopyroxene in contact with undersaturated host liquids to form olivine + clinopyroxene + glass. Textures such as symplectic intergrowth of chromite with silicate phases and variable recrystallization indicate a history of vertical movement of mantle material prior to inclusion of that material in upward-migrating magmas. HL mineral compositions suggest that they sample infusible residue remaining after a melting episode which may have produced the Samoan shields, whereas the DW group may represent early cumulates from those lavas. The two groups may form the oceanic analogs to the division between Cr-diopside and Al-augite types of xenoliths observed in continental settings.

Introduction

Ultramafic inclusions, or xenoliths, are commonly found in alkalic and Si-undersaturated basasltic lavas erupted in oceanic settings [e.g. White, 1966; Jackson and Wright, 1970; Tracey, 1980; Kirby and Green, 1980; Wright, 1985] and continental settings [e.g. Leggo and Hutchison, 1968; Dawson et al., 1970; Kutolin and Frolova, 1970; Frey and Green, 1974; Wilshire and Shervais, 1975; Pike, 1976; Varne, 1977; Frey and Prinz, 1978; Basu, 1979; Cohen et al., 1984]. Ultramafic nodules may have a variety of origins. These include the following, as discussed by White [1966]: clumps of phenocrysts formed in the enclosing lava; fragments of accumulated material precipitated from the enclosing lava (cognate inclusions) or some previous magma episode; fragments of infusible residue left behind from a melting event which may or may not have formed the enclosing lava; fragments of primary mantle which may or may not be the source of the enclosing lava; accidental fragments of totally unrelated mantle or crustal material. For each xenolith suite, these hypotheses must be evaluated using textural and mineralogical observations, mineral modes and compositions, bulk geochemical data, and geothermometric and geobarometric calculations. The study of xenoliths provides important clues to the nature of the earth's mantle and the dynamics of melt genesis and migration. In the case of the Samoan Islands that mantle appears to have unusually enriched geochemical characteristics which makes characterization of the xenolith suite particularly important [Wright, 1984; 1986; Wright and White, in press]. This paper will discuss the types, textures and mineralogy of ultramafic xenoliths from the Samoan Islands, as well as features such as metamorphic recrystallization, compositional and textural changes, and reactions between host lavas and xenoliths, which give clues to the history of the upper mantle below Samoa.

Location

The Samoan linear volcanic chain sits on the Pacific plate about 120 km north of the westward-trending portion of the Tonga Trench. The chain is composed of a series of large basaltic shield volcanoes, forming the islands (from east to west) of the Manua group, Tutuila, and Upolu (Fig. 1). Shield-building lavas have been postulated on the island of Savai'i on the basis of limited exposures, but these do not define a caldera or otherwise indicate the location of a central vent [Kear and Wood, 1959]. The shield volcanoes of Manua, Tutuila, and Upolu developed large central calderas within which alkalic post-caldera lavas were erupted [Stearns, 1944; Macdonald, 1944; Stice and McCoy, 1968; Natland, 1980; Natland and Turner, in press]. On Tutuila and Upolu, trachyte plugs were intruded along caldera ring faults and through the flanks of the shield volcanoes [Stearns, 1944]. No trachytes are found on Manua.

The shield volcanoes on Tutuila, Upolu, and presumably Savai'i have been capped by voluminous late-Pleistocene to historic lavas, erupted chiefly from a single, narrow rift (about 2 km wide in Upolu and 3.5 km wide in most of Savai'i) which trends 110°, parallel to the trend of the island chain. The line of vents extends the length of Savai'i and Upolu at least, and probably continues under water to a few vents on Tutuila (Fig. 1b). Stearns [1944] compared these eruptions on Tutuila to Hawaiian post-erosional volcanism, noting that they occurred after extinction of the associated shield volcanoes. Natland [1980] applied the term "post-erosional" to analogous flows on Upolu and Savai'i. Hawkins and Natland [1975] and Natland [1980] were able to demonstrate petrological similarities between Samoan and Hawaiian post-erosional lavas, and to distinguish them from the shield series.

Shield-building flows from Upolu and Tutuila have been dated at 2.45-2.80 Ma and 1.27-1.40 Ma, respectively. Post- caldera mugearites and trachytes followed at 1.54 Ma on Upolu and 1.03 Ma on Tutuila [Natland and Turner, in press]. The oldest post-erosional lavas are less than 1 Ma in Western Samoa and are Holocene in age on Tutuila [Stearns, 1944; Kear and Wood, 1959].

Rock Types

Ultramafic xenoliths occur in many Samoan lavas, including both shield-building and post-erosional flows and tuffs. Xenoliths were collected from every island or island group along the chain. Host rocks to the xenoliths include massive and scoriaceous lavas and bedded tuffs, cinder cones and dikes, alkali olivine basalts (AOB), olivine basanitoids, and olivine nephelinites. Most of the xenoliths are small (<10 cm) and angu-

Copyright 1987 by the American Geophysical Union.

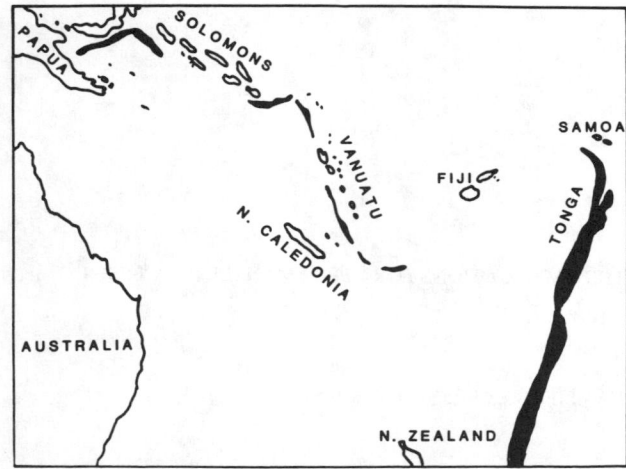

Fig. 1a. Map of the southwest Pacific, showing the Samoan Islands. Trenches are shown in black.

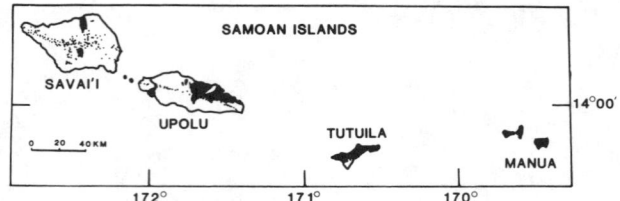

Fig. 1b. Map of the Samoan Islands. Subaerial exposures of shield lavas are shown as black patches; white areas are exposures of post-erosional lavas; post-erosional vents appear as dots.

lar, composed of coarsely crystalline olivine (OL) with lesser amounts of orthopyroxene (OPX), clinopyroxene (CPX) and spinel (SP). Grains vary from <1 mm to 7 mm in size. Many xenoliths, especially those included in massive flows, appear to be elongate and tabular, whereas those in scoria or tuff tend to be more equidimensional. A variety of rock types are represented in the Samoan xenolith suite. The majority of the Samoan xenoliths are assumed to derive from the mantle; only in the shield-building tuffs of Manua were dunites of clearly cumulate origin identified by their fresh, sugary texture and Fe-rich OL. These xenoliths were evidently scavenged from a high level magma chamber or conduit, and are related to the differentiation of the host AOB. They will not be discussed further.

The overwhelming majority of Samoan xenoliths were collected from the young, silica-undersaturated post-erosional flows of Savai'i, Upolu, and Tutuila [Wright, 1986]. The major and trace element evidence suggests that these lavas represent a deeper source than associated shield basalts [Natland, 1980]; it is not surprising, then, that the xenoliths included in the post-erosional flows reflect a larger variety of rock types and textural history than those included in shield-building lavas.

Twenty-six xenoliths from seven post-erosional flows were selected for detailed petrographic study; fourteen of these were further studied by electron microprobe. Most of the xenoliths studied are olivine-rich spinel lherzolites (<90% OL, <35% OPX, <15% CPX) and harzburgites (<3% CPX). One sample (82UL-47x) is unusually rich in OPX (estimated mode: 45%). Three (82SM-42a,b,c) have no OPX at all, but have up to 15% CPX, resulting in their classifications as dunite and olivine wehrlite (Table 1; Fig. 2). All of the samples are olivine-rich.

Mineral compositions and textures of the harzburgite and lherzolite

TABLE 1. Estimated Modes of Samoan Xenoliths

	OL	OPX	CPX	SP	Glass	Type
82TL-83xa	60-70	15-25		5		Harz[1]
82TL-83xb	60	20-25	3-5	10-12	<3	Lherz[2]
82UP-15xa	55-60	25	5-7	<3	<5	Lherz
82UP-15xb	70	10	10	5		Lherz
82UP-15xc	70	10-15	10	5-10		Lherz
82UP-15xd	65-70	15-20	5-10	3-5		Lherz
82UP-15xf	80	10		10		Harz
82UL-47x	40	45	5-10	3-5		Lherz
82SP-10xb	60-65	30	3	<3		Harz
82SP-10xxc	55-60	25	3-5	<3	<3	Harz
82SS-15xa	60-65	20-25	3-5	<3		Lherz
82SS-32xa	65-70	10	5-10	3-5	3-5	Lherz
82SM-42xa	80-85		10-15	<3	<3	Wehrl[3]
82SM-42xb	90		10	<3	<3	Wehrl
82SM-42xc	90-95		5-10	<3	<3	Dunite

[1]harzburgite; [2]lherzolite; [3]wehrlite

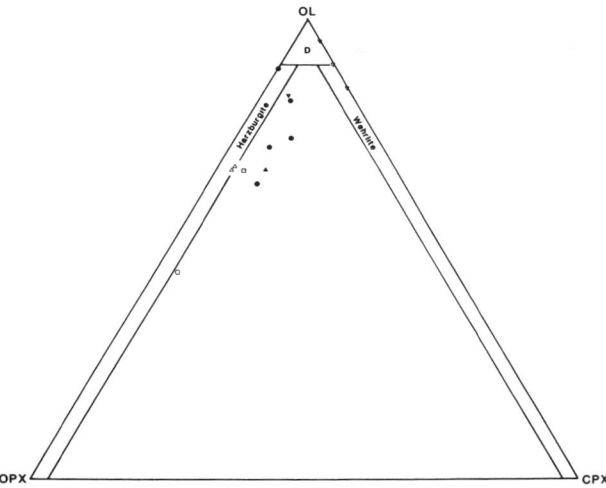

Fig. 2. Ternary plot of modal proportions of olivine, orthopyroxene and clinopyroxene in Samoan ultramafic xenoliths.

xenoliths are largely similar; these samples probably reflect similar origins and stress histories. The dunite-wehrlite group, however, can be clearly distinguished from the others by their lower Mg#'s, Al-rich and Cr-poor SP, and by interstitial and possibly cumulus textures. This will be discussed below. Most Samoan xenoliths have compositions and textures suggesting varying degrees of metamorphism in the upper mantle.

The Harzburgite-Lherzolite Group

Members of the harzburgite-lherzolite (HL) group have mineral assemblages (OL > OPX > CPX > chromite) and mineral compositions (silicate Mg#'s = 89-93) that suggest they represent depleted mantle or a relatively "refractory" residue from melting. However, there are many textural and compositional indications of reaction with the host lavas, including zonation of OL grains at the contact with the host lava, reaction of OPX with the silica-undersaturated host, and veins of fine-grained OL and CPX crystals within the xenoliths. In order to characterize the original compositions of these xenoliths before interaction with the host lavas, it is important to present analyses of interior grains (grains near the center of a xenolith), to identify reaction products, and to document the extent of mineral zonation and other compositional variation.

Representative analyses of xenolith constituent phases are given in Table 2. Little variation in composition was observed in large, interior grains: zonation was absent, and porphyroclasts differed little from coarsely recrystallized mosaic textured grains. Large compositional ranges are, however, observed in grains within fine-grained veins and granular reaction zones, as well as in larger grains in contact with the host.

The Dunite-Wehrlite Group

Members of the dunite-wehrlite (DW) group were found only at a quarry 8 km inland from the western tip of Savai'i. These samples have no OPX. Mg#'s for OL and CPX range from 82-85; these are much lower than the HL group (Table 2). SP grains are less common, and less Cr-rich than the HL chromite (CHR). The DW nodules contain Al-rich SP (with up to 51% Al_2O_3), which are not found in HL xenoliths, and occasional grains of titanomagnetite. CPX is also more aluminous in the DW group: whereas HL CPX generally contain < 4% Al_2O_3, most DW CPX fall in the range of 4-6%.

Textures

Samoan xenoliths contain textural evidence for a variety of processes such as metamorphic recrystallization and incipient partial melting, as well as symplectic textures which suggest a possible response to changing pressure and temperature, and other textures related to interactions between xenolith and host lava. These are discussed below.

The textural variation in the HL xenoliths equals their compositional variation. Textures vary tremendously amongst xenoliths included in a

TABLE 2a. Selected Samoan Xenolith Mineral Compositions: Harzburgites

SP-10xb	OL^1	OL^2	OPX^1	OPX^2	CPX^2	CHR^3
SiO_2	40.38	39.89	55.47	54.81	53.30	.03
TiO_2	.03	.02	.01	.13	.54	4.28
Al_2O_3	.00	.00	2.17	2.92	.62	7.85
Fe_2O_3						15.55
FeO	7.56	11.16	5.21	5.73	4.05	25.75
MnO	.14	.16	.15	.15	.14	.41
MgO	50.59	47.61	34.35	33.71	21.19	7.02
CaO	.10	.25	.86	1.07	17.93	.07
Na_2O	.00	.00	.11	.06	.43	.00
K_2O	.01	.00	.00	.01	.01	.03
P_2O_5	.10	.06	.08	.08	.07	.01
Cr_2O_3	.10	.06	.81	.61	.99	44.07
NiO	.16	.19	.08	.08	.07	.09
sum	99.17	99.40	99.22	99.32	99.27	99.87
Mg#	92.3	88.4	92.2	91.3	90.3	32.9

[1]grain in interior of xenolith; [2]grain in granular reaction zone; [3]cubic chromite

TABLE 2b. Selected Samoan Xenolith Compositions: Lherzolites

	OL[1]	OL[2]	OL[4]	OPX	CPX	CHR
			UP-15xd			
SiO_2	40.85	39.85	38.76	55.76	53.17	.00
TiO_2	.04	.03	.18	.03	.09	.08
Al_2O_3	.00	.06	.77	1.94	2.87	26.56
Fe_2O_3						7.91
FeO	8.29	10.70	17.47	4.93	2.49	11.06
MnO	.15	.21	.34	.15	.14	.21
MgO	51.01	48.46	41.33	33.32	16.69	16.43
CaO	.31	.41	.51	3.15	23.37	.01
Na_2O	.00	.00	.24	.14	1.08	.00
K_2O	.01	.00	.15	.04	.01	.00
P_2O_5	.01	.07	.03	.00	.03	.00
Cr_2O_3	.02	.08	.04	.50	.80	38.35
NiO	.36	.27	.17	.07	.05	.19
sum	101.05	100.14	99.98	100.03	100.77	100.80
Mg#	91.6	89.0	80.8	92.3	92.3	72.6

	OL[1]	OL[4]	OL[2]	OPX	CPX[5]	CPX[2]	CHR[2]	CHR[2]
				UL-47x				
SiO_2	40.35	39.88	38.99	54.99	53.24	52.63	1.41	2.04
TiO_2	.03	.03	.04	.06	.55	.66	5.55	14.74
Al_2O_3	.00	.00	.01	3.43	1.63	1.98	15.94	6.62
Fe_2O_3							10.69	10.01
FeO	8.97	14.43	17.96	5.70	2.76	4.64	22.81	33.10
MnO	.10	.21	.27	.11	.15	.15	.30	.37
MgO	50.40	46.49	43.17	33.75	17.69	18.67	10.55	7.32
CaO	.10	.11	.27	1.09	21.16	19.75	.31	.05
Na_2O	.01	.00	.00	.13	1.02	.63	.08	.55
K_2O	.02	.01	.01	.00	.07	.00	.07	.01
P_2O_5	.03	.06	.09	.02	.04	.00	.02	.00
Cr_2O_3	.08	.02	.09	.82	1.76	1.39	33.66	22.93
NiO	.35	.41	.23	.06	.05	.04	.11	.23
sum	100.42	101.63	101.14	100.16	100.12	100.54	101.50	97.96
Mg#	90.9	85.2	81.1	91.3	92.0	87.7	45.2	28.3

single flow. Most of the textures are metamorphic, in the terminology of Pike and Schwarzman [1977]. Many of the xenoliths display porphyroclastic texture [Mercier and Nicolas, 1975; Pike and Schwarzman, 1977]: small, recrystallized OL grains surround residual, anhedral, strained OL or OPX porphyroclasts (Plate 1). The recrystallized "matrix" often displays a preferred orientation parallel or subparallel to the long dimension of the porphyroclasts. Some xenoliths or parts of xenoliths show an equigranular mosaic texture composed of completely recrystallized, unstrained OL (and pyroxene) grains, "hollyleaf" SP, and regular, 120° triple junctions (Plate 2). This texture may or may not incorporate a preferred linear orientation. This corresponds to the mosaic equigranular texture of Mercier and Nicolas [1975] or, if preferred orientation is present, to the tabular equigranular texture of these authors.

Neoblast sizes range from 7 mm in some samples to 0.5-1.0 mm in others. This corresponds to minimum values for characteristic flow stress of 0.05 kb for the coarse-grained xenoliths and 0.2-0.3 kb for the finer-grained samples, using the relations of Post [1977] and Nicolas [1978]. These values represent mimimum stress estimates because annealing and cold-working may have operated to increase grain size subsequent to deformation [Post, 1977].

Five of the xenoliths, representing inclusions in four different flows, show distinctive "fingerprint patterns" of intergrown CHR and silicate minerals (Plate 3). The silicate is most often massive OPX or its granular melt products (see below), although massive OL or CPX are occasionally present as well.

Several xenoliths show signs of internal partial melting. It is not clear whether this melting occurred prior to the inclusion of the xenolith in the melt, or whether it reflects the heat derived from the enclosing magma, or melting in response to pressure release as the xenolith migrated upward.

According to Pike and Schwarzman [1977], pyroxene grains within the

TABLE 2b. (continued)

	OL core[1]	OL rim[4]	OL[2]	OL[2]	OL[6]	OPX[1]	CPX[2]	CHR[6]
				SS-32xa				
SiO_2	40.44	38.76	37.39	38.26	55.52	41.31	.05	.04
TiO_2	.00	.04	.33	.18	.03	5.53	7.39	15.23
Al_2O_3	.00	.02	.76	.28	1.78	10.79	14.79	12.20
Fe_2O_3							14.75	15.29
FeO	8.24	15.97	17.49	18.58	5.27	7.39	27.91	41.01
MnO	.11	.27	.23	.29	.16	.12	.35	.53
MgO	50.56	44.06	42.90	41.09	34.28	11.10	7.91	4.06
CaO	.03	.32	.35	.35	1.35	22.46	.07	.06
Na_2O	n.d.	n.d.	n.d.	n.d.	n.d.	n.d.	n.d.	n.d.
K_2O	n.d.	n.d.	n.d.	n.d.	n.d.	n.d.	n.d.	n.d.
P_2O_5	n.d.	n.d.	n.d.	n.d.	n.d.	n.d.	n.d.	n.d.
Cr_2O_3	.01	.00	1.18	.50	.57	.16	25.43	14.53
NiO	.36	.19	.16	.20	.13	.07	.18	.04
sum	99.76	99.63	100.79	99.73	99.08	98.93	98.85	98.89
Mg#	91.6	83.1	81.4	79.8	92.1	72.8	33.6	15.0

[1]grain in interior of xenolith; [2]grain in granular reaction zone; [3]cubic chromite; [4]grain at xenolith/host boundary; [5]grain in vein filling; [6]grain in symplectite.

xenolith are first to melt. They refer to this as pyrometamorphic texture. In the Samoan xenoliths, melting appears in internal OPX grains as a fine granular rim around the grain boundaries or, in one case, around a vesicle within an OPX porphyroclast (Plate 4). In some cases it may be argued that such granular areas simply reflect injection of host melt along tiny fractures in the xenolith, but some of these occurrences are clearly not in contact with host melt, indicating that P-T changes alone initiated melting.

In contrast to the porphyroclastic or equigranular mosaic textures of the HL group, the DW xenoliths are strongly inequigranular and relatively unrecrystallized, and lack symplectic textures. Large subhedral OL are surrounded by smaller subhedral OL and irregular, interstitial CPX. No preferred orientation is observed in any section. Most OL grains, both large and small, show strong undulatory extinction bands indicative of severely strained crystal lattices. Subgrain sizes are generally 0.5-1.0 mm, suggesting deviatoric stresses on the order of 0.25 kb [Nicolas, 1978]. Small grains appear to show as much strain as large ones, suggesting that

TABLE 2c. Selected Samoan Xenolith Mineral Compositions: Wehrlites

SM-42xa	OL[1]	CPX[1]	CHR[1]	CHR[1]
SiO_2	39.03	49.78	.00	2.06
TiO_2	.02	1.41	8.58	1.85
Al_2O_3	.00	3.62	10.84	43.62
Fe_2O_3			17.45	7.83
FeO	17.01	5.07	31.68	17.60
MnO	.24	.07	.42	.21
MgO	43.59	15.78	5.89	14.56
CaO	.11	22.94	.11	.22
Na_2O	.00	.43	n.d.	n.d.
K_2O	.01	.00	n.d.	n.d.
P_2O_5	.00	.00	n.d.	n.d.
Cr_2O_3	.06	.92	24.69	13.06
NiO	.21	.07	.21	.24
sum	100.29	100.09	99.87	101.25
Mg#	82.0	84.7	18.1	51.3

[1]grain in interior of xenolith.

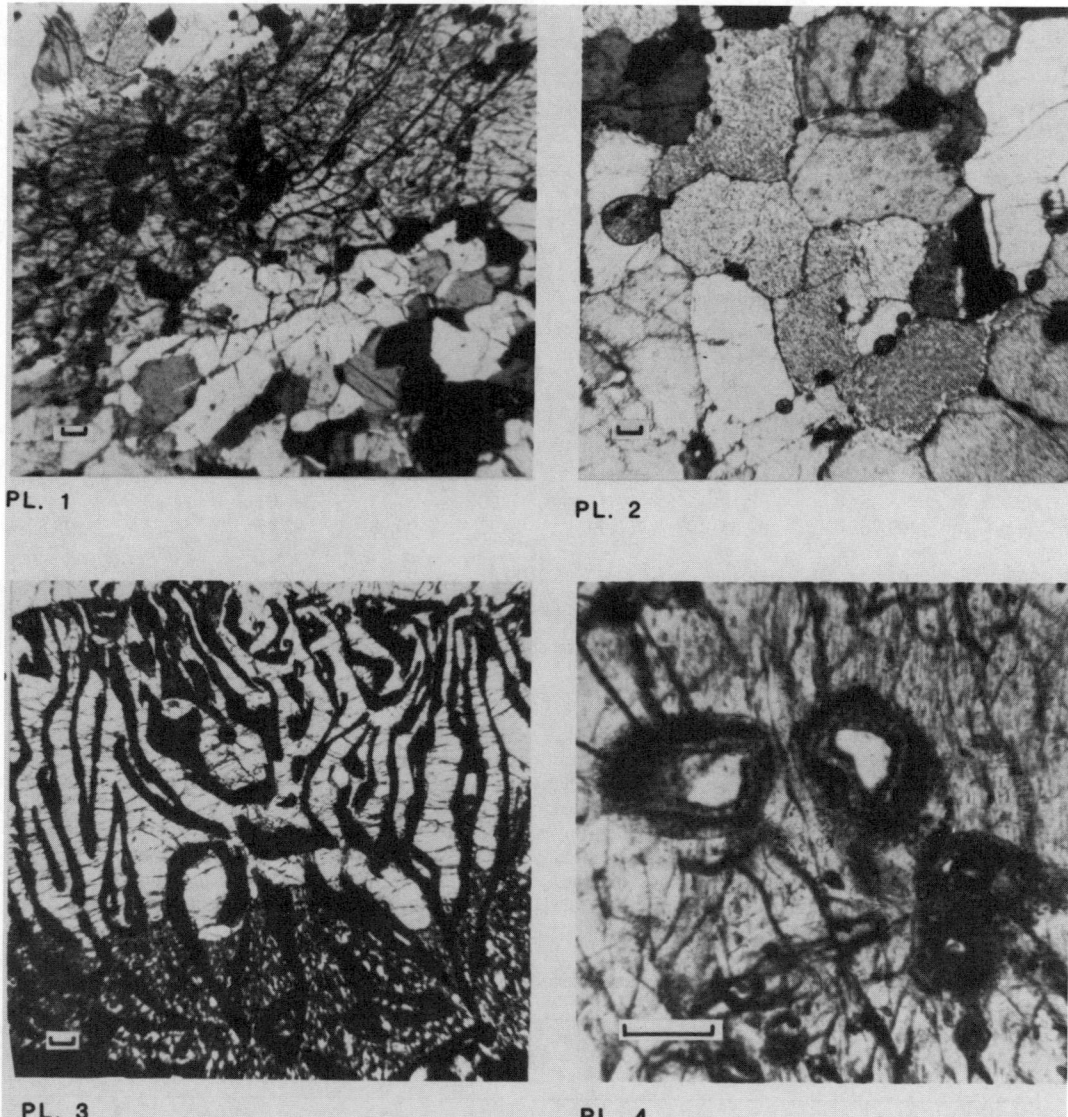

Plate 1. Example of porphyroclastic metamorphic texture. Highly fractured, unrecrystallized orthopyroxene grain about 2 mm long is surrounded by a recrystallized mosaic of olivine and clinopyroxene which shows preferred orientation parallel to the long axis of the porphyroclast. (82UP-15xc) Plate 2. Example of equigranular mosaic metamorphic texture. Unstrained, recrystallized grains of olivine about 0.75 mm in diameter show typical 120° grain boundary junctions and no preferred orientation. (82SP-10xc) Plate 3. Symplectic intergrowth of chromite (dark strands) with orthopyroxene (top half) and orthopyroxene reaction products (lower half). Symplectic texture ends at boundaries with olivine (top) and host lava (bottom). (82UP-15xa) Plate 4. Very fine-grained material around cavities in a large orthopyroxene porphyroclast, indicating incipient localized melting. (82UP-15xc) The scale in all plates is 10 microns.

the smaller grains are not simply the result of recrystallization in response to this deformation, since such recrystallization would be expected to eliminate signs of strain.

As in the HL group, apparent incipient melting has affected the pyroxene grains. DW CPX is "spongy," or filled with glass inclusions (Plate 5). In advanced stages of melting, interstitial pyroxene may begin to disaggregate the unmelted OL grains which compose most of the xenolith, finally seeping into the host melt (Plate 5). Disaggregated OL grains are frequently of the same size and shape as host phenocrysts, which means that phenocryst studies of the post-erosional lavas, even those with no apparent xenoliths, may be biased by the presence of xenocrysts.

Discussion

Interactions with Host Lavas

Many of the xenoliths in the post-erosional series rocks show signs of partial re-equilibration or reaction with the enclosing lavas. Minerals in

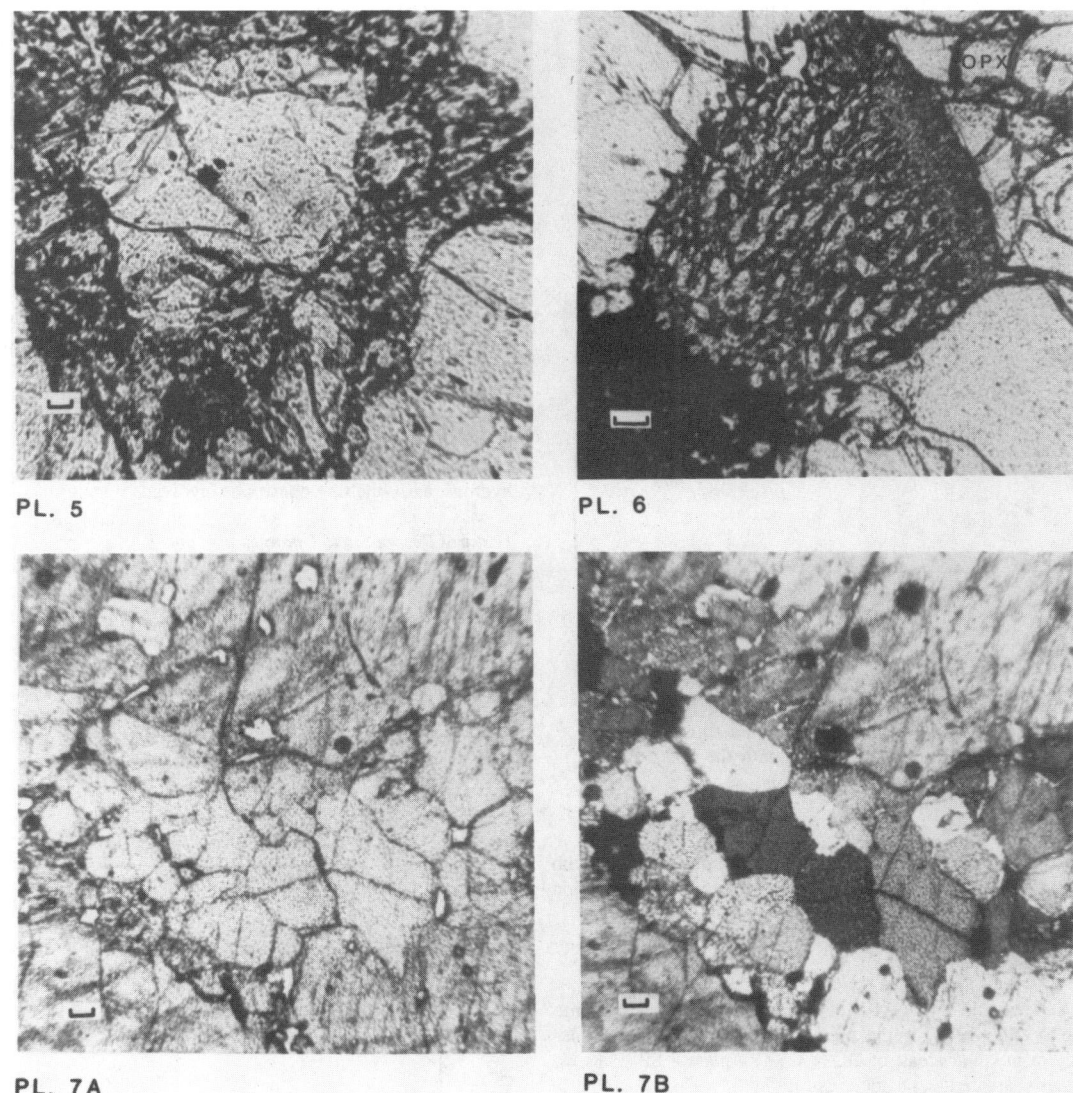

Plate 5. Cumulate olivine and interstitial clinopyroxene in tectonized cumulate wehrlite-dunite. Clinopyroxene is saturated with fine glass inclusions, suggesting incipient (re)melting. (82SM-42xa) Plate 6. Reaction of orthopyroxene in harzburgite xenolith with nephelinite host to form a fine-grained mass of olivine + clinopyroxene + glass + spinel. See text for explanation. (82UP-15xa) Plate 7a. Unfractured lens of recrystallized olivine, surrounded by highly fractured, unrecrystallized olivine and orthopyroxene. (82SP-10xb) Plate 7b. Same, crossed polars. The scale in all plates is 10 microns.

contact with the host frequently show zonation at their rims toward host rock phenocryst compositions. Similarly, grains isolated from the host lavas within a xenolith interior often have more magnesian compositions than grains of the same mineral on the edge of the xenolith. Individual mineral reactions are summarized below.

1. Chromian Spinel. Figure 3 is a plot of Cr vs. Al cations within SP. SP compositions from xenolith-bearing post-erosional lavas plot within a broad field, indicating a general fractionation trend from early-crystallizing Cr-, Al-rich SP to later-forming Cr- and Al-poor titanomagnetite [Wright, 1986]. Also plotted are core and rim compositions of xenolith SP, where the rims are near to, or in contact with, the host lava. In every case where the xenolith SP core composition differs markedly from the magmatic SP fractionation trend, the rim composition of the xenolith SP approaches that trend. This is true regardless of whether the xenolith SP fall on the high-Al or high-Cr side of the magmatic trend. In general, Cr-rich SP appear to have reacted with less fractionated liquids than the Cr-poor SP. This was also noted by Tracey [1980] in Tahitian xenoliths.

2. Olivine and Orthopyroxene. Evidence of equilibration between xenolith silicate minerals and the host lavas appears in Figure 4, a plot showing distribution of Fe and Mg between OL and OPX. Most xenolith OL grains fall in the range Fo 88-93, and the ratio $[Fe/(Fe+Mg)]_{OPX}/[Fe/(Fe+Mg)]_{OL}$ varies from 0.66 to 1.0, all reasonable mantle values. However, analyses of OL-OPX pairs near the rims of the xenoliths show that this OL is much more Fe-rich - values which in fact overlap the range in host OL compositions. OPX compositions do not

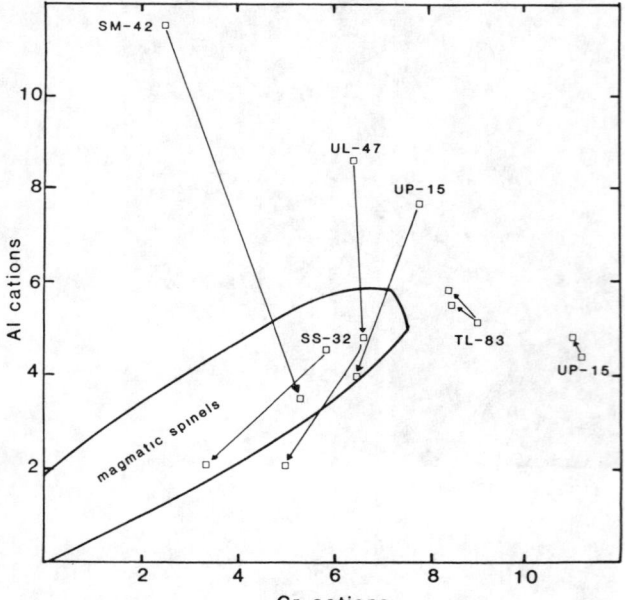

Fig. 3. Plot of Cr vs. Al cations in Samoan spinels, showing re-equilibration of xenolith spinels with host compositions. The field labeled "magmatic spinels" represents spinel compositions from post-erosional lavas. Pairs of points represent cores and rims of xenolith spinels, where rims are near to or in contact with the host. Arrows point to rim analyses.

The OPX reaction areas of one xenolith (82UP-15xa) were investigated in some detail using the electron microprobe. Analyses of the components are given in Tables 3 and 4. Most of the reaction products are homogeneous in composition, except for the interstitial glass, which varied drastically within 10-20 microns. It is clear from these analyses that some additional input is needed to produce the concentrations of Ti, K, Na, and P observed in the bulk composition of the granular area from an equal volume of OPX; hence a combination of melting and reaction of OPX with a basaltic liquid is required, as opposed to simple incongruent melting of OPX.

Frey and Green [1974] suggested that incongruent melting of a hydrous phase such as phlogopite or amphibole produced glass which they observed within xenoliths included in Victorian (Australia) basanites. The only Victorian glass analysis which resembles 82UP-15xa glass is found on the edge of the nodule, presumably near to or in contact with a host lava very similar to the Samoan host, rather than in the cores of xenoliths near to relict phlogopite. Since glass in Samoan nodules is largely restricted to faces in contact with the host melt, it seems more likely that input from the host enriched the xenolith glass in Na, K, etc., than that a hydrous, early-melting phase was involved.

Textural Responses to Changes in P and T

Some of the xenoliths are strongly fractured and sheared, and give evidence of deviatoric stress or substantial, rapid changes in total pressure; others, even in the same flow, show little evidence of such fracturing. Many of the larger, strained OL grains are cross-cut by streamers of bubbles, probably filled with CO_2 [Roedder, 1965]. Recrystallization of OL and pyroxene generally eliminates fractures, bubble streams, and strained extinction. In other cases (e.g. 82UP-15xd), pervasive fractures cross-cut

seem to be affected, probably because they were not in direct contact with the host lava. OPX in contact with host melts has without exception reacted to form OL and glass.

Reaction Melting of Orthopyroxene

One feature common to many OPX-bearing xenoliths from this suite and others [e.g. Varne, 1977] is the presence of patches of very fine-grained mosaics, or granular areas, of OL (+ CPX) + glass + SP (Plate 6). These occurrences share certain characteristics:
1. They usually occur between xenolith OPX and the host, i.e., where xenolith OPX grains come into contact with alkalic, Si-undersaturated host lavas.
2. Where the xenolith OPX is still visible, a "buffer zone" of very fine-grained CPX protects it from direct contact with the granular area.
3. The granular area always includes OL, and often CPX and glass as well.
4. SP take the form of euhedral inclusions in granular OL grains.

It has long been known that under certain P-T conditions enstatite melts incongruently to form forsterite and a silica liquid [Bowen and Anderson, 1914]. It has been suggested [White, 1966; Kutolin and Frolova, 1970] that the input of heat from the enclosing host magma may be sufficient to melt xenolith OPX, given local concentrations of H_2O, CO_2, and possibly alkalis to flux the melting. A more reasonable explanation is that OPX in contact with a basaltic liquid, which may be but need not be the alkalic host magma, reacted to form OL, occasional CPX, and liquid of variable composition. As has been noted, OPX is strongly incompatible with the highly Si-undersaturated post-erosional lavas, most of which are nepheline normative. It is likely, therefore, that of all the xenolith phases, OPX would readily react upon contact with these liquids.

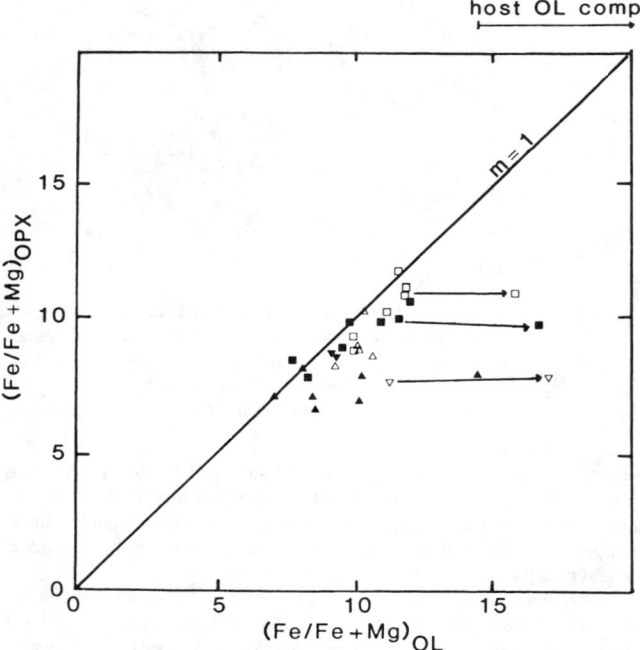

Fig. 4. Plot showing the distribution of Fe and Mg between olivine and orthopyroxene within Samoan xenoliths. Arrows point from olivine-orthopyroxene pairs within the xenolith interiors to pairs on the edges of the same xenoliths, showing re-equilibration of olivine compositions with the host lava compositions (shown in upper right).

TABLE 3. Orthopyroxene Reaction Products: UP-15xa

	OL	CPX	SP	glass	glass	glass	glass	Xen OPX	bulk comp.[1]
SiO_2	39.54	54.28	2.06	41.08	46.20	48.88	46.92	55.63	41.50
TiO_2	.02	.27	2.28	6.26	4.01	3.83	3.81	.03	.46
Al_2O_3	.00	1.95	17.81	9.71	18.43	16.94	16.72	2.25	1.88
FeO*	13.41	4.21	28.25	7.67	8.57	7.71	9.23	5.34	11.92
MnO	.25	.13	.32	.05	.17	.15	.20	.13	.22
MgO	46.87	20.45	12.02	11.19	2.80	3.04	3.38	34.53	38.87
CaO	.32	15.07	.31	22.99	8.95	7.68	8.31	1.11	3.46
Na_2O	.01	.77	.16	.70	4.73	4.47	4.31	.01	.18
K_2O	.01	.61	.16	.04	3.47	3.91	3.51	.00	.32
P_2O_5	.08	.00	.05	.04	2.13	1.70	1.95	.01	.18
Cr_2O_3	.10	1.04	38.42	.18	.04	.07	.03	.60	1.01
NiO	.19	.05	.14	.05	.00	.00	.00	.60	1.01
sum	100.80	98.83	103.00	99.96	99.48	98.38	98.36	99.64	100.23

[1]Bulk composition = .75(OL) + .15(CPX) + .08(GL) + .02(SP), based on estimate of modal abundances of reaction products.

even the smaller, recrystallized grains (Plate 7). This fracturing clearly post-dated at least one episode of recrystallization, and may well have occurred immediately prior to or during inclusion and transport of the xenoliths within the host lava.

The variation in textures between xenoliths close to each other in mineralogy and included in a single flow suggests that the stress regime in the upper mantle parent rock may have varied significantly within a fairly small volume due to localized movement. This situation is illustrated in 82UP-15xb (Plate 8), which consists of alternating coarse- and fine-grained zones separated by streamers of blocky CHR. The fine-grained sections are largely recrystallized with a preferred orientation parallel to the line of opaque grains, whereas the coarse-grained sector is somewhat strained. Both sections are fractured. I suggest that this sample represents a zone of shear, in which the coarse-grained material is a coherent, resistant lens and the fine-grained areas are shear zones taking up the motion around this lens. The CHR grains are thus metamorphically concentrated along the planes of greatest differential motion. This indicates that gradients of deformation may be very sharp within the mantle, enabling relatively closely spaced samples to reflect a variety of degrees of deformation.

Symplexis

Basu and MacGregor [1975] discussed CHR-silicate intergrowths (symplectites) which they found in harzburgites and lherzolites from kimberlites. These symplectites were generally intergrowths of SP and CPX, although they did observe some of SP and OPX. They noted that symplexis generally occurred between large OL and OPX grains, usually along OPX margins. However, they suggested that such intergrowths were exclusively restricted to kimberlites, whereas xenoliths in continental alkalic basalts contained SP only in the form of separate interstitial grains. This is clearly not the case in oceanic basalts, as is shown by the samples from Samoa (Plate 3). Even here, however, the post-erosional xenolith-bearing lavas appear on the basis of REE geochemistry [Wright and Batiza, 1986] to have come from somewhat deeper sources than most AOB, just as kimberlites reflect a deeper source than continental AOB.

It is not clear how these intergrowths form, although a number of mechanisms have been proposed [Dawson and Smith, 1975]. The most promising of these include:
1. Pressure-induced subsolidus recrystallization of chromite already present in the mantle rock [Dawson and Smith, 1975].
2. Subsolidus reaction and re-equilibration of low-P phases in response to rising pressure or falling temperature [Varne, 1977].
3. Breakdown or reaction of high-P phases in response to reduction in pressure [Boyd, 1971; Aoki and Prinz, 1974; Dawson and Smith, 1975] or rise in temperature [Dickey et al., 1971].

The first mechanism requires the existence of concentrated areas of CHR, which then recrystallize under conditions of directed stress into the characteristic form. CHR may be concentrated metamorphically in materials on scales both large [Evans, 1983] and small (Plate 8). However, studies of tectonically mobilized alpine peridotite [Thayer, 1969] show that CHR tends to deform as a solid, yielding to stress over a wide range of strain rates by granulation without recrystallization. Aoki and Prinz [1974] saw no chemical differences in SP from garnet lherzolites and SP lherzolites, which presumably represent different P-T environments. From this they concluded that SP do not recrystallize easily under normal mantle conditions.

TABLE 4. Host Compositions: 82UP-15

	OL	CPX	glass	bulk rock
SiO_2	39.34	43.93	44.79	41.83
TiO_2	.03	4.31	3.90	4.01
Al_2O_3	.03	8.25	16.65	10.90
FeO*	14.42	7.96	10.33	12.95
MnO	.23	.19	.25	.17
MgO	45.70	11.10	3.87	11.93
CaO	.22	20.76	8.80	9.64
Na_2O	.00	1.35	4.58	3.32
K_2O	.00	.55	3.29	1.98
P_2O_5	.07	.50	2.02	.99
Cr_2O_3	.05	.04	.04	n.d.
NiO	.22	.04	.00	n.d.
sum	100.29	98.97	98.52	97.72

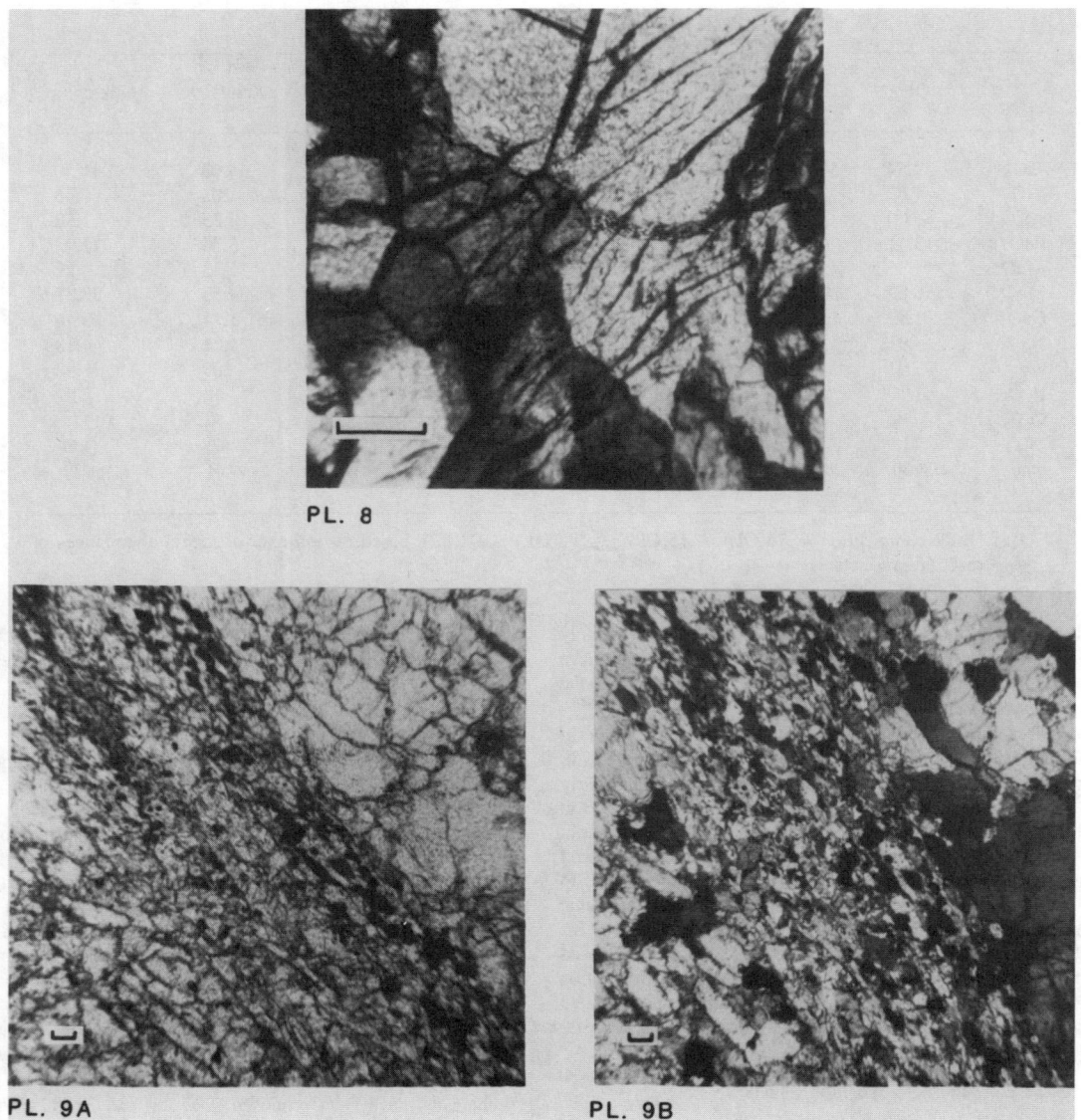

Plate 8. Fractures cross-cutting euhedral, recrystallized olivine grain boundaries, indicating that brittle deformation followed recrystallization. (82UP-15xd) Plate 9a. Juxtaposition of fine-grained, euhedral-subhedral, sheared harzburgite material and its coarse-grained, unrecrystallized equilivalent. The two domains are separated by a "stringer" of anhedral blocky chromite, metamorphically concentrated along this interface. The sheared material grades into a coarser mosaic texture away from the interface. (82UP-15xb) Plate 9b. Same, crossed polars. Scale in all plates is 10 microns.

On the basis of experimental studies in the $MgO-CaO-Al_2O_3-SiO_2$ system, Varne [1977] suggested that SP symplexis forms from reaction and exsolution involving pyroxenes and OL, occurring with pervasive recrystallization of the silicate phases as P increases or T decreases. It is important to note that the SP in his study, from xenoliths in Tasmanian basalts, are much more aluminous (54-64% Al_2O_3) and less Cr-rich than Samoan CHR, and thus are closer to the simple experimental system. However, if Varne's explanation is used, the re-equilibration process which produces symplexis cannot be the result of inclusion and transportation of the xenolith within the host magma, a process which would lower pressure and raise temperature.

The final mechanism involves exsolution of CHR from a Cr-rich phase such as garnet or Cr-diopside to form the symplectite. Most Samoan symplectites consist of CHR and low-Cr and -Al OPX, but it is not clear how Ca from the original garnet or CPX would be accommodated. There is no apparent Ca-bearing phase. One mechanism which avoids the problem is exsolution of CHR from a Cr- and Al-rich OPX stable at high pressure, in response to vertical movement or other drop in pressure. An analogous process was suggested by Green [1963] to explain symplectite with intergrowths of high-Al SP and Al-poor enstatite. He suggested that Al from early coarse-grained Al-enstatite is released during recrystallization to form these lower pressure phases. However, the SP in Green's study were true SP, not CHR.

If the symplectite were the residue left by partial incongruent melting of

TABLE 5. Xenolith Thermometry

Sample	Roeder et al., 1979 OL-SP	Lindsley, 1983 PX	Nickle et al., 1985 2PX	Rock Type
TL-83xa	811		993	H[1]
TL-83xb	1014	1115	1540	L[2]
UP-15xa	1010	1110		L
UP-15xb	845			L
UP-15xd	1028	910	1017	L
UP-15xf	1090			H
UL-47x	774	1150	1202	L
SP-10xb	532	1250	1358	H
SP-10xxc	758	1300	1378	H
SS-15xa	1042	1185	1214	L
SS-32xa	487			L
SM-42xa	550	1130	913	DW[3]
SM-42xb	853			DW
SM-42xc	688	1114		D[4]

[1]Harzburgite; [2]Lherzolite; [3]Dunite-Wehrlite; [4]Dunite. Values represent temperatures in degrees C.

Cr-diopside to form SP + liquid [Dickey et al., 1971], then the Ca would partition into the liquid phase, which has presumably migrated out of the residual mantle. However, Dickey et al. [1971] expected this mechanism to produce disseminated CHR grains.

The major problem with any mechanism involving reaction of a silicate phase to form CHR-silicate intergrowths is the large amount of Cr present in the CHR. These symplectic CHR contain 30-40% Cr_2O_3 and account for roughly 45% of the intergrowth. Thus, the entire intergrowth contains about 16% Cr_2O_3. Unless substantial migration of Cr occurred during the exsolution, it is difficult to imagine a parental silicate phase rich enough in Cr to produce the intergrowths by exsolution or recrystallization. However, if the liquid phase produced by partial incongruent melting of Cr-diopside migrated out of the residual mantle [Dickey et al., 1971], and is no longer represented in the intergrowth, the actual concentration of Cr in the original phase need not have been as high as 16%. In any case, if the parent material underwent pressure changes which resulted in the formation of symplectites, these must have occurred prior to its inclusion in the host.

Geothermometry

Three mineralogic geothermometers were used to calculate temperatures of equilibration for xenolith phases (Table 5):
1. the OL-SP thermometer of Roeder et al. [1979; this is a modification of the thermometer of Jackson, 1969], P = 1 atm;
2. the pyroxene thermometer of Lindsley [1983], P = 15 kb; and
3. the 2-pyroxene thermometer of Nickel et al. [1985], P = 20 kb.

Of the three methods, the OL-SP thermometer yields the lowest calculated temperatures (532-1090°C), and the 2-pyroxene method the highest temperatures (913-1540°C). The temperatures calculated with the pyroxene thermometer are intermediate and more uniform, ranging from 910-1300°C (six out of nine xenoliths fall between 1110 and 1185°C using this method). There is little correlation of calculated temperatures with rock types.

The discrepancies between the thermometers may partly result from the fact that the thermometers measure the temperature of last equilibration of different phases, and different phases do in fact equilibrate at different temperatures. However, some of the discrepancy must also be attributed to problems in applying the thermometers.

Thermometers which rely on thermodynamic data such as the OL-SP and 2-pyroxene thermometers are dependent on which data are selected from the literature, and on the assumptions of ideal and known solid solution behavior. Extra solid solution endmembers such as titaniferous compositions, which are typically found in the Samoan xenolith phases, are likely to be sources of error [Wright, 1986].

Re-equilibration between minerals during slow cooling of the plutonic source rock may yield lower values for the calculated temperature. This has been demonstrated in the case of subsolidus Fe and Mg exchange between OL and SP [Roeder et al., 1979].

As previously discussed, interactions of xenolith phases with the host melt occurred in the Samoan xenoliths (e.g. zoned crystals, incipient and reaction melting of pyroxenes). Such reactions can be expected to reset the thermometers. The effects of host-xenolith reactions should affect the pyroxene thermometers most strongly.

Geobarometry

There are no precise geobarometers for spinel lherzolites, although a new technique utilizing partitioning of Ca between OL and pyroxene appears promising [Adams and Bishop, in press]. The petrogenetic grid of MacGregor [1974] has been used with variable success in deriving geotherms based on ultramafic inclusions in kimberlites [e.g. Boyd and Nixon, 1973; Pike, 1976]. Use of this method for Samoan xenoliths yields pressures in the range 20-45 kb; this is outside the stability region for spinel lherzolites. A similar problem was reported by Pike [1976], who ascribed it to chemical interaction of the xenoliths with the host lava. In addition, the dependence of this method on accurate thermometry means that errors affecting the thermometric calculations are propagated into the barometric estimate.

Implications for the Origins of Samoan Xenoliths

When lherzolite undergoes partial melting, CPX and then OPX are the first phases to be consumed. Normally, CPX disappears first, leaving a harzburgite residue [Frey and Green, 1974]. It seems likely, therefore, that the Samoan HL xenoliths, most of which are poor in pyroxene (especially CPX) and rich in OL, are samples of a portion of the upper mantle left behind as infusible residue after an episode of partial melting. Such an origin is consistent with the relatively "depleted" composition, namely minerals with high Mg, Ni, and Cr and low Fe, Al, and Ti. HL OL compositions are in equilibrium with liquids having primitive Mg#'s of 69-78 [Roeder and Emslie, 1970].

The DW group, however, contains no OPX at all, and relatively minor amounts of interstitial CPX. They are therefore unlikely to represent residual mantle. Mineral constituents are relatively enriched in Al, Fe and Ti, and are relatively depleted in Cr and Ni. DW OL compositions indicate equilibration with liquids having Mg#'s of 58-59 [Roeder and Emslie, 1970], much less primitive ratios than the HL OL.

These two groups conform in a limited sense to the identification of Wilshire and Shervais [1975] of "Cr-diopside" and "Al-augite" type xenoliths (Groups I and II, respectively, in the terminology of Frey and Prinz [1978]). The Cr-diopside type of xenolith comprises mostly lherzolites and harzburgites, and contains magnesian OL and pyroxene (Mg# > 87), and Cr-rich SP. Metamorphic textures are common. The HL group of Samoa corresponds to this type.

The Al-augite type is enriched in Al, Ti, and Fe. Clinopyroxenites, websterites, and wehrlites are the most common rock types. Pyroxenes are Al- and Ti-rich, but Cr-poor. Aluminous SP are common. Mg#'s are generally less than 85. The DW group of Samoa may be analogous to this type.

However, both HL and DW xenoliths from Samoa are low in Al when compared to Al-augite xenoliths from San Carlos, Arizona and other localities in the western U.S. [Frey and Prinz, 1978; Wilshire et al., 1975]. For example, San Carlos Group II CPX contains 8-9% Al_2O_3 [Frey and Prinz, 1978], in contrast to 4-6% Al_2O_3 for DW CPX from Samoa. Samoan xenoliths are also markedly poor in Al when compared to abyssal peridotites [Dick and Bullen, 1984]. Even the "low Al" type of abyssal peridotite reported by these authors has OPX containing 2.4% Al_2O_3 and SP containing 25% Al_2O_3, whereas Samoan xenolith OPX has Al_2O_3 contents as low as 1%, and HL CHR with less than 15-20% Al_2O_3.

Frey and Prinz [1978] suggest that the Group I, or Cr-diopside type of xenolith represents accidental inclusions of infusible residual mantle not related to the host lava. Samoan HL xenoliths are remarkably uniform in mineral composition despite significant variations in host composition [Wright, 1986]. Although bulk chemical and isotopic data are not available for the Samoan xenoliths to test this hypothesis more carefully, I suggest that the HL group are analogous to the Cr-diopside type of xenolith, and are in fact unrelated to the post-erosional AOB, olivine basanitoids, and olivine nephelinites in which they are found.

Frey and Prinz [1978] suggest that Group II xenoliths, the Al-augite type, represent high-pressure cumulates derived from Si-undersaturated magmas. The Samoan DW xenoliths are free of OPX and are poorer in CPX than most examples of the Al-augite type. It is likely that these xenoliths do in fact represent cumulates, but they may not require high pressures of crystallization. No enstatite is present in these samples, and CPX and SP compositions, though more aluminous than the HL phases, are Al-poor compared to Group II xenoliths from the western U.S. This is consistent with a lower pressure of formation.

The DW xenoliths cannot be direct cumulates from the host lava, however. Changes in stress regime have occurred in the recent history of the cumulate mass, as is indicated by the severely "kinked" extinction patterns in all the OL. There has been insufficient time and energy for significant recrystallization to occur in response to this distortion of the crystal lattices. Cumulate material from the shield-building phase of Samoan volcanism is a possible candidate for the source of the DW xenoliths. Intrusion of subsequent post-erosional magmas is a plausible mechanism for the deformation of the cumulate pile.

Conclusions

Two fundamentally different types of ultramafic rock are represented in the Samoan xenolith suite: the harzburgite-lherzolite spectrum and the dunite-wehrlite group. The DW xenoliths were brought up in a single flow which included no other types of xenoliths, suggesting that it traversed material significantly different from the other flows. Chemically and isotopically, flows from this part of the chain are unique [Wright, 1986; Wright and White, in press].

The HL group of xenoliths may be analogous to the Cr-diopside type of Wilshire and Shervais [1975], whereas the DW group resemble the Al-augite group of these authors. The Samoan xenoliths do not conform precisely to these groupings, which are, after all, defined for xenoliths from continental settings, but may rather represent their oceanic analogs. The HL group are most likely residual material left behind in the mantle by a previous melting event, but the DW xenoliths appear to be cumulate in origin.

It is thought that the host lavas rose fairly directly to the surface, one of the lines of evidence being the presence of angular xenoliths. This suggests that some xenolith-host interactions, such as chemical exchange between the melt and grains at the xenolith boundaries and reaction melting of OPX in contact with the melt, may occur rapidly.

The xenolith textures show a history of vertical movement of the parent mantle prior to the inclusion of pieces of it in upward-moving melts. Evidence for this history includes the presence of CHR-silicate symplectic intergrowths, recrystallization and porphyroclastic textures, and strongly strained OL and OPX grains. Boyd and Nixon [1973] identified porphyroclastic and mosaic textures in xenoliths as being indicative of stress regimes at the top of the moving lithosphere. However, the changes in pressure-temperature conditions suggested by the symplectic intergrowths are more consistent with diapirism within the mantle.

That none of the xenoliths studied represent the source material for the Samoan post-erosional lavas is shown by the dearth of alkalis, Ti, Fe, and easily melted CPX. The HL group could, however, represent residual mantle produced in the generation of basaltic magmas by partial melting. A possible candidate for this melting event is the one which produced the Samoan shield edifices, 1-3 million years before the eruption of the post-erosional lavas. The evidence for diapirism is consistent with the formation of large shield volcanic systems.

Acknowledgments. I would like to thank Roy Fujita for assistance in the analytical work, and Cindy Evans, James Natland, and James Hawkins for helpful reviews of the manuscript in its original form as a portion of my Ph.D. dissertation. An anonymous reviewer was of great help in its conversion from chapter to paper. Carol Stein made preparation of the manuscript possible. This work was supported in part by NSF grant #EAR82-18781 to J. Natland.

References

Adams, G.E. and Bishop, F.C., The olivine-clinopyroxene geobarometer: experimental results in the CaO-FeO-MgO-SiO_2 system, *Contrib. Mineral. Petrol.*, in press, 1986.

Aoki, K. and Prinz, M., Chromian spinels in lherzolite inclusions from Itinome-gata, Japan, *Contrib. Mineral. Petrol.*, 46, pp. 249-256, 1974.

Basu, A.R., Geochemistry of ultramafic xenoliths from San Quintin, Baja California, in *The Mantle Sample: intrusions in kimberlites and other volcanics*, F.R. Boyd and H.O.A. Meijer, eds., AGU Mono., pp. 391-399, 1979.

Basu, A.R. and MacGregor, I.D., Chromite spinels from ultramafic xenoliths, *Geochim. et Cosmochim. Acta*, 39, pp. 937-945, 1975.

Bowen, N.L. and Anderson, O., The system MgO-FeO-SiO_2, *Am. J. Sci.*, 29, pp. 151-217, 1914.

Boyd, F.R., Pargasite-spinel peridotite xenolith from the Wesselton Mine, *Carn. Inst. Wash. Yearbk.*, 70, pp. 138-142, 1971.

Boyd, F.R. and Nixon, P.H., Structure of the upper mantle beneath Lesotho, *Carn. Inst. Wash. Yearbk.*, 72, pp. 431-445, 1973.

Cohen, R.S., O'Nions, R.K. and Dawson, J.B., Isotope geochemistry of xenoliths from East Africa: implications for development of mantle reservoirs and their interaction, *Earth Planet. Sci. Lett.*, *68*, pp. 209-220, 1984.

Dawson, J.B., Powell, D.G. and Reid, A.M., Ultrabasic xenoliths and lava from the Lashaine Volcano, northern Tanzania, *J. Petrol.*, *11*, pp. 519-548, 1970.

Dawson, J.B. and Smith, J.V., Chromite-silicate intergrowths in upper-mantle peridotites, *Phys. Chem. Earth*, *9*, pp. 339-350, 1975.

Dickey, J.S., Yoder, H.S., and Schairer, J.F., Chromium in silicate-oxide systems, *Carn. Inst. Wash. Yearbk.*, *70*, pp. 118-122, 1971.

Frey, F.A. and Green, D.H., The mineralogy, geochemistry and origin of lherzolite inclusions in Victorian basanites, *Geochim. et Cosmochim. Acta*, *38*, pp. 1023-1059, 1974.

Frey, F.A. and Prinz, M., Ultramafic inclusions from San Carlos, Arizona: petrologic and geochemical data bearing on their petrogenesis, *Earth Planet. Sci. Lett.*, *38*, pp. 129-176, 1978.

Green, D.H., Alumina content of enstatite in a Venezuelan high-temperature peridotite, *Geol. Soc. Am. Bull.*, *74*, pp. 1397-1402, 1963.

Hawkins, J.W. and Natland, J.H., Nephelinites and basanites of the Samoan linear volcanic chain: their possible tectonic significance, *Earth Planet. Sci. Lett.*, *24*, pp. 427-439, 1975.

Jackson, E.D., Chemical variation in coexisting chromite and olivine in the chromitite zones of the Stillwater Complex, *Econ. Geol. Monogr.*, *4*, pp. 41-71, 1969.

Jackson, E.D. and Wright, T.L., Xenoliths in the Honolulu volcanic series, Hawaii, *J. Petrol.*, *11*, pp. 405-430, 1970.

Kear, D. and Wood, B.L., The geology and hydrology of Western Samoa, *New Zealand Geol. Survey Bull.*, *63*, 92 pp, 1959.

Kirby, S.H. and Green, H. W., Dunite xenoliths from Hualalai Volcano: evidence for mantle diapiric flow beneath the island of Hawaii, *Am. J. Sci.*, *280-A*, pp. 550-575, 1980.

Kutolin, V.A. and Frolova, V.M., Petrology of ultrabasic inclusions from basalts of Minusa and Transbaikalian regions (Siberia, U.S.S.R.), *Contrib. Mineral. Petrol.*, *29*, pp. 163-179, 1970.

Leggo, P.J. and Hutchison, R., A Rb-Sr study of ultrabasic xenoliths and their basaltic host rocks from the Massif Central, France, *Earth Planet. Sci. Lett.*, *5*, pp. 71-75, 1968.

Lindsley, D.H., Pyroxene thermometry, *Am. Mineral.*, *68*, pp. 477-493, 1983.

Macdonald, G.A., Petrography of the Samoan Islands, *Geol. Soc. Am. Bull.*, *55*, pp. 1333-1362, 1944.

MacGregor, I.D., The system $MgO-Al_2O_3-SiO_2$: solubility of Al_2O_3 in enstatite for spinel and garnet peridotites, *Am. Mineral.*, *59*, pp. 110-119, 1974.

Mercier, J.-C. C. and Nicolas, A., Textures and fabrics of upper mantle peridotites as illustrated by xenoliths from basalts, *J. Petrol.*, *16*, pp. 454-486, 1975.

Natland, J.H., The progression of volcanism in the Samoan linear volcanic chain, *Am. J. Sci.*, *280-A*, pp. 709-735, 1980.

Natland, J.H. and Turner, D.L., Age progression and petrological development of Samoan shield volcanoes: evidence from K-Ar ages, lava compositions, and mineral studies, in *Geological Investigations of the Northern Melanesian Borderland*, T. Brocher, ed., in press, 1986.

Nickel, K.G., Brey, G.P. and Kogarko, L., Orthopyroxene-clinopyroxene equilibria in the system $CaO-MgO-Al_2O_3-SiO_2$ (CMAS): new experimental results and implications for two-pyroxene thermometry, *Contrib. Mineral. Petrol.*, *91*, pp. 44-53, 1985.

Nicolas, A., Stress estimates from structural studies in some mantle peridotites, *Phil. Trans. R. Soc. Lond.*, *A 288*, pp. 49-57, 1978.

Pike, J.E.N., Pressures and temperatures calculated from chromium-rich pyroxene compositions of megacrysts and peridotite inclusions, Black Rock Summit, Nevadaa , *Am. Mineral.*, *61*, pp. 725-731, 1976.

Pike, J.E.N. and Schwarzman, E.C., Classification of textures in ultramafic xenoliths, *J. Petrol.*, *85*, pp. 49-61, 1977.

Post, R.L., High-temperature creep of Mt. Burnet dunite, *Tectonophys.*, *42*, pp. 75-110, 1977.

Roedder, E., Liquid CO_2 inclusions in olivine-bearing nodules and phenocrysts from basalts, *Am. Mineral.*, *50*, pp. 1746-1782, 1965.

Roeder, P.L., Campbell, I.H., and Jamieson, H.E., A re-evaluation of the olivine-spinel geothermometer, *Contrib. Mineral. Petrol.*, *68*, pp. 325-334, 1979.

Stearns, H.T., Geology of the Samoan Islands, *Geol. Am. Soc. Bull.*, *55*, 1279-1332, 1944.

Stice, G.D. and McCoy, F.W., The geology of the Manu'a Islands, Samoa, *Pac. Sci.*, *22*, pp. 426-457, 1968.

Thayer, T.P., Gravity differentiation and magmatic re-emplacement of podiform chromite deposits, *Econ. Geol. Monogr.*, *4*, pp. 132-146, 1969.

Tracy, R.J., Petrology and genetic significance of an ultramafic xenolith suite from Tahiti, *Earth Planet. Sci. Lett.*, *48*, pp. 80-96, 1980.

Varne, R., On the origin of spinel lherzolite inclusions in basaltic rocks from Tasmania and elsewhere, *J. Petrol.*, *18*, pp. 1-23, 1977.

White, R.W., Ultramafic inclusions in basaltic rocks from Hawaii, *Contrib. Mineral. Petrol.*, *12*, pp. 245-314, 1966.

Wilshire, H.G. and Shervais, J.W., Al-augite and Cr-diopside ultramafic xenoliths in basaltic rocks from Western United States, *Phys. Chem. Earth*, *9*, pp. 257-272, 1975.

Wilshire, H.G., Meyer, C.E., Nakata, J.K., Calk, L.C., Shervais, J.W., Pike, J.E., and Schwarzman, E.C., Mafic and ultramafic xenoliths from volcanic rocks of the Western United States, U.S.G.S. Open-File Report 85-139, 1985.

Wright, E., Mapping of mantle heterogeneity below Samoa: sources of post-erosional lavas (abstr.), *EOS (Trans. Am. Geophys. Union)*, *65*, p. 1152, 1984.

Wright, E., Samoan ultramafic xenoliths: a record of upper mantle history (abstr.), *EOS (Trans. Am. Geophys. Union)*, *66*, p.1080, 1985.

Wright, E., Petrology and geochemistry of shield-building and post-erosional lava series on the islands of Samoa: implications for mantle heterogeneity and magma genesis, Ph.D. dissertation, University of California at San Diego, La Jolla, 1986.

Wright, E. and Batiza, R., REE geochemistry of the Samoan post-erosional lavas: evidence for a variably enriched mantle (abstr.), *EOS (Trans. Am. Geophys. Union)*, *67*, p. 1272, 1986.

Wright, E. and White, W.M., The origin of Samoa: new evidence from Sr, Nd, and Pb isotopes, *Earth Planet. Sci. Lett.*, *81*, pp.151-162, 1987.

PETROLOGIC EVOLUTION OF THE LOUISVILLE SEAMOUNT CHAIN

James W. Hawkins and Peter F. Lonsdale

Geological Research Division, Scripps Institution of Oceanography, La Jolla, CA 92093

Rodey Batiza

Department of Geological Sciences, Northwestern University, Evanston, IL 60201

Abstract. The Louisville Seamount Chain (LSC) extends for 4300 km from Osbourn Seamount, at the junction of the Tonga and Kermadec Trenches, southeasterly towards the Pacific-Antarctic Ridge. The chain is formed of 60 or more seamounts and guyots which are aligned along a trend concentric with the Emperor-Hawaii Chain. The Louisville Chain crosses at a low angle several fracture zones which are part of the Eltanin Fracture Zone system, but there is no apparent genetic relation between the two structures. Rocks collected from the Louisville Chain comprise a spectrum of rock types including alkalic basalt, hawaiite, and basanitoid. Some samples have compositions suggesting that they are transitional to tholeiitic basalt, but no true tholeiites have been collected from the seamounts. Osbourn Seamount, at the westernmost end of the chain, is capped with basanitoid; these have been dated as ~66 Ma. Clinopyroxene phenocrysts in basaltic composition pebbles and detrital grains of clinopyroxene have been recovered from DSDP site 204, north of Osbourn Seamount, at subbottom depths of 112 to 114 meters (Late? Cretaceous age). Some of these pyroxenes have compositions indicating a tholeiitic parental magma, some were derived from alkalic magmas. Osbourn Seamount or an older neighbor were likely sources of the clastic sediments. This is an indication that the early stages of seamount volcanism included tholeiitic magmas, magmatism subsequently evolved through alkalic and basanitic types. Samples dredged from the carapaces of seamounts east of Osbourn are mainly alkalic basalt, or hawaiite, or both. The young, eastern end of the chain near Long. 139°10'W has alkalic basalt lavas.

Modeling of trace element and REE data suggest that small amounts (e.g., 4%) melting of garnet lherzolite could have provided the parental alkalic basalt magmas. Basanitoids represent slightly higher (~9%) levels of melting. Element ratios of Ti/Zr, Nb/Zr, Y/Zr, Ba/La, La/Ce, La/Sm, Nb/La suggest that the mantle source for the LSC seamounts remained remarkably homogeneous through the ~66 m.y. recorded history of the chain. This is also supported by Nd and Sr isotope data for these samples. The mantle source must have been enriched in elements such as K, Rb, Ba, Y, REE relative to the source for N-MORB or to "primitive" mantle. The LSC seamounts have evolved through a petrologic sequence like that of the Hawaiian and Samoan Chains, but the long term homogeneity of the mantle source of LSC magmas is in marked contrast to the heterogeneous mantle implied by the petrology of Hawaiian and Samoan volcanoes. A hotspot origin for the LSC seems likely: there may be an active "Loihi counterpart" yet to be found at the southeastern end of the chain.

Introduction

Menard et al. [1964] drew attention to the northwesterly trend of a group of guyots in the southwestern Pacific basin that paralleled the Austral Chain; they pointed out that each guyot was an isolated volcano. These guyots form part of the Louisville Ridge (Figure 1) which is one of the major bathymetric features in the southwestern Pacific Ocean Basin. It is formed by a great arcuate chain, comprising numerous seamounts and bathymetric highs, that extends southeastward from the Tonga-Kermadec Trench system to the Pacific-Antarctic Ridge. Its total length is on the order of 4300 km, and it varies in width from 75 to 100 km. The submerged peaks aligned along the chain typically rise 2 to 4 km above the seafloor. The name "Louisville Ridge" implies that it is a more or less continuous bathymetric high, but in fact it is formed largely of individual submarine peaks plus a few elongated segments that represent several closely spaced (coalesced) peaks. The form of the seamounts suggests that all are submarine volcanoes, and all that have been sampled are indeed volcanic.

The Louisville Ridge intersects the Tonga-Kermadec Trench systems and causes the trench axes to shoal rapidly from about 7 km to about 5 km; Osbourn Seamount and a smaller satellite volcano block the trenches at this point and separate the nearly straight Kermadec Trench, that trends 020°, from the slightly arcuate Tonga Trench, that trends 025°. At the intersection between the trenches and the ridge there is a gap in the shallow and intermediate depth (<400 km) Wadati-Benioff Zone [*Billington*, 1980; *Giardini and Woodhouse*, 1984]. *Giardini and Woodhouse* [1986] find no convincing evidence for a "scar" deep in the Benioff Zone that would have been left by subduction of the Louisville Ridge. Neither is there a "positive correlation with continuous gaps of seismic activity....on the projected location of the subducted seamount." A submarine volcanic eruption on the Tonga Arc immediately west of the intersection (at Lat. 25°55'S, Long. 175°14'W) was reported on 17 October 1977; this suggests that the subduction of oceanic lithosphere is active at this latitude. The Louisville Ridge itself is aseismic [*Vogt et al.*, 1976]. It is not clear what happens to the seamounts of the "ridge" as they collide with the Tonga Arc, but *Vallier et al.* [1985] report the occurrence

Copyright 1987 by the American Geophysical Union.

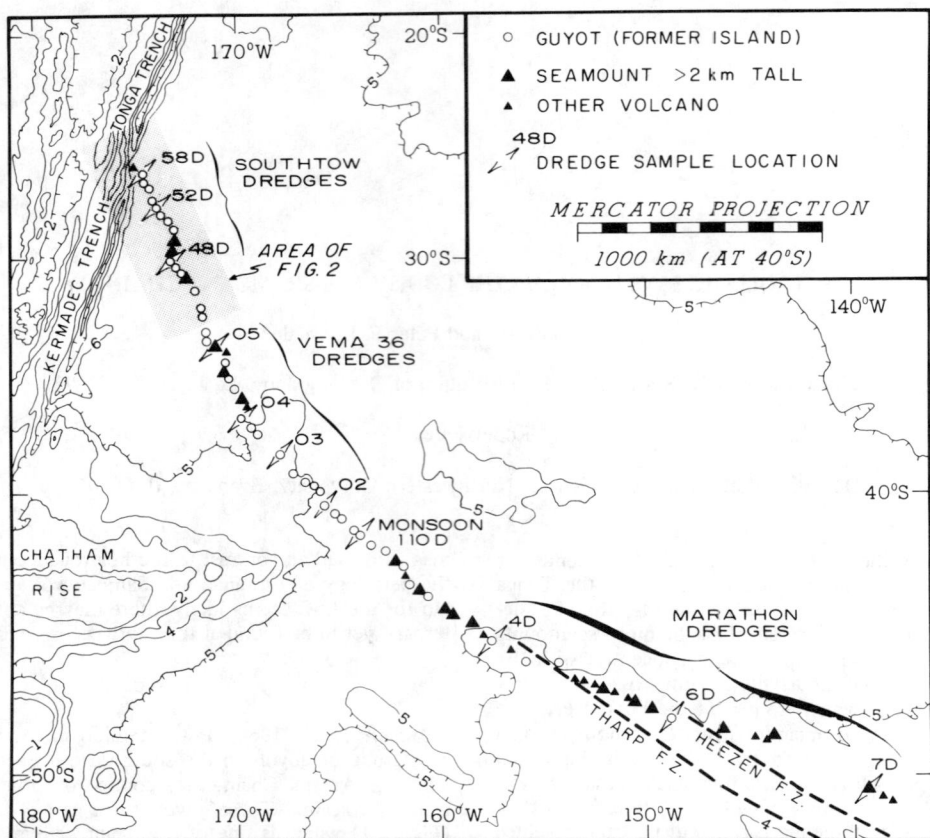

Fig. 1. Distribution of dredge samples along the Louisville Chain. Pattern of guyots and other seamounts is from *Lonsdale* [in press].

of Upper Cretaceous pelagic sediment (shales, radiolarian oozes and carbonates, D. Scholl, oral communication) near the intersection of the trench and the Louisville Ridge. This implies the presence of debris scraped off from a guyot or seamount. To date, however, there is no evidence for a train of seamount fragments along the west wall of the Tonga Trench as would be expected if there had been an oblique collision of the ridge. However, reconstructions of plate motions suggest that the ridge swept along the trench wall as the Lau Basin opened [*Dupont*, 1982; *Dupont and Herzer*, 1985]. Osbourn Seamount is broken up at its top and appears to be failing in tension as it approaches the trench [*Lonsdale*, 1986]. Is it possible that Osbourn Seamount is the oldest seamount of this chain and it has "just arrived" at the trench? The age of this seamount is about 66 Ma [*Watts et al.*, 1986] and if the Louisville Ridge is analogous to the Emperor-Hawaii Chain we would expect that there were older seamounts (e.g., >70 Ma) that must have been subducted or accreted at the trench. More dredging of the trench wall may provide evidence for accreted seamount fragments of older parts of the Louisville Ridge.

The name Louisville Ridge was first used for a 350 km long array of four seamounts--Currituck, Seafox, Louisville, and Burton--aligned on a trend that can be projected towards Osbourn Seamount [*U.S. Navy*, 1961]. *Hayes and Ewing* [1968] proposed to use the name for a 3500 km long feature that followed close to a great circle extending from Osbourn Seamount, at the junction of the Tonga and Kermadec Trenches (Lat. 26°S, Long. 175°W) to the Eltanin Fracture Zone near Lat. 53°S, Long. 135°W. They interpreted the bathymetric data as indicating that this feature was a more or less continuous ridge and proposed that it was an extension of the Eltanin Fracture Zone. Subsequent surveying and rock dredging [*Hawkins*, 1973] showed that the northwestern part of the "ridge" comprised a curvi-linear chain of seamounts, some with flat tops and some with sharp peaks, that were built atop a discontinuous pedestal that rose about 1000 m above the seafloor. More recently, Sea Beam surveying [*Lonsdale*, in press] showed that the same pattern prevails along the entire "ridge" although the volcanoes become more widely spaced towards the southeast. All of the dredged rocks are varieties of alkalic basalts and their differentiates. A "hotspot" origin for the seamount chain was proposed by *Hawkins* [1973] who noted that while it followed close to projections of the Eltanin Fracture Zone trend it lacked fracture zone morphology. *Clague and Jarrard* [1973] also proposed a hotspot origin for the ridge because its trend is approximately co-polar with the Emperor Chain; they suggested that it had an age similar to the Emperor Chain (70 to 42 Ma). *Molnar et al.* [1975] discounted the argument for a fracture zone origin for the ridge on the basis of morphology and on the basis of the seafloor age. They showed that because the Eltanin Fracture Zone was related to spreading on the Pacific-Antarctic Rise, which began 81 m.y. ago, the fracture zone could not be genetically related to features on the older crust beneath the Louisville Ridge.

The hotspot origin for the chain has also been supported by *Vogt et al.* [1976], *Jurdy* [1978], and *Epp* [1978]. With the advent of Seasat radar altimetry data many new seamounts have been

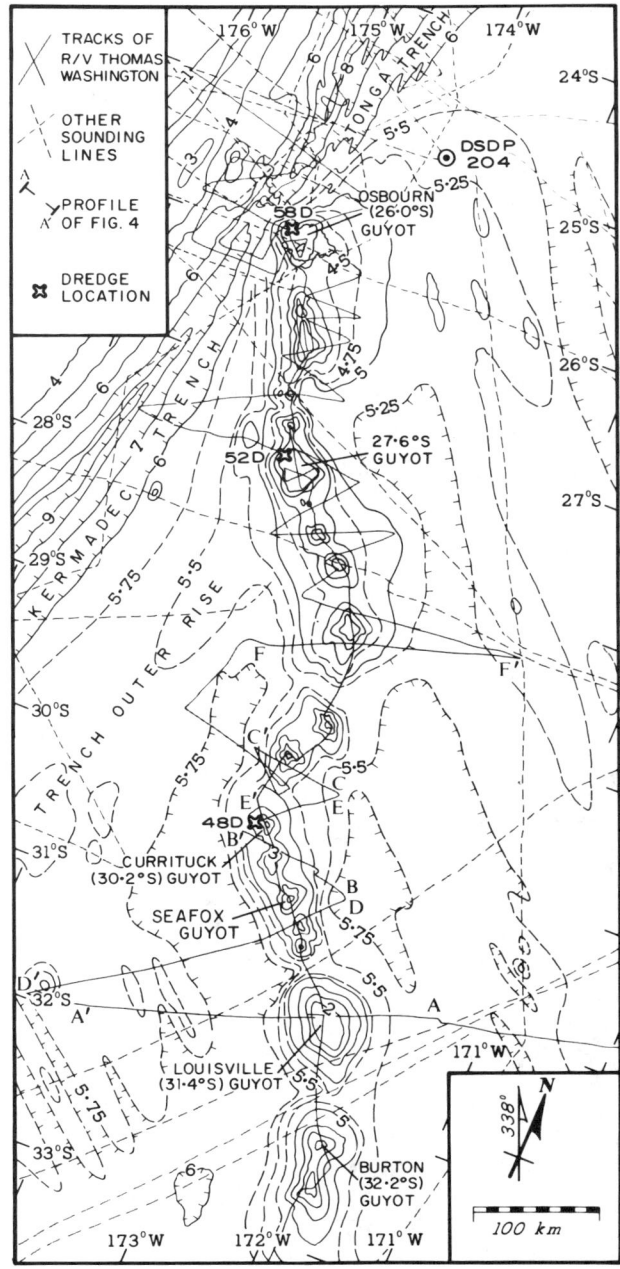

Fig. 2. Bathymetry and sample locations in the northwestern part of the Louisville Chain. The R/V THOMAS WASHINGTON tracks include a zig-zag of conventional profiles and a single longitudinal Sea Beam traverse.

recognized, and the trace of the Louisville Ridge with respect to the Eltanin Fracture Zone has been defined better [*Dixon and Parke*, 1983; *Sandwell*, 1984; *Cazenave and Dominh*, 1984; *Watts et al.*, 1985, 1986]. These authors reach different conclusions as to whether or not the Ridge is a hotspot trace or an extension of the Eltanin Fracture Zone, but the Seasat data show clearly that the "ridge" is actually a great chain of seamounts as Menard proposed in 1964. Radiometric dating of our samples and those collected by Lamont-Doherty Geological Observatory, and analysis of the timing of loading of the lithosphere plate by the seamounts relative to the age of the crust beneath them [*Watts et al.*, 1986], helps further to substantiate the origin of the ridge as due to off-axis intraplate volcanism. The age progression of dated samples, from 66 Ma on the west to "zero" age on the east offer a good test of the hotspot hypothesis. *Lonsdale*'s [in press] Sea Beam survey of this 4300 km long chain includes more than 60 seamounts, many more than indicated by the Seasat data (Figure 1). The "missing" seamounts in the Seasat data may be due to variable thinning of the lithosphere by hotspot activity resulting in Airy compensation for parts of the chain. The seamounts include flat-topped, sharp-peaked and large edifices formed by coalescence of volcanoes, and there are several small kinks in the trend of the chain (Figures 2, 3). The Sea Beam data also show that many of the discontinuities or overlaps in the spacing of peaks along the chain may be due to the chain crossing fracture zones that are nearly co-linear with the ridge. This brings us back to the original suggestion of *Hayes and Ewing* [1968] but, rather than the "ridge" being the extension of the Eltanin Fracture Zone, the local trend of the seamount chain may in part have been controlled by magma leakage along a series of subparallel major fractures through the lithosphere. It seems clear that the proper name for this great geological feature should be the "Louisville Seamount Chain". The older term "Louisville Ridge" seems so well established that it may persist, but in this paper we will use the more suitably descriptive name "Louisville Seamount Chain" and formally propose that it be adopted.

Geologic Setting

The overall trend of the chain is nearly concentric with the Emperor-Hawaii Chain, including the bend at about 40 Ma; this has suggested that both are the expressions of magma leaks due to hotspots relatively fixed with respect to the spin axis [e.g., *Clague and Jarrard*, 1973; *Epp*, 1978]. However, Lonsdale showed that in addition to a major change in trend at Lat. 37°30'S that coincides with rocks about 40 m.y. old (equivalent to the Emperor-Hawaii bend) there is another small bend at about 25 Ma. These bends may be due to changes in plate-motion vectors with time, or changes in the position of the mantle melting anomaly, or the locus of magma conduits (e.g., fracture zones) may have varied as the plate moved over the melt source. The discontinuous and sinuous form of the western part of the ridge appears to be related to deviations from an arcuate trend where the magma leaks were diverted into conduits controlled by crossings of fracture zone trends.

Bathymetric profiles for six crossings of the northwestern end of the chain are shown in Figure 4. These profiles were taken on the SIO SOUTHTOW expedition that collected most of the rock samples described in this report. These show the general depth accordance on both the north and south sides of the ridge, the sharp peaked or multiple peaked form of ridge crossings at depths greater than 1500 m, and the more rounded or flattened form of shallower crossings. The magnetic profiles taken on these crossings show high amplitude magnetic anomalies, some with negative anomalies at the "ridge" crest, some with positive anomalies. This variability in the patterns suggests that the seamounts formed during periods of alternate polarity of the earth's magnetic field. Similar data are shown by *Watts et al.* [1986].

Sample Sites

Our well spaced suite of samples (Figure 1) results from combining the yields of dredging on Scripps SOUTHTOW expedition [*Hawkins*, 1973] at the old end of the chain, Lamont-Doherty's

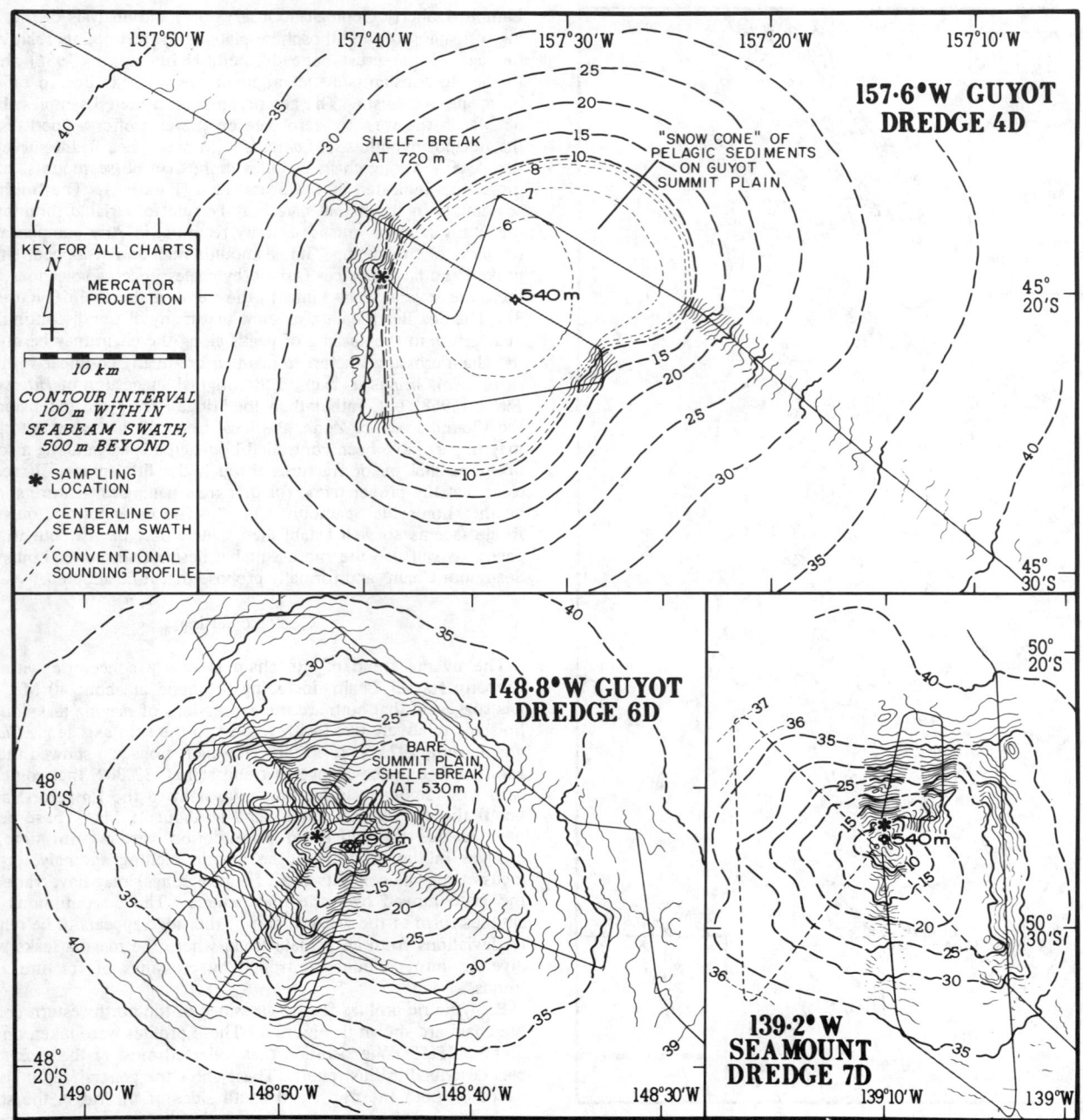

Fig. 3. Sampled volcanoes in the younger southeastern part of the chain. In this remote region there are no conventional echo-sounding profiles to supplement the incomplete Sea Beam surveys (except at the 139.2°W seamount, where Sea Beam data was not collected along our entire survey track because of a temporary failure of the system).

VEMA 36 [*Watts et al.*, in press] and Scripps MONSOON [*Menard et al.*, 1964] from the middle section, and Scripps MARATHON [*Lonsdale*, in press] from the young southeastern end. The SOUTHTOW and VEMA 36 dredge hauls (Table 1) covered a rather broad depth range on the outer slopes of large volcanoes, and probably collected talus representative of the principal rock outcrops. Some of the dredge hauls contained several types of lava (e.g., SOTW-58). The MONSOON and MARATHON dredge hauls were from seamount summits, either from the shelf-break of guyots or from the top of a sharp-crested peak (MTHN 7D); dredge locations are shown in Figure 3 and in Figure 2 of *Menard et al.* [1964], which refers to MONSOON 110D as MSN VII-9. MARATHON 4D collected mainly Miocene chalk from the guyot summit platform, but this sediment contained lithic fragments and

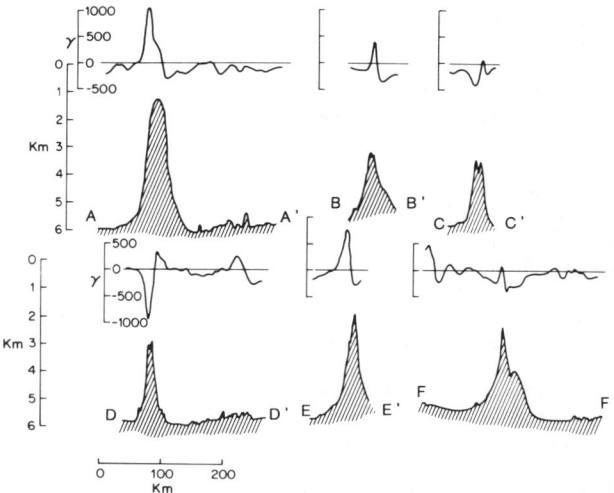

Fig. 4. Bathymetric and magnetic profiles across the northwestern part of the Louisville Seamount Chain. Profile locations are shown on Figure 2. Data from SIO SOUTHTOW Expedition.

bles and detrital clinopyroxene probably derived from Osbourn Guyot or one of its since-subducted neighbors.

Petrology

In this paper we present data for rocks dredged from the Louisville Chain that supports the proposal that it formed by off-ridge volcanism and that it could be due to "hotspot" magmatism. The dredged rocks are mainly alkalic basalt, differentiates (e.g., hawaiite) and basanitoid. The youngest rocks, from the eastern end of the chain (Figure 3), have some of the characteristics of alkalic basalts that are transitional to ocean island tholeiite. This is shown by their position close to the alkalic-tholeiitic boundary on an alkali-silica diagram (Figure 5).

With such a limited suite of samples it is unwise to attempt a detailed petrologic synthesis for the geologic history of the Louisville Chain, but we can at least make some inferences about its origin and evolution. The main conclusion we can draw from the data is that the chain is formed of submarine volcanoes capped mainly by alkalic basalts and their differentiates and that there is evidence to suggest that many of the seamounts have evolved through a "Hawaiian-type" volcanic sequence that included tholeiitic composition magmas early in their growth and subsequently have evolved through alkalic and silica undersaturated magma types. This sequence is typical of the linear volcanic chains such as the Samoan Chain [*Macdonald*, 1944; *Hawkins and Natland*, 1975; *Natland*, 1980], the Emperor-Hawaii Chain [*Macdonald and Katsura*, 1964], and the Marquesas [*Duncan et al.*, 1986].

clinopyroxene crystals that we were able to analyze. Another relevant sedimentary sample that we examined is a core of the northernmost Louisville apron at DSDP site 204 (Figure 2), where Upper Cretaceous (?) volcaniclastics contain basaltic peb-

The dredges only sampled talus derived from surface outcrops

TABLE 1. Louisville Seamount Chain, Sample Locations

Site	Lat.	Long.	Depth, m	Site Description
SOTW 48	30°10.2'S	173°25.7'W	3291	southeast side of
	30°08.4'S	173°23.7'W	2300	Currituck Guyot
SOTW 52	27°28.3'S	174°24.8'W	3593	west side of
	27°29.2'S	174°22.8'W	3480	seamount
SOTW 58	25°52.3'S	175°05.4'W	3270	northwest side of
	25°54.7'S	175°05.8'W	2443	Osbourn Seamount
MONS 110	41°27.6'S	164°17.0'W	1500	southeast side,
	41°26.5'S	164°14.8'W	950	Valerie Guyot
MTHN 4	45°19.0'S	157°39.0'W	1500	west side,
	45°19.4'S	157°38.8'W		157.6°W guyot
MTHN 6	48°12.1'S	148°48.4'W	720	west side,
	48°12.2'S	148°48.5'W		148.8°W guyot
MTHN 7	50°26.4'S	139°10.0'W	640	north side,
	50°26.4'S	139°10.0'W		139.2°W seamount
LV 2	40°47'S	165°21'W	1883	seamount
LV 3	38°19.5'S	167°43.7'W	1232	seamount
LV 4	36°57.0'S	169°50.0'W	2910	seamount
			1446	
LV 5	33°56.7'S	171°11.5'W	3704	seamount
			2760	
DSDP 204	24°57.27'S	174°06.69'W	5354	drill site

Identification: SOTW - SIO expedition SOUTHTOW, leg 09, 1972; MONS - SIO expedition MONSOON, leg 07, 1961; MTHN - SIO expedition MARATHON, leg 06, 1984; LV 2 - LDGO expedition VEMA 36-01, 1979; LV 3,4,5 - LDGO expedition VEMA 36-02, 1979; DSDP 204 - Deep Sea Drilling Project site 204, leg 21, 1971 - "upper" samples from core interval 113-113.5 m sub-bottom, "lower" samples from core interval 116-116.5 m sub-bottom

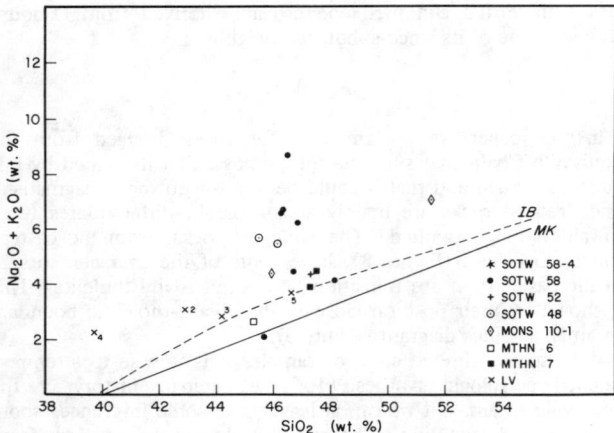

Fig. 5. Alkali-silica diagram showing data for Louisville Seamount Chain. Boundary I-B is based on *Irvine and Baragar* [1971], and M-K is based on *Macdonald and Katsura* [1964].

on the seamounts so we have no way of knowing the internal composition and magmatic sequence for individual seamounts. However, we have an age progression from ~66-70 Ma to "zero" age along the chain to give us insights to magmatic evolution. Some evidence for the early history of the northwesternmost part of the chain comes from basaltic pebbles near the bottom of DSDP hole 204. These pebbles were deposited in a sediment apron; the most likely source was a volcano of the Louisville Chain. The basaltic debris in DSDP core 204 are overlain by reworked Late Cretaceous sediments. This led *Burns et al.* [1973] to conclude a "Cretaceous (?Early) age" for the cores containing the pebbles. An Early Cretaceous age seems unlikely in view of the ~66 Ma age obtained for the "post-erosional" lavas of Osbourn Seamount [*Watts et al.*, in press], but a Late Cretaceous age is supported by the drill core data which has evidence for Eocene and younger sediments above the pebble-bearing layers. The composition of some of these pebbles is tholeiitic (silica-saturated basalt), and this supports the idea that the seamount magmas evolved from tholeiitic to alkalic composition. We still do not know the composition of the first magmas erupted, but there is evidence from small seamounts that the initial stages may be heterogeneous in composition and silica undersaturated magmas are important [*Hawkins and Natland*, 1975; *Moore et al.*, 1982]. The final evolutionary stages of ocean island (off-axis seamount) volcanism reverts to silica undersaturated magmas as is well known from the Hawaiian and Samoan volcanoes. Rocks from the Louisville Seamount Chain represent all parts of this ocean island magmatic evolutionary sequence and, even though we lack age-stratigraphic control, it seems likely that the ridge evolved like other linear volcanic chains.

All of the igneous rocks from the Louisville Chain are fine grained volcanic rocks with variable amounts of phenocrystic olivine, clinopyroxene and plagioclase. Nearly all of the samples show effects of alteration such as extensive replacement of olivine by serpentine and iddingsite, abundant groundmass chlorite, filling of vesicles and fractures by calcite or zeolites such as natrolite (derived from nepheline?). Chemical data show that most of the samples have high contents of water (e.g., up to 8%), moderate CO_2 (e.g., up to 0.3%), and alkali metal concentrations that are probably due to alteration imposed on rocks that initially had elevated alkali concentrations.

The Fe ratios measured on the samples show that they have been extensively altered by oxidation. Ratios Fe'''/Fe'' range from 0.5 to 5.5. In calculating the norms (Table 2), we used a ratio of 0.5 which is likely to be a maximum value for the original magmas even though values as low as 0.15 to 0.2 are typical of some Hawaiian basalts and may well have been true of the Louisville Chain samples. The Fe ratio used obviously affects the norm, and a lower ratio makes the norms appear even less saturated in silica. The Fe ratio also controls the apparent Mg number as discussed below. The P content of sample SOTW-9-48-2 is so high as to suggest phosphatic alteration perhaps due to near surface or reef/lagoonal phosphatization. The Y and REE abundances of this sample are also high and probably reflect their uptake during phosphatization. In general rocks from the western, older, end of the chain show the most extensive alteration, whereas relatively fresh basalts were collected at sites MTHN-6 and MTHN-7 at the "zero" age end of the chain. In spite of the alteration effects on the older samples, it is still possible to recognize their alkalic character by element abundances and element ratios especially those of the high field strength (HFS) elements. Petrographic characteristics such as the presence of groundmass Fe-rich olivine and mineralogic data such as clinopyroxene composition also are useful criteria.

The alkalic character of the Louisville Chain is shown on an alkali-silica plot (Figure 5). The chemical data for the samples are in Tables 2, 3, and 4, normative data are in Table 2, and mineral data are in Table 5. These data show that there are two broad categories of rocks present: the oldest (?) tholeiitic basalts that were the source of basalt pebbles cored at DSDP site 204 and all of the rest which are alkalic rock varieties. Some of the youngest samples have characteristics suggestive of a transition to tholeiitic composition (Figure 5). Two of the samples from dredge site SOTW-58 may be subalkalic or transitional according to this diagram, but their trace element chemistry argues for an alkalic composition. Alteration of these samples may account for their shift towards the more silicic composition suggested by this diagram. Within the alkalic rocks there are two series (Figure 6); most of the samples are characterized by high Na (expressed also in the normative nepheline that ranges up to 23%) and the other

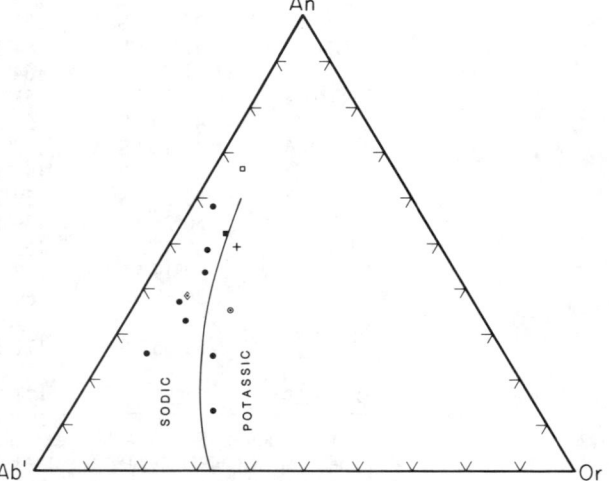

Fig. 6. Plot of normative An-Ab'-Or for Louisville Chain samples showing the predominance of sodic alkalic series rocks, after *Irvine and Baragar* [1971]. Ab' = Ab + 5/3 Ne.

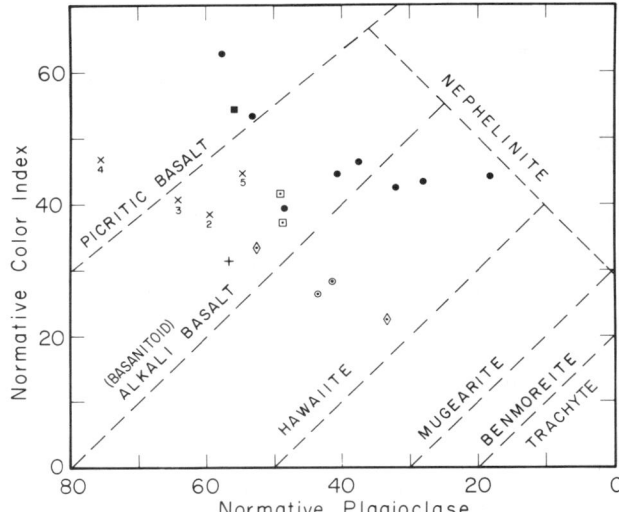

Fig. 7. Classification scheme for alkalic rocks showing Louisville Seamount Chain samples [*Irvine and Baragar*, 1971]. Symbols as in Figure 6.

by rocks with relatively higher K content. The latter lack normative nepheline and have about 10% normative orthoclase.

Rock classification of altered alkalic rock series is difficult because of changes in the original plagioclase composition and alkali, magnesium and silicon concentrations. Alteration effects tend to shift the rock compositions toward rocks more fractionated than the original magma, and changes in Fe-oxidation ratios affect the normative data. We have recalculated our data to volatile free compositions and used the classification scheme of *Irvine and Baragar* [1971] for mafic rocks. Normative and petrographic data were used to give appropriate names. The norms were calculated with Fe-oxidation ratios of 0.5 which probably is a maximum value for the original ratio. A value of 0.15 may be more appropriate but does not change the normative data appreciably other than to cause a small increase in normative OL and NE. The Louisville Chain rocks are mainly sodic alkalic rocks, as shown in Figure 6, and thus differ from "Atlantic" alkalic rock series which typically are enriched in potassium.

Relative enrichment of Na over K appears to be typical of Pacific Basin alkalic rock series such as those of the Samoan Chain [*Natland*, 1980] and sodic rocks are abundant in other Pacific chains, such as Hawaii and the Line Islands [*Schlanger et al.*, 1984], that have both Na- and K-rich alkalic rocks. The relatively high Na coupled with Si deficiency is seen in the abundance of nepheline in the norms. Several of the alkali basalts are classified as basanitoids because normative Ne is greater than 5%. It should be pointed out that nepheline is never present as a mineral but only as a normative constituent. It may be occult in the groundmass but could not be recognized optically or by X-ray diffraction.

The K-rich rocks show similarity to the magma series that formed Atlantic seamounts and islands such as Gough Island and Tristan da Cunha [*Le Maitre*, 1962; *Baker et al.*, 1964], although the K content of the Louisville Chain rocks is lower. The relatively minor importance of K-rich alkalic rocks in the Pacific, and the low levels of K in all of the Pacific alkalic series suggests a fundamental chemical difference in the sub-oceanic mantle of the Atlantic and Pacific basins. This may have implications to the role of recycled K-enriched crustal rocks in causing mantle heterogeneities.

The abundances of large ion lithophile (LIL) elements are also typical of alkalic series rocks (e.g., K, P, Ba, Sr, Rb, REE, Th, U). These abundances are similar to rocks from the Hawaiian and Samoan chains with the exception of Ba and Rb. The abundances of other low partition coefficient elements (Ti, Zr, Hf, Y, Nb) are enriched in Louisville Chain rocks relative to N-MORB values and resemble alkalic rocks of the linear volcanic chains. The trace element data for the Louisville Chain rocks are consistent with their being derived by small amounts (e.g., 10% or less) of fractional melting [*Gast*, 1968; *Sun and Hanson*, 1975]. *Kay and Gast* [1972] proposed that alkali-rich, silica undersaturated basalts are derived by small amounts of melting of hydrous garnet peridotite at the top of the asthenosphere. Our data are consistent with this model and, as discussed below, we postulate that the garnet peridotite source for the Louisville rocks was enriched in some LIL elements in order to give the observed concentrations of many of these elements even with low degrees of partial melting.

The alkalic rocks may be subdivided into picritic basalts, alkali basalt and hawaiite using the normative color index and normative plagioclase (Figure 7). Two samples, dredged from the easternmost end of the chain, may be transitional to subalkaline (Figure 5) silica saturated basalts such as tholeiitic rocks from Hawaii, but they are clearly distinct from N-MORB in major, minor, and trace element characteristics and have low partition coefficient (LPC) element abundances that are alkalic.

Mineralogy

Electron probe micro-analyses were made of the phenocrysts and groundmass minerals of the samples (Table 5 gives representative data). Many of the samples were moderately to heavily altered, but the clinopyroxene had resisted alteration and gave the best data for characterizing these rocks. In addition, X-ray diffraction analyses were made of all samples to determine alteration and vesicle-vein filling minerals.

Olivine is largely altered to iddingsite and serpentine, but those crystals still preserved show only minor range in composition (Fo_{77-80}) within samples or between different samples. The only exception to this is phenocrysts in MONS-110 (Valerie Guyot) that have cores of Fo_{85}. Olivine in the postulated primary sample

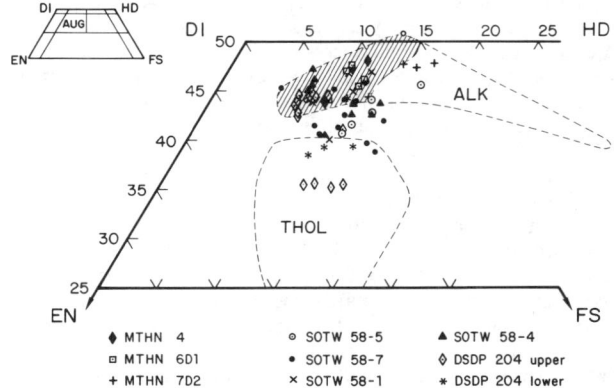

Fig. 8. Clinopyroxene data shown on part of the pyroxene quadrilateral. Fields for Hawaiian alkalic and tholeiitic pyroxenes from *Basaltic Volcanism Study Project* [1981]. Shaded area in alkalic field is for megacrysts.

TABLE 2. Chemical

Sample	SOTW 58-1	SOTW 58-10	SOTW 58-8	SOTW 58-9	SOTW 58-5	MTHN 6D1	MTHN 6D2 FRAC	SOTW 58-4	MTHN 7D2	SOTW 58-6	MONS 110-1
SiO_2	46.72	46.29	46.36	46.85	45.75	45.21	46.06	47.55	47.27	46.70	45.99
TiO_2	2.81	2.59	2.52	2.79	1.66	3.00	3.57	2.22	3.09	2.99	3.44
Al_2O_3	14.65	15.64	15.60	15.93	10.70	12.89	15.75	13.54	15.82	14.44	17.46
FeO*	11.47	11.80	11.46	11.37	12.78	13.04	12.28	11.64	11.79	13.73	10.25
MnO	0.23	0.17	0.18	0.20	0.33	0.18	0.20	0.19	0.21	0.33	0.21
MgO	7.54	7.15	7.13	6.45	22.10	12.21	7.13	10.19	8.31	7.78	6.63
CaO	10.58	8.48	8.38	9.75	4.61	10.38	11.49	10.39	9.08	9.01	10.72
Na_2O	3.94	4.34	4.36	5.37	1.77	2.23	2.62	2.51	3.22	3.67	3.21
K_2O	1.12	2.26	2.26	0.86	0.27	0.39	0.50	0.64	0.74	0.77	1.17
P_2O_5	0.47	0.28	0.28	0.39	0.24	0.55	0.40	0.31	0.72	0.42	0.72
TOTAL	99.53	99.00	98.53	99.96	100.21	100.08	100.00	99.18	100.25	99.84	99.80
H_2O^+	3.74	7.79	5.87	5.48	7.44		—	3.94		5.42	1.28
CO_2	0.07	.01	.01	.01	.01		—	0.01		.01	.36
Fe_2O_3	7.91	8.77	7.87	9.13	10.86	6.28	—	7.77	4.36	10.23	6.77
FeO	3.91	2.99	3.71	2.53	2.05	7.39	—	4.19	7.87	3.77	3.99
Type (1)	B	B	B	NH	PB	PB	AB	AB	AB	AB	AB
Type (2)	B	B	B	T	AB	AB	AB	AB	AB	AB	AB
OL	9.7	11.2	11.2	7.9	29.2	16.7	6.4	9.9	11.3	13.9	9.7
DI	24.4	19.2	19.0	23.2	0.7	20.3	19.7	20.6	13.0	17.1	14.8
HY	—	—	—	—	22.9	4.6	5.1	9.3	4.8	—	—
MT	6.2	6.4	6.2	6.1	6.8	7.0	6.6	6.3	6.3	7.3	5.5
IL	5.3	4.9	4.8	5.3	3.1	5.7	6.7	4.2	5.9	5.7	6.5
NE	6.6	11.1	10.9	12.4	—	—	—	—	—	1.3	2.3
AB	21.1	16.5	17.2	22.3	14.9	18.8	22.1	21.3	27.1	28.6	22.9
AN	19.0	16.6	16.5	16.8	20.3	23.9	29.6	23.9	26.4	20.6	29.7
OR	6.6	13.4	13.5	5.1	1.6	2.3	2.9	3.8	4.4	4.5	9.7
Q	—	—	—	—	—	—	—	—	—	—	—
AP	1.1	0.7	0.7	0.9	0.6	0.7	0.9	0.7	0.8	1.0	0.9
CC	—	—	—	—	—	—	—	—	—	—	0.8

Key to rock types: B = basanitoid; T = tephrite; NH = nepheline hawaiite; FeO* = total iron as FeO; AB = alkali basalt; PB = picritic basalt; F = foidite; H = hawaiite; M = mugearite; (1) after *Irvine and Baragar* [1971]; (2) after *Le Bas et al.* [1986]; FeO determined by titration; values shown for

(SOTW 58-4) is completely replaced by phyllosilicates. Plagioclase composition varies with rock type as expected. Basanitoid and alkali basalts range from $An_{60}Ab_{36}Or_2$ to $An_{75}Ab_{24}Or_1$; groundmass plagioclase is usually about 2 mol percent lower in An than core compositions of phenocrysts. The K content of the plagioclase is relatively low for alkalic rocks, but this follows the generally low K content of the rocks. The hawaiite samples have more sodic plagioclase, and they too are low in K (e.g., $An_{57-60}Ab_{32-37}Or_{2-2.6}$).

Clinopyroxene data are shown in Figures 8, 9, 10, and in Table 5d. The pyroxene is largely augite or salite (Figure 8); Al_2O_3 typically is in the range 4-7%, but some samples have up to 8%. For most samples, much of the Al is in the tetrahedral site (e.g., typically there is >.12 Al per 6 oxygen anions and several samples have >.25 Al per 6 oxygens). This is consistent with their crystallization from silica deficient magmas. Titanium is also enriched in these samples; TiO_2 ranges from about 1% to 3.8% but Na_2O is low (0.2 to 0.6%). They plot in the field for Ti-Al pyroxenes or the Ca-Tschermaks field on a plot of Ti-NaM_2-Al^{IV}. Both the high Ti and Al^{IV} coupled with relatively low Si are typical of clinopyroxenes crystallized from alkalic magmas [*Kushiro*, 1960; *LeBas*, 1962]. The relations between Si and Al for Louisville Chain clinopyroxenes and for the DSDP site 204 detritus are shown in Figures 9 and 10 which show that most of the samples are alkaline or peralkaline. Many of the detrital clinopyroxene from DSDP 204 plot in the tholeiitic field and have Al^{IV} <.14 per 6 oxygen and lower TiO_2 (<.85%). These pyroxenes give evidence for the nature of the earlier magmatism in either Osbourn Seamount or an older neighbor now accreted or subducted at the Tonga Trench. Most of the alkalic pyroxenes from the Louisville Chain plot in the same field as Hawaiian alkalic pyroxenes on the pyroxene quadrilateral (Figure 8). A similar coincidence is seen for the tholeiitic pyroxenes from Hawaii and some of the DSDP 204 grains.

We lack any igneous rock samples from the guyot dredged at MTHN-4, but the carbonate rocks have minor amounts of detrital pyroxene and plagioclase. Microprobe analyses of the clinopyroxene (Table 5d) show that it is alkalic and points to an alkalic basalt cap on this seamount as is found at all of the other dredge sites.

Clinopyroxene from SOTW 58-4, the postulated "primary" magma, are diopside-endiopside and have relatively high TiO_2 and low Al^{IV} (e.g., .14 per 6 oxygens). Some SOTW 58-4 phenocrysts have more than 1% Cr_2O_3 in their cores which decreases to 0.8% on the rims. The phenocrysts record crystallization under relatively low fO_2 where Cr entered the pyroxene rather than forming spinel. In contrast, MTHN 6D-1, a relatively "primitive" composition, has both chrome spinel and clinopyroxene having about 0.6% Cr_2O_3 suggesting either higher or variable fO_2. Aluminum in

and Normative Data

	SOTW 58-3	MTHN 7D1	LV-4	SOTW 58-7	LV-5	LV-3	SOTW 52-1	LV-2	SOTW 48-1	SOTW 48-2	MONS 110-B
	48.18	47.42	39.69	46.36	46.59	44.21	47.34	42.92	45.52	46.19	51.45
	2.90	3.22	5.05	2.60	3.59	3.72	3.36	2.81	3.84	3.62	2.34
	15.78	16.60	15.80	15.83	15.28	17.12	18.46	16.22	15.77	16.19	18.14
	11.04	11.56	17.22	10.37	16.39	13.45	11.41	13.68	12.21	11.85	9.97
	0.18	0.22	0.29	0.18	0.10	0.19	0.14	0.26	0.13	0.14	0.17
	6.52	6.45	6.19	5.98	5.82	4.82	3.80	3.74	3.19	3.01	3.06
	10.04	9.42	11.18	9.11	8.70	12.19	9.69	14.22	9.77	9.52	6.81
	3.25	3.35	1.30	5.47	2.62	2.29	2.96	2.51	3.51	3.39	4.95
	0.94	1.15	0.91	3.15	1.01	0.59	1.42	0.51	2.25	2.03	2.09
	0.50	0.63	0.65	0.23	0.27	0.54	0.84	2.52	2.85	2.96	1.09
	99.33	100.02	98.29	99.28	100.36	99.11	99.42	99.38	99.04	98.90	100.13
	2.60			8.13			2.51			4.83	1.30
	0.01			0.30			0.02		0.72	0.67	0.02
	6.11	5.30	12.90	9.70	14.03	9.69	8.05	12.12		11.15	8.30
	5.25	6.79	5.61	0.76	3.76	4.73	3.87	2.77		1.81	2.37
	AB	AB	PB	NH	AB	AB	AB	AB	H	H	H
	AB	AB	F	T	AB	PB	AB	T	H	H	M
	5.7	9.8	7.4	5.2	0.5	3.5	—	4.2	1.4	1.2	7.5
	16.8	13.1	13.6	27.7	11.7	18.1	7.9	18.7	3.8	0.6	4.5
	6.0	1.8	6.9	—	17.2	5.0	10.8	2.8	9.3	11.0	0.7
	5.9	6.2	9.3	5.6	8.7	7.2	6.1	7.4	6.5	6.5	5.3
	5.5	6.1	9.7	5.0	6.8	7.1	6.4	5.3	7.3	7.0	4.4
	—	—	—	21.8	—	—	—	—	—	—	—
	27.6	28.2	11.1	6.2	22.0	19.5	25.1	21.3	29.6	29.3	41.7
	25.8	26.8	35.0	9.4	26.7	34.8	32.9	31.5	20.6	23.5	21.0
	5.6	6.8	5.4	18.7	5.9	3.5	8.4	3.0	13.3	12.3	12.3
	—	—	—	—	—	—	0.4	—	—	—	—
	1.2	1.2	1.5	0.5	0.6	1.3	1.9	5.8	7.0	7.0	2.5
	—	—	—	—	—	—	—	—	1.6	1.6	—

FeO and Fe_2O_3 are for rock compositions readjusted for H_2O^+ and CO_2 content; Norms calculated assuming $Fe'''/Fe'' = 0.5$

octahedral coordination is variable in the Louisville Chain samples but generally is less than .05 Al^{VI} per 6 oxygens. *LeBas* [1962] suggests that higher pressure may favor Al^{VI} because of the observations that eclogitic pyroxenes have higher Al^{VI} and this may be related to a pressure induced decrease in the *a* and *b* cell dimensions. Application of these observations to the Louisville Chain pyroxenes suggests that nearly all crystallized at low pressure with the exception of some phenocryst cores (e.g., analyses 1, 4, Table 5d) which have about 1/6 of the Al in octahedral sites. These may reflect an early stage of crystallization at higher P while the melt was ascending from the mantle source region. Groundmass pyroxenes associated with these phenocrysts have low Al^{VI} as would be expected for low pressure crystallization.

Oxide minerals include Fe-Ti oxides, magnetite, and chrome spinel. Much of the magnetite appears to be an alteration product due to the breakdown of olivine to serpentine and to hydration and oxidation of intersertal glass. The Fe-Ti oxides are nearly euhedral grains that probably are primary. In some samples the Fe-Ti and Fe oxides account for about 10-12 modal percent of the rock. Chrome spinel was found as euhedral inclusions and epitaxial grains with olivine in MTHN-6D. It has low $Cr/(Cr + Al)$ that is typical of ocean floor basalts and has relatively high $Fe'''/(Cr + Al + Fe''')$.

Discussion of Petrogenesis

In considering the petrologic evolution of the Louisville Chain we first consider the range in magma compositions represented and ask whether or not any may be "primary" or unfractionated parental magmas. Magmas postulated as primary are recognized by high Mg number ($100 \, Mg/(Mg + Fe'')$), for example, >65, Ni > 100 ppm, Cr > 200 ppm, Sc 15-28 ppm, and Co 27-80 ppm [*Green*, 1971; *Sun and Hanson*, 1975; *Frey et al.*, 1978]. Variations in concentrations of low partition coefficient elements (e.g., Rb, Zr, LREE) are due to varied extent of melting or variable source characteristics or both. Abundances of Na, Al, HREE reflect both source composition and depth of melting. Sample SOTW-58-4, from Osbourn Seamount, is fine grained olivine-clinopyroxene-plagioclase-Fe-Ti oxide alkalic basalt with about 2-3 modal percent olivine micro-phenocrysts. It probably is close to a liquid composition. It has an Mg number of 70, 350 ppm Ni, and 10% normative olivine (calculated for $Fe'''/Fe'' = 0.5$). The Mg number would be 64 if a ratio of 0.15 were used. These data suggest that it is close to a "primary" magma composition; it is the least evolved sample we have, and we use it as an example of the parental magma for the seamounts of the chain. Another sample

TABLE 3. Trace

Sample	SOTW 58-10	SOTW 58-8	SOTW 58-9	SOTW 58-5	MTHN 6D1	SOTW 58-4	MTHN 7D2
Ni	116	156	104	892	313	350	99
Cr	—	—	—	—	573	—	263
Co	—	—	—	—	65	—	42
Sc	—	—	—	—	26	—	21
V	308	314	294	232	239	276	272
Zn	—	—	—	—	—	—	—
Sb	—	—	—	—	0.230	—	0.334
Rb	11	9	8	0.1	14	11	19
Cs	—	—	—	—	0.24	—	0.12
Ba	48	54	27	19	144	92	240
Sr	1560	327	765	53	678	340	1185
Hf	—	—	—	—	6.41	—	7.33
Zr	210	200	193	121	273	159	299
Nb	29	30	22	18	40	24	41
Y	31	32	31	20	28	27	33
Ta	—	—	—	—	2.51	—	2.63
Th	—	—	—	—	3.21	—	4.44
U	—	—	—	—	0.90	—	1.35

Ni, V, Rb, Ba, Sr, Zr, Nb, Y by x-ray fluorescence; other elements by INAA

that may be close to a primary composition is MTHN-6D1 from a young volcano at the eastern end of the chain. It has Mg number 71.5, but this is because it has 15 modal percent olivine (Fo_{80}) phenocrysts. When corrected for the olivine phenocrysts and the trace (0.2%) amounts of chromite ($Cr/(Cr + Al)$) = 0.47, the "liquid" composition has Mg number = 60.8, 6% normative olivine, 105 ppm Ni, 280 ppm Cr, 76 ppm Co, and 31 ppm Sc. A calculated phenocryst-free analysis of this sample is listed as MTHN-6D1 FRAC in Table 2.

Much of the variation in composition of Louisville Chain samples may be due to fractionation of olivine (Fo_{78-82}) and diopsidic augite which are the main phenocrysts in the alkali basalts and basanitoids. The control on melt composition by removal of olivine and clinopyroxene is shown in the plot of CaO vs MgO (Figure 11). This is only a qualitative representation because the samples have come from twelve different seamounts, each of

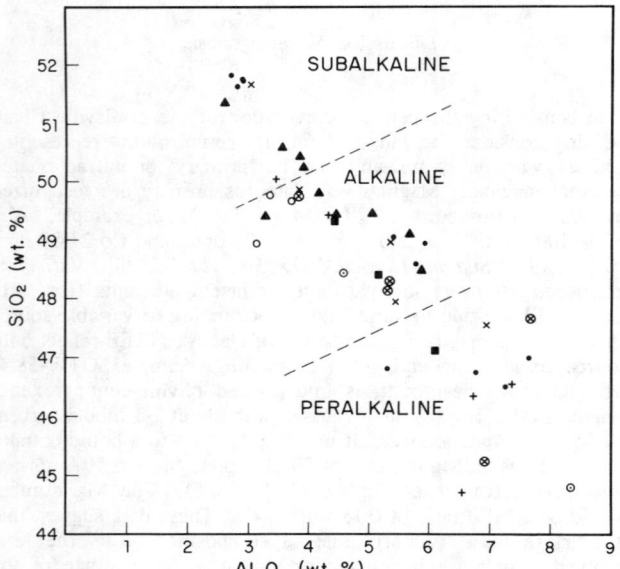

Fig. 9. Plot of SiO_2 vs. Al_2O_3 for Louisville Seamount Chain clinopyroxenes. Boundaries for magma types after *LeBas* [1962].

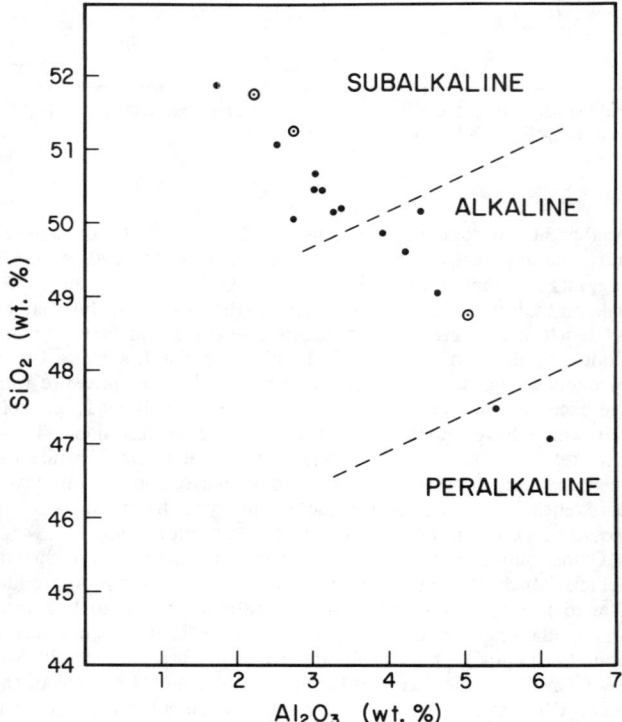

Fig. 10. Plot of SiO_2 vs. Al_2O_3 for DSDP site 204 clinopyroxene. Data are for microphenocrysts in basalt pebbles and individual detrital grains. Boundaries after *LeBas* [1962]. Symbols as in Figure 8.

Elements (ppm)

SOTW 58-6	SOTW 58-1	MONS 110-1	SOTW 58-3	MTHN 7D1	SOTW 58-7	SOTW 52-1	SOTW 48-2
124	182	162	92	101	82	56	94
—	509	418	—	215	—	109	88
—	46	62	—	46	—	33	39
—	30	23	—	21	—	27	21
350	299	302	314	284	165	356	270
—	93	97	—			117	153
—	—	—	—	0.175	—	—	—
12	15	19	22	25	12	25	89
—	0.43	0.72		0.12		0.59	5.85
72	143	194	125	265	128	202	135
233	634	667	481	681	3954	647	596
—	5.21	7.73		7.36		6.53	6.51
241	217	312	247	293	182	276	277
28	32	54	28	45	24	45	54
37	29	37	36	34	25	34	76
—	—	—	—	2.61	—	—	—
—	2.23	3.42	—	4.12	—	2.96	3.08
—	0.44	1.01	—	1.28	—	0.75	1.19

which probably had its own parental magma. The general negative correlation suggests that clinopyroxene was important in controlling major element chemistry even though it rarely is more abundant than olivine as a phenocryst. This may suggest that the melts represent mixing of successive batches of magma that have already lost pyroxene by fractional crystallization.

The co-variation between Ni and Zr shown in Figure 12 illustrates magma evolution by olivine fractionation. Most of the samples from Osbourn Seamount (SOTW 58) lie along the trend expected from removal of olivine from a postulated primary magma. The similarity in K_D for Ni and Zr in olivine and clinopyroxene makes this an insensitive test to discriminate between fractionation of olivine alone or olivine plus clinopyroxene. One sample, which has about 15% olivine phenocrysts, clearly shows the effect of olivine accumulation. Alkali basalt samples from the eastern end of the chain (Marathon expedition-MTHN) and Valerie Guyot (MONS-110) have distinct enrichment in Zr relative to Osbourn Seamount suggesting that they were derived from a source with higher Zr, or by a lower degree of melting of the source or both. Estimates of the extent of melting, discussed below, suggests that the basanitoids of Osbourn Seamount represent about 9% melting in contrast to 4 or 5% for the alkali basalts.

Data for rare earth elements (REE) are in Table 4 and are shown normalized to chondritic values in Figure 13. The least fractionated sample (SOTW 58-1) is a basanitoid from Osbourn Seamount, and the most fractionated is a hawaiite (SOTW 48-2) from Currituck Seamount. The latter has been phosphatized, and this probably accounts for the elevated La and Ce. The abundances and ratios for the Louisville Chain samples are similar to those reported for alkalic rocks of the Hawaiian Chain for which an undepleted mantle source has been proposed [*Chen and Frey*, 1985]. For example, Hawaiian series show a progressive increase from tholeiitic, to alkalic, to post-erosional (e.g., basanites) basalts in ratios such as La/Ce, La/Sm, Ba/Zr, Ba/La, and a progressive decrease in Zr/Nb. The Louisville Chain basaltic samples have La/Ce 0.43 to 0.46 (Hawaiian Kula and Hana series have 0.41 to 0.47); Louisville Chain La/Sm is 3.27 to 3.29 (Hawaii 3.29 to 4.03); Louisville Chain Zr/Nb is 5.9 to 8.8 (Hawaii 5.4 to 8.6). An important distinction is that the Louisville Chain samples all have lower Ba than comparable Hawaiian series rocks as is shown in Ba/Zr and Ba/La. For the Louisville Chain these ranges are, respectively, 0.16 to 0.90 and 4.8 to 7.3. Otherwise comparable Hawaiian alkalic series basalts have Ba/Zr 1.45 to 2.2 and Ba/La 13.0 to 16.1. The source for the Louisville Chain has much lower Ba relative to other low partition coefficient elements than the

TABLE 4. Rare Earth Elements (ppm)

	SOTW 58-1	MTHN 6D1	SOTW 52-1	MONS 110-1	MTHN 7D2	MTHN 7D1	SOTW 48-2
La	22.87	30.08	31.07	33.81	35.50	36.36	44.39
Ce	53.75	64.6	71.06	78.54	78.1	80.1	65.58
(Nd)	29	34	36	43	37	38	40
Sm	7.00	8.13	8.65	10.01	8.89	9.16	9.48
Eu	2.16	2.6	2.68	3.14	2.84	2.84	3.02
Tb	0.98	1.03	1.16	1.33	1.17	1.22	1.48
Yb	1.99	2.03	2.37	2.46	2.23	2.22	3.89
Lu	0.29	0.276	0.35	0.36	0.293	0.311	0.61
$[La/Sm]_{EF}$	2.06	2.33	2.26	2.13	2.51	2.50	2.95
La/Ce	0.43	0.47	0.44	0.43	0.45	0.45	0.67

Analyses by INAA. Nd values estimated from Nd/Sm data [*Cheng et al.*, this volume].

TABLE 5A.

	1	2	3	4	5	6	7	8
SiO_2	38.58	37.91	38.45	39.43	39.11	37.83	38.00	37.83
FeO	19.01	21.16	19.37	14.29	15.60	20.34	19.77	20.34
MnO	0.24	0.28	0.34	0.23	0.27	0.29	0.33	0.29
CaO	0.29	0.18	0.29	0.12	0.12	0.34	0.36	0.34
MgO	41.66	40.23	41.29	45.69	44.63	40.95	41.19	40.95
NiO	0.17	0.10	0.11	0.23	0.22	0.18	0.18	0.18
SUM	99.95	99.86	99.85	99.99	99.95	99.92	99.82	99.93
Fo	79.6	77.2	79.2	85.1	83.6	78.2	78.8	78.2

1. MNS 110-1 - core, microphenocryst; 2. MNS 110-1 - core, phenocryst; 3. MNS 110-1 - rim, phenocryst #2; 4. MNS 110-1 - core, phenocryst; 5. MNS 110-1 - rim, phenocryst #4; 6. MTHN 6D1 - core, phenocryst; 7. MTHN 6D1 - rim, phenocryst #6; 8. MTHN 6D1 - core, phenocryst; 9. MTHN 6D1 - rim, phenocryst #8; 10. MTHN 6D1 - core, phenocryst;

Hawaiian source and, to a lesser extent, Rb and K are lower as well. These differences in alkalis and alkaline earths are discussed in the following section.

Nature of the Mantle Source

Linear seamount chains are of great interest to petrologists because they are time transgressive sampling devices for magmas derived from the mantle at melting sites away from "mid-ocean" ridges. Some seamount chains may record melts from deep in the mantle that rise as magma plumes, others may represent melts from sources near the base of the lithosphere. Not all seamounts in a chain may be part of a progressive time sequence as the oceanic plate may have already had a seamount population before the trace of the chain was printed on it; but, if age control is available, we have the potential of tracking melt and source variation with time.

The temporal variation seen in some chains and in individual volcanoes, e.g., Hawaii [*Clague and Frey*, 1982] and Maui [*Chen and Frey*, 1983, 1985] may be due to variation in extent of melting or mixing of magmas from compositionally distinct sources. The Louisville Chain gives us an opportunity to study source- and melt-evolution over a time span of about 66 m.y. and over a distance of 4300 km.

The primary controls on differences between alkalic and tholeiitic magma series are believed to be fundamental differences in the chemistry of the mantle source and the extent of fractional melting [e.g., *Gast*, 1968; *Kay and Gast*, 1973; *Sun and Hanson*, 1975]. Subsequent modification of the magmas by fractional crystallization acts as an important secondary control. The ratio of pairs of low partition coefficient (LPC) elements having similar partition coefficients should not change significantly during fractional melting, or low levels of fractional crystallization of phases with low levels of LPC elements, and the ratio should reflect the element ratio of the source. Discriminant schemes for recognizing source characteristics and melting relations have been proposed that use ratios of LPC elements such as Ti, Zr, Nb, Y, and LREE [*Pearce and Cann*, 1973; *Pearce and Norry*, 1979]. These elements are generally considered to be immobile under conditions of low temperature alteration [*Cann*, 1970] and thus should be useful tracers of magma history even for the altered rocks of the Louisville Chain.

Chen and Frey [1983, 1985] have modeled the evolution of Hawaiian Chain basalts by proposing variable mixing of mantle sources similar to the MORB source with an undepleted "primitive" mantle source. We have used their proposed "recently enriched" mantle as a model for the Louisville Chain source and find that it is adequate for most trace elements although we can-

TABLE 5B.

	1	2	3	4	5	6	7	8
SiO_2	52.20	52.30	50.41	50.98	49.41	52.45	50.95	53.05
TiO_2	0.21	0.21	0.13	0.18	0.16	0.23	0.16	0.18
Al_2O_3	29.41	29.43	31.14	30.72	31.93	29.21	30.63	28.94
FeO	0.83	0.75	0.60	0.60	0.75	0.96	0.69	0.72
MgO	0.08	0.11	0.18	0.12	0.24	0.16	0.44	0.22
CaO	11.86	12.46	13.94	13.57	13.97	11.93	13.92	11.73
Na_2O	3.72	4.29	3.64	3.92	3.27	4.58	3.81	4.86
K_2O	1.69	0.45	0.23	0.26	0.24	0.40	0.18	0.36
SUM	100.00	100.00	100.27	100.36	99.98	99.96	100.76	100.06
An	57.5	59.9	67.1	64.6	69.3	57.6	66.2	56.0
Ab	32.7	37.4	31.6	33.5	29.3	40.1	32.8	42.0
Or	9.8	2.6	1.3	1.5	1.4	2.3	1.0	2.0

1. SOTW 9-48-2 - plagioclase lath; 2. SOTW 9-48-2 - microphenocryst; 3. MONS 110-1 - phenocryst core; 4. MONS 110-1 - rim of #3; 5. MONS 110-1 - phenocryst core; 6. MONS 110-1 - rim of #5; 7. SOTW 58-4 - plagioclase lath; 8. SOTW 58-4 - plagioclase lath

Olivine Analyses

9	10	11	12	13	14	15	16
38.00	37.88	38.14	38.43	38.73	38.49	38.38	37.38
19.77	20.64	19.26	18.70	18.65	18.90	18.83	21.93
0.32	0.26	0.29	0.25	0.28	0.29	0.24	0.31
0.36	0.34	0.37	0.43	0.22	0.29	0.21	0.38
41.19	40.70	41.60	41.76	41.91	41.79	42.03	39.52
0.18	0.12	0.23	0.16	0.16	0.08	0.15	0.09
99.82	99.94	99.89	99.73	99.95	99.84	99.84	99.61
78.8	77.9	79.4	79.9	80.0	79.8	79.9	76.3

11. MTHN 6D1 - rim, phenocryst #10; 12. MTHN 6D1 - groundmass; 13. MTHN 7D2 - core, phenocryst; 14. MTHN 7D2 - rim, phenocryst #12; 15. MTHN 7D2 - core, phenocryst; 16. MTHN 7D2 - skeletal groundmass grain

not fit our data to the model for alkalis, alkaline earths, U, and Th. We lack sufficient data to make a well-constrained model for the mantle source as has been done for the Hawaiian volcanoes [*Clague and Frey*, 1982; *Chen and Frey*, 1983, 1985], but our samples show many similarities to the Hawaiian lavas and we are encouraged by the fairly good fit to our data and a model based on a proposed enriched mantle source.

We recognize that we cannot generate a unique model to estimate the mantle source composition or to model its melting history. We lack information about the source mineralogy, the contribution of each phase to the melt ("P" in the melting equations), and the original concentration of each element in the source. We present here a qualitative model that can be tested and improved as more data for the chain become available.

Three main points come from our qualitative model: (1) The mantle source appears to have been relatively homogeneous throughout the 66 m.y. history of this 4300 km long chain; (2) the source resembles a postulate enriched mantle source except that it is slightly depleted in alkalis, alkaline earths, U, and Th; (3) this depletion suggests that the mantle source either has been partly depleted by a melting event or was not enriched by the same type material as the model enriched mantle.

In making our melting model we assumed that the source was peridotite and used published values of partition coefficients and original element concentration. Details are in the Appendix. The mantle source used has 0.6 olivine (OL), 0.25 orthopyroxene (OPX), 0.1 clinopyroxene (CPX), and 0.05 J where J equals garnet (GA), plagioclase (PL), or amphibole (AM). To test for the role of phlogopite we used 0.57 OL, 0.25 OPX, 0.1 CPX, 0.05 GA, 0.03 phlogopite.

Alkalic basalts and basanites have been interpreted as the result of small amounts of melting (<10%) of a peridotite source [e.g., *Gast*, 1968; *Kay and Gast*, 1973] and that their source was enriched in "incompatible" elements relative to the source for MORB. We have estimated the extent of melting of the peridotite source by using the concentration of highly incompatible elements such as Th, La, Ce, P in our relatively unfractionated samples and comparing them to concentrations in model sources. We used the relationship $C_L/C_O = F^{D-1}$ where C_O and C_L equal the concentrations of an element in the source and liquid, respectively, D equals bulk partition coefficient, and F equals the extent of melting. For low partition coefficient elements $C_L/C_O \sim 1/F$. We used *Chen and Frey*'s [1985] estimates of Th = 0.22 ppm, La = 1.35 ppm, Ce = 3.4 ppm, and P = 126 ppm for a recently enriched mantle. The "primitive" alkali basalts may represent 4 to 7% fractional melts, and basanites may represent about 9% melts

Plagioclase Analyses

9	10	11	12	13	14	15	16
49.95	50.60	48.89	47.61	52.70	52.13	51.98	52.01
0.12	0.14	0.13	0.15	0.26	0.12	0.11	0.19
31.83	31.18	32.25	32.39	28.87	30.59	30.49	30.07
0.58	0.65	0.60	0.80	1.01	0.44	0.47	0.67
0.20	0.21	0.10	0.12	0.22	0.07	0.06	0.14
14.90	14.39	15.83	16.23	12.20	12.90	12.89	13.28
3.15	3.51	2.87	2.52	4.41	4.39	4.37	4.21
0.09	0.17	0.18	0.19	0.35	0.24	0.20	0.24
100.82	100.85	100.84	100.01	100.02	100.87	100.56	100.82
72.0	68.7	74.5	77.3	59.2	61.1	61.3	62.7
27.5	30.4	24.6	21.7	38.7	37.5	37.0	36.0
0.5	0.9	1.0	1.0	2.0	1.4	1.1	1.4

9. SOTW 58-4 - phenocryst core; 10. SOTW 58-4 - rim of #9; 11. MTHN 6D1 - phenocryst core; 12. MTHN 6D1 - rim of #11; 13. MTHN 6D1 - groundmass lath; 14. MTHN 7D2 - phenocryst core; 15. MTHN 7D2 - rim of #14; 16. MTHN 7D2 - groundmass

TABLE 5C. Chrome Spinel Analyses

	1	2	3	4	5
Cr_2O_3	21.06	18.98	18.91	10.90	9.24
Al_2O_3	15.95	11.70	12.95	9.94	6.74
Fe_2O_3	4.42	14.97	18.60	16.24	16.69
FeO	41.35	34.51	31.31	42.24	45.95
MgO	9.80	8.95	9.17	7.18	5.49
MnO	0.34	0.32	0.28	0.39	0.37
CaO	0.04	0.08	0.03	0.05	0.10
TiO_2	6.72	10.29	8.49	12.90	15.26
TOTAL	99.68	99.80	99.74	99.84	99.84
Mg#	29.7	31.6	34.4	23.3	17.2
Cr#	43.0	37.5	33.8	26.4	26.0
Al#	48.5	34.4	34.6	36.0	28.3
Fe#	8.6	28.1	31.6	37.6	45.8
Fe'''/Fe''	.096	.391	.535	.346	.327

Microprobe analyses - Fe_2O_3 calculated by stoichiometry; Mg# = Mg/(Mg + Fe''); Cr# = Cr/(Cr + Al + Fe'''); Al# = Al/(Cr + Al + Fe'''); Fe# = Fe'''/(Cr + Al + Fe'''); 1. MTHN 6D1 - inclusion in olivine ($Fo_{79.4}$); 2. MTHN 6D1 - epitaxial grain on olivine ($Fo_{79.9}$); 3. MTHN 6D1 - inclusion in olivine ($Fo_{78.8}$); 4. MTHN 7D2 - inclusion in olivine; 5. MTHN 7D2 - inclusion in olivine

if these assumptions are used. Results of these calculations are in Table 6. Zr in the mantle source was estimated by using Th/Zr in the samples (0.010 to 0.015) as an approximation of the source ratio [*Clague and Frey*, 1982]. *Chen and Frey* [1985] give a source ratio of 0.017, and *Clague and Frey*'s [1982] estimate is 0.011. We use the Chen and Frey enriched mantle source estimate of 13 ppm Zr instead of the 18 ppm required by our Th/Zr data because our higher value leads to unreasonably high calculated Zr at low melt-

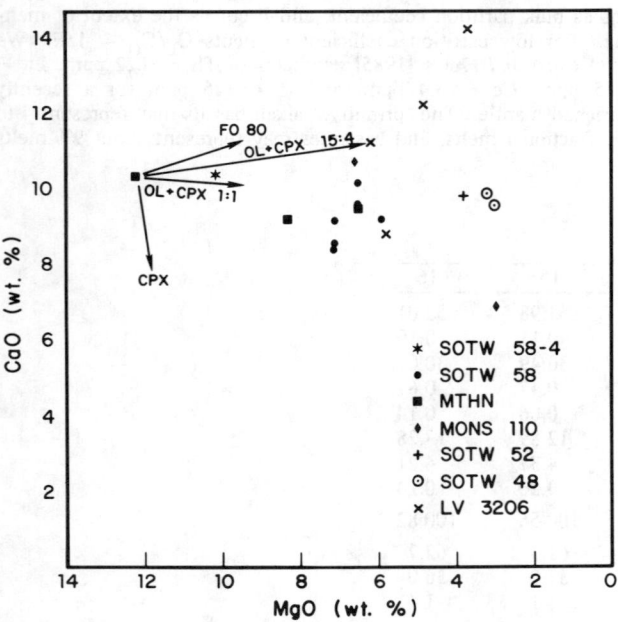

Fig. 11. CaO vs. MgO for Louisville Seamount Chain samples. Paths show fractionation trends for removal of olivine or clinopyroxene or both. OL:CPX ratio 15:4 corresponds to phenocryst proportions in MTHN 6D1 which is used as hypothetical parent composition.

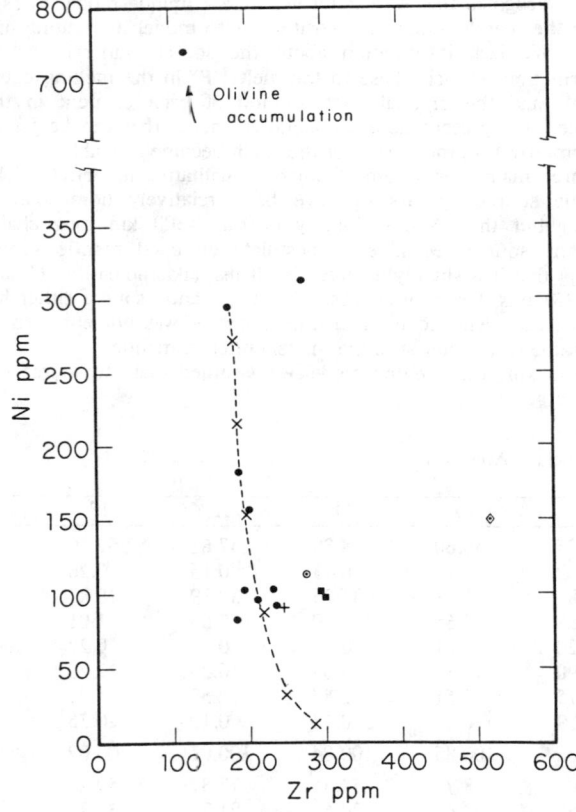

Fig. 12. Ni vs. MgO for Louisville Seamount Chain samples. Dashed line shows calculated path for fractionation of olivine from postulated parental magma (SOTW 58-4). Effect of olivine accumulation is shown to explain SOTW 58-5. Fractionation path was calculated for Rayleigh fractionation with K_D for nickel in olivine = 20, Xs mark 5% and subsequent 10%, 20% etc. fractionation intervals.

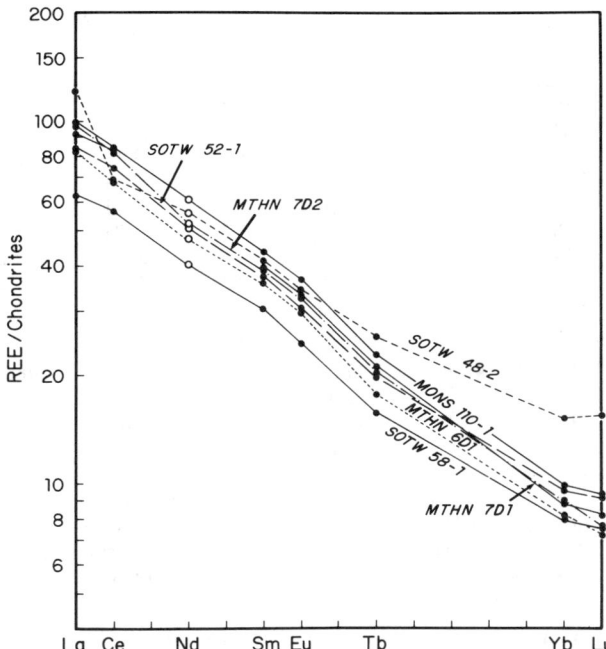

Fig. 13. REE analyses normalized to chondritic values for Louisville Chain samples. Analyses by INAA. Normalizing values used are from *Evensen et al.* [1978] recalculated to a volatile-free basis.

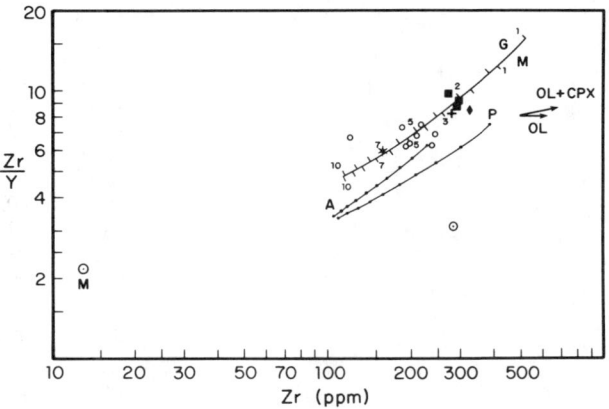

Fig. 15. Variation in Zr/Y vs. Zr for fractional melting models of mantle material M. Model mantle, melting ratio, and partition coefficients as in Figure 14.

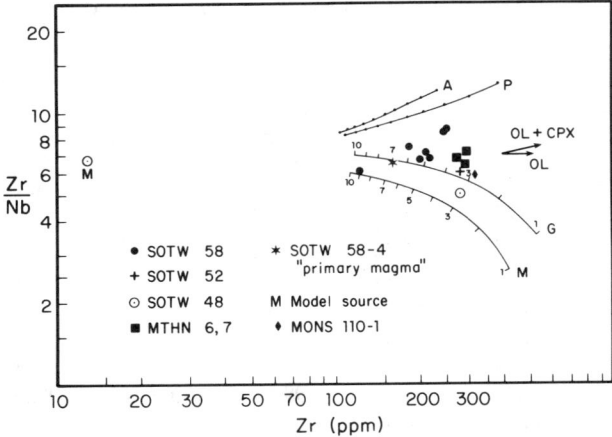

Fig. 14. Variation in Zr/Nb vs. Zr for fractional melting models of mantle material M. Mantle source was modeled for 0.6 olivine, 0.25 orthopyroxene, 0.1 clinopyroxene, and .05 J. Path P is for plagioclase as J, path A is for amphibole as J, and path G is for garnet as J. Tick marks represent 1 to 10% partial melts. Path M is for .057 olivine, 0.25 orthopyroxene, 0.1 clinopyroxene, .05 garnet, and .03 phlogopite. This path and the garnet path coincide but have different coordinates for melt increments. See Appendix for details of the melting model.

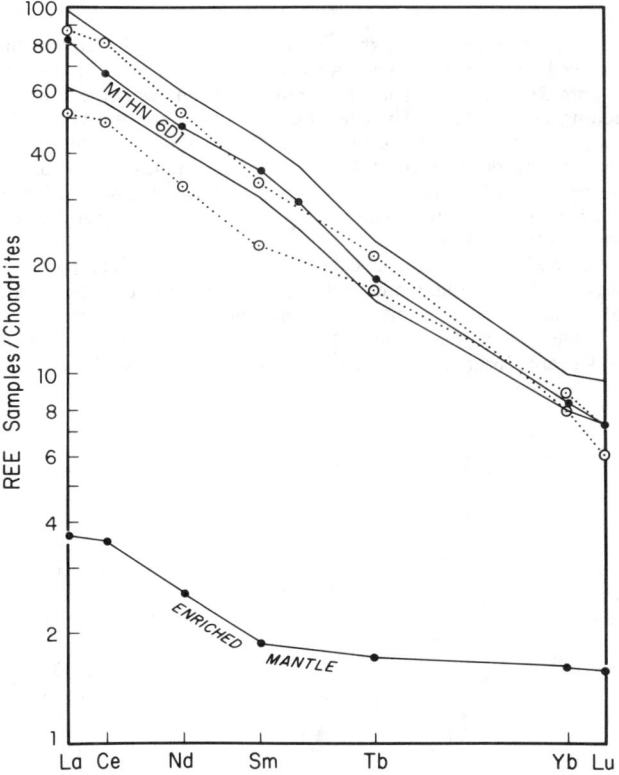

Fig. 16. Model for deriving REE pattern of postulated "primary" magma from an "enriched" mantle source [*Chen and Frey*, 1985]. Model melt data shown as open circles; solid lines define range in REE for analyzed samples from Louisville Seamount Chain. Lower curve is for 4% melting, upper curve is for 7% melting. The model melts for 4 and 7% melting of the source were derived from garnet lherzolite mantle (0.6 olivine, 0.25 orthopyroxene, 0.1 clinopyroxene, .05 garnet melting in proportions 0.1 OL, 0.1 OPX, 0.4 CPX, 0.4 GA. Partition coefficients for LREE from *Chen and Frey* [1985]; HREE from *Frey et al.* [1978] model 3.

TABLE 5D.

	1	2	3	4	5	6	7
SiO_2	45.39	49.38	51.09	50.27	50.45	49.43	51.39
TiO_2	3.18	1.63	1.04	0.93	1.05	1.53	0.97
Al_2O_3	8.07	3.82	3.00	3.92	3.87	3.30	2.61
FeO	7.34	7.64	5.56	4.45	4.76	8.89	7.27
MnO	0.15	0.30	0.15	0.10	0.13	0.23	0.24
MgO	13.64	17.00	16.89	16.06	16.29	14.94	17.20
CaO	21.68	19.74	21.68	23.22	22.12	20.68	20.20
Na_2O	0.38	0.45	0.24	0.25	0.26	0.35	0.23
Cr_2O_3	0.16	0.03	0.36	1.03	0.78	0.14	0.15
SUM	99.99	99.99	100.01	100.24	99.69	99.50	100.26
EN	40.0	42.9	47.4	45.6	46.7	42.9	48.0
FS	12.3	10.2	8.7	7.0	7.6	14.3	11.3
WO	46.7	40.0	43.7	47.3	45.6	42.7	40.6
Al^{IV}	.300	.253	.118	.148	.137	.141	.106

Al^{IV} = tetrahedrally coordinated aluminum calculated on basis of 6 oxygen anions per structural formula unit; 1. SOTW 58-1 - phenocryst core; 2. SOTW 58-1 - phenocryst core; 3. SOTW 58-1 - groundmass; 4. SOTW 58-4 - phenocryst core; 5. SOTW 58-4 - rim of #4; 6. SOTW 58-4 - groundmass; 7. SOTW 58-4 - microphenocryst

ing percent or requires high melting (e.g., >15%) to explain the observed Zr concentrations. An original mantle concentration of 13 ppm Zr gives melt concentrations consistent with the 5 to 9% melting derived from Th data. Mantle source concentrations for Nb (1.92 ppm) is increased from the Chen and Frey value of 1.8 ppm and is derived from Zr/Nb of our samples. The mantle source concentration for Y (6 ppm) follows *Clague and Frey* [1982] and is consistent with the C_O implied by the melting model for the 5 to 9% range.

We used the Zr, Nb, Y data to model the melt compositions derived from various mantle mineral assemblages (Figures 14 and 15). The best apparent fit comes from the garnet lherzolite model with melting in the range 5 to 7%. Not all of the data points shown are "primary" magmas and fractional crystallization of olivine and clinopyroxene may explain much of the displacement from the calculated curves of melt composition. The role of phlogopite in the source is not clear, the Zr-Y plots do not support a garnet lherzolite source with 3% phlogopite, but the Zr-Nb data are equivocal. The K, Rb, Ba, Sr data, as discussed below, suggest that residual phlogopite may explain the observed depletion in these elements.

The REE data for the Louisville Chain were compared with calculated fractional melts of a source with 2 to 3x enrichment of LREE relative to a chondritic source and nearly chondritic HREE (Figure 16). The LREE data are from the *Chen and Frey* [1985] recently enriched mantle; Yb and Lu are from *Clague and Frey* [1982] and Tb is 2x chondritic. Except for Tb, Yb and Lu, the calculated REE patterns for 5 and 7% melting bracket data for an

TABLE 5D.

	15	16	17	18	19	20
SiO_2	49.78	51.75	51.02	49.84	50.67	50.47
TiO_2	1.32	0.83	0.74	0.92	0.80	0.74
Al_2O_3	2.85	2.23	3.03	3.99	3.03	3.03
FeO	9.69	7.29	5.22	5.35	4.66	5.22
MnO	0.21	0.25	0.95	0.10	2.03	0.95
MgO	15.90	18.27	17.13	16.37	16.90	17.13
CaO	19.57	19.70	20.67	21.69	20.94	20.67
Na_2O	0.37	0.20	0.23	0.29	0.29	0.23
Cr_2O_3	0.10	0.22	0.49	0.78	0.99	0.49
SUM	99.80	100.73	99.47	99.34	100.31	98.92
EN	44.8	50.0	49.0	46.8	48.9	46.0
FS	15.3	11.1	8.3	8.5	7.5	12.8
WO	39.7	38.7	42.5	44.5	43.5	41.0
Al^{IV}	.125	.096	.119	.148	.130	.119

15. SOTW 58-7 - microphenocryst; 16. DSDP 204 - lower, groundmass (THOL); 17. DSDP 204 - lower, groundmass (THOL); 18. DSDP 204 - upper, microphenocryst (ALK); 19. DSDP 204 - upper, microphenocryst (THOL); 20. DSDP 204 - upper, microphenocryst (THOL)

Clinopyroxene Analyses

8	9	10	11	12	13	14
46.52	50.01	44.70	48.66	46.55	51.11	49.69
2.98	1.56	3.70	1.78	2.48	0.93	1.47
7.32	3.40	6.52	5.89	7.60	2.87	3.72
8.19	8.07	10.12	7.65	7.44	6.51	7.81
0.21	0.23	0.16	0.22	0.15	0.15	0.19
14.06	16.33	12.36	15.69	14.60	17.23	16.44
20.52	19.91	21.22	20.53	20.50	20.56	20.29
0.36	0.24	0.45	0.34	0.30	0.23	0.30
0.37	0.34	0.30	0.23	0.41	0.43	0.29
100.54	100.09	99.52	100.99	100.03	100.04	100.19
42.0	46.4	37.1	45.1	43.5	48.3	46.4
13.7	12.8	17.0	12.3	12.4	10.2	12.3
44.1	40.7	45.8	42.4	44.0	41.4	41.1
.269	.143	.291	.208	.265	.115	.156

8. SOTW 58-5 - phenocryst; 9. SOTW 58-5 - phenocryst; 10. SOTW 58-5 - phenocryst; 11. SOTW 58-9 - phenocryst core; 12. SOTW 58-9 - rim of #11; 13. SOTW 58-9 - groundmass; 14. SOTW 58-7 - groundmass

alkali basalt sample from the eastern end of the chain and lie within the spread of all of the data we have. The problems with modeling Tb, Yb and Lu are due to uncertainties about K_D, especially for garnet, the amount of garnet in the source, and the extent to which it melts and influences P in the melting equations. These same uncertainties also apply to Y.

The Louisville Seamount Chain has evolved through stages similar to the Hawaiian Chain, and there are many similarities in rock chemistry and mineralogy for the two suites. There are several distinct differences between the two chains that point to some major differences in their source characteristics. These include a general depletion in K, Rb, Sr, Ba, U, Th for Louisville Chain samples relative to Hawaii; remarkable uniformity in element ratios that characterize the source throughout the magmatic history of the Louisville Chain; and a parallel homogeneity in Nd and Sr isotope ratios [Cheng et al., 1986]. Some of the element abundance differences are shown in Figure 17 where the recently enriched mantle source [Chen and Frey, 1985] and our model source are both normalized to the source for NMORB. The composition of the Louisville Chain mantle source was derived by using the melting equation (see Appendix) and appropriate values of each element to match the "primitive" samples such as SOTW 58-4 and MTHN 6D1 and 7D2 for 4, 5, and 7% partial melts. There are obvious pitfalls in this technique because small variations in melting, mantle mineralogy and "P" will control the ratio C_L/C_O. The plot is at best a qualitative estimate of differences between this non-unique model and another proposed enriched mantle source. The relative depletion in the more incompatible elements may mean that residual phlogopite in the source causes depletion in the melts [e.g., Clague and Frey, 1982] or that the

(CONT.)

21	22	23	24	25	26	27	28
47.84	45.17	49.56	45.23	49.17	47.48	43.21	48.00
1.86	3.48	1.56	3.59	1.91	2.32	4.59	2.25
6.72	7.97	3.28	6.91	3.81	5.23	8.21	4.53
5.46	7.06	7.18	7.93	6.35	6.37	9.39	8.27
0.12	0.15	0.19	0.15	0.15	0.14	0.19	0.22
15.05	13.33	15.98	13.27	15.47	14.54	12.20	14.71
21.51	21.60	21.02	22.42	22.48	22.89	21.97	21.57
0.50	0.42	0.31	0.49	0.44	0.40	0.55	0.37
0.76	0.71	0.09	0.19	0.23	0.62	0.25	0.10
99.81	99.90	99.19	100.18	100.01	99.99	100.57	100.02
44.7	40.5	45.4	39.2	43.9	42.2	36.6	42.1
9.3	12.3	11.7	13.2	10.2	10.2	15.8	13.3
46.0	47.2	42.9	47.6	45.9	47.6	47.4	44.5
.227	.307	.144	.297	.167	.224	.362	.199

21. MTHN 4-1 - pyroxene grain in pelagic limestone; 22. MTHN 4-1 - pyroxene grain in pelagic limestone; 23. MTHN 4-1 - pyroxene grain in pelagic limestone; 24. MTHN 6-1 - groundmass; 25. MTHN 6-1 - phenocryst core; 26. MTHN 6-1 - phenocryst rim of #25; 27. MTHN 7-2 - groundmass; 28. MTHN 7-2 - groundmass

TABLE 6. Calculated Extent of Melting (%)

	Th	La	Ce	P	Mg#
SOTW 58-1	9.9	5.9	6.3	6.3	63.7
SOTW 58-4	9.2	9.2	9.8	9.5	70.1
MONS 110-1	6.4	4.0	4.3	4.0	63.4
MTHN 6D1	6.9	4.5	5.3	5.4	71.5
MTHN 7D1	5.3	3.7	4.2	4.7	59.9
MTHN 7D2	4.9	3.8	4.4	4.1	65.3

% melt estimated from $C_L/C_O = F^{D-1}$ for Th, La, Ce, P; values used for C_O: Th 0.22 ppm, La 1.35 ppm, Ce 3.4 ppm, P 126 ppm [*Chen and Frey*, 1985]; Th, La, Ce values for SOTW 58-4 were calculated from ratios Th/Zr, Ba/La, La/Ce of SOTW 58-1 and measured values of Ba and Zr in SOTW 58-4; Mg# = atomic ratio Mg/(Mg + Fe") for Fe'''/Fe" = 0.5

source itself has this depletion. Source depletion could be the result of earlier partial melting episodes ("tholeiitic" substructure of seamounts capped by the alkalic lavas we sampled?), or the Louisville source was not as enriched in these elements as the recently enriched model source.

Temporal variations in Hawaiian lavas show a change in chemistry from older tholeiitic lavas to younger alkalic and post-erosional (basanitic) lavas. *Chen and Frey* [1985] showed how mixing of small amounts of a small fractional melt of a tholeiitic source with melts from an undepleted ("primitive") mantle source could explain the isotopic and trace element signature of the Hawaiian volcanic series. In contrast, the Louisville Chain samples show little or no variation in potential tracers of the source composition. For example, Zr/Nb varies from 6.8 at 66 Ma old Osbourn Seamount to 7.3 at the "zero age" seamount (MTHN 7D). The basanites at the west end of the chain have La/Ce = 0.43, La/Sm = 3.27, Nb/La = 1.40, Ba/La = 6.25, and Sm/Nd = 0.302. The alkali basalts at the easternmost end of the chain have, respectively, 0.45, 3.97, 1.24, 7.28, and 0.251 for these elements. *Cheng et al.* [1986] show that $^{143}Nd/^{144}Nd$ at the old western end is 0.512822 (ϵ = +6.7) and $^{87}Sr/^{86}Sr$ is 0.70357; the young eastern end has $^{143}Nd/^{144}Nd$ = 0.512938 (ϵ = +7.3) and $^{87}Sr/^{86}Sr$ = 0.70374. There is little variation in element or isotope ratios for the other seamounts between these end points. In contrast, Hawaiian samples show an increase in La/Ce, Ba/La, Nb/La, Rb/Sr, and $^{143}Nd/^{144}Nd$. A possible explanation may be that we have only sampled the latest stages in the evolution of each seamount and would see a wider range in composition if we could see the evolution of each volcanic center. Nevertheless, the source characteristics for the final stages of each Louisville Seamount seems to have varied but little over 66 m.y.

The homogeneity of isotope ratios throughout the Louisville Chain supports the inference we make from trace element data [*Cheng et al.*, 1986]. This homogeneity contrasts with the wide range in isotope ratios and element ratios seen in the Hawaiian Chain and in individual islands [*Chen and Frey*, 1983, 1985]; in the Marquesas [*Vidal et al.*, 1984; *Duncan et al.*, 1986]; the Samoan and Society Islands [*White and Hoffman*, 1982; *Wright*, 1986; *Wright and White*, 1986]. These data require heterogeneity in mantle sources and the existence of isotopically distinct mantle domains having variable dimensions and longevity. The well documented "mantle array" (as seen in Nd and Sr isotope ratios [*Richard et al.*, 1977]) and "mantle plane" (as seen in Pb, Nd and Sr isotope ratios [*Zindler et al.*, 1982]) are becoming broad zones as more data are acquired. Mixing of melts from domains in a multicomponent mantle are implied. Helium isotope data [e.g., *Rison and Craig*, 1982] are a tracer of yet another mobile phase (postulated as derived from a mantle plume source) that penetrates and mixes with less mobile domains.

We conclude from our data that there has been a very large, relatively homogeneous, and long-lived mantle source at the melting anomaly that fed the Louisville Chain. We lack samples from enough seamounts in the chain to test this hypothesis rigorously, but it would be an unusual coincidence if our sample sites just happened to find material derived from similar sources in an otherwise heterogeneous mantle.

Summary

Linear volcanic chains are part of an important component of the oceanic lithosphere generated within oceanic plates rather than at spreading ridges. A "hotspot" origin has been proposed for many of them [*Okal and Batiza*, 1986]. The relative proportion of off-ridge to ridge axis volcanism has been debated, but off-ridge volcanism may be the site of origin of up to 10% of the oceanic crust [*Batiza*, 1982]. The Louisville Seamount Chain is an example of a great linear chain of submarine volcanoes extending from the Tonga-Kermadec trench system over 4300 km to the southeast. The chain cuts across the fabric of the ocean crust and crosses members of the Eltanin Fracture Zone system at a low angle. The Louisville Chain is concentric with the Emperor-Hawaii chain and shares similar changes in trend including a bend that occurred at about 43 Ma [*Lonsdale*, in press]. At the western end of the chain Osbourn Seamount, capped by ~66 m.y. old "post-erosional" lavas, is built on pre-Late Cretaceous crust. A seamount with "zero age" marks the southeastern end of the chain. A hotspot origin for the chain seems to be a viable explanation.

The morphology of the seamounts shows that many were emergent and now have planed off tops that have been submerged to varied depths depending on their age. These guyots are capped by

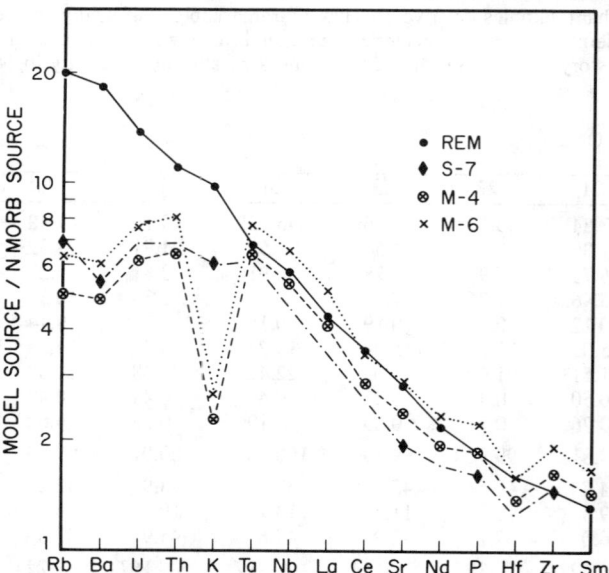

Fig. 17. Composition of an "enriched" mantle source (REM) normalized to an N-MORB source [*Chen and Frey*, 1985]. S-7 is model source for SOTW 58-4 at 7% melting; M-4 is source for MTHN 6D1 at 4% melting; M-5 is source for MTHN 6D1 at 5% melting.

limestones with fauna indicating formation at higher latitudes (e.g., Bryozoans) [Lonsdale, in press].

The composition of volcanic rocks dredged from the seamounts shows that they are mainly alkalic series lavas including alkali basalt, hawaiite and basanitoid. The latter are typical of "post-erosional" lavas from other oceanic islands. Detrital clinopyroxene and clinopyroxene phenocrysts in basalt pebbles have been recovered from DSDP site 204 north of the western end of the chain. These samples include clinopyroxene that crystallized from "tholeiitic" magmas indicating that some of the larger and older seamounts (such as Osbourn) must have evolved through a tholeiitic shield building stage. Detrital pyroxene indicating an origin in alkalic basalt magmas is also found in the DSDP core. Collectively the rock and mineral data indicate a petrogenetic evolution that paralleled the classic Hawaiian sequence.

The chemical data for the samples suggests that "primary" magmas may have been derived by small amounts (e.g., 4%) of melting of an enriched garnet lherzolite mantle. The mantle source must have been enriched in K, Rb, Ba, Y, and REE relative to the MORB source or to "primitive" mantle.

The chemistry of the samples, especially the ratios for refractory high field strength elements, gives evidence for a remarkably homogeneous mantle source throughout more than 60 m.y. of seamount generation. This homogeneity, shown by trace element ratios (e.g., Zr/Y, Zr/Nb, Ba/La, La/Ce), is also supported by Nd and Sr isotope studies [Cheng et al., 1986]. This geochemical signature is a striking contrast to the more heterogeneous mantle source suggested for the Samoan and Hawaiian Island Chains. The geology of the known parts of this chain prompts the speculation that an active "Loihi counterpart" may yet be found to the southeast of our dredge site MTHN-7.

Appendix

1. Melting model for non-modal melting:

$$C_L/C_O = \frac{1}{D_O + F(1-P)} \quad [Shaw, 1970]$$

C_L = element concentration in liquid

C_O = initial element concentration in unmelted source rock

F = degree of melting

D_O = bulk distribution coefficient

P = sum fractions of total liquid contributed by each phase during melting

2. Mantle sources:
   A. 0.6 olivine, 0.25 orthopyroxene, 0.1 clinopyroxene, 0.05 J, where J = garnet or plagioclase or amphibole. Melt proportion 0.1, 0.1, 0.4, 0.4
   B. 0.57 olivine, 0.25 orthopyroxene, 0.1 clinopyroxene, 0.05 garnet, 0.03 phlogopite. Melt proportions 0.1, 0.1, 0.3, 0.3, 0.2

3. Distribution coefficients:

   Rb, Ba, K, Sr, La, Ce, Nd, Sm, Th, Ta, Nb, P, Hf, Zr [Chen and Frey, 1985] lowest values for Nd and Sm were used

   Nb, Y, Zr for phlogopite [Pearce and Norry, 1979]

   Tb, Yb, Lu, Y [Frey et al., 1978]

4. Values for C_O, enriched mantle:

Rb, Ba, Th, K, Ta, Nb, Sr, Nd, P, Hf, Zr, Sm, Nd [Chen and Frey, 1985]

Yb, Y [Clague and Frey, 1982]

Lu, Tb 2x chondritic [Frey et al., 1978]

U 2.5x chondritic

Acknowledgments. We dedicate this paper to the memory of our friend and colleague Bill Menard. Support for data collection and samples was provided by NSF GA-30315 (to J.H.) and ONR USN N00014-80-C-0440 (to P.L.). Analytical work was supported by research awards (to J.H.) from the University of California San Diego Academic Senate and the Scripps Industrial Associates Fund. We thank A. Zindler and K. Park for giving us samples from the VEMA Expedition to include with this study. Reviews by C. Y. Chen and B. Dalrymple were most helpful in improving an earlier version of the manuscript.

References

Baker, P. E., I. Gass, P. Harris, and R. W. LeMaitre, The volcanological report of the Royal Society expedition to Tristan da Cunha, *Phil. Trans. Roy. Soc. London, Ser. A, 256,* 439–578, 1964.

Basaltic Volcanism Study Project, *Basaltic Volcanism on the Terrestrial Planets,* New York, Pergamon, 1268 pp., 1981.

Batiza, R., Abundances, distribution and sizes of volcanoes in the Pacific Ocean and implications for the origin of non-hotspot volcanoes, *Earth Planet. Sci. Lett., 60,* 195–206, 1982.

Billington, S., The morphology and tectonics of the subducted lithosphere in the Tonga-Fiji-Kermadec region from seismicity and focal mechanism solutions, Ph.D. thesis, Cornell University, Ithaca, 1980.

Burns, R. E., J. E. Andrews, G. J. van der Lingen, M. Churkin, J. S. Galehouse, G. H. Packham, T. A. Davies, J. P. Kennett, P. Dumitrica, A. R. Edwards, and R. P. von Herzen, Site 204, *Init. Rep. Deep Sea Drill. Proj., 21,* 33–56, 1973.

Cann, J. R., Rb, Sr, Y, Zr, and Nb in some ocean floor basaltic rocks, *Earth Planet. Sci. Lett., 19,* 7–11, 1970.

Cazenave, K. A., and K. Dominh, Geoid heights over the Louisville Ridge (South Pacific), *J. Geophys. Res., 89,* 11171–11180, 1984.

Chen, C. Y., and F. Frey, Origin of Hawaiian tholeiite and alkalic basalt, *Nature, 302,* 785–789, 1983.

Chen, C. Y., and F. A. Frey, Trace element and isotopic geochemistry of lavas from Haleakala volcano, East Maui Hawaii: Implications for the origin of Hawaiian basalts, *J. Geophys. Res., 90,* 8743–8768, 1985.

Cheng, Q., K. H. Park, J. D. Macdougall, A. Zindler, G. W. Lugmair, J. Hawkins, P. Lonsdale, and H. Staudigel, Isotopic evidence for a hotspot origin of the Louisville Seamount Chain, *J. Geophys. Res.,* this issue.

Clague, D. A., and F. A. Frey, Petrology and trace element geochemistry of the Honolulu volcanics, Oahu: Implications for the oceanic mantle below Hawaii, *J. Petrol., 23,* 447–504, 1982.

Clague, D. A., and R. D. Jarrard, Tertiary plate motion deduced from the Hawaiian-Emperor Chain, *Geol. Soc. Am. Bull., 84,* 1135–1154, 1973.

Dixon, T. H., and M. E. Parke, Bathymetry estimates in the southern oceans from Seasat altimetry, *Nature, 304,* 406–411, 1983.

Duncan, R. A., M. T. McCulloch, H. Barsczus, and D. R. Nelson, Plume versus lithospheric sources for melts at Ua Pou, Marquesas Islands, *Nature, 322,* 534–538, 1986.

Dupont, J., Morphologie et structures superficielles de l'arc insulaire des Tonga-Kermadec, in *Contrib. a l'etude geodynamique du Sud-Ouest Pacifique: Paris, ORSTOM 147*, 263–282, 1982.

Dupont, J., and R. Herzer, Effect of subduction of the Louisville Ridge on structure and morphology of the Tonga Arc, in D. W. Scholl and T. L. Vallier (compilers and eds.), *Geology and Offshore Resources of Pacific Island Arcs - Tonga Region*, Circum Pacific Council for Energy and Mineral Resources Earth Science Series, v. 2, Circum Pacific Council for Energy and Mineral Resources, Houston, TX, 323–332, 1985.

Epp, D., Age and tectonic relationships among volcanic chains on the Pacific plate, Ph.D. thesis, Univ. of Hawaii, Honolulu, 1978.

Evensen, M. N., P. J. Hamilton, and R. K. O'Nions, Rare earth abundances in chondritic meteorites, *Geochim. Cosmochim. Acta, 42*, 1199–1212, 1978.

Frey, F., D. H. Green, and S. D. Roy, Integrated models of basalt petrogenesis: A study of quartz tholeiites to olivine melilites from southeast Australia utilizing geochemical and experimental petrologic data, *J. Petrol., 19*, 463–513, 1978.

Gast, P. W., Trace element fractionation and the origin of tholeiitic and alkaline magma types, *Geochim. Cosmochim. Acta, 32*, 1057–1086, 1968.

Giardini, D., and J. H. Woodhouse, Deep seismicity and modes of deformation in the Tonga subduction zone, *Nature, 319*, 551–555, 1986.

Green, D. H., Composition of basaltic magmas as indicators of conditions of origin: Application to oceanic volcanism, *Phil. Trans. R. Soc. London, Ser. A, 268*, 707-725, 1971.

Hawkins, J. W., Geology of the Louisville Ridge - a possible hotspot trace, *Eos Trans. AGU, 54*, 1221, 1973.

Hawkins, J., and J. Natland, Nephelinites and basanites of the Samoan linear volcanic chain: Their possible tectonic significance, *Earth Planet. Sci. Lett., 24*, 427–439, 1975.

Hawkins, J. W., P. Lonsdale, and R. Batiza, Petrologic evolution of the Louisville "Ridge", *Eos Trans. AGU, 66*, 405, 1985.

Hayes, D. E., and M. Ewing, The Louisville Ridge - A possible extension of the Eltanin Fracture Zone, in *Antarctic Oceanology I*, edited by J. L. Reid, pp. 223–228, Amer. Geophys. Union, Antarctic Research Vol. 15, Washington, D. C., 1971.

Irvine, T. N., and W. Baragar, A guide to the chemical classification of the common volcanic rocks, *Canad. J. Earth. Sci., 8*, 523–548, 1971.

Jordan, T. H., H. W. Menard, and D. K. Smith, Density and size distribution of seamounts in the Eastern Pacific inferred from wide-beam sounding data, *J. Geophys. Res., 88*, 10508–10518, 1983.

Jurdy, D. M., An alternative model for early Tertiary absolute plate motions, *Geology, 6*, 469–472, 1978.

Kay, R. W., and P. W. Gast, The rare earth content and origin of alkali-rich basalts, *J. Geol., 81*, 653–682, 1973.

Kushiro, I., Si-Al relations in clinopyroxenes from igneous rocks, *Am. J. Sci., 258*, 548–554, 1960.

LeBas, M. J., The role of aluminum in igneous clinopyroxenes with relation to their parentage, *Am. J. Sci., 260*, 267–288, 1962.

LeBas, M. J., R. W. LeMaitre, A. Streckeisen, and B. Zanettin, Chemical classification of volcanic rocks based on the total alkali-silica diagram, *J. Petrol., 27*, 745–750, 1986.

LeMaitre, R. W., Petrology of volcanic rocks, Gough Island, South Atlantic, *Geol. Soc. Am. Bull., 73*, 1309–1340, 1962.

Lonsdale, P., Geography and history of the Louisville hotspot chain in the Southwest Pacific, *J. Geophys. Res.*, in press.

Macdonald, G. A., Petrography of the Samoan Islands, *Geol. Soc. Am. Bull., 55*, 1333–1362, 1944.

Macdonald, G., and T. Katsura, Chemical composition of Hawaiian lavas, *J. Petrol., 5*, 82–133, 1964.

Menard, H. W., S. M. Smith, and T. E. Chase, Guyots in the Southwestern Pacific Basin, *Geol. Soc. Am. Bull., 75*, 145–148, 1964.

Molnar, P., T. Atwater, J. Mammerickx, and S. Smith, Magnetic anomalies, bathymetry and the tectonic evolution of the South Pacific since the Late Cretaceous, *Geophys. J. R. Astron. Soc., 40*, 383–420, 1975.

Moore, J. G., D. A. Clague, and W. R. Normark, Diverse basalt types from Loihi Seamount, Hawaii, *Geology, 10*, 88–92, 1982.

Natland, J., The progression of volcanism in the Samoan linear volcanic chain, *Am. J. Sci., 280-A*, 709–735, 1980.

Okal, E., and R. Batiza, Hotspots: The first 25 years, *J. Geophys. Res.*, this issue.

Pearce, J. A., and J. R. Cann, Tectonic setting of basic volcanic rocks determined using trace element analyses, *Earth Planet. Sci. Lett., 5*, 47–51, 1973.

Pearce, J. A., and M. J. Norry, Ti, Zr, and Nb variations in volcanic rocks, *Contrib. Min. Pet., 69*, 33–47, 1979.

Richard, P., N. Shimizu, and C. J. Allegre, $^{143}Nd/^{144}Nd$, a natural tracer: An application to oceanic basalts, *Earth Planet. Sci. Lett., 31*, 269–278, 1976.

Rison, W., and H. Craig, Helium-3: Coming of age in Samoa, *Eos Trans. AGU, 63*, 1144, 1982.

Sandwell, D., A detailed view of the South Pacific geoid from satellite altimetry, *J. Geophys. Res., 89*, 1089–1104, 1984.

Schlanger, S. O., M. Garcia, B. Keating, J. Naughton, W. Sager, J. Haggerty, J. Philpotts, and R. Duncan, Geology and geochronology of the Line Islands, *J. Geophys. Res., 89*, 11261–11272, 1984.

Shaw, D. M., Trace element fractionation during anatexis, *Geochim. Cosmochim. Acta, 34*, 237–243, 1970.

Sun, S. S., and G. N. Hanson, Evolution of the mantle: Geochemical evidence from alkali basalt, *Geology, 3*, 297–302, 1975.

U. S. Navy, Map of the world, *Hydrographic Office Misc., 15-254*, 1961.

Vallier, T. L., R. M. O'Connor, D. W. Scholl, A. J. Stevenson, and P. J. Quinterno, Petrology of rocks dredged from the landward slope of the Tonga Trench, in *Geology and Offshore Resources of Pacific Island Arcs - Tonga Region*, edited by D. W. Scholl and T. L. Vallier, Circum-Pacific Council for Energy and Mineral Resources, Houston, TX, 109–120, 1985.

Vidal, P., C. Chauvel, and R. Brousse, Large mantle heterogeneity beneath French Polynesia, *Nature, 307*, 536–538, 1984.

Vogt, P., A. Lowrie, D. R. Bracey, and R. N. Hey, Subduction of aseismic ridges: Effects on shape, seismicity, and other characteristics of consuming plate boundaries, *Geol. Soc. Am. Spec. Paper 172*, 59 pp., 1976.

Watts, A. B., J. Weissel, R. Duncan, and R. Larson, The origin of the Louisville Ridge and its relation to the Eltanin Fracture Zone, *Eos Trans. AGU, 66*, 360, 1985.

Watts, A. B., J. K. Weissel, R. A. Duncan, and R. L. Larson, The origin of the Louisville Ridge and its relationship to the Eltanin Fracture Zone system, *J. Geophys. Res.*, in press.

White, W. M., and A. W. Hoffman, Sr and Nd isotope geochemistry of oceanic basalts and mantle evolution, *Nature, 296*, 821–825, 1982.

Wright, E., Petrology and geochemistry of shield-building and post-erosional lava series of Samoa: Implications for mantle heterogeneity and magma genesis, Ph.D. thesis, Univ. of California San Diego, La Jolla, 1986.

Wright, E., and W. M. White, The origin of Samoa: New evidence from Sr, Nd, and Pb isotopes, *Earth Planet. Sci. Lett.*, in press.

Zindler, A., E. Jagoutz, and S. Goldstein, Nd, Sr and Pb isotopic systematics in a three-component mantle: A new perspective, *Nature, 298*, 519–523, 1982.

PETROLOGY AND CHEMISTRY OF LAVAS FROM SEAMOUNTS FLANKING THE EAST
PACIFIC RISE AXIS, 21°N: IMPLICATIONS CONCERNING THE MANTLE
SOURCE COMPOSITION FOR BOTH SEAMOUNT AND ADJACENT EPR LAVAS

James F. Allan and Rodey Batiza

Department of Geological Sciences, Northwestern University, Evanston, Illinois 60201

Peter Lonsdale

Marine Physical Laboratory, Scripps Institution of Oceanography, La Jolla, California 92093

Abstract. The 1982 PLUTO expedition collected lava samples from 3 seamounts and two small pillow cones that flank the East Pacific Rise near 21°N on crust $2.5-8 \times 10^5$ years old. The lavas are typically aphyric to porphyritic N-type and T-type MORBs, with a range in Mg# of 0.68-0.46, 1.1-2.1% TiO_2, 13.8-17.7% Al_2O_3, 9.9-12.6% CaO, 2.5-4.0% Na_2O, 10-190 ppm Ni, 1.8-8.1 ppm La, and $(La/Sm)_N$ of 0.36-1.22. Phenocrysts assemblages are pl+ol, pl, or ol+pl, with groundmass clinopyroxene and groundmass titanomagnetite as common phases. Cr-spinel may occur as inclusions in olivine or plagioclase or as loose crystals in the groundmass. The lavas from two of the seamounts, Green and Red, define distinct fractionation trends in CaO/Al_2O_3 vs Mg# and $Na_2O/(Na_2O+CaO)$ vs Mg#. These trends are not correlated with $(La/Sm)_N$, effectively precluding the derivation of lavas from these seamounts from a single bulk source. Lavas from individual volcanoes and from the entire data set define binary mixing lines when considering the REE, LILE, and HIFS, consistent with a mixed source of enriched and depleted material. Variable $(La/Sm)_N$ and sparse $^{87}Sr/^{86}Sr$ and $^{143}Nd/^{144}Nd$ data are consistent with source trace element heterogeneity for individual seamounts; the differing fractionation trends and the differing parental lavas that they require within individual seamounts may be related to either or both major element and mineralogical (i.e., spinel lherzolite vs plagioclase lherzolite) source heterogeneity. Comparable trace element data show that the seamount lavas are more diverse than the 21°N EPR lavas (seamount Ti/Zr is 65-215, EPR Ti/Zr is 84-107). The youthfulness of the seamount lavas (Late Pleistocene) and the proximity of the seamounts to the EPR imply that the seamount and adjacent EPR lavas share a common source, one that has compositional heterogeneities volumetrically large enough to be preserved in the seamount lavas.

Introduction

Well located lava samples were collected by transponder-navigated dredging, 10 ALVIN submersible dives, and accidental bottom encounters by the ANGUS towed camera system from 5 central volcanoes located within 30 km of the spreading axis in the mouth of the Gulf of California. This part of the East Pacific Rise (EPR) is the medium-spreading (64 mm/yr) boundary between the Pacific and Rivera plates. Between the Tamayo and Rivera transform faults this spreading center is segmented by three small (~10 km) offsets (Figure 1) that were created by a change of spreading direction in the past 2 m.y., and have a subsequent history of along-ridge propagation (Lonsdale, in press). The 800 m high seamount F, whose cratered topography is described by Batiza et al. [1984], overlies 1.0 Ma Rivera crust on the southeast flank of the EPR, midway between the 22°g N and 21.3°N offsets. Two other 800 m high volcanoes, Green (or "B") and Red (or "E"), are the "Larson's Seamounts" mapped by Larson [1972] and Lonsdale et al. [1982] on the northwest (Pacific) flank of the EPR. Bathymetric maps of both are given in Figure 2. Both volcanoes have incomplete 2 km wide calderas with walls up to 150 m high. The caldera floor of Red seamount has several pillow cones with 50-100 m of relief, while seamount Green has a nested pair of pit craters with a combined depth of 200 m. These seamounts and the 100-150 m high pillow cones C1 and C2 form a lineament that strikes 080°g to the Rise hydrothermal field [Rise Project Group, 1980] on the spreading axis midway between its 21.3°g N and 20.5°N offsets. The formation of these seamounts is likely associated with intense magma injection at the adjacent spreading ridge, and the northward-pointing V formed by the seamounts and the EPR axis likely reflects the northward propagation of intense magmatic activity at the EPR.

The absolute ages of the seamount edifices are unknown. Red seamount is at the edge of the central magnetic anomaly [Larson, 1972] and overlies crust 0.7-0.8 Ma in age; the interpolated age of the crust centered under Green seamount is 0.4 Ma. Hydrothermal sulfide and oxide deposits indicative of Late Quaternary to Recent volcanic activity have been described by Lonsdale et al. [1982] and Alt et al. [1987] from Green seamount, and hydrothermal oxide deposits that are forming from active vents have been described by the same authors from Red seamount. Alt et al. [1987] report two $^{230}Th/^{234}U$ disequilibrium ages on Green seamount opal-rich sulfide deposits of 69±15 and 139±23 thousand years. These ages provide an estimate of the timing of caldera and pit crater formation, constrain the timing of the most recent hydrothermal activity, and imply that most of the volcanic edifice of Green seamount was built in less than 260,000 years.

Chemical analyses of several samples from each of the volcanoes have been previously presented in Batiza and Vanko [1984], Batiza et al. [1984], and Lonsdale and Batiza [1980]. These 5 volcanoes

Copyright 1987 by the American Geophysical Union.

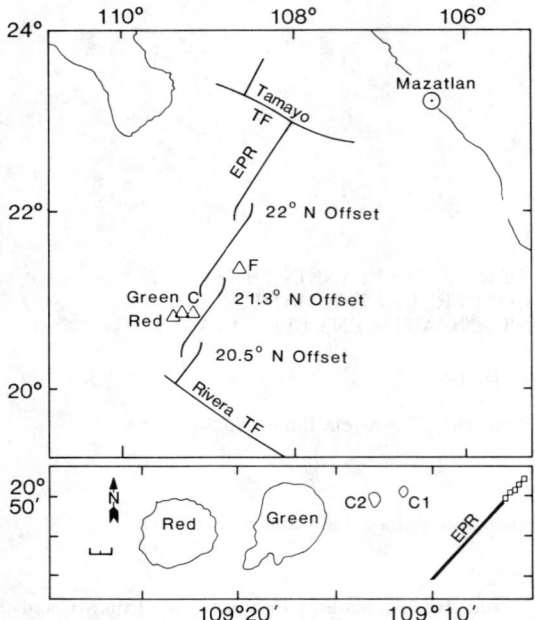

Fig. 1. Location of seamounts and cones studied, with offsets of the EPR marked. Hydrothermal vents on EPR [Speiss et al., 1980] denoted by open squares; lower map after Lonsdale et al. [1980].

are part of a much larger Pacific seamount group discussed by Batiza and Vanko [1984]. Our purpose here is to take a close petrological look at these individual volcanoes that are geographically adjacent to the EPR. We have several goals: 1) to delineate the magma evolutionary processes, such as the relative effects of fractionation at depth or in within-edifice magma chambers, that have affected the seamount lavas; 2) to approximate the ultimate magma source characteristics that are reflected in lavas from individual seamounts; and 3), to extend these deductions towards delineating the characteristics of the adjacent EPR MORB source.

Petrography

The PLUTO lavas were collected predominantly from pillowed lava and pahoehoe (sheet) flows [Ballard et al., 1979], from talus slopes, or from fractured outcrops. All are tholeiites. Based on preliminary petrographic and analytic study, 22 representative samples were chosen for more extensive mineralogical study on the electron probe. Table 1 gives the results of point counting on these 22 samples, and lists the groundmass phases observed. The size nomenclature used throughout this paper is as follows: phenocrysts are any crystal larger than 0.5 mm; microphenocrysts are any crystal 0.25-0.5 mm in size; and groundmass crystals are those smaller than 0.25 mm. The microphenocryst-groundmass boundary correlates well with the natural size break observed between smaller skeletal plagioclase and euhedral-subhedral, thicker-bodied plagioclase; the size range shown by olivine is less well defined and hence the size distinction is more arbitrary.

Most samples range from sparsely phyric to porphyritic (Table 1). Plagioclase is the dominant phenocryst and microphenocryst in all of these lavas except for Ang-2, which is dominated by olivine. In most phyric samples, crystal clots of intergrown phenocrysts and microphenocrysts of plagioclase or plagioclase + olivine are common. The observed phenocryst+microphenocryst assemblages are pl and pl+ol; clinopyroxene occurs only in the groundmass. Some lavas contain euhedral Cr-rich spinel as inclusions in olivine or plagioclase, or as loose groundmass crystals. Unidentified iron- and copper-rich sulfide minerals are present as rare, small ($<30\mu$) irregular groundmass grains, and are likely magmatic [Mathez, 1976]. Some lavas that have plagioclase as the sole phenocryst or microphenocryst phase lack any olivine or contain olivine as only very small ($>100\mu$) groundmass grains, implying that plagioclase may have been the sole liquidus phase immediately before eruption. Such samples were previously reported by Batiza and Vanko [1984] and Thompson et al. [1985].

Groundmass textures of the aphyric to porphyritic lavas are similar to those observed in other oceanic basalts [e.g., Bryan, 1972; Natland, 1978, 1980; Kirkpatrick, 1978]. Typically, both pillow and pahoehoe fragments have a sparsely crystalline, glassy rim, followed by a spherulitic zone of quench phases, which may then evolve into a coarser microlitic zone in the interior of the sample. Rock fragments studied commonly lacked 1 or more of the above zones, and some microcrystalline samples contain only a poorly-developed spherulitic texture.

Samples without well-developed flow banding are typically rich in sheaf spherulites in the spherulitic zones, and contain bow-tie to radial clusters of plagioclase microlites in the microlitic zone. Groundmass olivine and clinopyroxene are commonly intergrown with plagioclase in these radial clusters, and in coarser groundmasses may develop into micro-glomeroporphyritic clusters. These textures indicate cotectic crystallization of these phases [Bryan, 1979; Batiza and Vanko, 1984]. In samples with strong flow orientation, the clusters are flattened; in some, a crude pilotaxitic to trachytic texture of feldspar microlites is developed. Unlike the MORBs studied by Natland [1980], no clear relationship was noted between groundmass textures and rock composition. No systematic compositional relationship was noted for vesicularity, which varied widely among the PLUTO lavas. Indeed, vesicles within individual samples could be either more or less abundant in the glassy rims than in the crystalline interiors.

One of the probed samples (1182-6) is much more coarsely crystalline than the others, and contained intergranular, intersertal, seriate and subophitic textures, with a dark, turbid mesostasis between some of the coarse crystals. Subhedral plagioclase laths and anhedral to subhedral clinopyroxene crystals, both up to 1 mm in length, dominate the rock, with olivine and magnetite occurring as smaller, anhedral grains between the larger crystals. No orthopyroxene or sub-calcic augite was observed. Most visible crystals are well above 100 μ in size.

Most of the lavas are very fresh, with only small amounts of a yellowish celadonitic clay mineral and reddish hydrated iron oxides lining a few vesicles and cracks. Two of the lavas (1182-6 and 1179-12) are altered more pervasively, and the above alteration minerals line or fill most of their vesicles, and have replaced some of the mesostasis in 1182-6. Irregular manganese oxide grains averaging 30μ in size are found in the groundmass of 6-7.

Mineralogy

All analyses were obtained on a JEOL 733 superprobe equipped with 3 automated spectrometers. Sample currents during analysis were 0.015 μamps for plagioclase and 0.03 μamps for all other phases; counting times ranged from 20-30 seconds for all elements.

Cr-Rich Spinel

Orange-brown chromium-rich spinel is restricted to lavas with $Mg/(Mg+Fe^{2+})$ higher than 0.60, and are not found in lavas from Seamount F. Like those described from other Pacific seamounts

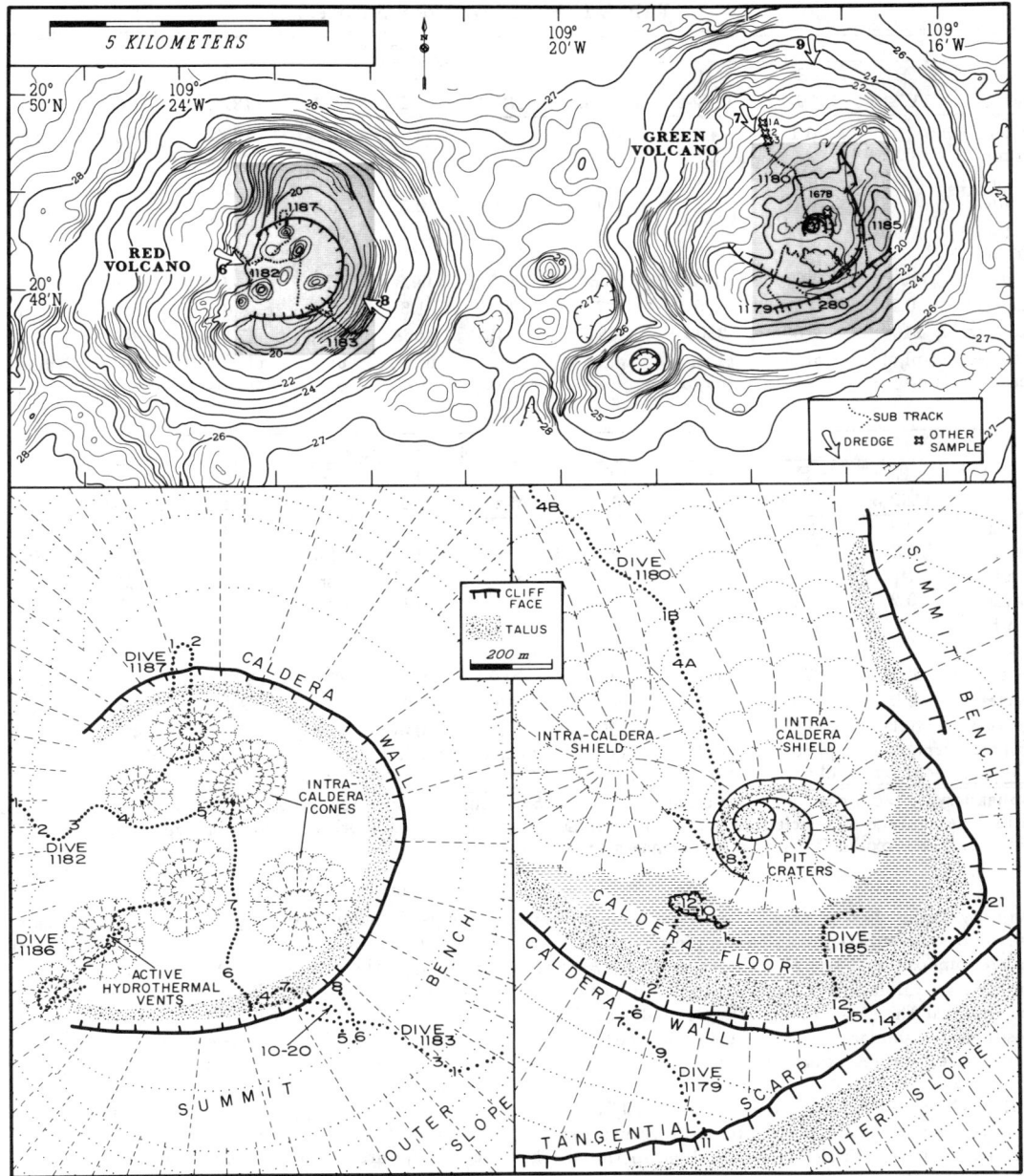

Fig. 2. Location of analyzed samples from Red and Green seamounts. Upper panel shows position of dredge samples, ANGUS sample 167B, and all dive tracks (including DSRV TURTLE dive 280 [Lonsdale and Batiza, 1980]. Contour interval is 20 m within Seabeam swaths, 100 m beyond the area of multibeam coverage (and on steep slopes). Lower panels show enlargements of the summit area (stippled on bathymetric chart) with numbers denoting sample locations along the transponder-navigated dive tracks. The active hydrothermal vents at bottom left are those described by Lonsdale et al. [1982].

[Batiza and Vanko, 1984], most Cr-rich spinels from the PLUTO seamounts have $Cr/(Cr+Al)$ less than 0.5. No high-Al spinels or reversely-zoned spinels with high-Al cores possibly indicative of high pressure origin [Sigurdsson, 1977; Sigurdsson and Schilling, 1976; Fisk and Bence, 1980] were found.

Cr-rich spinels are occasionally found as euhedral inclusions within plagioclase and olivine phenocrysts and microphenocrysts, or as grains adhered to their edges. Isolated euhedral spinels are occasionally found in samples 6-7 and 7-2, and are abundant in Ang-2. The inclusions and loose crystals range in size from 10-

TABLE 1. Pluto Lava Modal Analyses

	Volcanic Center										
Rock	B 1179-6	B 1179-12	B 1179-2	B 1180-4B	B 1185-1	B 7-2	B 9-1	C1 1181-1	C1 1181-2	E 1182-1	E 1182-3
Plag ph		0.1	4.8	1.0		tr	0.4	13.4	18.1	11.2	0.1
mph	0.3	tr	2.6	0.7	tr	0.1	2.7	2.1	1.5	1.1	0.3
Ol ph		0.6									
mph		0.1		0.1		0.5	0.2	0.8	tr		
Cpx ph											
mph											
gmass	99.7	99.9	91.9	98.3	99.9	99.8	97.9	84.0	79.8	86.2	99.6
% vesicles	0.1	1.7	2.0	3.7	2.3	1.3	0.4	3.8	2.2	2.8	3.2
Point counts	2108	3168	2305	2651	1542	1668	1393	1770	2349	2903	2180
Groundmass phases	pl,ol	pl,ol	pl,ol, cpx,ox	pl,ol	pl,ol, cpx,ox, sp	pl,ol, cpx	pl,ol, ox	pl,ol, cpx,ox	pl,ol, cpx,ox	pl,ol, cpx,ox	pl,ol, ox

	Volcanic Center										
Rock	E 1182-5	E 1182-6	E 6-2	E 6-3	E 6-5	E 6-6	E 6-7	E 8-4	E Ang167A	E Ang2	F 5-2
Plag ph	0.6	1.0					0.2	5.9	0.2	0.4	0.2
mph	0.3	7.8	tr	0.1		tr	1.3	0.3	0.1	0.5	0.4
Ol ph							tr		1.3		
mph	0.2	0.1				0.1	tr		3.8		
Cpx ph											
mph	3.3	0.7									
gmass	98.8	87.0	99.9	100	99.9	98.5	93.7	99.7	94.0	99.4	
% vesicles	0.9	2.8	3.1	2.1	6.0	4.3	0.4	2.0	2.8	1.3	3.3
Point counts	2033	1112	1287	1900	1114	2045	1922	2632	1925	2253	2580
Groundmass phases	pl,ol, cpx,ox	pl,cpx, ol,ox	pl,ol, cpx,ox	pl,ol, cpx,ox	pl,cpx, ox	pl,ol, cpx,ox	pl,ol, cpx,sp	pl,ol, cpx	pl,cpx, ol,ox	pl,ol	pl,ox sp

ph=phenocryst, >0.5 mm; mph=microphenocryst, 0.25-0.5 mm, gmass=groundmass, <0.25 mm. Ph, mph, and gmass calculated as a percentage of vesicle-free rock. Groundmass phases are pl=plagioclase, ol=olivine, cpx=clinopyroxene, sp=Cr-rich spinel, and ox=oxide; feathery quench phases are not noted.

80μ, the majority being $25-50\mu$ across. Analysed spinels from lavas from volcanoes Green, C1, and Red are plotted in Figure 3, and form broad compositional trends. The range of Mg# of the spinels within a rock exhibit only a loose correlation with the host rock and host mineral chemistry (Table 2). Groundmass Cr-rich spinel compositions are similar to those of inclusions within either olivine or plagioclase. Representative Cr-rich spinel analyses are given in Table 3.

Zoning within Cr-spinels in most cases is minimal, although some spinels have narrow rims of magnetite, representing a spinel crystallization gap between Cr-rich spinel and magnetite [Sack, 1982]. An exception occurs in Ang 2-2, where a single large, 70μ spinel is strongly zoned (Ang 2-3, Ang 2-6; Table 3) from a Cr-rich, Mg-poor core to an Al-rich, Mg-rich rim. Other spinels within this rock exhibit similar but less marked zoning (Ang 2-21 and Ang 2-22) or else little zoning (Ang 2-10, Ang 2-11). Slight spinel zoning in most other lavas (1179-2-48, 1179-2-49, Table 3) follows the same trend of increase in Mg# and decrease in Cr/(Cr + Al) from core to rim. If this zoning is due only to simple epitaxial growth in equilibrium, it implies that spinel crystallization within most of these lavas may start at any point within the trend shown in Figure 3a, and then proceed towards lower Cr/(Cr + Al) and higher Mg#. This trend is the same as that observed by Fisk and Bence [1980] both naturally in FAMOUS basalt 527-1-1 and experimentally at 1 bar in the same lava where increasing oxygen fugacity with crystallization caused lower Cr/(Cr + Al) (i.e., their groups II and III). It is opposite to other trends projected for low pressure coexisting olivine and Cr-rich spinel fractionation at constant f_{O_2}, where Cr/(Cr + Al) and Mg/(Mg + Fe^{2+}) are expected to decrease with crystallization [Irvine, 1965 and 1976; Dick and Bullen, 1984]. The PLUTO trend is also different from that expected when plagioclase is co-precipitating with spinel, due to Al depletion in the melt by the precipitating plagioclase [Fisk and Bence, 1980]. For example, zoned spinels from DSDP Hole 396B have increasing Cr/(Cr+Al) and decreasing Mg# from core to rim (opposite to the PLUTO trend), and have been interpreted to have co-precipitated with both olivine and plagioclase [Dick and Bryan, 1979]. In the absence of other crystallizing phases, generalized and local depletion of Cr in the melt causes spinel Cr to decrease and Al to increase [Thy, 1983]; the strong Mg-Al coupled substitution [Engi, 1983] may account for the increase in Mg# in the rims of the zoned spinels and perhaps for the trend as a whole. The PLUTO spinel trend may at least be partially explained by assimilation of wallrock material during crystallization, effectively buffering lava MgO content (H.J.B. Dick, pers. comm., 1986), although xenoliths are lacking from the lavas. It is also possible that the strongly zoned Cr-rich spinel in Ang-2 is a xenocryst, obtained by assimilation or magma mixing.

Overall, the spinels overlap or are slightly lower in Cr/(Cr + Al) for a given Mg/(Mg+Fe^{2+}) than for Cr-rich spinels described from the Mid-Atlantic ridge [Sigurdsson and Schilling, 1976; Sigurdsson, 1977; Dick and Bryan, 1978; Fisk and Bence, 1980], and like the

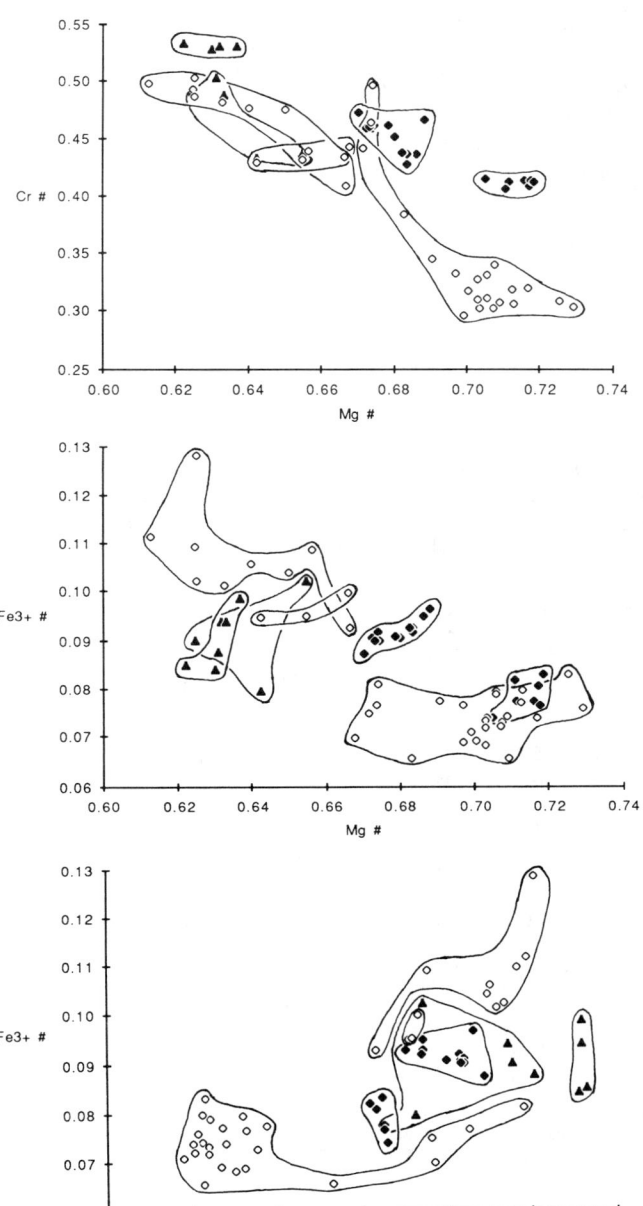

Fig. 3. Microprobe Cr-rich spinel analyses. Cr# refers to Cr/(Cr+Al), Fe^{3+}# refers to $Fe^{3+}/(Cr+Al+Fe^{3+})$, and Mg# refers to $Mg/(Mg+Fe^{2+})$. Closed diamonds represent spinels from Green seamount, open diamonds represent spinels from Red seamount, and closed triangles represent spinels from cone C1. Compositional fields defined by spinels from single lavas are circled.

MAR spinels are higher in Al_2O_3, lower in TiO_2, and have higher $Mg/(Mg + Fe^{2+})$ ratios than spinels from Kilaeau [Evans and Wright, 1972] and from Hawaiian tholeiites in general [Basaltic Volcanism Study Group, 1980]. Spinel Al_2O_3, which varies from 22.9% to 38.6% by weight, only poorly correlates with host rock Al_2O_3, in contrast to spinels from Mid-Atlantic Ridge lavas studied by Sigurdsson and Schilling [1976] and perhaps reflects variation in f_{O_2} [Hill and Roeder, 1974]. Cr_2O_3 in spinels varies from 24.0-40.1 % by weight, and again shows only a slight overall correlation with host rock Cr_2O_3. Minor element variations in Cr-spinel in weight percent are: TiO_2, 0.46 to 1.36; MnO, <0.05 to 0.50; and NiO, <0.05 to 0.40.

On average, spinel $Fe^{3+}/(Fe^{3+}+Al+Cr)$ shows a very general inverse correlation with $Mg/(Mg+Fe^{2+})$ and little correlation with $Cr/(Cr + Al)$ (Figures 2b and 2c). On the $Fe^{3+}/(Fe^{3+}+Al+Cr)$ vs. $Mg/(Mg+Fe^{2+})$ plot, there is a suggestion that the spinels within individual lavas show correlated $Fe^{3+}/(Fe^{3+}+Al+Cr)$ and Mg# increases, in contrast to the spinel trend for all lavas that shows decreasing $Fe^{3+}/(Fe^{3+}+Al+Cr)$ with Mg#. Indeed, calculated Fe^{3+} is typically slightly enriched in the rims relative to cores, implying an increase in lava oxygen fugacity [Irvine, 1965; Hill and Roeder, 1974; Batiza and Vanko, 1984] and a crystallization trend of increasing $Fe^{3+}/(Fe^{3+}+Al+Cr)$ and Mg# in the spinels of a single sample. Nevertheless, it must be realized that these core-rim differences in calculated Fe^{3+} and $Fe^{3+}/(Fe^{3+}+Al+Cr)$ often fall within analytical error. Batiza and Vanko [1984] showed for East Pacific seamount lavas a well-constrained increase in $Fe^{3+}/(Fe^{3+}+Al +Cr)$ with decreasing Mg#, and correlated this with alkalinity of the host rock. The range of spinel $Fe^{3+}/(Fe^{3+}+Al+Cr)$ for a given Mg# observed in this study is much broader than Batiza and Vanko [1984] observed, and here we find no relationship between host lava composition and spinel $Fe^{3+}/(Fe^{3+}+Al+Cr)$, perhaps because the PLUTO lavas occupy a more restricted range of alkalinity.

One of the lavas (1181-2) contains two apparent populations of spinels (1181-2-38 and 1181-2-42 in Table 3). Spinels from both populations are found as inclusions within one crystal of plagioclase. While the coupled increase in Al_2O_3 and MgO and decrease in Cr_2O_3 in 1181-2-42 relative to 1181-2-38 is consistent with the above proposed MgO-enrichment, Cr_2O_3-depletion crystallization trend, the reduction in TiO_2 by half is perplexing, as no spinels in other lavas show this effect. The lowering of TiO_2 may be related to the strong antipathy of Al_2O_3 to TiO_2 in spinels [Sack, 1982].

Plagioclase

Plagioclase is abundant in all analyzed lavas, and typically occurs as skeletal groundmass microlites or as subhedral to euhedral microphenocrysts and phenocrysts up to 4 mm in size. Phenocrysts and microphenocrysts may be quite calcic (to An89), with phenocrysts typically slightly more calcic than microphenocrysts. The cores of both are usually more calcic than their respective rims and coexisting groundmass crystals (Figure 4). Nevertheless, in more primitive basalts where only microlitic groundmass plagioclase is present, groundmass plagioclase may be quite calcic (e.g., 1185-1, Figure 4). We follow Bryan [1972] and Batiza and Vanko [1984] in proposing that the sodic rim and groundmass plagioclase represent low-pressure plagioclase growth during or immediately prior to eruption. Representative analyses are given in Table 4.

Some large, An-rich, subhedral plagioclase phenocrysts and microphenocrysts contain abundant ovoid to elongate crystallized melt inclusions, and are sometimes bounded by An-rich, scalloped rims indicative of resorption. These crystals typically contain complex or simple reverse compositional zoning, as shown by a traverse across a plagioclase phenocryst in 1179-12 (Figure 5). Other subhedral, melt-inclusion-ridden crystals may have sodic, skeletal feldspar growing from the crystal boundaries; one from 1182-3 in Figure 5 is an example. As found by Dungan and

TABLE 2. Pertinent Whole-Rock and Mineral Data for Cr-Rich Spinels

Rock	Lava Mg#	Lava Cr PPM	Lava Al_2O_3	Olivine Fo Mol%	Plagioclase Ar Mol%	Spinel $Mg/Mg+Fe^{2+}$	Spinel $Cr/Cr+Al$	# Analyses Spinel
Ang 2	63.4	274	17.66	87-86	83-65	.67-.63	.30-.50	26
1182-1	60.9	281	15.68	86-85	86-69	.61-.67	.48-.50	19
1181-1	62.8	349	15.52	96-76	88-65	.62-.63	.53	4
1181-2	64.8	331	15.62	87-85	89-65	.63-.66	.43-.50	5
1179-2	65.9	292	17.67	87-86	84-58	.67-.69	.43-.47	12
7-2	65.9	315	16.66	87	84-66	.71-.72	.41-.42	7
6-7	61.8	254	16.10	86-85	81-69	.64-.67	.43	3
								66

Rhodes [1978], Kuo and Kirkpatrick [1982], and Batiza and Vanko [1984], plagioclase next to melt inclusions is often relatively sodic, indicating exchange between the melt inclusion and host feldspar. It is unclear whether the melt inclusions in these lavas were trapped during rapid crystal growth or represent corrosion, as melt inclusions are equally common within zoned and unzoned cores of euhedral plagioclase. Complex or simple reverse zoning also occurs within euhedral to subhedral phenocrysts and microphenocrysts that may or may not contain melt inclusions (1179-6, Figure 5, has no melt inclusions). In some lavas, most phenocrysts and microphenocrysts show reverse zoning, often quite sharp in character. Intense oscillatory zoning rarely occurs in euhedral phenocrysts. Deeply embayed and corroded calcic cores jacketed with thick sodic rims, such as those described by Batiza and Vanko

TABLE 3. Representative Chromium-Rich Spinel Analyses

Spinel	Ang2-3 gmass c	Ang2-6 gmass r	Ang2-21 gmass c	Ang2-22 gmass r	Ang2-10 inc ol	Ang2-11 inr ol	1179-2-48 inc pl	1179-2-49 inr pl	1182-1-31 inc pl
SiO_2	0.07	0.10	0.09	0.10	0.11	0.24	0.07	0.07	0.07
TiO_2	0.4	0.51	0.55	0.56	0.53	0.58	0.78	0.78	0.096
Al_2O_3	27.94	37.21	35.77	37.58	38.58	38.35	26.97	27.50	30.15
Cr_2O_3	36.03	26.16	26.38	24.97	24.84	23.99	36.14	35.09	31.12
FeO	19.28	18.02	18.76	18.53	18.56	18.60	20.29	20.26	21.01
MnO	0.21	0.46	0.08	0.20	0.17	0.15	0.18	0.22	0.07
NiO	0.16	0.29	0.25	0.31	0.18	0.24	0.10	0.10	0.10
MgO	15.33	16.09	16.54	17.23	16.97	16.62	15.31	15.35	15.35
CaO	0.01	0.07	0.05	0.16	0.08	0.15	0.11	0.19	0.28
Total	99.57	99.72	98.47	99.64	100.02	98.92	99.95	99.56	99.11
Fe_2O_3*	6.75	6.83	7.21	7.71	6.74	6.52	7.65	7.88	8.18
FeO*	13.20	11.87	12.27	11.59	12.49	12.73	13.40	13.17	13.65
Total	100.25	100.40	99.19	100.41	100.70	99.57	100.72	100.35	99.93
Cr/(Cr+Al)	0.464	0.320	0.331	0.308	0.302	0.296	0.473	0.461	0.409
$Mg/(Mg+Fe^{2+})$	0.674	0.717	0.706	0.726	0.708	0.699	0.671	0.675	0.667
$Fe^{3+}/(Fe^{3+}+Al+Cr)$	0.076	0.074	0.079	0.083	0.072	0.071	0.087	0.090	0.093

	1181-2-38 inc pl	1181-2-42 inc pl	1181-1-34 inc pl	1181-1-35 inr pl	1181-1-37 gmass r	7-2-8 gmass
SiO_2	0.04	0.23	0.06	0.08	0.14	0.06
TiO_2	0.95	0.54	0.86	0.83	0.63	0.86
Al_2O_3	25.48	28.34	23.56	22.98	30.94	22.93
Cr_2O_3	36.50	32.80	39.39	38.76	31.59	38.71
FeO	21.98	21.87	21.13	21.83	18.34	21.47
MnO	0.25	0.22	0.27	0.20	0.14	0.27
NiO	0.07	0.15	0.13	0.19	0.14	0.12
MgO	14.04	14.72	14.04	14.09	16.31	13.85
CaO	0.11	0.49	0.04	0.14	0.30	0.21
Total	99.42	99.35	99.48	99.10	98.58	98.48
Fe_2O_3*	7.74	8.96	7.18	8.37	7.28	7.90
FeO*	7.74	8.96	7.18	8.37	7.28	7.90
Total	100.20	100.26	100.20	99.94	99.31	99.27
Cr/(Cr+Al)	0.490	0.437	0.529	0.531	0.406	0.531
$Mg/(Mg+Fe^{2+})$	0.625	0.655	0.630	0.637	0.711	0.632
$Fe^{3+}/(Fe^{3+}+Al+Cr)$	0.090	0.102	0.098	0.098	0.082	0.093

* Calculated after Carmichael [1967].
inc=inclusion, c=core, r=rim, pl=in plagioclase, ol=in olivine, gmass=in groundmass.

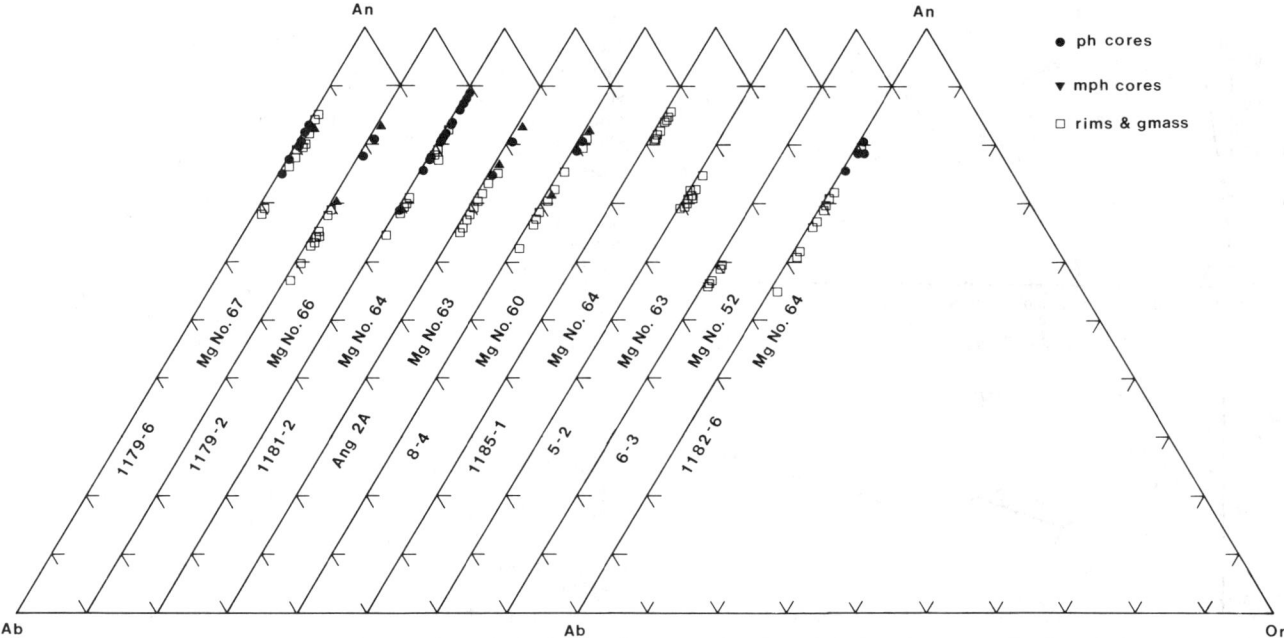

Fig. 4. Microprobe point analyses of plagioclase from representative lava samples. Closed circles, phenocryst cores; closed triangles microphenocryst cores; open squares, rims and groundmass grains. Analyses are plotted on a molecular basis in Albite-Anorthite-Orthoclase ternary diagram.

TABLE 4. Representative Plagioclase Analyses

	7-2-10	7-2-11	7-2-6	1179-2-5	1179-2-6	1179-2-9	1179-6-6	1179-6-7	Ang167A-18	6-7-11
Size	phc	phr	gmass	phc	phr	gmass	phc	phr	gmass	gmass
SiO_2	47.0	51.1	49.55	47.85	50.79	52.09	47.0	45.6	50.6	54.74
TiO_2	n.d.	n.d.	0.05	0.01	0.07	0.06	0.04	.03	0.13	n.a.
Al_2O_3	33.5	31.0	31.20	32.72	30.38	29.22	32.8	33.8	30.5	27.50
Fe_2O_3*	0.31	0.78	0.74	0.51	0.59	0.87	0.41	0.47	0.61	1.16
MgO	0.17	0.27	0.34	0.21	0.29	0.32	0.18	0.19	0.19	0.44
CaO	17.3	14.8	15.00	16.03	14.15	12.91	16.8	17.5	13.6	11.65
Na_2O	1.78	2.97	3.07	2.38	3.63	4.12	1.94	1.62	3.73	4.70
K_2O	n.d.	0.01	0.03	0.01	0.02	0.01	0.01	0.02	0.06	0.08
Total	100.1	101.0	99.98	99.72	99.92	99.60	99.2	99.2	99.4	100.26
An%	84.3	73.3	72.8	78.8	68.2	63.4	82.7	85.6	66.6	57.5
Or%	0.0	0.1	0.2	0.1	0.1	0.1	0.1	0.1	0.3	0.5
	8-4-1	8-4-2	8-4-4	Ang2-10	Ang2-11	Ang167A-1	1182-3-8	Ang2-2	1185-1-1E	1182-5-2A
Size	phc	phr	mphc	phc	phr	phc	mphr	gmass	gmass	phc
SiO_2	47.0	47.77	46.66	48.89	50.86	50.9	47.3	50.51	47.77	54.20
TiO_2	n.d.	0.02	0.05	0.03	0.05	0.04	0.05	0.36	n.a.	n.a.
Al_2O_3	32.77	33.06	33.30	31.88	29.78	30.2	33.2	28.47	32.41	29.10
Fe_2O_3*	0.43	0.49	0.58	0.36	0.86	0.56	0.70	1.60	0.48	0.61
MgO	0.19	0.17	0.14	0.18	0.35	0.20	0.19	0.79	0.20	0.16
CaO	16.48	16.26	16.70	15.29	13.90	14.1	16.3	13.96	16.74	11.01
Na_2O	2.12	2.23	1.94	2.76	3.74	3.55	2.25	3.62	1.64	5.20
M_2O	n.d.	0.06	0.01	0.02	0.02	0.03	n.d.	0.05	0.02	0.06
Total	98.99	100.06	99.38	99.40	99.56	99.6	99.99	99.36	99.26	100.34
An%	81.1	79.8	82.6	75.3	67.2	68.6	80.0	67.9	84.8	53.7
Or%	0.0	0.4	0.1	0.1	0.1	0.2	0.0	0.3	0.1	0.3

* All Fe recalculated to Fe_2O_3.

n.a.=not analyzed, n.d.=not detected, ph=phenocryst, mph=microphenocryst, gmass=groundmass, c=core, r=rlm.

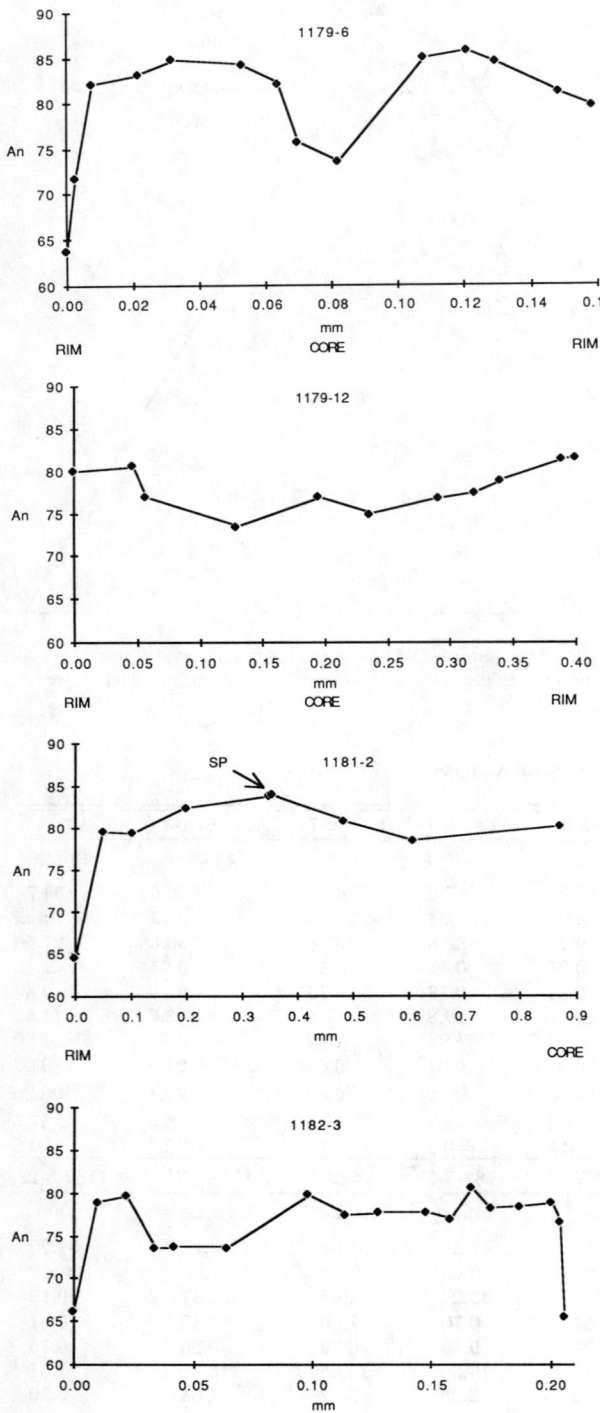

Fig. 5. Microprobe compositional traverses through representative reversely zoned plagioclase crystals. Composition shown in percentage molecular An content. SP with arrow denotes location of spinel in 1181-2 traverse. Estimated 1 sigma counting error is 0.002 (An/(An+Ab)).

[1984] (Fig. 4B) were not found. Inclusions of euhedral spinel were found in all types of calcic (>An75) plagioclase phenocrysts and microphenocrysts. One curious phenocryst in 1181-2 contains 3 spinel inclusions, all of which lie at the exact reversal in compositional zoning of the phenocryst (Figure 5).

Generally, Fe_2O_3, TiO_2, K_2O and MgO are higher in groundmass plagioclase grains and crystal rims relative to phenocryst or microphenocryst cores, MgO least consistently so. Fe_2O_3 is a substantial component in the analyses of some groundmass grains and crystal rims, and sometimes exceeds 1% by weight. Maximum minor element contents in plagioclase are as follows: Fe_2O_3, 1.60%; MgO, 0.79%; TiO_2, 0.36%; and K_2O, 0.12%. These concentrations are somewhat higher than those observed by Bryan [1974] for plagioclase in other submarine basalts.

Olivine

Euhedral to subhedral phenocrysts and microphenocrysts, and skeletal to euhedral groundmass olivine crystals are common within the seamount lavas, and occasionally contain Cr spinel and crystallized melt inclusions. Phenocrysts may reach 1.5 mm in size. Representative olivine analyses are given in Table 5 and plotted in Figure 6.

Compositional zoning of olivine is minimal, and olivine rims and groundmass crystals are typically only slightly more Fe-rich than the cores of phenocrysts and microphenocrysts. The compositional range of olivine grains contained within a single lava rarely exceeds 2-3 molecular % Fo (Figure 6). Most olivine phenocrysts and microphenocrysts within lavas 1181-1, 8-4, and 1182-5 (Table 5) exhibit slight reverse zoning. This may be due to increased oxygen fugacity upon eruption, as observed by Luhr and Carmichael [1981] for olivines within subaerial potassic basalt flows, and is in agreement with the calculated $Fe^{3+}/(Fe^{3+}+Al+Cr)$ zonation in the spinels of 1181-1. Alternatively, this reverse zoning could reflect magma mixing. One large (900μ) subhedral olivine phenocryst from 1181-1 (1181-1-12, 13, Table 5) exhibits very strong reverse zoning; its relatively fayalitic core (Fo 77) indicates that it is a xenocryst, acquired from conduit wallrock assimilation or from magma mixing prior to eruption.

Ni within the olivines may reach 0.53% by weight, and varies in abundance among crystals within a single sample, with little relation to crystal size. The range of Ni exhibited by olivine within a sample is roughly correlated with the Ni content of the host lava. MnO in olivine varies from 0.16 to 0.45% and CaO varies from 0.29 to 0.47%, and both are roughly constant for olivines of a single lava. Groundmass grains and crystal rims have slightly higher MnO and CaO contents relative to the phenocryst and microphenocryst cores, perhaps reflecting quench growth or kinetic effects [Adams and Bishop, 1985].

Roeder and Emslie [1970] and Roeder [1974] experimentally determined the distribution coefficient of Mg-Fe partitioning between olivine and host liquid to be approximately 0.30. Assuming a host lava $Fe^{3+}/Fe^{3+}+Fe^{2+}$ ratio of 0.15 (approximately the NNO oxygen buffer), the PLUTO olivines reflect Mg-Fe K_D's that are principally in the range of 0.26 to 0.31, with an average of about 0.28. If the oxygen fugacity of the PLUTO lavas was equivalent to the FMQ buffer, then the average K_D will be about 0.30. Nevertheless, Bender et al. [1978] determined that this distribution coefficient for MORBs is actually 0.30-0.27, with lower coefficients representing lower pressures and higher temperatures, and Perfit and Fornari [1983] obtained distribution coefficients of 0.24-0.29 in lavas at QFM from the Eastern Galapagos Rift.

TABLE 5. Representative Olivine Analyses

Olivine	1181-1-12	1181-1-13	1181-3-3	1181-2-4	6-2-1	Ang2-1	Ang2-2A	Ang2-22	1182-5-3	1182-5-4
Size	phc	phr	mphc	mphr	gmass	mphc	mphr	gmass	mphc	mphr
SiO_2	37.82	38.90	39.45	39.38	38.29	40.08	40.03	39.70	37.95	38.55
FeO	21.69	14.21	13.01	13.73	20.66	12.61	13.29	12.87	23.31	23.24
MnO	0.37	0.22	0.20	0.26	0.31	0.22	0.25	0.22	0.40	0.43
NiO	0.09	0.32	0.41	0.11	n.d.	0.30	0.28	0.25	0.04	n.d.
MgO	40.00	45.74	45.86	45.04	39.50	46.32	45.91	46.36	37.37	37.84
CaO	0.29	0.35	0.31	0.31	0.44	0.29	0.31	0.31	0.35	0.31
Total	100.26	99.74	99.24	98.83	99.20	99.82	99.81	99.72	99.42	100.37
Mg#	0.767	0.852	.863	.854	.773	0.867	0.860	0.865	0.741	0.743
KD*	0.513	0.293	.283	.305	0.312	0.266	0.280	0.270	0.299	0.296
Olivine	1182-6-1A	1179-6-1	1179-2-1	1179-2-2						
Size	gmass	gmass	phc	phr						
SiO_2	34.78	39.79	39.69	39.74						
FeO	41.08	12.22	12.63	12.56						
MnO	n.d.	0.24	0.20	0.21						
NiO	n.d.	0.19	0.21	0.26						
MgO	23.50	46.68	45.91	45.96						
CaO	0.42	0.33	0.32	0.34						
Total	99.78	99.45	99.02	99.07						
Mg#	0.504	0.872	0.866	0.867						
KD*		.293								

* After Roeder and Emslie (1970), assuming host lava glass. $Fe^{2+}/(Fe^{3+} = Fe^{2+}) = 0.15$, not calculated when no quench glass available. Crystal sizes as in Table 4. n.d.=not detected.

Clinopyroxene

Orthopyroxene was not found in any of the PLUTO lavas, but clinopyroxene is common. In all lavas except 1182-6, clinopyroxene is confined to the groundmass and occurs as anhedral grains as large as 100μ, but is typically smaller than 40μ. Clinopyroxene is usually subordinate to olivine and is absent (except as a quench phase) in some lavas (Table 1), but it greatly predominates over olivine in the evolved lavas Ang167A and 6-5. In the coarser grained sample 1182-6, clinopyroxene occurs as slightly pleochroic, anhedral, light brownish-green grains up to 500μ long. They are commonly elongate in shape, exhibit subophitic texture, and greatly predominate over olivine.

Representative clinopyroxene analyses from the PLUTO lavas are given in Table 6 and plotted in Figure 6. The PLUTO clinopyroxenes are variable in composition, and range from Mg-rich salites and diopsidic augites to augites approaching the subcalcic augite-augite compositional boundary [Poldervaart and Hess, 1951]. Sector and radial zoning is common. The clinopyroxenes are generally similar in composition to other groundmass clinopyroxenes described from oceanic tholeiites [e.g., Batiza, 1978; Batiza and Vanko, 1984; Perfit and Fornari, 1983; Shibata et al., 1979; Mazzullo and Bence, 1976] but are generally less rich in the Wo component than clinopyroxenes from basalts recovered during DSDP Leg 64 in the Gulf of California [Perfit et al., 1982].

Two compositional trends within the PLUTO clinopyroxenes are apparent. One trend extends from near the salite-diopside-endiopside-augite join towards the Fs apex. The other trend extends parallel to the augite-endiopside join, and is especially visible in Ang167A (Figure 6). The latter trend was also noted by Shibata et al. [1979] in clinopyroxenes from the Oceanographer Fracture Zone, who suggested that such a trend could be produced by variations in cooling rate; Perfit and Fornari [1983] ascribed similar pyroxene trends in Galapagos Rift basalts to kinetic effects.

Within an individual lava, clinopyroxene TiO_2 and Al_2O_3 correlate inversely with clinopyroxene MgO, although there is significant scatter. This observation agrees with the theoretical predictions of Sack and Carmichael [1984], concerning Fe^{2+}-Mg and $TiAl_2$-$MgSi_2$ coupled substitution. Clinopyroxene TiO_2 in the PLUTO samples ranges from 0.9 to 3.1% and Al_2O_3 ranges from 1.7 to 10.0%, while Na_2O varies from 0.22 to 0.89% and MnO varies from 0.13 to 0.47% by weight. Clinopyroxene Cr_2O_3 is highly variable and ranges up to 0.35% by weight, and only weakly correlates with the host lava's Cr content.

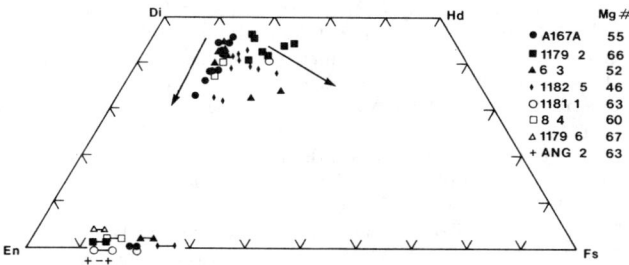

Fig. 6. Olivine and clinopyroxene analyses of representative lavas plotted in lower half of En-Fs-Wo ternary. Symbols represent microprobe point analyses of clinopyroxene or range in olivine composition; closed circles denote analyses from A167A; closed squares, 1179-2; closed triangles, 6-3; closed diamonds, 1182-5; open circles, 1181-1; open squares, 8-4; open triangles, 1179-6; and crosses, Ang-2.

TABLE 6. Representative Clinopyroxene Analyses

	1179-2-4	1179-2-2	1181-1-1	8-4-4	Ang167A-3	1182-5-5	1182-5-8	1182-5-6	1182-6-26	1182-6-2A
SiO_2	47.08	48.61	46.73	48.47	48.85	49.78	46.92	46.07	49.36	51.12
TiO_2	2.32	1.43	2.36	2.41	1.77	1.51	2.46	3.02	1.93	0.95
Al_2O_3	5.56	2.75	4.74	9.99	6.19	4.51	7.07	6.67	3.41	1.67
Cr_2O_3	0.35	0.06	0.17	0.12	0.20	0.11	0.11	0.07	0.05	0.05
FeO	10.78	14.70	14.06	8.38	8.42	11.03	10.13	10.62	10.96	10.39
MnO	0.25	0.34	0.32	0.14	0.17	0.26	0.20	0.27	0.34	0.32
MgO	11.85	10.73	11.64	13.31	15.97	17.12	13.42	12.62	14.10	15.83
CaO	20.89	20.37	18.64	16.90	18.39	15.59	19.28	19.74	19.22	18.25
Na_2O	0.42	0.40	0.35	0.89	0.27	0.30	0.41	0.45	0.36	0.29
Total	99.50	99.39	99.01	100.61	100.23	100.21	100.00	99.53	99.73	98.87
Mg#	.662	.565	.596	.739	.772	.734	.702	.679	.696	.731
Wo	.456	.436	.407	.403	.390	.325	.421	.433	.406	.377
En	.360	.319	.353	.441	.471	.496	.407	.385	.414	.455
Fs	.184	.245	.240	.156	.139	.179	.172	.182	.181	.168

	6-2-3B	6-3-2B	6-3-4B	6-2-1A
SiO_2	50.68	46.82	8.20	50.00
TiO_2	1.28	2.87	2.00	0.97
Al_2O_3	3.69	7.06	3.06	3.94
Cr_2O_3	0.14	0.04	n.d.	0.13
FeO	6.63	8.01	16.49	7.37
MnO	0.23	0.15	.46	0.39
MgO	16.20	13.94	12.36	16.01
CaO	20.65	20.52	16.07	19.41
Na_2O	0.34	0.34	0.47	0.27
Total	99.84	99.75	99.11	99.09
Mg#	.813	.756	.572	.795
Wo	.427	.445	.348	.409
En	.466	.420	.373	.469
Fs	.107	.135	.279	.121

n.d.=not detected.

Opaque Oxides

Granular and skeletal disseminated magnetite is a common constituent within the crystalline groundmass of many of the seamount lavas. Ilmenite was not identified. In a few of the coarser groundmasses, particularly in 1179-2, euhedral magnetite may exceed 10μ in size but in most samples is less than 5μ across. In the intergranular lava 1182-6, anhedral magnetite typically exceeds 100μ in size. Magnetites from 1182-6 and from 1179-2 are titanomagnetites, with TiO_2 contents ranging from 19.9 to 22.6% in 1182-6 and 7.1 to 11.3% in 1179-2. Representative analyses are given in Table 7. Titanomagnetite composition is relatively constant in 1182-6 (Figure 7), and is similar to other magnetites described from MORBs [Mazzulo and Bence, 1976; Perfit and Fornari, 1983; Basaltic Volcanism Study Group, 1981], particularly in TiO_2 content. In contrast are the low TiO_2 titanomagnetites from 1179-2, which exhibit a broader range in composition than those of 1182-6. Al_2O_3 (1.6-2.7% in 1182-6, 2.1-3.9% in 1179-2), MgO (1.2-2.6% in 1182-6, 1.7-2.6% in 1179-2), and MnO (0.5-0.9% in 1182-6, 0.4-0.5% in 1179-2) are other important components of the titanomagnetites; NiO and Cr_2O_3 are always less than 0.1%.

Whole Rock Chemistry

Major and trace-element analyses of lavas from volcanoes Green, C1, C2, Red, and F are given in Tables 8 and 9. Additional information regarding flow morphology and field occurrence is given in the appendix. Major elements given in Table 8 represent wide beam (50μ) electron probe analyses on quenched glass; trace elements were analysed from hand-picked quenched glass separates using neutron activation techniques. Samples that lacked quenched glass were ground in an alumina shatterbox and analyzed by both X-ray fluorescence and neutron activation, and are given in Table 9. Their high ferric/ferrous ratios measured by titration imply post-eruptive oxidation during cooling [Carmichael et al., 1985; Christie et al., 1986].

Selected major and trace element contents of the seamount basalt glasses are plotted in Figure 8, and the ranges of chondrite-normalized [Haskin et al., 1968] rare-earth element abundances for each seamount are plotted in Figure 9. Major element analyses of quenched glass were used for plotting, as glassy rinds are the most representative and least altered material reflecting the composition of the erupting magma [Byerly et al., 1976]. They correspond to N- and T-type MORBs as described by Sun et al. [1979]. The great majority are ol- and hy-normative (calculated assuming $Fe^{3+}/Fe^{3+} + Fe^{2+} = 0.15$), with only a few that are slightly (<1%) quartz normative (5-2, 1178-2, and 1178-4 from seamount F) or nepheline-normative (7-2 and 1180-4B from Green seamount). The quartz-normative lavas have low Na_2O and LREE enrichments and the Ne-normative lavas have relatively high Na_2O and LREE enrichments. Generally, the seamount lavas are quite similar in major element content to those from the adjacent East Pacific Rise [Newman et al., 1983; Rise Project Group, 1980; Juteau et al., 1980; Moore et al., 1977], but each volcano exhibits distinct compositional trends. The lavas of seamount F are considerably less enriched than the other seamounts in Na, Ti,

TABLE 7. Representative Groundmass Titanomagnetite Analyses

	1179-2-51	1179-2-31	1182-6-21	1182-6-19
SiO_2	0.11	0.09	0.09	0.10
TiO_2	9.21	11.87	19.89	22.14
Al_2O_3	2.42	2.06	2.67	1.84
Cr_2O_3	0.04	0.03	0.47	0.07
FeO	79.81	77.92	71.31	71.11
MnO	0.36	0.37	0.54	0.73
NiO	0.01	0.05	n.d.	n.d.
MgO	2.64	1.68	2.56	1.35
CaO	0.08	0.18	0.04	0.09
Total	94.68	94.35	97.57	97.43
Fe_2O_3*	49.22	43.19	28.43	23.44
FeO*	35.52	39.05	45.72	49.12
Total	99.61	98.68	100.42	99.88
Recalculated Mole Percent **				
FeO	53.9	56.5	59.8	61.4
Fe_2O_3	33.6	28.1	16.7	13.7
TiO_2	12.6	15.4	23.4	24.9
Usp	36.0	45.1	67.8	73.2
Mt	64.0	54.9	32.2	26.8

* Analyses recalculated after Carmichael (1967).
** For pure titanomagnetite.
n.d.=not detected.

Ta, Th, and the LREE while Green and Red seamounts are distinct from F and overlap in composition. The lavas of Red seamount exhibit a much greater compositional range than the others, even containing Fe-Ti basalt compositions [Melson et al., 1976].

Correlations between lava chemistry and sample location on individual seamounts are generally poor, and no relationship exists between lava flow morphology or texture and composition. The most evolved sampled lavas from both Red and Green seamounts are associated with intracaldera features, such as intracaldera lava cones, intracaldera shield volcanoes, and caldera lava fill, that represent relatively recent volcanism on the seamounts (Figure 2). The most evolved lavas in the PLUTO data set all come from the summit region of Red seamount.

None of the lavas from the PLUTO expedition contain more than 8.5% MgO by weight, contain more than 190 ppm Ni, or have a Mg # higher than 0.68. If most previous estimates of the composition of likely mantle melts are accurate [e.g., Frey et al., 1978; Sato, 1977; Green, 1971; Rhodes and Dungan, 1979; Presnall et al., 1979] then virtually all of the basalts in this study have undergone magmatic evolution since their initial formation as partial melts. Nevertheless, their estimates of primitive mantle melts allow for more Fe-rich and Ni-poor compositions. For example, Hebert et al. [1983] have proposed that liquid in equilibrium with ultramafic rocks from the Garrett Transform Fault, East Pacific Rise had an Mg# of about 0.7 and Ni contents of only 150 ppm, while Bryan et al. [1981] propose that lavas with Mg#'s as low as 0.65 may represent primitive MORBs. If these latter estimates are correct, only small amounts of fractionation or assimilation may have affected the most primitive of the PLUTO lavas. In the PLUTO lavas, Sc and Cr correlate poorly with MgO, perhaps reflecting variable amounts of clinopyroxene and spinel fractionation. In contrast, Ni correlates relatively well with MgO.

A characteristic of Green and Red seamounts is the diversity of the LREE, even for lavas of similar MgO content (Table 8) within a given seamount. Equally striking are the two distinct sub-parallel compositional groups or trends shown by the lavas of Green in TiO_2, Al_2O_3, Na_2O and CaO vs. MgO (Figure 8), with the the Na_2O trend showing some scatter. Two similar groups are visible in the more primitive (MgO > 7.0, Mg# > 0.60) lavas from Red seamount, although the differences between the groups are not as great. These correlate with one another; low Ca occurs with high Ti, Na, and Al. These same groups are even more marked on plots of CaO/Al_2O_3 vs. Mg# and $Na_2O/(Na_2O+CaO)$ vs. Mg# (Figure 10), which serve as proxies for normative plagioclase composition and content. Of great interest is the fact that the lavas in each group have highly variable $(La/Sm)_N$ or $(La/Ce)_N$ ratios. For example, the high CaO/Al_2O_3 trend of lavas from Green have $(La/Sm)_N$ ranging from 0.51-0.93.

Geothermometry

Rim and groundmass compositions of plagioclase and olivine were used together with quenched glass compositions (assuming $Fe^{3+}/Fe^{3+}+Fe^{2+} = 0.15$) to calculate magmatic temperatures. A variety of geothermometers were used, including those based on olivine-glass compositions [Roeder and Emslie, 1970; Roeder, 1974; Glazner, 1984; Bender et al.'s 1978 modification of Roeder and Emslie, 1970], plagioclase-glass compositions [Kudo and Weill, 1970; Mathez, 1973; Drake, 1976; Glazner, 1984], and bulk melt composition [Fisk et al., 1980], calibrated using lavas from the Reykjanes Ridge and Iceland). Results from several of these geothermometers are presented in Figure 11.

The results show a decrease in calculated eruption temperatures corresponding with a decrease in Mg#. Most lavas have calculated temperatures between 1210°g and 1140°C. Plagioclase-liquid and Mg# calculated temperatures are systematically but variably (10-80°g C) higher than olivine-liquid temperatures. Batiza and Vanko [1984] obtained similar results from other East Pacific seamount lavas, with the difference being most pronounced in evolved alkali basalts. They proposed that the temperature difference between the two geothermometers reflects the effects of

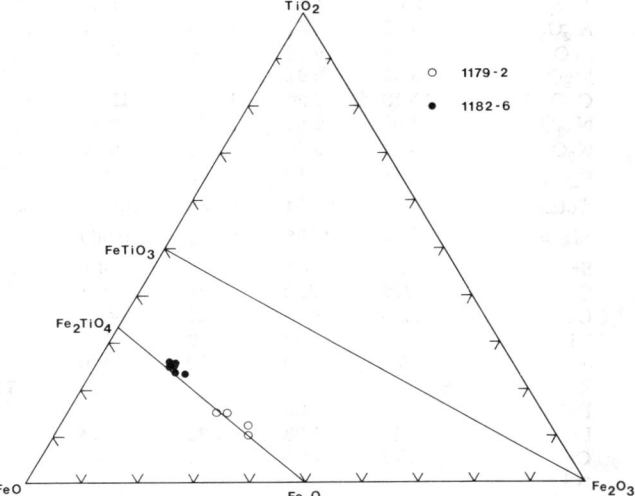

Fig. 7. Microprobe point analyses of titanomagnetite plotted on a molecular basis in the Fe_2O_3-TiO_2-FeO tetrahedron. Open circles represent titanomagnetite from 1179-2, and closed circles represent titanomagnetite from 1182-6.

TABLE 8. Quench Glass Analyses

Volcano Sample	Green 1179-1	Green 1179-10	Green 1179-11	Green 1179-12	Green 1179-6	Green 1179-7	Green 1179-9	Green 1180-1A	Green 1180-1B	Green 1180-2	Green 1180-3	Green 1180-4A
SiO_2	50.58	50.95	49.73	50.88	49.55	49.1	50.13	49.91	49.81	50.17	50.52	49.38
TiO_2	1.42	1.52	1.24	1.51	1.27	1.22	1.5	1.44	2.01	1.4	1.4	1.12
Al_2O_3	15.15	15.22	16.9	15.28	16.79	17.02	15.03	15.66	15.38	15.43	15.56	16.81
FeO	9.58	9.76	8.81	9.51	8.6	8.62	9.46	9.66	10.42	9.4	9.27	8.45
MgO	7.34	7.01	8.4	6.96	8.16	8.52	7.08	7.41	6.64	7.59	7.31	8.52
CaO	12.09	12.29	12	12.37	11.95	11.98	12.22	12.1	11.28	12.01	12.29	12.07
Na_2O	2.78	2.79	2.81	2.81	2.87	2.84	2.76	2.7	3.53	2.78	2.72	2.59
K_2O	0.18	0.2	0.12	0.2	0.16	0.11	0.22	0.19	0.24	0.2	0.19	0.09
P_2O_5	0.17	0.16	0.17	0.15	0.17	0.17	0.2	0.15	0.22	0.2	0.16	0.15
Total	99.29	99.9	100.18	99.67	99.52	99.58	98.6	98.82	99.53	99.18	99.42	99.18
Mg #	0.616	0.601	0.667	0.606	0.666	0.675	0.611	0.627	0.572	0.629	0.623	0.679
Sc			40.8	42.6	34.1		42.4	41.8	41.7			34.3
Cr			256	310	307		320	327	240			338
Co			38.7	39.8	42.4		40.2	40.9	39.1			43.1
Ni			60	70	150		80	70	70			130
Sr			160	200	100		130	140	190			90
Zr			110	140	40		90	70	140			
Ba			56	22			39	28	37			12
La			7.35	5.25	2.78		5.21	5.31	8.08			2.37
Ce			19.1	14.8	8.64		14.3	14.2	22.7			7.91
Nd												
Sm			4.32	3.45	2.88		3.46	3.45	4.91			2.55
Eu			1.51	1.25	1.06		1.28	1.26	1.72			0.99
Tb			0.95	0.86	0.71		0.78	0.87	1.04			0.71
Yb			3.39	2.98	2.44		2.9	2.84	3.71			2.49
Lu			0.52	0.46	0.37		0.45	0.46	0.53			0.35
Hf			3.46	2.72	2.15		2.77	2.78	4.21			1.94
Ta			0.63	0.4	0.18		0.39	0.43	0.56			0.18
Th			0.74	0.36			0.38	0.39	0.47			0.08
U												
$(La/Sm)_N$			0.93	0.84	0.53		0.83	0.84	0.9			0.51

Volcano Sample	Green 1180-4B	Green 1180-8	Green 1185-1	Green 1185-12	Green 1185-2	Green 7-1	Green 7-2	Green 9-1	Green 9-6	Green Ang 2	C1 1181-1	C1 1181-2
SiO_2	49.71	50.91	50.33	49.51	50.5	48.72	49.79	48.89	49.46	48.84	50.53	50.21
TiO_2	2.05	1.49	1.37	1.27	1.41	1.79	1.17	1.31	1.35	1.28	1.3	1.24
Al_2O_3	15.47	15.31	15.98	17.02	15.93	16.81	16.66	16.61	16.41	17.66	15.52	15.62
FeO	9.94	9.42	9.24	8.77	9.28	9.23	8.88	9.11	8.89	9.77	9.63	9.34
MgO	6.56	6.92	7.8	8.46	7.82	7.2	8.19	8.05	7.92	8.08	7.76	7.96
CaO	11.13	12.26	12.04	11.92	12.04	11.22	12.12	11.98	12.02	11.37	12.48	12.56
Na_2O	3.66	2.82	2.72	2.85	2.73	3.35	2.73	2.81	2.82	3.04	2.73	2.52
K_2O	0.24	0.22	0.2	0.09	0.19	0.25	0.1	0.12	0.11	0.13	0.09	0.08
P_2O_5	0.17	0.19	0.2	0.2	0.18	0.26	0.11	0.12	0.12	0.14	0.17	0.12
Total	98.93	99.54	99.88	100.09	100.08	98.83	99.75	100	99.1	100.31	100.21	99.65
Mg #	0.581	0.606	0.639	0.669	0.639	0.621	0.659	0.65	0.651	0.634	0.628	0.641
Sc	41.4	42.1	40.3	34.8	40.1	35.8	35.4	34.3		35	40.9	40.4
Cr	229	322	328	311	326	263	315	304		273.6	349	330
Co	38.4	39.7	46.4	41.8	41.1	40	42.6	41.7		47.7	41.1	40.4
Ni	50	60	70	120	110	110	110	120		190	120	110
Sr	260	140	170	120	150	220	140	100		170	50	80
Zr	160	90		70	110	140	70	80		140	90	
Ba	44	36		15	40	39	27	28			6	22
La	7.81	5.23	5.31	2.74	5.12	6.4	2.65	3.07		4.11	2.08	2.05
Ce	23.1	14.6	13.8	9.1	14.2	17.9	8.73	9.94		11.7	7.54	6.99
Nd			9.1									
Sm	4.95	3.43	3.34	2.95	3.35	3.98	2.65	2.93		2.82	2.91	2.86
Eu	1.67	1.28	1.21	1.1	1.23	1.42	1.02	1.08		1.1	1.09	1.06
Tb	1.03	0.85	0.72	0.78	0.92		0.62			0.64	0.81	0.79
Yb	3.75	2.96	2.76	2.54	2.68	3.12	2.46	2.51		2.6	2.99	2.92
Lu	0.56	0.44	0.4	0.37	0.41	0.46	0.37	0.36		0.38	0.44	0.45

TABLE 8. (continued)

Volcano	Green	Green	Green	Green	Green	Green	Green	Green	Green	Green	C1	C1
Sample	1180-4B	1180-8	1185-1	1185-12	1185-2	7-1	7-2	9-1	9-6	Ang 2	1181-1	1181-2
Hf	4.12	2.8	2.63	2.17	2.51	3.32	2.1	2.32		2.12	2.2	2.06
Ta	0.51	0.44	0.34	0.17	0.4	0.39	0.15	0.17		0.22	0.07	0.13
Th	0.46	0.34	0.34	0.1	0.33	0.36	0.09	0.09		0.13	0.03	
U	0.18											
(La/Sm)N	0.87	0.84	0.87	0.51	0.84	0.88	0.55	0.58		0.8	0.39	0.39

	Between C1 and C2					C2	C2	C2	C2	Red	Red	Red
Volcano												
Sample	1181-3	1181-4	1181-8	1181-7	1181-8	1181-5	1181-6	1181-7	Ang 167A	1182C	1182-1	1182-2
SiO_2	51.02	50.57	50.36	50.55	50.1	50.21	50.44	50.64	50.3	50.76	50.36	49.93
TiO_2	1.25	1.21	1.22	1.29	1.58	1.82	1.79	1.23	2.07	1.47	1.73	1.56
Al_2O_3	15.73	15.64	15.71	15.38	15.39	15.33	15.44	15.71	14.5	15.3	15.68	15.31
FeO	9.36	9.39	9.31	9.49	9.65	10.04	10.18	9.32	11.15	9.81	9.53	9.84
MgO	7.95	7.97	8.09	8	7.32	6.83	6.97	8.02	6.49	7.4	7.08	7.36
CaO	12.45	12.55	12.5	12.57	11.83	11.41	11.45	12.52	11.1	12.14	11.64	11.92
Na_2O	2.53	2.5	2.6	2.64	3.09	3.22	3.25	2.52	3.19	3.02	3.37	3.03
K_2O	0.07	0.05	0.05	0.07	0.15	0.29	0.32	0.07	0.23	0.11	0.3	0.11
P_2O_5	0.16	0.13	0.15	0.16	0.13	0.2	0.26	0.18	0.18	0.14	0.18	0.21
Total	100.52	100.01	99.66	100.16	99.35	99.35	100.1	100.21	99.21	100.15	99.87	99.27
Mg #	0.64	0.64	0.646	0.639	0.614	0.589	0.586	0.643	0.55	0.613	0.609	0.611
Sc	40	40.1				36.3	41.6		43.7		46.6	42
Cr	360	365				271	258		167.6		282	292
Co	41.5	41.3				41	39.5		42.4		41.5	40.8
Ni	150	120				110	120		90		120	100
Sr	70	80				210	160		140		160	190
Zr		60				120	140		140		80	50
Ba	12					37	64		51			29
La	1.78	1.81				5.58	7.46		7.45		6.82	3.67
Ce	6.37	6.34				15.5	19.9		19.8		17.6	11.2
Nd									16.3		14.1	
Sm	2.72	2.68				3.65	4.39		5.04			3.56
Eu	1.01	1.02				1.36	1.56		1.77		1.46	1.29
Tb	0.74	0.75				0.9	0.94		1.13		0.84	0.93
Yb	2.84	2.84				2.9	3.42		4.31		2.9	3.12
Lu	0.4	0.42				0.42	0.5		0.62			0.48
Hf	1.84	1.93				2.92	3.38		3.94		3.1	2.86
Ta	0.11	0.1				0.45	0.66		0.48		0.47	0.22
Th						0.36	0.62		0.5		0.92	
U									0.08			
(La/Sm)N	0.36	0.37				0.84	0.93		0.81			0.57

Volcano	Red	Red	Red	Red	Red	Red	Red	Red	Red	Red	Red	Red
Sample	1182-3	1182-4	1182-5	1182-7	1183-1	1183-10	1183-13	1183-19	1183-20	1183-3	1183-5	1183-6
SiO_2	50.13	50.12	49.95	49.15	50.46	49.99	49.62	50.1	50.13	50.67	50.08	49.66
TiO_2	1.56	1.51	2.54	1.44	1.8	1.7	1.53	1.48	1.52	1.77	1.51	1.53
Al_2O_3	15.33	15.53	13.77	16.87	15.25	15.63	16.6	16.92	16.76	15.34	16.68	16.72
FeO	9.66	9.85	12.8	9.23	9.79	9.57	9.06	9.52	9.24	10.14	9.36	9.34
MgO	7.4	7.4	5.22	7.75	6.76	6.97	7.58	7.92	7.61	6.9	7.76	7.73
CaO	11.99	12.02	9.9	11.38	11.29	11.51	11.31	11.41	11.34	11.42	11.39	11.38
Na_2O	3.01	3	3.95	3.06	3.34	3.34	3.08	3.09	3.1	3.34	3.06	3.14
K_2O	0.11	0.12	0.25	0.34	0.19	0.27	0.21	0.2	0.2	0.21	0.22	0.2
P_2O_5	0.15	0.18	0.25	0.18	0.24	0.22	0.17	0.21	0.19	0.25	0.22	0.2
Total	99.34	99.73	98.63	99.4	99.12	99.2	99.16	100.85	100.09	100.04	100.28	99.9
Mg #	0.616	0.612	0.461	0.638	0.592	0.604	0.637	0.636	0.633	0.588	0.635	0.634
Sc	41.9	42.2	39	33.6	42.3		36.1	35.7	35		36.4	
Cr	273	293	57	275	262		267	252	300		272	
Co	40.4	41.3	41.7	39.2	38.6		41	40	41.5		40.9	
Ni	80	80	10	120	60		90	120	140		130	

TABLE 8. (continued)

Volcano	Red	Red	Red	Red	Red	Red	Red	Red	Red	Red	Red	Red
Sample	1182-3	1182-4	1182-5	1182-7	1183-1	1183-10	1183-13	1183-19	1183-20	1183-3	1183-5	1183-6
Sr	120	110	140	210	200		160	220	170		170	
Zr		90	160	110			150	120	80		80	
Ba	40		35	59	38		48	49	33		27	
La	3.6	3.64	6.48	8	5.77		5.81	5.5	4.09		5.68	
Ce	11.8	11.4	19.9	19	17.1		15.3	15.6	11.9		15.7	
Nd												
Sm	3.58	3.58	5.92	3.57	4.16		3.63	3.57	3.05		3.67	
Eu	1.31	1.33	2.09	1.31	1.51		1.35	1.3	1.17		1.36	
Tb	0.86	0.94	1.53	0.72	0.96		0.81	0.8	0.71		0.93	
Yb	3.22	3.17	5.01	2.53	3.34		2.82	2.68	2.52		2.72	
Lu	0.49	0.47	0.78	0.39	0.49		0.41	0.45	0.35		0.42	
Hf	2.6	2.75	4.73	2.77	3.47		2.87	2.88	2.45		2.96	
Ta	0.19	0.23	0.45	0.81	0.37		0.42	0.46	0.3		0.45	
Th	0.14		0.34	0.92	0.27		0.36	0.59	0.24		0.39	
U				0.06				0.09				
(La/Sm)N	0.55	0.56	0.6	1.23	0.76		0.88	0.85	0.74		0.85	

Volcano	Red	Red	Red	Red	Red	Red	Red	Red	Red	Red	Red	Red
Sample	1183-8	1187-1	1187-2	6-1	6-2	6-3	6-4	6-5	6-6	6-8	6-8	8-1
SiO_2	50.11	49.81	49.3	50.49	50.58	50.24	50.08	50.72	50.38	49.42	50.3	50.25
TiO_2	1.76	1.56	1.59	2.06	2.04	2.06	1.63	2.02	2.09	1.59	2.1	1.69
Al_2O_3	15.55	16.53	16.57	14.58	14.63	14.44	16.33	14.62	14.29	16.1	14.14	15.9
FeO	9.35	9.01	8.98	12.18	12.02	11.73	9.6	12.11	11.57	9.46	11.9	9.77
MgO	6.77	7.54	7.6	6.14	6.08	6.14	7.39	6.15	6.12	7.3	5.93	7.18
CaO	11.47	11.43	11.47	10.77	10.75	10.88	11.66	10.79	10.77	11.51	10.54	11.46
Na_2O	3.28	3.12	3.15	3.72	3.67	3.62	3.24	3.72	3.71	3.17	3.35	3.21
K_2O	0.27	0.21	0.21	0.23	0.23	0.21	0.23	0.21	0.24	0.24	0.23	0.22
P_2O_5	0.23	0.16	0.18	0.16	0.16	0.23	0.2	0.16	0.21	0.21	0.2	0.2
Total	98.79	99.37	99.05	100.33	100.16	99.55	100.36	100.5	99.38	99	98.69	99.88
Mg #	0.603	0.637	0.64	0.514	0.515	0.523	0.618	0.516	0.526	0.618	0.511	0.606
Sc		36.2	35.9	41.3	42.4	41.8	36.1	42.8	41.9	36.4		
Cr		268	268	30	32.2	30	270	32.4	31	254		
Co		41	40.5	40.8	43.5	41.2	39.8	44	41.9	39.8		
Ni		130	110	30	10	40	130	30		90		
Sr		220	180	120	170	150	200	170	130	220		
Zr		110	120	120	150	140	80	140	120	60		
Ba			22	28	38	34	38		17	41		
La		5.82	5.69	5.53	5.87	5.56	5.69	5.95	5.61	5.58		
Ce		15.5	15.4	16.2	15.6	16.6	14.9	15.8	16.4	15.7		
Nd					10.4			9.9				
Sm		3.69	3.63	4.91	4.86	4.76	3.69	4.78	4.8	3.67		
Eu		1.34	1.33	1.71	1.74	1.7	1.3	1.74	1.75	1.32		
Tb		0.86	0.87	1.14	0.97	1.17	0.81	1.05	1.16	0.82		
Yb		2.65	2.65	3.91	3.96	4.06	2.71	3.91	4.01	2.88		
Lu		0.41	0.41	0.62	0.58	0.61	0.4	0.58	0.63	0.42		
Hf		2.85	2.84	3.72	3.7	3.78	2.86	3.69	3.81	2.92		
Ta		0.46	0.44	0.45	0.38	0.46	0.45	0.41	0.42	0.46		
Th		0.47	0.36	0.36	0.33	0.36	0.31	0.33	0.45	0.13		
U										0.06		
(La/Sm)N		0.87	0.86	0.62	0.66	0.64	0.85	0.68	0.64	0.83		

elevated H_2O and other volatiles in the melts on plagioclase and olivine composition. This argument is supported by the general observation that the more evolved lavas show the greatest temperature discrepancies. Alternatively, empirical activity models for forsterite and anorthite derived from high-pressure experiments [Glazner et al., 1985] predict that the olivine-liquid and plagioclase-liquid compositions used in the geothermometry calculations will yield similar temperatures at pressures of 8-10 kbar (A. Glazner, pers. comm., 1986), although only compositions from groundmass crystals were used.

Discussion

Although no alkali basalts were found on any of the seamounts, there is a great deal of compositional diversity among the lavas studied, even among those that have erupted from a single

TABLE 8. (continued)

Volcano Sample	Red 8-2	Red 8-4	F 1178-5	F 1178-6	F 1178-6 Dup	F 4-1	F 4-10	F 4-11	F 4-12	F 4-13	F 4-14	F 4-2
SiO_2	50.31	50.14	50.54	49.71		49.78	50.58	50.14	50.08	50.08	50.55	50.02
TiO_2	1.66	1.68	1.02	0.95		1.07	1.15	1.13	1.1	1.15	1.19	1.13
Al_2O_3	15.48	15.75	15.14	16.28		16.15	15.77	15.59	15.78	15.68	15.66	15.77
FeO	9.69	9.86	9.6	8.7		9.22	9.19	9.45	9.44	9.43	9.62	9.18
MgO	7.05	7.01	8.24	8.87		8.51	8.18	8.27	8.34	8.14	7.94	8.18
CaO	11.44	11.53	12.91	12.86		12.47	12.54	12.69	12.6	12.54	12.83	12.55
Na_2O	3.27	3.27	2.91	2.86		2.43	2.46	2.46	2.47	2.44	2.4	2.42
K_2O	0.18	0.18	0.04	0.05		0.06	0.07	0.06	0.07	0.05	0.06	0.05
P_2O_5	0.18	0.17	0.1	0.1		0.1	0.1	0.1	0.1	0.11	0.11	0.12
Total	99.26	99.59	99.76	99.64		99.79	100.04	99.89	99.98	99.62	100.36	99.42
Mg #	0.604	0.599	0.643	0.681		0.659	0.651	0.647	0.649	0.644	0.634	0.651
Sc		40.2		37.2	37.1							
Cr		278		372	392							
Co		40.2		45.1	45.5							
Ni		80		150	100							
Sr		170		60								
Zr		110		50	90							
Ba		25										
La		5.19		1.41	1.71							
Ce		15.1		5.12	5.6							
Nd												
Sm		3.89		2.11	2.15							
Eu		1.45		0.82	0.85							
Tb		0.84		0.6	0.62							
Yb		3.15		2.39	2.26							
Lu		0.48		0.35	0.36							
Hf		3.2		1.6	1.55							
Ta		0.34		0.06	0.05							
Th		0.26										
U												
(La/Sm)N		0.73		0.37	0.36							

seamount. Much of the diversity correlated with changes in Mg# is likely due to crystal fractionation, but fractionation alone cannot account for the major and trace element diversity independent of Mg# nor for the diversity among the most primitive lavas. After studying numerous seamounts on the flanks of the East Pacific Rise, Batiza and Vanko [1983] and Batiza [1985] concluded that the melts constructing the seamounts were derived from the same source as the EPR basalts, but these seamount melts bypassed the sub-axial magma chambers beneath some portions of the EPR. If so, it is reasonable to suppose that a variety of lavas that originated from chemically heterogeneous and physically different mantle sources could be erupted from the same seamount edifice. In this way, diverse lavas from a heterogeneous source can be erupted because they are not mixed and homogenized in a magma chamber as may occur beneath portions of the EPR.

Batiza and Vanko [1984] conclude that seamounts likely tap a relatively small region of the mantle where the extent of melting is small [also see Cohen and O'Nions, 1982 and Hedge, 1978], perhaps reflecting a lower-temperature regime near fractures and transform faults [Sleep, 1975]. The diversity of lavas seen in the seamounts is similar to that observed at the EPR near certain transform faults such as the Tamayo Fracture Zone (Bender et al., 1978; Langmuir et al., 1986], a diversity that likely results from low but variable amounts of melting of a heterogeneous mantle source [Carlson et al., 1978; Johnson, 1979; Batiza and Johnson, 1980]. In the ensuing discussion, we will present evidence demonstrating that mixing and fractionation were important petrogenetic processes during the genesis of the PLUTO lavas, but that different parental lavas derived from a heterogeneous source are required to produce the range of lavas seen within single seamounts of the Larson group. We will then discuss how this lava diversity serves as a guide to the extent of mantle heterogeneity beneath the adjacent East Pacific Rise.

Evidence for Mixing

Trace element plots indicate that simple mixing between endmembers relatively enriched in LREE and other incompatible elements and endmembers depleted in the same elements is an important process in the development of lavas erupted from the PLUTO seamounts. The PLUTO lavas define simple binary mixing lines when considering ratios of the REE, high field strength elements, and other incompatible elements. Several examples are given in Figure 12. Companion plots to these ratio-ratio plots buttress the argument that these represent true general mixing lines [Langmuir et al., 1978]. It is important to note that the position of individual lavas on any of the mixing plots is independent of their MgO content and are preserved from plot to plot. From the plots shown in Figure 12, it is impossible to say whether the binary mixing lines result simply from mixing of discrete melts at the source (mixing of sources), from mixing of melts enroute to the surface or shortly before eruption, or from incorporation of wallrock.

Although individual seamounts define distinct mixing lines, these mixing lines are not displaced from one another, thus indi-

TABLE 8. (continued)

Volcano Sample	F 4-20	F 4-21	F 4-3	F 4-4	F 4-5	F 4-6	F 4-6 Dup	F 4-7	F 4-7 Dup	F 4-8	F 4-8 Dup	F 4-9	F 5-2	Estimated Errors
SiO_2	49.84	50	50.28	49.71	50.14	50.09	49.97	49.98	50.6	50.54	49.9	50.26	50.92	
TiO_2	1.1	1.09	1.14	1.13	1.12	1.11	1.16	1.08	1.23	1.12	1.09	1.12	1.07	
Al_2O_3	15.82	15.89	16.11	16.13	16.01	15.91	15.79	16.12	15.32	15.96	15.92	16.15	14.59	
FeO	9.25	9.23	9.22	9.17	9.16	9.29	9.43	9.19	9.93	9.31	8.81	9.2	9.75	
MgO	8.43	8.26	8.31	8.37	8.45	8.48	7.6	8.44	7.88	8.34	8.06	8.47	7.94	
CaO	12.51	12.52	12.67	12.48	12.59	12.46	12.68	12.5	12.38	12.64	12.5	12.66	12.78	
Na_2O	2.36	2.35	2.46	2.47	2.42	2.42	2.57	2.43	2.5	2.5	2.47	2.42	2.33	
K_2O	0.05	0.03	0.06	0.06	0.06	0.06	0.05	0.05	0.05	0.06	0.05	0.06	0.02	
P_2O_5	0.09	0.1	0.11	0.08	0.1	0.1	0.12	0.08	0.12	0.11	0.12	0.11	0.09	
Total	99.45	99.47	100.36	99.6	100.05	99.92	99.37	99.87	100.01	100.58	98.92	100.45	99.49	
Mg #	0.657	0.652	0.654	0.657	0.659	0.657	0.628	0.658	0.641	0.653	0.657	0.659	0.631	
Sc	38.6	39.5											43.9	0.4
Cr	350	360											230	2
Co	53.6	44.9											44.9	0.4
Ni	120	110											80	27
Sr	110	70											50	33
Zr	90													42
Ba	23												0.07	
La	2.19	1.85											12	12
Ce	7.85	6.42											1.31	0.08
Nd													5.02	0.4
Sm	2.51	2.5												3.1
Eu	0.95	0.96											2.3	0.06
Tb	0.7	0.71											0.89	0.03
Yb	2.59	2.58											0.61	0.05
Lu	0.37	0.38										2.74	0.09	
Hf	1.86	1.86											0.42	0.02
Ta	0.08												1.69	0.11
Th	0.01												0.07	0.02
U														0.06
														0.08
$(La/Sm)_N$	0.48	0.41											0.31	

cating very similar end members for the mixtures. Similarly, the PLUTO mixing lines fall on the same binary mixing lines defined in Batiza and Vanko [1984] for the much larger group of 22 East Pacific seamounts. Batiza and Vanko [1984] inferred that the mixing lines reflect mixing of relatively enriched and depleted melt sources within a mantle heterogeneous on the order of kilometers, an interpretation in accord with $^{87}Sr/^{86}Sr$, $^{143}Nd/^{144}Nd$, and $^{3}He/^{4}He$ ratios obtained from the same data set [Zindler et al., 1984; Graham et al., in prep.), and from similar sparse isotopic data on the PLUTO lavas.

Magma mixing is suggested by the sharp reverse zoning commonly seen in some PLUTO An-rich plagioclase phenocrysts [Dungan and Rhodes, 1978; Rhodes et al., 1979], and by the reverse zoning observed in some olivines. Of special interest is the reversely-zoned plagioclase phenocryst in PLUTO lava 1181-2 where two slightly different populations of spinels are found as inclusions (Figure 5). The spinels in this crystal occur where zoning changes from reverse to normal. This change in zoning pattern reflects changing magmatic conditions, and cannot be accounted for by movement of the magma from high to low pressure, as the activity of Ab in plagioclase increases with pressure [Green et al., 1980; Mahood and Baker, 1986]. Rather, the adherence of the spinels to the plagioclase at the change in compositional zoning may reflect magma mixing, with the two sets of spinels perhaps reflecting crystallization from two different magmas.

Figure 13 shows the PLUTO glass compositions projected from PLAGIOCLASE onto the plane OLIVINE-SILICA-DIOPSIDE using the algorithm of Walker et al. [1979]. All compositions plot well above the 10-20 kbar cotectics estimated from experimental data by Stolper [1980]. In addition, many lavas, including all from seamount F, cluster around the 1 bar cotectic; a few plot well into the high-Ca pyroxene field, possibly indicating that substantial low pressure mixing or assimilation has occurred [Walker et al., 1979].

The seamounts Green, Red, and F contain calderas, representing collapse features associated with large magma conduits and chambers within the volcanic edifice [Batiza at al., 1984; Fornari et al., 1984; Simkin, 1972]. These chambers and conduits reflect an environment in which low-pressure mixing and assimilation can occur. The multi-kilometer size of the calderas implies the existence of extensive magmatic plumbing systems within the seamounts that could accommodate magma for substantial amounts of time.

Fractionation

Although it is uncertain whether any PLUTO lavas can be considered primary, some may be representative of parental liquids to

TABLE 9. Whole-Rock Analyses

Seamount Sample	Green 1185-15	Green 1179-2	Green 1185-21	Green 1185-14	Green 1185-14 Duplicate	Red 1182-6	Red 1183-4	Red 1183-7	Red 1186-2	F 1178-2	F 1178-3	F 1178-7	F 1178-4	F 1178-1
SiO_2		49.7		48.7	49.1	49.6	48.8	49.4		50.5	49.7		50.4	49.3
TiO_2		1.24		1.24	1.25	1.59	1.56	1.58		1.45	1.26		1.12	1.03
Al_2O_3		17.67		16.52	16.69	16.06	15.88	15.96		16.3	14.96		17.11	15.51
Fe_2O_3		2.03		1.45	2.57	1.96	2.5	3.11		2.85	2.85		4.32	1.83
FeO	8.34	6.1	8.35	7.26	6.25	7.06	6.68	5.66	10.75	6.02	8.11	8.66	3.75	7.4
MnO		0.15		0.16	0.15	0.16	0.16	0.14		0.16	0.18		0.15	0.18
MgO		7.3		8.76	8.3	7.61	7.25	6.8		6.82	7.37		6.62	8.76
CaO		12.79		11.83	12.1	11.49	11.5	11.88		12.01	11.81		12.57	12.8
Na_2O	2.83	2.73	2.91	2.67	2.76	3.16	3.14	3.14	3.76	2.59	2.29	2.59	2.46	2.09
K_2O		0.15		0.11	0.15	0.23	0.33	0.33		0.08	0.1		0.08	0.06
P_2O_5		0.11		0.11	0.11	0.18	0.18	0.17		0.1	0.1		0.07	0.08
H_2O^+		0.32		0.4	0.76	0.1	0.46	0.57		0.85	0.37		1.13	0.49
H_2O^-														
CO_2		0.09		0.05	0.08	0.06	0.67	0.14		0.06	0.11		0.05	0.04
Total		100.38		99.26	100.27	99.26	99.11	98.99		99.77	99.21		99.83	99.57
Mg #		0.659		0.682	0.67	0.644	0.63	0.628		0.625	0.591		0.645	0.67
Sc	35.1	35.4	34.9	34.9	37	37.4	36.9	37.6	41.5	46.4	44.2	44.3	42.4	39.7
Cr	296	292	292	299	254	411	254	254	33	183	366	302	405	366
Co	41.7	40.3	41.3	40.9	38.9	41.5	38.9	43	41.2	33.4	43.6	44.9	40.3	43.6
Ni	170	120	180	130	70	190	70	80	80	50	40	40	50	
Sr	120	140	110	140	160	200	160	200	150					90
Zr		90	60		110	110	100	130	130			70	90	
Ba	21		30		56	53	60	49	50					
La	2.75	2.8	2.81	2.91		5.98	5.95	5.98	6.04	5.5	2.4	1.76	1.91	1.71
Ce	9.46	8.87	9.03	9.29		15.6	16.3	15.6	15.5	16.3	7.01	6.64	7.25	6.25
Sm	2.87	2.84	2.92	2.87		3.73	3.8	3.73	3.98	4.79	2.96	2.86	2.69	2.23
Eu	1.11	1.05	1.08	1.07		1.37	1.38	1.37	1.38	1.7	1.15	1.1	0.98	0.92
Tb	0.72	0.69	0.69	0.67		0.87	0.92	0.87	0.89	1.14	0.73	0.79	0.69	0.58
Yb	2.62	2.54	2.46	2.52		2.88	2.9	2.88	2.97	4.08	2.87	3.28	2.73	2.18
Lu	0.38	0.39	0.39	0.38		0.41	0.44	0.41	0.44	0.6	0.43	0.47	0.42	0.34
Hf	2.3	2.22	2.28	2.21		3.1	3.24	3.1	2.99	3.78	2.36	2.18		1.97
Ta	0.12	0.17	0.14	0.16		0.51	0.52	0.51	0.45	0.46			0.08	0.08
Th	0.21	0.11	0.08	0.11		0.36	0.36	0.36	0.44	0.4				
U		0.24	0.08		0.4	0.28	0.4	0.28	0.16	2.21		0.35	0.64	
$(La/Sm)_N$	0.53	0.54	0.53	0.56		0.88	0.86	0.88	0.83	0.63	0.45	0.34	0.39	0.42
V*		230		222	226	251	250	249		314	305		270	258
Cr*		313		304	329	256	261	329			146		417	370
Co*		41		38	43	42	38	49		40	40		39	41
Ni*		115		149	185	102	103	170			67		72	92
Cu*		118		126	111	109	108	112		84	107			122
Zn*		79		80	74	78	82	88			92			77
Rb*		4		6	9	5	8	10			10		7	3
Sr*		170		169	180	260	230	238		129	109		117	121
Y*		28		26	26	30	31	29		30	33		23	25
Zr*		81		77	76	115	115	114		71	69		62	56

Major elements by broad-beam electron probe, T. O'Hearn, analyst; trace elements by INAA, D. Vanko, R. Batiza, and P. Castillo, analysts. Estimated INAA errors (Korotev, in press a and b) also shown.

Major elements, trace elements with asterick analyzed by XRF, H.-U. Schminke, analyst; other trace elements by INAA, D. Vanko, R. Batiza, and P. Castillo, analysts. Note that 1185-14 has a duplicate analysis shown.

other lavas from the seamounts. In order to test possible genetic relationships involving fractionation, magma mixing, and assimilation, a two-tiered modeling strategy was followed. The first tier involved the use of a least-squares mixing program based on the methods of Bryan et al. [1969], using only the compositions of phenocryst phases and lavas actually observed in the PLUTO suite. Analyzed compositions of lavas were taken to represent actual magmatic values. If results from this modeling were acceptable (i.e., $\Sigma r^2 < 1.0$), the values of 7 trace elements were predicted by Rayleigh fractionation [Arth, 1976], using the crystal-liquid partition coefficients given in Table 10. Examples of successful results are given in Table 11.

The results show that some lavas within individual seamounts may be related to one another by crystal fractionation, and that crystal fractionation may indeed explain the pattern of general Fe enrichment seen in the seamount lavas. The seamount environment, with its isolated magma bodies in the form of small edifice or sub-edifice magma chambers, provides the necessary thermal isolation (cooling without magma replenishment or eruption) for the large amounts of fractionation [Natland, 1980] needed to produce the ferrobasalts of Red seamount. Nevertheless, the ferrobasalt fractionation models investigated require that a great deal of clinopyroxene fractionation occur, when petrographic evidence and experimental evidence [Fisk et al., 1980; Dungan et al., 1978;

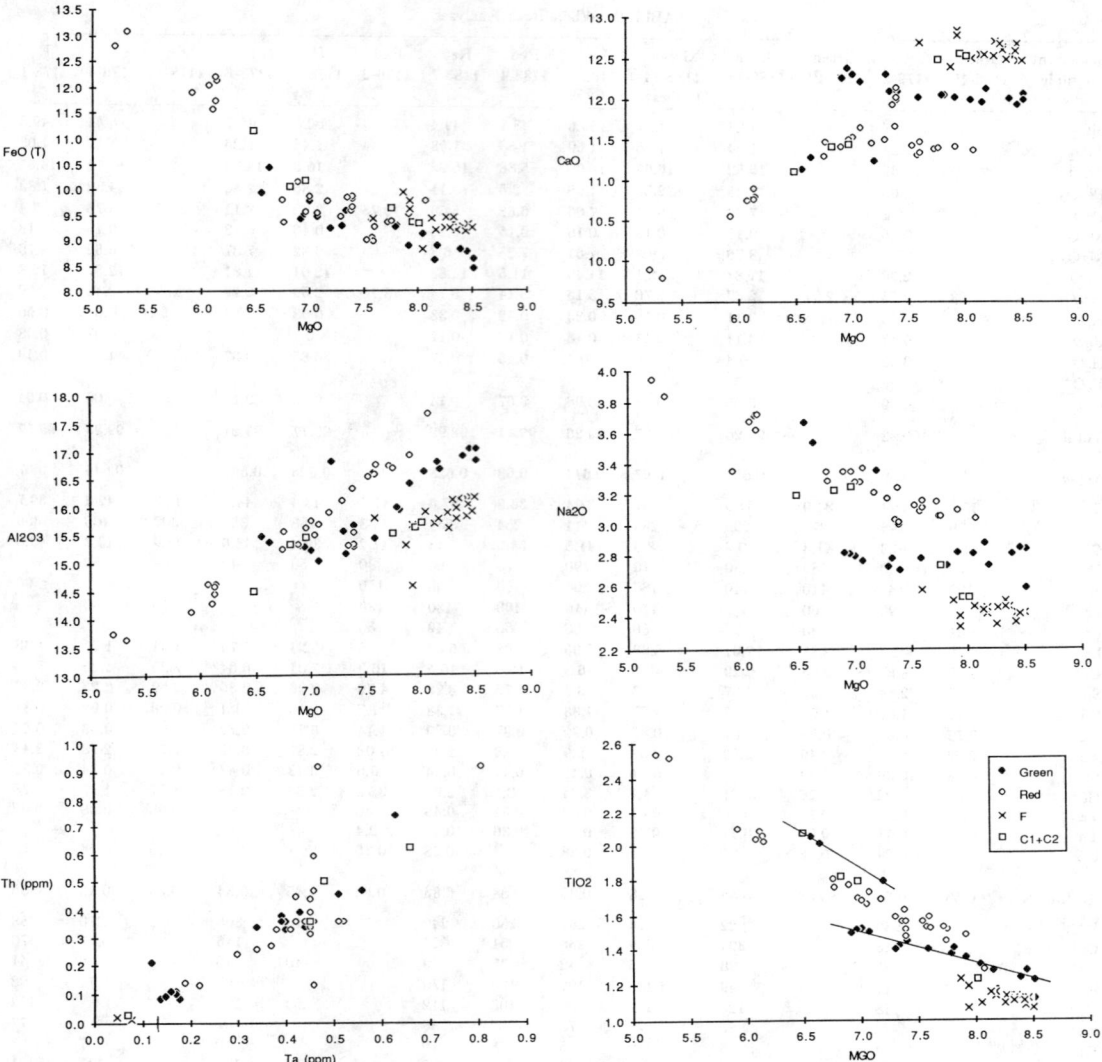

Fig. 8. Quenched glass compositions from different PLUTO volcanoes. Major element oxides plots are in weight percent, and show fractionation-related enrichment and depletion trends with respect to MgO. Closed diamonds represent lavas from Green seamount, open diamonds represent lavas from Red seamount, crosses represent lavas from seamount F, and open squares represent lavas from cones C1 and C2. Note the two distinct compositional groups within the lavas of Green seamount, with approximate fractionation trends drawn as straight lines. Ta and Th are given in ppm; note the relatively depleted nature of these elements in seamount F, and the wide variation of these elements in Green and Red seamounts.

Fujii et al., 1978; Fukuyama and Hamuro, 1979; Grove and Bryan, 1983] show that clinopyroxene is the last silicate phase to crystallize at low pressures. Clinopyroxene fractionation agrees with the MgO- and Mg#-depletion trend exhibited by the most evolved Red seamount lavas (Figures 8 and 10). The lack of clinopyroxene phenocrysts or microphenocrysts in the non-intergranular lavas implies that this clinopyroxene fractionation could not have occurred at low pressures (the clinopyroxene paradox of Fisk et al., [1980]). Indeed, most of the models investigated benefitted substantially from including clinopyroxene as a fractionating phase. The explanations that Fisk et al. [1980] offer to explain the clinopyroxene paradox fit this data set as well: clinopyroxene fractiona-

tion may occur at depth where it stably coexists with olivine and plagioclase (>6 Kb; Kushiro and Thompson [1972]; Bence and Hibberson [1975]; Bender et al. [1978]; Fujii et al. [1978]), or that clinopyroxene in the model is a proxy for magma mixing or assimilation. Other possibilities are that clinopyroxene phenocryst segregation may be unusually effective, or that melt inclusions in precipitating olivine and plagioclase may play a role in determining the liquid line of descent.

The Fe enrichment of the Red seamount lavas may be related to sub-volcanic edifice crystal fractionation processes. South of the PLUTO seamounts, and just south of the Clipperton Fracture Zone, a chain of seamounts extends to the west from the EPR on

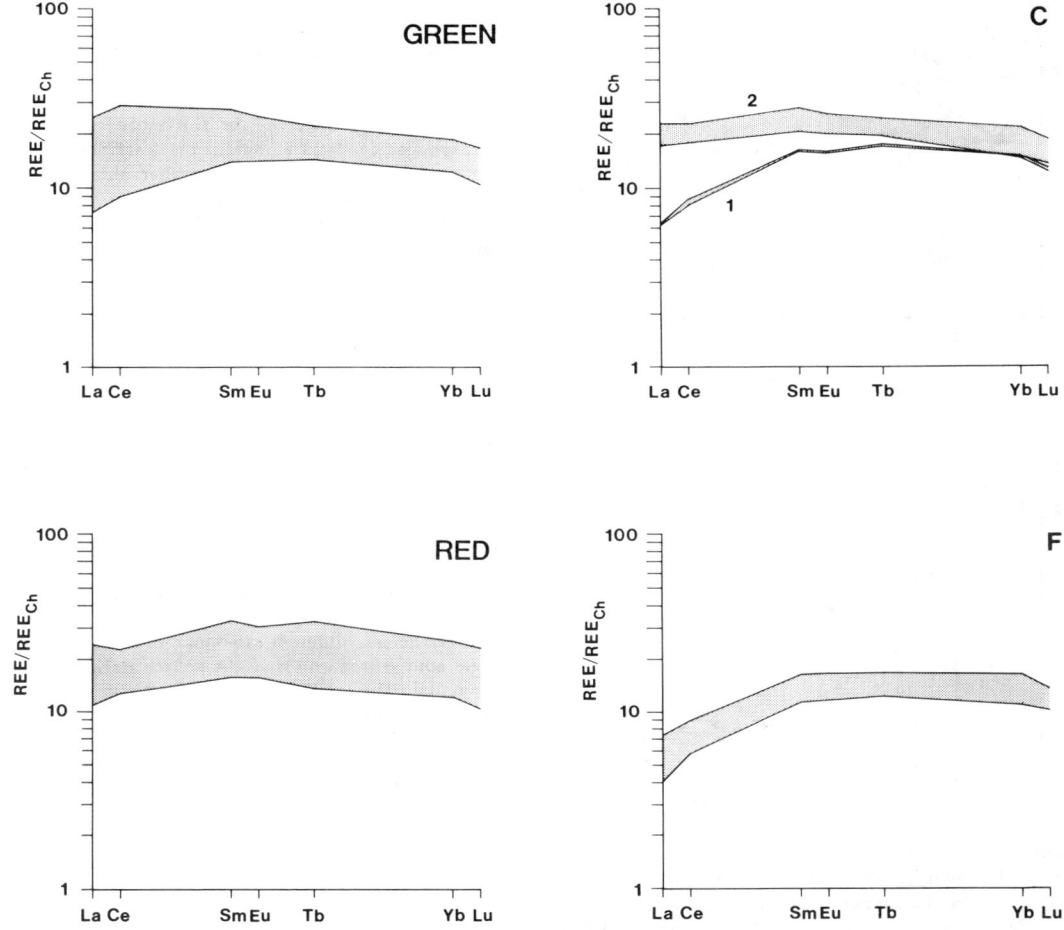

Fig. 9. Range in chondrite-normalized [Haskin et al., 1968] REE contents of individual volcanoes of the Larson seamount group. Note the compositional overlap between lavas from Green and Red seamounts, and the relatively depleted nature of the lavas of F.

crust ranging from $1\text{-}7 \times 10^5$ years in age [Fornari et al., 1985; Fornari et al., 1984]. These seamounts are notable in that much smaller, independent volcanic cones occur at their bases or in the near vicinity. These cones exhibit a range in Fe enrichment similar to that seen in the major seamounts [Perfit et al. [1985]; unpublished data]; a range nearly as great as seen in Red seamount, indicating that within edifice magma chamber fractionation may not be necessary to produce significant amounts of Fe enrichment.

The crystal fractionation modeling shows that both parent and daughter must fall within the same compositional groups shown in Figures 8 and 10 and must share similar $(La/Sm)_N$ ratios for fractionation to successfully explain parent-daughter evolution. Several successful models stipulating simple fractionation to explain lava evolution within individual seamounts are given in Table 11. In contrast, lavas lying in different compositional groups or trends (Figure 10) cannot be related by simple crystal fractionation or by simple mixing between observed lavas. For example, fractionation models relating lavas from the two CaO/Al_2O_3 compositional trends observed in Green seamount required adding either plagioclase or clinopyroxene to the parent to obtain reasonable results. For Green seamount, no combination of fractionation and mixing of observed lavas can produce the two trends.

In summary, crystal fractionation is likely the major process causing the enrichment and depletion trends as seen in the major element compositional groups as shown in Figures 8 and 10. The discrete enrichment and depletion trends represent approximate fractionation paths of lavas derived from a range of parental lavas of similar major element composition, although mixing of primitive and evolved melts has also played a minor role within these trends. The presence of several compositionally discrete major element trends in the data requires that a variety of parental magmas of differing composition be invoked, even for a single seamount. The diverse $(La/Sm)_N$ ratios observed in single enrichment or depletion trends (e.g., the high-Ca, low-Al, low-Na, low-Ti trend of Green seamount with $(La/Sm)_N$ clustering at 0.5 or 0.85) clearly show that multiple parents with variable $(La/Sm)_N$ are required to produce the range of lavas seen in an individual seamount.

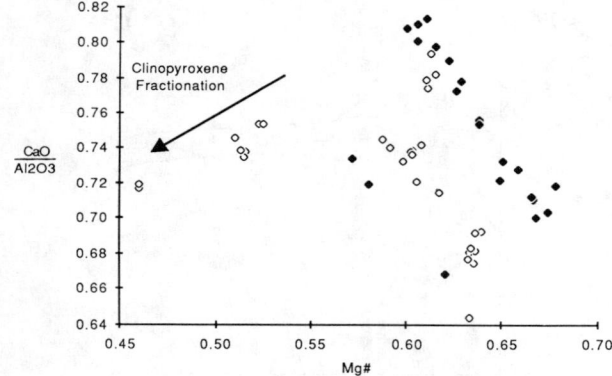

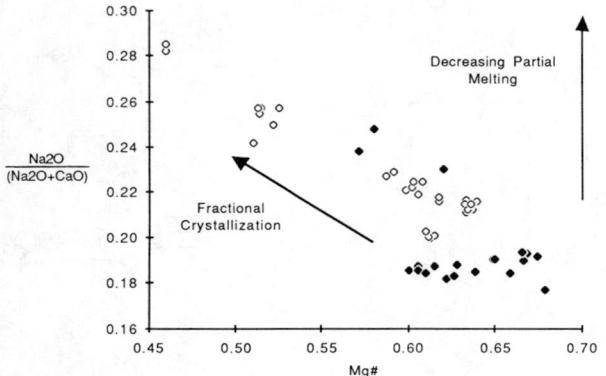

Fig. 10. Symbols as in Figure 8. Note the parallel but differing fractionation-related compositional groups or trends in both Green and Red seamounts. Groups cannot be related to one another by mixing of observed lavas. One arrow indicates compositional trend in primitive lavas resulting from decreasing amounts of partial melting from a single source (after Schouten et al. [1986]); the other arrow denotes clinopyroxene fractionation.

Evidence for Source Region Heterogeneity

The diversity of LREE contents in the more primitive lavas (Mg# > 0.65, La 1.48-7.35 ppm) of the PLUTO suite implies that the lavas represent large variations in the amount of partial melting of a mantle source. Fresh, well-characterized spinel lherzolite from Zabargad Island, Red Sea [Bonatti et al., 1986] was chosen as a model source for the PLUTO lavas. The Zabargad peridotite body has been interpreted as representative of oceanic mantle before extraction of basaltic oceanic crust [Bonatti et al., 1986], and spinel lherzolite from the body is quite similar to pyrolite in both major and trace element content [Ringwood, 1979]. La, Sm, Yb, and Ni abundance for various amounts of partial melting were calculated by both batch [Arth, 1976] and fractional melting [Shaw, 1970; Allègre and Minster, 1978] using both modal and non-modal melting models. Non-modal models used included those designed to leave trace amounts of all phases in the source at 20% melting, and those based upon experimental determination of relative source phase contribution to the melt (melting equation of Presnall et al. [1979]; melting of CMAS + Na at 11 and 20 kb,

Hoover and Presnall [1982 and in prep.]). Crystal-liquid K_D's were the same as those used in the crystal fractionation modeling.

Results from all melting models gave roughly comparable results, and an example showing calculated La contents and $(La/Sm)_N$ vs. % batch partial melting is given in Figure 14. The range of LREE observed in the more primitive PLUTO lavas corresponds to 3-20% batch or fractional partial melting of LREE-depleted Zabargad spinel lherzolite Z-37 [Bonatti et al., 1986]. In all models, predicted values of Ni were higher (200-260 ppm) than observed in the PLUTO lavas (>190 ppm, most 150 ppm or less).

Veining of the Zabargad peridotite body by LREE-enriched amphibole lherzolite, similar to other ultramafic localities such as St. Paul's Rocks [Melson et al., 1972; Roden et al., 1984] and at the Causon complex, France [Conquere, 1971], has been interpreted by Bonatti et al [1986] to represent metasomatic processes or crystallization of impregnating alkali basalt liquids. Batch modal melting of Zabargad amphibole peridotite Z-35 indicates that the modeled trace element concentrations of the most LREE-enriched primitive PLUTO lavas can be produced by 25% partial melting. More bulk melting in the spinel lherzolite source would be allowed to produce the high La and $(La/Sm)_N$ PLUTO lavas if the source contained both depleted material (spinel lherzolite) and small amounts of enriched material (amphibole lherzolite), a proposal in accord with the binary mixing behavior (Figure 12) exhibited by the PLUTO lavas.

Nevertheless, different amounts of bulk partial melting of an single source, regardless if the source itself is heterogeneous, cannot explain the existence of differing trends in CaO/Al_2O_3 vs Mg# and $Na_2O/(Na_2O+CaO)$ vs Mg#, when the individual trends contain lavas that have a variety of $(La/Ce)_N$ or $(La/Sm)_N$ ratios. Fujii and Scarfe [1985] and Jacques and Green [1980] have experimentally determined that $Na_2O/(Na_2O+CaO)$ decreases and

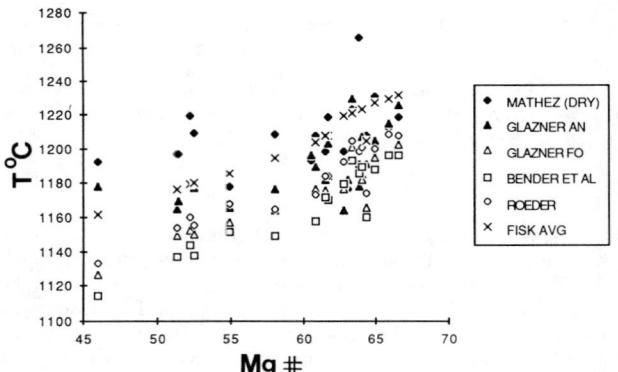

Fig. 11. Geothermometry of PLUTO lavas. Temperatures are in degrees C, and Mg# refers to $Mg/(Mg+Fe^{2+})$ of lava, where $Fe^{2+}/(Fe^{2+}+Fe^{3+}) = 0.85$. Closed triangles and closed diamonds refer to plagioclase-liquid temperatures (Glazner [1984] and Mathez [1973], respectively); open triangles, open diamonds, and open squares refer to olivine-liquid temperatures (Glazner [1984], Roeder [1974], and Bender et al. [1978], respectively); and crosses represent the average temperature of lavas based on comparison of their Mg# with experimentally-determined liquidi of lavas from Reykjanes Ridge and Iceland [Fisk et al., 1980]. Plagioclase-liquid and Mg# calculated temperatures are consistently higher than olivine-liquid temperatures, a possible consequence of H_2O and other volatiles.

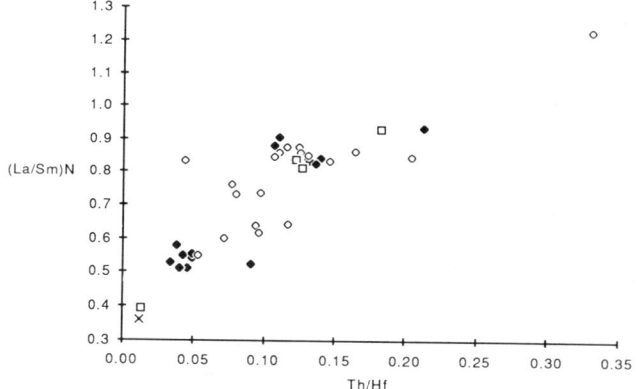

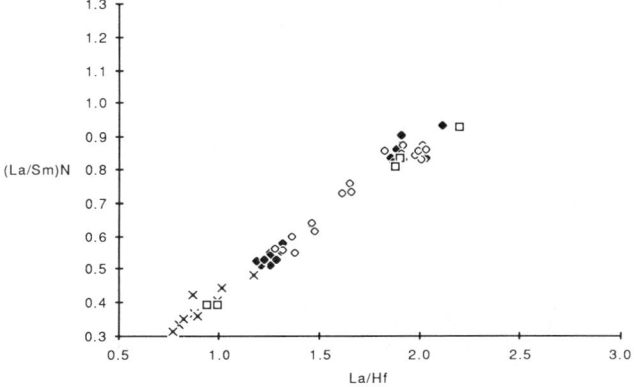

Fig. 12. Plots showing apparent binary mixing behavior for PLUTO lavas. Symbols as in Fig. 8. La/Sm normalized to chondrite values [Haskin et al., 1968].

CaO/Al_2O_3 increases with increasing amounts of partial melting of both spinel and plagioclase lherzolite at a single pressure. $Na_2O/(Na_2O+CaO)$ for a given Mg# has been used as a measure of the amount of source partial melting [Schouten et al., 1986], and it and CaO/Al_2O_3 should correspond with $(La/Sm)_N$ for relatively primitive lavas if there is only a single bulk source. In the PLUTO lavas, both $Na_2O/(Na_2O+CaO)$ and CaO/Al_2O_3 for a given Mg# are independent of $(La/Sm)_N$, as is normative plagioclase. These data imply that the parental lavas for the seamounts as a whole and for the individual Green and Red seamounts must have been derived from a variety of mantle sources.

Several explanations may be offered to explain why the incompatible trace element content of the PLUTO lavas is independent of major element composition. Complex melting [Langmuir et al., 1978; O'Hara, 1985], especially of a heterogeneous source, is difficult to ascertain, as is wallrock interaction with ascending magma (H.J.B. Dick, pers. comm., 1986); nevertheless, both processes may help produce the compositional trends. A more easily modeled alternative explanation is that the differing trends are produced by melting sources that are different in either bulk chemical composition or in mineralogy, an idea previously proposed by Bryan and Dick [1982] to define varying liquidus trends from Mid-Atlantic MORBs.

There is currently great debate about the ultimate source depth of primitive MORBs, primarily centering on whether they are derivatives from picritic lavas in equilibrium with spinel lherzolite at pressures of 15 Kb or greater [e.g., Green et al., 1979; Stolper, 1980; Jaques and Green, 1980; Elthon and Scarfe, 1980, 1984; O'Hara, 1968], or whether primitive MORBs represent partial melts derived from spinel or plagioclase lherzolite at depths of 7-11 Kbar [Presnall et al., 1979; Presnall and Hoover, 1984; Fujii and Bougault, 1983; Takahashi and Kushiro, 1983; Kushiro, 1973; Fujii and Scarfe, 1985]. While acknowledging the uncertainty about the proposed MORB source depths, it is important to consider whether the two different compositional groups or trends observed in Green seamount could be produced simply by melting spinel lherzolite in one case and plagioclase lherzolite in the other. Various depths of MORB mantle source melting have been proposed previously by Dmitriev et al. [1984] to explain high TiO_2-Na_2O-MgO and low TiO_2-Na_2O populations observed in abyssal basalts worldwide. Klein and Langmuir [1986 and in press] noted a positive correlation of axial spreading ridge depth with Na_2O and TiO_2 and a negative depth correlation with CaO/Al_2O_3 in erupted MORBs. They attributed these observations to greater depths of initial partial mantle melting and to greater extents of partial melting that occur beneath shallower spreading ridges where the upper oceanic mantle is hotter. Applied to the PLUTO lavas, their ideas would ascribe the high CaO/Al_2O_3, low $Na_2O/(Na_2O+CaO)$ lava group of Green seamount to derivation

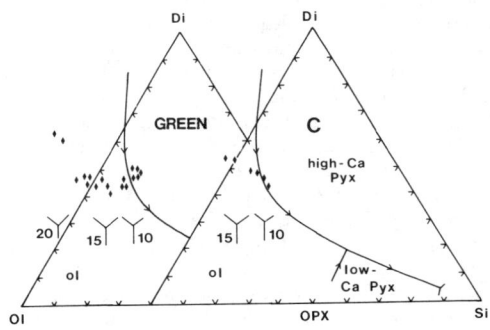

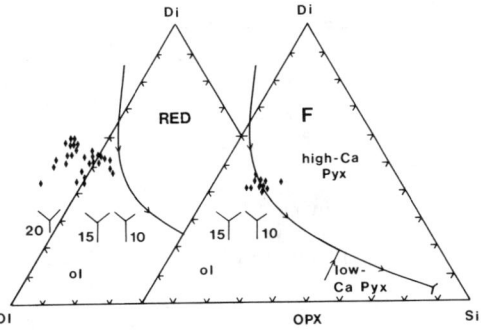

Fig. 13. PLUTO quench glasses plotted in OLIVINE-SILICA-DIOPSIDE pseudo-ternary of Walker et al. [1978], projected from PLAGIOCLASE. Also shown is the 1 bar pseudo-cotectic of Walker et al. [1979], and the 10, 15, and 20 kbar cotectics of Stolper [1980]. Note that many lavas from volcanoes B and F and the cones C1 and C2 plot along the 1 bar pseudocotectic, and some plot within the high-Ca pyroxene field, possibly indicating low-pressure mixing [Walker et al., 1979].

TABLE 10. Trace Element Crystal-Liquid Partition Coefficients Used in Modelling

	Ol	Opx	Cpx	Sp	Plag	Amph
Sc	0.26	1.65	5	0.54	0.017-0.065	
Ni	12	3-5	2-4	5	0.04	2.9
Sr	0.0005	0.0002	0.072	0	2-3	0.46
Zr	0.01	0.01	0.01	0.01	0	
La	0.0005	0.0005	0.02	0.0058	0.23	0.1-0.45
Sm	0.0019-0.0048	0.0028-0.0147	0.14-0.736	0.007	0.08	0.7-1.1
Yb	0.004	0.286	0.20	0.0041	0.03	0.3-0.9

References: Chen and Frey [1985], Ottonello et al. [1985], Ottonello [1980], Green and Pearson [1985a,b], Frey et al. [1978], Irving [1978], Mysen [1978], Arth [1976], and Drake and Weill [1975].

from melts that are a product of greater amounts of partial melting at greater depths than melts which produced Green seamount's low CaO/Al_2O_3, high $Na_2O/(Na_2O+CaO)$ lava trend. This model, however, assumes a single or similar mantle sources and cannot explain the independence of the LREE with respect to the major element compositions in the PLUTO lavas.

To help test the hypothesis that the PLUTO lavas could be derived from plagioclase lherzolite, Zabargad spinel lherzolite Z-37 was transformed to plagioclase lherzolite by least squares mixing using pyroxene compositions observed in Zabargad plagioclase lherzolite, olivine compositions from Zabargad spinel lherzolite, and plagioclase from the PLUTO lavas (Table 12). The K_D's used to model melting of this "plagioclase lherzolite" were the same as used earlier for fractionation, and batch melting was modeled modally and using the melting results of Hoover and Presnall [1982, in prep.] at 9 kb. Results show that smaller amounts (<2.5%) of partial melting are required to produce the La content of the least depleted PLUTO lavas as compared to spinel lherzolite. These results also indicate that batch melting of the Z-37 "plagioclase" lherzolite is not a viable source for the entire PLUTO suite, as the predicted La and $(La/Sm)_N$ values are too low (<5.2 ppm La and <0.53 $(La/Sm)_N$ at 2.5% partial melting; Figure 14) due to the relatively high (0.23) La K_D used for plagioclase liquid partitioning. This conflict may be overcome if the plagioclase lherzolite source contains LREE-enriched material, such as the amphibole lherzolite discussed above, or if <5% fractional melting is invoked.

Given that a plagioclase lherzolite containing small amounts of amphibole lherzolite is an acceptable source for the PLUTO lavas, will the CaO/Al_2O_3 and $Na_2O/(Na_2O+CaO)$ ratios of a melt change if the source is plagioclase lherzolite instead of spinel lherzolite? Jaques and Green [1980] have calculated equilibrium melt compositions for various amounts of partial melting (11-44%) of two starting compositions: pyrolite minus 40% olivine, and Tinaquillo lherzolite minus 40% olivine. For both pyrolite and the lherzolite at a given degree of partial melting, their results at 15, 10, and 5 kb show a general increase in melt CaO/Al_2O_3 with depth, but also indicate that melt $Na_2O/(Na_2O+CaO)$ remains fairly constant. Some of the increase in CaO/Al_2O_3 may be related to a slight positive pressure dependence of the solubility of Al_2O_3 in pyroxene that the data of Jacques and Green suggest (Klein and Langmuir, in press). Ranges of the calculated ratios were 0.63-1.03 for CaO/Al_2O_3 and 0.06-0.27 for $Na_2O/(Na_2O+CaO)$.

Simple mixing calculations, using the melting equations of Presnall et al. [1979] (9.6 kbar) and Hoover and Presnall [1982 and in prep.] (9, 9.6, 11, and 20 kbar) provide another means of testing this hypothesis. The starting mantle composition used in the calculations was Zabargad Island lherzolite Z-37, and all phase compositions used were from the Zabargad ultramafic rocks [Bonatti et al., 1986], with the exception of plagioclase from the PLUTO samples. The Na_2O, Al_2O_3, and CaO contents of the plagioclase and spinel lherzolite mixes were closely matched to those measured by Bonatti et al. [1986], and care was taken that the spinel lherzolite

TABLE 11. Fractionation Models

	Seamount					
	B	B	B	B	E	E
	1180-4A to 9-1		7-1 to 1180-18		6-1 to 1182-5	
Mg#	0.68	0.65	0.62	0.57	0.51	0.46
	Wt% Phase Removed					
Olivine	2.59 (Fo86)		3.35 (Fo83)		2.45 (Fo79)	
Clinopyroxene	3.15 (En47, Wo43)				4.47 (En47, Wo43)	
Plagioclase	8.17 (An75)		11.07 (An75)		9.18 (An70)	
	Trace Element Fit					
	Predicted	Observed	Predicted	Observed	Predicted	Observed
Sc	32.9-33.2	34.3	41.1-41.4	41.7	37.5-38.0	39.0
Ni	90-100	120	80	70	20	20
Sr	80-90	100	180-200	190	110-120	140
Zr		160		140		
La	2.70	3.07	7.28	8.08	6.43	6.48
Sm	2.87-2.93	2.93	4.61	4.91	5.60-5.76	5.92
Yb	2.86	2.51	3.63	3.71	4.60	5.01
$(La/Sm)_N$	0.51-0.52	0.57	0.87	0.90	0.61-0.63	0.60

Trace elements are in ppm.

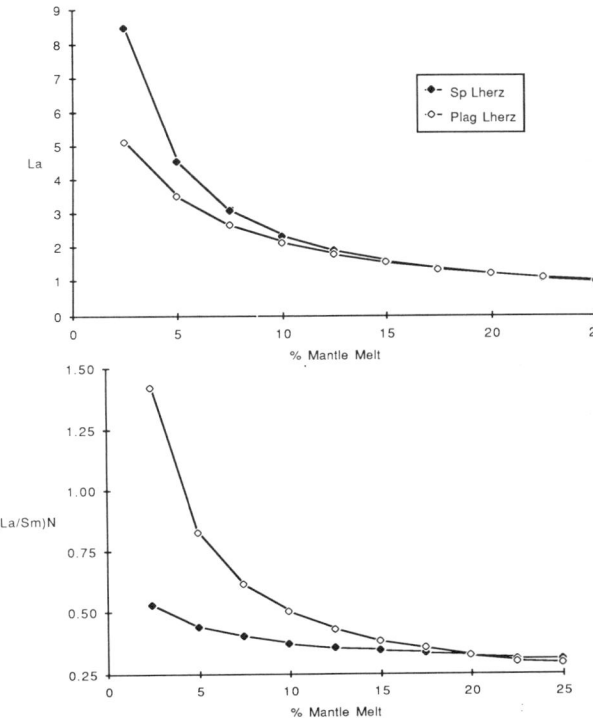

Fig. 14. Plot showing representative batch melting models [Arth, 1976] of Zabargad Island Z-37 spinel lherzolite and "plagioclase" lherzolite, where calculated La (in ppm) and $(La/Sm)_N$ is plotted against % partial melting. Batch melting of pure (non-enriched) Z-37 lherzolite with plagioclase lherzolite mineralogy cannot reproduce the La and $(La/Sm)_N$ of the PLUTO lavas, except at under 2.5% partial melting.

TABLE 12. Sample Mixes Used in Melting Calculations

"Plagioclase Lherzolite" Mix		Spinel lherzolite Mix	
Phase	Amount (wt%)	Phase	Amount (wt%)
Z98C Opx	19.4	Z37 Opx	32.6
Z98 Cpx	7.1	Z34Cpx	15.7
Z37 Ol	63.6	Z37Ol	48.8
Pluto An75 Plag	10.1	Z37 Spinel	2.8
Fit		Fit	
Obs	Pred	Obs	Pred
Si 44.40	44.36	Si 44.4	45.10
Ti 0.20	0.20	Ti 0.20	0.18
Al 4.01	4.08	Al 4.01	4.02
Fe 8.48	8.32	Fe 8.48	8.38
Mg 38.19	38.64	Mg 38.19	37.67
Ca 3.29	3.32	Ca 3.29	3.32
Na 0.34	0.32	Na 0.34	0.35
residuals^2 = 0.22		residuals^2 = 0.78	

mixes approximated the mode of Z-37 calculated by Bonatti et al. [1986]. Examples of lherzolite mixes used in the modeling are given in Table 12. The mixing results, summarized in Table 13, indicate that melting of plagioclase lherzolite may indeed produce melts of lower CaO/Al_2O_3 than will spinel lherzolite, if the large degrees of partial melting required by the melting models (~30%) are attained. It should be noted that the predicted CaO/Al_2O_3 of the spinel melting models is higher than the observed PLUTO lava values. The modeling is ambiguous with regard to $Na_2O/(Na_2O+CaO)$; the predicted values of $Na_2O/(Na_2O+CaO)$ for melts derived from spinel lherzolite and plagioclase lherzolite overlap. Indeed, a major weakness of the modeling is the assumption that Na partitioning between clinopyroxene and melt and between plagioclase and melt will be identical, an assumption that is almost certainly wrong. If the clinopyroxene-melt distribution coefficient for Na is close to 0.2 for MORB at 10 kbar as Bender et al. [1978] suggest, then the mixing calculations may not be valid. Nevertheless, the mixing calculations bear out the assumption that the CaO/Al_2O_3 of melts derived during the clinopyroxene-dominated melting of spinel lherzolite should be different from those derived by the plagioclase-dominated melting of plagioclase lherzolite. In summary, heterogeneous sources are clearly required to produce the variety of lavas erupted from Larson's seamounts, but it is still uncertain whether mineralogical source heterogeneity could produce the range of parental lavas required to derive the PLUTO lava suite.

Conclusions and Implications for Adjacent EPR Source

The close proximity of the seamounts to the adjacent EPR, and the general similarity of the seamount and EPR lavas implies that lavas from both features share a similar, if not common, source. Seamount basalts as a rule show a greater range in trace element and isotopic composition than do MORBs from the immediate vicinity [Batiza and Vanko, 1984] (exceptions are near transform faults, overlapping spreading centers, and small, non-overlapping ridge offsets as discussed by Langmuir et al. [1985] and Thompson et al. [1985]), implying that the MORB sources are more heterogeneous than indicated by the homogeneous nature of MORB chemistry [Natland, 1980b]. The lack of published REE data precludes an involved comparison of lavas from the Red and Green seamounts and from the EPR axis at 21°N, but it is instructive to realize that the range in Ti/Zr exhibited in the seamount lavas (INAA data, 65-215; X-ray fluorescence data, 81-122) is greater than that observed in the 21°N EPR axis lavas (84-107, Newman et al. [1983]; Speiss et al., [1980]).

TABLE 13. Calculated Melting Results

Depth	Lherzolite	CaO/Al_2O_3	$Na_2O/(Na_2O+CaO)$
9Kb	plagioclase lherzolite	0.78-0.77	0.12-0.10
9.6Kb	spinel-plagioclase lherzolite	0.75	0.11
9.6Kb	spinel lherzolite	1.10-1.00	0.10
11Kb	spinel lherzolite	1.07-1.16	0.10
20Kb	spinel lherzolite	0.89-1.12	0.10

Melting models are: Hoover and Presnall (1982, in prep.) for 9Kb, 9.6Kb spinel-lherzolite, 11Kb, and 20Kb; Presnall et al. [1979] for 9.6Kb spinel lherzolite.

We believe that the seamounts may serve as a window for studying the complexity of the source region for the adjacent East Pacific Rise. The source for both the adjacent EPR and for individual seamounts is compositionally heterogeneous, containing both LREE-enriched and LREE-depleted material. The source may also be mineralogically heterogeneous, with melts originating and equilibrating with spinel lherzolite, spinel-plagioclase lherzolite, and plagioclase lherzolite. The diversity of lavas erupted by the seamounts shows that 21°N EPR MORB melt sources and processes are more complex than would be inferred if only lavas from the EPR are examined, reflecting the "homogenization" [Cohen and O'Nions, 1982; Batiza, 1984] that the EPR lavas have undergone through more extensive mixing in sub-axial magma chambers.

APPENDIX. Analysed Rock Samples

Sample #	Seamount	Depth (m)	Rock Description	Location of Outcrop
Dredge 4	F	~2450	Hyaloclastite	Outer Slope
Dredge 5	F	~2050	Hyaloclastite, Pillow Fragments	Summit Bench
Dredge 6	Red	~2150	Pillow Fragments	Outer Slope*
Dredge 7	Green	~2150	Pillow Fragments	Outer Slope*
Dredge 8	Red	~2150	Basalt Fragments	Outer Slope*
Dredge 9	Green	~2400	Pillow Fragments	Outer Slope*
Angus 167A	C2	~2400	Pillow Fragment	Pillow Cone
Angus 2	Green	~1950	Pillow Fragment	Intra-Caldera Shield
1178-1	F	2225	Pillow Fragment**	Pit-Crater Talus
1178-2	F	2266	Pillow Fragment	Pit-Crater Talus
1178-3	F	2213	Pillow Fragment**	Pit-Crater Talus
1178-4	F	2113	Pillow Fragment**	Caldera Floor
1178-5	F	2096	Hyaloclastite	Base of Caldera Wall
1178-6	F	2120	Glassy Mass**	Caldera Floor
1178-7	F	2119	Pillow Fragment**	Caldera Floor
1179-1	Green	1985	Pillow Rind	Caldera Floor
1179-2	Green	1945	Pillow Fragment	Caldera Wall
1179-6	Green	1867	Glassy Pillow Fragment	Summit Bench
1179-7	Green	1867	Glassy Pillow Fragment	Summit Bench
1179-9	Green	1876	Glass Fragments	Summit Bench
1179-10	Green	1981	Slab with Lava Drips	Collapse in Caldera Floor
1179-11	Green	1915	Glassy Pillow Fragment	Tangential Scarp
1179-12	Green	1984	Slab with Lava Drips	Collapse in Caldera Floor
1180-1A	Green	2161	Glassy Mass	Outer Slope*
1180-1B	Green	1984	Glassy Mass	Intra-Caldera Shield
1180-2	Green	2146	Pillow Fragment	Outer Slope*
1180-3	Green	2139	Glassy Chunks-Sheet Flow	Outer Slope*
1180-4A	Green	1987	Glassy Chunks-Sheet Flow	Intra-Caldera Shield
1180-4B	Green	2115	Pillow Fragment	Outer Slope*
1180-8	Green	1966	Glassy Slab-Sheet Flow	Pit-Crater Wall
1181-1	C1	2377	Pillow	Pillow Cone
1181-2	C1	2376	Pillow	Pillow Cone
1181-3		2521	Pillow	Lava Plain Between C1&C2
1181-4		2523	Glassy Crust-Sheet Flow	Lava Plain Between C1&C2
1181-5	C2	2502	Glassy Pillow Fragment	Base of Pillow Cone
1181-6	C2	2485	Glassy Mass-Pillow Lava	Base of Pillow Cone
1181-7	C2	2380	Glassy Pillow Fragment	Summit of Pillow Cone
1181-8	C2	2522	Glassy Bud Piece	Lava Plain Between C1&C2
1181-B		2509	Box Core	Lava Plain Between C1&C2
1181-T		2504	Tube Core	Lava Plain Between C1&C2
1182-1	Red	2118	Slab w/Lava Drips-Sheet Flow	Outer Slope*
1182-2	Red	2102	Glassy Mass-Sheet Flow	Top of Outer Slope*
1182-3	Red	2103	Glassy Fragment	Caldera Floor
1182-4	Red	2097	Glassy Mass-Pillow Lava	Caldera Floor
1182-5	Red	2069	Pillow Fragment	Foot of Pillow Cone
1182-6	Red	2074	Basalt Fragment	Caldera Floor
1182-7	Red	2044	Glassy Slab	Caldera Floor
1182-C	Red	Unknown	Alvin Cradle Sample	Red Summit Caldera
1183-1	Red	2040	Glass Pieces	Outer Slope
1183-3	Red	2030	Glassy Piece	Outer Slope
1183-4	Red	1980	Basalt Fragment	Caldera Talus
1183-5	Red	1941	Glass Crusts	Summit Bench
1183-6	Red	1943	Glass Crusts	Summit Bench
1183-7	Red	1979	Basalt Fragment	Caldera Wall Talus
1183-8	Red	1899	Hyaloclastite	Summit Bench
1183-10	Red	1903	Glassy Slab/Hyaloclastite	Summit Bench
1183-13	Red	1912	Glassy Piece	Summit Bench
1183-19	Red	1940	Glassy Piece	Summit Bench
1183-20	Red	1940	Glassy Pillow Rind	Summit Bench
1185-1	Green	1989	Glassy Pillow	Caldera Floor
1185-2	Green	1989	Glassy Slab	Caldera Floor near 1185-1
1185-12	Green	1835	Glassy "Bubble"	Top of Caldera Wall
1185-14	Green	1835	Pillow Fragment	Summit Bench
1185-15	Green	1836	Pillow Fragment	Top of Caldera Wall
1185-21	Green	1836	Basalt Fragment	Summit Bench
1186-2	Red	2034	Hyaloclastite	Intra Caldera Cone
1187-1	Red	1982	Glass Pieces	Summit Bench
1187-2	Red	1983	Glassy Bud	Summit Bench

* = sector of outer slope subject to spillover from flows from caldera.
** = with hyaloclastite coating.

Acknowledgments. We are indebted to the crews of the R/V New Horizon and LULU, and to the ALVIN pilots and crew. We would like to thank P. Castillo, D. Vanko, M. Perfit, C. Langmuir, D. Graham, J. Alt, D. Lindstrom, H. Dick, M. Fisk, R. Sack, J. Luhr, D. Baker, J. Hoover, A. Glazner, R. Dymek, and J. Pasteris for compelling discussions concerning this research. Thoughtful and extended reviews were provided by M. Perfit, and M. Fisk. Early versions of this manuscript were reviewed by P. Castillo, M. Sultan, J. Alt, D. Lindstrom, T. Smith, and S. Alioto. A. Heatherington collected a substantial portion of the microprobe data, D. Vanko collected much of the trace element data, and S. Alioto assisted in the collation and reduction of both microprobe and whole-rock data. D. Kremser assisted in the collection of the microprobe data. We also would like to express our gratitude to W. Melson and T. O'Hearn of the Smithsonian Institution for providing the major element glass analyses and discussion of the data, to H.-U. Schmincke for the XRF whole-rock analyses, and to R. Korotev, M. Lindstrom, and L. Haskin for help in obtaining and understanding the INAA results. This research was supported by NSF grants OCE-8308980, OCE-8415270, and OCE-8508042, and ONR grant 10-14-80-C-0856.

References

Adams, G.E., and F.C. Bishop, An experimental investigation of thermodynamic mixing properties and unit-cell parameters of forsterite-monticellite solid solutions, *Am. Min.*, 70, 714-722, 1985.

Allégre, C.J., and J.F. Minster, Quantitative models of trace element behavior in magmatic processes, *Earth Planet. Sci. Lett.*, 38, 1-25, 1978.

Alt, J.C., Lonsdale, P., Haymon, R., and Muehlenbachs, K., Hydrothermal Sulfide and oxide deposits on seamounts near 21°N, East Pacific Rise, *Geol. Soc. Am. Bull.*, in press.

Arth, J. G., Behavior of trace elements during magmatic processes-a summary of theoretical models and their applications, *J. Res. U. S. Geol. Survey*, 4, 41-47, 1976.

Ballard, R. D., R. T. Holcomb, and T. H. van Andel, The Galapagos Rift at 86°W, 3, Sheet flows, collapse pits, and lava lakes of the rift valley, *J. Geophys. Res.*, 84, 5407-5422, 1979.

Basaltic Volcanism Study Project, *Basaltic volcanism on the terrestrial planets*, Pergamon Press, New York, 1981.

Batiza, R., Geology, petrology, and geochemistry of Isla Tortuga, a recent tholeiitic island in the Gulf of California, *Geol. Soc. Am. Bull.*, 89, 1309-1324, 1978.

Batiza, R., A general hypothesis for the origin of seamounts at and near mid-ocean ridges (abstract), *EOS Trans. AGU*, 66, 1079, 1985.

Batiza, R., $^{87}Sr/^{86}Sr$ diversity, spreading/eruption rate, mantle heterogeneity and mixing in ocean basalts, *Nature*, 309, 440-441.

Batiza, R., and J. R. Johnson, Trace element and isotopic evidence for magma mixing in alkalic and transitional basalts near the East Pacific Rise at 8°N, *Init. Rep. Deep Sea Drill. Proj.*, 54, 63-69, 1980.

Batiza, R., and D. Vanko, Volcanic development of small oceanic central volcanoes on the flanks of the East Pacific Rise inferred from narrow beam echo sounder surveys, *Mar. Geol.*, 54, 53-90, 1983.

Batiza, R., and D. Vanko, Petrology of young Pacific seamounts, *J. Geophys. Res.*, 89, 11235-11260, 1984.

Batiza, R., D. J. Fornari, D. Vanko, and P. Lonsdale, Craters, calderas, and hyaloclastites: Common features of young Pacific seamounts, *J. Geophys. Res.*, 89, 8371-8390, 1984.

Bender, J. F., F. N. Hodges, and A. E. Bence, Petrogenesis of basalts from the project FAMOUS area: Experimental study from 0 to 15 kbars, *Earth Planet. Sci. Lett.*, 41, 277-302, 1978.

Bender, J. F., C. H. Langmuir, and G. N. Hanson, Petrogenesis of basalts from the Tamayo region, East Pacific Rise: Evidence that partial melting is responsible for systematic variations in glass chemistry with distance from a transform fault, *J. Petrol*, 25, 213-254, 1984.

Bonatti, E., G. Ottonello, and P. R. Hamlyn, Peridotites from the island of Zabargad (St. John), Red Sea: Petrology and Geochemistry, *J. Geophys. Res.*, 91, 599-631, 1986.

Bryan, W. B., Mineralogical studies of submarine basalts, *Ann. Rep. Director Geophys. Lab., Yearbook* 71, 396-403, 1972.

Bryan, W.B., Fe-Mg relationships in sector-zoned submarine basalt plagioclase, *Earth Planet. Sci. Lett.*, 24, 157-165, 1974.

Bryan, W. B., Regional variation and petrogenesis of basalt glasses from the FAMOUS area, Mid-Atlantic Ridge, *J. Petrol.*, 20, 293-325, 1979.

Bryan, W. B., and H. J. B. Dick, Contrasted basalt liquidus trends: Evidence for mantle major element heterogeneity, *Earth Planet. Sci. Lett.*, 58, 15-26, 1982.

Bryan, W. B., L. W. Finger, and F. Chayes, A least-squares approximation for estimating the compositions of a mixture, *Carnegie Inst. Washington Year Book*, 67, 244-247, 1969.

Bryan, W. B., G. Thompson, and J. N. Ludden, Compositional variation in normal MORB from 22°-25°N: Mid-Atlantic Ridge and Kane Fracture Zone, *J. Geophys. Res.*, 86, 11815-11836, 1981.

Byerly, G. R., W. G. Melson, and P. R. Vogt, Rhyodacites, andesites, ferrobasalts, and ocean tholeiites from the Galapagos Spreading Center, *Earth Planet. Sci. Lett.*, 30, 215-221, 1976.

Byerly, G. R., W. G. Melson, J. A. Nelen, and E. Jarosewich, Abyssal basaltic glasses as indicators of magma compositions, in: B. Mason, ed., Mineral Sciences Investigations, 1974-1975, *Smithsonian Contrib. Earth Sci.*, 19, 22-30, 1976.

Carlson, R.W., J.D. Macdougall, and G.W. Lugmair, Differential Sm/Nd evolution in oceanic basalts, *Geophys. Res. Lett.*, 5, 229-232, 1978.

Carmichael, I. S. E., The iron-titanium oxides of salic volcanic rocks and their associated ferromagnesian silicates, *Contrib. Mineral. Petrol.*, 14, 36-64, 1967.

Carmichael, I.S.E, D. M. Christie, and C. H. Langmuir, Ferric/ferrous ratios and oxygen fugacities of MORB glasses, *EOS Trans. Am. Geophys. Union*, 66, 46, 1108, 1985.

Chen, C.-Y., and F. A. Frey, Trace element and isotopic geochemistry of lavas from Haleakala Volcano, east Maui, Hawaii: Implications for the origin of Hawaiian basalts, *J. Geophys. Res.*, 90, 8743-8768, 1985.

Christie, D.M., I.S.E. Carmichael, and C.H. Langmuir, Oxidation states of mid-ocean ridge basalt glasses, *Earth Planet. Sci. Lett.*, submitted March 1986.

Cohen, R. S., and R. K. O'Nions, The lead, neodynium and strontium isotope structure of ocean ridge basalts, *J. Petrol.*, 23, 299-324, 1982.

Conquere, F., La lherzolite a amphibole du gisement de Cassou (Ariege, France), .ul Contrib. Mineral. Petrol., 30, 296-313, 1971.

Dick, H. J. B., and T. Bullen, Chromium spinel as a petrogenetic indicator in abyssal and alpine-type peridotites and spatially associated lavas, *Contrib. Mineral. Petrol.*, 86, 54-76, 1984.

Dick, H. J. B., and W. B. Bryan, Variation of basalt phenocryst mineralogy and rock compositions in DSDP hole 396B, *Initial Rep. Deep Sea Drill Proj.*, 46, 215-225, 1979.

Dmitriev, L. V., A. V. Sobolev, A. V. Uchanov, T. V. Malysheva, and W. G. Melson, Primary differences in oxygen fugacity and depth of melting in the mantle source regions for oceanic basalts, *Earth Planet. Sci. Lett.*, *70*, 303-310, 1984.

Drake, M. J., Plagioclase-melt equilibria, *Geochim. Cosmochim. Acta*, *40*, 457-465, 1976.

Drake, M. J., and D. F. Weill, The partition of Sr, Ba, Ca, Y, Eu^{2+}, Eu^{3+}, and other REE between plagioclase feldspar and magmatic silicate liquid: An experimental study, *Geochim. Cosmochim. Acta*, *39*, 689-712, 1975.

Dungan, M. A., and J. M. Rhodes, Residual glasses and melt inclusions in basalts from DSDP legs 45 and 46: Evidence for magma mixing, *Contrib. Mineral. Petrol.*, *67*, 417-431, 1978.

Dungan, M. A., J. M. Rhodes, and P. Long, The petrology and geochemistry of basalts from Site 396, Legs 45 and 46 of the Deep Sea Drilling Project, *Init. Rep. Deep Sea Drill Proj.*, *46*, 89, 1978.

Elthon, D., and C. M. Scarfe, High pressure phase equilibria of a high-magnesia basalt: Implications for the origin of mid-ocean ridge basalt, *Carnegie Inst. Wash. Yearbook*, *79*, 277-281, 1980.

Elthon, D., and C. M. Scarfe, High-pressure phase equilibria of a high-magnesia basalt and the genesis of primary oceanic basalts, *Am. Mineral.*, *69*, 1-15, 1984.

Engi, M., Equilibria involving Al-Cr spinel: Mg-Fe exchange with olivine. Experiments, thermodynamic analysis, and consequences for geothermometry, *Am. J. Sci.*, *283-A*, 29-71, 1983.

Evans, B. W., and T. L. Wright, Composition of liquidus chromite from the 1959 (Kilauea Iki) and 1965 (Makaopuhi) eruptions of Kilauea Volcano, Hawaii, *Am. Min.*, *57*, 217-230.

Fisk. M. R., and A. E. Bence, Experimental crystallization of chrome spinel in FAMOUS basalt 527-1-1, *Earth Planet. Sci. Lett.*, *48*, 111-123, 1980.

Fisk, M. R., J. -G. Schilling, and H. Sigurdsson, An experimental investigation of Iceland and Reykjanes Ridge tholeiites, I, Phase relations, *Contrib. Min. Petrol.*, *74*, 361-374, 1980.

Fornari, D. J., W. B. F. Ryan, and P.J. Fox, The evolution of craters and calderas on young seamounts: Insights from SeaMARC I and Seabeam sonar surveys of a small seamount group near the axis of the East Pacific Rise at ~10°N, *J. Geophys. Res.*, *89*, 11069-11083, 1984.

Fornari, D.J., R. Batiza, R. Haymon, T. Simkin, L. Levin, J. Allan, T. Smith, A. Barone, and E. Kappel, Structure and morphology of young seamounts near the axis of the East Pacific Rise at 09 53'N based on ALVIN dive observations and Sea Beam bathymetric surveys (abstract), *EOS Trans. AGU*, *66*, 1079, 1985.

Frey, F. A., D. H. Green, and S. D. Roy, Integrated models of basalt petrogenesis: A study of quartz tholeiites to olivine melilites from southeast Australia utilizing geochemical and experimental petrologic data, *J. Petrol.*, *19*, 463-513, 1978.

Fujii, T., and H. Bougault, Melting relations of a magnesian abyssal tholeiite and the origin of MORBs, *Earth Planet. Sci. Lett.*, *62*, 283-295, 1983.

Fujii, T., and C.M. Scarfe, Composition of liquids coexisting with spinel lherzolite at 10 kbar and the genesis of MORBs, *Contrib. Mineral. Petrol.*, *90*, 18-28, 1985.

Fujii, T., I. Kushiro, and M. Hamuro, Melting relations and viscosity of an olivine tholeiite, *Init. Rep. Deep Sea Drill. Proj.*, *45*, 513-517, 1978.

Fukuyama, H. and K. Hamuro, Melting relations of Leg 46 basalts at atmospheric pressure, *Init. Rep. Deep Sea Drill. Proj.*, *46*, 235-239, 1979.

Glazner, A. F., Activities of olivine and plagioclase components in silicate melts and their application to geothermometry, *Contrib. Mineral. Petrol.*, *88*, 260-268, 1984.

Glazner, A.F., Crystal-melt thermobarometry: Application to alkali basalt evolution, the depth of magma chambers, and basalt underplating of continental crust, *EOS Trans. Am. Geophys. Union*, *66*, 46, 1121, 1985.

Graham, D. W., W. J. Jenkins, M. D. Kurz, and R. Batiza, Helium isotopic disequilibrium and geochronology of glassy submarine basalts, in prep.

Green, D. H., Compositions of basaltic magmas as indicators of conditions of origin: Application to oceanic volcanism, *Philos. Trans. R. Soc. London Ser. A*, *268*, 707-725, 1971.

Green, D. H., W. O. Hibberson, and A. L. Jaques, Petrogenesis of mid-ocean ridge basalts, in: McElhinney, M. W., ed., *The Earth: Its Origin, Structure, and Evolution*, London, Academic Press, 265-299, 1979.

Green, T. H., and N. J. Pearson, Rare earth element partitioning between clinopyroxene and silicate liquid at moderate to high pressure, *Contrib. Mineral. Petrol.*, *91*, 24-36, 1985a.

Green, T. H., and N J. Pearson, Experimental determination of REE partition coefficients between amphibole and basaltic to andesitic liquids at high pressure, *Geochim. Cosmochim. Acta*, *49*, 1465-1468, 1985b.

Grove, T. L., and W. B. Bryan, Fractionation of pyroxene-phyric MORB at low pressure: An experimental study, *Contrib. Mineral. Petrol.*, *84*, 293-309, 1983.

Haskin, L. A., F. A. Frey, R. A. Schmitt, and R. H. Smith, Meteoric, solar, and terrestrial rare-earth distributions, *Phys. Chem. Earth*, *7*, 167-321, 1968.

Hebert, R., D. Bideau, and R. Hekinian, Ultramafic and mafic rocks from the Garret Transform Fault near 13°30'S on the East Pacific Rise: Igneous petrology, *Earth Planet. Sci. Lett.*, *65*, 107-125, 1983.

Hedge, C. E., Strontium isotopes in basalts from the Pacific Ocean basin, *Earth Planet. Sci. Lett.*, *38*, 88-94, 1978.

Hill, R. H., and P. L. Roeder, The crystallization of spinel from basaltic liquid as a function of oxygen fugacity, *J. Geol.*, *82*, 709-722, 1974.

Irvine, T. N., Chrome spinel as a petrogenetic indicator, 1. Theory, *Can. J. Earth Sci.*, *2*, 648-672, 1965.

Irvine, T. N., Chromium spinel as a petrogenetic indicator: Part 2, Petrological applications, *Can. J. Earth Sci.*, *4*, 71-103, 1967.

Irving, A. J., A review of experimental studies of crystal/liquid trace element partitioning, *Geochim. Cosmochim. Acta*, *42*, 743-770, 1978.

Jaques, A. L., and D. H. Green, Anhydrous melting of peridotite at 0-15 kb pressure and the genesis of tholeiitic basalts, *Contrib. Mineral. Petrol.*, *73*, 287-310, 1980.

Johnson, J. R., Transitional basalts and tholeiites from the East Pacific Rise, 9°N, *J. Geophys. Res.*, *84*, 1635-1651, 1979.

Juteau, T., J. P. Eissen, J. Francheteau, D. Needham, P. Choukroune, C. Rangin, M. Seguret, R. D. Ballard, P. J. Fox, W. R. Normark, A. Carranza, D. Cordoba, and J. Guerrero, Homogeneous basalts from the East Pacific Rise at 21°N: Steady state magma reservoirs at moderately fast spreading centers, *Oceanologica Acta*, *3*, 487-503, 1980.

Kirkpatrick, R. J., Petrology of basalts: Hole 296B DSDP leg 46, *Initial Rep. Deep Sea Drill. Proj.*, *46*, 164-178, 1978.

Klein, E.M., and C.H. Langmuir, Global correlations between basalt chemistry and axial depth, *EOS Trans. Am. Geophy. Union*, *67*, 16, 356, 1986.

Klein, E.M., and C.H. Langmuir, Ocean ridge basalt chemistry, axial depth, crustal thickness and temperature variations in the mantle, *J. Geophys. Res.*, submitted April 1986.

Korotev, R.L., Chemical homogeneity of National Bureau of Standards Coal Flyash (SRM 1633a), *J. Radioanaly. Nuclear Chem.*, in press (a).

Korotev, R.L., National Bureau of Standards Coal Flyash (SRM 1633a) as a multielement standard for instrumental neutron activation analysis, *J. Radioanaly. Nuclear Chem.*, in press (b).

Kudo, A. M., and D. F. Weill, An igneous plagioclase thermometer, *Contrib. Mineral. Petrol., 25*, 5265, 1970.

Kuo, L. -C., and R. J. Kirkpatrick, Pre-eruption history of phyric basalts from DSDP Legs 45 and 46: Evidence from morphology and zoning patterns of plagioclase, *Contrib. Mineral. Petrol., 79*, 13-27, 1982.

Kushiro, I., Origin of some magmas in oceanic and circum-oceanic regions, *Tectonophysics, 17*, 211-212, 1973.

Kushiro, I., and R. Thompson, Origin of some abyssal tholeiites from the Mid-Atlantic Ridge, *Carnegie Inst. Washington Yrbk. 71*, 403-406, 1972.

Langmuir, C. H., J. F. Bender, A. E. Bence, and G. N. Hanson, Petrogenesis of basalts from the FAMOUS area: Mid-Atlantic Ridge, *Earth Planet. Sci. Lett., 36*, 133-156, 1977.

Langmuir, C. H., R. D. Vocke, and G. N. Hanson, A general mixing equation with application to Icelandic basalts, *Earth Planet. Sci. Lett., 37*, 380-392, 1978.

Langmuir, C. H., J. F. Bender, R. Batiza et al., Petrologic and tectonic segmentation of the East Pacific Rise between 6° and 14°N (abstract), *EOS Trans. AGU, 66*, 1107, 1985.

Langmuir, C. H., J. F. Bender, and R. Batiza, Petrologic and tectonic segmentation of the East Pacific Rise, 5°30'-14°30'N, *Nature, 322*, 422-429.

Larson, R. L., Bathymetry, magnetic anomalies, and plate tectonic history of the mouth of the Gulf of California, *Geol. Soc. Am. Bull., 83*, 3345-3360, 1972.

Lindstrom, D. J., Experimental study of the partitioning of the transition metals between clinopyroxene and coexisting silicate liquids, Ph.D. thesis, University of Oregon, 1976.

Lindstrom, D. J., and D. F. Weill, Partitioning of transition metals between diopside, and coexisting silicate liquids-I. nickel, cobalt, and manganese, *Geochim. Cosmochim Acta, 42*, 817-832, 1978.

Lonsdale, P., and R. Batiza, Submersible study of hyaloclastite and lava flows on young seamounts at the mouth of the Gulf of California, *Geol. Soc. Am. Bull., 91*, 545-554, 1980.

Lonsdale, P., R. Batiza, and T. Simkin, Metallogenesis at seamounts on the East Pacific Rise, *Marine Technol. Soc. J., 16*, 54-61, 1982.

Luhr, J. F., and I. S. E. Carmichael, The Colima Volcanic Complex, Mexico: Part II. Late-Quaternary cinder cones, *Contrib. Mineral. Petrol., 76*, 127-147, 1981.

Mahood, G., and D. Baker, Experimental constraints on depth of fractionation of mildly alkalic basalts and associated felsic rock: Pantelleria, Strait of Sicily, *Contrib. Mineral. Petrol., 93*, 251-264, 1986.

Mathez, E. A., A refinement of the Kudo-Weill plagioclase thermometer and its application to basaltic rocks, *Contrib. Mineral. Petrol., 41*, 61-72, 1973.

Mathez, E. A., Sulfur solubility and magmatic sulfides in submarine basalt glass, *J. Geophys. Res., 81*, 4269-4276, 1976.

Mazzullo, L. J., and A. E. Bence, Abyssal tholeiites from DSDP Leg 34: The Nazca Plate, *J. Geophys. Res., 81*, 4237-4351, 1976.

Melson, W. G., S. R. Hart, and G. Thompson, St. Paul's Rocks, equatorial Atlantic: Petrogenesis, radiometric ages and implications on sea floor spreading, *Geol. Soc. Am. Mem. 132*, 241-272, 1972.

Melson, W. G., T. L. Vallier, T. L. Wright, G. Byerly, and J. Nelen, Chemical diversity of abyssal volcanic glass erupted along Pacific, Atlantic, and Indian Ocean sea-floor spreading centers, in: Sutton, G. H., M. H. Manghnani, and R. Moberly, eds., The geophysics of the Pacific Ocean basin and its margin, *Geophys. Mon. 19*, American Geophysical Union, 351-367, 1976.

Moore, J. G., W. R. Normark, G. R. Hess, and C. E. Meyer, Petrology of basalt from the East Pacific Rise near 21° north latitude, *J. Res. U. S. Geol. Survey, 5*, 753-759, 1977.

Myson, B. O., Experimental determination of rare earth element partitioning between hydrous silicate melt, amphibole, and garnet peridotite minerals at upper mantle pressures and temperatures, *Geochim. Cosmochim Acta, 42*, 1255-1264, 1978.

Natland, J. H., Crystal morphologies in basalt from DSDP site 395, 23°N, 46°W, Mid-Atlantic Ridge, *Initial Rep. Deep Sea Drill. Proj., 45*, 423-445, 1978.

Natland, J. H., Crystal Morphologies in basalts dredged and drilled from the East Pacific Rise near 9°N and the Sequeiros fracture zone, *Initial Rep. Deep Sea Drill. Proj., 54*, 605-634, 1980a.

Natland, J. H., Effect of axial magma chambers beneath spreading centers in the composition of basaltic rocks, *Initial Rep. Deep Sea Drill. Proj., 54*, 833-850, 1980b.

Newman, S., R. C. Finkel, and J. D. MacDougall, $^{230}Th/^{238}U$ disequilibrium systematics in oceanic tholeiites from 21°N on the East Pacific Rise, *Earth Planet. Sci. Lett., 65*, 17-33, 1983.

O'Hara, M. J., The bearing of phase equilibria studies in synthetic and natural systems on the origin and evolution of basic and ultra basic rocks, *Earth Sci. Rev., 4*, 69-133, 1968.

O'Hara, M. J., Are ocean floor basalts primary magma?, *Nature, 220*, 683-686, 1968.

O'Hara, M. J., Importance of the "shape" of the melting regime during partial melting of the mantle, *Nature, 314*, 58-62, 1985.

Ottonello, G., Rare earth abundances and distribution in some spinel peridotite xenoliths from Assab (Ethiopia), *Geochim. Cosmochim. Acta, 44*, 1885-1901, 1980.

Ottonella, G, W. G. Ernst, and J. L Joron, Rare earth and 3d transition element geochemistry of peridotitic rocks: I. Peridotites from the western Alps, *J. Petrol., 25*, 343-372, 1984.

Perfit, M. R., A. D. Saunders, and D. J. Fornari, Phase chemistry, fractional crystallization, and magma mixing in basalts from the Gulf of California, Deep Sea Drilling Project Leg 64, *Init. Rep. Deep Sea Drill. Proj., 64*, 649-666, 1982.

Perfit, M. R. and Fornari, D. J., Geochemical studies of abyssal lavas recovered by DSRV ALVIN from Eastern Galapagos Rift, Inca Transform, and Ecuador Rift 2. Phase chemistry and crystallization history, *J. Geophys. Res., 88*, 10530-10550, 1983.

Perfit, M. R., R. Batiza, J. Allan, T. Smith, and D. J. Fornari, Geochemistry of basalts from a seamount group at 09 53'N near the East Pacific Rise: Possible implications for off-axis magma chambers (abstract), *EOS Trans. Am. Geophys. Union, 66*, 1079, 1985.

Poldervaart, A., and H. H. Hess, Pyroxenes in the crystallization of basaltic magma, *J. Geol., 59*, 472-479, 1951.

Presnall, D. C., J. R. Dixon, T. H. O'Donnell, and S. A. Dixon, Generation of mid-ocean ridge tholeiite, *J. Petrol., 20*, 3-35, 1979.

Presnall, D. C., and J. D. Hoover, Composition and depth of origin of primary mid-ocean ridge basalts, *Contrib. Mineral. Petrol., 87*, 170-178, 1984.

Rhodes, J. M., and M. A. Dungan, The evolution of ocean-floor basaltic magmas, in: Deep drilling results in the Atlantic Ocean: Oceanic crust, *Maurice Ewing Ser. 2*, Am. Geophys. Union, 262-272, 1979.

Rhodes, J. M., M. A. Dungan, D. P. Blanchard, and P. E. Long, Magma mixing at mid-ocean ridges: Evidence from basalts drilled near 22°N on the Mid-Atlantic Ridge, *Tectonophysics, 55*, 35-61, 1979.

Ringwood, A. E., *Origin of the earth and the moon*, Springer-Verlag, New York, 1979.

Rise Project Group, Hot springs and geophysical experiments on the East Pacific Rise, *Science, 207*, 1421-1433, 1980.

Roden, M., S. R. Hart, and F. A. Frey, REE and Sr, Nd, and Pb isotopic chemistry of St. Paul's rocks: The metamorphic and metasomatic development of an alkali basalt source, *Contrib. Mineral. Petrol.*, *85*, 376-390, 1984.

Roeder, P. L., Activity of iron and olivine solubility in basaltic liquids, *Earth Planet. Sci. Lett.*, *23*, 397-411, 1974.

Roeder, P. L., and R. F. Emslie, Olivine-liquid equilibrium, *Contrib. Mineral. Petrol.*, *29*, 275-289, 1970.

Sack, R. O., Spinels as petrogenetic indicators: Activity-composition relations at low pressures, *Contrib. Mineral. Petrol.*, *79*, 169-186, 1982.

Sack, R. O., and I. S. E. Carmichael, Fe^2-Mg^2 and $TiAl_2$-$MgSi^2$ exchange reactions between clinopyroxenes and silicate melts, *Contrib. Mineral. Petrol.*, *85*, 103-115, 1984.

Sato, H., Nickel content of basaltic magmas: Identification of primary magmas and a measure of the degree of olivine fractionation, *Lithos*, *10*, 113-120, 1977.

Schouten, H., H. J. B. Dick, J. A. Whitehead, and K. D. Klitgord, Whole-mantle upwelling under spreading centers (abstract), *EOS Trans. Am. Geophys. Union*, *67*, 16, 359, 1986.

Shaw, D. M., Trace element fractionation during anatexis, *Geochim. Cosmochim. Acta*, *34*, 237-243, 1970.

Shibata, T., S. E. Delong, and D. Walker, Abyssal tholeiites from the Oceanographer Fracture Zone, 1, Petrology and fractionation, *Contrib. Mineral. Petrol.*, *70*, 89-102, 1979.

Sigurdsson, H., Spinels in leg 37 basalts and peridotites: Phase chemistry and zoning, *Initial Rep. Deep Sea Drill. Proj.*, *37*, 883-891, 1977.

Sigurdsson, H., and J. -G. Schilling, Spinels in Mid-Atlantic Ridge basalts: Chemistry and occurrence, *Earth Planet. Sci.*, *29*, 7-20, 1976.

Simkin, T., Origin of some flat-topped volcanoes and guyots, *Geol. Soc. Am. Mem.*, *132*, 183-193, 1972.

Sleep, N. H., Formation of oceanic crust: Some thermal constraints, *J. Geophys. Res.*, *80*, 4037-4042, 1975.

Stolper, E. A., A phase diagram for mid-ocean ridge basalts: Preliminary results and implications for petrogenesis, *Contrib. Mineral. Petrol.*, *74*, 13-27, 1980.

Sun, S. S., R. W. Nesbitt, and A. Y. Sharaskin, Geochemical characteristics of mid-ocean ridge basalts, *Earth Planet. Sci. Lett.*, *44*, 119-138, 1979.

Takahashi, E., and I. Kushiro, Melting of a dry peridotite at high pressures and basalt magma genesis, *Am. Mineral.*, *68*, 859-879, 1983.

Thompson, G., W. B. Bryan, R. Ballard, K. Hamuro, and W.G. Melson, Axial processes along a segment of the East Pacific Rise 10-12°N, *Nature*, *318*, 6045, 429-433, 1985.

Thy, P., Phase relations in transitional and alkalic basalt glasses from Iceland, *Contrib. Mineral. Petrol.*, *82*, 232-251, 1983.

Thy, P., Spinel minerals in transitional and alkalic basaltic glasses, *Contrib. Mineral. Petrol.*, *83*, 141-149, 1983.

Walker, D., R. J. Kirkpatrick, J. Longhi et al., Crystallization history of lunar picritic basalt sample 12002: Phase-equilibria and cooling rate studies, *Geol. Soc. Am. Bull.*, *87*, 646-656, 1976.

Walker, D., T. Shibata, and S. E. Delong, Abyssal tholeiites from the Oceanographer Fracture Zone, II, Phase equilibria and mixing, *Contrib. Mineral. Petrol.*, *70*, 111-125, 1979.

Zindler, A., H. Staudigel, and R. Batiza, Isotope and trace element geochemistry of young Pacific seamounts: Implications for the scale of upper mantle heterogeneity, *Earth Planet. Sci.*, *70*, 175-195, 1984.

ISOTOPIC EVIDENCE FOR A HOTSPOT ORIGIN OF THE LOUISVILLE SEAMOUNT CHAIN

Q. Cheng[1], K.-H. Park[2], J.D. Macdougall[1], A. Zindler[2], G.W. Lugmair[1], H. Staudigel[1], J. Hawkins[1], and P. Lonsdale[1]

[1]Scripps Institution of Oceanography, La Jolla, California
[2]Lamont-Doherty Geological Observatory, Palisades, New York

Abstract. The Louisville Seamount Chain (LSC) is the longest seamount chain in the South Pacific and in many ways resembles the Hawaiian-Emperor chain, suggesting a hotspot origin. Fifteen samples from ten LSC seamounts spanning the length of the LSC and covering a time span of more than 65 My were analyzed for Nd, Sr and Pb isotopic compositions. Since most of the samples are old and altered, systematic leaching experiments were conducted in order to study seawater alteration effects and to obtain age-corrected Sr and Nd isotopic compositions. These experiments show that even fresh appearing samples have elevated $^{87}Sr/^{86}Sr$ due to seawater Sr addition, and that highly altered samples may contain substantial amounts of seawater Nd, possibly hosted in secondary oxides or phosphate phases. However, after appropriate leaching, reliable, age-corrected $^{87}Sr/^{86}Sr$ and $^{143}Nd/^{144}Nd$ initial ratios can be obtained. The data for leached samples show very narrow ranges in Sr, Nd and Pb isotopic compositions ($^{87}Sr/^{86}Sr$ from .7032 to .7038; $^{143}Nd/^{144}Nd$ from .51282 to .51294; $^{206}Pb/^{204}Pb$ from 19.128 to 19.452) both for different rock types within the same seamount and for the LSC chain as a whole. The LSC seamounts record a chemical plume signature that is distinct from that of MORB sources and is very homogeneous on a large scale over a long period of time. The data also imply a stationary source region for the long-lived upwelling mantle plume, thus favoring a mantle structure which is at least partly non-convective and a likely deep mantle origin for the hotspot plume as proposed by Morgan [1971, 1972a,b]. No appreciable mixing occurred between the LSC and MORB sources, which may have implications for the mechanism of plume transport.

1. Introduction

Seamounts and guyots of the Louisville Seamount Chain (LSC), also called the Louisville Ridge (LVR), were first discovered by various ships of the U.S. Navy sailing to and from New Zealand in connection with the exploration of Antarctica, and were reported by Menard et al. [1964]. Various surveys and studies of LSC have been made since then [Hawkins, 1973; Watts et al., 1985; Lonsdale, 1986]. A number of uncharted seamounts and other geographic features such as submarine plateaus and fracture zones have also been discovered in this region using satellite altimeter data [Dixon and Parke, 1983; Sandwell, 1984; Cazenave and Dominh, 1984]. These data show that the LSC is the longest seamount chain in the Southern Pacific. There has been much

Copyright 1987 by the American Geophysical Union.

debate about its origin. Hayes and Ewing [1971] interpreted the LSC as the northwestern continuation of the Eltanin Fracture Zone (EFZ), as did Larson and Chase [1972], and Chase [1971]. However, the topography of the LSC is very different from that of the EFZ, as noted by Hawkins [1973], Molnar et al. [1975] and Dixon and Parke [1983]. Based on the lack of typical fracture zone morphology, Hawkins [1973] proposed that the LSC may be related to magma leaks from a "hot spot". The new bathymetric data also show that the chain crosses the EFZ at the southeastern end, although a "pre-Eltanin fracture zone" can be traced further north parallel to the LSC [Lonsdale, 1986]. Casenave and Dominh [1984] also noticed a large offset of the LSC and the Tharp fracture zone near 150°W. Shallow depth anomalies near the southeastern end of the LSC [Casenave et al., 1983; Schroeder, 1984] indicate mantle upwelling or a thermal anomaly in the underlying mantle. K-Ar dating of LSC seamounts by Duncan [Watts et al., 1985, 1986] documents a general age progression from the SE to the NW from ~0.5 My to ~70 My. All of these observations seem to preclude the possibility that the LSC is the continuation of the EFZ. Rather, it resembles many other linear chains or aseismic ridges in the Pacific and thus is likely to owe its existence to the same processes which produced, for example, the Hawaiian chain: a hotspot origin, the hypothesis which has been invoked to interpret many linear island chains. The LSC has considerable importance in the study of regional plate tectonic history, the underlying mantle structure and composition in that area, and the origin of seamount chains in general.

The main objectives of this investigation were: to study the composition of the LSC mantle source by analyzing Nd, Sr and Pb isotopic compositions of the seamounts and comparing these data with those of other oceanic island and seamount chains; to examine isotopic variation along the chain since the large age range of the LSC seamounts allows us to study long term (more than 65 My) variations in the mantle source; and to use the isotopic data to help understand the processes which generated the LSC, particularly with respect to the structure and evolution of its mantle source.

2. Geological Setting and Sampling

The Louisville Seamount Chain is a 4300 km long, aseismic seamount chain which extends from the Tonga-Kemadec Trench at the northwestern end (175°W, 26°S) to near the southern East Pacific Rise at the southeastern end (139°W, 50°S). Figure 1 shows the regional bathymetry and our sample locations. At least 75 volcanoes [Lonsdale, 1986] exist in the entire chain; most of them are guyots with small, flattened summits, and are believed

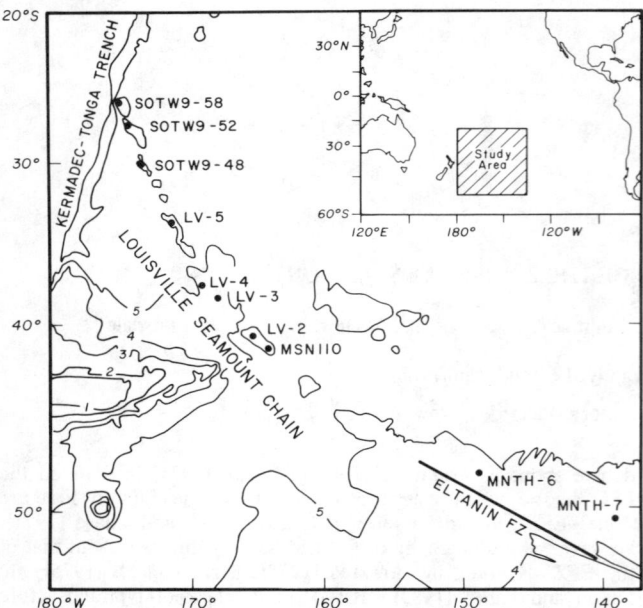

Fig. 1. Map showing the Louisville Seamount Chain, with dredge locations indicated. Detailed information about cruises, seamount ages and locations, and rock types analyzed is presented in Table 1.

originally to have been subaerial. Although most of the seamounts or guyots have a local relief of 3500 to 4500 m, which is greater than that of most drowned ancient islands in the Pacific [Menard et al., 1964], the entire erupted volume is considerably smaller than that of the Hawaiian-Emperor seamount chain [Lonsdale, 1986]. However, the total length of the LSC and its spatial pattern are in general comparable with the Hawaiian-Emperor chain: the bend near 37.5°S is analogous to the ~45 My bend of the latter and its age has been confirmed by K-Ar dating [Watts et al., 1985, 1986]; likewise, the trend of the LSC can be described, to first order, by small circles about Pacific absolute motion poles derived from the Hawaiian-Emperor chain [Clague and Jarrard, 1973; Epp, 1978; Lonsdale, 1986].

Sea-floor spreading in the South Pacific started approximately 81 My ago when New Zealand split away from West Antarctica [Molnar et al., 1975]. This event may coincide with the southeastern migration of the Pacific-Phoenix spreading center and its alignment with the proto New Zealand-Antarctic rift zone. The Eltanin Fracture Zone developed at that time because of the difference in half-spreading rate between Pacific-Phoenix (Aluk) (10 cm/yr) and Pacific-Antarctic (4.5 cm/yr) spreading centers [Larson et al., 1979]. At present, a 1000 km offset separates the EPR and PAR (Pacific-Antarctic Ridge) across the EFZ. This offset diminishes at magnetic anomaly 34, corresponding to an age of 80 My [Larson et al., 1972]. Prior to anomaly 34, the magnetic pattern is not well established because it enters the Cretaceous quiet zone; thus, the sea-floor age beyond 80 My is not well known. One DSDP sample (site 204) near Osbourn seamount, located ~100 km east of the Tonga Trench, gives a Late Cretaceous age of about 100 My based on reworked fossil assemblages [Edwards, 1973]. Sediment cover around the bases of most Louisville Ridge seamounts is very thin, usually less than 50 m thick [Hayes and Ewing, 1971; Lonsdale, 1986], in contrast to some other volcano chains such as the Walvis Ridge [Ewing et al.,

1966]. Elastic thickness estimates for the lithosphere along the LSC suggest that the seamounts may have formed on a 50-70 My-old plate [Casenave and Dominh, 1984]. If the trend of increasing elastic thickness northward proposed by Casenave and Dominh [1984] can be confirmed, it may indicate that seamounts in the northern portion of the chain formed on slightly older and thicker seafloor than those of the southern portion and that the adjacent spreading center may have been migrating toward the fixed Louisville hotspot. However, additional data are required to draw a firm conclusion. The present site of the proposed hotspot is uncertain; two young seamounts at 139.2°W and 138.1°W are the most probable candidates.

More than 15 dredged samples from ten LSC seamounts were collected during Scripps Institution of Oceanography (SIO) and Lamont-Doherty Geological Observatory (LDGO) cruises. These dredged samples cover the length of the LSC and a time span of more than 65 My. Sample locations are given in Figure 1 and Table 1.

3. Analytical Techniques

Fifteen samples were analyzed for Sr and Nd isotopes; a number of samples were analyzed at both SIO and LDGO to establish the basis for interlaboratory comparison. A subset of these samples were analyzed for Pb at LDGO. These samples have also been analyzed for major and trace elements by Hawkins et al. [this issue]. As the samples are all altered by seawater to different extents, systematic, multi-step leaching experiments were conducted on two specimens at SIO (SOTW9-48-2 and MSN110-1) to determine the degree of seawater influence on isotopic compositions. Details of these experiments are described below.

All samples measured at SIO were leached with 6N HCl plus 5% HF in an ultrasonic bath (corresponding to the last step in the leaching experiments). For the phyric, less altered sample SOTW9-52-1, the two youngest, fresh looking samples MTHN7-D-1 and MTHN6-D-1, and clinopyroxenes of MTHN6-D-1 and SOTW9-52-1, only 2N HCl leaching for less than 30 minutes was employed to remove surface contamination. Samples measured at LDGO were washed with pure water to remove fine minerals, leached with 6N HCl in an ultrasonic bath and usually followed by hot 6N HCl leaching overnight (~100°C). Pb measurements were done on unleached or mildly leached powders. The chemical separation and isotopic analysis procedures employed at Scripps are those of Lugmair et al. [1975] and Carlson [1980] with minor modifications. Nd and Sr analytical procedures used at LDGO are patterned after those described by Hart and Brooks [1977] for Sr, Richard et al. [1976] and Zindler et al. [1979] for Nd; Pb procedures are modified after Chen [1977].

Isotopic fractionation corrections, estimated precisions and standard reference values for both laboratories are given in Table 4.

4. Seafloor Alteration Effects

It has been recognized for a long time that $^{87}Sr/^{86}Sr$ ratios in submarine basalts can be substantially changed due to seawater alteration [e.g. Hart, 1971; Chapman et al., 1975; Spooner, 1976; Staudigel and Hart, 1983]. However, no significant modifications in $^{143}Nd/^{144}Nd$ ratios of altered oceanic basalts have been reported. Owing to the very low concentrations of REE in seawater and their immobility, it is generally assumed that the effects of low temperature alteration on REE patterns and Nd isotopes are negligible.

However, a systematic study on dredged Atlantic basalts with an

TABLE 1. List of Dredged Samples Studied

Sample	Location	Depth (m)	Age[1] (My)	Age[2] (My)	Rock Type[3]	Cruise
MTHN7-D-1	50°26.4'S 139°10'W	640	1.1	0.5 ± .4	Alkalic Basalt	SIO, SMRTHN 1984
MTHN6-D-1	48°12.1'S 148°48.4'W	720	11	12.5 ± .4	Alkalic Basalt	Same
MSN110-1	41°27'S 164°16'W	1000	32.8	34.4 ± .6 36.6 ± .6	Alkalic Basalt	SIO, MONSOON 1961
MSN110-B	Same	1080	32.8	Same	Alkalic Basalt	Same
LV-2	40°47'S 165°21'W	1883	35.4	—	Alkalic Basalt	LDGO, VEMA 1979
LV-3	38°19.5'S 167°43.7'W	1232	42.2	45.5 ± .5	Alkalic Basalt	LDGO, VEMA 1979
LV-4	36°57'S 169°50'W	1446-2910	45.9	44.6 ± .5 43.9 ± 2.4	Picritic Basalt	Same
LV-5	33°56.7'S 171°11.5'W	2760-3704	51.8	53.3 ± 2.6	Alkalic Basalt	Same
SOTW9-48-2	30°10.2'S 173°25.7'W	3291	62.3	61.2 ± .9	Hawaiite	SIO, SOTW09 1972
SOTW9-52-1	27°28.3'S 174°24.8'W	3593	63.6	66.7 ± 1.4 70.1 ± 1.4	Hawaiite	Same
SOTW9-58-1	25°52.3'S 175°5.4'W	3270	66.6	65.9 ± .6 66.6 ± .6	Basanitoid	Same
SOTW9-58-3	Same	Same	Same	—	Alkalic Basalt	Same
SOTW9-58-5	Same	Same	Same	—	Alkalic Basalt	Same
SOTW9-58-7	Same	Same	Same	—	Olivine Neph.	Same
SOTW9-58-9	Same	Same	Same	—	Basanitoid	Same

1. From tectonic reconstruction [Lonsdale, 1986]. 2. From K/Ar dating [Watts et al., in press]. 3. From Hawkins et al., this issue.

age span from 0-57 My [Ludden and Thompson, 1979] demonstrated the possibility of REE mobility during prolonged low temperature alteration, especially for the light REE. Staudigel and Hart [1983] also found REE loss during palagonitization of basalt glasses. Thus, REE exchange with seawater may be a significant process for rocks which have been exposed to large volumes of seawater over long time periods. Our systematic leaching experiments suggest that this is the case for some of the LSC samples.

Most of our dredged samples are old surficial rocks; some are vesicular and highly altered and therefore likely to have been affected. Our isotopic data reveal that not only $^{87}Sr/^{86}Sr$, but also $^{143}Nd/^{144}Nd$ ratios have been altered by exchange with seawater, as shown in Figures 3 and 4 and Table 2 and discussed below.

4.1. Leaching Experiments

Leaching experiments were carried out at Scripps on two LSC samples during this study in order to: (1) make a systematic survey of the effects of different leaching conditions on seawater-altered samples; (2) observe the behavior of Rb/Sr systematics during leaching (this has particular relevance for age corrections of $^{87}Sr/^{86}Sr$ ratios in old, alkali-enriched rocks); (3) study the effects of alteration on Sm/Nd systematics, both on $^{143}Nd/^{144}Nd$ and Sm/Nd ratios; (4) find optimum leaching conditions for different types and degrees of alteration; and (5) recover the maximum amount of information on the original isotopic compositions of the samples.

The experiments were designed in stepwise fashion from mild to heavy leaching. Two samples, SOTW9-48-2 and MSN110-1, differing in chemical composition, texture, age and degree of alteration, were examined. Two slightly different leaching procedures were used for the two different samples as shown in Figure 2. In brief, for the highly altered sample (SOTW9-48-2) we used consecutive acid leaching steps, while for the relatively fresh one (MSN110-1), parallel acid leaching using different HCl normalities was carried out. Fine powders were used for all leaching experiments and measurements were made on the leached residue after each step. Enough reagent-solution was added in all cases to insure a high solution/powder ratio. Leaching time was generally one hour in an ultrasonic bath, but was sometimes longer depending on the sample size and degree of alteration. Solutions and suspended fine materials were decanted several times during this treatment until the solution became clear and colorless. Sonification physically helps to remove fine-grained

TABLE 2. Leaching Experiments[1]

Sample/Step	Reagents	Time	$^{87}Sr/^{86}Sr$	$^{143}Nd/^{144}Nd$	Nd	Sm	Sr	Rb	Rb/Sr	Sm/Nd
MSN110-1										
1	None	—	0.704116 ± 26	0.512910 ± 18	43.3	9.58	722	12.0	0.0166	0.222
2	Water	60 min	0.703954 ± 26	0.512949 ± 18	41.1	9.13	722	13.0	0.0180	0.222
3	2N HCl	60 min	0.703705 ± 26	0.512936 ± 14	18.7	4.95	735	12.6	0.0171	0.264
4	4N HCl	60 min	0.703709 ± 26	0.512938 ± 14	19.1	5.03	745	12.8	0.0171	0.264
5	6N HCl	60 min	0.703682 ± 26	0.512925 ± 14	20.4	5.29	768	13.9	0.0182	0.259
6	Step 5 + 5% HF	5 min	0.703659 ± 26	0.512930 ± 14	20.5	5.42	825	12.1	0.0146	0.265
SOTW9-48-2										
1	None	—	0.704783 ± 36	0.512795 ± 14	53.0	11.28	610	81.7	0.1338	0.213
2	Water	4 hrs	0.704598 ± 26	0.512779 ± 18	53.6	11.43	673	63.5	0.0944	0.213
3	1M $NH_2OH \cdot HCl$	60 min	0.704388 ± 26	0.512788 ± 14	54.9	11.69	644	61.7	0.0958	0.213
4	1M α-HIBA	60 min	0.704491 ± 26	0.512782 ± 20	53.9	11.41	664	63.8	0.0961	0.212
5	1M $Na_2S_2O_4$	2 days (50°C)	0.704143 ± 26	0.512782 ± 14	41.0	8.72	698	50.9	0.0730	0.213
6	2N HCl	20 min	0.704110 ± 26	0.512876 ± 16	14.1	3.02	590	55.6	0.0942	0.214
7	Step 6 + 2N HCl	40 min	0.703765 ± 26	0.512936 ± 16	2.73	0.54	675	51.0	0.0756	0.199
8	Step 7 + 6N HCl	60 min	0.703692 ± 26	0.512922 ± 32	2.74	0.55	756	23.3	0.0309	0.200
9	Step 8 + 5% HF	5 min	0.703632 ± 26	0.512937 ± 14	5.95	1.12	1240	8.6	0.0069	0.188

1. Isotopic standard values and normalizations are the same as reported in Table 4. All isotope and concentration data are measured on residues after leaching. Concentration data (ppm) are by isotope dilution mass spectrometry.

alteration products and also reduces surface tension, allowing acid to penetrate into small vesicles and cracks; the combined effect thus seems to dissolve and remove alteration products along grain rims, vesicle and crack walls. Since sonification will also pack the leaching powders, frequent shaking is required to prevent formation of "cakes". Residues were finally washed by sonifying in pure water and then dried for dissolution. Microscopic inspection of the leached residues usually showed clean crystal assemblages, mainly consisting of plagioclase, olivine, pyroxene and opaque minerals.

SOTW9-48-2. This sample is a vesicular, aphyric alkalic basalt (Hawaiite) with an age of about 62 My (see Table 1). It is composed of fine-grained plagioclase, olivine, clinopyroxene and devitrified glass. Olivine has been altered to iddingsite, suggesting that the seamount from which the sample was dredged may originally have been subaerial. Vesicles comprise about 50% by volume and are filled with carbonates or opal, or coated with smectite and ferromanganese material. Analcite appears in some vesicles as microcrystals. In the groundmass and within individual plagioclase crystals abundant black acicular crystals occur forming grid and radial structures. Energy dispersive x-ray analyses of these fine-grained phases using the electron probe showed the presence of Fe, Ti, Ca and P. We infer that they are Fe-Ti oxides intergrown with microcrystalline carbonate and phosphate precipitated during alteration of the groundmass and along crystal planes in feldspar. In addition, the bulk rock chemical data [Hawkins et al., this issue] show high P_2O_5, suggesting the presence of secondary phosphates which are a likely site for the rare earths.

The flow chart of leaching steps is shown in Fig. 2(a) and results are given in Table 2. Step 1 is an unleached powder, measured as a baseline for comparison. This step gives the highest $^{87}Sr/^{86}Sr$ (.70478) and Rb content (81.7 ppm) and a high REE concentration. In Step 2, powder was sonified in distilled water and fine-grained suspended materials (mostly clays) were removed by frequent decanting. This step had two purposes: first, to remove water-soluble components and fine-grained clay particles and Fe-oxides, and second, to supply powders for later steps

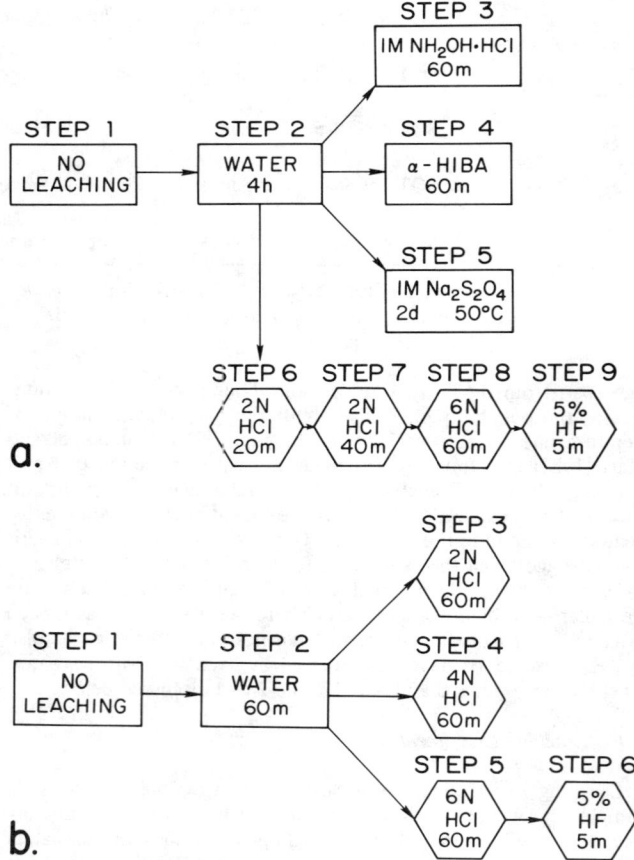

Fig. 2. Flow charts showing leaching procedures for: (a) SOTW9-48-2 and (b) MSN110-1. Arrows designate consecutive steps. Hexagonal boxes indicate acid treatment.

TABLE 3. Weight Loss During Leaching Experiment for MSN110-1

Step	Weight before (g)	Weight after (g)	Loss (%)
2 (Water)[1]	17.53	9.67	45
3 (2N HCl)	0.85	0.75	12
4 (4N HCl)	1.47	1.28	13
5 (6N HCl)	4.93	4.17	15
6 (6N HCl + 5% HF)	2.94	2.57	13

1. Includes decanting of fines as discussed in text.

so that variations caused by water-soluble components and clays could be eliminated. This step reduces $^{87}Sr/^{86}Sr$ and Rb/Sr while Sm and Nd contents and the Nd isotope ratio remain unchanged, indicating that phases containing seawater Sr and high Rb/Sr have been removed. In Step 3, a mild reducing reagent, hydroxylamine-hydrochloride ($NH_2OH \cdot HCl$), was used with the hope of dissolving ferromanganese oxides [Arrhenius, 1963; Arrhenius et al., 1978], which are believed to be a carrier of seawater REE [Piper, 1974], without disturbing intrinsic Nd. However, no change was observed in either REE content or $^{143}Nd/^{144}Nd$ under our conditions. Step 4 used a strong chelating agent, α-hydroxyisobutyric acid (α-HIBA), (($CH_3)_2C(OH)CO_2H$), to extract exchangeable REE, but again neither concentrations nor $^{143}Nd/^{144}Nd$ were changed, indicating that the REE are not in readily exchangeable sites. Step 5 employed the strong reducing reagent sodium dithionite ($Na_2S_2O_4$). (Note: in order to test the efficiency of the sodium dithionite for dissolving oxide phases, a corollary experiment was done prior to this step in which three rock chips with both manganese oxide coating and bright yellow smectite were soaked in $1M\ Na_2S_2O_2$, $1M\ NH_2OH \cdot HCl$ and $1M\ \alpha$-HIBA solution respectively for one week. Both MnO_2 and smectite dissolved in the $1M\ Na_2S_2O_4$ solution; MnO_2 dissolved and smectite partly dissolved in the $1M\ NH_2OH \cdot HCl$ solution; and neither MnO_2 nor smectite dissolved in $1M\ \alpha$-HIBA solution). The leaching was carried out at ~50°C for two days. Residual material was examined under the microscope and it was noted that most of the bright yellow smectite was dissolved, but that the black acicular crystals still were present. Isotopic compositions of the residue showed a large reduction in $^{87}Sr/^{86}Sr$ and Rb/Sr; the Nd concentration was reduced by ~20%, but surprisingly $^{143}Nd/^{144}Nd$ did not change at all. Step 6 started hydrochloric acid (2N) leaching for 20 minutes. During this step, $^{143}Nd/^{144}Nd$ increased from .512782 to .512876, and both Nd and Sm concentrations decreased sharply. Step 7 continued Step 6 for a total length of 60 minutes, and resulted in further changes in both Nd isotopic ratio and Nd and Sm concentrations. Steps 8 and 9 continued with more concentrated HCl and HF, respectively. The last two steps resulted in essentially no change in Nd isotopic composition from Step 7, although $^{87}Sr/^{86}Sr$ continued to decrease. The Rb/Sr systematics for the last three steps in fact yielded an isochronous relation, suggesting complete removal of the seawater component.

MSN110-1. This rock is a massive, phyric, relatively fresh alkalic basalt with an age of ~33 My (see Table 1). Phenocrysts are composed of relatively fresh plagioclase, olivine and clinopyroxene. Plagioclase is the major phenocryst phase (>80%). Olivine grains have iddingsite rims. The matrix is composed of microcrystalline plagioclase, olivine and clinopyroxene.

The leaching flow chart for this rock is shown in Figure 2(b) and analytical data are given in Table 2. Weight loss measurements through various steps are also presented in Table 3.

No reducing or complexing agents were used with this relatively fresh sample. During water leaching and decanting of suspended materials (Step 2), about 45% of the original material was lost. Although a large reduction in $^{87}Sr/^{86}Sr$ occurred, no obvious changes were observed for $^{143}Nd/^{144}Nd$, Nd, Sm, Sr or Rb concentrations. During subsequent HCl leaches (Steps 3-5), $^{87}Sr/^{86}Sr$ decreased significantly. Although $^{143}Nd/^{144}Nd$ did not change outside our standard uncertainty, the Nd and Sm concentrations decreased about 50% and Sm/Nd increased from ~0.222 to ~0.263. An average of ~13% additional material by weight was lost during each of the HCl leaching steps, accounting for about 50% of the Nd in the whole rock. By mass balance calculations, this indicates that acid leachable components (most likely originally glassy interstitial material) contain ~174 ppm Nd, about 8 to 9 times higher than that of residues, with a Sm/Nd ratio of ~0.11, about half that of the residue. On the other hand, both Sr and Rb concentrations stayed nearly constant, although there is a trend of slightly increasing Sr concentrations. During the final HF leaching step, no further changes in Sm/Nd systematics were observed, but Rb/Sr decreased substantially, which may be a result of dissolution or partial dissolution of low Sr phases, and thus responsible for the slightly low measured $^{87}Sr/^{86}Sr$ of this step.

4.2. Discussion

Rb/Sr Systematics. Both SOTW9-48-2 and MSN110-1 show a decreasing trend in $^{87}Sr/^{86}Sr$ as leaching proceeds. After strong acid leaching, constant (MSN110-1) or convergent (SOTW9-48-2) $^{87}Sr/^{86}Sr$ ratios are obtained which may represent "true" values for the residue material.

Except for HF leaching, the relatively fresh MSN110-1 has similar Rb/Sr and Rb and Sr concentrations for both the unleached powder and leached residues. This indicates that the acid-leachable portion either contains essentially the same concentrations of Rb and Sr as those of leached residues or it contains extremely small amounts of Rb and Sr, so that its removal does not affect the measured values. The change in Rb/Sr during the HF leaching step may have resulted from the selective dissolution of other phases. The bulk of the seawater component, as reflected by $^{87}Sr/^{86}Sr$, appears to have been removed by the one hour 2N HCl leach; subsequent more severe acid leaching reduced the $^{87}Sr/^{86}Sr$ only slightly. The linear trend from Steps 3-6 in Figure 4c appears to be a mixing line between a major phase (plagioclase) and minor phases, generated by removal of mineral phases during stepwise leaching.

For the highly altered SOTW9-48-2, the situation is more complicated. Both Rb concentration and Rb/Sr were lowered substantially during the first step, indicating that the suspended and water-soluble materials removed possess higher Rb concentration and Rb/Sr than the bulk rock and that the secondary products preferentially incorporate Rb relative to Sr. During Steps 3 to 6, $^{87}Sr/^{86}Sr$ decreased continuously, but Rb/Sr only changed slightly. For Steps 7, 8 and 9, data form a linear array on the Sr evolution diagram. The "isochron" formed by this array corresponds to an age of 46 ± 13 My (Fig. 3a) which within error is close to the ages determined by other methods (61-62 My; see Table 1). Thus, assuming that most of the seawater component has been removed, this "isochron" may be due to internal growth of radiogenic Sr in different phases with different Rb/Sr ratios and different susceptibilities to acid leaching. Unlike MSN110-1, this sample showed a continuous decrease in Rb/Sr ratio during acid leaching. After Step 9, Rb/Sr is too small for age corrections on $^{87}Sr/^{86}Sr$ to be significant.

Our leaching experiments were designed to remove chemically low temperature alteration phases. At the same time some magmatic phases are removed, mostly the fine grained groundmass

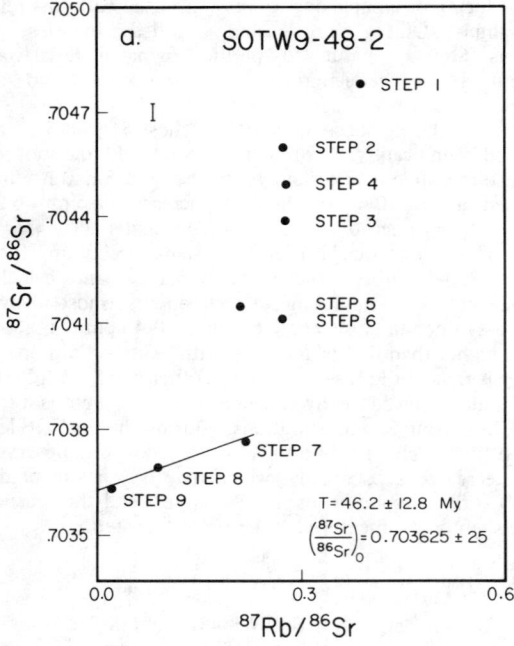

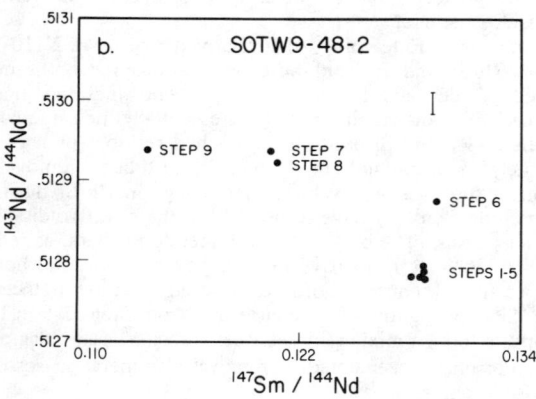

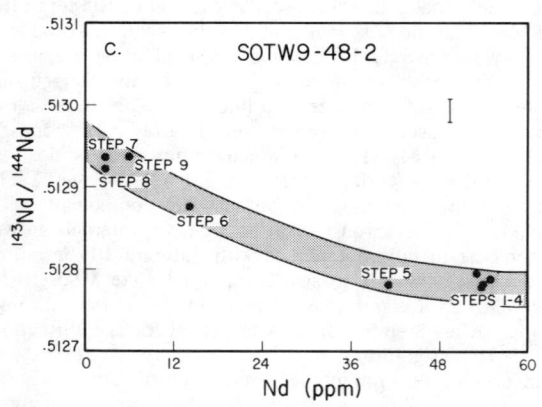

Fig. 3. Leaching results for SOTW9-48-2. (a) $^{87}Rb/^{86}Sr$ vs. $^{87}Sr/^{86}Sr$ diagram. Both $^{87}Rb/^{86}Sr$ and $^{87}Sr/^{86}Sr$ decrease as leaching proceeds. The last three acid leaching steps (7-9) fall along a linear array which, if interpreted as an isochron, corresponds to an age close to K/Ar and plate reconstruction ages [Watts et al., 1986; Lonsdale, 1986]. This may result from chemical separation of mineral phases as discussed in the text. (b) $^{147}Sm/^{144}Nd$ vs. $^{143}Nd/^{144}Nd$ diagram. Steps 1-5 and Steps 7-9 form two separate groups, with Step 6 falling in between them. This is clearly not an isotopic evolution trend, and is probably a leaching effect. Acid leached residues are more LREE enriched than acid leachable components, based on Sm/Nd. (c) Nd concentration vs. $^{143}Nd/^{144}Nd$ variation forms an approximately hyperbolic mixing curve between the high concentration, seawater influenced component (A) and the low concentration, unaltered residual component (U).

and residual glass. These phases are enriched in incompatible elements like Rb, and thus the leached residue has a lower Rb/Sr ratio and less radiogenic ^{87}Sr than the unleached bulk rock. Its final elemental ratios largely depend on the compositions and proportions of residual mineral phases. However, one might consider the possibility of selective removal of Rb from residual magmatic phases, thus disturbing the Rb-Sr isotope systematics. In this case Rb/Sr of a mineral assemblage separated by chemical means would differ from one separated by physical means, and would not fall on the whole rock-mineral isochron. Different leaching methods may have different effects on Rb-Sr systematics. We believe that the disturbances of Rb/Sr ratios by our leaching condition must be minor because: (1) no significant and systematic changes in Rb/Sr ratio of residues have been observed during different acid treatments of MSN110-1; (2) the Rb/Sr isotope systematics of leached bulk rocks are consistent with mineral data from the same rock (MTHN6-D-1 and SOTW9-52-1); and (3) direct comparison of fresh glass and leached whole-rock powder of two old DSDP drilled basalts gave identical age-corrected $^{87}Sr/^{86}Sr$ and $^{143}Nd/^{144}Nd$ ratios (see discussion below). For these reasons we believe that the Rb/Sr ratios of leached bulk rocks obtained by this leaching method closely approximate the Rb/Sr of the residual magmatic mineral assemblage left behind after leaching and that the initial isotopic ratios calculated from these data are close to the initial magmatic $^{87}Sr/^{86}Sr$.

Sm/Nd Systematics. The $^{143}Nd/^{144}Nd$ ratio in seawater varies both between and within ocean basins, ranging from $\epsilon(0) = -14$ to $\epsilon(0) = +1$ [Piepgras and Wasserburg, 1980, 1982]. In the South Pacific the range is narrower, $\epsilon = -7$ to $\epsilon(0) = -2$ [Staudigel et al., 1985]. Thus the effect of seawater alteration on the Nd isotopic composition of oceanic rocks will depend on local seawater composition; however, in general, it will result in decreased $^{143}Nd/^{144}Nd$. Although present day seawater contains only about 3×10^{-6} ppm Nd, the Nd concentration in ferromanganese nodules and in oceanic phosphates may be several hundred ppm [Piepgras and Wasserburg, 1980, 1982; Piper, 1974; Shaw and Wasserburg, 1985]. Thus, depending on the degree of secondary mineralization, phosphates and ferromanganese oxides could dominate the Nd budget of altered oceanic basalts.

The untreated MSN110-1 sample (Step 1) has a marginally lower $^{143}Nd/^{144}Nd$ than subsequent leached residues, but falls within analytical uncertainties of most of those values in spite of large changes in concentration. For this relatively fresh sample, seawater alteration appears to have had a negligible effect on Nd isotopic composition. This result is in agreement with the conventional view that for relatively fresh rocks seawater effects on the Nd isotopic ratio are insignificant. However, in the case of highly altered SOTW9-48-2, the seawater effect is substantial. The difference between isotopic values for leached and unleached aliquots is as large as three ϵ units. Figure 3(c) shows the negatively sloping trend on a ^{143}Nd/^{144}Nd versus Nd concentration diagram produced by the various leaching steps; this diagram clearly shows the correlation between seawater-introduced Nd and ^{143}Nd/^{144}Nd ratios. A second sample (LV-5) also showed a large difference in Nd isotopic composition for unleached and leached aliquots (^{143}Nd/^{144}Nd from 0.512777 to 0.512825). The seawater contamination may have occurred in two ways, both consistent with the petrography of SOTW9-48-2: (1) formation of secondary phases containing very high concentrations of Nd with seawater isotopic ratios, such as ferromanganese oxides and phosphates (apatite); the high P_2O_5 contents of some samples from LSC seamounts [Hawkins et al., this issue] indicate that some of these rocks may have been phosphatized when they were at shallower depths, thus strongly supporting this argument; and (2) incorporation or exchange of seawater Nd during alteration of matrix glass, which contains relatively large amounts of REE. Our mild leaches (Steps 2-4) did not remove seawater Nd, implying that seawater Nd is not primarily absorbed by clays or in exchangeable sites. Instead, it appears to be strongly held in non-exchangeable sites as a structural substitute.

To answer quantitatively how the seawater affects measured Nd isotopic compositions is not an easy task. For example, Step 5 partly dissolved surficial ferromanganese oxides, smectites and perhaps some other alteration products. As a consequence, the Nd content of the residual material was lowered by ~20%, but ^{143}Nd/^{144}Nd did not change. Whether alteration took place in multiple stages with isotopic zonation (e.g. ferromanganese oxides should have the seawater value, palagonite may be intermediate) or whether all alteration products have reached equilibrium is not quite clear, and since acid leach undoubtedly also removes some of the Nd that once belonged to the groundmass, it is impossible to determine accurately seawater effects from leached residues, but an approximate estimate of the Nd budget distribution can be made from the data for sequential leaching steps. Assume that the water-leached residue in Step 2 represents a mixture (M) of an "unaltered" (U) intrinsic component and an "altered" (A) component. The latter must itself be a mixture of seawater and intrinsic Nd. Values for concentration and isotope ratios can be assigned from the leaching data: for M, Nd = 54 ppm, ^{143}Nd/^{144}Nd = .512779; for U, Nd is unknown and ^{143}Nd/^{144}Nd = .512936; for A, Nd = (54 ppm - Nd content of U) and ^{143}/^{144}Nd is unknown. Based on ^{143}Nd/^{144}Nd, the residue from Step 6, with 14.1 ppm Nd, still contains some seawater Nd. However, that from Steps 7 and 8, with 2.7 ppm Nd, appears to be free of a seawater component. If it is assumed that all seawater Nd has been removed at some point during Step 7, say, at an intermediate Nd concentration of 7-8 ppm, then component U contains less than 15% of the total Nd. By mass balance, component A thus has ^{143}Nd/^{144}Nd = .512752, or ϵ (0) = 3.6. Thus the bulk Nd of the unleached sample is controlled by component A, and even removal of 20% (Step 5) does not change the isotopic ratio significantly. If the isotopic composition of seawater Nd in the LSC area has not changed substantially over the past 60 My, it can be assigned a value of ~.5123 [Staudigel et al., 1985]. The seawater Nd comprises approximately 25% of the total Nd in this sample, i.e. about 13 ppm. If seawater contains 3×10^{-6} ppm [Piepgras and Wasserburg, 1980, 1982], then an effective minimum water-rock ratio of 4.5×10^6 is required. Whatever the phases holding seawater Nd, one hour leaching in 2N HCl, in addition to the initial water leaching and decanting of fine particles, seems to have removed all secondary Nd. Further leaching does not change ^{143}Nd/^{144}Nd.

Both MSN110-1 and SOTW9-48-2 showed changes in Sm/Nd ratios during leaching. For MSN110-1, the residues have higher Sm/Nd than the acid-leachable components, while in SOTW9-48-2 the opposite is true. This observation presumably reflects different partitioning of Sm and Nd in different phases, and the final proportions of these phases in the residue. Thus neither Sm/Nd nor elemental concentrations measured on leached residues are representative of the unaltered whole rock composition. Since seawater REE and other elements [Ludden and Thompson, 1979; this study; Staudigel and Hart, 1983] are exchanged during alteration, chemical data for the unleached samples, particularly those which are highly altered, may also not reflect the original composition. Therefore, for highly altered samples, chemical data for both leached and unleached samples must be used with caution in petrological interpretation.

For sample MSN110-1, no preferential leaching of Nd relative to Sm (Table 2) was observed during acid leaching steps 3-6. This result agrees with Rb/Sr systematics (Table 2), implying that changes in Rb/Sr and Sm/Nd ratios in leaching steps may be due to phase removal rather than chemical fractionation during leaching. The measured Rb/Sr and Sm/Nd ratios of leached residues therefore may be useful for age corrections on ^{87}Sr/^{86}Sr and ^{143}Nd/^{144}Nd isotopic ratios.

Alteration depends on a variety of parameters, including time of exposure to seawater as well as rock texture and composition. It should be emphasized that seawater effects on Nd isotopes are significant only for extremely altered samples, and are generally unimportant for moderately altered oceanic basalts.

4.3. Further Evidence for the Validity of Leaching

Additional evidence came from direct comparison of fresh glass and leached whole-rock powder of two old DSDP drilled basalts. Sample 462A-56-1 (9-10) is from the Nauru Basin and has an age of ~110 My; sample 238-58-1 (123-136) is from the Central Indian Ridge with an age of ~38 My. Both rocks have small amounts of fresh glass remaining in their rims and highly altered interiors (clay, carbonate and smectite). The glasses were carefully hand-picked, briefly leached in HCl and measured by J. Mahoney [this issue]. We measured the altered whole-rock powders after leaching in 6N HCl and 5% HF, as was done for the LSC samples. The data are presented in Table 5. The age-corrected ^{87}Sr/^{86}Sr and ^{143}Nd/^{144}Nd values for both the fresh glass and the leached powders are essentially the same.

5. Data Measured on Leached Samples

Data measured on the same samples in the two laboratories using different leaching methods in general agree quite well. Table 4 shows the measured and age-corrected Sr and Nd isotopic data on leached residues, and Pb isotopic data on unleached samples.

The most striking feature of the isotopic data for the Louisville Seamount Chain is the consistency of Sr, Nd and Pb isotopic compositions despite the wide variety of rock types and long temporal and spatial span represented. The total range of Sr, Nd and Pb isotopic ratios for the whole chain is considerably less than for most single oceanic islands [e.g. White and Hofmann, 1982; Zindler et al., 1982; Stille et al., 1983; Chen and Frey, 1983; Vidal et al., 1984; Duncan et al., 1986] and much smaller than for the Hawaiian Island chain [e.g. White and Hofmann, 1982; references compiled in Zindler et al., 1982; also see Figs. 4-5 in Staudigel et

TABLE 4. LSC

Sample		$^{87}Sr/^{86}Sr$	Rb^2	Sr^2	$(^{87}Sr/^{86}Sr)_i$	$^{143}Nd/^{144}Nd$
MTHN7-D-1	SIO	0.703741 ± 26	—	—		0.512939 ± 14
	LDGO	0.703747 ± 40	27.16	693		0.512953 ± 21
MTHN6-D-1	SIO	0.703808 ± 26	—	—		0.512904 ± 14
"	cpx	0.703753 ± 26	0.6287	75.71	0.703749	0.512920 ± 20
	LDGO	0.703714 ± 29	15.35	610.3		0.512871 ± 19
MSN110-1	SIO	0.703659 ± 26	12.07	824.7	0.703639	0.512930 ± 14
	LDGO	0.703638 ± 22	13.63	682		0.512933 ± 18
MSN110-B	SIO	0.703675 ± 38	44.89	754.6	0.703595	0.512932 ± 14
LV-2	LDGO	0.703205 ± 40	11.14	612		0.512897 ± 26
		0.703152 ± 32				
LV-3	LDGO	0.703538 ± 36	8.5	633		0.512942 ± 34
		0.703584 ± 45				
LV-4	LDGO	0.703340 ± 59	26.7	574.0		0.512918 ± 19
LV-5	LDGO	0.703867 ± 43	26.97	164.0		0.512825 ± 22
	SIO	0.703810 ± 26				0.512855 ± 26
SOTW9-48-2	SIO	0.703632 ± 26	8.562	1240	0.703614	0.512930 ± 14
"		0.703630 ± 26	2.066	1663	0.703627	0.512937 ± 14
	LDGO	0.703657 ± 36	87.06	568		—
SOTW9-52-1	SIO	0.703396 ± 26	26.13	620.4	0.703286	0.512888 ± 14
"	cpx	0.703289 ± 26	0.5384	66.85	0.703268	0.512912 ± 14
"	pl	0.703274 ± 26	1.014	1121	0.703272	0.512872 ± 44
SOTW9-58-1	SIO	0.703601 ± 30	1.528	127.1	0.703568	0.512902 ± 14
SOTW9-58-3	SIO	0.703561 ± 26	10.41	370.9	0.703484	0.512904 ± 18
SOTW9-58-5	SIO	0.703505 ± 64	0.5213	23.08	0.703443	0.512908 ± 14
SOTW9-58-7	SIO	0.703525 ± 38	0.6185	78.71	0.703504	0.512936 ± 14
SOTW9-58-9	SIO	0.703562 ± 32	0.1883	43.07	0.703550	0.512934 ± 14

1. All Sr and Nd isotope ratios are measured from leached residues and are age-corrected using tectonic reconstructed ages (Table 1) based on parent/daughter ratios measured from leached residues. All isotopic ratios are measured from whole rock samples except as otherwise mentioned. cpx - clinopyroxene; pl - plagioclase. All Pb isotopic ratios were measured at LDGO from unleached or lightly leached whole rock powders. Reported values are relative to NBS 981; $^{206}Pb/^{204}Pb$ = 16.9371, $^{207}Pb/^{204}Pb$ = 15.4913 and $^{208}Pb/^{204}Pb$ = 36.7213. All LDGO Sr and Nd isotopic ratios have been normalized through common standards to agree with SIO standard values for ease of comparison. At SIO, isotopic data are fractionation-corrected to $^{87}Sr/^{86}Sr$ = 0.1194 and $^{148}NdO/^{144}NdO$ = 0.242436.

al., 1984]. This is particularly remarkable as many island and seamount chains in the southern hemisphere demonstrate very large ranges in isotopic composition. For the LSC, $^{87}Sr/^{86}Sr$ varies only from 0.70321 to 0.70381, $^{143}Nd/^{144}Nd$ from 0.512821 to 0.512938 and $^{206}Pb/^{204}Pb$ from 19.128 to 19.452 (Table 4). For most of the seamounts, only one sample is available. However, multiple flow units with different chemical characteristics [Hawkins, this issue] were dredged from two localities: Osbourn seamount (SOTW9-58) and Valerie Guyot (MSN110). The Sr and Nd isotopic data for these units also show little variability (Table 4).

6. Discussion

6.1. Multiple Flow Units on Single Seamount

Different rock types often occur within a single volcanic structure. Petrologic studies on the Hawaiian Islands reveal that most islands evolved in stages from a possibly alkalic or basanitic "zero stage" [Moore et al., 1982] to a tholeiitic shield building stage, and, usually after a hiatus, into an alkali basaltic and finally nephelinitic, post-erosional stage [MacDonald, 1968]. One theory, based on geochemistry [Gast, 1968; Schilling and Winchester, 1968], is that oceanic alkalic basalts are formed from the same source which produces tholeiites, but involve smaller degrees of partial melting at greater depth. However, isotopic data show that some associated oceanic alkalic and tholeiitic basalts are from a common source [Lanphere et al., 1980; Feigenson et al., 1983; Stille et al., 1983], while others are not [Lanphere, 1983; Chen and Frey, 1983, 1985].

We analyzed five samples from Osbourn seamount (SOTW9-58-1, 3, 5, 7, 9) and two from Valerie Guyot (MSN110-1, B) which, based on their chemical differences [see Hawkins et al., this issue], are ascribed different flow units. Those from Osbourn seamount range from alkalic basalt to silica-undersaturated olivine nephelinite and basanite, apparently covering the spectrum of post-shield-building, and possibly post-erosional, stages if the Hawaiian analogue applies. Initial $^{143}Nd/^{144}Nd$ ratios of all five flow units are the same within our standard uncertainty range, while the $^{87}Sr/^{86}Sr$ variability is slightly outside standard uncertainties, but values cluster very closely. This variation could be indigenous, but may also be due to incomplete removal of seawater effects or small errors associated with the age correction. For Valerie Guyot, the two flow units have essentially identical Nd and Sr isotopic compositions. In both cases, the measured values are similar to those measured for other LSC seamounts. No tholeiites have been dredged from the LSC. However, the transitional basalts [Hawkins et al., 1985] dredged from the youngest seamounts of the LSC chain (MTHN7-D-1 and MTHN6-D-1) have the same $\epsilon(t)$ values as those of alkalic basalts from other parts of the chain. Considering

Isotopic Data[1]

Sm[2]	Nd[2]	^{143}Nd/^{144}Nd$_i$	ϵ (t)	^{206}Pb/^{204}Pb	^{207}Pb/^{204}Pb	^{208}Pb/^{204}Pb
4.319	17.20	0.512938	7.3			
5.076	21.32			19.203 ± 19	15.615 ± 16	38.921 ± 31
7.745	33.58	0.512894	6.7			
4.553	13.82	0.512906	6.9			
7.029	30.63			19.422 ± 17	15.625 ± 14	39.239 ± 40
5.424	20.47	0.512896	6.7			
7.820	33.45			19.332 ± 10	15.626 ± 8	39.127 ± 18
3.286	12.794	0.512899	6.8			
5.715	22.79			19.128 ± 6	15.574 ± 5	38.676 ± 13
7.278	31.61			19.214 ± 6	15.601 ± 4	38.991 ± 15
8.837	40.38			19.229 ± 13	15.616 ± 8	38.995 ± 24
9.473	43.87			19.300 ± 15	15.622 ± 10	39.052 ± 20
0.8188	4.399	0.512884	7.7			
1.119	5.947	0.512891				
6.819	12.68			19.452 ± 18	15.632 ± 17	39.216 ± 39
5.751	62.02	0.512832	6.8			
4.313	13.26	0.512830	6.7			
0.1702	1.166	0.512835	6.8			
4.064	13.42	0.512822	6.6			
5.029	15.94	0.512821	6.6			
4.098	14.18	0.512832	6.8			
4.258	12.37	0.512845	7.1			
5.575	17.29	0.512849	7.2			

LDGO data are fractionation-corrected to ^{87}Sr/^{86}Sr = 0.1194 and ^{146}Nd/^{144}Nd = 0.721900. Measured standard values at SIO are: ^{87}Sr/^{86}Sr = 0.710260 ± 26 for NBS 987 Sr and ^{143}Nd/^{144}Nd = 0.511859 ± 14 for La Jolla Nd standard. Uncertainties of SIO data represent total range; where the uncertainties for individual sample runs were less than this standard range, they are reported as the latter. A value of ^{143}Nd/^{144}Nd = 0.512566 corresponds to a present day epsilon value of zero for Juvinas. 2. All concentration data (ppm) are by isotope dilution mass spectrometry. SIO data for leached residue; LDGO data for unleached powder.

the absolute values and small ranges of Nd, Sr and Pb isotopic ratios, both between seamounts and for several rock types from a single seamount, a common, non-MORB source for all rock types from the LSC is indicated. This source has been quite homogeneous over its lifetime. Additional support for a homogeneous source comes from highly incompatible elemental ratios of the same samples [Hawkins et al., this issue], which also show remarkably consistent values over the entire chain. It is statistically unlikely that these randomly selected samples with a wide range in chemical composition and from different locations with different ages, would have similar Sr, Nd and Pb isotopic compositions and incompatible element ratios unless their source is truly homogeneous. It is thus unlikely that the observed homogeneity is an artifact of sampling. It is always possible that our current data fields would be broadened if more data were collected, but to first order, our sample collection must be representative of the entire LSC.

6.2. Mantle Source

Figure 5 shows the isotopic field of LSC samples on the ^{143}Nd/^{144}Nd versus ^{87}Sr/^{86}Sr plot. Also shown are some selected data from other oceanic intraplate volcanoes. In general, the LSC

TABLE 5. Comparison of Glass and Leached Powder[1]

Sample	Age (My)	^{143}Nd/^{144}Nd	^{87}Sr/^{86}Sr	^{147}Sm/^{144}Nd	^{87}Rb/^{86}Sr	Age Corrected ^{143}Nd/^{144}Nd	Age Corrected ^{87}Sr/^{86}Sr
238-58-1 (123-136)	38						
Glass		0.513022 ± 14	0.703465 ± 26	0.2312	0.07024	0.512977	0.70344
Leached Residue		0.513027 ± 14	0.703408 ± 26	0.2454	0.01537	0.512966	0.70340
462A-56-1 (9-10)	110						
Glass		0.512975 ± 14	0.703666 ± 26	0.2047	0.04400	0.512828	0.70360
Leached Residue		0.512993 ± 14	0.703629 ± 26	0.2211	0.00827	0.512834	0.70362

1. Glass data are from *J. Mahoney* [this issue; personal communication].

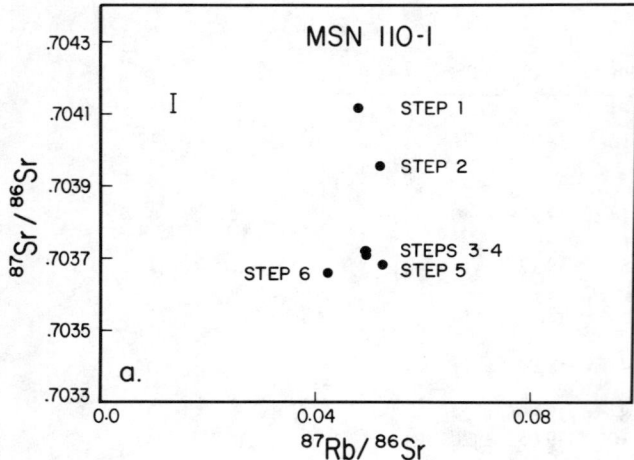

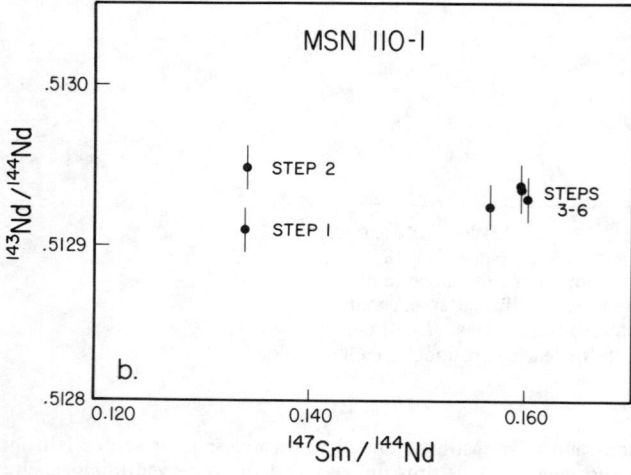

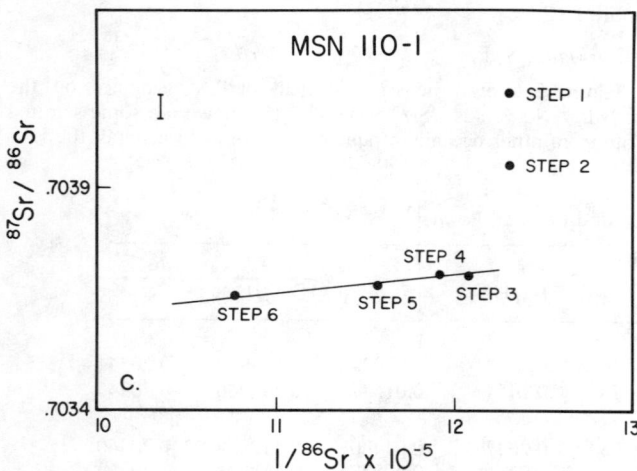

has a time-integrated depleted source relative to "primitive" mantle, but is slightly more enriched than the Hawaiian Islands and is quite similar to Bouvet Island. Figure 6 shows that the LSC data plot centrally in the $^{87}Sr/^{86}Sr$ versus $^{206}Pb/^{204}Pb$ diagram. On all plots, LSC data are restricted to small fields, the smallest among observed island or seamount chains. Therefore, the LSC source is relatively homogeneous over a time scale of more than 65 My, and slightly depleted compared to the chondritic reference value.

Such a source may be envisioned as a single homogeneous mantle source, or a consistent mixture of depleted, "primitive" and/or enriched components. In the latter case, isotopically distinct mantle reservoirs must have mixed very reproducibly, as has been discussed by Zindler and Hart [1986] for the PREMA mantle component, during at least the last 65 My. In the former case, a single homogeneous source with LSC or PREMA isotopic characteristics, whatever its previous history was, has remained isolated and unfractionated in the mantle for more than 65 My. Lacking unequivocal evidence for either case, the assumption of a homogeneous source appears less difficult to envision than a constant, reproducible mixing process over 65 My. For this reason we prefer the former interpretation for LSC source, and our following discussions are based on this assumption.

6.3. Implications for the Hotspot Theory

The LSC data on their own do little to constrain the physical and chemical structure of the mantle. It is in the framework of a hotspot origin of oceanic islands that they have important implications for mantle properties and the hotspot theory itself. First, a single homogeneous mantle source could exist on a large scale and over a long period of time. The LSC data faithfully documented such a mantle feature through upwelling chemical plume, which is distinct from the MORB source, and has not been seriously altered by interaction with lithospheric or other sublithospheric components as has been proposed for other island chains [Oskarsson et al., 1982; Chen and Frey, 1983, 1985; Staudigel et al., 1984]. Taking the total erupted volume of the LSC as 200×10^3 km^3 [Lonsdale, 1986] and assuming 10% melting of the source, the estimated LSC source is $> 2 \times 10^6$ km^3, which is about one-fifth of that estimated to be supplying the Hawaiian Emperor chain [Shaw et al., 1980].

Secondly, the data show that a single, relatively homogeneous mantle source, and its access to the surface, have survived for a long time, on the order of 100 My. This requires rather constant dynamic conditions in the source region. The fact that hotspot localities have remained roughly stationary relative to one another for the last 200 My led Morgan [1971, 1972a, b] to propose that hotspot plumes have deep roots in the mantle, unaffected by mantle convection. Mantle "blobs" would be transformed into schlier-

Fig. 4. Leaching results for sample MSN110-1. (a) $^{87}Rb/^{86}Sr$ vs. $^{87}Sr/^{86}Sr$ diagram. $^{87}Sr/^{86}Sr$ decreased from Step 1 to Step 3, but no large decline was observed after Step 3. Rb/Sr ratios did not change except for Step 6. This may result from selective dissolution during leaching and may in part be responsible for the slightly lower $^{87}Sr/^{86}Sr$ ratio as discussed in the text. (b) $^{147}Sm/^{144}Nd$ vs. $^{143}Nd/^{144}Nd$ diagram. No obvious variations of $^{143}Nd/^{144}Nd$ were observed after acid leaching despite a large change in Sm/Nd ratios. In contrast to the SOTW9-48-2 case, Sm/Nd increased with progressive leaching. (c) In the $^{87}Sr/^{86}Sr$ vs. $1/^{86}Sr$ diagram, the progressively acid-leached residues form a linear array. This line is interpreted as a mixing line between a major phase (pl) and minor phases in the rock.

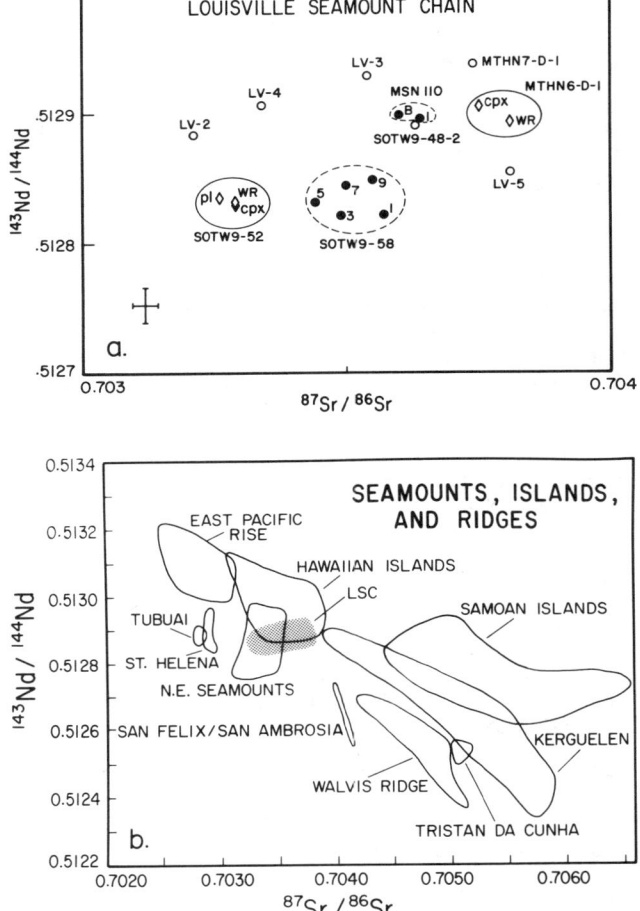
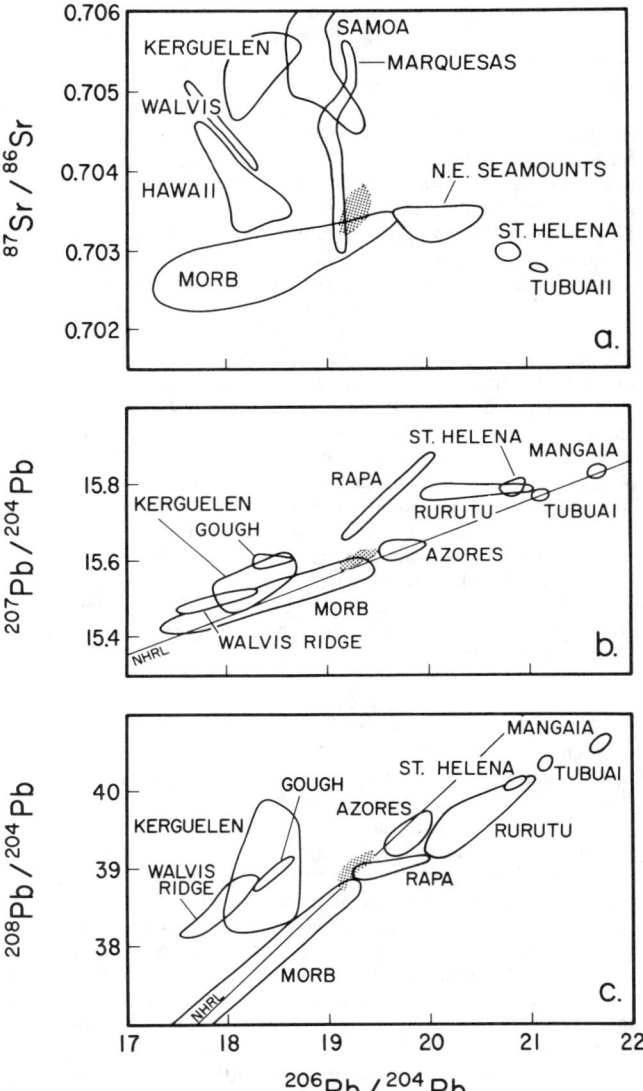

Fig. 5. ^{143}Nd/^{144}Nd vs. ^{87}Sr/^{86}Sr diagram. (a) Data for LSC seamounts show a narrow range and no MORB source involvement. Solid circles enclosed by a dashed line are multiple flows from single seamounts. Diamonds enclosed by a solid line are leached whole rock (WR) residue, clinopyroxene (CPX) and/or plagioclase (PL) from single samples. (b) LSC seamount data (shaded area) are compared to selected OIB and MORB data. Data are from DePaolo and Wasserburg [1976], O'Nions et al. [1977], Lanphere et al. [1980], Dosso and Murthy [1980], Zindler et al. and references therein [1982], White and Hofmann [1982], Richardson et al. [1982], Stille et al. [1983], Chen and Frey [1983, 1985], Staudigel et al. [1984], Vidal et al. [1984], Hart et al. [1986] and Gerlach et al. [1986].

Fig. 6. LSC seamount data (shaded areas) are compared to selected OIB and MORB data. (a) ^{87}Sr/^{86}Sr vs. ^{206}Pb/^{204}Pb; (b) ^{207}Pb/^{204}Pb vs. ^{206}Pb/^{204}Pb; and (c) ^{208}Pb/^{204}Pb vs. ^{206}Pb/^{204}Pb. NHRL is the Northern Hemisphere Reference Line [Hart, 1984]. Data are from Tatsumoto [1978], Dosso et al. [1979], Sun [1980], Allegre et al. [1980], Dosso and Murthy [1980], Zindler et al. [1982], Richardson et al. [1982], Hart [1984], Vidal et al. [1984], Hart et al. [1986] and Palacz and Saunders [1986].

en or streaks within a few hundred million years in convecting regions [McKenzie, 1979; Richter and Ribe, 1979], and thus could not act as a long-term hotspot sources. Parmentier and co-workers [1975] found that relatively narrow mantle plumes are possible flow solutions if convection is confined to the upper mantle and if heat is primarily supplied from below. Also, seismic data derived from body waves indicate that some hotspots seem to have "hot roots" extending well into the lower mantle [Richard, 1984, and references therein]. The LSC data provide geochemical evidence that this feature originates as a chemical plume tapping a relatively stationary source, probably in the non-convecting region of the lower mantle. This observation thus favors the hotspot theory in which the hotspot plumes originate from the deep mantle [Morgan, 1971, 1972a], and implies a layered mantle structure in which the lower mantle or part of the lower mantle is not convective. In this case, while a 100-200 km thick cumulative layer [Hofmann and White, 1982] and/or upper-lower mantle, mantle-core boundary layers of unknown thickness could be stationary, a stagnant lower mantle seems to be equally plausible. An alternative is that part or all of the lower mantle convects very slowly, being practically stagnant on a time scale of several hundred million years, the lifetime of hotspots.

The third important aspect of the LSC data relates to the mechanism by which a chemical plume (diapir, jet, blob, etc.) ascends through the mantle. The observed variability of isotopic ratios for oceanic islands has been attributed to either internal heterogeneity of the source or mixing with MORB source material [Stille et al., 1983; Chen and Frey, 1983; Staudigel et al., 1984; Mahoney et al., 1983]. The LSC isotopic data permit neither of these. Griffiths [1986a, b] found experimentally that rising diapirs driven by a temperature difference along (thermals) entrain materials from their surroundings, while diapirs driven by compositional difference (intrinsic) do not. Depending on the ratio of the chemical to the thermal buoyancy contribution, the amount of entrainment will vary. If this result is applicable to the mantle plume, the lack of evidence for mixing in the case of LSC suggests that the LSC plume is not a "thermal" but a "chemical" plume. This may also in part explain the observed isotopic and chemical features of oceanic islands, namely, some islands and island chains clearly show plume-MORB source mixing (e.g. Hawaii); while others do not (e.g. LSC). Thus, some heterogeneities observed in islands or seamounts may be caused by mixing, and their source regions could be more homogeneous than previously thought, examples may be St. Helena and Kerguelen [White, pers. comm.].

7. Conclusions

Leaching experiments have shown that low temperature seawater alteration can change not only $^{87}Sr/^{86}Sr$ but also $^{143}Nd/^{144}Nd$ for submarine samples, especially old exposed vesicular rocks. The degree of alteration is very much dependent on rock texture, age and geological setting. Different leaching approaches can be used to circumvent this problem. In general, strong acid leaching removes all secondary effects, even for highly altered rocks. Reliable age corrected $^{87}Sr/^{86}Sr$ and $^{143}Nd/^{144}Nd$ initial ratios can be obtained after proper leach treatment, but whole rock chemical data from extremely altered rocks may not reflect the original composition for either acid-leached or unleached fractions. Using the experience gained from the leaching experiments, isotopic compositions were measured for samples from ten LSC seamounts, including the oldest and youngest in the chain. The data show only very small variations in Sr, Nd and Pb isotopic compositions both for different rock types within the same seamount and for the LSC seamount chain as a whole. This result implies the existence of a long-lived upwelling mantle plume originating from a stationary source, and thus favors a layered mantle structure in which the lower mantle or part of the lower mantle is not or very slowly convecting. No appreciable mixing occurred between the LSC and MORB sources, which may have implications for the mechanism of plume transport.

Acknowledgments. The authors thank W. White for his thoughtful reviews and comments; P. Hey and M.B. Hiller for typing the manuscript and R. Zdvorak and E. Hegemier for drawing the illustrations. We also thank J. Mahoney for discussion and comments on an earlier draft and C. MacIsaac for laboratory assistance. This research was supported by NSF grants OCE 8416095 (JDM and GWL), OCE 8410615 (AZ), GA-30315 (JH), OCE 8515641 (HS), and ONR USN N00014-80-0440 (PL). LDGO Contribution 4149.

References

Allegre, C.J., O. Brevart, B. Dupre and J.F. Minster, Isotopic and chemical effects produced in a continuously differentiating convecting earth mantle, *Phil. Trans. R. Soc. London A297*, 447–477, 1980.

Arrhenius, G., Pelagic Sediments, in *The Sea*, ed. M.N. Hill, Interscience, 655–727, 1963.

Arrhenius, G., K. Cheung, S. Crane, M. Fisk, J. Frazer, J. Korkisch, T. Mellin, S. Nakao, A. Tsai and G. Wolf, Counterions in marine manganates, *Colloques Internationaux de C.N.R.S., No. 289*, 332–356, 1978.

Carlson, R.W., Crust-mantle differentiation on the earth and moon: evidence from isotopic studies for contrasting mechanisms and duration, Ph.D. thesis, Univ. of Calif. at San Diego.

Casenave, A. and K. Dominh, Geoid heights over the Louisville Ridge (South Pacific), *J. Geophys. Res.* 89, 11171–11179, 1984.

Casenave, A., B. Lago and K. Dominh, Thermal parameters of the oceanic lithosphere estimated from geoid height data, *J. Geophys. Res.* 88, 1105–1118, 1983.

Chapman, H.J., E.T.C. Spooner and J.D. Smewing, $^{87}Sr/^{86}Sr$ enrichment of ophiolitic rocks from Troodos, Cyprus indicates seawater interaction, *EOS* 56, 1074, 1975.

Chase, C.G., Tectonic history of the Fiji Plateau, *Geol. Soc. Am. Bull.* 82, 3087–3110, 1971.

Chen, C.-Y. and F.A. Frey, Origin of Hawaiian tholeiite alkalic basalts, *Nature* 302, 785–, 1983.

Chen, C.-Y. and F.A. Frey, Trace element and isotopic geochemistry of lavas from Haleakala volcano, East Maui, Hawaii: Implications for the origin of Hawaiian basalts, *J. Geophys. Res.* 90, 8743–8768, 1985.

Chen, J.H, Uranium-lead isotope ages from the Southern Sierra Nevada batholith and adjacent areas, California, Ph.D. Thesis, University of California, Santa Barbara, 183 pp., 1977.

Clague, D.A. and R.D. Jarrard, Tertiary plate motion deduced from Hawaiian Emperor Chain, *Geol. Soc. Am. Bull.* 84, 1135–1154, 1973.

DePaolo, D.J. and G.J. Wasserburg, Nd isotopic variations and petrogenetic models, *Geophys. Res. Lett.* 3, 249–252, 1976.

Dixon, T.H. and M.E. Parke, Bathymetry estimates in the southern oceans from Seasat altimetry, *Nature* 304, 406–411, 1983.

Dosso, L. and V.R. Murthy, A Nd isotopic study of the Kerguelen islands: Inferences on enriched oceanic mantle sources, *Earth Planet. Sci. Lett.* 48, 268–276, 1980.

Dosso, L., P. Vidal, J.M. Cantagrel, J. Lameyre, A. Marot and S. Zimine, Kerguelen: Continental fragment or oceanic island?: Petrology and isotopic geochemistry evidence, *Earth Planet. Sci. Lett.* 43, 46–60, 1979.

Duncan, R.A., M.T. McCulloch, H.G. Barsczus and D.R. Nelson, Plume versus lithospheric sources for melts at Ua Pou, Marquesas Islands, *Nature* 322, 534–538, 1986.

Edwards, A.R., Calcareous nannofossils from the Southwest Pacific, *Init. Rept. DSDP, Leg 21*, 641–691, 1973.

Epp, D., Age and tectonic relationship among volcanic chains on the Pacific plate, Ph.D. dissertation, Univ. of Hawaii, Honolulu, HI, 1978.

Ewing, M., Z. Le Pichon and J. Ewing, Crustal structure of the mid-ocean ridges, *J. Geophys. Res.* 71, 319–339, 1966.

Feigenson, M.D., A.W. Hofmann and F.J. Spera, Case studies on the origin of basalt II: The transition from tholeiitic to alkalic volcanism on Kohala volcano, Hawaii, *Contr. Mineral. Petrol.* 84, 382–389, 1983.

Gast, P.W., Trace element fractionation and origin of tholeiitic and alkaline magma types, *Geochim. Cosmochim. Acta* 32, 1057–1086, 1968.

Gerlach, D.C., S.R. Hart, V.W.J. Morales and C. Palacios, Mantle heterogeneity beneath the Nazca plate: San Felix and Juan Fernandez islands, *Nature* 322, 165–169, 1986.

Griffiths, R.W., Dynamics of mantle thermals with constant buoyancy or anomalous internal heating, *Earth Planet. Sci. Lett.* 78, 435–446, 1986a.

Griffiths, R.W., Differing effects of compositional and thermal buoyancies on the evolution of mantle diapirs, *Phys. Earth Planet. Int.* 43, 261–273, 1986b.

Hart, S.R., K, Rb, Cs, Sr and Ba contents and Sr isotopic composition of ocean floor basalts, *Phil. Trans. R. Soc. London A268*, 573–587, 1971.

Hart, S.R., A large-scale isotope anomaly in the Southern Hemisphere mantle, *Nature* 309, 753–757, 1984.

Hart, S.R. and C. Brooks, The geochemistry and evolution of the early precambrian mantle, *Contr. Mineral. Petrol.* 61, 109–128, 1977.

Hart, S.R., D.C. Gerlach and W.M. White, A possible new Sr-Nd-Pb mantle array and consequences for mantle mixing, *Geochim. Cosmochim. Acta* 50, 1551–1557, 1986.

Hawkins, J.W., Geology of the Louisville Ridge--a possible hot spot trace (abst.) *EOS* 54, 1221, 1973.

Hawkins, J.W., P. Lonsdale and R. Batiza, Petrologic evolution of the Louisville "Ridge" (abst.), *EOS* 66, 405, 1985.

Hawkins, J.W., P. Lonsdale and R. Batiza, Petrologic evolution of the Louisville seamount chain, this issue.

Hayes, D.E. and M. Ewing, The Louisville Ridge--a possible extension of the Eltanin Fracture Zone, in *Antarctic Oceanology I*, ed. Reid, J.I., 223–228, Antarctic Res. Series 15, Am. Geophys. Un., 1971.

Hofmann, A.W. and W.M. White, Mantle plumes from ancient oceanic crust, *Earth Planet. Sci. Lett.*, 57, 421–436, 1982.

Lanphere, M.A., $^{87}Sr/^{86}Sr$ ratios for basalt from Loihi Seamount, Hawaii, *Earth Planet. Sci. Lett.* 66, 380–387, 1983.

Lanphere, M.A. and G.B. Dalrymple, Age and strontium isotopic composition of the Honolulu volcanic series, Oahu, Hawaii, *Am. J. Sci. 280A*. 736–751, 1980.

Lanphere, M.A., G.B. Dalrymple and D.A. Clague, Rb-Sr systematics of basalts from the Hawaiian-Emperor volcanic chain, *Init. Rept. DSDP, Leg 55*, 695–706, 1980.

Larson, R.L. and C.G. Chase, Late Mesozoic evolution of the western Pacific Ocean, *Geol. Soc. Am. Bull.* 83, 3627–3644, 1972.

Larson, R.L., S.C. Cande, J.H. Bodine and A.B. Watts, The origin of the Eltanin Fracture Zone (abst.), *EOS* 60, 957, 1979.

Lonsdale, P., Geography and history of the Louisville hot spot chain in the southwest Pacific, *J. Geophys. Res.*, in press.

Ludden, J.N. and G. Thompson, An evaluation of the behavior of the rare earth elements during the weathering of seafloor basalt, *Earth Planet. Sci. Lett.* 43, 85–92, 1979.

Lugmair, G.W., N.B. Scheinin and K. Marti, Sm-Nd age and history of Apollo 17 basalt 75075: Evidence for early lunar differentiation of the lunar exterior, Proc. 6th Lunar Sci. Conf., *Geochim. Cosmochim. Acta* 6, 1419–1429, 1975.

MacDonald, G.A., Composition and origin of the Hawaiian lavas, *Mem. Geol. Soc. Am.* 116, 477–522, 1968.

Mahoney, J.J., An isotopic survey of Pacific oceanic plateaus: implications for their nature and origin, this issue.

Mahoney, J.J., J.D. Macdougall and G.W. Lugmair, Kerguelen hotspot source for Rajmahal Traps and Ninetyeast Ridge?, *Nature* 303, 385–389, 1983.

McKenzie, D.P., Finite deformation during fluid flow, *Geophys. J.R. Astron. Soc.*, 58, 689–715, 1979.

Menard, H.W., S.M. Smith and T.E. Chase, Guyots in the southwestern Pacific basin, *Geol. Soc. Am. Bull.* 75, 145–148, 1964.

Morgan, W.J., Convection plumes in the lower mantle, *Nature* 230, 42–43, 1971.

Morgan, W.J., Deep mantle convection plumes and plate motions, *Amer. Ass. Petrol. Geol. Bull.* 56, 203–213, 1972a.

Morgan, W.J., Plate motions and deep mantle convection, *Geol. Sci. Am. Mem.* 132, 7–22, 1972b.

Molnar, P., T. Atwater, J. Mammerickx and S.M. Smith, Magnetic anomalies, bathymetry and the tectonic evolution of the south Pacific since the late Cretaceous, *Geophys. J.R. Astron. Soc.* 40, 383–420, 1975.

Moore, J.G., D.A. Clague and W.R. Normark, Diverse basalt types from Loihi Seamount, Hawaii, *Geology* 10, 88–92, 1982.

O'Nions, R.K., P.J. Hamilton and N.M. Evenson, Variations in $^{143}Nd/^{144}Nd$ and $^{87}Sr/^{86}Sr$ ratios in oceanic basalts, *Earth Planet. Sci. Lett.* 34, 13–22, 1977.

Oskarsson, N., S. Steinthorsson and G.E. Sigvaldason, Iceland geothermal anomaly: Origin, volcanotectonics, chemical fractionation, and isotope evolution of the crust, *J. Geophys. Res.* 90, 10011–10025, 1985.

Palacz, Z.A. and A.D. Saunders, Coupled trace element and isotope enrichment in the Cook-Austral-Samoa islands, southwest Pacific, *Earth Planet. Sci. Lett.* 79, 270–280, 1986.

Parmentier, E.M., D.L. Turcotte and K.E. Torrance, Numerical experiments on the structure of mantle plumes, *J. Geophys. Res.* 80, 4417–4424, 1975.

Piepgras, D.J. and G.J. Wasserburg, Neodymium isotopic variations in seawater, *Earth Planet. Sci. Lett.* 50, 128–138, 1980.

Piepgras, D.J. and G.J. Wasserburg, Isotopic composition of neodymium in waters from the Drake Passage, *Science* 217, 207–214, 1982.

Piper, D.Z., Rare earth elements in ferromanganese nodules and other marine phases, *Geochim. Cosmochim. Acta* 38, 1007–1022, 1974.

Richard, A.K., Developing a big picture of Earth's mantle, *Science* 225, 702–703, 1984.

Richard, P., N. Shimizu and C.J. Allegre, $^{143}Nd/^{144}Nd$, a natural tracer: an application to oceanic basalts, *Earth Planet. Sci. Lett.* 31, 269–278, 1976.

Richardson, S.H., A.J. Erlank, A.R. Duncan and D.L. Reid, Correlated Nd, Sr and Pb isotope variation in Walvis Ridge basalts and implications for the evolution of their mantle source, *Earth Planet. Sci. Lett.* 59, 327–342, 1982.

Richter, F.M. and N.M. Ribe, On the importance of advection in determining the local isotopic composition of the mantle, *Earth Planet. Sci. Lett.* 43, 212–222, 1979.

Sandwell, D.T., A detailed view of the south Pacific geoid from satellite altimetry, *J. Geophys. Res.* 89, 1089–1104, 1984.

Schilling, J.-G. and J.W. Winchester, Rare earth contribution to the origin of Hawaiian lavas, *Contrib. Mineral. Petrol.* 23, 27–37, 1969.

Schroeder, W., The empirical age-depth relation and depth anomalies in the Pacific Ocean basin, *J. Geophys. Res.*, 89, 9837–9883, 1984.

Shaw, H.F. and G.J. Wasserburg, Sm-Nd in marine carbonates and phosphates: Implication for Nd isotopes in seawater and crustal age, *Geochim. Cosmochim. Acta* 49, No. 2, 503–512, 1985.

Shaw, H.R., E.D. Jackson and K.E. Bargar, Volcanic periodicity along the Hawaiian-Emperor chain, *Am. J. Sci.* 280A, 667–708, 1980.

Spooner, E.T.C., The strontium isotopic composition of seawater and seawater-oceanic crust interaction, *Earth Planet. Sci. Lett.* 31, 167–174, 1976.

Staudigel, H. and S.R. Hart, Alteration of basaltic glass: Mechanisms and significance for the oceanic crust-seawater budget, *Geochim. Cosmochim. Acta* 47, 337–350, 1983.

Staudigel, H., A. Zindler, S.R. Hart, T. Leslie, C.-Y. Chen and D. Clague, The isotope systematics of a juvenile intraplate volcano: Pb, Nd and Sr isotope ratios of basalts from Loihi Seamount, Hawaii, *Earth Planet. Sci. Lett.* 69, 13–29, 1984.

Staudigel, H., P. Doyle and A. Zindler, Sr and Nd isotope systematics in fish teeth, *Earth Planet. Sci. Lett.*, 76, 45–56, 1985.

Stille, P., D.M. Unruh and M. Tatsumoto, Pb, Sr, Nd and Hf isotopic evidence of multiple sources for Oahu, Hawaii basalts, *Nature* 304, 25–29, 1983.

Sun, S.S., Lead isotopic study of young volcanic rocks from mid-ocean ridges, ocean islands and island arcs, *Phil. Trans. R. Soc. London*, Ser. A297, 409–445, 1980.

Tatsumoto, M., Isotopic composition of lead in oceanic basalt and its implication to mantle evolution, *Earth Planet. Sci. Lett.*, 38, 63–87, 1978.

Vial, P., C. Chanvel and R. Brousse, Large mantle heterogeneity beneath French Polynesia, *Nature* 307, 536–538, 1984.

Watts, A.B., J.K. Weissel, R. Duncan and R.L. Larson, The origin of the Louisville Ridge and its relationship to the Eltanin fracture zone system (abstr.), *EOS* 66, 360, 1985.

Watts, A.B., J.K. Weissel, R.A. Duncan and R.L. Larson, The origin of the Louisville Ridge and its relationship to the Eltanin Fracture Zone system, *J. Geophys. Res.*, in press, 1986.

White, W.M., Sources of oceanic basalts: Radiogenic isotopic evidence, *Geology* 13, 115–118, 1985.

White, W.M. and A.W. Hofmann, Sr and Nd isotope geochemistry of oceanic basalts and mantle evolution, *Nature* 296, 821–825, 1982.

Zindler, A. and S.R. Hart, Chemical geodynamics, *Ann. Rev. Earth Planet. Sci.* 14, 493–571, 1986.

Zindler, A., S.R. Hart, F.A. Frey and S.P. Jakobsson, Nd and Sr isotope ratios and rare earth element abundances in Reykjanes Peninsula basalt: Evidence for mantle heterogeneity beneath Iceland, *Earth Planet. Sci. Lett.* 45, 249–262, 1979.

Zindler, A., E. Jagoutz and S. Goldstein, Nd, Sr and Pb isotopic systematics in a three-component mantle: A new perspective, *Nature* 298, 519–523, 1982.

^{40}Ar/^{39}Ar AGE, PETROLOGY, AND TECTONIC SIGNIFICANCE OF SOME SEAMOUNTS IN THE GULF OF ALASKA

G. Brent Dalrymple, David A. Clague, and Tracy L. Vallier

U.S. Geological Survey, Menlo Park, California 94025

H. William Menard

Scripps Institution of Oceanography, La Jolla, California 92093

Abstract. New petrographic, geochemical, and ^{40}Ar/^{39}Ar age data on Welker Guyot, Patton Seamount, Murray Guyot, Miller Seamount, and Pathfinder Seamount, when considered with previously published data, show that the majority of seamounts in the Gulf of Alaska formed by mid-plate, rather than ridge-associated, volcanic processes. Lavas recovered by dredging from Welker, Patton, Murray, and Pathfinder include alkalic basalt, hawaiite, mugearite, benmoreite, and trachyte, which are typical of mid-plate volcanoes. Lavas from Miller Seamount are tholeiitic basalt and basalt transitional between tholeiitic and alkalic basalt, which are typical of volcanoes associated with accretionary processes at spreading ridges. These genetic associations are confirmed by the age data, which show that Miller was constructed on younger crust than the other four seamounts. ^{40}Ar/^{39}Ar age spectra show the following ages for the five seamounts: Welker 14.9±0.3 m.y., Patton 29.7±0.3 m.y., Murray 27.6±0.2 m.y., Miller 25.8±2.1 m.y., and Pathfinder 23.1±0.2 m.y. Welker Guyot is too old to be part of the hot spot trace proposed by Turner et al. [1980] for other dated volcanoes in the Pratt-Welker chain unless the velocity of volcanic propagation changed just before and after Welker formed. It seems more likely that the volcanoes in this chain were formed by at least two episodes of mid-plate volcanism as well as volcanism associated with spreading ridges. The ^{40}Ar/^{39}Ar ages of Patton and Murray are much older than the 2-8 m.y. age suggested by their shallow depth and basement swell height; they apparently sit on crust that has been recently thermally rejuvenated. The volcanic "chains" in the Gulf of Alaska were formed by multiple episodes of intermittent mid-plate volcanism and by volcanism associated with spreading ridges rather than by the persistent volcanic activity typically associated with hot-spot chains elsewhere on the Pacific Plate. Their apparent alignment is in part fortuitous.

Copyright 1987 by the American Geophysical Union.

Introduction

The Gulf of Alaska contains about three dozen major seamounts and guyots whose relief above the sea floor exceeds 1000 m (Figure 1). Murray [1941, 1946] speculated that these seamounts are volcanoes and noted that they form three ranges that are similar in alignment and direction to the Hawaiian and other island chains to the southwest. Menard and Dietz [1951], on the basis of more detailed bathymetry, confirmed the volcanic origin of the seamounts and, following Hess [1946], proposed that the guyots were former volcanic islands that had been flattened by wave erosion and submerged. They, too, noted the approximate alignment of the volcanoes along three sub-parallel chains and named the northern one the Pratt-Welker chain.

Following Wilson's [1963] hypothesis that the Hawaiian Islands were formed progressively as the lithosphere moved over a fixed source of lava within the mantle, Morgan [1972a,b] suggested that the Pratt-Welker, Hawaiian-Emperor, Tuamotu-Line, and Austral-Gilbert-Marshall chains were generated by rotation of the Pacific plate over four fixed hot spots, which he proposed were caused by thermal plumes in the asthenosphere. Morgan located the Pratt-Welker hot spot near Cobb Seamount on the west flank of the Juan de Fuca Ridge. Based on geometry and the existence of a continuous acoustic basement ridge, Silver et al. [1974] agreed that the Pratt-Welker chain, which they called the Kodiak-Bowie chain, is a continuous chain of volcanoes and proposed that the hot spot is located on the spreading ridge at or near the Dellwood Knolls. They noted that the curvature of the Pratt-Welker and other Gulf of Alaska chains was concave away from, instead of toward, the proposed pole of rotation and suggested that this reversed curvature was due to slow relative motion between the Hawaiian and Pratt-Welker hot spots.

Turner et al. [1973, 1980] dated six volcanoes to test the hot-spot hypothesis for the origin of the Pratt-Welker chain. They found that alkali basalt and

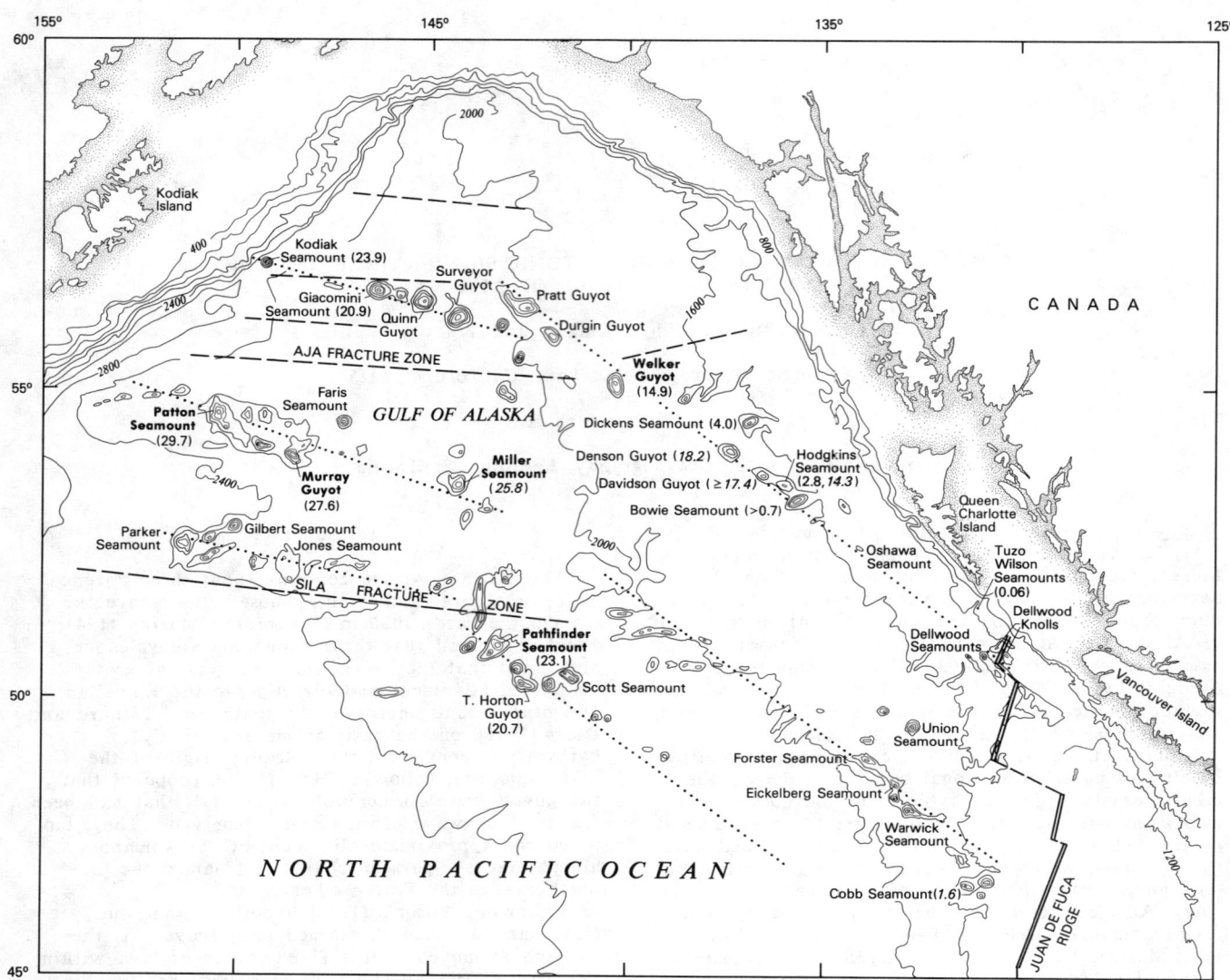

Fig. 1. Bathymetric map showing major seamounts, fracture zones (dashed lines), and spreading ridges (shaded bars) in and near the Gulf of Alaska. Seamounts and guyots included in the present study are shown in bold lettering. Dotted lines show the alignment of seamounts proposed by Smoot [1985]. Contour interval 400 fm. After Chase et al. [1970].

trachyte from Kodiak, Giacomini, Dickins, Hodgkins, and Bowie seamounts are age progressive with a volcanic propagation rate of 4.4 cm/yr or 0.88°m.y. about a pole of rotation at about 70°N and 95°W. This rotation rate is somewhat slower and the pole position closer to the Pacific Plate than those found for other age-progressive chains in the Pacific [Clague and Jarrard, 1973; Jackson, 1976; Jarrard and Clague, 1977; McDougall and Duncan, 1980]. In addition, the summit depths of these volcanoes are consistent with the relatively shallow depths predicted from thermal rejuvenation and subsequent reageing of the lithosphere after passage over a hot spot [Parsons and Sclater, 1977; Detrick and Crough, 1978; Crough, 1983]. Transitional basalt from Denson, Davidson, and Hodgkins, however, are older than predicted and the summit depths of Denson and Davidson are greater than expected for a hot spot origin. On the basis of these findings, Turner et al. [1980] concluded that the Pratt-Welker Guyot chain had a complex origin, with some of the seamounts formed over a hot spot just southeast of Bowie Seamount and others generated at or near the spreading ridge. Cousens et al. [1985] suggested that the Pratt-Welker hot spot was near the Tuzo Wilson Seamounts because of the occurrence there of hawaiite.

Lambeck et al. [1984] used geoid height anomalies to determine the effective flexural rigidity of the crust beneath each of the Pratt-Welker seamounts and, from this, their state of isostatic compensation. They found that Denson, Davidson, and Hodgkins are locally compensated, as expected for near-ridge generated volcanoes, whereas the others were more regionally compensated, which is consistent with their origin as mid-plate volcanoes that formed on older but thermally rejuvenated crust. They agreed with Turner et al. [1980] that the volcanoes of the chain were due to at least two mechanisms of origin.

Duncan and Clague [1985], using some preliminary ages from this study, reevaluated the data for the Pratt-Welker chain and for the Cobb-Eickelberg chain, a presumed chain to the south of Pratt-Welker that includes Cobb, T. Horton, Miller and Murray. They found that the age-distance data for both chains were complex and concluded that the rates of relative motion for the Pratt-Welker and Cobb-Eickelberg chains were more nearly 6-7 cm/yr ($0.95°$/m.y.) about a pole of rotation at $68°N, 75°W$.

In contrast to most previous workers, Smoot [1985] proposed that the seamounts in the Gulf of Alaska originated primarily as a result of volcanism at spreading ridges and that they constitute three older and three younger sub-parallel volcanic chains (Figure 1). He speculated that the bends separating the older and younger chains result from the "jamming" of the subduction mechanism of the western Aleutian Trench about 17 m.y. ago, which resulted in a clockwise rotation of the spreading vector of about $23°$.

We have acquired geochemical and $^{40}Ar/^{39}Ar$ age data on 5 additional volcanoes in an effort to clarify the origin of seamounts in the Gulf of Alaska (Fig. 1). Of particular interest in our study are the seamounts to the south of the Pratt-Welker chain, for which few data are available. Three of the seamounts sampled (Patton, Murray, and Miller) lie along a lineament to the south of the Aja fracture zone that is sub-parallel to the western portion of the Pratt-Welker chain (Figure 1). Pathfinder Seamount is in the central portion of a third sub-parallel lineament that includes Parker and Scott seamounts. Pathfinder is slightly to the northwest of T. Horton Guyot, which, on the basis of its age and depth, appears to have been generated by mid-plate volcanism [Turner et al., 1980]. Both Turner et al. [1980] and Lambeck et al. [1984] concluded that the origin of Welker Guyot, which is geographically part of the Pratt-Welker chain, is ambiguous as both its summit platform depth and degree of isostatic compensation are intermediate between mid-plate and ridge-generated volcanoes.

Dredging

The samples were dredged at 11 sites on six seamounts during cruises by the U. S. Geological Survey vessels SEA SOUNDER and S.P. LEE in 1979 (cruise S6-79) and 1980 (cruise L3-80) (Table 1). The rocks in the dredge hauls were sorted on shipboard to separate the ice-rafted debris from the in situ volcanic rocks. In general, the in situ volcanic rocks formed a compositionally consistent group of lava flow fragments and volcaniclastic sedimentary rocks. Rounded, striated, and faceted rocks were presumed to be ice rafted and were discarded. In addition, Mn crusts on ice-rafted rocks tended to be very thin or absent in contrast to the relatively thick Mn crusts on the in situ volcanic rocks [Koski, in press].

Further sorting of in situ from iced-rafted rocks was done on the basis of thin section examination; approximately one dozen samples that appeared to represent allochthonous rocks were eliminated from further study. Two analyzed samples, one from Gilbert and another from Welker, were later rejected because their major-element chemistry resembled that of island-arc andesite rather than ocean-island tholeiitic or alkalic rocks.

We recovered in situ volcanic rocks in two dredges from Welker, four from Patton, two from Pathfinder, and one each from Miller and Murray (Table 1). Ice-rafted debris dominated both dredge hauls from Welker but 19 rock fragments from dredge 1 and 33 from dredge 2 appeared to be in situ volcanic flow and volcaniclastic rocks, the former including hawaiite, mugearite, and benmoreite. The single dredge from Miller Seamount recovered more than 20 specimens of volcanic rock, volcanic breccia, conglomerate, and siltstone. The lavas include tholeiitic basalt and basalt transitional between tholeiitic and alkalic basalt; all have been altered by submarine weathering. The samples from Murray Guyot are fragments of pillow lava plus volcanigenic sandstone, siltstone, and hyaloclastite. The lavas are all hawaiite.

Three of the four successful dredges on Patton Seamount recovered primarily ice-rafted debris with a minor quantity of in situ volcanic rocks, but about 45 kg of in situ volcanic rock, including pillow lava fragments, volcanic breccia, and tuff, were recovered in dredge 9, cruise S6-79. Hawaiite is the dominant lava type although mugearite and benmoreite were also recovered.

The two dredges from Pathfinder Seamount contained an assortment of lavas including alkalic basalt, hawaiite, and trachyte; the trachyte was confined to the shallower of the two dredges. The dredge from Gilbert Seamount contained only ice-rafted material.

Except where ambiguous, we refer to individual samples by dredge and specimen number (e.g., 1-10) and omit the cruise designator (S6-79 and L3-80).

Petrography and Chemistry

We determined whole-rock major- and selected trace-element compositions for 37 samples from Welker (Table 2), Miller (Table 3), Murray (Table 4), Patton (Table 5), and Pathfinder (Table 6) seamounts. Despite careful sampling of the dredge contents to select the freshest samples, most of the analyzed samples are moderately altered. Many of the samples have interstitial glass replaced by clays or phosphorite. Most of the samples studied are encased in thick crusts of Mn-oxides which have also penetrated the rocks along fractures, [Koski, in press]. Despite the alteration, a number of samples have glassy selvages on pillow fragments or glassy fragments in hyaloclastite. Microprobe analyses of these glasses from Welker, Miller, Patton, and Pathfinder seamounts are listed in Table 7.

TABLE 1. Location and Depths of Dredged Samples

Dredge No.	Seamount	Latitude	Longitude	Water Depth (m)
6-79-1	Welker	55° 06.4'N	140° 27.7'W	2200-2100
S6-79-2	Welker	55° 07.5'N	140° 25.6'W	1400
S6-79-4	Miller	53° 32.6'N	144° 22.4'W	2100
S6-79-5	Murray	53° 56.5'N	148° 31.5'W	2200
S6-79-6	Patton	54° 30.9'N	150° 33.8'W	1800-1700
S6-79-8	Patton	54° 35.9'N	150° 22.1'W	750-700
S6-79-9	Patton	54° 39.6'N	150° 11.8'W	1500-1300
L3-80-7	Patton	54° 31.0'N	150° 31.3'W	450
L3-80-3	Pathfinder	50° 56.3'N	143° 16.1'W	850
L3-80-4	Pathfinder	50° 58.7'N	143° 22.6'W	1150
L3-80-5	Gilbert	52° 48.3'N	150° 07.9'W	2300-1800

Relative rare-earth-element (REE) compositions commonly are little changed by moderate alteration, even in volcanic glass (Staudigel and Hart, 1983), and have proved to be valuable in evaluating the original composition of altered submarine volcanic rocks. Twenty-nine of the samples in this study were analyzed by instrumental neutron activation analysis (INAA) and the REE results are listed in Tables 8 and 9.

Welker Guyot

Dredge 1 recovered benmoreite (samples 1-6, 1-10, and 1-12) and hawaiite (samples 1-2, 1-13, and 1-15) which occur both as angular (pillow?) fragments and as monolithic volcanic breccia and hyaloclastite. The benmoreite contains rare microphenocrysts of olivine, plagioclase, and titanomagnetite and even more rare clinopyroxene and amphibole in a glassy matrix. The hawaiite contains about 2% olivine, altered to iddingsite, and 4% large, zoned plagioclase phenocrysts in a highly altered groundmass that is partly replaced by phosphorite.

Dredge 2 recovered abundant volcanic breccia, fragments of hawaiite similar to that in dredge 1, and mugearite. The hawaiite fragments contain about 2% olivine replaced by fibrous clay, and 4% plagioclase phenocrysts in an altered glassy groundmass. Samples 2-13, 2-19, and 2-26 represent this lithology; sample 2-23 is similar but contains more abundant phenocrysts, especially of olivine. The mugearite fragments contain about 10% plagioclase, 2% olivine, 1% clinopyroxene, and rare titanomagnetite microphenocrysts; sample 2-25 is the sole analyzed example of this lithology.

The volcanic breccia recovered in dredge 2 contains a range of lithologies including phyric and aphyric hawaiite; mugearite with 5% plagioclase, 1% clinopyroxene, and rare titanomagnetite and apatite;

TABLE 2. Whole-Rock Analyses of Samples From Welker Guyot (S6-79)

	1-2	1-6	1-12	1-13	1-15	2-13	2-19	2-25	2-26
SiO_2	46.0	56.1	53.0	42.5	47.9	48.1	48.1	51.0	47.0
Al_2O_3	17.4	16.9	17.3	17.9	17.7	18.6	18.6	18.5	19.0
Fe_2O_3	8.58	7.30	7.14	10.4	6.37	4.15	8.13	7.56	5.42
FeO	1.80	2.15	2.35	1.21	3.88	4.92	2.71	2.36	4.39
MgO	3.21	1.45	1.53	2.93	3.16	2.90	2.54	1.73	2.61
CaO	8.94	4.21	3.94	10.3	9.90	8.57	9.02	6.78	8.24
Na_2O	4.20	6.02	5.42	3.62	4.01	3.84	3.93	4.67	4.16
K_2O	1.45	2.84	2.80	0.88	1.24	1.59	1.48	2.21	1.61
H_2O^+	1.63	0.41	3.01	2.11	1.05	1.54	0.95	1.01	1.59
H_2O^-	2.62	0.87	1.83	2.73	1.31	2.23	1.37	1.20	2.46
TiO_2	2.44	1.17	1.21	2.72	2.50	2.98	2.86	2.05	3.10
P_2O_5	0.96	0.45	0.40	2.14	0.85	0.56	0.84	0.86	0.54
MnO	0.13	0.22	0.25	0.59	0.21	0.15	0.15	0.15	0.14
CO_2	0.19	0.10	0.15	0.35	0.15	0.04	0.10	0.06	0.04
Total	99.6	100.1	100.3	100.4	100.2	100.2	100.8	100.1	100.3
Ba	400	830	730	320	310	280	300	400	280
Nb	42	68	78	52	44	40	44	46	50
Rb	-	-	-	40	-	25	19	-	-
Sr	660	490	755	755	745	645	675	635	675
Zr	280	575	605	280	265	305	280	435	295
Y	98	64	56	180	52	42	57	40	42
Ni	17	6	10	91	31	25	34	22	29
V	210	40	20	200	250	220	220	140	250
Ga	31	32	30	24	28	29	29	31	32

Analysts: L. Espos for x-ray fluorescence major oxides and Rb, Sr, and Zr; M. Taylor for H_2O^+, H_2O^-, CO_2, and FeO; and C. Heropoulos for emission spectroscopy Ba, Nb, Y, V, and Ga; not analyzed -. Oxides in wt %, trace elements in ppm.

TABLE 3. Whole-Rock Analyses of Samples From Miller Seamount (S6-79)

	4-3	4-4	4-5	4-10	4-12
SiO_2	47.6	47.4	43.2	48.2	48.2
Al_2O_3	15.7	15.9	16.3	16.1	16.3
Fe_2O_3	5.70	5.30	9.71	5.82	6.83
FeO	4.89	5.59	2.05	4.84	3.85
MgO	5.00	5.07	4.72	4.97	5.13
CaO	12.7	12.6	14.1	12.3	12.5
Na_2O	3.36	3.17	3.04	3.26	3.33
K_2O	0.45	0.39	0.39	0.47	0.39
H_2O^+	0.40	0.51	1.26	0.52	0.46
H_2O^-	1.01	1.11	1.38	1.42	0.90
TiO_2	1.81	1.83	1.58	1.83	1.84
P_2O_5	0.88	0.85	2.15	0.55	0.63
MnO	0.14	0.16	0.22	0.13	0.14
CO_2	0.18	0.24	0.44	0.09	0.13
Total	99.8	100.1	100.5	100.5	100.6
Ba	52	76	170	44	52
Nb	<20	<20	<20	<20	<20
Rb	-	<10	-	11	-
Sr	270	255	295	260	270
Zr	95	95	65	80	95
Y	37	40	37	32	36
Ni	40	30	85	30	45
V	260	270	270	250	250
Ga	18	20	17	15	14

Analysts: same as Table 2. Not analyzed -.
Oxides in wt %, trace elements in ppm.

TABLE 4. Whole-Rock Analyses of Samples From Murray Guyot (S6-79)

	5-3	5-4	5-10	5-11
SiO_2	47.3	45.8	47.5	46.2
Al_2O_3	15.0	15.2	14.8	14.9
Fe_2O_3	10.6	11.2	10.7	11.3
FeO	2.90	2.83	2.82	2.87
MgO	3.11	3.32	3.35	3.43
CaO	7.91	7.73	7.96	7.59
Na_2O	4.00	3.68	4.05	3.72
K_2O	1.65	1.55	1.64	1.72
H_2O^+	1.38	1.72	1.34	1.60
H_2O^-	2.27	2.59	2.25	3.18
TiO_2	2.68	2.64	2.61	2.63
P_2O_5	1.31	1.26	1.32	1.28
MnO	0.13	0.13	0.12	0.11
CO_2	0.35	0.10	0.13	0.09
Total	100.6	99.8	100.6	100.6
Ba	250	220	240	230
Nb	32	38	32	30
Rb	-	140	-	-
Sr	415	410	390	405
Zr	310	270	280	280
Y	70	65	61	59
Ni	6	12	<2	6
V	73	68	58	66
Ga	24	25	22	28

Analysts; same as Table 2. Not analyzed -
Oxides in wt %, trace elements in ppm.

TABLE 6. Whole-Rock Analyses of Samples From Pathfinder Seamount (L3-80)

	3-5	3-5A	3-13	4-6	4-10	4-11	4-19	4-20
SiO_2	60.3	60.8	59.2	46.6	48.0	48.2	44.7	44.5
Al_2O_3	17.9	18.5	17.7	15.9	15.7	13.9	15.7	15.9
Fe_2O_3	3.80	2.35	5.17	8.42	7.31	8.76	8.74	9.48
FeO	2.09	1.91	1.84	3.40	4.04	4.81	2.57	3.98
MgO	0.55	0.45	0.70	4.84	4.16	4.38	3.29	3.29
CaO	2.71	2.83	2.56	9.74	10.6	9.87	10.8	11.4
Na_2O	6.55	6.68	6.30	3.20	3.16	3.46	3.04	3.20
K_2O	3.29	3.09	3.26	0.64	0.85	0.95	0.66	0.77
H_2O^+	0.53	0.66	0.80	1.44	0.77	0.73	1.65	1.28
H_2O^-	0.93	0.86	1.34	2.94	1.27	0.94	2.98	0.95
TiO_2	0.52	0.52	0.52	2.22	2.98	3.92	2.22	3.05
P_2O_5	0.12	0.12	0.11	0.43	0.48	0.51	1.37	1.55
MnO	0.11	0.14	0.14	0.12	0.13	0.18	0.40	0.18
CO_2	0.01	0.01	0.01	0.03	0.01	0.01	0.16	0.15
Total	99.4	98.9	99.6	99.9	99.8	100.4	99.4	99.7
Ba	439	461	444	56	114	132	993	120
Nb	108	116	94	18	26	32	18	26
Rb	15	12	18	39	38	14	34	14
Sr	175	190	180	297	335	309	391	388
Zr	1010	1076	694	174	218	261	180	222
Y	98	119	64	36	33	41	36	38
Ni	22	15	27	65	78	38	75	63
V	<20	<20	38	300	348	458	282	440
Ga	35	48	31	14	18	18	15	17

Analysts: same as listed in Table 5. Oxides in wt %, trace elements in ppm.

TABLE 5. Whole-Rock Analyses of Samples From Patton Seamount

	S6-79							L3-80			
	6-1	6-2	6-4	6-5	6-6	9-4	9-8	7-4	7-5	7-8	7-11
SiO_2	51.1	55.3	47.0	49.1	40.9	43.8	46.2	51.1	37.4	49.3	51.0
Al_2O_3	15.0	16.6	16.4	15.4	14.1	18.0	13.3	16.6	14.4	16.8	16.7
Fe_2O_3	9.44	5.83	10.1	9.16	10.0	8.53	7.77	5.09	7.85	6.90	9.12
FeO	2.35	3.60	3.72	2.42	2.40	2.92	7.92	5.77	2.11	4.68	2.77
MgO	2.21	1.42	2.07	2.00	2.17	2.91	4.22	2.30	1.52	2.60	2.32
CaO	5.03	4.89	5.66	7.29	11.7	10.3	8.70	7.10	15.8	7.66	6.75
Na_2O	4.03	4.85	3.47	4.42	3.62	3.61	2.71	4.18	3.79	4.15	4.80
K_2O	2.39	2.39	1.29	1.85	1.61	0.88	0.92	1.90	0.92	1.47	1.93
H_2O^+	2.44	1.49	3.65	2.05	3.06	1.63	1.40	1.49	1.96	1.24	0.90
H_2O^-	3.03	2.23	3.61	3.03	3.58	1.98	2.59	0.99	1.57	1.70	0.75
TiO_2	1.41	1.03	1.63	1.42	1.33	2.71	3.57	2.31	2.01	2.26	2.24
P_2O_5	1.12	0.26	1.22	1.71	4.68	2.12	0.61	0.56	6.99	0.85	0.63
MnO	0.18	0.13	0.24	0.17	0.50	0.59	0.20	0.17	0.27	0.18	0.15
CO_2	0.20	0.43	0.21	0.39	0.76	0.65	0.05	0.02	1.14	0.01	0.01
Total	99.9	100.4	100.3	100.4	100.4	100.6	100.2	99.6	97.7	99.8	100.1
Ba	880	720	550	390	640	430	120	388	4154	404	410
Nb	52	46	40	46	54	<20	<20	51	48	55	50
Rb	-	40	13	-	-	10	21	37	24	27	69
Sr	285	305	315	380	450	395	245	368	1309	417	375
Zr	690	775	725	555	575	140	250	357	327	370	329
Y	150	90	96	130	160	110	52	51	90	58	48
Ni	25	5	30	15	70	40	30	37	54	38	31
V	20	<10	29	38	44	300	320	178	236	196	210
Ga	33	33	24	26	24	26	26	25	15	19	23
Cr	15	-	-	35	40	-	-	23	95	33	32

Analysts: same as Table 2 for dredges 6 and 9 from cruise S6-79. For L3-80, dredge 7 samples the analysts are: J. Wahlberg, J. Taggart and J. Baker for x-ray fluorescence major oxides; H Neiman, F. Newman, and E. Engleman for H_2O^+, H_2O^-, CO_2, FeO; R. Johnson, H.J. Rose, B. McCall, G. Sellers, and J. Lindsay for x-ray fluorescence Ba, Nb, Rb, Sr, Zr, Y; B. King for energy-dispersive x-ray fluorescence Ni and V; R. Lerner for emission spectroscopy Ga and Cr. Not analyzed -. Oxides in wt %, trace elements in ppm.

TABLE 7. Microprobe Analyses of Volcanic Glass, Gulf of Alaska Seamounts

Sample No. Rock Type	Welker (S6-79)		Miller (S6-79)	Patton (S6-79)					Pathfinder (L3-80)
	1-10 Benmoreite	2-23 Hawaiite	4-9 Tholeiitic Basalt	6-1A Benmoreite	6-3	8-1	9-4 Hawaiite	9-11A	4-19 Alkalic Basalt
SiO_2	55.6	49.4	49.7	57.1	57.5	47.8	48.9	48.9	48.9
Al_2O_3	16.5	14.3	16.0	14.8	14.5	15.6	13.6	11.8	16.2
FeO*	8.56	13.3	10.9	9.60	9.54	13.3	14.2	16.3	11.7
MgO	1.39	3.68	7.94	0.98	0.95	4.25	3.09	3.80	6.20
CaO	3.66	7.55	11.1	3.91	3.83	7.85	7.34	8.23	9.88
Na_2O	6.01	4.11	2.46	4.98	5.33	3.57	3.05	2.91	3.37
K_2O	2.97	1.98	0.09	3.00	3.05	1.64	1.63	1.03	0.59
P_2O_5	0.46	1.08	0.06	0.35	0.32	0.86	1.32	0.64	0.29
TiO_2	1.04	4.03	1.35	1.13	1.12	3.82	2.69	4.39	2.35
MnO	0.26	0.22	0.18	0.28	0.28	0.21	0.28	0.26	0.18
S	0.01	0.03	0.04	0.05	0.07	0.06	-	-	0.10
Total	96.5	99.7	99.8	96.2	96.5	99.0	96.1	98.3	99.8

Analyst: W. Bohrson. *Total Fe as FeO.

mugearite with rare plagioclase, clinopyroxene, and titanomagnetite; trachyte with sanidine, aegerine-augite, and titanomagnetite; and abundant porphyritic hawaiite like that in dredge 1. These breccia fragments were too small to analyze.

Whole-rock chemical analyses (Table 2) and microprobe analyses of glass (Table 7) demonstrate the effects of marine alteration and of contamination by encrusting Mn-oxides. Sample 1-13 has higher P_2O_5, CaO, H_2O, Fe_2O_3/FeO, Y, and REE (except Ce) and lower MgO, K_2O, and SiO_2 than less altered samples 1-2 and 1-15 of the same lithology. In addition, the higher MnO, Ni, and Zn in sample 1-13 reflect Mn-oxide contamination.

Chondrite-normalized REE plots (Figure 2a) show the increase in REE abundances and the degree of light-REE enrichment progressing from hawaiite to benmoreite. In addition, the effects of phosphatization and Mn-oxide contamination are evident when sample 1-13 is compared with its less altered equivalent, sample 1-15.

Miller Seamount

Four lithologies are present in the samples recovered from Miller; they are tholeiitic basalt and basalt transitional between tholeiitic and alkalic basalt. The most abundant lithology is an aphyric transitional basalt that varies in texture from glassy to intersertal and has about 15% vesicles. Samples 4-2, 4-3, 4-4, 4-10, and 4-12 represent this lithology. These samples have had complete replacement of glass by clays and variable but small amounts of phosphorite.

Sample 4-2 contains about 15% small, round vesicles in a variolitic to pilotaxitic groundmass consisting of about 40% plagioclase laths, 20% iddingsite after olivine, 15% clinopyroxene, 10% Fe-Ti oxides, and 15% clay after glass. Sample 4-10 contains about 10% vesicles, commonly lined with glassy material, set in an intergranular groundmass. The groundmass mineralogy is the same in sample 4-2 except that the clays are variable in abundance (0-30%) and are bright yellow. Sample 4-12 is similar to 4-10 except that there are 15% vesicles and the secondary clays are dark orange-brown in color.

Sample 4-5, which represents the second lithologic type, is an altered, glassy, transitional basalt that contains plagioclase glomerocrysts, rare iddingsite pseudomorphs after olivine, and rare red-brown Cr-spinel. The third lithology, also transitional basalt, is similar to the first except that the groundmass

TABLE 8. Washington University INAA Analyses (ppm)

	Welker (S6-79)		Miller (S6-79)		Murray (S6-79)		Patton (L3-80)			Pathfinder (L3-80)		
	1-15	2-19*	4-3	4-12	5-3	5-10	7-4*	7-8*	7-11*	3-5*	4-10	4-11*
Sc	18.5	18.7	43.5	45.6	21.3	20.3	23.2	2.27	23.1	6.5	35.4	41.6
Cr	27.6	28.2	123.9	112.0	2.6	1.7	18.5	23.7	22.3	0.8	123.0	40.9
Co	26.8	21.9	33.3	41.5	18.1	17.1	21.4	17.5	19.0	1.4	49.3	60.0
Rb	17.5	23	10.4	13.4	44	91	35	26	58	24.5	35.5	5
Cs	0.174	0.75	0.35	0.31	10.3	10.2	0.66	0.78	4.12	0.30	3.12	0.25
La	32.2	38.7	9.6	7.44	40.9	39.7	41.3	40.1		64.1	17.8	22.5
Ce	74.9	76.7	20.7	21.7	98.1	94.2	86.9	89.8	88.4	152.7	44.2	54.0
Nd	46.1	45.3	16.2	15.1	62.6	59.7	49.2	50.1	49.8	84.0	28.2	35.4
Sm	9.44	9.95	4.68	4.54	14.79	14.23	11.0	11.37	11.13	17.86	7.46	8.98
Eu	3.01	3.09	1.63	1.64	4.52	4.37	3.81	3.93	3.98	4.21	2.39	2.86
Tb	1.41	1.50	0.91	1.08	2.51	2.32	1.94	1.93	1.87	3.27	1.37	1.7
Yb	2.86	3.71	2.71	2.83	5.56	5.43	5.09	5.38	5.01	9.98	3.42	4.75
Lu	0.433	0.576	0.44	0.416	0.85	0.82	0.783	0.826	0.764	1.48	0.517	0.718
Hf	7.05	7.68	3.33	3.41	10.5	10.0	9.82	10.16	10.17	28.05	6.10	7.50
Ta	2.58	2.64	0.56	0.55	3.13	3.06	2.87	3.01	2.98	5.76	1.64	1.97
Th	2.69	3.1	0.39	0.42	3.98	3.81	3.93	4.31	4.52	7.66	1.53	1.89
U	0.73	1.52	2.38	0.46	1.6	1.79	1.36	1.09	1.76	0.44	0.96	1.67

*Same samples also analyzed at the U.S. Geological Survey, data in Table 9. Analysts: P. Castillo and R. Batiza.

TABLE 9. U.S. Geological Survey INAA Data (ppm)

	Welker[1] (S6-79)				Miller[1] (S6-79)		Murray[1] (S6-79)		Patton[1] (S6-79)			
	1-12	1-13	2-13	2-19*	4-4	4-10	5-4	5-11	6-2	6-4	9-4	9-8
Sc	11	19	18	18	41	41	20	20	19	22	30	34
Cr	2.5	25	21	16	112	104	1	0.4	1.4	1.9	242	38
Co	12	35	24	21	48	35	21	12	2	9	26	37
La	58	66	31	38	8	7	39	38	67	65	20	20
Ce	151	82	76	76	24	22	96	95	145	148	28	50
Nd	65	60	43	44	19	17	56	55	72	72	26	30
Sm	12.5	11.0	9.9	10.5	4.2	3.9	15.0	14.1	15.6	16.4	5.8	7.8
Eu	4.27	4.05	3.04	3.17	1.65	1.51	4.50	4.34	5.32	6.10	2.03	2.57
Tb	1.75	2.32	1.42	1.52	0.97	0.90	2.44	2.29	2.89	2.89	1.33	1.55
Yb	5.0	7.6	3.1	3.8	2.9	2.6	5.5	5.4	8.3	9.1	4.5	4.7
Lu	0.69	1.16	0.45	0.56	0.43	0.40	0.77	0.76	1.17	1.28	0.67	0.73
Hf	13.2	6.4	6.8	6.6	2.9	2.8	9.0	8.8	17.4	16.0	3.7	6.0
Ta	6.2	2.8	2.9	2.9	0.6	0.7	3.4	3.2	6.0	5.6	1.0	2.0
Th	6.7	3.0	3.1	3.0	0.6	0.5	3.9	3.7	8.1	7.3	1.3	2.2
Zn	121	178	112	129	108	110	210	185	215	254	200	169

	Patton[2] (L3-80)				Pathfinder[2] (L3-80)							Pathfinder[3] (L3-80)
	7-4	7-5	7-8	7-11*	3-5*	3-13	4-6	4-10	4-11	4-19	4-20	3-5A
Sc	23	21	23	22	6.5	7.1	28	34	38	27	35	6.5
Cr	19	109	30	30	3.6	40	110	119	40	104	145	0.8
Co	25	58	19	18	3	20	34	47	36	54	38	20
La	38	66	43	38	65	63	17	17	20	18	19	87
Ce	86	85	90	85	153	139	33	45	51	34	43	184
Nd	49	67	53	57	79	79	29	29	30	24	28	92
Sm	10.8	14.6	11.4	10.8	17.8	17.0	6.0	7.2	8.0	5.8	7.2	19.2
Eu	3.88	4.71	4.08	3.92	4.71	4.59	1.97	2.45	2.71	1.97	2.39	4.75
Tb	1.89	2.79	2.09	1.74	3.35	2.74	1.28	1.39	1.56	1.11	1.53	4.01
Yb	5.1	7.5	5.5	5.0	10.5	6.2	3.0	3.4	4.1	3.2	3.4	14.4
Lu	0.73	1.15	0.85	0.73	1.47	0.89	0.46	0.53	0.61	0.49	0.53	1.93
Hf	8.5	8.5	9.0	8.3	23.9	23.7	4.1	5.4	6.1	4.1	5.5	25.1
Ta	3.4	3.2	3.5	3.2	6.8	6.8	1.2	1.9	2.2	1.3	1.9	7.5
Th	4.6	4.1	4.6	4.4	7.9	7.9	1.3	1.6	1.8	1.2	1.5	8.4
Zn	142	239	167	172	129	160	217	149	153	184	164	153

[1] Rare-earth-element abundances corrected for interlaboratory bias to be consistent with data from Washington University. Data reported here are determined values multiplied by 0.914 for La, 1.053 for Ce, 0.909 for Sm, 1.055 for Eu, and 1.032 for Tb.
[2] Rare-earth-element abundances corrected for interlaboratory bias to be consistent with data from Washington University. Data reported here are determined values multiplied by 0.914 for La, 1.053 for Ce, 1.128 for Sm, 1.055 for Eu, 1.66 for Tb, and 0.952 for Yb.
[3] Rare-earth-element abundances as determined.
* Same samples also analyzed at Washington University, data in Table 8. Analysts: L. Schwarz and G.A. Wandless; Project Leader: P Baedecker.

contains abundant iddingsite pseudomorphs after olivine instead of groundmass clinopyroxene. The fourth lithology is a tholeiitic basalt vitrophyre that contains phenocrysts of olivine, plagioclase, and nearly opaque Cr- spinel. A microprobe analysis of glass (Table 7, sample 4-9) indicates that this sample is chemically similar to mid-ocean ridge basalt.

The analyzed transitional basalt from Miller Seamount has the lowest K_2O content and is the least light-REE enriched. The REE patterns have nearly flat light- to middle-REE and somewhat fractionated heavy-REE (Figure 2b). These characteristics are similar to those observed in Hawaiian tholeiitic basalt [e.g., Basaltic Volcanism Study Project, 1981]. Similar rare-earth patterns have been reported for small seamounts formed near spreading centers [Batiza and Vanko, 1984]. Tholeiitic basalt sample 4-9 was not analyzed for REE so we cannot assess how similar it is to mid-ocean ridge basalt.

Murray Guyot

Nearly all samples recovered from Murray Guyot are vesicular, sparsely phyric to aphyric hawaiite. Most samples contain rare phenocrysts of plagioclase, clinopyroxene, and titanomagnetite, and have 30-50% small (1mm), round vesicles; a few samples have about 15% large (3mm) vesicles. The hyaloclastite recovered from Murray also appears to be hawaiite in composition. The high water contents (2.9 to 3.3%) and high Fe_2O_3/FeO ratios (3.65 to 3.96) reflect the moderate submarine alteration of the samples (Table 4). In all of the samples the abundant (25%) groundmass glass is replaced by clays. As a group, these are the most altered of the dated samples.

All four samples have nearly identical REE patterns (Figure 2c) with less light-REE-enriched patterns than observed by Cousens et al. [1985] for hawaiite from the Tuzo Wilson Seamounts. The hawaiite from Murray has $[La/Sm]_N$ 1.5 and $[La/Lu]_N$ 5 whereas that from Tuzo Wilson Seamounts has $[La/Sm]_N$ 3.4 and $[La/Lu]_N$ 13.

Patton Seamount

Dredge 6 recovered hawaiite, mugearite, and benmoreite. The hawaiite contains sparse microphenocrysts of olivine, titanomagnetite, and

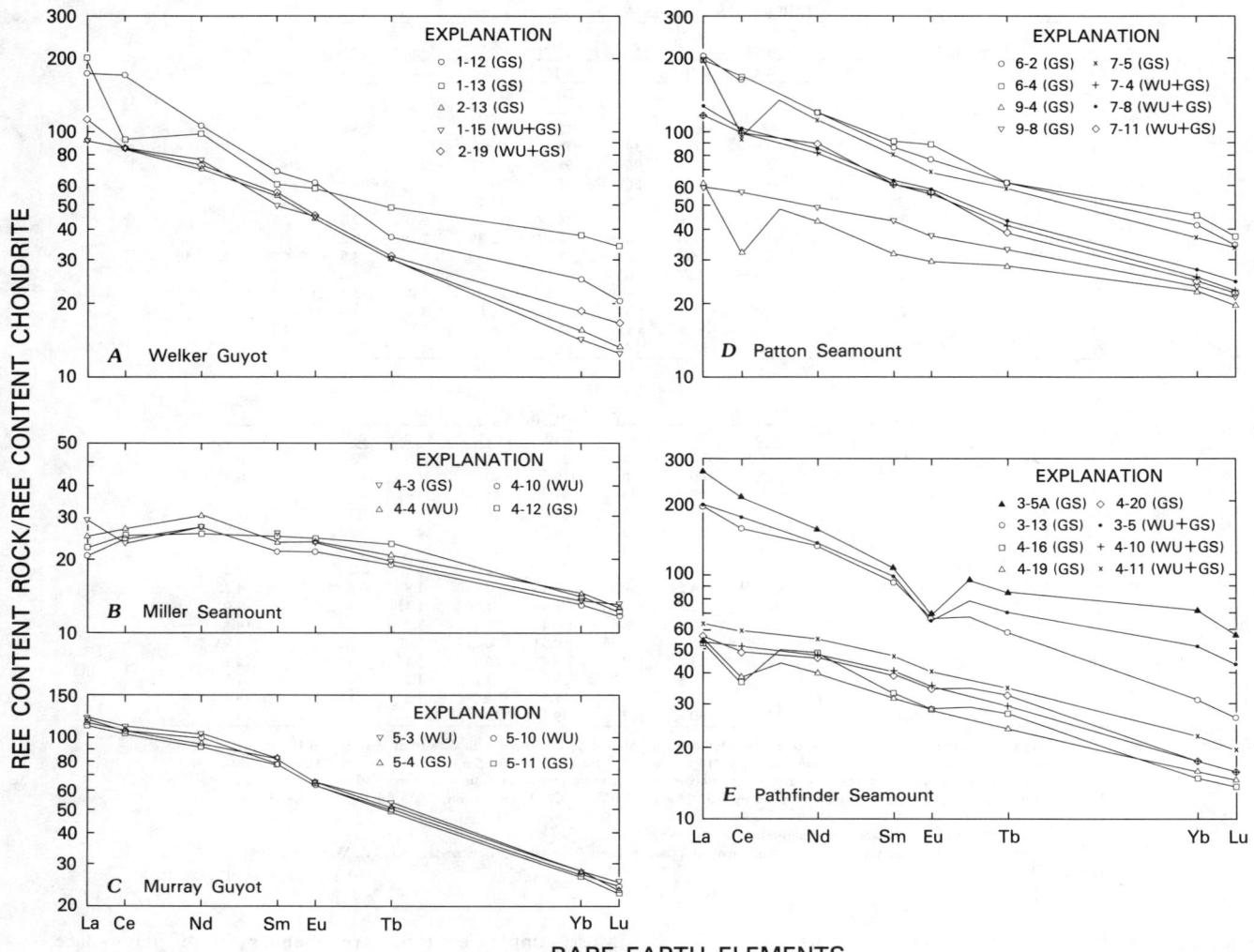

Fig. 2. Chondrite-normalized rare-earth-element plot of samples from: (a) Welker Guyot. The large negative Ce anomaly is caused by addition of phosphorite that contains abundant REE except Ce. Analytical data from Tables 8 and 9. (b) Miller Seamount. All four samples are the same transitional basalt lithology. Analytical data from Tables 8 and 9. (c) Murray Guyot. All four samples are the same hawaiite lithology. Analytical data from Tables 8 and 9. (d) Patton Seamount. Sample 7-5 is the same lithology as samples 7-4, 7-8, and 7-11. The negative Ce anomaly and elevated REE abundances reflect addition of marine phosphorite. Sample 9-4 also has added phosphorite and prior to phosphatization was the least light-REE enriched of the Patton samples. (e) Pathfinder Seamount. The three trachyte samples have small negative Eu anomalies that probably reflect fractionation of anorthoclase. The highly variable heavy-REE abundances in the trachyte are probably due to accumulation of clinopyroxene. Samples 4-6 and 4-19 have moderate negative Ce anomalies due to either addition of phosphorite (4-19) or exchange with seawater (4-6).

plagioclase in a pilotaxitic groundmass (sample 6-4). The benmoreite contains plagioclase, titanomagnetite, and rare clinopyroxene and olivine in a glassy subtrachytic groundmass (samples 6-1, 6-5, 6-6); samples 6-1 and 6-3 have perlitic glassy groundmasses and sample 6-6 has altered glassy groundmass partly replaced by phosphorite. Sample 6-7 is a crystal-rich

hawaiite that contains about 15% plagioclase, 3% olivine, and 2% green and brown clinopyroxene. This hawaiite is similar to that recovered in dredge 7 from cruise L3-80. Dredge 8 contained monolithic hawaiite hyaloclastite in which the angular fragments contain plagioclase and olivine phenocrysts (Table 7). Dredge 9 recovered hawaiite fragments and monolithic hawaiite hyaloclastite. Samples 9-8 and 9-11A (glass analysis in table 7) contain olivine, clinopyroxene, and plagioclase microphenocrysts, whereas sample 9-4 contains plagioclase, olivine altered to iddingsite, and rare titanomagnetite.comparison of the whole-rock and glass analyses of sample 9-4 demonstrate that the whole-rock composition has been modified by phosphatization of interstitial glass.

The hawaiite samples from dredge 7 (7-4, 7-5, 7-8, and 7-11) are chemically and petrographically similar. The glassy groundmass of sample 7-5 is extensively replaced by phosphorite and the elevated Mn, Ni, and Cr contents reflect slight contamination by encrusting Mn-oxide. The addition of marine phosphorite resulted in elevated P, Ba, Sr, Y, and all the REE except Ce. The dredge 7 hawaiite contains about 15% plagioclase, 3% olivine, and 2% clinopyroxene phenocrysts and microphenocrysts. Much of the plagioclase displays resorbed margins and contains abundant glass inclusions. The pyroxene occurs as both green and brown crystals, commonly green cores are enclosed by brown rims. Sample 7-11 has a more crystalline groundmass that contains rare pale reddish amphibole. Hyaloclastite, breccia, and volcanic sandstone contain small fragments of aphyric hawaiite, mugearite, and aegerine trachyte. These fragments are too small to analyze.

All of the samples from Patton have light-REE-enriched patterns typical of alkalic basalt, hawaiite, mugearite, and benmoreite from Hawaii [Clague, in press]. Prior to phosphatization, sample 9-4 had the least light-REE enriched pattern, followed by hawaiite sample 9-8 ($[La/Sm]_N=1.4$, $[La]_N=58$, hawaiite samples 7-4, 7-8, and 7-11 ($[La/Sm]_N=2.0$ and $[La]_N=114-130$), and benmoreite sample 6-2 and hawaiite sample 6-4 ($[La/Sm]_N=2.3$ and $[La]_N=200$), which have nearly identical REE patterns. Sample 6-4 has a slight positive Eu anomaly indicating accumulation of plagioclase. The large increase in $[La/Sm]_N$ from the least to the most evolved lava indicates that clinopyroxene was a major phase in the fractionating mineral assemblage. The strong enrichment in REE in sample 6-4 compared to other hawaiite samples indicates that the Patton Seamount lava is differentiated from a variety of alkalic basalt parental compositions.

Pathfinder Seamount

Dredge 3 recovered numerous fragments of trachyte that are, in general, only slightly altered (Table 6). The trachyte samples are fine-grained and contain microphenocrysts of anorthoclase, acmite, and titanomagnetite set in a groundmass of the same minerals with variable amounts of glass replaced by clay. Sample 3-4 has about 10% bright yellow clay whereas sample 3-5A is nearly holocrystalline.

Dredge 4 recovered three distinct lithologies that range from alkalic basalt to hawaiite in composition. The alkalic basalt includes analyzed samples 4-6 and 4-19. The glassy rind of sample 4-19 contains about 5% olivine and 10% plagioclase microphenocrysts; chrome spinel is absent. Another sample of this lithology contains a single small gabbro xenolith in which the plagioclase contains many small glass inclusions. The interiors of the pillow fragments are extensively altered; all olivine and about 30% of the groundmass are replaced by clay and phosphorite. The bulk analyses are of this weathered material. The microprobe glass analysis (Table 7) gives a more reliable measure of the composition of this alkalic basalt than do the whole-rock analyses.

The second lithology in dredge 4, represented by samples 4-10 and 4-20, is a slightly vesicular hawaiite that contains <1% phenocrysts of plagioclase and iddingsite pseudomorphs after olivine. Many of the plagioclase phenocrysts have corroded margins and are crowded with glass inclusions. The groundmass consists of plagioclase, colorless clinopyroxene, titanomagnetite, and about 10% clay after glass. The third lithology in dredge 4, represented by sample 4-11, is a dense mafic hawaiite that contains <1% plagioclase microphenocrysts. The groundmass consists of plagioclase, abundant titanaugite, abundant Fe-Ti oxides, and rutile. Interstitial glass is absent from the center of the fragment and no alteration is observed in thin section.

The chemical analyses show that the trachyte is nearly identical to that from Kodiak Seamount described by Forbes and Hoskin [1969] and is slightly more mafic and less potassic than its Hawaiian counterpart [Clague, in press].

The glass and whole-rock analyses of sample 4-19 show that phosphatization has modified the pillow interior as P_2O_5 is 0.25% in the glassy rind and 1.37% in the whole-rock. This phosphatization also is evident in the REE pattern of sample 4-19 (Figure 2e), which displays a prominent negative Ce anomaly.

The relatively unaltered hawaiite and mafic hawaiite have light-REE-enriched patterns with $[La/Sm]_N=1.3-1.4$ and $[La/Lu]_N=3.3-3.4$. These samples are not as light-REE enriched as hawaiite from Murray Seamount. The REE patterns of alkalic basalt samples 4-6 and 4-19 have been modified so severely by alteration that no reliable petrogenic information can be extracted.

The dredge 3 trachyte REE patterns are typically light-REE enriched with $[La/Sm]_N=2.0-2.3$. The heavy-REE however, are highly variable with $[La/Lu]_N=4.4-7.3$. The variable heavy-REE abundances indicate that a phase with a strong affinity for the heavy REE, probably aegirine-augite, has fractionated. All the trachyte samples display large negative Eu anomalies indicating extensive fractionation of plagioclase and probably anorthoclase.

Magma Supply Rates and Eruption Depths

Two conclusions can be drawn from the present chemical data. First, the presence of differentiated alkalic lava on the mid-plate seamounts indicates that during the end of the volcanic cycle eruption rates were rather low and that a magma storage system existed within or beneath the volcanoes. In Hawaii, these types of lava erupt infrequently during the waning stage of volcanism that follows the main edifice-building stage [Clague, in press]. These volcanoes must have had an edifice-building stage with high eruption rates in order to develop the magma storage zone in which differentiation occurs during the waning (alkalic) stage. It is not clear whether these volcanoes had a tholeiitic edifice-building stage such as occurs on Hawaii, or whether the main edifice is constructed of alkalic basalt as proposed for the Caroline Islands [Mattey, 1982]. The relatively small size of the Gulf of Alaska seamounts can be used to argue that the edifice is largely constructed of alkalic basalt since volume, eruption rate, and lava composition are related in Hawaii [Clague and Dalrymple, 1987; Clague, in press].

Second, the S data from the microprobe glass analyses (Table 7) can be used to assess the degree of volatile degassing, which accompanies subaerial or shallow-water eruption. Basalt erupted in deep water generally contains 0.08% to about 0.14% S [Moore and Fabbi, 1981]. Concentrations lower than this probably result from degassing during vesiculation. Alkalic basalt sample 4-19 from Pathfinder Seamount is the only glass that is clearly undegassed and therefore erupted well below sea-level. The tholeiitic basalt glass from Miller Seamount is partially degassed, indicating that it erupted below sea-level but in shallow water. These data confirm that Miller Seamount was either an island or a shallow bank at the time it was volcanically active. This observation is consistent with the interpretation of Hess [1946] that some of the Gulf of Alaska seamounts were eroded at sea level to form their flat (guyot) summits.

K-Ar and $^{40}Ar/^{39}Ar$ Methods and Results

Methods

Whole rock samples for $^{40}Ar/^{39}Ar$ dating were small cores, 6 mm diameter by approximately 1 cm long, weighing from 0.50 to 0.76 g. Plagioclase separates weighed from 0.30 to 0.38 g. The samples were sealed in air in quartz vials and irradiated in the core of the U.S. Geological Survey TRIGA reactor (GSTR) for 24 to 30 hours where they received a neutron dose of approximately 2.4×10^{18} to 3×10^{18} nvt. The effective neutron flux constant, J, was measured with our standard monitor biotites SB-2 and SB-3, which are from the same rock and have an age of 162 m.y. Further details of the GSTR flux characteristics, the monitor mineral, sample encapsulation and geometry, and the corrections for interfering K- and Ca-derived Ar isotopes are given by Dalrymple and Lanphere [1971] and Dalrymple et al.[1981].

Ar extractions for both total fusion and incremental heating were done in a conventional Ar extraction line using radio-frequency induction heating following bakeout at 280°C [Dalrymple and Lanphere, 1969]. Temperatures for incremental heating experiments were estimated using previously calibrated RF settings and an optical pyrometer; they are accurate to no more than about 50°C. Samples were held at each temperature for 30 minutes.

For conventional whole-rock K-Ar measurements (Table 10) a small block of material was crushed and sieved to a size of 0.5 to 1.0 mm. One aliquant was used for the Ar analysis and another was pulverized to a fine powder for duplicate K_2O analyses. Argon and K_2O analyses were by isotope dilution and flame photometry, respectively, using methods previously described [Dalrymple and Lanphere, 1969; Ingamells, 1970]. Ar mass analyses for both $^{40}Ar/^{39}Ar$ and conventional measurements were done with the computerized multiple collector mass spectrometer described by Stacey et al. [1981].

$^{40}Ar/^{39}Ar$ incremental heating data were reduced as both age spectra and isochrons; the results are summarized in Figures 3-5 and Table 11.* Plateau ages are presented as weighted means, where each increment age is weighted by the inverse of its variance, rather than as a simple arithmetic mean. The weighting allows increments with different analytical errors to be combined into a single mean without the poorer data having a disproportionate effect on the result. The error in the weighted mean is given by $(1/\Sigma(1/\sigma_i^2))$, where σ_i^2 are the estimated variances of the individual increment ages [Taylor, 1982]. We have used the York-2 least-squares cubic fit with correlated errors [York, 1969] and both the $^{40}Ar/^{36}Ar$ vs $^{39}Ar/^{36}Ar$ and the $^{36}Ar/^{40}Ar$ vs $^{39}Ar/^{40}Ar$ correlation diagrams to determine "isochron" ages. Roddick et al. [1980] and McDougall [1985] have suggested that the latter method is superior to the former because it minimizes the effects of correlated errors, which are large when the ^{40}Ar and ^{39}Ar data are normalized to the very small quantity of ^{36}Ar. We have found that the difference in results obtained from the two methods is negligible. In every instance the age, composition of trapped (atmospheric) $^{40}Ar/^{36}Ar$, goodness of fit (SUMS/(N-2)), and the errors obtained are virtually identical when the correlation coefficients are determined using the method recommended by York [quoted in Ozima et al., 1977]. The only difference we have found between the two methods is that the $^{36}Ar/^{40}Ar$ vs $^{39}Ar/^{40}Ar$ solution converges faster than the $^{40}Ar/^{36}Ar$ vs $^{39}Ar/^{36}Ar$ solution. The identical results obtained by both methods demonstrates that the York-2 cubic fit with correlated errors does precisely what it was designed to do, i.e., it compensates for correlated errors.

Results

Conventional K-Ar and $^{40}Ar/^{39}Ar$ total fusion ages (Table 10) were obtained primarily to determine minimum ages and to assess the effects of submarine alteration on the K-Ar system. As expected for altered rocks the K-Ar ages on samples from Miller Seamount are substantially younger than the $^{40}Ar/^{39}Ar$ total fusion ages. Elsewhere we have suggested that this is probably the result of ^{39}Ar loss from alteration products (e.g., clays) during irradiation or bakeout, which has the effect of increasing the $^{40}Ar/^{39}Ar$ ages [Clague et al., 1975; Dalrymple and Clague, 1976].

---

*Complete incremental heating data as well as $^{40}Ar/^{36}Ar$ vs $^{39}Ar/^{36}Ar$ and $^{36}Ar/^{40}Ar$ isochron diagrams, and K/Ca spectra are on microfiche at the back of this volume.

TABLE 10. $^{40}Ar/^{39}Ar$ Total Fusion Age and Conventional K-Ar Data for Samples From Seamounts in the Gulf of Alaska

Sample No.	Material	J	$^{40}Ar/^{39}Ar$	$^{37}Ar/^{39}Ar$ (a)	$^{36}Ar/^{39}Ar$	$^{36}Ar_{Ca}$ (%)	$^{39}Ar_{Ca}$ (%)	$^{40}Ar_K$ (%)	$^{40}Ar_R$ (%) (b)	Calculated Age (10^6 years) (c)
				Weker Guyot (S6-79)						
2-25	mugearite	0.006066	1.841	1.308	0.00215	16.6	<0.1	0.3	70.9	14.3 ± 0.2
	plagioclase	0.005933	5.515	19.63	0.0195	27.4	1.2	0.1	24.0	14.3 ± 0.8
				Miller Seamount (S6-79)						
4-2	basalt	0.006066	6.473	42.85	0.0254	46.0	2.7	<0.1	37.3	27.0 ± 1.6
4-10	basalt	0.005933	12.53	41.65	0.0465	24.4	2.6	<0.1	17.0	23.2 ± 2.5
4-12	basalt	0.006066	12.05	33.54	0.0414	22.0	2.1	<0.1	20.8	27.8 ± 2.2
				Murray Guyot (S6-79)						
5-1A	hawaiite	0.006135	3.525	2.074	0.00461	12.2	0.1	0.2	65.9	25.6 ± 0.3
5-1B	hawaiite	0.006135	19.16	2.801	0.0587	1.3	0.2	<0.1	10.7	22.5 ± 2.0
5-3	hawaiite	0.006135	11.82	4.146	0.0335	3.4	0.3	<0.1	19.0	24.8 ± 1.6
5-5	hawaiite	0.006135	12.09	2.785	0.0339	2.2	0.2	<0.1	18.9	25.1 ± 1.2
5-6	hawaiite	0.006135	10.73	5.112	0.0298	4.7	0.3	<0.1	21.6	25.6 ± 1.5
				Patton Seamount (L3-80)						
7-4	plagioclase	0.005779	16.21	13.26	0.0496	7.3	0.8	<0.1	16.1	27.2 ± 2.9
7-8	plagioclase	0.005779	11.91	14.35	0.0357	10.9	0.9	<0.1	21.0	26.1 ± 0.8
	plagioclase	0.004716	18.17	14.28	0.0526	7.4	0.9	<0.1	20.7	32.0 ± 2.7
7-11	hawaiite	0.005868	9.57	1.722	0.0231	2.0	0.1	<0.1	30.0	30.2 ± 0.5
				Pathfinder SeamounT (L3-80)						
3-4	trachyte	0.006856	2.568	0.3773	0.00231	4.4	<0.1	0.2	74.3	23.5 ± 0.2
3-5	trachyte	0.006856	4.998	0.3714	0.0104	1.0	<0.1	0.1	38.7	23.8 ± 0.2
4-11	hawaiite	0.005720	3.764	5.965	0.00680	23.9	0.4	0.2	59.2	22.9 ± 0.7

Sample No.	Material	K_2O (d) (wt. %)	Argon weight (gms)	$^{40}Ar_R$ (mol/gm)	$^{40}Ar_R$ (%)	Calculated Age (10^6 years) (c)
			Welker Guyot (S6-79)			
1-9	plagioclase	0.187 ± 0.004(2)	4.990	3.422 x 10^{-12}	6.6	12.7 ± 1.8
2-25	plagioclase	0.265 ± 0.004(2)	5.006	4.672	16.3	12.2 ± 0.6
			Miller Seamount (S6-79)			
4-2	basalt	0.426 ± 0.004(2)	6.703	4.640	26.1	7.6 ± 0.2
4-10	basalt	0.239 ± 0.001(2)	2.362	3.007	33.7	8.7 ± 0.4
4-12	basalt	0.436 ± 0.003(2)	6.305	4.836	16.8	7.7 ± 0.2

(a) Corrected for ^{37}Ar decay, half-life = 35.1 days.
(b) Subscripts indicate radiogenic (R), calcium-derived (Ca), and potassium-derived (K) argon.
(c) $\lambda_\varepsilon + \lambda'_\varepsilon = 0.581 \times 10^{-10} yr^{-1}$, $\lambda_\beta = 4.962 \times 10^{-10} yr^{-1}$. Errors are estimates of the standard deviation of analytical precision (Dalrymple and Lanphere, 1969, 1971).
(d) Calculated standard deviation. Number of measurements in parentheses.

308 GULF OF ALASKA SEAMOUNTS

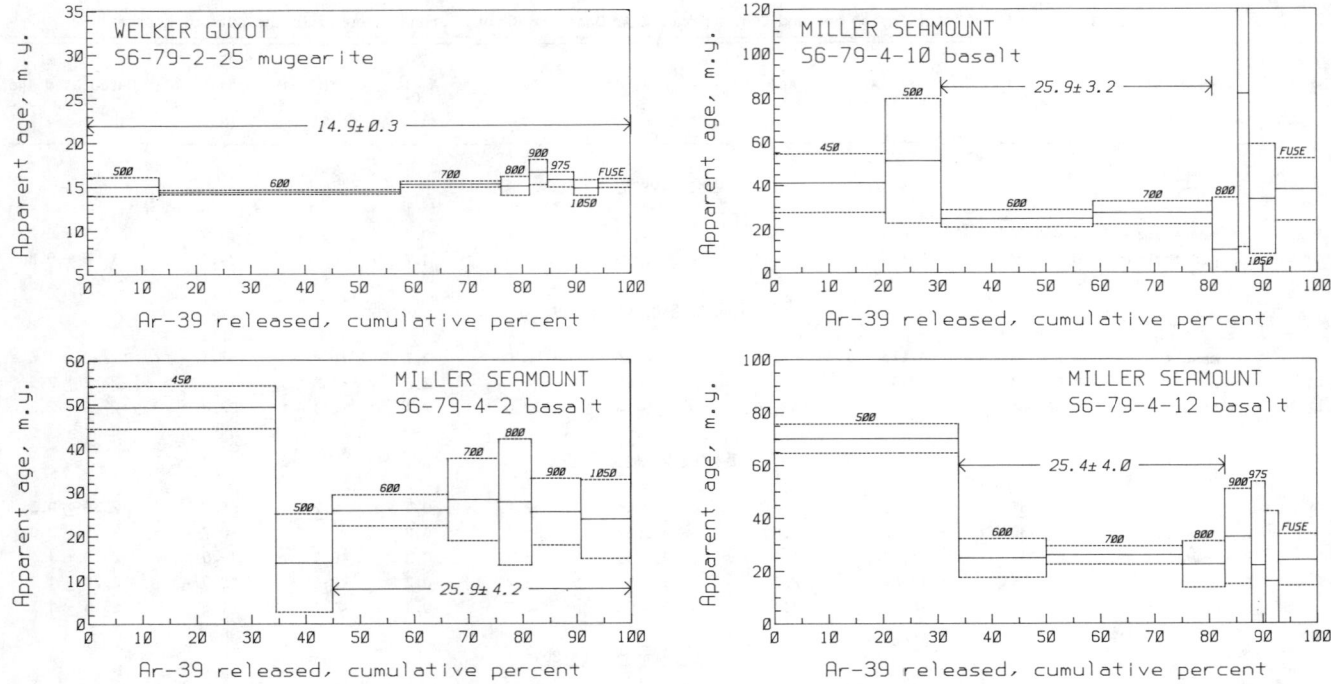

Fig. 3. $^{40}Ar/^{39}Ar$ age spectra for mugearite from Welker Guyot and basalt from Miller Seamount. Dashed lines indicate the estimated standard deviation of precision about the calculated ages (solid lines) for each gas increment. Temperatures for each increment are in degrees C.

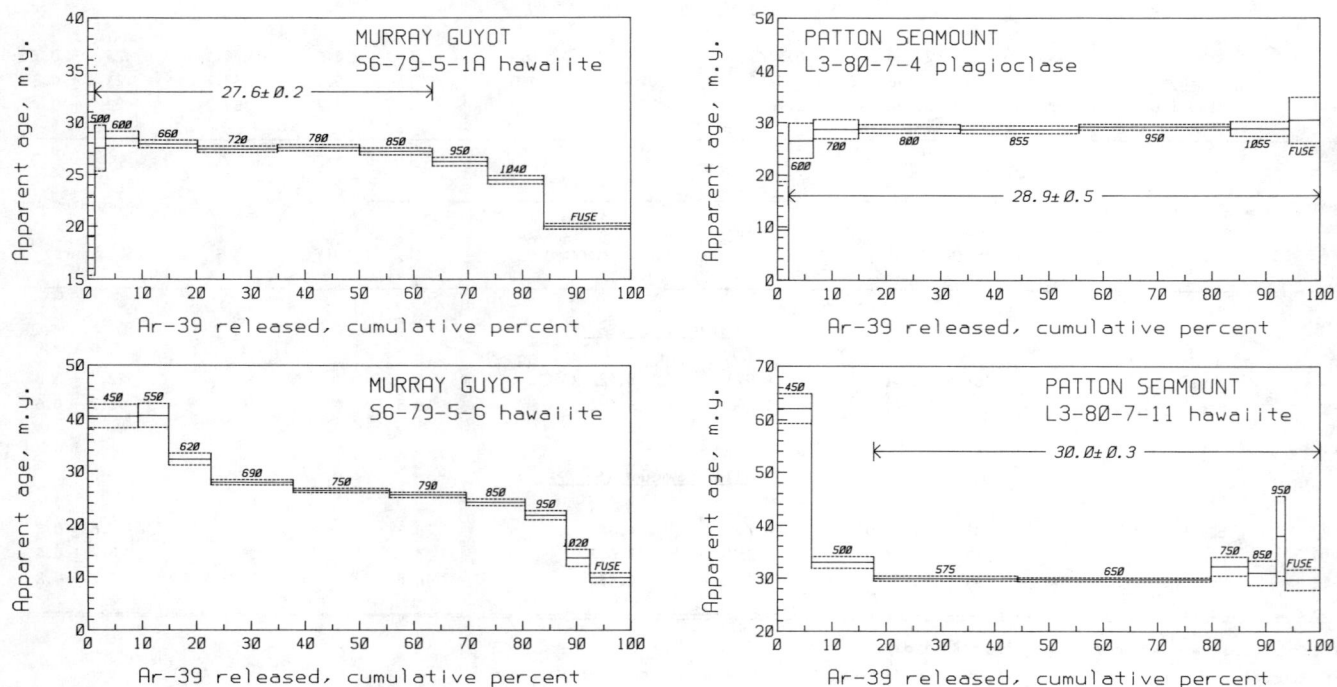

Fig. 4. $^{40}Ar/^{39}Ar$ age spectra for hawaiite and plagioclase from Murray Guyot and Patton Seamount. Symbols as in Figure 2.

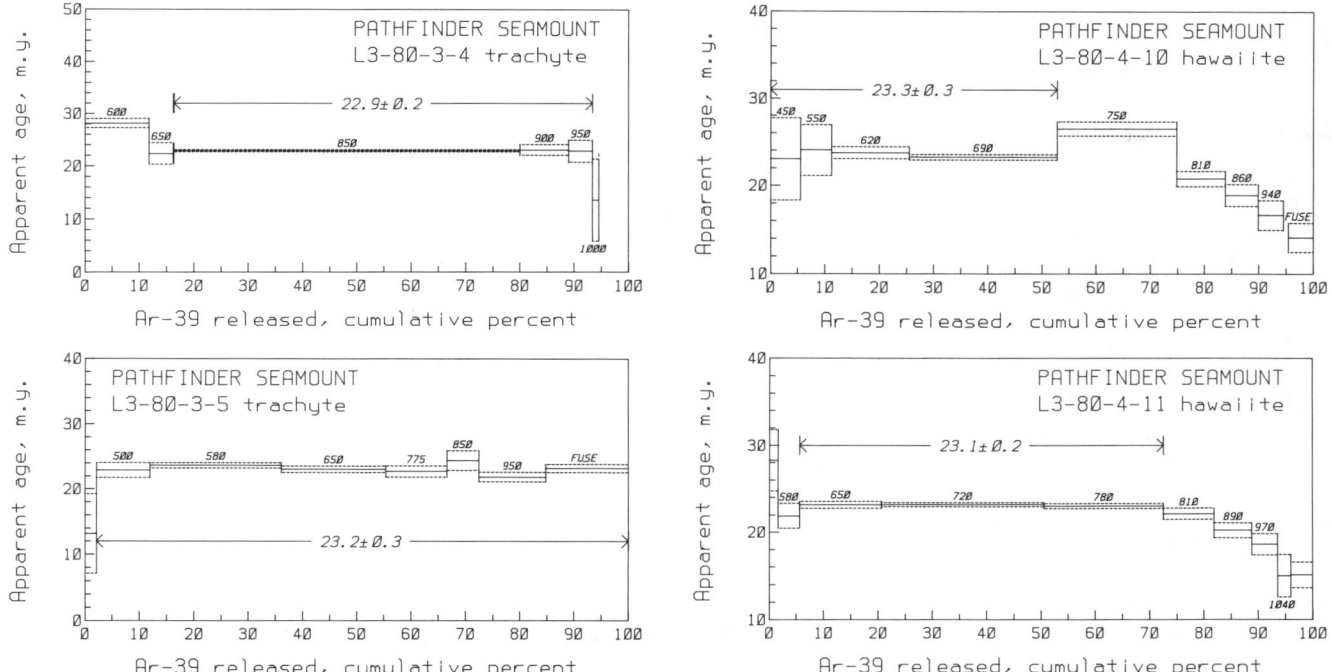

Fig. 5. ^{40}Ar/^{39}Ar age spectra for trachyte and hawaiite from Pathfinder Seamount. Symbols as in Figure 2.

Commonly, the ^{40}Ar/^{39}Ar total fusion ages for rocks altered in the submarine environment are consistent with ages based on ^{40}Ar/^{39}Ar incremental heating plateaus. This is true for Welker, Miller, Patton, and Pathfinder (Tables 10 and 11). The total fusion ages for the Murray samples, however, are about 10% lower than the age spectrum plateau age for sample 5-1A, indicating that total fusion ages must be interpreted cautiously in the absence of age spectrum data. The ^{40}Ar/^{39}Ar total fusion age for plagioclase from Welker Guyot is likewise older than the conventional K-Ar age. This indicates that the plagioclase is slightly altered even though there is no obvious microscopic indication of alteration. Thus, even fresh appearing feldspar separates from lavas altered in the submarine environment are not necessarily reliable chronometers for conventional K-Ar dating.

Based on incremental heating data for 12 samples from the five seamounts (Table 11), we consider the best ages for the seamounts to be:

Welker Guyot	14.9 ± 0.3 m.y.
Miller Seamount	25.8 ± 2.1
Murray Guyot	27.6 ± 0.2
Patton Seamount	29.7 ± 0.3
Pathfinder Seamount	23.1 ± 0.2

The age for Welker Guyot is based on data from a single sample of mugearite. This sample, however, gives an age spectrum plateau over all gas increments (Figure 3), a concordant isochron age, and a ^{40}Ar/^{36}Ar ratio equivalent, within the errors, with the air ratio of 295.5 (Table 11).

The errors for individual increments in the age spectra of the three samples from Miller Seamount are quite high because of relatively low amounts of radiogenic ^{40}Ar and relatively high amounts of Ca-derived ^{36}Ar (Table 11). As a result, the age spectra lack precision. The high temperature gas increments, however, have plateaus and concordant isochron ages that are consistent and have a weighted mean of 25.8 ± 2.1 m.y. (Fig. 3). In selecting increments for plateaus for the Miller samples, we have omitted those with very large errors even though they are not statistically different from contiguous increments. The exclusion of these data, however, does not significantly change the results (Table 11).

Murray Guyot is not particularly well dated. Hawaiite sample 5-6 has the type of age spectrum that has been interpreted as due to redistribution of ^{39}Ar, perhaps due to recoil associated with the ^{39}K(n,p)^{39}Ar reaction [Fleck et al., 1977]; it has no plateau (Figure 4). The other sample (5-1A) has a plateau at 27.6 ± 0.2 m.y. consisting of the low and intermediate temperature increments. The isochron age for these same increments is concordant with the plateau age. At higher temperatures, the increments decrease in apparent age, perhaps because of ^{39}Ar loss due to recoil from fine-grained phases. We have taken the plateau age of this sample to represent the age of the seamount.

The two samples from Patton Seamount (Figure 4), one plagioclase and one hawaiite, each have concordant plateau and isochron ages, and the ages from the two samples are not different at the 95 percent level of confidence. We have, therefore, used

TABLE 11. Summary of Age Spectrum and Isochron Analyses From $^{40}Ar/^{39}Ar$ Incremental Heating Experiments on Seamounts From the Gulf of Alaska. Asterisks Indicate Data Shown as Figures

Sample No.	Material	Increments Used	Age Spectrum Wt. Mean Age(my)	^{39}Ar (%)	Isochron Age (my)	$^{40}Ar/^{36}Ar$ Intercept	SUMS/(N-2)
			Welker Guyot (S6-79)				
2-25	mugearite	*All	14.9 ± 0.3	100	14.9 ± 0.4	297.2 ± 6.5	2.00
			Miller Seamount (S6-79)				
4-2	basalt	500-1050	25.2 ± 4.0	66	27.6 ± 3.2	289.5 ± 6.7	0.22
		*600-1050	25.9 ± 4.2	55	24.9 ± 4.8	298.0 ± 12.9	0.08
4-10	basalt	*600-700	25.9 ± 3.2	50	---	---	--
4-12	basalt	600-FUSE	25.4 ± 4.0	66	25.8 ± 3.7	294.4 ± 5.7	0.12
		*600-800	25.4 ± 4.0	49	26.2 ± 4.3	293.9 ± 7.7	0.15
			Murray Guyot (S6-79)				
5-1A	hawaiite	*500-850	27.6 ± 0.2	62	27.5 ± 0.2	297.0 ± 1.7	1.13
		660-850	27.5 ± 0.2	54	27.2 ± 0.3	309.4 ± 12.6	1.00
5-6	hawaiite	*450-FUSE	no plateau	--	---	---	--
			Patton Seamount (L3-80)				
7-4	plagioclase	*600-FUSE	28.9 ± 0.5	98	29.1 ± 0.6	293.0 ± 6.1	0.25
		700-1055	29.0 ± 0.5	88	29.0 ± 0.8	295.3 ± 9.2	0.23
7-11	hawaiite	*575-FUSE	30.0 ± 0.3	82	29.3 ± 0.6	312.4 ± 12.8	0.49
		575-850	30.0 ± 0.4	74	29.1 ± 0.8	318.1 ± 20.7	0.61
		575-650	29.9 ± 0.3	62	---	---	--
			Pathfinder Seamount (L3-80)				
3-4	trachyte	*850-950	22.9 ± 0.2	77	22.9 ± 0.2	296.7 ± 13.7	0.02
3-5	trachyte	*500-FUSE	23.2 ± 0.3	98	23.2 ± 0.4	295.3 ± 2.0	1.20
		500-775	23.3 ± 0.4	64	23.5 ± 0.4	294.6 ± 1.7	0.76
4-10	hawaiite	*450-690	23.3 ± 0.3	53	23.3 ± 0.2	295.8 ± 0.6	0.31
		620-690	23.3 ± 0.3	41	---	---	--
4-12	hawaiite	580-780	23.1 ± 0.2	71	23.2 ± 0.2	273.6 ± 19.0	0.38
		*650-780	23.1 ± 0.2	67	23.2 ± 0.2	276.9 ± 34.9	0.75

the weighted mean age of the two plateau ages for the age of Patton.

The incremental heating experiments on Pathfinder samples 3-4 and 4-10 yielded poor data because of experimental difficulties (Figure 5). Trachyte sample 3-5, however, has a plateau at 23.2 ± 0.3 m.y. over all but one of the gas increments and a concordant isochron age. Hawaiite 4-11 has a low to intermediate temperature plateau with an age of 23.1 ± 0.2 m.y. We have used the weighted mean of these two plateaus for the age of Pathfinder.

Discussion and Conclusions

The five newly dated seamounts and guyots bring to 15 the number of radiometrically dated volcanoes in the Gulf of Alaska. These data are summarized in Table 12. Two of these, Bowie Seamount and Davidson Guyot, have only minimum ages [Turner et al., 1980]. Some compositional data are available for lavas from 13 of the seamounts and petrographic data exist for several others.

The difference in age between an individual

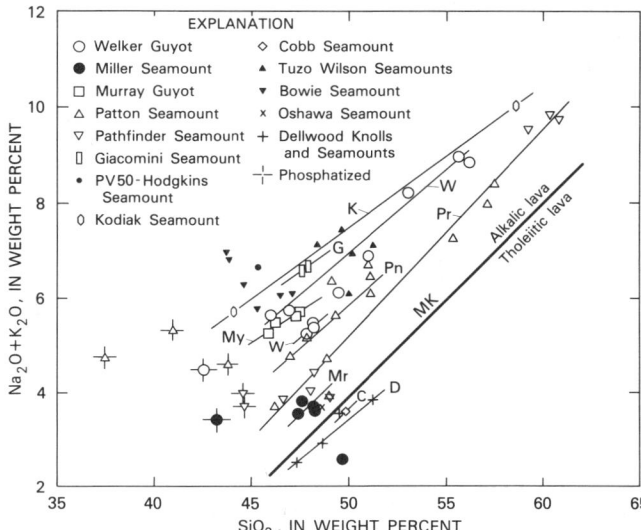

Fig. 6. Alkali-silica diagram showing whole rock and glass analyses of samples in Tables 2-7 and other published analyses of samples from seamounts in the Gulf of Alaska. [Forbes et al., 1969; Forbes and Hoskin, 1969; Engel et al., 1965; Cousens et al., 1984, 1985]. The line labelled MK separates Hawaiian tholeiitic and alkalic lavas. Tholeiitic and transitional composition lavas occur on seamounts formed at or near spreading centers whereas alkalic lavas occur on seamounts in the northerly Pratt-Welker chain.

volcano and the crust on which it formed is one indicator of whether the volcano is the result of mid-plate or near-ridge volcanic processes. The lava composition is a second indicator. Previous studies of the petrology of seamounts in the Gulf of Alaska [Forbes and Hoskin, 1969; Forbes et al., 1969; Macleod and Pratt, 1973; Cousens et al., 1984, 1985; Forbes, unpub. data cited in Turner et al., 1980] suggest that basalt transitional between tholeiitic and alkalic basalt occurs on seamounts that formed at or near spreading centers whereas alkalic basalt and associated differentiated lava (hawaiite, mugearite, benmoreite, trachyte) occur on seamounts formed by mid-plate volcanism. The occurrence of hawaiite from the Tuzo Wilson seamounts is used by Cousens et al. [1985] to infer that the hypothesized Pratt-Welker hot-spot is located nearby (Figure 1).

Our new chemical analyses are plotted on an alkali-silica diagram (Figure 6) with published data on samples from other seamounts in the Gulf of Alaska. In a general way, the degree of alkalinity is positively correlated with the degree of light-REE enrichment so that more alkaline lavas have higher $[La/Sm]_N$ ratios than less alkaline lavas. For our analyzed samples, lavas from Welker Guyot are the most light-REE enriched whereas those from Miller Seamount are the least light-REE enriched (Figure 7). The samples do not, however, plot on simple curves as expected from mixing of two components. This suggests that the lavas result from different degrees of melting and subsequent fractionation, and possibly from different mantle source rocks. Detailed petrogenetic modeling was not pursued because of the limited number and altered state of the samples.

For purposes of discussion, we have grouped the data into the Pratt-Welker, Patton-Murray, and Pathfinder-Horton "chains".

Pratt-Welker

This lineament includes 9 dated volcanoes from Kodiak Seamount to the Tuzo Wilson Seamounts. Distances along the chain in Table 12 are measured from the ridge segment that bisects the Dellwood Knolls. As noted by previous workers [Turner et al., 1980, Lambeck et al., 1984], the volcanoes in the Pratt-Welker chain do not have a single mode of origin. Their petrology, ages, and degree of isostatic compensation indicate that Denson, Davidson, and the older (14.3 m.y.) phase of Hodgkins originated near a spreading ridge on crust about 3-4 million years old. Volcanism was renewed on Hodgkins at least once, 2.8 million years ago, at which time the volcano erupted differentiated lava more typical of mid-plate volcanism. In contrast, Dickens, Giacomini, and Kodiak were clearly formed by mid-plate volcanism. They are younger than the underlying crust by 16-21 m.y., are regionally compensated, and have erupted alkalic lava. The petrology of volcanic rocks recovered from Bowie Seamount indicates that it also had a mid-plate origin [Turner et al., 1980]. Age

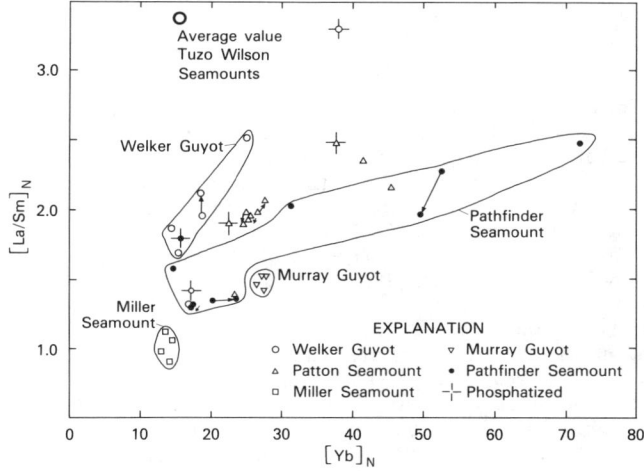

Fig. 7. Chondrite-normalized La/Sm plotted against chondrite normalized Yb. The most light-REE enriched samples are the most alkaline samples in Fig. 3, whereas the least light-REE enriched samples are transitional basalts from Miller Seamount. The fractionation trend for samples from Welker Seamount has a large increase in $[La/Sm]_N$ for a rather small increase in $[Yb]_N$ indicating that clinopyroxene is a major component of the fractionating mineral assemblage.

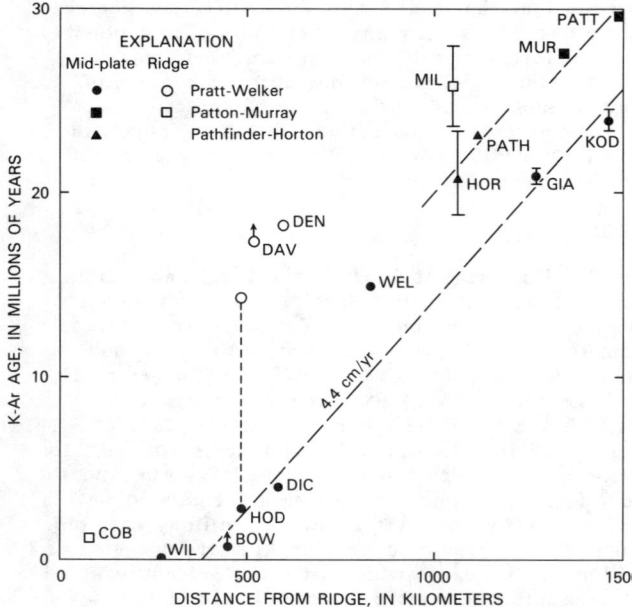

Fig. 8. Age versus distance for seamounts and guyots in the Gulf of Alaska. Data are labeled with first 3 or 4 letters of seamount names (Table 13). Vertical dashed line connects two distinct ages from Hodgkins Seamount; arrows indicate minimum ages. The distances for each of the three "chains" are measured from their respective ridge segments and so are not on a common distance base. The volcanic propagation rate of 4.4 cm/yr (sloping lines) is from Turner et al. [1980].

information for Bowie is somewhat ambiguous but suggests that the seamount is quite young. Bowie is reversely magnetized, indicating an age greater than 0.73 m.y. but a sample from the pinnacle has a K-Ar age of 0.075 ± 0.100 million years [Michkofsky, 1969, cited in Turner et al., 1980; Herzer, 1971].

Welker Guyot was considered of unknown origin by both Turner et al. [1980] and Lambeck et al. [1984] on the basis of summit depth and degree of isostatic compensation. The samples we recovered from Welker are hawaiite and mugearite whose K-Ar age of 14.9 ± 0.3 million years shows that Welker formed well away from the ridge on crust about 9 m.y. old and is of mid-plate origin. It does not, however, fit on the age-distance trend formed by Kodiak, Giacomini, Dickens, Hodgkins (recent volcanism), and Bowie (Figure 8). Thus, Welker must be accounted for either by a non-constant rate of volcanic propagation, i.e., a higher velocity immediately prior to Welker followed by a lower velocity immediately after, or by another episode of mid-plate volcanism distinct from the one that formed the other dated volcanoes of the Kodiak-Bowie chain. We think that a variable rate of volcanic propagation sufficient to account for the age of Welker is unlikely because large changes are required, i.e., a minimum of 7.0 cm/yr prior to Welker and a maximum of 2.6 cm/yr after, and changes of this magnitude have not been observed for other hot spot chains in the Pacific [Duncan and Clague, 1985; Clague and Dalrymple, 1987]. The alternative suggestion that Welker is part of a hot spot trace that includes Kodiak and Giacomini and ends near the Dellwood Knolls [Duncan and Clague, 1985] is equally problematic because it leaves the origin of Dickens, Hodgkins and Bowie to a second hot spot. In addition, rocks recovered from Dellwood Knolls are among the least alkalic of those analyzed (Figure 6) indicating that Dellwood probably is of ridge rather than of hot-spot origin. The Welker data are also at odds with the proposal by Smoot [1984] that Welker belongs to a linear chain that extends from Pratt Guyot to the Dellwood Knolls (Figure 1).

The Pratt-Welker "chain" is more complicated than envisioned by Morgan [1972a, b]. Its volcanoes cannot be accounted for by passage of the Pacific Plate over a single, persistent hot-spot. Some of the volcanoes in the lineament (Denson, Davidson, Hodgkins) formed near a spreading ridge and have simply been incorporated into the chain by the propagating volcanism as suggested by Clague and Dalrymple [1975] for several volcanoes in the Hawaiian chain. It seems likely that the remaining volcanoes originated during at least two, and probably more, distinct episodes of mid-plate volcanism, none of which could have had a lifetime of more than a few million years.

Even though Kodiak, Giacomini, Dickens, Hodgkins, and Bowie appear to fit a linear volcanic propagation trend (Figure 8) there is a hiatus in the "chain" between Durgin and Dickens that represents some 8-12 m.y. of time. This gap is occupied only by Welker Guyot, which is much too old to fit the propagation trend. The hiatus, the age of Welker, and the shape of the chain (convex poleward) argue against the hypothesis [Morgan, 1972a, b; Turner et al., 1980] that the mid-plate volcanoes of the Pratt-Welker chain are the product of a single hot spot. The seamounts from Kodiak thru Durgin may have formed over a single hot spot with a lifetime of 7-8 m.y. but only Kodiak and Giacomini have been studied so that continuity of this chain segment is untested. It seems unlikely that Welker is part of this lineament because the angular propagation rate obtained from Kodiak, Giacomini, and Welker is much higher than predicted from other Pacific hot spot chains. Similar difficulties with rate and geometry are encountered if Welker is combined with Dickens, Hodgkins, and Bowie. Thus, from the present data it seems possible that the mid-plate volcanoes of the Pratt-Welker chain are the product of at least three episodes of hot spot volcanism, i.e., Kodiak-Durgin, Welker, and Dickens-Bowie. At present we see no compelling reason to extend the Dickens-Bowie segment westward of Bowie.

The complex origin of the Pratt-Welker chain obviates the need for a moving hot spot to account for the apparent convex-poleward curvature of the chain proposed by Silver et al. [1974].

Patton-Murray

The age and petrology of lava from Miller Seamount indicate that it formed near a spreading ridge. Patton and Murray were formed on crust 11-12

TABLE 12. Summary of Age-Distance Data for Seamounts and Guyots in the Gulf of Alaska

Volcano	Distance From Ridge (km)	K-Ar Age (my)	Age of Crust (my)	Crust age-Seamount age	Ref.
Tuzo Wilson	275	0.055 ± 0.055	5	5	(1)
Bowie	450	>0.73	17	<16	(2)
Cobb	80	1.6 ± 0.3	2.4	0.8	(3)
Hodgkins	485	2.8, 14.3	18	15,4	(4)
Dickins	585	4.0 ± 0.2	20	16	(4)
Welker	830	14.9 ± 0.3	24	9	(5)
Davidson	520	>=17.4 ± 1.7	19	<2	(4)
Denson	595	18.2 ± 2.0	21	3	(4)
T. Horton	1060	20.7 ± 2.0	32	11	(4)
Giacomini	1270	20.9 ± 0.4	40	19	(6)
Pathfinder	1115	23.1 ± 0.2	34	11	(5)
Kodiak	1465	23.9 ± 0.6	45	21	(6)
Miller	1050	25.8 ± 2.1	31	5	(5)
Murray	1345	27.6 ± 0.2	39	11	(5)
Patton	1490	29.7 ± 0.3	42	12	(5)

References: (1) Cousens et al. [1985]; (2) Michkofsky [1969] cited in Turner et al. [1980]; (3) Dymond et al. [1968]; (4) Turner et al. [1980]; (5) This paper; (6) Turner et al. [1973].
Crustal ages from Naugler and Wageman [1973], Wilson [1985] and Harland et al. [1982].
Underlined volcanoes are known to have erupted alkalic lavas and are thought to have been formed by mid-plate, rather than ridge, volcanism.

m.y. old (Table 12) and their lava includes hawaiite and benmoreite. They appear, therefore, to be the result of mid-plate rather than near-ridge volcanism. The two volcanoes are age-progressive (Figure 8) but too close to each other to yield a meaningful volcanic propagation rate. Duncan and Clague [1985] suggested that these volcanoes belong to a chain that includes Cobb and Eickelberg seamounts but the geometry of this proposed chain is not convincing, especially with Miller Seamount eliminated (Figure 1).

A further puzzle is that the summit depths and basement swell heights of Patton and Murray are too shallow for their ages. Both of these volcanoes rise from a basement swell that has a local relief of 840-1350 m above crust 39-42 m.y. old. In addition, the summit platforms are at relatively shallow depths of 450 and 750 m, respectively. These data suggest that Patton Seamount and Murray Guyot are quite young, perhaps 2-8 m.y. old, which is contrary to the K-Ar data. The crust may be elevated several hundred meters by flexure within 100-200 km of a trench axis [Caldwell et al., 1976]. This might account for the summit depth of Patton, which is about 190 km from the trench axis, but it cannot explain the summit depth of Murray or the height of the swell above basement. A more likely explanation is that the basement beneath these two seamounts has been thermally rejuvenated within the past few million years. The discrepancy between seamount age and the ages estimated from bathymetry suggest caution in using the latter to "date" seamounts.

Pathfinder-Horton

The K-Ar age of Pathfinder Seamount is slightly greater than the age determined for T. Horton Guyot by Turner et al. [1980]. Both of these volcanoes formed on crust about 11 m.y. old, both have produced highly differentiated alkalic lavas, and both are the products of mid-plate volcanism. It is not known, however, whether or not these two volcanoes are part of a hot spot trace as data on other volcanoes in the lineament (e.g., Parker, Gilbert, and Scott) are lacking.

The age, petrologic, bathymetric, geometric, and satellite data indicate that the majority of the seamounts and guyots in the Gulf of Alaska formed by mid-plate rather than the near-ridge volcanic processes invoked by Smoot [1985]. Evidence for sustained hot-spot volcanism and the lengthy linear volcanic chains it produces, however, is presently lacking. While some of the mid-plate volcanoes may be part of a linear chain (e.g., Kodiak and Giacomini), other mid-plate volcanoes appear to be either isolated (e.g., Welker) or associated with only a few others (e.g., Patton and Murray) and thus are the result of "hot spots" that were active for only a few million years. Alternatively, these volcanoes may be the result of mid-plate volcanism that depends on zones of weakness in the lithosphere [Batiza, 1981] rather than a persistent hot-spot capable of penetrating the lithosphere.

The evidence shows that Smoot's [1985] hypothesis for 6 chains in the Gulf of Alaska (Fig 1) is incorrect. Pathfinder and T. Horton, for example, are not part of a younger chain but are approximately the same age as Giacomini and clearly older that Smoot's proposed "bend". Also, neither Welker nor Miller are part of the chains he proposes. Finally, reorganization of subduction and spreading in the Gulf of Alaska 17 m.y. ago would be recorded in the magnetic anomaly pattern, and they are not.

Based on studies of the Hawaiian-Emperor, Marquesas, Society Islands, and other well-documented volcanic chains it has been presumed that all hot-spots are persistent, form easily recognizeable linear chains, and possess significant geographic stability. Data from seamounts in the Gulf of Alaska, however, show that some hot-spots are short-lived and produce only a few volcanoes before ceasing activity. We see no reason why this phenomenon should be unique to the Gulf of Alaska.

Acknowledgements. We thank David Scholl and Andy Stevenson for their assistance with cruise logistics and dredging operations, Michael Underwood for shipboard and onland assistance with sample descriptions and selections, Andy Stevenson for navigation plots and encouragement, Elliot Kollman and James Saburomaru for assistance with the K-Ar and $^{40}Ar/^{39}Ar$ analyses, and the staff of the U.S.G.S. TRIGA reactor for providing the 2×10^{21} fast neutrons necessary for this study. We are also grateful to our colleagues Richard Gordon, Malcolm Pringle and Randy Koski who reviewed the manuscript and offered suggestions for improvement.

References

Basaltic Volcanism Study Project, Basaltic Volcanism on the Terrestrial Planets, Pergamon Press, New York, 1286 p, 1981.
Batiza, R., Lithospheric age dependence of off-ridge volcano production in the North Pacific, Geophys. Res. Lett., 8, 853-856, 1981.
Batiza, R. and D. Vanko, Petrology of young Pacific Seamonts, J. Geophys. Res., 89, 11,235-11,260, 1984.
Caldwell, J.G., W.F. Haxby, D.E. Karig, and D.L. Turcott, On the applicabililty of a universal elastic trench profile, Earth Planet. Sci. Lett., 31, 239-246, 1976.

Chase, T.E., H.W. Menard, and J. Mammerickx, Bathymetry of the North Pacific, Charts 3 and 4, La Jolla, Calif., Inst. Marine Resources, Scripps Inst. Oceranog., 1970.
Clague, D.A. Hawaiian alkaline volcanism, J. Geol. Soc. London, in press.
Clague, D.A., and G.B. Dalrymple, Cretaceous K-AR agests of volcanic rocks from the Muscians Seamounts and the Hawaiian Ridge, Geophys. Res. Lett., 2, 305-308, 1975.
Clague, D.A. and G.B. Dalrymple, The Hawaiian-Emperor volcanic chain: Part 1. Geologic Evolution, U.S. Geol. Surv. Prof. Pap., 1350, 5-54, 1987.
Clague, D.A., and R.D. Jarrard, Tertiary Pacific plate motion deduced from the Hawaiian-Emperor chain, Geol. Soc. Amer. Bull., 84, 1135-1154, 1973.
Cousens, B.L., R.L. Chase, and J.G. Schilling, Basalt geochemistry of the Explorer Ridge area, northeast Pacific Ocean, Can. J. Earth Sci., 21, 157-170, 1984.
Cousens, B.L., R.L. Chase, and J.G. Schilling, Geochemistry and origin of volcanic rocks from Tuzo Wilson and Bowie seamounts, northeast Pacific Ocean, Can. J. Earth Sci., 22, 1609-1617, 1985.
Crough, S.T., Hotspot swells, Ann. Rev. Earth Planet. Sci., 11, 165-193, 1983.
Dalrymple, G.B., E.C. Alexander, Jr., M.A. Lanphere, and G.P. Kraker, Irradiation of samples for $^{40}Ar/^{39}Ar$ dating using the Geological Survey TRIGA reactor, U.S. Geol. Surv. Prof. Pap. 1176, 55 p, 1981.
Dalrymple, G.B., and Clague, D.A., Age of the Hawaiian - Emperor bend, Earth Planet. Sci. Lett., 31, 313-329, 1976.
Dalrymple, G.B., and M.A. Lanphere, Potassium-Argon Dating, San Francisco, W.H. Freeman Co., 258 pp., 1969.
Dalrymple, G.B., and M.A. Lanphere, $^{40}Ar/^{39}Ar$ technique of K-Ar dating: A comparison with the conventional technique, Earth Planet. Sci. Lett., 12, 300-308, 1971.
Detrick, R.S., and S.T. Crough, Island subsidence, hot spots, and lighospheric thinning, J. Geophys. Res., 83, 1236-1244, 1978.
Duncan, R.A., and D.A. Clague, Pacific plate motion recorded by linear volcanic chains, in A.E.M. Nairn, F.G. Stehli, and S. Uyeda, eds., The Ocean Basins and Margins, 7A, 89-121, 1985.
Dymond, J.R., N.D. Watkins, and Y.R. Nayudu, Age of Cobb Seamount, J. Geophys. Res., 73, 3977-3979, 1968.
Engel, A.E.J., C.E. Engel, and R.G. Havens, Chemical characteristics of oceanic basalts and the upper mantle, Geol. Soc. Am. Bull., 76, 719-734, 1965.
Fleck, R.J., J.F. Sutter, and D.H. Elliot, Interpretation of discordant $^{40}Ar/^{39}Ar$ age-spectra of Mesozoic tholeiites from Antarctica, Geochim. Cosmochim. Acta, 41, 15-32, 1977.
Forbes, R.B., R.C. Duyale, T. Katsura, H. Matsumoto, and H. Haramura, Dredged basalt from Giacomini Seamount, Nature, 221, 849-850, 1969.
Forbes, R.B. and C.M. Hoskin, Dredged trachyte and basalt from Kodiak Seamount and the adjacent Aleutian trench, Science, 166, 502-504, 1969.
Harland, W.B., A.V. Cox, P.G. Llewellyn, C.A.G. Pickton, A.G. Smith, and R. Walters, A

Geologic Time Scale, Cambridge, Cambridge Univ. Press, 131 pp., 1982.

Herzer, R.H., Bowie Seamount, a recently active, flat-topped seamount in the northeast Pacific Ocean, Can J. Earth Sci., 8, 676-687, 1971.

Hess, H.H., Drowned ancient islands of the Pacific, Amer. J. Sci., 244, 772-791, 1946.

Ingamells, C.O., Lithium metaborate flux in silicate analysis, Anal. Chim. Acta, 52, 332-334.

Jackson, E.D., Linear volcanic chains on the Pacific Plate, in G.H. Sutton, M.H. Manghani, and R. Moberly, eds., The Geophysics of the Pacific Ocean Basin and its Margin, Geophys. Mon. 19, Washington, D.C., Amer. Geophys. Union, 319-335, 1976.

Jarrard, R.D. and D.A. Clague, Implications of Pacific island and ieamount ages for the origin of volcanic chains, Rev. Geophys. Space Phys., 15, 57-76, 1977.

Koski, R.A., Ferromanganese deposits from the Gulf of Alaska Seamount Province: Mineralogy, chemistry, and origin, Can. J. Earth Sci., in press.

Lambeck, K., C.L. Penny, S.M. Nakiboglu, and R. Coleman, Subsidence and flexure along the Pratt-Welker seamount chani, J. Geodynam., 1, 29-60, 1984.

MacLeod, N.S., and R.M. Pratt, Petrology of volcanic rocks recovered on leg 18, in L.D. Kulm et al., Initial Reports of the Deep Sea Drilling Project, Vol. 18, United States Government Printing Office, Washington, D.C., 935-945, 1973.

Mattey, D.P., The minor and trace element geochemistry of volcanic rocks from Truk, Ponope and Kusaie, Eastern Caroline Islands: The evolution of a young hotspot trace across old Pacific Ocean Crust, Contrib. Min. and Petrol., 80, 1-13, 1982.

McDougall, I., L-Ar and $^{40}Ar/^{39}Ar$ dating of the hominid-bearing Pliocena-Pleistocene sequence at Koobi Fore, Lake Turkana, northern Kenya, Geol. Soc. Amer. Bull., 96, 159-175, 1985.

McDougall, I., and R.A. Duncan, Linear volcanic chains--recording plate motions?, Tectonophys., 63, 275-295, 1980.

Menard, H.W., and R.S. Dietz, Submarine geology of the Gulf of Alaska, Geol. Soc. Amer. Bull. 62, 1263-1285, 1951.

Moore, J.G., and B.P. Fabbi, An estimate of the juvenile sulfur content of basalt, Contrib. Min. and Petrol. 33, 118-127, 1971.

Morgan, W.J., Deep mantle convection plumes and plate motions, Amer. Assoc. Petrol. Geol. Bull., 56, 203-213, 1972a.

Morgan, W.J., Plate motions and deep mantle convection, in R. Shagan et al., eds., Studies in Earth and Space Sciences, Geol. Soc. Amer. Mem. 132 (Hess Volume), 7-22, 1972b.

Murray, H.W., Submarine mountains in the Gulf of Alaska, Geol. Soc. Amer. Bull., 52, 333-362, 1941.

Murray, H.W., Submarine relief of the Aleutian Trench, Trans. Amer. Geophys. Union, 27, 871-875, 1946.

Naugler, F.P., and J.M. Wageman, Gulf of Alaska: Magnetic anomalies, fracture zones, and plate interactions, Geol. Soc. Amer. Bull., 84, 1575-1583, 1973.

Ozima, M., M. Honda, and K. Saito, ^{40}Ar-^{39}Ar ages of guyots in the western Pacific and discussion of their evolution, Roy. Astron. Soc. Geophys. J., 51, 475-485, 1977.

Parsons, B., and J.G. Sclater, An analysis of the variation of ocean floor bathymetry and heat flow with age, J. Geophys. Res., 82, 803-827, 1977.

Roddick, J.C., R.A. Cliff, and D.C. Rex, The evolution of excess argon in alpine biotities- ^{40}Ar-^{39}Ar analysis, Earth Planet. Sci. Lett., 48, 185-203, 1980.

Silver, E.A., R. von Huene, and J.K. Crouch, Tectonic significance of the Kodiak-Bowie seamount-chain, northeastern Pacific, Geology, 2, 147-150, 1974.

Smoot, N.C., Observations on Gulf of Alaska seamount chain by multi-beam sonar, Tectonophys., 115, 235-246, 1985.

Stacey, J.S., N.D. Sherrill, G.B. Dalrymple, M.A. Lanphere, and N.V. Carpenter, A five-collector system for the simultaneous measurement of argon isotope ratios in a static mass spectrometer, Int. Jour. Mass Spec. Ion Phys., 39, 167-180, 1981.

Staudigel, H. and S.R. Hart, Alteration of basaltic glass: Mechanisms and significance for the oceanic crust-seawater budget, Geochim. Cosmochim. Acta, 47, 337-350, 1983.

Taylor, J.R., An Introduction to Error Analysis, Mill Valley, California, University Science Books, 270 pp., 1982.

Turner, D.L., R.B. Forbes, and C.W. Naeser, Radiometric ages of Kodiak Seamount and Geacomini Guyot, Gulf of Alaska: Implications for circum-Pacific tectonics, Science, 182, 579-581, 1973.

Turner, D.L., R.D. Jarrard, and R.B. Forbes, Geochronology and origin of the Pratt-Welker seamount chain, Gulf of Alaska: A new pole of rotation for the Pacific plate, J. Geophys. Res., 85, 6547-6556, 1980.

Wilson, D.S., 1985, Tectonic history of the Juan de Fuca Riege, Ph.D thesis, Stanford University, 105 pp.

Wilson, J.T., A possible origin of the Hawaiian Islands, Can. J. Phys., 41, 863-870, 1963.

York, D., Least squares fitting of a straight line with correlated errors, Earth Planet Sci. Lett., 5, 320-324, 1969.

Oceanographic and Biological Studies

A REVIEW OF THE EFFECTS OF SEAMOUNTS ON BIOLOGICAL PROCESSES

George W. Boehlert

Southwest Fisheries Center Honolulu Laboratory, National Marine
Fisheries Service, NOAA, 2570 Dole St., Honolulu, HI 96822-2396

Amatzia Genin

Scripps Institution of Oceanography, A-008, University of California, La Jolla, CA 92093

Abstract. Seamounts interacting with oceanic currents create flow complexities which depend upon current speed, stratification, latitude, and seamount morphology. Seamount effects, which include internal wave generation, eddy formation, local upwelling, and closed circulation patterns called Taylor columns, have important effects upon pelagic and benthic ecosystems over seamounts. The biological effects of these current-topography interactions are poorly understood. Flow acceleration on upper flanks of seamounts may lead to low sedimentation but areas of high standing stocks of benthic fauna, particularly filter feeders. Other effects extend into the water column; nutrient enrichment and enhanced primary productivity occur over some seamounts. Longer observational periods will be necessary to understand the time-varying nature of such enhanced productivity and the extent to which it remains at the seamount or is advected away. At higher trophic levels, unusual patterns of distribution and abundance occur at some seamounts. Maintenance of high standing stocks of seamount-associated micronekton and demersal fishes suggests that seamounts are locations for high rates of energy transfer. The energy driving this biological productivity may either be generated from in situ processes or be advected from elsewhere and concentrated at the seamount; interdisciplinary studies will be necessary to better understand these ecosystems.

Introduction

Seamounts represent a major physical feature of all ocean basins. For marine biota, they may be considered as islands separated by deep ocean areas; seamounts were thus the topic of many biogeographic studies [Wilson and Kaufman, 1987]. Biological communities at seamounts, however, may differ qualitatively and quantitatively from their continental shelf or slope counterparts at similar water depths [Hubbs, 1959]. In the open ocean, seamounts interact with ocean currents and create variability in the physical flow field. Several studies have described these effects on the Gulf Stream [Vastano and Warren, 1976] and the Kuroshio [Roden et al., 1982; Roden, 1987]. The physical effects include local small- and mesoscale phenomena including the shedding of mesoscale eddies which alter flow patterns for significant distances downstream of the seamounts [Royer, 1978]. Biological effects of these physical complexities are not well understood [Genin and Boehlert 1985; Boehlert, 1986]. Discovery of seamount fishery [Uchida and Tagami, 1984] and mineral resources [Manheim, 1986], however, has caused increased interest in seamount oceanography and its effects on biota [Darnitsky et al., 1984; Genin and Boehlert, 1985; Uchida et al., 1986].

The effects of sea floor topography on ocean currents have been a topic of interest to physical oceanographers for several decades. This area has recently been reviewed by Hogg [1980] and was the topic of a monograph by Kozlov [1983]. Semistationary eddies or Taylor columns above seamounts have been theoretically predicted and experimentally demonstrated in the laboratory [Taylor, 1917; Huppert and Bryan, 1976] and have been observed over some seamounts [Darnitsky, 1980; Owens and Hogg, 1980; Richardson, 1980]. Unfortunately, oceanographic surveys generally have station patterns inappropriate to detect these open-ocean, small-scale or mesoscale phenomena [Roden 1986]. Still, past theoretical and observational studies on the physics of topographic effects are available to serve as a background for biological studies.

Many studies have suggested that ecosystems at certain banks or seamounts are highly productive [Uda and Ishino 1958; Fedosova, 1974; Zaika and Kovalev, 1984; Tseitlin, 1985]. The ideas which explain such high productivity are typically based upon either local enhancement and subsequent

Copyright 1987 by the American Geophysical Union.

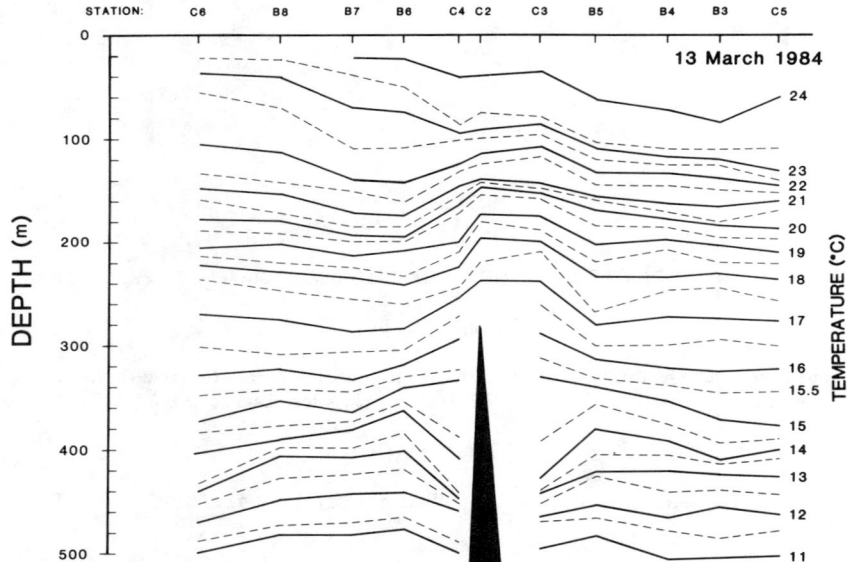

Fig. 1. Temperature structure at Minami-Kasuga Seamount (lat. 21°6'N, long. 143°8'E) along a west-east transect showing uplifted isotherms over the summit of the seamount. Note that the vertical scale is 50 times greater than the horizontal scale. (From Genin and Boehlert, 1985.)

retention of productivity or advection and concentration of food produced elsewhere. Some support exists for each of these hypotheses. Differences often exist between the pelagic ecosystems of waters above seamounts and adjacent, oceanic waters, including nutrient concentrations [Kozlov et al., 1982], chlorophyll [Genin and Boehlert, 1985], plankton biomass [Bezrukov and Natarov, 1976], ichthyoplankton [Nellen, 1973], and micronekton [Boehlert and Seki, 1984]. In the case of advected productivity, however, seamount populations may not be limited by local production, but rather by physical aggregation mechanisms [Isaacs and Schwartzlose, 1965; Darnitsky et al., 1984], which have been shown to exist in gyres and near reefs and coastal headlands [Alldredge and Hamner, 1980; Olson and Backus, 1985]. Benthic ecosystems on seamounts and islands may similarly differ from corresponding systems on continental shelves and slopes but have typically been less well studied. In many cases, unusual or even unique faunas exist [Simpson and Heydorn, 1965; Littler et al., 1986]. In addition, more recent studies have investigated the relationship of benthic fauna to current speeds and seamount-induced physical variability [Genin et al., 1986]. In this paper we review the effects of seamounts on biological processes, particularly as they affect pelagic and benthic ecosystems and fisheries productivity.

The Pelagic Ecosystem at Seamounts

Much of the impact of seamounts on pelagic ecosystems may be traced to current-topography interactions, which have been summarized in this volume by Roden [1987]. Where seamounts act as obstacles to current flow, compression of streamlines will occur due to flow acceleration. Local deflections of isotherms, usually in the form of uplifting, have been observed above several seamounts at different locations and depths [Meincke, 1971; Vastano and Warren, 1976]. Taylor columns represent an interesting phenomenon pertinent to seamounts; associated theory [Taylor, 1923; Huppert and Bryan, 1976] predicts such deflections as a result of the encounter between a current and a seamount. Under certain conditions of current, stratification, and topography, a closed streamlined anticyclonic vortex, or Taylor column, is expected to remain trapped above the seamount [Hogg, 1973; Huppert, 1975]. Such trapping may enhance nutrients shallower in the water column and if the residence time of a water mass above the seamount is sufficiently long, result in enhanced primary productivity and transfer into higher trophic levels. In this section we consider evidence for such enhancement and the role it plays in different trophic levels.

Nutrients and Primary Productivity

The uplifting of isotherms over seamounts is distinct and occurs with sufficient frequency to provide support for Taylor column dynamics. As an example, isotherms over Minami-Kasuga Seamount in the Mariana Archipelago [Genin and Boehlert, 1985] showed a clear uplift (Fig. 1) which did not reach the surface. Such upwelling at seamounts, like coastal upwelling, will transport nutrients into the euphotic zone where the primary production is nutrient-limited; an analogous situation exists around islands in stratified seas, where increased tidal mixing may stimulate primary productivity [Simpson et al., 1982]. Observations on a variety of seamounts support this contention; Bezrukov and Natarov [1976] suggested that vertical velocities on the order of 0.00003 to 0.0008 $cm \cdot sec^{-1}$ exist over various seamounts and that differences in the magnitude of upwelling may explain variability in seamount productivity. Vortices associated with seamounts can produce physical structures much like open-ocean cold core rings, except they remain centered over the seamount. Kozlov et al. [1982] describe a "columnar distribution" of temperature, salinity, silicate, and phosphate over one of the summits of Milwaukee Seamount in the southern Emperor Chain, in which elevated nutrient levels corresponding to the values at the seamount flanks reach high into the water column. Two visits, one month apart, to Pulkovskaya Seamount in the South Pacific suggested that vortices existed around the twin peaks and "satellite" vortices remained in surrounding waters. Again, signals were apparent in salinity, temperature, and silicate; silicate concentration at the summit depth of 500 m extended to the surface, with values nearly double that in surrounding waters [Kozlov et al., 1982]. Darnitsky et al. [1984] studied nutrients over Wanganella Bank near New Zealand during six visits from 1974 to 1977. Although upwelling and the resultant nutrient enrichment were clearly observed twice, the water was stratified with no apparent seamount effect during four other transects.

A shorter time scale was addressed in a study by Genin and Boehlert [1985], who conducted a series of transects to describe temperature and chlorophyll distribution over Minami-Kasuga Seamount. On the first of three surveys made within a month, uplifted isotherms formed a subsurface cold dome above the seamount (Fig. 1). The vertical displacement of the uplifted isotherms gradually decreased with distance above the seamount, from a 50 m uplift of the 17° isotherm close to the substratum, to a decay of the cold anomaly at about 80 m depth (180 m above the seamount top). Different deflection trends of isotherms in the vicinity of the substratum around the seamount slope formed a "boundary zone" comprising three distinctive layers composed of downward deflected isotherms from approximately 500 m to about 420 m, a relatively well mixed "transition zone" (Fig. 1) between the 14.5° and 15° isotherms (approximately 50 m above the previous layer), and an upwelling layer shallower than 340 m. These layers may be related to energy dissipation in the benthic boundary layer and agree with the statement by Bezrukov and Natarov [1976] that there is typically a change in the sign of vertical velocity between 300 and 600 m on the flanks of seamounts. On this first survey, calculations based upon seamount morphology suggested that conditions favoring maintenance of a Taylor column were present.

Three chlorophyll profiles taken within the cold dome showed a distinctive maximum between 80 and 100 m depth, whereas the chlorophyll maximum layer at the four control stations was comparatively diffuse (Fig. 2). The causal relationships between the localized upwelling and the biological response are corroborated by the confinement of the chlorophyll increase to depths below 80 m, the uppermost edge of the cold dome. The chlorophyll concentrations at shallower depths above the seamount and at the control stations varied little throughout the area. These results clearly contrast with data from the second and third surveys in which neither cold dome nor chlorophyll increases were detectable along the same transects. These observations suggest that varying strength of oncoming currents result in a varying time scale for presence of the uplifted isotherms. Estimates of the time necessary for the formation of the observed chlorophyll maximum from the first survey, however, suggest a minimum residence time of the hypothesized Taylor column on the order of days [Genin and Boehlert, 1985].

The vertical extent and residence time of seamount-induced upwelling will determine the magnitude of its effect on local biological processes in overlying waters. Unfortunately, the temporal sampling scale of the studies described above is inadequate to determine the temporal dynamics clearly, and knowledge of regional currents is frequently lacking; moreover, the time scales will vary from seamount to seamount, which will have an effect on the manner in which any enhanced primary productivity may reach higher trophic levels. In oligotrophic oceans, phytoplankton production would increase if the uplifted isotherms penetrated into the euphotic zone, replenishing its depleted water with nutrients, as noted by Kozlov et al. [1982] and in the first survey by Genin and Boehlert [1985]. Entrapment on the order of days would probably affect only the primary producers, and hence, a patch of relatively high chlorophyll concentrations would be associated with the seamount. A longer residence time, on the order of several weeks, may locally affect the growth and abundance of zooplankton species; months would be necessary for micronekton [Pudyakov and Tseitlin, 1986]. Lagrangian current observations made above the Emperor Seamounts [Cheney et al., 1980] and the Corner Rise Seamounts [Richardson, 1980] suggested entrapment periods up to several weeks within seamount-generated anticyclonic eddies. Much longer periods (on the order of several months) were inferred from hydrographic and Eulerian current measurements above a deep seamount in the North Atlantic [Owens and Hogg, 1980]. If local enrichment persists for long periods and is a recurrent phenomenon, nektonic organisms may be attracted to or aggregated in these habitats [Uda and Ishino, 1958; Boehlert and Seki, 1984; Uchida and Tagami, 1984]. An analogy may be drawn to demersal plankton in nearshore reef systems [Hobson and Chess, 1978; Alldredge and King, 1985].

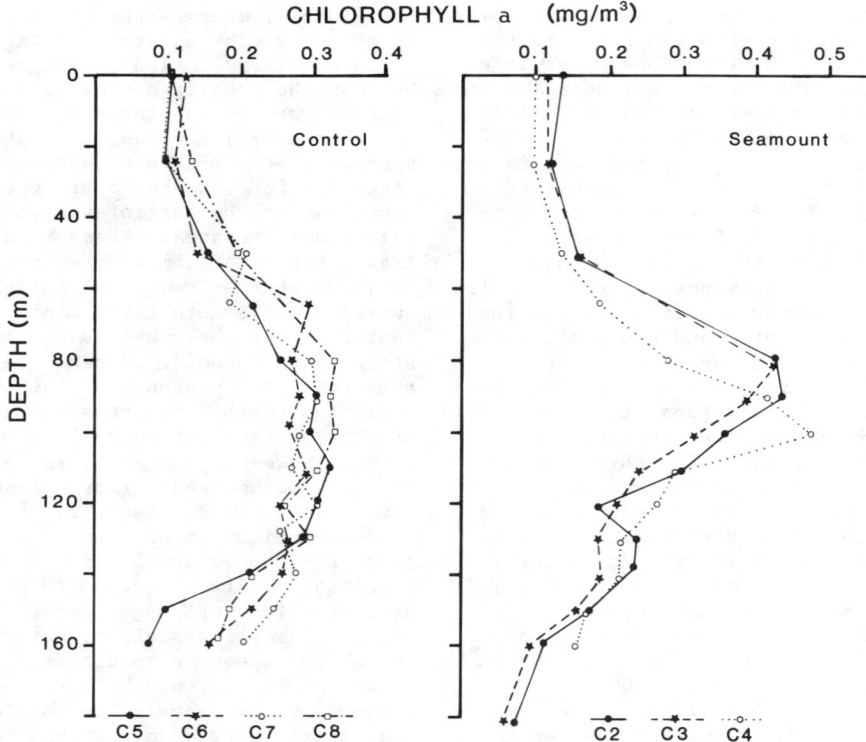

Fig. 2. Chlorophyll a profiles above Minami-Kasuga Seamount taken concurrently with the temperature transects shown in Figure 1. Three stations were occupied over the top of the seamount (right) and at control stations which were 10 km from the seamount summit (left). (From Genin and Boehlert 1985.)

Zooplankton and Nekton

Evidence concerning densities of planktonic organisms above seamounts is often conflicting. Sorokin and Sorokina [1985] noted no differences between waters above seamounts and surrounding waters with respect to bacterioplankton. Many surveys in the regions of seamounts, however, indicate two- to eightfold increases in zooplankton abundance in waters over seamounts [Fedosova 1974]; Zaika and Kovalev [1984] summarize results from a variety of Soviet papers. Zooplankton samples were taken by Genin and Boehlert [1985] in two of their three surveys, one during elevated and the other under normal chlorophyll levels. Zooplankton displacement volume was greater above the seamount only on the first survey; in contrast to the chlorophyll signal, however, zooplankton volumes were higher within the cold dome and above it, possibly indicative of the more vertically mobile nature of zooplankton [Genin and Boehlert 1985]. Whereas the studies referred to above have typically considered zooplankton biomass, it may be more appropriate to consider specific taxa, which may be either more abundant or relatively depleted in waters above seamounts [Hirota and Boehlert, 1985].

A specific component of the plankton studied above seamounts has been the ichthyoplankton. In the North Pacific, Borets and Sokolovsky [1978] observed no differences in ichthyoplankton abundance or species composition above seamounts as compared to distant waters; Belyanina [1985] had similar results in the Indian Ocean. Nellen [1973], however, in a study on the Great Meteor Seamount, noted increased abundance of neritic species and depletion of others, most typically midwater fish larvae, above the seamount. Boehlert [1985] described ichthyoplankton densities from winter and summer cruises at Southeast Hancock Seamount. Fish larvae at this open-ocean seamount are dominated by midwater rather than neritic species. In the summer, daytime samples showed no difference between the seamount and reference stations with the exception of the 50-100 m stratum (Fig. 3A). At night, however, the densities at the reference station were significantly increased as compared to daytime values, but not in the samples taken over the seamount. Samples taken on a winter cruise showed a different pattern from that in the summer (Fig. 3B); ichthyoplankton densities over the seamount were much greater than at the reference station, and the pattern held for night and day. These data

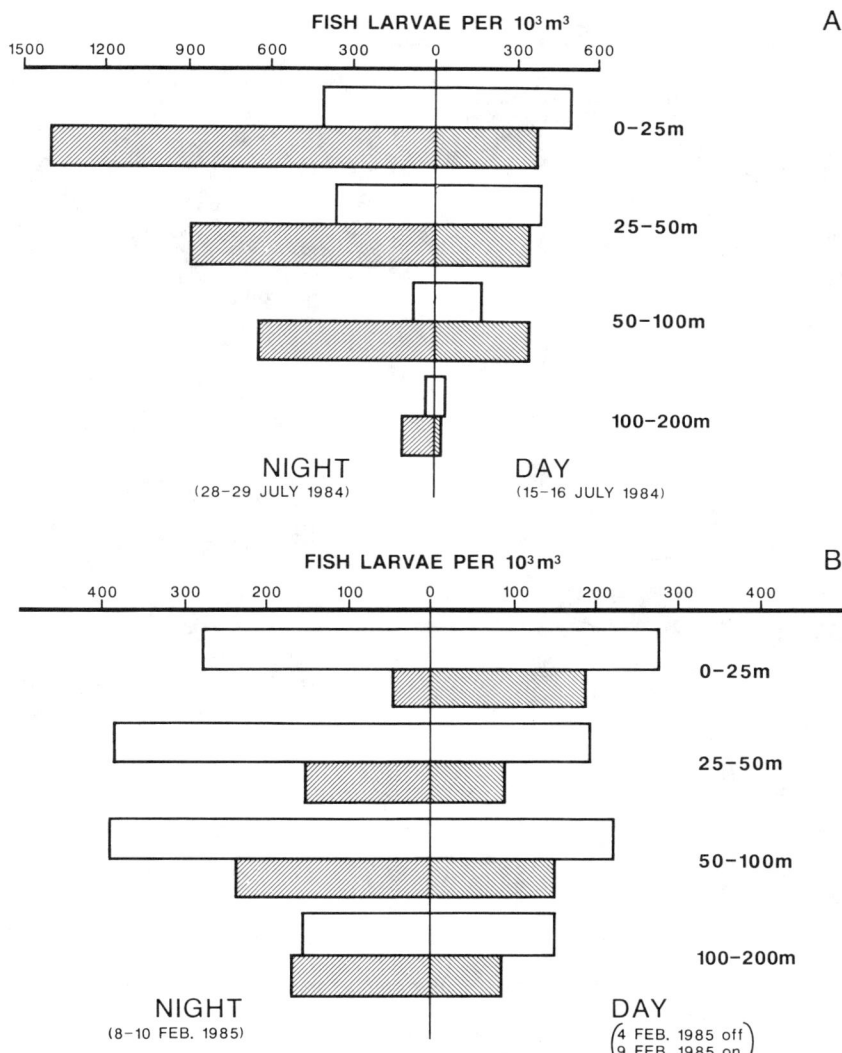

Fig. 3. Comparison of ichthyoplankton densities above Southeast Hancock Seamount (lat. 29°8'N, long. 178°5'E) with those at reference stations 20 km away. Samples were taken at discrete depths with an opening-closing Tucker trawl. A. Summer 1984. B. Winter 1985. Daytime densities are on the right, nighttime on the left, with each value the mean of duplicate samples. Densities above the seamount are represented by the upper (solid) bar, densities at the reference station by the lower (cross-hatched) bar. (Presented in Boehlert, 1985.)

suggest that some phenomena differing between winter and summer (or an aliased time scale) impact the abundance of these taxa.

As compared to the passive planktonic species, micronekton and nekton have more control over their movements. Fewer studies over seamounts have been conducted on these species, but Uda and Ishino [1958] suggested that aggregations of such animals may result in enhancement of fishing grounds. Densities may be estimated using hydroacoustic observations and net sampling. Some organisms normally rare in open-ocean areas may be abundant on seamounts. The sternoptychid fish, Maurolicus muelleri, typically associated with continental shelf-slope breaks, has been observed in abundance over South Atlantic and North Pacific seamounts [Linkowski, 1983; Boehlert and Seki, 1984]. Kozlov et al. [1982] noted vertical columns of scattering layers over two seamounts in the North Pacific but mistakenly considered them to be simply vertical manifestations of the oceanic scattering layers arrayed vertically like the "columnar" distributions of temperature and nutrients. Hydroacoustic observations at night above Southeast Hancock Seamount [Boehlert and Seki, 1984] showed pronounced scattering (Fig. 4).

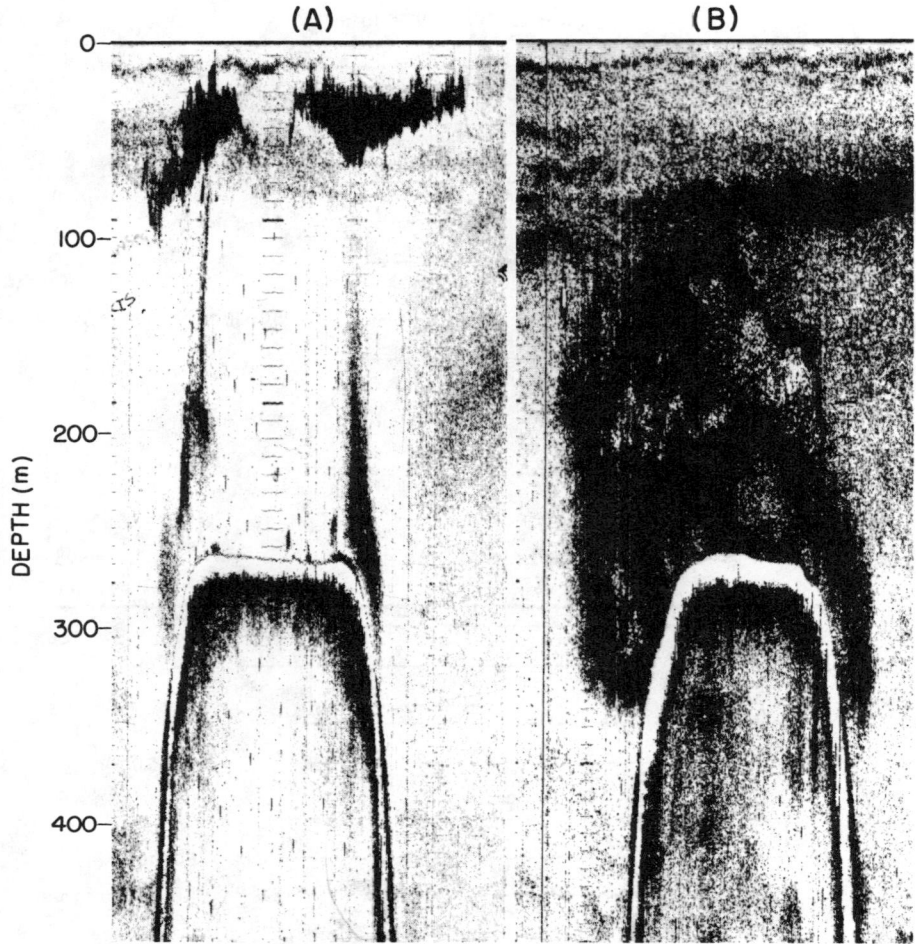

Fig. 4. Acoustic transects over Southeast Hancock Seamount on 17-18 July 1984 taken with a 38 kHz echo sounder. Each transect, from west to east (left to right) near the central axis of the seamount, took approximately 25 min. The distance across the flat portion of the seamount is approximately 1.8 km. A. 1931 h. Note the scattering layers rising off the seamount flanks to a depth of 40-60 m; net samples show these early layers to be predominantly Maurolicus muelleri. Sunset was at 1907. B. 0330 h. The layer has developed over the seamount extending from the flanks upwards to near 100 m; it developed this configuration at approximately 2130 and remained in a similar configuration throughout the night, until dispersing in early morning. These scattering targets may have been larger fishes or squids not sampled by our midwater trawl. (Presented in Boehlert and Seki, 1984.)

Scatterers typically remained on the flanks of the seamount by day, but began streaming vertically upward to depths near 50 m early in the evening (Fig. 4A), followed by consolidation of the shallow layers, a slight sinking of the top layer, and expansion downwards until the scattering layer extended from the summit of the seamount upwards to approximately 100 m depth (Fig. 4B). By contrast, no deep scattering layers in surrounding oceanic waters displayed either such high density or this type of behavior, suggesting that organisms specific to the region of the seamount were responsible for the acoustic traces. Subsequent hauls with midwater trawls demonstrated differences in abundance and species composition between waters above the seamount and at the reference stations. Maurolicus muelleri and the lophogastrid mysid, Gnathophausia longispina, dominated the catch over the seamounts. A third species, the sepiolid squid, Iridoteuthis iris, was characteristic of the deeper portions of the seamount scattering layer (Fig. 5A). In waters away from the seamount, oceanic taxa were generally more abundant and the three seamount taxa were either

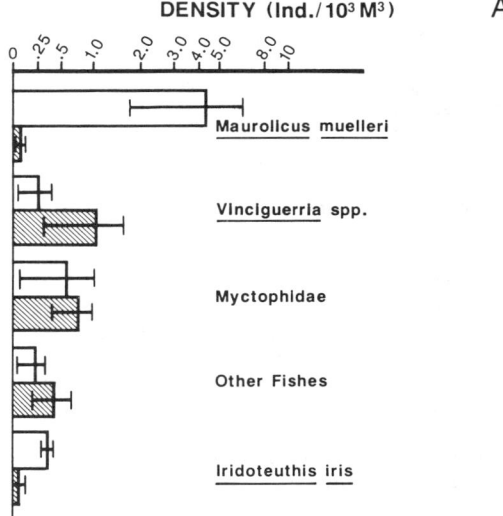

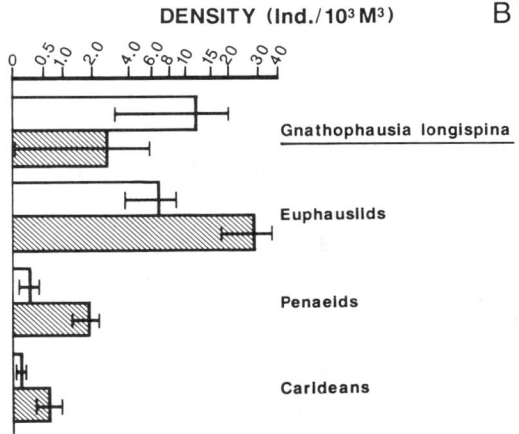

Fig. 5. Comparison of densities of selected micronekton taxa captured above Hancock Seamount with those taken at reference stations 5 to 20 km away in summer, 1984. Twelve samples were taken above the seamount and six at reference stations with a 6-ft Isaacs-Kidd midwater trawl. A. Fishes and squid. B. Crustacea. Two values are represented for each taxon; the upper (solid) bar indicates mean density (± 2 S.E.) from the tows over the seamount while the lower (cross-hatched) bar indicates mean densities in off-seamount tows; note that abundances are on a log scale. (Presented in Boehlert and Seki 1984.)

absent or in low abundance (Fig. 5B). It would appear that this seamount, and others described above, have important effects upon the pelagic ecosystem. A better understanding of the local physical and biological oceanography will be necessary to determine the nature and cause of these effects.

Ecology of Seamount Benthos

Evidence that seamounts are inhabited by unique, and sometimes rich, benthic communities was first obtained in the surveys of Vema Seamount (South Atlantic) and Bowie and Cobb Seamounts (northeast Pacific), all shallow seamounts where scuba diving was used [Simpson and Heydorn, 1965; Scagel, 1970; Birkeland, 1971]. Developments in deep-sea photography allowed the first visual examination of deeper seamounts. Some of the first photographs [Heezen and Hollister, 1971] showed current-swept beds inhabited by corals, sea pens, anemones, sponges, crinoids, and other sessile suspension feeders on Eltanin Seamount (southeast Pacific, 162 m), Kelvin Seamounts (western North Atlantic, 1,419 m, 903 m), and Ampere Seamount (North Atlantic, 143 m, 529 m). Other studies have revealed dense populations of the gorgonian coral, Ellisella flagellum, seen in photographs taken on Josephine and Great Meteor Seamounts (east Atlantic, 200-300 m; Grasshoff, 1972] and the high abundance of sponges, hydroids, bryozoans, and serpulid tubeworms on the top of Patton Seamount (Gulf of Alaska, 433 m; Raymore, 1982].

Most of the photographic investigations noted above were rather limited in spatial coverage, with photographs taken at only a few locations on each seamount. Only with the use of more advanced photographic instruments could the distributional patterns of deep seamount benthos be studied. Genin et al. [1986] used the Deep Tow [Spiess and Tyce, 1973] and Grigg et al. [1987] used towed sleds to take hundreds of photographs along several transects on different parts of seamounts. Manned submersibles have also been used recently in seamount studies, allowing detailed surveys of megafauna as well as small meiofauna [Levin et al., 1986; Lissner and Dorsey, 1986]. Submersible investigations, which allow detailed observations and even experimental manipulations, hold great promise for understanding seamount benthos.

Seamounts are highly diverse habitats. A single seamount usually extends over a large depth interval, sometimes from the euphotic zone to the abyss. Substrata of seamounts vary from exposed rocky bottom to a continuous thick layer of sediments. The latter is usually found on the top of deep guyots and in topographic depressions, whereas rocky outcrops and extensive hard-bottom areas characterize the steep flanks as well as the tops of shallow guyots [Karig et al., 1970; Lonsdale et al., 1972; Raymore, 1982; Genin et al. 1986]. Sediments on seamounts can vary in grain size and can be rippled at one site and smooth at another. The sediment distribution pattern can be greatly affected by the topographically-induced current regime, creating sometimes a moat around the seamount base [Roberts et al., 1974]. Types of hard bottom on seamounts are highly variable, ranging from carbonate rocks and pillow basalt to rocks encrusted with a hard ferromanganese layer. Remarkably different substrata can even be found on a single seamount. In spite of this great variability, some unique environmental conditions seem to lead to common biological characteristics of seamount benthos. These features include the clarity of overlying waters and extended light penetration, the presence of deep rocky substratum, and the exposure to strong currents. The effects of these conditions on the structure of biological communities on seamounts are the focus of this section.

Shallow Seamounts--Effects of Water Clarity and Isolation

Far away from sources of terrigenous turbidity, mid-ocean seamounts (like many oceanic islands) are characterized by exceptionally clear overlying waters, where the attenuation of light is far lower than in coastal waters. Consequently, benthic autotrophs may occur in greater depths. The deepest known plant life, for example, has recently been discovered on San Salvador Seamount in the Bahamas, where an undescribed species of coralline alga was found at 268 m [Littler et al. 1986]. The flat top of this seamount contains a rich and exceptionally diverse multi-layer community of macroalgae with planar algal cover (understory and canopies) exceeding 100%. On Tanner and Cortes Banks (off southern California), a dominant macroalga, Eisenia arborea, grows as deep as 40 m, whereas its lower limit at coastal sites in the Southern California Bight is between 5 and 12 m depth [Lewbel et al., 1981; Lissner and Dorsey, 1986]. Macroalgal species on these and other banks exhibit similar depth extensions [Scagel, 1970; Lissner and Dorsey, 1986]. Most of these species are usually found in the lower intertidal or upper subtidal zones. This extension was also the case with some intertidal animals, such as the mussel, Mytilus californianus, found in relatively greater depths on Bowie Seamount [Scagel, 1970] and on a submerged pinnacle off the northwest coast of Washington [Paine, 1976]. Depth extensions of animals were attributed to biological factors, such as the rarity or absence of predators [Paine, 1976]. The asteroid, Pisaster ochraceus, determines the lower limit of Mytilus in coastal regions but is rare on the submerged pinnacle due to the lack of an intertidal zone. Small recruits of Pisaster are found primarily in the lower intertidal zone where they feed on small barnacles [Paine, 1976].

In addition to extensions of depth ranges, distinctive differences between animal communities on seamounts and those at adjacent coastal sites at corresponding depths have been described on several shallow seamounts [Birkeland, 1971; Lewbel et al., 1981]. Suspension feeders are typically in much greater abundance on Tanner and Cortes Banks than in corresponding coastal regions [Lewbel et al., 1981]. The scallop, Hinnites multirugosus, dominates the entire primary substratum on vertical surfaces of Cobb Seamount, whereas it exhibits a scattered distribution in coastal areas of the northeast Pacific [Birkeland 1971]. Tunicates, which frequently dominate rocky areas on the coasts of Washington, are represented by a single species on Cobb Seamount, and neither hydroids nor barnacles have been observed on the seamount. On the other hand, the community on Cobb Seamount differs from that on Bowie Seamount; barnacles and hydroids are found on the latter but not on the former, and different molluscs are dominant at each site. Such changes are probably caused by inter-site differences of ecological conditions combined with differences of colonization history. The presence of brooding species (the asteroid Leptasterias) and species with no planktonic larvae (the gastropod Searlesia dira) on Cobb Seamount [Birkeland, 1971] suggests that rare colonization events can affect the structure of the community on each seamount. Propagules of the brooding asteroids, for example, probably reached Cobb Seamount with drifting kelp [Birkeland, 1971].

Deep Seamounts--Effects of Substratum and Currents

The most distinctive characteristic of deep seamounts is the occurrence of extensive areas of hard substratum. Unfortunately, most information on the abundance of deep hard-bottom species on seamounts is incomplete, largely due to the small number of detailed surveys conducted. Furthermore, most of the observations were obtained with dredges or photography, so that very little is known about the abundance of smaller organisms. Large suspension feeders, including sponges, horny corals (gorgonians), black corals (antipatharians), ahermatypic scleractinian corals, anemones, tunicates, brisingid seastars, and crinoids, are the dominant taxa which have been observed. Their abundance generally decreases with depth [Grigg et al., 1987]. Photographs taken shallower than 1,000 m usually exhibit several taxa in each frame, sometimes forming dense communities (Fig. 6, and Heezen and Hollister, 1971; Grasshoff, 1972; Raymore, 1982; Genin et al., 1986). Rich gorgonian fields occur on several seamounts (depth <1,000 m) in the Emperor Seamount chain (northwest Pacific). The discovery of these fields in the late 1970's caused a sharp decline in prices of precious corals on the world market [Grigg, 1984].

In oligotrophic oceans, even shallow seamounts, such as Cross Seamount near Hawaii (summit depth 300 m), exhibit sparse communities [Grigg et al. 1987], whereas relatively high densities of large suspension feeders are sometimes found in greater depths on seamounts located in fertile waters (e.g., on Kelvin Seamount at 1419 m depth; Heezen and Hollister, 1971). In addition to the fertility of overlying waters, differences in the abundance of organisms on different seamounts can be related to local environmental conditions and to availability of sources of larvae (i.e., the presence of adult populations upstream of a sea-

Fig. 6. Antipatharians, sponges, and other suspension feeders near a satellite peak at 700 m depth on Jasper Seamount in the northeast Pacific. Stichopathes sp., the whip-like black coral, is the most abundant megafaunal species between 600 and 1,000-m depth.

mount; Lutjeharms and Heydorn, 1981b; Grigg et al., 1987].

The presence of several satellite peaks on Jasper Seamount allowed Genin et al. [1986] to separate the effects of depth and topography on the abundance of animals. It was expected that passive suspension feeders would be generally more abundant at shallower depths, where the concentration of particulate food in the impinging waters is greater. The observations, however, showed that within a certain depth range the distance from a peak is a key factor in determining animal densities. The densities of a dominant species on Jasper Seamount, the black coral, Stichopathes sp., were significantly higher near peaks than in mid-slope areas at corresponding depths (Fig. 7). A similar increase in the densities of corals on the upper part of a slope, near a peak, has been observed at ca. 2,000 m depth on Horizon Guyot (central North Pacific, A. Genin and K. L. Smith, Jr., unpubl. manuscr., 1986). Other distributional patterns of large suspension feeders on seamounts further support the hypothesis that the abundance of animals on seamounts is determined by factors related to the local topography. These patterns can be separated into three spatial scales, namely patterns observed on the entire area of a seamount, patterns on topographic features such as knobs and pinnacles, and small-scale patterns such as those seen within a photograph. The large-scale patterns include the above-mentioned increased densities near peaks. They can be divided into patterns on narrow tapering peaks and those on wide or flat peaks. Densities on narrow peaks are greatest near the crest, whereas densities on flat tops of guyots and on gently sloping peaks are higher near the rim than near the center (Fig. 8 and Genin et al., 1986,

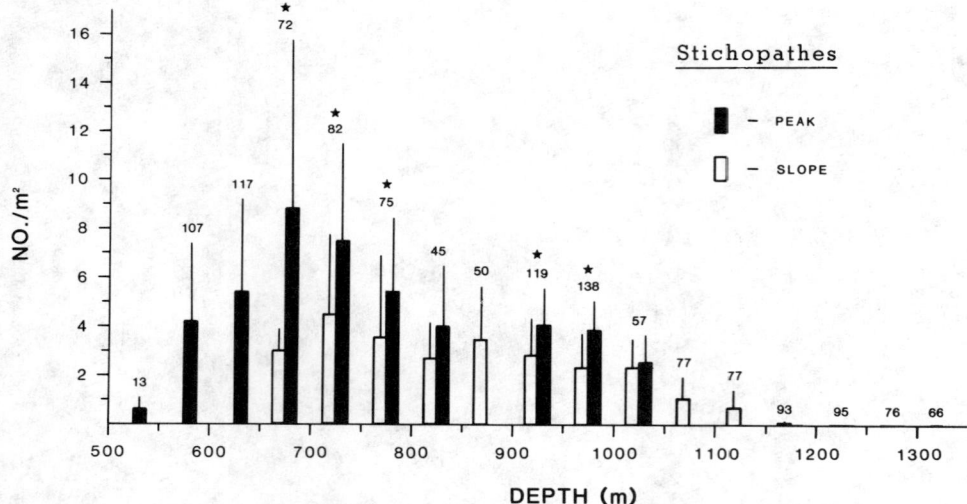

Fig. 7. Densities of <u>Stichopathes</u> (mean ± s.d.) at different depth intervals on Jasper Seamount. The photographs were divided into those near peaks (solid bars) and those >150 m below a peak (open bars). Stars indicate the intervals in which the mean near-peak density is significantly higher than the mean mid-slope density ($P < 0.001$, Mann-Whitney U test). The number of photographs taken at each depth interval is indicated above the corresponding bar. (From Genin et al., 1986.)

Jasper Seamount; Grigg et al., 1987, Cross Seamount). A similar increase of coral densities was observed along the rim of Fieberling Guyot (eastern North Pacific, ca. 500 m depth; A. Genin, unpubl. data). On the scales of tens of meters, animal densities are usually greater on topographic prominences, such as pinnacles and knobs, than in surrounding areas (e.g., Fig. 8). On the smaller scale, suspension feeders are frequently aggregated on upper parts of rocks, and small animals were found on protruding parts of larger organisms, such as sponges.

The occurrence of similar distributional patterns on different seamounts, combined with hydrodynamic theories and observations, suggests that a topographically induced current regime is a key factor in determining the abundance of suspension feeders on deep hard-bottom seamounts. Two different mechanisms may enhance currents near the edges of wide peaks. First, the flow of waters impinging on the flank may be upwelled above a seamount's top. Due to conservation of potential vorticity, an anticyclonic motion is induced, resulting in an accelerated flow on the left side of a seamount (looking downstream) and deceleration near the center and on the right [Huppert, 1975; Huppert and Bryan, 1976]. Alternating tidal flows would thereby cause intermittent acceleration periods near the edges and recurrent deceleration near the center of wide peaks and guyots. The other mechanism is related to the reflection of internal waves along a sloping bottom, where intensification of the flow occurs, especially for those waves with frequencies within an octave of a critical frequency defined by the bottom slope, stratification, and Coriolis parameter [Wunsch 1969; Eriksen, 1982, 1985]. Such an intensification is not expected to be distinctive on the flat or gently sloping areas at the center of guyots and wide peaks, where animal densities are low.

Existing physical theories do not predict the occurrence of stronger currents near a crest of a peak as compared with a mid-slope site at the same depth and on a similar slope angle. Hydrographic observations, however, suggest that the upwelling above such peaks is confined to the proximity of the crest and does not occur over mid-slope areas [Bezrukov and Natarov, 1976; Fukasawa and Nagata 1978; Genin and Boehlert, 1985; Roden and Taft 1985]. Short-term current measurements made by Genin et al. [1986] on Jasper Seamount also showed differences between a peak and a mid-slope site; the average current speed near a peak was about twice the mean speed recorded at a mid-slope site at the same depth. The mid- and small-scale increases of densities of suspension feeders on knobs, pinnacles, and on the top of protruding rocks can be similarly explained by an exposure to enhanced currents as these structures protrude to higher elevations above the bottom and are therefore exposed to more energetic zones of the benthic boundary layer [Butman, 1986; Grant and Madsen, 1986]. Even on such small-scale features, however, variability in colonization rates may be related to small-scale flow structure [Nowell and Jumars, 1984]. Genin et al. [1986] proposed two different mechanisms through which intensified currents can induce higher animal densities. In the "settlement pathway," a site is colonized by relatively more recruits simply because more

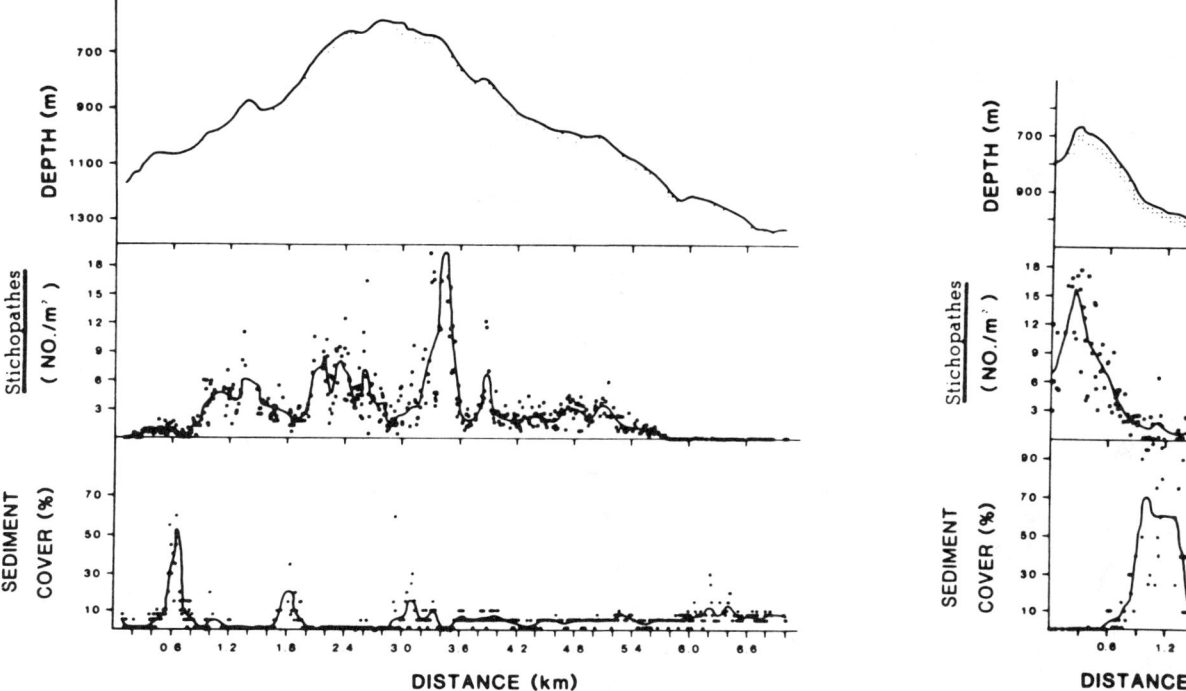

Fig. 8. Bathymetry, densities of <u>Stichopathes</u>, and sediment cover across two satellite peaks on Jasper Seamount. Each dot indicates the animal density or sediment cover in a single photograph. Solid lines indicate 9-point running means. Note that the animal densities follow the bathymetric line on the sharp peak (C) whereas lower densities are found near the center of the wide peak (A) than near its edges. Animal densities are relatively higher on small topographic prominences such as those at 1.4 and 3.9 km along the transect. Note the sharp increase of sediment cover in the topographic depression near peak C. (From Genin et al., 1986.)

water, and thereby more larvae, flow through per unit of time; in the "feeding pathway," more water flows past suspension feeders at sites characterized by stronger currents, resulting in increased feeding and growth rates and possibly higher survival rates of small recruits. The actual mechanisms involved are yet to be experimentally tested.

Very little is known about soft-bottom fauna on deep seamounts. Unlike hard-bottom epifauna, infauna in sedimentary substrata cannot be observed by photography. In a recent study of deep (1,000 to 3,000 m) seamounts in the Pacific Ocean off Mexico, Levin et al. [1986] used a submersible to investigate the effects of giant protozoans (xenophyophores) on local soft-bottom communities. Xenophyophores are abundant on seamounts where they agglutinate sediments to form large tests (up to 25 cm diameter) which protrude above the sediment. Sediments immediately surrounding these organisms exhibit higher densities and diversities of metazoan species relative to control sediments collected at distances of 1 m from those protozoans. Levin et al. [1986] propose that xenophyophores contribute to maintenance of high benthic diversity by altering hydrodynamic conditions and by providing metazoans with substratum, food, and refuge. The diversity of soft-bottom habitats on seamounts has not been compared with the surrounding deep sea; this would make an interesting investigation from a submersible, since a wide depth range occurs at a single site on soft-bottom seamounts.

The Role of Seamounts in Fisheries Productivity

Seamounts and banks may aggregate resident demersal and transient, pelagic organisms which can support fisheries [Uda and Ishino, 1958; Uchida et al., 1986]. Polovina [1985] compared seamounts with bank and island systems and found higher densities of the same species on the seamounts. A variety of demersal resources in high

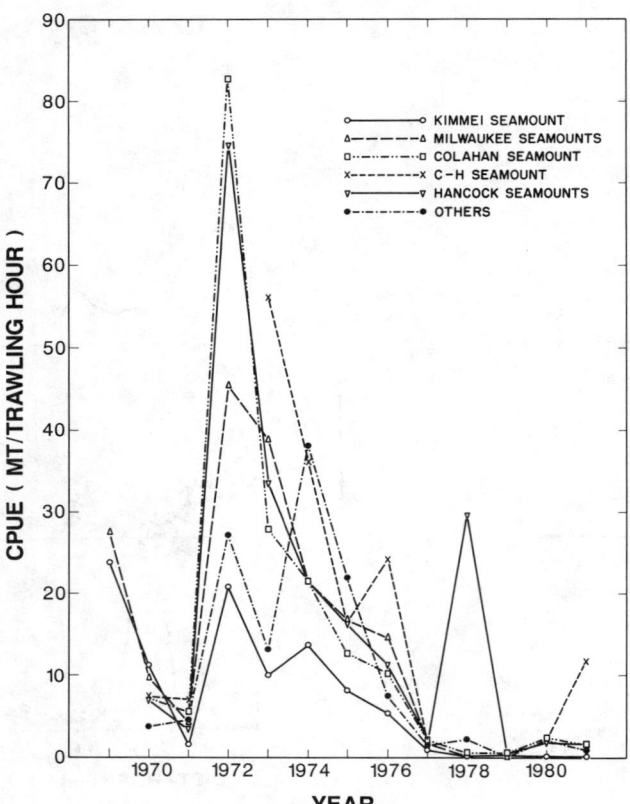

Fig. 9. Annual data on catch-per-unit-effort (an index of abundance) of Japanese trawlers for pelagic armorhead on several of the southern Emperor-northern Hawaiian Ridge seamounts, 1969-81. These data show the sharp decline in stock abundance. The Japanese catch was about one-fifth that of the Soviets; combined, they took approximately one million metric tons of this species off these seamounts during this period. (From Wetherall and Yong, 1986.)

abundance has been noted on seamounts including fishes [Sasaki, 1986], lobsters [Lutjeharms and Heydorn, 1981a], crabs [Hughes, 1981; Alton, 1986] and precious corals [Grigg, 1986; Genin et al. 1986]. Pelagic species such as tunas and squid may seasonally feed in waters above seamounts [Inoue, 1983; Yasui, 1986], as do some marine mammals [Hui, 1985]. In the open ocean, seamounts thus function as sites of increased production or aggregation of higher trophic level organisms.

A specific example of high fisheries productivity is provided in the southern Emperor and northern Hawaiian Ridge seamounts. Between 1967 and 1975, nearly one million metric tons of pelagic armorhead, <u>Pseudopentaceros wheeleri</u>, were taken by Soviet and Japanese trawlers, and standing stocks were estimated at nearly 400,000 metric tons [Borets, 1975; Sasaki, 1986]. Japanese data on catch per unit effort (Fig. 9) demonstrate extremely high catch rates which declined drastically in later years of the fishery. Some of the same physical mechanisms which alter the patterns of distribution and abundance of the taxa as described earlier for Hancock Seamount may be invoked to explain the availability of the energy necessary to maintain high densities of fish here and at other seamounts. First, convergent flow resulting in accumulation and greater flux of oceanic plankton and micronekton may provide prey [Isaacs and Schwartzlose, 1965; Darnitsky et al. 1984; Tseitlin, 1985]. Secondly, as described earlier, locally enhanced productivity may be retained in the region of the seamount. A Taylor column or other stationary water mass could retain this productivity, but the residence times of such features are unknown. Energy for the high biomass demersal fish resources, however, appears to be derived from oceanic rather than seamount-derived sources. This assertion is supported by diet studies of pelagic armorhead [Fedosova, 1976], species on seamounts in the Indian Ocean [Parin and Prutko, 1985], and elsewhere [Kashkin, 1984]. Simulation models of seamount fish populations [Tseitlin, 1985; Pudyakov and Tseitlin, 1986] suggest that such allochthonous energy inputs are necessary for population maintenance.

An intriguing question about these animal resources, given that most have pelagic larvae, is the mechanism of recruitment back to the seamount. One of the first suggestions of such a mechanism invoked the concept of stationary Taylor columns over seamounts for maintenance of pelagic larvae [Shomura and Barkley 1980]. This hypothesis is an extension of the ideas on the conservation of insular plankton described by Boden [1952]. Maintenance of pelagic larvae in closed circulations above large bank systems has recently been demonstrated in several locations [Dooley 1984; Sundby, 1984; Smith and Morse, 1985]. Others have suggested that seamount populations are derived from upstream source populations; the distances proposed have been as great as 1,100 nmi [Lutjeharms and Heydorn, 1981b]. In either of these cases, however, physical variability can lead to interannual variability in recruitment strength; such fluctuations may be characteristic of seamount resources [Lutjeharms and Heydorn 1981a; Wetherall and Yong, 1986]. Given the small geographic extent of seamounts and the variability in recruitment, great care must be taken to manage seamount resources and prevent overexploitation [Boehlert, 1986; Sasaki, 1986].

Conclusions and Suggestions for Future Research

As we have described in this paper, seamounts are sites where physical perturbations result in development of unique ecosystems. Understanding variability in the biological productivity of seamounts is a challenging research problem which will require interdisciplinary research. Mesoscale physical oceanographic studies will be necessary to define the conditions for development of eddies, Taylor columns, and other features of flow complexity. Small-scale studies of upwelling, turbulent mixing, and benthic boundary layer effects will better characterize the local conditions near the seamount. Concurrent studies of biological oceanography of the water column over seamounts can define the variability of nutrients and primary productivity and their residence times. By understanding the seasonal and interannual variability of these phenomena, we should be able to better define the importance of enhanced productivity to higher trophic levels and to determine the role of currents in concentrating or increasing the flux of allochthonous energy sources. In addition to these temporal components of variability, comparative studies of seamounts can provide an understanding of spatial variability. Given information on bottom topography and ocean currents, perhaps we can develop generalities or predictive capabilities concerning seamount productivity. In this comparative vein, we should consider other topographic features, including banks, coastal headlands, and islands, where related phenomena may occur.

Benthic communities on seamounts may provide an initial indication of productivity, since the benthos may serve as an integrator of productivity of the overlying water column; sediments, where they occur on or around seamounts, may provide a historical record of the patterns of such productivity. Most studies of seamount benthos, however, have been observational or descriptive. A greater understanding of factors structuring the communities on deep seamounts will undoubtedly require the use of submersibles. The remarkable changes of environmental conditions over relatively small distances on seamounts, combined with manipulative capabilities of research submersibles, could prove most useful in conducting controlled experiments to define the mechanisms which structure deep-sea communities.

Finally, the local modification of physical and biological conditions by mid-ocean seamounts provides a unique opportunity in marine research. Experimental manipulations commonly performed in marine intertidal and subtidal research have significantly contributed to the understanding of key ecological processes. Such manipulations cannot typically be performed on scales large enough to be applicable to the open ocean. Warm- and cold-core rings have provided natural experiments in which isolated pelagic populations have been studied [Backus et al., 1981; Olson and Backus, 1985]. Seamount-induced upwelling and eddy generation may provide similar "manipulations." Processes related to the formation and maintenance of the deep chlorophyll maximum, for example, may be studied with the temporally varying upwelling induced by seamounts. In addition, relationships between different time scales of physical events and the associated biological response at different trophic levels can contribute significantly to our understanding of marine ecosystems.

Acknowledgments. We thank the many people who helped in compiling the great deal of literature surveyed in this paper, particularly Vladimir Darnitsky, who provided much of the Soviet literature, and Wilvan G. Van Campen, who tirelessly provided translations. We also thank E. O. Hartwig, P. A. Jumars, and R. E. Young for providing reviews of the manuscript. Finally, it was Bill Menard who first introduced the junior author to the subject of "seamount biology" during a geology class; his curiosity and enthusiasm have been inspirational.

References

Alldredge, A. L., and W. M. Hamner. Recurring aggregations of zooplankton by a tidal current. Estuarine Coastal Marine Science 10, 31-37, 1980.

Alldredge, A. L., and J. M. King. The distance demersal zooplankton migrate above the benthos: Implications for predation. Marine Biology (Berlin) 84, 253-260, 1985.

Alton, M. S. Fish and crab populations of Gulf of Alaska seamounts, in The Environment and Resources of Seamounts in the North Pacific, R. N. Uchida, S. Hayasi, and G. W. Boehlert (eds.), Proceedings of the Workshop on the Environment and Resources of Seamounts in the North Pacific, pp. 45-51. U.S. Department of Commerce, NOAA Technical Report NMFS 43, 1986.

Backus, R. H., G. R. Flierl, D. R. Kester, D. B. Olson, P. L. Richardson, A. C. Vastano, P. H. Wiebe, and J. H. Wormuth. Gulf Stream cold-core rings: their physics, chemistry, and biology. Science 212, 1091-1100, 1981.

Belyanina, T. N. Preliminary data on ichthyoplankton of seamount regions of the northwestern Indian Ocean. Okeanologiya, SSSR 25, 1013-1016, 1985.

Bezrukov, Y. F., and V. V. Natarov. Formation of abiotic conditions over the submarine eminences of some regions of the Pacific Ocean. Izvestiya Tikhookeanskiy Nauchno-Issledovatel'skiy Institut Rybnogo Khozyaystva i Okeanografii (TINRO) (Pacific Research Institute of Fisheries and Oceanography 100, 93-99. (Transl. by W. G. Van Campen, 1983; in the files of NMFS Honolulu Laboratory.) 1976.

Birkeland, C. Biological observations on Cobb Seamount. Northwest Science 45, 193-199, 1971.

Boden, B. P. Natural conservation of insular plankton. Nature 169, 697-699, 1952.

Boehlert, G.W. Effects of Southeast Hancock Seamount on the pelagic ecosystem. [Abstr.] EOS, Transactions of the American Geophysical Union 66, 1336, 1985.

Boehlert, G. W. Productivity and population maintenance of seamount resources and future research directions, in Environment and Resources of Seamounts in the North Pacific, R. N. Uchida, S. Hayasi, and G. W. Boehlert (eds.), pp. 95-101. U.S. Department of Commerce, NOAA Technical Report NMFS 43, 1986.

Boehlert, G. W., and M. P. Seki. Enhanced micronekton abundance over mid-Pacific seamounts. EOS, Transactions of the American Geophysical Union 65, 928, 1984.

Borets, L. A. Some results of studies on the biology of the boarfish (Pentaceros richardsoni Smith). Investigations of the Biology of Fishes and Fishery Oceanography, No. 6, Izvestiya Tikhookeanskiy Nauchno-Issledovatel'skiy Institut Rybnogo Khozyaystva i Okeanografii (TINRO) Pacific Research Institute of Fisheries and Oceanography, Vladivostok, 1975.

Borets, L. A., and A. S. Sokolovsky. Species composition of ichthyoplankton of the Hawaiian submarine ridge and Emperor Seamounts. Izvestiya Tikhookeanskiy Nauchno-Issledovatel'skiy Institut Rybnogo Khozyaystva i Okeanografii (TINRO) Pacific Research Institute of Fisheries and Oceanography 102, 43-50, 1978.

Butman, C. A. Larval settlement of soft-sediment invertebrates: some predictions based on an analysis of near-bottom velocity profiles. in Marine Interfaces Ecohydrodynamics, J. C. J. Nihoul (ed.), p. 487-513. Proceedings of the 17th International Liege Colloquium on Ocean Hydrodynamics, Elsevier, Amsterdam, 1986.

Cheney, R. E., P. L. Richardson, and K. Nagasaka. Tracking a Kuroshio cold ring with a free-drifting surface buoy. Deep-Sea Research 27, 641-654, 1980.

Darnitsky, V. B. On the synoptic variability of the geostrophic circulation in areas of underwater rises in the North Pacific Ocean. Problems in Oceanography (State Committee of the USSR for Hydrometeorology and Environmental Monitoring) 86, 63-70, 1980.

Darnitsky, V. B., B. L. Boldyrev, and A. F. Volkov. Environmental conditions and some ecological characteristics of fishes from the central North Pacific seamounts, in Proceedings, Conditions of Formation of Commercial Fish Concentrations, Ministry of Fisheries, U.S.S.R., All-Union Research Institute of Marine Fisheries and Oceanography (VNIRO), pp. 64-77. Moscow. 1984.

Dooley, H. D. Aspects of oceanographic variability on Scottish fishing grounds. Ph.D. Thesis, University of Aberdeen, Scotland, 154 pp., 1984.

Eriksen, C. C. Observations of internal wave reflection off sloping bottoms. Journal of Geophysics Research 87, 525-538, 1982.

Eriksen, C. C. Implications of ocean bottom reflection for internal wave spectra and mixing. Journal of Physical Oceanography 15, 1145-1156, 1985.

Fedosova, R. A. Distribution of some copepod species in the vicinity of the underwater Hawaiian Ridge. Oceanology 14, 724-727, 1974.

Fedosova, R. A. Some data on the feeding of boarfish, Pentaceros richardsoni Smith, on the banks of the Hawaiian Ridge. Izvestiya Tikhookeanskiy Nauchno-Issledovatel'skiy Institut Rybnogo Khozyaystva i Okeanografii (TINRO) Pacific Research Institute of Fisheries and Oceanography (TINRO) Trudy 7, 29-36, 1976.

Fukasawa, M., and Y. Nagata. Detailed oceanic structure in the vicinity of the shoal Kokushosone. Journal of Oceanographical Society of Japan 34, 41-49, 1978.

Genin, A., and G. W. Boehlert. Dynamics of temperature and chlorophyll structures above a seamount: an oceanic experiment. Journal of Marine Research 43, 907-924, 1985.

Genin, A., P. K. Dayton, P. F. Lonsdale, and F. N. Spiess. Corals on seamount peaks provide evidence of current acceleration over deep-sea topography. Nature 322, 59-61, 1986.

Grant, W. D., and O. S. Madsen. The continental-shelf bottom boundary layer. Annual Review of Fluid Mechanics 18, 265-305, 1986.

Grasshoff, M. Die gorgonaria des ostlichen Nordatlantik und des Mittelmeeres. I. Die familie Ellisellidae (Cnidaria: Anthozoa). Meteor Forschungsergerbnisse Reihe D - Biologie D10, 73-87.

Grigg, R. W. Resource management of precious corals: a review and application to shallow water reef building corals. Marine Ecology 5, 57-74, 1984.

Grigg, R. W. Precious corals: An important seamount fisheries resource, in The Environment and Resources of Seamounts in the North Pacific. R. N. Uchida, S. Hayasi, and G. W. Boehlert (eds.), Proceedings of the Workshop on the Environment and Resources of Seamounts in the North Pacific, pp. 43-44. U.S. Department of Commerce, NOAA Technical Report NMFS 43, 1986.

Grigg, R. W., A. Malahoff, E. H. Chave, and J. Landahl. Seamount oceanography: Benthic Ecology and Potential Environmental Impact from Manganese Crust Mining in Hawaii, in Seamounts, Islands, and Atolls, B. Keating, P. Fryer, R. Batiza, and G. Boehlert (eds.), American Geophysical Union, 1987.

Heezen, B. C., and C. D. Hollister. The face of the deep. Oxford University Press, N.Y., 1971.

Hirota, J., and G. W. Boehlert. Feeding of Maurolicus muelleri at Southeast Hancock Seamount and its effects on the zooplankton community. EOS, Transactions of the American Geophysical Union, 66, 1336, 1985.

Hobson, E. S., and J. R. Chess. Trophic relationships among fishes and plankton in the lagoon at Enewetak Atoll, Marshall Islands. Fishery Bulletin, U.S. 76, 133-153, 1978.

Hogg, N. G. On the stratified Taylor column. Journal of Fluid Mechanics 58, 517-537, 1973.

Hogg, N. G. Effects of bottom topography on ocean currents, in Global Atmospheric Research Program (GARP) Publication Series 23, pp. 167-205. World Meteorological Organization-International Council of Scientific Unions.

Hubbs, C. L. Initial discoveries on fish faunas on seamounts and offshore banks in the eastern Pacific. Pacific Science 13, 311-316, 1959.

Hughes, S. E. Initial U.S. exploration of nine Gulf of Alaska seamounts and their associated fish and shellfish resources. Marine Fisheries Review 43, 1, 26-33, 1981.

Hui, C. A. Undersea topography and the comparative distributions of two pelagic cetaceans. Fishery Bulletin, U.S. 83, 472-475, 1985.

Huppert, H. E. Some remarks on the initiation of inertial Taylor columns. Journal of Fluid Mechanics 67, 397-412, 1975.

Huppert, H. E., and K. Bryan. Topographically generated eddies. Deep-Sea Research 23, 655-679, 1976.

Inoue, M. Exploitation of fishing grounds of southward migrants of fall skipjacks in the northwestern Pacific Ocean. [In Jpn., Engl. summ.] Journal of the Faculty of Marine Science and Technology, Tokai University 17, 121-130, 1983.

Isaacs, J. D., and R. A. Schwartzlose. Migrant sound scatterers: Interactions with the sea floor. Science 150, 1810-1813, 1965.

Karig, D. E., M. N. A. Peterson, and G. G. Shor. Sediment-capped guyots in the mid-Pacific mountains. Deep-Sea Research 17, 373-378, 1970.

Kashkin, H. I. Mesopelagic micronekton as a factor in fish productivity on oceanic banks. in Frontal Zones in the Southeastern Pacific Ocean, pp. 285-291. Nauka Press, Moscow, 1984.

Kozlov, V. F. Models of Topographic Vortices in the Ccean. Pacific Oceanological Institute, Academy of Sciences of the USSR. Nauka, Moscow, 199 pp., 1983.

Kozlov, V. F., V. B. Darnitsky, and M. I. Ermakov. An experiment in modeling topographic vortices over underwater mountains. Problems in Oceanography (State Committee of the USSR for Hydrometeorology and Environmental Monitoring) 96, 3-25, 1982.

Levin, L. A., D. J. Demaster, L. D. McCann, and C. L. Thomas. Effects of giant protozoans (class: Xenophyophorea) on deep-seamount benthos. Marine Ecology Progress Series 29, 99-104, 1986.

Lewbel, G. S., A. Wolfson, T. Gerrodette, W. H. Lippincott, J. L. Wilson, and M. M. Littler. Shallow-water benthic communities on California's outer continental shelf. Marine Ecology Progress Series 4, 159-168, 1981.

Linkowski, T. B. Some aspects of the biology of Maurolicus muelleri (Sternoptychidae) from the South Atlantic. International Council for the Exploration of the Sea, ICES CM, H:17, 1983.

Lissner, A. L., and J. H. Dorsey. Deep-water biological assemblages of a hard-bottom bank-ridge complex of the southern California continental borderland. Bulletin Southern California Academy of Sciences 85, 87-101, 1986.

Littler, M. M., D. S. Littler, S. M. Blair, and J. N. Norris. Deep-water plant communities from an uncharted seamount off San Salvador Island, Bahamas: distribution, abundance, and primary productivity. Deep-Sea Research 33, 881-892, 1986.

Lonsdale, P., W. R. Normark, and W. A. Newman. Sedimentation and erosion on Horizon Guyot. Geological Society of America Bulletin 83, 289-316, 1972.

Lutjeharms, J. R. E., and A. E. F. Heydorn. Recruitment of rock lobster on Vema Seamount from the islands of Tristan da Cunha. Deep-Sea Research 28A, 1237, 1981a.

Lutjeharms, J. R. E., and A. E. F. Heydorn. The rock-lobster (Jasus tristani) on Vema Seamount: Drifting buoys suggest a possible recruiting mechanism. Deep-Sea Research 28A, 631-636, 1981b.

Manheim, F. T. Marine cobalt resources. Science 232, 600-608, 1986.

Meincke, J. Observation of an anticyclonic vortex trapped above a seamount. Journal of Geophysical Research 76, 7432-7440, 1971.

Nellen, W. Untersuchungen zur Verteilung von Fischlarven und Plankton im Gebiet der Grossen Meteor Forschungsergebnisse Reihe D - Biologie 13, 47-69, 1973.

Nowell, A. R. M., and P. A. Jumars. Flow environments of aquatic benthos. Annual Review Ecology and Systematics 15, 303-328, 1984.

Olson, D. B., and R. H. Backus. The concentrating of organisms at fronts: a cold-water fish and a warm-core Gulf Stream ring. Journal of Marine Research 43, 113-137, 1985.

Owens, W. B., and N. G. Hogg. Oceanic observations of stratified Taylor columns near a bump. Deep-Sea Research 27A, 1029-1045, 1980.

Paine, R. T. Biological observations on a subtidal Mytilus californianus bed. Veliger 19, 125-130, 1976.

Parin, N. V., and V. G. Prutko. Thalassal mesobenthopelagic ichthyocoen over the Equator Submarine Rise in the western tropical Indian Ocean. Okeanologiya, SSSR 25, 1017-1020, 1985.

Polovina, J. J. Variation in catch rates and species composition in handline catches of deep-water snappers and groupers in the Mariana Archipelago. Proceedings of the Fifth International Coral Reef Congress, Tahiti 5, 515-520, 1985.

Pudyakov, Y. A., and V. B. Tseitlin. Simulation model of separate fish populations inhabiting submarine rises. Journal of Ichthyology (English translation of Voprosy Ikhtiologii) 26, 145-150, 1986.

Raymore, P. A., Jr. Photographic investigations on three seamounts in the Gulf of Alaska. Pacific Science 36, 15-34, 1982.

Richardson, P. L. Anticyclonic eddies generated near the Corner Rise seamounts. Journal of Marine Research 38, 673-686, 1982.

Roberts, D. G., N. G. Hogg, D. G. Bishop, and C. G. Flewellen. Sediment distribution around moated seamounts in the Rockall Trough. Deep-Sea Research 21, 175-184, 1974.

Roden, G. I. Aspects of oceanic flow and thermohaline structure in the vicinity of seamounts, in The Environment and Resources of Seamounts in the North Pacific, pp. 3-12. R. N. Uchida, S. Hayasi, and G. W. Boehlert (eds.), U.S. Department of Commerce, NOAA Technical Report NMFS 43, 1986.

Roden, G. I. Effect of seamounts and seamount

chains on ocean circulation and thermohaline structure, in Seamounts, Islands, and Atolls, B. Keating, P. Fryer, R. Batiza, and G. Boehlert (eds.), American Geophysical Union, 1987.

Roden, G. I., and B. A. Taft. Effect of the Emperor Seamounts on the mesoscale thermohaline structure during the summer of 1982. Journal of Geophysical Research 90, 839-855, 1985.

Roden, G. I., B. A. Taft, and C. C. Ebbesmeyer. Oceanographic aspects of the Emperor Seamounts region. Journal Geophysical Research 87, 9537-9552, 1982.

Royer, T. C. Ocean eddies generated by seamounts in the North Pacific. Science 199, 1063-1064, 1978.

Sasaki, T. Development and present status of Japanese trawl fisheries in the vicinity of seamounts, in The Environment and Resources of Seamounts in the North Pacific, R. N. Uchida, S. Hayasi, and G. W. Boehlert (eds.), pp. 21-30. U.S. Department of Commerce, NOAA Technical Report, NMFS 43, 1986.

Scagel, R. F. Benthic algae of Bowie Seamount. Syesis 3, 15-16, 1970.

Shomura, R. S., and R. A. Barkley. Ecosystem dynamics of seamounts--a working hypothesis, in The Kuroshio IV. Proceedings of the Fourth Symposium for the Cooperative Study of the Kuroshio and Adjacent Regions, the Japan Academy, Tokyo, Japan, 14-17 February 1979, pp. 789-790. Saikon Publisher, Tokyo, Japan, 1980.

Simpson, E. S. W., and A. E. F. Heydorn. Vema Seamount. Nature 207, 249-251, 1965.

Simpson, J. H., P. P. Tett, M. L. Argote-Espinoze, A. Edwards, K. J. Jones, and G. Sividge. Mixing and phytoplankton growth around an island in a stratified (shelf) sea. Continental Shelf Research 1, 15-31, 1982.

Smith, W. G., and W. W. Morse. Retention of larval haddock Melanogrammus aeglefinus in the Georges Bank region, a gyre-influenced spawning area. Marine Ecology Progress Series 24, 1-13, 1985.

Sorokin, Y. I., and O. V. Sorokina. Bacterioplankton in the seamount regions in the western part of the Indian Ocean. Okeanologiya, SSSR 25, 1006-1012, 1985.

Spiess, F. N., and R. C. Tyce. The marine physical laboratory deep tow instrument system. Scripps Institution of Oceanography Reference 73-74, 1973.

Sundby, S. Influence of bottom topography on the circulation at the continental shelf off northern Norway. Fiskeridirektoratets Skrifter Serie Havundersokelser 17, 501-519, 1984.

Taylor, G. I. Notion of solids in fluids when the flow is not irrotational. Proceedings of the Royal Society A93, 99-113, 1917.

Taylor, G. I. Experiments on the motion of solid bodies in rotating fluids. Proceedings of the Royal Society of London B Biological Sciences 104A, 213-218, 1923.

Tseitlin, V. B. The energetics of the fish population inhabiting the underwater mountain. Okeanologiya 25, 308-311, 1985.

Uchida, R. N., S. Hayasi, and G. W. Boehlert (eds.). Environment and resources of seamounts in the North Pacific. U.S. Department of Commerce, NOAA Technical Report NMFS 43, 105 pp. 1986.

Uchida, R. N., and D. T. Tagami. Groundfish fisheries and research in the vicinity of seamounts in the North Pacific Ocean. Marine Fisheries Review 46, 2, 1-17, 1986.

Uda, M., and M. Ishino. Enrichment pattern resulting from eddy systems in relation to fishing grounds. Journal of the Tokyo University of Fisheries 44, 105-119, 1958.

Vastano, A. C., and B. A. Warren. Perturbations to the Gulf Stream by Atlantis II Seamount. Deep-Sea Research 23, 681-694, 1976.

Wetherall, J. A., and M. Y. Y. Yong. Problems in assessing the pelagic armorhead stock on the central North Pacific Seamounts, in The Environment and Resources of Seamounts in the North Pacific, R. N. Uchida, S. Hayasi, and G. W. Boehlert (eds.), Proceedings of the Workshop on the Environment and Resources of Seamounts in the North Pacific, pp. 73-85. U.S. Department of Commerce, NOAA Technical Report NMFS 43, 1986.

Wilson, R. R., and R. S. Kaufman. Seamount biota and biogeography, in Seamounts, Islands, and Atolls, B. Keating, P. Fryer, R. Batiza, and G. Boehlert (eds.), American Geophysical Union, 1987.

Wunsch, C. Progressive internal waves on slopes. Journal of Fluid Mechanics 35, 131-144, 1969.

Yasui, M. Albacore, Thunnus alalunga, pole-and-line fishery around the Emperor Seamounts, in The Environment and Resources of Seamounts in the North Pacific, R. N. Uchida, S. Hayasi, and G. W. Boehlert (eds.), pp. 37-40. U.S. Department of Commerce, NOAA Technical Report, NMFS 43.

Zaika, V. E., and A. V. Kovalev. The study of the ecosystems of submarine mountains. Biologiya Morya (Vladivostok) 1984, 3-8, 1984.

EFFECT OF SEAMOUNTS AND SEAMOUNT CHAINS ON OCEAN CIRCULATION AND THERMOHALINE STRUCTURE

Gunnar I. Roden

School of Oceanography, University of Washington

Abstract. Aspects of effects of seamounts and seamount chains on oceanic flow and thermohaline structure are discussed on the basis of recent theoretical and observational findings. The flow patterns resulting from the flow-topography interaction are complex and occur on scales from local to planetary. They depend on a variety of parameters involving the rotation of the earth and its variation with latitude, stratification, structure of the basic flow, friction, and the height, shape, orientation, and spacing of the seamounts. Internal wave reflection, tidal amplification, eddy trapping, mesoscale geopotential height perturbations, and deflection and modification of the incident flow are some of the more conspicuous features that have been observed. On some seamounts, bottom intensified Taylor columns and trapped thermohaline fronts are suggested. Highly idealized models anticipate vortex pair generation in the initial state, complex eddy-mean flow and eddy-eddy interaction in the intermediate state, and permanent flow deflection, eddy trapping, and wake generation in the final state. While the simplified models anticipate some of the observed features, the dynamics of interaction between realistically shaped seamounts and time varying, spatially nonuniform flow are not fully understood at present.

Introduction

Seamounts are ubiquitous geomorphological features of the ocean floor. They come in various shapes and sizes and occur singly or in groups, sometimes arranged along elongated arcs to form the peaks of underwater mountain ranges. Many seamounts have steep slopes and are high, occupying a large fraction of the ocean's depth. Many of them have flat tops with superposed minor topographic irregularities and are known as guyots. Much of the present knowledge of the distribution, number, and characteristics of seamounts and guyots is based on the pioneering work of H. William Menard (Menard and Ladd, 1963) who, after the end of the Second World War, was able to persuade both the reluctant fishermen and naval authorities to release the positions and descriptions of seamounts and seamount chains, previously held secret for fishing and military reasons.

Seamounts are embedded in a stratified ocean on a rotating earth and interact with the impinging flow. They affect the ocean circulation and thermohaline structure and are known to enhance boundary mixing (Armi and Millard, 1976; Eriksen, 1985), amplify the baroclinic and barotropic components of tidal flow (Meincke, 1971), generate internal wavetrains (Eriksen, 1982; Kaneko et al., 1986) and eddies (Richardson, 1980), give rise to Taylor columns (Owens and Hogg, 1980; Roden, 1984a), cause flow deflection and intensification (Gould et al., 1981), trap drifting buoys and advected eddies (Cheney et al., 1980), and lead to the formation of large-amplitude geopotential height perturbations in their vicinity (Roden and Taft, 1985), enhance biological productivity and improve fish catch (Brainard, 1986). Not all the seamount effects on circulation are local. Western boundary currents impinging and crossing seamount chains often undergo large deflections in their path that can be seen both in the geopotential topography (Roden, 1984b) and in satellite tracked drifter trajectories (Vastano et al., 1985). In some gaps, topographic steering and rectification of the deep flow have been observed (Rattray, 1985).

Despite the observed seamount effects on circulation, the detailed dynamics of topography-flow interaction are not fully understood at present. In principle, an obstacle in a moving rotating fluid distorts the flow field and leads to forced vertical motion as well as the formation of topography induced gradients of velocity and bottom stress. These, in turn, generate vorticity, deformation, and divergence in the flow field. Thus, one can expect to find in the vicinity of a seamount a variety of phenomena, such as changes in the path and intensity of current, confluence and convergence lines, waves, and eddies, some of them trapped and others transient. The dynamics of the formation, modification, and decay of these features are highly

Copyright 1987 by the American Geophysical Union.

complex and involve a delicate balance among the rotation of the earth, the stratification, the temporal and spatial structure of the incident or large scale flow, the orientation, height, and shape of the seamounts, and the frictional forces. Changes in one or several of the above-mentioned parameters can alter drastically the results of flow-topography interaction. Still more complex situations arise when the large scale flow impinges on a group or ridge of seamounts. A potential then exists for the topographically generated perturbations to interact with each other. The resulting flow patterns are not necessarily the same as those that would emerge from the current interating with each of the seamounts in the group separately. On a smaller scale, irregularities in the shape of individual seamounts, such as numerous peaks, also cause perturbations which interact with all scales of motion.

Theoretical investigations of seamount effects on circulation have dealt of necessity with highly idealized flows and obstacle shapes in homogeneous or simply stratified fluids, and a fairly large literature exists on the subject. Taylor (1917) was among the first to investigate the effect of an obstacle in rotational flow in a homogeneous liquid and found that for certain flow parameters closed circulations appeared atop the obstacle. These were later called Taylor columns by Hide (1961) and subsequent investigators. Johnson (1982) investigated analytically the effect of elliptically shaped seamounts placed at various angles to uniform flow in a homogeneous fluid and found that flow intensification takes place on the left side of the seamount looking in the downstream direction. Verron and LeProvost (1985, 1986) used a numerical model to study time variable quasi-geostrophic barotropic flow over a low amplitude circular seamount in the presence of dissipation both on an f-plane (constant Coriolis parameter) and a beta-plane (constant variation of Coriolis parameter with latitude) for a variety of flow parameter ranges. They found, in agreement with earlier investigators (Ingersoll, 1969; McCartney, 1975), that fundamental differences exist between the flow patterns on f- and beta-planes. In the former case, the topographically generated disturbances are similar for eastward and westward flow and remain essentially confined to the vicinity of seamounts after the transients have died out. In the latter case, the flow direction becomes crucial. For eastward flow, Rossby wakes are generated so that the influence of the seamounts is felt far downstream. For westward flow, such wakes are not formed and the disturbances remain in the vicinity of the seamount. Inclusion of friction reduces the amplitude of the disturbances and reduces the speed of transients so that some of them remain in the vicinity of the seamount.

All of the above investigations refer to a homogeneous fluid. The chief drawback with this approach is that the real ocean is stratified and that the topography effect on circulation is exaggerated in the homogeneous case. Stratification, in general, inhibits vertical motion and limits the vertical extent of topographically generated disturbances. Fluid particles displaced from their original position will, by the action of buoyancy forces, tend to return to their original position even if they have to make long excursions around seamounts and accelerate in the process. Stratification also permits the presence of depth variable baroclinic flows and affects the restoring force for Rossby waves so that the results of topography-flow interaction will differ, in princple, from the homogeneous case. Detailed theoretical studies of realistic high amplitude seamounts penetrating deeply into a continuously stratified fluid and interacting with vertically and horizontally sheared flows have yet to be made. For the simple case of a low amplitude circular seamount in a hyperbolically stratified fluid on a beta-plane Zyryanov (1981) found that Taylor columns are bottom intensified, inclined cones displaced from the seamount center. In a pioneering numerical study of topographically generated eddies Huppert and Bryan (1976) considered an idealized low amplitude circular seamount in a two-layer fluid on an f-plane with time variable but spatially constant upstream flow and found that the evolution of flow redistributed vorticity and temperature in such a way that a cold-core anticyclonic eddy remained over the seamount, while warm core cyclonic eddies were shed from atop the seamount. For strong flows the warm core eddies drifted away, while for weak flows they remained in the vicinity of the seamount. The application of the above findings to realistic seamounts and flows is still an open question, though some of the observed flow features and thermohaline structures around seamounts appear to support partially the theoretical and numerical conclusions (Brainard, 1986).

Geological Aspects of Seamount Effects on Circulation

Knowledge of how seamounts and seamount chains interact with the circulation is important geologically, because it affects sedimentation rates, species distribution, and paleoclimatological interpretations. Firstly, sedimentation rates are affected by mean flow deflection, eddy generation, and wave trapping. Intensified flow often leads to sediment erosion and decelerating or stagnating flow to sediment deposition. Because the flow patterns over seamounts are complex, patchiness in sediment accumulation occurs. Asymmetrical deposition and erosion atop seamounts and scoured flow channels near their bases have been observed by Lowrie and Heezen (1967) and Johnson et al. (1971). The tops of other seamounts are virtually devoid of any sediment, suggesting strong erosive processes (Pratt, 1967).

Secondly, the complex flow patterns resulting from the interaction with topography can have large effects on the seamount biota. Endemic biological populations can be maintained by trapped eddies with lifetimes of a few weeks or more (Genin and Boehlert, 1985). New colonists can be brought in by the impinging currents and old ones dispersed downstream by eddies swept from the seamount. This produces asymmetry and patchiness, so that the number and composition of the biota upstream, atop, and downstream of the seamount is not necessarily the same. The implications for the geological interpretations of micropaleontological records based on few samples are obvious.

Thirdly, in reconstructing the paleo-ocean circulation it is important to know not only the paleoclimate, but also the paleo-distribution of major seamount chains. Seamount chains are known to deflect major ocean currents that carry heat poleward (Roden and Taft, 1985; Richardson, 1980) and generate eddies and waves (Rhines, 1969; Verron and LeProvost, 1985) in the present-day ocean and there is every reason to believe that similar processes occurred in the geological past.

The purpose of the present paper is to discuss aspects of seamount and seamount chain effects on the ocean circulation based on recent theoretical and observational findings and to elucidate the salient features. Though the discussion is based entirely on the present-day ocean, the results are relevant also for understanding seamount effects on the flow in the geological past.

Theoretical Aspects of Flow Around Seamounts

Most seamounts have typical horizontal scales between 20 km and 200 km. For a fluid particle traveling with a characteristic speed of 0.1 ms^{-1}, it takes from 2 to 23 days to cross such distances. Because the crossing time of fluid particles is long compared to the inertial period of the earth's rotation ($T_i = 2\pi/f$, where f is the Coriolis parameter, is about a day in midlatitudes), rotational effects dominate the dynamics of flow around seamounts. The flow patterns that result from seamount-current interaction on a rotating earth with variable Coriolis parameter are quite different than would result from an identical interaction on a constant Coriolis parameter earth. This is so, because the change of Coriolis parameter with latitude provides a restoring force for a new class of motion, Rossby waves.

Many seamounts have large amplitudes relative to the surrounding water depth and extend deeply into the stratified part of the fluid. The dynamic effects of the stratification are large, ranging from the suppression of local vertical velocities to the providing of restoring forces for a new type of shear induced planetary waves that rival classical Rossby waves, with which they are sometimes lumped together as generalized Rossby waves. In almost all oceanic areas the stratification varies with depth. The combination of large amplitude seamounts and depth variable stratification gives rise to intricate dynamic balances that depend upon depth (Rhines and Bretherton, 1974; Veronis, 1981). Therefore, the flow patterns resulting from the seamount-flow interaction in the strongly stratified upper layers can be expected to differ from those in the weakly stratified lower layers.

In the following, a few illustrative examples will be given for simple quasigeostrophic flows in homogeneous and stratified fluids, both for the case of a constant Coriolis parameter and a variable Coriolis parameter.

I. Homogeneous Flows

The homogeneous models of quasigeostrophic flow over topography are crude in that they ignore the effects of density stratification, which is present almost always in the real ocean. Nevertheless, such models are useful for illuminating the physical principles involved, for cases of barotropic motion. One of the fundamental theorems of rotating flow in a frictionless fluid is the conservation of potential vorticity, Q, which states that along a fluid trajectory $Q = (f+\zeta)/D = $ constant, where f is the Coriolis parameter, ζ the relative vorticity, and D is depth. The theorem states that as the depth decreases, the absolute vorticity must decrease. On an f-plane this implies generation of anticyclonic relative vorticity by vortex compression as the fluid ascends the leading edge of the seamount. Thus, in the initial state, a pair of oppositely rotating eddies is found in the vicinity of the seamount. This is common to all theories. As time progresses, the two eddies interact with each other and with the mean flow in a complicated manner to produce numerous transient and trapped features, the details of which vary greatly. In the final steady state, after the transients have died away, f-plane solutions are characterized by a typical vorticity field with an anticyclonic eddy trapped over the seamount. When the Coriolis parameter varies with latitude, the flow patterns depend upon the direction of the mean flow. For eastward mean flows, Rossby waves are generated and the flow pattern consists of a trapped anticyclonic eddy over the seamount and an extensive wake on its downstream side. For westward mean flows, a wake does not exist and only a trapped anticyclonic eddy is found (Verron and LeProvost, 1985).

A. Quasigeostrophic steady-state flow over isolated elliptical topography on an f-plane. The case was investigated by Johnson (1982) for

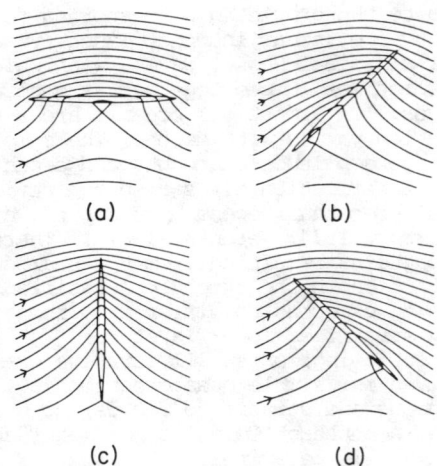

Fig. 1. Quasigeostrophic flow past an elliptic cylinder inclined at an angle to the oncoming flow, for (a) $\alpha=0$, (b) $\alpha=\pi/4$, (c) $\alpha=\pi/2$, and (d) $\alpha=3\pi/4$, according to Johnson (1982).

uniform impinging flow in a homogeneous ocean with the objective of finding out how an elliptically shaped seamount placed at various angles to the flow deflects and blocks the flow and where closed circulation regions--Taylor columns--occur. The theory is based on quasigeostrophic potential vorticity, with the relevant parameters of (1) ellipse aspect ratio $\gamma = L/l$, where L and l are the lengths of the major and minor axis, respectively, (2) the blocking parameter $B = hfl/DU$, where h is the seamount height, D the water depth, f the Coriolis parameter, and U the speed of the impinging flow, and (3) the angle α between the directions of the far field approaching flow and the major axis of the ellipse. Change of any of the three parameters leads to different flow patterns; for example, Taylor columns will form only when B exceeds a critical value of order one (Hide, 1961). A typical case for $\gamma = 25$, $B = 1.2$, and $\alpha = 0$, $\pi/4$, $\pi/2$, $3\pi/4$ are given in Figure 1. In all cases the deflection by the seamount is anticyclonic and there is flow intensification on the left side of the seamount when looking in the downstream direction. For a seamount orientation perpendicular to the incoming flow (c), the flow pattern is symmetric with respect to the major axis of the ellipse; for all other orientations, asymmetric patterns result. Taylor columns (identified by the small streamline loop in the figure) occur atop the seamount, near its center when the ellipse is oriented in the direction of the approaching flow, and near its southern end for other orientations. The region affected by the flow topography interaction is of the order of L, the length of the major axis of the ellipse.

Changing the values of B affects the occurrence and location of Taylor columns. For $B<0(1)$ no Taylor columns form; for $B=0(1)$ they occur over the seamount; and for $B>0(1)$ they can occur in the flow, off the seamount. Changing the values of γ essentially affects the symmetry of flow; as $\gamma\rightarrow 1$ the perturbations of flow become more and more symmetric around the seamount. Changing the direction of U from eastward to westward does not affect the findings discussed above; the resulting flow patterns are the mirror image of those shown in Figure 1. The last statement is a strict consequence of the f-plane approximation and will not hold where this assumption is violated.

B. Evolution of quasigeostrophic flow over isolated circular Gaussian topography on an f-plane. This instructive case was studied in a numerical model by Verron and LeProvost (1985) for flow initiated from rest in a homogeneous ocean in the presence of dissipation. The goal was to study the evolution of transient and steady perturbations caused by seamount-flow interaction and to assess the importance of friction. The model is based on the quasi-geostrophic vorticity equation applied to a zonal channel with open ends and a rigid lid (to filter out gravity and Kelvin waves). The relevant model parameters are (1) the blocking parameter $B = hfL/DU$, which measures the dynamical effect of the topography, (2) the nondimensional bottom friction parameter $r = r_o/UL$, where r_o is the dimensional bottom friction, and (3) the nondimensional lateral friction parameter $A = A_h/UL$, where A_h is the classical horizontal turbulent viscosity. By varying the parameters, and time, different flow patterns result. Despite the diversity of patterns, a few evolutionary features are common. During the initiation period ($t \ll L/U$), two vortices form, an anticyclonic one on the upstream and a cyclonic one on the downstream side of the seamount. The primary physical processes during this period are vortex compression and vortex stretching. During the intermediate period ($t = 0(L/U)$), the two eddies tend to rotate anticyclonically around the seamount and interact with each other as well as with the incoming flow to give rise to a great variety of perturbations, many of them transitory. Here, two physical processes are dominant, nonlinear vorticity interaction and advection by the incoming flow. During the final period ($t \gg L/U$) the transients die down and a permanent flow deflection with one or more (depending on the choice of parameters) trapped eddies is observed in the vicinity of the seamount. A few typical examples, based on the work of Verron and LeProvost (1985), are shown in Figures 2 and 3.

a. Small blocking parameter (Figure 2, top). In this case (B=4, r=0, A=0.025) advection processes dominate over vorticity interaction, the initially formed anticyclonic eddy slowly moves to the top of the seamount, while the cyclonic eddy is carried downstream by the mean flow. In the final stage, a single trapped anticyclonic eddy remains atop the seamount.

b. Moderate blocking parameter (Figure 2,

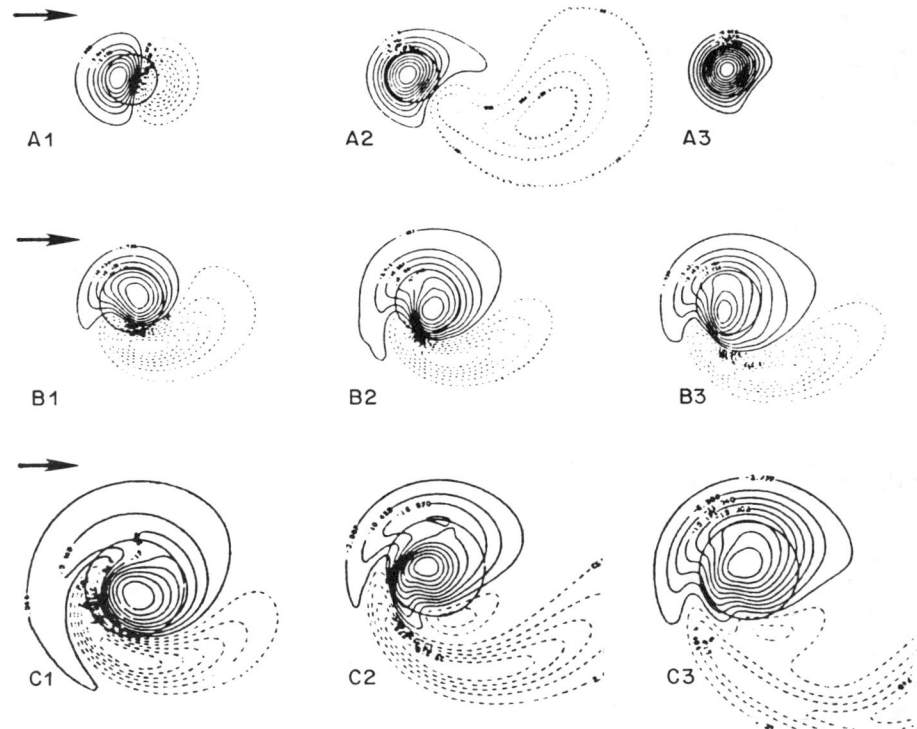

Fig. 2. Evolution of the vorticity for quasigeostrophic flow past a circular cylinder for various nondimensional times T. Anticyclonic vorticity is indicated by solid contours, cyclonic vorticity by dashed ones. Arrow indicates incoming flow. Top: Strong advection and weak blocking (A1) T=0.36; (A2) T=2.88; (A3) T=7.20. Middle: vorticity interaction with moderate blocking (B1) T=0.92; (B2) T=1.38; (B3) T=1.84. Bottom: vorticity interpenetration and strong blocking (C1) T=1.08; (C2) T=1.94; (C3) T=3.24, after Verron and LeProvost (1985). For all cases the initiation period of the flow is at left, the intermediate period at the center, and the final period at right.

middle). Here (B=12.5, r=0, A=0.01) vorticity interaction and advection processes are equally important. The initially formed cyclonic and anticyclonic eddies stay in the vicinity of the seamount and, after some rotational movement, become temporarily entrapped in the transverse position, with the anticyclonic center over the seamount and the cyclonic center to the right of it. The flow configuration remains stable over the advective time scale L/U. Eventually advection effects take over and the cyclonic eddy moves downstream as in the previous case.

c. Strong blocking parameter (Figure 2, bottom). For strong blocking (B=18, r=0, A=0.005) vorticity interaction dominates over advection processes. The resulting flow patterns are exceedingly complex. After initial formation, the two eddies rotate and come to a transverse position, as before. Then the cyclonic eddy is enwrapped in the anticyclonic one; both begin to oscillate and may become unstable, at which time vorticity splitting into smaller scales is observed. This results in the occurrence of multiple eddies in the vicinity of the seamount, some of which may subsequently coalesce and be carried away by the mean current. The figure shows the enwrapment on the left and the appearance of satellite cyclonic eddies in the middle and on the right.

d. Single and double vortex entrapment by a seamount and the role of friction. The streamline patterns for flow past a circular shaped Gaussian seamount are shown in Figure 3 for two parameter sets (B=10, r=0, A=0.01) and (B=15.6, r=0, A=0.02). In the first case, for weak horizontal friction, the classical case is obtained: when the flow becomes steady, the streamlines are deflected anticyclonically around the seamount and a single anticyclonic eddy is trapped near its center. In the second case, for stronger horizontal friction, the flow splits, making an anticyclonic northward loop and a cyclonic southward loop, before rejoining farther downstream. Simultaneously, a vortex pair is trapped by the seamount, with an anticyclonic eddy in the north and a cyclonic eddy in the south. Trapping of

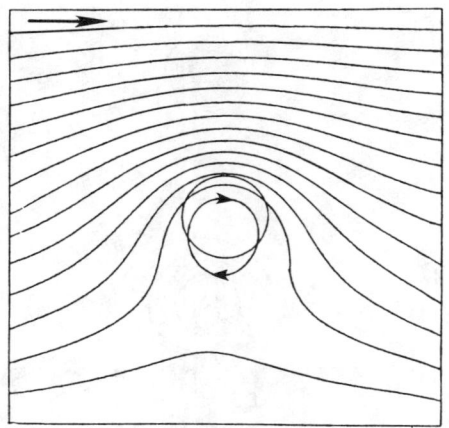 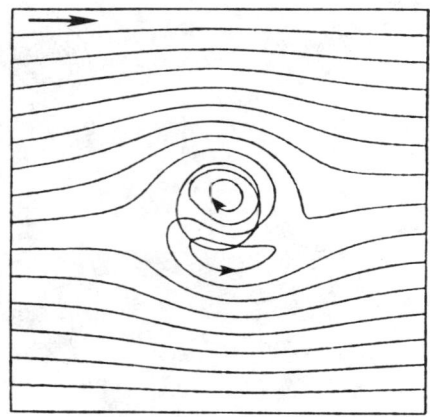

Fig. 3. Quasigeostrophic streamlines of flow past a circular cylinder showing single (left) and double (right) vorticity entrapment, after Verron and LeProvost (1985).

vortex pairs occurs also for seamounts of different shape. Kozlov (1981) investigated elliptically shaped seamounts and found that in addition to the anticyclonic eddy trapped over the seamount, there occurred a cyclonic trapped eddy in deep water south of the seamount.

e. *Eddy shedding from a seamount in the presence of unsteady mean flow.* Verron (1986) studied the interaction of a circular seamount with temporally varying mean flow in the presence of lateral friction. He found that, under certain circumstances, both cyclonic and anti-cyclonic eddies are shed from the seamount. This is thought to result from increased vorticity dissipation over topography, which locally affects the balance of potential vorticity on the advective time scale (L/U) and a periodic prevalence of advective effects, which sweep away the eddies trapped by the seamount, including Taylor columns.

All the above examples were for quasi-geostrophic flow on an f-plane in the case of no density stratification. In such models the effect of topography on flow is exaggerated compared to what is likely to occur in the real stratified ocean.

II. Stratified Flow

Stratification, in general, has two effects: it reduces the topographic effect upon flow and, in combination with a variable Coriolis parameter, supports a new class of motion, Rossby waves, which can interact with the topography (in a fluid with geographically varying stratification, Rossby waves are sustained not only by beta, the change of Coriolis parameter with latitude, but also by the horizontal and vertical curvature of the mean flow, which is pronounced in many frontal regions). The resulting flow patterns are exceedingly complex, and only a few idealized cases have been investigated so far.

A. *Quasigeostrophic steady-state flow over isolated cylindrical topography on a beta-plane in a stratified ocean.* The problem was investigated analytically by McCartney (1975) for a two-layer ocean with uniform velocity in each layer and a seamount that does not penetrate into the upper layer. The relevant parameters are (1) the blocking parameter $B = hfL/dU$, where d is the thickness of the lower layer, L is the seamount diameter, and the other variables are as before, (2) the stratification parameter (Burger number) $S = g\Delta\rho D/\rho f^2 L^2$ where g is the acceleration of gravity, D is the total water depth, and $\Delta\rho$ is the density difference between the two layers, and (3) the beta parameter $b = \beta L^2/U$ where β is the latitudinal change of the Coriolis parameter. The latter parameter measures, in essence, the importance of the curvature of the earth in the dynamics. For typical flow speeds observed in the ocean, $O(0.1 \text{ ms}^{-1})$, the beta effect becomes important for seamounts with diameters of more than 50 km. When this is the case, two more parameters are necessary to specify the flow regime, (4) the direction of impinging flow in the upper layer, and (5) the direction of impinging flow in the lower layer. The dramatic effect of flow direction on the type of perturbations caused by the seamount is shown in Figure 4, where the streamlines are for the lower layer, based on the parameter set (B=6, S→∞, b=|U|). In the case of eastward flow, the perturbation patterns upstream and downstream of the seamount are decidedly asymmetrical. A large amplitude wake is present downstream, but not upstream. Two eddies occur, a trapped anticyclonic eddy on the seamount, its center shifted westward, and a cyclonic eddy downstream from the seamount in deep water. In the case of westward flow, a downstream wake does not develop, and the flow patterns on either side of the seamount are similar. The effect of stratification is to weaken the topographically generated flow in the

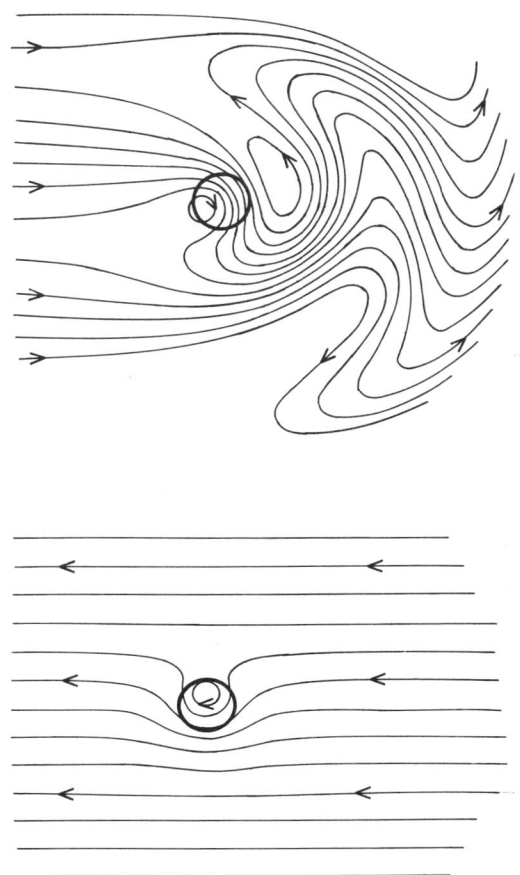

Fig. 4. Quasigeostrophic streamlines of flow past a cylindrical seamount on a beta-plane in the lower layer of a two-layer fluid for eastward flow (left) and westward flow (right), after McCartney (1975).

upper layer. The topographically generated eddies are thus bottom intensified. For $S \to \infty$, the eddies are not felt in the upper layer at all. The above conclusions are valid when the flow directions in both layers are the same. When the flow directions in the two layers are not the same, complex flow patterns develop. No detailed studies of these patterns appear to have been made.

B. <u>Quasigeostrophic steady-state flow over two cylindrical seamounts on a beta-plane in a stratified ocean</u>. This was investigated by Zyryanov (1981) for the case of one and two low amplitude ($h/D = 0.1$) seamounts in a continuously stratified ocean with a hyperbolic vertical density gradient and horizontally uniform impinging flow. The objectives were to determine the perturbations caused by flow-seamount interaction, to study the shapes and locations of eddies, and to assess the effects of the second seamount. As before, the relevant parameters are the direction of the flow U, the blocking parameter B, the stratification parameter S, and the beta-effect parameter b. A typical example valid for the parameter set (B=0(10), S=0(1), b=0.43, U=1 eastward) is shown in Figure 5, where the left and right panels refer to the northern and southern hemispheres, respectively. As expected, anticyclonic eddies over topography (Taylor columns), cyclonic eddies in deep water, and large amplitude Rossby waves in lee of the seamounts are found. The centers of the Taylor columns are shifted with respect to the seamount centers, to the southwest in the northern and to the northwest in the southern hemisphere. The shapes of the Taylor columns, for the stratification used, are vertically inclined cones with elliptic cross-sections. As the stratification increases the apex of the cones shrinks, so that the columns become more and more bottom trapped. In the case of two seamounts, Taylor columns occur on each of them. The circulation around the first seamount is reduced compared to the single seamount case and the cyclonic deep water eddy is shifted to the vicinity of the second seamount. The above results are valid for the stratification parameter of 0(1). For very strong stratification, the solutions indicate that an oppositely rotating cyclonic eddy may occur above the anticyclonic Taylor column eddy.

The flow patterns shown in Figure 5 depend not

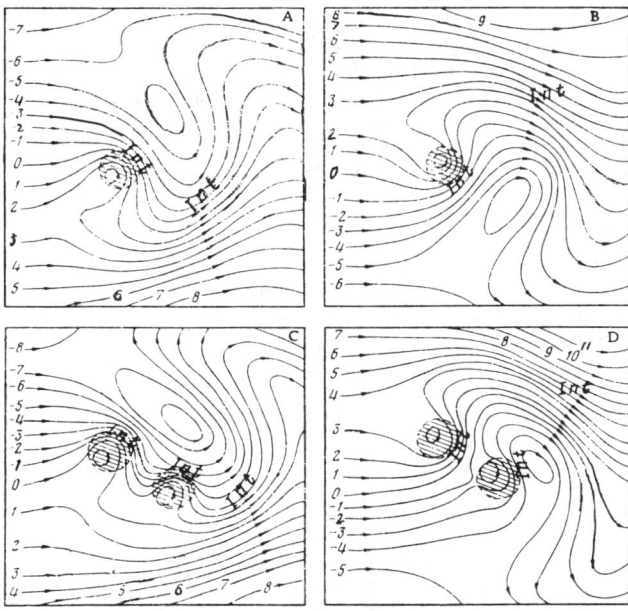

Fig. 5. Quasigeostrophic streamlines of flow past one and two circular seamounts in the northern (left) and southern (right) hemispheres for a continuously stratified fluid with a hyperbolic vertical density gradient profile, showing regions of flow intensification (Int), after Zyryanov (1981).

only on the hemisphere and number of seamounts, but also on the relative position of the seamounts to each other. For a single seamount, the flow patterns in the northern and southern hemispheres are symmetric, as expected. For two seamounts, Zyryanov's (1981) calculations show an asymmetry between the hemispheres, which can be explained as the combined effect of the change of the relative position of the seamounts with a change in hemisphere. Had he kept the relative position of the seamounts constant (second seamount equatorward of the first), the flow patterns would have remained symmetric. This indicates that when several seamounts are involved, the flow patterns from one hemisphere cannot be transferred to the other without exercising due care.

C. Comments on the quasigeostrophic flow. The above theoretical examples all deal with the quasigeostrophic assumption and low amplitude seamounts and so, to a certain extent, are atypical of the real ocean. The effect of the quasigeostrophic assumption is to filter out surface gravity waves, inertial waves, and Kelvin waves, so that the trapping of these waves by topography is neglected. Laboratory studies by Heikes and Maxworthy (1982) have shown that such waves can be generated by a cylindrically shaped object in a tank and hence, possibly, by seamount chains in the ocean.

The choice of low amplitude seamounts is made usually for mathematical convenience. Analytical solutions are hard to come by when the seamount height is a sizeable fraction of the ocean's depth and penetrates deeply into the stratified fluid. Numerical studies of high amplitude seamount effects in a stratified nongeostrophic fluid are just beginning and no far-reaching conclusions can be drawn as yet from the available results. Hurlburt and Thompson (1984) used a two-layeer primitive equation box model with a 20 km resolution to investigate the influence of the New England seamount chain upon an idealized Gulf Stream and found that even in this oversimplified case which overstates the effect of topography on the upper ocean the seamount chain deflects the path of the Gulf Stream, changes the amplitude of its meanders, and generates numerous warm core eddies on its upstream side.

Observations of Seamount Effects on Circulation

The variety of flow patterns and thermohaline structures observed in the vicinity of seamounts and seamount chains is large. This is so, because seamounts of different shape, height, and groupings interact with complex impinging flows to produce a multitude of observable features on scales varying from local to planetary. Scale changes also occur during this process. For example, the interaction of large scale flow with large scale topography, such as between the Kuroshio and the Emperor seamount chain, not only modifies the large scale flow, but also gives rise to intense secondary circulations that are of the mesoscale and submesoscale. The presence of multiple scales and of the time variability complicates the observational approach to studying seamount effects. To resolve mesoscale features requires high resolution quasisynoptic sampling with a grid spacing not larger than 10 km and a time interval not exceeding a few days. Resolution of submesoscale features requires even finer sampling grids and shorter time intervals. At the same time, a large enough domain must be covered by the grid to define the incoming flow and to investigate the far field seamount effects. In the future, the observational approach may well involve a judicious mix of shipboard CTD and acoustic Doppler current measurements, moored profiling instrumentation, acoustically tracked subsurface and satellite tracked surface drifters, satellite IR imagery (most useful in weakly stratified flows, where the seamount effect extends to the surface) and satellite altimetry (useful to study the variability, but not the absolute value of geopotential height near seamounts). At present, such a complete list of observations does not exist. The available information is limited to occasional shipboard surveys and a small number of surface drifter tracks, current moorings, and acoustic scattering measurements. Thus, the observational evidence of seamount effects on circulation is far from complete. The largest problem is the lack of synopticity and repetition of many shipboard surveys. The problem becomes more severe as the scale of sampling decreases. In view of the aforesaid, the conclusions drawn below are preliminary and subject to revision as new and better data become available.

A. Early observations. One of the earliest references of seamount effects on the thermohaline structure is due to Sverdrup (1941) who noticed that isopycnals dome atop Altair seamount in the Atlantic (Figure 6, left) and that the doming intensity decreases upward from the seamount top. Superficially, the observation resembles what in modern theory is called a stratified Taylor column. This implies anticyclonic flow around the seamount in the steady state (Huppert and Bryan, 1976). Sverdrup (1941), by neglecting the barotropic flow component, thought however that the rotational flow around the dome of high density was a "counterclockwise whirl". The coarse station spacing of the early observations precludes more definite conclusions to be drawn and points out the need for a better sampling strategy. The sampling resolution was improved when continuously profiling temperature-salinity-depth sensors became available and satellite navigation was introduced. It was soon found out that many of the large amplitude perturbations near seamounts had surprisingly small horizontal scales and were bottom trapped (Meincke, 1971). At Josephine seamount in the Atlantic, for example, the diameter of the cold core dome is only 10 km, which

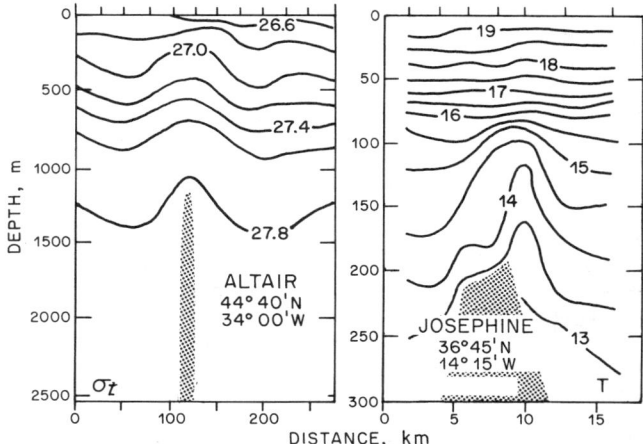

Fig. 6. Early observations of density and temperature structure near Atlantic seamounts, after Sverdrup (1941) and Meincke (1971).

is of the order of the width of the seamount top (Figure 6, right) and the roof of the dome lies at the lower boundary of the shallow thermocline. The implication is that the presence of the dome cannot be detected from temperature measurements at the sea surface, nor can it be found from coarse grid hydrographic measurements in the vicinity of the seamount, which may explain the paucity of reports of seamount effects on the thermohaline structure prior to the 1960s.

B. Benthic boundary layers above seamounts. No detailed observations of benthic boundary layers above seamounts appear to have been made, despite their obvious importance in understanding small scale processes occurring on the seamount tops and flanks. Elsewhere, Armi and Millard (1976) made a study of the benthic boundary layer over the Hatteras abyssal plain and found that the thickness of this layer varied between 10 m and 100 m, increasing with the speed of the mean flow, averaged over a day. The observed boundary layer thickness was much larger than that estimated from turbulent bottom Ekman layer heights, which gave values between 1 and 10 m. A benthic boundary layer was observed also at the fringes of the abyssal plain where the topography was rough. The vertical structure of this layer was considerably more complicated than observed over flat bottom. The benthic boundary layer appears to be of dynamic origin, involving poorly understood nonlinear and frictional processes.

C. Internal waves and internal wavetrains in the vicinity of seamounts. Bell (1975) and Wunsch and Webb (1979) investigated internal waves in the deep ocean and found that the internal wave field near seamounts and other topographic features differed from that observed over a flat bottom. Near seamounts, the internal waves were amplified and the flow patterns decidedly anisotropic. The authors initially thought that the seamounts were the source of the increased wave energy, but later concluded that the seamounts merely distorted the existing deep sea internal wave field. Eriksen (1982, 1985) conclusively demonstrated that reflection of internal waves by seamounts causes amplification of energy and shear, particularly near the critical frequency $\sigma_c^2 = N^2 \sin^2\alpha + f^2 \cos^2\alpha$ (N is the Väisälä frequency, f the Coriolis parameter, and the bottom slope) at which an incident ray is reflected parallel to the sloping bottom, unable to carry away the energy. Moored current meter observations near Muir seamount in the Sargasso Sea indicated that the vertical scale of the energy amplification is of the order of 100 m and that there is intensification of horizontal kinetic energy near the critical frequency. The reflection of internal waves by seamounts is a highly nonlinear and dissipative process that leads to boundary layer mixing and the formation of benthic boundary layers. Kunze and Sanford (1986) focused on near-inertial wave interactions with topography and mean flow near Caryn seamount in the Sargasso Sea and found from velocity profiler measurements that enhanced upward moving near-inertial wave energy occurs within 100 m of the seamount's top.

Kaneko et al. (1986) investigated in calm weather the interaction of the Tsushima current with the Shichiri-Ga-Sone seamounts by a combination of hydrographic, turbidity, and towed echosounder (200 kHz) measurements. The latter gave return signals from various oceanic scatterers that were amplified by a factor of 10 and color coded according to signal strength. A simplified black-and-white version of the original color echogram is shown in Figure 7 where the shading indicates strong acoustic signals. An internal wavetrain with an amplitude of about 10 m is clearly seen at the base of a well mixed surface layer, where the acoustic signal strength changes rapidly. On the upstream side of the seamounts, the wavelength is 400 m, on the downstream side 2 km. The subsurface wavetrain induced a similar low amplitude disturbance at the sea surface, which was recorded photographically by the

Fig. 7. Internal wavetrain upstream of Shichiri-Ga-Sone seamount, as revealed by acoustic scattering measurements, after Kaneko et al. (1986).

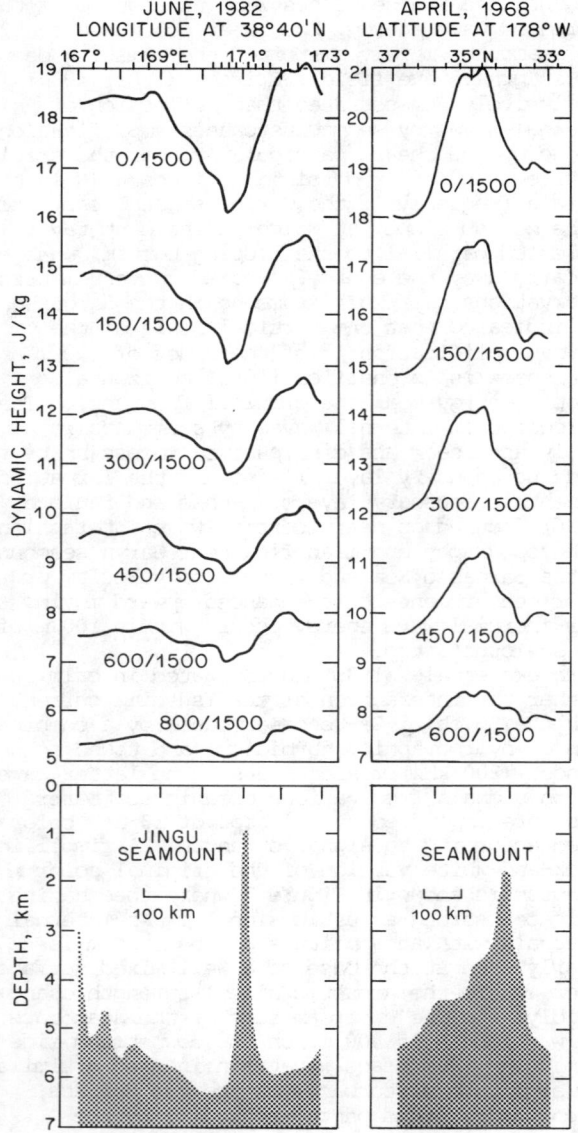

Fig. 8. Mesoscale perturbations of dynamic height in the vicinity of seamounts as a function of increasing pressure. The numbers refer to pressure levels (db) with respect to the 1500 db reference pressure.

authors. The dynamics of the seamount-flow interaction are not fully understood, though it is known that strong flow over small amplitude ridges can generate internal wavetrains and solitons (Farmer and Smith, 1980; Maxworthy, 1979).

D. **Amplification of tidal flow and temperature perturbations near seamounts.** Meincke (1971) and Horn et al. (1971) made a thorough study of the stratification and the time variability of flow and temperature on and around Great Meteor seamount in the Atlantic, using expendable bathythermographs and moored current meters over a period of 46 days. They found in the records clear indication of tidal flow. The tidal perturbations of velocity and temperature over the seamount top were higher by a factor of four relative to surrounding deep ocean, for all frequencies observed. The residual currents, after elimination of the tides, showed predominantly (33 out of 46 days) anticyclonic flow above the seamount top. The horizontal coherence of current fluctuations observed at different locations atop the seamount was high for the semi-diurnal tidal component, but low for the diurnal one.

The residual currents resulting from tidal-flow seamount interaction do not have to be anticyclonic over seamount tops. Pingree and Maddock (1985) investigated in a numerical model (barotropic, f-plane, with bottom friction) the residual currents resulting from the interaction of a circular bank with oscillatory rotary mean flow. They found that while the effect of the earth's rotation is always anticyclonic (in the northern hemisphere), the frictionally induced Eulerian residual currents can be anticyclonic or cyclonic, depending upon the sense of rotation of the rotary far field flow. When the far field flow is anticyclonic, the effects of the earth's rotation and of bottom friction are of the same sign and the residual currents are anticyclonic. When the far field flow is cyclonic, the two effects are opposed and, if friction dominates, the residual currents are cyclonic.

E. **Mesoscale perturbations near seamounts.** Mesoscale (here defined to encompass features between 1 and 10 baroclinic Rossby radii of deformation, or roughly 50 km to 500 km) perturbations of large amplitude are often observed near seamounts. They involve disturbances of geopotential height and baroclinic flow, as well as density and sound speed structures, which result from the interaction of horizontally and vertically sheared flows with topography of various height and size. The resulting flow patterns are highly complex. Because the impinging flow and the topographic shape are different for each seamount, the mesoscale perturbations generated by the interaction also differ and, in general, findings from one seamount cannot be extrapolated to the next. In the following, a few salient examples are given for large-amplitude seamounts in the central and western North Pacific.

A. **Geopotential topography perturbations.** The geopotential height field and its variation with depth in the vicinity of two large seamounts are shown in Figure 8. A pronounced depression is observed about 40 km west of Jingu seamount and a large rise is found 50 km north of an unnamed seamount near the Date Line. In both cases the perturbation amplitudes from the sourrounding terrain are about 3 J/kg (equivalent to a geo-

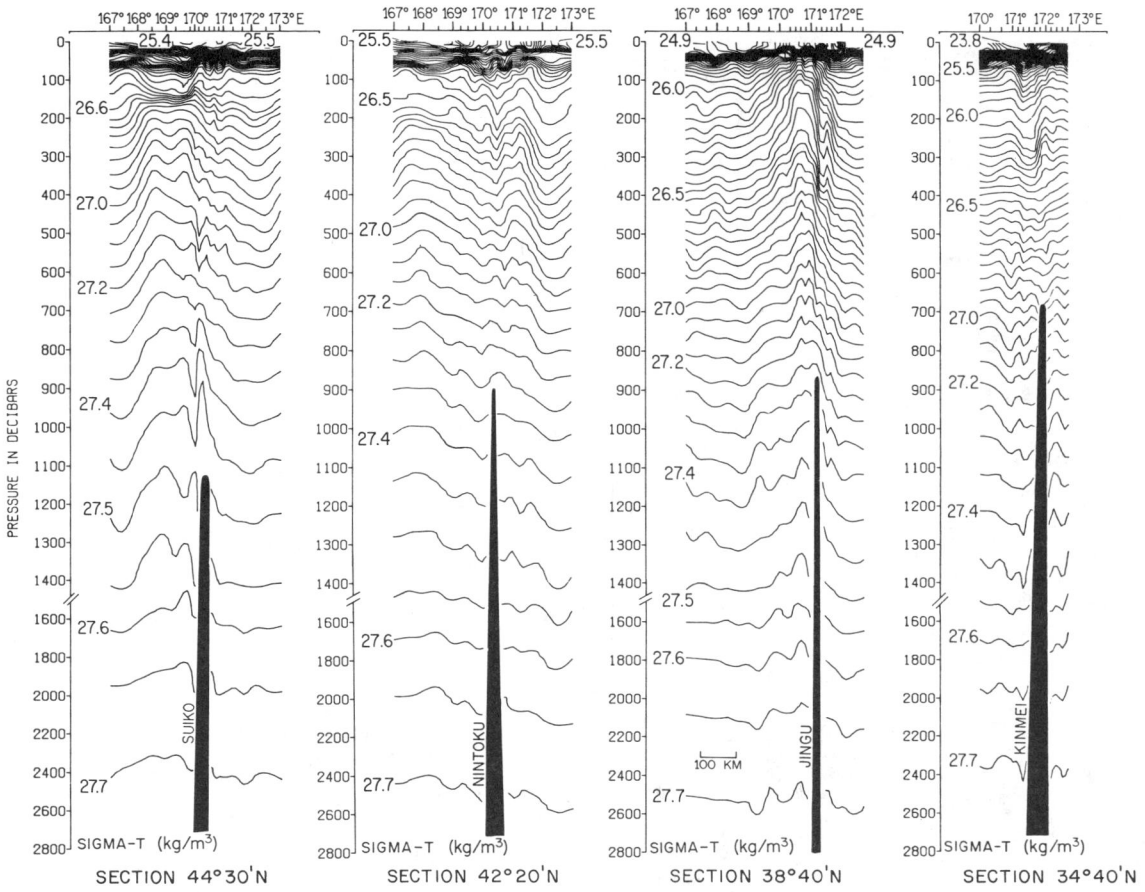

Fig. 9. Mesoscale perturbations of density in the vicinity of the Emperor seamounts, after Roden and Taft (1985).

metrical distance of 0.3 m) at the sea surface and diminish with increasing pressure, to about 1/2 of the surface avlue at 450 db and 1/4 of this value at 800 db. The perturbation widths are of the order of 200-250 km. At Jingu seamount, the shape of the depression is clearly asymmetric, with the steeper slope toward the seamount side. This implies enhanced northward flow on the left side of the seamount (Roden and Taft, 1985), and is anticipated in some quasigeostrophic theories for certain parameter ranges (Johnson, 1982). Because the geopotential height sections across these seamounts were occupied only once, nothing can be said about the lifetimes of these perturbations. To monitor changes in the shape of geopotential height perturbations, satellite altimeter information could be employed. The absolute shape of the geopotential surface, on the other hand, cannot be so obtained with present technology, because of the large uncertainties in determining the shape of the local geoid near seamounts.

b. Density and baroclinic flow perturbations. Complex density and baroclinic flow structures are observed near high amplitude seamounts. Typical examples of the density structure are shown in Figure 9 for several of the Emperor seamounts. At Suiko, the outstanding feature is the large amplitude, small horizontal scale perturbation above the seamount top, which is clearly bottom intensified and probably a manifestation of a lightly inclined Taylor column, as anticipated by Zyryanov's (1981) theoretical work. At Nintoku, there is an indication of an increased amplitude density disturbance between 100 and 500 db, but no sign of a Taylor column. At Jingu, the main feature is the 250 km wide asymmetric dome just west of the seamount, located between its top and the bottom of the shallow pycnocline at 100 db. Because the diameter of this dome is much wider than the seamount width and the domint is most pronounced between 100 and 500 db, rather than above the seamount top, the feature probably represents an intense eddy or current meander and not a Taylor column. At Kinmei, the large density disturbance in the upper 400 db is caused by an omega-shaped loop of the Kuroshio extension (discussed below).

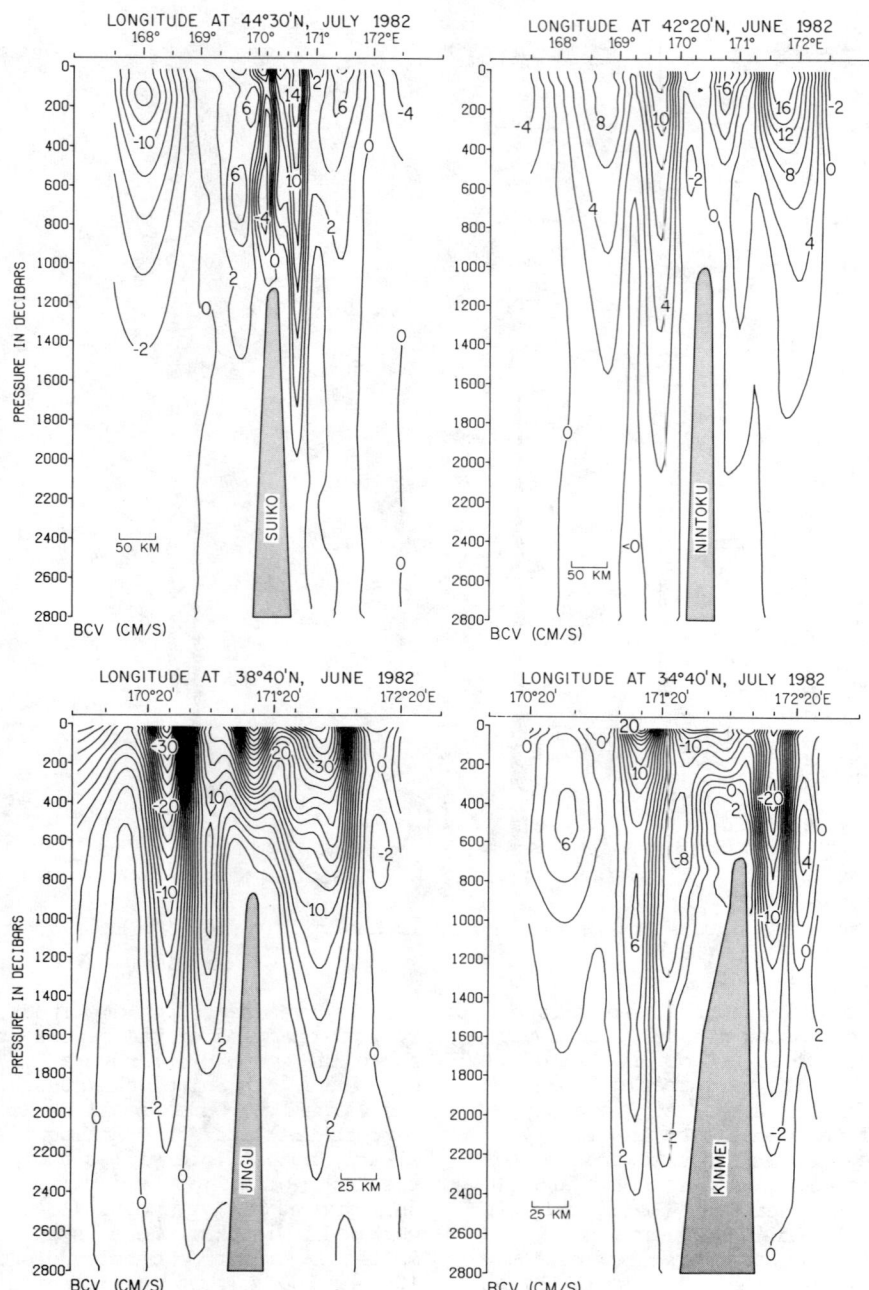

Fig. 10. Mesoscale perturbations of the northward component (positive) of baroclinic flow in the vicinity of the Emperor seamounts. The location of the seamounts is shown in Figure 12.

The density sections across the sea permit one to compute the vertical structure of the meridianal baroclinic flow component. This is shown in Figure 10 for flow relative to 2800 db. The dominant horizontal scale is of the order of the seamount's width. Numerous jet-like features with deep roots extending to 2000 m occur along the flanks of the seamounts. Above the tops of some seamounts complex flows and counterflows and eddy-like structures are observed. Maximum speeds of the baroclinic meridional flow component vary typically between 0.15 and 0.35 ms^{-1}. Beyond these common features, the details of the velocity structure vary greatly from one seamount to the next. At Suiko, the far-field flow is southward. The flow above both flanks is north-

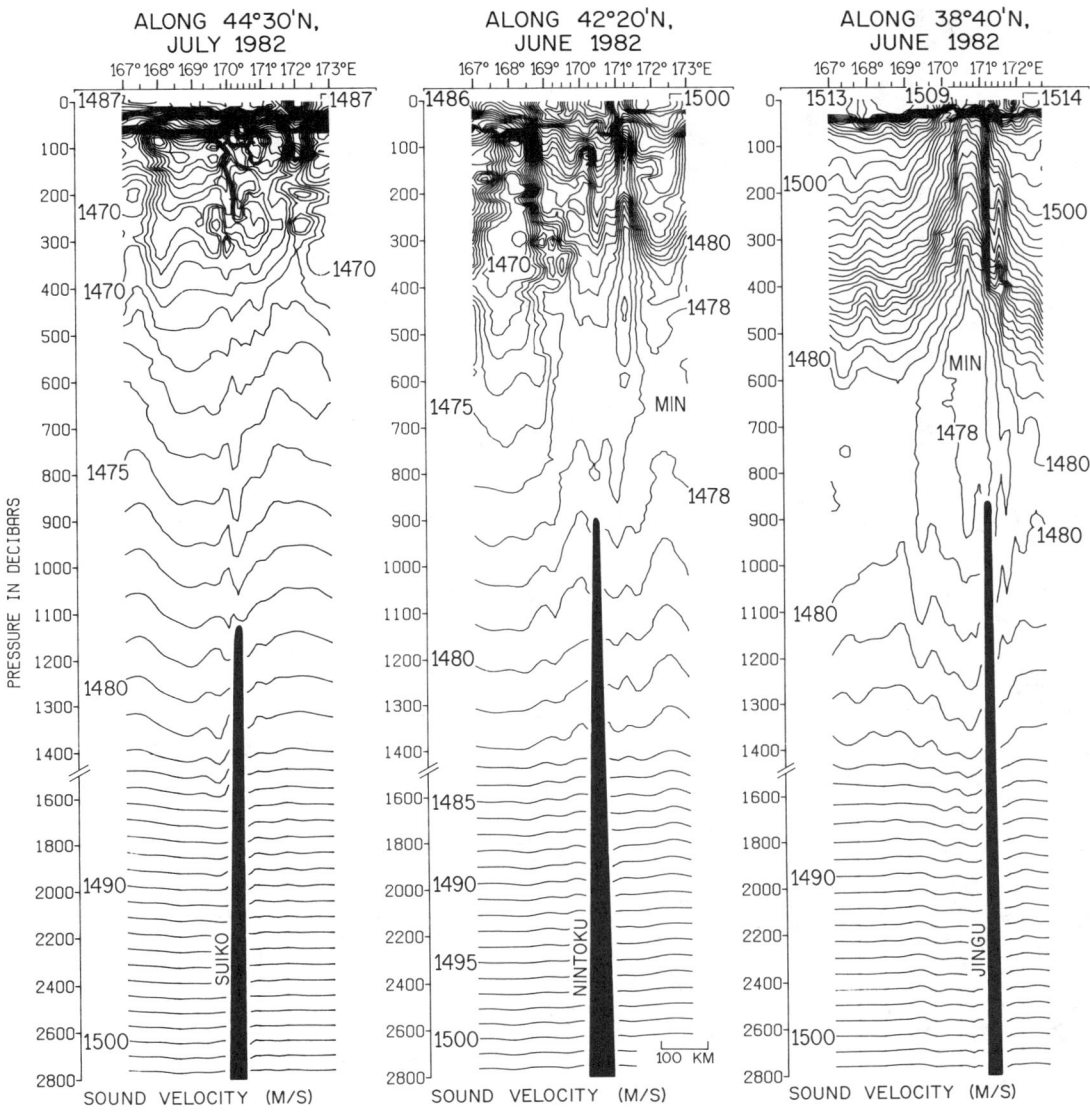

Fig. 11. Mesoscale perturbations of sound velocity in the vicinity of the Emperor seamounts, after Roden (1984a).

ward, while atop the seamount iself there is a narrow region of southward flow between 200 and 1100 db. At Nintoku, northward flow occurs on the western and southward flow on the eastern flank. Atop the seamount, a region of southward flow is observed between 400 and 700 db. At Jingu, there is intense cyclonic flow west of the seamount and strong northward flow to the east. At Kinmei, the deep intense northward flow in the west and the deep southward flow in the east are caused by an anticyclonic loop of the Kuroshio extension. Atop this seamount, the flow is northward between 300 and 600 db, and southward between 0 and 300 db.

The large variability of baroclinic flow over short distances makes it difficult to interpret direct current measurements made at a few points in the vicinity of seamounts. The horizontal coherence of current fluctuations around seamounts is generally low, except for certain tidal frequencies (Meincke, 1971).

c. Sound speed perturbations near seamounts. The perturbations caused by seamount-flow interaction also affect the sound speed field, knowledge of which is important for converting sonic depth to true depth in the accurate mapping of seamounts. Sound speed perturbations near the Emperor seamounts were inestigated by Roden (1984) and show many large amplitude mesoscale perturbations, ranging from pronounced fronts to secondary sound channels and eddy-like features (Figure 11). Most of the intense fronts are

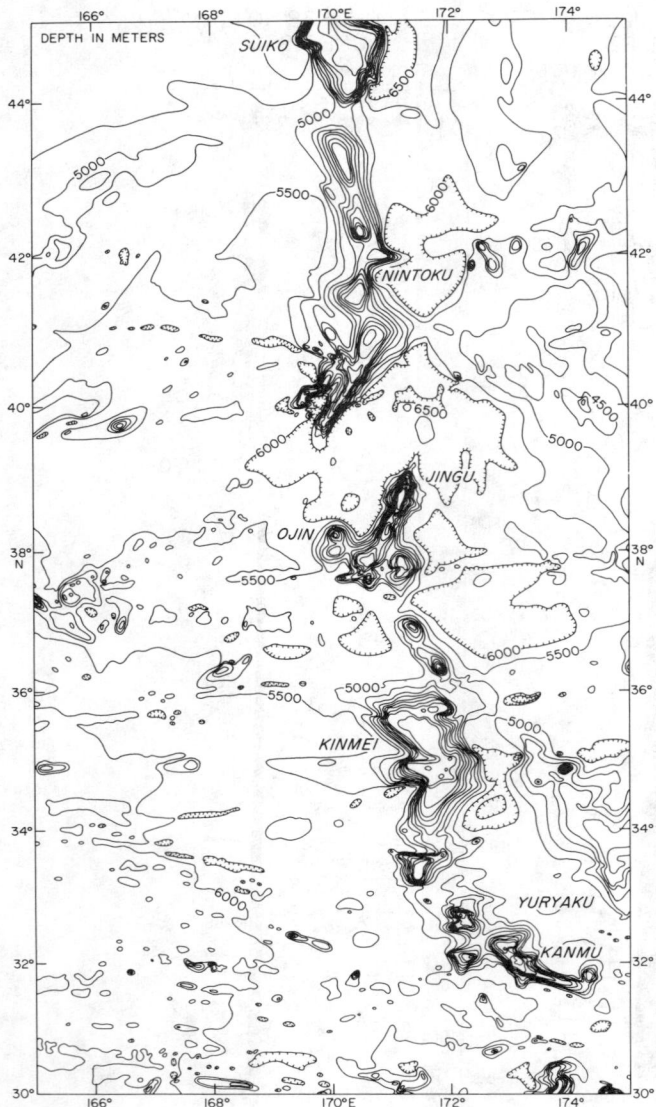

Fig. 12. Topograhic map, with depths in meters, of the Emperor seamounts region. After maps No. 6303 and 6304 of the Japan Maritime Safety Agency (1968).

found in the upper 400 m. Several large perturbations occur above the seamount tops. Because sound speed is a nonlinear function of temperature, pressure, and salinity, care has to be used in the dynamic interpretation of these features. Consider a Taylor column the top of which lies below the Sofar axis, where the vertical temperature and sound speed gradients are of opposite sign. In the temperature, salinity, and density fields, the Taylor column is represented by bottom intensified uplift of the isolines (as suggested by the doming of the isopycnals over Suiko seamount in Figure 9). In the sound speed field, the same Taylor column is represented by a downwarp of the isosons (Figure 10).

Observations of Seamount Chain Effects on Circulation

Seamount chains can be regarded as large amplitude comblike structures with gaps and missing teeth embedded in a stratified ocean. A typical example is the Emperor seamount chain which is about 100 km wide, 2400 km long, and has peaks that extend to within a few hundred meters of the ocean surface (Figure 12). The flow impinging on such planetary scale topographic structures is nonuniform and may consist of more than one current system. The circulation patterns resulting from the interaction are exceedingly complex and depend, in addition to blocking, stratification, and beta-effect parameters discussed above, also on the relative spacings and dimensions of the individual peaks and gaps. Among the better known effects are boundary current deflections and attenuations, eddy generation and front trapping, as well as flow rectification and intensification in gaps. A few examples are given below.

A. <u>Deflection of the Kuroshio extension and of the subarctic current by the Emperor seamount chain</u>. The horizontal distribution of temperature, salinity, and dynamic height at 150 m in the Emperor seamounts region is shown in Figure 13. The subsurface depth was selected in order to bring out more cleearly the thermohaline fronts. The Kuroshio extension, located near $35°35'N$ at $167°E$, approaches the seamounts in a southeasterly direction. About 50 km from the seamounts the current is deflected northward. The angle of deflection varies between 45 and 90 degrees, with the larger angles occurring near the northern, shallower part of Kinmei seamount. Over this seamount the current performs an omega shaped loop and weakens in the process. Downstream of the seamount, the Kuroshio extension reintensifies, though not to its upstream strength.

The subarctic current, located near $41°N$ at $167°E$, approaches Nintoku seamount on a southeasterly course. Over the southern part of this seamount, the current is deflected and flows northward to about $42°30'N$, where it turns eastward. Then the current splits, with one branch turning southeastward to complete an anticyclonic loop and the other branch continuing eastward.

The baroclinic flow approaching Jingu seamount in a southeastward direction is deflected northward upon encountering a shallow ridge. A pronounced eddy with a diameter of 150 km is located about 50 km west of the seamount.

The thermohaline fronts follow the current boundaries. The Kuroshio extension temperature

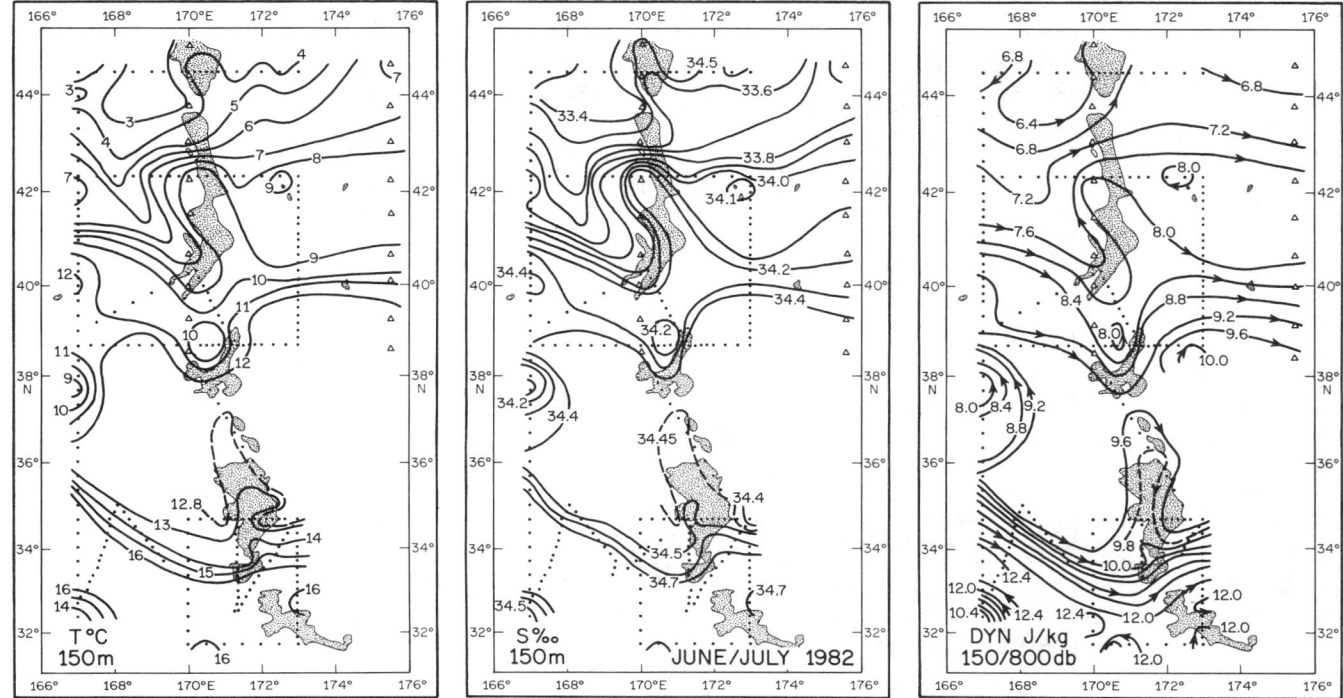

Fig. 13. Temperature, salinity, and relative dynamic height in the vicinity of the Emperor seamounts. The names of the large seamounts are, from north to south: Suiko, Nintoku, Jingu, and Kinmei. Dots and triangles refer to station positions of the R/V Thomas G. Thompson (Roden and Taft, 1985) and the R/V Hokusei Maru (University of Hokkaido, 1983).

and salinity fronts weaken over Kinmei seamount compared to the upstream intensity while the subarctic tmperature and salinity fronts over Nintoku seamount appear to intensify with respect to the intensities obesrved upstream. The subarctic fronts over Nintoku Seamount are remarkably stable from year to year at almost the same location (Figure 14).

The deflection of the impinging currents by the Emperor seamount chain is seen not only in maps of dynamic height, but also in the path of satellite tracked tsurface drifters (Figure 15). The results indicate that the latitude at which the drifters cross the seamount chain varies from year to year. According to Vastano et al. (1985) drifters originally released in the Kuroshio extension upstream crossed the seamount chain between $39°$ and $40°N$, in the region of a deep gap. A few years later, Nitani (Roden et al., 1982) found that drifters released upstream in the Kuroshio extension went around Kinmei seamount, crossing the chain at $36°N$. In all four cases the drifters made a basically anticyclonic loop when crossing the chain. Outside the chain, small cyclonic loops of uncertain origin were observed in some of the drifter records.

B. Deflection of the Gulf Stream by the New England seamount chain. The influence of the New England Seamount Chain on the Gulf Stream was investigated by several authors. Vastano and Warren (1976) studied baroclinic flow patterns in the vicinity of Kelvin and Atlantis II seamounts and found the patterns to be highly time variable, with frequent indications of large flow deflections and isotherm distortions near these seamounts. Richardson (1981) used satellite tracked surface drifters and found large anticyclonic and cyclonic current deflections near and increased Gulf Stream meanders downstream of the New England seamounts. Cornillon (1986), using satellite IR imagery to track the northern boundary of the Gulf Stream, concluded, however, that there was no significant meander amplitude increase downstream of these seamounts. Because satellite drifters and satellite IR devices do not necessarily describe the same phenomenon, the discrepancy in findings is not surprising. Future use of acoustically tracked subsurface drifters may help solve the problem.

C. Eddy trapping and generation by seamount groups. Two cases of drifter trapping by seamount groups are shown in Figure 16, one in the

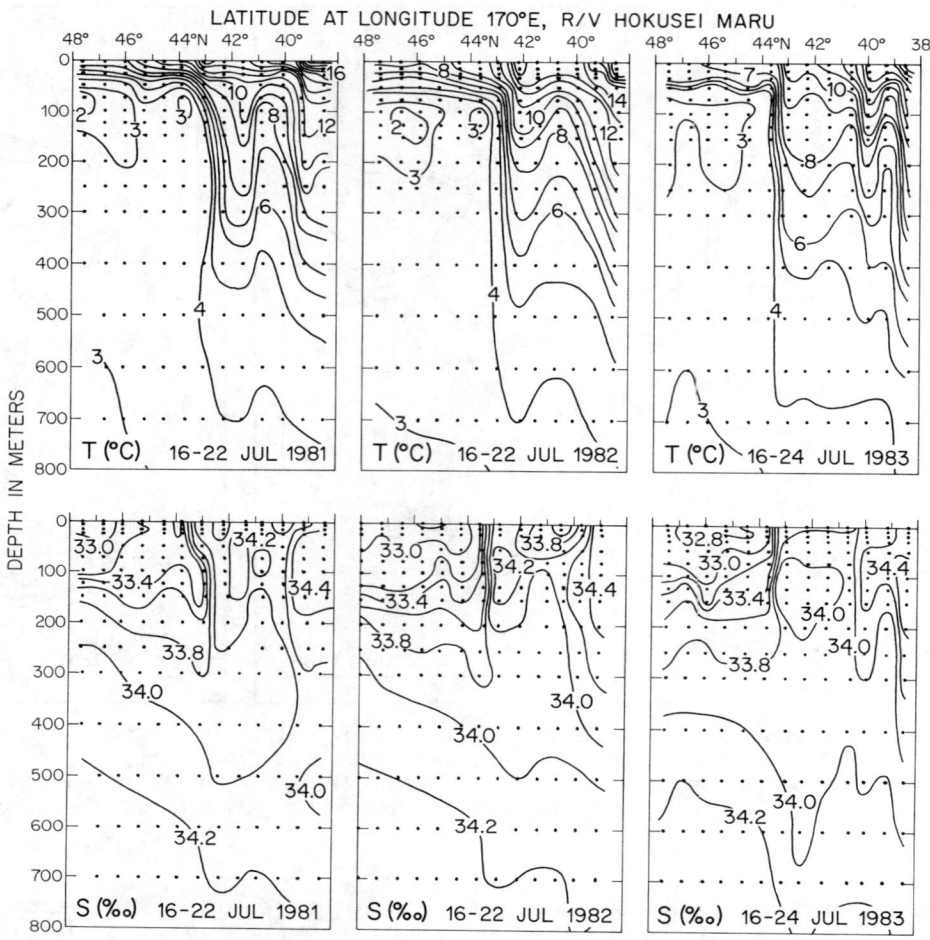

Fig. 14. Vertical thermohaline structure and its interannual variation based on observations of the R/V Hokusei Maru (University of Hokkaido, 1983-1985). The large thermohaline front is located over the northern part of Nintoku seamount.

Atlantic and the other in the Pacific. At the Corner Rise seamounts (Richardson, 1980), the trajectories suggest that an anticyclonic eddy was generated over the seamounts, which entrapped the drifters. The particular drifter shown remained in the vicinity of the seamounts for 86 days. The eddy slowly moved southwestward with a speed of a few centimeters per second and performed numerous loops with speeds of a few tens of centimeters per second.

At the Jenkins Seamounts group (Cheney et al., 1980) the trajectories also suggest the presence of a moving anticyclonic eddy, perhaps generated by the 20 km wide, 2 km high unnamed dotted seamount in the western part of the group. The eddy stayed in the vicinity of this isolated seamount for a period of six weeks and in the general area of the Jenkins seamount group for 56 days. The loop diameters ranged from 5 to 65 km. A maximum peripheral speed of 0.7 ms^{-2} was observed during the largest loop.

D. Flow rectification in gaps of the Emperor seamount chain. The Emperor seamount chain is 2400 km long and rises from 3 to 5 km above the deep ocean floor (Figure 12). It is broken by one main gap, about 150 km wide and 6000 m deep between Nintoku and Jingu seamounts, and numerous smaller ones, which are narrower and less deep. The main gap provides open communication for waters of the western and eastern basins of the North Pacific below about 1000 m. A year-long time series of low-pass filtered currents (Hamann and Taft, 1987) is shown in Figure 17 for three depth levels. Near the top of the seamounts (950 m) the currents are mainly oscillatory and vary considerably in strength from season to season. As the depth increases (1650 m), northward and northeastward components predominate and the current intensities vary less with time. At still greater depths (3950 m) the currents set almost uniformly along the main axis of the gap toward the northeast and the speeds are rather

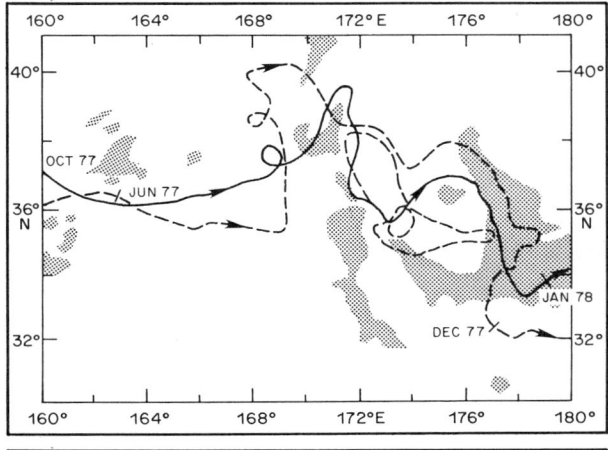

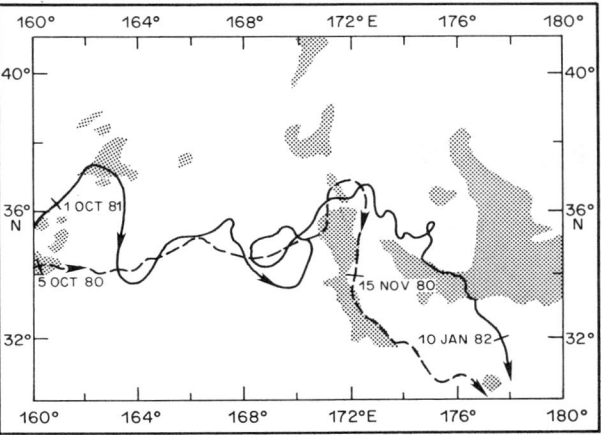

Fig. 15. Paths of satellite tracked drifters in the vicinity of the Emperor seamounts showing the deflection of the Kuroshio extension, based on American and Japanese measurements, after Roden et al., 1982, and Vastano et al., 1985.

constant. This flow rectification with increasing depth is a characteristic example of topographic steering of deep flow in gaps and has been observed elsewhere. Rattray (1985) investigated the effect of bathymetry upon deep flow in Drake Passage and found enhanced deep flows with increased baroclinicity in and downstream of gaps through the main ridge.

Conclusions

The following conclusions can be drawn from the theoretical and observational findings discussed above:

1. The effects of seamounts and seamount chains upon the oceaenic circulation and thermohaline structure are complex and depend on a variety of topographic and flow parameters involving the rotation of the earth and its variation with latitude, stratification, structure of the approaching flow and its direction, height, shape, orientation of seamounts, and the spacing of peaks and gaps in seamount chains. Depending upon the parameters chosen, diverse flow patterns are obtained with features varying in scale from local to planetary.

2. Observed seamount effects on circulation and thermohaline structure include generation of internal wave trains, amplification of tidal flow, bottom intensified Taylor columns, trapping of eddies and fronts, large-amplitude, mesoscale geopotential height perturbations, and deflection and modification of western boundary currents.

3. The dynamics of flow-topography interaction are poorly understood at present for seamounts of realistic height and shape embedded in non-uniform, time varying stratified flow. Highly idealized f-plane models generally predict double-vortex generation in the vicinity of the seamount, which interact with each other and the mean flow. Ultimately, when the steady state is

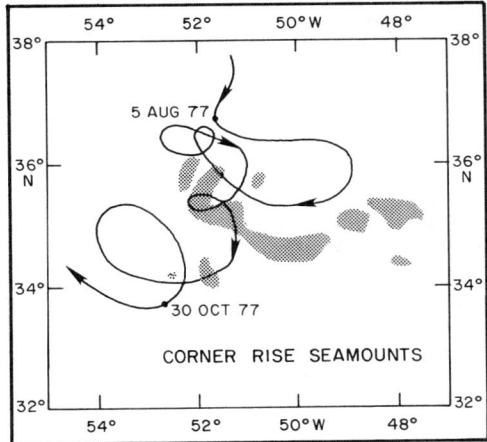

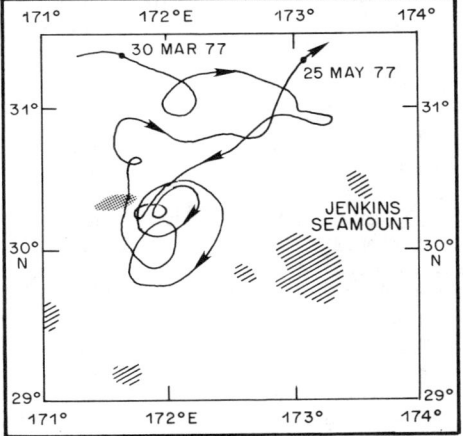

Fig. 16. Paths of satellite tracked drifters in the vicinity of Corner Rise seamounts (Richardson, 1980) and Jenkins seamounts (Cheney et al., 1980) showing anticyclonic eddy motion.

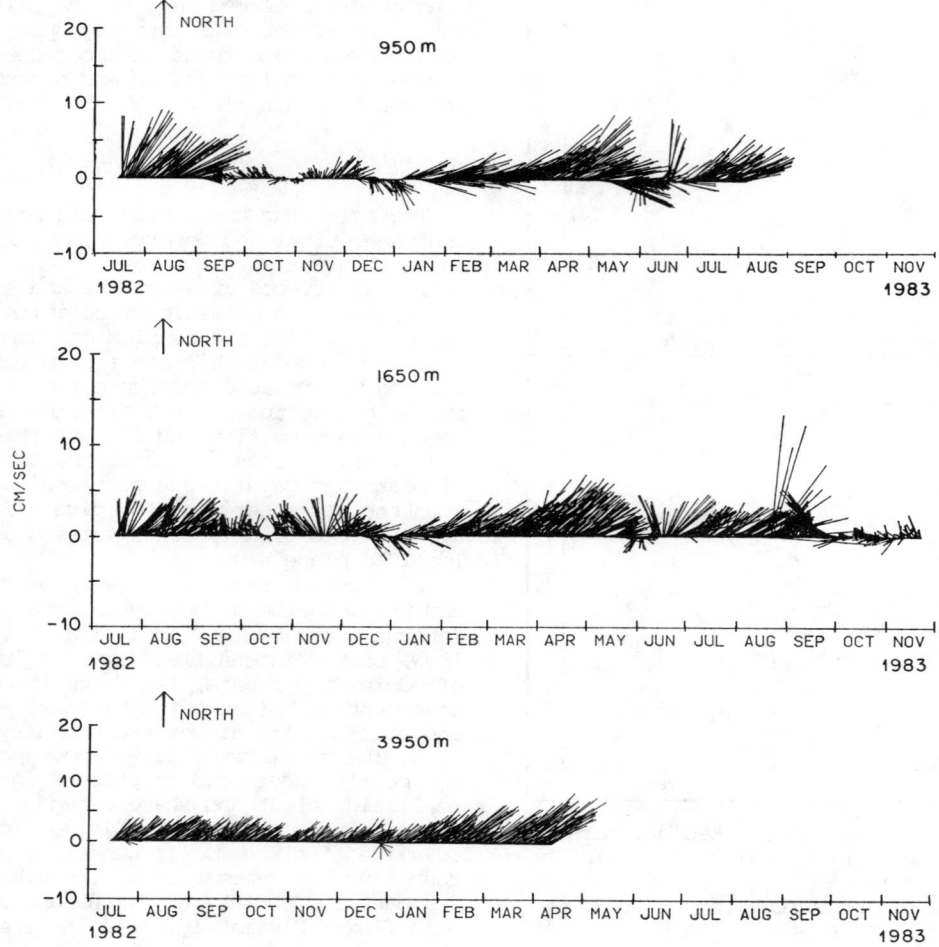

Fig. 17. Temporal variability of measured and low-pass filtered currents in the main gap between the northern and southern Emperor seamounts, with sticks indicating the speed and direction of flow, after Pillsbury et al. (1985) and Hamann and Taft (1987).

reached, the flow around the seamount is clockwise and a trapped anticyclonic eddy (Taylor column) appears near its top, for a certain parameter range. Observational evidence for steady state anticyclonic deflections and Taylor columns is mixed, probably because a steady state is rarely encountered in the real ocean. While anticyclonic flow deflections around seamounts are frequently observed in drifter tracks and isotherm distortions, cyclonic deflections also occur. The evidence for Taylor columns is scant; only a few have been identified indirectly, based on thermohaline structure. Idealized beta-plane models bring out the added effect of Rossby waves, which occur on the downstream side for eastward, but not westward mean flow. Unambiguous evidence for the existence of leeside Rossby waves in the ocean does not exist. Though an increase in meander amplitude has been observed downstream of the New England seamount chain, it is not clear what their origin is. Furthermore, in a realistic ocean Rossby waves can be exited by the shear of the basic flow, in which case upstream as well as downstream effects will occur. For the transient stage, the models predict cyclonic and anticyclonic eddies generated by the seamounts. These eddies can become temporarily entrapped by the seamounts, oscillate, penetrate each other, break into smaller eddies and coalesce, or be swept away by the mean flow, depending upon the flow conditions. Few observations of such transient features exist.

From the complicated paths of drifters in the vicinity of seamounts and from convoluted temperature structures seen in satellite infrared images it appears, however, that such flow phenomena are quite likely to occur.

4. Future progress in the understanding of seamount effects on circulation and thermohaline structure is likely to come from a combined observational and modeling approach. On the observational side the greatest need is for high resolution measurements of the flow and thermohaline structure by complimentary methods involving surface and subsurface drifters in sufficient numbers to determine the Lagrangian flow, moored arrays and vertical profiles to investigate temporal and spatial near field variability, and satellite altimeter and infrared imagery to assess the meso and layer scale variability. On the modeling side, the need is for dealing with seamounts of realistic height in a continuously stratified ocean in the presence of nonuniform incident flow and lateral boundaries. The models ought to be initialized, updated, and verified using suitable field observations.

Acknowledgements. The author dedicates this article to the memory of H. William Menard, whose pioneering interest in seamounts stimulated not only geologists, but also physical oceanographers concerned with seamount effects on circulation. Thanks are due the scientific and operation crew of the R/V Thomas G. Thompson, Captain Clampitt for outstanding performance under sometimes adverse weather conditions. William J. Fredericks efficiently produced the computer plots and Lennart E. Roden helped diligently to transfer the early cruise data from punched cards to magnetic tape. This research was funded by National Science Foundation Grant OCE81-17047 and Office of Naval Research Contract N00014-84-C-0252. Contribution No. 1679 from the School of Oceanography, University of Washington, Seattle, WA 98195.

References

Armi, L. and R.C. Millard, The bottom boundary layer of the deep ocean, J. Geophys. Res., 81, 4983-4990, 1976.

Bell, T.H., Topographically generated interval waves in the open ocean, J. Geophys. Res., 80, 320-327, 1975.

Brainard, R.E., Fisheries aspects of seamounts and Taylor columns. Thesis, Department of Oceanography, Naval Postgraduate School, Monterey, CA, 88 pp., 1986.

Cheney, R.E., P.L. Richardson and K. Nagasaka, Tracking a Kuroshio ring with a free drifting buoy, Deep-Sea Res., 27, 641-654, 1980.

Cornillon, P., The effect of the New England Seamounts on Gulf Stream meandering as observed from satellite IR imagery, J. Phys. Oceanogr., 16, 1986.

Eriksen, C.C., Observations of internal wave reflection off sloping bottoms, J. Geophys. Res., 87, 525-538, 1982.

Eriksen, C.C., Implications of ocean bottom reflection for internal wave spectra and mixing, J. Phys. Oceanogr., 15, 1145-1156, 1985.

Farmer, D.M. and J.D. Smith, Tidal interaction of stratified flow with a sill in Knight Inlet, Deep-Sea Res., 27A, 239-254, 1980.

Genin, A. and G.W. Boehlert, Dynamics of temperature and chlorophyll structures above a seamount: an oceanic experiment, J. Mar. Res., 43, 907-924, 1985.

Gould, W.J., R. Hendry and H.E. Huppert, An abyssal topographic experiment, Deep-Sea Res., 28, 409-440, 1981.

Hamann, I. and B.A. Taft, The Kuroshio Extension near the Emperor seamounts, J. Geophys. Res., in press, 1987.

Heikes, K.E. and T. Maxworthy, Observations of inertial waves in a homogeneous rotating fluid, J. Fluid Mech., 125, 319-345, 1982.

Hide, R., Origin of Jupiter's Great Red Spot, Nature, 190, 895-896, 1961.

Horn, W., Die zeitliche Veränderlichkeit der Temperatur der ozeanischen Deckschicht in Gebiet der Grossen Meteorbank, Meteor Forschungsergebneisse A, 9, 47-57, 1971.

Hurlburt, H.E. and J.D. Thompson, Preliminary results from a numerical study of the New England seamount chain influence upon the Gulf Stream, in Predictability of Fluid Motions, edited by G. Holloway and B.J. West, pp. 489-503, American Institute of Physics, New York, 1984.

Huppert, H.E. and K. Bryan, Topographically generated eddies, Deep-Sea Res., 23, 655-679, 1976.

Ingersoll, A.P., Inertial Taylor columns and Jupiter's Great Red Spot, J. Atm. Sci., 26, 744-752, 1969.

Japan Maritime Safety Agency, Bathymetric Charts of the Adjacent Seas of Nippon, numbers 6303, 6304, Tokyo, 1968.

Johnson, E.R., Quasigeostrophic flow over isolated elongated topography, Deep-Sea Res., 29, 1085-1097, 1982.

Johnson, G.L., P.R. Vogt, and E.D. Schneider, Morphology of the northeastern Atlantic and Labrador Sea, Deut. Hydrograph. Z., 24, 49-73, 1971.

Kaneko, A., H. Honji, K. Kawatate, S. Mizuno, A. Masuda and T. Miita, A note on internal wavetrains and the associated undulation of the sea surface observed upstream of seamounts, J. Oceanogr. Soc., Japan, 42, 75-82,, 1986.

Kozlov, V.F., On a stationary problem of topographic cyclogenesis in a homogeneous rotating fluid, Izvestiya, Atmospheric and Oceanic Physics, 17, 878-882, 1981.

Kunze, E. and T.B. Sanford, Near inertial wave interactions with mean flow and bottom topography near Caryn seamount, J. Phys. Oceanogr., 16, 109-120, 1986.

Lowrie, A. and B.C. Heezen, Knoll and sediment drift near Hudson Canyon, Science, 157, 1552-1553, 1967.

Maxworthy, T., A note on internal solitary waves produced by tidal flow over a three-dimensional ridge, J. Geophys. Res., 84, 338-346, 1979.

McCartney, M., Inertial Taylor columns on a beta-plane, J. Fluid Mech., 68, 71-95, 1975.

Meincke, J., Der Einfluss der Grossen Meteorbank auf Schichtung und Zirkulation der ozeanischen Deckschicht, Meteor Forschungsergebnisse A, 67-94, 1971.

Menard, H.W. and H.S. Ladd, Oceanic islands, seamounts, guyots and atolls, in The Sea, 3, edited by M.N. Hill, pp. 365-385, Interscience, 1963.

Owens, W.B. and N.G. Hogg, Oceanic observations of stratified Taylor columns near a bump, Deep-Sea Res., 27, 1029-1045, 1980.

Pillsbury, R.D., J.S. Bottero, E.A. Seifert and D.C. Rott, A compilation of observations from moored current meters, 25; Currents, temperature and pressure collected near the Emperor Seamounts, Oregon State University Data Report 118, Ref. 85-13, 116 pp., 1985.

Pingree, R.D. and L. Maddock, Rotary currents and residual circulation around banks and islands, Deep-Sea Res., 32, 929-947, 1985.

Pratt, R.M., Photography of seamounts, in Deep Sea Photography, edited by J.B. Hersey, The Johns Hopkins Oceanographic Studies 3, pp. 145-158, Johns Hopkins Press, 1967.

Rattray, M., The effect of bathymetry on the deep flow in Drake Passage, Deep-Sea Res., 32, 127-147, 1985.

Rhines, P.B., Slow oscillations in an ocean of varying depth, part 2: islands and seamounts, J. Fluid Mech., 37, 191-205, 1969.

Rhines, P.B. and F.P. Bretherton, Topographic Rossby waves in a rough bottomed ocean, J. Fluid Mech., 61, 583-607, 1974.

Richardson, P.L., Anticyclonic eddies generated near the Corner Rise seamounts, J. Mar. Res., 38, 673-686, 1980.

Richardson, P.L., Gulf Stream trajectories measured with free drifting buoys, J. Phys. Oceanogr., 11, 999-1010, 1981.

Roden, G.I., Mesoscale sound speed fronts in the central and western North Pacific and in the Emperor seamounts region, J. Phys. Oceanogr., 14, 1659-1669, 1984a.

Roden, G.I., Mesoscale oceanic fronts of the North Pacific, Annales Geophysicae, 2, 399-410, 1984b.

Roden, G.I., B.A. Taft and C.C. Ebbesmeyer, Oceanographic aspects of the Emperor seamounts region, J. Geophys. Res., 87, 9537-9552, 1982.

Roden, G.I. and B.A. Taft, Effect of the Emperor seamounts on the mesoscale thermohaline structure during the summer of 1982, J. Geophys. Res., 90, 839-855, 1985.

Sverdrup, H.U., The influence of bottom topography on ocean currents, Applied Mechanics, Theodore von Karman Anniversary Volume, 66-75, 1941.

Taylor, G.I., Motion of solids in fluids when the flow is not irrotational, Proc. Roy. Soc. London A, 93, 99-113, 1917.

University of Hokkaido, Data record of oceanographic observations and exploratory fishing, No. 26 (1983), No. 27 (1984), No. 28 (1985), Hakodate, Japan.

Vastano, A.C. and B.A. Warren, Perturbations to the Gulf Stream by Atlantis II seamount, Deep-Sea Res., 23, 681-694, 1976.

Vastano, A.C., D.E. Hagan and G.J. McNally, Lagrangian observations of surface circulation at the Emperor seamount chain, J. Geophys. Res., 90, 3325-3331, 1985.

Veronis, G., Dynamic of large-scale ocean circulation, in Evolution of Physical Oceanography, edited by B.A. Warren and C. Wunsch, pp. 140-183, 1981.

Verron, J. and C. LeProvost, A numerical study of quasi-geostrophic flow over isolated topography, J. Fluid Mech., 154, 231-252, 1985.

Verron, J., Topographic eddies in temporally varying oceanic flows, Geophys. Astrophys. Fluid Dynamics, 35, 257-276, 1986.

Wunsch, C. and S. Webb, The climatology of deep ocean internal waves, J. Phys. Oceanogr., 9, 225-243, 1979.

Zyryanov, V.N., A contribution to the theory of Taylor columns in a stratified ocean, Izvestiya, Atmospheric and Ocean Physics, 17, 793-800, 1981.

G.I. Roden, School of Oceanography, WB-10, University of Washington, Seattle, WA 98195.

SEAMOUNT BIOTA AND BIOGEOGRAPHY

Raymond R. Wilson, Jr.[1] and Ronald S. Kaufmann

Marine Biology Research Division, A-002, Scripps Institution of Oceanography,
University of California, San Diego, La Jolla, CA 92093

Abstract. A review of the literature and unpublished data has identified 1045 species of plants, invertebrates and fishes collected from more than 100 seamounts worldwide at depths of 29 to 3800 m. Cnidarians and decapod crustaceans among invertebrates, and scorpaenids and morids among fishes, were the most widely distributed groups on seamounts, according to published reports. Biota of seamounts is dominated by organisms inhabiting the nearest continental areas, especially at high latitudes. On shallow seamounts (<1000 m) provincial species with distributions limited to the region in which the seamount is located and widespread/cosmopolitan species are nearly equally represented. On deeper seamounts, the widespread/cosmopolitan categories dominate. Seamounts appear to provide "stepping stones" for trans-oceanic dispersal in both the Atlantic and Pacific oceans. Dispersal onto seamounts probably occurs both actively (swimming) and passively (drift of pelagic and planktonic stages). Seamount endemism is estimated maximally at 15.4% among invertebrates and 11.6% among fishes. Population divergence and possibly speciation have occurred on seamounts of varying depths and distances from continental margins.

Introduction

The presence of flora and fauna on seamounts has long intrigued marine naturalists, especially with regard to the origin of seamount biota. Hubbs [1959] formulated a few of the more intriguing questions about the nature of seamount biota: "What species inhabit the individual banks, and in what regularity and abundance? Do banks and seamounts...provide stepping stones for the transgression of narrow to broad oceanic areas, even supposedly the vast eastern Pacific barrier that separates Indo-Pacific and the American faunas...? How did these species become dispersed to and established on these structures? To what degree has isolation on the banks and seamounts led to speciation?"

Although these questions persist the emergence of plate tectonics as a unifying theory of geology adds another: What effect does the geologic history of a seamount have on the composition of its biota? This paper addresses these questions on the nature of seamount biota and offers some answers to them. The basis for doing so is a thorough review of published reports on organisms collected from seamounts worldwide and the use of available unpublished data from various sources. The first section reviews the distribution of seamounts for which biological data exists and the collected biota in terms of diversity and regularity on seamounts. The second section reviews the biogeographic affinities of seamount species as reported in papers discussing them. The possible origins of these biogeographic patterns are discussed in terms of dispersal, vicariance and speciation. Since a knowledge of fishes is more within our joint expertise than that of any other group, fish zoogeography is treated in greatest detail.

"Seamounts", as used here, include guyots, large plateaus, submarine mountains (both isolated and in ridges) and some banks. All seamounts from which biological samples were collected, including unnamed ones, were given 3-character abbreviations and assigned to an oceanic region (e.g. the northeastern Pacific or the southwestern Atlantic) for referencing purposes. Positions, depths and distances to the nearest continental shelf at the 200 m or 100 fm isobath, and the number of species collected were recorded as possible for each.

Published reports of species collected on seamounts were used to compile a data base of nominal, extant species which were then referred to appropriate higher taxa. Except for those species caught in anchored traps, midwater animals caught over seamounts, such as arrow

---
[1]Present Address: Marine Science Department, University of South Florida, 140 Seventh Avenue South, St. Petersburg, FL 33701

Copyright 1987 by the American Geophysical Union.

356 SEAMOUNT BIOTA AND BIOGEOGRAPHY

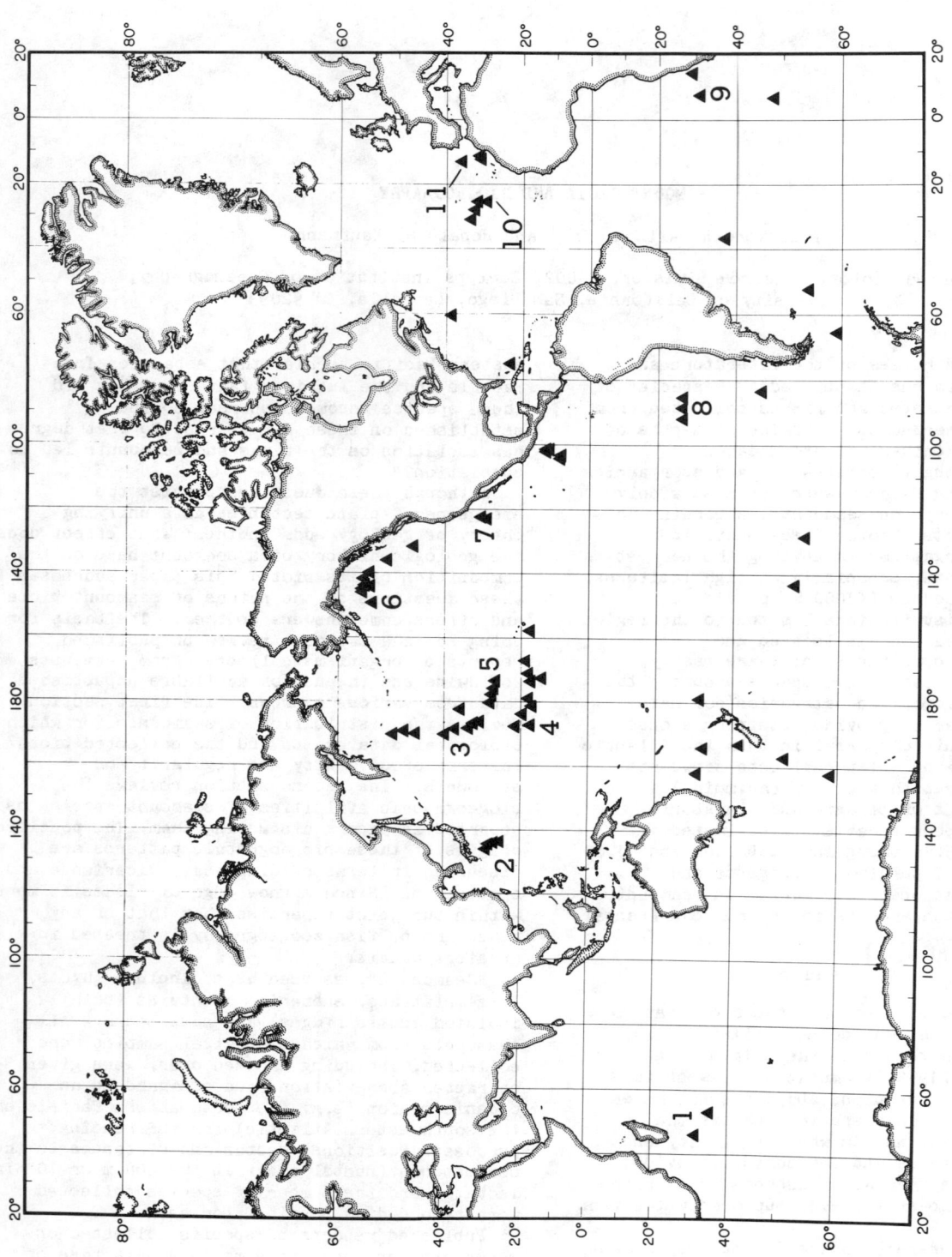

Fig. 1. Distribution of seamounts yielding biological data. Numbers refer to seamounts discussed in the text: (1) Walters Shoal and UN2, (2) Kyushu-Palau Ridge, (3) Emperor Seamount Chain, (4) Mid-Pacific Mountains, (5) Northern Hawaiian Ridge, (6) Seamounts in the Gulf of Alaska, (7) Seamounts in the Baja California Seamount Province, (8) Shoal Guyot and area of the Nazca and Sala-y-Gomez ridges, (9) Vema, (10) Great Meteor and seamounts of the Atlantis-Great Meteor Seamount Chain, (11) Josephine. Not all sampled seamounts are plotted in the Emperor Chain and Hawaiian Ridge to preserve clarity.

worms, lanternfishes, and hatchetfishes, were not included. Although we have concentrated on benthic species, some species typically caught over seamounts are included. This data base is available from the first author on request. No special effort was made to determine the current status of specific invertebrate or plant names included in the data base. The current taxonomic status of fish names were determined as possible, but not every name could be verified.

Any species list derived from published literature is effectively limited to taxa which are of interest to certain specialists. Since the lack of published information on certain groups does not establish their absence on seamounts, we do not wish to imply that the true representation of taxa on seamounts is necessarily reflected by their representation in the data base. The greatest utility of this data base will be to give an overview of taxa presently known from seamounts and serve as a source of information for future studies of seamount biota.

Review of Sampled Seamounts and Biota

Seamounts

Biological samples have been taken from at least 100 seamounts in all oceans except the Arctic (Fig. 1, Table 1). At least half of these lie between 200 and 1000 m depth (51%) and nearly half are within 1000 km of a continental shelf (47%) (Table 1). Most (ca. 63%) seamounts yielding biological data are in the North Pacific Ocean, divided mostly among 5 major seamount groups in three regions: the Kyushu-Palau Ridge in the western Pacific, the Emperor Seamount Chain, the Hawaiian Ridge and the Mid-Pacific, Mountains in the central Pacific and the Gulf of Alaska Seamounts in the sub-Arctic eastern Pacific. Those in the central region, located at more than 2000 km from a continental shelf, are the most remote. Atlantic seamounts collectively represent about 17% of the total sample. More than half of these are in the northeastern Atlantic at 268 to 1580 km from the North African and Iberian shelves. The remaining 20% of sampled seamounts are scattered about the South Pacific (18%) and Indian oceans (2%).

Many of the seamounts appear to have been haphazardly sampled or else incompletely reported upon (e.g. 1 species known), whereas others, particularly Vema and Great Meteor, have been sampled repeatedly and have been the focus of much research [e.g. Hesthagen, 1970; Thiel, 1970; Berrisford, 1969]. Sampling and reporting of seamount biota in the North Pacific ranges from haphazard to extensive. This uneven sampling and reporting has a tremendous influence on the data base of known species, a fact which should be remembered throughout the following discussions. For example, most publications concerned with seamount-dwelling species examined only a single taxonomic group.

Sampling gear has included various kinds of trawls, rock dredges, epibenthic sleds, baited traps and baited hooks [Hesthagen, 1970; Thiel, 1970; Solomon-Raju and Rosenblatt, 1971; Rehder and Ladd, 1973; Wilson et al., 1985]. In addition, submersibles [Schwartz and Lingbloom, 1973; Levin et al., 1986; Littler et al., 1986], SCUBA [Heydorn, 1969; Scagel, 1970; Birkeland, 1971] and camera systems have been used. Camera systems include still-frame cameras [Thiel, 1970; Raymore, 1982] and free-vehicle video cameras [Wilson et al., 1985]. The main limitation of camera systems is that specific identification of organisms is not always possible without concomitant collections.

Plants and Invertebrates

Over 596 species of invertebrates in 16 phyla have been reported from at least 59 seamounts ranging from 27 to 3800 m depth. Of these, 92 (15.4%) were new species. In addition, 55 species of plants (3 newly described species) representing three divisions of algae were present on four seamounts from 27 to 268 m depth. Some groups appear to be widely distributed on seamounts (e.g. arthropods, cnidarians, molluscs; Table 2), whereas others are known from very few seamounts, e.g. chlorophytes, phaeophytes, rhodophytes, ctenophores, nematodes, sipunculids, echiurids, entoprocts, brachiopods (Table 2).

The limited occurrence of algae appears to be a result of inadequate light levels on most seamount crests since only nine of the more than 100 seamounts reported in this paper have crest depths shallower than 100 m and at least sixty are deeper than 300 m. The deepest recorded algae was found at 268 m [Littler, et al., 1985]. Most of the algae reported from seamounts typically occur intertidally [Scagel, 1970; Birkeland, 1971; Herlinveaux, 1971] and apparently can inhabit shallow seamounts if water clarity is high [Scagel, 1970; Herlinveaux, 1971; Littler et al., 1985]. Non-intertidal algae found on seamounts tend to be either deep-water species or shallow-water forms typically found in shaded, low-light environments [Littler et al., 1986].

Similar distributional unevenness observed among the invertebrate fauna may be attributed to variation in the sampling and reporting of collected specimens. Of the 596 invertebrate species described from 59[+] seamounts, just five seamounts (Cobb, Cross, Great Meteor, the Hess Plateau, and Vema) accounted for 430 (72%). In addition, there were 37 seamounts for which fewer than ten species were reported. Some groups appear underrepresented on seamounts relative to their perceived abundance elsewhere. Although ophiuroids are widespread and plentiful

TABLE 1. Summary of seamounts from which biological specimens were collected

Oceanic Region	Seamount	Abbrev.	Position	Depth (m)	Km to nearest shelf*	Species Reported	Reference**
Indian Ocean (IND)	Unnamed #2	UN2	34°54'S, 53°14'E	164	1212	8	14
	Walters Shoal	WAL	33°13'S, 43°51'E	42	768	5	33, 51
North-Central Pacific (NCP)	Academician	ACD	28°50'N, 178°53'E	-***	>2000	18	8
	Agassiz	AGZ	17°51'N, 178°25'E	1544	>2000	12	59, 61, 72, 74
	Allison	ALL	18°35'N, 179°37'W	1500	>2000	10	59, 61, 74
	Colahan	COL	31°02'N, 175°54'E	-	>2000	40	8, 30, 57
	Cross	CRS	18°40'N, 158°17'W	2745	>2000	47	23
	Darwin	DAR	21°53'N, 171°17'E	1284	>2000	7	59, 61, 68, 72, 74
	Emperor	EMR	Unspecified seamounts	-	-	5	2, 8, 24, 31, 75
	Equator	EQU	29°42'N, 179°22'E	-	>2000	15	8
	Hamilton	HAM	19°55'N, 177°13'E	1413	>2000	12	72, 74
	Hancock	HCK	28°47'N, 179°04'E	265	>2000	60	8, 30, 70
	Hayot	HAY	18°02'N, 173°35'E	1360	>2000	1	9
	Hess	HSS	17°53'N, 174°25'W	1674	>2000	15	59, 61, 72, 74
	Hess Plateau	HSP	36°10'N, 178°00'E	3800	>2000	128	49, 73
	Horizon Guyot	HZN	19°20'N, 169°00'W	1422	>2000	29	59, 61, 72, 74
	Jingu	JNG	38°34'N, 171°02'E	786	1700	15	8
	Kanmu	KMU	32°00'N, 172°50'E	355	>2000	1	50
	Hawaiian Ridge	HWR	Various unspecified	<300	>2000	33	30, 70
	Karandash	KAR	30°22'N, 177°33'E	-	>2000	13	8
	Kinmei	KMI	35°20'N, 171°41'E	350	>2000	44	8, 31, 50
	Koko	KOK	34°50'N, 172°20'E	427	1850	25	30
	Ladd	LAD	28°30'N, 176°43'W	75	>2000	31	30, 70
	Lira	LRA	36°48'N, 171°21'E	-	1630	8	8
	Milwaukee	MIL	31°50'N, 172°45'E	288	>2000	63	8, 30
	Multipeak	MLP	42°16'N, 170°27'E	-	1466	7	8
	Nero Bank	NRO	28°02'N, 178°18'W	72	>2000	28	30, 61, 70, 72
	Nintoku	NKU	40°38'N, 170°15'E	934	1520	11	8
	Papanin	PAP	46°15'N, 169°35'E	-	1032	6	8
	Pedestal	PED	30°16'N, 178°41'E	-	>2000	26	8
	Sio	SIO	18°18'N, 171°06'E	1692	>2000	10	59
	Suiko	SKO	44°34'N, 170°43'E	1079	1303	8	8
	Turnif	TNF	28°55'N, 178°36'W	-	>2000	13	8
	Vityaz	VIT	13°37'N, 173°27'W	1220	>2000	2	9
	Zapadnaya	ZAP	28°52'N, 179°31'E	-	>2000	21	8
Northeastern Atlantic (NEA)	Atlantis	ATL	34°05'N, 30°00'W	275	1580	7	65
	Dacia	DAC	31°01'N, 13°40'W	85	268	1	46
	Irving	IRV	32°00'N, 28°00'W	210	1340	17	65
	Gettysburg	GET	36°30'N, 11°32'W	200	218	1	46
	Great Meteor	GMR	30°07'N, 28°27'W	210	1340	108	3, 4, 5, 15, 16, 17, 21, 22, 26, 42, 43, 44, 62, 65, 71
	Jer	JER	Unspecified	235	?	28	65
	Josephine	JSE	36°40'N, 14°17'W	148	425	45	3, 5, 12, 22, 26, 44, 62
	Plato	PTO	33°08'N, 29°30'W	500	1520	28	65
	Small Meteor	SMR	29°30'N, 29°00'W	227	1360	16	71
	Unnamed #1	UN1	Unspecified	280	?	20	65
Northeastern Pacific (NEP)	Bonanza	BON	31°11'N, 122°15'W	2776	296	1	37, 38
	Bowie	BOE	53°20'N, 135°40'W	27	170	20	25, 63
	Baja A	BCA	12°45'N, 102°35'W	1775	514	1	37
	Baja B	BCB	13°20'N, 102°30'W	1790	472	2	37
	Cobb	COB	46°48'N, 130°50'W	59	398	52	7, 64
	Dickens	DIC	54°31'N, 136°56'W	410	185	3	29
	DTD	DTD	10°04'N, 104°40'W	1529	870	15	38
	Durgin	DUR	55°50'N, 141°51'W	617	320	11	29
	Giacomini	GIA	56°27'N, 146°42'W	661	268	6	29, 60
	Green	GRN	30°49'N, 109°16'W	1547	307	4	38
	Hoke	HOK	32°04'N, 126°56'W	985	615	3	38
	Jasper	JSP	30°30'N, 123°00'W	576	381	1	19, 20
	MIB	MIB	09°55'N, 104°28'W	1513	866	13	38
	MOK	MOK	09°57'N, 104°35'W	1700	867	12	38
	NW Bonanza	NWB	31°11'N, 122°14'W	2739	290	3	38
	Patton	PAT	54°34'N, 150°29'W	180	238	23	29, 60, 69
	Pratt	PRT	56°14'N, 142°32'W	693	305	3	29
	Quinn	QNN	56°18'N, 145°13'W	671	331	17	29, 60
	Surveyor	SVR	56°03'N, 144°19'W	540	389	20	29
	Volcano D	VOD	12°57'N, 103°12'W	2100	516	13	38
	Volcano 5	VO5	12°56'N, 103°29'W	975	547	12	38
	Volcano 6	VO6	12°45'N, 102°35'W	1547	498	12	38
	Volcano 7	VO7	13°20'N, 102°30'W	788	443	12	38
	Welker	WLK	55°07'N, 140°21'W	693	324	12	29
Northwestern Atlantic (NWA)	San Pablo	SPO	39°00'N, 60°00'W	1313	550	1	10
	San Salvador	SAN	24°14'N, 74°29'W	81	110	18	39, 40

TABLE 1. (continued)

Oceanic Region	Seamount	Abbrev.	Position	Depth (m)	Km to nearest shelf*	Species Reported	Reference**
Northwestern Pacific (NWP)	Seamounts in Kyushu-Palau Ridge	KPR	29°52'N, 133°20'E 28°05'N, 134°39'E 27°54'N, 134°42'E 26°45'N, 135°23'E 26°08'N, 135°47'E 25°09'N, 135°41'E	470 530 685 320 350 530	220 to 472	142	52
Southeastern Atlantic (SEA)	Meteor	MET	48°10'S, 08°20'E	560	1575	1	10
	Tripp	TRP	29°36'S, 14°15'E	150	33	2	32, 33
	Vema	VEM	31°38'S, 08°20'E	63	670	197	6, 27, 32, 33, 36, 41, 47, 48, 58, 66, 67
Southeastern Pacific (SEP)	Antarctic Seamounts	ANT	54°49'S, 129°48'W 53°56'S, 140°19'W	549 460	>1600 >1800	2	10 10
	Chilean Seamount	CHI	46°04'S, 83°55'W	298	576	1	11
	in Heezen Fracture Zone	HEE	54°50'S, 129°50'W	567	>1600	2	10, 11
	Nazca Ridge	NAZ	25°45'S, 85°22'W	320	1475	18	13, 34, 35, 54, 55, 56, 76
	Drake Passage	DRK	59°49'S, 68°52'W	512	352	3	10, 11
	Sala-y-Gomez Ridge	SAL	25°18'S, 93°34'W	260	2350	4	54, 56
	Shoal Guyot	SHO	25°44'S, 85°25'W	250	1480	17	1, 28, 77, 78
Southwestern Atlantic (SWA)	Rio Grande Plateau	RIO	30°00'S, 38°00'W	1000	1065	47	53
	Scotia	SCO	54°09'S, 52°08'W	419	380	1	11
Southwestern Pacific (SWP)	Gifford	GIF	26°30'S, 159°58'E	-	597	1	18
	Hjort	HRT	59°19'S, 158°29'E	800	1304	10	4
	Hunter	HNT	30°47'S, 156°15'E	280	272	1	18
	Seamount in Kermadec Ridge	KER	32°30'S, 179°12'W	508	600	1	10
	Seamounts in Macquarie Ridge	MAQ	51°00'S, 162°01'E 51°07'S, 162°01'E	351 1665	416 423	8	10, 45
	Seamount off New Zealand	WNZ	40°15'S, 168°16'E	913	255	1	10
	Seamount in Norfolk Ridge	NFR	32°35'S, 167°23'E	82	452	3	18
	Seamounts in South Pacific	SPS	various, unspecified			2	10

* Estimated to the 100 fm or 200 m isobath

** 1) Allison et al. [1967], 2) Barsukov and Fedorov [1975], 3) Bartsch [1973a], 4) Bartsch [1973b], 5) Bartsch [1973c], 6) Berrisford [1969], 7) Birkeland [1971], 8) Borets [1986], 9) Britaev [1981], 10) Cairns [1982a], 11) Cairns [1982b], 12) Diehl [1970], 13) Dolganov [1984], 14) Duhamel [1984], 15) Ehrich [1977], 16) Emschermann [1971], 17) Fricke [1985], 18) Fujii [1986], 19) Genin et al. [1986], 20) Genin, unpublished data, 21) Grasshoff [1972a], 22) Grasshoff [1972b], 23) Grigg et al., this volume, 24) Habe [1979], 25) Herlinveaux [1971], 26) Hesthagen [1970], 27) Heydorn [1969], 28) Hubbs [1959], 29) Hughes [1981], 30) Humphreys et al. [1984], 31) Kanayama [1981], 32) Kensley [1980], 33) Kensley [1981], 34) Kotlyar [1982a], 35) Kotlyar [1982b], 36) Levi [1969], 37) Levin et al. [1986], 38) Levin, unpublished data, 39) Littler et al. [1985], 40) Littler et al. [1986], 41) Lutjeharms and Heydorn [1981], 42) Maul [1972a], 43) Maul [1972b], 44) Maul [1976], 45) McKnight [1984], 46) Mikhaylin [1977], 47) Millar [1968], 48) Millard [1966], 49) Murray [1895], 50) Nakabo et al. [1983], 51) Newman [1980], 52) Okamura et al. [1982], 53) Pakhorukov [1976], 54) Parin [1982], 55) Parin [1983], 56) Parin [1984], 57) Parin and Mikhaylin [1982], 58) Penrith [1967], 59) Rao and Newman [1972], 60) Raymore [1982], 61) Rehder and Ladd [1973], 62) Rice and Williamson [1977], 63) Scagel [1970], 64) Schwartz and Lingbloom [1973], 65) Shcherbachev et al. [1985], 66) Sieg [1981], 67) Simpson and Heydorn [1965], 68) Solomon-Raju and Rosenblatt [1971], 69) Somerton [1981], 70) Uchida and Tagami [1984], 71) Weigmann [1974], 72) Wilson, unpublished data, 73) Wilson and Waples [1983], 74) Wilson et al. [1985], 75) Yabe [1983], 76) Zevina [1983], 77) Zullo and Newman [1964], 78) Zullo et al. [1964].

*** Depth not reported

in soft bottom deep-sea environments [Smith, 1983], they have been reported from only twelve of the 59+ seamounts on which invertebrates were collected. Thirteen species from five seamounts were identified; "ophiuroids present" was noted in the remaining cases. Crinoids have been similarly ignored although a widely distributed group on seamounts (A. Genin, Scripps Institution of Oceanography, personal communication). Only eleven species have been described in the references examined, with the group's presence recorded for only 17 seamounts. This apparent lack of literature reporting ophiuroids and crinoids on seamounts is probably not indicative of their true abundance in these biotopes. Seamounts that have been thoroughly

TABLE 2. Summary of Seamount Algae and Invertebrate Fauna.
Number of newly-described species in parentheses.

Taxa	No. of Species Represented	Seamounts Represented	Regions	Depths (m)
K. Plantae				
D. Chlorophyta	12 (0)	COB, SAN, VEM	NEP, NWA, SEA	59 – 268
D. Phaeophyta	11 (1)	BOE, COB, SAN, VEM	NEP, NWA, SEA	27 – 268
D. Rhodophyta	32 (2)	BOE, COB, SAN, VEM	NEP, NWA, SEA	27 – 268
K. Animalia				
P. Protista				
C. Sarcodina	99 (0)	BCA, BCB, BON, HSP, SAN, SHO, VEM, V07	NCP, NEP, NWA, SEA, SEP	63 – 3800
O. Foraminifera	99 (0)	BCA, BCB, BON, HSP, SAN, SHO, VEM, V07	NCP, NEP, NWA, SEA, SEP	63 – 3800
O. Xenophyophorea	93 (0)	HSP, SAN, SHO, VEM	NCP, NWA, SEA, SEP	63 – 3800
P. Porifera	6 (0)	BCA, BCB, BON, V07	NEP	788 – 3140
	68 (14)	AGZ, CRS, DAR, DTD, GMR, HAM, HSP, HSS, HZN, JSE, MIB, MOK, PAT, QNN, SAN, SAS, VEM, V95, V06, V07	NCP, NEA, NEP, NWA, SEA	40 – 3800
P. Cnidaria	75 (5)	AGZ, ANT, CHI, COB, CRS, DAR, DRK, DTD, GIA, GMR, GRN, HAM, HEE, HOK, HRT, HSP, HSS, HZN, JSE, JSP, KER, MAQ, MET, MIB, MOK, NRO, PAT, SAS, SCO, SPO, SPS, VEM, VOD, V06, V07, WNZ	NCP, NEA, NEP, NWA, SEA, SEP, SWA, SWP	40 – 3800
C. Hydrozoa	26 (1)	CHI, COB, DRK, GMR, HEE, JSE, PAT, SCO, VEM	NEA, NEP, SEA, SEP, SWA	59 – 567
C. Scyphozoa	?	AGZ, GMR, HAM, HSS, HZN, JSE, NRO	NCP, NEA	40 – 1674
C. Anthozoa	49 (4)	AGZ, ANT, COB, CRS, DAR, DTD, GIA, GMR, GRN, HAM, HEE, HOK, HRT, HSP, HSS, HZN, JSP, KER, MAQ, MET, MIB, MOK, PAT, SAS, SPO, SPS, VEM, VOD, V05, V06, V07, WNZ	NCP, NEA, NEP, NWA, SEA, SEP, SWP	59 – 3800
O. Actiniaria	3 (0)	COB	NEP	59
O. Scleractinia	18 (0)	AGZ, ANT, CRS, DAR, HEE, HRT, HSS, HZN, KER, MAQ, MET	NCP, NWA, SEA, SEP, SWP	63 – 1674
	?	SPO, SPS, VEM, WNZ		
O. Ceriantharia	8 (3)	CRS, DTD, HSP, JSP, MIB, SAS, VOD, V05, V06, V07	NEP	661
O. Antipatharia	1 (0)	AGZ, DAR, DTD, GRN, HAM, HSS, HZN, MIB, MOK, V05	NCP, NEP	330 – 3800
O. Alcyonacea	1 (1)	HSP, PAT	NCP	1125 – 2025
O. Pennatulacea	17 (0)	CRS, DTD, GMR, HOK, JSE, MIB, MOK, PAT, SAS, VOD, V05, V06, V07	NCP, NEA, NEP	180 – 3800
O. Gorgonacea			NCP, NEA, NEP	148 – 3050
O. Zoantharia	1 (0)	CRS	NCP	350-380
P. Ctenophora	1 (0)	COB	NEP	59
P. Nematoda	?	GMR, JSE	NEA	
P. Sipuncula	4 (0)	COB, JSE, VEM	NEA, NEP, SEA	148 – 210
P. Mollusca	72 (15)	COB, ALL, BOE, COB, DAR, DIC, DTD, DUR, EMR, GIA, GMR, HAM, HSP, HSS, HZN, JSE, MIB, MOK, NRO, PAT, QNN, SAS, SHO, SVR, VEM, VOD, V05, V06, V07, WLK	NCP, NEA, NEP, SEA, SEP	59 – 148
				27 – 3800
C. Polyplacophora	1 (0)	BOE, PAT	NEP	27 – 180
C. Aplacophora	?	GMR, JSE	NEA	148 – 210
C. Gastropoda	37 (9)	AGZ, ALL, COB, EMR, GIA, GMR, HSP, HSS, HZN, JSE, NRO, PAT, SHO, VEM	NCP, NEA, NEP, SEA, SEP	40 – 3800
C. Bivalvia	17 (3)	BOE, COB, DAR, GMR, HAM, HSP, HSS, HZN, JSE, NRO, PAT, SHO	NCP, NEA, NEP, SEA, SEP	27 – 3800
C. Scaphopoda	3 (3)	AGZ, DTD, HSP, MIB, MOK, SAS, VOD, V05, V06, V07	NCP, NEP	788 – 3800
C. Cephalopoda	14 (0)	AGZ, DAR, DIC, DUR, GMR, HAM, HSS, HZN, NRO, PAT, QNN, SVR, VEM, WLK	NCP, NEA, NEP, SEA	40 – 1674
P. Echiura	?	GMR	NEA	210
P. Annelida	29 (3)	COB, DTD, GMR, GRN, HAM, HAY, HSP, HZN, JSE, MIB, MOK, NRO, PAT, QNN, SAS, SHO, VEM, VIT, VOD, V05, V06, V07	NCP, NEA, NEP, SEA, SEP	40 – 3800
C. Polychaeta	29 (3)	COB, DTD, GMR, GRN, HAM, HAY, HSP, HZN, JSE, MIB, MOK, NRO, PAT, QNN, SAS, SHO, VEM, VIT, VOD, V05, V06, V07	NCP, NEA, NEP, SEA, SEP	40 – 3800

P. Arthropoda	163 (43)	AGZ, ALL, COB, CRS, DAR, DIC, DTD, DUR, GIA, GMR, HAM, HOK, HSP, HSS, HZN, JSE, MIB, MOK, NAZ, PAT, PRT, QNN, SAS, SHO, SIO, SMR, SVR, TRP, VEM, VOD, V05, V06, V07, WAL, WLK			
sP. Chelicerata	18 (10)	GMR, JSE		NEA	148 – 210
C. Arachnida	18 (10)	GMR, JSE		NEA	148 – 210
O. Acarina	18 (10)	GMR, JSE		NEA	148 – 210
F. Halacaridae	18 (10)	GMR, JSE		NEA	148 – 210
C. Pycnogonida	?	GMR, JSE		NEA	148 – 210
sP. Crustacea	145 (33)	AGZ, ALL, COB, CRS, DAR, DIC, DTD, DUR, GIA, GMR, HAM, HOK, HSP, HSS, HZN, JSE, MIB, MOK, NAZ, PAT, PRT, QNN, SAS, SHO, SIO, SMR, SVR, TRP, VEM, VOD, V05, V06, V07, WAL, WLK		IND, NCP, NEA, NEP, SEA, SEP	59 – 3800
C. Ostracoda	7 (7)	GMR, HSP, JSE		NCP, NEA	148 – 3800
C. Copepoda	?	GMR, JSE		NEA	148 – 210
C. Cirripedia	29 (14)	AGZ, ALL, COB, CRS, DAR, GMR, HSP, HZN, JSE, NAZ, SHO, SIO, WAL		IND, NCP, NEA, NEP, SEP	59 – 3800
C. Malacostraca	109 (12)	AGZ, COB, CRS, DAR, DIC, DTD, DUR, GIA, GMR, HAM, HOK, HSP, HSS, HZN, JSE, MIB, MOK, PAT, PRT, QNN, SAS, SHO, SMR, SVR, TRP, VEM, VOD, V05, V06, V07, WAL, WLK		IND, NCP, NEA, NEP, SEA, SEP	59 – 3800
SO. Eucarida	86 (3)	AGZ, COB, CRS, DAR, DIC, DTD, DUR, GIA, GMR, HAM, HOK, HZN, JSE, MIB, MOK, PAT, PRT, QNN, SAS, SHO, SMR, SVR, TRP, VEM, VOD, V05, V06, V07, WAL, WLK		IND, NCP, NEA, NEP, SEA, SEP	59 – 3100
O. Euphausiacea	18 (0)	GMR, SMR		NEA	210 – 227
O. Decapoda	68 (3)	AGZ, COB, CRS, DAR, DIC, DTD, DUR, GIA, GMR, HAM, HOK, HZN, JSE, MIB, MOK, PAT, PRT, QNN, SAS, SHO, SVR, TRP, VEM, VOD, V05, V06, V07, WAL, WLK		IND, NCP, NEA, NEP, SEA, SEP	59 – 3100
SO. Peracarida	23 (9)	AGZ, COB, GMR, HAM, HSP, HSS, JSE, PAT, QNN, SVR, VEM		NCP, NEA, NEP, SEA	63 – 3800
O. Mysidacea	3 (0)	GMR, HAM, HSP, JSE		NEA, NEP	148 – 693
O. Cumacea	1 (1)	GMR, HSP		NCP, NEA	148 – 3800
O. Tanaidacea	1 (1)	VEM		SEA	63
O. Isopoda	12 (7)	GMR, HSP, JSE, VEM		NCP, NEA, SEA	63 – 3800
O. Amphipoda	6 (0)	GMR, HAM, HSS, HZN, JSE, PAT, SHO, VEM		NCP, NEA	148 – 1674
P. Ectoprocta	4 (0)	COB, GMR, JSE		NEA, NEP, SEA, SEP	59 – 210
P. Entoprocta	1 (1)	GMR		NEA	210
P. Brachiopoda	1 (0)	HSP, PAT		NCP, NEP	180 – 3800
P. Chaetognatha	?	GMR, JSE		NCP, NEA, NEP, SEA, SEP	148 – 210
P. Echinodermata	63 (6)	AGZ, BON, COB, CRS, DAR, DTD, GIA, GMR, GRN, HAM, HOK, HSP, HSS, HZN, VEM, VOD, V05, V06, V07	MOK, MIB, NRO, NWB, PAT, QNN, SAS	NCP, NEA, NEP, SEA, SEP, SWP	40 – 3800
C. Crinoidea	11 (0)	AGZ, HZN, MAQ, MIB, NWB, CRS, DTD, GRN, HAM, HOK, V05, V06, MIB, MOK, PAT, QNN, SHO, VEM, V07	HSS, HZN, JSE, JSP,	NCP, NEA, NEP, SEA, SWP	63 – 3090
C. Asteroidea	19 (1)	COB, CRS, DTD, GMR, HAM, HOK, HSP, HSS, HZN, JSE, MAQ, VEM, SAS, VOD, V05, V06, V07		NCP, NEA, NEP, SMP	59 – 3800
C. Ophiuroidea	13 (1)	AGZ, COB, CRS, DAR, DTD, GMR, HAM, HSS, HZN, JSE, MAQ, MIB, VEM NRO, SAS, SHO, VOD, V05, V06		NCP, NEA, NEP, SEA, SWP	59 – 3800
C. Echinoidea	13 (3)	COB, CRS, DAR, DTD, GMR, HAM, HOK, MIB, MOK, MIB, MOK, VEM		NCP, NEA, NEP, SEP	40 – 2990
C. Holothuroidea	7 (1)	CRS, DTD, GIA, HSP, HZN, MIB, MOK, QNN, SAS, VEM, VOD, V05, V06, V07		NCP, NEP, SEA	63 – 3800
P. Chordata	361 (46)	GMR, HSP, JSE, VEM		NCP, NEA, SEA	63 – 3800
sP. Urochordata	16 (5)	GMR, HSP, JSE, VEM		NCP, NEA, SEA	63 – 3800
C. Ascidiacea	15 (5)	HSP, JSE, VEM		NCP, NEA, SEA	63 – 3800
C. Thaliacea	1 (0)	GMR		NEA	210
C. Larvacea	?	GMR, JSE		NEA	148 – 210
sP. Vertebrata	449 (52)	[See Table 3]		IND, NCP, NEA, NEP, NWP, SEA, SEP, SWA	27 – 3800

*K = Kingdom, D = Division, P = Phylum, sP = Subphylum, C = Class, SO = Superorder, O = Order, F = Family

TABLE 3. Summary of Seamount Ichthyofauna. Number of newly-described species is in parentheses.

Sub-Class and Family	Family Common Name	No. of Species Represented	Seamounts Represented	Regions	Depths (m)
Holocephali					
Chimaeridae	Chimaerids	5 (17)	HZN, KMI, KOK, MIL, PTO, RIO	NCP, NEA, SWA	288 – 1422
Elasmobranchii					
Hexanchidae	Cow sharks	2 (0)	GMR, HCK, IRV, JER, KMI, KPR, UN1	NCP, NEA, NWP	210 – ca. 400
Chlamydoselachidae	Frill shark	1 (0)	COL, MIL	NCP	288
Lamnidae	Lamnid sharks	2 (0)	HCK, KPR	NCP, NWP	265 – ca. 400
Odontaspididae	Sand tigers	1 (0)	PED	NCP	?
Scyliorhinidae	Cat sharks	4 (0)	JNG, KPR, MPL, PTO	NCP, NEA, NWP	ca. 400 – 786
Carcharhinidae		1 (0)	COB, HCK	NCP, NEP	59 – 265
Squalidae	Dog fish sharks	26 (57)	ACD, COL, HCK, HWR, JER, JNG, KAR, KMI, KOK, KPR, LAD, LRA, MIL, MLP, NAZ, NRO, PED, PTO, RIO, TUN, UN1, ZAP	NCP, NEA, NWP, SEP	72 – 1422
Rajidae	Skates	3 (0)	GMR, JSE	SWA	148 – 210
Dasyatidae	Sting rays	3 (0)	HCK, KPR	NCP, NWP	265 – ca. 400
Teleostei					
Albulidae	Bonefishes	1 (0)	KPR	NWP	ca. 400
Notacanthidae	Spiny eels	1 (0)	RIO	SWA	1000
Halosauridae	Halosaurs	6 (0)	AGZ, ATL, GMR, HAM, HSS, HZN, RIO, UN1	NCP, NEA, SWA	275 – 1544
Xenocongridae	False morays	1 (0)	GMR	NEA	210
Muraenidae	Moray eels	6 (0)	EMR, IRV, LAD, NRO	NCP, NEA	72 – 260
Nemichthyidae	Snipe eels	1 (0)	KPR	NWP	ca. 400
Synaphobranchidae	Cutthroat eels	8 (0)	DAR, HAM, HCK, HSP, HSS, HZN, KPR, RIO	NCP, NWP, SWA	265 – 3800
Nettastomidae	Duckbill eels	2 (0)	HAM, KPR	NCP, NWP	ca. 400 – 1413
Congridae	Conger eels	12 (1)	ACD, COL, EMR, GMR, HCK, IRV, JSE, KMI, KPR, LAD, MIL, PED, PTO	NCP, NEA, NWP	75 – 500
Serrivomeridae	Sawtooth eels	1 (0)	KPR	NWP	ca. 400
Alepocephalidae	Slick heads	21 (17)	JNG, NKU, PAP, PTO, RIO, UN1	NCP, NEA, SWA	280 – 1000
Aulopidae	Aulopus	2 (0)	ACD, EQU, GMR, JSE	NCP, NEA	148 – 210
Chlorophthalmidae	Greeneyes	17 (1)	ATL, CRS, GMR, HAM, HCK, HZN, JER, KMI, KPR, MIL, PTO, RIO	NCP, NEA, NWP, SWA	210 – 2745
Synodontidae	Lizardfishes	1 (0)	UN1	SWA	1000
Moridae	Codlings	27 (87)	ACD, COL, EQU, DAR, DUR, GIA, GMR, HAM, HCK, HZN, JER, JNG, JSE, KAR, KMI, KOK, KPR, LAD, LRA, MIL, MLP, NKU, NRO, PAP, PED, PTO, RIO, SKO, SVR, UN1, WLK, ZAP	NCP, NEA, NEP, NWP, SEP, SWA	72 – 1422
Gadidae	Cods	1 (0)	GMR, JSE	SWA	1000
Macrouridae	Grenadiers	39 (5)	ATL, COL, CRS, HCK, HSP, HSS, HZN, JER, JNG, KMI, KPR, MIL, NKU, PAP, PAT, PED, PTO, QNN, RIO, SKO, SVR, UN1, WLK, ZAP	NCP, NEA, NEP, NWP, SWA	148 – 3800
Bythitidae	Brotulas	3? (1)	GMR, KPR	NEA, NWP	210 – ca. 400
Carapidae	Pearlfishes	2 (0)	GMR, JSE	NCP, NEA	148 – 210
Ophidiidae	Cusk eels	3 (0)	AGZ, GMR, RIO	NCP, NEA, SWA	210 – 1544
Lophiidae	Goosefishes	2 (0)	COL, CRS, HCK, KAR, KMI, KOK, KPR, PED, PTO	NCP, NEA, NWP	265 – 2745
Chaunacidae	Sea toads	5 (27)	COL, GMR, JER, KMI, KPR, MIL, PTO	NCP, NEA, NWP	210 – 500
Ogcocephalidae	Batfishes	7 (32)	HZN, KPR, MIL	NCP, NWP	288 – 1422
Trachipteridae	Ribbonfishes	2 (0)	KPR, MIL	NCP, NWP	288 – ca. 400
Ateleopodidae	Slimeheads	4 (3?)	CRS, KPR	CRS, NWP	ca. 400 – 2745
Diretmidae	Spinyfins	5 (0)	COL, HCK, KMI, KOK, KPR, MIL, PED, TNF, ZAP	NCP, NWP	265 – 427
Berycidae	Alfonsins	2 (0)	KOK, RIO	NCP, SWA	427 – 1000
Holocentridae	Squirrelfishes	2 (0)	ACD, ATL, COL, CRS, EQU, HCK, JER, KMI, KOK, KPR, LRA, MIL, PED, PTO, UN1, ZAP	NCP, NEA, NWP	235 – 2745
Polymixiidae	Beardfishes	5 (2?)	KPR	NWP	ca. 400
Labridae	Wrasses	6 (1)	ACD, COL, CRS, EQU, GMR, HCK, IRV, JER, KMI, KOK, KPR, MIL, NAZ, NRO, PTO, TNF, UN1, ZAP	NCP, NEA, NWP, SEP	72 – 500
			EMR, JSE, KPR, LAD, NRO	NCP, NEA, NWP	72 – 427

Family	Common name	N	Codes	Region	Depth
Zeidae	Dories	7 (0)	ACD, ATL, COL, EQU, HCK, IRV, JER, KAR, KMI, KOK, KPR, MIL, PED, PTO, TNF, UN1, ZAP	NCP, NEA, NWP	210 – 500
Oreosomatidae	Oreos	1 (0)	JNG, KMI, EQU, JER, LRA, NKU, SKO	NCP	350 – 1079
Grammicolepididae	Grammicolepidids	1 (0)	ACD	NCP, NEA	235
Fistulariidae	Cornetfishes	1 (0)	LAD	NCP	75
Caproidae	Boarfishes	5 (0)	ACD, EQU, GMR, HCK, HWR, IRV, JER, JSE, KMI, KOK, KPR, MIL, PED	NCP, NEA, NWP	148 – 427
Macrorhamphosidae	Snipefishes	4 (0)	COL, GMR, HCK, JSE, KMI, KPR, MIL, PED, RIO	NCP, NEA, NWP, SWA	148 – 1000
Scorpaenidae	Scorpionfishes	34 (5)	BOE, COB, COL, CRS, DUR, EMR, GIA, GMR, HWR, IRV, JER, JNG, JSE, KMI, KOK, KPR, SVR, UN1, UN2, MIL, MLP, NKU, NRO, PAT, PTO, QNN, RIO, SKO, VEM, WLK, ZAP	IND, NCP, NEA, NEP, NWP, SEA, SWA	27 – 1079
Triglidae	Sea robins	9 (27)	COL, HCK, KAR, KPR, MIL	NCP, NWP, SEP	250 – ca. 400
Platycephalidae	Flatheads	1 (0)	COL, KMI, KPR	NCP, NWP	350 – ca. 400
Hoplichthyidae	Ghost Flatheads	2 (0)	HCK, KPR	NCP, NWP	265 – ca. 400
Anoplopomatidae	Sablefishes	2 (0)	DUR, KOK, PAT, SVR, WLK	NCP, NEP	180 – 693
Icelidae	Icelids	1 (0)	EMR, KOK	NEP	427
Cottidae	Sculpins	1 (0)	COB	SWA	59
Psychrolutidae	Psychrolutids	1 (0)	RIO	NEP, SWA	1000
Cyclopteridae	Lump fishes	2 (0)	SVR, KPR, PTO, UN1, UN2, VEM	IND, NEA, NWP, SEA	540 – 1000
Perchichthyidae	Basses	3 (0)	JER, KPR	IND, NCP, NEA, NWP	63 – 500
Serranidae	Basses	20 (0)	ACD, COL, EMR, EQU, GIF, MIL, NFR, NRO, PED, TNF, PTO, UN1	SEA, SWP	63 – ca. 400
Priacanthidae	Bigeyes	2 (0)	ACD, EMR, HCK, KAR, KMI, KPR, MIL, KOK, KPR, ZAP	NCP, NWP	72 – ca. 400
Apogonidae	Cardinalfishes	6 (0)	COL, CRS, HCK, KAR, KOK, KPR, MIL, KOK	NCP, NEA, NWP	280 – 2745
Pomatomidae	Bluefishes	1 (0)	KPR	NWP	ca. 400
Carangidae	Jacks	4 (0)	ACD, ATL, COL, EMR, GMR, HCK, HWR, IRV, JER, JSE, KAR, KPR, LAD, NRO, PED, TNF, VEM, ZAP	NCP, NEA, NWP, SEA	72 – ca. 400
Coryphaenidae	Dolphins	1 (0)	KPR, VEM	NWP, SEA	63 – ca. 400
Bramidae	Pomfrets	4 (0)	HCK, KPR	NCP, NWP	265 – ca. 400
Emmelichthyidae	Rovers	6 (1)	ACD, COL, EMR, EQU, HCK, KAR, KMI, KPR, MIL, NAZ, PED, TNF, UN2, VEM, ZAP	IND, NCP, NWP, SEA, SEP	63 – ca. 400
Mullidae	Goatfishes	2 (0)	HWR	NCP	<300
Lutjanidae	Snappers	10 (0)	ACD, EMR, HCK, HWR, KPR, KMI, KPR, LAD, NRO, PED, TNF, ZAP	NCP, NWP	72 – ca. 400
Chaetodontidae	Butterflyfishes	3 (1)	HWR, KPR, LAD	NCP, NWP	ca. 400
Acanthuridae	Surgeonfishes	1 (0)	HWR	NCP	
Pentacerotidae	Armorheads	2 (0)	EMR, HCK, KMI, KPR, LAD, MIL	NCP, NWP	75 – ca. 400
Pomacentridae	Damselfishes	1 (0)	TNF	NCP	?
Chelidodactylidae	Morwongs	3 (1)	HWR, UN2, VEM	IND, NCP, SEA	63
Zoarcidae	Eelpouts	2 (0)	EMR, WLK	NCP, NEP	693
Uranoscopidae	Stargazers	1 (17)	KPR	NWP	ca. 400
Percophididae	Duckbills	5 (1)	CRS, KPR, MIL	NCP, NWP	ca. 400 – 2745
Mugiloididae	Sandperches	2 (0)	CRS, HCK, KPR, PED	NCP, NWP	265 – 2745
Callionymidae	Dragonets	4 (1)	COL, GMR, JSE, KMI, KMU, MIL	NCP, NEA	148 – 355
Draconettidae	Dragonets	5 (0)	GMR, JSE, KPR, SAL, NAZ	NEA, NWP, SEP	148 – ca. 400
Scombrolabracidae		1 (0)	IRV, KPR	NCP, NWP	260 – ca. 400
Gempylidae	Snake mackerels	5 (0)	ACD, COL, EQU, GMR, HCK, IRV, JER, KAR, KPR, LAD, MIL, NRO	NCP, NEA, NWP	72 – ca. 400
Trichiuridae	Cutlassfishes	6 (1)	PED, TNF, UN2, ZAP, EMR, GET, GMR, IRV, JER, JSE, KMI, KPR, LRA, MIL	IND, NCP, NEA, NWP	85 – 500
Scombridae	Mackerels & Tunas	2 (0)	COL, DAC, EMR	NCP, SWP	63 – 235
Centrolophidae	Medusafishes	4 (0)	GMR, HCK, IRV, JER, VEM, KAR, KMI, KOK, KPR, LAD, MIL, PED, PTO, UN1	NCP, NEA, NWP	75 – 500
Ariommatidae	Ariommatids	1 (0)	ACD, COL, EQU, HCK, JER, KAR, KMI, KPR, MIL, PED, TNF, ZAP	NCP	265 – ca. 400
Stromateidae	Butterfishes	2 (0)	VEM	SEA	63
Bothidae	Left-eyed flounders	11 (37)	COL, GMR, HCK, JSE, KMI, KOK, KPR, MIL, KPR, PAT, PRT	NCP, NEA, NWP, SEP	148 – ca. 400
Pleuronectidae	Right-eyed flounders	4 (1)	HCK, KMI, MIL, TNF, KPR, NAZ, PED, ZAP	NCP, NEP	180 – ca. 400
Triacanthidae	Triacanths	1 (0)	LAD	NCP	265
Ballistidae	Triggerfishes	1 (0)	LAD, NFR	NCP	75
Ostraciontidae	Boxfishes	2 (0)	HWR, KPR, LAD, VEM, ZAP	NCP, SWP	75 – 82
Tetraodontidae	Puffers	3 (0)		NCP, NWP, SEA	63 – ca. 400
Molidae	Molas	1 (0)	COB	NEP	59

sampled (Cobb, Great Meteor, Josephine, the Hess Plateau, Vema) support representatives of one or both taxa.

The three most widely distributed invertebrate phyla are the Cnidaria (75 species from 37+ seamounts in 8 regions), Mollusca (72 species from seamounts in 5 regions) and Arthropoda (163 species from 35 seamounts in 6 regions). Protists and sponges were also numerically quite abundant (99 and 68 species, respectively), but these two phyla were reported from far fewer seamounts (8 and 26, respectively) than any of the three previously mentioned phyla. Cnidarians were found at depths ranging from 72 m (Nero Bank) to 3800 m (Hess Plateau); however, no hydrozoans were collected from depths greater than 567 m (seamount in the Heezen Fracture Zone). Scyphozoans were collected as deep as 1674 m (Hess guyot) while anthozoans were found on many seamounts deeper than 1000 m, and as deep as 3800 m. The relative thoroughness with which some of the deeper seamounts have been sampled (e.g. Hess Plateau and the Mid-Pacific Mountains) argues for the reality of these differences in vertical distribution.

Molluscs were collected on seamounts ranging from 27 m (Bowie) to 3800 m depth. Over half (51%) of the species reported were gastropods, but numerous bivalves (24%) and cephalopods (19%) were also collected. No cephalopods were collected below 1700 m (deepest record from 1674 m on Hess Guyot), although specimens have been photographed at 3000 m [Barnes, 1980] and deeper [K. L. Smith, Scripps Institution of Oceanography, personal communication]. Polyplacophorans were rare, having been reported only from two northeast Pacific seamounts [Scagel, 1970; Raymore, 1982]. One species, Cryptochiton stelleri, is a common denizen of the rocky intertidal, as are many chitons. Thus its presence on seamounts is more remarkable than would be its absence. Several scaphopods were found on two seamounts in the central North Pacific, at depths of 1544 m (Agassiz Guyot) and 3800 m as well as on several deep seamounts in the northeastern Pacific. Scaphopods are known inhabitants of the deep-sea benthos [Barnes, 1980], and their distribution on seamounts is probably more widespread than indicated in the literature.

Arthropods were the most numerically dominant invertebrate phylum on seamounts, with a depth range of 59 m (Cobb) to 3800 m. The bulk (145 of 163) of the species reported were crustaceans, primarily decapods (68 of 145). These decapods were conspicuous components of the epibenthic seamount (invertebrate) megafauna [Kensley, 1980, 1981; Hughes, 1981; Raymore, 1982; Wilson et al., 1985], with some species (e.g. Lithodes couesi, Chionoecetes tanneri) occurring on both soft and hard substrates [Raymore, 1982]. Deep-sea crustaceans are often highly motile, opportunistic scavengers, and thus are able to actively respond to baited traps and baited video cameras, such as those used by various researchers [Heydorn, 1969; Hughes, 1981; Raymore, 1982; Wilson et al., 1985].

Most seamount crustaceans are cosmopolitan species typical of depths at which the seamount collections have been made, although some species (e.g. Notostomus auriculatus, Gennadas gilchristi, Funchalia villosa) are true mesopelagics not usually associated with land masses [Kensley, 1980]. Few of the seamount crustaceans are truly benthic, however, and most are capable of excursions into the water column (e.g. isopods and amphipods). This makes them available for capture in midwater trawls and in baited traps located some distance above the bottom.

Fishes

Fishes were collected from more than 60 seamounts located in all regions except the northwestern Atlantic Ocean. Certainly fishes are present on seamounts in this region, but no reports of them have come to our attention. In all, 449 nominal species (exclusive of midwater species) in 92 families and two subclasses are known to be associated with seamounts (Table 3). The family Macrouridae (grenadiers) with 39 species was the best represented in terms of diversity. The next six were: Scorpaenidae (scorpionfishes, 34 species), Moridae (codlings, 27 species), Squalidae (dogfishes, 26 species), Alepocephalidae (slickheads, 21 species), Serranidae (seabasses, 20 species), and Chlorophthalmidae (17 species).

Scorpionfishes was the most widely distributed family, present on 33 seamounts in 7 regions. Next were: codlings (29 seamounts, 6 regions), seabasses (26 seamounts, 6 regions), grenadiers (29 seamounts, 5 regions), dogfishes (24 seamounts, 5 regions), rovers (Emmelichthyidae; 15 seamounts, 5 regions), jacks (Carangidae; 21 seamounts, 4 regions) and chlorophthalmids (13 seamounts, 4 regions). Cutlassfishes (15 seamounts, 4 regions) and snake mackerels (7 seamounts, 4 regions) were also widely distributed, but this was largely due to a single widespread species in each family, Lepidopus caudatus (cutlassfish) and Promethichthys prometheus (snake mackerel). Slickheads had a rather limited distribution in relation to their diversity because 14 of 21 species were collected from one seamount, the Rio Grande Plateau [Pakhorukov, 1976].

The Macrouridae, Scorpaenidae, Alepocephalidae, Moridae, Squalidae and Chloropthalmidae comprise 6.5% of the fish families reported from seamounts but collectively contain 36.5% of the species. Their importance probably reflects the fact that over 60% of the seamounts were sampled at greater than 300 m depth, whether on the summit, on a slope, or near the base. The Macrouridae, Alepocephalidae, Moridae and Chloropthalmidae contain mostly or exclusively deep-water species (>200 m depth) and the Scorpaenidae and Squalidae contain some deep-water species. In all, perhaps 12 of the families in Table 3 contain exclusively deep-water species while some 16 have deep-water representatives, with the remainder primarily known from shallower shelf waters.

The strong presence of the aforementioned six families may be due in part to the large number of species they contain. The Macrouridae contains minimally 260 species, Scorpaenidae 310 species, Moridae 70 species, Alepocephalidae 60 species, Chloropthalmidae 38 species and Squalidae 71 species [Nelson, 1984]. On the other hand, there are other large families with deep-water/cold-water representatives that appear poorly represented on these seamounts. The Zoarcidae (eelpouts) contains some 150 species, but only two have been reported from seamounts. The family Ophidiidae (cuskeels) with at least 164 species and the Bythididae (brotulids) with at least 103 species [Nelson, 1984] are represented by 6 species on 3 seamounts.

Seamount Biogeography

Biogeographic Patterns

The seamount biota is divisible into four main biogeographic categories: provincial, widespread to cosmopolitan, exotic and endemic. Provincials are simply those species restricted to the region in which the seamount is located; widespread to cosmopolitan species occur both in and beyond the immediate region or are found worldwide and exotics are those rarely or never before found in the immediate region. Strictly speaking, endemics would be those species confined to a particular seamount, or perhaps several seamounts of a particular group (e.g. Mid-Pacific Mountains). Many species classified as endemics probably meet this definition. However, in some poorly-studied groups where species distributions are not well known the term endemic may also be applied to species first collected on a seamount but which have subsequently been discovered elsewhere, unknown to us. Thus, the endemic categories may be overestimated in many cases.

The biogeographic affinities of Vema Seamount are perhaps the best studied to date. Vema is a relatively isolated peak located about 670 km off the west coast of South Africa. It has a minimum age of 11 m.y. and was probably exposed during the Pleistocene [Simpson and Heydorn, 1965]. Collections on the shallow summit (63 m) produced 22 species of algae, more than 105 species of benthic invertebrates (Table 1) and 14 species of fishes [Penrith, 1967; Berrisford, 1969]. The algae have affinities with South Africa, but the extent was not determined. The invertebrates of Berrisford's [1969] report were referred to 7 zoogeographic groups, reducible to the 4 main groups given above. Endemic species (mostly sponges and ascidians) made up the largest category (28%), followed by cosmopolites (27%), species restricted to Vema and South Africa (25%) (provincial), Indo-Pacific species (10%) (exotic), species restricted to West Africa and Europe (6%) (provincial) and species mainly in West and South Africa, but with some overlap in Europe (4%) (widespread). The rock lobster, _Jasus tristani_, was the only species restricted to Vema and the nearby Tristan da Cunha Islands (provincial). Among the fishes there were: one endemic species, nine species common to Vema and South Africa, eight of which were considered wide-ranging pelagic forms (e.g. _Coryphaena hippurus_ and _Sphoeroides cutaneous_) and three species common to Vema and the Tristan da Cunha Islands. A subsequent analysis of additional decapod and isopod fauna from Tripp and Vema seamounts [Kensley, 1980] revealed similar zoogeographic affinities.

The provincial and widespread/cosmopolitan categories on Vema each comprise about 31% of the species total while the endemic category is about 28%. However, the high level of endemism on Vema is heavily influenced by the poorly known sponges and ascidians and might yield a distorted picture [Berrisford, 1969]. The provincial and widespread/cosmopolitan categories strongly dominate the biota, and if the Indo-Pacific species were considered widespread rather than exotic, this one category would make up nearly 50% of the total fauna.

Sampled seamounts of the Kyushu-Palau Ridge in the northwestern Pacific are much deeper than Vema (320 - 685 m versus 63 m) but are closer to shallow continental shelf water (220 to 472 km distant versus 670 km for Vema (Table 1). These collections have yielded at least 142 species of fishes [Okamura et al., 1982]. Although no zoogeographic analysis for this ichthyofauna was offered, there were useful distributional notes for 137 species collected on the ridge [Okamura et al., 1982]. According to these notes, approximately 38% of the 137 fishes are provincial (limited to the western Pacific between the Philippines, Japan and Hawaii), about 36% widespread/cosmopolitan (Australia, New Zealand, Indian and Atlantic Oceans), 26% apparently endemic (i.e. newly-reported species known only from the Kyushu-Palau Ridge) and < 1% exotic. Since fishes are well known as a group, this estimate of endemism is relatively reliable.

The fishes on northeastern Atlantic seamounts, particularly Great Meteor, comprise similar categories. Great Meteor is further from a continent (1340 km) than either Vema or the Kyushu-Palau Ridge, but lies at an intermediate depth of 210 m. It is an extinct Cretaceous volcano with a limestone cap flattened by wave action sometime before the Pliocene, 2 to 5 m.y. BP [von Rad, 1974]. It has been at its present summit depth probably since the end of the Pleistocene. Two expeditions to Great Meteor yielded at least 61 species of invertebrates and 35 species of fishes [Maul, 1976; Ehrich, 1977]. Among the fishes the two largest categories were species not restricted to the Atlantic Ocean (34%) (widespread/cosmopolitan) and those with Mediterranean-East Atlantic distributions (34%) (provincial). Next were widespread Atlantic species (14%) (widespread/cosmopolitan), endemics (9%), Northwest African species (6%) (provincial) and western Atlantic species (3%) (exotic). Great Meteor ichthyofauna was most similar to that of the African shelf between Gibraltar and Cape Blanc (28 species in common) and showed slightly less similarity with the ichthyofauna of Madeira (24 species in common) and the Canary Islands (17 species in common) [Ehrich, 1977]. The closest Atlantic relative of *Protogrammus sousai*, the endemic callionymid on Great Meteor, occurs in the western North Atlantic [Fricke, 1985].

Shcherbachev et al. [1985] also studied the zoogeography of fishes caught on Great Meteor as well as those obtained from six additional northeastern Atlantic seamounts which are part the Atlantis-Great Meteor Seamount Chain (Table 1). Most collections were made between 210 and 1400 m, with a few below 3000 m. They identified four vertical zones associated with seamounts: 1) epipelagic - the water above those seamounts with summits less than 300 m depth, 2) sublittoral- 150 to 350 m on the seamount, 3) mesobenthic - 300 to 800 m on seamount slopes, 4) abyssobenthic - near the seamount base.

The epipelagic and sublittoral zones yielded 30 species, 15 in common with Ehrich's [1977] list, while the sublittoral ichthyofauna contained 27 species grouped into four main categories: subtropical northeastern Atlantic species (52%) (provincial), widespread eastern Atlantic species (19%) (widespread/cosmopolitan), species with extra-Atlantic distributions (19%) (widespread/cosmopolitan) and boreal East Atlantic species (11%) (provincial).

The dominance of provincial species in the sublittoral appeared to give way to species with broad distributions at greater depths on the seamounts. The mesobenthic zone included 50 species, 17 in common with Ehrich's [1977] list, and while provincial species with eastern Atlantic distributions dominated the upper mesobenthic zone, the mid-mesobenthic contained only 2 of 16 species considered to be eastern Atlantic. The lower mesobenthic zone contained exclusively species widely distributed in the Atlantic, or with extra-Atlantic distributions. The same was true of the abyssobenthic zone [Shcherbachev et al., 1985].

The affinities of biota on deep seamounts even further from continental shelves continue the same trends. Wilson et al. [1985] studied the zoogeography of bathyal (1413-1674 m) seamounts in the Mid-Pacific Mountains, which are more than 2000 km from a continental shelf (Table 1). Horizon Guyot is the largest of these and yielded the most biological data. It is a volcanic ridge of Cretaceous age which probably has never risen to the sea surface [Lonsdale et al., 1972]. The distributions revealed that among 14 fish species identified, three were provincial (21%) and 11 were widespread/cosmopolitan (79%) and there were no exotics nor endemics. The widespread/cosmopolitan category contained circumtropical species and those with Atlantic to Indo-West Pacific distributions. The batfish, *Haleutopsis* n. sp., was thought to be an endemic on Horizon Guyot, but it has since been discovered in unreported collections from the Indian Ocean (M. Bradbury, San Francisco State University, personal communication). Among 25 invertebrates identified to species, one was provincial (4%), 14 were widespread/cosmopolitan (56%), 8 were apparent endemics (36%) and one was exotic (4%). Widespread species were distributed in the Indo-West Pacific, whereas the exotic was considered an eastern Pacific species.

Borets [1986] analyzed the zoogeography of ichthyofauna collected from 16 remote seamounts in the northern Hawaiian Ridge and southern Emperor Chain of the central North Pacific. These seamounts were formed at the Hawaiian melting anomoly beneath the island of Hawaii and have been moving north or northwest with the Pacific lithospheric plate and gradually subsiding for approximately the past 70 m.y.; older seamounts are to the North and younger ones to the South [e.g., Scott and Rotondo, 1983]. Seamounts of the Hawaiian Ridge extend northwesterly some 3500 km from the island of Hawaii to Colahan Seamount (31°20'N, 175°54'E). The Emperor seamounts begin at the Milwaukee Seamount Group (31°50'N, 172°45'E) and extend northward some 2300 km to Meiji Seamount [Jackson et al., 1980 cited in Humphreys et al., 1984] (Fig. 2). There is an apparent faunal break at the 180th meridian which bisects the Hawaiian Ridge. Collections from seamounts northwest of this meridian are dominated by deep-water demersal and benthic fishes, whereas those southeast of it are represented by subtropical species [Humphreys et al., 1984].

Borets' [1986] collections were from seamounts spanning the 17 degrees of latitude between 28°50'N and 46°15'N (Fig. 2). Depths of collections ranged from 200 to 2500 m. From his distributional notes on the total sample of 96 species representing 51 families [Borets, 1986, Table 2] we determined the largest category to be provincial species: those limited to the tropical or subtropical West Pacific and the Hawaiian region, or belonging to the Pacific rim

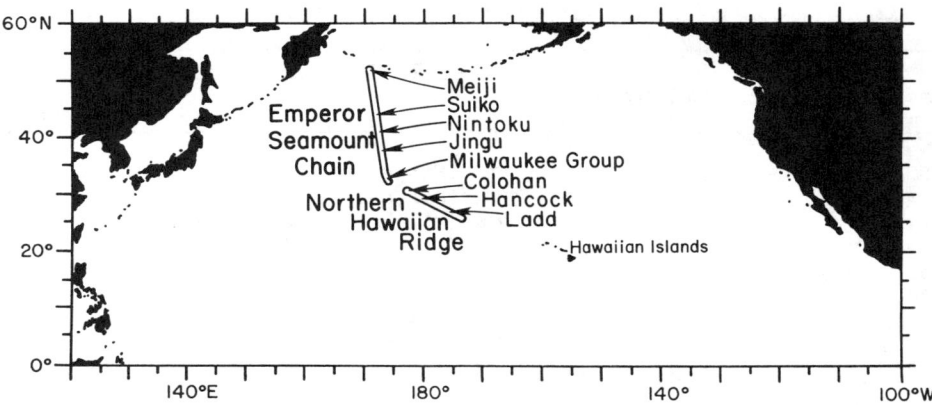

Fig. 2. Region of the Emperor Seamount Chain and the Northern Hawaiian Ridge showing sampled seamounts in the studies of Borets [1986] and Humphreys et al. [1984].

boreal fauna (41%). Next came the widespread/cosmopolitan category comprised mostly of broadly tropical species (35%), the endemic category (22%) and the exotic category (1%) represented by one eastern Pacific chlorophthalmid, Chlorophthalmus proridens.

The 27 species collected from the five northern-most seamounts (between 46°15'N and 38°15'N) contained 59% provincial elements from the Pacific rim distributed between northern Japan and northern Baja California. The rest were widespread/cosmopolitan tropical (34%) and endemic (7%) species. The eleven southernmost seamounts produced 72 mostly tropical and subtropical species. The provincial and widespread/cosmopolitan categories were nearly equal at 39% and 37.5% and followed in importance by the endemic (22%) and exotic (1.5%) categories.

Borets [1986] also identified six "ichthyocenes" similar to those of Shcherbachev et al. [1985] which were related to the species' habitat depths. Borets' [1986] sublittoral ichthyocene had four species (two endemic), the mesobathyal 26 species (15 endemic), the bathybenthic 9 species (two endemic), the epipelagic four species (one endemic), the mesopelagic 35 species (two endemic) and the bathypelagic 18 species (none endemic). Although the same absence of endemism is evident in Borets' samples from the greater seamount depths as that observed in Shcherbachev et al.'s [1985] deep collections, the composition of Borets' bathypelagic ichthyocene is about 40% provincial elements from the boreal North Pacific rather than widespread species.

Available data suggest that northeastern Pacific (i.e., Gulf of Alaska) seamounts are dominated by provincial elements, with a much smaller contribution in evidence from widespread species. For example, some 17 algal, 42 (identified) invertebrate and 18 fish species have been reported from shallow (<1000 m) seamounts in the Gulf of Alaska, all of which lie within 400 km of a continental shelf (Table 1). No rigorous biogeographic analyses have been performed, but it is evident that only North Pacific boreal (e.g. Oregon to the Sea of Okhotsk and northern Japan) and northeastern Pacific (Alaska to Baja California) elements are present among the fishes, since as yet no exotic or cosmopolitan species have been reported. The high latitudes at which the Gulf of Alaska Seamounts (above 50° North latitude) lie might be responsible for the lack of cosmopolitan species since the many widespread subtropical species are probably excluded due to the cold water.

Although several seamounts in the subtropical northeastern Pacific have been sampled (Table 1) for both fishes (E. Fujii, Tokai Regional Fisheries Research Laboratory, Tokyo, Japan, unpublished manuscript) and benthic invertebrates (L. Levin, North Carolina State University, Raleigh, North Carolina, unpublished data), biogeographic analyses remain to be performed. The little data available to us on fishes from seamounts in the Baja California Seamount Province (e.g., Jasper and Hoke, Table 1) indicate mostly provincial elements of the California Current fauna with perhaps two widespread subtropical species not part of the nearby shelf or slope fauna (Fujii, unpublished manuscript).

The biogeographic composition of ichthyofauna of the central North Pacific seamounts agrees with that of the eastern North Atlantic seamounts in that the provincial category decreases relative to the widespread/cosmopolitan category at greater depths. Seamounts from both regions are heavily dominated by species typically found in the vicinity of the seamount, whether restricted to a portion of the region (provincials) or present because of a generally widespread distribution (Table 4). Exotic species are typically rare

TABLE 4. Summary of the biogeographic composition of some seamounts

Seamount or Seamount Group	Biogeographic Category			
	Widespread/ cosmopolitan	Provincial	Endemic	Exotic
Emperor Chain	34% (Fishes)	59% (Fishes)*	7% (Fishes)	0%
Hawaiian Ridge	37.5% (Fishes)	39% (Fishes)	22% (Fishes)	1.5% (Fishes)
Mid-Pacific Mountains	79% (Fishes) 56% (Invert.)	21% (Fishes) 4% (Invert.)	0% (Fishes) 36% (Invert.)	0% (Fishes) 4% (Invert.)
Kyushu-Palau Ridge	36% (Fishes)	38% (Fishes)	26% (Fishes)	<1% (Fishes)
Great Meteor	48% (Fishes)	40% (Fishes)	9% (Fishes)	3% (Fishes)
Great Meteor-Atlantis Seamount Chain	38% (Fishes)	62% (Fishes)*	0%	0%
Vema	31% (Invert.)	31% (Invert.)	28% (Invert.)	10% (Invert.)

*Influenced by boreal elements.

whereas endemic species appear to vary in importance. Seamounts in high latitudes will probably prove to generally have more provincial species than those in low latitudes at similar depths. Thus, latitude, depth and distance from the continent appear to be factors which most influence the balance between the provincial and widespread/cosmopolitan categories. Although remote, the central Pacific seamounts of the Hawaiian Ridge appear to be largely within the domain of Indo-West Pacific shelf and slope fauna. However, Fujii [1986] revealed that 21 of 28 demersal fishes (80%) obtained from various seamounts and ridges on the Pacific lithospheric plate were oceanic, restricted to seamounts and insular slopes and shelves. Thus, there might an important fraction of seamount ichthyofauna which is not simply an extension of the nearby shelf and slope biota.

Origins of Biogeographic Patterns

Stepping-stone dispersal and vicariance. Hamilton [1956] proposed that seamounts may once have served as "island stepping stones" for the dispersal of fauna throughout the Pacific Ocean basin. By asking whether seamounts might be present-day "stepping stones", Hubbs [1959] expanded this idea. The stepping stone concept has two components requiring distinction. One is that the fauna of subsiding islands (or seamounts) successively transfers itself, either whole or in part, to nearby younger islands, thereby crossing deep ocean basins by having used sunken islands of past geologic times as "stepping stones." The other component is that islands and seamounts may serve as "way stations" for expanding populations, allowing species to disperse across expansive deep ocean basins in small "steps." Both components are dispersalistic in nature, but the first transpires on a scale of millions of years whereas the second may require only tens or hundreds of generations. Hubbs' [1959] view of seamount biogeography was entirely dispersalistic, perhaps owing to the fact that the field of plate tectonics and modern theories of vicariant biogeography were not yet developed. Nevertheless, the stepping stone concept remains a valid one and is discussed here in light of current knowledge and contemporary ideas.

Although seamount fauna remain poorly investigated, some biogeographic patterns are evident and some practical discussion of their origination is possible. For example, it is clear that the fauna of central Pacific seamounts (i.e., the Mid-Pacific Mountains, the Hawaiian Ridge and the Emperor Chain) is allied with that of the Indo-West Pacific. This connection has been documented for gastropods, barnacles, caridean shrimps and fishes of the Mid-Pacific Mountains [Rao and Newman, 1972; Rehder and Ladd, 1973; Wilson, et al., 1985] and for fishes of the Hawaiian Ridge and Emperor Chain [e.g., Uchida and Tagami, 1984; Humphreys et al., 1984; Borets, 1986]. Shorefish fauna show the essentially same alliance. For example, Springer [1982] noted that all families of shorefishes with non-marginal representation on the Pacific Plate (N=111) are widely distributed in the Indo-West Pacific, if not even more widely. However, only some 62% of all Indo-West Pacific shorefish families are present non-marginally on the Pacific Plate, indicating absence of complete homogeneity between the Pacific plate and the West Pacific. Probably all but two of the 70 fish families present on central North Pacific seamounts are widely distributed in the Indo-West Pacific with some extending into the North Atlantic. The two exceptions are from the North Pacific boreal fauna with both species ranging from northern Japan along the Pacific rim to California. These are the skilfish, *Erilepis zonifer* (Family Anoplopomatidae) and the ragfish, *Icosteus aenigmaticus* (Family Icosteidae) [Humphreys et al., 1984; Borets, 1986].

Springer [1982] reported ten monotypic genera of shorefish as endemic to the Pacific plate out of some 461 present non-marginally. Three of these are part of the Hawaiian fauna but are not restricted there. There are at least 136 fish genera represented on seamounts of the central North Pacific inclusive of the Mid-Pacific Mountains, Northern Hawaiian Ridge and Emperor Chain. Among these we know of one endemic genus, the monotypic Adelosebastes from the Emperor Chain [Eschmeyer et al., 1979; Kanayama, 1981]. Springer [1982] estimated specific endemism at 29% among Hawaiian shore fishes whereas that figure is about 22% for seamount fishes of the Northern Hawaiian Ridge and southern Emperor Chain [Borets, 1986].

Pacific island biogeography is complex, with different islands showing varying levels of faunal affinities with one another, although all are essentially part of the Indo-West Pacific faunal pool, which is highly diverse. The biogeographic history of Pacific island faunas, particularly the Hawaiian, receives much discussion from contemporary biogeographers. (See Springer [1982] and Newman [1986] for recent summaries.) The relative proximity of seamounts in the Hawaiian Ridge and the Mid-Pacific Mountains to the Hawaiian Islands (Fig. 1), and the large endemic category of fishes, approximately 22% on the Hawaiian Ridge, make portions of this debate relative to seamount biogeography even though it is mostly concerned with tropical and subtropical biota.

Newman [1986] has dismissed the possibility that the Mid-Pacific Mountains served as island stepping stones for contemporary Hawaiian shore fauna, although it is clear that they presently serve to disseminate bathyal species by providing shallow habitats in a deep basin [Wilson et al., 1985]. Moveover, the plethora of seamounts on the western portion of the Pacific plate [Heezen and Tharp, 1977] appears to offer many stepping stones for population expansion of deep-living Indo-West Pacific species into the central Pacific. Newman [1986] supports the idea that dispersal via island stepping stones accounts for some of the faunal similarities between the Hawaiian and southeastern Pacific island fauna. Alternatively, Rotondo et al. [1981] and Springer [1982] have proposed that Hawaiian and southeastern Pacific faunal similarities can be explained by "island integration" whereby islands carrying endemic biota from the southeastern Pacific merged with islands forming at the Hawaiian melting anomaly. When this occurred, the respective faunas combined and merged. Newman [1986], however, contests island integration as proposed by Rotondo et al. [1981] and Springer [1982] on the grounds that Hawaiian barnacles, corals and fishes are predominantly of Tertiary age, and thus too young to have been left over from the Cretaceaous seamounts and islands which figure in the island integration scenario. Extending the concept of island integration to one of "seamount integration" probably would not help explain the biogeography of central Pacific seamount fauna for the same reason.

One faunal component of the Emperor seamounts exempt from the above considerations is North Pacific boreal species whose distributions follow the Pacific rim from northern Japan to northern Baja California. These are the dogfish shark Somniosus pacificus, the codling Antimora microlepis, the grenadiers Coryphaenoides acrolepis and C. pectoralis, the ragfish Icosteus aenigmaticus and the skilfish Erilepas zonifer. These six species along with Chlorophthalmus proridens represent the only eastern Pacific elements of the central North Pacific seamount ichthyofauna. A stepping stone (dispersalistic) hypothesis accounts for their presence on seamounts.

The southern extent in the Emperor Seamount Chain of all except A. microlepis is Jingu Seamount, more than 1500 km distant from a continental slope (Table 1, Fig. 2). A. microlepis is known from the Mid-Pacific Mountains [Small, 1981; Wilson et al., 1985] more than 2000 km from a slope. Emperor seamounts get deeper as they near the Kamchatka Trench thus moving into the depth range of these species, and are progressively older than seamounts to the south. (See references cited in Scott and Rotondo [1983].) Since the seamounts have been converging for some 70 my [Scott and Rotondo, 1983] toward the continental margin inhabited by these species, there has been no possibility of vicariant isolation and movement away from the continent. In contrast, Emperor seamounts probably form a corridor which allows these boreal, Pacific rim species into the central Pacific by serving as stepping stones for population expansion.

There is also a biogeographic connection between the Indo-West Pacific and a southeastern Pacific seamount and two submarine ridges. The seamount is Shoal Guyot which lies at about 250 m some 1480 km west of the Chilean Shelf (Table 1). It is one in a nearly continuous line of guyots on the East Pacific Rise extending between the Nacza Ridge and Easter Island, and has an estimated age of about 29.2 m.y. based on magnetic anomaly data [Newman and Foster, 1983]. On Shoal Guyot this biogeographic connection is seen among barnacles [Zullo and Newman, 1964; Zullo et al., 1964], echinoids [Allison et al., 1967] and a fish [Hubbs, 1959]. On Nazca and Sala-y-Gomez ridges it occurs among dragonet fishes and codlings of the genus Physiculus [Parin, 1982, 1984]. Species of genera which are widely distributed in the Atlantic and Indo-West Pacific are also present on Nazca and Sala-y-Gomez ridges although these genera remain unknown from the closer continental margins of western America. Examples are the beardfish Polymixia yuri and the rover Emmelichthys elongatus [Kotlyar, 1982a,b] (Figs. 3 and 4). A similar biogeographic connection between the

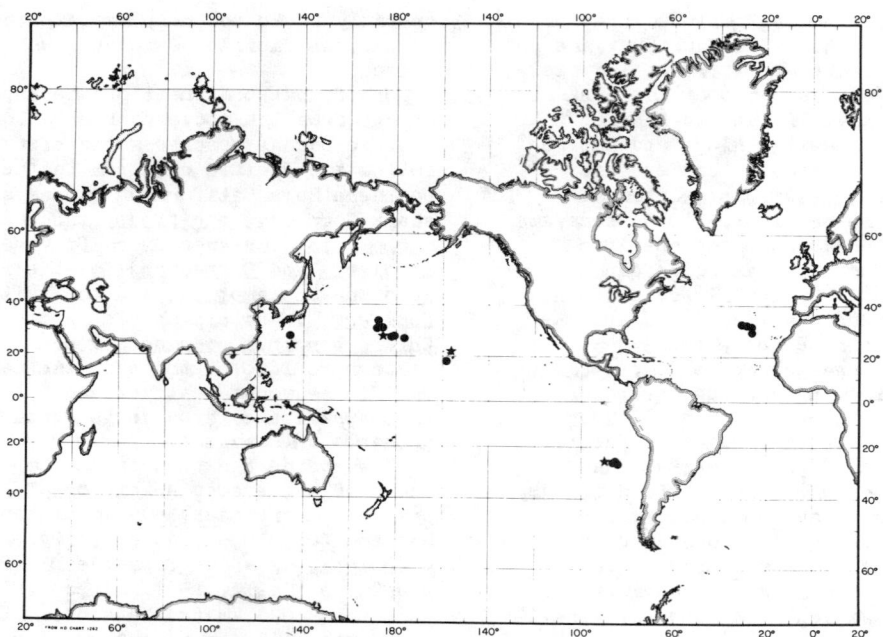

Fig. 3. Distribution of the beardfish genus *Polymixia* (dots) and the codling species *Laemonema rhodochir* (stars) as represented on seamounts. *Polymixia* species and *L. rhodochir* are not present on the close continental shelves and slopes of the western Americas.

Indo-West Pacific and the eastern tropical Pacific has been known for many years among island and shelf fauna [Ekman, 1953; Briggs, 1961], although Hubbs [1959] produced the first record of it from a seamount. Studies of island and shore fauna have since shown the eastern tropical Pacific to contain several Indo-West Pacific species or close relatives [Emerson, 1967; Rosenblatt et al., 1972; Briggs, 1974], some of which are restricted in the eastern Pacific to offshore islands [Briggs, 1974, pp. 102-104].

An interesting component of this West Pacific-South East Pacific alliance is the affinity between endemic species of the southeastern Pacific islands and those of the Hawaiian group [Rehder, 1980; Springer, 1982; Newman, 1986] which is extended to the Sala-y-Gomez Ridge by the presence of the codling fish *Laemonema rhodochir*, a species otherwise known only from the Hawaiian region and possibly from the Kyushu-Palau Ridge south of Japan [Parin, 1984] (Fig. 3), and *Chlorophthalmus proridens* known from the Hawaiian region and the Nacza Ridge [Borets, 1986]. The nearly continuous line of seamounts, islands and insular slopes connecting the northwestern and southeastern Pacific [Heezen and Tharp, 1977] are possible stepping stones for the dispersal of deep-living western Pacific elements into the southeastern Pacific, thus accounting for their presence on Shoal Guyot as well as on Nazca and Sala-y-Gomez ridges. On the other hand, this dispersalistic mechanism does not explain all aspects of the insular affinities [Newman, 1986] and other explanations have been offered. For example, this connection may represent a North-South disjunct (antitropical) distribution as discussed by Springer [1982] which is vicariant and does not rely upon dispersal via stepping stones. It may best account for the distribution of *L. rhodochir* and *C. proridens*.

The presence on seamounts and ridges of "exotic" species remote from their apparent distributional centers might, but does not necessarily, suggest a "stepping stone" function for seamounts in both the Pacific and Atlantic oceans. The occurrence of the dragonet fish *Centrodraco acanthopoma* on Great Meteor and Josephine seamounts illustrates this point. *C. acanthopoma* was unknown in the eastern Atlantic until collected on Great Meteor and Josephine seamounts and Madeira [Maul, 1976; Ehrich, 1977]. It is absent on the North African and Iberian shelves [Ehrich, 1977; Nakabo, 1981] but has recently been reported from Kyushu-Palau Ridge south of Japan, the first record in the West Pacific [Nakabo, 1981; Okamura et al., 1982]. The situation parallels that of *Pterygotrigla picta* from Shoal Guyot [Hubbs, 1959] and the Juan Fernandez Islands (R. H. Rosenblatt, Scripps Institution of Oceanography, personal communication) in that both species are absent from the continental areas nearest the

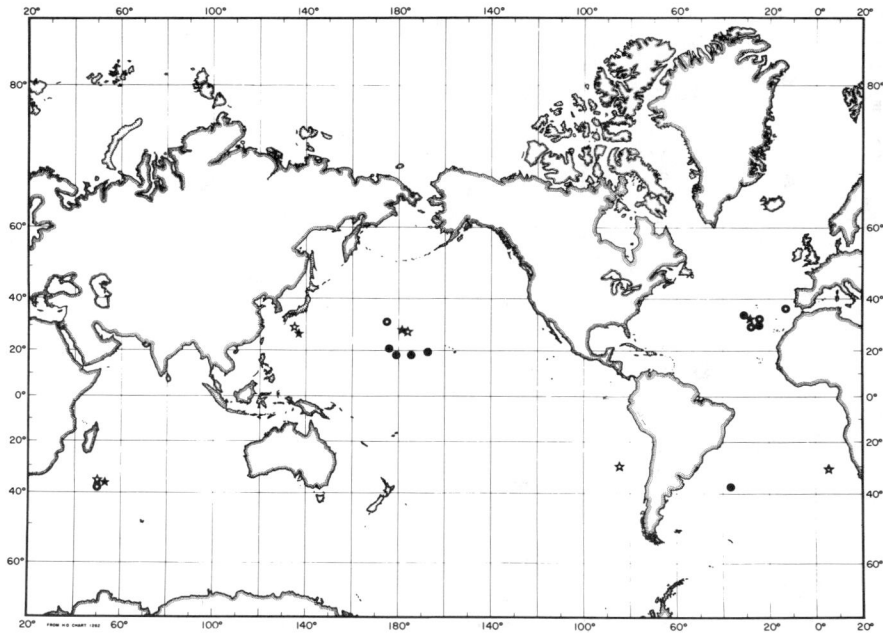

Fig. 4. Distribution of the fish family Emmelichthyidae (open stars), the fish genera Aldrovandia (dots) and Helicolenus (open stars in filled dots) and the fish species Promethichthys prometheus (filled stars) as represented on seamounts. All groups are absent in the eastern North Pacific. Not all records plotted in Emperor Chain to preserve clarity.

seamount(s) on which they occur. This pattern therefore contrasts with the more common one discussed above (Table 4) where seamount species are also present on the nearest continental shelf or slope. The possibility that exotic species may colonize "remote seamounts" suggests their capacity to reach the nearby continental shelves as well, but perhaps cannot become established on them unless some catastrophe creates "niche space." In such a scenario seamounts would be serving as stepping stones for dispersal.

On the other hand, the present-day distribution of C. acanthopoma also suggests an alternative biogeographic explanation. The species is restricted to the continental shelf of the eastern United States, to Madeira Island and Great Meteor and Josephine seamounts in the eastern North Atlantic and to the Kyushu-Palau Ridge in the North Pacific south of Japan [Nakabo, 1981]. C. acanthopoma might formerly have been widespread on continental slopes and simply went extinct everywhere except on the shelf of the eastern U.S.A. and on seamounts between 200 and 600 m depth at subtropical latitudes. However, Great Meteor Seamount is an extinct volcano of Cretaceous age which originated on the eastern shoulder of the mid-Atlantic Ridge and had reached the sea surface by the early Miocene [von Rad, 1974]. Since it has always been oceanic its past and present fauna must have dispersed there at some point, although it is an open question as to whether Great Meteor (or other seamounts) has served as a stepping stone for transgressing the subtropical North Atlantic from either direction.

Although seamounts certainly extend the ranges of certain species far beyond the limits of continental shelves and slopes many species and even entire genera represented on seamounts in more than one region (including the central North Pacific) apparently have not been able to "step across" to the northeastern Pacific (Figs. 3, 4 and 5). Among fishes these genera include Antigonia, Aldrovandia [McDowell, 1973, p. 89; Wilson et al., 1985] Beryx [Woods and Sonoda, 1973], Helicolenus [Eschmeyer and Hureau, 1971], Promethichthys (monotypic), Synaphobranchus [Wilson et al., 1985], Polymixia [Kotlyar, 1982b] and all Emmelichthyid genera [Springer, 1982]. Particularly enigmatic is the scorpaenid genus Helicolenus which is distributed worldwide, including in the southeastern Pacific, but is totally absent in the northeastern Pacific [Eschmeyer and Hureau, 1971] although present on the Emperor seamounts [Abe and Eschmeyer, 1972; Kanayama, 1981] (Fig. 4). Perhaps the relative paucity of seamounts in northeastern Pacific compared to the southeastern Pacific is a factor [e.g., Heezen and Tharp, 1977], there being essentially no

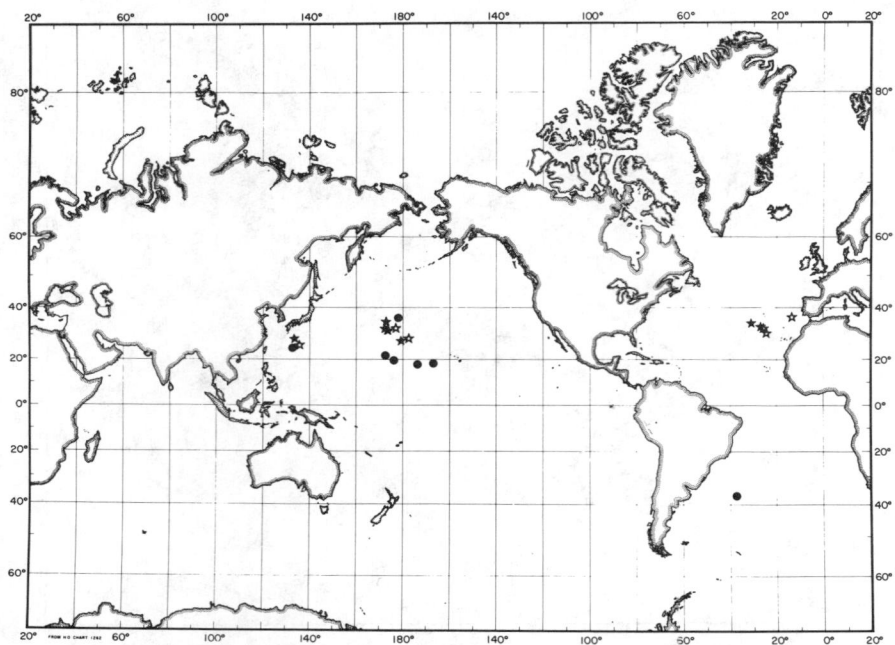

Fig. 5. Distribution of the fish family Synaphobranchidae (dots) and the fish genera *Antigonia* (open stars) and *Beryx* (filled stars) as represented on seamounts. All groups are absent in the eastern North Pacific. Not all records plotted in Emperor Chain to preserve clarity.

well-positioned stepping stones to aid the transgression envisioned by Hubbs [1959]. Although these genera may never have arrived in the northeastern Pacific, the possibility that they did arrive but have gone extinct cannot be ruled out.

Dispersal by currents. Currents alone may play a significant role in the dispersal of species found on seamounts, since seamounts tend to be geographically isolated from the land masses which probably serve as distribution sources. Genin et al., [1986] have postulated that seamounts structure local current regimes, which in turn are factors governing community structure and faunal composition on the seamounts themselves. Thus, seamounts may be efficient "traps" for organisms transported by currents through the overlying water column. In some cases this may lead to species distributions which reflect the prevailing current patterns.

One example of current-influenced distribution involves the South Atlantic rock lobster, *Jasus tristani*. *J. tristani* occurs on Tristan da Cunha, Gough Island and Vema Seamount [Simpson and Heydorn, 1965; Berrisford, 1969; Heydorn, 1969; Kensley, 1980, 1981; Lutjeharms and Heydorn, 1981; Fig. 6], and there has been considerable speculation on the mechanism by which this species spread from Tristan da Cunha and Gough Island (the presumed distribution centers) to the isolated Vema. In one experiment, weather buoys released in the vicinity of Tristan da Cunha and Gough Island passed over or near Vema after drifting for 146-227 days [Lutjeharms and Heydorn, 1981]. Although these results are not conclusive, they do suggest that *J. tristani* larvae could drift from Tristan da Cunha and/or Gough Island to Vema Seamount in surface currents.

Additional support for the drift theory is seen in the distribution of the scorpaenid fish, *Sebastes capensis*, which occurs on both Tristan da Cunha and Gough Island as well as on the western coast of South Africa [Eschmeyer and Hureau, 1971]. Eschmeyer and Hureau [1971] suggested dispersal paths for *S. capensis* similar to those proposed by Heydorn [1969] and Lutjeharms and Heydorn [1981] for *J. tristani*. Another scorpaenid, *Helicolenus mouchezi*, is also found on Tristan da Cunha and Gough Island, but is not known from either Vema or South Africa. However, *H. mouchezi* has been collected from seamount UN2 (1212 km southeast of South Africa; Table 1), Amsterdam Island and St. Paul Island (Fig. 6). Its distribution indicates a dispersal path similar to that proposed for *J. tristani* and *S. capensis*, with larvae being carried by a more southerly current, possibly the West Wind Drift, the northern portion of which forms part of a cyclonic gyre in the southwest Indian Ocean (Fig. 6).

This gyre may also provide Indian Ocean and Indo-West Pacific species with a means of reaching the Atlantic Ocean [Kensley, 1981]. This might explain the presence on Vema of

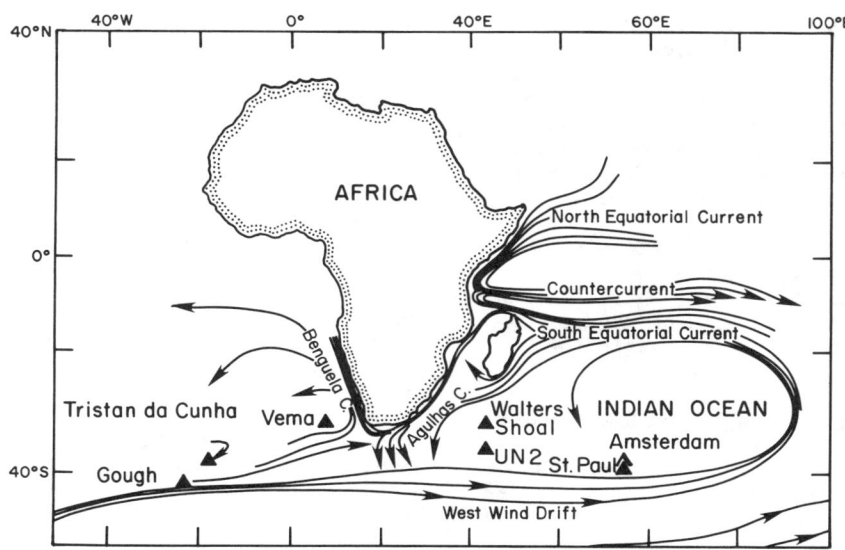

Fig. 6. Ocean current patterns in the vicinity of Tristan de Cunha, Gough, St. Paul and Amsterdam islands, Vema and UN2 seamounts and Walters Shoal which may account for the distribution of some crustacean and fish species on seamounts in the southeastern Atlantic. Figure is redrawn and modified from Kensley [1981].

Gennadas gilchristi, a species typically found in the Agulhas Basin and the southwest Indian Ocean, as well as the occurrence of the Indo-Pacific decapod Platypodia granulosa on Walters Shoal. According to Kensley's [1981] model, "the westward-flowing North and South Equatorial currents could bring the larval planktonic or pelagic forms toward the East African coast, both north and south of Madagascar." The southern portion of these currents would thus pass near or over Walters Shoal (Fig. 6), while the southernmost component might reach Vema as well as areas of southwestern Africa. Although Kensley [1981] proposes the transport of "larval planktonic or pelagic forms", adults and non-pelagic stages may also be distributed by currents.

One possible means of dispersal is by attachment of adult or larval phases to floating objects, to pelagic organisms, to birds' feet, or to man-made structures (e.g. in the ballast tanks or on the hulls of ships) [Hertlein and Emerson, 1953; Emerson, 1967]. This mechanism may account for the presence of the brooding starfish, Leptasterias hexactis, and the egg-laying gastropod, Searlesia dira, on Cobb Seamount [Birkeland, 1971]. Neither of these species has a planktonic stage in its life history, but Nereocystis, a subtidal phaeophyte which often breaks free from the substrate [Ricketts et al., 1968], and driftwood were observed floating over the crest of Cobb [Birkeland, 1971]. Leptasterias is known to crawl over kelp in pursuit of prey [Birkeland, 1971], thus the possibility of being carried to Cobb on a mat of Nereocystis exists. This "floating raft" mechanism of dispersal may be important in the distribution of species which lack planktonic stages in their life histories.

Endemism and speciation. Determining the extent of speciation on seamounts is difficult. Although consideration of the number of endemic species may offer a clue, there remains the problem of knowing whether an endemic species has evolved in situ as a result of isolation or is a "relict" of a species that was once widespread but which is now restricted to one seamount or a group of seamounts. This possibility was discussed above for C. acanthopoma but there are other cases. For example, the barnacle genus Scillalepas is now confined to deep continental areas, ridges (Mid-Atlantic Ridge) or plateaus (e.g., Walters Shoal in the Indian Ocean), but was formerly widespread in the shallow seas of the late Mesozoic [Newman, 1980]. One does not know whether the species on Walters Shoal was left there, or speciated there.

Although an estimate of endemism might put an upper limit on the extent of speciation, there are at least two potential sources of error in determining this figure. The first is that some species reported as seamount endemics may actually exist in unsampled areas or in unreported collections, as with the batfish Halieutopsis n. sp. mentioned above. The second is that some species reported as new seamount endemics are later found to be previously known species with much wider distributions, as with the two Foetroepus species of Nakabo et al. [1983] from two Emperor seamounts which have since been referred to the synonymy of

Synchiropus altivelis, an Indo-West Pacific dragonet fish [Fricke, 1983]. Since little effort was made to verify the current taxonomic standing of each newly reported species, both sources of error are present in our estimate of seamount endemism, which is 11.6% for fishes and 15.4% for invertebrates, based on the number of new species minus those now known to be otherwise.

One measure of potential speciation is population differentiation between seamounts or between seamounts and continental shelves. Few authors have attempted this kind of study. Grasshoff [1972a] found important variation between populations of the horny coral, *Ellisella flagellum*, on Josephine and Great Meteor seamounts. *E. flagellum* on Great Meteor were larger, lacked the color variation and had a different composition of spicule types than on Josephine. These differences were attributed to genetic divergence rather than the presence of ecophenotypes.

Different morphotypes of the frostfish, *Lepidopus caudatus*, which has an antitropical distribution in the eastern Atlantic, are present on different northeastern Atlantic seamounts [Mikhyalin, 1977]. Gettysburg Seamount supports the southern morphotype whereas Dacia and the Azores seamounts support the northern. In discussing this observation, Rosenblatt and Wilson [1987] suggested that two frostfish species occur in the northeastern Atlantic, since differences distinguishing northern- and southern-type *L. caudatus* were being maintained in sympatry. However, it is not clear how important geographic isolation between seamounts may have been in this speciation process.

Using discriminant function analysis, Ehrich [1977] discovered significant morphometric variation between seamount and shelf populations of three fishes present on Great Meteor Seamount and the West African shelf: *Antigonia capros* (Caproidae), *Capros aper* (Caproidae) and *Callionymus phaeton* (Callionymidae). He favored the explanation that this divergence resulted from relative genetic isolation of the seamount populations rather than from ecophenotypic variation, arguing that larvae recruiting to Great Meteor would originate primarily from adults on the seamount itself. A similar comparison between populations of the snipefish, *Macrorhamphosus scolopax*, revealed comparatively little variation between Great Meteor and shelf populations. This lack of divergence was attributed to reduced isolation as a result of the long pelagic larval phase in *M. scolopax*.

In conclusion, we refer once again to the questions posed by Hubbs [1959]. Clearly, there is fair diversity of species present on seamounts, ranging from protists to fishes and numbering over 1000 species by our present count which is drawn from few seamounts. Some species probably have used seamounts as "stepping stones" for the transgression of oceanic regions, but there is no direct evidence of it and the extent to which this may have occurred is uncertain. Although it seems that dispersal via both passive (drifting) and active (swimming) is how most species have become established on seamounts, recency of this dispersal is not necessarily implied. Successful dispersals might have occurred during prior geographic configurations and survived to present times. Seamounts probably do facilitate speciation through isolation, but the degree to which it occurs is still difficult to assess.

Acknowledgements. We thank John C. Briggs of the University of South Florida, St. Petersburg, Florida, William A. Newman, Richard H. Rosenblatt and Kenneth L. Smith, Jr. of the Scripps Institution of Oceanography, La Jolla, California, and four referees for reading an earlier draft of this manuscript and making many useful comments. The manuscript benefitted considerably from discussions of biogeography with William A. Newman, but any errors of fact or interpretation contained herein are solely those of the authors. We also thank Lisa A. Levin of North Carolina State University, Raleigh, North Carolina, for sharing her unpublished data on specimens from eastern Pacific seamounts. This work was completed during tenure as an NSF postdoctoral fellow at the Scripps Institution of Oceanography while on leave of absence from the University of South Florida, St. Petersburg, Florida (RRW). RSK acknowledges support from K. L. Smith, Scripps Institution of Oceanography.

References

Abe, T. and W. N. Eschmeyer, A new species of the scorpionfish genus *Helicolenus* from the north Pacific Ocean, *Proc. Calif. Acad. Sci.*, 34, 47-53, 1972.

Allison, E. C., J. W. Durham, and L. W. Mintz, New southeast Pacific echinoids, *Occ. Pap. Calif. Acad. Sci.*, 62, 1-23, 1967.

Barnes, R. D., *Invertebrate Zoology*, Fourth Ed., W.B. Saunders, Philadelphia, 1089 pp., 1980.

Barsukov, V. V. and V. V. Fedorov, Species of the genus *Hozukius* (Scorpaenidae, Sebastinae) from the guyots of the Hawaiian submarine ridge, *J. Ichthyol.*, 15, 869-875, 1975.

Bartsch, I., Halacaridae (Acari) von der Josephinebank und der Grossen Meteorbank aus dem ostlichen Nordatlantik. I. Die Halacaridae aus den Schleppnetzproben, "Meteor" *Forsch. Reihe D*, 13, 37-46, 1973a.

Bartsch, I., Halacaridae (Acari) von der Josephinebank und der Grossen Meteorbank aus dem ostlichen Nordatlantik. II. Die Halacaridae aus den Bodengreiferproben, "Meteor" *Forsch. Reihe D*, 15, 51-78, 1973b.

Bartsch, I., *Copidognathus raekor*, eine neue Halacaride (Acari) von der Grossen

Meteorbank, "Meteor" Forsch. Reihe D, 16, 65-68, 1973c.

Berrisford, C. D., Biology and zoogeography of the Vema seamount: a report on the first biological collection made on the summit, Trans. Roy. Soc. S. Afr., 38, 387-398, 1969.

Birkeland, C., Biological observations on Cobb seamount, Northwest Sci., 45, 193-199, 1971.

Borets, L. A., Ichthyofauna of the Northwestern and Hawaiian submarine ranges, J. Ichthyol., 26, 1-13, 1986.

Briggs, J. C., The east Pacific barrier and the distribution of marine shore fishes, Evolution, 15, 545-554, 1961.

Briggs, J. C., Marine Zoogeography, McGraw-Hill, New York, 475 pp., 1974.

Britaev, T. A., Two new species of commensal polynoids (Polychaeta, Polynoidae) and bibliography on polychaetes, symbionts of Coelenterata, Zool. Zh., 60, 817-824, 1981.

Cairns, S. D., Antarctic and subantarctic Scleractinia, Ant. Res. Ser., 34, 1-74, 1982a.

Cairns, S. D., A new subfamily of operculate stylasterine (Coelenterata: Hydrozoa) from the subantarctic, J. Nat. Hist., 16, 71-82, 1982b.

Diehl, M., Die neue, okologisch Extreme Sand-Ascidie von der Josephinebank: Seriocarpa rhizoides Diehl 1969 (Ascidiacea, Styelidae), "Meteor" Forsch. Reihe D, 7, 43-58, 1970.

Dolganov, V. N., A new shark from the family Squalidae caught on the Nazca Submarine Ridge, Zool. Zh., 63, 1589-1591, 1984 (In Russian, English summary).

Duhamel, G., Ichtyofaune d'un haut-fond (34°54'S, 53°14'E) de l'ocean Indien sudouset, Cybium, 8, 91-94, 1984.

Ehrich, S., Die Fischfauna der Grossen Meteorbank, "Meteor" Forsch. Reihe D, 25, 1-23, 1977.

Ekman, S. Zoogeography of the Sea, Sidgwick and Jackson, London, 417 pp., 1953.

Emerson, W. K., Indo-Pacific faunal elements in the tropical eastern Pacific, with special reference to the mollusks, Venus, Jap. J. Malacol., 25, 85-93, 1967.

Emschermann, P., Loxomespilon perezi- Ein Entoproctenfund im Mittelatlantik. Uberlegungen zur Benthosbesiedlung der Grossen Meteorbank, Mar. Biol., 9, 51-62, 1971.

Eschmeyer, W. N. and J. C. Hureau, Sebastes mouchezi, a senior synonym of Helicolenus tristanensis, with comments on Sebastes capensis and zoogeographical considerations, Copeia, 1971, 576-579, 1971.

Eschmeyer, W. N., T. Abe and S. Nakano, Adelosebastes latens, a new genus and species of scorpionfish from the North Pacific Ocean (Pisces, Scorpaenidae), U O, 30, 77-84, 1979.

Fricke, R., Revision of the Indo-Pacific genera and species of the dragonet family Callionymidae, Thes. Zool., 3, 1-774, 1983.

Fricke, R., Protogrammus, a new genus of callionymid fishes, with a redescription of P. sousai from the eastern Atlantic., Jap. J. Ichthyol., 32, 294-298, 1985.

Fujii, E., Zoogeographical features of fishes in the vicinity of seamounts, In: Uchida, R. N., S. Hayasai and G. W. Boehlert (eds.), Environment and resources of seamounts in the North Pacific, U. S. Depart. Commer. NOAA Tech. Rep. NMFS, 43, 67-69, 1986.

Genin, A., P. K. Dayton, P. F. Lonsdale, and F. Spiess, Corals on seamount peaks provide evidence of current acceleration over deep-sea topography, Nature, 322, 59-61, 1986.

Grasshoff, M., Infraspezifische Variabilitat und isolierte Populationen der Hornkoralle Ellisella flagellum (Cnidaria: Anthozoa: Gorgonaria)- Auswerte der "Atlantische Kuppenfahrten 1967" von F.S. "Meteor", "Meteor" Forsch. Reihe D, 10, 65-72, 1972a.

Grasshoff, M., Die Gorgonaria des ostlichen Nordatlantik und des Mittelmeeres. I. die Familie Ellisellidae (Cnidaria: Anthozoa)-Auswertung der "Atlantischen Kuppenfahrten 1967" von F.S. "Meteor", "Meteor" Forsch. Reihe D, 10, 73-87, 1972b.

Grigg, R. W., A. Malahoff, E. H. Chave and J. Landahl, Seamount oceanography: benthic ecology and potential environmental impact from manganese crust mining in Hawaii, In: this volume, 1987.

Habe, T., A new Fusitriton from the Emperor Seamounts in the North Pacific, Venus, Jap. J. Malacol., 38, 79-81, 1979.

Hamilton, E. L., Sunken islands of the mid-Pacific Mountains, Geol. Soc. Amer., Memoir, 64, 1-97, 1956.

Heezen, B. C. and M. Tharp, World Ocean Floor (Map), United States Navy, Office of Naval Research, 1977.

Hertlein, L. G. and W. K. Emerson, Mollusks from Clipperton Island (eastern Pacific) with the description of a new species of gastropod, Trans. San Diego Soc. Nat. Hist., 11, 345-364, 1953.

Herlinveaux, R. H., Oceanographic features of and biological observations at Bowie seamount, Fish. Res. Bd Can. Tech. Rep., 273, 1-35, 1971.

Hesthagen, I., On the near-bottom plankton and benthic invertebrate fauna of the Josephine Seamount and the Great Meteor Seamount, "Meteor" Forsch. Reihe D, 8, 61-70, 1970.

Heydorn, A. E., The South Atlantic rock lobster Jasus tristani at Vema Seamount, Gough Island and Tristan da Cunha, S. Afr. Div. Sea Fish. Inves. Rep., 73, 1-20, 1969.

Hubbs, C. L., Initial discoveries of fish faunas on seamounts and offshore banks in the eastern Pacific, Pac. Sci., 13, 311-316, 1959.

Hughes, S. E., Initial exploration of nine Gulf of Alaska seamounts and their associated fish and shellfish resources, Mar. Fish. Rev., 43, 26-33, 1981.

Humphreys, R. L., Jr., D. T. Tagami and M. P. Seki, Seamount fishery resources within the southern Emperor-Northern Hawaiian Ridge area, Proc. Res. Inv. NWHI, 1, 283-327, 1984.

Jackson, E. D., I. Koisumi, G. B. Dalrymple, D. A. Clague, R. J. Kirkpatrick and H. G. Greene, Introduction and summary of results from DSDP Leg 55, the Hawaiian-Emperor hotspot experiment, In: Jackson, E. D. et al. (eds.), Initial reports of the deep-sea drilling project, 55, 5-31, Washington, D. C., U. S. Gov. Print. Off., 1980.

Kanayama, T., Scorpaenid fishes from the Emperor Seamount Chain, Res. Inst. N. Pac. Fish. Hokkaido Univ., Spec. Vol., 119-129, 1981.

Kensley, B., Decapod and isopod crustaceans from the west coast of southern Africa, including seamounts Vema and Tripp, Ann. S. Afr. Mus., 83, 13-32, 1980.

Kensley, B., On the zoogeography of Southern African decapod crustacea, with a distributional checklist, Smithson. Contri. Zool., 338, 1-64, 1981.

Kotlyar, A. N., A new species of the genus Emmelichthys (Emmelichthyidae, Osteichthyes) from the southwestern [sic] part of the Pacific Ocean, Byull. Mosk. O-Va Ispyt. (Biol.), 87, 48-52, 1982a (In Russian).

Kotlyar, A. N., Polymixia yuri sp. n. (Beryciformes, Polymixiidae) from the southeast Pacific, Zool. Zh., 61, 1380-1384, 1982b (In Russian, English summary).

Levi, C., Sponges of the Vema Seamount (South Atlantic), Bull. Mus. Nat. Hist. Natur., 41, 952-973, 1969.

Levin, L. A., D. J. DeMaster, L. D. McCann, and C. L. Thomas, Effects of giant protozoans (Class: Xenophyophorea) on deep-seamount benthos, Mar. Ecol. Prog. Ser., 29, 99-104, 1986.

Littler, M. M., D. S. Littler, S. M. Blair, and J. N. Norris, Deepest known plant life discovered on an uncharted seamount, Science, 227, 57-59, 1985.

Littler, M. M., D. S. Littler, S. M. Blair and J. N. Norris, Deep-water plant from an uncharted seamount off San Salvador Island, Bahamas: distribution, abundance, and primary productivity, Deep-Sea Res., 33, 881-892, 1986.

Lonsdale, P., W. R. Normark and W. A. Newman, Sedimentation and erosion on Horizon Guyot, Bull. Geol. Soc. Amer., 83, 289-316, 1972.

Lutjeharms, J. R. and A. E. Heydorn, The rock-lobster Jasus tristani on Vema Seamount: drifting buoys suggest a possible recruiting mechanism, Deep-Sea Res. 28, 631-636, 1981.

Maul, G. E., On a new species of the genus Callionymus from the Great Meteor Seamount, (Percomorphi, Callionymidae), Bocagiana, 30, 1-8, 1972a.

Maul, G. E., On a new species of eel of the genus Gnathophis (Apodes, Congridae) from the Meteor Seamount, Bocagiana, 31, 1-7, 1972b.

Maul, G. E., The fishes taken in bottom trawls by R.V. Meteor during the 1967 seamounts cruises in the northeast Atlantic, "Meteor" Forsch. Reihe D, 22, 1-69, 1976.

McDowell, S. B., Family Halosauridae, In: Cohen, D. M. (ed.-in-chief), Fishes of the Western North Atlantic, Mem. Sears Found. Mar. Res., 1, part 6, 32-123, 1973.

McKnight, D. G., Echinoderms from Macquarie Island and the Macquarie Ridge, NZOI Rec., 4, 139-147, 1984.

Mikhaylin, S. V., The intraspecific variability of the frostfish Lepidopus caudatus, J. Ichthyol., 17, 201-210, 1977.

Millar, R. H., A collection of ascidians from the Vema Seamount, Trans. Royal Soc. S. Afr., 38, 1-21, 1968.

Millard, N. A., Hydroids of the Vema Seamount, Ann. S. Afr. Mus., 48, 489-496, 1966.

Murray, J., A summary of the scientific results of the voyage of H.M.S. Challenger, station 246 (Hess Plateau), Rep. Sci. Res. Voyage H.M.S. Challenger During the Years 1872-1876, 961-966, 1895.

Nakabo, T., Revision of the draconettidae, Japan. J. Ichthol., 28, 355-367, 1981.

Nakabo, T., E. Yamamoto, and C. Chen, Two new species of the genus Foetorepus (Callionymidae) from the Emperor Seamounts, North-central Pacific, Jap. J. Ichthyol. 29, 349-354, 1983.

Nelson, J., Fishes of the World, Second Edition, Jonh Wiley and Sons, New York, 523 pp., 1984.

Newman, W. A., A review of extant Scillaelepas (Cirripedia: Scalpellidae) including recognition of new species from the North Atlantic, Western Indian Ocean and New Zealand, Tethys, 9, 379-398, 1980.

Newman, W. A., Origin of the Hawaiian marine fauna: Dispersal and vicariance as indicated by barnacles and other organisms, Crustacean Issues, 4, 21-49, 1986.

Newman, W. A. and B. A. Foster, The rapanuian faunal district (Easter and Sala y Gomez): in search of ancient archipelagos, Bull. Mar. Sci., 33, 633-644, 1983.

Okamura, O., K. Amakoa and F. Mitani, Fishes of the Kyushu-Palau Ridge and Tosa Bay, Japan Fisheries Resource Conservation Association, Tosho Printing Co., LTD., Tokyo, 435 pp., 1982.

Pakhorukov, N. P., Preliminary list of the bathyal bottom fishes of the Rio Grande Rise, Trudy. Akad. Nauk. Inst. Okeanol. SSSR, 104, 318-331, 1976 (In Russian, English summary).

Parin, N. V., New species of the genus Draconetta and a key for the family Draconettidae (Osteichthyes), Zool. Zh., 61, 544-563, 1982 (In Russian, English summary).

Parin, N. V., Two new species of sinistral flounders (Bothidae, Pleuronectiformes) from the Nazca Ridge, Byul. Mosk. O-Va Ispyt. Prir. (Biol.), 88, 90-96, 1983 (In Russian).

Parin, N. V., Three new species of the genus Physiculus and other fishes (Moridae, Gadiformes) from the submarine seamounts of

Parin, N. V. and S. V. Mikhaylin, Lepidopus calcar, a new trichiurid fish from the Hawaiian underwater ridge, Jap. J. Ichthyol., 29, 27-30, 1982.

Penrith, M. J., The fishes of Tristan da Cunha, Gough Island and the Vema Seamount, Ann. S. Afr. Mus., 48, 523-548, 1967.

Rad, E. von, Great Meteor and Josephine Seamounts (eastern North Atlantic): Composition and origin of bioclastic sands, carbonate and pyroclastic rocks, "Meteor", Forsch. Reihe C, 19, 1-61, 1974.

Rao, M. V. and W. A. Newman, Thoracic Cirripedia from guyots of the Mid-Pacific Mountains, Trans. San Diego Soc. Nat. Hist., 17, 69-94, 1972.

Raymore, P. A., Jr, Photographic investigations on three seamounts in the Gulf of Alaska, Pac. Sci. 36, 15-34, 1982.

Rehder, R. A., The marine mollusks of Easter Island (Isla de Pascua) and Sala-y-Gomez, Smith. Contr. Zool., 289, 1-167, 1980.

Rehder, R. A. and H. S. Ladd, Deep and shallow-water mollusks from the central Pacific, Tohoku Univer. Sci. Rep., 6, 37-51, 1973.

Rice, A. L. and D. I. Williamson, Planktonic stages of Crustacea Malacostraca from Atlantic seamounts, "Meteor" Forsch. Reihe D, 26, 28-64, 1977.

Ricketts, E. F., J. Calvin and J. W. Hedgpeth, Between Pacific Tides, Fourth Ed., Stanford University Press, Stanford, 614 pp., 1968.

Rosenblatt, R. H. and R. R. Wilson, Jr, Cutlassfishes of the genus Lepidopus with two new eastern Pacific species, Jap. J. Ichthyol., 33, 1987 (in press).

Rosenblatt, R. H., J. E. McCosker, and I. Rubinoff, Indo-West Pacific fishes from the Gulf of Chiriqui, Panama, Contr. Sci. Nat. Hist. Mus. Los Angeles Co., 234, 1-18, 1972.

Rotondo, G. M., V. G. Springer, G. A. Scott and S. O. Schlanger, Plate movement and island integration- a possible mechanism in the formation of endiemic biotas with special reference to the Hawaiian Islands, Syst. Zool., 30, 12-21, 1981.

Scagel, R. F., Benthic algae of Bowie Seamount, Syesis, 3, 15-16, 1970.

Schwartz, M. L. and K. L. Lingbloom, Research submersible reconnaissance of Cobb Seamount, Geology, 1, 31-32, 1973.

Scott, G. A. and G. M. Rotondo, A model to explain the differences between Pacific Plate island-atoll types, Coral Reefs, 1, 139-150, 1983.

Shcherbachev, Y. N., E. I. Kukuev, and V. I. Shlibanov, Composition of the benthic and demersal ichthyocenoses of the submarine mountains in the southern part of the North Atlantic range, J. Ichthyol., 25, 110-125, 1985.

Sieg, J., A new species of the genus Paratanais (Crustacea- Tanaidacea), P. spinanotandus, from Seamount Vema, Proc. Biol. Soc. Wash., 94, 1271-1278, 1981.

Simpson, E. S. and A. E. Heydorn, Vema Seamount, Nature, 207, 249-251, 1965.

Small, G. J., A review of the bathyal fish genus Antimora (Moridae: Gadiformes), Proc. Calif. Acad. Sci., 42, 341-348, 1981.

Smith, K. L., Metabolism of two dominant epibenthic echinoderms in the Santa Catalina Basin, Mar. Biol., 72, 249-256, 1983.

Solomon-Raju, N. and R. H. Rosenblatt, New records of a parasitic eel, Simenchelys parasiticus, from the central North Pacific with notes on its metamorphic form, Copeia, 1971, 312-313, 1971.

Somerton, D. A., Fusitriton oregonensis from the Patton Seamount in the Gulf of Alaska, Veliger, 24, 185-186, 1981.

Springer, V. G., Pacific plate biogeography, with special reference to shorefishes, Smithson. Contri. Zool., 367, 1-182, 1982.

Thiel, H., Bericht uber die Benthosuntersuchungen wahrend der "Atlantischen Kuppenfahrten 1967" von F.S. "Meteor", "Meteor" Forsch. Reihe D, 7, 23-42, 1970.

Uchida, R. N. and D. T. Tagami, Groundfish fisheries and research in the vicinity of seamounts in the North Pacific Ocean, Mar. Fish. Rev., 46, 1-17, 1984.

Weigmann, R., Untersuchungen zum Vorkommen der Euphausiaceen (Crustacea) im Beriech der Grossen Meteorbank, "Meteor" Forsch. Reihe D, 17, 17-32, 1974.

Wilson, R. R., Jr and R. S. Waples, Distribution, morphology and biochemical genetics of Coryphaenoides armatus and C. yaquinae (Pisces:Macrouridae) in the central and eastern North Pacific, Deep-Sea Res., 30, 1127-1145, 1983.

Wilson, R. R., Jr, K. L. Smith, Jr and R. H. Rosenblatt, Megafauna associated with bathyal seamounts in the central North Pacific Ocean, Deep-Sea Res., 32, 1243-1254, 1985.

Woods, L. P. and P. M. Sonada, Order Berycomorphi (Beryciformes), In: Cohen, D. M., Fishes of the Western North Atlantic, Mem. Sears Found. Mar. Res., 1, part 6, 263-396, 1973.

Yabe, M., A new cottoid fish of the family Ercuniidae, Marukawichthys pacificus, from the central North Pacific, Japan. J. Ichthyol., 30, 18-26, 1983.

Zevina, G. B., The cirripedia from peaks of the Nazca ridge mountains (Pacific Ocean), Zool. Zh., 62, 1635-1642, 1983 (In Russian, English summary).

Zullo, V. A., R. F. Kaar, J. W. Durham, and E. C. Allison, The echinoid genus Salenia in the eastern Pacific, Paleontology, 7, 331-349, 1964.

Zullo, V. A. and W. A. Newman, Thoracic cirripedia from a southeast Pacific guyot, Pac. Sci., 18, 355-372, 1964.

SEAMOUNT BENTHIC ECOLOGY AND POTENTIAL ENVIRONMENTAL IMPACT FROM MANGANESE CRUST MINING IN HAWAII

Richard W. Grigg

Hawaii Institute of Marine Biology, University of Hawaii, Honolulu, HI 96822

A. Malahoff and E. H. Chave

Department of Oceanography, University of Hawaii, Honolulu, HI 96822

J. Landahl

National Marine Fisheries Service, NOAA, Seattle, WA 98111

Abstract. The benthic megafauna on Cross Seamount (18°40'N and 158°17'W) is characterized by patterns of low diversity and abundance. Various factors that might account for this include geographic isolation, small habitat area and unfavorable environmental conditions. The seamount is isolated both geographically and due to weak surrounding bottom currents. Small habitat area in combination with isolation, may restrict colonization of the seamount to species that produce only long-lived larvae. The progeny of such species, would in turn be expected to be swept away before settling, resulting in parent populations low in abundance. Unfavorable environmental conditions including sluggish bottom currents may also reduce recruitment by failing to maintain substrata free of sediment. Highest population densities were found concentrated on large rocky outcrops and summit rim areas probably subjected to accelerated water flow. In zones characterized by thick ferromanganese crust deposits, patterns of abundance were particularly low suggesting the possibility of larval avoidance of such areas. The dominant faunal elements are gorgonian corals and solitary anemones. Two species of precious coral were discovered although neither in commercial abundance. The low biotic diversity and abundance and commercial insignificance of the benthic megafauna on Cross Seamount suggests that environmental impacts produced by manganese crust mining operations in this region of the Hawaiian EEZ would be minimal to this portion of the biota. Further study is needed to better ascertain the abundances of bottom commercial fishes and crustacean resources as well as pelagic species and the extent of potential impact to these organisms from crust mining.

Copyright 1987 by the American Geophysical Union.

Introduction

Although seamounts are one of the most abundant features on the floor of the deep ocean, surprisingly little is known about their biological oceanography [Genin et al. 1986; Genin and Boehlert, 1985; Boehlert, 1985; Roden and Taft, 1985; Wilson et al. 1985; Roden et al. 1982]. Over 10,000 seamounts have been charted in the Pacific Ocean alone [Menard, 1964]. Clearly numerous scientific problems exist, both basic and applied, which are in need of more research. Some of the most important include: 1) identifying seamount resource potential - both fisheries and metalliferous crust deposits; 2) understanding patterns of zonation of the benthos and causative factors; 3) assessing potential environmental impacts of crust mining on the biota of seamounts in the EEZ of the United States (200 mile Exclusive Economic Zone); 4) determining the effects of seamounts on oceanographic processes of surrounding waters, particularly currents, and the distribution of nutrients, plankton and fish populations; 5) understanding the zoogeographic importance of seamounts as "stepping stones" in the dispersal of deep-sea communities; and 6) identifying the origin and geochronology of seamounts and the paleoceanography of their overlying waters.

In this paper, which is a report on the results of an intensive biogeological reconnaissance of Cross Seamount in the Hawaiian 200 mile Exclusive Economic Zone (Figure 1), various aspects of the above problems are considered. The primary objective of the reconnaissance was to describe patterns of distribution and abundance of the benthic biota on Cross Seamount for the purpose of: 1) evaluating biological resource potential; 2) determining potential environmental impacts of cobalt-rich ferromanganese crust mining should future economics

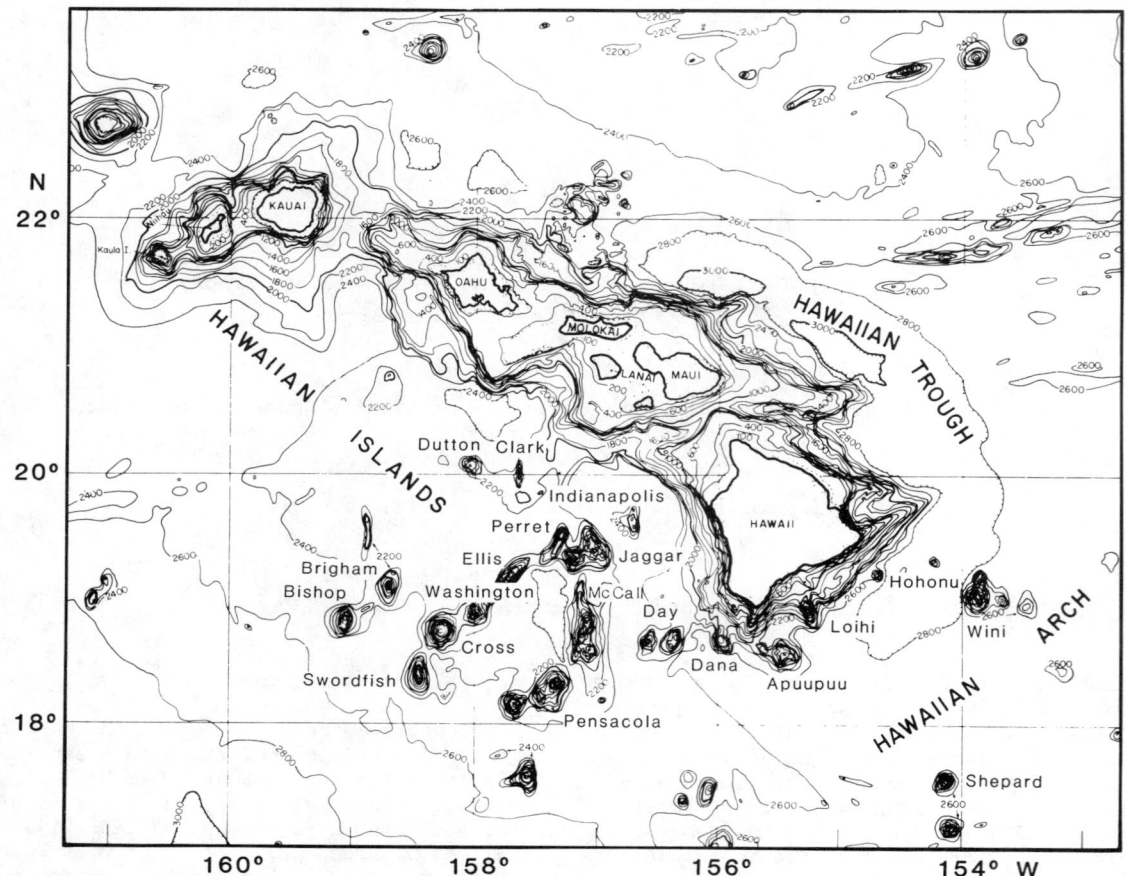

Fig. 1. Map of the major Hawaiian Islands and West Hawaiian seamounts.

create the demand for certain strategic metals; 3) identifying major factors controlling the abundance of megafaunal benthic populations; and 4) determining the zoogeographic implications of the abundance and diversity of the benthic megafauna. The geophysical history, chronology and paleoceanography of Cross Seamount were also studied but will be reported on in a companion paper.

Description of the Site

Cross Seamount is situated 250 km almost due south of the island of Oahu in the Hawaiian Archipelago at 18°40'N and 158°17'W (Figure 1). It is one of 13 seamounts collectively referred to as the Hawaiian or west Hawaiian seamounts. All are situated "off axis" to the ridge, meaning their origin appears to be independent of the Hawaiian hot-spot. Research concurrent with this study suggests that Cross Seamount formed about 80 million years ago at or near the crest of an ancestral East Pacific Rise [Malahoff et al. 1985]. Since formation, the seamount has drifted northwest about 8000 km due to movement of the Pacific Plate. The summit depth (350 m) and its flat surface morphology (5.5 km^2) indicate a history of truncation by wave erosion at sea level followed by a long period of vertical subsidence and then more recent uplift associated with movement over the Hawaiian swell. The presence of rounded cobbles, boulders, and eroded talus interspersed between thin deposits of sand on the summit support this interpretation. To date, no limestone or reefal deposits of any kind have been found on the summit or sides. The only exception to the otherwise flattened surface morphology of the summit is a cluster of 20- to 30-meter high basalt dikes near the eastern edge of the seamount top (see Figure 3). The flanks of the seamount consist of alternating ridges and valleys which slope at first steeply and then more gradually to a depth of 4000 meters. The valleys contain an abundance of talus, indicative of significant past mass wasting [Malahoff, 1985].

Methods

Patterns of distribution and abundance of the benthic biota of Cross Seamount were studied using bottom photography and several methods of dredging. For bottom photography, a camera sled tethered by

TABLE 1. Depth and Position of Camera Transects and Dredge Hauls

	Depth (m)		Position	
No.	Beginning	End	Beginning	End

Transect

I	415	2400	18°42.5', 158°17.5°	18°37.4', 158°19.0'
II	410	1650	18°43.5', 158°16.0'	18°46.5', 158°15.0'
III	385	~3400	18°43.0', 158°16.0'	18°50.0', 158°14.0'
IV	2100	3000	18°15.0', 158°47.5'	18°49.5', 158°15.2'
V	1500	3800	18°43.0', 158°20'	18°43.0', 158°25.0'
VI	410	650	18°42.0', 158°17.5'	18°41.5', 158°19.0'
VII	370	800	18°43.5', 158°16.0'	18°43.5', 158°14.6'
VIII	390	~3500	18°42.0', 158°16.5'	18°40.0', 158°9.6'
IX	380	~3200	18°43.'0, 158°16.0'	158°22.5', 18°44.5'

Coral Tangle

1	445	560	18°41.3', 158°18.0'	-
2	700	1000	18°39.1', 158°18.7'	-
3	390	420	18°43.0', 158°15.0'	18°43.5, 158°16.0'
4	3300	3300	18°50.1', 158°8.8'	18°48.7, 158°11.2'
5	1325	1800	18°48.0', 158°13.0'	18°47', 158°14.1'
6	530	600	18°44.7', 158°16.2'	18°44.4', 158°16.4'
7	390	500	18°42.0', 158°16.0'	18°41.6', 158°18.2'
8	1800	1900	18°42.8, 158°20.5'	18°41.7', 158°19.3'
9	465	465	18°43.5', 158°17.7'	18°42.8', 158°18.9'
10	430	465	18°43.6', 158°16.7'	18°43.2', 158°18.4'
11	1400	1400	18°41.3', 158°11.5	18°41.3', 158°11.5'
12	500	585	18°42.0', ?	18°42', ?
13	1275	1650	18°41.0', 158°13.0'	18°42.2', 158°11.9'
14	410	420	18°42.2', 158°14.6'	18°42.2', 158°14.6'
15	900	925	18°43.2', 158°12.81'	18°43.5, 158°12.7'

Rock Dredge

1	1750	2125	18°39', 158°19.5	18°38.5, 158°19.0'
2	1850	2100	18°47.0', 158°14.0'	18°47.0', 158°15.0'
3	350	385	18°43.5', 158°16.0'	18°43.0', 158°16.5'
4	350	450	18°43.0', 158°16.0'	18°43.0', 18°17.5'
5	600		18°44.0', 158°15.0'	-
6	900	1300	18°44.5', 158°18.0'	18°44.0', 158°19.0'
7	1000	1500	18°46.0', 158°17.0'	18°45.2', 158°17.5'
8	2550	~3200	18°46.5', 158°20.0'	18°46.5', 158°21.5'

wire to the support vessel consisting of two down-looking Benthos cameras (model #377) mounted in partial stereo with Benthos strobes (model #383) was used. A pinger (Benthos model #2216) with 12 Khz output was mounted within the sled in order to provide accoustic control of the height of the camera sled off the bottom. The dredge used for rock collection was a 1.5 ton "Preussag Mega dredge." It was deployed primarily to sample cobalt-manganese crust deposits but also proved effective in some cases for collecting large gorgonians. Tangle dredges originally designed for the harvest of precious corals, [Grigg et al. 1973] were used to collect attached macrobenthos. The coral dredges consist very simply of a metal cylinder (0.6 m long, 0.4 diam) filled with concrete and equipped with 5 pad-eyes for the attachment of tangle netting. The coral dredges are designed to ride over the bottom without hanging-up so as to cover broad areas. The weight serves to detach the macrobenthos while the nets entangle specimens.

Stations were positioned in order to provide the broadest possible coverage of Cross Seamount. Particular attention was focused on zones of known biotic abundance [400 m, Grigg and Bayer, 1976] and areas of thick Mn-crust deposits (800-2400 m). In total, 9 camera transects, 15 coral tangle hauls and rock dredge stations were successfully completed. The photo transects produced about 7800 35 mm transparencies of the bottom ranging in depth from 385 m to 3800 m. The depth range covered by the coral and rock dredges was 390-3300 m and 350-3200 m, respectively (Table 1).

The photo transects covered approximately 250,000

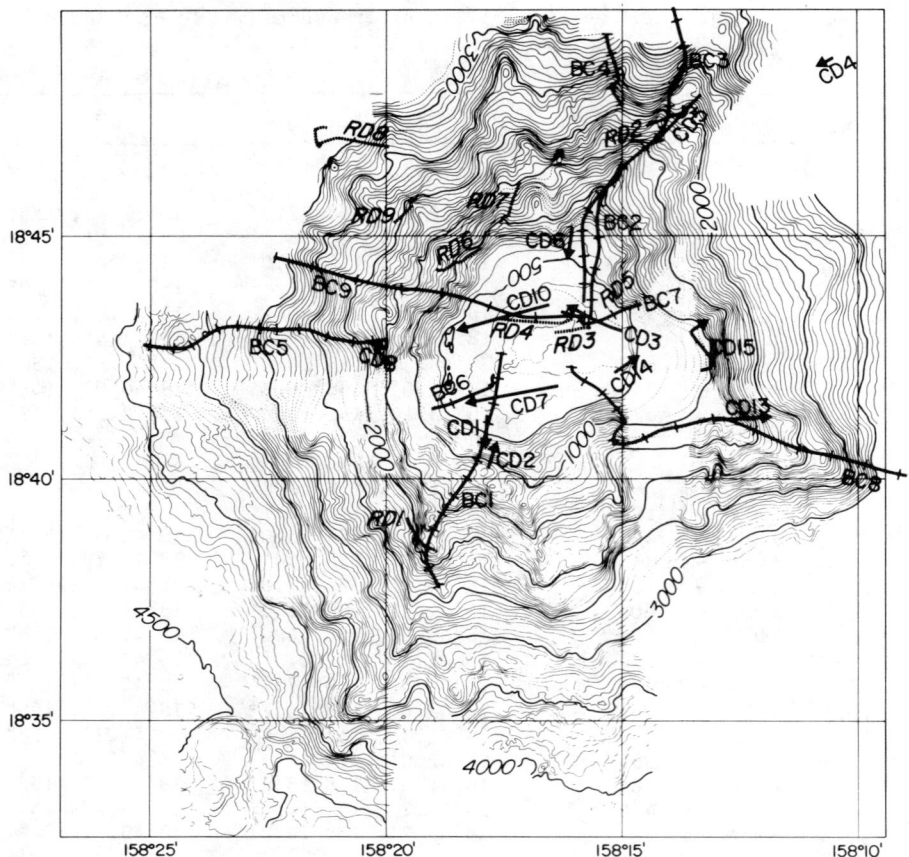

Fig. 2. Bathymetric map of Cross Seamount showing position of all photo-transects and dredge hauls.

m^2 of bottom area. The total area of bottom photographed was calculated as the sum of bottom area covered by individual pictures, each of which was determined as a function of the height of the camera off the bottom. Each slide produced was carefully analyzed for species composition, abundance and approximate size of all benthic organisms and bottom fish. The entire area on each photograph was analyzed. All measures of abundance were normalized to counts per m^2. When the camera was towed more than 6.5 meters above the substrate, biological identifications to meaningful taxonomic levels were usually not possible. Therefore, a cutoff point of 6.5 meters was selected for biological data analysis. Sediment cover was estimated as the percent of the bottom in each slide covered by sediment.

Identification of the biota in the photo-transects was aided by the contents of the coral and rock dredge hauls. The location of both coral and rock dredge hauls generally corresponded to location of photo-transect tracks (Figure 2).

A Seabeam map of Cross Seamount produced in June, 1985 by Preussag [P. Halback, pers. comm. 1985] was used to locate stations (Figure 2).

Photo-transect filmstrips were processed and analyzed aboard ship and used to select dredging stations. All camera and dredge haul data were collected between September 9-18, 1985, on board the University of Hawaii research vessel "Moana Wave." Measurements of bottom current on the summit and flanks of Cross Seamount were obtained from meters deployed between 4-4-85 and 7-17-85 by E. Noda and Associates [E. Noda and R.C.Y. Koh, E. Noda and Associates, Honolulu, Hawaii, 1985].

Results

In general, the benthic megafauna and bottom fish (unaffected by avoidance) on Cross Seamount are low in diversity and abundance (Figure 3). In total, 3,124 organisms representing 61 species were counted in 2,100 bottom photographs taken at camera heights off the bottom of 6.5 m or less. The total bottom area covered by these photographs was 22,770 m^2. The average density of all organisms, counted on these transects was 0.14 organisms per m^2. In addition to low diversity and abundance, patterns of distribution for some organisms were extremely patchy. For example, the two most abundant benthic

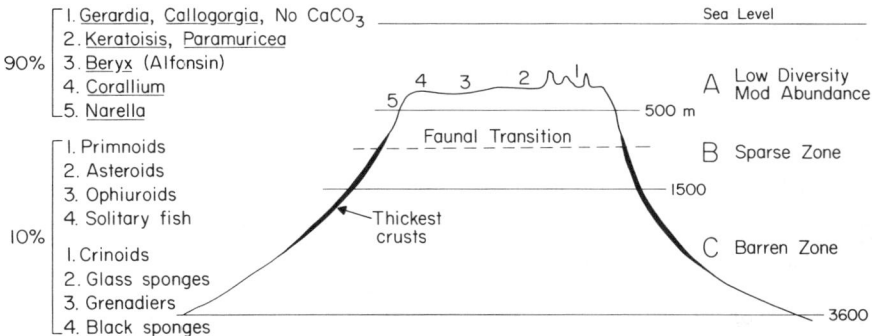

Fig. 3. Schematic cross section of Cross Seamount illustrating the truncated summit, summit dikes, the distribution and thickness of Mn-cobalt rich crusts and biotic zonation.

organisms on Cross Seamount, a solitary black anemone and a bamboo coral, Keratoisis sp., were found in dense aggregations (up to 5 m²) on the summit concentrated in the region of the basalt dikes. Both species exhibited highly clumped patterns of distribution with variance to mean ratios for abundance [Greig-Smith, 1964] ranging up to 18.5 for the black anemone ($p<0.001$), and 75.1 ($p<0.001$), for Keratoisis.

Vertical zonation was another striking pattern in the distribution of the biota (Figures 3-5). Eighty-one percent (2545 organisms) of the fauna was observed at depths shallower than 500 meters. Below 500 meters, the abundance of all organisms decreased by an order of magnitude. Between 501 and 1500 m, only 463 organisms (15%) were counted in the bottom photographs. Below 1500 meters depth, 116 or less than 4% of the total organisms counted were present. Within the range of 350-1700 meters two general zones of abundance seemed evident, one associated with the summit around 400 meters and the other between 600-1000 meters Figure 4 a-c). This pattern was found to hold for the benthic megafauna and bottom fishes although fishes were more evenly distributed with depth (Figure 4c). Bottom fishes were more than an order or magnitude less abundant than benthic invertebrate species. Considering the bottom fauna overall, no significant differences in abundance were found to exist between the north or south sides of the seamount (Figure 5a and b).

Of the 61 species groups enumerated (Table 3) the dominant faunal elements were solitary anemones and gorgonian corals. Thirteen species of gorgonians were either photographed or collected. The only fish to be observed in abundance was the alfonsin Beryx sp. Several aggregations containing over 100 individuals were seen swimming close to the bottom over the summit. In the area of the dikes near the northeastern rim of the seamount, patches of rock were observed with dense aggregations of a small but delicate and highly branched bamboo coral Keratoisis sp. On the dikes per se, large colonies of the gold corals Gerardia sp. and Callogorgia gilberti were consistently present at depths between 350-380 m (Figure 6). A similar pattern of larger than average seafans situated on bottom prominences was evident at greater depths on the seamount. For example, on Phototransect 9, an area of large outcrops near 1250 m contained very large (∼1.0 m) primnoid gorgonians (Narella sp.) (Figure 7) but was surrounded by an otherwise barren hard-ground.

Another pattern of abundance was an increase in density of gorgonians associated with the rim of the seamount. This was particularly true for the pink corals Corallium secundum and Corallium regale. Both species were most abundant along the edges of

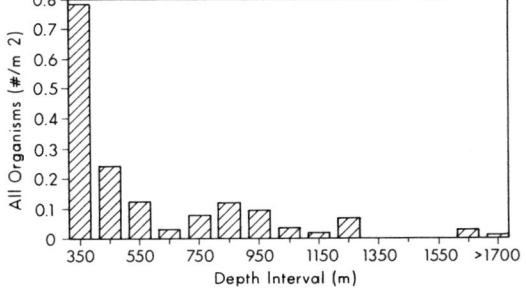

Fig. 4a. Vertical zonation of biota (all organisms) on Cross Seamount.

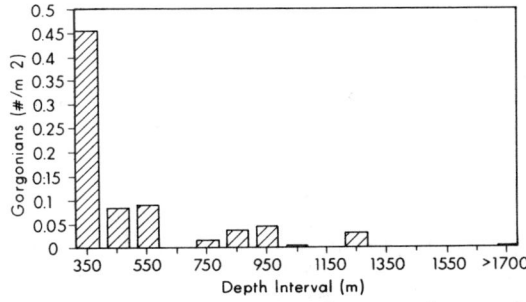

Fig. 4b. Vertical zonation of biota (gorgonians) on Cross Seamount.

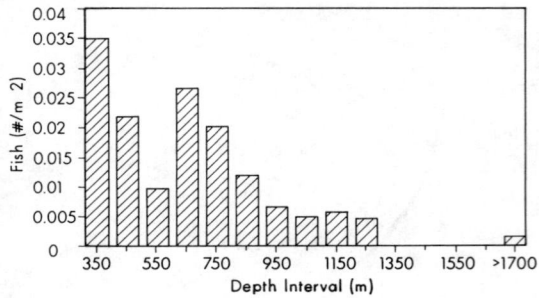

Fig. 4c. Vertical zonation of biota (fishes) on Cross Seamount.

the southwest, west and north rims. Both exhibited highly patchy patterns of distribution with variance to mean ratios of abundance greatly in excess of 1.0 (random distribution).

Organisms visible in the bottom photographs were universally more abundant on hard than soft substrata. Sediment cover on the bottom gradually increased with depth and decreasing slope. A broad apron of sediment surrounds the seamount and in some areas contains talus sheets and rubble mounds of what appears to be fragments of exfoliated crust material.

Other major faunal macrobenthic groups represented on Cross Seamount but in low abundance were echinoderms, sponges and arthropods. Echinoderms included species of the starfish genera Ceremaster, Henricia, Brissingia, and Pentagonaster, the urchin Stereocidaris sp., two feather stars (crinoids), and two sea cucumbers. Hexactanellid (glass) sponges and pandalid shrimp were solitary and rare but consistently present at depths below 1500 meters. Various other groups such as tube sponges, antipatharians, dendrophyllid corals, and sea pens were sporadically observed (see Table 3 for a complete listing).

Among the fishes, the most common groups next to alfonsins were eels (190 counted), banded fish (130) - mostly chlorophthalmids and platycephalids, and scorpaenids (56). Epigonus sp. and Owstonia sp. were occasionally observed and triglid, lophiid, polymixiid, and ateleopodid fishes were rare. At depths greater than 1000 meters only grenadier fish, eels, carapids, paralepidids and morids were observed.

Discussion

The most significant characteristic of the benthic megafauna of Cross Seamount is its relative low diversity and abundance. Even at depths of 350-500 m, where along the Hawaiian Ridge the benthos is relatively abundant and diverse [Grigg and Bayer, 1975], few species were encountered. For example, considering only gorgonians which are the most dominant faunal element on Cross Seamount, only 13 species out of a total of 93 known from deep water in Hawaii were found on Cross Seamount. Other groups appeared to be equally underrepresented [disharmonic, sensu; MacArthur and Wilson, 1967]. The abundance of all megabenthic organisms observed in all bottom photographs on Cross Seamount was only 0.14 org./m^2 (3124/22,700 m^2). This compares to an average density of 2.5 org./m^2 for all megabenthic species in the Makapuu coral bed, off Oahu, Hawaii (Hawaii Undersea Research Laboratory Voice Transcript Archive, Unpublished). This comparison, however, may not be entirely valid because the Makapuu coral bed exists within a depth zone of known high abundance. For example, of 59 species of gorgonians collected by the Sango Expedition from dredge hauls ranging in depth between 189 and 1275 m, 51 or 86% were found within the 400±100 m depth zone [Grigg and Bayer, 1976]. It is therefore important to base comparisons on comparable depth zones (e.g. 400±100 m). Using only Corallium, the pink corals, the genus for which the best information is available, the difference in average density between comparable depth zones in the two areas is about 30 (0.001 for Cross Seamount versus 0.030 for Makapuu) [Grigg, 1976, Table 4]. If Corallium is representative of the biota in general, benthic populations on Cross Seamount would appear to be at least an order of magnitude less abundant than at equivalent depths along the Hawaiian Ridge.

The mean density of the black coral, Stichopathes sp., on Jasper Seamount in the northeast Pacific (observed in 1359 bottom photographs ranging in depth between 200 and 1300 m) was 2.8 organisms/m^2 [Genin et al. 1986], 20 times more dense than all the organisms on Cross Seamount.

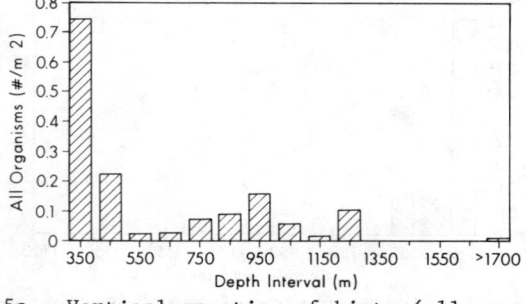

Fig. 5a. Vertical zonation of biota (all organisms) on north side of Cross Seamount.

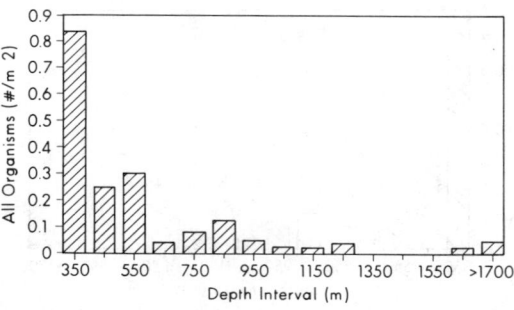

Fig. 5b. Vertical zonation of biota (all organisms) on south side of Cross Seamount.

TABLE 2. Similarities and Differences Between Cross and Jasper Seamounts

	Jasper Seamount (Genin et al, 1986)	Cross Seamount (Present paper)
Location	30°22'N, 122°43'W	18°40'N, 158°17'W
Age	?	80 MA
Diameter	30 Km	24 Km
Floor depth	4100 m	4000 m
Height off bottom	3500 m	3600 m
Summit depth	600 m	360 m
Summit type	Multi-peaked	Truncated with dikes one side
Substratum	Basalt with thin pockets of sediment	Basalt, thin sand deposits Mn-crusts 800-2400 m
Mean current summit	4.9 cm/sec	12.8 cm/sec
Current direction summit	Predominantly south	Predominantly north
Survey method	Bottom photography (1359 frames)	Bottom photography (7800 frames) dredging
Depth range surveyed	600-1400 m	350-3800 m
Most common benthic organism	*Stichopathes* sp. (black coral)	*Keratoisis* sp. bamboo coral solitary anemone
Highest coral density	Near summit, tops of pinnacles	Near summit, on dikes and rim of guyot
Correlation between benthic density and sediment cover	Negative, $p<0.01$	Negative, $p<0.01$
No. taxa identified	2	61

Fig. 6. *Gerardia* sp. and *Callogorgia gilberti* on dikes at 350-380 m depth on Cross Seamount.

Fig. 7. Large outcrops at 1240 m on Cross Seamount with colonies of primnoid gorgonians (Narella sp.).

Other similarities and differences between benthic communities on Cross Seamount and Jasper Seamount are given in Table 2. The dominant faunal elements at each site consist of various species of anthozoa [Grigg and Bayer, 1976; Genin et al. 1986; also see Kukenthal, 1924 and Nutting, 1908, 1910-11]. On both seamounts, the highest densities of benthic organisms were near the summits, particularly on large rocky prominences. A strong negative correlation between abundance and sediment cover exists on both seamounts.

Various factors may play a role in accounting for the low diversity and sparse abundance patterns of benthic populations on Cross Seamount. First, Cross Seamount, situated about 160 km south of the Hawaiian Ridge, is relatively isolated from the Hawaiian Chain and other seamounts at comparable depths. Bottom current may further isolate the seamount in terms of larval settlement. Progressive vector diagrams for currents measured on the summit and flank of Cross Seamount suggest that water flow at the bottom is consistently to the

TABLE 3. Species Groups Identified From Photographs and Dredge Hauls on Cross Seamount

Phylum	Class or Order	Family or Species	Depth	Method Recorded*
Profera	C. Hexactanellida	Unidentified species 1	700-1600	CD
		Unidentified species 2	530-600	CD
	C. Demospongiae	Unidentified species 1	530-600	CD
Cnidaria	O. Gorgonacea	Corallium secundum	390-500	CD,P
		Corallium regale	390-500	CD,P
		Acanthogorgia sp.	445-485	CD
		Paramuricea hawaiiensis	330-1100	CD
		Pseudothesea sp.	400-450	CD
		Paracis miyajimai	400-450	CD
		Lepidisis sp.	1200-1600	CD
		Keratoisis sp.	375-420	CD
		Callogorgia gilberti	380	RD
		Narella sp. 1	445-485	CD,P
		Narella sp. 2	700-1600	CD
		Calyptrophora sp.	900-1000	CD
		Metallogorgia sp.	>1500	P

TABLE 3. (continued)

Phylum	Class or Order	Family or Species	Depth	Method Recorded*
	O. Zoantharia	Gerardia sp.	380	RD
	O. Antipatharia	Parantipathes sp.	430-465	CD
		Antipathes sp.	330-420	CP
		Cirrhipathes spiralis	330-420	CP
	O. Scleractinea	Madrepora kauaiensis	530-600	CD
		Javania lamproticum	400-465	CD
		Dendrophyllia cf. oahuensis	330-500	CD
		Enallopsammia rostrata	390-1100	CD
	O. Actinaria	Unidentified black anemone	350-1200	P
Echinodermata	C. Asteroidea	Pentagonaster ammophilus	400-500	P
		Calliastar pedicellaris	1300-1600	CD
		Ceremaster bowersi	390-500	CP,P
		Hippasterina spinosa	400-465	CD
		Henricia pauperima	330-420	CD
		Brissingia sp.	350-600	P
	C. Crinoidea	Tricometra vexator	700-1100	CD
		Naumatochrinus hawaiiensis	1134-1292	CD
	C. Ophiuroidea	Asteroschema cf. glaucum	900-1000	P,CD
		Asteroschema cf. ajax	700-1100	CD,P
		Ophiothrix sp.	330-420	CD
	C. Echinoidea	Stereocidaris hawaiiensis	445-485	CD
Arthropoda	C. Cirripedia	Lepas sp. (gooseneck barnacle)	330-420	CD
		Balanus sp. (barnacle)	330-420	CD
	C. Crustacea	Plesionika sp.	370-380	P
		Eumunida smithii	370-380	P
Chordata	C. Osteichthyes	Neomerinthe rufuscens	330-420	P,RD
		Beryx sp.	400-600	P
		Ijimaia plicatellus	400-500	P
		Chrionema chryseres	300-500	P
		C. squammiceps	300-600	P
		Chloropthalmus proridens	400-600	P
		Neopercis roseoviridis	300-500	P
		Epigonus glossodontis	400-500	P
		Macrouridae	692-2216	P
		Unidentified species 1		
		Unidentified species 2		
		Lophiomus miacanthus	400-600	P
		Moridae	300-600	
		Unidentified species 1		
		Unidentified species 2		
		Unidentified species 3		
		Owstonia sp.	300-600	P
		Polymixia berndti	400-500	P
		Paralepadidae	1055-2032	P
		Carapidae	1055-2032	P
		Scorpaenidae	300-500	P
		Triglidae	398-412	P
		Congridae	400-1350	P
	C. Chondrichthyes	Squalus sp.	1175-1186	P

*P = Photograph
RD = Rock dredge
CD = Coral dredge

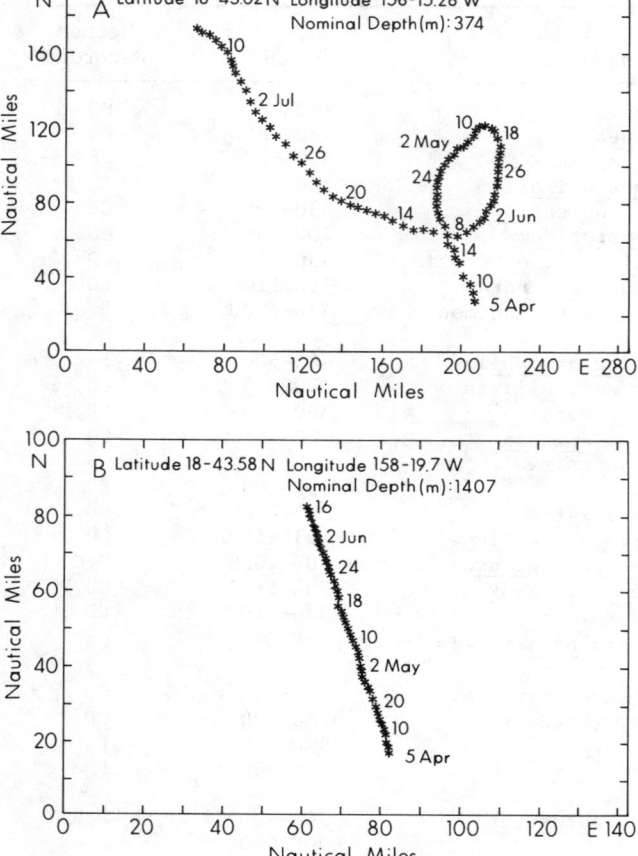

Fig. 8. Progressive vector diagrams of bottom currents at 384 m (top) and 1417 m (bottom) measured between April 5, 1985 and July 17, 1985 (top) and April 5, 1985 and June 15, 1985 (bottom). Maximum and average currents were 37.9 cm/sec and 12.8 cm/sec (top) and 28.8 cm/sec and 4.8 cm/sec (bottom) [E. Noda, Unpublished].

north or northeast (Figure 8). Given this pattern of flow, colonization would occur only from the south which is from an area almost devoid of seamounts at comparable depths for over 600 miles. That the diversity and abundance of benthic populations on Cross Seamount is not lower than observed possibly indicates that bottom currents may periodically vary in direction. Even so, the sluggish speeds of the bottom current measured on Cross Seamount (mean velocity at summit = 12.8 cm/sec. [E. Noda and R.C.Y. Koh, E. Noda and Associates, Honolulu, Hawaii, 1985], would contribute to isolating it from potential surrounding colonization sites. Bottom currents of this speed would only carry passive larvae about 70 km per week, possibly creating a selection pressure for species with long lived planktonic larvae.

Small habitat area could also be a factor causing low abundance patterns. If only species capable of producing long lived larvae successfully establish on Cross Seamount, these species in turn may fail to produce recruits that can settle before being swept away by even weak bottom currents. The combination of isolation and small habitat area should therefore favor the selection of species with longevous vagile larvae. Bottom currents on the order of those measured on Cross would be expected to carry planktonic larvae away from the seamount in about one day. Thus only species which produce short-lived larvae (<1 day) would increase in abundance due to within habitat recruitment. Hence, small isolated seamounts might generally be characterized by species which fail to self-seed. Such species would be similar to Fugitive Species in terms of dispersal capabilities [MacArthur and Wilson, 1967], but may differ by not necessarily being poor competitors. If this kind of life history phenomena does characterize most species on Cross Seamount, then low abundance patterns could well be due to the lack of positive feedback between parent populations and recruitment. Recruitment may be totally dependent on outside colonization.

Low diversity and abundance may also be a result of unfavorable environmental conditions on Cross Seamount. Bottom currents may affect settlement and growth of the benthos by controlling the number of larvae (settlement pathway) or amount of food (feeding pathway) passing a given site per unit time [Genin et al. 1986]. On Jasper Seamount in the northeastern Pacific, Genin and his co-workers (1986) found that the black coral, Stichopathes sp., is significantly more abundant on sites with accelerated flow (seamount peaks, crests and prominences). The same pattern of increased size and density of gorgonians on bottom prominences was found on Cross Seamount. Highest densities occurred at depths near the summit where measures of bottom current averaged three times greater than along the flank of the seamount at 1400 m [E. Noda and R.C.Y. Koh, E. Noda and Associates, Honolulu, Hawaii, 1985]. The "coral bed" with a very high density of gorgonians which exists off Makapuu, Oahu at 400 m depth (2.5 col/m^2) is also situated in an area of relatively strong bottom current. Bottom currents of up to 150 cm/sec have been frequently encountered in the Makapuu precious coral bed [Boh Bartko, University of Hawaii, Unpublished data, 1982]. While accelerated flow may enhance settlement and/or growth in certain restricted areas on Cross Seamount, the converse may account for sparsity of the fauna. More generally, weak bottom current may also fail to maintain substrata free of sediment, a factor known to inhibit the settlement of many invertebrates [Wilson, 1958]. A strong inverse relation between the abundance of gorgonian corals and sediment cover (Kendall Tau r = -0.73, p<0.1), was found at all depths (Figure 9), illustrating the effect of sediment cover on recruitment and/or survival. Another environmental parameter of possible significance is the presence of manganese cobalt-rich crusts at depths between

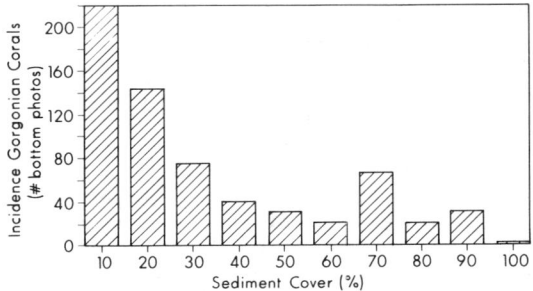

Fig. 9. Gorgonian density vs. sediment cover on Cross Seamount, all depths integrated. Kendall Tau = -0.73, p<0.01.

800 and 2400 meters on Cross Seamount. It is possible that the scarcity of megafauna at these depths is due to larval avoidance possibly caused by metal oxides or surface dwelling microbes such as foraminifera.

While the lack of biotic diversity and abundance may be negative from the standpoint of commercial resources, this characteristic may be viewed as beneficial from the standpoint of not creating potential negative environmental impacts associated with marine mining. The only species of commercial value found on Cross Seamount were the alfonsin fish, Beryx sp., the precious pink corals, Corallium secundum, and C. regale, and the gold coral, Gerardia sp. All are present in abundance too low to be of commercial importance and all exist at many other locales in the Hawaiian Archipelago. Gerardia is found Pacific wide. No species unique to Cross Seamount were observed or collected during the expedition. To the extent Cross Seamount is representative of other seamounts in the southeastern Hawaiian EEZ, these results suggest that environmental impacts to benthic megafaunal populations from mining cobalt-rich ferromanganese crusts would be negligible. This may not be true for seamounts located in the central and northern portion of the Hawaiian Archipelago where sizable beds of precious coral and large bottom fish resources are known to exist. It is also clear that more work is needed regarding the environmental effects of bottom and surface mining plumes on water column biota (plankton and fish) and primary productivity.

Summary and Conclusions

1) The diversity and abundance of the benthic biota on Cross Seamount is low relative to other hard bottom habitats at similar depths along the Hawaiian Ridge and some seamounts in the eastern Pacific.

2) Two zones of relative abundance exist on Cross Seamount, one near the summit about 400 meters depth, and the other between 600-100 meters.

3) In general, the megafaunal is more abundant and individual organisms are larger on major rock outcrops. These areas are probably subjected to accelerated water motion, suggesting a favorable effect due to current.

4) The most abundant benthic species are characterized by aggregated patterns of distribution.

5) Factors which may account for the low diversity and abundance of the benthic megafauna include: i) isolation of the seamount due to surrounding geography and bottom currents; ii) small habitat area and possible selection of species with longevous larvae not likely to self-seed; iii) unfavorable environmental conditions including weak bottom currents which may reduce recruitment and survival and fail to maintain substrata free of sediment; and iv) possible larval avoidance in zones of thick ferromanganese crusts.

6) The results of this work are of additional significance in terms of evaluating possible negative environmental impacts associated with mining cobalt-rich manganese crusts in the Hawaiian EEZ. Assuming that Cross Seamount is representative of other seamount mining sites, the sparse nature of the benthic megafauna found on Cross Seamount, particularly at depths where the crusts are thickest, reduces the potential for negative environmental impact to at least this portion of the biota. More research is needed to determine the potential impacts of mining to mobile and water column species as well as surface primary productivity.

Acknowledgements. We would like to thank the captain and crew of the research vessel "Moana Wave" for their excellent support in the field. The work was supported by grants from the National Sea Grant Program, the Office of Minerals Management (MMS) of the Department of Interior and the State Department of Planning and Economic Development, Ocean Resources Branch. The data base produced by the study was relied upon by MMS in the preparation of a draft EIS on potential crust mining in the Hawaiian EEZ. Charles Morgan coordinated the preparation of the Draft EEZ and also provided valuable assistance in the analysis of the data contained in this paper. We also thank Charles Morgan and Amatzia Genin for critically reviewing the paper.

References

Boehlert, G. W. Effects of Southeast Hancock Seamount on the pelagic ecosystem. EOS, 66(51), 1336, 1985.

Genin, A. and G. W. Boehlert. Dynamics of temperature and chlorophyll structures above a seamount: An oceanic experiment. J. Mar. Res., 43, 907-924, 1985.

Genin, A., Dayton, P. K., Lonsdale, P. F. and F. N. Spiess. Coral seamount peaks provide evidence of current acceleration over deep sea topography. Nature, 322, 59-61, 1986.

Greig-Smith, P. Quantitative plant ecology. Butterworth and Co., London, 246 pp., 1964.

Grigg, R. W. Fishery management of precious and stony corals in Hawaii. UNIHI-SEAGRANT-AR-73-01, 76 pp., 1973.

Grigg, R. W. and F. M. Bayer. Present knowledge of

the systematics and zoogeography of the Order Gorgonacea in Hawaii. Pacific Science, 30, 167-175, 1976.

Grigg, R. W., Bartko, B. and C. Brancart. A new system for the commercial harvest of precious coral. UNIHI-SEAGRANT-AR-73-01, 6 pp., 1973.

Kukenthal, W. Gorgonaria. Das Tierreich. 47, 1-0478, 1924.

Malahoff, A., Grigg, R. W., Vonderhaar, D., Kelly, K. and A. Arquit. Mass wasting and manganese crust growth on Cross Seamount, Hawaii, EOS, 66 (46), 1083-1084, 1985.

MacArthur, R. H. and E. O. Wilson. The theory of island biogeography. Monographs in population biology. Princeton University Press, Princeton, NJ, 203 pp., 1967.

Menard, H. W. Marine geology of the Pacific. Academic Press, NY, 1964.

Nutting, C. C. Descriptions of the Alcyonaria collected by the U. S. Bureau of Fisheries Albatross in the vicinity of the Hawaiian Islands in 1902. Proc. U. S. Nat. Mus. 34(1624):543-601.

Roden, G. I. and B. A. Taft. Effect of the Emperor Seamounts on mesoscale thermohaline structure during the summer of 1982. J. Geophys. Res., 90, 839-855, 1985.

Roden, G. I., B. A. Taft and C. C. Ebbesmeyer. Oceanographic aspects of the Emperor Seamounts region. J. Geophys. Res., 87, 9537-9552, 1982.

Wilson, D. P. Some problems in larval ecology related to the localized distribution of bottom animals. p. 87-104 in A. A. Buzzati-Traverso, ed. Perspectives in marine biology. U. C. Press, Berkeley and Los Angeles, 1958.

Wilson, R. W., Jr., K. L. Smith and R. H. Rosenblatt. Megafauna associated with bathal seamounts in the central North Pacific Ocean. Deep-Sea Res. 32:1243-1254, 1985.

LITHOSPHERIC THINNING UNDER THE ATLANTIS-METEOR SEAMOUNT COMPLEX (NORTH ATLANTIC)

J. Verhoef

Geological Survey of Canada, Atlantic Geoscience Center, Bedford Institute of Oceanography, PO Box 1006, Dartmouth, NS, Canada, B2Y 4A2

B. J. Collette

Vening Meinesz Laboratorium, PO Box 80.021, 3508 TA Utrecht, The Netherlands

Abstract. The Atlantis-Meteor Seamount Complex, a group of submarine volcanoes located about 700 km to the south of the Azores, was investigated on the basis of seismic, magnetic and gravity data. The depths in the area around the seamount complex are too shallow compared to the standard cooling curve for oceanic lithosphere. The free-air anomalies in the area are predominantly positive. Thermal lithospheric rejuvenation caused by the injection of heat into the lithosphere, embodied by intrusive masses, has been proposed as a unifying concept. A flexural study was carried out and resulted in estimates of the elastic thickness of the lithosphere under the various seamounts. Assuming that these values represent the lithospheric thicknesses under the seamounts at the time of loading, the ages of the seamounts are found to range from 38 to 66 Ma. This is in conflict with the Early Miocene to Late Oligocene age of the seamount complex inferred from a sediment model-study, a subsidence analysis, and two available K-Ar determinations. It is argued that the excessive ages found in the flexural study are due to the neglecting of the effect of thermal lithospheric rejuvenation on the elastic thickness of the lithosphere (lithospheric thinning). Lithospheric thinning will become evident as a decrease of the flexural rigidity and, therefore, means a resetting of the age of the lithoshere when loaded. As a result, the computed ages of the seamounts become too large. It appears that the degree of lithospheric thinning under the seamounts of the Atlantis-Meteor Seamount complex is by no means uniform.

Introduction

The Atlantis-Meteor Seamount Complex, a group of submarine volcanoes, is located some 700 km to the south of the Azores (see inset of Figure 1).

Copyright 1987 by the American Geophysical Union.

This large seamount complex was investigated on the basis of data obtained during the Kroonvlag-project [Collette et al., 1984], of results of two surveys in the area carried out in 1979 and 1980 [Verhoef and Collette, 1985], of published data, especially on Great Meteor Seamount [cf. Hinz, 1969 and Fleischer et al., 1970] and of additional gravity data obtained from the N.O.A.A. National Geophysical and Solar-Terrestrial Data Center.

Like many volcanic complexes in the oceans the Atlantis-Meteor Complex is surrounded by a positive depth anomaly, i.e. the depths in the area are too shallow compared to the standard curve for the cooling of oceanic lithosphere [Parsons and Sclater, 1977]. The area forms the southernmost part of the North Atlantic Gravity High [Cochran and Talwani, 1977 and 1978], which extends from Iceland to about $30°N$ and which comprises areas of different plate tectonic setting. In discussing the regional positive gravity anomaly of the area Cochran and Talwani [1977 and 1978] stressed the general relationship between positive depth anomalies, regional positive gravity anomalies and the occurrence of intra-plate volcanism. Detrick and Crough [1978] proposed lithospheric rejuvenation as a common link between these phenomena: the injection of heat by intrusive volcanism in the lithosphere resets the thermal clock. This would result in oceanic lithosphere appearing to be younger, i.e. the ocean floor becomes too shallow and its subsidence thereafter is faster than one would expect from the real age.

The emplacement of a volcanic load on the lithosphere causes it to deform over a broad region. The regionality of this deformation depends primarily on the effective elastic thickness of the oceanic lithosphere, estimates of which can be obtained from the observed gravity anomalies over volcanic loads. These estimates represent the elastic thickness of the lithosphere at the time the loading occurred. The results of several studies of flexure of oceanic lithosphere

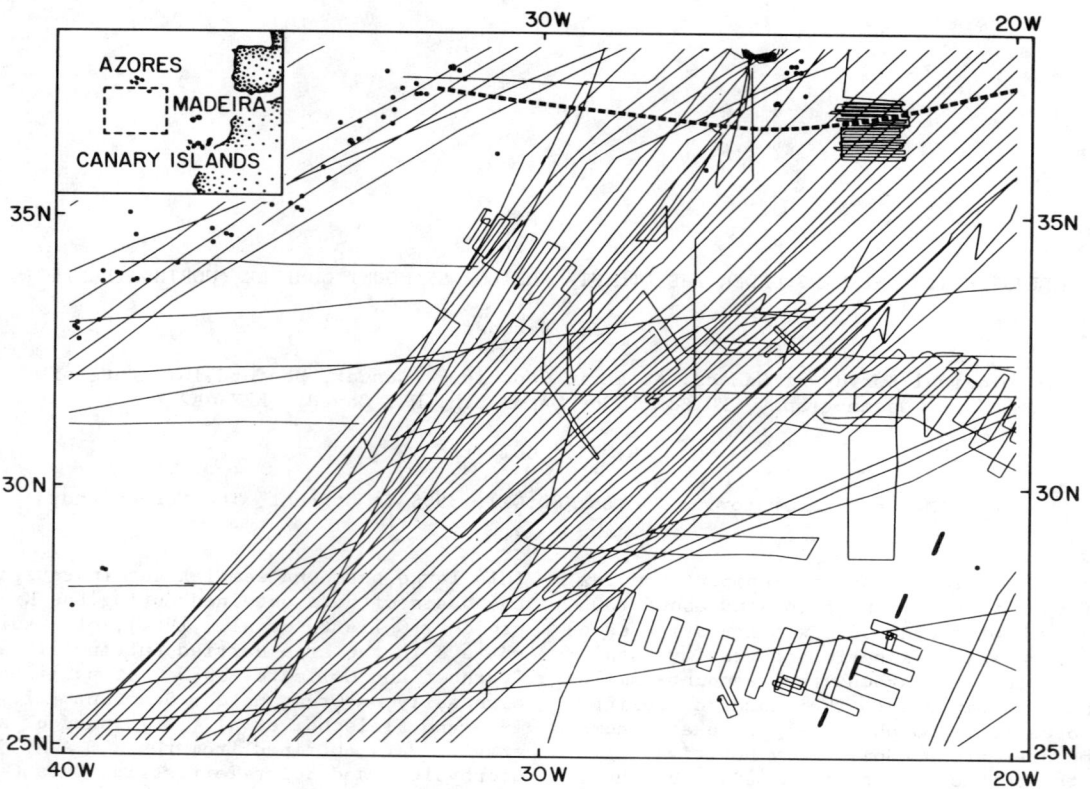

Fig. 1. Tracklines with seismic and magnetic data. The heavy dashes denote the East Azores Fracture Zone. The Mid-Atlantic Ridge is indicated by the earth-quake epicenters (solid circles).

caused by surface loads led to the suggestion that the effective elastic thickness of oceanic lithosphere increases with increasing age [e.g Watts, 1978; Watts et al., 1980; Cazenave et al., 1980; Bodine et al., 1981 and McNutt and Menard, 1982]. Therefore, it should be possible to estimate the age of a seamount from the effective elastic thickness of the lithosphere under it, using a relation proposed by Bodine et al. [1981].

The question that is relevant is whether and to what degree lithospheric rejuvenation will affect the mechanical properties of the lithosphere. Bodine et al. [1981] assume that the effects are negligible, McNutt [1984] explicitly states the contrary. If these effects are substantial, the value of age determination of seamounts based upon the computation of lithospheric thickness becomes questionable and ages obtained in this way become maximum estimates.

The present paper focuses on the conclusions that can be drawn from the study of the gravity anomalies on the state of the oceanic lithosphere under the Atlantis-Meteor Seamount Complex. We will present values for the thickness of the lithosphere under all subgroups of the Atlantis-Meteor Seamount Complex. The ages of the seamounts based on the lithospheric thickness as reflected in the gravity anomalies will be compared with other age data. It will appear that the ages as obtained from the elastic thickness are too high and, therefore, that the mechanical properties of the lithosphere are reset by the rejuvenation process, albeit not in a uniform way.

The average track spacing in the central part of the study area is about 25 km for the seismic and magnetic data (see Figure 1) and about 40 km for the gravity data (Figure 4). This data coverage is such that a three dimensional approach seems suitable, making it necessary to obtain grid values from the data. We applied a gridding algorithm that uses a digital Butterworth filter to avoid spatial aliasing [Slootweg, 1978, cf. Verhoef et al., 1986]. The cut-off wavelength of this filter must be related to the mean track-spacing. With this process a contour-file can be generated, unbiased by the track-line geometry. The method has the disadvantage that along-track details with wavelengths shorter than the mean track-spacing are reduced in amplitude. For the gridding and subsequent contouring of the data a cut-off wavelength of 55 km was used for the bathymetry and 80 km for the gravity. As these wavelengths are outside the diagnostic waveband, i.e. the wavelength band in which the observed gravity can reliably detect differences in the elastic thickness of the oceanic lithosphere,

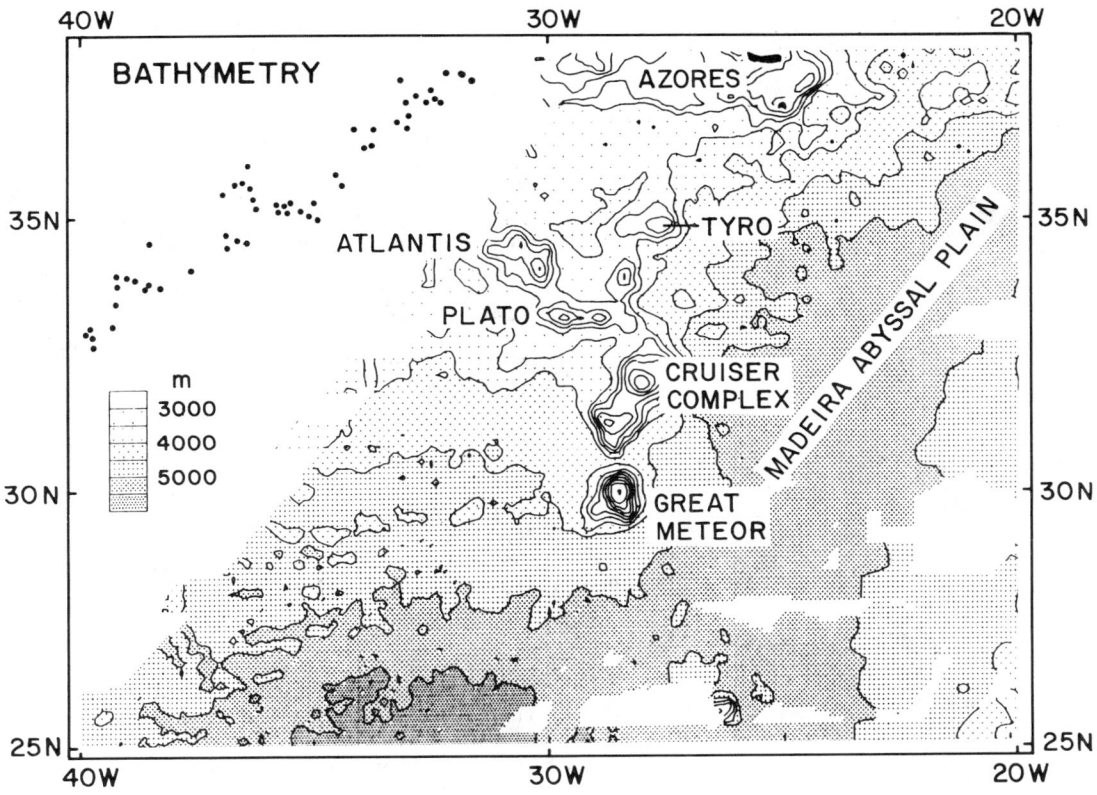

Fig. 2. Contoured bathymetry based upon the tracklines of Figure 1. The contour interval is 500 m. The cut-off wavelength of the filter used in the gridding algorithm is 55 km, roll-off 6 dB/octave.

defined by Ribe and Watts [1982] to be between wavelengths of 80 and 250 km, the filtering of the wavelengths below 55 km and 80 km will not substantially influence the results.

Bathymetry

Figure 2 shows the general bathymetric contours of the area. In general, there is a gradual deepening toward the east, with increasing distance from the Mid-Atlantic Ridge. The depth contours show the Atlantis-Meteor Seamount Complex as a general rising of the sea floor. To the north, between 24°W and 27°W this topographic high grades to the Azores. The regional NE-SW course of the depth contours, parallel to the Mid-Atlantic Ridge, can be seen in the Madeira Abyssal Plain. In the far eastern part of the area the sea floor again rises, firstly due to the increase of the thickness of the Madeira Abyssal Plain sediments and secondly, due to the presence of Madeira and the Canary Islands. Clearly recognizable in the contour chart are the elevated blocks forming the different seamount groups of the Atlantis-Meteor Seamount Complex.

The relatively dense spacing of the track lines in the area around the Atlantis-Meteor Seamount Complex (Figure 1 shows the track lines with seismic and magnetic data and Figure 4 those with gravity data) led to the discovery of a feature of the seamount complex that was not recognized before. Previously the volcanic complex had appeared as an amorphous group of seamounts on the bathymetric charts of the area. The denser network revealed that the complex consists of linear elements of about 100 km in length, which are arranged in a general NW-SE direction and which can be subdivided into the following four subgroups [cf. Verhoef and Collette, 1983 and 1985]. Figure 3A shows line drawings of the continuous seismic reflection profiles across Great Meteor Seamount, the most southeastern part of the seamount complex. Centered at about 30°N/ 28°30' W, this seamount rises up to about 275 m below sea level. The seismic reflection profiles show that this seamount has a flat surface and is a tablemount. Tablemounts are covered by reef sediments and debris thereof on the slopes. Hinz [1969] detected sedimentary thicknesses of more than 0.3 seconds on top of Great Meteor Seamount. The seismic reflection profiles show that the seamount is elongated in a NW-SE direction with a length in that direction of about 100 km.

Between 30°45' N and 32°50' N and around 28°W lies the Cruiser complex, which consists of Cruiser, Irving and Hyeres seamounts (Figures 3B).

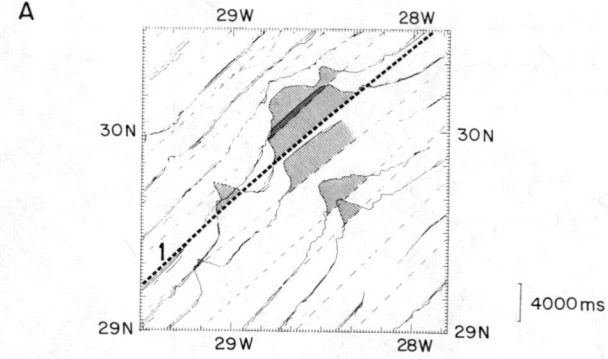

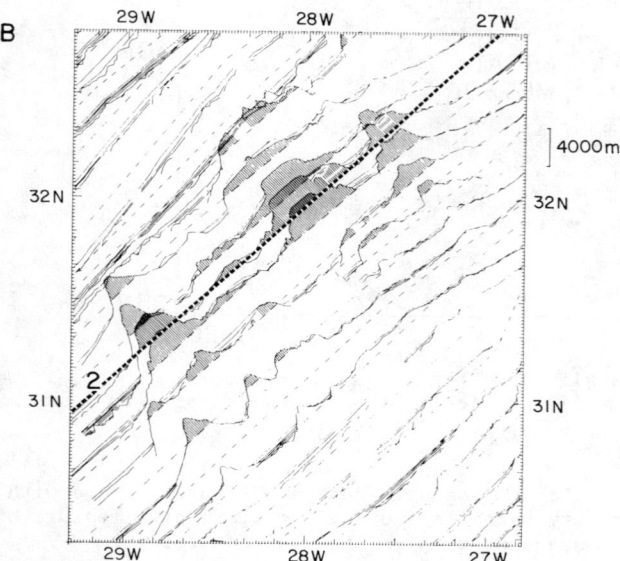

Fig. 3. Line drawings of seismic reflection profiles over a): Great Meteor Seamount and b): Cruiser, Irving and Hyeres seamounts (Cruiser complex). The offset is 3333 ms (2500 m). Parts less deep than 2500 m have been shaded. The profiles marked 1 and 2 are shown in Figure 10.

The most northeastern structure is Cruiser seamount with a minimum depth of 590 m below sea level, a general strike of 320 and a length of about 70 km in that direction. Cruiser seamount contains no flat surface. Irving seamount is situated around 32°N/ 28°W. It rises up to 250 m below sea level and is a tablemount. The direction of elongation of Irving seamount is about NW-SE and its length is about 100 km.

Between Irving and Hyeres seamounts several strucures are found which are not as high as the other seamounts but with similar directions. Hyeres seamount is the most southwestern structure of the complex and has a recorded minimum depth of 330 m. No flat surfaces have been recorded over this seamount. Coming from the northwest Hyeres seamount rises up from the sea floor in a very abrupt way (see Figure 3B) and breaks up into two branches to the southeast. Hyeres seamount has a strike of 305 and a length of about 100 km.

Inside the Cruiser complex several sedimentary basins are found, e.g. the one between Cruiser and Irving seamounts. In several places sedimentary cover has been observed on the seamount, e.g. over the northwestern part of Irving seamount and over Cruiser seamount.

To the northwest of the Cruiser Complex, the Plato group is found (see Figure 2) with Plato and Tyro seamounts, and further to the north west the Atlantis subgroup. Both Plato, which actually consists of two en-echelon elements, and the Atlantis group exhibit features with a more WNW-ESE strike. These two subgroups were described in a paper on their magnetization [Williams et al., 1983].

The lineated structure and the mosaic pattern of the Atlantis-Meteor Seamount Complex led Verhoef and Collette [1983 and 1985] to assume a tectonic origin for the complex under the influence of a general NE-SW extension.

The Gravity Data

The more than 220,000 km of track lines with the gravity data in the area around the Atlantis-Meteor Seamount Complex are given in Figure 4. Verhoef [1984] performed a cross-over analysis of the gravity data set in order to investigate its internal consistency. Different gravity meters, some without cross-coupling devices, as well as different navigation systems were used in collecting the data. The standard deviation of the differences at the more than 1700 crossings is 8 mGal, a value, although appreciable, which is not unusually high for such an inhomogeneous data set [cf. Prince and Forsyth, 1984].

The free-air anomalies along the ship-tracks were contoured by computer, using the same algorithm as described above. The resulting contours (Figure 5) show strong positive anomalies correlating with the topographic highs of the seamounts and, in the northern part, with the Azores Islands. The large positive anomalies over the seamount subgroups are surrounded by relative-ly negative anomalies, with a possible exception of the Meteor group.

In the northwestern part of the area the Mid-Atlantic Ridge shows as a fairly large and broad positive anomaly. This anomaly is inter-sected at about 35°N/ 36°W by a roughly E-W trending anomaly associated with the Oceanographer Fracture Zone. The coverage over the Mid-Atlantic Ridge farther south is insufficient to delineate the other fracture zones.

With the exception of the negative anomaly around the Cruiser complex, the area of the seamounts and the region to the W and N of them is characterized by a regional positive gravity anomaly of 20 to 40 mGal. The Madeira Abyssal Plain, further to the east, has a predominantly

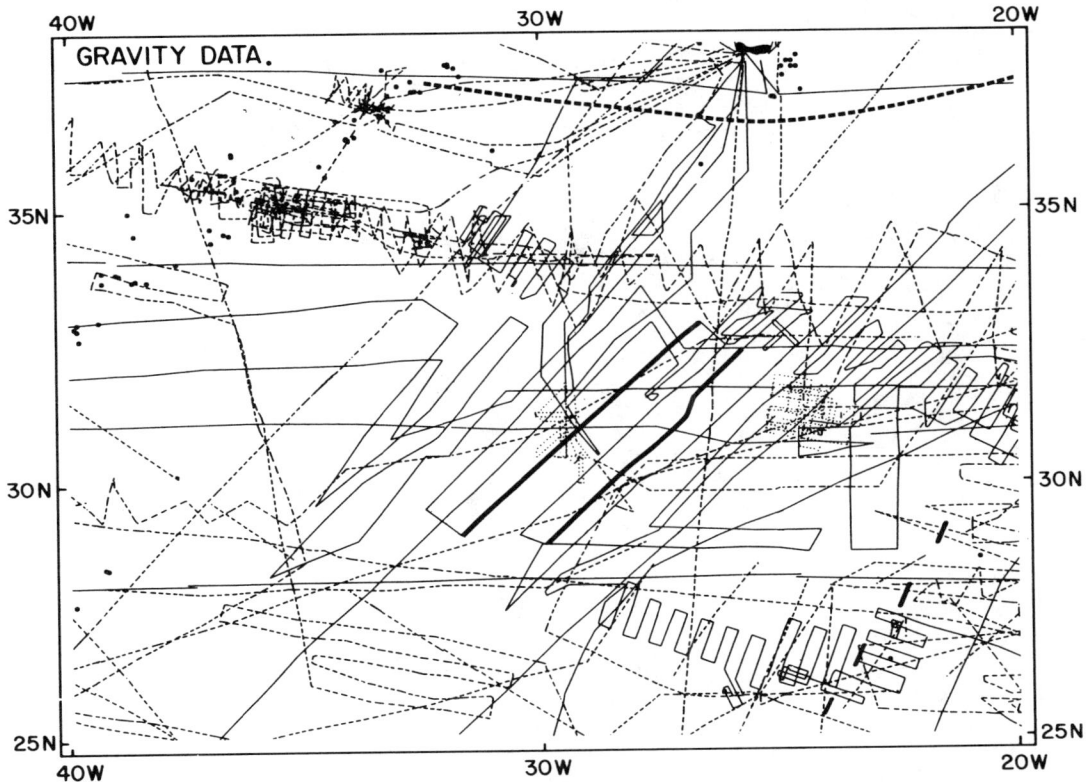

Fig. 4. Tracklines with gravity data. Solid lines: Vening Meinesz Laboratorium. Dashes: NOAA data center. Dotted lines: Geological Survey of the Netherlands. Solid circles: earthquake epicenters. Heavy dashes: East Azores Fracture Zone. Heavy lines: profiles shown in Figure 10.

negative gravity anomaly (about -20 mGal). In the eastern part of the area shown in Figure 5 the gravity anomalies become positive again, due to the presence of Madeira and the Canary Islands.

Near 27°N and east of 36°W the regional positive gravity anomaly is bounded to the south by a line which seems to follow the fracture zone pattern. This change in sign is in agreement with the change from positive to negative depth anomaly (see Figure 7) as was already noted by Cochran and Talwani [1977 and 1978].

Structural Pattern

The sea floor spreading pattern, i.e. the fracture zones and the identified sea floor spreading anomalies, of the study area is given in Figure 6. This pattern is based upon an analysis of seismic and magnetic data in a much larger area in the central North Atlantic, between 10°N and 38°N [Collette et al., 1984]. For the reconstruction of the pattern in the Atlantis-Meteor area the magnetic anomalies were corrected for the effect of the seamounts [Verhoef and Collette, 1985]. The seamounts are superimposed on the pre-existing fracture zone pattern which they partly conceal. The gaps in the fracture zone pattern were filled using a synthetic flow-line pattern [Collette et al., 1984]. For the continu-ation of the fracture zones to the Mid-Atlantic Ridge the same flow-line pattern was used. For the continuation to the east up to the Mesozoic magnetic anomaly M0 a simpli-fied flow-line pattern was used, based on an analysis of the spreading pattern in the Creta-ceous Magnetic Quiet Zone [Slootweg and Collette, 1985]. To the north of the East Azores Fracture Zone the magnetic anomaly identifications of Laughton and Whitmarsh [1974] and Searle [1980] were used.

From the identification of the sea floor spreading anomalies it becomes possible to deter-mine the age of the ocean floor under the differ-ent seamounts of the Atlantis-Meteor Seamount Complex. This age forms the upper limit to the age of the seamounts in question and would be their real age if the seamounts originated at the spreading axis. Table 1, column 1 lists the ages under the center of the seamounts, as obtained by linear interpolation between the sea floor spread-ing anomalies using the time scale of Lowrie and Alvarez [1981].

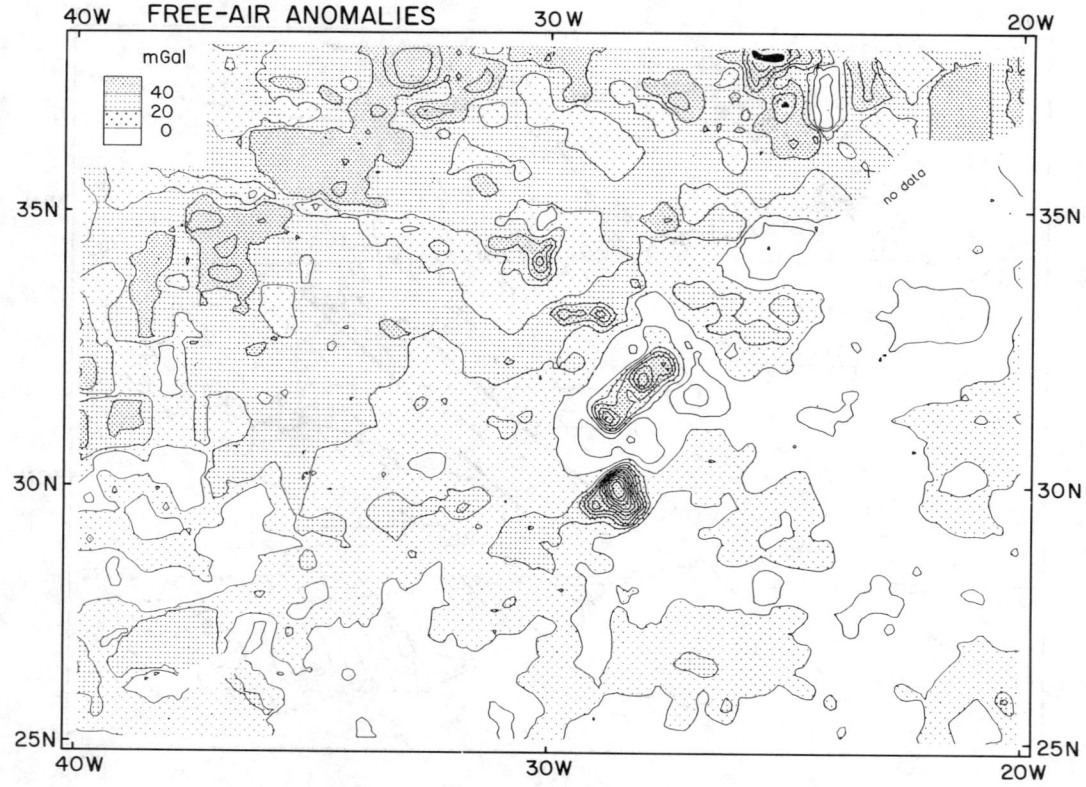

Fig. 5. Free-air gravity anomalies (computer contoured) with a contour interval of 20 mGal. The cut-off wavelength of the filter used in the gridding algorithm is 80 km, roll-off 6 dB/ octave.

Depth Anomaly Map

The depth anomaly at a certain point on the ocean floor of given age is defined by Menard [1973] as the difference between the real depth at that point, corrected for the loading of sediments if necessary, and the depth calculated from the standard depth-age curve [Parsons and Sclater, 1977]. A positive depth anomaly denotes a point which is too shallow.

Figure 7 is a contour map of the depth anomalies of the area. The depth anomaly was calculated along all available seismic profiles. The age of the ocean floor at each point was calculated from Figure 6. The correction for sediment loading was done by adding 600 m to the water depth for every second (two-way travel time) of sediment thickness [Crough, 1983]. A peculiar difficulty arose from the occurrence of a highly reflective horizon around the seamounts [Verhoef, 1985], probably consisting of volcanoclastic sediments which date from the time that the larger seamounts became subaereal and developed into tablemounts. Within the heavy line of Figure 7 the shielding effect of this horizon is so large that no reflections from the oceanic basement were recorded. Neither do the seismic sections yield information on the moats which can be expected around the seamounts. In the absence of information on the oceanic basement the depth to the deepest reflector was taken for the sediment thickness. Therefore, the positive depth anomalies close to the seamounts represent maximum values.

Like the free-air anomaly map, the depth anomaly contours of Figure 7 denote the seamount area as one of positive values. Not only the seamounts themselves stand out clearly, as is only natural, but also a wide area around the seamounts with values of 500 m or more. This regional depth anomaly merges to the north with the Azores high. In the Madeira Abyssal Plain a small negative occurs. Farther east the positive depth anomalies of the Madeira Tore Rise and of the Canary Island can be seen. Comparable to the free-air anomaly map, the positive depth anomaly is bounded to the south by a line at about 27°N which follows the general trend of the fracture zone pattern.

Isostatic Anomaly Maps and Thickness of the Lithosphere

For the study of the isostatic equilibrium of the area isostatic anomalies will be calculated, after correcting for the indirect effect and for

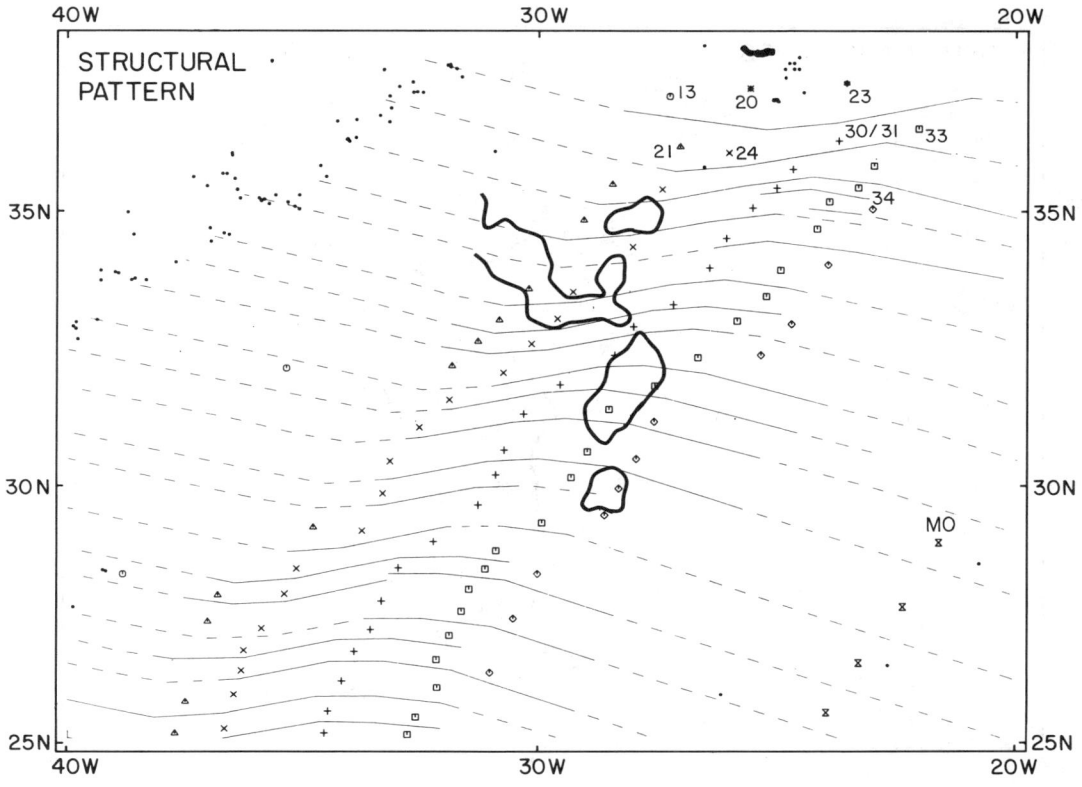

Fig. 6. Regional structural pattern. Continuous lines indicate fracture zones, dashes extensions thereof. Identified sea floor spreading anomalies are indicated by different symbols. Heavy dashes denote the generalized 3000 m depth contours from Figure 2.

the topography, and assuming a regional compensation with varying degree of regionality. From the degree of regionality, i.e. from the elastic response of the lithosphere, the flexure of which causes the regional compensation, the elastic thickness under the various seamounts from the Atlantis-Meteor Seamount Complex can be calculated. The age of the lithosphere at the time of loading may be inferred from the elastic thickness.

Since the free-air anomalies refer to the reference ellipsoid, and measurements are made at

TABLE 1. Results of Flexure Study

	(1) Age of Oceanfloor (Ma)	(2) Elastic Thickness at Time of Loading (km)	(3) Computed Age of Lithosphere at Time of Loading (Ma)	(4) Resulting Age of Seamount (Ma)	(5) Theoretical Elastic Thickness (km)	(6) Effective Thinning (km)	(%)
Great Meteor	84	18 ± 5	33 ± 10	51 ± 21	23.8	6 ± 5	(24 ± 21)
Cruiser complex	76	10 ± 5	10 ± 5	66 ± 10	22.1	12 ± 5	(55 ± 23)
Plato (east)	58	12 ± 5	15 ± 6	43 ± 13	17.8	6 ± 5	(32 ± 28)
Tyro	53	10 ± 5	10 ± 5	43 ± 10	16.4	6 ± 5	(39 ± 30)
Plato (west)	52	8 ± 4	7 ± 3	45 ± 7	16.1	8 ± 4	(50 ± 25)
Atlantis	43	7 ± 4	5 ± 3	38 ± 6	13.2	6 ± 4	(45 ± 30)

(1) Age under center of seamount; (2) value obtained from flexure study; (3) obtained with relation of Bodine et al. [1981]; (4) computed as (1) - (3); (5) value calculated with the assumption that the age of the seamounts is 25 Ma, using the relation of Bodine et al. [1981]; (6) computed as (5) - (2).

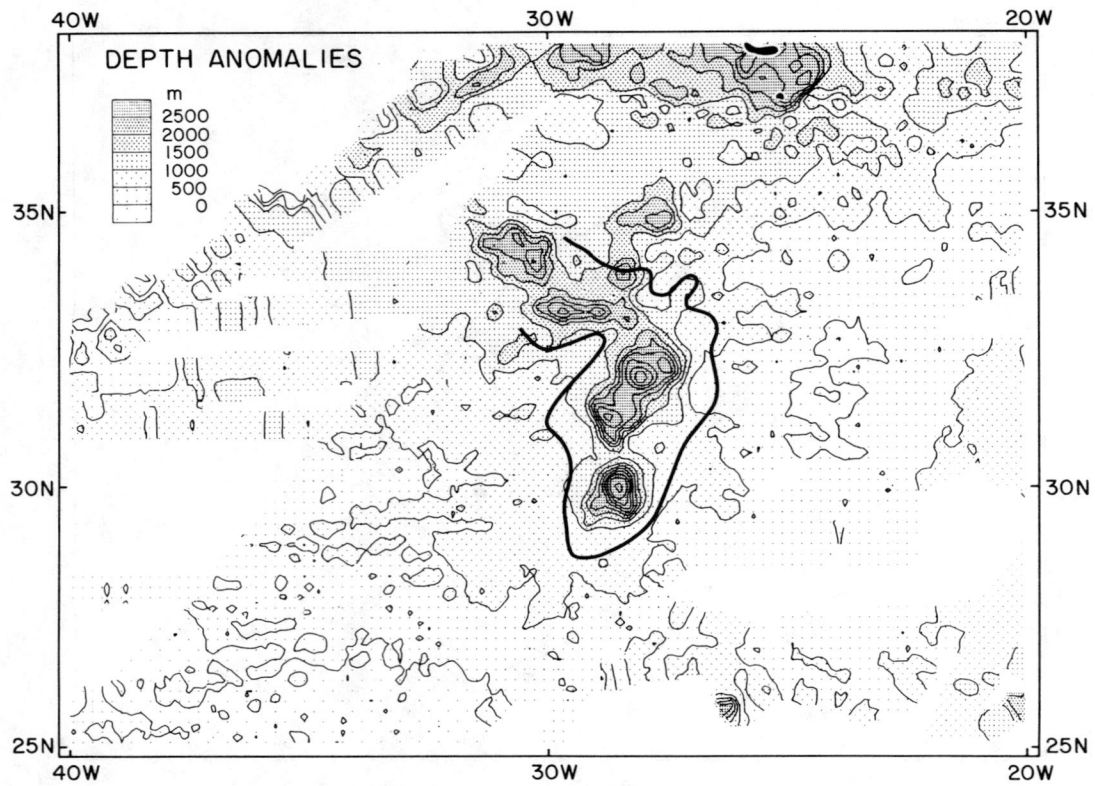

Fig. 7. Depth anomaly map with a contour interval of 500 m. The cut-off wavelength of the filter used in the gridding algorithm is 55 km, roll-off 6 dB/octave. Heavy solid line represents area within which no basement depth could be detected due to the occurrence of a highly reflective horizon.

sea level (or the geoid, neglecting sea surface topography), a correction may be applied for the difference, the indirect effect [e.g. Chapman and Bodine, 1979]. Verhoef [1984] calculated this correction for the area around the seamount complex using the spherical harmonic coefficients of the geopotential up to and including order and degree 30 as given by Gaposchkin [1980]. Its value varies over the area involved from about 3 mGal in the southwest to about 13 mGal in the northeast. The observed free-air anomalies were corrected for this effect.

A further correction was made for the effect of the Mid-Atlantic Ridge. In this study all values have been reduced to the cooling or Sclater curve, which enables one to directly correlate deviations from the standard depth-age relationship, i.e. depth anomalies, with their corresponding gravity anomalies. Therefore, the gravity anomalies must be corrected for the gravity effect of the cooling curve. For this the empirical gravity-age relation of Cochran and Talwani [1977] was used, which gives a value of about 20 mGal at the spreading center and decreases to about zero for ages larger than 40 Ma. The gravity anomalies were corrected for this effect, using the structural pattern of Figure 6 for determining the ages.

The computations for the topographic and the isostatic corrections were performed on a spherical earth, assuming a density of the crust of 2.83 g/cm^3. The actual computations comprised all topography within a radius of 7.85 degrees (up to and including Hayford zone 11). For the nearby topography (within a radius of 2.5 degrees), the equation for the gravity effect of a parallelepiped by Talwani [1973] was used, with a correction for the curvature of the earth. For topography between 2.5 and 7.85 degrees the mass-line equation of Kükkamaki [1955] was used. Beyond the radius of 7.85 degrees the combined effect of topography and isostasy was taken from the map of Niskanen and Kivioja [1951] for the Hayford zones 1-10 for the Airy-Hiskanen compensation system with a normal crustal thickness of 30 km, which corresponds to an oceanic crustal thickness of (30-3.7 h) km, where h is the waterdepth [e.g Heiskanen and Vening Meinesz, 1958]. This is allowed since at this distance the difference between regional and local compensation becomes negligible. Variations in the normal crustal thickness only result in a less than 2 mGal difference for this contribution in this part of the Atlantic.

For determining the flexure, the topographic

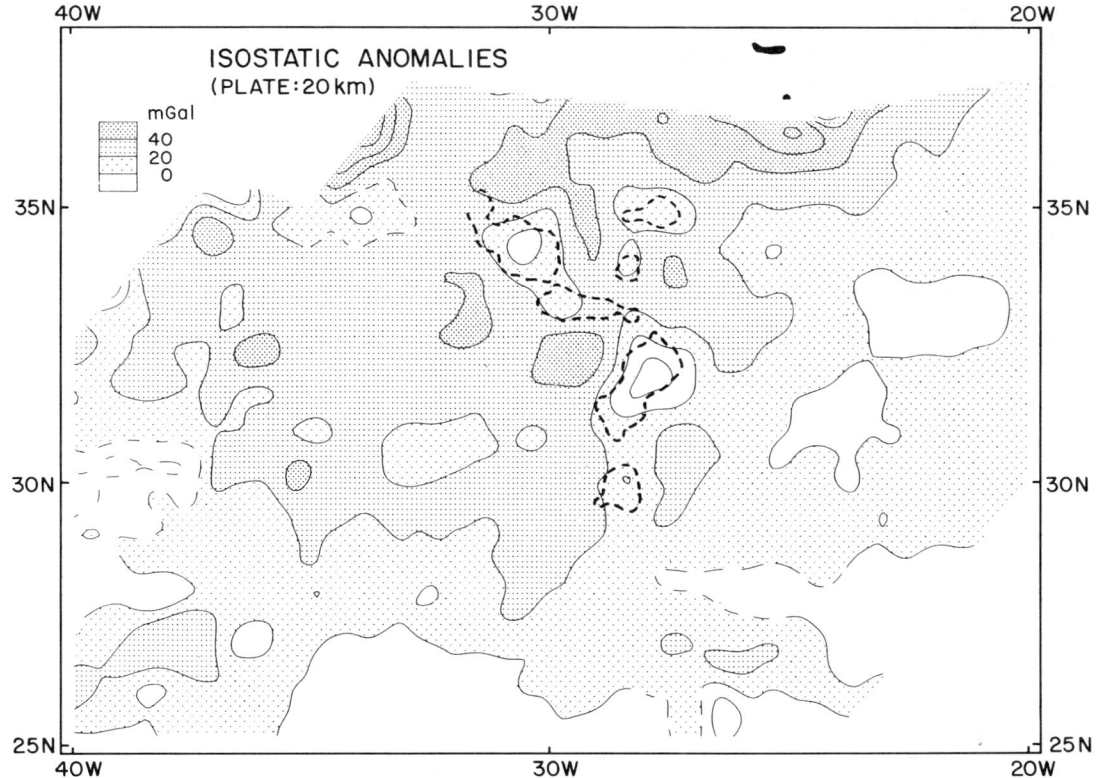

Fig. 8. Regional isostatic anomalies for an effective elastic thickness of 20 km. Contours have been smoothed with a Gaussian filter, halfwidth: 45 km. Isostatic anomalies have only been calculated to the east of the Mid-Atlantic Ridge and to the south of the East Azores Fracture Zone. Dashes indicate the generalized 3000 m contours.

load was convolved with the response function of an elastic plate to a point load, expressed in Kelvin functions. The convolution was done in the Fourier domain, using standard 2D-FFT techniques [Verhoef, 1984]. A Young's modulus of $8.5 \; 10^{10} \; N/m^2$ and a Poisson ratio of 0.25 were assumed, differrent values for the thickness of the lithosphere of 7, 10, 15, 20 and 30 km were taken. The attraction of the isostatic compensation, defined by the flexure for these different values, was computed in the same way as the effect of the topography within the radius of 7.85 degrees. We took the lower side of the crust with undeflected lithosphere at 10 km and assumed a density contrast of $- 0.6 \; g/cm^3$.

The determination of the load in the case of a seamount is complicated by the fact that the deflection or moat around the base of the seamount is usually filled in by sediments and/or volcanic debris. If we only take the visible part of the load, then the load is underestimated. A simple way out is to assume that the density of the fill-in is equal to that of the load [e.g. Lambeck, 1981]. In that case we take as the load that part of the seamount above a reference level and correct for the load of the fill-in by an appropriate choice of the flexural parameter [cf. Verhoef, 1984]. We remind that, in this study the cooling curve was chosen as the reference level. Topography deviating from this curve constitutes the load, i.e. the load is formed by the depth anomaly given in Figure 7. At the same time the topography corrections were performed for the same amount of material, taking the correct depths into account [Verhoef, 1984].

Figure 8 and 9 give the isostatic anomalies assuming elastic thicknesses of respectively 20 and 10 km. Both Figures show a regional positive isostatic anomaly with an amplitude of more than 20 mGal. For an elastic thickness of 20 km, the anomaly over Great Meteor Seamount has disappeared (Figure 8). All other seamounts clearly show as local minima in the isostatic anomalies. This means that for these latter seamounts the assumed flexure is too small. With a value for the elastic thickness of 10 km the negative anomaly over the Cruiser Complex diminishes, but over Great Meteor a positive anomaly appears (Figure 9)

Rather than choosing the best fitting elastic thickness for each seamount directly from the contourcharts of the anomalies, we calculated from the grid values the isostatic anomalies along

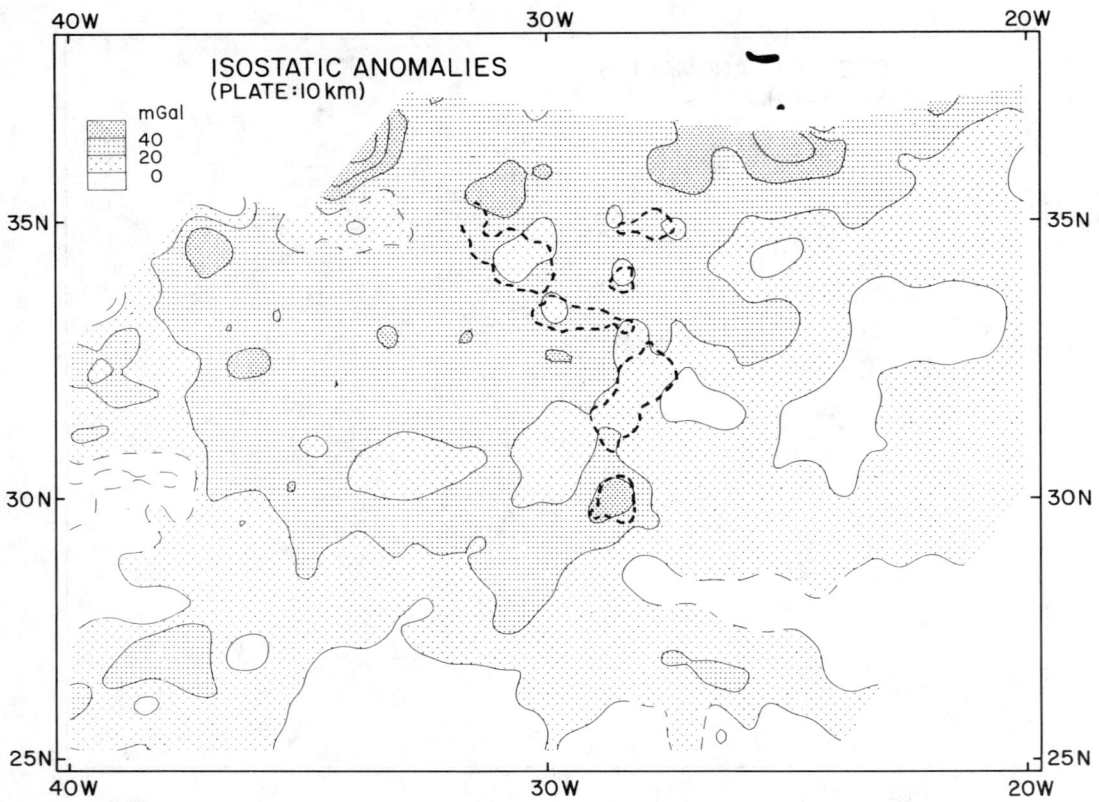

Fig. 9. Regional isostatic anomalies for an effective elastic thickness of 10 km. Contours have been smoothed with a Gaussian filter, halfwidth: 45 km. Dashed indicate generalized 3000 m contours.

selected profiles across each seamount. Figure 10 shows as an example profiles across Great Meteor Seamount and the Cruiser complex. Part of the errors in the resulting elastic thickness for the different seamounts are based upon the change in the local isostatic anomalies, due to variation of the assumed elastic thickness, as can be seen in Figure 10. There are other errors involved and they are due to the uncertainty in the observed free-air anomalies, the oversimplification of assuming a constant density for the seamounts, the effects of the applied filter in the gridding and the assumption of the same density for the infill and the load. The latter errors are not easy to quantify and our estimations of an extra 2 km uncertainty in the calculated elastic thickness are based upon two dimensional admittance calculations on simple models (see discussion).

The resulting elastic thicknesses for all the different subgroups of the Atlantis-Meteor Seamount Complex are given in Table 1, column 2. The outcome for Great Meteor seamount confirms earlier computations by Watts et al. [1975]. The much thinner lithosphere under the Cruiser complex came as a surprise, since the oceanic crust under this complex is not significantly younger (cf. Table 1, column 1). This outcome would mean that the Cruiser complex is much older than Great Meteor Seamount. We shall investigate this in the next section.

A further remark concerns the regional positive which shows in the isostatic anomaly maps. The gravity positive largely coincides with the regional depth anomaly, with the 20 mGal contour roughly following the 500 m depth anomaly contour. This configuration points to a deep-seated Airy type compensation of the long wavelength topography. This is confirmed by an admittance study [Verhoef and Collette, 1985], which shows an increase of the experimental admittances for wavelengths larger than about 700 km instead of the further decrease predicted by a plate model compensation. This increase can be explained by a deep seated Airy compensation. The present data does not allow a good estimate of the depth involved, but the deep compensation of the long-wavelength topography is evidence for the presence of lower than normal densities in the upper mantle. This forms an indication that the depth anomaly resulted from lithospheric rejuvenation. The data are insufficient to determine whether the Atlantis-Meteor depth anomaly gradually merged

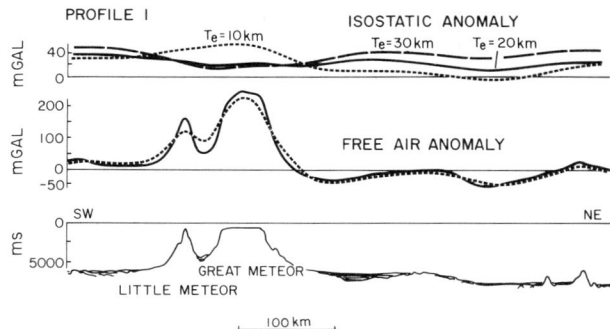

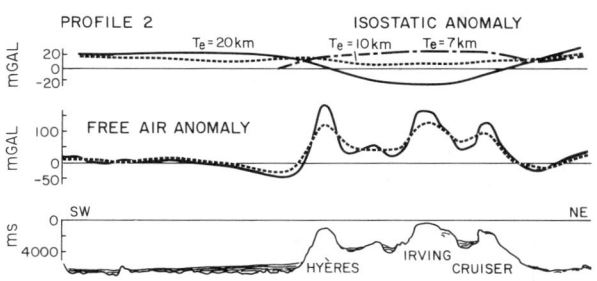

Fig. 10. Line drawings of continuous seismic reflection profiles, free-air gravity and isostatic anomalies over Great Meteor seamount and the Cruiser complex. For locations of the profiles see Figures 3 and 4. The free-air anomalies are given as observed (solid lines) and as interpolated from the grid values of the contour file. The differences are caused by the filter used in the gridding algorithm.

into the present anomalous depths of the Mid-Atlantic Ridge at these latitudes, or whether we are dealing with two separate events.

Comparison of Ages

Assuming that the thicknesses found by the flexure study represent the thickness of the lithosphere at the time of loading, and by converting this thickness into age and subtracting this age from the age of the crust under the seamount, a value follows for the age of the seamount itself. This has been done for the seamounts of the Atlantis-Meteor complex. For the conversion of lithospheric thickness into age (Table 1, column 3), we applied the relation given by Bodine et al. [1981]. They determined how the flexural parameters and the rheological properties of the oceanic lithosphere are related and used a yield stress envelope model, constrained by data from experimental rock mechanics. Assuming a uniform temperature structure for the oceanic lithosphere based on the cooling plate model Bodine et al. [1981] found that for loads in the interior of the plate the effective elastic thickness (T_e, in km) may be approximated by: $T_e = a \sqrt{t}$, in which t is the age in Ma and a, a constant. With the value for the Young's modulus used in this paper, a becomes 3.1 ± 0.5. Column 4 of Table 1 gives the ages defined in this way; they vary from 38 to 66 Ma.

There are only a few direct age determinations available for the Atlantis-Meteor Seamount Complex. Wendt et al. [1976] published two K-Ar ages of 11 and 16 Ma for Great Meteor. Pratt [1963] derived a minimum Miocene age of this seamount from the occurrence of Miocene foraminifera on terraces and in reworked sediments. Fermont and Troelstra [1983] indicate an Early Miocene age for Cruiser Seamount on the basis of the fossil content of reworked sediments.

Verhoef and Collette [1985] computed maximum ages from the depth of peaks belonging to tablemounts, which do not show signs of erosion or reef growth. Since these peaks were never above sea level, their depth below sea level is a direct measure for their maximum subsidence since their formation. Since no sea level fluctuations were taken into account, nor possible effects of rejuvenation on the subsidence, which would result in a faster subsidence for these peaks, these ages are maximum estimates. Verhoef and Collette [1985] arrived at values of 28 to 35 Ma. Finally, Verhoef [1985] presented a sedimentation model for the area around the Atlantis-Meteor complex, in which the distribution of calcareous sediment thicknesses are computed from the history of subsidence of each point in the area. He arrived at the conclusion that the depth anomaly, related to the seamount complex, cannot be much older than 25 Ma.

Closer age determinations of the seamounts cannot be made reliably from the magnetic anomalies, since the variation of the paleomagnetic pole during the Cenozoic and the Late Cretaceous is not large enough to produce appreciable phase-shift differences in this part of the Atlantic [Williams et al., 1983].

Taking all this evidence together, a Late Oligocene/Early Miocene age (about 22 Ma) for the bulk of the complex seems fairly possible. Allowing a few million years for the growth of the seamounts, 25 Ma is a fair estimate for the maximum age. This is much less than the ages derived from our flexure studies. In addition, there are no indications that the Cruiser Complex is older than the other seamounts.

Thinning of the Lithosphere

The discrepancies between the geologically probable age of the Atlantis-Meteor Seamount Complex and the ages derived from flexure are consistent; the latter being too large. Therefore, it seems plausible that there is another process involved which seemingly reduces the obtained age of the lithosphere at the time of loading. The aforementioned process of thermal rejuvenation, as proposed by Detrick and Crough [1978], could have the effect of also resetting the mechanical parameters of the lithosphere.

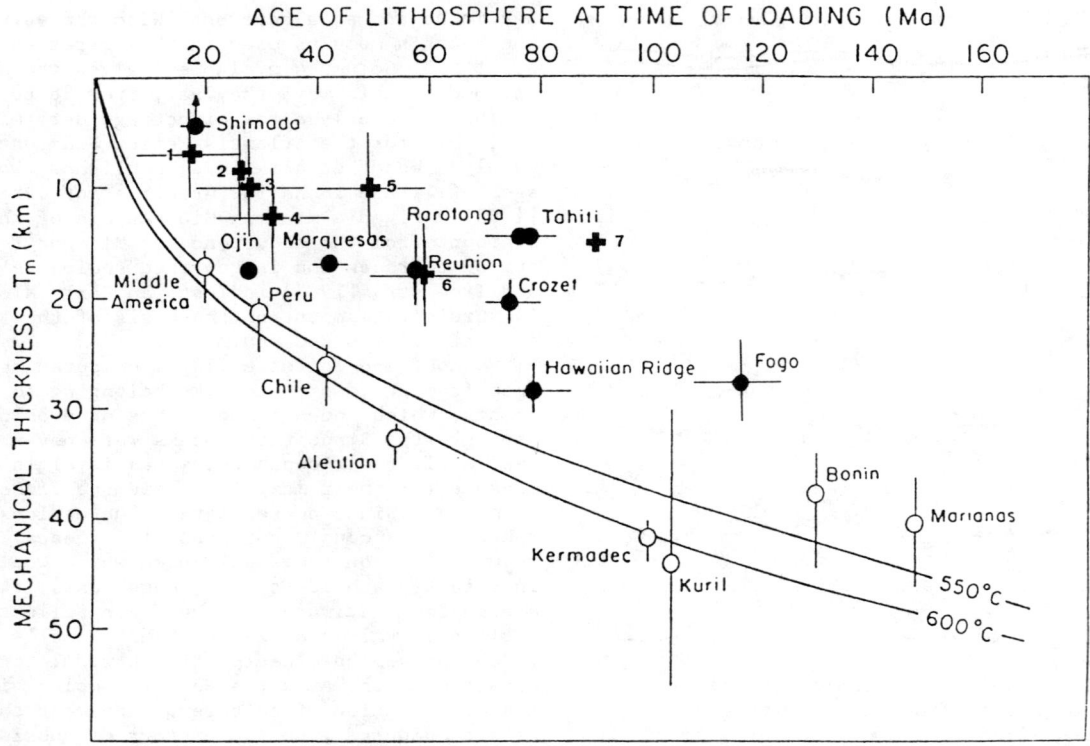

Fig. 11. Lithospheric thickness as a function of age for seamounts (solid circles) and for flexed lithosphere near trenches (values are corrected for the effect of finite yield strength, open circles). After McNutt [1984, Figure 4b], extended with the new result for Fogo [McNutt, 1987]. Included are the present results for 1: Atlantis subgroup, 2: Plato Seamount (west), 3: Tyro Seamount, 4: Plato Seamount (east), 5: Cruiser Complex, 6: Great Meteor Seamount, and 7: Canary Islands [Danobeitia, 1985]. The elastic thicknesses are from Table 1, column 2. For the age of the seamounts 1-6 we took (25 +/- 10) Ma and subtracted that value from the age of the oceanfloor (Table 1, column 1) to obtain ages for the lithosphere at the time of loading. The value for the Canary Islands was obtained from the present age of 150 Ma for the oceanfloor and a Tertiary age (60 Ma) of the islands [after Danobeita, 1985].

Assuming that lithospheric thinning indeed occurred we computed the amount of it. We took for the best estimate of the ages of the seamounts 25 Ma. Column 5 of Table 1 lists the theoretical thickness of the lithosphere under the seamounts 25 Ma ago. Columns 6 of Table 1 then gives the effective thinning. There is a considerable variation. Great Meteor Seamount is lowest with 24% thinning. Less certain are the low values for the eastern part of Plato seamount. The percentages for the other seamounts fall in the range of about 40 to 55%. This means that if lithospheric thinning is real, the amount of thinning is variable in the area of the Atlantis-Meteor Seamount Complex.

McNutt [1984] arrived at the conclusion that thinning of the oceanic lithosphere under seamounts occurs globally on the basis of a survey of published data on lithospheric thicknesses versus age of seamounts and a comparison with data on lithospheric bending near subduction zones. We reproduce as Figure 11 a synopsis of this paper, supplemented with the results of the present study and of a study by Danobeitia [1985] on the Canary Islands. Also included in this Figure is the new result of 28 ± 4 km for Fogo [McNutt, in press 1987]. For the age of the lithosphere at the time of loading we took the values from Table 1, column 1 and subtracted our best estimate of 25 ± 10 Ma for the age of the seamounts from it. Figure 11 shows that for seamounts in general the thermal clock of the lithosphere appears to be reset. At the same time, the data show a large dispersion, comparable to our findings.

Discussion and Conclusions

The degree of thinning, given in Table 1, is by no means uniform in the seamount area, percentages range from 24% to 55%. Factors that could explain this variability are:

- For our computations a uniform age for all

seamounts of 25 Ma was assumed. This may be an over-simplification. A smaller age of, say 15 Ma, for Great Meteor Seamount increases the percentage of thinning to 30%. However there is no evidence to support age differences of this size.

- It is not inconceivable that the deformation of the lithosphere under large linear seamounts can be better described as warping under the influence of an end-load, as suggested on different grounds for Hawaii by Vening Meinesz [1948, p.98], Walcott [1970] and Watts et al. [1985], and as considered for Louisville Ridge by Watts and Ribe [1984]. This would lead to a different interpretation of the flexure and would increase the calculated elastic thickness under the seamount in question. This situation might apply to the Cruiser complex and reduce the high value of 55 % effective thinning for this complex. Verhoef [1984] investigated the possibility whether the bending moments under the Cruiser complex might reach values comparable to those at trenches and therefore, the calculated elastic thickness under the complex gives too low a value [cf. McNutt, 1984]. Verhoef [1984] found that for the same elastic thickness the bending stresses under the Cruiser complex are not significantly different from those under the Great Meteor Seamount. A different elastical behaviour cannot, therefore, be attributed to the size of the load as such.

- Models that have been proposed for lithospheric thinning assume that the temperature of the lower part of the lithosphere is instantaneously increased to the solidus [e.g. Crough, 1978; Von Herzen et al., 1984; Menard and McNutt, 1982]. McNutt [1984] also considers as an alternative a model in which the reheating is uniform, thus the temperature structure of the lithosphere after rejuvenation corresponds exactly to that of normal lithosphere of a younger age. The observed reduction in elastic plate thickness is caused by the shallowing of an isotherm (usually assumed to be the 600°C isotherm). On young, thin lithosphere the 600°C isotherm is not very far from the base of the lithosphere and therefore it is possible to get a large percentage of thinning. On very old lithosphere, the cold, lower plate insulates the 600°C isotherm from the heating below and a lesser percentage of elastic thinning is predicted. This effect is in qualitative agreement with the trend in the data presented in this paper, with an exception formed by the Cruiser complex.

- Large seamounts might have a larger effect on the temperature structure of the underlying lithosphere than smaller ones. Therefore, effects of thinning under large volcanic complexes could be larger than those under smaller ones. The Cruiser complex, which has the largest thinning (about 55%) is the largest seamount in the area, not only as a topographic feature but also with regard to the buried part (about 6 km for the Cruiser complex and 3 km for the Great Meteor seamount, cf. Verhoef, 1984).

- It has been suggested that the presence of dykes and remnant magma chambers at greater depth, if of sufficient volume, might lead to a hybrid character of the isostatic compensation, adding an Airy-type component to the regional compensation [e.g. Suyenaga, 1979 and Watts et al., 1985]. Watts et al. [1985] show that the flexed oceanic crust beneath the south-eastern Hawaiian-Emperor seamount chain is underlain by a 4 km thick deep crustal body.

In the present computations the density of the sediment infill of the moats has been taken to be the same as that of the crust (2.8 g/cm^3). This affects the gravity computations in two ways. Firstly, the negative gravity anomalies around the seamounts are entirely attributed to the depression of the Moho, which is only partly correct. This leads to an overestimation of the lithospheric depression to be accounted for in the flexure calculations. Secondly, the load available for depressing the lithosphere is overestimated. Danobeitia [1985] devised an iterative method to compute these effects for a three dimensional load in the absence of seismic data. From his results it follows that neglecting density differences in the moats leads to an overestimation of the calculated elastic thickness. Therefore, the two effects are opposite, reducing the influence of the lower density of the moats on the calculated elastic thickness. Detailed calculations of the total effect as a function of the size and shape of the load are underway [Danobeitia et al., in preparation].

In the calculations of the elastic plate thickness it was assumed that all topography above the Sclater curve constitutes the load. For the longer wavelength depth anomalies it was found that they are probably due to density anomalies in the upper mantle associated with lithospheric thinning and therefore, are caused by a loading below rather than by loading above the elastic plate. The effect of loading of an elastic plate from below could be dealt with using the linear filter technique of McNutt and Shure [1986], but as long as the regional depth anomalies are broad compared to the wavelength of the seamounts the determination of the elastic plate thickness remains unaffected.

The mentioned uncertainties regard more the details of the 3-D flexure study of the Atlantis-Meteor Seamount Complex than the outcome. There seems to be reason to conclude that thermal lithospheric rejuvenation led to considerable (24 to 55%) thinning of the lithosphere under the seamount complex. Details of the thinning process have still to be specified.

A final remark concerns the cause behind the extension of the Atlantis-Meteor area. A deformation of the area will show up in the frozen-in flowlines, i.e. in the fracture zones. As no inconsistencies were found in the reconstruction of the fracture zone pattern [cf. Collette et al., 1984], the accuracy of the reconstruction forms an upper limit to a hypothetical extension. It is estimated that the error of the reconstruction is between 10 and 20 km in a NE-SW direction. Therefore, although there is no evidence for a large extension of the area, an extension of restricted dimensions may have occurred. Possible causes of the extension of the area are a change of sea floor spreading direction leading to a major reorganization of the spreading or the occurrence of a (temporary) plate boundary through the area connecting the Mid-Atlantic Ridge with the Mediterranean area via the Canary Islands and NW-Africa. The latter suggestion would classify the Atlantis-Meteor Seamount Complex as the expression of a secondary plate boundary which might have been active between anomaly 33 and anomaly 22 time [cf. W.R. Roest, PhD thesis, in preparation].

Acknowledgements. The surveys of 1979 and 1980 formed part of the Vaarplan-project of the Netherlands Council of Oceanic Research of the Royal Netherlands Academy of Arts and Sciences. We acknowledge the assistance from colleagues, technical staff and students in the data collection and processing. We thank the Geological Survey of the Netherlands for the permission to incorporate data of the detailed surveys in the area. We thank J. Woodside and R. Boutilier for their comments on an earlier version of the manuscript and M. C. McNutt and J. Kellogg for their reviews of the manuscript and their many useful suggestions. Geological Survey of Canada, contribution no: 45286.

References

Bodine, J. H., M. S. Steckler and A. B. Watts, Observations of flexure and the rheology of the oceanic lithosphere., J Geophys. Res., 86, 3695-3707, 1981.

Cazenave, A., B. Lago, K. Dominh and K. Lambeck, On the response of the oceanic lithosphere from Geos-3 satellite radar altimeter observations., Geophys. J. R. astr. Soc., 63, 233- 252, 1980.

Chapman, M. E. and J. H. Bodine, Considerations of the indirect effect in marine gravity modelling., J. Geophys. Res., 84, 3889- 3893, 1979.

Cochran, J. R. and M. Talwani, Free-air gravity anomalies in the world's oceans and their relationship to residual elevation, Geophys. J. R. astr. Soc., 50, 495-552, 1977.

Cochran, J. R. and M. Talwani, Gravity anomalies, Regional Elevation and the deep structure of the North Atlantic, J. Geophys. Res., 83, 4907-4925, 1978.

Collette, B. J., A. P. Slootweg, J. Verhoef and W. R. Roest, Geophysical investigations of the floor of the Atlantic Ocean between 10°and 38°N (Kroonvlag-project), Proc. Kon. Ned. Akad. Wet., series B, 87, 1-76, 1984.

Crough, S. T., Thermal origin of mid-plate hot-spot swells, Geophys. J. R. astr. Soc., 55, 451-469, 1978.

Crough, S. T., The correction for sediment loading on the seafloor, J. Geophys. Res., 88, 6449-6455, 1983.

Danobeitia, J. J., Estudio Geofisico submarino en el eare del Archipielago Canario, Ph.D. Thesis, University of Madrid, pp. 168, 1985.

Detrick, R. S. and S.T. Crough, Island subsidence, hot spots and lithospheric thinning., J. Geophys. Res., 83, 1236-1244, 1978.

Fermont, W. J. J. and S. R. Troelstra, Early Miocene larger foraminifera from the Cruiser-Hyeres seamount complex (Eastern North Atlantic), Proc. Kon. Ned. Akad. Wet., series B, 86, 243-253, 1983.

Fleischer, U., O. Meyer and H. Schaaf, On the structure of the submarine tablemounts south of the Azores as derived from gravimetric-magnetic N-S profile across the Grosse Meteor Bank, Meteor Forschungsergebnisse, Reihe C, 3, 37-48, 1970.

Gaposchkin, E. M., Global gravity field to degree and order 30 from Geos 3 satellite altimetry and other data, J. Geophys. Res., 85, 7221-7234, 1980.

Heiskanen, W. A. and F. A. Vening Meinesz, The earth and its gravity field, McGraw-Hill, New York, pp 470, 1958.

Hinz, K., The Great Meteor Seamount. Results of seismic reflection measurements with a pneumatic sound source, and their geological interpretation, Meteor Forschungsergebnisse, Reihe C, 2, 63-77, 1969.

Kükkamaki, J., Gravimetric reductions with electronic computers, Publ. Isos. Inst. I.A.G. (Helsinki), no 30, 1955.

Lambeck K., Flexure of the oceanic lithosphere from island uplift, bathymetry and geoid height observations: the Soceity Islands, Geophys. J. R. astr. Soc., 67, 91-114, 1981.

Laughton, A. S. and R. B. Whitmarsh, The Azores-Gibraltar plate boundary, in: Geodynamics of Iceland and the North Atlantic area, edited by L. Kristjansson, pp. 63-81, D. Reidel, Dordrecht, 1974.

Lowrie, W. and W. Alvarez, One hundred million years of geomagnetic polarity history, Geology, 9, 392-397, 1981.

McNutt, M. K., Lithospheric flexure and thermal anomalies, J. Geophys. Res., 89, 11180-11194, 1984.

McNutt, M. K., Thermal and mechanical properties of the Cape Verde Rise, J. Geophys. Res., in press, 1987.

McNutt, M. K. and H.W. Menard, Constraints on yield strength in the oceanic lithosphere derived from observations of flexure, Geophys. J. R. astr. Soc., 71, 363-394, 1982.

McNutt, M. K. and L. Shure, Estimating the compensation depth of the Hawaiian swell with linear filters, J. Geophys. Res., 91, 13915-13923, 198

Menard, H. W., Depth anomalies and the bobbing motion of drifting islands, J. Geophys. Res., 78, 5128-5138, 1973.

Menard, H. W. and M. K. McNutt, Evidence for and consequences of thermal rejuvenation, J. Geophys. Res., 87, 8570-8580, 1982.

Niskanen, E. and L. Kivioja, Topographic-isostatic

world maps of the effect of the Hayford zones 10 to 1 for the Airy- Heiskanen and Pratt-Hayford systems, Publ. Isos. Inst. I.A.G. (Helsinki), no. 28, 1951.

Parsons, B. and J. G. Sclater, An analysis of the variation of ocean floor bathymetry and heat flow with age, J. Geophys. Res., 82, 803-828, 1977.

Pratt, R. M., Great Meteor Seamount, Deep Sea Res., 10, 17-25, 1963.

Prince, R. A. and D. W. Forsyth, A simple objective method for minimizing crossover errors in marine gravity data, Geophysics, 49, 1070-1084, 1984.

Ribe, N. M. and A.B. Watts, The distribution of intraplate volcanism in the Pacific Ocean Basin: a spectral approach, Geophys. J. R. astr. Soc., 71, 333-362, 1982.

Searle, R. C., Tectonic pattern of the Azores spreading centre and triple junction, Earth Planet. Sci. Lett., 51, 415-434, 1980.

Slootweg, A. P., Computer contouring with a digital filter, Mar. Geophys. Res., 3, 401-405, 1978.

Slootweg, A. P. and B.J. Collette, Crustal structure and spreading history of the central North Atlantic in the Cretaceous Magnetic Quiet Zone (African Plate), Proc. Kon. Ned. Akad. Wet. series B, 88, 1985.

Suyenaga, W., Isostasy and flexure of the lithosphere under the Hawaiian Islands, J. Geophys. Res., 84, 5599-5604, 1979.

Talwani, M., Computer usage in the computation of gravity anomalies, in: Methods in computational physics, 13, edited by B. Bolt, 343-389, Academic New York, 1973.

Vening Meinesz, F. A., Gravity expeditions at sea, 1923-1938, vol. 4, Publ. Neth. Geod. Comm., Delft, pp.233, 1948.

Verhoef, J., Geophysical study of the Atlantis-Meteor seamount complex, Ph.D. Thesis, Geologica Ultraiectina, 38, pp 153, 1984.

Verhoef, J., The Sedimentation pattern around the Atlantis-Meteor Seamount Complex: a model study, Earth. Planet. Sci. Lett., 73, 117- 128, 1985.

Verhoef, J. and B. J. Collette, A tear fault system beneath the Atlantis-Meteor Seamount Group, Ann. Geoph., 1, 199-206, 1983.

Verhoef, J. and B. J. Collette, A geophysical investigation of the Atlantis-Meteor Seamount Complex, Proc. Kon. Ned. Akad. Wet., series B, 88, 427-479, 1985.

Verhoef, J, B. J. Collette, P. R. Miles, R. C. Searle, J-C. Sibuet and C. A. Williams, Magnetic anomalies in the Northeast Atlantic Ocean ($35°$ - $50°$ N), Mar. Geophys. Res., 8, 1-25, 1986.

Von Herzen, R. P., R. S. Detrick, S. T. Crough, D. Epp and U. Fohn, Thermal origin of the Hawaiian swell: heat flow evidence and thermal models, J. Geophys. Res., 87, 6711-6723, 1982.

Walcott, R.I., Flexure of the lithosphere at Hawaii, Tectonophysics, 9, 435-446, 1970.

Watts, A. B., An analysis of isostasy in the world's oceans, 1: Hawaiian-Emperor seamount chain, J. Geophys. Res., 83, 5989- 6004, 1978.

Watts, A. B., J. H. Bodine and M. S. Steckler, Observations of flexure and the state of stress in the oceanic lithosphere, J. Geophys. Res., 85, 6369-6376, 1980.

Watts, A. B., J. R. Cochran and G. Selzer, Gravity anomalies and flexure of the lithosphere: a three-dimensional study of the Great Meteor Seamount, North East Atlantic, J. Geophys. Res., 80, 1391-1399, 1975.

Watts, A. B. and N. M. Ribe, On geoid heights and flexure of the lithosphere at seamounts, J. Geophys. Res., 89, 11152-11171, 1984.

Watts, A. B., U. S. ten Brink, P. Buhl and T. M. Brocher, A multychannel seismic study of the lithospheric flexure across the Hawaiian-Emperor seamount chain, Nature, 315, 105-112, 1985.

Wendt, I. H. Kreuzer, P. Muller, U. Von Rad and H. Raschka, K-Ar ages of basalts from Great Meteor and Josephine Seamounts (Eastern North Atlantic), Deep Sea Res., 23, 849-862, 1976.

Williams, C. A., J. Verhoef and B. J. Collette, Magnetic analysis of some large seamounts in the North Atlantic, Earth Planet. Sci. Lett., 63, 399-407, 1983.

551.4608 Se16k　　　　c.1
150101　000
Seamounts, islands, and atolls
3 9315 00113176 9
MANCHESTER COLLEGE LIBRARY

FUNDERBURG LIBRARY
MANCHESTER COLLEGE

WITHDRAWN
from
Funderburg Library

551.4608 Se16k
Seamounts, islands, and atolls

551.4608 Se16k
Seamounts, islands, and atolls

DEMCO